Get the Job Done with Human Resources Online...

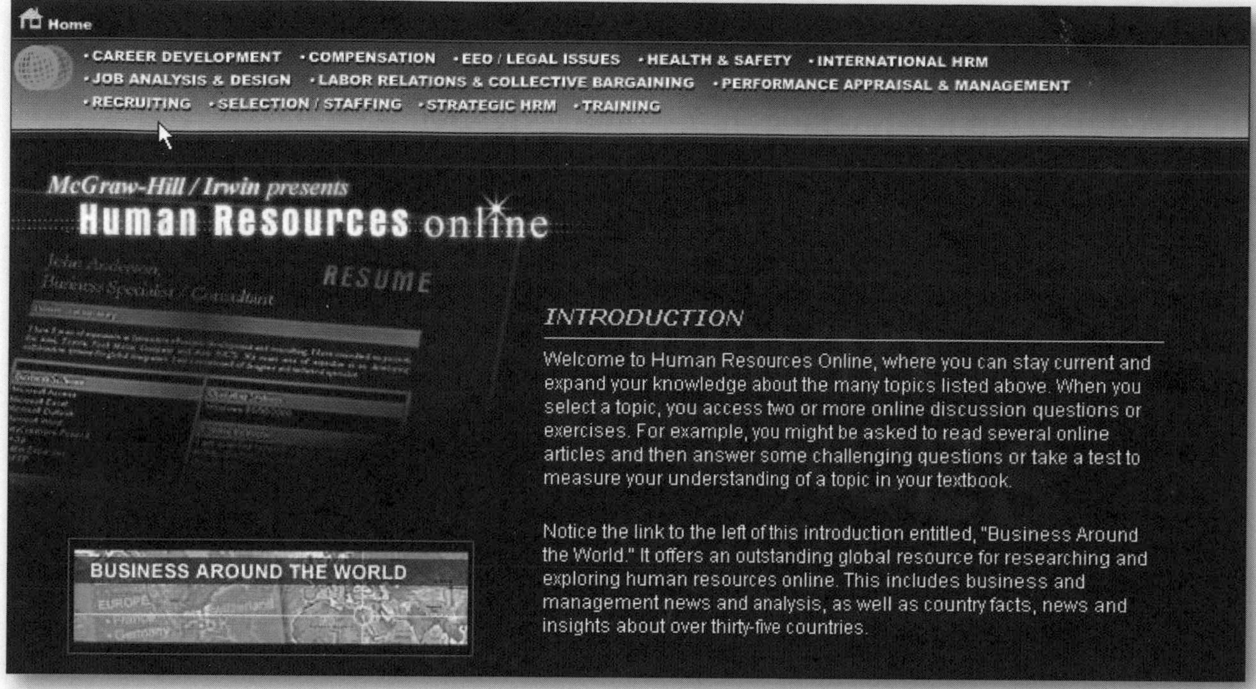

Stay current and expand your knowledge in the field of human resource management by completing approximately twenty online exercises in such areas as

- training and employee development
- selection and recruitment
- compensation and benefits
- labor relations
- employee separation and retention

In each exercise, you will review one or more online resources, such as articles covering a recent HRM trend, and then answer some challenging questions.

This exciting new resource will not only help you understand the concepts in the course, but it will reinforce the objectives and skills you'll need in your professional career.

Human Resource Management

GAINING A COMPETITIVE ADVANTAGE

Human Resource Management

GAINING A COMPETITIVE ADVANTAGE

Fourth Edition

RAYMOND A. NOE
The Ohio State University

JOHN R. HOLLENBECK
Michigan State University

BARRY GERHART
University of Wisconsin—Madison

PATRICK M. WRIGHT
Cornell University

Boston Burr Ridge, IL Dubuque, IA Madison, WI New York San Francisco St. Louis
Bangkok Bogotá Caracas Kuala Lumpur Lisbon London Madrid Mexico City
Milan Montreal New Delhi Santiago Seoul Singapore Sydney Taipei Toronto

McGraw-Hill Higher Education

A Division of The ***McGraw-Hill*** *Companies*

HUMAN RESOURCE MANAGEMENT: GAINING A COMPETITIVE ADVANTAGE

Published by McGraw-Hill/Irwin, a business unit of The McGraw-Hill Companies, Inc., 1221 Avenue of the Americas, New York, NY, 10020.

The book is printed on acid-free paper.

domestic 2 3 4 5 6 7 8 9 0 DOW/DOW 0 9 8 7 6 5 4 3 2
international 2 3 4 5 6 7 8 9 0 DOW/DOW 0 9 8 7 6 5 4 3 2

ISBN 0-07-246994-3

Publisher: *John E. Biernat*
Senior editor: *John Weimeister*
Developmental editor: *Sarah Reed*
Senior marketing manager: *Ellen Cleary*
Marketing coordinator: *Dana L. Woo*
Senior project manager: *Pat Frederickson*
Senior production supervisor: *Michael R. McCormick*
Director of design BR: *Keith J. McPherson*
Producer, media technology: *Mark Molsky*
Supplement producer: *Vicki Laird*
Photo research coordinator: *Jeremy Cheshareck*
Photo researcher: *Jennifer Blankenship*
Cover image: *© Photodisc 2002*
Typeface: *10.5/12 Goudy*
Compositor: *ElectraGraphics, Inc.*
Printer: *R. R. Donnelley & Sons Company*

Library of Congress Cataloging-in-Publication Data

Human resource management : gaining a competitive advantage / Raymond A. Noe . . . [et al.]—4th ed.
p. cm.
Includes index.
ISBN 0-07-246994-3 (alk. paper)—
ISBN 0-07-119864-4 (international ed: alk. paper)
1. Personnel management—United States. I. Noe, Raymond A.
HF5549.2.U5 H8 2003
658.3—dc21

2002025533

INTERNATIONAL EDITION ISBN 0-07-119864-4

www.mhhe.com

To my parents,
Raymond and Mildred,
and my children, Ray,
Tim, and Melissa
—R. A. N.

To my parents, Harold
and Elizabeth, my wife,
Patty, and my children,
Jennifer, Marie,
Timothy, and Jeffrey
—J. R. H.

To my parents, Robert
and Shirley, my wife,
Heather, and my
children, Chris and
Annie
—B. G.

To my parents, Patricia
and Paul, my wife,
Mary, and my sons,
Michael and Matthew
—P. M. W.

About the Authors

Raymond A. Noe is the Robert and Anne Hoyt Professor of Management at The Ohio State University. He was previously a professor in the Department of Management at Michigan State University and the Industrial Relations Center of the Carlson School of Management, University of Minnesota. He received his BS in psychology from The Ohio State University and his MA and PhD in psychology from Michigan State University. Professor Noe conducts research and teaches undergraduate as well as MBA and PhD students in human resource management, managerial skills, quantitative methods, human resource information systems, training, employee development, and organizational behavior. He has published articles in the *Academy of Management Journal, Academy of Management Review, Journal of Applied Psychology, Journal of Vocational Behavior,* and *Personnel Psychology.* Professor Noe is currently on the editorial boards of several journals including *Personnel Psychology, Journal of Business and Psychology, Journal of Training Research,* and *Journal of Organizational Behavior.* Professor Noe has received awards for his teaching and research excellence, including the Herbert G. Heneman Distinguished Teaching Award in 1991 and the Ernest J. McCormick Award for Distinguished Early Career Contribution from the Society for Industrial and Organizational Psychology in 1993. He is also a fellow of the Society for Industrial and Organizational Psychology.

John R. Hollenbeck is Professor of Management at the Eli Broad Graduate School of Business Administration at Michigan State University. He received his PhD in management and organizational behavior from New York University in 1984. Professor Hollenbeck is the editor of *Personnel Psychology* and has served on the editorial boards of *Academy of Management Journal, Organizational Behavior and Human Decision Processes,* the *Journal of Management,* and the *Journal of Applied Psychology.* Professor Hollenbeck has been recognized for both his research and teaching. He was the first recipient of the Ernest J. McCormick Award for Distinguished Early Career Contributions to the field of Industrial and Organizational Psychology in 1992 and was the 1987 Teacher–Scholar Award winner at Michigan State University. Dr. Hollenbeck's research focuses on self-regulation theories of work motivation, employee separation and acquisition processes, and team decision making and performance.

Barry Gerhart is the John and Barbara Keller Distinguished Chair in Business at University of Wisconsin—Madison. He was previously Professor in the Owen School of Management at Vanderbilt University and Associate Professor and Chairman of the Department of Human Resource Studies, School of Industrial and Labor Relations at Cornell University. He received his BS in psychology from Bowling Green State University in 1979 and his PhD in industrial relations from the University of Wisconsin—Madison in 1985. His research is in the areas of compensation/rewards, staffing, and employee attitudes. Professor Gerhart has worked with a variety of organizations, including TRW, Corning, and Bausch & Lomb. His work has appeared in the *Academy of Management Journal*, *Industrial Relations*, *Industrial and Labor Relations Review*, *Journal of Applied Psychology*, *Personnel Psychology*, and *Handbook of Industrial and Organizational Psychology*, and he has served on the editorial boards of the *Academy of Management Journal*, *Industrial and Labor Relations Review*, and the *Journal of Applied Psychology*. He was a corecipient of the 1991 Scholarly Achievement Award, Human Resources Division, Academy of Management.

Patrick M. Wright is Professor of Human Resource Studies and Director of the Center for Advanced Human Resource Studies in the School of Industrial and Labor Relations at Cornell University. He was formerly Associate Professor of Management and Coordinator of the Master of Science in Human Resource Management program in the College of Business Administration and Graduate School of Business at Texas A & M University. He holds a BA in psychology from Wheaton College and an MBA and a PhD in organizational behavior/human resource management from Michigan State University. He teaches, conducts research, and consults in the areas of personnel selection, employee motivation, and strategic human resource management. His research articles have appeared in journals such as the *Academy of Management Journal*, *Journal of Applied Psychology*, *Organizational Behavior and Human Decision Processes*, *Journal of Management*, and *Human Resource Management Review*. He has served on the editorial boards of *Journal of Applied Psychology* and *Journal of Management* and also serves as an ad hoc reviewer for *Organizational Behavior and Human Decision Processes*, *Academy of Management Journal*, and *Academy of Management Review*. In addition, he has consulted for a number of organizations, including Whirlpool Corporation, Amoco Oil Company, and the North Carolina State government.

The excitement of e-business, a new president, the fall of the dot-coms, an economy in recession, the tragic events of September 11, 2001, America's war on terrorism—many historical episodes have occurred since the third edition of *Human Resource Management: Gaining a Competitive Advantage*. As a result of these events, many of us have examined our personal and professional priorities and perhaps spent more time in quiet reflection to give thanks for what we have or to consider the value of freedom and democracy. Security, whether in the context of personal safety or employment, has taken on greater meaning.

The events that have occurred also have forced most companies to reexamine their business priorities and place more emphasis on providing value to customers, shareholders, and employees. Traditionally, the concept of *value* has been considered a function of finance or accounting. However, we believe that how human resources are managed is crucial to the long-term value of a company and ultimately to its survival. Our definition of *value* includes not only profits but also employee growth and satisfaction, additional employment opportunities, protection of the environment, and contributions to community programs. Organizations' resources are stretched tighter than ever, and allocating those resources wisely is imperative. For that reason, all functions in an organization must work together to contribute whatever they can; and all functions, particularly human resource management, are increasingly being scrutinized for the value they add.

We believe that all aspects of human resource management—including how companies interact with the environment; acquire, prepare, develop, and compensate human resources; and design and measure work—can help companies meet their competitive challenges and create value. Meeting challenges is necessary to create value and to gain a competitive advantage.

The Competitive Challenges

The challenges organizations face today can be grouped into four categories:

- **The new economy challenge.** Changes in the economy, including the development of e-business and growth in professional and services jobs, have made it increasingly important for companies to find and keep talented employees. Companies in today's economy use mergers and acquisitions, growth, and downsizing to successfully compete. While companies rely on employees with high math, verbal, and information skills (that is, knowledge workers) to be productive, innovative, and creative, work is demanding, and companies cannot guarantee job security, especially in an economic recession. The human resource management challenge is how to build a committed, productive workforce in turbulent economic conditions that offer opportunity for financial success but can also quickly turn sour, making every employee expendable. To successfully compete in the new economy, companies are providing more flexible work schedules, training and development opportunities, and incentive-based compensation plans. Companies are also using electronic HRM applications to give employees more ownership of the employment relationship through the ability to enroll in and participate in training programs, change benefits, and communicate with coworkers and customers online.

- **The global challenge.** Increasingly, organizations are finding that to survive they must compete with organizations around the world. Companies must both defend their domestic markets from foreign competitors and broaden their scope to encompass global markets. Recent threats to and successes of U.S. businesses have proven that globalization is a continuing challenge.
- **The challenge of meeting stakeholders' needs.** The key to success in today's business environment is to simultaneously meet investor or financial needs and those of other stakeholders including customers, employees, and the community. Companies are challenged to reach financial objectives through meeting customer needs and employee needs. Innovation, cost reduction, and quality objectives that relate directly to the financial success or failure of the firm are influenced by human resource management practices. Forward-looking businesses are capitalizing on the strengths of a diverse workforce. Businesses are realizing the advantages they have in attracting, retaining, and motivating employees through ethical and responsible actions. Successful companies have human resource management practices that motivate and reward employees to provide high-quality products and services.
- **The high-performance work systems challenge.** Using new technologies such as computer-aided manufacturing, virtual reality, expert systems, and the Internet can give companies an edge. New technologies can result in employees' "working smarter" as well as providing higher-quality products and services to customers. However, companies that have seen the greatest gains from new technology have human resource management practices that support the use of technology. Work, training programs, and reward systems often need to be reconfigured to support employees' use of new technology. Thus the three links of high-performance work systems are (1) human resources and their capabilities, (2) new technology and its opportunities, and (3) efficient work structures and policies that allow employees and technology to interact. The strength of each of these links determines an organization's competitiveness.

We believe that organizations must successfully deal with these challenges to create and maintain value, and the key to facing these challenges is a motivated, well-trained, and committed workforce.

The Changing Role of the Human Resource Management Function

The human resource management (HRM) profession and practices have undergone substantial change and redefinition. Many articles written in both the academic and practitioner literature have been critical of the traditional HRM function. Unfortunately, in many organizations HRM services are not providing value but instead are mired down in managing trivial administrative tasks. Where this is true, HRM departments can be replaced with new technology or outsourced to a vendor who can provide higher-quality services at a lower cost. Although this recommendation is indeed somewhat extreme (and threatening to both HRM practitioners and those who teach human resource management!), it does demonstrate that companies need to ensure that their HRM functions are creating value for the firm.

Technology should be used where appropriate to automate routine activities, and managers should concentrate on HRM activities that can add substantial value to the company. Consider employee benefits: Technology is available to automate the process by which employees enroll in benefits programs and to keep detailed records of benefits usage. This use of technology frees up time for the manager to focus on activities that can create value for the firm (such as how to control health care costs and reduce workers' compensation claims).

Although the importance of some HRM departments is being debated, everyone agrees on the need to successfully manage human resources for a company to maximize its competitiveness. Three themes emerge from our conversations with managers and our review of research on HRM practices. First, in today's flatter organizations, managers themselves are becoming more responsible for HRM practices. Second, most managers believe that their HRM departments are not well respected because of a perceived lack of competence, business sense, and contact with operations. Third, many managers believe that for HRM practices to be effective they need to be related to the strategic direction of the business. This text emphasizes how HRM practices can and should contribute to business goals and help to improve product and service quality and effectiveness.

Our intent is to provide students with the background to be successful HRM professionals, to manage human resources effectively, and to be knowledgeable consumers of HRM products. Managers must be able to identify effective HRM practices to purchase these services from a consultant, to work with the HRM department, or to design and implement them personally. The text emphasizes how a manager can more effectively manage human resources and highlights important issues in current HRM practice.

We think this book represents a valuable approach to teaching human resource management for several reasons:

- The text draws from the diverse research, teaching, and consulting experiences of four authors. They have taught human resource management to undergraduates, traditional day MBA students as a required and elective course, and more experienced managers and professional employees in weekend and evening MBA programs. The teamwork approach gives a depth and breadth to the coverage that is not found in other texts.
- Human resource management is viewed as critical to the success of a business. The text emphasizes how the HRM function, as well as the management of human resources, can help companies gain a competitive advantage.
- The book discusses current issues such as e-HRM, finding and keeping talented employees, diversity, and use of teams, all of which have a major impact on business and HRM practice.
- Strategic human resource management is introduced early in the book and integrated throughout the text.
- Examples of how new technologies are being used to improve the efficiency and effectiveness of HRM practices are provided throughout the text.

Organization

Human Resource Management: Gaining a Competitive Advantage includes an introductory chapter (Chapter 1) and five parts.

Chapter 1 provides a detailed discussion of the global, new economy, stakeholder, and work system challenges that influence companies' abilities to successfully meet the needs of shareholders, customers, employees, and other stakeholders. We discuss how the management of human resources can help companies meet the competitive challenges.

Part 1 includes a discussion of the environmental forces that companies face in attempting to capitalize on their human resources as a means to gain competitive advantage. The environmental forces include the strategic direction of the business, the legal environment, and the type of work performed, and physical arrangement of the work.

A key focus of the strategic human resource management chapter is highlighting the role that staffing, performance management, training and development, and compensation play in different types of business strategies. A key focus of the legal chapter is enhancing managers' understanding of laws related to sexual harassment, affirmative action, and accommodations for disabled employees. The various types of discrimination and ways they have been interpreted by the courts are discussed. The chapter on analysis and design of work emphasizes how work systems can improve company competitiveness by alleviating job stress and by improving employees' motivation and satisfaction with their jobs.

Part 2 deals with the acquisition and preparation of human resources, including human resource planning and recruitment, selection, and training. The human resource planning chapter illustrates the process of developing a human resource plan. Also, the strengths and weaknesses of staffing options such as outsourcing, use of contingent workers, and downsizing are discussed. Strategies for recruiting talented employees are emphasized. The selection chapter emphasizes ways to minimize errors in employee selection and placement to improve the company's competitive position. Selection method standards such as validity and reliability are discussed in easily understandable terms without compromising the technical complexity of these issues. The chapter discusses selection methods such as interviews and various types of tests (including personality, honesty, and drug tests) and compares them on measures of validity, reliability, utility, and legality.

We discuss the components of effective training systems and the manager's role in determining employees' readiness for training, creating a positive learning environment, and ensuring that training is used on the job. The advantages and disadvantages of different training methods are described, such as e-learning.

Part 3 explores how companies can determine the value of employees and capitalize on their talents through retention and development strategies. The performance management chapter examines the strengths and weaknesses of performance management methods that use ratings, objectives, or behaviors. The employee development chapter introduces the student to how assessment, job experiences, formal courses, and mentoring relationships are used to develop employees. The chapter on retention and separation discusses how managers can maximize employee productivity and satisfaction to avoid absenteeism and turnover. The use of employee surveys to monitor job and organizational characteristics that affect satisfaction and subsequently retention is emphasized.

Part 4 covers rewarding and compensating human resources, including designing pay structures, recognizing individual contributions, and providing benefits. Here we explore how managers should decide the pay rate for different jobs, given the company's compensation strategy and the worth of jobs. The advantages and disadvantages of merit pay, gainsharing, and skill-based pay are discussed. The benefits chapter highlights the different types of employer-provided benefits and discusses how benefit costs can be contained. International comparisons of compensation and benefit practices are provided.

Part 5 covers special topics in human resource management, including labor–management relations, international HRM, and managing the HRM function. The collective bargaining and labor relations chapter focuses on traditional issues in labor–management relations, such as union structure and membership, the organizing process, and contract negotiations; it also discusses new union agendas and less adversarial approaches to labor–management relations. Social and political changes, such as introduction of the euro currency in the European Community, are discussed in the chapter on global human resource management. Selecting, preparing, and rewarding employees for foreign assignments are also discussed. The text concludes with a chapter that emphasizes how HRM practices should be aligned to help the company meet its business objectives. The chapter emphasizes that the HRM function needs to have a customer focus to be effective.

Video cases at the end of each part integrate the concepts presented. These cases are intended to give students practice dealing with real HRM issues that companies are facing.

Acknowledgments

Although this book enters its fourth edition, it is important to acknowledge those who started it all. The first edition of this book would not have been possible if not for the entrepreneurial spirit of two individuals. Bill Schoof, president of Austen Press, gave us the resources and had the confidence that four unproven textbook writers could provide a new perspective for teaching human resource management. John Weimeister, our editor, provided us with valuable marketing information, coordinated all of the book reviews, helped us in making major decisions regarding the book, and made writing this book an enjoyable process. We were fortunate to have the opportunity in the fourth edition to work with John again. Also, Sarah Reed joined our team as developmental editor for the first time. Sarah's suggestions, patience, gentle prodding, and organizational ability kept the author team focused and allowed us to meet publication deadlines. Dana Woo, our marketing coordinator, deserves kudos for her ideas and efforts in creating excitement for the new edition. Amit Shah of Frostburg State University wrote a first-class Instructor's Manual and PowerPoint presentation, and he developed the quiz questions for the Student CD. Roy Johnson of Iowa State University developed the new quizzes for the Online Learning Center. Fred Heidrich of Black Hills State University developed a high-quality Test Bank. Also, many thanks go to Interactive Learning LLC and Nick Kaufman Productions for their help with content for the Student CD and videos.

We would also like to thank the professors who gave of their time to review the text in this and previous editions. Their helpful comments and suggestions during manuscript reviews and focus groups have greatly helped to shape the book from edition to edition:

Alison Barber
Michigan State University

Walter Coleman
Florida Southern College

John Hannon
SUNY—Buffalo

Robert Figler
University of Akron

Bob Graham
Sacred Heart University

Fred Heidrich
Black Hills State University

Ken Kovach
George Mason University

Nick Mathys
DePaul University

Mark Roehling
Michigan State University

Mary Ellen Rosetti
Hudson Valley Community College

Cynthia Sutton
Indiana University—South Bend

Steve Thomas
Southwest Missouri State University

Dan Turban
University of Missouri—Columbia

Richard Arvey
University of Minnesota

Ron Beaulieu
Central Michigan University

Chris Berger
Purdue University

Sarah Bowman
Idaho State University

Charles Braun
University of Kentucky

Georgia Chao
Michigan State University

Michael Crant
University of Notre Dame

John Delery
University of Arkansas

Tom Dougherty
University of Missouri

Cynthia Fukami
University of Denver

Dan Gallagher
James Madison University

Donald G. Gardner
University of Colorado at Colorado Springs

Terri Griffith
Washington University

Bob Hatfield
Indiana University

Rob Heneman
Ohio State University

Wayne Hockwater
Florida State University

Denise Tanguay Hoyer
Eastern Michigan University

Natalie J. Hunter
Portland State University

Gwen Jones
Fairleigh Dickinson University

Marianne Koch
University of Oregon

Tom Kolenko
Kennesaw State College

Larry Mainstone
Valparaiso University

Nicholas Mathys
DePaul University

Cheri Ostroff
Teachers College Columbia University

Robert Paul
Kansas State University

Sam Rabinowitz
Rutgers University

Katherine Ready
University of Wisconsin

Mike Ritchie
University of South Carolina

Josh Schwarz
Miami University, Ohio

Christina Shalley
Georgia Tech

Richard Simpson
University of Utah

Scott Snell
Cornell University

Charles Vance
Loyola Marymount University

Raymond A. Noe
John R. Hollenbeck
Barry Gerhart
Patrick M. Wright
December 2001

A Guided Tour

The Fourth Edition of **Human Resource Management: Gaining a Competitive Advantage** was developed to teach students how to face and meet a variety of challenges within their organizations and how to gain a competitive advantage for their companies.

Throughout this text, special boxed areas focus on four distinct categories—in order to teach readers about all the aspects of human resource management. These boxes are found in every chapter and provide excellent real-business examples to underscore key concepts throughout the text.

Please take a moment to learn about this new edition and its exciting enhancements by paging through this visual guide outlining the text's new features.

NEW

"Competing in the New Economy" boxes provide examples of how companies are using HRM practices to successfully compete in the digital age. Successful companies use technology such as the Web to streamline HRM practices, bring training and performance feedback to employees' desktops, and get employees more involved in making choices about compensation and benefits; they also focus on practices that encourage employees to be innovative, creative, and satisfied. Topical coverage includes e-HRM, e-commerce, knowledge workers, off-site workers, knowledge management, and more.

COMPETING IN THE NEW ECONOMY

E-Learning Helps Build Management Talent

To succeed in the new economy, companies need to identify employees with managerial talent and help managers develop skills needed to be more effective. To attract and retain talented employees who are in short supply, companies must offer training and development opportunities on the Web to meet the needs of geographically dispersed force dealing with many demands. IBM's "Basic Bl Managers" program uses e-learning and face-to-fac classroom experiences. Th program helps managers derstand their responsibili managing performance, e ployee relations, diversity, multicultural issues. It mov the learning of all basic m agement skills to the Web using classroom experienc more complex manageme sues. It also gives manag and their bosses greater r sponsibility for developme while the company provid support in the form of unl access to development ac ties and support networks learning model includes f levels:

- Management quick views: These provide practical information on over 40 common management topics related to how to conduct business, leadership and management competencies, productivity, and HRM issues.
- Interactive learning modules and simulations: These inter-

nity. Through challenging activities and assignments managers gain increased awareness of themselves, their work teams, and IBM.

The program recognizes the roles of the boss as coach, supporter, and role model. The boss is involved in the program

382

COMPETING THROUGH GLOBALIZATION

Stock Options Heat Up in Europe

One way to recognize employees' contributions to their company is to offer them stock options, which allow them to buy shares of the firm's stock in the future at a previously set price. Although this practice has been widespread in the United States for a number of years, European businesses are now embracing the idea as a method of retaining the best employees and competing in a global marketplace. In fact, European companies that have North American operations have been feeling the greatest pressure to join the stock option club for some time. For instance, executives at the French telecommunications equipment manufacturer Alcatel SA recently realized that they needed to broaden the scope of their compensation when they began to buy North American firms like Canada's Newbridge Networks. Afraid that failing to do so would mean qualified employees would quickly leave the newly acquired firm, Alacatel announced a plan that would award options to 35 percent of its engineers and middle managers outside the United States (the rate inside the United States is 75 percent).

The major difference between the way U.S. and European firms award stock options is that the European companies usually link them to specific performance goals, such as a company's share price increase compared with its competitors'. German law actually requires this, and British firms such as Barclays are beginning to enforce stricter guidelines. Belgium and Switzerland still discourage the use of stock options through high taxes, but Italy and Norway have passed legislation and tax changes that make stock options more attractive to firms and their employees. As competition in the European market increases, experts predict that companies not offering options will have a harder time recruiting the best employees.

Back in the United States, there may be a silver lining for new employees who are now receiving their options. With the faltering stock market driving prices down, these workers are now locking in low share prices that will probably earn them handsome profits in years to come as the stock market recovers. If they and their companies perform well, everyone will win.

SOURCE: "Taxation of European Stock Options," *The European Commission* (June 26, 2001), http://europa.eu.int; D. Woodruff, "Europe, a Latecomer, Embraces Options Even as Market Swoons," *The Wall Street Journal* (May 15, 2001), www.wsj.com; "Eager Europeans Press Their Noses to the Glass," *BusinessWeek Online* (April 19, 1999), www.businessweek.com.

How Does Pay Influence Labor Force Composition?

Traditionally, using pay to recognize employee contributions has been thought of as a way to influence the behaviors and attitudes of current employees, whereas pay level and benefits have been seen as a way to influence so-called membership behaviors: decisions about whether to join or remain with the organization. However, there is increasing recognition that individual pay programs may also affect the nature and composition of an organization's workforce.[12] For example, it is possible that an organization that links pay to performance may attract more high performers than an

497

"Competing through Globalization" boxes examine the effective HRM practices that U.S. businesses have used to deal with global threats and create global successes.

"Competing by Meeting Stakeholders' Needs" boxes discuss the continuous challenges that companies face of how to reach their financial objectives and meet the needs of multiple stakeholders, including shareholders, employees, and the community.

COMPETING BY MEETING STAKEHOLDERS' NEEDS

Has Downsizing Become a Way of Life?

One would have great difficulty ignoring the massive "war for talent" that went on during the late 1990s, particularly with the notable dot-com craze. Firms during this time sought to become "employers of choice," to establish "employment brands," and to develop "employee value propositions" as ways to ensure that they would be able to attract and retain talented employees. However, what few probably noticed was that in spite of the hiring craze, this was also a time of massive layoffs. In fact, 1998, the height of the war for talent, also saw the largest number of layoffs in the decade.

This new trend seems to represent a "churn" of employees, in which firms lay off those with outdated skills or cut whole businesses that are in declining markets while simultaneously building businesses and employee bases in newer, high-growth markets. For example, IBM cut 69,256 people and increased its workforce by 16,000 in 1996.

The important question facing firms is, How can we develop a reputation as an employer of choice, and engage employees to the goals of the firm, while constantly laying off a significant portion of our workforce? How firms answer this question will determine how they can compete by meeting the stakeholder needs of their employees.

SOURCE: J. Laabs, "Has Downsizing Missed Its Mark?" *Workforce*, April, 1999, pp. 31–38.

Number of layoffs during the 1990s

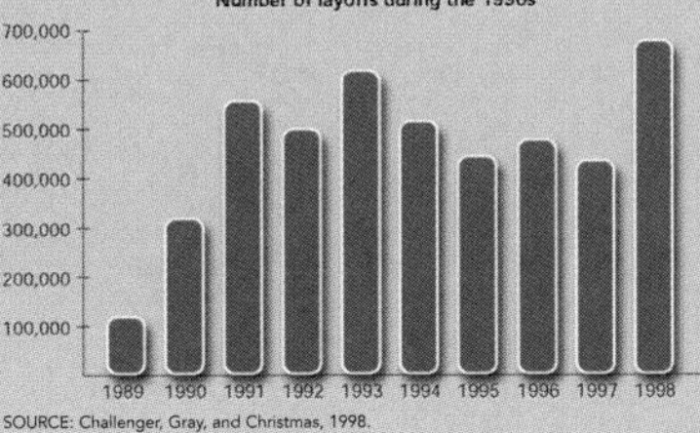

SOURCE: Challenger, Gray, and Christmas, 1998.

people while churning employees in response to changing skill requirements demanded by the dynamic competitive environment.

Research has indicated that few companies have fully integrated HRM into the strategy formulation process.[22] As we've mentioned before, companies are beginning

64

"Competing through High-Performance Work Systems" boxes give examples of companies that developed new technologies and efficient work structures and policies that made them more competitive.

COMPETING THROUGH HIGH-PERFORMANCE WORK SYSTEMS

Team-Based Job Redesign and Error Prevention

When Reggie Peterson showed up at the emergency department of his local university medical center, he was displaying flulike symptoms. He was tested and examined first by a nurse, who suspected he had meningitis, an inflammation of the brain. A doctor who subsequently examined him diagnosed the problem as simple flu and sent him home, recommending rest and plenty of fluids. Six hours later, Peterson died of spinal meningitis. Unfortunately, the nurse who suspected meningitis was not working alongside the doctor, and because she was earlier chastised by this same doctor for not "sticking to nursing" she never shared her opinions with him.

According to a recent study by the Institute of Medicine, an arm of the National Academy of Sciences, this type of medical error occurs all too frequently in today's hospitals and medical centers. Our widely distributed, fragmented health care system, along with secretive and unpublicized errors, makes it hard for the general public to appreciate the problem. However, if all the errors in U.S. hospitals were aggregated daily, the Institute of Medicine likened the situation to that of a 747 airplane crashing *every single day.*

One solution to this problem offered by the National Academy of Sciences was to organize work around teams, as opposed to individual doctors and nurses. For example, Suburban Hospital in Bethesda, Maryland, has adopted a team-based approach in its Intensive Care Unit (ICU). Each team includes an ICU specialist, a pharmacist, a nutritionist, a social worker, a nurse, a respiratory specialist, and a chaplain who go room-to-room each morning, visiting every patient—sometimes accompanied by a family member. The team meets with each patient's bedside nurse to discuss and debate the best action for this patient from all possible angles.

This focus on teamwork has a long tradition in other high-pressure work contexts such as aviation and the military, and it is increasingly being adopted in many businesses and industries. Indeed, enhanced communication technologies such as e-mail, teleconferencing, and videoconferencing have allowed the creation of "virtual teams" that work together despite being separated in space and time. The use of these technologies eliminates the need for travel and truly allows organizations to put together the best teams possible, free of traditional constraints.

At Suburban Hospital, this team-based approach is credited with reducing errors, shortening the time patients spend in the small (12-bed) ICU unit, and improving the communication between patients, their families, and the medical staff. It also has reduced the time patients spend on ventilators by 25 percent, which is critical because the use of ventilators increases the chances of pneumonia, which, in turn, greatly increases both costs and the chance of patients dying. Indeed, the cost savings from avoiding complications more than offsets the increased expense associated with team formation, and this does not even calculate the reduced amount of human suffering. As Dr. Joseph Fontan, an ICU specialist at Suburban, notes, "It's good to have people with different backgrounds and opinions looking at the same problem—it makes a huge difference because small problems that can turn into big ones are headed off early."

Source: J. Appleby and R. Davis, "Teamwork Used to Be a Money Saver; Now It's a Lifesaver," *USA Today* (March 1, 2001), pp. B1–B2; L. Kohn, J. Corrigan, and M. Donaldson, *To Err Is Human: Building a Safer Health System* (Washington, DC: National Academy Press, 2001); C. M. Solomon, "Managing Virtual Teams," *Workforce* (June 2001), pp. 61–65.

143

Objectives

After reading this chapter, you should be able to:

1. Discuss how to align a company's strategic direction with its human resource planning.
2. Determine the labor demand for workers in various job categories.
3. Discuss the advantages and disadvantages of various ways of eliminating a labor surplus and avoiding a labor shortage.
4. Describe the various recruitment policies organizations adopt to make job vacancies more attractive.
5. List the various sources from which job applicants can be drawn, their relative advantages and disadvantages, and the methods for evaluating them.
6. Explain the recruiter's role in the recruitment process, the limits the recruiter faces, and the opportunities available.

While most other airlines were laying off employees in the fall of 2001, Southwest Airlines was able to avoid any layoffs. Other cuts needed to be made, but the employees remained at the forefront of their company. What advantages and disadvantages may occur because of these decisions?

Enter the World of Business

Southwest Airlines: Focused on Take-Offs, Not Layoffs

In the summer of 2001, the airline industry was facing severe problems due to slumping business travel and vacationer demand. In fact, Northwest Airlines announced draconian cuts in both schedules and service; Midway Airlines declared bankruptcy in August of that year, citing "calamitous" decline in air traffic. However, as bad as things were, they soon got worse.

The September 11, 2001, terrorist attacks on New York and Washington, D.C., devastated the whole nation, but few segments of the economy felt the impact as dramatically as the already struggling airline industry. Even after reducing scheduled flights by more than 20 percent, most planes were taking off with fewer than half their seats filled, and airline shares lost a third of their value on the stock exchange. Most airlines needed to cut costs drastically in order to make ends meet, and over 100,000 employees were eventually laid off from American Airlines, United Airlines, US Airways, Continental Airlines, and America West.

Southwest Airlines bucked this trend, however. Indeed, despite the regular ups and downs of the airline industry, in its 30 years of operation, Southwest has never laid off employees; remarkably, it was able to maintain this record even during the difficult Fall 2001 period. Southwest's no-layoff policy is one of the core values that underlie its human resource strategy, and insiders stress that it is one of the main reasons why the Southwest workforce is so fiercely loyal, productive, and flexible.

The high productivity of these workers helps keep labor costs low, and these savings are passed on to consumers in the form of lower prices that are sometimes half those offered by competitors. High levels of job security also promote a willingness on the part of Southwest employees to be innovative on the job without fearing that they will be punished for any mistakes. Southwest also finds that satisfied employees help create satisfied customers and can even help in recruiting new employees when economic conditions are conducive to growth.

In order to keep this perfect no-layoff record in 2001, Southwest executives assembled into an emergency command and control center in Dallas and brain-

Learning objectives at the beginning of each chapter inform students about the key concepts they should understand after reading through the chapter.

The **chapter-opening vignettes** present a real business problem or issue that provides background for the issues discussed in the chapter.

NEW

"Finding and Keeping the Best Employees" information appears throughout the text, showing the various strategies through which companies hire and retain talent.

provide vouchers or discounts for employees to use at existing child care facilities (5 percent of companies). At the highest level, firms provide child care at or near their worksites (9 percent of companies). Toyota's Child Development Program provides 24-hours-a-day care for children of workers at its Georgetown, Kentucky, plant. This facility is designed to meet the needs of employees working evening and night shifts who want their children to be on the same schedule. In this facility, the children are kept awake all night. At the end of the night shift, the parents pick up their children and the whole family goes home to bed.[39]

An organization's decision to staff its own child care facility should not be taken lightly. It is typically a costly venture with important liability concerns. Moreover, the results, in terms of reducing absenteeism and enhancing productivity, are often mixed. One reason for this is that many organizations are "jumping on the day care bandwagon" without giving much thought to the best form of assistance for their specific employees.[40] Organizations that fail to do an adequate needs assessment often wind up purchasing the wrong alternative. For example, one *Fortune* 500 company found that less than 2 percent of its workforce used a flexible spending account that had been adopted as the chief company policy on child care. The waste and inefficiency of this practice could have been avoided had a more thorough needs analysis been conducted before the program was implemented.[41]

As an alternative example, Memphis-based First Tennessee Bank, which was losing 1,500 days of productivity a year because of child care problems, considered creating its own on-site day care center. Before acting, however, the company surveyed its employees. This survey indicated that the only real problem with day care occurred when the parents' regular day care provisions fell through because of sickness on the part of the child or provider. Based on these findings, the bank opted to establish a sick-child care center, which was less costly and smaller in scope than a full-time center and yet still solved the employees' major problem. As a result, absenteeism dropped so dramatically that the program paid for itself in the first nine months of operation.[42]

Finding and Keeping the Best Employees

PriceWaterhouseCoopers (PWC), the accounting and consulting firm, has seen many of its clients turn to cost cutting as the economy slows. That, in turn, has led PWC to examine its own expenses, including those in the area of employee benefits. But that overhaul has not touched one key benefit: flexible work arrangements. Employees are still free to leave work early or to telecommute to help them balance work and nonwork responsibilities. Even as employers slash jobs and cut small perquisites such as free food and drinks, they continue to provide programs that help employees juggle work and personal lives—mostly because they believe these programs help retain valued workers, who are being asked to do more as workforce reductions eliminate positions but not necessarily work. At Cisco Systems, which has also faced difficult financial times, telecommuting continues to be a core benefit, and its day care center at company headquarters in San Jose, California, continues to operate at capacity. Cisco feels that these benefits enhance productivity, which is all the more important given difficult times. These companies are looking ahead to a future that will once again bring growth; they want to be ready by retaining a group of dedicated and productive employees to take advantage of that opportunity when it comes.

SOURCE: "Benefits and the Bottom Line," *The News and Observer*, Raleigh, NC (October 14, 2001).

CHAPTER 5 Human Resource Planning and Recruitment **209**

characteristics of the job will "inoculate" them to such characteristics seems unwarranted, based on the research conducted to date.[91] Thus we return to the conclusion that an organization's decisions about personnel policies that directly affect the job's attributes (pay, security, advancement opportunities, and so on) will probably be more important than recruiter traits and behaviors in affecting job choice.

Enhancing Recruiter Impact. Although research suggests that recruiters do not have much influence on job choice, this does not mean recruiters cannot have an impact. Most recruiters receive little training.[92] Recent research has attempted to find conditions in which recruiters do make a difference. Based on this research, an organization can take several steps to increase the impact that recruiters have on those they recruit.

First, recruiters can provide timely feedback. Applicants react very negatively to delays in feedback, often making unwarranted attributions for the delays (such as, the organization is uninterested in my application). Second, recruiters need to avoid behaviors that might convey the wrong organizational impression.[93] Table 5.5 lists quotes from applicants who felt that they had had extremely bad experiences with recruiters. Third, recruiting can be done in teams rather than by individuals. As we have seen, applicants tend to view line personnel (job incumbents and supervisors) as more credible than personnel specialists, so these kinds of recruiters should be part of any team. On the other hand, personnel specialists have knowledge that is not shared by line personnel (who may perceive recruiting as a small part of their "real" jobs), so they should be included as well.

A Look Back

The chapter opener showed how Southwest Airlines steadfastly refused to lay off workers, despite the pressure applied by the external environment. This one instance of behavior, however, was simply an extension of a long-term culture that used methods other than layoffs as a means of managing a labor surplus.

Questions

1. Based on this chapter, what steps can other firms that want to emulate Southwest take in order to avoid layoffs? That is, what are some alternatives to lay offs for avoiding a labor surplus?
2. How does the way a firm reacts to a labor shortage affect its ability to successfully manage a labor surplus?

Summary

Human resource planning uses labor supply and demand forecasts to anticipate labor shortages and surpluses. It also entails programs that can be utilized to reduce a labor surplus (such as downsizing and early retirement programs) and eliminate a labor shortage (like bringing in temporary workers or expanding overtime). When done well, human resource planning can enhance the success of the organization while minimizing the human suffering resulting from poorly anticipated labor surpluses or shortages. Human resource recruiting is a buffer activity that creates an applicant pool that the organization can draw from in the event of a labor shortage that is to be filled with new hires. Organizational recruitment programs affect applications through personnel policies (such as promote-from-within policies or due process provisions) that affect the attributes of the vacancies themselves. They can also

CHAPTER 3 The Legal Environment: Equal Employment Opportunity and Safety **105**

employees perceive the company's affirmative action policies. If the OFCCP finds that the contractors or subcontractors are not complying with the executive order, then its representatives may notify the EEOC (if there is evidence that Title VII has been violated), advise the Department of Justice to institute criminal proceedings, request that the Secretary of Labor cancel or suspend any current contracts, and forbid the firm from bidding on future contracts. This last penalty, called *debarment*, is the OFCCP's most potent weapon.

Having discussed the major laws defining equal employment opportunity and the agencies that enforce these laws, we now address the various types of discrimination and the ways these forms of discrimination have been interpreted by the courts in a number of cases.

Types of Discrimination

How would you know if you had been discriminated against? Assume that you have applied for a job and were not hired. How do you know if the organization decided not to hire you because you are unqualified, because you are less qualified than the individual ultimately hired, or simply because the person in charge of the hiring decision "didn't like your type"? Discrimination is a multifaceted issue. It is often not easy to determine the extent to which unfair discrimination affects an employer's decisions.

Legal scholars have identified three theories of discrimination: disparate treatment, disparate impact, and reasonable accommodation. In addition, there is protection for those participating in discrimination cases or opposing discriminatory actions. In the act, these theories are stated in very general terms. However, the court system has defined and delineated these theories through the cases brought before it. A comparison of the theories of discrimination is given in Table 3.3.

Disparate Treatment

Disparate treatment exists when individuals in similar situations are treated differently and the different treatment is based on the individual's race, color, religion, sex, national origin, age, or disability status. If two people with the same qualifications apply for a job and the employer decides whom to hire based on one individual's race, the individual not hired is a victim of disparate treatment. In the disparate treatment case the plaintiff must prove that there was a discriminatory motive—that is, that the employer *intended* to discriminate.

Disparate treatment
A theory of discrimination based on different treatments given to individuals because of their race, color, religion, sex, national origin, age, or disability status.

Whenever individuals are treated differently because of their race, sex, or the like, there is disparate treatment. For example, if a company fails to hire women with school-age children (claiming the women will be frequently absent) but hires men with school-age children, the applicants are being treated differently based on sex. Another example would be an employer who checks the references and investigates the conviction records of minority applicants but does not do so for white applicants. Why are managers advised not to ask about marital status? Because in most cases, a manager will either ask only the female applicants or, if the manager asks both males and females, he or she will make different assumptions about females (such as "She will have to move if her husband gets a job elsewhere") and males (such as "He's very stable"). In all these examples, notice that (1) people are being treated differently and (2) there is an actual intent to treat them differently.[16]

NEW

A new end-of-chapter segment, **"A Look Back,"** encourages students to recall the chapter's opening vignette and apply it to what they have just learned.

CHAPTER 2 Strategic Human Resource Management **83**

way with both the flight attendants and the mechanics. In addition, labor costs have been driven up as a result of the union activity. The pilots signed a lucrative five-year contract that will place them at the highest pay in the industry. In an effort to head off the organizing drive, the mechanics were recently given raises to similarly put them at the industry top. Now the flight attendants are seeking industry-leading pay irrespective of but certainly encouraged by the union drive.[70]

The Delta Air Lines story provides a perfect example of the perils that can await firms that fail to adequately address human resource issues in the formulation and implementation of strategy.

Questions

1. How does the experience of Delta Air Lines illustrate the interdependence between strategic decisions of "how to compete" and "with what to compete?" Consider this with regard to both strategy formulation and strategy implementation.
2. If you were in charge of HRM for Delta Air Lines now, given the issues described in the "A Look Back" section, what would be your major priorities? How would you approach and solve these issues?

NEW

Key terms are highlighted and defined in the margin in order to help students learn the language of HRM.

Summary

A strategic approach to human resource management seeks to proactively provide a competitive advantage through the company's most important asset: its human resources. The HRM function needs to be integrally involved in the formulation of strategy to identify the people-related business issues the company faces. Once the strategy has been determined, HRM has a profound impact on the implementation of the plan by developing and aligning HRM practices that ensure that the company has motivated employees with the necessary skills. Finally, the emerging strategic role of the HRM function requires that HR professionals in the future develop business, professional–technical, change management, and integration competencies. As you will see more clearly in later chapters, this strategic approach requires more than simply developing a valid selection procedure or state-of-the-art performance management systems. Only through these competencies can the HR professional take a strategic approach to human resource management.

Discussion Questions

1. Pick one of your university's major sports teams (like football or basketball). How would you characterize that team's generic strategy? How does the composition of the team members (in terms of size, speed, ability, and so on) relate to that strategy? What are the strengths and weaknesses of the team? How do those dictate the team's generic strategy and its approach to a particular game?
2. Do you think that it is easier to tie human resources to the strategic management process in large or in small organizations? Why?
3. Consider one of the organizations you have been affiliated with. What are some examples of human resource practices that were consistent with that organization's strategy? What are examples of practices that were inconsistent with its strategy?
4. How can strategic management within the HRM department ensure that HRM plays an effective role in the company's strategic management process?
5. What types of specific skills (such as knowledge of financial accounting methods) do you think HR professionals will need to have the business, professional–technical, change management, and integrative competencies necessary in the future? Where can you develop each of these skills?
6. What are some of the key environmental variables that you see changing in the business world today? What impact will those changes have on the HRM function in organizations?

Discussion questions at the end of each chapter help students learn the concepts presented in the chapter and understand potential applications of the chapter material.

CHAPTER 1 Human Resource Management: Gaining a Competitive Advantage **45**

contributes most to helping a company gain a competitive advantage? Which area do you believe contributes the least? Why?

4. What is the balanced scorecard? Identify the four perspectives included in the balanced scorecard. How can HRM practices influence the four perspectives?
5. Is HRM becoming more strategic? Explain your answer.
6. Explain the implications of each of the following labor force trends for HRM: (1) aging workforce, (2) diverse workforce, (3) skill deficiencies.
7. What role do HRM practices play in a business decision to expand internationally?
8. Is business emphasis on quality a fad? Why or why not? What might a quality goal and high-performance work systems have in common in terms of HRM practices?
9. What disadvantages might result from outsourcing HRM practices? From employee self-service? From increased line manager involvement in designing and using HR practices?

Web Exercise

In this chapter we discuss four competitive challenges that companies face (the new economy, global competition, managing stakeholders, and high-performance work systems). Go to the Society for Human Resource Management (SHRM) home page on the Web. SHRM is an important professional society for human resource management. The address is **www.shrm.org**. Here you will find current articles related to HRM issues. SHRM also publishes *HR Magazine*, a business magazine for human resource managers.

Questions

1. How are companies dealing with the competitive challenges? Use Web resources to find an article that relates to how a company is dealing with the competitive challenges. Go to "HR Channels." Click on any of the HR practices listed to find an article.
2. Summarize the main topic of the article.
3. Identify how it relates to one of the competitive challenges discussed in the chapter.

Managing People: From the Pages of *BusinessWeek*

BusinessWeek The Human Factor

Julie Jones jumped at the chance to take a sabbatical when Accenture Ltd. (ACN) offered one in June. Although she had been a consultant in the firm's Chicago office for just two and a half years, the 25-year-old expert in accounts payable software had long wanted to work for AmeriCorps, the national volunteer group. So in July, Jones, who's single, headed out to Los Angeles for a year to join an AmeriCorps group that helps nonprofits with technology problems. Accenture, the former consulting arm of Andersen Worldwide, will pay 20 percent of her salary, plus benefits, and let her keep her work phone number, laptop, and e-mail. "This gives me the security of knowing I'll have a job when I come back," says Jones.

Accenture hopes the program will offer it some security, too. The economic slowdown has pinched the company's business, forcing it to rein in costs. But after years of scrambling to find scarce talent, Accenture is reluctant to lay off workers it hopes to need when the economy turns north again. Accenture did cut 600 support staff jobs in June. But to retain skilled employees, it cooked up the idea of partially paid sabbaticals, such as the one Jones is taking. About 1,000 employees took up the offer, which allows them to do whatever they want for 6 to 12 months, says Larry Solomon, Accenture's managing partner in charge of internal operations. "This is a way to cut costs that gives us the ability to hang onto people we spent so much time recruiting and training," he says.

Plenty of other employers are feeling the same way. The slumping economy has put pressure on companies to slash expenses and boost sagging profits. But the United States has just sailed through five years of labor shortfalls on a scale not seen in more than three decades. What's more, the unemployment rate, while rising, remains at historically low levels. Many employers are wary about dumping too many workers just to find themselves scrambling later to refill the positions.

Even companies that have handed out pink slips often did so with caution rather than abandon. When Charles Schwab Corp. (SCH) first saw business deteriorate last fall, it put projects on hold and cut back on such expenses as travel and entertainment to avoid layoffs, says human resources vice president Ruth K. Ross. In December, as it became clear that more was needed, top executives all took pay cuts: 50 percent for the company's two co-CEOs, 20 percent for executive vice presidents, 10 percent for senior vice presidents, and 5 percent for vice presidents.

Schwab took further steps this year before finally cutting staff. It encouraged employees to take unused vaca-

CHAPTER 13 Employee Benefits **559**

Discussion Questions

1. The opening vignette described how relationships between employers and employees are changing. What are the likely consequences of this change? Where does the social responsibility of employers end, and where does the need to operate more efficiently begin?
2. Your company, like many others, is experiencing double-digit percentage increases in health care costs. What suggestions can you offer that may reduce the rate of cost increases?
3. Why is communication so important in the employee benefits area? What sorts of programs can a company use to communicate more effectively? What are the potential positive consequences of more effective benefits communication?
4. What are the potential advantages of flexible benefits and flexible spending accounts? Are there any potential drawbacks?
5. Although benefits account for a large share of employee compensation, many feel there is little evidence on whether an employer receives an adequate return on the benefits investment. One suggestion has been to link benefits to individual, group, or organization performance. Explain why you would or would not recommend this strategy to an organization.

Web Exercise

The Health Insurance Portability and Accountability Act (HIPAA) of 1996 is a major health care reform mandate that sets minimum standards to improve the access, portability, and renewability of health insurance coverage. Visit **www.hcfa.gov** (the Web site for HIPAA), which answers some commonly asked questions for small employers about the provisions of HIPAA. Click on HIPAA, then Employers.

Questions

1. What does *portability* mean?
2. What is a preexisting condition? How does HIPAA affect how businesses can apply preexisting condition exclusions to employees?
3. How does HIPAA benefit small employers?

Managing People: From the Pages of *BusinessWeek*

BusinessWeek Dr. Goodnight's Company Town

The war for talent has businesses transforming their corporate campuses into country clubs—offering everything from five-star lunches to concierges willing to arrange employee lawn mowing and haircuts. But long before the words "labor crunch" put employee perks in vogue, SAS Institute Inc. founder James Goodnight was lavishing money on programmers instead of headhunters. It worked: SAS turnover is 4 percent in an industry for which 20 percent is typical. The Cary (North Carolina)-based company may compete against PeopleSoft Inc. and Oracle Corp., but SAS employees aren't asked to mimic their Silicon Valley brethren's sleep-starved lifestyle. Goodnight, a shy billionaire who until recently drove a Buick Roadmaster wagon, believes in leaving the office at 5 P.M. sharp. Dinner, he says, should be spent with your family, not at your desk.

THE PERK FACTORY. Goodnight remembers working as a programmer for NASA—a place so cheap it wouldn't even spring for workers' sodas. Insulted, he vowed to do things differently. Today he's become a Willy Wonka to his workers, creating a corporate perk factory where even the plain and peanut-filled M&M's, replenished like clockwork every Wednesday, are free. Goodnight believes that if you treat people as if they make a difference, they will. The turnover savings he reaps from his largesse are huge: an estimated $75 million a year. This means Goodnight can afford all those banana trees and cracker-and-cheese–stocked snack rooms. It may be too Stepford-like for cynics, but the T-shirt- and Teva-sporting SAS employees say they wouldn't have it any other way.

On-site benefits at the Institute include day care, Montessori school, the Atrium, and lunchtime entertainment. For $25 a month, the center will take babies after SAS's six-week paid maternity leave. Sixty percent of the employees use the on-site day care; parents can visit or pick up their kids for lunch. Employees also get private offices and open spaces for impromptu meetings and breaks.

The perks aren't limited to the on-site stuff. Goodnight offers discounts on everything from land in his ritzy subdivision to memberships at his country club. Employees make only industry-average salaries, but they get a generous year-end bonus, profit sharing, and an extra week of paid vacation at Christmas. Employees can also enjoy

End-of-chapter **Internet exercises** require students to use their Web skills to further understand the value of the Internet for managing human resources, and as a professional resource.

BusinessWeek **cases** look at incidents and real companies as reported by the nation's number one business weekly, and encourage students to critically evaluate each problem and apply the chapter concepts.

End-of-part **video cases** and accompanying questions challenge students to view HRM issues and problems from multiple perspectives.

VIDEO CASE

Developing a Diverse Workforce

Most jobs start with an interview, whether it's conducted in person, by phone, or even online. Interpersonal dynamics can affect those interviews, so a human resource manager who is looking to develop a diverse workforce to meet company needs must be able to ask the right questions of a candidate and listen to the answers in an objective, controlled manner. The ultimate goal is to evaluate the candidate fairly and accurately so that he or she fits well with job requirements. As you'll see in the video, two managers for the Beck 'n' Call company are interviewing two job applicants, and how they conduct the interviews and evaluate the applicants will affect both the organization and the individuals—in the composition of the company's workforce and the way those employees later develop in their positions. Both racial and gender issues enter into play in this scenario.

The U.S. workforce is becoming increasingly diverse. Experts estimate that by 2006 the American workforce will be 72 percent Caucasian, 11 percent African American, 12 percent Hispanic, and 5 percent Asian and other ethnic or cultural groups. Companies that want to grow and remain competitive need to utilize the talents, experience, and knowledge of workers from different backgrounds and cultures. If they do not, they may miss a golden opportunity to reach a larger customer base. The customer base for Beck 'n' Call is growing more and more diverse, with African American and Hispanic communities increasing in population where Beck 'n' Call is located. So it makes sense to recruit, develop, and retain employees who can relate to this broadening customer base and meet their needs in specific ways.

Managers at all companies, whether product or service oriented, can reap the rewards of diversity for their organizations if they practice *ethnorelativism*—the belief that groups and subcultures are inherently equal. The first step toward this belief may be consciously recognizing their own tendencies toward *ethnocentrism*—the belief that their own cultures are superior. Once a person recognizes and acknowledges his or her own attitudes and stereotypical beliefs, he or she can open up to new ideas and begin to change. For instance, conducting a structured employment interview with questions that are standardized and focused on accomplishing defined goals will help promote ethnorelativism as opposed to ethnocentrism. In addition, the interview should contain questions that allow the job applicant to respond and demonstrate his or her competencies in ways that are job related, not personal. Hunches and gut feelings should play a tiny part in such an interview, because once a job applicant becomes an employee, it's the concrete evidence of performance that counts, not whether the interviewer and employer went to the same college or like the same sports teams.

After employees are hired, it is important to give them opportunities to develop their skills and advance. This practice not only enhances the employee–employer relationship but also boosts overall productivity of the company. Managers must also be aware of the possibility of a "glass ceiling," an invisible barrier that separates female employees or those of different cultural or ethnic backgrounds from top levels of the organization. One way to guard against barriers to advancement is to examine workforce composition and statistics. Do certain groups of employees top out at middle management positions? Is there a cluster of women and minorities near the bottom of the employment ladder? Is upper management made up entirely of Caucasian males? If so, why? Do all employees receive equal training and opportunities for advancement, or do some receive preferential treatment, even if it isn't obvious? Some studies indicate that companies may also have "glass walls," which are invisible barriers to important lateral moves within the company. These barriers are just as important as the glass ceiling because a glass wall can prevent an employee from receiving training or experience in certain areas that would enable him or her to move up eventually. Studies confirm the existence of the glass ceiling and glass walls; one showed recently that 97 percent of the top U.S. managers are Caucasian and 95 percent of them are male. Limiting career advancement for certain groups undermines morale at a

455

Supplements for Students and Instructors

Instructor's Manual/Transparency Masters
(0072470070)

The Instructor's Manual contains a lecture outline and notes, answers to the discussion questions, additional questions and exercises, teaching suggestions, paper and project topics, video case notes and answers, and answers to the end-of-chapter case questions. Transparency masters are also included in the IM. Amit Shah of Frostburg State University wrote the 4th edition Instructor's Manual and revised the transparency masters.

Test Bank
(0072470062)

The print test bank has been revised and updated to reflect the content of the 4th edition of the book. Each chapter includes multiple choice, true/false, and essay questions. Fred Heidrich of Black Hills State University authored the 4th edition Test Bank.

Instructor Presentation CD-ROM
(007247002x)

This multimedia CD-ROM allows instructors to create dynamic classroom presentations by incorporating PowerPoint, videos, and every available print supplement.

Brownstone's Diploma for Windows
(0072469994)

This test generator allows instructors to add and edit questions, create new versions of the test, and more.

Videos
(0072469986)

Five new videos on HRM issues accompany this edition. The accompanying video cases are included in the text at the end of each part.

PowerPoint
(0072469978)

This presentation program features 10-20 slides for each chapter, which are also found on the Instructor CD-ROM. Amit Shah of Frostburg State University revised the PowerPoint presentation.

Online Learning Center
(www.mhhe.com/noe4e)

This text-specific website follows the text chapter by chapter. OLC content is ancillary and supplementary germane to the textbook; as students read the book, they can go online to take self-grading quizzes, review material, or work through interactive exercises. OLCs can be delivered multiple ways—professors and students can access them directly through the textbook website, through PageOut, or within a course management system (i.e., WebCT, Blackboard, TopClass, or eCollege).

Student CD-ROM
(0072533056)

This NEW CD-ROM contains chapter review questions, self-assessment exercises, flashcards to review key terms, and a link to Human Resources Online. Students will stay current and expand their knowledge in the field of human resources by completing approximately 20 online exercises in such areas as training and employee development, selection and recruitment, compensation and benefits, labor relations, employee separation and retention, as well as training and employee development. In each exercise, students will review one or more online resources, such as articles covering a recent HRM trend. They will then answer some challenging questions. For the busy instructor, Human Resources Online includes password-protected teaching notes that provide insights and answers to each question.

PowerWeb

Harness the assets of the Web to keep your course current with PowerWeb! This online resource provides high quality, peer-reviewed content including up-to-date articles from leading periodicals and journals, current news, weekly updates with assessment, interactive exercises, Web research guide, study tips, and much more! Visit www.dushkin.com/powerweb or access through the OLC at www.mhhe.com/noe4e.

Brief Contents

Contents

1 Chapter

Human Resource Management: Gaining a Competitive Advantage

Objectives
After reading this chapter, you should be able to:

1. Discuss the roles and activities of a company's human resource management function.
2. Discuss the implications of the new economy and e-business for human resource management.
3. Discuss how human resource management affects a company's balanced scorecard.
4. Discuss what companies should do to compete in the global marketplace.
5. Identify the characteristics of the workforce and how they influence human resource management.
6. Discuss human resource management practices that support high-performance work systems.
7. Provide a brief description of human resource management practices.

At The Container Store, the focus is on keeping employees loyal, motivated, trained, and compensated well. In turn, there is a very low turnover rate and a high rate of customer satisfaction.

Enter the World of Business

Kodak and The Container Store: Human Resource Management Excellence Takes Different Forms

The management of human resources is critical to company success. But the way that human resources are managed takes many different forms. Eastman Kodak, based in Rochester, New York, is prepared to expand its market share of the imaging industry by helping consumers and commercial customers use computerized formats for displaying pictures. Although the snapshots taken to record birthdays, anniversaries, graduations, and important family events remain the core of Kodak's business, the company has expanded into other markets for its imaging products, including X rays, microfilm, satellite photography, and large film format for the motion picture industry. Kodak has 80,650 employees worldwide with just over half in U.S. locations. Kodak's defined HRM staff includes a director of human resources for the consumer division, HRM directors of five geographic regions, and four office staff. They are currently working with managers on three HRM challenges: building employee confidence in the future following a period of layoffs, effectively competing for talent, and understanding the implications of e-business in Kodak's traditional culture. Kodak was forced to abandon its policy of lifetime employment in the early 1990s with workforce downsizing. Today few Kodak employees are under 30, and a large proportion are nearing retirement age. Kodak's worldwide operations are key to its future success. The company is trying to move from a culture of producing what it could invent to a culture of inventing products that consumers are demanding. Consistency and continuity ensure that everyone is working toward the same goals. Given the worldwide demand for talent, human resource managers at Kodak have had to strive for work schedules, dress codes, and a work atmosphere that create the kind of place talented workers will choose.

The Container Store, a retailer of boxes, bags, racks, and shelves that organize everything from shoes to spices, has become respected for its commitment to employees and has gained many rewards for its HRM leadership. The Dallas-based company has 2,000 employees in 11 states.

The store interiors have an open layout, which is divided into sections marked with brightly colored banners such as Closet, Kitchen, Office, and Laundry. Wherever you look in the store, someone in a blue apron is ready to help solve the tiniest of storage problems to the most intimidating organizational challenges. The company has been ranked as the best U.S. organization to work for by *Fortune* and has received other awards for its outstanding people management strategies (such as *The Workforce* magazine Optimas Award in 2001).

The company attributes its success to a 15–20 percent turnover rate in an industry where 100 percent turnover is common. The Container Store culture is directly responsible for the low turnover rate and employees providing high levels of customer service. The company's few uncomplicated guidelines, such as always being flexible, are based on a set of humanistic philosophies that emphasize treating others as you want to be treated. A strong customer service philosophy allows employees to take ownership of the company and make decisions they believe will benefit customers. The company treats employees with respect, and in turn employees enthusiastically serve customers. Employees' ability to create a customized organizational product solution for each customer is the key to increased sales.

The Container Store does not have a large HRM department. In fact, until recently HRM was viewed as working against the company culture. According to Elizabeth Barrett, vice president of operations, the company has always trusted supervisors to attract, motivate, and retain employees. Managers are responsible for many traditional HRM tasks because they are closest to employees. The Container Store believes that people have to fit into the company's culture to succeed. The company has a focused people strategy: hire for fit, train comprehensively, and pay and support for long tenure. Forty-one percent of new employees are recommended by current employees. Many new employees are the company's customers, are usually college educated, and want their quality of life at work to reflect their lifestyle, beliefs, and values. The company invests more than 235 hours of training in first-year employees, well above the industry average of 7 hours per year. After their first year, employees receive an average of 160 hours of training each year. The company spends considerable time measuring the direct impact of training on store sales. Most retailers focus primarily on merchandise. The Container Store managers believe that loyal employees will pay off handsomely with increased sales and customer service. So they pay store employees 50 to 100 percent above the industry average, share financial information with everyone, and offer benefits to both full- and part-time employees.

The company now has a semiformal HRM structure with recruiting, training, payroll, and benefits departments. HR managers are also given responsibility for other areas of the company, such as store operations, and are required to take store-level positions so they can better understand the company's purpose—to serve customers. Most HRM employees start out as salespeople so they will understand more about serving customer needs. Despite the new HRM structure, managers take the lead in recruiting and evaluating potential employees as well as in the extensive employee training. The company has seen its human resource strategy pay off. The Container Store is continuing to expand strategically from coast to coast and beyond, and the company grows at an average annual rate of 20–25 percent. In 2001 sales were expected to reach $262 million.

SOURCE: Based on R. Laglow, "Container Store Does Great HRM—Even Without an HR Department," *HR Executive*, August 2001, p. 23; J. Labbs, "Thinking outside the Box at The Container Store," *Workforce*, March 2001, pp. 34–38; C. Cole, "Kodak Snapshops," *Workforce*, June 2000, pp. 64–72; Visit The Container Store's website at **www.containerstore.com**.

Introduction

Both Kodak and The Container Store illustrate the key role that human resource management (HRM) plays in determining the effectiveness and competitiveness of U.S. businesses. **Competitiveness** refers to a company's ability to maintain and gain market share in its industry. Both Kodak's and The Container Store's human resource management practices have helped the companies provide services the customer values. The value of a product or service is determined by its quality and how closely the product fits customer needs.

Competitiveness
A company's ability to maintain and gain market share in its industry.

Competitiveness is related to company effectiveness, which is determined by whether the company satisfies the needs of stakeholders (groups affected by business practices). Important stakeholders include stockholders, who want a return on their investment; customers, who want a high-quality product or service; and employees, who desire interesting work and reasonable compensation for their services. The community, which wants the company to contribute to activities and projects and minimize pollution of the environment, is also an important stakeholder. Companies that do not meet stakeholders' needs are unlikely to have a competitive advantage over other firms in their industry.

Human resource management (HRM) refers to the policies, practices, and systems that influence employees' behavior, attitudes, and performance. Many companies refer to HRM as involving "people practices." Figure 1.1 emphasizes that there are several important HRM practices. The strategy underlying these practices needs to be considered to maximize their influence on company performance. As the figure shows, HRM practices include analyzing and designing work, determining human resource needs (HR planning), attracting potential employees (recruiting), choosing employees (selection), teaching employees how to perform their jobs and preparing them for the future (training and development), rewarding employees (compensation), evaluating their performance (performance management), and creating a positive work environment (employee relations). The HRM practices discussed in this chapter's opening highlighted how effective HRM practices support business goals and objectives. That is, effective HRM practices are strategic! Effective HRM has been shown to enhance company performance by contributing to employee and customer satisfaction, innovation, productivity, and development of a favorable

Human resource management (HRM)
Policies, practices, and systems that influence employees' behavior, attitudes, and performance.

FIGURE 1.1
Human Resource Management Practices

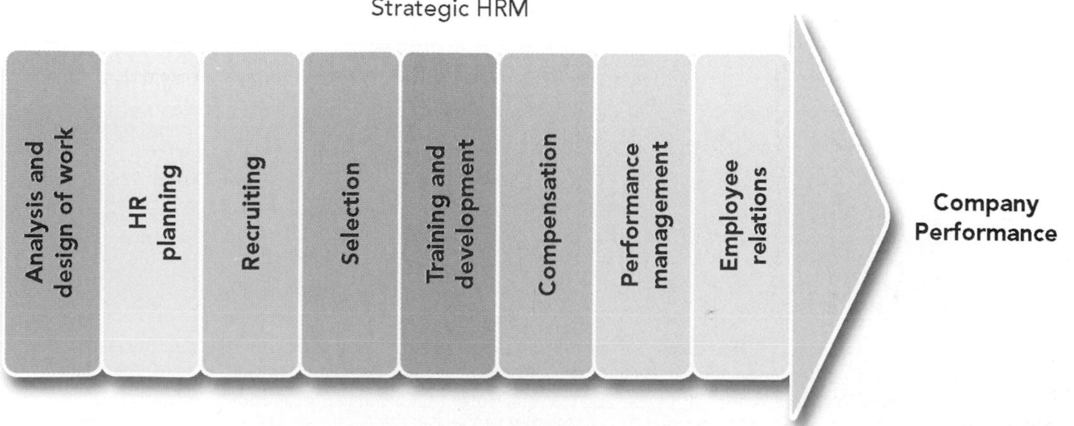

reputation in the firm's community.[1] The potential role of HRM in company performance has only recently been recognized.

As the opening examples illustrate, many companies such as Kodak have human resource management departments. However, others such as The Container Store see HRM as the daily responsibility of managers. Even at companies like Kodak HRM is also a day-to-day activity of managers. We begin by discussing the roles and skills that a human resource management department and/or managers need for any company to be competitive. The second section of the chapter identifies the competitive challenges that U.S. companies currently face, which influence their ability to meet the needs of shareholders, customers, employees, and other stakeholders. We discuss how these competitive challenges are influencing HRM. The chapter concludes by highlighting the HRM practices covered in this book and the ways they help companies compete.

What Responsibilities and Roles Do HR Departments Perform?

Only recently have companies looked at HRM as a means to contribute to profitability, quality, and other business goals through enhancing and supporting business operations.

Table 1.1 shows the responsibilities of human resource departments. The average ratio of HR department staff to total number of employees has been 1.0 for every 100 employees served by the department. The median HR department expenditure per employee was $813, with wholesale and retail trade organizations spending the least ($282) and finance, insurance, real estate, advanced manufacturing, and communications and information companies the most ($1,300). As with other business func-

TABLE 1.1
Responsibilities of HR Departments

Employment and recruiting	Interviewing, recruiting, testing, temporary labor coordination
Training and development	Orientation, performance management skills training, productivity enhancement
Compensation	Wage and salary administration, job descriptions, executive compensation, incentive pay, job evaluation
Benefits	Insurance, vacation leave administration, retirement plans, profit sharing, stock plans
Employee services	Employee assistance programs, relocation services, outplacement services
Employee and community relations	Attitude surveys, labor relations, publications, labor law compliance, discipline
Personnel records	Information systems, records
Health and safety	Safety inspection, drug testing, health, wellness
Strategic planning	International human resources, forecasting, planning, mergers and acquisitions

SOURCE: Based on SHRM-BNA Survey No. 66, "Policy and Practice Forum: Human Resource Activities, Budgets, and Staffs, 2000–2001." Bulletin to Management, Bureau of National Affairs Policy and Practice Series, June 28, 2001. Washington, DC: Bureau of National Affairs.

tions, HR expenditures relative to operating costs have been fairly stable over the past few years.

The HR department is solely responsible for outplacement, labor law compliance, record keeping, testing, unemployment compensation, and some aspects of benefits administration. The HR department is most likely to collaborate with other company functions on employment interviewing, performance management and discipline, and efforts to improve quality and productivity. Large companies are more likely than small ones to employ HR specialists, with benefits specialists being the most prevalent. Other common specializations include recruitment, compensation, and training and development.[2]

The chapter opening vignette showed that no two human resource departments have the same roles and responsibilities. Many different roles and responsibilities can be performed by the HR department depending on the size of the company, the characteristics of the workforce, the industry, and the value system of company management. The HR department may take full responsibility for human resource activities in some companies, whereas in others it may share the roles and responsibilities with managers of other departments such as finance, operations, or information technology. In some companies the HR department advises top-level management; in others the HR department may make decisions regarding staffing, training, and compensation after top managers have decided relevant business issues.

The roles and responsibilities of the HR department are summarized in Figure 1.2. The vertical dimension represents the *focus* of a future or strategic orientation versus a day-to-day operational orientation. The *activities* are shown as people versus process along the horizontal dimension.[3] The figure shows that the HR function can play roles in the management of strategic human resources (strategic partner), the management of company infrastructure (administrative expert), the management of transformation and change (change agent), and the management of employee contribution (employee advocate). These roles are discussed next.

The role of HRM has evolved over time. As we saw in the opening vignettes, it has now reached a crossroads. Although it began as a purely administrative function, most HRM executives now see the function's major role as much more strategic.

FIGURE 1.2
HR Roles in Building a Competitive Organization

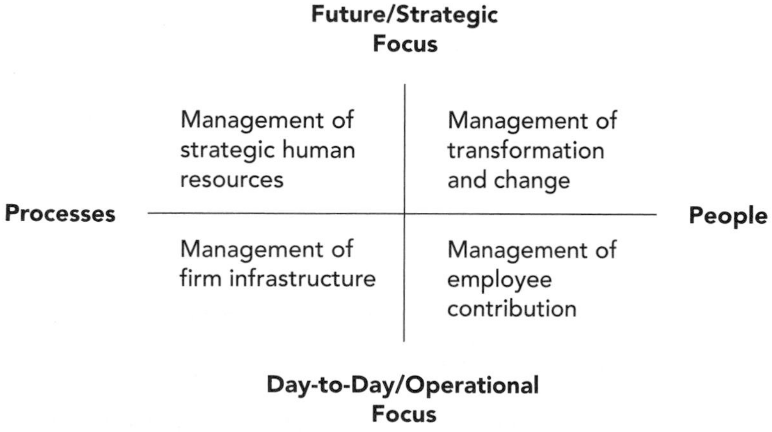

Future/Strategic Focus

Processes		**People**
Management of strategic human resources	Management of transformation and change	
Management of firm infrastructure	Management of employee contribution	

Day-to-Day/Operational Focus

SOURCE: Reprinted with permission of Harvard Business School Press. From *Human Resource Champions*, by D. Ulrich. Boston, MA, 1998, page 24.

However, this evolution has resulted in a misalignment between the skills and capabilities of members of the function and the new requirements placed on it. Virtually every HRM function in top companies is going through a transformation process to play this new strategic role while successfully fulfilling its other roles.

Strategic Partner. One of the most important roles that HRM can play today is that of a strategic partner. Aligning HRM strategies to business strategies is important to help the company execute its business strategy.[4]

For example, when Continental Airlines began its turnaround, Gordon Bethune proposed a four-pronged strategy of Fly to Win (achieve the top quartile in industry margins), Fund the Future (reduce debt), Make Reliability a Reality (have an industry-leading product), and Working Together (have a company where employees enjoy coming to work every day). Ken Carrig, VP of HR at Continental, helped to lead HRM to develop systems and plans that would ensure the execution of strategy. For example, they kept the base pay low relative to competitors (to create a labor cost advantage) but then heavily leveraged the variable pay to create an opportunity for employees to earn above the industry average if company performance improved. This variable pay consisted of (1) an on-time bonus where all employees received a $65 bonus check in any month in which Continental was in the industry's top three in on-time arrivals and (2) a profit-sharing plan that paid out if Continental returned to profitability. These incentives played a critical role in moving Continental to the top of the industry in on-time performance as well as profitability.[5]

Administrative Expert. Playing the role of administrative expert requires designing and delivering efficient and effective HRM systems, processes, and practices.[6] These include systems for selection, training, developing, appraising, and rewarding employees.

Continental also exemplifies this efficient delivery of HR systems. As part of its effort to turn the airline around, the HRM function examined its delivery of HRM systems and found a number of inefficiencies. Through outsourcing and streamlining of its processes, it achieved HRM operating ratios (such as HR FTEs to total FTEs, and HR expense to total expense) far below the industry average. In fact, this efficiency saved the company $4.5 million per year.[7]

Employee Advocate. The employee advocate role entails managing the commitment and contributions of employees.[8] No matter how skilled workers may be, if they are alienated or angry, they will not contribute their efforts to the firm's success, nor will they stay with the firm for long. Thus the role of employee advocate is of great importance for firms seeking to gain competitive advantage through people.

For example, in its role as employee advocate within Continental, the HRM function developed a number of communication mechanisms both for informing employees of company developments and plans, and for informing company officers of employee concerns. One such mechanism was the town meeting, where CEO Bethune would meet with large groups of employees to let them ask questions and air their grievances. Employees' commitment and trust grew as they saw their concerns being taken seriously by the leadership of the company.[9]

Change Agent. The final role, change agent, requires that HRM help transform organizations to meet the new competitive conditions. In today's fast-changing competitive world, firms need to both constantly change and develop a capacity for change. HR managers must help identify and manage processes for change.[10]

Continental's turnaround required both massive changes in operating performance and large-scale change in the culture of the organization. Increasing operating performance required developing more realistic schedules as well as getting employees committed to meeting those schedules. Realistic schedules were created and reviewed by employee committees, and their participation and the on-time incentive increased their determination to meeting the schedules. The culture of antagonism and mistrust had to be replaced by one of cooperation and trust. The profit-sharing plans, revamping of the top management team (36 of 48 officers were fired), burning of the 800-page employee manual, and town meetings all contributed to changing the culture at Continental.[11]

What Skills Do HRM Professionals Need?

Figure 1.3 shows the competencies that HRM professionals need to be successful. These competencies are organized according to the four roles (strategic partner, administrative expert, employee advocate, and change agent). These competencies include the ability to consider current and future business goals and how HRM can contribute, as well as being able to analyze turnover, retention, productivity, and customer service problems to recommend potential HRM solutions (strategic partner). They also include overcoming resistance to new HRM policies and procedures, technology, and work designs (change agent); coaching and counseling employees and representing their views to management (employee advocate); and designing and delivering effective HRM systems and understanding how technology can make HRM systems more efficient and less costly (administrative expert).[12]

How Is the HRM Function Changing?

The amount of time that the HRM function devotes to administrative tasks is decreasing, and its roles as a strategic business partner, change agent, and employee

FIGURE 1.3
Human Resource Roles and Competencies

SOURCE: Adapted from "The Changing Human Resource Function," *The Conference Board*, 1990 (New York: The Conference Board Inc.), p. 11.

advocate are increasing.[13] HR managers face two important challenges: shifting their focus from current operations to strategies for the future[14] and preparing non-HR managers to develop and implement human resource practices (recall The Container Store's HRM philosophy from the chapter opener).

The role of HRM in administration is decreasing as technology is used for many administrative purposes, such as managing employee records and allowing employees to get information about and enroll in training, benefits, and other programs. Advances in technology such as the Internet have decreased the HRM role in maintaining records and providing self-service to employees.[15] **Self-service** refers to giving employees online access to information about HR issues such as training, benefits, compensation, and contracts; enrolling online in programs and services; and completing online attitude surveys. For example, MCI Worldcom has moved beyond using technology for online employee directories, handbooks, and employee record updates.[16] Using the Internet, employees at MCI Worldcom can purchase stock and reallocate retirement account investments, fill out electronic forms, and view electronic pay stubs before they are paid. They can also view streaming video of managers providing briefings or discussing strategic issues, see best practices, and sign up for training courses they will participate in using their desktop computers.

Self-service
Giving employees online access to HR information.

Outsourcing of the administrative role has also occurred. **Outsourcing** refers to the practice of having another company (a vendor, third-party provider, or consultant) provide services. Outsourcing is being used for payroll administration and for training, selecting, and recruiting employees. For example, Bank of America signed a 10-year contract with Exult Inc. to manage much of the bank's HR function.[17] Among the functions being outsourced are payroll, accounts payable, and benefits. Other services being handled by Exult include delivery of HR services and a call center for human resource and benefits information. Recruiting, compensation, and legal counsel will remain at the Bank of America. HR managers inside Bank of America are free to work on strategy and vision and focus on HRM responsibilities that add value to the business.

Outsourcing
The practice of having another company provide services.

Traditionally, the HRM department (also known as "Personnel" or "Employee Relations") was primarily an administrative expert and employee advocate. The department took care of employee problems, made sure employees were paid correctly, administered labor contracts, and avoided legal problems. The HRM department ensured that employee-related issues did not interfere with the manufacturing or sales of products or services. Human resource management was primarily reactive; that is, human resource issues were a concern only if they directly affected the business. Although that still remains the case in many companies that have yet to recognize the competitive value of human resource management, other companies believe that HRM is important for business success and therefore have expanded the role of HRM as a change agent and strategic partner.

Other roles such as practice development and strategic business partnering have increased. One of the most comprehensive studies ever conducted regarding HRM concluded that "human resources is being transformed from a specialized, stand-alone function to a broad corporate competency in which human resources and line managers build partnerships to gain competitive advantage and achieve overall business goals."[18] HR managers are increasingly included on high-level committees that are shaping the strategic direction of the company. These managers report directly to the CEO, president, or board of directors and propose solutions to business problems.

For example, the vice president–relationship leader of human resources for Corporate Services at American Express spends considerable time during his workday on

TABLE 1.2

Questions Used to Determine if Human Resources Are Playing a Strategic Role in the Business

1. What is HR doing to provide value-added services to internal clients?
2. What can the HR department add to the bottom line?
3. How are you measuring the effectiveness of HR?
4. How can we reinvest in employees?
5. What HR strategy will we use to get the business from point A to point B?
6. What makes an employee want to stay at our company?
7. How are we going to invest in HR so that we have a better HR department than our competitors?
8. From an HR perspective, what should we be doing to improve our marketplace position?
9. What's the best change we can make to prepare for the future?

SOURCE: Data from A. Halcrow, "Survey Shows HR in Transition," *Workforce* (June 1988), p. 74.

HR projects supporting business initiatives.[19] He spends two hours reviewing service delivery and drivers of employee satisfaction. Service delivery and drivers of employee satisfaction are inherent in a Corporate Services vision statement known as "The Stand." (Three goals of "The Stand" include making people successful, inspiring customer loyalty, and continually transforming industries. Corporate Services' progress toward reaching these goals is assessed by an annual employee survey.) Issues discussed in the two-hour meeting include how "The Stand" relates to competencies and behaviors as well as team training effectiveness, with a review of the current reward structure. Later in the day, he mentors a new director–relationship leader who supports government services and the corporate purchasing card group. (American Express services more than 1 million federal employees who use the Government Card when they travel.) He conducts an orientation with her that emphasizes the need to (1) understand the government services business and (2) gain an understanding of the key HRM challenges and start to develop an effective working relationship.

Table 1.2 provides several questions that managers can use to determine if HRM is playing a strategic role in the business. If these questions have not been considered, it is highly unlikely that (1) the company is prepared to deal with competitive challenges or (2) human resources are being used to help a company gain a competitive advantage! We will discuss strategic human resource management in more detail in Chapter 2.

Why have HRM roles changed? Managers see HRM as the most important lever for companies to gain a competitive advantage over both domestic and foreign competitors. We believe this is because HRM practices are directly related to companies' success in meeting competitive challenges. In the next section we discuss these challenges and their implications for HRM.

The HRM Profession

There are many different types of jobs in the HRM profession. Table 1.3 shows various HRM positions and their salaries. The salaries vary depending on education and experience as well as the type of industry. As you can see from Table 1.3, some positions involve work in specialized areas of HRM like recruiting, training, or labor and

TABLE 1.3
Median Salaries for HRM Positions

POSITION	SALARY
Organization development executive	$155,100
Corporate labor/industrial relations directors	153,000
EEO/diversity managers	90,000
HR managers	88,800
Technical trainers	58,100
Manager, professional recruiters	59,200
Human resource information system specialist	52,000

SOURCE: Based on Society for Human Resource Management—Mercer Survey 2001 as reported in the Bureau of National Affairs website, www.bna.com, August 28, 2001.

industrial relations. HR generalists usually make between $50,000 and $70,000 depending on their experience and education level. Generalists usually perform the full range of HRM activities including recruiting, training, compensation, and employee relations.

A college degree is held by the vast majority of HRM professionals, many of whom also have completed postgraduate work. Business typically is the field of study (human resources or industrial relations), although some HRM professionals have degrees in the social sciences (economics or psychology), the humanities, and law programs. Those who have completed graduate work have master's degrees in HR management, business management, or a similar field. Professional certification in HRM is less common than membership in professional associations. A well-rounded educational background will likely serve a person well in an HRM position. As one HR professional noted, "One of the biggest misconceptions is that it is all warm and fuzzy communications with the workers. Or that it is creative and involved in making a more congenial atmosphere for people at work. Actually it is both of those some of the time, but most of the time it is a big mountain of paperwork which calls on a myriad of skills besides the 'people' type. It is law, accounting, philosophy, and logic as well as psychology, spirituality, tolerance, and humility."[20]

The primary professional organization for HRM is the Society for Human Resource Management (SHRM). SHRM is the world's largest human resource management association with more than 160,000 professional and student members throughout the world. SHRM provides education and information services, conferences and seminars, government and media representation, and online services and publications (such as *HR Magazine*). You can visit SHRM's website to see their services at www.shrm.org.

Competitive Challenges Influencing Human Resource Management

Four competitive challenges that companies now face will increase the importance of human resource management practices: the challenge of the new economy, the global challenge, the challenge of meeting stakeholders' needs, and the high-performance work system challenge. These four challenges are shown in Figure 1.4.

FIGURE 1.4

Competitive Challenges Influencing U.S. Companies

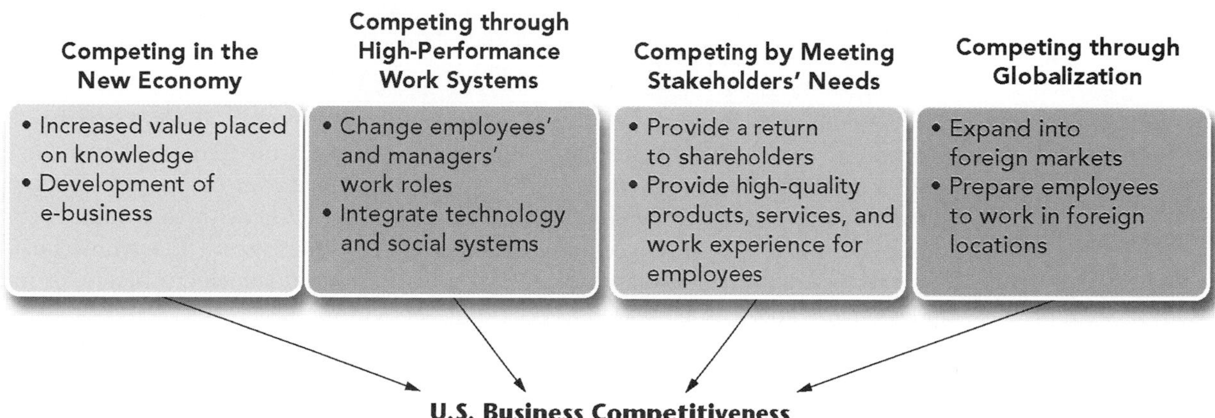

Competing in the New Economy

Several changes in the economy have important implications for human resource management. Some key statistics about the economy and the workforce are shown in Table 1.4. These include the changing structure of the economy, the development of e-business, and more growth in professional and service occupations. Growth in these occupations means that skill demands for jobs have changed, with knowledge becoming more valuable. Not only have skill demands changed, but remaining competitive in a global economy requires demanding work hours and changes in

TABLE 1.4

Summary of Key Labor Statistics Influencing HRM

- The economy is expected to add 20 million new jobs.
- The jobless rate is expected to remain low by historical standards (5 percent or less).
- Professional specialty and service occupations are expected to account for 46 percent of the total job growth between 1996 and 2006.
- 70 percent of the fastest-growing occupations require postsecondary education and training.
- There will be a shortage of 4.6 million workers, of which 3.5 million will need college-level skills.
- 38 percent of job applicants tested for basic skills lack the reading, writing, and math skills needed for the jobs they are seeking.
- Immigration will add 1 million persons to the workforce each year through 2006.
- The projected median age of the labor force by 2010 is 40.

SOURCE: Based on "BLS Releases New 1998–2008 Employment Projections," from the U.S. Bureau of Labor Statistics website, **http://stats.bls.gov**; H. N. Fullerton, "Labor Force Projections to 2008: Steady Growth and Changing Composition," *Monthly Labor Review,* November 1999, pp. 19–32; N. Saunders and B. Su, "U.S. Economy to 2008: A Decade of Continued Growth," *Monthly Labor Review,* November 1999, pp. 5–18; and J. Day, *Population Projections of the United States by Age, Sex, Race, and Hispanic Origin: 1995 to 2050,* U.S. Bureau of the Census Current Population Reports, P25-1130 (Washington, DC: U.S. Government Printing Office, 1996), p. 1.

traditional employment patterns. The creation of new jobs, aging employees leaving the workforce, slow population growth, and a lack of employees who have the skills needed to perform the jobs in greatest demand means that demand for employees will exceed supply. This has created a "war for talent" that has increased the attention companies pay to attracting and retaining human resources.

Electronic business (e-business)
Any process that a business conducts electronically.

Development of Electronic Business (E-Business). The way business is conducted has changed rapidly during the past few years and will continue to do so. Many companies are connecting to the Internet to gain an advantage over competitors. About one-third of all American teens and adults are online regularly, with that number expected to grow as Internet access increases and its cost decreases.[21] **Electronic business (e-business)** includes any process that a business conducts electronically. It includes buying and selling, as well as providing services such as

- Business to consumer transactions (such as purchasing books and tickets, and services conducted online, such as banking).
- Business to business (transactions between companies such as manufacturers, retailers, wholesalers, and construction firms).
- Consumer to consumer (individuals buying and selling goods and services through auctions).[22]

E-business relies on the Internet to enable buyers to obtain product information online, directly order products and services, receive after-sale technical assistance, and view the status of orders and deliveries. Internet sites may also have e-mail, which allows the customer and seller to communicate with each other. Companies are also creating customer service centers that use e-mail or live telephone connections to provide assistance, advice, or product information not found on their websites. The development of e-business has created electronic HRM applications that let employees enroll in and participate in training programs, change benefits, and communicate with coworkers online. We will discuss e-HRM in more detail later in the chapter.

Consumer reaction to the Internet has been slower than expected. To win the hearts of consumers, e-commerce has to be better, cheaper, and faster than traditional retailing, entertainment, or information sources.[23] One thing the Internet can do better than any other medium is search through information. Companies that take advantage of this feature lower the costs of making sales and therefore improve profits.[24] Some e-businesses, such as those in the online travel business dealing with purchasing airline tickets, hotel rooms, and rental cars online, have been successful. The profitable companies provide services that are information-intensive, rely on old economy roots, and have little or no physical transportation of products. For example, eBay takes a cut of each sale on its site but is not directly involved transporting items between buyers and sellers. Monster.com charges companies to post job openings and see resumes but does not set up interviews between job candidates and employees. Travel websites such as Travelocity.com earn a commission if the customer purchases a ticket or rents a car or a hotel room. Other old economy businesses with strong brand recognition, such as FTD, the floral delivery service, have successfully used the Internet to complement telephone and flower store business. FTD can rely on local retailers to receive and ship orders using their own delivery vehicles. The Internet has given customers a new way to place orders.

COMPETING IN THE NEW ECONOMY

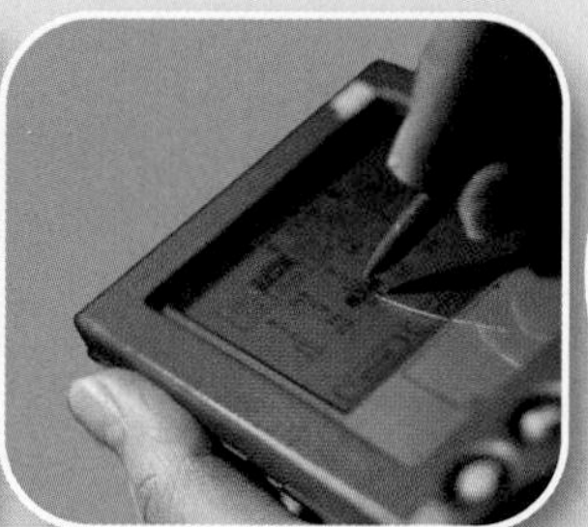

HRM at Dot-Coms: Hyperchallenges, Hyperspeed, and Many Rewards

There are many HRM challenges in a dot-com company. They include the need to quickly identify and hire talented employees, work through the stresses of a downsizing or business restructuring, and respond to and reduce the chances of potential legal problems. For example, within the first six months of Jessica Keim's tenure as HR manager for Multex.com, an online financial services firm, the company grew from 350 to 500 employees by acquiring two companies. Potential legal problems exist because young, inexperienced managers of many dot-coms have created a fraternity-party culture that is needed for innovation and creativity but may cultivate sexual harassment. It's also not unusual to find incomplete personnel folders or poor documentation about when and why employees were terminated. This occurs because to be successful dot-coms have to focus so intently on bringing a product or service to market and making sales to survive that they do not have time to develop HRM policies, procedures, or standards. Also, the work environment tends to be casual, dress codes may be loose, and work schedules are flexible. HRM needs to maintain a balance between accommodating the unique needs of an unstructured and creative workforce and enforcing necessary policies and procedures. Managers and employees often don't know how to nurture or mentor people, so counseling is needed. One HR professional summarized the experience as being like "a counselor at a day care camp."

Despite these challenges, dot-coms offer a dynamic, exciting HRM work environment. Their small size allows HR professionals to speak directly to the CEO. Because of the important role that HRM practices such as recruiting, selection, and compensation play in a growing company, HRM is asked to get involved with strategic decision making. As Beth Skrzyniarz, vice president of HRM for NetFolio Inc., an Internet-based investment advisor firm, says, "You're invited to sit at the table a lot more . . . you are heard a lot more than you would be in a big corporation." Because of the numerous HRM needs of small dot-coms, HRM sees its decisions implemented, quickly sees the impact on the business, and receives personal recognition for successful actions. Successful candidates for HRM positions in dot-com companies are flexible and resilient to chaos and like challenge. They have a passion for the Internet and e-commerce. HR professionals are expected to work without much structure and be confident in their decisions. They need to be able to constantly refine the HRM services the company offers to meet or exceed those of the competition. The dot-com environment is challenging but offers the opportunity to work with intelligent, energetic, and enthusiastic people. The pace is fast, and decisions can be made quickly without a lot of red tape. HRM professionals have the opportunity to build the HR function from scratch, something that is virtually impossible in a large, more established company.

SOURCE: L. Grensing-Pophal, "Are You Suited for a Dot-Com?" *HR Magazine*, November 2000, pp. 75–80.

What are the HRM demands in e-business? The Competing in the New Economy box above highlights human resource management at dot-com companies, which are considered e-businesses.

Structure of the Economy. The competition for labor is affected by the growth and decline of industries, jobs, and occupations. Competition for labor is also influenced by the number and skills of persons available for full-time work. Figure 1.5 shows expected job openings due to new jobs (growth and job openings resulting from having to replace employees due to retirement, disability, or leaving the workforce to attend school or stay at home). Most of the new job growth in professional specialties is expected among teachers, librarians, and counselors; computer, mathematical, and operations research occupations; and health assessment and treatment occupations. Computer-related positions, such as computer engineers, computer support specialists, system analysts, and computer database administrators, are projected to be four of the fastest-growing jobs in the economy.[25] The largest number of job openings will be in occupations requiring a bachelor's degree and on-the-job training. Employees with the most education will have greater opportunities in the job market and better chances of landing higher-paid jobs. Retail will continue to provide jobs for unskilled workers.[26]

Service occupations make up the next fastest-growing job group, with an expected addition of 46 million jobs. This has important implications for HRM. Research

FIGURE 1.5

Job Openings Due to Growth and Replacement Needs by Major Occupational Group, Projected 1998–2008.

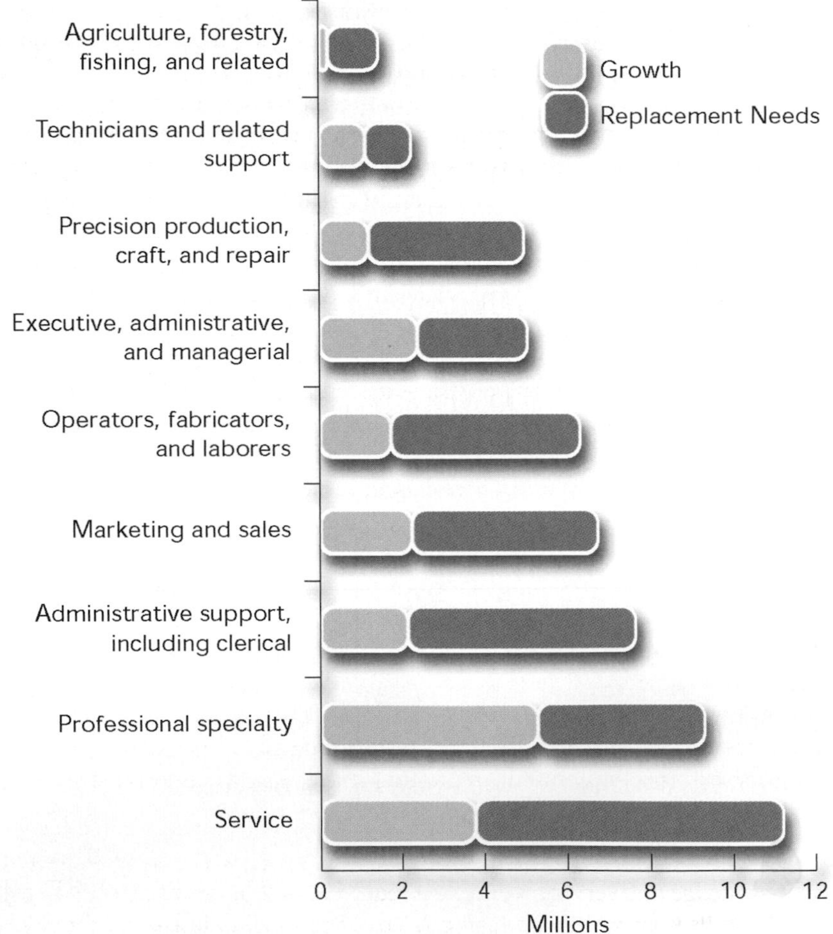

SOURCE: "Tomorrow's Jobs" in the *2000–01 Occupational Outlook Handbook,* chart 11. From website **http://stats.bls.gov/oco/oco2003.htm**.

shows that employee perceptions of HRM practices are positively related to customer evaluation and service quality. To maximize customer service, companies with service jobs should consider creating both a positive experience for the customer and progressive HRM policies.

Increased Value Placed on Knowledge. By one estimate, up to 75 percent of the source of value in a company is intangible **intellectual capital,** which refers to the creativity, productivity, and service provided by employees.[27] Effective management of people is key to boosting the value of intellectual capital. This includes understanding what the company is about, what it does, the expectations for performance, how and why performance will be rewarded, and how employee talents will be developed. Today more companies are interested in developing intellectual capital to gain an advantage over competitors. As a result, companies are trying to attract, develop, and retain knowledge workers. **Knowledge workers** are employees who own the means of producing a product or service. Such employees cannot simply be ordered to perform tasks; rather, they must share knowledge and collaborate on solutions. Knowledge workers contribute specialized knowledge that their managers may not have, such as information about customers. Managers depend on them to share information. Knowledge workers have many job opportunities; if they choose, they can leave a company and take their knowledge to a competitor. Knowledge workers are in demand because of the growth of service-producing jobs requiring them. This includes jobs in health services, business services, social services, engineering, and management.

Intellectual capital
Creativity, productivity, and service provided by employees.

Knowledge workers
Employees who own the means of producing a product or service.

To completely benefit from employees' knowledge requires a management style that focuses on developing and empowering employees. **Empowerment** means giving employees responsibility and authority to make decisions regarding all aspects of product development or customer service.[28] Employees are then held accountable for products and services; in return, they share the resulting rewards and losses. HRM practices related to performance management, training, work design, and compensation are important. For empowerment to succeed, managers must be trained to link employees to resources within and outside the company (people, websites, and so on), help employees interact with staff throughout the company, and ensure that employees are updated on important issues and cooperate with each other. Employees must also be trained to use the Internet, e-mail, and other tools for communicating, collecting, and sharing information.

Empowerment
Giving employees responsibility and authority to make decisions.

As more companies become knowledge-based, they must promote and capture learning at the employee, team, and company levels. Buckman Laboratories, for example, is known for its knowledge management practices.[29] Buckman Laboratories develops and markets specialty chemicals. Buckman's CEO, Robert Buckman, has developed an organizational culture, technology, and work processes that encourage the sharing of knowledge. Employees have laptop computers so they can share information anywhere and anytime via the Internet. The company set up rewards for innovation and knowledge creation and exchange by measuring performance based on the percentage of sales of new products. Buckman also changed the focus of the company's information systems department, renaming it the "knowledge transfer department" to better match the service it is supposed to provide.

Skill Requirements. As the occupational structure of the U.S. economy has shifted to emphasize knowledge and service work, skill requirements have changed.[30] The demand for specific skills is being replaced by a need for cognitive skills—mathematical and verbal reasoning ability—and interpersonal skills related to being able to work in teams or to interact with customers in a service economy (such as patients, students, vendors, and suppliers). Many jobs, especially those in e-business, require employees to have technology-related skills (like using the Internet, spreadsheets, and statistical software packages). Cognitive and interpersonal skills are important because in the service-oriented economy employees must take responsibility for the final product or service. Variety and customization requires employees who are creative and good problem solvers. Continuous innovation requires the ability to learn, especially as technology changes jobs. To add novelty and entertainment value for customers, workers must be creative.

Most companies relate these skills to educational attainment, using a college degree as a standard to screen prospective new employees. However, some companies who are unable to find qualified employees rely on training to correct skill deficiencies after hiring.[31] Other companies team up with universities, community colleges, and high schools to design and teach courses ranging from basic reading to design blueprint reading. The skills gap has decreased competitiveness because it makes it difficult for companies to upgrade technology, reorganize work, and empower employees, which are key elements in high-performance work systems.

Changes in the Employment Relationship. Economic downturns will continue to occur, resulting in layoffs in all industries. For example, recently Xerox laid off 12,000 employees and Cisco Systems 3,000 employees. Due to excessive optimism about the Internet, nearly 600 dot-coms such as e-Tots Inc and Webvan Group Inc. (which delivered groceries ordered over the Internet) have gone out of business since January 2000. Layoffs and bankruptcies have played a major role in changing the employment relationship. The **psychological contract** describes what an employee expects to contribute and what the company will provide to the employee for these contributions.[32] Unlike a sales contract, a psychological contract is not written. Traditionally, companies expected employees to contribute time, effort, skills, abilities, and loyalty. In return, companies would provide job security and opportunities for promotion. However, in the new economy a new type of psychological contract is emerging.[33] The competitive business environment demands frequent changes in the quality, innovation, creativeness, and timeliness of employee contributions and the skills needed to provide them. This has led to company restructuring, mergers and acquisitions, layoffs, and longer hours for many employees. Companies demand excellent customer service and high productivity levels. Employees are expected to take more responsibility for their own careers, from seeking training to balancing work and family. In exchange for top performance and working longer hours without job security, employees want companies to provide flexible work schedules, comfortable working conditions, more autonomy in accomplishing work, training and development opportunities, and financial incentives based on how the company performs. Employees realize that companies cannot provide employment security, so they want employability—that is, they want their company to provide training and job experiences to help ensure that employees can find other employment opportunities. The human resource management challenge is how to build a committed, productive workforce in turbulent economic conditions that offer opportunity for financial success but can also quickly turn sour, making every employee expendable.

Psychological contract
Expectations of employee contributions and what the company will provide in return.

As a result of this changing psychological contract, companies are using more alternative work arrangements. **Alternative work arrangements** include independent contractors, on-call workers, temporary workers, and contract company workers. The Bureau of Labor Statistics estimates that there are 12.2 million "nontraditional workers," including 8.2 million independent contractors, 2 million on-call workers, 1.2

Alternative work arrangements
Independent contractors, on-call workers, temporary workers, and contract company workers who are not full-time employed by the company.

million temporary workers, and approximately 800,000 contract company workers (workers employed by a company that provides them to other companies under a contract). These alternative work arrangements constitute about 10 percent of employees.[34]

More workers in alternative employment relationships are choosing these arrangements. Most independent contractors and contract workers have chosen this type of arrangement, whereas temporary agency workers and on-call workers prefer traditional full-time employment. There is some debate whether nontraditional employment relationships are good or bad. Some labor analysts argue that alternative work arrangements are substandard jobs characterized by low pay, fear of unemployment, poor health insurance and retirement benefits, and dissatisfying work. Others claim that these jobs provide flexibility for both companies and employees in a tight labor market. Alternative work arrangements allow companies to more easily modify their hiring levels and are more cost-effective when demand for products and service fluctuates. Alternative arrangements also allow employees to balance work with nonwork activities.

Demanding Work, but with More Flexibility. The globalization of the world economy and the development of e-commerce have made the notion of a 40-hour work week obsolete. As a result, companies need to be staffed 24 hours a day, seven days a week. Employees in manufacturing environments and service call centers are being asked to move from 8- to 12-hour days or to work afternoon or midnight shifts. Similarly, professional employees face long hours and and work demands that spill over into their personal lives. E-mail, pagers, and cell phones bombard employees with information and work demands. In the car, on vacation, on planes, and even in the bathroom, employees can be interrupted by work demands. More demanding work results in greater employee stress, less satisfied employees, loss of productivity, and higher turnover—all of which are costly for companies.

Many companies are taking steps to provide more flexible work schedules, protect employees' free time, and more productively use employees' work time. Workers consider flexible schedules a valuable way to ease the pressures and conflicts of trying to balance work and nonwork activities. Employers are using flexible schedules to recruit and retain employees and to increase satisfaction and productivity. For example, International Paper plants need to run paper-producing machinery 24 hours a day, seven days a week. The challenge for the company was to devise a schedule that keeps the machines running while allowing employees to balance work and rest. At its plant in DePere, Wisconsin, employees are asked to rotate between daytime work hours to nighttime shifts and back again. Typically, such rotating shifts force employees to continually adjust to different sleep patterns and disrupt social activities. At the DePere plant, shifts have been extended from 8 to 12 hours. The typical rotation follows a pattern of four days on, two off, three on, three off, three on, and four off. This means employees work only 190 days a year and can balance the demands of work and family life. As another example, in response to the loss of talented computer service employees who were forced to answer calls late at night and on weekends, Hewlett-Packard redesigned work schedules to allow employees to volunteer to work either during the week or on weekends. As a result, turnover rates decreased and customer response times improved.[35] To protect employees' nonwork time, some companies, such as the consulting firm Ernst & Young, allow employees to wait until they return to work to answer weekend or vacation voice mail and e-mail messages.[36] At SCJohnson in Racine, Wisconsin, employees often had to take work home on the weekends because they were so tied up in meetings from Monday through Friday that they had to finish duties on their own time.[37] SCJohnson now completely bans all meetings for two Fridays each month. The policy helps employees rest on at least two weekends and work at home on those Fridays because they won't be afraid of missing a meeting.

Finding and Keeping the Best Employees

There are several ways that companies are trying to win the war for talent; all involve HRM practices. They include finding creative ways to avoid layoffs and retirement, creating a positive work environment, and expanding the search for talent to the global labor force.

Companies are coming up with creative ways to avoid layoffs or remain connected to laid-off talented employees whom they worked hard to recruit.[38] For example, Sun Microsystems is trying to avoid layoffs by closing plants over the summer. Cisco Systems is paying some laid-off employees one-third of their previous salaries and will continue to provide full benefits, including health insurance, use of a laptop, and access to the company gym. After a year the employees will get an additional two months' salary to help pay for a job search inside Cisco. Charles Schwab is promising a $75,000 rehiring bonus to any of the 2,100 employees laid off who return within 18 months. Many companies are considering rehiring retired employees on a part-time basis or as consultants, and rather than offering all-or-none retirement programs, they are allowing employees to gradually phase out of work. For example, Monsanto Corporation has developed its own in-house temporary employment agency, the Retiree Resource Corporation (RRC), to utilize retirees' talents.[39]

Macy's West has developed a comprehensive retention strategy that includes (1) advising managers on how to run meetings and conduct performance evaluations in a way that will motivate associates, (2) flexible schedules, (3) development opportunities to prepare associates to be managers.[40] Executives at Macy's are also held accountable for retention among the employees who report to them.

Consider how SAS Institute is trying to win the war for talent by giving employees the opportunity to do interesting work in a comfortable environment that permits them to have both jobs and lives.[41] SAS Institute is a privately held worldwide company that develops and markets statistical software. By any criteria, SAS is successful; 80 percent of the *Fortune* 500 companies use its software. SAS Institute operates on the basis of trust. The company has no sick days or sick leave policy. Employees can take as many days as they need; if they take advantage of the policy they are fired. The company's approach to performance management involves setting high expectations and giving employees the freedom to meet the expectations. SAS Institute is most famous for its generous, family-friendly benefits and pleasant physical environment. Every employee has a nice private office with computer equipment. Company policy is for employees to work 35 hours a week or a 9-to-5 day with an hour for lunch or exercise. The company is closed after 5 P.M. The company also has an on-site medical facility, on-site day care, a fitness center, and a liberal snack policy. Every Wednesday afternoon, plain and peanut M&Ms are distributed to snack areas on every floor in every building (the company uses 22.5 tons of M&Ms per year). Not surprisingly, SAS Institute has a low turnover rate. Many other high-tech and pharmaceutical companies are located close to SAS's headquarters in Cary, North Carolina, so competition for talented employees is high. However, SAS Institute's work environment encourages employees to stay even if they have opportunities at other companies. SAS's business strategy will soon make it a publicly traded company. Although SAS Institute will face challenges, its HRM practices will continue to give the company a competitive advantage.

Companies are relying on the global labor market to find employees with specific talent. In India, computer programmers and call center employees work part-time on contracts for numerous companies around the world. Companies such as Conseco, an insurance firm, are finding that by outsourcing or contracting business to India, they can find a greater supply of better-educated persons than in the United States.[42] The Indian employees are excited about the type of customer service work offered and are loyal and eager to learn, taking the initiative to improve business processes and please their customers. In the United States it is difficult to find and retain the same type of employees. The cost of doing business in India (such as wages and benefits) are much cheaper, so this outsourcing helps improve the bottom line. Companies are also moving business operations to where employees are available.[43] In Ireland more than 100 international companies have set up telemarketing operations, and the country is attracting employees from all over Europe.

The Global Challenge

Companies are finding that to survive they must compete in international markets as well as fend off foreign corporations' attempts to gain ground in the United States. To meet these challenges, U.S. businesses must develop global markets, use their practices to improve global competitiveness, and better prepare employees for global assignments.

Development of Global Markets. Anecdotal evidence suggests that the most admired and successful companies in the world have not only created multinational corporations, but have created organizations with workforces and corporate cultures that reflect the characteristics of the global markets in which they operate.[44] Examples of these companies include General Electric, Coca-Cola, Microsoft, Walt Disney, Intel, Toyota Motors, ABB Asea Brown Boveri, and Hewlett-Packard.

These companies' key priorities include traditional business objectives such as customer focus and innovation. However, a distinguishing characteristic is that these companies believe that people are their most important asset. Believing that employees are the key to success translates into human resource management practices such as rewarding employee performance, measuring employee satisfaction, using an intensive employee selection process, promotion from within, and investing in employee development.

Globalization has affected not only businesses with international operations. Companies without international operations buy or use goods that have been produced overseas, hire employees with diverse backgrounds, and compete with foreign-owned companies operating within and outside the United States. More companies are entering international markets by exporting their products overseas, building manufacturing facilities in other countries, entering into alliances with foreign companies, and engaging in e-commerce. Globalization is not limited to a particular sector of the economy or product market. For example, Procter & Gamble is targeting feminine hygiene products to new markets such as Brazil. The demand for steel in China, India, and Brazil is expected to grow at three times the U.S. rate. Developing nations such as Taiwan, Indonesia, and China may account for over 60 percent of the world economy by 2020.[45] Consider the market for Western goods from computers to hamburgers in China. China has a population of 1.2 billion with 200 million people living in cities! And in Latin America, governments are selling state-owned businesses to private investors, and foreign investment is welcome. Global business expansion has been made easier by technology. The Internet allows data and information to be instantly accessible and sent around the world. Using the Internet, e-mail, and videoconferencing, business deals can be completed between companies thousands of miles apart. Mark Braxton, chief technology officer for GM OnStar-Europe, believes that new technologies will open up opportunities for underdeveloped villages and communities in Africa, Asia, Europe, the United States, Central America, and South America by allowing employers to consider locating telephone service centers where companies would never have considered putting them.[46] Economically deprived communities in Ireland, Brazil, and Mexico are being equipped with satellite links that give them access to universities, local government offices, and businesses. This is not to say that developing these markets will be easy. Political instability, poor roads and communications, and poor economies increase the risks involved in doing global business in developing countries.

Despite the risks, many U.S. competitors are willing to gamble and are realizing high returns. They are reacting decisively to global changes and are positioning themselves as active participants in areas of the world that are expected to grow most rapidly. For example, ABB Asea Brown Boveri AG (Europe's largest engineering company and a competitor of General Electric) was one of the first Western companies to react to the Asian monetary crisis.[47] With over 219,000 employees worldwide, ABB was considered a global company well before the Asian monetary crisis. But to capitalize on the crisis, the company underwent a massive restructuring plan involving layoffs in Europe and North America and production shifts to low-cost countries in Asia. The company also did away with its regional reporting structure and organized its businesses along global lines. ABB hopes to beat its rivals by capitalizing on Asia's low production costs, which are half of European costs.

Training has an important role in ABB's global business success. One of the biggest problems that ABB has to overcome is resistance to the idea that Asian countries can match the standards of European or North American factories and complete work on time. Plant managers at its electrical motor facility in Shanghai, China, have been trained in ABB quality standards by ABB employees on assignment in China (employees known as *expatriates*).

Competitiveness in Global Markets through HRM Practices. While many large firms such as Exxon, Ford, and Procter & Gamble are already multinational corporations that span the globe, many medium-sized and small businesses are becoming increasingly international. To succeed in the global marketplace, the challenge for all businesses—regardless of size—is to understand cultural differences and invest in human resources. Consider how Starbucks Coffee handled its recent expansion into Beijing, China.[48] Competition for local managers exceeds the available supply. As a result, companies have to take steps to attract and retain managers. Starbucks researched the motivation and needs of the potential local management workforce. The company found that managers were moving from one local Western company to another for several reasons. In the traditional Chinese-owned companies, rules and regulations allowed little creativity and autonomy. Also, in many joint U.S.–China ventures, local managers were not trusted. To avoid local management turnover, in its recruiting efforts Starbucks emphasized its casual culture and opportunities for development. Starbucks also spends considerable time in training. New managers are sent to Tacoma, Washington, to learn the corporate culture as well as the secrets of brewing flavorful coffee.

To compete in the world economy, U.S. companies need to put greater effort into selecting and retaining talented employees, employee training and development, and dismantling traditional bureaucratic structures that limit employees' ability to innovate and create.[49]

Preparing Employees for International Assignments. Besides taking steps to ensure that employees are better used, U.S. companies must do a better job of preparing employees and their families for overseas assignments. The failure rate for expatriates is higher than that for European and Japanese expatriates.[50] U.S. companies must carefully select employees to work abroad based on their ability to understand and respect the cultural and business norms of the host country, their language skills, and their technical ability. (See the "Competing through Globalization" box.) Additionally, U.S. companies must be willing to train and develop foreign employees to win foreign business. Several companies (such as Boeing and CSX Corporation) bring foreign workers to the United States for training and then return them to their home countries.[51] For example, Boeing brings workers from India and Poland to the United States. They return home with needed knowledge in aircraft design and manufacturing.

The Challenge of Meeting Stakeholders' Needs

As we mentioned earlier, company effectiveness and competitiveness are determined by whether the company satisfies the needs of stakeholders. Stakeholders include stockholders (who want a return on their investment), customers (who want a high-quality product or service), and employees (who desire interesting work and reasonable compensation for their services). The community, which wants the company to contribute to activities and projects and minimize pollution of the environment, is also an important stakeholder.

The Balanced Scorecard: Measuring Performance to Stakeholders

The **balanced scorecard** gives managers an indication of the performance of a company based on the degree to which stakeholder needs are satisfied; it depicts the company from the perspective of internal and external customers, employees, and shareholders.[52] The balanced scorecard is important because it brings together most of the features that a company needs to focus on to be competitive. These include being customer-focused, improving quality, emphasizing teamwork, reducing new product and service development times, and managing for the long term.

Balanced scorecard
A means of performance measurement that gives managers a chance to look at their company from the perspectives of internal and external customers, employees, and shareholders.

The balanced scorecard differs from traditional measures of company performance by emphasizing that the critical indicators chosen are based on the company's business strategy and competitive demands. Companies need to customize their balanced scorecards based on different market situations, products, and competitive environments.

Using the Balanced Scorecard to Manage Human Resources. Communicating the scorecard to employees gives them a framework that helps them see the goals and strategies of the company, how these goals and strategies are measured, and how they influence the critical indicators. For example, Chase Manhattan Bank used the balanced scorecard to change the behavior of customer service representatives.[53] Before the company implemented the scorecard, if a customer requested a change in a banking service, the representative would have simply met the customer's need. Based on knowledge of the scorecard, the customer service representative might now ask if the customer is interested in the bank's other services such as financial planning, mortgages, loans, or insurance.

COMPETING THROUGH GLOBALIZATION

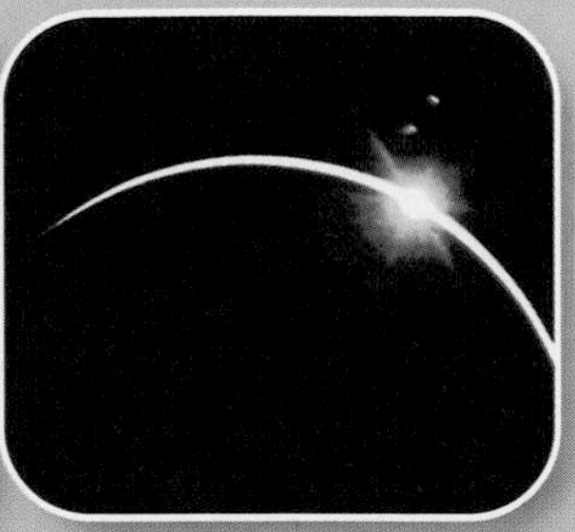

Success in Global Fast Food Depends on Careful Choice for Overseas Assignments

As companies expand globally, they are spending more time and energy assessing employees' cultural fit for overseas assignments. Research and practice indicate that the biggest mistake companies make is choosing people who have the technical skills needed to perform the job, but ignoring personality characteristics and family support. One estimate is that the cost of each failed overseas assignment ranges from $200,000 to $500,000. These costs relate to lost productivity, relocation, recruitment, and severance (buyout of employment) for the unsuccessful employee. Overseas assignments typically fail because the employee or family becomes homesick, or the employee cannot cope with the nuances of interacting with others in a different culture.

Tricon Restaurants International, based in Dallas, Texas, has 100 expatriates; 20 are Americans working overseas. Tricon is the franchiser for over 10,000 overseas Kentucky Fried Chicken, Pizza Hut, and Taco Bell Restaurants. Rather than choosing candidates who are merely excited about overseas assignment and who have the technical skills to perform the job, Tricon is taking a closer look at whether the candidates have the necessary personality characteristics, especially their ability to adapt to different situations, and the family support needed to succeed in overseas assignments. To identify employees for overseas assignments, Tricon interviews candidates about the position, the country's culture, and its marketplace. If there is any doubt whether the candidate can make the adjustment, a consulting firm is hired to further assess whether the candidate has the personality needed to succeed in an overseas assignment. Some of the personality characteristics needed include empathy, adaptability, and the ability to interact with others (sociability). If candidates pass the interview, a 360-degree feedback survey, which asks peers and their manager about their strengths and weaknesses, is used to evaluate their skills. If the evaluation is positive, candidates and their families are sent overseas for a week. During the visit, local managers evaluate the candidate while the family evaluates the community. The family spends time touring local schools, potential housing locations, and meeting with other expatriates in the country who help them understand the local culture and environment. If the local managers find the candidate acceptable, the candidate, with input from family, can accept or reject the position.

SOURCE: Based on C. Patton, "Match Game," *Human Resource Executive*, 2001, pp. 36–41.

The balanced scorecard should be used to (1) link human resource management activities to the company's business strategy and (2) evaluate the extent to which the HRM function is helping the company meet its strategic objectives. Measures of HRM practices primarily relate to productivity, people, and process.[54] Productivity measures involve determining output per employee (such as revenue per employee). Measuring people includes assessing employees' behavior, attitudes, or knowledge. Process measures focus on assessing employees' satisfaction with people systems within the company. People systems can include the performance management system, the compensation and benefits system, and the development system. The "Competing by

COMPETING BY MEETING STAKEHOLDERS' NEEDS

For Employee Retention the Venue Makes a Difference

The U.S. Bureau of Labor Statistics reports that the typical American worker holds nine different jobs before age 32. Turnover cannot be eliminated, and it can be positive. Turnover creates promotion opportunities and allows for the recruitment of new talent. But excessive turnover can disrupt customer service, innovation, and productivity, especially if the employees who leave take with them valuable industry-specific knowledge and customer relationships. At Athleta Corporation, a retail catalog and online sports apparel company founded in 1997 in Petaluma, California, the workforce is so committed to the company that turnover is less than 1 percent, productivity is increasing, and the company grew 500 percent last year. Athleta offers clothing from companies like Patagonia, She-Beest, and Adidas, and it also designs its own line of Athleta Essentials bodywear and technical apparel for running and cycling. The work environment has contributed to employee retention. The CEO has created a culture in which most of the 60 employees set their own work schedules and can take personal time during the day. Work gets done because employees seek to learn other employees' jobs (cross-training) and fill in for each other during the day. Employees who take time off for personal reasons willingly work odd hours. The work environment is about enjoying work, and team support is the rule. That team also includes a number of canines, so if you visit Athleta, you'll likely be greeted by a pack of friendly dogs curious to see what treats you've brought them. The dogs offer excellent running company and the occasional wrestling match or game of fetch to reduce stress. Athleta encourages people to take time out and participate in some type of physical activity during the day. The open space preserve behind the company facility is used by runners; part of a storage area is a makeshift gym, complete with weights, mats, and a treadmill. Group fitness classes, including kick-boxing and circuit training, are also offered so employees can sweat, laugh, and sometimes grimace in pain together—team building at its finest!

SOURCE: Based on the Athleta Corporation website, www.athleta.com, 9/22/01; and K. Dobbs, "Knowing How to Keep Your Best and Brightest," *Workforce*, April 2001, pp. 56–60.

Meeting Stakeholders' Needs" box shows how people systems can contribute to competitive advantage. For HRM activities to contribute to a company's competitive advantage, managers need to consider the questions shown in Table 1.5 and be able to answer them!

For example, at Tellabs, a company that provides communication service products (such as optical networking) around the world, key results tracked on the balanced scorecard include revenue growth, customer satisfaction, time to market for new products, and employee satisfaction.[55] Every employee has a bonus plan; bonuses are tied to performance as measured by the scorecard. The performance appraisal process measures employee performance according to departmental objectives that support the scorecard. At quarterly meetings, how employee performance is evaluated according to the scorecard is shared with every employee, and the information is also available on the company Intranet website.

TABLE 1.5
The Balanced Scorecard

PERSPECTIVE	QUESTIONS ANSWERED	EXAMPLES OF CRITICAL INDICATORS
Customer	How do customers see us?	Time, quality, performance, service, cost
Internal	What must we excel at?	Processes that influence customer satisfaction, availability of information on service and/or manufacturing processes
Innovation and learning	Can we continue to improve and create value?	Improve operating efficiency, launch new products, continuous improvement, empowering of workforce, employee satisfaction
Financial	How do we look to shareholders?	Profitability, growth, shareholder value

Meeting Customer Needs for Quality

To compete in today's economy, whether on a local or global level, companies need to provide a quality product or service. If companies do not adhere to quality standards, their ability to sell their product or service to vendors, suppliers, or customers will be restricted. Some countries even have quality standards that companies must meet to conduct business there. **Total Quality Management (TQM)** is a companywide effort to continuously improve the ways people, machines, and systems accomplish work.[56] Core values of TQM include the following:[57]

Total quality management (TQM)
A cooperative form of doing business that relies on the talents and capabilities of both labor and management to continually improve quality and productivity.

- Methods and processes are designed to meet the needs of internal and external customers.
- Every employee in the company receives training in quality.
- Quality is designed into a product or service so that errors are prevented from occurring, rather than being detected and corrected.
- The company promotes cooperation with vendors, suppliers, and customers to improve quality and hold down costs.
- Managers measure progress with feedback based on data.

There is no universal definition of quality. The major differences in its various definitions relate to whether customer, product, or manufacturing process is emphasized. For example, quality expert W. Edwards Deming emphasized how well a product or service meets customer needs. Phillip Crosby's approach emphasizes how well the service or manufacturing process meets engineering standards. Table 1.6 contrasts the HRM practices in companies recognized for successfully implementing TQM with traditional management practices. To ensure the success of TQM, companies need to create an environment that supports innovation, creativity, and risk taking to meet customer demands. Participative problem solving involving managers, employees, and customers should be used. Employees should not be afraid to communicate information regarding customer needs to managers.

Malcolm Baldrige National Quality Award
An award established in 1987 to promote quality awareness, to recognize quality achievements of U.S. companies, and to publicize successful quality strategies.

The emphasis on quality is seen in the establishment of the **Malcolm Baldrige National Quality Award** and the ISO 9000:2000 quality standards. The Baldrige award, created by public law, is the highest level of national recognition for quality that a U.S. company can receive. To become eligible for the Baldrige, a company must complete a detailed application that consists of basic information about the firm, as well

TABLE 1.6

HRM Practices in Total Quality Companies

In companies that successfully implemented TQM, the corporate climate emphasized collective and cross-functional work, coaching and enabling employees, customer satisfaction, and quality, rather than the traditional emphasis on individualism, hierarchy, and profit.

HUMAN RESOURCE MANAGEMENT CHARACTERISTICS	TRADITIONAL MODEL	TOTAL QUALITY MODEL
Communications	Top-down	Top-down Horizontal, lateral Multidirectional
Voice and involvement	Employment at will Suggestion systems	Due process Quality circles Attitude surveys
Job design	Efficiency Productivity Standard procedures Narrow span of control Specific job descriptions	Quality Customization Innovation Wide span of control Autonomous work teams Empowerment
Training	Job-related skills Functional, technical	Broad range of skills Cross-functional Diagnostic, problem solving
Performance measurement and evaluation	Productivity Individual goals Supervisory review Emphasize financial performance	Productivity and quality Team goals Customer, peer, and supervisory review Emphasize quality and service
Rewards	Competition for individual merit increases and benefits	Team and group-based rewards Financial rewards, financial and nonfinancial recognition
Health and safety	Treat problems	Prevent problems Safety programs Wellness programs Employee assistance programs
Selection and promotion	Selection by manager	Selection by peers
Career development	Narrow job skills Promotion based on individual accomplishment Linear career path	Problem-solving skills Promotion based on group facilitation Horizontal career path

SOURCE: *Academy of Management Executive,* by R. Blackburn and B. Rosen. Copyright © 1993 by Academy of Management. Reproduced with permission of Academy of Management via Copyright Clearance Center.

as an in-depth presentation of how it addresses specific criteria related to quality improvement. The categories and point values for the Baldrige award are found in Table 1.7. It is important to note that human resources is recognized as an important criterion. The award is not given for specific products or services. Three awards may be given annually in each of these categories: manufacturing, service, small business,

TABLE 1.7

Categories and Point Values for the Malcolm Baldrige National Quality Award Examination

Category	Points
Leadership The way senior executives create and sustain corporate citizenship, customer focus, clear values, and expectations and promote quality and performance excellence	**125**
Information and Analysis Management and effectiveness of the use of data and information to support customer-driven performance and market excellence	**85**
Strategic Planning The way the company sets strategic direction, how it determines plan requirements, and how plan requirements relate to performance management	**85**
Human Resource Focus Company's efforts to develop and utilize the workforce and to maintain an environment conducive to full participation, continuous improvement, and personal and organizational growth	**85**
Process Management Process design and control, including customer-focused design, product and service delivery, support services, and supply management	**85**
Business Results Company's performance and improvement in key business areas (product, service, and supply quality, productivity, and operational effectiveness and related financial indicators)	**450**
Customer and Market Focus Company's knowledge of the customer, customer service systems, responsiveness to customer, and customer satisfaction	**85**
Total Points	**1,000**

SOURCE: Based on Malcolm Baldrige National Quality Award 2000 Award Criteria (Gaithersburg, MD: National Institute of Standards and Technology, 2000).

education, and health care. All applicants for the Baldrige Award undergo a rigorous examination that takes from 300 to 1,000 hours. Applications are reviewed by an independent board of 400 examiners who come primarily from the private sector. Each applicant receives a report citing strengths and opportunities for improvement.

HRM practices, especially training, play an important role in improving quality. Operations Management International Inc. (OMI) is a 2000 Baldrige Award winner in the service category. OMI operates and maintains more than 160 public- and private-sector wastewater and water treatment facilities in 29 states and Brazil, Canada, Egypt, Israel, Malaysia, New Zealand, the Philippines, and Thailand. OMI's primary services are processing raw wastewater to produce clean, environmentally safe effluent and processing groundwater and surface water to produce clean, safe drinking water. Ninety-four percent of its customers are public, including cities and counties; 5 percent are industrial; and 1 percent are international communities or companies. Four strategic objectives—customer focus, business growth, innovation, and market leadership—enable OMI to design management systems and processes that consistently achieve high performance, reduce operating costs, and satisfy customers and associates. Training is key to the success of the company. OMI provides a broad array of training opportunities for its workforce, including a six-day Obsessed with Quality orientation program, OMI University for management and leadership development, on-the-job training, and mentoring. OMI's expenditures on training and tuition almost doubled from 1996 to 2000. Overall research suggests that the Baldrige award has had a positive impact in overall corporate performance (including better employee relations and increased productivity, customer satisfaction, and market share).[58]

The **ISO 9000:2000** standards were developed by the International Organization for Standardization in Geneva, Switzerland.[59] ISO 9000 is the name of a family of standards (ISO 9001, ISO 9004) that includes requirements such as how to establish quality standards and document work processes to help workers understand quality system requirements. ISO 9000:2000 has been adopted as a quality standard in nearly 100 countries, including Austria, Switzerland, Norway, Australia, and Japan. The ISO 9000:2000 standards apply to companies in many different industries—for example, manufacturing, processing, servicing, printing, forestry, electronics, steel, computing, legal services, and financial services. ISO 9001 is the most comprehensive standard because it covers product or service design and development, manufacturing, installation, and customer service. It includes the actual specification for a quality management system. ISO 9000 provides a guide for companies that want to improve.

ISO 9000:2000
Quality standards adopted worldwide.

Why are standards useful? A customer may want to check that a product ordered from a supplier meets the purpose for which it is required. One of the most efficient ways to do this is having the specifications of the product defined in an international standard. That way, even if they are based in different countries, both supplier and customer are both using the same references. Today many products require testing for conformance with specifications or compliance with safety or other regulations before they can be put on many markets. Even simpler products may require supporting technical documentation that includes test data. One example of an ISO standard is on the inside cover of this book and nearly every other book. On the inside cover there is something called an *ISBN*, which stands for International Standard Book Number. Publishers and booksellers are familiar with ISBNs because they are the method through which books are ordered and bought. Try buying a book on the Internet, and you will soon learn the value of the ISBN—there is a unique number for the book you want! And it is based on an ISO standard.

In addition to competing for quality awards and seeking ISO certification, many companies are using the Six Sigma process. The **Six Sigma process** refers to a system of measuring, analyzing, improving, and then controlling processes once they have been brought within the narrow Six Sigma quality tolerances or standards. The objective of Six Sigma is to create a total business focus on serving the customer—that is, deliver what customers really want when they want it. For example, at General Electric introducing the Six Sigma quality initiative meant going from approximately 35,000 defects per million operations (which is average for most companies, including GE) to fewer than 4 defects per million in every element of every process GE businesses perform—from manufacturing a locomotive part to servicing a credit card account to processing a mortgage application to answering the telephone.[60] Training is an important component of the process. Six Sigma involves highly trained employees known as Champions, Master Black Belts, Black Belts, and Green Belts who lead and teach teams focused on an ever-growing number of quality projects. The quality projects improve efficiency and reduce errors in products and services. Today GE has over 100,000 employees trained in Six Sigma and working on over 6,000 quality projects. Since 1996, when the Six Sigma quality initiative was started, it has produced more than $2 billion in benefits for GE.

Six Sigma process
System of measuring, analyzing, improving, and controlling processes once they meet quality standards.

Composition of the Labor Force

Company performance on the balanced scorecard is influenced by the characteristics of its labor force. The labor force of current employees is often referred to as the **internal labor force.** Employers identify and select new employees from the external labor market through recruiting and selection. The **external labor market** includes persons actively seeking employment. As a result, the skills and motivation of a company's internal labor force are influenced by the composition of the available labor market (the external labor market). The skills and motivation of a company's internal labor force determine the need for training and development practices and the effectiveness of the company's compensation and reward systems.

Internal labor force
Labor force of current employees.

External labor market
Persons outside the firm who are actively seeking employment.

The Bureau of Labor Statistics, a part of the U.S. Department of Labor, tracks changes in the composition of the U.S. labor force and projects employment trends.[61] Over the 1996–2006 period, the labor force is projected to increase by 15 million from 134 million to 149 million workers. This is an increase of 11 percent, less than the 14 percent increase between 1986 and 1996. The composition of the labor force will change because of shifts in the U.S. population. The youth labor force (ages 16 to 24) is expected to grow more rapidly than the overall labor force for the first time in 25 years. The labor force aged 45 to 64 will grow faster than any other age group as the baby boom generation (born from 1946 to 1964) continues to age. An aging workforce means that employers will increasingly face HRM issues such as career plateauing, retirement planning, and retraining older workers to avoid skill obsolescence. Companies will struggle with how to control the rising costs of benefits and health care. Growth in the youth labor force suggests that employers will have to find ways to attract, train, and retain younger employees.

As Figure 1.6 shows, the U.S. workforce is becoming increasingly diverse. It is projected that by 2006 the workforce will be 72 percent white, 11 percent black, 12 percent Hispanic, and 5 percent Asian and other minorities. Labor force participation of women in all age groups is expected to increase, while men's participation rates are expected to continue to decline for all age groups under 45 years. The Asian and other labor force and Hispanic labor force are projected to increase faster than other groups because of immigration and higher-than-average birthrates.

FIGURE 1.6
Changes in the U.S. Workforce, 1996 and 2006

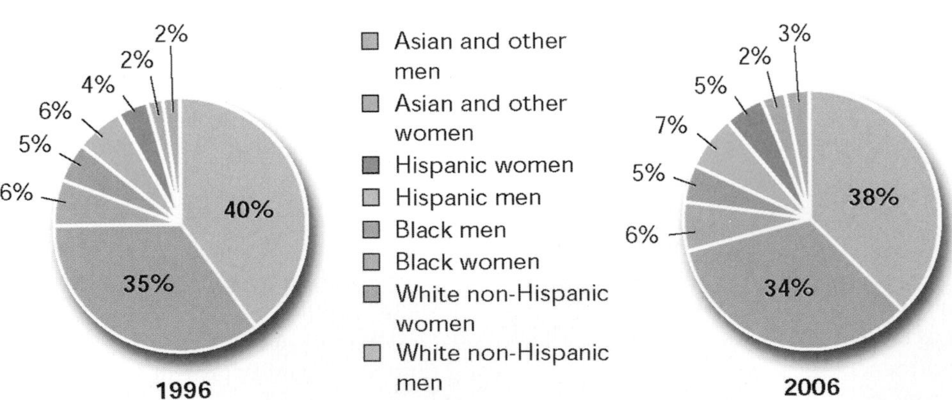

SOURCE: Bureau of Labor Statistics, "BLS Releases New 1996–2006 Employment Projections," www.bls.gov/new.release/ecopro.nws.htm. Numbers rounded to nearest percentage may not add to 100%.

Immigration is an important factor contributing to the diversity of the workforce. Immigrants will likely account for an additional 1 million persons in the workforce each year through 2006.[62] About 70 percent of these new workers will be Hispanics and Asians. There is considerable disagreement regarding the impact of immigration on employment prospects for U.S.-born workers and the U.S. economy. The U.S. economy has benefited by acquiring talented, intelligent workers from other countries, but it is unclear whether an influx of skilled workers from other countries lowers wages or increases unemployment for U.S.-born employees. Immigrants who enter the United States illegally (from formerly communist countries, for example) tend to have less education and depend more on the welfare system than those who enter legally.[63]

The heterogeneous composition of the workforce challenges companies to create HRM practices that ensure that the talents, skills, and values of all employees are fully utilized to help deliver high-quality products and services.

Managing Diversity. Because the workforce is predicted to become more diverse in terms of age, ethnicity, and racial background, it is unlikely that one set of values will characterize all employees.[64] For example, Generation Yers (born between 1976 and 1995) begin their career with the assumption they will frequently change jobs. They place a high value on money as well as on helping others. "Baby busters" (employees born between 1965 and 1975) value unexpected rewards for work accomplishments, opportunities to learn new things, praise, recognition, and time with the manager. "Traditionalists," employees born between 1925 and 1945, tend to be uncomfortable challenging the status quo and authority. They value income and employment security.

Most employees, however, value several aspects of work regardless of their background. Employees view work as a means to self-fulfillment—that is, a means to more fully use their skills and abilities, meet their interests, and allow them to live a desirable life-style.[65] One report indicated that employees who are given opportunities to fully use and develop their skills, receive greater job responsibilities, believe the promotion system is fair, and have a trustworthy manager who represents the employee's best interests are more committed to their companies.[66] Fostering these values requires companies to develop HRM practices that provide more opportunity for individual contribution and entrepreneurship.[67] Because many employees place more value on the quality of nonwork activities and family life than on pay and production, employees will demand more flexible work policies that allow them to choose work hours and locations where work is performed.

The implications of the changing labor market for managing human resources are far-reaching. Because labor market growth will be primarily in female and minority populations, U.S. companies will have to ensure that employees and human resource management systems are free of bias to capitalize on the perspectives and values that women and minorities can contribute to improving product quality, customer service, product development, and market share. Managing cultural diversity involves many different activities, including creating an organizational culture that values diversity, ensuring that HRM systems are bias-free, facilitating higher career involvement of women, promoting knowledge and acceptance of cultural differences, ensuring involvement in education both within and outside the company, and dealing with employees' resistance to diversity.[68] Table 1.8 presents ways that managing cultural diversity can provide a competitive advantage. Traditionally, in many U.S. companies the costs of poorly managing cultural diversity were viewed mainly as increased legal

TABLE 1.8

How Managing Cultural Diversity Can Provide Competitive Advantage

1. Cost argument	As organizations become more diverse, the cost of a poor job in integrating workers will increase. Those who handle this well will thus create cost advantages over those who don't.
2. Resource acquisition argument	Companies develop reputations on favorability as prospective employers for women and ethnic minorities. Those with the best reputations for managing diversity will win the competition for the best personnel. As the labor pool shrinks and changes composition, this edge will become increasingly important.
3. Marketing argument	For multinational organizations, the insight and cultural sensitivity that members with roots in other countries bring to the marketing effort should improve these efforts in important ways. The same rationale applies to marketing to subpopulations within domestic operations.
4. Creativity argument	Diversity of perspectives and less emphasis on conformity to norms of the past (which characterize the modern approach to management of diversity) should improve the level of creativity.
5. Problem-solving argument	Heterogeneity in decisions and problem-solving groups potentially produces better decisions through a wider range of perspectives and more thorough critical analysis of issues.
6. System flexibility argument	An implication of the multicultural model for managing diversity is that the system will become less determinate, less standardized, and therefore more fluid. The increased fluidity should create greater flexibility to react to environmental changes (i.e., reactions should be faster and cost less).

SOURCE: *Academy of Management Executive,* by T.H. Cox and S. Blake. Copyright © 1991 by Academy of Management. Reproduced with permission of Academy of Management via Copyright Clearance Center.

fees associated with discrimination cases. However, as Table 1.8 illustrates, the implications of successfully managing a diverse workforce go beyond legal concerns. How diversity issues are managed has implications for creativity, problem solving, retaining good employees, and developing markets for the firm's products and services. To successfully manage a diverse workforce, managers must develop a new set of skills, including

1. Communicating effectively with employees from a wide variety of cultural backgrounds.
2. Coaching and developing employees of different ages, educational backgrounds, ethnicity, physical ability, and race.
3. Providing performance feedback that is based on objective outcomes rather than values and stereotypes that work against women, minorities, and handicapped persons by prejudging these persons' abilities and talents.
4. Creating a work environment that makes it comfortable for employees of all backgrounds to be creative and innovative.[69]

Many U.S. companies have already made a commitment to ensuring that diversity in their workforce is recognized and effectively used for competitive advantage. A recent survey of HR professionals found that the most common diversity initiatives included recruiting efforts to increase diversity within the organization and training programs.[70] Ninety-one percent believed that their company's diversity initiative helped the company maintain a competitive advantage. And 75 percent believed this was accomplished by improving both the corporate culture and employee satisfaction.

Texaco developed a state-of-the-art diversity program after the company had to pay more than $175 million to settle a racial discrimination lawsuit.[71] The lawsuit made public accusations that company executives were using racial slurs. Prior to the lawsuit, Texaco's diversity program consisted of a workshop presented to top executives on practical tips for managing a diverse workforce. Today all Texaco employees are required to attend a two-day diversity "learning experience" that emphasizes awareness of what it feels like to be excluded, develops employee sensitivity to others, and improves communications skills needed for interacting with diverse peers. However, managing diversity at Texaco goes far beyond attending workshops; it is part of a culture change. As you will see in Chapter 7, Texaco's diversity effort includes programs designed to stop discrimination in hiring, retention, and promotion.

The bottom line is that to gain a competitive advantage in the next decade, companies must harness the power of the diverse workforce. These practices are needed not only to meet employee needs but to reduce turnover costs and ensure that customers receive the best service possible. The implication of diversity for HRM practices will be highlighted throughout this book. For example, from a staffing perspective, it is important to ensure that tests used to select employees are not biased against minority groups. From a work design perspective, employees need flexible schedules that allow them to meet nonwork needs. From a training perspective, it is clear that all employees need to be made aware of the potential damaging effects of stereotypes. From a compensation perspective, new benefits such as elder care and day care need to be included in reward systems to accommodate the needs of a diverse workforce.

Legislation and Litigation

Five main areas of the legal environment have influenced human resource management over the past 25 years.[72] These areas include equal employment opportunity legislation, employee safety and health, employee pay and benefits, employee privacy, and job security.

Employers and the courts continue to struggle with identifying what constitutes religious discrimination. Employers are being asked to juggle the demands of workers who want to express their faith with those who find such expressions offensive.[73]

The increased use of and access to electronic databases by employees and employers suggest that in the near future legislation will be needed to protect employee privacy rights. Currently no federal legislation outlines how employee databases should be used to protect privacy and confidentiality.

Legislation mandating access to technology for physically challenged employees will likely be debated. The Americans with Disabilities Act (ADA) covers access of disabled persons to the physical work environment and attempts to eliminate discrimination against physically challenged persons in hiring and other HRM practices. (We will discuss the ADA in detail in Chapter 3.) However, no law helps eliminate disabled persons' disadvantages in access to technology such as the Internet, cell phones, and other electronic devices. Disabled people's computer usage and Internet access are only about half that of persons without disabilities. Legislation will probably soon be considered to incorporate accessibility into technology.[74] Such accessibility might include adding screen readers to websites, providing voice recognition technology to computer users, or changing computer design to make them easier to use for employees with limited mobility.

There is also likely to be continued discussion about legislation to prohibit discrimination by employers and health insurers against employees based on their genetic makeup. Advances in medicine and genetics allow scientists to predict from DNA samples a person's likelihood of contracting certain diseases. To reduce health care costs, companies may want to use this information to screen out job candidates or reassign current employees who have a genetic predisposition to a disease that is triggered by exposure to certain working conditions. Legislation is being debated that permits genetic testing only to monitor the adverse effects of exposure to hazardous workplace exposures (such as chemicals) and prohibits the requirement to provide or request predictive genetic information.

Although women and minorities are advancing into top management ranks, "glass ceilings" are still keeping women and minorities from getting the experiences necessary to move to top management positions. A recent survey showed that 97 percent of top U.S. managers are white and at least 95 percent of them are male.[75] We are likely to see more challenges to sex and race discrimination focusing on lack of access to training and development opportunities that are needed to be considered for top management positions.

An area of litigation that will continue to have a major influence on HRM practices involves job security. As companies are forced to close plants and lay off employees because of restructuring, technology changes, or financial crisis, cases dealing with the illegal discharge of employees have increased. The issue of what constitutes employment at will—that is, employment that can be terminated at any time without notice—will be debated. As the age of the workforce increases, the number of cases dealing with age discrimination in layoffs, promotions, and benefits will likely rise. Employers' work rules, recruitment practices, and performance evaluation systems will need to be revised to ensure that these systems do not falsely communicate employment agreements the company does not intend to honor (such as lifetime employment) or discriminate on the basis of age.

Ethical Considerations

Many decisions related to managing human resources are characterized by uncertainty. Ethics can be considered the fundamental principles by which employees and companies interact.[76] These principles should be considered in making business decisions and interacting with clients and customers. Recent surveys suggest that the general public and managers do not have positive perceptions of the ethical conduct of U.S. businesses. For example, in a survey conducted by *The Wall Street Journal*, 4 out of 10 executives reported they were asked to behave unethically.[77]

As a result of unfavorable perceptions of U.S. business practices and an increased concern for better serving the customer, U.S. companies are becoming more aware of the need for all company representatives to act responsibly.[78] They have an interest in the way their employees behave because customer, government agency, and vendor perceptions of the company play an important role in maintaining the relationships necessary to sell products and services.

Ethical, successful companies can be characterized by four principles.[79] First, in their relationships with customers, vendors, and clients, these companies emphasize mutual benefits. Second, employees assume responsibility for the actions of the company. Third, such companies have a sense of purpose or vision the employees value and use in their day-to-day work. Finally, they emphasize fairness; that is, another person's interests count as much as their own.

The Raytheon Company has a checklist including several questions that is distributed to each employee to use when considering whether an action is ethical:[80]

- Is the action legal?
- Is it right?
- Who will be affected?
- Does it fit with Raytheon's values?
- How will I feel afterward?
- How will it look in the newspaper?
- Will it reflect poorly on the company?

Raytheon reinforces its ethics codes with formal training programs, a toll-free "ethics line," and full-time ethics offices and officers in all of its major business units. Mandatory one-hour ethics training for all employees uses case studies to make employees aware of the ethical problems that may occur at work.

Human resource managers must satisfy three basic standards for their practices to be considered ethical.[81] First, HRM practices must result in the greatest good for the largest number of people. Second, employment practices must respect basic human rights of privacy, due process, consent, and free speech. Third, managers must treat employees and customers equitably and fairly. Throughout the book we will highlight ethical dilemmas in human resource management practices.

The High-Performance Work System Challenge

For U.S. companies to compete with foreign competitors, they will have to learn to better utilize employees' talents and skills and new technology. The challenge that companies face is how to integrate technology and structure to gain a competitive advantage—that is, competing through **high-performance work systems.** High-performance work systems maximize the fit between the company's social system (employees) and its technical system.[82]

High-performance work systems
Work systems that maximize the fit between employees and technology.

Technological advances in manufacturing, transportation, telecommunications, and microprocessors are changing how work is performed, managers' and employees' roles, and organizational structure. Technology also has made human resource information databases more available and accessible and has created a need to develop HRM practices that integrate technology with people.

Change in Employees' Work Roles and Skill Requirements. New technology causes changes in basic skill requirements and work roles and often results in combining jobs.[83] For example, computer-integrated manufacturing uses robots and computers to automate the manufacturing process. The computer allows the creation of different products that meet market demands simply by reprogramming the computer. As a result, laborer, material handler, operator–assembler, and maintenance jobs may be merged into one position. Computer-integrated manufacturing requires employees to monitor equipment and troubleshoot problems with sophisticated equipment, share information with other employees, and understand the interaction between components of the manufacturing process.[84]

Technology is often a means to achieve product diversification and customization. As a result, employees need job-specific product knowledge and basic learning skills to keep up with product development and design improvements. To customize products and services, employees must listen to and communicate with customers. Interpersonal skills, such as negotiation and conflict management, and problem-solving skills are more important than physical strength, coordination, and fine-motor skills, which were previously required for many manufacturing and service jobs.

Increase in the Use of Teams to Perform Work. As the information needed to improve product quality and customer service becomes more available to employees at the point of sale or point of production because of advances in microprocessing systems, employees are expected to make more decisions concerning how their jobs are performed. One of the most popular methods of increasing employee responsibility and control is work teams. Work teams involve employees with various skills, who interact to assemble a product or provide a service. Work teams frequently assume many of the activities usually reserved for managers, such as selecting new team members, planning work schedules, and coordinating activities with customers and other units within the firm. Work teams also perform inspection and quality-control activities while the product or service is being completed, an important component for achieving total quality. Due to technological advances work teams may also be virtual teams. *Virtual team* refers to a team that has little or no face-to-face interaction, relying on telecommunications and information technology to collaborate on projects and services.

Besides the potential motivational advantages of work teams, labor costs can also be reduced for companies adopting teams. A number of companies are reorganizing assembly operations—abandoning the assembly line in favor of hybrid operations combining mass production with jobs in which employees perform multiple tasks, use many skills, control the pace of work, and assemble the entire final product.[85] One example of this type of teamwork is Compaq Computer's assembly cells. In manufacturing sites in Scotland and Texas, computers are built by four-person teams. One person assembles parts, another builds components, and two people assemble the computer unit. The new teams helped raise labor productivity 51 percent. The "Competing through High-Performance Work Systems" box highlights BP Exploration's use of virtual teams.

Changes in the Nature of Managerial Work. To gain the maximum benefit from the introduction of new technology in the workplace, managers must be able to move away from the military model of management, which emphasizes controlling, planning, and coordinating activities, and instead focus on creating work conditions that facilitate employee creativity and innovation. Because of advances in technology, information is more readily accessible to employees at all levels of the company, and decision making increasingly is decentralized. As a result, it is difficult, and certainly not effective, for managers to attempt to directly control interactions between work teams or between work teams and customers.

The manager's job will increasingly be to empower employees. Empowerment means giving employees responsibility and authority to make decisions regarding all aspects of product development or customer service.[86] Employees are then held accountable for products and services and, in return, share the rewards and failures that result. For empowerment to succeed, managers must serve in a linking and coordinating role.[87] The linking role involves representing employees (or teams) by ensuring that adequate resources are provided to perform the work (external link-

COMPETING THROUGH HIGH-PERFORMANCE WORK SYSTEMS

Developing Electronic Relationships at Work

Virtual teams reduce travel expenses and allow employees to be fast and competitive in disseminating information. BP Exploration, the division of BP that explores for and produces oil and gas, organized its regional operating centers into 42 autonomous business units. BP wanted these units to be freed to develop the processes and solutions appropriate to their specific problems; best practices and innovations could be shared in other places in the company. As a result, BP launched a project called "The Virtual Teamwork Program," designed to develop effective ways for team members to collaborate across different locations. The program's goal was to build a network of people to allow knowledgeable people to communicate. The hardware and software used for the program included desktop videoconferencing equipment, multimedia e-mail, shared chalkboards, document scanners, groupware, and a Web browser. This equipment was chosen because it captured the richness of communications, allowing human interactions to be as real as possible. Training showed employees how to use the technology and helped them understand how it could make them more effective. The trainers, known as coaches because the learning process was interactive, and employees communicated using virtual team stations to demonstrate the system's value for collaborative work and knowledge exchange. The emphasis was on personal contact and human needs. Eighty percent of the coaches' time was devoted to helping team members link their business objectives to the system capabilities and helping them to consider new ways of working made possible by the equipment. One example of the program's success comes from the North Sea. When an equipment failure occurred on a North Sea drilling ship, the ship's engineers used the video equipment and a satellite link to transmit images of the faulty equipment to a drilling equipment expert miles away. He quickly diagnosed the problem and guided the engineers to make the necessary repairs.

SOURCE: Based on T. Davenport and L. Prusak, *Working Knowledge* (Boston: Harvard Business School Press, 1998).

ing), facilitating interactions across departments (informal linking), and ensuring that employees are updated on important issues and cooperate by sharing information and resources (internal linking). In addition, managers who successfully perform the internal linking role must be available and willing to help employees deal with problems daily.

Although strong interpersonal and communications skills are required by both managers and employees, managers have to be able to either answer technical issues or, more likely, refer employees to persons within or outside the firm who can provide insight into technical problems. This means that managers have to be more aware of various resources available within the company and the community.

Changes in Company Structure. The traditional design of U.S. companies emphasizes efficiency, decision making by managers, and dissemination of information from the top of the company to lower levels. However, this structure will not be effective in the current work environment, in which personal computers give employees immediate access to information needed to complete customer orders or modify product lines. In the adaptive organizational structure, employees are in a constant state of learning and performance improvement. Employees are free to move wherever they are needed in the company. The adaptive organization is characterized by a core set of values or a vital vision that drives all organizational efforts.[88] Previously established boundaries between managers and employees, employees and customers, employees and vendors, and the various functions within the company are abandoned. Employees, managers, vendors, customers, and suppliers work together to improve service and product quality and to create new products and services. Line employees are trained in multiple jobs, communicate directly with suppliers and customers, and interact frequently with engineers, quality experts, and employees from other functions.

Increased Availability of Human Resource Management Databases and e-HRM. Improvements in technology related to computers and software have also had a major impact on the use of information for managing human resources. Large quantities of employee data (including training records, skills, compensation rates, and benefits usage and cost) can be easily stored on personal computers and manipulated using user-friendly spreadsheets or statistical software packages. A **human resource information system (HRIS)** is a system used to acquire, store, manipulate, analyze, retrieve, and distribute information related to the company's human resources.[89] From the manager's perspective, an HRIS can be used to support strategic decision making, to avoid litigation, to evaluate programs or policies, or to support daily operating concerns.

Human resource information systems (HRIS)
A system used to acquire, store, manipulate, analyze, retrieve, and distribute HR information.

Performance management, succession planning, and training and employee-development applications are becoming increasingly important. For example, projections of the level of skills that will be available in the future workforce suggest that math and reading competencies will be below the level required by new jobs. Changing technology can easily make the skills of technical employees obsolete. These trends demand that employees' skills and competencies be monitored carefully. Complicating this need for information is the fact that many employees are geographically dispersed across several locations within the same city or country, or across countries. In response to these needs companies have implemented global human resource management systems. Northern Telecom Limited (a Canadian telecommunications company that has facilities in 90 countries, including the United Kingdom, China, and the United States) needed access to information about employees located worldwide. The company has created a central database built on a common set of core elements. Anyone with authorization can view employee records from around the globe. Head count, salary, and recruiting data are continually updated as changes are made around the world. Although the system is customized to specific country needs, several common data fields and elements are used globally. Northern Telecom's system has enabled managers around the world to obtain up-to-date employee data to meet customer needs and address internal staffing issues.[90]

Electronic human resource management (e-HRM)
The processing and transmission of digitized information used in HRM.

Electronic human resource management (e-HRM) refers to the processing and transmission of digitized information used in HRM, including text, sound, and visual images, from one computer or electronic device to another. E-HRM has the potential to change all traditional human resource management functions. Table 1.9 shows the implications of e-HRM. For example, employees do not have to be in the same geographic area to work together. Use of the Internet lets companies search for talent

TABLE 1.9
Implications of e-HRM for HRM Practices

HRM PRACTICE	IMPLICATIONS OF E-HRM
Analysis and design of work	Employees in geographically dispersed locations can work together in virtual teams using video, e-mail, and the Internet.
Recruiting	Post job openings online; candidates can apply for jobs online.
Training	Online learning can bring training to employees anywhere, anytime.
Selection	Online simulations, including tests, videos, and e-mail, can measure job candidates' ability to deal with real-life business challenges.
Compensation and benefits	Employees can review salary and bonus information and seek information about and enroll in benefit plans.

without geographic limitations. Recruiting can include online job postings, applications, and candidate screening from the company's website or the websites of companies that specialize in online recruiting, such as Monster.com or HotJobs.com. Employees from different geographical locations can all receive the same training over the company's intranet. Because the globalization of business requires employees to be located throughout the world, to meet customer demands employees need to work in teams with members who have different functional skills and are in different places. This global reach allows companies to reduce travel and lodging costs associated with having to find and identify potential recruits or bring geographically dispersed employees to one location for meetings and training. It also can increase the speed with which employees can bring a product to market by facilitating communications between employees on virtual teams using Internet discussion forums, video- and audioconferencing, and global scheduling. For example, at Procter & Gamble a team of employees from two different divisions, paper and cleaning agents, developed the Swiffer, a "broom" containing disposable cloths, in just 10 months—half the usual time. The team used the Internet to analyze markets, demographics, and cost information; it also had the ability and authority to access any of the company's engineers, who are located in 23 sites around the world.[91]

Competitiveness in High-Performance Work Systems. Unfortunately, many managers have tended to consider technological and structural innovations independent of each other. That is, because of immediate demands for productivity, service, and short-term profitability, many managers implement a new technology (such as a networked computer system) or a new work design (like service teams organized by product) without considering how a new technology might influence the efficiency or effectiveness of the way work is organized.[92] Without integrating technology and structure, a company cannot maximize production and service.

Human resource management practices that support high-performance work systems are shown in Table 1.10. The HRM practices involved include employee selection, performance management, training, work design, and compensation. These practices are designed to give employees skills, incentives, knowledge, and autonomy. Research studies suggest that high-performance work practices are usually associated

TABLE 1.10

How HRM Practices Support High-Performance Work Systems

- Teams perform work.
- Employees participate in selection.
- Employees receive formal performance feedback and are actively involved in the performance improvement process.
- Ongoing training is emphasized and rewarded.
- Employees' rewards and compensation relate to the company's financial performance.
- Equipment and work processes are structured and technology is used to encourage maximum flexibility and interaction among employees.
- Employees participate in planning changes in equipment, layout, and work methods.
- Work design allows employees to use a variety of skills.
- Employees understand how their jobs contribute to the finished product or service.

SOURCE: Based on J. A. Neal and C. L. Tromley, "From Incremental Change to Retrofit: Creating High-Performance Work Systems," *Academy of Management Executive* 9 (1995), pp. 42–54; M. A. Huselid, "The Impact of Human Resource Management Practices on Turnover, Productivity, and Corporate Financial Performance," *Academy of Management Journal* 38 (1995), pp. 635–72.

with increases in productivity and long-term financial performance.[93] Research also suggests that it is more effective to improve HRM practices as a whole, rather than focus on one or two isolated practices (such as the pay system or selection system).[94] There may be a best HRM system, but whatever the company does, the practices must be aligned with each other and be consistent with the system if they are to positively affect company performance.[95] We will discuss this alignment in more detail in Chapters 2 and 16.

GE Fanuc Automation North America is a good example of the holistic approach needed for high-performance work practices to be effective. This joint venture between General Electric Company and FANUC Ltd. of Japan has developed a high-involvement workforce. Based in Charlottesville, Virginia, the joint venture employs 1,500 people. Recognition of the company's commitment to quality is reflected in its being one of the first U.S. firms to become a certified ISO 9000 manufacturer.

GE Fanuc Automation achieved its reputation and recognition for quality as a result of the use of high-performance work practices. Central to its practices is the idea that employees closest to the work have the best improvement ideas. As a result, employees must be encouraged to voice their opinions and make changes.

How does the company use high-performance work practices? The facility has three layers of management, and over 40 work teams set their own goals and measure success factors based on the overall business goals. Each team spends at least one hour per week measuring the goals and discussing new ways to be effective. To ensure team effectiveness, all employees receive more than 100 hours of training. Employees are also guaranteed that they will never lose their jobs due to an idea developed by the teams. Managers (known as coaches) are evaluated based on their support of the teams. Each functional team within the business has a dedicated HR manager who helps the team develop its strategies, accompanies the team on sales calls, and does whatever she can to help the team.[96]

Meeting Competitive Challenges through HRM Practices

We have discussed the global, stakeholder, new economy, and high-performance work system challenges U.S. companies are facing. We have emphasized that management of human resources plays a critical role in determining companies' success in meeting these challenges. HRM practices have not traditionally been seen as providing economic value to the company. Economic value is usually associated with equipment, technology, and facilities. However, HRM practices have been shown to be valuable.[97] Compensation, staffing, training and development, performance management, and other HRM practices are investments that directly affect employees' motivation and ability to provide products and services that are valued by customers. Research has shown that companies that attempt to increase their competitiveness by investing in new technology and becoming involved in the quality movement also invest in state-of-the-art staffing, training, and compensation practices.[98] Figure 1.7 shows examples

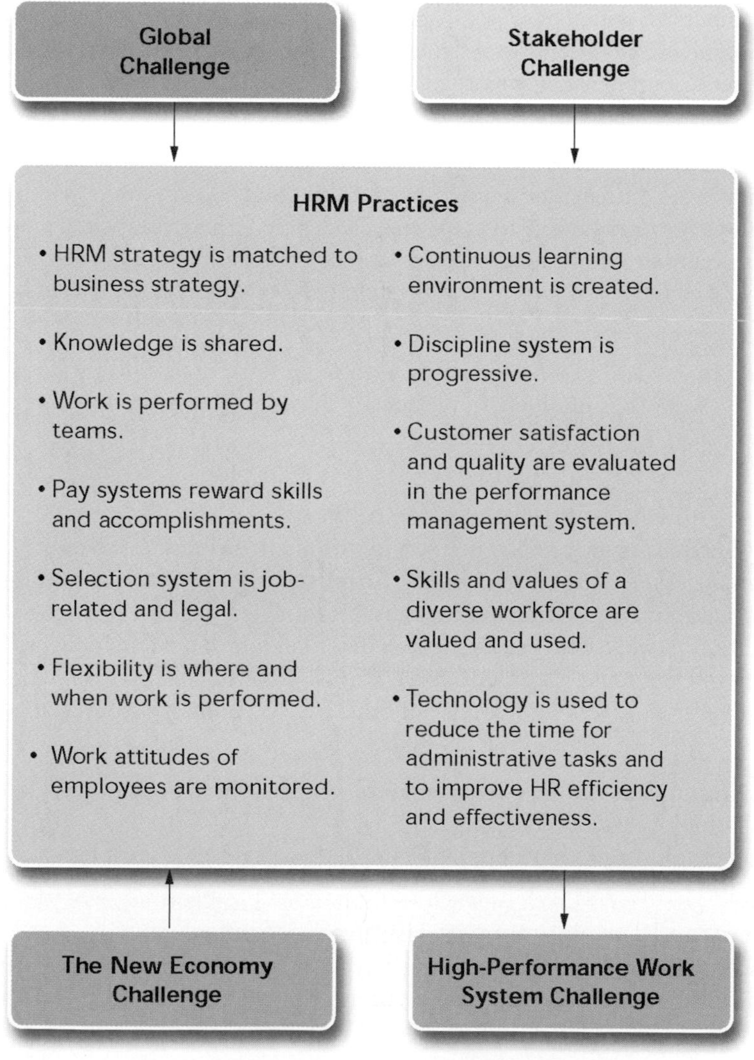

FIGURE 1.7
Examples of How HRM Practices Can Help Companies Meet Competitive Challenges

FIGURE 1.8
Major Dimensions of HRM Practices Contributing to Company Competitiveness

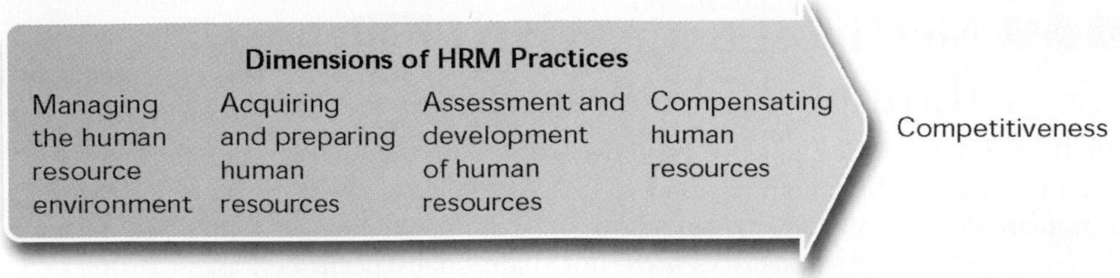

Dimensions of HRM Practices				
Managing the human resource environment	Acquiring and preparing human resources	Assessment and development of human resources	Compensating human resources	Competitiveness

of human resource management practices that help companies deal with the four challenges. For example, to meet stakeholder needs, companies need to identify through their selection processes whether prospective employees value customer relations and have the levels of interpersonal skills necessary to work with fellow employees in teams. To meet all four challenges, companies need to capitalize on the diversity of values, abilities, and perspectives that employees bring to the workplace.

HRM practices that help companies deal with the four competitive challenges can be grouped into the four dimensions shown in Figure 1.8. These dimensions include the human resource environment, acquiring and preparing human resources, assessment and development of human resources, and compensating human resources. In addition, some companies have special issues related to labor management relations, international human resource management, and managing the human resource function.

Managing the Human Resource Environment

Managing internal and external environmental factors allows employees to make the greatest possible contribution to company productivity and competitiveness. Creating a positive environment for human resources involves

- Linking HRM practices to the company's business objectives—that is, strategic human resource management.
- Ensuring that HRM practices comply with federal, state, and local laws.
- Designing work that motivates and satisfies the employee as well as maximizes customer service, quality, and productivity.

Acquiring and Preparing Human Resources

Customer needs for new products or services influence the number and type of employees businesses need to be successful. Terminations, promotions, and retirements also influence human resource requirements. Managers need to predict the number and type of employees who are needed to meet customer demands for products and services. Managers must also identify current or potential employees who can successfully deliver products and services. This area of human resource management deals with

- Identifying human resource requirements—that is, human resource planning, recruiting employees, and selecting employees.
- Training employees to have the skills needed to perform their jobs.

Assessment and Development of Human Resources

Managers need to ensure that employees have the necessary skills to perform current and future jobs. As we discussed earlier, because of new technology and the quality movement, many companies are redesigning work so that it is performed by teams. As a result, managers and employees may need to develop new skills to succeed in a team environment. Companies need to create a work environment that supports employees' work and nonwork activities. This area of human resource management addresses

- Measuring employees' performance.
- Preparing employees for future work roles and identifying employees' work interests, goals, values, and other career issues.
- Creating an employment relationship and work environment that benefits both the company and the employee.

Compensating Human Resources

Besides interesting work, pay and benefits are the most important incentives that companies can offer employees in exchange for contributing to productivity, quality, and customer service. Also, pay and benefits are used to reward employees' membership in the company and attract new employees. The positive influence of new work designs, new technology, and the quality movement on productivity can be damaged if employees are not satisfied with the level of pay and benefits or believe pay and benefits are unfairly distributed. This area of human resource management includes

- Creating pay systems.
- Rewarding employee contributions.
- Providing employees with benefits.

Special Issues

In some companies, employees are represented by a labor union. Managing human resources in a union environment requires knowledge of specific laws, contract administration, and the collective bargaining process.

Many companies are globally expanding their business through joint ventures, mergers, acquisitions, and establishing new operations. Successful global expansion depends on the extent to which HRM practices are aligned with cultural factors as well as management of employees sent to work in another country. Human resource management practices must contribute to organizational effectiveness.

Human resource management practices of both managers and the human resource function must be aligned and contribute to the company's strategic goals. The final chapter of the book explains how to effectively integrate human resource management practices.

Organization of This Book

The topics in this book are organized according to the four areas of human resource management and special issues. Table 1.11 lists the chapters covered in the book.

The content of each chapter is based on academic research and examples of effective company practices. Each chapter includes examples of how the human resource management practice covered in the chapter helps a company gain a competitive advantage by addressing global, stakeholder, new economy, or high-performance work system challenges.

TABLE 1.11

Topics Covered in This Book

I	The Human Resource Management Environment
	2 Strategic Human Resource Management
	3 The Legal Environment: Equal Employment Opportunity and Safety
	4 The Analysis and Design of Work
II	Acquisition and Preparation of Human Resources
	5 Human Resource Planning and Recruitment
	6 Selection and Placement
	7 Training
III	Assessment and Development of Human Resources
	8 Performance Management
	9 Employee Development
	10 Employee Separation and Retention
IV	Compensation of Human Resources
	11 Pay Structure Decisions
	12 Recognizing Employee Contributions with Pay
	13 Employee Benefits
V	Special Topics in Human Resource Management
	14 Collective Bargaining and Labor Relations
	15 Managing Human Resources Globally
	16 Strategically Managing the HRM Function

A Look Back

The chapter opening vignette illustrated two different approaches to managing human resources. Kodak has a large human resource function, whereas The Container Store, a much smaller organization than Kodak, has a smaller human resource function and expects managers to actively participate in human resource activities such as recruiting.

Questions

1. Consider the HRM practice dimensions shown in Figure 1.8. For each dimension describe the role of managers and the HR function.
2. Should line managers play an important role in HRM regardless of the size of the company? Explain.

Discussion Questions

1. Traditionally, human resource management practices were developed and administered by the company's human resource department. Line managers are now playing a major role in developing and implementing HRM practices. Why do you think non-HR managers are becoming more involved in developing and implementing HRM practices?
2. Staffing, training, compensation, and performance management are important HRM functions. How can each of these functions help companies succeed in the new economy? Meet stakeholders' needs? High-performance work system challenges? Global challenges?
3. This book covers four human resource management practice areas: managing the human resource environment, acquiring and preparing human resources, assessment and development of human resources, and compensating human resources. Which area do you believe

contributes most to helping a company gain a competitive advantage? Which area do you believe contributes the least? Why?
4. What is the balanced scorecard? Identify the four perspectives included in the balanced scorecard. How can HRM practices influence the four perspectives?
5. Is HRM becoming more strategic? Explain your answer.
6. Explain the implications of each of the following labor force trends for HRM: (1) aging workforce, (2) diverse workforce, (3) skill deficiencies.
7. What role do HRM practices play in a business decision to expand internationally?
8. Is business emphasis on quality a fad? Why or why not? What might a quality goal and high-performance work systems have in common in terms of HRM practices?
9. What disadvantages might result from outsourcing HRM practices? From employee self-service? From increased line manager involvement in designing and using HR practices?

Web Exercise

In this chapter we discuss four competitive challenges that companies face (the new economy, global competition, managing stakeholders, and high-performance work systems). Go to the Society for Human Resource Management (SHRM) home page on the Web. SHRM is an important professional society for human resource management. The address is **www.shrm.org**. Here you will find current articles related to HRM issues. SHRM also publishes *HR Magazine*, a business magazine for human resource managers.

Questions

1. How are companies dealing with the competitive challenges? Use Web resources to find an article that relates to how a company is dealing with the competitive challenges. Go to "HR Channels." Click on any of the HR practices listed to find an article.
2. Summarize the main topic of the article.
3. Identify how it relates to one of the competitive challenges discussed in the chapter.

Managing People: From the Pages of *BusinessWeek*

BusinessWeek The Human Factor

Julie Jones jumped at the chance to take a sabbatical when Accenture Ltd. (ACN) offered one in June. Although she had been a consultant in the firm's Chicago office for just two and a half years, the 25-year-old expert in accounts payable software had long wanted to work for AmeriCorps, the national volunteer group. So in July, Jones, who's single, headed out to Los Angeles for a year to join an AmeriCorps group that helps nonprofits with technology problems. Accenture, the former consulting arm of Andersen Worldwide, will pay 20 percent of her salary, plus benefits, and let her keep her work phone number, laptop, and e-mail. "This gives me the security of knowing I'll have a job when I come back," says Jones.

Accenture hopes the program will offer it some security, too. The economic slowdown has pinched the company's business, forcing it to rein in costs. But after years of scrambling to find scarce talent, Accenture is reluctant to lay off workers it hopes to need when the economy turns north again. Accenture did cut 600 support staff jobs in June. But to retain skilled employees, it cooked up the idea of partially paid sabbaticals, such as the one Jones is taking. About 1,000 employees took up the offer, which allows them to do whatever they want for 6 to 12 months, says Larry Solomon, Accenture's managing partner in charge of internal operations. "This is a way to cut costs that gives us the ability to hang onto people we spent so much time recruiting and training," he says.

Plenty of other employers are feeling the same way. The slumping economy has put pressure on companies to slash expenses and boost sagging profits. But the United States has just sailed through five years of labor shortfalls on a scale not seen in more than three decades. What's more, the unemployment rate, while rising, remains at historically low levels. Many employers are wary about dumping too many workers just to find themselves scrambling later to refill the positions.

Even companies that have handed out pink slips often did so with caution rather than abandon. When Charles Schwab Corp. (SCH) first saw business deteriorate last fall, it put projects on hold and cut back on such expenses as travel and entertainment to avoid layoffs, says human resources vice president Ruth K. Ross. In December, as it became clear that more was needed, top executives all took pay cuts: 50 percent for the company's two co-CEOs, 20 percent for executive vice presidents, 10 percent for senior vice presidents, and 5 percent for vice presidents.

Schwab took further steps this year before finally cutting staff. It encouraged employees to take unused vacation and to take unpaid leaves of up to 20 days. Management designated three Fridays in February and March as voluntary days off without pay for employees who didn't have clients to deal with. Only in March, after the outlook darkened yet again, did Schwab announce 2,000 layoffs out of a workforce of 25,000. Even then, the severance package includes a $7,500 "hire-back" bonus that any employee will get if they're rehired within 18 months. "We felt the markets will turn at some point, and the cost of hiring people back with the bonus is small compared to what it would be to pay for recruiting and retraining new employees," says Ross.

Employers also are trying to protect their core workers by axing temps and contract employees. Throughout the 1990s, many companies built up buffer workforces so they could more easily adjust staffing levels. Since 1990 the number of temporary employees tripled, to a peak of 3.6 million last fall. But since then their ranks have fallen by half a million as companies have tried to adjust to slower sales.

Slashing work hours is another way to reduce payroll without lopping off heads. The workweek has edged steadily downward as the economy slowed, to 34.3 hours for most of this year. Manufacturers, hit the hardest by the economic slump, have dialed back the most. Factory overtime has fallen by about 15 percent from last year, to four hours a week in June. The factory workweek has plunged by a similar amount, to 40.7 hours. "Businesses have aggressively cut hours worked, which is the first thing you do if you want to hang onto staff," says Mark M. Zandi, chief economist at Economy.com Inc. in West Chester, Pennsylvania.

The result of all these trends has been a relatively modest upturn in unemployment. The jobless rate has jumped up to 4.5 percent since hitting a 30-year low of 3.9 percent last fall. But that's still below the 5 percent or even 6 percent that most experts had considered full employment for some two decades. It's also much lower than the spike that occurred during the last recession, in 1991. Back then, unemployment soared from a low of 5 percent to a peak of 7.8 percent. The rate probably will continue to inch higher throughout the year as companies face up to the fact that the sales volumes they had geared up for in 2000 aren't going to materialize. But if the consensus among economists is right, labor, especially the more skilled kind, will remain scarce for the foreseeable future. "Even if we get unemployment up over 5 percent, it won't free up more nurses or computer programmers," says David A. Wyss, chief economist at Standard & Poor's, a unit of *BusinessWeek*'s publisher, The McGraw-Hill Companies. "There aren't enough of them to go around."

Even high-tech workers are likely to remain in demand. Employers will have about 900,000 job openings this year for programmers, software engineers, tech-support personnel, and similar workers, according to an April survey by the Information Technology Association of America (ITAA), an industry group based in Arlington, Virginia. That's down sharply from 1.6 million openings in 2000. But the survey found that even this year, companies believe that they will be unable to fill nearly half of those jobs, or 420,000 positions. "Demand for workers remains strong," the report concluded.

Part of the reason is that most of these posts aren't at high-tech companies, which have borne the brunt of the sharp falloff in demand for computers and telecom equipment. Roughly 90 percent of the country's 10.4 million tech workers are employed by non–high-tech companies, the ITAA found in its survey. Employers say they will have a total of about 640,000 openings this year.

Still, even battered tech companies would like to hire 260,000 skilled workers this year—and expect to be able to find just half of those they need, according to the survey. "We're still hiring for some critical areas, like electrical engineers," says Matt McKinney, a spokesman for Texas Instruments Inc., which announced 2,500 layoffs in April. "Every year, the universities graduate fewer students in these areas, so the available talent pool is shrinking. Yet demand still goes up."

Absent a full-blown recession, though, skilled workers are likely to remain in short supply. The same may not hold true at the bottom of the labor market, which is unlikely to see solid wage growth without a return to the extraordinary growth levels of 2000. That leaves the United States facing renewed social cleavages as those on the top continue to gain while the rest struggle to keep up.

SOURCE: Reprinted from August 27, 2001 issue of *BusinessWeek* by special permission.

Questions

1. How can companies offer some degree of job security to employees in this type of economy? Should they offer job security? Explain.
2. What HRM practices may be useful for attracting scarce skilled workers?

Notes

1. A.S. Tsui and L.R. Gomez-Mejia, "Evaluating Human Resource Effectiveness," in *Human Resource Management: Evolving Rules and Responsibilities*, ed. L. Dyer (Washington, DC: BNA Books, 1988), pp. 1187–227; M.A. Hitt, B.W. Keats, and S.M. DeMarie, "Navigating in the New Competitive

Landscape: Building Strategic Flexibility and Competitive Advantage in the 21st Century," *Academy of Management Executive 12*, no. 4 (1998), pp. 22–42; J.T. Delaney and M.A. Huselid, "The Impact of Human Resource Management Practices on Perceptions of Organizational Performance," *Academy of Management Journal* 39 (1996), pp. 949–69.
2. SHRM-BNA Survey No. 66, "Policy and Practice Forum: Human Resources Activities, Budgets, and Staffs: 2000–2001." Bulletin to Management, Bureau of National Affairs Policy and Practice Series, June 28, 2001 (Washington, DC: Bureau of National Affairs).
3. D. Ulrich, *Human Resource Champions* (Boston: Harvard Business School Press, 1998).
4. Ulrich, *Human Resource Champions*.
5. K. Carrig, "Reshaping Human Resources for the Next Century: Lessons from a High-Flying Airline," *Human Resource Management* 36, no. 2 (1997), pp. 277–89.
6. Ulrich, *Human Resource Champions*.
7. Carrig, "Reshaping Human Resources for the Next Century."
8. Ulrich, *Human Resource Champions*.
9. Carrig, "Reshaping Human Resources for the Next Century."
10. Ulrich, *Human Resource Champions*.
11. Carrig, "Reshaping Human Resources for the Next Century."
12. Ulrich, *Human Resource Champions*.
13. A. Halcrow, "Survey Shows HRM in Transition," *Workforce*, June 1998, pp. 73–80: J. Laabs, "Why HR Can't Win Today," *Workforce*, May 1998, pp. 62–74; C. Cole. "Kodak Snapshots," *Workforce*, June 2000, pp. 65–72.
14. Towers Perrin, *Priorities for Competitive Advantage: An IBM Study Conducted by Towers Perrin*, 1992.
15. S. Greengard, "Building a Self-Service Culture That Works," *Workforce*, July 1998, pp. 60–64.
16. S. Greengard, "Technology Finally Advances HR," *Workforce*, January 2000, pp. 38–41.
17. E. Zimmerman, "B of A and Big-Time Outsourcing," *Workforce*, April 2001, pp. 50–54.
18. Towers Perrin, *Priorities for Competitive Advantage: An IBM Study Conducted by Towers Perrin*, 1992.
19. B.P. Sunoo, "A Day in the Life of John Harvey: Positioning HR for the Fast Track," *Workforce*, June 1988, pp. 64, 66, 68.
20. J. Wiscombe, "Your Wonderful, Terrible HR Life," *Workforce*, June 2001, pp. 32–38.
21. "Two-Thirds of Americans Online," *CyberAtlas* (May 10, 2000), **http://cyberatlas.internet.com**.
22. D. Hecker, "Employment Impact of Electronic Business," *Monthly Labor Review*, May 2001, pp. 3–16.
23. R.D. Blackwell and K. Stephan, *Customers Rule! Why the E-Commerce Honeymoon Is Over and Where Winning Businesses Go from Here* (New York: Crown Publishing, 2001).
24. J. Angwin, "Latest Dot-Com Fad Is a Bit Old-Fashioned: It's Called 'Profitability,' " *The Wall Street Journal* (August 14, 2001), pp. A1, A6.
25. U.S. Bureau of Labor Statistics Employment Projections, Table 3b. "The Ten Fastest-Growing Occupations, 1998–2008." From **http://stats.bls.gov**.
26. A. Saveri, "The Realignment of Workers and Work in the 1990s." In *New Directions in Career Planning in the Workplace*, ed. J.M. Kummerow (Palo Alto, CA: Consulting Psychologists Press, 1991, pp. 117–53.
27. E. Zimmerman, "What Are Employees Worth?" *Workforce*, February 2001, pp. 32–36.
28. Conseco website (June 2001) **www.conseco.com**.
29. "CIO Panel: Knowledge-Sharing Roundtable," *Information Week Online*, "News in Review," April 26, 1999 (from *Information Week* website, **www.informationweek.com**); Buckman Laboratories website, **www.buckman.com**.
30. A. Carnevale and D. Desrochers, "Training in the Dilbert Economy," *Training & Development*, December 1999, pp. 32–36.
31. "Industry Report 2000," *Training*, October 2000, p. 48.
32. D.M. Rousseau, "Psychological and Implied Contracts in Organizations," *Employee Rights and Responsibilities Journal* 2 (1989), pp. 121–29.
33. D. Rousseau, "Changing the Deal While Keeping the People," *Academy of Management Executive* 11 (1996), pp. 50–61; M.A. Cavanaugh and R. Noe, "Antecedents and Consequences of the New Psychological Contract," *Journal of Organizational Behavior* 20 (1999), pp. 323–40.
34. M. DiNatale, "Characteristics of and Preferences for Alternative Work Arrangements, 1999," *Monthly Labor Review*, March 2001, pp. 28–49.
35. C. Johnson, "Don't Forget Your Shift Workers," *HR Magazine*, February 1999, pp. 80–84.
36. J. Cook, "Keeping Work at Work," *Human Resource Executive*, July 2001, pp. 68–71.
37. Cook, "Keeping Work at Work."
38. K. Clark, "You're Laid Off! Kind of. Firms Look beyond Pink Slips," *US News and World Report* (July 2, 2001), pp. 50–53.
39. L. Phillon and J. Brugger. "Encore! Retirees Give Top Performance as Temporaries," *HR Magazine*, October 1994, pp. 74–77.
40. N. Breuer, "Shelf Life," *Workforce*, August 2000, pp. 29–34.
41. C.A. O'Reilly III and J. Pfeffer, "Hidden Value" (Boston: Harvard Business School Press, 2000).

42. Conseco website (June 2001), **www.conseco.com**.
43. Society for Human Resource Management, "Globalization and the Human Resources Profession: Workplace Visions" (no. 5, 2000).
44. J. Kahn, "The World's Most Admired Companies," *Fortune* (October 26, 1998), pp. 206–26; A. Fisher, "The World's Most Admired Companies," *Fortune* (October 27, 1997), p. 232.
45. C. Hill, *International Business* (New York: Irwin/McGraw-Hill, 1997).
46. M. Braxton, "HR's Role in a New Global Economy," *HRTX iLinx*, May/June 2001, pp. 1, 14.
47. C. Fleming and L. Lopez, "No Boundaries," *The Wall Street Journal* (September 9, 1998), p. R16.
48. J.L. Young, "Starbucks expansion into China is slated." *The Wall Street Journal* (October 5, 1998), p. B13C.
49. K. Roberts, E.E. Kossek, and C. Ozeki, "Managing the Global Workforce: Challenges and Strategies," *Academy of Management Executive* 12 (1988), no. 4, pp. 93–106.
50. R.L. Tung, "Expatriate Assignments: Enhancing Success and Minimizing Failure," *Academy of Management Executive* 1 (1987), pp. 117–26.
51. G.P. Zachary, "Stalled U.S. Workers' Objections Grow as More of Their Jobs Shift Overseas," *The Wall Street Journal* (October 9, 1995), pp. A2, A9.
52. R.S. Kaplan and D.P. Norton, "The Balanced Scorecard—Measures That Drive Performance," *Harvard Business Review*, January–February 1992, pp. 71–79; R.S. Kaplan and D.P. Norton, "Putting the Balanced Scorecard to Work," *Harvard Business Review*, September–October 1993, pp. 134–47.
53. M. Gendron, "Using the Balanced Scorecard," *Harvard Business Review*, October 1997, pp. 3–5.
54. D. Ulrich, "Measuring Human Resources: An Overview of Practice and a Prescription for Results," *Human Resource Management* 36 (1997), pp. 303–20.
55. E. Raimy, "A Plan for All Seasons," *Human Resource Executive*, April 2001, pp. 34–38.
56. J.R. Jablonski, *Implementing Total Quality Management: An Overview* (San Diego: Pfeiffer, 1991).
57. R. Hodgetts, F. Luthans, and S. Lee, "New Paradigm Organizations: From Total Quality to Learning World-Class," *Organizational Dynamics*, Winter 1994, pp. 5–19.
58. General Accounting Office, *Management Practices: U.S. Companies Improve Performance through Quality Efforts* (GAO/NSIAD-91-190) (Washington, DC: U.S. General Accounting Office, 1991).
59. S.L. Jackson, "What You Should Know about ISO 9000," *Training*, May 1992, pp. 48–52; Bureau of Best Practices, *Profile of ISO 9000* (Boston: Allyn & Bacon, 1992); "ISO 9000 International Standards for Quality Assurance," *Design Matters* **www.iso9000y2k.com**, a website containing ISO 9000:2000 documentation.
60. General Electric 1999 Annual Report. At **www.ge.com/annual99**.
61. H.N. Fullerton, "Labor Force 2006: Slowing Down and Changing Composition," *Monthly Labor Review*, November 1997, pp. 23–28. Also see the Bureau of Labor Statistics employment projections on the Web at **www.bls.gov/news.release/ecopro.nws.htm**.
62. M. Cohen, *Labor Shortages as America Approaches the Twenty-first Century* (Ann Arbor: University of Michigan Press, 1995); "Human Resources and Their Skills," in *The Changing Nature of Work*, ed. A. Howard (San Francisco: Jossey-Bass, 1995), pp. 211–22; H. Fullerton, "Another Look at the Labor Force," *Monthly Labor Review*, November 1993, pp. 31–40.
63. M. Mandel, "It's Really Two Immigrant Economies," *Business Week* (June 20, 1994), pp. 74–78.
64. C.M. Solomon, "Managing the Baby Busters," *Personnel Journal*, March 1992, pp. 52–59; J. Wallace, "After X Comes Y," *HR Magazine* (April 2001), p. 192.
65. B. Wooldridge and J. Wester, "The Turbulent Environment of Public Personnel Administration: Responding to the Challenge of the Changing Workplace of the Twenty-first Century," *Public Personnel Management* 20 (1991), pp. 207–24; J. Laabs, "The New Loyalty: Grasp It. Earn It. Keep It," *Workforce*, November 1998, pp. 34–39.
66. "Employee Dissatisfaction on Rise in Last 10 Years, New Report Says," *Employee Relations Weekly* (Washington, DC: Bureau of National Affairs, 1986).
67. D.T. Hall and J. Richter, "Career Gridlock: Baby Boomers Hit the Wall," *The Executive* 4 (1990), pp. 7–22.
68. T.H. Cox and S. Blake, "Managing Cultural Diversity: Implications for Organizational Competitiveness," *The Executive* 5 (1991), pp. 45–56.
69. M. Loden and J.B. Rosener, *Workforce America!* (Homewood, IL: Business One Irwin, 1991).
70. "Impact of Diversity Initiatives on the Bottom Line Survey," *SHRM/Fortune*, June 2001.
71. H. Rosin, "Cultural Revolution at Texaco," *The New Republic* (February 2, 1998), pp. 15–18; K. Labich, "No More Crude at Texaco," *Fortune* (September 6, 1999), pp. 205–12.
72. J. Ledvinka and V.G. Scarpello, *Federal Regulation of Personnel and Human Resource Management*, 2nd ed. (Boston: PWS-Kent, 1991).
73. M.A. Jacobs, "Courts Wrestle with Religion in Workplace," *The Wall Street Journal* (October 10, 1995), p. B1.

74. J. Britt, "Disability Advocates Aim at Technology Barriers," *HR News* 20 (2001), no. 9, pp. 1, 9.
75. S. Nelton, "Nurturing Diversity," *Nation's Business*, June 1995, pp. 25–27.
76. M. Pastin, *The Hard Problems of Management: Gaining the Ethics Edge* (San Francisco: Jossey-Bass, 1986).
77. R. Ricklees, "Ethics in America," *The Wall Street Journal* (October 31–November 3, 1983), p. 33.
78. C. Lee, "Ethics Training: Facing the Tough Questions," *Training* (March 31, 1986), pp. 33, 38–41.
79. Pastin, *Hard Problems of Management*.
80. D. Fandray, "The Ethical Company," *Workforce*, December 2000, pp. 75–77.
81. G.F. Cavanaugh, D. Moberg, and M. Velasquez, "The Ethics of Organizational Politics," *Academy of Management Review* 6 (1981), pp. 363–74.
82. J.A. Neal and C.L. Tromley, "From Incremental Change to Retrofit: Creating High-Performance Work Systems," *Academy of Management Executive* 9 (1995), pp. 42–54.
83. P. Choate and P. Linger, *The High-Flex Society* (New York: Knopf, 1986); P.B. Doeringer, *Turbulence in the American Workplace* (New York: Oxford University Press, 1991).
84. K. Miller, *Retraining the American Work Force* (Reading, MA: Addison-Wesley, 1989).
85. M. Williams, "Some Plants Tear Out Long Assembly Lines, Switch to Craft Work," *The Wall Street Journal* (October 24, 1994), pp. A1, A4.
86. T.J. Atchison, "The Employment Relationship: Untied or Re-tied," *Academy of Management Executive* 5 (1991), pp. 52–62.
87. D. McCann and C. Margerison, "Managing High-Performance Teams," *Training and Development Journal* (November 1989), pp. 52–60; S. Sheman, "Secrets of HP's 'Muddled' Team," *Fortune* (March 18, 1996), pp. 116–20.
88. T. Peters, "Restoring American Competitiveness: Looking for New Models of Organizations," *The Executive* 2 (1988), pp. 103–10.
89. M.J. Kavanaugh, H.G. Guetal, and S.I. Tannenbaum, *Human Resource Information Systems: Development and Application* (Boston: PWS-Kent, 1990).
90. S. Greengard, "When HRMS Goes Global: Managing the Data Highway," *Personnel Journal*, June 1995, pp. 91–106.
91. M. Stepanek, "Using the Net for Brainstorming," *BusinessWeek e.biz* (December 13, 1999).
92. R.N. Ashkenas, "Beyond the Fads: How Leaders Drive Change with Results," *Human Resource Planning* 17 (1994), pp. 25–44.
93. M.A. Huselid, "The Impact of Human Resource Management Practices on Turnover, Productivity, and Corporate Financial Performance," *Academy of Management Journal* 38 (1995), pp. 635–72; U.S. Dept. of Labor, *High-Performance Work Practices and Firm Performance* (Washington, DC: U.S. Government Printing Office, 1993).
94. B. Becker and M.A. Huselid, "High-Performance Work Systems and Firm Performance: A Synthesis of Research and Managerial Implications," in *Research in Personnel and Human Resource Management* 16, ed. G.R. Ferris (Stamford, CT: JAI Press, 1998), pp. 53–101.
95. B. Becker and B. Gerhart, "The Impact of Human Resource Management on Organizational Performance: Progress and Prospects," *Academy of Management Journal* 39 (1996), pp. 779–801.
96. G. Flynn, "HR Leaders Stay Close to the Line," *Workforce*, February 1997, p. 53; GE Fanuc Corporate Profile, "World Class Excellence," Internet address **www.ge.com/gemis/gefanuc**.
97. W.F. Cascio, *Costing Human Resources: The Financial Impact of Behavior in Organizations*, 3rd ed. (Boston: PWS-Kent, 1991).
98. S.A. Snell and J.W. Dean, "Integrated Manufacturing and Human Resource Management: A Human Capital Perspective," *Academy of Management Journal* 35 (1992), pp. 467–504; M.A. Youndt, S. Snell, J.W. Dean Jr., and D.P. Lepak, "Human Resource Management, Manufacturing Strategy, and Firm Performance," *Academy of Management Journal* 39 (1996), pp. 836–66.

The Human Resource Environment

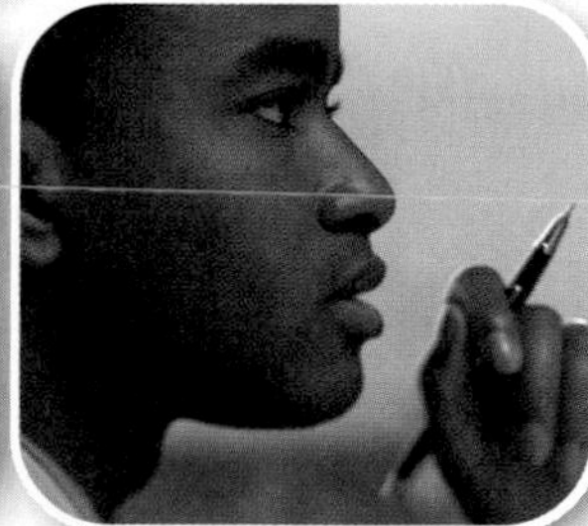

Chapter 2
Strategic Human Resource Management

Objectives
After reading this chapter, you should be able to:

1. Describe the differences between strategy formulation and strategy implementation.
2. List the components of the strategic management process.
3. Discuss the role of the HRM function in strategy formulation.
4. Describe the linkages between HRM and strategy formulation.
5. Discuss the more popular typologies of generic strategies and the various HRM practices associated with each.
6. Describe the different HRM issues and practices associated with various directional strategies.
7. List the competencies the HRM executive needs to become a strategic partner in the company.

Delta's "Leadership 7.5" strategy cut down on costs but resulted in diminished quality, customer service, and employee morale. How might HRM have had an impact on this strategy?

Enter the World of Business

Strategy and HRM at Delta Air Lines

In 1994 top executives at Delta Air Lines faced a crucial strategic decision. Delta, which had established an unrivaled reputation within the industry for having highly committed employees who delivered the highest-quality customer service, had lost over $10 per share for two straight years. A large portion of its financial trouble was due to the $491 million acquisition of Pan Am in 1991, which was followed by the Gulf War (driving up fuel costs) and the early 1990s recession (causing people to fly less). Its cost per available seat mile (what it costs to fly one passenger one mile) was 9.26 cents, among the highest in the industry. In addition, it was threatened by new discount competitors with significantly lower costs—in particular, Valujet, which flew out of Delta's Atlanta hub. How could Delta survive and thrive in such an environment? Determining the strategy for doing so was the top executives' challenge.

Chairman and Chief Executive Officer Ron Allen embarked upon the "Leadership 7.5" strategy, whose goal was to reduce the cost per available seat mile to 7.5 cents, comparable with Southwest Airlines. Implementing this strategy required a significant downsizing over the following three years, trimming 11,458 people from its 69,555-employee workforce (the latter number representing an 8 percent reduction from two years earlier). Many experienced customer service representatives were laid off and replaced with lower-paid, inexperienced, part-time workers. Cleaning service of planes as well as baggage handling were outsourced, resulting in layoffs of long-term Delta employees. The numbers of maintenance workers and flight attendants were reduced substantially.

The results of the strategy were mixed as financial performance improved but operational performance plummeted. Since it began its cost cutting, its stock price more than doubled in just over two years and its debt was upgraded. On the other hand, customer complaints about dirty airplanes rose from 219 in 1993 to 358 in 1994 and 634 in 1995. On-time performance was so bad that passengers joked that Delta stands for "Doesn't Ever Leave The Airport." Delta slipped from fourth to seventh among the top 10 carriers in baggage handling. Employee morale hit an all-time low, and unions were beginning to make headway toward organizing some of Delta's employee groups. In 1996 CEO Allen was quoted as saying, "This has tested our people. There have been some morale problems. But so be it. You go back to the question of survival, and it makes the decision very easy."

Shortly after, employees began donning cynical "SO BE IT" buttons. Delta's board saw union organizers stirring blue-collar discontent, employee morale destroyed, the customer service reputation in near shambles, and senior managers exiting the company in droves. Less than one year later, Allen was fired despite Delta's financial turnaround. His firing was "not because the company was going broke, but because its spirit was broken."

SOURCE: M. Brannigan and E. De Lisser, "Cost Cutting at Delta Raises the Stock Price but Lowers the Service," *The Wall Street Journal* (June 20, 1996), pp. A1, A8; M. Brannigan and J. White, "So Be It: Why Delta Air Lines Decided It Was Time for CEO to Take Off," *The Wall Street Journal* (May 30, 1997), p. A1.

Introduction

As the Delta example just illustrated, business organizations exist in an environment of competition. They can use a number of resources to compete with other companies. These resources are physical (such as plant, equipment, technology, and geographic location), organizational (the structure, planning, controlling, and coordinating systems, and group relations), and human (the experience, skill, and intelligence of employees). It is these resources under the control of the company that provide competitive advantage.[1]

The goal of strategic management in an organization is to deploy and allocate resources in a way that gives it a competitive advantage. As you can see, two of the three classes of resources (organizational and human) are directly tied to the human resource management function. As Chapter 1 pointed out, the role of human resource management is to ensure that a company's human resources provide a competitive advantage. Chapter 1 also pointed out some of the major competitive challenges that companies face today. These challenges require companies to take a proactive, strategic approach in the marketplace.

To be maximally effective, the HRM function must be integrally involved in the company's strategic management process.[2] This means that human resource managers should (1) have input into the strategic plan, both in terms of people-related issues and in terms of the ability of the human resource pool to implement particular strategic alternatives; (2) have specific knowledge of the organization's strategic goals; (3) know what types of employee skills, behaviors, and attitudes are needed to support the strategic plan; and (4) develop programs to ensure that employees have those skills, behaviors, and attitudes.

We begin this chapter by discussing the concept of strategy and by depicting the strategic management process. Then we discuss the levels of integration between the HRM function and the strategic management process in strategy formulation. Next we review some of the more common strategic models and, within the context of these models, discuss the various types of employee skills, behaviors, and attitudes, and the ways HRM practices aid in implementing the strategic plan. Finally, we discuss the new competencies needed by HRM executives to fulfill the strategic role of HRM.

What Is Strategic Management?

Many authors have noted that in today's competitive market, organizations must engage in strategic planning to survive and prosper. *Strategy* comes from the Greek word *strategos*, which has its roots in military language. It refers to a general's grand design behind a war or battle. In fact, *Webster's New American Dictionary* defines *strategy* as the "skillful employment and coordination of tactics" and as "artful planning and management."

Strategic management is a process, an approach to addressing the competitive challenges an organization faces. It can be thought of as managing the "pattern or plan that integrates an organization's major goals, policies, and action sequences into a cohesive whole."[3] These strategies can be either the generic approach to competing or the specific adjustments and actions taken to deal with a particular situation.

First, business organizations engage in generic strategies that often fit into some strategic type. One example is "cost, differentiation, or focus."[4] Another is "defender, analyzer, prospector, or reactor."[5] Different organizations within the same industry often have different generic strategies. These generic strategy types describe the consistent way the company attempts to position itself relative to competitors.

However, a generic strategy is only a small part of strategic management. The second aspect of strategic management is the process of developing strategies for achieving the company's goals in light of its current environment. Thus, business organizations engage in generic strategies, but they also make choices about such things as how to scare off competitors, how to keep competitors weaker, how to react to and influence pending legislation, how to deal with various stakeholders and special interest groups, how to lower production costs, how to raise revenues, what technology to implement, and how many and what types of people to employ. Each of these decisions may present competitive challenges that have to be considered.

Strategic management is more than a collection of strategic types. It is a process for analyzing a company's competitive situation, developing the company's strategic goals, and devising a plan of action and allocation of resources (human, organizational, and physical) that will increase the likelihood of achieving those goals. This kind of strategic approach should be emphasized in human resource management. HR managers should be trained to identify the competitive issues the company faces with regard to human resources and think strategically about how to respond.

Strategic human resource management (SHRM)
A pattern of planned human resource deployments and activities intended to enable an organization to achieve its goals.

Strategic human resource management (SHRM) can be thought of as "the pattern of planned human resource deployments and activities intended to enable an organization to achieve its goals."[6] For example, many firms have developed integrated manufacturing systems such as advanced manufacturing technology, just-in-time inventory control, and total quality management in an effort to increase their competitive position. However, these systems must be run by people. SHRM in these cases entails assessing the employee skills required to run these systems and engaging in HRM practices, such as selection and training, that develop these skills in employees.[7] To take a strategic approach to HRM, we must first understand the role of HRM in the strategic management process.

Strategy formulation
The process of deciding on a strategic direction by defining a company's mission and goals, its external opportunities and threats, and its internal strengths and weaknesses.

Components of the Strategic Management Process

The strategic management process has two distinct yet interdependent phases: strategy formulation and strategy implementation. During **strategy formulation** the strategic planning groups decide on a strategic direction by defining the company's

FIGURE 2.1
A Model of the Strategic Management Process

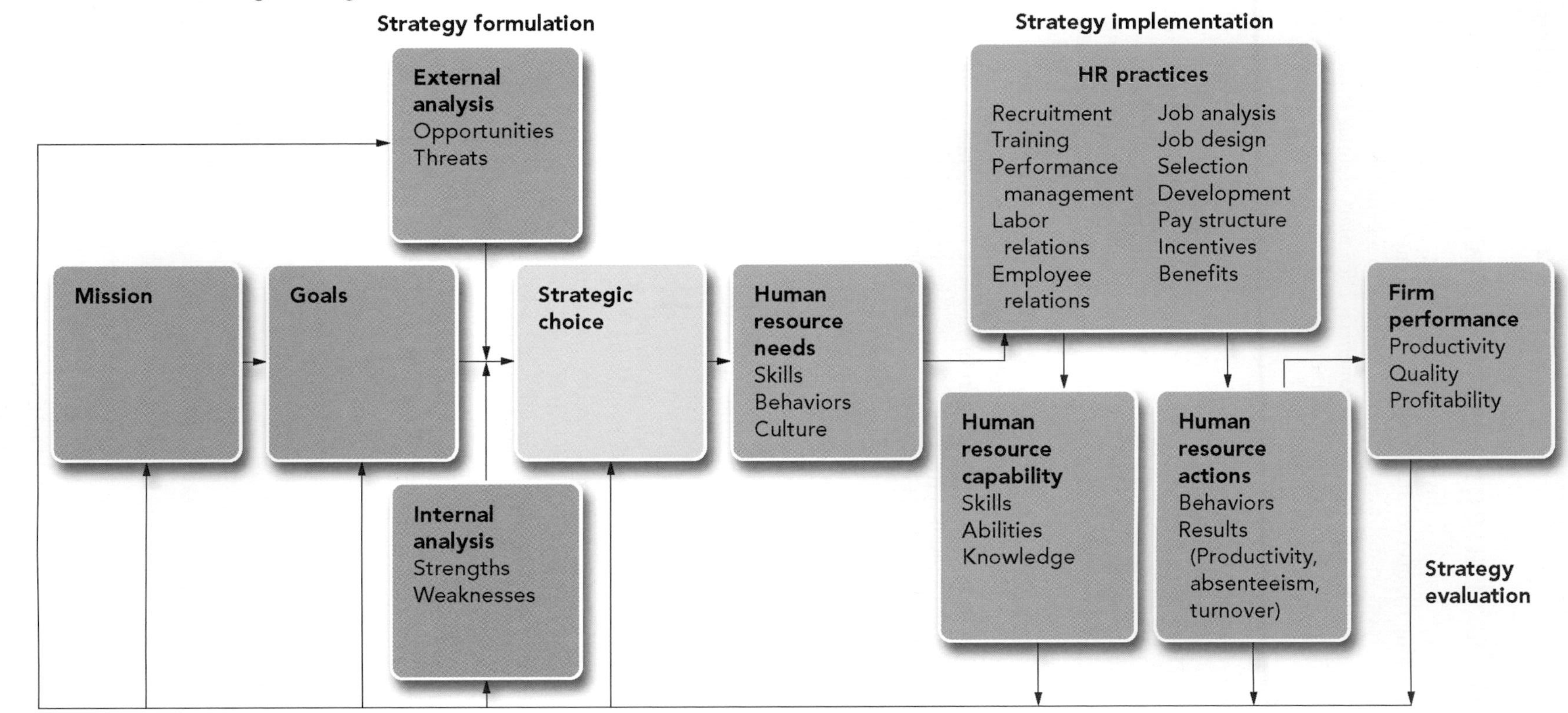

mission and goals, its external opportunities and threats, and its internal strengths and weaknesses. They then generate various strategic alternatives and compare those alternatives' ability to achieve the company's mission and goals. During **strategy implementation,** the organization follows through on the chosen strategy. This consists of structuring the organization, allocating resources, ensuring that the firm has skilled employees in place, and developing reward systems that align employee behavior with the organization's strategic goals. Both of these strategic management phases must be performed effectively. It is important to note that this process does not happen sequentially. As we will discuss later with regard to emergent strategies, this process entails a constant cycling of information and decision making. Figure 2.1 presents the strategic management process.

Strategy implementation
The process of devising structures and allocating resources to enact the strategy a company has chosen.

In recent years organizations have recognized that the success of the strategic management process depends largely on the extent to which the HRM function is involved.[8]

Linkage between HRM and the Strategic Management Process

The strategic choice really consists of answering questions about competition—that is, how the firm will compete to achieve its missions and goals. These decisions consist of addressing the issues of where to compete, how to compete, and with what to compete, which are described in Figure 2.2. Although these decisions are all important, strategic decision makers often pay less attention to the "with what will we compete" issue, resulting in poor strategic decisions. For example, PepsiCo in the 1980s acquired the fast food chains of Kentucky Fried Chicken, Taco Bell, and Pizza Hut ("where to compete" decisions) in an effort to increase its customer base. However, it failed to adequately recognize the differences between its existing workforce (mostly professionals) and that of the fast food industry (lower-skilled people and high schoolers) as well as its ability to manage such a workforce. This was one reason that PepsiCo, in 1998, spun off the fast food chains. In essence, it had made a decision about where to compete without fully understanding what resources it would take to compete in that market.

Boeing illustrates how failing to address the "with what" issue resulted in problems in its "how to compete" decisions. When the aerospace firm's consumer products division entered into a price war with Airbus Industrie, it was forced to move away from its traditional customer service strategy toward emphasizing cost reduction.[9] The strategy was a success on the sales end as Boeing received large numbers of orders for aircraft from firms such as Delta, Continental, Southwest, and Singapore Airline. However, it had recently gone through a large workforce reduction (thus, it didn't have enough people to fill the orders) and did not have the production technology to

1. Where to compete?
   In what market or markets (industries, products, etc.) will we compete?
2. How to compete?
   On what criterion or differentiating characteristic(s) will we compete? Cost? Quality? Reliability? Delivery?
3. With what will we compete?
   What resources will allow us to beat our competition?
   How will we acquire, develop, and deploy those resources to compete?

FIGURE 2.2
Strategy—Decisions about Competition

COMPETING THROUGH HIGH-PERFORMANCE WORK SYSTEMS

Boeing Begins a Comeback

As mentioned in the chapter, Boeing's strategic change to compete on cost caused the company significant financial and operational difficulty. As Airbus has continued to eat away at Boeing's market share, Boeing has now begun to create the systems and structures to enable them to fight back.

One way of building cost-competitive processes is through the implementation of lean manufacturing concepts. The basic idea behind these concepts is to examine everything from component design to the machinery used in production toward a goal of enabling workers to increase productivity using less space and movement. For instance, one of the converted 737 lines in Renton, Washington, consists of a moving line where a tug pulls the plane at two inches a minute for two shifts a day. Rather than running back and forth for tools and parts, workers move on a floatlike contraption with the plane, and the tools and parts are wheeled to waiting spots on the line. Emergency call boxes are placed at several spots on the line so workers can alert support departments to problems. (In one group a flashing light accompanies a recording of Aretha Franklin's "Rescue Me" to call for help.)

So far these efforts have proved successful. Assembly of the 777 has been reduced to 37 days from 71, and the 737 is down to 11 days with a goal of 5. Overall inventories have been reduced by 42 percent, and profit margin in the commercial airplane division hit 10.2 percent in the first half of 2001, up from 1 percent in 1998.

SOURCE: J. L. Lunsford, "Boeing Rethinks How It Builds Planes with Help from Its "Moonshine Shop," *The Wall Street Journal* (September 5, 2001), p. 1.

enable the necessary increase in productivity. The result of this failure to address "with what will we compete" in making a decision about how to compete resulted in the firm's inability to meet delivery deadlines and the ensuing penalties it had to pay to its customers.

The "Competing through High-Performance Work Systems" box describes how Boeing has used work design to compete on cost against Airbus.

Role of HRM in Strategy Formulation

As the preceding examples illustrate, often the "with what will we compete" questions present ideal avenues for HRM to influence the strategic management process. This might be through either limiting strategic options or forcing thoughtfulness among the executive team regarding how and at what cost the firm might gain or develop the human resources (people) necessary for such a strategy to be successful. For example, HRM executives at PepsiCo could have noted that the firm had no expertise in managing the workforce of fast food restaurants. The limiting role would have been for these executives to argue against the acquisition because of this lack of resources. On the other hand, they might have influenced the decision by educating top executives as to the costs (of hiring, training, and so on) associated with gaining people who had the right skills to manage such a workforce.

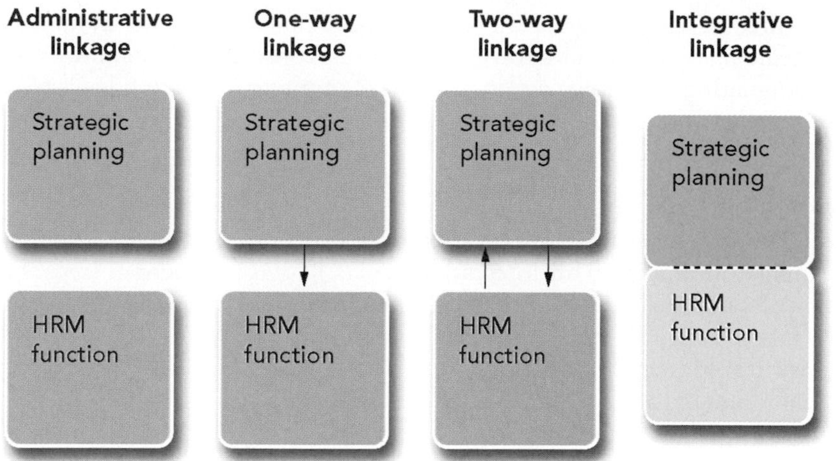

FIGURE 2.3
Linkages of Strategic Planning and HRM

SOURCE: Adapted from K. Golden and V. Ramanujam, "Between a Dream and a Nightmare: On the Integration of the Human Resource Function and the Strategic Business Planning Process," *Human Resource Management* 24 (1985), pp. 429–51.

A firm's strategic management decision-making process usually takes place at its top levels, with a strategic planning group consisting of the chief executive officer, the chief financial officer, the president, and various vice presidents. However, each component of the process involves people-related business issues. Therefore, the HRM function needs to be involved in each of those components. One recent study of 115 strategic business units within *Fortune* 500 corporations found that between 49 and 69 percent of the companies had some link between HRM and the strategic planning process.[10] However, the level of linkage varied, and it is important to understand these different levels.

Four levels of integration seem to exist between the HRM function and the strategic management function: administrative linkage, one-way linkage, two-way linkage, and integrative linkage.[11] These levels of linkage will be discussed in relation to the different components of strategic management. The linkages are illustrated in Figure 2.3.

Administrative Linkage

In administrative linkage (the lowest level of integration), the HRM function's attention is focused on day-to-day activities. The HRM executive has no time or opportunity to take a strategic outlook toward HRM issues. The company's strategic business planning function exists without any input from the HRM department. Thus, in this level of integration, the HRM department is completely divorced from any component of the strategic management process in both strategy formulation and strategy implementation. The department simply engages in administrative work unrelated to the company's core business needs.

One-Way Linkage

In one-way linkage, the firm's strategic business planning function develops the strategic plan and then informs the HRM function of the plan. Many believe this level of integration constitutes strategic HRM—that is, the role of the HRM function is to design systems and/or programs that implement the strategic plan. Although one-way linkage does recognize the importance of human resources in implementing the strategic plan, it precludes the company from considering human resource issues while formulating the strategic plan. This level of integration often leads to strategic plans that the company cannot successfully implement.

Two-Way Linkage

Two-way linkage allows for consideration of human resource issues during the strategy formulation process. This integration occurs in three sequential steps. First, the strategic planning team informs the HRM function of the various strategies the company is considering. Then HRM executives analyze the human resource implications of the various strategies, presenting the results of this analysis to the strategic planning team. Finally, after the strategic decision has been made, the strategic plan is passed on to the HRM executive, who develops programs to implement it. The strategic planning function and the HRM function are interdependent in two-way linkage.

Integrative Linkage

Integrative linkage is dynamic and multifaceted, based on continuing rather than sequential interaction. In most cases the HRM executive is an integral member of the senior management team. Rather than an iterative process of information exchange, companies with integrative linkage have their HRM functions built right into the strategy formulation and implementation processes. It is this role that we will discuss throughout the rest of this chapter.

Thus, in strategic HRM, the HRM function is involved in both strategy formulation and strategy implementation. The HRM executive gives strategic planners information about the company's human resource capabilities, and these capabilities are usually a direct function of the HRM practices. This information about human resource capabilities helps top managers choose the best strategy because they can consider how well each strategic alternative would be implemented. Once the strategic choice has been determined, the role of HRM changes to the development and alignment of HRM practices that will give the company employees having the necessary skills to implement the strategy. In addition, HRM practices must be designed to elicit actions from employees in the company. In the next two sections of this chapter we show how HRM can provide a competitive advantage in the strategic management process.

Strategy Formulation

Five major components of the strategic management process are relevant to strategy formulation.[12] These components are depicted in Figure 2.4. The first component is the organization's mission. The mission is a statement of the organization's reason for being; it usually specifies the customers served, the needs satisfied and/or the values received by the customers, and the technology used. The mission statement is often accompanied by a statement of a company's vision and/or values. For example, Table 2.1 on page 62 illustrates the mission and values of Merck & Co., Inc.

Goals
What an organization hopes to achieve in the medium- to long-term future.

An organization's **goals** are what it hopes to achieve in the medium- to long-term future; they reflect how the mission will be operationalized. The overarching goal of most profit-making companies in the United States is to maximize stockholder

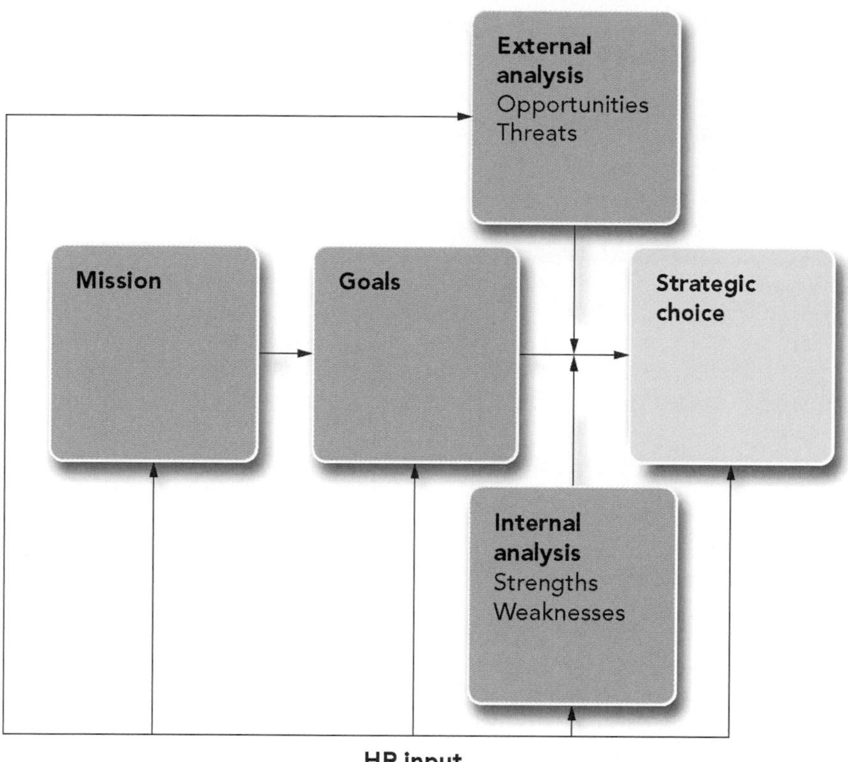

FIGURE 2.4
Strategy Formulation

SOURCE: Adapted from K. Golden and V. Ramanujam, "Between a Dream and a Nightmare," *Human Resource Management* 24 (1985), pp. 429–451. Reprinted with permission.

wealth. But companies have to set other long-term goals in order to maximize stockholder wealth.

External analysis consists of examining the organization's operating environment to identify the strategic opportunities and threats. Examples of opportunities are customer markets that are not being served, technological advances that can aid the company, and labor pools that have not been tapped. Threats include potential labor shortages, new competitors entering the market, pending legislation that might adversely affect the company, and competitors' technological innovations.

External analysis
Examining the organization's operating environment to identify strategic opportunities and threats.

Internal analysis attempts to identify the organization's strengths and weaknesses. It focuses on the quantity and quality of resources available to the organization—financial, capital, technological, and human resources. Organizations have to honestly and accurately assess each resource to decide whether it is a strength or a weakness.

Internal analysis
The process of examining an organization's strengths and weaknesses.

External analysis and internal analysis combined constitute what has come to be called the *SWOT* (strengths, weaknesses, opportunities, threats) *analysis*. After going through the SWOT analysis, the strategic planning team has all the information it needs to generate a number of strategic alternatives. The strategic managers compare these alternatives' ability to attain the organization's strategic goals; then they make their **strategic choice.** The strategic choice is the organization's strategy; it describes the ways the organization will attempt to fulfill its mission and achieve its long-term goals.

Strategic choice
The organization's strategy; the ways an organization will attempt to fulfill its mission and achieve its long-term goals.

Many of the opportunities and threats in the external environment are people-related. With fewer and fewer highly qualified individuals entering the labor market,

TABLE 2.1
Merck & Co.'s Mission and Values

MISSION STATEMENT
Merck & Co., Inc. is a leading research-driven pharmaceutical products and services company. Merck discovers, develops, manufactures and markets a broad range of innovative products to improve human and animal health. The Merck-Medco Managed Care Division manages pharmacy benefits for more than 40 million Americans, encouraging the appropriate use of medicines and providing disease management programs.
Our Mission
The mission of Merck is to provide society with superior products and services—innovations and solutions that improve the quality of life and satisfy customer needs—to provide employees with meaningful work and advancement opportunities and investors with a superior rate of return.
Our Values
1. **Our business is preserving and improving human life.** All of our actions must be measured by our success in achieving this goal. We value above all our ability to serve everyone who can benefit from the appropriate use of our products and services, thereby providing lasting consumer satisfaction.
2. **We are committed to the highest standards of ethics and integrity.** We are responsible to our customers, to Merck employees and their families, to the environments we inhabit, and to the societies we serve worldwide. In discharging our responsibilities, we do not take professional or ethical shortcuts. Our interactions with all segments of society must reflect the high standards we profess.
3. **We are dedicated to the highest level of scientific excellence and commit our research to improving human and animal health and the quality of life.** We strive to identify the most critical needs of consumers and customers; we devote our resources to meeting those needs.
4. **We expect profits, but only from work that satisfies customer needs and benefits humanity.** Our ability to meet our responsibilities depends on maintaining a financial position that invites investment in leading-edge research and that makes possible effective delivery of research results.
5. **We recognize that the ability to excel—to most competitively meet society's and customers' needs—depends on the integrity, knowledge, imagination, skill, diversity, and teamwork of employees, and we value these qualities most highly.** To this end, we strive to create an environment of mutual respect, encouragement, and teamwork—a working environment that rewards commitment and performance and is responsive to the needs of employees and their families.

SOURCE: www.merck.com/overview/philosophy.html.

organizations compete not just for customers but for employees. It is HRM's role to keep close tabs on the external environment for human resource–related opportunities and threats, especially those directly related to the HRM function: potential labor shortages, competitor wage rates, government regulations affecting employment, and so on. For example, as discussed in Chapter 1, U.S. companies are finding that more and more high school graduates lack the basic skills needed to work, which is one source of the "human capital shortage."[13] However, not recognizing this environmental threat, many companies have encouraged the exit of older, more skilled workers while hiring less skilled younger workers who require basic skills training.[14]

An analysis of a company's internal strengths and weaknesses also requires input from the HRM function. Today companies are increasingly realizing that their human resources are one of their most important assets. In fact, one estimate is that over one-third of the total growth in U.S. GNP between 1943 and 1990 was the result of increases in human capital. A company's failure to consider the strengths and weaknesses of its workforce may result in its choosing strategies it is not capable of pursuing.[15] However, some research has demonstrated that few companies have achieved this level of linkage.[16] For example, one company chose a strategy of cost reduction through technological improvements. It built a plant designed around a computer-integrated manufacturing system with statistical process controls. Though this choice may seem like a good one, the company soon learned otherwise. It discovered that its employees could not operate the new equipment because 25 percent of the workforce was functionally illiterate.[17]

Thus, with an integrative linkage, strategic planners consider all the people-related business issues before making a strategic choice. These issues are identified with regard to the mission, goals, opportunities, threats, strengths, and weaknesses, leading the strategic planning team to make a more intelligent strategic choice. Although this process does not guarantee success, companies that address these issues are more likely to make choices that will ultimately succeed.

Recent research has supported the need to have HRM executives integrally involved in strategy formulation. One study of U.S. petrochemical refineries found that the level of HRM involvement was positively related to the refinery manager's evaluation of the effectiveness of the HRM function.[18] A second study of manufacturing firms found that HRM involvement was highest when top managers viewed employees as a strategic asset and associated with reduced turnover.[19] However, both studies found that HRM involvement was unrelated to operating unit financial performance.

Delta Air Lines and HRM's Role in Strategy Formulation

Returning to the story of Delta's Leadership 7.5 strategy discussed at the opening of this chapter, how might an HRM executive have influenced the decision to adopt the strategy? She or he could have pointed out that Delta had one source of sustainable competitive advantage (one that provided value, was rare, and was impossible or costly for its competitors to imitate):[20] its highly committed workforce, which delivered the highest level of customer service in the industry.[21] In fact, Delta employees were so committed to the airline that in the 1980s the employees pitched in and bought the airline a new airplane. Thus the limiting role would have been to point out the absurdity of throwing away its one source of sustainable competitive advantage.

However, one lesson for all business decision makers is to never say no unless one can present a better alternative. Thus an HRM executive could have proposed an alternative strategy that would have reduced cost without sacrificing its workforce. For example, a workforce that buys a plane would certainly be willing to generate ways for the airline to run more efficiently. They might also have ideas regarding how to make any necessary workforce reductions and perhaps would be willing to take temporary pay cuts to help the firm get back on its feet. This would be an example of a strategy that sought to deploy rather than destroy the firm's source of competitive advantage. The "Competing by Meeting Stakeholders' Needs" box describes the dilemma firms face in simultaneously trying to create competitive advantage through

COMPETING BY MEETING STAKEHOLDERS' NEEDS

Has Downsizing Become a Way of Life?

One would have great difficulty ignoring the massive "war for talent" that went on during the late 1990s, particularly with the notable dot-com craze. Firms during this time sought to become "employers of choice," to establish "employment brands," and to develop "employee value propositions" as ways to ensure that they would be able to attract and retain talented employees. However, what few probably noticed was that in spite of the hiring craze, this was also a time of massive layoffs. In fact, 1998, the height of the war for talent, also saw the largest number of layoffs in the decade.

This new trend seems to represent a "churn" of employees, in which firms lay off those with outdated skills or cut whole businesses that are in declining markets while simultaneously building businesses and employee bases in newer, high-growth markets. For example, IBM cut 69,256 people and increased its workforce by 16,000 in 1996.

The important question facing firms is, How can we develop a reputation as an employer of choice, and engage employees to the goals of the firm, while constantly laying off a significant portion of our workforce? How firms answer this question will determine how they can compete by meeting the stakeholder needs of their employees.

SOURCE: J. Laabs, "Has Downsizing Missed Its Mark?" *Workforce*, April, 1999, pp. 31–38.

Number of layoffs during the 1990s

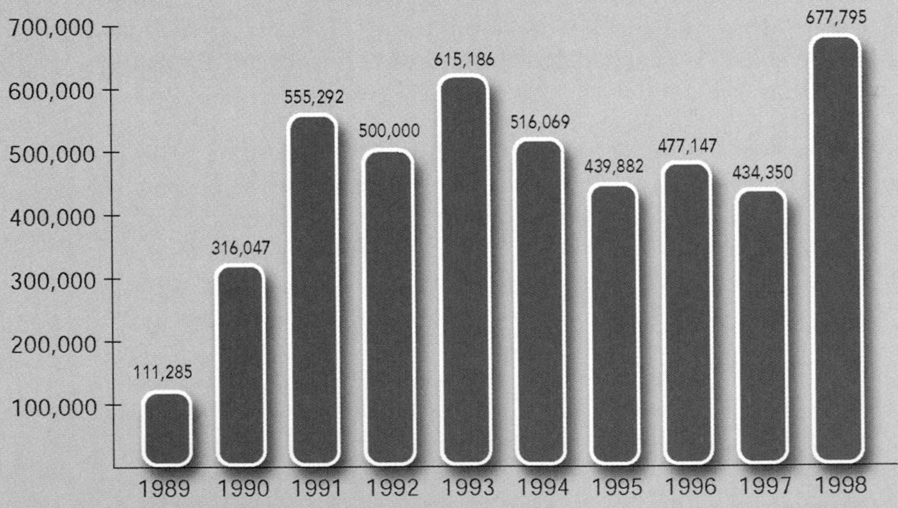

SOURCE: Challenger, Gray, and Christmas, 1998.

people while churning employees in response to changing skill requirements demanded by the dynamic competitive environment.

Research has indicated that few companies have fully integrated HRM into the strategy formulation process.[22] As we've mentioned before, companies are beginning to recognize that in an intensely competitive environment, managing human resources strategically can provide a competitive advantage. Thus companies at the administrative linkage level will either become more integrated or face extinction. In addition, companies will move toward becoming integratively linked in an effort to manage human resources strategically.

It is of utmost importance that all people-related business issues be considered during strategy formulation. These issues are identified in the HRM function. Mechanisms or structures for integrating the HRM function into strategy formulation may help the strategic planning team make the most effective strategic choice. Once that strategic choice is determined, HRM must take an active role in implementing it. This role will be discussed in the next section.

Strategy Implementation

After an organization has chosen its strategy, it has to execute that strategy—make it come to life in its day-to-day workings. The strategy a company pursues dictates certain HR needs. For a company to have a good strategy foundation, certain tasks must be accomplished in pursuit of the company's goals, individuals must possess certain skills to perform those tasks, and these individuals must be motivated to perform their skills effectively.

The basic premise behind strategy implementation is that "an organization has a variety of structural forms and organizational processes to choose from when implementing a given strategy," and these choices make an economic difference.[23] Five important variables determine success in strategy implementation: organizational structure; task design; the selection, training, and development of people; reward systems; and types of information and information systems.

As we see in Figure 2.5, HRM has primary responsibility for three of these five implementation variables: task, people, and reward systems. In addition, HRM can also directly affect the two remaining variables: structure and information and decision processes. First, for the strategy to be successfully implemented, the tasks must be

FIGURE 2.5
Variables to Be Considered in Strategy Implementation

FIGURE 2.6
Strategy Implementation

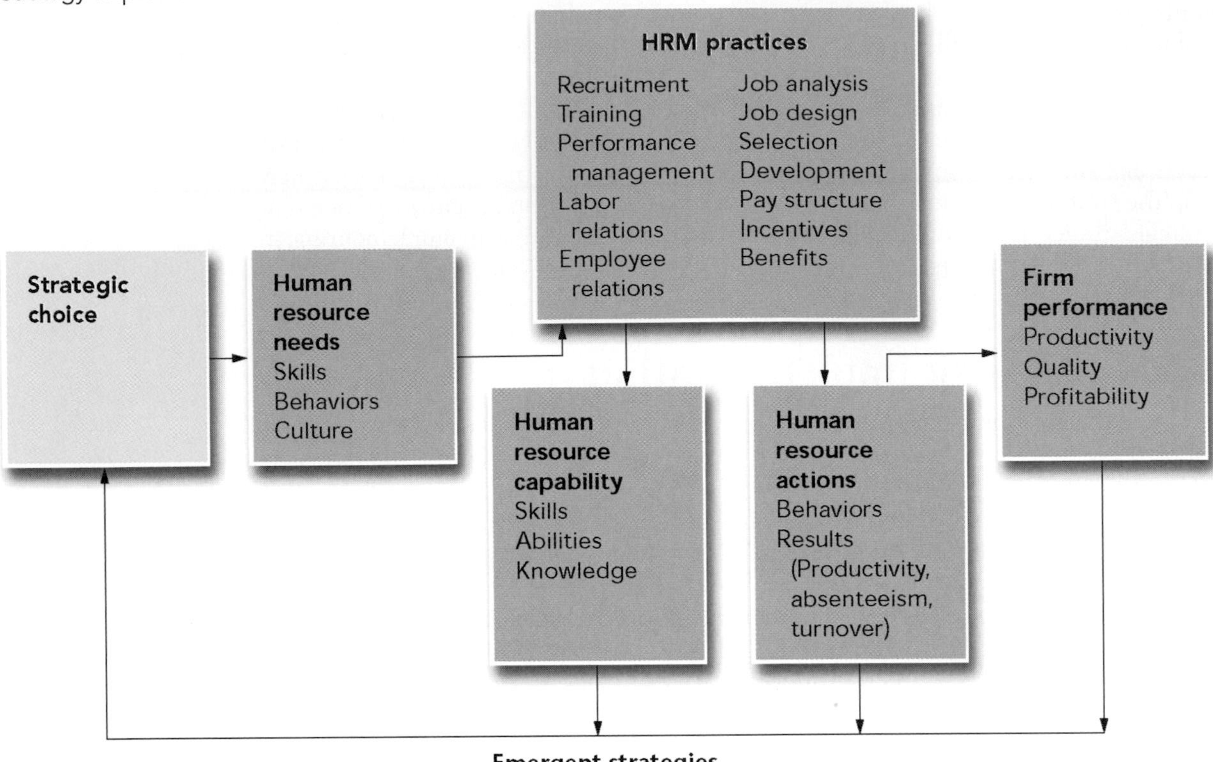

designed and grouped into jobs in a way that is efficient and effective.[24] In Chapter 4 we will examine how this can be done through the processes of job analysis and job design. Second, the HRM function must ensure that the organization is staffed with people who have the necessary knowledge, skill, and ability to perform their part in implementing the strategy. This goal is achieved primarily through recruitment, selection and placement, training, development, and career management—topics covered in Chapters 5, 6, 7, and 9. In addition, the HRM function must develop performance management and reward systems that lead employees to work for and support the strategic plan. The specific types of performance management systems are covered in Chapter 8, and the many issues involved in developing reward systems are discussed in Chapters 11 through 13. In other words, the role of the HRM function becomes one of (1) ensuring that the company has the proper number of employees with the levels and types of skills required by the strategic plan[25] and (2) developing "control" systems that ensure that those employees are acting in ways that promote the achievement of the goals specified in the strategic plan.[26]

How does the HRM function do this? As Figure 2.6 shows, it is through administering HRM practices: job analysis/design, recruitment, selection systems, training and development programs, performance management systems, reward systems, and labor relations programs. The details of each of these HRM practices are the focus of the rest of this book. However, at this point it is important to present a general overview of the HRM practices and their role in strategy implementation. We will then discuss the various strategies companies pursue and the types of HRM systems congruent with those strategies. First we focus on how the strategic types are implemented; then we discuss the HRM practices associated with various directional strategies.

HRM Practices

The HRM function can be thought of as having six menus of HRM practices, from which companies can choose the ones most appropriate to implementing their strategy. Each of these menus refers to a particular functional area of HRM: job analysis/design, recruitment/selection, training and development, performance management, pay structure/incentives/benefits, and labor/employee relations.[27] These menus are presented in Table 2.2.

TABLE 2.2
Menu of HRM Practice Options

Job Analysis and Design		
Few tasks	↔	Many tasks
Simple tasks	↔	Complex tasks
Few skills required	↔	Many skills required
Specific job descriptions	↔	General job descriptions
Recruitment and Selection		
External sources	↔	Internal sources
Limited socialization	↔	Extensive socialization
Assessment of specific skills	↔	Assessment of general skills
Narrow career paths	↔	Broad career paths
Training and Development		
Focus on current job skills	↔	Focus on future job skills
Individual orientation	↔	Group orientation
Train few employees	↔	Train all employees
Spontaneous, unplanned	↔	Planned, systematic
Performance Management		
Behavioral criteria	↔	Results criteria
Developmental orientation	↔	Administrative orientation
Short-term criteria	↔	Long-term criteria
Individual orientation	↔	Group orientation
Pay Structure, Incentives, and Benefits		
Pay weighted toward salary and benefits	↔	Pay weighted toward incentives
Short-term incentives	↔	Long-term incentives
Emphasis on internal equity	↔	Emphasis on external equity
Individual incentives	↔	Group incentives
Labor and Employee Relations		
Collective bargaining	↔	Individual bargaining
Top-down decision making	↔	Participation in decision making
Formal due process	↔	No due process
View employees as expense	↔	View employees as assets

SOURCE: Adapted from R. S. Schuler and S. F. Jackson, "Linking Competitive Strategies with Human Resource Management Practices," *Academy of Management Executive* 1 (1987), pp. 207–19; and C. Fisher, L. Schoenfeldt, and B. Shaw, *Human Resource Management*, 2nd ed. (Boston: Houghton Mifflin, 1992).

Job analysis
The process of getting detailed information about jobs.

Job design
The process of defining the way work will be performed and the tasks that will be required in a given job.

Recruitment
The process of seeking applicants for potential employment.

Selection
The process by which an organization attempts to identify applicants with the necessary knowledge, skills, abilities, and other characteristics that will help it achieve its goals.

Training
A planned effort to facilitate the learning of job-related knowledge, skills, and behavior by employees.

Development
The acquisition of knowledge, skills, and behaviors that improve an employee's ability to meet changes in job requirements and in client and customer demands.

Job Analysis and Design

Companies produce a given product or service (or set of products or services), and the manufacture of these products requires that a number of tasks be performed. These tasks are grouped together to form jobs. **Job analysis** is the process of getting detailed information about jobs. **Job design** addresses what tasks should be grouped into a particular job. The way that jobs are designed should have an important tie to the strategy of an organization because the strategy requires either new and different tasks or different ways of performing the same tasks. In addition, because many strategies entail the introduction of new technologies, this impacts the way that work is performed.[28]

In general, jobs can vary from having a narrow range of tasks (most of which are simplified and require a limited range of skills) to having a broad array of complex tasks requiring multiple skills. In the past, the narrow design of jobs has been used to increase efficiency, while the broad design of jobs has been associated with efforts to increase innovation. However, with the advent of total quality management methods and a variety of employee involvement programs such as quality circles, many jobs are moving toward the broader end of the spectrum.[29]

Employee Recruitment and Selection

Recruitment is the process through which the organization seeks applicants for potential employment. **Selection** refers to the process by which it attempts to identify applicants with the necessary knowledge, skills, abilities, and other characteristics that will help the company achieve its goals. Companies engaging in different strategies need different types and numbers of employees. Thus the strategy a company is pursuing will have a direct impact on the types of employees that it seeks to recruit and select.[30]

Employee Training and Development

A number of skills are instilled in employees through training and development. **Training** refers to a planned effort to facilitate the learning of job-related knowledge, skills, and behavior by employees. **Development** involves acquiring knowledge, skills, and behavior that improve employees' ability to meet the challenges of a variety of existing jobs or jobs that do not yet exist. Changes in strategies often require changes in the types, levels, and mixes of skills. Thus the acquisition of strategy-related skills is an essential element of the implementation of strategy. For example, many companies have recently emphasized quality in their products, engaging in total quality management programs. These programs require extensive training of all employees in the TQM philosophy, methods, and often other skills that ensure quality.[31]

Through recruitment, selection, training, and development, companies can obtain a pool of human resources capable of implementing a given strategy.[32]

Performance Management

Performance management is used to ensure that employees' activities and outcomes are congruent with the organization's objectives. It entails specifying those activities and outcomes that will result in the firm's successfully implementing the strategy. For example, companies that are "steady state" (not diversified) tend to have evaluation systems that call for subjective performance assessments of managers. This stems from the fact that those above the first-level managers in the hierarchy have extensive knowledge about how the work should be performed. On the other hand, diversified companies are more likely to use quantitative measures of performance to evaluate managers because top managers have less knowledge about how work should be performed by those below them in the hierarchy.[33]

Similarly, executives who have extensive knowledge of the behaviors that lead to effective performance use performance management systems that focus on the behaviors of their subordinate managers. However, when executives are unclear about the specific behaviors that lead to effective performance, they tend to focus on evaluating the objective performance results of their subordinate managers.[34]

Performance management
The means through which managers ensure that employees' activities and outputs are congruent with the organization's goals.

Pay Structure, Incentives, and Benefits

The pay system has an important role in implementing strategies. First, a high level of pay and/or benefits relative to that of competitors can ensure that the company attracts and retains high-quality employees, but this might have a negative impact on the company's overall labor costs.[35] Second, by tying pay to performance, the company can elicit specific activities and levels of performance from employees.

In a study of how compensation practices are tied to strategies, researchers examined 33 high-tech and 72 traditional companies. They classified them by whether they were in a growth stage (greater than 20 percent inflation-adjusted increases in annual sales) or a maturity stage. They found that high-tech companies in the growth stage used compensation systems that were highly geared toward incentive pay, with a lower percentage of total pay devoted to salary and benefits. On the other hand, compensation systems among mature companies (both high-tech and traditional) devoted a lower percentage of total pay to incentives and a high percentage to benefits.[36]

Labor and Employee Relations

Whether companies are unionized or not, the general approach to relations with employees can strongly affect their potential for gaining competitive advantage. In the late 1970s Chrysler Corporation was faced with bankruptcy. Lee Iacocca, the new president of Chrysler, asked the union for wage and work-rule concessions in an effort to turn the company around. The union agreed to the concessions, in return receiving profit sharing and a representative on the board. Within only a few years, the relationship with and support from the union allowed Chrysler to pull itself out of bankruptcy to record profitability.[37]

Companies can choose to treat employees as an asset that requires investment of resources or as an expense to be minimized.[38] They have to make choices about how much employees can and should participate in decision making, what rights employees have, and what the company's responsibility is to them. The approach a company takes in making these decisions can result in it either successfully achieving its short- and long-term goals or ceasing to exist.

Recent research has begun to examine how companies develop sets of HRM practices that maximize performance and productivity. For example, one study of automobile assembly plants around the world found that plants that exhibited both high productivity and high quality used "HRM best practices," such as heavy emphasis on recruitment and hiring, compensation tied to performance, low levels of status differentiation, high levels of training for both new and experienced employees, and employee participation through structures such as work teams and problem-solving groups.[39] Another study found that HRM systems composed of selection testing, training, contingent pay, performance appraisal, attitude surveys, employee participation, and information sharing resulted in higher levels of productivity and corporate financial performance, as well as lower employee turnover.[40]

Strategic Types

As we previously discussed, companies can be classified by the generic strategies they pursue. It is important to note that these generic "strategies" are not what we mean by a strategic plan. They are merely similarities in the ways companies seek to compete in their industries. Various typologies have been offered, but we will focus on the two generic strategies proposed by Porter: cost and differentiation.[41]

According to Michael Porter of Harvard, competitive advantage stems from a company's being able to create value in its production process. Value can be created in one of two ways. First, value can be created by reducing costs. Second, value can be created by differentiating a product or service in such a way that it allows the company to charge a premium price relative to its competitors. This leads to two basic strategies. According to Porter, the "overall cost leadership" strategy focuses on becoming the lowest-cost producer in an industry. This strategy is achieved by constructing efficient large-scale facilities, by reducing costs through capitalizing on the experience curve, and by controlling overhead costs and costs in such areas as research and development, service, sales force, and advertising. This strategy provides above-average returns within an industry, and it tends to bar other firms' entry into the industry because the firm can lower its prices below competitors' costs. For example, IBM-clone computer manufacturers like Dell and Compaq have captured an increased share of the personal computer market by offering personal computers at lower cost than IBM and Apple.

The "differentiation" strategy, according to Porter, attempts to create the impression that the company's product or service is different from that of others in the industry. The perceived differentiation can come from creating a brand image, from technology, from offering unique features, or from unique customer service. If a company succeeds in differentiating its product, it will achieve above-average returns, and the differentiation may protect it from price sensitivity. For example, IBM has consistently emphasized its brand image and its reputation for superior service while charging a higher price for its computers.

HRM Needs in Strategic Types

While all of the strategic types require competent people in a generic sense, each of the strategies also requires different types of employees with different types of behaviors and attitudes. As we noted earlier in Figure 2.1, different strategies require employees with specific skills and also require these employees to exhibit different "role behaviors."[42] **Role behaviors** are the behaviors required of an individual in his or her role as a job holder in a social work environment. These role behaviors vary on a number of dimensions. Additionally, different role behaviors are required by the different strategies. For example, companies engaged in a cost strategy require employees to have a high concern for quantity and a short-term focus, to be comfortable with stability, and to be risk averse. These employees are expected to exhibit role behaviors that are relatively repetitive and performed independently or autonomously.

Role behaviors
Behaviors that are required of an individual in his or her role as a jobholder in a social work environment.

Thus companies engaged in cost strategies, because of the focus on efficient production, tend to specifically define the skills they require and invest in training employees in these skill areas. They also rely on behavioral performance management systems with a large performance-based compensation component. These companies promote internally and develop internally consistent pay systems with high pay differentials between superiors and subordinates. They seek efficiency through worker participation, soliciting employees' ideas on how to achieve more efficient production.

On the other hand, employees in companies with a differentiation strategy need to be highly creative and cooperative; to have only a moderate concern for quantity, a long-term focus, and a tolerance for ambiguity; and to be risk takers. Employees in these companies are expected to exhibit role behaviors that include cooperating with others, developing new ideas, and taking a balanced approach to process and results.

Thus differentiation companies will seek to generate more creativity through broadly defined jobs with general job descriptions. They may recruit more from outside, engage in limited socialization of newcomers, and provide broader career paths. Training and development activities focus on cooperation. The compensation system is geared toward external equity, as it is heavily driven by recruiting needs. These companies develop results-based performance management system and divisional–corporate performance evaluations to encourage risk taking on the part of managers.[43]

A recent study of HRM among steel minimills in the United States found that mills pursuing different strategies used different systems of HRM. Mills seeking cost leadership tended to use control-oriented HRM systems that were characterized by high centralization, low participation, low training, low wages, low benefits, and highly contingent pay, whereas differentiator mills used "commitment" HRM systems, characterized as the opposite on each of those dimensions.[44] A later study from the same sample revealed that the mills with the commitment systems had higher productivity, lower scrap rates, and lower employee turnover than those with the control systems.

Directional Strategies

As discussed earlier in this chapter, strategic typologies are useful for classifying the ways different organizations seek to compete within an industry. However, it is also necessary to understand how increasing size (growth) or decreasing it (downsizing) affects the HRM function. For example, the top management team might decide that they need to invest more in product development or to diversify as a means for growth. With these types of strategies, it is more useful for the HRM function to aid in evaluating the feasibility of the various alternatives and to develop programs that support the strategic choice.

Companies have used five possible categories of directional strategies to meet objectives.[45] Strategies emphasizing market share or operating costs are considered "concentration" strategies. With this type of strategy, a company attempts to focus on what it does best within its established markets and can be thought of as "sticking to its knitting." Strategies focusing on market development, product development, innovation, or joint ventures make up the "internal growth" strategy. Companies with an internal growth strategy channel their resources toward building on existing strengths. Those attempting to integrate vertically or horizontally or to diversify are exhibiting an **"external growth" strategy,** usually through mergers or acquisitions. This strategy attempts to expand a company's resources or to strengthen its market position through acquiring or creating new businesses. Finally, a "divestment," or downsizing, strategy is one made up of retrenchment, divestitures, or liquidation.

External growth strategy
An emphasis on acquiring vendors and suppliers or buying businesses that allow a company to expand into new markets.

These strategies are observed among companies facing serious economic difficulties and seeking to pare down their operations. The human resource implications of each of these strategies are quite different.

Concentration Strategies

Concentration strategy
A strategy focusing on increasing market share, reducing costs, or creating and maintaining a market niche for products and services.

Concentration strategies require that the company maintain the current skills that exist in the organization. This requires that training programs provide a means of keeping those skills sharp among people in the organization and that compensation programs focus on retaining people who have those skills. Appraisals in this strategy tend to be more behavioral because the environment is more certain, and the behaviors necessary for effective performance tend to be established through extensive experience.

Internal Growth Strategies

Internal growth strategy
A focus on new market and product development, innovation, and joint ventures.

Internal growth strategies present unique staffing problems. Growth requires that a company constantly hire, transfer, and promote individuals, and expansion into different markets may change the necessary skills that prospective employees must have. In addition, appraisals often consist of a combination of behaviors and results. The behavioral appraisal emphasis stems from the knowledge of effective behaviors in a particular product market, and the results appraisals focus on achieving growth goals. Compensation packages are heavily weighted toward incentives for achieving growth goals. Training needs differ depending on the way the company attempts to grow internally. For example, if the organization seeks to expand its markets, training will focus on knowledge of each market, particularly when the company is expanding into international markets. On the other hand, when the company is seeking innovation or product development, training will be of a more technical nature, as well as focusing on interpersonal skills such as team building. Joint ventures require extensive training in conflict resolution techniques because of the problems associated with combining people from two distinct organizational cultures.

Mergers and Acquisitions

Increasingly we see both consolidation within industries and mergers across industries. For example, British Petroleum's recent agreement to acquire Amoco Oil represents a consolidation, or reduction in number of firms within the industry. On the other hand, Citicorp's merger with Traveller's Group to form Citigroup represents firms from different industries (pure financial services and insurance) combining to change the dynamics within both. Whatever the type, one thing is for sure—mergers and acquisitions are on the increase, and HRM needs to be involved. In addition, these mergers more frequently consist of global megamergers, in spite of some warnings that these might not be effective (See the "Competing through Globalization" box).

According to a report by the Conference Board, "people issues" may be one of the major reasons that mergers do not always live up to expectations. Some companies now heavily weigh firm cultures before embarking on a merger or acquisition. For example, prior to acquiring ValueRx, executives at Express Scripts, Inc., interviewed senior executives and middle managers at the potential target firm in order to get a sense of its culture.[46] In spite of this, fewer than one-third of the HRM executives sur-

COMPETING THROUGH GLOBALIZATION

Questioning the Value of Global Megamergers

It seems to have become accepted wisdom that it's *good* to become bigger in a globalizing economy. Recent mergers such as Exxon and Mobil, BP and Amoco, Daimler-Benz and Chrysler, and even the failed attempt to merge GE and Honeywell were based on the logic that globalization will result in industries becoming more concentrated. The big winners will be the big companies, so the lesson is to get big fast, and global megamergers such as those noted are the quickest way to do so.

However, recent work seems to question the value of these megamergers. In addition to all the obstacles that face any merger, the logic itself may be flawed. First, evidence does not lead to the conclusion that industries are becoming more concentrated. In fact, industries such as oil and automobiles, those characterized by huge mergers, have become significantly *less* concentrated over the past 50 years. Second, industry concentration can actually destroy value rather than create it. Value can be created if the mergers reduce production costs, reduce risk, or increase volume, but these goals are seldom attained in any way that offsets the costs of the mergers.

Interestingly, one reason that these global megamergers have increased has a significant human resource component. As shareholders require top-line (revenue) growth of 10–15 percent per year, firms in industries seeing only 2–3 percent growth can achieve growth only through mergers and acquisitions. When virtually all the organizational rewards (bonuses, promotions, stock option values, and so on) are tied to revenue growth, it is not surprising that top managers will engage in such activity, even though it may not create true value for shareholders.

SOURCE: P. Ghemawat and F. Ghadar, "The Dubious Logic of Global Megamergers," *Harvard Business Review*, July–August 2000.

veyed said that they had a major influence in how mergers are planned, yet 80 percent of them said that people issues have a significant impact after the deals are finalized.[47]

In addition to the desirability of HRM playing a role in evaluating a merger opportunity, HRM certainly has a role in the actual implementation of a merger or acquisition. Training in conflict resolution is also necessary when companies engage in an external growth strategy. All the options for external growth consist of acquiring or developing new businesses, and these businesses often have distinct cultures. Thus many HRM programs face problems in integrating and standardizing practices across the company's businesses. The relative value of standardizing practices across businesses must be weighed against the unique environmental requirements of each business and the extent of desired integration of the two firms. For example, with regard to pay practices, a company may desire a consistent internal wage structure to maintain employee perceptions of equity in the larger organization. In a recent new business developed by IBM, the employees pressured the company to maintain the same wage structure as IBM's main operation. However, some businesses may function in environments where pay practices are driven heavily by market forces. Requiring these businesses to adhere to pay practices in other environments may result in an ineffective wage structure.

Finding and Keeping the Best Employees

Cisco Systems recognizes that when it acquires a new company, in large part, it is acquiring the human assets of that company. If the key people in the acquired company leave, then the acquisition was a tremendous failure. Thus Cisco first aims to screen potential acquisitions to ensure that the vision of the leader in that company and the company's direction are similar to Cisco's. In the acquisition discussion, it tries to make clear to the employees to be acquired that there will be massive change into the Cisco way of doing things. This is to ensure that employees are not surprised once they become part of Cisco. Third, during the integration, Cisco emphasizes that only one culture will survive and that it will be Cisco's. Fourth, it finds significant roles for the top executives and the top technical talent in order to give them challenging opportunities. By giving such people a major role, Cisco is much better than most firms at being able to retain the top talent after an acquisition.

SOURCE: C. O'Reilly, J. Pfeffer, *Hidden Value: How Great Companies Achieve Extraordinary Results with Ordinary People* (Cambridge, MA: HBS Press, 2000).

Downsizing

Downsizing
The planned elimination of large numbers of personnel, designed to enhance organizational effectiveness.

Of increasing importance to organizations in today's competitive environment is HRM's role in **downsizing** or "rightsizing." The number of organizations undergoing downsizing has increased significantly. In fact, from 1988 to 1993, 1.4 million executives, managers, and administrators were laid off during downsizing, compared with only 782,000 from 1976 to 1981.[48] Table 2.3 lists some major company downsizings as well as statements from the companies' annual reports about the reasons behind the downsizing.

TABLE 2.3
Company Downsizings and Reasons Given

COMPANY	ANNUAL REPORT STATEMENT	TRANSLATION IN LAYOFFS
Sears	"Our dramatic downsizing certainly attracted a lot of attention over the last 18 months."	50,000
IBM	"Shortly after I [CEO Louis Gerstner] joined the company, I set as my highest priority to right-size the company as quickly as we could."	35,000
Boeing	"Boeing continues to take the steps necessary to adjust to the market downturn."	28,000
Kodak	"The fundamentals show that we are making real progress in reducing our cost base."	12,000
GE	"[Our] plan includes explicit programs that will result in the closing, downsizing and streamlining of certain production, service and administrative facilities worldwide."	10,000

SOURCE: "Bumstead, You're Downsized!" *Time* (April 1994): 143(16), p. 22. Reprinted by permission.

TABLE 2.4
Effects of Downsizing on Desired Outcomes

DESIRED OUTCOME	PERCENTAGE THAT ACHIEVED DESIRED RESULT
Reduced expenses	46%
Increased profits	32
Improved cash flow	24
Increased productivity	22
Increased return on investment	21
Increased competitive advantage	19
Reduced bureaucracy	17
Improved decision making	14
Increased customer satisfaction	14
Increased sales	13
Increased market share	12
Improved product quality	9
Technological advances	9
Increased innovation	7
Avoidance of a takeover	6

In spite of the increasing frequency of downsizing, research reveals that it is far from universally successful for achieving the goals of increased productivity and increased profitability. For example, Table 2.4 illustrates the results of a survey conducted by the American Management Association indicating that only about one-third of the companies that went through downsizings actually achieved their goal of increased productivity. Another survey by the AMA found that over two-thirds of the companies that downsize repeat the effort a year later.[49] Also, research by the consulting firm Mitchell & Company found that companies that downsized during the 1980s lagged the industry average stock price in 1991.[50] Thus it is important to understand the best ways of managing downsizings, particularly from the standpoint of HRM.

Downsizing presents a number of challenges and opportunities for HRM. In terms of challenges, the HRM function must "surgically" reduce the workforce by cutting only the workers who are less valuable in their performance. Achieving this is difficult because the best workers are most able (and often willing) to find alternative employment and may leave voluntarily prior to any layoff. For example, in 1992 General Motors and the United Auto Workers agreed to an early retirement program for individuals between the ages of 51 and 65 who have been employed for 10 or more years. The program provided those who agreed to retire their full pension benefits, even if they obtained employment elsewhere, and as much as $13,000 toward the purchase of a GM car.[51]

Early retirement programs, although humane, essentially reduce the workforce with a "grenade" approach. This type of reduction does not distinguish between good and poor performers but rather eliminates an entire group of employees. In fact, recent research indicates that when companies downsize by offering early retirement programs, they usually end up rehiring to replace essential talent within a year. Often the company does not achieve its cost-cutting goals because it spends 50 to 150 percent of the departing employee's salary in hiring and retraining new workers.[52]

Another HRM challenge is to boost the morale of employees who remain after the reduction; this is discussed in greater detail in Chapter 5. Survivors may feel guilt over keeping their jobs when their friends have been laid off, or they may envy their friends who have retired with attractive severance and pension benefits. Their reduced satisfaction with and commitment to the organization may interfere with work performance. Thus the HRM function must maintain open communication with remaining employees to build their trust and commitment rather than withholding information.[53] All employees should be informed of the purpose of the downsizing, the costs to be cut, the duration of the downsizing, and the strategies to be pursued. In addition, companies going through downsizing often develop compensation programs that tie the individual's compensation to the company's success. Employee ownership programs often result from downsizing, and gainsharing plans such as the Scanlon plan (discussed in Chapter 12) originated in companies facing economic difficulties.

In spite of these challenges, downsizing provides opportunities for HRM. First, it often allows the company to "get rid of dead wood" and make way for fresh ideas. In addition, downsizing is often a unique opportunity to change an organization's culture. In firms characterized by antagonistic labor–management relations, downsizing can force the parties to cooperate and to develop new, positive relationships.[54] Finally, downsizing can demonstrate to top-management decision makers the value of the company's human resources to its ultimate success. The role of HRM is to effectively manage the process in a way that makes this value undeniable. We discuss the implications of downsizing as a labor force management strategy in Chapter 5.

Delta Air Lines and HRM's Role in Strategy Implementation

As was described in the opening vignette, HRM issues were significant components to Delta's Leadership 7.5 strategy. While the effectiveness of the strategy has already been questioned, HRM seemed to play a significant role in its implementation. Because labor costs are the largest single controllable cost for an airline, significant cost reductions had to have HRM implications; thus costs were cut approximately $1.6 billion through workforce reductions. These reductions were achieved through buyouts, early retirement, extended leaves, and layoffs. In many cases experienced, highly paid, long-term Delta employees were replaced by less experienced but also much lower-paid employees, either full-time, part-time, or contract. For example, cleaning of the airplanes prior to this strategy was performed in-house by employees earning $7.80 an hour to start, with full benefits and travel privileges. This allowed Delta to often hire college graduates who were willing to take on such jobs to get a foot in the door at Delta. These employees were replaced with outside contractors, who received lower wages, few benefits, and no travel privileges, resulting in much lower labor costs. However, the downside was that Delta soon faced "smelly lavatories, soiled carpets, sticky tray tables, and littered seat pockets."[55]

The negative outcomes of the strategy in terms of employee morale, customer service, and operational performance have been discussed. A vast majority of these stemmed from the strategy itself, but one wonders if the same strategy might have been implemented differently with less negative impact. For example, significant communications with employees regarding the need for restructuring might have provided more legitimacy to the downsizing effort. In addition, seeking to provide outplacement services to laid-off employees might have eased their transition out of the

COMPETING IN THE NEW ECONOMY

Cisco Stumbles

Cisco Systems has been viewed as one of the most successful new economy companies based on its incessant, rapid growth. The company supplies the routers and other electronic network modules that enabled the transfer of information via the Internet when bandwidth was small and Internet use was rapidly accelerating. At one point in the spring of 2000 its market capitalization exceeded that of any other company, including Microsoft and GE. However, since then its shares have fallen by 80 percent, and this fall exemplifies the concept of "Internet speed" and how it is impacting businesses.

As late as November 2000, Cisco projected order growth at a 70 percent annual rate, yet within six months it experienced a decline in orders. As the economy softened, many customers cut back on orders. In addition, this time frame saw the shakeout of a number of dot-coms; although they made up only 5 percent of Cisco's orders, they comprised a much larger percentage of Cisco's projected growth rates. The new economy information technology enabled many customers to quickly sense and respond to the lessening demand in their markets.

However, Cisco, in spite of its vaunted internal ordering system, seemed to either ignore or miss the softening of orders, and continued its expansion plans. Soon, unable to be ignored any longer, the weak economy popped Cisco's bubble. In April 2001 Cisco announced that it would be laying off 8,500 full-time and temporary employees after hiring 5,000 during the previous five months.

SOURCE: S. Thurm, "Even as Rivals Began to Stumble, Cisco Believed Itself to Be Immune," *Wall Street Journal* (April 18, 2001), p. 1.

firm. HRM might have developed programs aimed at boosting the morale of Delta's survivors. However, it is unlikely that such measures would have had a significant positive influence given the severity of the cuts. Again, it highlights the strategic importance of HRM having an impact on the strategy formulation as well as implementation processes if people are to be deployed as a source of competitive advantage.

Strategy Evaluation and Control

A final component to the strategic management process is that of strategy evaluation and control. Thus far we have focused on the planning and implementation of strategy. However, it is extremely important for the firm to constantly monitor the effectiveness of both the strategy and the implementation process. This monitoring makes it possible for the company to identify problem areas and either revise existing structures and strategies or devise new ones. In this process we see emergent strategies appear as well as the critical nature of human resources in competitive advantage. The "Competing in the New Economy" box describes how Cisco's failure to effectively monitor its environment and adjust its business and human resource strategies appropriately resulted in its recent stumble.

COMPETING THROUGH HIGH-PERFORMANCE WORK SYSTEMS

Motorola's Strategy Uses All Its Resources

When Motorola embarks on a project, the organization employs every resource it has to plan and implement its strategy. In a high-technology field in which products, customers' needs, markets, and technology itself are constantly changing, Motorola and companies like it need to rely on internal and external growth strategies, as well as intended and emergent strategies. To complete these strategies, they must rely on people—their technical skill, motivation, and innovative ways of thinking.

We can view a microcosm of Motorola's use of high-performance work systems (teamwork, empowerment, training, and education development of new technology, and so forth) to move its strategy forward in its new Harvard, Illinois, location. One reason Motorola chose this location for a $100 million plant was the concentration of qualified workers. (The company normally hires only 1 in 10 applicants. Here 65 percent of the applicants were hired.) Another reason for the choice of location was its proximity to a nearby cellular subscriber operation. (Employees from the existing operation were recruited to help employees at the new plant get things up and running.) The size of the lot—300 acres—was another factor. (Motorola can expand the plant if necessary.) All these considerations were part of the intended strategy.

Motorola's strategy does not stop at its own doors. At Harvard, the organization has reached out to local schools, focusing just as hard on the quality of education and training of future workers as it does on the development and manufacture of its products. With its Learning Leadership Teams, Motorola conducts meetings and programs to help teachers and administrators develop curricula that will launch students into a rapidly changing 21st century, preparing them to compete and succeed at their jobs. Teams of teachers then work with students, who also complete learning projects in

The Role of Human Resources in Providing Strategic Competitive Advantage

Thus far we have presented the strategic management process as including a step-by-step procedure by which HRM issues are raised prior to deciding on a strategy and then HRM practices are developed to implement that strategy. However, we must note that human resources can provide a strategic competitive advantage in two additional ways: through emergent strategies and through enhancing competitiveness. (See the "Competing through High-Performance Work Systems" box.)

Emergent Strategies

Having discussed the process of strategic management, we also must distinguish between intended strategies and emergent strategies. Most people think of strategies as teams. "Our message to our employees is that schools have to change, and we have to help them change." Not every educator greeted this encroachment with enthusiasm. "At first, what we were thinking was, Don't tell us what to do," says Fred Schroeder, assistant superintendent for the state's fourth-largest school district. "[But] we started talking with them and found out that their value orientation is not to criticize but to help."

Motorola also reaches out to its suppliers, working closely with them and insisting on striving for the highest quality. Motorola actually acts as a partner to its suppliers, providing training at its own Motorola University. "They are very demanding in terms of their quality standards and what they expect from suppliers, but they help you to become a better company," notes John Krehbeil, president of Molex. "They help educate your organization in a number of different areas." The establishment of Motorola University was part of the strategy of former chairman Robert Galvin. "In starting Motorola University, Bob Galvin realized he had to continually reinvest in the company," explains James Schwarz, president of Omni Circuits Inc.

Motorola is the undisputed technological leader in cellular communications, and there are some solid reasons for this. First, its strategy is always forward-thinking. "I think it's their commitment to research and development," observes Joe Fristenksy, a telecommunications industry analyst for Frost & Sullivan in California. Second, the organization's emergent strategy compares favorably with its intended strategy; Motorola actually does what it says it is going to do. "While other people are dreaming about, 'Well, maybe we can do this,' they look over, and Motorola is already halfway there. They get ahead of everybody else, which forces the rest of the pack to play catch-up," says Fristenksy. Third, quality is a driving force, not only in the development and production of its products but in the development of its people (employees, suppliers, and students in the community). "They're never happy; they're never satisfied. They always have to get better," says Schwarz.

Critics may charge that some of Motorola's strategy is paternalistic, designed to give the organization as much control as possible over people who are part of its environment. But the fact remains that Motorola relies heavily on the way its people function in a high-performance work system to maintain its competitive advantage in the market. Having the technology to produce the new generation of digital cellular communications is not of great value unless people understand the ways it will change their world.

SOURCE: J. Rondy, "Makeover by Motorola," *Illinois Business*, 3rd quarter 1995, pp. 41–49. Reprinted by permission.

being proactive, rational decisions aimed toward some predetermined goal. The view of strategy we have presented thus far in the chapter focuses on intended strategies. *Intended strategies* are the result of the rational decision-making process used by top managers as they develop a strategic plan. This is consistent with the definition of *strategy* as "the pattern or plan that integrates an organization's major goals, policies, and action sequences into a cohesive whole."[56] The idea of emergent strategies is evidenced by the feedback loop in Figure 2.1.

Most strategies that companies espouse are intended strategies. For example, when Compaq was founded, the company had its strategy summarized in its name, an amalgam of the words *computer*, *compact*, and *quality*. Thus the intended strategy was to build compact portable computers that were completely free of any defect, and all of the company's efforts were directed toward implementing that strategy. Following that strategy allowed Compaq to become one of the fastest-growing companies in the world, commanding 20 percent of the world market in 1991. In 1992 Compaq's performance began to falter again, sparking new CEO Eckhard Pfieffer to change Compaq's strategy to one focused on being a low-cost producer. This strategic change resulted in Compaq becoming the leading PC maker in the world in 1994.[57]

Emergent strategies, on the other hand, consist of the strategies that evolve from the grass roots of the organization and can be thought of as what organizations actually do, as opposed to what they intend to do. Strategy can also be thought of as "a pattern in a stream of decisions or actions."[58] For example, when Honda Motor Company first entered the U.S. market with its 250 cc and 305 cc motorcycles in 1959, it believed that no market existed for its smaller 50 cc bike. However, the sales on the larger motorcycles were sluggish, and Japanese executives running errands around Los Angeles on Honda 50s attracted a lot of attention, including that of a buyer with Sears, Roebuck. Honda found a previously undiscovered market as well as a new distribution outlet (general retailers) that it had not planned on. This emergent strategy gave Honda a 50 percent market share by 1964.[59]

The distinction between intended and emergent strategies has important implications for human resource management. The new focus on strategic HRM has tended to focus primarily on intended strategies. Thus HRM's role has been seen as identifying for top management the people-related business issues relevant to strategy formulation and then developing HRM systems that aid in the implementation of the strategic plan.

However, most emergent strategies are identified by those lower in the organizational hierarchy. It is often the rank-and-file employees who provide ideas for new markets, new products, and new strategies. HRM plays an important role in facilitating communication throughout the organization, and it is this communication that allows for effective emergent strategies to make their way up to top management. This fact led Philip Caldwell, Ford's chairman in the early 1980s, to state, "It's stupid to deny yourself the intellectual capability and constructive attitude of tens of thousands of workers."[60]

Enhancing Firm Competitiveness

A related way in which human resources can be a source of competitive advantage is through developing a human capital pool that gives the company the unique ability to adapt to an ever-changing environment. Recently managers have become interested in the idea of a "learning organization," in which people continually expand their capacity to achieve the results they desire.[61] This requires the company to be in a constant state of learning through monitoring the environment, assimilating information, making decisions, and flexibly restructuring to compete in that environment. Companies that develop such learning capability have a competitive advantage. Although certain organizational information-processing systems can be an aid, ultimately the people (human capital) who make up the company provide the raw materials in a learning organization.

Thus the role of human resources in competitive advantage should continue to increase because of the fast-paced change characterizing today's business environment. It is becoming increasingly clear that even as U.S. automakers have increased the quality of their cars to compete with the Japanese, these competitors have developed such flexible and adaptable manufacturing systems that they can respond to customer needs more quickly.[62] This flexibility of the manufacturing process allows the emergent strategy to come directly from the marketplace by determining and responding to the exact mix of customer desires. It requires, however, that the company have people in place who have the skills to similarly adapt quickly.[63] As George Walker, president of Delta Wire, stated, "Anyone can come in and buy machines like I have. The difference is the knowledge of your workers."[64] This statement exemplifies the increasing importance of human resources in developing and maintaining competitive advantage.[65]

Strategic Human Resource Executives

For a reader who is just getting a first glimpse of the HRM function, it is impossible to portray what a vastly different role HRM must play today compared to 20 or even 10 years ago. As noted earlier, HRM has traditionally played a largely administrative role—simply processing paperwork plus developing and administering hiring, training, appraisal, compensation, and benefits systems—and all of this has been unrelated to the strategic direction of the firm. In the early 1980s HRM took on more of a one-way linkage role, helping to implement strategy. Now strategic decision makers are realizing the importance of people issues and so are calling for HRM to become the "source of people expertise" in the firm.[66] This requires that HR managers possess and use knowledge of how people can and do play a role in competitive advantage as well as the policies, programs, and practices that can leverage the firm's people as a source of competitive advantage. This leads to an entirely new set of competencies for today's strategic HR executive.

In the future, HR professionals will need four basic competencies to become partners in the strategic management process.[67] (See Figure 2.7.) First, they will need "business competence"—knowing the company's business and understanding its economic financial capabilities. This calls for making logical decisions that support the company's strategic plan based on the most accurate information possible. Because in almost all companies the effectiveness of decisions must be evaluated in terms of dollar values, the HR executive must be able to calculate the costs and benefits of each alternative in terms of its dollar impact.[68] In addition, it requires that the nonmonetary impact be considered. The HR executive must be fully capable of identifying the social and ethical issues attached to HRM practices.

FIGURE 2.7
Human Resource Competencies

Second, HR professionals will need "professional–technical knowledge" of state-of-the-art HRM practices in areas such as staffing, development, rewards, organizational design, and communication. New selection techniques, performance appraisal methods, training programs, and incentive plans are constantly being developed. Some of these programs can provide value, whereas others may be no more than the products of today's HRM equivalent of snake oil. HR executives must be able to critically evaluate the new techniques offered as state-of-the-art HRM programs and use only those that will benefit the company.

Third, they must be skilled in the "management of change processes," such as diagnosing problems, implementing organizational changes, and evaluating results. Every time a company changes its strategy in even a minor way, the entire company has to change. These changes result in conflict, resistance, and confusion among the people who must implement the new plans or programs. The HR executive must have the skills to oversee the change in a way that ensures its success. In fact, one survey of *Fortune* 500 companies found that 87 percent of the companies had their organization development/change function as part of the HR department.[69]

Finally, these professionals must also have "integration competence," meaning the ability to integrate the three other competencies to increase the company's value. This requires that, although specialist knowledge is necessary, a generalist perspective must be taken in making decisions. This entails seeing how all the functions within the HRM area fit together to be effective and recognizing that changes in any one part of the HRM package are likely to require changes in other parts of the package. For example, a health care company in central Texas was attempting to fill a position in the X-ray department. It was able to identify qualified candidates for the position, but none of the candidates accepted the offer. It was not until the company examined its total package (pay, benefits, promotion opportunities, and so on) and changed the composition of the package that it was able to fill the position.

The new strategic role for HRM presents both opportunities and challenges. HRM has the chance to profoundly impact the way organizations compete through people. On the other hand, with this opportunity come serious responsibility and accountability. HRM functions of the future must consist of individuals who view themselves as business people who happen to work in an HRM function, rather than HRM people who happen to work in a business.

A Look Back

As we saw at the outset of this chapter, Delta's Leadership 7.5 strategy destroyed the firm's core competence of a highly experienced, highly skilled, and highly committed workforce that delivered the highest quality customer service in the industry. We examined how HRM might have affected the strategy to point out the negative impact that this strategy would have on the firm. We also explored how, given the strategy and competitive environment, Delta might have sought to implement the cost cutting differently to reduce the cost structure but preserve its source of differentiation.

The present state of Delta provides further support to these conclusions. With the family atmosphere dissolved and the bond between management and rank-and-file employees broken, employees have begun to seek other ways to gain voice and security. As of Fall 2001 Delta has two union organizing drives under way with both the flight attendants and the mechanics. In addition, labor costs have been driven up as a result of the union activity. The pilots signed a lucrative five-year contract that will place them at the highest pay in the industry. In an effort to head off the organizing drive, the mechanics were recently given raises to similarly put them at the industry top. Now the flight attendants are seeking industry-leading pay irrespective of but certainly encouraged by the union drive.[70]

The Delta Air Lines story provides a perfect example of the perils that can await firms that fail to adequately address human resource issues in the formulation and implementation of strategy.

Questions

1. How does the experience of Delta Air Lines illustrate the interdependence between strategic decisions of "how to compete" and "with what to compete?" Consider this with regard to both strategy formulation and strategy implementation.
2. If you were in charge of HRM for Delta Air Lines now, given the issues described in the "A Look Back" section, what would be your major priorities? How would you approach and solve these issues?

Summary

A strategic approach to human resource management seeks to proactively provide a competitive advantage through the company's most important asset: its human resources. The HRM function needs to be integrally involved in the formulation of strategy to identify the people-related business issues the company faces. Once the strategy has been determined, HRM has a profound impact on the implementation of the plan by developing and aligning HRM practices that ensure that the company has motivated employees with the necessary skills. Finally, the emerging strategic role of the HRM function requires that HR professionals in the future develop business, professional–technical, change management, and integration competencies. As you will see more clearly in later chapters, this strategic approach requires more than simply developing a valid selection procedure or state-of-the-art performance management systems. Only through these competencies can the HR professional take a strategic approach to human resource management.

Discussion Questions

1. Pick one of your university's major sports teams (like football or basketball). How would you characterize that team's generic strategy? How does the composition of the team members (in terms of size, speed, ability, and so on) relate to that strategy? What are the strengths and weaknesses of the team? How do those dictate the team's generic strategy and its approach to a particular game?
2. Do you think that it is easier to tie human resources to the strategic management process in large or in small organizations? Why?
3. Consider one of the organizations you have been affiliated with. What are some examples of human resource practices that were consistent with that organization's strategy? What are examples of practices that were inconsistent with its strategy?
4. How can strategic management within the HRM department ensure that HRM plays an effective role in the company's strategic management process?
5. What types of specific skills (such as knowledge of financial accounting methods) do you think HR professionals will need to have the business, professional–technical, change management, and integrative competencies necessary in the future? Where can you develop each of these skills?
6. What are some of the key environmental variables that you see changing in the business world today? What impact will those changes have on the HRM function in organizations?

Web Exercise

This chapter emphasized that for companies to gain a competitive advantage they must integrate HRM into the company's business strategy. Go to Honeywell's home page at **www.honeywell.com**.

Questions

1. What types of businesses is the company involved in?
2. What is the company's growth and productivity strategy?
3. What are the implications of the company's growth and productivity strategy for how the company manages its human resources? Make sure you describe the implications for recruitment and selection, training, performance management, and compensation.

Managing People: From the Pages of *BusinessWeek*

BusinessWeek SAP: Less Ego, More Success

Hasso Plattner, Its Hard-Driving Co-CEO, Discovered He Couldn't Fix His Company Alone

When German software giant SAP (SAP) runs into a glitch, Hasso Plattner, its red-meat-for-breakfast co-CEO, figures out what is wrong and fixes it with his own bare hands, if necessary. That's how he responded in February 1999, after he got the bad news at an executive retreat that the company was hopelessly behind on the Internet. Unless SAP did something fast, this would end its era of dominance as the leading maker of run-the-company software applications for the world's big corporations.

Plattner reacted like a man shot out of a cannon. In a matter of days, a series of frenetic brainstorming sessions yielded a brand-new strategy, which he personally christened mySAP.com. SAP's array of software programs would be made Net-ready before the end of the year, and millions of office workers from Berlin to Bangkok would tap into the Net and their own companies' networks on computer screens with SAP's logo on them. "We want to be the portal through which businesspeople access everything," he said later. "It's like AOL—for corporations."

It was a grand vision befitting one of the software industry's most successful leaders. Problem was, it didn't work. When mySAP.com arrived seven months later, customers were confused about what the products did, and the $50 million ad campaign flopped. In the company's crucial Americas region, revenues actually declined 3 percent in the first quarter of 2000. So Plattner did something completely out of character: he admitted that he and SAP couldn't handle this on their own.

FLEXIBILITY. What followed is one of the most surprising personal odysseys in the annals of tech. As one of the top two executives at SAP since its 1972 founding, Plattner had built a corporate culture in his own image: engineering-focused, headstrong, and determined to do it all without help. That stiff spine made SAP into the third-largest software company in the world. But Plattner realized after mySAP.com was slow to take off that it wasn't enough just to Web-ize his products. Unless he and his company started doing things differently, both could be washed up. Now he's busting apart the edifice he built piece by piece—keeping what's good and rejecting the rest.

It's all about being flexible. SAP used to build nearly all its core technology itself. Now it has deals with upstart Commerce One Inc. (CMRC) for business-to-business Web software. Convinced that its way was always best, SAP used to strong-arm customers to buy one massive conglomeration of bolted-together software programs—applications that did everything from managing financials and human resources to planning and manufacturing. Now SAP makes it easier for customers to pick and choose between SAP products and software sold by others. And Plattner once figured he could have the last word on marketing. Today he relies on a pro—Martin Homlish, formerly of Sony Corp. (SNE)—and took the surprising step of moving marketing from Germany to Manhattan.

His efforts are starting to pay off. In the first quarter, SAP's revenues grew a more than respectable 29 percent, to $1.36 billion. And SAP logged $106 million in profits, more than double the quarter a year earlier. Analysts forecast the company will meet its goal of attaining better than 21 percent revenue growth for the first three quarters of this year. ABN AMRO expects SAP's profits to rise from $596 million last year to $800 million this year and $1.1 billion the next. A humbler Plattner is making his company a force to fear in e-business.

That's humbler, not humbled. Plattner can't suppress his I-told-you-sos. "People say we're back," says Plattner, a pit bull of a man with a squared-off jaw. "We were never gone." He predicts corporations will buy e-business software to make themselves more efficient and to goose revenue growth. As evidenced by SAP's strengthening sales, he believes they're relying more on large, well-established software makers such as SAP, rather than the upstarts.

If he's right, the corporate computing world is about to be turned on its head. For much of the 1990s, big companies dominated the landscape. After browser maker Netscape Communications Corp. (AOL) burst on the scene with its vision of Internet computing, the biggies seemed to be on a path to irrelevance. Dozens of upstarts emerged as the darlings of corporate software buyers. Ariba Inc. was the pioneer of procurement over the Web. Commerce One was first to set up exchanges linking buyers and sellers over the Net. Now the old gunfighters are staging a counterattack, and the upstarts are hurting. In April Ariba laid off one-third of its staff. Lawrence J. Ellison, chairman of SAP rival Oracle Corp., also says corporate customers now prefer dealing with established companies. "It will be us and SAP, SAP and us," he predicts.

Still, it will be extremely difficult for Plattner to remake SAP into one of the leaders in the next era of computing. Thanks to the dot-com collapse, he has a chance to make up lost ground. Indeed, he has retooled before. In the late 1980s, when SAP was a maker of software for mainframe computers, he transformed it within two years into a maker of applications running on networks. Back then, though, he was the pioneer. Now he's playing catch-up. His challenge is to leapfrog nimble competitors and start setting the pace again.

FANTASTIC FOUR? Plattner is acutely aware of his problem, and he's working on it. He has targeted a quartet of product areas that he hopes will spark growth: customer management, supply-chain management, e-marketplaces, and corporate portals, which allow employees of corporations to tap easily into internal data through the Web.

Besides, he's happiest when he's wrestling with a challenge. That spirit permeates his life—from the boardroom to his world-class racing yacht, *Morning Glory*. He'll keep fighting even when the stakes are impossibly low. For instance, last year, during a break from the annual meeting of the company's investment arm, SAP Ventures, Plattner arranged a race between teams of investors in rented yachts in San Diego harbor. At one point, with Plattner at the helm, his boat was on a collision course with another. "Hasso's yelling at the other guy that we had the right of way. In the end, the other guy turned off. We missed by a few feet," recalls Gordon Hull, a venture capitalist at CMEA Ventures in San Francisco. "He's got nerves of steel. I wouldn't want to compete with him."

"STREET FIGHTER." That out-there personality seems rooted in his childhood. Born in 1944 in Berlin, Plattner's earliest memories are of sailing with his parents, Horst and Inge, on the lakes around the rubble-strewn city. His father, an eye surgeon, did not fight in the war. Still, there was a sense of peril. Plattner remembers seeing British jets landing with provisions during the 1948 airlift that broke Russia's Berlin blockade, and he saw one plane crash. Rather than becoming fearful, he grew up confident. "I'm a Berliner—fast, loud, obnoxious, industrious, brutally open," he brags.

The battler in him emerged during adolescence. After his parents divorced, he was sent at age 15 to a strict, military-style boarding school in Bavaria. It was like moving from Manhattan to Texas overnight. "I had to become a street fighter," he recalls during a recent dinner of beef-cheek ravioli at Babbo, a trendy New York restaurant. Despite jet lag and an overstuffed day of meetings, Plattner is full of energy. His eyes grow wide and he fingers scars on his wrist and hand as he tells how upperclassmen picked on him because he was a city slicker. "Once I pushed a big guy into a glass cabinet, and it shattered. I still have the scars," he says.

Other early influences shaped Plattner's career. He worshiped John F. Kennedy. "He had a vision," Plattner says, shifting into a nasal Boston accent to mimic Kennedy's voice: "We want to get to the moon in 10 years." For a kid growing up in beaten-down Germany, Kennedy represented the promise of a new, can-do era. When Kennedy was shot, Plattner was devastated. "I couldn't believe it," he says. "I went to bed and listened to the radio." Plattner followed in the footsteps of a grandfather and studied engineering—intent on being where the action was.

The future, it turned out, was to be built on electronics. In college Plattner studied telecommunications because a computer science program wasn't available. Upon graduating, he got a job as a sales consultant for IBM in Mannheim, Germany. That didn't last long. He left with four colleagues in 1972 to form SAP after they were rebuffed by IBM when they suggested creating a financial software package for corporations. Their novel idea: to replace expensive custom applications with off-the-shelf packages. Since then Plattner has been the company's cheerleader and visionary, mapping out technology and strategy while the original chairman, Dietmar Hopp, managed the business. Plattner became the number one executive in 1998 when Hopp resigned and has remained SAP's spark plug.

Sometimes, though, he has been the sludge that clogs up its engine. This is the dark side of Plattner. Even though customers complained for years about how difficult SAP's products were to use, Plattner didn't launch a campaign to fix that until 1998. He long refused to believe that marketing was important, and that cost SAP dearly in the competition with image-savvy Ellison. Plattner's pride in SAP sometimes blossoms into full-blown arrogance. At a software industry conference in Monterey, California, in 1998, "Hasso shocked people by saying he didn't believe SAP had to form alliances with anybody," recalls Mark B. Hoffman, CEO of Commerce One.

Plattner's change of heart has been remarkable. In early 2000, even as he was forming SAPMarkets, an independent e-marketplace subsidiary in San Francisco, he accepted an invitation from Hoffman to talk about creating a partnership between SAPMarkets and Commerce One. Ultimately, over several months of talks, the two decided on an unusually close relationship in which they would co-engineer a new suite of integrated products. Plattner recalls that a high school art teacher taught him to be flexible. "He said: 'When you reach the point that you don't change your mind anymore, you know you're old," recalls Plattner. Now it's one of Plattner's mantras. "We have to be able to adapt to new situations," he says.

Plattner's ongoing project is turning SAP's engineering culture inside out. In spite of his push for alliances and a program of setting up nimble, independent subsidiaries, the organization remains insular and slow to change its ways. His goal is to make sure SAP's products are created with maximum input from customers—rather than in cloistered isolation by engineers at the labs in Walldorf, Germany. SAP's engineering groups are now plugged into the sales organizations. SAP America, for instance, has lined up 100 customers to be "development partners" that actually help write code. Customers appreciate the way Plattner is operating. Enporion, an e-marketplace for the utilities industry, uses software from Commerce One and SAP. "I give Hasso Plattner a lot of credit," says Michael Johnson, its chief information officer. "He saw he had to transform his company [so it could] address e-commerce between companies and between industries."

CORPORATE COOKERY. That kind of overhaul takes dogged persistence. Inside SAP, Plattner is like a chef—constantly stirring the pot. He spends about one-third of his work time in California, one-third on the road visiting customers and SAP offices, and the rest back at headquarters in Walldorf. At the home office, he typically arrives around 10 A.M., often with a new idea he wants to try out on his colleagues. The planned schedule usually gets thrown out, replaced by impromptu meetings in his fourth-floor office.

While Plattner believes in obtaining consensus among his lieutenants, he doesn't care how much he irritates people along the way. In fact, his confrontational style is deliberate. "He creates stressful situations. He fuels the discussions with provocative statements. Sometimes he's rigid, even rude. But it's about getting people engaged so they can be creative," says Wolfgang Kemna, CEO of SAP America, a 13-year SAP veteran. Co-CEO Henning Kagermann, whom Plattner elevated to work alongside him in 1998, is his counterweight in the organization—calm and efficient.

Since he vowed to change his ways, Plattner doesn't try to do everyone else's jobs. Kagermann, for instance, runs sales and finance. That's not to say that Plattner sits back passively and watches how others work. He has been the acting CEO of SAPMarkets since it was formed. And Plattner personally manages the relationship with Commerce One, making sure it doesn't fall apart—which happens to most high-tech alliances. "He's absolutely the change leader at SAP," says Jack Barr, a former top sales executive at SAP America who is now head of sales at e-commerce start-up Atlas Commerce Inc. "He's the guy who saw what was happening and would drive in that direction."

With a 10 percent stake in SAP worth $4.5 billion, Plattner has been richly rewarded. Now he's giving some of his money away to help places with big problems—including $6 million to combat AIDS in South Africa and $55 million to the University of Potsdam in former East Germany. "I want to engage in battles and win them," he says. "You have goals. Now the goal is to pass Siebel."

At the rate Siebel Systems is growing, though, that will remain an unattainable goal for a long time. But given Plattner's ferocious personality, it's unlikely he'll give up trying.

Source: *BusinessWeek* online, **www.businessweek.com** (October 23, 2001).

Questions:

1. SAP's CEO (and his ego) seems to have had a huge role in determining the strategy over the past years. What have been the problems with the strategy as it was formulated? What could HRM's role have been in influencing it?
2. What is the new strategy? How will HRM play a role in its implementation?

Notes

1. J. Barney, "Firm Resources and Sustained Competitive Advantage," *Journal of Management* 17 (1991), pp. 99–120.
2. L. Dyer, "Strategic Human Resource Management and Planning," in *Research in Personnel and Human Resources Management*, ed. K. Rowland and G. Ferris (Greenwich, CT: JAI Press, 1985), pp. 1–30.
3. J. Quinn, *Strategies for Change: Logical Incrementalism* (Homewood, IL: Richard D. Irwin, 1980).
4. M. Porter, *Competitive Strategy: Techniques for Analyz-*

ing Industries and Competitors (New York: Free Press, 1980).

5. R. Miles and C. Snow, *Organizational Strategy, Structure, and Process* (New York: McGraw-Hill, 1978).
6. P. Wright and G. McMahan, "Theoretical Perspectives for Strategic Human Resource Management," *Journal of Management* 18 (1992), pp. 295–320.
7. S. Snell and J. Dean, "Integrated Manufacturing and Human Resource Management: A Human Capital Perspective," *Academy of Management Journal* 35 (1992), pp. 467–504.
8. J. Butler, G. Ferris, and N. Napier, *Strategy and Human Resource Management* (Cincinnati, OH: Southwestern Publishing Co., 1991).
9. F. Biddle and J. Helyar, "Behind Boeing's Woes: Chunky Assembly Line, Price War with Airbus," *The Wall Street Journal* (April 24, 1998), pp. A1, A16.
10. K. Martell and S. Carroll, "How Strategic Is HRM?" *Human Resource Management* 34 (1995), pp. 253–67.
11. K. Golden and V. Ramanujam, "Between a Dream and a Nightmare: On the Integration of the Human Resource Function and the Strategic Business Planning Process," *Human Resource Management* 24 (1985), pp. 429–51.
12. C. Hill and G. Jones, *Strategic Management Theory: An Integrated Approach* (Boston: Houghton Mifflin, 1989).
13. W. Johnston and A. Packer, *Workforce 2000: Work and Workers for the Twenty-first Century* (Indianapolis, IN: Hudson Institute, 1987).
14. "Labor Letter," *The Wall Street Journal* (December 15, 1992), p. A1.
15. P. Wright, G. McMahan, and A. McWilliams, "Human Resources and Sustained Competitive Advantage: A Resource-Based Perspective," *International Journal of Human Resource Management* 5 (1994), pp. 301–26.
16. P. Buller, "Successful Partnerships: HR and Strategic Planning at Eight Top Firms," *Organizational Dynamics* 17 (1988), pp. 27–42.
17. M. Hitt, R. Hoskisson, and J. Harrison, "Strategic Competitiveness in the 1990s: Challenges and Opportunities for U.S. Executives," *The Executive* 5 (May 1991), pp. 7–22.
18. P. Wright, G. McMahan, B. McCormick, and S. Sherman, *Strategy, Core Competence, and HR Involvement as Determinants of HR Effectiveness and Refinery Performance*. Paper presented at the 1996 International Federation of Scholarly Associations in Management, Paris, France.
19. N. Bennett, D. Ketchen, and E. Schultz, *Antecedents and Consequences of Human Resource Integration with Strategic Decision Making*. Paper presented at the 1995 Academy of Management Meeting, Vancouver, BC, Canada.
20. J. Barney and P. Wright, "On Becoming a Strategic Partner: The Role of Human Resources in Gaining Competitive Advantage," *Human Resource Management* 37, no. 1 (1998), pp. 31–46.
21. M. Brannigan and J. White, "So Be It: Why Delta Air Lines Decided It Was Time for CEO to Take Off," *The Wall Street Journal* (May 30, 1997), p. A1.
22. Golden and Ramanujam, "Between a Dream and a Nightmare."
23. J. Galbraith and R. Kazanjian, *Strategy Implementation: Structure, Systems, and Process* (St. Paul, MN: West Publishing, 1986).
24. B. Schneider and A. Konz, "Strategic Job Analysis," *Human Resource Management* 27 (1989), pp. 51–64.
25. P. Wright and S. Snell, "Toward an Integrative View of Strategic Human Resource Management," *Human Resource Management Review* 1 (1991), pp. 203–25.
26. S. Snell, "Control Theory in Strategic Human Resource Management: The Mediating Effect of Administrative Information," *Academy of Management Journal* 35 (1992), pp. 292–327.
27. R. Schuler, "Personnel and Human Resource Management Choices and Organizational Strategy," in *Readings in Personnel and Human Resource Management*, 3rd ed., ed. R. Schuler, S. Youngblood, and V. Huber (St. Paul, MN: West Publishing, 1988).
28. J. Dean and S. Snell, "Integrated Manufacturing and Job Design: Moderating Effects of Organizational Inertia," *Academy of Management Journal* 34 (1991), pp. 776–804.
29. E. Lawler, *The Ultimate Advantage: Creating the High Involvement Organization* (San Francisco: Jossey-Bass, 1992).
30. J. Olian and S. Rynes, "Organizational Staffing: Integrating Practice with Strategy," *Industrial Relations* 23 (1984), pp. 170–83.
31. G. Smith, "Quality: Small and Midsize Companies Seize the Challenge—Not a Moment Too Soon," *Business Week* (November 30, 1992), pp. 66–75.
32. J. Kerr and E. Jackofsky, "Aligning Managers with Strategies: Management Development versus Selection," *Strategic Management Journal* 10 (1989), pp. 157–70.
33. J. Kerr, "Strategic Control through Performance Appraisal and Rewards," *Human Resource Planning* 11 (1988), pp. 215–23.
34. S. Snell, "Control Theory in Strategic Human Resource Management."
35. B. Gerhart and G. Milkovich, "Employee Compensation: Research and Practice," in *Handbook of Industrial and Organizational Psychology*, 2nd ed., ed.

M. Dunnette and L. Hough (Palo Alto, CA: Consulting Psychologists Press, 1992), pp. 481–569.
36. D. Balkin and L. Gomez-Mejia, "Toward a Contingency Theory of Compensation Strategy," *Strategic Management Journal* 8 (1987), pp. 169–82.
37. A. Taylor, "U.S. Cars Come Back," *Fortune* (November 16, 1992), pp. 52, 85.
38. S. Cronshaw and R. Alexander, "One Answer to the Demand for Accountability: Selection Utility as an Investment Decision," *Organizational Behavior and Human Decision Processes* 35 (1986), pp. 102–18.
39. P. MacDuffie, "Human Resource Bundles and Manufacturing Performance: Organizational Logic and Flexible Production Systems in the World Auto Industry," *Industrial and Labor Relations Review* 48 (1995), pp. 197–221; P. McGraw, "A Hard Drive to the Top," *U.S. News and World Report* 118 (1995), pp. 43–44.
40. M. Huselid, "The Impact of Human Resource Management Practices on Turnover, Productivity, and Corporate Financial Performance," *Academy of Management Journal* 38 (1995), pp. 635–72.
41. M. Porter, *Competitive Advantage* (New York: Free Press, 1985).
42. R. Schuler and S. Jackson, "Linking Competitive Strategies with Human Resource Management Practices," *Academy of Management Executive* 1 (1987), pp. 207–19.
43. R. Miles and C. Snow, "Designing Strategic Human Resource Management Systems," *Organizational Dynamics* 13, no. 1 (1984), pp. 36–52.
44. J. Arthur, "The Link between Business Strategy and Industrial Relations Systems in American Steel Mini-Mills," *Industrial and Labor Relations Review* 45 (1992), pp. 488–506.
45. A. Thompson and A. Strickland, *Strategy Formulation and Implementation: Tasks of the General Manager*, 3rd ed. (Plano, TX: BPI, 1986).
46. G. Fairclough, "Business Bulletin," *The Wall Street Journal* (March 5, 1998), p. A1.
47. P. Sebastian, "Business Bulletin," *The Wall Street Journal* (October 2, 1997), p. A1.
48. J.S. Champy, *Reengineering Management: The Mandate for New Leadership* (New York: Harper Business, 1995).
49. S. Pearlstein, "Corporate Cutback Yet to Pay Off," *Washington Post* (January 4, 1994), p. B6.
50. K. Cameron, "Guest Editor's Note: Investigating Organizational Downsizing—Fundamental Issues," *Human Resource Management* 33 (1994), pp. 183–88.
51. N. Templin, "UAW to Unveil Pact on Slashing GM's Payroll," *The Wall Street Journal* (December 15, 1992), p. A3.
52. J. Lopez, "Managing: Early-Retirement Offers Lead to Renewed Hiring," *The Wall Street Journal* (January 26, 1993), p. B1.
53. A. Church, "Organizational Downsizing: What Is the Role of the Practitioner?" *The Industrial–Organizational Psychologist* 33, no. 1 (1995), pp. 63–74.
54. N. Templin, "A Decisive Response to Crisis Brought Ford Enhanced Productivity," *The Wall Street Journal* (December 15, 1992), p. A1.
55. M. Brannigan and E. De Lisser, "Cost Cutting at Delta Raises the Stock Price but Lowers the Service," *The Wall Street Journal* (June 20, 1996), pp. A1, A8.
56. J. Quinn, *Strategies for Change*.
57. H. Mintzberg, "Patterns in Strategy Formulation," *Management Science* 24 (1978), pp. 934–48.
58. R. Pascale, "Perspectives on Strategy: The Real Story behind Honda's Success," *California Management Review* 26 (1984), pp. 47–72.
59. N. Templin, "A Decisive Response to Crisis."
60. P. Senge, *The Fifth Discipline* (New York: Doubleday, 1990).
61. T. Stewart, "Brace for Japan's Hot New Strategy," *Fortune* (September 21, 1992), pp. 62–76.
62. C. Snow and S. Snell, *Staffing as Strategy*, vol. 4 of *Personnel Selection* (San Francisco: Jossey-Bass, 1992).
63. T. Batten, "Education Key to Prosperity—Report," *Houston Chronicle* (September 7, 1992), p. 1B.
64. P. Wright, "Human Resources as a Competitive Weapon," *Applied Advances in Strategic Management* 2 (1991), pp. 91–122.
65. G. McMahan, University of Texas at Arlington, personal communications.
66. G. McMahan and R. Woodman, "The Current Practice of Organization Development within the Firm: A Survey of Large Industrial Corporations," *Group and Organization Studies* 17 (1992), pp. 117–34.
67. D. Ulrich and A. Yeung, "A Shared Mindset," *Personnel Administrator*, March 1989, pp. 38–45.
68. G. Jones and P. Wright, "An Economic Approach to Conceptualizing the Utility of Human Resource Management Practices," *Research in Personnel/Human Resources* 10 (1992), pp. 271–99.
69. R. Schuler and J. Walker, "Human Resources Strategy: Focusing on Issues and Actions," *Organizational Dynamics*, Summer 1990, pp. 5–19.
70. M. Brannigan, "Delta Lifts Mechanics' Pay to Top of Industry Amid Push by Union, *Wall Street Journal Interactive* (August 16, 2001); M. Adams, "Delta May See Second Big Union, *USA Today* (August 27, 2001), p. 1B.

3 Chapter

The Legal Environment: Equal Employment Opportunity and Safety

Objectives
After reading this chapter, you should be able to:

1. Identify the three branches of government and the role each plays in influencing the legal environment of human resource management.
2. List the major federal laws that require equal employment opportunity and the protections provided by each of these laws.
3. Discuss the roles, responsibilities, and requirements of the federal agencies responsible for enforcing equal employment opportunity laws.
4. Identify the four theories of discrimination under Title VII of the Civil Rights Act and apply these theories to different discrimination situations.
5. Identify behavior that constitutes sexual harassment and list things that an organization can do to eliminate or minimize it.
6. Discuss the legal issues involved with preferential treatment programs.
7. Identify the major provisions of the Occupational Safety and Health Act (1970) and the rights of employees that are guaranteed by this act.

Home Depot has been criticized for not hiring enough women to work as merchandise employees. What can Home Depot do to avoid complaints that they are gender stereotyping?

Enter the World of Business

Home Depot's Bumpy Road to Equality

Home Depot is the largest home products firm selling home repair products and equipment for the "do-it-yourselfer." Founded 20 years ago, it now boasts 100,000 employees and more than 500 warehouse stores nationwide. The company's strategy for growth has focused mostly on one task: build more stores. In fact, an unwritten goal of Home Depot executives was to position a store within 30 minutes of every customer in the United States. They've almost made it. In addition, Home Depot has tried hard to implement a strategy of providing superior service to its customers. The company has prided itself on hiring people who are knowledgeable about home repair and who can teach customers how to do home repairs on their own. This strategy, along with blanketing the country with stores, has led to the firm's substantial advantage over competitors, including the now-defunct Home Quarters (HG) and still-standing Lowe's.

But Home Depot has run into some legal problems. During the company's growth, a statistical anomaly has emerged. About 70 percent of the merchandise employees (those directly involved in selling lumber, electrical supplies, hardware, and so forth) are men, whereas about 70 percent of operations employees (cashiers, accountants, back office staff, and so forth) are women. Because of this difference, several years ago a lawsuit was filed on behalf of 17,000 current and former employees as well as up to 200,000 rejected applicants. Home Depot explained the disparity by noting that most female job applicants have experience as cashiers, so they are placed in cashier positions; most male applicants express an interest or aptitude for home repair work such as carpentry or plumbing. However, attorneys argued that Home Depot was reinforcing gender stereotyping by hiring in this manner.

More recently, five former Home Depot employees sued the company, charging that it had discriminated against African American workers at two stores in southeast Florida. The five alleged that they were paid less than white workers, passed over for promotion, and given critical performance reviews based on race. "The company takes exception to the charges and believes they are without merit," said Home Depot spokesman Jerry Shields. The company has faced other racial discrimination suits as well, including one filed by the Michigan Department of Civil Rights.

To avoid such lawsuits in the future, Home Depot could resort to hiring and promoting by quota, ensuring an equal distribution of employees across all job categories—something that the company has wanted to avoid because it believes such action would undermine its competitive advantage. However, the company has taken steps to broaden and strengthen its own nondiscrimination policy by adding sexual orientation to the written policy. In addition, company president and CEO Bob Nardelli announced in the fall of 2001 that Home Depot would take special steps to protect benefits for its more than 500 employees who serve in the Army reserves and had been activated. "We will make up any difference between their Home Depot pay and their military pay if it's lower," said Nardelli. "When they come home [from duty], their jobs and their orange aprons are waiting for them."

SOURCE: "Home Depot Says Thanks to America's Military; Extends Associates/Reservists' Benefits, Announces Military Discount," company press release (October 9, 2001); S. Jaffe, "New Tricks in Home Depot's Toolbox?" *BusinessWeek Online* (June 5, 2001), www.businessweek.com; "HRC Lauds Home Depot for Adding Sexual Orientation to its Non-Discrimination Policy," *Human Rights Campaign* (May 14, 2001), www.hrc.org; "Former Home Depot Employees File Racial Discrimination Lawsuit," *Diversity at Work*, June 2000, www.diversityatwork.com; "Michigan Officials File Discrimination Suit against Home Depot," *Diversity at Work*, February 2000, www.diversityatwork.com; M. Boot, "For Plaintiffs' Lawyers, There's No Place Like Home Depot," *The Wall Street Journal*, interactive edition (February 12, 1997).

Introduction

In the opening chapter we discussed the environment of the HRM function, and we noted that several environmental factors affect an organization's HRM function. One is the legal environment, particularly the laws affecting the management of people. As the troubles at Home Depot indicate, legal issues can cause serious problems for a company's success and survival. In this chapter we first present an overview of the U.S. legal system, noting the different legislative bodies, regulatory agencies, and judicial bodies that determine the legality of certain HRM practices. We then discuss the major laws and executive orders that govern these practices.

One point to make clear at the outset is that managers often want a list of "dos and don'ts" that will keep them out of legal trouble. They rely on rules such as "Don't ever ask a female applicant if she is married" without understanding the "why" behind these rules. Clearly, certain practices are illegal or inadvisable, and this chapter will provide some valuable tips for avoiding discrimination lawsuits. However, such lists are not compatible with a strategic approach to HRM and are certainly not the route to developing a competitive advantage. They are simply mechanical reactions to the situations. Our goal is to provide an understanding of how the legislative, regulatory, and judicial systems work to define equal employment opportunity law. Armed with this understanding, a manager is better prepared to manage people within the limits imposed by the legal system. Doing so effectively is a source of competitive advantage. Doing so ineffectively results in competitive disadvantage. The "Competing in the New Economy" box illustrates the kinds of legal problems faced by firms without HR

COMPETING IN THE NEW ECONOMY

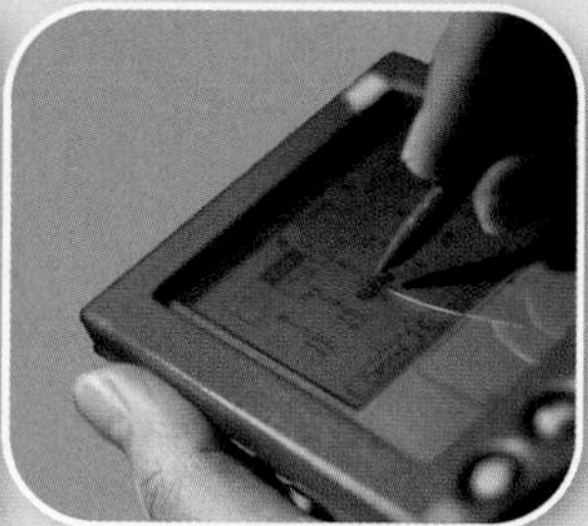

Lack of Professional HRM Spells Trouble for Downsizing Dot-Coms

The dot-com craze saw spiraling salaries as small start-ups drew workers away from large established firms with huge stock option packages that presented the hope of becoming a millionaire quickly. However, the years 2000 and 2001 saw the dot-com bubble burst in a way few ever predicted. Firms that had lured potential employees with bundles of money soon provided pink slips instead. This craze demonstrated the importance of having not only a valid business model but also seasoned HR professionals to help manage the people side of the business.

Whereas large firms possess skilled, experienced HR staff who have considerable knowledge of legal repercussions of various decisions, the smaller Internet businesses lacked this valuable resource. Consequently, when the time for layoffs came, they were often performed in ways that made former employees furious (rather than disappointed) and elicited a number of lawsuits. The most angry employees were those lured from secure old economy jobs that were left with no severance or other benefits. For example, Cynthia Dell'Isola left her previous employer to join Foodline.com for a 20 percent salary increase. Just three weeks later the company eliminated her job as part of a restructuring that affected more than 50 other employees.

Often such shabby treatment results in lawsuits. Dale Hopkins lost her job as president of iwin.com during a widespread reduction. She filed suit against the company alleging she was fired without cause in a layoff in which 70 percent of those laid off were women. An iwin.com spokesperson says that she was let go as part of a structural layoff, and that gender had nothing to do with it. However, when a company is struggling with profitability, expensive lawsuits certainly present problems.

As the shakeout in the new economy begins to stabilize, companies will learn from their mistakes and find better ways to manage employees in the bad times as well as the good. Experienced, knowledgeable HR professionals will be a resource they can draw on to do this more effectively.

SOURCE: K.J. Dunham, "When Dot-Coms Cut the Cord," *The Wall Street Journal* (October 17, 2000), p. B1.

professionals and managers that understand the legal ramifications of many organizational decisions.

The Legal System in the United States

The foundation for the U.S. legal system is set forth in the U.S. Constitution, which affects HRM in two ways. First, it delineates a citizen's constitutional rights, on which the government cannot impinge.[1] Most individuals are aware of the Bill of Rights, the first 10 amendments to the Constitution; but other amendments, such as the Fourteenth Amendment, also influence HRM practices. The Fourteenth Amendment, called the *equal protection clause*, states that all individuals are entitled to equal protection under the law.

Second, the Constitution established three major governing bodies: the legislative, executive, and judicial branches. The Constitution explicitly defines the roles and responsibilities of each of these branches. Each branch has its own areas of authority, but these areas have often overlapped, and the borders between the branches are often blurred.

Legislative Branch

The legislative branch of the federal government consists of the House of Representatives and the Senate. These bodies develop laws that govern many HRM activities. Most of the laws stem from a perceived societal need. For example, during the civil rights movement of the early 1960s, the legislative branch moved to ensure that various minority groups received equal opportunities in many areas of life. One of these areas was employment, and thus Congress enacted Title VII of the Civil Rights Act. Similar perceived societal needs have brought about labor laws such as the Occupational Safety and Health Act, the Employee Retirement Income Security Act, the Age Discrimination in Employment Act, and, more recently, the Americans with Disabilities Act of 1990 and the Civil Rights Act of 1991.

Executive Branch

The executive branch consists of the president of the United States and the many regulatory agencies the president oversees. Although the legislative branch passes the laws, the executive branch affects these laws in many ways. First, the president can propose bills to Congress that, if passed, would become laws. Second, the president has the power to veto any law passed by Congress, thus ensuring that few laws are passed without presidential approval—which allows the president to influence how laws are written.

Third, the regulatory agencies, under the authority of the president, have responsibility for enforcing the laws. Thus a president can influence what types of violations are pursued. For example, many laws affecting employment discrimination are enforced by the Equal Employment Opportunity Commission under the Department of Justice. During President Jimmy Carter's administration, the Department of Justice brought a lawsuit against Birmingham, Alabama's, fire department for not having enough black firefighters. This suit resulted in a consent decree that required blacks to receive preferential treatment in hiring and promotion decisions. Two years later, during Ronald Reagan's administration, the Department of Justice sided with white firefighters in a lawsuit against the city of Birmingham, alleging that the preferential treatment required by the consent decree discriminated against white firefighters.[2]

Fourth, the president can issue executive orders, which sometimes regulate the activities of organizations that have contracts with the federal government. For example, Executive Order 11246, signed by President Lyndon Johnson, required all federal contractors and subcontractors to engage in affirmative action programs designed to hire and promote women and minorities within their organizations. Fifth, the president can influence the Supreme Court to interpret laws in certain ways. When particularly sensitive cases come before the Court, the attorney general, representing the executive branch, argues for certain preferred outcomes. For example, one recent court case involved a white female schoolteacher who was laid off from her job in favor of retaining a black schoolteacher with equal seniority and performance with the reason given as "diversity." The white woman filed a lawsuit in federal court and the Bush administration filed a brief on her behalf, arguing that diversity was not a legitimate reason to use race in decision making. She won in federal court, and the school district appealed. The Clinton administration, having been elected in the meantime, filed a brief on behalf of the school district, arguing that diversity was a legitimate defense.

Finally, the president appoints all the judges in the federal judicial system, subject to approval from the legislative branch. This affects the interpretation of many laws.

Judicial Branch

The judicial branch consists of the federal court system, which is made up of three levels. The first level consists of the U.S. District Courts and quasi-judicial administrative agencies. The district courts hear cases involving alleged violations of federal laws. The quasi-judicial agencies, such as the National Labor Relations Board (or NLRB, which is actually an arm of the executive branch, but serves a judicial function), hear cases regarding their particular jurisdictions (in the NLRB's case, disputes between unions and management). If neither party to a suit is satisfied with the decision of the court at this level, the parties can appeal the decision to the U.S. Courts of Appeals. These courts were originally set up to ease the Supreme Court's caseload, so appeals generally go from the federal trial level to one of the 13 appellate courts before they can be heard by the highest level, the Supreme Court. The Supreme Court must grant certiorari before hearing an appealed case. However, this is not usually granted unless two appellate courts have come to differing decisions on the same point of law or if the case deals with an important interpretation of constitutional law.

The Supreme Court serves as the court of final appeal. Decisions made by the Supreme Court are binding; they can be overturned only through legislation. For example, Congress, dissatisfied with the Supreme Court's decisions in certain cases such as *Wards Cove Packing* v. *Atonio*, overturned those decisions through the Civil Rights Act of 1991.[3]

Having described the legal system that affects the management of HR, we now explore some laws that regulate HRM activities, particularly equal employment opportunity laws. We first discuss the major laws that mandate equal employment opportunity in the United States. Then we examine the agencies involved in enforcing these laws. This leads us into an examination of the four theories of discrimination, with a discussion of some relevant court cases. Finally, we explore some equal employment opportunity issues facing today's managers.

Equal Employment Opportunity

Equal employment opportunity (EEO) refers to the government's attempt to ensure that all individuals have an equal chance for employment, regardless of race, color, religion, sex, age, disability, or national origin. To accomplish this, the federal government has used constitutional amendments, legislation, and executive orders, as well as the court decisions that interpret these laws. (However, equal employment laws are not the same in all countries.) The major EEO laws we discuss are summarized in Table 3.1.

Equal employment opportunity (EEO)
The government's attempt to ensure that all individuals have an equal opportunity for employment, regardless of race, color, religion, sex, age, disability, or national origin.

TABLE 3.1
Summary of Major EEO Laws and Regulations

ACT	REQUIREMENTS	COVERS	ENFORCEMENT AGENCY
Thirteenth Amendment	Abolished slavery	All individuals	Court system
Fourteenth Amendment	Provides equal protection for all citizens and requires due process in state action	State actions (e.g., decisions of government organizations)	Court system
Civil Rights Acts (CRAs) of 1866 and 1871 (as amended)	Grants all citizens the right to make, perform, modify, and terminate contracts and enjoy all benefits, terms, and conditions of the contractual relationship	All individuals	Court system
Equal Pay Act of 1963	Requires that men and women performing equal jobs receive equal pay	Employers engaged in interstate commerce	EEOC
Title VII of CRA	Forbids discrimination based on race, color, religion, sex, or national origin	Employers with 15 or more employees working 20 or more weeks per year; labor unions; and employment agencies	EEOC
Age Discrimination in Employment Act of 1967	Prohibits discrimination in employment against individuals 40 years of age and older	Employers with 15 or more employees working 20 or more weeks per year; labor unions; employment agencies; federal government	EEOC
Rehabilitation Act of 1973	Requires affirmative action in the employment of individuals with disabilities	Government agencies; federal contractors and subcontractors with contracts greater than $2,500	OFCCP
Americans with Disabilities Act of 1990	Prohibits discrimination against individuals with disabilities	Employers with more than 15 employees	EEOC
Executive Order 11246	Requires affirmative action in hiring women and minorities	Federal contractors and subcontractors with contracts greater than $10,000	OFCCP
Civil Rights Act of 1991	Prohibits discrimination (same as Title VII)	Same as Title VII, plus applies Section 1981 to employment discrimination cases	EEOC

Constitutional Amendments

Thirteenth Amendment

The Thirteenth Amendment of the Constitution abolished slavery in the United States. Though one might be hard-pressed to cite an example of race-based slavery in the United States today, the Thirteenth Amendment has been applied in cases where the discrimination involved the "badges" (symbols) and "incidents" of slavery.

Fourteenth Amendment

The Fourteenth Amendment forbids the states from taking life, liberty, or property without due process of law and prevents the states from denying equal protection of the laws. Passed immediately after the Civil War, this amendment originally applied only to discrimination against blacks. It was soon broadened to protect other groups such as aliens and Asian-Americans, and more recently it has been applied to the protection of whites in allegations of reverse discrimination. In *Bakke* v. *California Board of Regents*, Alan Bakke alleged that he had been discriminated against in the selection of entrants to the University of California at Davis medical school.[4] The university had set aside 16 of the available 100 places for "disadvantaged" applicants who were members of racial minority groups. Under this quota system, Bakke was able to compete for only 84 positions, whereas a minority applicant was able to compete for all 100. The court ruled in favor of Bakke, noting that this quota system had violated white individuals' right to equal protection under the law.

One important point regarding the Fourteenth Amendment is that it is applicable only to "state actions." This means that only the decisions or actions of the government or of private groups whose activities are deemed state actions can be construed as violations of the Fourteenth Amendment. Thus, one could file a claim under the Fourteenth Amendment if one were fired from a state university (a government organization) but not if one were fired by a private employer.

Congressional Legislation

The Reconstruction Civil Rights Acts (1866 and 1871)

The Thirteenth Amendment eradicated slavery in the United States, and the Reconstruction Civil Rights Acts were attempts to further this goal. The Civil Rights Act passed in 1866 was later broken into two statutes. Section 1982 granted all persons the same property rights as white citizens. Section 1981 granted other rights, including the right to enter into and enforce contracts. Courts have interpreted Section 1981 as granting individuals the right to make and enforce employment contracts. The Civil Rights Act of 1871 granted all citizens the right to sue in federal court if they felt they had been deprived of some civil right. Although these laws might seem outdated, they are still used because they allow the plaintiff to recover both compensatory and punitive damages.

In fact, these laws came to the forefront in a Supreme Court case: *Patterson* v. *McClean Credit Union*.[5] The plaintiff had filed a discrimination complaint under Section 1981 for racial harassment. After being hired by McClean Credit Union, Patterson failed to receive any promotions or pay raises while she was employed there. She was also told that "blacks work slower than whites." Thus she had grounds to prove discrimination and filed suit under Section 1981, arguing that she had been

COMPETING THROUGH HIGH-PERFORMANCE WORK SYSTEMS

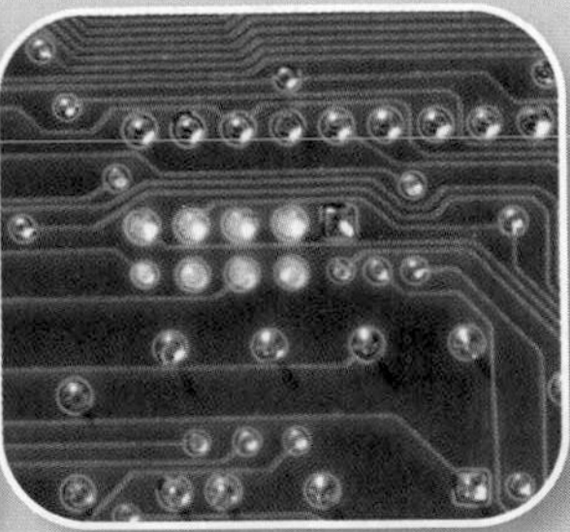

Bonne Bell Leverages Seniors in the Talent Wars

Finding and Keeping the Best Employees

In 1996 Bonne Bell, the maker of a number of cosmetics popular among teenage girls, faced a tight labor market and a strong growth in demand for its products in Canada. Jess Bell, the president and son of the founder, had an epiphany. Being 76 years old himself, he increasingly felt that working with younger people made him feel self-conscious about his own ability to keep pace. So he created an entire production department of older workers.

He figured that having a line comprised entirely of older workers would allow them to compete at their own level, rather than against those much younger and more energetic. He also thought older workers would not necessarily want to listen to either the conversations or the music of 20-year-olds. Juliana Carlton, 65, supervises eight employees on the line and notes, "I raised my kids. It's my turn to be with people my own age group. We can talk to each other. We don't have to compete."

The experiment began with taking three older packaging machines and two conveyors out of storage so as not to invest much in new equipment in case the idea did not work. The senior workers tend to have more flexible hours to adapt to many of the aches and pains that accompany growing old. The employees listen to oldies like Frank Sinatra while they work. The department began with 16 people but has now grown to 50 workers on each shift. Pay starts at $7.50 an hour and moves to $8 after a year. The workers get 72 hours of paid time off but no health care coverage, which helps keep costs down. The average age of the assembly line workers is 70, and the oldest just turned 90.

Each worker has his or her own reasons for working. Some workers need the extra $600 a month to pay bills. Some need the money to help take care of their parents. But for others, working provides a sense of connection and self-esteem. Many are mothers who are not as integral to their grown children's lives as they once were. Mrs. Carlton states, "Instead of sitting around, I wanted to do something with my life."

So far, this experiment has been a success. The group has saved the company more than $1 million since it was launched while meeting shipment goals and experiencing almost zero turnover.

SOURCE: C. Ansberry, "Bonne Bell Retires Stereotypes with Seniors-Only Department," *The Wall Street Journal* (February 5, 2001), p. 1.

Vietnam Era Veteran's Readjustment Act of 1974

Similar to the Rehabilitation Act, this act requires federal contractors and subcontractors to take affirmative action toward employing Vietnam veterans (those serving between August 5, 1964, and May 7, 1975). The Office of Federal Contract Compliance Procedures, discussed later in this chapter, has authority to enforce this act.

Civil Rights Act of 1991

The Civil Rights Act of 1991 (CRA 1991) amends Title VII of the Civil Rights Act of 1964, Section 1981 of the Civil Rights Act of 1866, the Americans with Disabilities Act, and the Age Discrimination in Employment Act of 1967. One major change

EMPLOYER SIZE	DAMAGE LIMIT
14 to 100 employees	$ 50,000
101 to 200 employees	100,000
201 to 500 employees	200,000
More than 500 employees	300,000

TABLE 3.2
Maximum Punitive Damages Allowed under the Civil Rights Act of 1991

in EEO law under CRA 1991 has been the addition of compensatory and punitive damages in cases of discrimination under Title VII and the Americans with Disabilities Act. Before CRA 1991, Title VII limited damage claims to equitable relief such as back pay, lost benefits, front pay in some cases, and attorney's fees and costs. CRA 1991 allows compensatory and punitive damages when intentional or reckless discrimination is proven. Compensatory damages include such things as future pecuniary loss, emotional pain, suffering, and loss of enjoyment of life. Punitive damages are meant to discourage employers from discriminating by providing for payments to the plaintiff beyond the actual damages suffered.

Recognizing that one or a few discrimination cases could put an organization out of business, thus adversely affecting many innocent employees, Congress has put limits on the amount of punitive damages. Table 3.2 depicts these limits. As can be seen, damages range from $50,000 to $300,000 per violation, depending on the size of the organization. Punitive damages are available only if the employer intentionally discriminated against the plaintiff(s) or if the employer discriminated with malice or reckless indifference to the employee's federally protected rights. These damages are excluded for an employment practice held to be unlawful because of its disparate impact.[10]

The addition of damages to CRA 1991 has had two immediate effects. First, by increasing the potential payoff for a successful discrimination suit, it has increased the number of suits filed against businesses. Second, organizations are now more likely to grant all employees an equal opportunity for employment, regardless of their race, gender, religion, or national origin. Many organizations have felt the need to make the composition of their workforce mirror the general population to avoid costly lawsuits. This act adds a financial incentive for doing so.

Americans with Disabilities Act (ADA) of 1990

One of the most far-reaching acts concerning the management of human resources is the Americans with Disabilities Act. This act protects individuals with disabilities from being discriminated against in the workplace. It prohibits discrimination based on disability in all employment practices such as job application procedures, hiring, firing, promotions, compensation, and training—in addition to other employment activities such as advertising, recruitment, tenure, layoff, leave, and fringe benefits. Because this act is so new, we will cover its various stipulations individually.

Americans with Disabilities Act (ADA) of 1990
A 1990 act prohibiting individuals with disabilities from being discriminated against in the workplace.

The ADA defines a disability as a physical or mental impairment that substantially limits one or more major life activities, a record of having such an impairment, or being regarded as having such an impairment. The first part of the definition refers to individuals who have serious disabilities—such as epilepsy, blindness, deafness, or paralysis—that affect their ability to perform major life activities such as walking, seeing, performing manual tasks, learning, caring for oneself, and working. The second part refers to individuals who have a history of disability, such as someone who has had cancer but is currently in remission, someone with a history of mental illness, and someone with a history of heart disease. The third part of the definition, "being regarded as having a disability," refers, for example, to an individual who is severely disfigured and is denied employment because an employer fears negative reactions from others.[11]

Thus the ADA covers specific physiological disabilities such as cosmetic disfigurement and anatomical loss affecting the neurological, musculoskeletal, sensory, respiratory, cardiovascular, reproductive, digestive, genitourinary, hemic, or lymphatic systems. In addition, it covers mental and psychological disorders such as mental retardation, organic brain syndrome, emotional or mental illness, and learning disabilities. However, conditions such as obesity, substance abuse, eye and hair color, and lefthandedness are not covered.[12]

Executive Orders

Executive orders are directives issued and amended unilaterally by the president. These orders do not require congressional approval, yet they have the force of law. Two executive orders directly affect HRM.

Executive Order 11246

President Johnson issued this executive order, which prohibits discrimination based on race, color, religion, sex, and national origin. Unlike Title VII, this order applies only to federal contractors and subcontractors. Employers receiving more than $10,000 from the federal government must take affirmative action to ensure against discrimination, and those with contracts greater than $50,000 must develop a written affirmative action plan for each of their establishments within 120 days of the beginning of the contract. The Office of Federal Contract Compliance Procedures enforces this executive order.

Executive Order 11478

President Richard M. Nixon issued this order, which requires the federal government to base all its employment policies on merit and fitness, and specifies that race, color, sex, religion, and national origin should not be considered. (The U.S. Office of Personnel Management is in charge of this.) The order also extends to all contractors and subcontractors doing $10,000 worth of business with the federal government. (The relevant government agencies have the responsibility to ensure that the contractors and subcontractors comply with the order.)

Enforcement of Equal Employment Opportunity

As discussed previously, the executive branch of the federal government bears most of the responsibility for enforcing all EEO laws passed by the legislative branch. In addition, the executive branch must enforce the executive orders issued by the president. The two agencies responsible for the enforcement of these laws and executive orders are the Equal Employment Opportunity Commission and the Office of Federal Contract Compliance Procedures, respectively.

Equal Employment Opportunity Commission (EEOC)

An independent federal agency, the EEOC is responsible for enforcing most of the EEO laws, such as Title VII, the Equal Pay Act, and the Americans with Disabilities Act. The EEOC has three major responsibilities: investigating and resolving discrimination complaints, gathering information, and issuing guidelines.

Equal Employment Opportunity Commission (EEOC)
The government commission to ensure that all individuals have an equal opportunity for employment, regardless of race, color, religion, sex, age, disability, or national origin.

Investigation and Resolution

Individuals who feel they have been discriminated against must file a complaint with the EEOC or a similar state agency within 180 days of the incident. Failure to file a complaint within the 180 days results in the case's being dismissed immediately, with certain exceptions, such as the enactment of a seniority system that has an intentionally discriminatory purpose.

Once the complaint is filed, the EEOC takes responsibility for investigating the claim of discrimination. The complainant must give the EEOC 60 days to investigate the complaint. If the EEOC either does not believe the complaint to be valid or fails to complete the investigation, the complainant may sue in federal court. If the EEOC determines that discrimination has taken place, its representatives will attempt to provide a reconciliation between the two parties without burdening the court system with a lawsuit. Sometimes the EEOC enters into a consent decree with the discriminating organization. This decree is an agreement between the agency and the organization that the organization will cease certain discriminatory practices and possibly institute additional affirmative action practices to rectify its history of discrimination.

If the EEOC cannot come to an agreement with the organization, there are two options. First, it can issue a "right to sue" letter to the alleged victim, which certifies that the agency has investigated and found validity in the victim's allegations. Second, although less likely, the agency may aid the alleged victim in bringing suit in federal court.

Information Gathering

The EEOC also plays a role in monitoring the hiring practices of organizations. Each year organizations with 100 or more employees must file a report (EEO-1) with the EEOC that provides the number of women and minorities employed in nine different job categories. The EEOC computer analyzes these reports to identify patterns of discrimination that can then be attacked through class-action suits.

Issuance of Guidelines

A third responsibility of the EEOC is to issue guidelines that help employers determine when their decisions are violations of the laws enforced by the EEOC. These guidelines are not laws themselves, but the courts give great deference to them when hearing employment discrimination cases.

For example, the *Uniform Guidelines on Employee Selection Procedures* is a set of guidelines issued by the EEOC, the Department of Labor, the Department of Justice, and the U.S. Civil Service Commission.[13] This document provides guidance on the ways an organization should develop and administer selection systems so as not to violate Title VII. The courts often refer to the *Uniform Guidelines* to determine whether a company has engaged in discriminatory conduct or to determine the validity of the procedures it used to validate a selection system. Another example: Since the passage of the ADA, employers have been somewhat confused about the act's implications for their hiring procedures. Therefore, the EEOC issued guidelines in the *Federal Register* that provided more detailed information regarding what the agency will consider legal and illegal employment practices concerning disabled individuals. Although companies are well advised to follow these guidelines, it is possible that courts will interpret the ADA differently from the EEOC. Thus, through the issuance of guidelines the EEOC gives employers directions for making employment decisions that do not conflict with existing laws.

Office of Federal Contract Compliance Programs (OFCCP)

The OFCCP is the agency responsible for enforcing the executive orders that cover companies doing business with the federal government. Businesses with contracts for more than $50,000 cannot discriminate in employment based on race, color, religion, national origin, or sex, and they must have a written affirmative action plan on file.

Utilization analysis
A comparison of the race, sex, and ethnic composition of an employer's workforce with that of the available labor supply.

These plans have three basic components.[14] First, the **utilization analysis** compares the race, sex, and ethnic composition of the employer's workforce with that of the available labor supply. For each job group, the employer must identify the percentage of its workforce with that characteristic (female, for example) and identify the percentage of workers in the relevant labor market with that characteristic. If the percentage in the employer's workforce is much less than the percentage in the comparison group, then that minority group is considered to be "underutilized."

Goals and timetables
The part of a written affirmative action plan that specifies the percentage of women and minorities that an employer seeks to have in each job group and the date by which that percentage is to be attained.

Second, the employer must develop specific **goals and timetables** for achieving balance in the workforce concerning these characteristics (particularly where underutilization exists). Goals and timetables specify the percentage of women and minorities that the employer seeks to have in each job group and the date by which that percentage is to be attained. These are not to be viewed as *quotas*, which entail setting aside a specific number of positions to be filled only by members of the protected class. Goals and timetables are much more flexible, requiring only that the employer have specific goals and take steps to achieve those goals. In fact, one study that examined companies with the goal of increasing black employment found that only 10 percent of them actually achieved their goals. Although this may sound discouragingly low, it is important to note that these companies increased their black employment more than companies that set no such goals.[15]

Action steps
The written affirmative plan that specifies what an employer plans to do to reduce underutilization of protected groups.

Third, employers with federal contracts must develop a list of **action steps** they will take toward attaining their goals to reduce underutilization. The company's CEO must make it clear to the entire organization that the company is committed to reducing underutilization, and all management levels must be involved in the planning process. For example, organizations can communicate job openings to women and minorities through publishing the company's affirmative action policy, recruiting at predominantly female or minority schools, participating in programs designed to increase employment opportunities for underemployed groups, and removing unnecessary barriers to employment. Organizations must also take affirmative steps toward hiring Vietnam veterans and individuals with disabilities.

The OFCCP annually audits government contractors to ensure that they actively pursue the goals in their plans. These audits consist of (1) examining the company's affirmative action plan and (2) conducting on-site visits to examine how individual employees perceive the company's affirmative action policies. If the OFCCP finds that the contractors or subcontractors are not complying with the executive order, then its representatives may notify the EEOC (if there is evidence that Title VII has been violated), advise the Department of Justice to institute criminal proceedings, request that the Secretary of Labor cancel or suspend any current contracts, and forbid the firm from bidding on future contracts. This last penalty, called *debarment,* is the OFCCP's most potent weapon.

Having discussed the major laws defining equal employment opportunity and the agencies that enforce these laws, we now address the various types of discrimination and the ways these forms of discrimination have been interpreted by the courts in a number of cases.

Types of Discrimination

How would you know if you had been discriminated against? Assume that you have applied for a job and were not hired. How do you know if the organization decided not to hire you because you are unqualified, because you are less qualified than the individual ultimately hired, or simply because the person in charge of the hiring decision "didn't like your type"? Discrimination is a multifaceted issue. It is often not easy to determine the extent to which unfair discrimination affects an employer's decisions.

Legal scholars have identified three theories of discrimination: disparate treatment, disparate impact, and reasonable accommodation. In addition, there is protection for those participating in discrimination cases or opposing discriminatory actions. In the act, these theories are stated in very general terms. However, the court system has defined and delineated these theories through the cases brought before it. A comparison of the theories of discrimination is given in Table 3.3.

Disparate Treatment

Disparate treatment exists when individuals in similar situations are treated differently and the different treatment is based on the individual's race, color, religion, sex, national origin, age, or disability status. If two people with the same qualifications apply for a job and the employer decides whom to hire based on one individual's race, the individual not hired is a victim of disparate treatment. In the disparate treatment case the plaintiff must prove that there was a discriminatory motive—that is, that the employer *intended* to discriminate.

Disparate treatment
A theory of discrimination based on different treatments given to individuals because of their race, color, religion, sex, national origin, age, or disability status.

Whenever individuals are treated differently because of their race, sex, or the like, there is disparate treatment. For example, if a company fails to hire women with school-age children (claiming the women will be frequently absent) but hires men with school-age children, the applicants are being treated differently based on sex. Another example would be an employer who checks the references and investigates the conviction records of minority applicants but does not do so for white applicants. Why are managers advised not to ask about marital status? Because in most cases, a manager will either ask only the female applicants or, if the manager asks both males and females, he or she will make different assumptions about females (such as "She will have to move if her husband gets a job elsewhere") and males (such as "He's very stable"). In all these examples, notice that (1) people are being treated differently and (2) there is an actual intent to treat them differently.[16]

TABLE 3.3
Comparison of Discrimination Theories

TYPES OF DISCRIMINATION	DISPARATE TREATMENT	DISPARATE IMPACT	REASONABLE ACCOMMODATION
Show intent?	Yes	No	Yes
Prima facie case	Individual is member of a protected group, was qualified for the job, and was turned down for the job, and the job remained open	Statistical disparity in the effects of a facially neutral employment practice	Individual has a belief or disability, provided the employer with notice (request to accommodate), and was adversely affected by a failure to be accommodated
Employer's defense	Produce a legitimate, nondiscriminatory reason for the employment decision or show bona fide occupational qualification (BFOQ)	Prove that the employment practice bears a manifest relationship with job performance	Job-relatedness and business necessity, undue hardship, or direct threat to health or safety
Plaintiff's rebuttal	Reason offered was merely a "pretext" for discrimination	Alternative procedures exist that meet the employer's goal without having disparate impact	
Monetary damages	Compensatory and punitive damages	Equitable relief (e.g., back pay)	Compensatory and punitive damages (if discrimination was intentional or employer failed to show good faith efforts to accommodate)

To understand how disparate treatment is applied in the law, let's look at how an actual court case, filed under disparate treatment, would proceed.

The Plaintiff's Burden

As in any legal case, the plaintiff has the burden of proving that the defendant has committed an illegal act. This is the idea of a "prima facie" case. In a disparate treatment case, the plaintiff meets the prima facie burden by showing four things:

1. The plaintiff belongs to a protected group.
2. The plaintiff applied for and was qualified for the job.
3. Despite possessing the qualifications, the plaintiff was rejected.
4. After the plaintiff was rejected, the position remained open and the employer continued to seek applicants with similar qualifications, or the position was filled by someone with similar qualifications.

Although these four things may seem easy to prove, it is important to note that what the court is trying to do is rule out the most obvious reasons for rejecting the plaintiff's claim (for example, the plaintiff did not apply or was not qualified, or the position was already filled or had been eliminated). If these alternative explanations are ruled out, the court assumes that the hiring decision was based on a discriminatory motive.

The Defendant's Rebuttal

Once the plaintiff has made the prima facie case for discrimination, the burden shifts to the defendant. The burden is different depending on whether the prima facie case presents only circumstantial evidence (there is no direct evidence of discrimination such as a formal policy to discriminate, but rather discriminatory intent must be inferred) or direct evidence (a formal policy of discrimination for some perceived legitimate reason). In cases of circumstantial evidence, the defendant simply must produce a legitimate, nondiscriminatory reason, such as that, although the plaintiff was qualified, the individual hired was more qualified.

However, in cases where direct evidence exists, such as a formal policy of hiring only women for waitress jobs because the business is aimed at catering to male customers, then the defendant is more likely to offer a different defense. This defense argues that for this job, a factor such as race, sex, or religion was a **bona fide occupational qualification (BFOQ)**. For example, if one were hiring an individual to hand out towels in a women's locker room, being a woman might be a BFOQ. However, there are very few cases in which race or sex qualify as a BFOQ, and in these cases it must be a necessary, rather than simply a preferred, characteristic of the job.

Bona fide occupational qualification (BFOQ)
A job qualification based on race, sex, religion, and so on that an employer asserts is a necessary qualification for the job.

UAW v. *Johnson Controls, Inc.*, illustrates the difficulty in using a BFOQ as a defense.[17] Johnson Controls, a manufacturer of car batteries, had instituted a "fetal protection" policy that excluded women of childbearing age from a number of jobs in which they would be exposed to lead, which can cause birth defects in children. The company argued that sex was a BFOQ essential to maintaining a safe workplace. The Supreme Court did not uphold the company's policy, arguing that BFOQs are limited to policies that are directly related to a worker's ability to do the job.

The Plaintiff's Rebuttal

If the defendant provides a legitimate, nondiscriminatory reason for its employment decision, the burden shifts back to the plaintiff. The plaintiff must now show that the reason offered by the defendant was not in fact the reason for its decision but merely a "pretext" or excuse for its actual discriminatory decision. This could entail providing evidence that white applicants with very similar qualifications to the plaintiff have often been hired while black applicants with very similar qualifications were all rejected. To illustrate disparate treatment, let's look at the first major case dealing with disparate treatment, *McDonnell Douglas Corp.* v. *Green.*

McDonnell Douglas Corp. v. Green. This Supreme Court case was the first to delineate the four criteria for a prima facie case of discrimination. From 1956 to 1964, Green had been an employee at McDonnell Douglas, a manufacturing plant in St. Louis, Missouri, that employed about 30,000 people. In 1964 he was laid off during a general workforce reduction. While unemployed, he participated in some activities that the company undoubtedly frowned upon: a "lock-in," where he and others placed a chain and padlock on the front door of a building to prevent the employees from leaving; and a "stall-in," where a group of employees stalled their cars at the gates of the plant so that no one could enter or leave the parking lot. About three weeks after the lock-in, McDonnell Douglas advertised for qualified mechanics, Green's trade, and he reapplied. When the company rejected his application, he sued, arguing that the company didn't hire him because of his race and because of his persistent involvement in the civil rights movement.

In making his prima facie case, Green had no problem showing that he was a member of a protected group, that he had applied for and was qualified for the job (having already worked in the job), that he was rejected, and that the company continued to advertise the position. The company's defense was that the plaintiff was not hired because he participated in the lock-in and the stall-in. In other words, the company was merely refusing to hire a troublemaker.

The plaintiff responded that the company's stated reason for not hiring him was a pretext for discrimination. He pointed out that white employees who had participated in the same activities (the lock-in and stall-in) were rehired, whereas he was not. The court found in favor of the plaintiff.

This case illustrates how similarly situated individuals (white and black) can be treated differently (whites were hired back whereas blacks were not) with the differences in treatment based on race. As we discuss later, most plaintiffs bring cases of sexual harassment under this theory of discrimination, sexual harassment being a situation where individuals are treated differently because of their sex.

Mixed-Motive Cases

In a mixed-motive case, the defendant acknowledges that some discriminatory motive existed but argues that the same hiring decision would have been reached even without the discriminatory motive. In *Hopkins* v. *Price Waterhouse*, Elizabeth Hopkins was an accountant who had applied for partnership in her firm. Although she had brought in a large amount of business and had received high praise from her clients, she was turned down for a partnership on two separate occasions. In her performance reviews, she had been told to adopt more feminine dress and speech and received many other comments that suggested gender-based stereotypes. In court, the company admitted that a sex-based stereotype existed but argued that it would have come to the same decision (not promoted Hopkins) even if the stereotype had not existed.

One of the main questions that came out of this case was, Who has the burden of proof? Does the plaintiff have to prove that a different decision would have been made (that Hopkins would have been promoted) in the absence of the discriminatory motive? Or does the defendant have to prove that the same decision would have been made?

According to CRA 1991, if the plaintiff demonstrates that race, sex, color, religion, or national origin was a motivating factor for any employment practice, the prima facie burden has been met, and the burden of proof is on the employer to demonstrate that the same decision would have been made even if the discriminatory motive had not been present. If the employer can do this, the plaintiff cannot collect compensatory or punitive damages. However, the court may order the employer to quit using the discriminatory motive in its future employment decisions.

Disparate impact
A theory of discrimination based on facially neutral employment practices that disproportionately exclude a protected group from employment opportunities.

Disparate Impact

The second type of discrimination is called **disparate impact.** It occurs when a facially neutral employment practice disproportionately excludes a protected group from employment opportunities. A facially neutral employment practice is one that lacks obvious discriminatory content yet affects one group to a greater extent than other groups, such as an employment test. Although the Supreme Court inferred disparate impact from Title VII in the *Griggs* v. *Duke Power* case, it has since been codified into the Civil Rights Act of 1991.

There is an important distinction between disparate impact and disparate treatment discrimination. For there to be discrimination under disparate treatment, there has to be intentional discrimination. Under disparate impact, intent is irrelevant. The important criterion is that the consequences of the employment practice are discriminatory.

For example, if, for some practical reason, you hired individuals based on their height, you may not have intended to discriminate against anyone, and yet using height would have a disproportionate impact on certain protected groups. Women tend to be shorter than men, so fewer women will be hired. Certain ethnic groups, such as those of Asian ancestry, also tend to be shorter than those of European ancestry. Thus, your facially neutral employment practice will have a disparate impact on certain protected groups.

This is not to imply that simply because a selection practice has disparate impact, it is necessarily illegal. Some characteristics (such as height) are not equally distributed across race and gender groups; however, the important question is whether the characteristic is related to successful performance on the job. To help you understand how disparate impact works, let's look at a court proceeding involving a disparate impact claim.

The Plaintiff's Burden

In a disparate impact case, the plaintiff must make the prima facie case by showing that the employment practice in question disproportionately affects a protected group relative to the majority group. To illustrate this theory, let's assume that you are a manager who has 60 positions to fill. Your applicant pool has 80 white and 40 black applicants. You use a test that selects 48 of the white and 12 of the black applicants. Is this a disparate impact? Two alternative quantitative analyses are often used to determine whether a test has adverse impact.

The **four-fifths rule** states that a test has disparate impact if the hiring rate for the minority group is less than four-fifths (or 80 percent) of the hiring rate for the majority group. Applying this analysis to the preceding example, we would first calculate the hiring rates for each group:

Whites = 48/80 = 60%

Blacks = 12/40 = 30%

Then we would compare the hiring rate of the minority group (30%) with that of the majority group (60%). Using the four-fifths rule, we would determine that the test has adverse impact if the hiring rate of the minority group is less than 80% of the hiring rate of the majority group. Because it is less (that is, 30%/60% = 50%, which is less than 80%), we would conclude that the test has adverse impact. The four-fifths rule is used as a rule of thumb by the EEOC in determining adverse impact.

The **standard deviation rule** uses actual probability distributions to determine adverse impact. This analysis uses the difference between the expected representation (or hiring rates) for minority groups and the actual representation (or hiring rate) to determine whether the difference between these two values is greater than would

Four-fifths rule
A rule that states that an employment test has disparate impact if the hiring rate for a minority group is less than four-fifths, or 80 percent, of the hiring rate for the majority group.

Standard deviation rule
A rule used to analyze employment tests to determine disparate impact; it uses the difference between the expected representation for minority groups and the actual representation to determine whether the difference between the two is greater than would occur by chance.

occur by chance. Thus, in our example, 33% (40 of 120) of the applicants were blacks, so one would expect 33% (20 of 60) of those hired to be black. However, only 12 black applicants were hired. To determine if the difference between the expected representation and the actual representation is greater than we would expect by chance, we calculate the standard deviation (which, you might remember from your statistics class, is the standard deviation in a binomial distribution):

$$\sqrt{\text{Number hired} \times \frac{\text{Number of minority applicants}}{\text{Number of total applicants}} \times \frac{\text{Number of nonminority applicants}}{\text{Number of total applicants}}}$$

or in this case:

$$\sqrt{60 \times \frac{40}{120} \times \frac{80}{120}} = 3.6$$

If the difference between the actual representation and the expected representation (20 – 12 = 8 in this case) of blacks is greater than 2 standard deviations (2 × 3.6, = 7.2 in this case), we would conclude that the test had adverse impact against blacks, because we would expect this result less than 1 time in 20 if the test were equally difficult for both whites and blacks.

The *Wards Cove Packing Co.* v. *Atonio* case involved an interesting use of statistics. The plaintiffs showed that the jobs in the cannery (lower-paying jobs) were filled primarily with minority applicants (in this case, American Eskimos). However, only a small percentage of the noncannery jobs (those with higher pay) were filled by nonminorities. The plaintiffs argued that this statistical disparity in the racial makeup of the cannery and noncannery jobs was proof of discrimination. The federal district, appellate, and Supreme Courts all found for the defendant, stating that this disparity was not proof of discrimination.

Once the plaintiff has demonstrated adverse impact, he or she has met the burden of a prima facie case of discrimination.[18]

Defendant's Rebuttal

According to CRA 1991, once the plaintiff has made a prima facie case, the burden of proof shifts to the defendant, who must show that the employment practice is a "business necessity." This is accomplished by showing that the practice bears a relationship with some legitimate employer goal. With respect to job selection, this relationship is demonstrated by showing the job relatedness of the test, usually by reporting a validity study of some type, to be discussed in Chapter 6. For now, suffice it to say that the employer shows that the test scores are significantly correlated with measures of job performance.

Measures of job performance used in validation studies can include such things as objective measures of output, supervisor ratings of job performance, and success in training.[19] Normally, performance appraisal ratings are used, but these ratings must be valid for the court to accept the validation results. For example, in *Albermarle Paper* v. *Moody*, the employer demonstrated that the selection battery predicted performance (measured with supervisors' overall rankings of employees) in only some of the 13 occupational groups in which it was used. In this case, the court was especially critical of the supervisory ratings used as the measure of job performance. The court stated, "There is no way of knowing precisely what criteria of job performance the supervisors were considering."[20]

Plaintiff's Rebuttal

If the employer shows that the employment practice is the result of some business necessity, the plaintiff's last resort is to argue that other employment practices could sufficiently meet the employer's goal without adverse impact. Thus, if a plaintiff can demonstrate that selection tests other than the one used by the employer exist, do not have adverse impact, and correlate with job performance as highly as the employer's test, then the defendant can be found guilty of discrimination. Many cases deal with standardized tests of cognitive ability, so it is important to examine alternatives to these tests that have less adverse impact while still meeting the employer's goal. At least two separate studies reviewing alternative selection devices such as interviews, biographical data, assessment centers, and work sample tests have concluded that none of them met both criteria.[21] It seems that when the employment practice in question is a standardized test of cognitive ability, plaintiffs will have a difficult time rebutting the defendant's rebuttal.

***Griggs* v. *Duke Power*.** To illustrate how this process works, let's look at the *Griggs* v. *Duke Power* case.[22] Following the passage of Title VII, Duke Power instituted a new system for making selection and promotion decisions. The system required either a high school diploma or a passing score on two professionally developed tests (the Wonderlic Personnel Test and the Bennett Mechanical Comprehension Test). A passing score was set so that it would be equal to the national median for high school graduates who had taken the tests.

The plaintiffs met their prima facie burden showing that both the high school diploma requirement and the test battery had adverse impacts on blacks. According to the 1960 census, 34 percent of white males had high school diplomas, compared with only 12 percent of black males. Similarly, 58 percent of white males passed the test battery, whereas only 6 percent of blacks passed.

Duke Power was unable to defend its use of these employment practices. A company vice president testified that the company had not studied the relationship between these employment practices and the employees' ability to perform the job. In addition, employees already on the job who did not have high school diplomas and had never taken the tests were performing satisfactorily. Thus Duke Power lost the case.

It is interesting to note that the court recognized that the company had not intended to discriminate, mentioning that the company was making special efforts to help undereducated employees through financing two-thirds of the cost of tuition for high school training. This illustrates the importance of the *consequences*, as opposed to the *motivation*, in determining discrimination under the disparate impact theory.

Reasonable Accommodation

Reasonable accommodation presents a relatively new theory of discrimination. It began with regard to religious discrimination, but has recently been both expanded and popularized with the passage of the ADA. Reasonable accommodation differs from these two theories in that rather than simply requiring an employer to refrain from some action, reasonable accommodation places a special obligation on an employer to affirmatively *do* something to accommodate an individual's disability or

Reasonable accommodation
Making facilities readily accessible to and usable by individuals with disabilities.

religion. This theory is violated when an employer fails to make reasonable accommodation, where that is required, to a qualified person with a disability or to a person's religious observation and/or practices.

Religion and Accommodation

Often individuals with strong religious beliefs find that some observations and practices of their religion come into direct conflict with their work duties. For example, some religions forbid individuals from working on the sabbath day when the employer schedules them for work. Others might have beliefs that preclude them from shaving, which might conflict with a company's dress code. Although Title VII forbids discrimination on the basis of religion just like race or sex, religion also receives special treatment requiring employers to exercise an affirmative duty to accommodate individuals' religious beliefs and practices. As Figure 3.2 shows, the number of religious discrimination charges has consistently increased over the past few years, jumping significantly in 1997.

In cases of religious discrimination, an employee's burden is to demonstrate that he or she has a legitimate religious belief and provided the employer with notice of the need to accommodate the religious practice, and that adverse consequences occurred due to the employer's failure to accommodate. In such cases, the employer's major defense is to assert that to accommodate the employee would require an undue hardship.

Examples of reasonably accommodating a person's religious obligations might include redesigning work schedules (most often accommodating those who cannot work on their sabbath), providing alternative testing dates for applicants, not requiring union membership and/or allowing payment of "charitable contributions" in lieu of union dues, or altering certain dress or grooming requirements. Note that although an employer is required to make a reasonable accommodation, it need not be the one that is offered by the employee.[23]

In one recent case, Wal-Mart agreed to settle with a former employee who alleged that he was forced to quit in 1993 after refusing to work on Sunday. Wal-Mart has agreed to pay the former employee unspecified damages, to instruct managers on employee's rights to have their religious beliefs accommodated, and to prepare a computer-based manual describing employees' rights and religious harassment.[24]

FIGURE 3.2
Religious Discrimination Complaints, 1991–2000

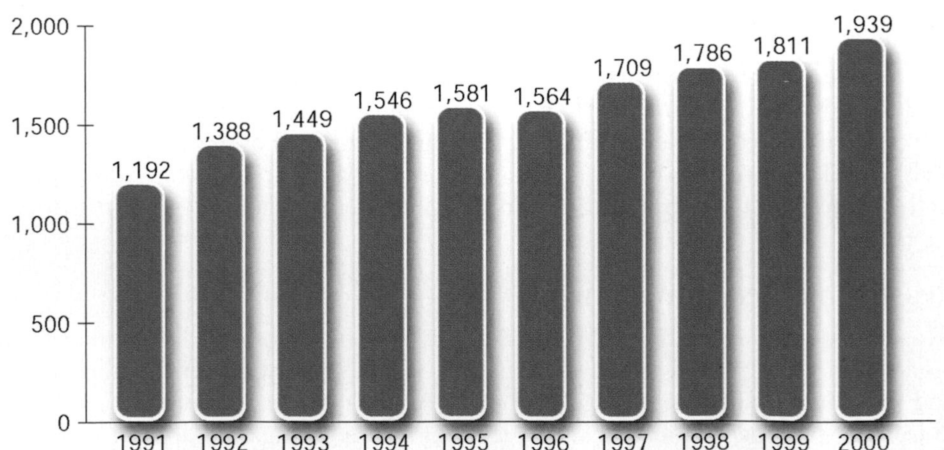

SOURCE: www.eeoc.gov/stats/religion.html

Disability and Accommodation

As previously discussed, the ADA made discrimination against individuals with disabilities illegal. However, the act itself states that the employer is obligated not just to refrain from discriminating, but to take affirmative steps to accommodate individuals who are protected under the act.

Under disability claims, the plaintiff must show that she or he is a qualified applicant with a disability and that adverse action was taken by a covered entity. The employer's defense then depends on whether the decision was made without regard to the disability or in light of the disability. For example, if the employer argues that the plaintiff is not qualified, then it has met the burden, and the question of reasonable accommodation becomes irrelevant.

If, however, the decision was made "in light of" the disability, then the question becomes one of whether the person could perform adequately with a reasonable accommodation. This leads to three potential defenses. First, the employer could allege job-relatedness or business necessity through demonstrating, for example, that it is using a test that assesses ability to perform essential job functions. However, then the question arises of whether the applicant could perform the essential job functions with a reasonable accommodation. Second, the employer could claim an undue hardship to accommodate the individual. In essence, this argues that the accommodation necessary is an action requiring significant difficulty or expense. Finally, the employer could argue that the individual with the disability might pose a direct threat to his own or others' health or safety in the workplace. This requires examining the duration of the risk, the nature and severity of potential harm, the probability of the harm occurring, and the imminence of the potential harm.

What are some examples of reasonable accommodation with regard to disabilities? First is providing readily accessible facilities such as ramps and/or elevators for disabled individuals to enter the workplace. Second, job restructuring might include eliminating marginal tasks, shifting these tasks to other employees, redesigning job procedures, or altering work schedules. Third, an employer might reassign a disabled employee to a job with essential job functions he or she could perform. Fourth, an employer might accommodate applicants for employment who must take tests through providing alternative testing formats, providing readers, or providing additional time for taking the test. Fifth, readers, interpreters, or technology to offer reading assistance might be given to a disabled employee. Sixth, an employer could allow employees to provide their own accommodation such as bringing a guide dog to work.[25] Note that most accommodations are inexpensive. A study by Sears Roebuck & Co. found that 69 percent of all accommodations cost nothing, 29 percent cost less than $1,000, and only 3 percent cost more than $1,000.[26] In addition, the "Competing through Globalization" box illustrates how accommodating disabled individuals can actually provide competitive advantage.

Retaliation for Participation and Opposition

Suppose you overhear a supervisor in your workplace telling someone that he refuses to hire women because he knows they are just not cut out for the job. Believing this to be illegal discrimination, you face a dilemma. Should you come forward and report this statement? Or if someone else files a lawsuit for gender discrimination, should you

COMPETING THROUGH GLOBALIZATION

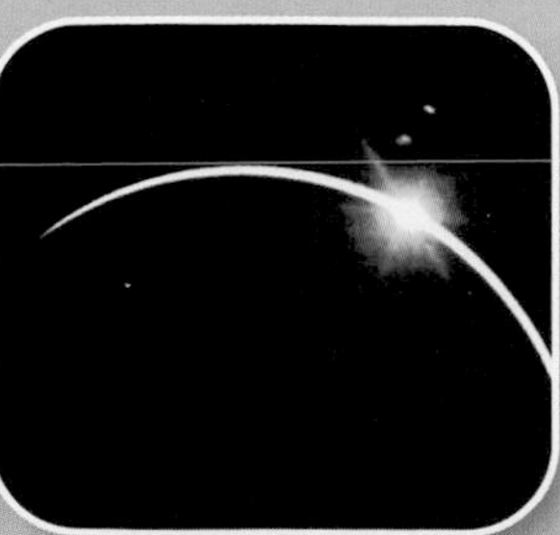

Blind Feeding the Blind

Many teachers use an exercise where students must walk around blindfolded for a few hours to help appreciate the situation of those who truly are blind. However, until recently, nobody actually made a business out of this.

At the Blind Cow restaurant in Zurich, Switzerland, nothing looks good to eat. The reason is not that the food is bad, but because patrons dine in total darkness. Rev. Jorge Spielman, a 37-year-old blind pastor, came up with the idea while tending bar at a public exhibit in Zurich. The exhibit required sighted people to grope their way through various dark rooms to experience what it is like to be blind. He and four blind colleagues decided to create a restaurant that would help sighted people appreciate the situation of the blind while providing jobs for the blind and visually impaired.

A blind waitress leads diners to their tables, asking one guest to place both hands on her shoulders, and other guests to do likewise to the guest in front of them. She explains the rules: no flashlights, no iridescent watches, and no wandering. Waitresses and waiters should be called by shouting, and guests who need to use the restrooms must be led by a waitress. The staff all wear bells to allow them to avoid colliding with one another while carrying hot plates of food.

The restaurant has been an unarguable success. Although Rev. Spielman worried that the novelty would wear off after a few months, a year after its opening the restaurant was still booked solid for the following three months. In addition, the breakage of dishes and glasses is no different from other restaurants because guests are extremely careful. In fact, the business has been such a success that the owners are now considering expanding into big U.S. cities like New York and Los Angeles.

Such expansion could succeed because the atmosphere provides for a variety of novel experiences. For instance, a group of three couples dined there, and when the ladies went to the restroom, the men changed places. When they returned, the men planted kisses on their "new" dates; not all the women noticed that the lips kissing them were unfamiliar ones. In addition, the restaurant was the site for a "blind date." The lady arrived early and sipped a drink until the man was led to her table. Unfortunately, according to the staff, they departed separately. Finally, Rev. Spielman has some ideas to keep the restaurant fresh. He plans to make Monday night "date night," bringing in guest speakers to discuss sex and relationships. He explains, "People can ask all kinds of questions in the dark."

SOURCE: J. Costello, "Swill Eatery Operated by the Blind Keeps Diners Completely in the Dark," *The Wall Street Journal* (November 28, 2001), p. 1.

testify on behalf of the plaintiff? What happens if your employer threatens to fire you if you do anything?

Title VII of the Civil Rights Act of 1964 protects you. It states that employers cannot retaliate against employees for either "opposing" a perceived illegal employment practice or "participating in a proceeding" related to an alleged illegal employment practice. *Opposition* refers to expressing to someone through proper channels that you believe that an illegal employment act has taken place or is taking place. *Participation* refers to actually testifying in an investigation, hearing, or court proceeding regarding an illegal employment act. Clearly, the purpose of this provision is to protect employees from employers' threats and other forms of intimidation aimed at discouraging the employees from bringing to light acts they believe to be illegal.

These cases can be extremely costly for companies because they are alleging acts of intentional discrimination, and therefore plaintiffs are entitled to punitive damages. For example, a 41-year-old former Allstate employee who claimed that a company official told her that the company wanted a "younger and cuter" image was awarded $2.8 million in damages by an Oregon jury. The jury concluded that the employee was forced out of the company for opposing age discrimination against other employees.[27]

This does not mean that employees have an unlimited right to talk about how racist or sexist their employers are. The courts tend to frown on employees whose activities result in a poor public image for the company unless those employees had attempted to use the organization's internal channels—approaching one's manager, raising the issue with the HRM department, and so on—before going public.

Current Issues Regarding Diversity and Equal Employment Opportunity

Because of recent changes in the labor market, most organizations' demographic compositions are becoming increasingly diverse. A study by the Hudson Institute projected that 85 percent of the new entrants into the U.S. labor force over the next decade will be females and minorities.[28] Integrating these groups into organizations made up predominantly of able-bodied white males will bring attention to important issues like sexual harassment, affirmative action, and the "reasonable accommodation" of employees with disabilities.

Sexual Harassment

Clarence Thomas's Supreme Court confirmation hearings in 1991 brought the issue of sexual harassment into increased prominence. Anita Hill, one of Thomas's former employees, alleged that he had sexually harassed her while she was working under his supervision at the Department of Education and the Equal Employment Opportunity Commission. Although the allegations were never substantiated, the hearing made many people more aware of how often employees are sexually harassed in the workplace and, combined with other events, resulted in a tremendous increase in the number of sexual harassment complaints being filed with the EEOC, as we see in Figure 3.3. In addition, after President Clinton took office and faced a sexual harassment lawsuit by Paula Corbin Jones for his alleged proposition to her in a Little Rock hotel room, the number of sexual harassment complaints took another jump from 1993 to 1994—again, potentially due to the tremendous amount of publicity regarding sexual harassment. In spite of all the publicity about President Clinton's affair with intern Monica Lewinsky and subsequent lying about it under oath in his deposition for the Paula Jones case and possibly before a grand jury (resulting in his impeachment), as well as his alleged groping of White House volunteer Kathleen Willey, the number of sexual harassment complaints has not risen dramatically.

FIGURE 3.3
Sexual Harassment Charges, 1991–2000

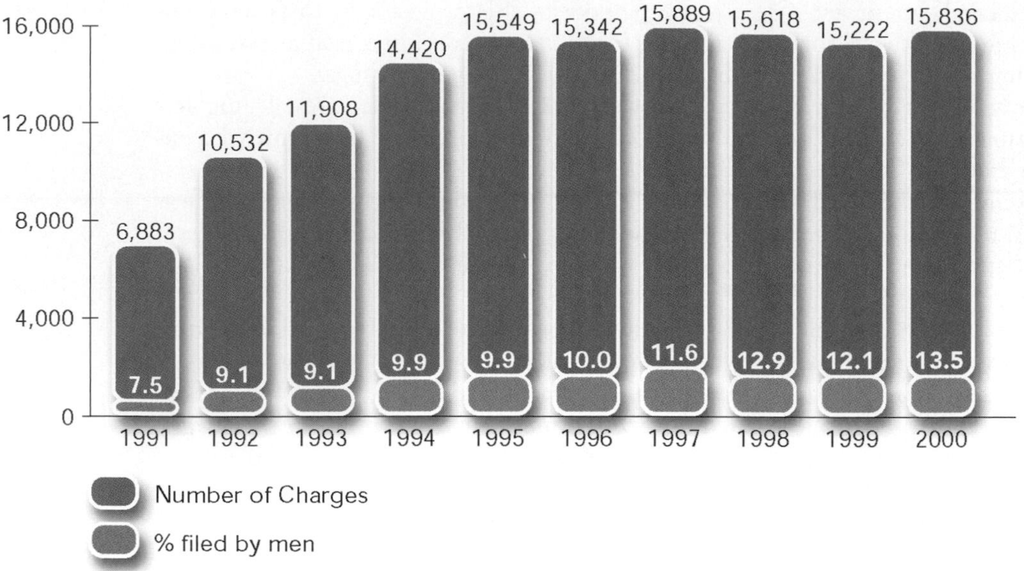

SOURCE: www.eeoc.gov/stats/harass.html

Sexual harassment refers to unwelcome sexual advances. (See Table 3.4.) It can take place in two basic ways. "Quid pro quo" harassment occurs when some kind of benefit (or punishment) is made contingent on the employee's submitting (or not submitting) to sexual advances. For example, a male manager tells his female secretary that if she has sex with him, he will help her get promoted, or he threatens to fire her if she fails to do so; these are clearly cases of quid pro quo sexual harassment.

The *Bundy* v. *Jackson* case illustrates quid pro quo sexual harassment.[29] Sandra Bundy was a personnel clerk with the District of Columbia Department of Corrections. She received repeated sexual propositions from Delbert Jackson, who was at the time a fellow employee (although he later became the director of the agency). She later began to receive propositions from two of her supervisors: Arthur Burton and James Gainey. When she raised the issue to their supervisor, Lawrence Swain, he dismissed her complaints, telling her that "any man in his right mind would want

TABLE 3.4
EEOC Definition of Sexual Harassment

Unwelcome sexual advances, requests for sexual favors, and other verbal or physical contact of a sexual nature constitute sexual harassment when
1. Submission to such conduct is made either explicitly or implicitly a term of condition of an individual's employment,
2. Submission to or rejection of such conduct by an individual is used as the basis for employment decisions affecting such individual, or
3. Such conduct has the purpose or effect of unreasonably interfering with an individual's work performance or creating an intimidating, hostile, or offensive working environment.

SOURCE: EEOC guideline based on the Civil Rights Act of 1964, Title VII.

to rape you," and asked her to begin a sexual relationship with him. When Bundy became eligible for a promotion, she was passed over because of her "inadequate work performance," although she had never been told that her work performance was unsatisfactory. The U.S. Court of Appeals found that Bundy had been discriminated against because of her sex, thereby extending the idea of discrimination to sexual harassment.

A more subtle, and possibly more pervasive, form of sexual harassment is "hostile working environment." This occurs when someone's behavior in the workplace creates an environment that makes it difficult for someone of a particular sex to work. Many plaintiffs in sexual harassment lawsuits have alleged that men ran their fingers through the plaintiffs' hair, made suggestive remarks, and physically assaulted them by touching their intimate body parts. Other examples include having pictures of naked women posted in the workplace, using offensive sexually explicit language, or using sex-related jokes or innuendoes in conversations.[30]

Note that these types of behaviors are actionable under Title VII because they treat individuals differently based on their sex. In addition, although most harassment cases involve male-on-female harassment, any individual can be harassed. For example, male employees at Jenny Craig recently alleged that they were sexually harassed, and a federal jury recently found that a male employee had been sexually harassed by his male boss.[31]

There are three critical issues in these cases. First, the plaintiff cannot have "invited or incited" the advances. Often the plaintiff's sexual history, whether she or he wears provocative clothing, and whether she or he engages in sexually explicit conversations are used to prove or disprove that the advance was unwelcome. However, in the absence of substantial evidence that the plaintiff invited the behavior, courts usually lean toward assuming that sexual advances do not belong in the workplace and thus are unwelcome. In *Meritor Savings Bank* v. *Vinson*, Michelle Vinson claimed that during the four years she worked at a bank she was continually harassed by the bank's vice president, who repeatedly asked her to have sex with him (she eventually agreed) and sexually assaulted her.[32] The Supreme Court ruled that the victim's voluntary participation in sexual relations was not the major issue, saying that the focus of the case was on whether the vice president's advances were unwelcome.

A second critical issue is that the harassment must have been severe enough to alter the terms, conditions, and privileges of employment. Although it has not yet been consistently applied, many courts have used the "reasonable woman" standard in determining the severity or pervasiveness of the harassment. This consists of assessing whether a reasonable woman, faced with the same situation, would have reacted similarly. The reasonable woman standard recognizes that behavior that might be considered appropriate by a man (like off-color jokes) might not be considered appropriate by a woman.

The third issue is that the courts must determine whether the organization is liable for the actions of its employees. In doing so, the court usually examines two things. First, did the employer know about, or should he or she have known about, the harassment? Second, did the employer act to stop the behavior? If the employer knew about it and the behavior did not stop, the court usually decides that the employer did not act appropriately to stop it.

To ensure a workplace free from sexual harassment, organizations can follow some important steps. First, the organization can develop a policy statement that makes it very clear that sexual harassment will not be tolerated in the workplace. Second, all

COMPETING BY MEETING STAKEHOLDERS' NEEDS

Inland Steel Faces Affirmative Action

The idea of affirmative action is easy to understand: to increase minority representation in the workforce at all levels of employment. (A company that achieves successful integration of minorities at all levels should also be more competitive than one that does not because it draws from a larger labor pool.) The reality, however, is as complex as human relations itself.

Take, for example, Inland Steel Industries, Inc. (a large manufacturing corporation located in the Midwest), whose jobs until recently were held mostly by white men. Antidiscrimination laws, a changing population, and affirmative action—all facts of an employer's life—have changed the face of Inland Steel. Social responsibility lies in helping employees adjust to the diverse workplace, so that everyone views diversity as a positive thing. This is not an easy task when people believe their paychecks and career opportunities are at stake. But Inland Steel has been trying to face such a challenge.

A major problem in trying to apply affirmative action is that there is no textbook for doing so. Organizations must develop their own methods by trial and error. Also, people's perceptions of affirmative action—what it is and how it will affect them—differ. For instance, one person might view affirmative action as applicable to all minorities as well as women. Another might view it as appropriate only to certain groups. Franklin Turner, a black male and a buyer for an Inland Steel subsidiary, claims, "Broadening the definition of *minority* has diluted it. It confuses the issue." He says that the promotion policy at his company places women (both white and black) ahead of black men. Instead of being a beneficiary of affirmative action, he sees himself as a victim.

Minorities, women, and white males get caught in a standoff. Consider these three different views by employees of the same company. Nathaniel Lott, a black male and a district sales rep for the same subsidiary, says, "Minorities are required to prove themselves to an extent not required of nonminorities." Paula Dent, a

employees, new and old, can be trained to identify inappropriate workplace behavior. Third, the organization can develop a mechanism for reporting sexual harassment that encourages people to speak out. Fourth, management can prepare to take prompt disciplinary action against those who commit sexual harassment as well as appropriate action to protect the victims of sexual harassment.[33]

Affirmative Action and Reverse Discrimination

Few would disagree that having a diverse workforce in terms of race and gender is a desirable goal, if all individuals have the necessary qualifications. In fact, many organizations today are concerned with developing and managing diversity. (See the "Competing by Meeting Stakeholders' Needs" box.) To eliminate discrimination in the workplace, many organizations have affirmative action programs to increase minority representation. Affirmative action was originally conceived as a way of taking extra effort to attract and retain minority employees. This was normally done by ex-day-shift supervisor who is a black female, observes, "What I'm doing is not strictly on my own ability but is also filling a need of the company. . . . I felt I was qualified, but that doesn't always open doors. Sometimes the powers that be don't see the qualifications." Pat Goeringer, a second-shift supervisor who doesn't feel that affirmative action has necessarily benefited her, comments, "I think white males have a right to complain about reverse discrimination, because they might get passed up. I think it's wrong to blame white males for everything that's gone wrong. . . . It's not fair."

Inland Steel started its affirmative action program after four black workers approached general manager Steve Bowsher, saying that they were tired of racist jokes and behavior by others on the job and that they felt they had been passed over for opportunities to advance. "I didn't have a clue," recalls Bowsher. "Hey, I'm a tall white person. The world was set up for me." But Bowsher listened and took action. He arranged classes for employees to discuss race and sex discrimination. He evaluated the pay that minority and female workers were receiving to make sure it was equal to that of white male workers. He banned racist and sexist jokes, pinup calendars on office walls, and company-paid country club memberships at clubs that practiced racial discrimination. Those who did not comply were fired. What were his reasons? "I've got to be the one to fix it because I have the power," he explains. Bowsher also actively recruits minorities for employment at Inland.

Fostering cooperation rather than suspicion among workers can only have a healthy effect on business. A company that has a unified (not homogeneous) workforce will be much more productive and profitable than one that is constantly dealing with the hostility of splinter groups. Inland Steel has created its own "textbook" rules for accomplishing this. First, support for affirmative action must come from top management. Second, affirmative action programs must be monitored, and managers must be made accountable for what happens. Third, a company must reach out to women and minorities if it wants to hire them. Just as important, it must provide training and guidance in their careers. Fourth, people must respect each other on the job, understanding their similarities and differences.

"[Affirmative action] is an ongoing journey because there are so many pieces," says Vivian Cosey, head of human resources at Inland's Ryerson Coil Processing plant. "It's not like learning an algebraic equation or even a foreign language." But it is a vital step toward gaining a competitive advantage.

SOURCE: T. Jones, J. Poe, and S. Franklin, "Progress and Problems of a Workplace Remedy," *Chicago Tribune* (September 3, 1995), pp. 1, 12; J. Poe, S. Franklin, and T. Jones, "True Equity Proves Elusive," *Chicago Tribune* (September 4, 1995), pp. 1, 6; S. Franklin, T. Jones, and J. Poe, "A Commitment to Action," *Chicago Tribune* (September 5, 1995), pp. 1, 8.

tensively recruiting minorities on college campuses, advertising in minority-oriented publications, and providing educational and training opportunities to minorities.[34] However, over the years, many organizations have resorted to quotalike hiring to ensure that their workforce composition mirrors that of the labor market. Sometimes these organizations act voluntarily; in other cases, the quotas are imposed by the courts or by the EEOC. Whatever the impetus for these hiring practices, many white and/or male individuals have fought against them, alleging what is called *reverse discrimination*.

An example of an imposed quota program is found at the fire department in Birmingham, Alabama. Having admitted a history of discriminating against blacks, the department entered into a consent decree with the EEOC to hold 50 percent of positions at all levels in the fire department open for minorities even though minorities made up only 28 percent of the relevant labor market. The result was that some white applicants were denied employment or promotion in favor of black applicants who scored lower on a selection battery. The federal court found that the city's use of the inflexible hiring formula violated federal civil rights law and the constitutional guarantee of equal protection. The appellate court agreed, and the Supreme Court refused to hear the case, thus making the decision final.

The entire issue of affirmative action should evoke considerable attention and debate over the next few years. Although most individuals support the idea of diversity, few argue for the kinds of quotas that have to some extent resulted from the present legal climate. In fact, one recent survey revealed that only 16 percent of the respondents favored affirmative action with quotas, 46 percent favored it without quotas, and 28 percent opposed all affirmative action programs. One study found that people favor affirmative action when it is operationalized as recruitment, training, and attention to applicant qualifications but oppose it when it consists of discrimination, quotas, and preferential treatment.[35] Affirmative action and quotas constituted an important topic of debate for the 1996 presidential candidates, and there is reason to believe that some changes in the legal system will be observed over the next few years.

Outcomes of the Americans with Disabilities Act

The ADA was passed with the laudable goals of providing employment opportunities for the truly disabled who, in the absence of legislation, were unable to find employment. Certainly, some individuals with disabilities have found employment as a result of its passage. However, as often occurs with legislation, the impact is not necessarily what was intended. First, there has been increased litigation. The EEOC reports that over 91,000 complaints have been filed since passage of the act. Approximately 50 percent of the complaints filed have been found to be without reasonable cause. For example, in July 1992 GTE Data Services fired an employee for stealing from other employees and bringing a loaded gun to work. The fired employee sued for reinstatement under the ADA, claiming that he was the victim of a mental illness and thus should be considered disabled.[36]

A second problem is that the kinds of cases being filed are not what Congress intended to protect. Although the act was passed because of the belief that discrimination against individuals with disabilities occurred in the failure to hire them, 52.2 percent of the claims deal with firings, 28.9 percent with failure to make reasonable accommodation, and 12.5 percent with harassment. Only 9.4 percent of the complaints allege a failure to hire or rehire.[37] In addition, although the act was passed to protect people with major disabilities such as blindness, deafness, lost limbs, or paralysis, these disabilities combined account for a small minority of the disabilities claimed. As we see in Table 3.5, the biggest disability category is "other," meaning that the plaintiff claims a disability that is not one of the 35 types of impairment listed in the EEOC charge data system. The second largest category is "back impairment," accounting for 16.1 percent of all charges, followed by mental-illness-related claims at 12.2 percent.

Finally, it does not appear that the act has had its anticipated impact on the employment of Americans with disabilities. According to the National Organization on Disability, a private group, only 31 percent of working-age Americans with disabilities were employed as of December 1993, compared with 33 percent in 1986, before the law was passed.

For these reasons, Congress has explored the possibility of amending the act to more narrowly define the term *disability*.[38] The debate continues regarding the effectiveness of the ADA. The "Competing by Meeting Stakeholders' Needs" box (see

TABLE 3.5
Types of Complaints Filed under the ADA

	1992	1993	1994	1995	1996	1997	1998	1999	TOTAL
Number of complaints	1,048	15,274	18,859	19,798	18,046	18,108	17,806	17,007	125,946
% dealing with									
Back	20.8%	20.0%	19.4%	17.5%	16.1%	14.9%	12.9%	12.2%	16.1%
Emotional/psychiatric	9.1	9.9	12.4	13.2	15.0	15.3	18.3	15.8	12.2
Neurological	15.6	14.0	10.9	10.1	10.4	9.9	10.0	10.7	11.1
Extremities	5.3	4.2	9.3	10.8	11.1	10.6	11.0	11.0	9.8
Heart	4.6	5.2	4.3	3.7	3.5	3.7	3.8	3.8	4.0
Diabetes	5.0	3.4	3.5	3.5	3.7	3.7	3.7	4.0	3.7
Substance abuse	3.5	3.8	3.3	3.6	2.8	2.3	2.2	1.7	2.9
Hearing	4.6	3.2	3.0	2.7	2.6	2.8	2.9	2.9	2.9
Blood disorders	2.4	2.6	2.5	2.8	2.4	2.8	2.8	2.4	2.8
Vision	4.6	3.2	2.7	2.3	2.3	2.4	2.4	2.5	2.5
Cancer	2.9	2.6	2.4	2.1	2.2	2.5	2.6	2.3	2.4
Asthma	1.7	1.8	1.7	1.7	1.7	1.5	1.7	1.8	1.7

SOURCE: EEOC.

page 122) discusses how some view the effectiveness of the ADA for promoting employment and public access opportunities to disabled Americans.

Employee Safety

Like equal employment opportunity, employee safety is regulated by both the federal and state governments. However, to fully maximize the safety and health of workers, employers need to go well beyond the letter of the law and embrace its spirit. With this in mind, we first spell out the specific protections guaranteed by federal legislation and then discuss various kinds of safety awareness programs that attempt to reinforce these standards.

The Occupational Safety and Health Act (OSHA)

Although concern for worker safety would seem to be a universal societal goal, the **Occupational Safety and Health Act of 1970 (OSHA)**—the most comprehensive legislation regarding worker safety—did not emerge in this country until the early 1970s. At that time, there were roughly 15,000 work-related fatalities every year.

OSHA authorized the federal government to establish and enforce occupational safety and health standards for all places of employment engaging in interstate commerce. The responsibility for inspecting employers, applying the standards, and levying fines was assigned to the Department of Labor. The Department of Health was assigned responsibility for conducting research to determine the criteria for specific operations or occupations and for training employers to comply with the act. Much of this research is conducted by the National Institute for Occupational Safety and Health (NIOSH).

Occupational Safety and Health Act (OSHA)
The law that authorizes the federal government to establish and enforce occupational safety and health standards for all places of employment engaging in interstate commerce.

COMPETING BY MEETING STAKEHOLDERS' NEEDS

Evaluating the ADA

Just over 10 years have passed since the Americans with Disabilities Act (ADA) was signed into law with the goals of increasing employment and public access opportunities for disabled Americans. One obvious question arises as to its effectiveness, and a variety of different answers can be found, depending on your perspective.

On the negative side, evidence mounts that people with disabilities are actually worse off than they were 10 years ago. Of the nation's estimated 54 million people with disabilities, over 70 percent are unemployed. In addition, during this time both employment and earnings have fallen while the rest of the nation experienced the lowest unemployment of the decade and rising earnings. Between 1989 and 1998 average inflation-adjusted income dropped 4 percent for disabled workers while it rose 5 percent for workers overall. A number of reasons have been offered for this, but one deals with the design of work. The trend has been toward broadening jobs through requiring workers to perform a greater variety of tasks, yet more narrowly defined jobs are often better suited to accommodating the disabled. In addition, supervisors seem to lack training in how to work with and accommodate disabled employees.

On the positive side, it appears that employers are not actively discriminating against the disabled. Susan Bruyere, Director of Cornell's Program on Employment and Disability, says that the ADA's greatest contribution is in helping HR professionals to address the needs of disabled workers through exploring ways to make accommodations. Evidence seems to support this. Of the 125,946 cases filed in 1999, half were dismissed by the EEOC as having "no reasonable cause." Of the remaining cases that went to trial, employers won 95.7 percent in 1999.

Some argue that a number of these suits seem to be filed "frivolously" in an effort to enrich trial lawyers. In fact, during the past five years, over 1,800 suits have been filed in South Florida alone (over 200 by the same law firm representing the same individual). Critics allege that attorneys seek minor ADA violations from small businesses, and because under the ADA businesses in violation are responsible for legal fees, most of these small businesses opt to cut their losses and settle, giving in to what amounts to legal extortion. Although advocates for the disabled argue that such lawsuits are the best way to gain compliance with the ADA, critics respond that this would be more believable if efforts were made to work with business owners to correct violations before suing.

Thus the jury is still out on the ADA's effectiveness. Perhaps the next 10 years will reveal a stronger case for either its effectiveness or ineffectiveness in increasing employment and access for the disabled.

SOURCE: S.J. Wells, "Is the ADA working?" *HR Magazine*, April 2001, pp. 38–46; Editorial Board of the Sun-Sentinel, Editorial, *South Florida Sun-Sentinel* (August 28, 2001), www.sun-sentinel.com.

Employee Rights under OSHA

The main provision of OSHA states that each employer has a general duty to furnish each employee a place of employment free from recognized hazards that cause or are likely to cause death or serious physical harm. This is referred to as the **general duty clause.** Some specific rights granted to workers under this act are listed in Table 3.6.

TABLE 3.6

Rights Granted to Workers under the Occupational Safety and Health Act

Employees have the right to
1. Request an inspection.
2. Have a representative present at an inspection.
3. Have dangerous substances identified.
4. Be promptly informed about exposure to hazards and be given access to accurate records regarding exposures.
5. Have employer violations posted at the work site.

General duty clause
The provision of the Occupational Health and Safety Act that states that an employer has an overall obligation to furnish employees with a place of employment free from recognized hazards.

The Department of Labor recognizes many specific types of hazards, and employers are required to comply with all the occupational safety and health standards published by NIOSH.

A recent example is the development of OSHA standards for occupational exposure to blood-borne pathogens such as the AIDS virus. These standards identify 24 affected industrial sectors, encompassing 500,000 establishments and 5.6 million workers. Among other features, these standards require employers to develop an exposure control plan (ECP). An ECP must include a list of jobs whose incumbents might be exposed to blood, methods for implementing precautions in these jobs, post-exposure follow-up plans, and procedures for evaluating incidents in which workers are accidentally infected.

Although NIOSH publishes numerous standards, it is clearly not possible for regulators to anticipate all possible hazards that could occur in the workplace. Thus, the general duty clause requires employers to be constantly alert for potential sources of harm in the workplace (as defined by the standards of a reasonably prudent person) and to correct them. For example, managers at Amoco's Joliet, Illinois, plant realized that over the years some employees had created undocumented shortcuts and built them into their process for handling flammable materials. These changes appeared to be labor saving but created a problem: workers did not have uniform procedures for dealing with flammable products. This became an urgent issue because many of the experienced workers were reaching retirement age, and the plant was in danger of losing critical technical expertise. To solve this problem, the plant adopted a training program that met all the standards required by OSHA. That is, it conducted a needs analysis highlighting each task new employees had to learn and then documented these processes in written guidelines. New employees were given hands-on training with the new procedures and were then certified in writing by their supervisor. A computer tracking system was installed to monitor who was handling flammable materials, and this system immediately identified anyone who was not certified. The plant met requirements for both ISO 9000 standards and OSHA regulations and continues to use the same model for safety training in other areas of the plant.[39]

OSHA Inspections

OSHA inspections are conducted by specially trained agents of the Department of Labor called *compliance officers*. These inspections usually follow a tight "script." Typically, the compliance officer shows up unannounced. For obvious reasons, OSHA's regulations prohibit advance notice of inspections. The officer, after presenting credentials, tells the employer the reasons for the inspection and describes, in a general way, the procedures necessary to conduct the investigation.

There are four major components of an OSHA inspection. First, the compliance officer reviews the employer's records of deaths, injuries, and illnesses. OSHA requires this kind of record keeping from all firms with 11 or more full- or part-time employees. Second, the officer, typically accompanied by a representative of the employer (and perhaps by a representative of the employees), conducts a "walkaround" tour of the employer's premises. On this tour, the officer notes any conditions that may violate specific published standards or the less specific general duty clause. The third component of the inspection, employee interviews, may take place during the tour. At this time, any person who is aware of a violation can bring it to the attention of the officer. Finally, in a closing conference the compliance officer discusses the findings with the employer, noting any violations. The employer is given a reasonable time frame in which to correct these violations. If any violation represents imminent danger (that is, could cause serious injury or death before being eliminated through the normal enforcement procedures), the officer may, through the Department of Labor, seek a restraining order from a U.S. District Court. Such an order compels the employer to correct the problem immediately.

Citations and Penalties

If a compliance officer believes that a violation has occurred, he or she issues a citation to the employer that specifies the exact practice or situation that violates the act. The employer is required to post this citation in a prominent place near the location of the violation—even if the employer intends to contest it. Nonserious violations may be assessed up to $1,000 for each incident, but this may be adjusted downward if the employer has no prior history of violations or if the employer has made a good-faith effort to comply with the act. Serious violations of the act or willful, repeated violations may be fined up to $10,000 per incident. Fines for safety violations are never levied against the employees themselves. The assumption is that safety is primarily the responsibility of the employer, who needs to work with employees to ensure that they use safe working procedures.

In addition to these civil penalties, criminal penalties may also be assessed for willful violations that kill an employee. Fines can go as high as $20,000, and the employer or agents of the employer can be imprisoned. Criminal charges can also be brought against anyone who falsifies records that are subject to OSHA inspection or anyone who gives advance notice of an OSHA inspection without permission from the Department of Labor.

The Effect of OSHA

OSHA has been unquestionably successful in raising the level of awareness of occupational safety. Yet legislation alone cannot solve all the problems of work site safety. Indeed, the number of occupational illnesses increased fivefold between 1985 and 1990, according to a survey by the Bureau of Labor Statistics.[40] Many industrial accidents are a product of unsafe behaviors, not unsafe working conditions. Because the act does not directly regulate employee behavior, little behavior change can be expected unless employees are convinced of the standards' importance.[41] This has been recognized by labor leaders. For example, Lynn Williams, president of the United Steelworkers of America, has noted, "We can't count on government. We can't count on employers. We must rely on ourselves to bring about the safety and health of our workers."[42]

Because conforming to the statute alone does not necessarily guarantee safety, many employers go beyond the letter of the law. In the next section we examine various kinds of employer-initiated safety awareness programs that comply with OSHA requirements and, in some cases, exceed them.

Safety Awareness Programs

Safety awareness programs go beyond compliance with OSHA and attempt to instill symbolic and substantive changes in the organization's emphasis on safety. These programs typically focus either on specific jobs and job elements or on specific types of injuries or disabilities. There are three primary components to a safety awareness program: identifying and communicating hazards, reinforcing safe practices, and promoting safety internationally.

Safety awareness programs
Employer programs that attempt to instill symbolic and substantive changes in the organization's emphasis on safety.

Identifying and Communicating Job Hazards

Employees, supervisors, and other knowledgeable sources need to sit down and discuss potential problems related to safety. The **job hazard analysis technique** is one means of accomplishing this.[43] With this technique, each job is broken down into basic elements, and each of these is rated for its potential for harm or injury. If there is consensus that some job element has high hazard potential, this element is isolated and potential technological or behavioral changes are considered.

Job hazard analysis technique
A breakdown of each job into basic elements, each of which is rated for its potential for harm or injury.

Another means of isolating unsafe job elements is to study past accidents. The **technic of operations review (TOR)** is an analysis methodology that helps managers determine which specific element of a job led to a past accident.[44] The first step in a TOR analysis is to establish the facts surrounding the incident. To accomplish this, all members of the work group involved in the accident give their initial impressions of what happened. The group must then, through group discussion, reach a consensus on the single, systematic failure that most contributed to the incident as well as two or three major secondary factors that contributed to it.

Technic of operations review (TOR)
Method of determining safety problems via an analysis of past accidents.

An analysis of jobs at Burger King, for example, revealed that certain jobs required employees to walk across wet or slippery surfaces, which led to many falls. Specific corrective action was taken based on analysis of where people were falling and what conditions led to these falls. Now Burger King provides mats at critical locations and has generally upgraded its floor maintenance. The company also makes slip-resistant shoes available to employees in certain job categories.[45]

Communication of an employee's risk should take advantage of several media. Direct verbal supervisory contact is important for its saliency and immediacy. Written memos are important because they help establish a "paper trail" that can later document a history of concern regarding the job hazard. Posters, especially those placed near the hazard, serve as a constant reminder, reinforcing other messages.

In communicating risk, it is important to recognize two distinct audiences. Sometimes relatively young or inexperienced workers need special attention. Research by the National Safety Council indicates that 40 percent of all accidents happen to individuals in the 20-to-29 age group and that 48 percent of all accidents happen to workers during their first year on the job.[46] The employer's primary concern with respect to this group is to inform them. However, the employer must not overlook experienced workers. Here the key concern is to remind them. Research indicates that long-term exposure and familiarity with a specific threat lead to complacency.[47] Experienced employees need retraining to jar them from complacency about the real dangers associated with their work. This is especially the case if the hazard in question poses a greater threat to older employees. For example, falling off a ladder is a greater threat to older workers than to younger ones. Over 20 percent of such falls lead to a fatality for workers in the 55-to-65 age group, compared with just 10 percent for all other workers.[48]

Reinforcing Safe Practices

One common technique for reinforcing safe practices is implementing a safety incentive program to reward workers for their support and commitment to safety goals. Initially, programs are set up to focus on improving short-term monthly or quarterly goals or to encourage safety suggestions. These short-term goals are later expanded to include more wide-ranging, long-term goals. Prizes are typically distributed in highly public forums (like annual meetings or events). These prizes usually consist of merchandise rather than cash because merchandise represents a lasting symbol of achievement. A good deal of evidence suggests that such programs are effective in reducing injuries and their cost.[49]

Whereas the safety awareness programs just described focus primarily on the job, other programs focus on specific injuries or disabilities. Lower back disability (LBD), for example, is a major problem that afflicts many employees. LBD accounts for approximately 25 percent of all workdays lost, costing firms nearly $30 billion a year.[50] Human resource managers can take many steps to prevent LBD and rehabilitate those who are already afflicted. Eye injuries are another target of safety awareness programs. The National Society to Prevent Blindness estimates that 1,000 eye injuries occur every day in occupational settings.[51] A 10-step program to reduce eye injuries is outlined in Table 3.7. Similar guidelines can be found for everything from chemical burns to electrocution to injuries caused by boiler explosions.[52]

Promoting Safety Internationally

Given the increasing focus on international management, organizations also need to consider how to best ensure the safety of people regardless of the nation in which they operate. Cultural differences may make this more difficult than it seems. For example,

TABLE 3.7

A 10-Step Program for Reducing Eye-Related Injuries

1. Conduct an eye hazard job analysis.
2. Test all employees' vision to establish a baseline.
3. Select protective eyewear designed for specific operations.
4. Establish a 100 percent behavioral compliance program for eyewear.
5. Ensure that eyewear is properly fitted.
6. Train employees in emergency procedures.
7. Conduct ongoing education programs regarding eye care.
8. Continually review accident prevention strategies.
9. Provide management support.
10. Establish written policies detailing sanctions and rewards for specific results.

SOURCE: T.W. Turrif, "NSPB Suggests 10-Step Program to Prevent Eye Injury," *Occupational Health and Safety* 60 (1991), pp. 62–66.

a recent study examined the impact of one standardized corporationwide safety policy on employees in three different countries: the United States, France, and Argentina. The results of this study indicated that the same policy was interpreted differently because of cultural differences. The individualistic, control-oriented culture of the United States stressed the role of top management in ensuring safety in a top-down fashion. However, this policy failed to work in Argentina, where the collectivist culture made employees feel that safety was everyone's joint concern; therefore, programs needed to be defined from the bottom up.[53]

A Look Back

At the outset of the chapter we discussed the litigation problems Home Depot faced by apparently segregating women to cashier positions and men to customer service positions. In settling the suit the company agreed to pay $65 million to women who had been steered to cashier's jobs and had been denied promotions. In addition, the company promised that every applicant would get a "fair shot." Home Depot's solution to this has been to leverage technology to make better hiring decisions that ensure they are able to maximize their diversity.

Home Depot instituted its Job Preference Program, an automated hiring and promotion system, across its 900 stores at a cost of $10 million. It has set up kiosks where potential applicants can log on to a computer, complete an application, and undergo a set of prescreening tests. This process weeds out unqualified applicants. Then the system prints out test scores along with structured interview questions and examples of good and bad answers for the managers interviewing those who make it through the prescreening. In addition, the Home Depot system is used for promotions. Employees are asked to constantly update their skills and career aspirations so they can be considered for promotions at nearby stores.

The system has been an unarguable success. Managers love it because they are able to get high-quality applicants without having to sift through mounds of résumés. In addition, the system seems to have accomplished its main purpose. The number of female managers has increased 30 percent and the number of minority managers by 28 percent since the introduction of the system. In fact, David Borgen, the co-counsel for the *plaintiffs* in the original lawsuit, states, "No one can say it can't be done anymore, because Home Depot is doing it bigger and better than anyone I know."

Questions

1. If Home Depot was correct in that it was not discriminating, but simply filling positions consistent with those who applied for them (and very few women were applying for customer service positions), given your reading of this chapter, was the firm guilty of discrimination? If so, under what theory?
2. How does this case illustrate the application of new technology to solving issues that have never been tied to technology? Can you think of other ways technology might be used to address diversity/EEO/affirmative action issues?

Summary

Viewing employees as a source of competitive advantage results in dealing with them in ways that are ethical and legal as well as providing a safe workplace. An organization's legal environment—particularly the laws regarding equal employment opportunity and safety—has a particularly strong effect on its HRM function. HRM is concerned with the management of people, and government is concerned with protecting individuals. One of HRM's major challenges, therefore, is to perform its function within the legal constraints imposed by the government. Given the multimillion-dollar settlements resulting from violations of EEO laws (and the moral requirement to treat people fairly regardless of their gender or race), as well as the penalties for violating OSHA, HR and line managers need a good understanding of the legal requirements and prohibitions in order to manage their businesses in ways that are sound, both financially and ethically. Organizations that do so effectively will definitely have a competitive advantage.

Discussion Questions

1. Disparate impact theory was originally created by the court in the *Griggs* case before finally being codified by Congress 20 years later in the Civil Rights Act of 1991. Given the system of law in the United States, from what branch of government should theories of discrimination develop?
2. Disparate impact analysis (the four-fifths rule, standard deviation analysis) is used in employment discrimination cases. The National Assessment of Education Progress conducted by the U.S. Department of Education found that among 21- to 25-year-olds, (a) 60 percent of whites, 40 percent of Hispanics, and 25 percent of blacks could locate information in a news article or almanac; (b) 25 percent of whites, 7 percent of Hispanics, and 3 percent of blacks could decipher a bus schedule; and (c) 44 percent of whites, 20 percent of Hispanics, and 8 percent of blacks could correctly determine the change they were due from the purchase of a two-item restaurant meal. Do these tasks (locating information in a news article, deciphering a bus schedule, and determining correct change) have adverse impact? What are the implications?
3. Many companies have dress codes that require men to wear suits and women to wear dresses. Is this discriminatory according to disparate treatment theory? Why?
4. Cognitive ability tests seem to be the most valid selection devices available for hiring employees, yet they also have adverse impact against blacks and Hispanics. Given the validity and adverse impact, and considering that race norming is illegal under CRA 1991, what would you say in response to a recommendation that such tests be used for hiring?
5. How might the ADA's reasonable accommodation requirement affect workers such as law enforcement officers and firefighters?
6. The reasonable woman standard recognizes that women have different ideas than men of what constitutes appropriate behavior. What are the implications of this distinction? Do you think it is a good or bad idea to make this distinction?
7. Employers' major complaint about the ADA is that the costs of making reasonable accommodations will make them less competitive relative to other businesses (especially foreign ones) that do not face these requirements. Is this a legitimate concern? How should employers and society weigh the costs and benefits of the ADA?
8. Many have suggested that OSHA penalties are too weak and misdirected (aimed at employers rather than employees) to have any significant impact on employee safety. Do you think that OSHA-related sanctions need to be strengthened, or are existing penalties sufficient? Defend your answer.

Web Exercise

The Fair Measures Management Law Consulting Group provides training and legal services for managers, HR managers, business owners, and employees. Their website has up-to-date information on court case decisions and legal interpretations of employment laws related to sexual harassment, wrongful termination, discrimination, and disability. Visit their website at **www.fairmeasures.com**. Choose one of the legal areas to investigate (sexual harassment, wrongful termination, or the like). Click on the legal area. Find the most recent court decisions and interpretations for the area by clicking on "FM eNews." The articles are arranged by title. Click on any one of the article titles to view the article.

Questions

1. Read the article you have chosen.
2. Summarize its implications for HRM practices. Make sure you identify any new legal interpretations or changes in interpretations.

Managing People: From the Pages of *BusinessWeek*

BusinessWeek Racism in the Workplace

In an Increasingly Multicultural United States, Harassment of Minorities Is on the Rise

When Wayne A. Elliott was transferred in 1996 from a factory job to a warehouse at Lockheed Martin Corporation's sprawling military aircraft production facilities in Marietta, Georgia, he says he found himself face to face with naked racism. Anti-black graffiti were scrawled on the restroom walls. His new white colleagues harassed him, Elliott recalls, as did his manager, who would yell at him, call him "boy," and tell him to "kiss my butt." He complained, but Elliott says the supervisor was no help. Instead he assigned Elliott, now 46, to collecting parts to be boxed, which involves walking about 10 miles a day. Meanwhile, the eight whites in his job category sat at computer terminals and told him to get a move on—even though Elliott outranked them on the union seniority list.

The atmosphere got even uglier when Elliott and a few other blacks formed a small group in 1997 called Workers Against Discrimination, which led to the filing of two class actions. One day, he and the other two black men among the 30 warehouse workers found "back-to-Africa tickets" on their desks. They reported this, but the Lockheed security officials who responded took the three victims away in their security cars as if they were the wrongdoers, he says, and interrogated them separately.

Then, one day in 1999, according to Elliott, a hangman's noose appeared near his desk. "You're going to end up with your head in here," Elliott recalls a white coworker threatening. Another noose appeared last November, he says. He and the other whites "hassle me all the time now, unplugging my computer so I lose work, hiding my bike or chair; it's constant," says Elliott, who gets counseling from a psychologist for the stress and says he has trouble being attentive to his two children, ages 7 and 8, when he's at home.

Racial hatred is not confined to small Southern cities such as Marietta. In addition to high-profile suits at Lockheed, Boeing, and Texaco, dozens of other household names face complaints of racism in their workforce. Noose cases have been prosecuted in cosmopolitan San Francisco and in Detroit, with a black population among the largest in the nation.

It's true that minorities' share of the workforce grew over the decade, which could have led to a corresponding rise in clashes. Yet racial harassment charges have jumped by 100 percent since 1990, while minority employment grew by 36 percent. What's more, most charges involve multiple victims, so each year the cases add up to tens of thousands of workers—mostly blacks, but also Hispanics and Asians.

It's hard to reconcile such ugly episodes with an American culture that is more accepting of its increasing diversity than ever before. To some extent, the rise in harassment cases may actually reflect America's improved race relations. Because more minorities believe that society won't tolerate blatant bigotry anymore, they file EEOC charges rather than keep quiet out of despair that their complaints won't be heard, says Susan Sturm, a Columbia University law professor who studies workplace discrimination. Many cases involve allegations of harassment that endured for years.

Multimillion-dollar settlements of racial discrimination or harassment claims at such companies as Coca-Cola and Boeing also give victims greater hope that a remedy is available. Such suits became easier in 1991, after Congress passed a law that allowed jury trials and compensatory and punitive damages in race cases. "It's like rape, which everyone kept silent about before," says Boeing human resources chief James B. Dagnon. "Now, prominent individuals are willing to talk publicly about what happened, so there's a safer environment to speak up in."

But many experts say they are seeing a disturbing increase in incidents of harassment. Minority workers endure the oldest racial slurs in the book. They're asked if they eat "monkey meat," denigrated as inferior to whites, or find "KKK" and other intimidating graffiti on the walls at work.

Even office workers are not exempt. In May 2001, 10 current and former black employees at Xerox Corporation offices in Houston filed harassment charges with the EEOC. One, Linda Johnson, says she has suffered racial slurs from a coworker since 1999, when glaucoma forced her to quit the sales department and become a receptionist. Last year a white colleague doctored a computer photo of her to make her look like a prostitute, she says. After she complained, her boss printed out the picture and hung it in his office, her charge says. "I tried to do what company procedures suggested and complain to my supervisor, then on up to human resources at headquarters," says Johnson, 47. "But they just sweep it under the rug." Xerox declined to comment on her case.

Worse yet are hangman's nooses, a potent symbol of mob lynchings in America's racial history. The EEOC has handled 25 noose cases in the past 18 months, "something that only came along every two or three years before," says Ida L. Castro, outgoing EEOC chairwoman. Management lawyers concur that racial harassment has jumped sharply. "I've seen more of these cases in the last few years than in the previous 10, and it's bad stuff," says Steve Poor, a partner at Seyfarth, Shaw, Fairweather & Geraldson, a law firm that helps companies defend harassment and discrimination suits.

Some lay the blame on blue-collar white men who think affirmative action has given minorities an unfair advantage. Their feelings may be fueled by the long-term slide in the wages of less skilled men, which have lagged inflation since 1973. Since many whites see little evidence of discrimination anymore, the small number who harbor racist views feel more justified in lashing out at minorities, whom they perceive as getting ahead solely due to their race, says Carol M. Swain, a Vanderbilt University law professor who is writing a book about white nationalism.

SILENCE. Incidents of open racism at work occur below the national radar because all the parties have powerful incentives to keep it quiet. Plaintiffs' lawyers don't want employees to go public before a trial for fear of prejudicing their case in court. Management and plaintiffs' lawyers alike say it takes tremendous nerve to file a suit or EEOC charges, given the likelihood that coworkers or bosses will strike back. Since 1990, the number of minorities filing charges of retaliation with the EEOC after they complained about racial mistreatment has doubled, to 20,000 a year.

Companies have an even greater desire to avoid bad publicity. Many suits end when employers settle. They routinely buy employees' silence with extra damage award money.

Because racial harassment allegations can be so embarrassing, they pose a difficult challenge for companies. Some quickly go on the offensive and take steps to change. Other employers hunker down for a fight, arguing that allegations are inaccurate or exaggerated. Northwest Airlines Corporation, for example, is fighting charges made by black construction workers who found a noose last July at the airline's new terminal under construction at Detroit Metro Airport. Northwest also recently settled two noose-related suits, although it denied liability. Northwest spokeswoman Kathleen M. Peach says the noose incidents do not "rise to the level of harassment. You have to ask was it a joke at a construction site? Or was it in a cargo area where a lot of ropes are used? It's not as cut-and-dried as it seems."

Some employers dismiss nooses and slurs as harmless joking. This seems to be the view taken by Lakeside Imports Incorporated, New Orleans' largest Toyota Motor Corporation dealer. Last August, it signed a consent decree with the EEOC to settle charges brought by six black salesmen in its 50-person used car department. The men said that their manager, Chris Mohrman, hit and poked them with two 3 1/2-foot-long sticks with derogatory words on them that he called his "[racial epithet] sticks."

Lakeside brushed aside the incident, according to case depositions. Mohrman's manager at the time, a white man named David Oseng, had hired the black salesmen. When he heard what was going on, Oseng said in his deposition, he told the dealership's top brass. Oseng said the top two managers "told me they were tired of all the problems with the [racial epithet]s. And if we hired another [racial epithet], [I] would be terminated."

Lakeside lawyer Ralph Zatzkis says the dealer didn't admit any guilt and denies that anything serious happened. He says the sticks, which the EEOC obtained by subpoena, did have writing on them, but "those weren't racial remarks." Zatzkis dismissed the episode as "horseplay." Mohrman and the black salesmen left Lakeside and couldn't be reached. Zatzkis says Lakeside's top managers declined to comment.

Frivolous harassment charges do occur, say experts, but they're rare. "It takes a lot of energy to raise a complaint, and you can make major mistakes assuming what the employees' motives are," warns Haven E. Cockerham, head of human resources at R.R. Donnelley & Sons Company, which is fighting a class action for alleged racial discrimination and harassment that included claims of whites donning KKK robes.

Consider Adelphia Communications Corporation, a $2.9 billion cable-TV company based in Coudersport, Pennsylvania. In February the EEOC filed suit on behalf of Glenford S. James, a 12-year veteran, and other black employees in the company's Miami office. A manager there racially harassed minorities "on a daily basis" after he took over in August 1999, the suit says. The manager twice put a noose over James's door, it says. Once, says the complaint, the manager told an employee to "order monkey meat or whatever they eat" for James.

In a suit filed in June, James says that Adelphia didn't stop the problem until he complained to the EEOC in May 2000. Then the manager was terminated or resigned. Adelphia declined to comment. However, its brief in the EEOC suit admits that the manager displayed a noose and "made inappropriate statements of a racial nature." The brief says Adelphia "promptly and severely disciplined" the manager "as a result of his actions." The manager couldn't be reached.

REVENGE. Whites who stand up for coworkers also can run into trouble. Ted W. Gignilliat, a worker at the Marietta facility of Lockheed since 1965, says he was harassed so badly for speaking up about two nooses that he had to take a leave of absence. He says he was threatened, his truck was broken into, and he got anonymous phone calls at work and at home—one telling him he would "wind up on a slab, dead." In March 2000, a psychologist told Gignilliat to stop work; he went on disability leave until May of this year. He now works as an alarm room operator in the plant's fire station. "It's in the middle of the security office, with guards, but I feel they will retaliate against me again for stepping forward," says Gignilliat.

Usually, of course, minorities bear the brunt of revenge. Roosevelt Lewis, who delivers Wonder bread for an Interstate Bakeries Corporation bakery in San Francisco, says his white superiors have been making his life miserable ever since he and other blacks filed a race suit in 1998. A jury awarded them $132 million last year (later reduced by a judge to $32 million). Lewis says this only exacerbated the behavior. "They're trying to make you insubordinate, to create an excuse to fire you," charges Lewis. He says he has complained to higher-ups, but the hassling continues.

Jack N. Wiltrakis, Interstate's head of human resources, says the company has a hotline to headquarters in Kansas City but has received no complaints. "If they have a problem, it's incumbent on them to tell us," he says. Interstate, which has 34,000 workers in 64 bakeries around the United States, has been sued for race problems in New York, Orlando, Indianapolis, and Richmond, Virginia. It has settled the two cases, denying liability, and is still fighting the others, including Lewis's. Wiltrakis says the suits haven't prompted Interstate to launch new policies.

In the end, racist behavior by employees lands at the door of corporate executives. They face a dilemma: if they admit there's a problem, the company is exposed to lawsuits and negative publicity. But denial only makes matters worse. Until more employers confront the rise of ugly racism head on, Americans will continue to see behavior they thought belonged to a more ignominious age.

SOURCE: *BusinessWeek* online, **www.businessweek.com** (October 23, 2001).

Questions:

1. Do you think racism still exists in the workplace? Why or why not?
2. What can firms do to ensure that racism does not pervade their organizations?

Notes

1. J. Ledvinka, *Federal Regulation of Personnel and Human Resource Management* (Boston: Kent, 1982).
2. *Martin* v. *Wilks*, 49 FEP Cases 1641 (1989).
3. *Wards Cove Packing Co.* v. *Atonio*, FEPC 1519 (1989).
4. *Bakke* v. *Regents of the University of California*, 17 FEPC 1000 (1978).
5. *Patterson* v. *McLean Credit Union*, 49 FEPC 1814 (1987).
6. J. Friedman and G. Strickler, *The Law of Employment Discrimination: Cases and Materials*, 2nd ed. (Mineola, NY: The Foundation Press, 1987).
7. "Labor Letter," *The Wall Street Journal* (August 25, 1987), p. 1.
8. J. Woo, "Ex-workers Hit Back with Age-Bias Suits," *The Wall Street Journal* (December 8, 1992), p. B1.
9. W. Carley, "Salesman's Treatment Raises Bias Questions at Schering-Plough," *The Wall Street Journal* (May 31, 1995), A1.
10. Special feature issue: "The New Civil Rights Act of 1991 and What It Means to Employers," *Employment Law Update* 6 (December 1991), pp. 1–12.
11. "ADA: The Final Regulations (Title I): A Lawyer's Dream/An Employer's Nightmare," *Employment Law Update* 16, no. 9 (1991), p. 1.
12. "ADA Supervisor Training Program: A Must for Any Supervisor Conducting a Legal Job Interview," *Employment Law Update* 7, no. 6 (1992), pp. 1–6.
13. Equal Employment Opportunity Commission, *Uniform Guidelines on Employee Selection Procedures*, Federal Register 43 (1978), pp. 38290–315.
14. Ledvinka, *Federal Regulation*.
15. R. Pear, "The Cabinet Searches for Consensus on Affirmative Action," *The New York Times* (October 27, 1985), p. E5.
16. *McDonnell Douglas* v. *Green*, 411 U.S. 972 (1973).
17. *UAW* v. *Johnson Controls, Inc.* (1991).
18. Special feature issue: "The New Civil Rights Act of 1991," pp. 1–6.
19. *Washington* v. *Davis*, 12 FEP 1415 (1976).
20. *Albermarle Paper Company* v. *Moody*, 10 FEP 1181 (1975).
21. R. Reilly and G. Chao, "Validity and Fairness of Some Alternative Employee Selection Procedures," *Personnel Psychology* 35 (1982), pp. 1–63; J. Hunter and R. Hunter, "Validity and Utility of Alternative

Predictors of Job Performance," *Psychological Bulletin* 96 (1984), pp. 72–98.

22. *Griggs* v. *Duke Power Company*, 401 U.S. 424 (1971).
23. B. Lindeman and P. Grossman, *Employment Discrimination Law* (Washington, DC: BNA Books, 1996).
24. M. Jacobs, "Workers' Religious Beliefs May Get New Attention," *The Wall Street Journal* (August 22, 1995), pp. B1, B8.
25. Lindeman and Grossman, *Employment Discrimination Law*.
26. J. Reno and D. Thornburgh, "ADA—Not a Disabling Mandate," *The Wall Street Journal* (July 26, 1995), p. A12.
27. Woo, "Ex-workers Hit Back."
28. W. Johnston and A. Packer, *Workforce 2000* (Indianapolis, IN: Hudson Institute, 1987).
29. *Bundy* v. *Jackson*, 641 F.2d 934, 24 FEP 1155 (D.C. Cir., 1981).
30. L.A. Graf and M. Hemmasi, "Risqué Humor: How It Really Affects the Workplace," *HR Magazine*, November 1995, pp. 64–69.
31. B. Carton, "At Jenny Craig, Men Are Ones Who Claim Sex Discrimination," *The Wall Street Journal* (November 29, 1995), p. A1; "Male-on-Male Harassment Suit Won," *Houston Chronicle* (August 12, 1995), p. 21A.
32. *Meritor Savings Bank* v. *Vinson* (1986).
33. R. Paetzold and A. O'Leary-Kelly, "The Implications of U.S. Supreme Court and Circuit Court Decisions for Hostile Environment Sexual Harassment Cases," in *Sexual Harassment: Perspectives, Frontiers, and Strategies*, ed. M. Stockdale (Beverly Hills, CA: Sage); R.B. McAfee and D.L. Deadrick, "Teach Employees to Just Say 'No'!" *HR Magazine*, February 1996, pp. 586–89.
34. C. Murray, "The Legacy of the 60's," *Commentary*, July 1992, pp. 23–30.
35. D. Kravitz and J. Platania, "Attitudes and Beliefs about Affirmative Action: Effects of Target and of Respondent Sex and Ethnicity," *Journal of Applied Psychology* 78 (1993), pp. 928–38.
36. J. Mathews, "Rash of Unintended Lawsuits Follows Passage of Disabilities Act," *Houston Chronicle* (May 16, 1995), p. 15A.
37. C. Bell, "What the First ADA Cases Tell Us," *SHRM Legal Report* (Winter), pp. 4–7.
38. K. Mills, "Disabilities Act: A Help, or a Needless Hassle," *B/CS Eagle* (August 23, 1995), p. A7.
39. V.F. Estrada, "Are Your Factory Workers Know-It-All?" *Personnel Journal*, September 1995, pp. 128–34.
40. R.L. Simison, "Safety Last," *The Wall Street Journal* (March 18, 1986), p. 1.
41. J. Roughton, "Managing a Safety Program through Job Hazard Analysis," *Professional Safety* 37 (1992), pp. 28–31.
42. M.A. Verespec, "OSHA Reform Fails Again," *Industry Week* (November 2, 1992), p. 36.
43. R.G. Hallock and D.A. Weaver, "Controlling Losses and Enhancing Management Systems with TOR Analysis," *Professional Safety* 35 (1990), pp. 24–26.
44. H. Herbstman, "Controlling Losses the Burger King Way," *Risk Management* 37 (1990), pp. 22–30.
45. L. Bryan, "An Ounce of Prevention for Workplace Accidents," *Training and Development Journal* 44 (1990), pp. 101–2.
46. J.F. Mangan, "Hazard Communications: Safety in Knowledge," *Best's Review* 92 (1991), pp. 84–88.
47. T. Markus, "How to Set Up a Safety Awareness Program," *Supervision* 51 (1990), pp. 14–16.
48. J. Agnew and A.J. Saruda, "Age and Fatal Work-Related Falls," *Human Factors* 35 (1994), pp. 731–36.
49. R. King, "Active Safety Programs, Education Can Help Prevent Back Injuries," *Occupational Health and Safety* 60 (1991), pp. 49–52.
50. J.R. Hollenbeck, D.R. Ilgen, and S.M. Crampton, "Lower Back Disability in Occupational Settings: A Review of the Literature from a Human Resource Management View," *Personnel Psychology* 45 (1992), pp. 247–78.
51. T.W. Turriff, "NSPB Suggests 10-Step Program to Prevent Eye Injury," *Occupational Health and Safety* 60 (1991), pp. 62–66.
52. D. Hanson, "Chemical Plant Safety: OSHA Rule Addresses Industry Concerns," *Chemical and Engineering News* 70 (1992), pp. 4–5; K. Broscheit and K. Sawyer, "Safety Exhibit Teaches Customers and Employees about Electricity," *Transmission and Distribution* 43 (1992), pp. 174–79; R. Schuch, "Good Training Is Key to Avoiding Boiler Explosions," *National Underwriter* 95 (1992), pp. 21–22.
53. M. Janssens, J.M. Brett, and F.J. Smith, "Confirmatory Cross-Cultural Research: Testing the Viability of a Corporation-wide Safety Policy," *Academy of Management Journal* 38 (1995), pp. 364–82.

Chapter 4

The Analysis and Design of Work

Objectives

After reading this chapter, you should be able to:

1. Analyze a work-flow process, identifying the output, activities, and inputs in the production of a product or service.
2. Understand the importance of job analysis in strategic and human resource management.
3. Choose the right job analysis technique for a variety of human resource activities.
4. Identify the tasks performed and the skills required in a given job.
5. Understand the different approaches to job design.
6. Comprehend the trade-offs among the various approaches to designing jobs.

Competing in the new economy has forced many companies, like IBM, to restructure their human resource departments into single, centralized groups. Even though these new departments consist of far fewer people, technology and corporate intranets enable such offices to replace local units while still remaining efficient, cost-effective, and most important, responsive.

Enter the World of Business

From Big Blue to Efficient Blue

IBM was long known as "Big Blue" because of its size, in terms of both the number of employees and the amount of revenue and costs associated with its operations. However, as the old saying goes, "the bigger they are, the harder they fall." In 1993 IBM racked up over $8 billion in losses when it was blindsided by the switch in consumer preferences from mainframe computers to smaller, networked personal computers.

The new incoming CEO, Lou Gerstner, needed to engineer one of the greatest turnarounds in modern business; he started with a new vision of what the company would become, as well as a strategy for getting where the company needed to be. The strategy had both an external aspect, focused on changing from an old-fashioned manufacturing company to a modern service provider, and an internal aspect of restructuring operations to reduce costs and promote efficiencies.

Nowhere was this internal strategy change felt more strongly than in the human resource division. In 1993, the HRM function at IBM was large, decentralized, and regionally based, with branch offices all over the world employing over 3,500 people. By the year 2000 there was only one single, centralized unit located in Raleigh, North Carolina, and this unit employed fewer than 1,000 people.

The key to the successful downsizing effort was its emphasis on matching size changes with changes in structure and the substitution of technology for labor. Instead of interacting face-to-face with the local human resources office, all communication would be technologically mediated and directed to the central Raleigh facility via telephone, e-mail, or fax. Moreover, user-friendly software was developed to help employees answer their questions without any other human involvement.

The sprawling, geographically dispersed units were replaced with an efficient three-tier system. The first tier was composed of broadly trained human resource generalists who received telephone calls from any of IBM's 700,000 HRM "customers" (employees) and tried to respond to any queries that could not be handled via the automated system. The second tier, a smaller number of highly trained specialists (such as in 401k plans, OSHA requirements, or selection standards), took any calls that exceeded the knowledge level of the generalists. Finally, the third tier consisted of even a smaller number of top executives charged with keeping the HRM practices in line with the overall corporate strategy being developed by Gerstner.

Amazingly, despite the radical downsizing of this unit, employee satisfaction with service actually increased to over 90 percent, and Gerstner singled out the reengineering of this department as a success story that should serve as a benchmark to the rest of the company's divisions. Moreover, the restructuring and redesign of these IBM jobs have formed a "blue"-print for many other HRM departments in other organizations.

SOURCE: S.N. Mehta, "What Lucent Can Learn from IBM," *Fortune* (June 25, 2001), p. 40; G. Flynn, "Out of the Red, Into the Blue," *Workforce* (March 2000), pp. 50–52; P. Gilster, "Making Online Self-Service Work," *Workforce* (January, 2001), pp. 54–61; J. Hutchins, "The U.S. Postal Service Delivers an Innovative HR Strategy," *Workforce* (October 2000), pp. 116–118.

Introduction

In Chapter 2 we discussed the processes of strategy formulation and strategy implementation. Strategy formulation is the process by which a company decides how it will compete in the marketplace; this is often the energizing and guiding force for everything it does. Strategy implementation is the way the strategic plan gets carried out in activities of organizational members. We noted five important components in the strategy implementation process, three of which are directly related to the human resource management function and one of which we will discuss in this chapter: the task or job.[1]

Many central aspects of strategy formulation address how the work gets done, in terms of both individual job design as well as the design of organizational structures that link individual jobs to each other and the organization as a whole. The way a firm competes can have a profound impact on the ways jobs are designed and how they are linked via organizational structure. In turn, the fit between the company's structure and environment can have a major impact on the firm's competitive success.

For example, if a company wants to compete via a low-cost strategy, it needs to maximize efficiency. Efficiency is maximized by breaking jobs down into small, simple components that are executed repetitively by low-wage, low-skilled workers. Efficiency is also enhanced by eliminating any redundancy of support services, so that jobs are structured into functional clusters where everyone in the cluster is performing similar work. (Thus all marketing people work together in a single unit, all engineering personnel work together in a single unit, and so on.) People working together within these functional clusters learn a great deal about how the function can be used to leverage their skills into small amounts of increased efficiency via continuous, evolutionary improvements. In our opening story, when IBM moved all of its regional human resources people into a single centralized location in North Carolina, it was trying to achieve this type of efficiency.

On the other hand, if a company wants to compete via innovation, it needs to maximize flexibility. Flexibility is maximized by aggregating work into larger, holistic pieces that are executed by teams of higher-wage, higher-skilled workers. Flexibility is also enhanced by giving the units their own support systems and decision-making authority to take advantage of local opportunities in regional or specialized product markets. People working together in these cross-functional clusters generate a greater number of creative and novel ideas that can be leveraged into more discontinuous, revolutionary improvements. Thus, although IBM's new centralized structure may be more efficient, it is less able to take advantage of opportunities or identify threats that might occur in local areas (such as a change in the state labor laws of California) in the same manner that it might have been able to back when it was decentralized.

Thus, it should be clear from the outset of this chapter that there is no "one best way" to design jobs and structure organizations. The organization needs to create a fit between its environment, competitive strategy, and philosophy on the one hand, with its jobs and organizational design on the other. As the story that opened this chapter shows, IBM was out to maximize efficiencies in its HRM department because this was not seen as its core business. At the same time it was centralizing human resource management, however, IBM was decentralizing its sales staff to take better advantage of unique opportunities in different sectors of the computer systems market (creating separate, autonomous sales units for small business sales, large accounts, government accounts, and educational customers).

This chapter discusses the analysis and design of work and, in doing so, lays out some considerations that go into making informed decisions about how to create and link jobs. The chapter is divided into three sections, the first of which deals with "big-picture" issues related to work-flow analysis and organizational structure. The remaining two sections deal with more specific, lower-level issues related to job analysis and job design.

The fields of job analysis and job design have extensive overlap, yet in the past they have been treated differently.[2] Job analysis has focused on analyzing existing jobs to gather information for other human resource management practices such as selection, training, performance appraisal, and compensation.[3] Job design, on the other hand, has focused on redesigning existing jobs to make them more efficient or more motivating to jobholders.[4] Thus job design has had a more proactive orientation toward changing the job, whereas job analysis has had a passive, information-gathering orientation. However, as we will show in this chapter, these two approaches are interrelated.

Work-Flow Analysis and Organization Structure

In the past, HR professionals and line managers have tended to analyze or design a particular job in isolation from the larger organizational context. *Work-flow design* is the process of analyzing the tasks necessary for the production of a product or service, prior to allocating and assigning these tasks to a particular job category or person. Only after we thoroughly understand work-flow design can we make informed decisions regarding how to initially bundle various tasks into discrete jobs that can be executed by a single person.

Organization structure refers to the relatively stable and formal network of vertical and horizontal interconnections among jobs that constitute the organization. Only after we understand how one job relates to those above (supervisors), below (subordinates), and at the same level in different functional areas (marketing versus production) can we make informed decisions about how to redesign or improve jobs to benefit the entire organization.

Finally, work-flow design and organization structure have to be understood in the context of how an organization has decided to compete. Both work-flow design and organization structure can be leveraged to gain competitive advantage for the firm, but how one does this depends on the firm's strategy and its competitive environment.

Work-Flow Analysis

As we noted in Chapter 1, the institution of the Malcolm Baldrige National Quality award resulted in the development of many TQM programs in U.S. businesses. A theme common to nearly all quality programs is the need to identify clearly the outputs of work, to specify the quality standards for those outputs, and to analyze the processes and inputs necessary for producing outputs that meet the quality standards.[5] This conception of the work-flow process is useful for TQM because it provides a means for the manager to understand all the tasks required to produce a high-quality product as well as the skills necessary to perform those tasks. This work-flow process is depicted in Figure 4.1. In this section we present an approach for analyzing the work process of a department as a means of examining jobs in the context of an organization.

FIGURE 4.1
Developing a Work-Unit Activity Analysis

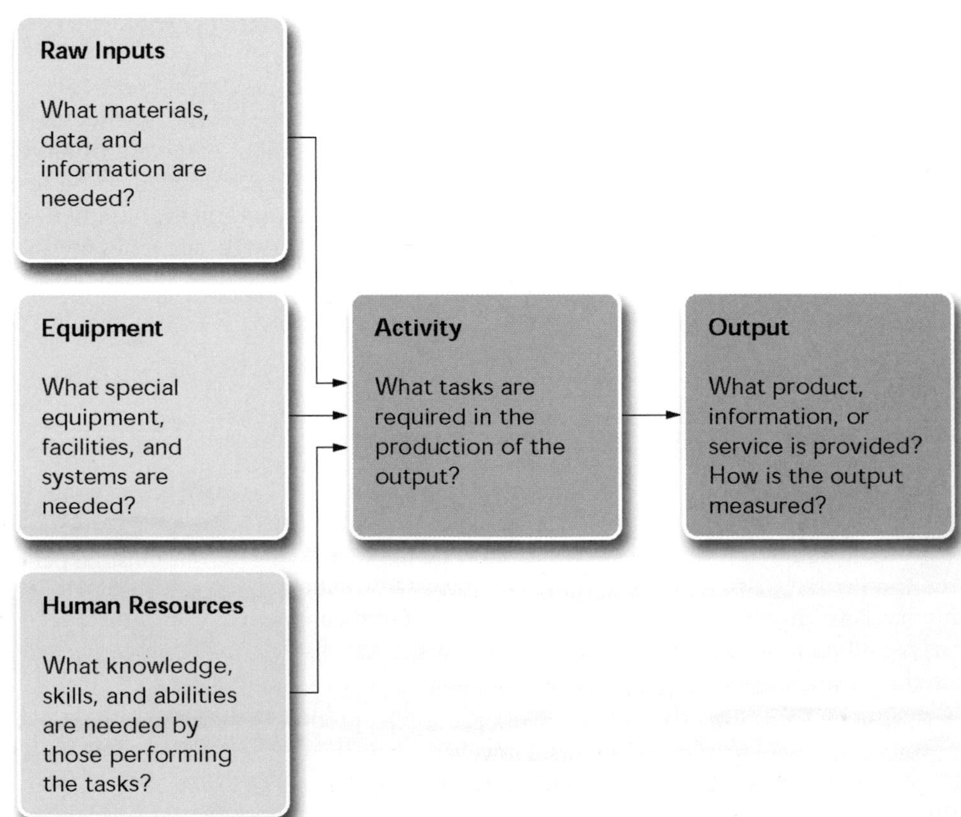

Analyzing Work Outputs

Every work unit—whether a department, team, or individual—seeks to produce some output that others can use. An output is the product of a work unit and is often an identifiable thing, such as a completed purchase order, an employment test, or a hot, juicy hamburger. However, an output can also be a service, such as the services provided by an airline that transports you to some destination, a housecleaning service that maintains your house, or a baby-sitter who watches over your children.

We often picture an organization only in terms of the product that it produces, and then we focus on that product as the output. For example, we could easily identify the output of IBM in the 1980s as being computers—a physical object. As a provider of services, IBM now produces output that is more difficult to conceptualize. Moreover, even producing computers requires many work units, each generating a variety of outputs; and each of these work units has a number of individuals who generate some work output. Thus an important determinant of the effectiveness of any organization is the efficiency and effectiveness with which it produces the many products within the various work units.

However, merely identifying an output or set of outputs is not sufficient. Once these outputs have been identified, it is necessary to specify standards for the quantity or quality of these outputs. For example, a recently developed productivity improvement technique known as ProMES (productivity measurement and evaluation system) focuses attention on both identifying work-unit outputs and specifying the levels of required performance for different levels of effectiveness.[6] With ProMES, the members of a work unit identify each of the products (outputs) of the work unit for the various customers. They then evaluate the effectiveness of each level of products in the eyes of their customers.

The identification of work outputs has only recently gained attention among HRM departments. As discussed in Chapter 2, HR executives have begun to understand the role of the HRM department as they have attempted to analyze their customers inside the company and the products that those customers desire from the HRM function.[7] This has given HR managers a clearer understanding of the specific products that they supply to the company and allows them to focus on producing high-quality products. Without an understanding of the output of a work unit, any attempt at increasing work-unit effectiveness will be futile.

Analyzing Work Processes

Once the outputs of the work unit have been identified, it is possible to examine the work processes used to generate the output. The work processes are the activities that members of a work unit engage in to produce a given output. Every process consists of operating procedures that specify how things should be done at each stage of the development of the product. These procedures include all the tasks that must be performed in the production of the output. The tasks are usually broken down into those performed by each person in the work unit.

Again, to design work systems that are maximally efficient, a manager needs to understand the processes required in the development of the products for that work unit. Often, as work loads increase within a work group, the group will grow by adding positions to meet these new requirements. However, when the work load lightens, members may take on tasks that do not relate to the work unit's product in an effort to appear busy. Without a clear understanding of the tasks necessary to the production of an output, it is difficult to determine whether the work unit has become overstaffed. Understanding the tasks required allows the manager to specify which tasks are to be carried out by which individuals and eliminate tasks that are not necessary for the desired end. This ensures that the work group maintains a high level of productivity.

For example, Microsoft, currently the most successful computer software company in the world, strategically manages the design of the total work-flow process for competitive advantage. To maintain the sense of being an underdog, Microsoft deliberately understaffs its product teams in "small bands of people with a mission." This ensures both a lean organization and high levels of motivation.[8] Other organizations keep staffing levels low by substituting technology for labor in the production process. Indeed, as the "Competing through Globalization" box shows, in an age of globalization, this type of substitution may be critical in keeping U.S. jobs from moving overseas.

Although this substitution was often focused formerly on production employees, more recently, the focus has been on eliminating midlevel managers. For example, at Unifi Inc., a textile producer, factory equipment is connected via high-speed data lines so that shop floor data can be relayed in real time to analysts at corporate headquarters, eliminating the need for local supervisors.[9] This kind of remote monitoring is becoming especially popular in multinational corporations as a means of standardizing work outputs. Although not all employees respond positively to technological changes in the nature of work, such changes are becoming increasingly critical in competing in the contemporary business environment.[10]

Analyzing Work Inputs

The final stage in work-flow analysis is to identify the inputs used in the development of the work unit's product. For example, assume that you were assigned a paper titled "The Importance of Human Resources to Organizational Performance." The output of your work process will be a paper that you will turn in to the professor. To produce this paper, you must perform a number of tasks, such as conducting research, reading articles, and writing the paper. What, however, are the inputs? As shown in Figure 4.1, these inputs can be broken down into the raw materials, equipment, and human skills needed to perform the tasks. *Raw materials* consist of the materials that will be converted into the work unit's product. Thus, for your assignment, the raw materials would be the information available in the library regarding the various effects of human resources on organizational performance.

Equipment refers to the technology and machinery necessary to transform the raw materials into the product. As you attempt to develop your paper, you may use the library computer search system to get a list of recent articles on the relationship between human resources and organizational performance. In addition, once you sit down to write, you will most likely have to use either a word processor or a personal computer to put your thoughts on paper.

The final inputs in the work-flow process are the *human skills* and efforts necessary to perform the tasks. Many skills are required of you in producing your paper. For example, you need to know how to use the library computer search facilities, you need some typing skill (or the phone number of a good typist), and you definitely need the ability to reason and write. Of course, in many situations where the work that needs to be done is highly complex, no single individual is likely to have all the required skills. In these situations, the work may be assigned to a team, and team-based job design is becoming increasingly popular in contemporary organizations.[11] In addition to

COMPETING THROUGH GLOBALIZATION

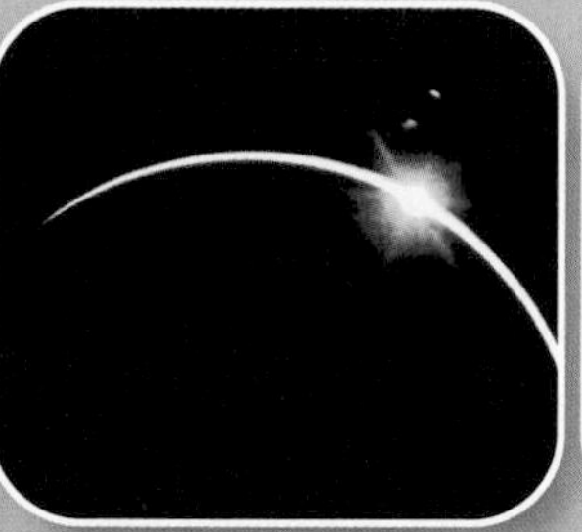

Low-Skill Jobs: Move Them or Improve Them?

If you were to travel to China and visit any subcontractor's factory in the athletic shoe industry, such as Nike or Reebok, you might think you had also ventured back in time to the 19th century. Teenage girls with little education and few skills work six 12-hour days each week, stooped over sewing machines much like those your great-grandparents might have used. The fact that these women work for 20 to 40 cents an hour certainly keeps production costs lower than one could ever hope to obtain in the United States, where the federal minimum wage is now over $5 an hour.

Because of this cost differential, many employers of low-skilled labor have moved jobs out of this country into other countries such as China, Vietnam, and Mexico in order to achieve competitive advantage in the marketplace. Although this may help the company's shareholders and keep prices down for consumers, many U.S. workers have been displaced from their jobs in this process. In addition, moving jobs to whatever country is willing to tolerate the most abusive work practices puts no pressure on employers to raise employment standards for those working in sweatshops.

The degree to which workers, both U.S. and foreign, are going to let this continue is now being questioned. Violent riots and protests were seen at the 1999 and 2000 World Trade Organization and International Monetary Fund/World Bank meetings. Statistics from the U.S. Commerce Department indicate that over 1 million Americans lose their jobs every year to globalization, and as one analyst has noted, a strong majority of the U.S. public feels that U.S. trade policies have not adequately addressed the concerns of American workers.

In the midst of all this controversy, however, one U.S. company is rewriting the rules of competitive advantage. Instead of *moving* their low-skill jobs to low-wage, low-labor-standard countries, New Balance Athletic Shoes Inc. is *improving* the jobs. The New Balance factory in Norridgewock, Maine, stands as a stark contrast to those in China. Well-educated employees, cross-trained in all tasks and working in teams, use automated equipment that operates over 20 sewing machines simultaneously. Most remarkably, these workers earn over $14 an hour rather than the 40 cents made by those working offshore.

New Balance can afford to pay these wages because it uses technology to increase the efficiency of its workers. Compared to Chinese facilities that produce one pair of shoes every three hours, the New Balance factory in Maine produces one pair of shoes every 20 minutes. Although the labor costs per shoe are still lower in China than in Maine ($1.30 versus $4.00 a pair), this is only a small percentage for a shoe that sells for $70. Moreover, New Balance can offset this by reduced transportation costs, faster order refilling, and more flexible style changes. This competitive strategy means that New Balance must constantly be on the watch for labor-saving technological developments, however, because as Herb Spivak, head of operations, notes, "Asian labor is so inexpensive that they can waste it—ours is so dear that we have to come up with techniques to be very efficient."

SOURCE: D. Shook, "Why Nike Is Dragging Its Feet," *BusinessWeek Online* (March 19, 2001); A. Bernstein, "Backlash: Behind the Anxiety over Globalization," *BusinessWeek* (April 20, 2000), pp. 38–43; A. Bernstein, "Low Skilled Jobs: Do They Have to Move?" *BusinessWeek* (February 26, 2001).

providing a wider set of skills, team members can back each other up, share work when any member becomes overloaded, and catch each others' errors. Indeed, as the "Competing through High-Performance Work Systems" box shows, this aspect of teams is becoming increasingly important in many high-risk organizations in the medical, military, and aviation industries. Teams are not a panacea, however, and for teams to be effective, it is essential that the level of task interdependence (how much they have to cooperate) matches the level of outcome interdependence (how much they share the reward for task accomplishment).[12]

It is important to note that a flawed product can be caused by deficiencies at any phase in production. For example, if you fail to spell-check your paper before turning it in, you may receive a lower grade. Similarly, if you cannot obtain the best raw materials (if you cannot find the right articles), do not use the proper equipment (the computer is down), or do not possess the necessary skills (you do not write well), your paper will receive less than the maximum grade.

Organization Structure

Whereas work-flow design provides a longitudinal overview of the dynamic relationships by which inputs are converted into outputs, organization structure provides a cross-sectional overview of the static relationships between individuals and units that create the outputs. Organization structure is typically displayed via organizational charts that convey both vertical reporting relationships and horizontal functional responsibilities.

Dimensions of Structure

Two of the most critical dimensions of organization structure are centralization and departmentation. **Centralization** refers to the degree to which decision-making authority resides at the top of the organizational chart as opposed to being distributed throughout lower levels (in which case authority is *decentralized*). **Departmentalization** refers to the degree to which work units are grouped based on functional similarity or similarity of work flow.

Centralization
Degree to which decision-making authority resides at the top of the organizational chart.

Departmentalization
Degree to which work units are grouped based on functional similarity or similarity of work flow.

For example, a school of business could be organized around functional similarity so that there would be a marketing department, a finance department, and an accounting department, and faculty within these specialized departments would each teach their area of expertise to all kinds of students. Alternatively, one could organize the same school around work-flow similarity, so that there would be an undergraduate unit, a graduate unit, and an executive development unit. Each of these units would have its own marketing, finance, and accounting professors who taught only their own respective students and not those of the other units.

Structural Configurations

Although there are an infinite number of ways to combine centralization and departmentalization, two common configurations of organization structure tend to emerge in organizations. The first type, referred to as a *functional structure*, is shown in Figure 4.2. A functional structure, as the name implies, employs a functional departmentalization scheme with relatively high levels of centralization. High levels of centralization tend to go naturally with functional departmentalization because individual units in the structures are so specialized that members of the unit may have

COMPETING THROUGH HIGH-PERFORMANCE WORK SYSTEMS

Team-Based Job Redesign and Error Prevention

When Reggie Peterson showed up at the emergency department of his local university medical center, he was displaying flulike symptoms. He was tested and examined first by a nurse, who suspected he had meningitis, an inflammation of the brain. A doctor who subsequently examined him diagnosed the problem as simple flu and sent him home, recommending rest and plenty of fluids. Six hours later, Peterson died of spinal meningitis. Unfortunately, the nurse who suspected meningitis was not working alongside the doctor, and because she was earlier chastised by this same doctor for not "sticking to nursing" she never shared her opinions with him.

According to a recent study by the Institute of Medicine, an arm of the National Academy of Sciences, this type of medical error occurs all too frequently in today's hospitals and medical centers. Our widely distributed, fragmented health care system, along with secretive and unpublicized errors, makes it hard for the general public to appreciate the problem. However, if all the errors in U.S. hospitals were aggregated daily, the Institute of Medicine likened the situation to that of a 747 airplane crashing *every single day.*

One solution to this problem offered by the National Academy of Sciences was to organize work around teams, as opposed to individual doctors and nurses. For example, Suburban Hospital in Bethesda, Maryland, has adopted a team-based approach in its Intensive Care Unit (ICU). Each team includes an ICU specialist, a pharmacist, a nutritionist, a social worker, a nurse, a respiratory specialist, and a chaplain who go room-to-room each morning, visiting every patient—sometimes accompanied by a family member. The team meets with each patient's bedside nurse to discuss and debate the best action for this patient from all possible angles.

This focus on teamwork has a long tradition in other high-pressure work contexts such as aviation and the military, and it is increasingly being adopted in many businesses and industries. Indeed, enhanced communication technologies such as e-mail, teleconferencing, and videoconferencing have allowed the creation of "virtual teams" that work together despite being separated in space and time. The use of these technologies eliminates the need for travel and allows organizations to put together the best teams possible, free of traditional constraints.

At Suburban Hospital, this team-based approach is credited with reducing errors, shortening the time patients spend in the small (12-bed) ICU unit, and improving the communication between patients, their families, and the medical staff. It also has reduced the time patients spend on ventilators by 25 percent, which is critical because the use of ventilators increases the chances of pneumonia, which, in turn, greatly increases both costs and the chance of patients dying. Indeed, the cost savings from avoiding complications more than offsets the increased expense associated with team formation, and this does not even calculate the reduced amount of human suffering. As Dr. Joseph Fontan, an ICU specialist at Suburban, notes, "It's good to have people with different backgrounds and opinions looking at the same problem—it makes a huge difference because small problems that can turn into big ones are headed off early."

SOURCE: J. Appleby and R. Davis, "Teamwork Used to Be a Money Saver; Now It's a Lifesaver," *USA Today* (March 1, 2001), pp. B1–B2; L. Kohn, J. Corrigan, and M. Donaldson, *To Err Is Human: Building a Safer Health System* (Washington, DC: National Academy Press, 2001); C. M. Solomon, "Managing Virtual Teams," *Workforce* (June 2001), pp. 61–65.

FIGURE 4.2
The Functional Structure

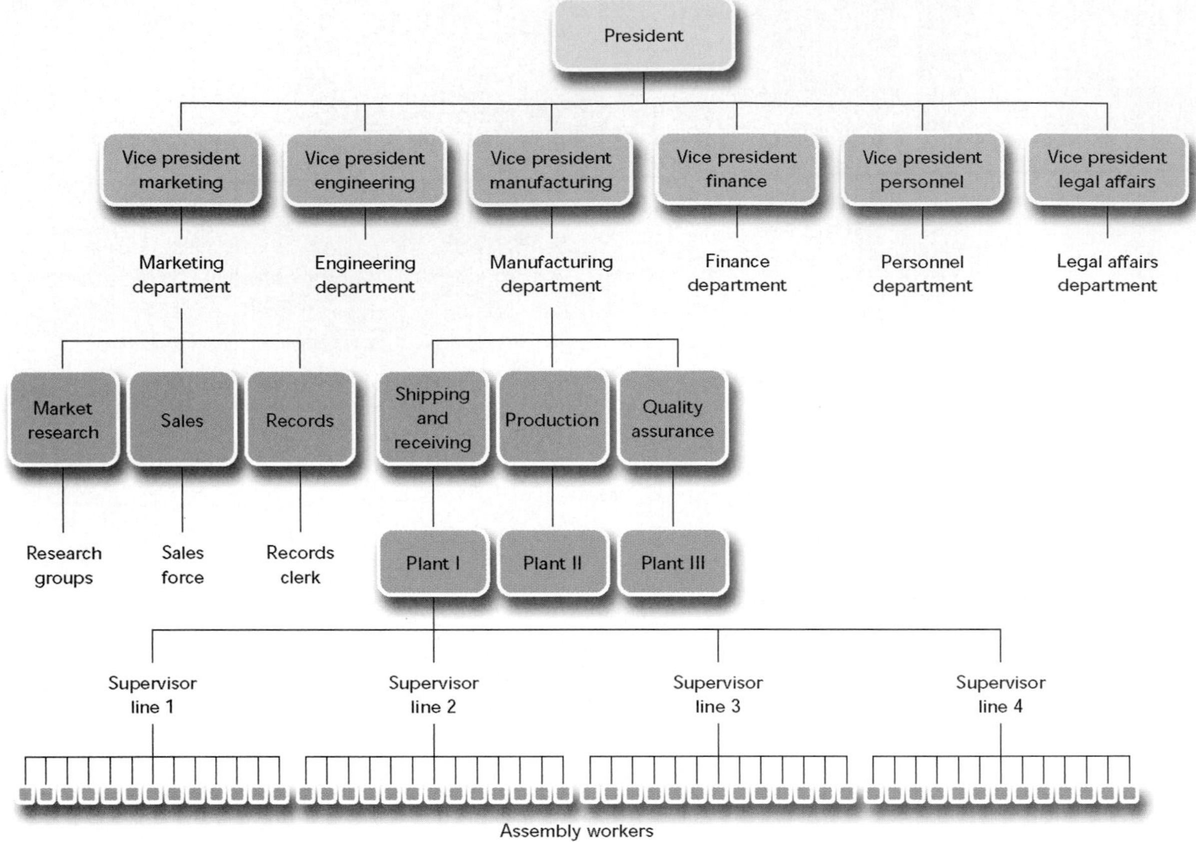

SOURCE: Adapted from J. A. Wagner and J. R. Hollenbeck, *Organizational Behavior: Securing Competitive Advantage,* 3rd ed. Prentice-Hall. Reprinted with permission.

a weak conceptualization of the overall organization mission. Thus, they tend to identify with their department and cannot always be relied on to make decisions that are in the best interests of the organization as a whole.

Alternatively, a second common configuration is a *divisional structure*, three examples of which are shown in Figures 4.3, 4.4, and 4.5. Divisional structures combine a work-flow departmentalization scheme with relatively low levels of centralization. Units in these structures act almost like separate, self-sufficient, semi-autonomous organizations. The organization shown in Figure 4.3 is divisionally organized around different products; the organization shown in Figure 4.4 is divisionally organized around geographic regions; and the organization shown in Figure 4.5 is divisionally organized around different clients.

Because of their work-flow focus, their semi-autonomous nature, and their proximity to a homogeneous consumer base, divisional structures tend to be more flexible and innovative. They can detect and exploit opportunities in their respective consumer base faster than the more centralized functionally structured organizations. The perceived autonomy that goes along with this kind of structure also means that most employees prefer it and feel they are more fairly treated than when they are

FIGURE 4.3

Divisional Structure: Product Structure

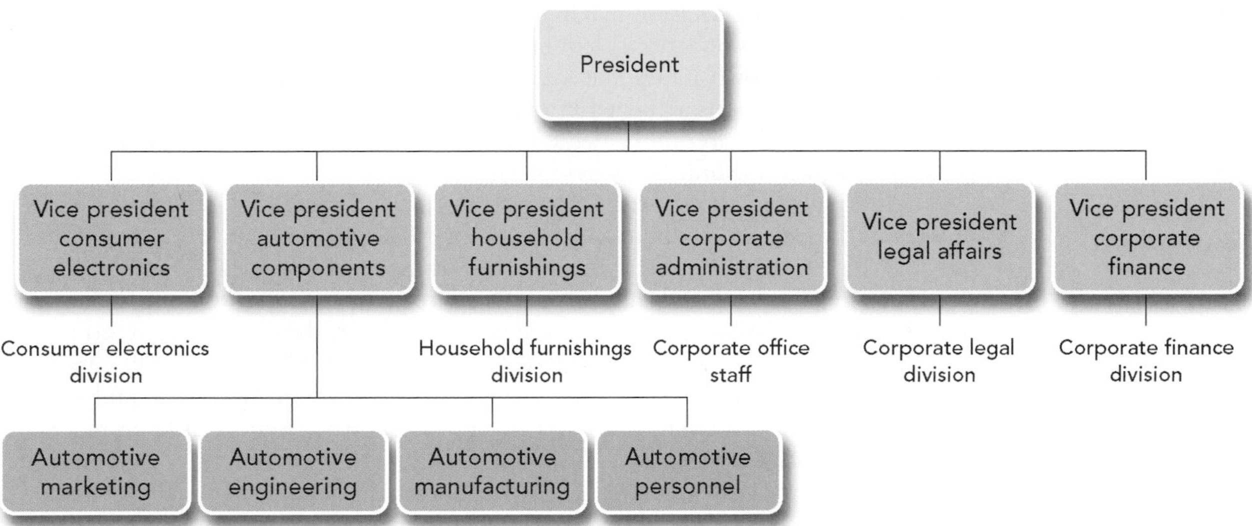

SOURCE: Adapted from J. A. Wagner and J. R. Hollenbeck, *Organizational Behavior: Securing Competitive Advantage*, 3rd ed. Prentice-Hall. Reprinted with permission.

FIGURE 4.4

Divisional Structure: Geographic Structure

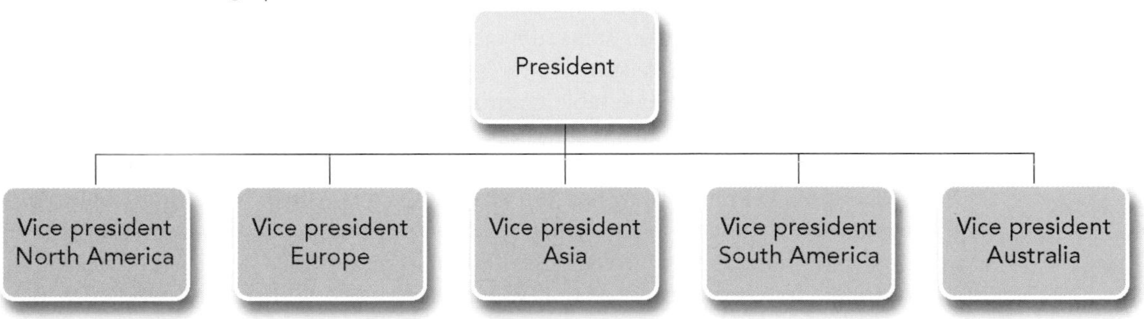

SOURCE: Adapted from J. A. Wagner and J. R. Hollenbeck, *Organizational Behavior: Securing Competitive Advantage*, 3rd ed. Prentice-Hall. Reprinted with permission.

FIGURE 4.5

Divisional Structure: Client Structure

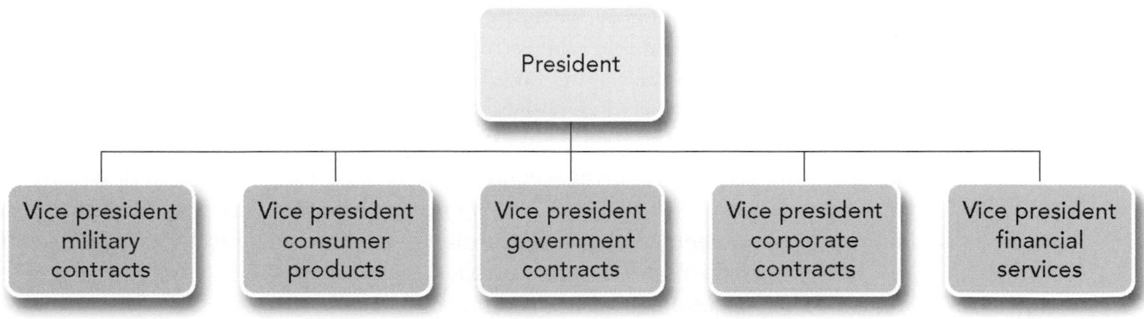

SOURCE: Adapted from J. A. Wagner and J. R. Hollenbeck, *Organizational Behavior: Securing Competitive Advantage*, 3rd ed. Prentice-Hall. Reprinted with permission.

subject to centralized decision-making structures.[13] However, on the downside, divisional structures are not very efficient because of the redundancy associated with each group carrying its own functional specialists. Also, divisional structures can "self-cannibalize" if the gains achieved in one unit come at the expense of another unit (for example, if sales in one General Motors unit like Oldsmobile come at the expense of another GM unit like Chevrolet).

Alternatively, functional structures are very efficient, with little redundancy across units, and provide little opportunity for self-cannibalization. As you may recall from our opening story, IBM was trying to avoid these kinds of inefficiencies when it shifted from a decentralized divisional structure to a more centralized functional structure for its human resource management. However, these structures tend to be inflexible and insensitive to subtle differences across products, regions, or clients. So, for example, in 1999, when Microsoft changed its structure, it went from a relatively centralized and functional form to a decentralized divisional form in order to increase its flexibility in different markets. Prior to the shift, Microsoft had two divisions split along technology lines—one for applications and one for operating systems. The new structure created six semi-autonomous units: one for conducting research and five others aimed directly at different sectors of the market, including corporate customers, knowledge workers, corporate programmers, home applications, and small business owners.[14] Thus, in general, no one structure is always the best.

Functional structures are most appropriate in stable, predictable environments, where demand for resources can be well anticipated and coordination requirements between jobs can be refined and standardized over consistent repetitions of activity. This type of structure also helps support organizations that compete on cost, because efficiency is central to make this strategy work. Divisional structures are most appropriate in unstable, unpredictable environments, where it is difficult to anticipate demands for resources, and coordination requirements between jobs are not consistent over time. This type of structure also helps support organizations that compete on differentiation or innovation, because flexible responsiveness is central to making this strategy work. Indeed, in the words of Microsoft founder Bill Gates, "we are now holding the leaders of our new business divisions accountable to think and act as if they are independent businesses so that will give us the flexibility to respond more quickly to changes in technology and the marketplace."[15]

Structure and the Nature of Jobs

Finally, moving from big-picture issues to lower-level specifics, the type of organization structure also has implications for the design of jobs. Jobs in functional structures need to be narrow and highly specialized, and people tend to work alone. Workers in these structures (even middle managers) tend to have little decision-making authority or responsibility for managing coordination between themselves and others. Jobs in divisional structures need to be more holistic, with people working in teams that tend to have greater decision-making authority.

In our next section we cover specific approaches for analyzing and designing jobs. Although all of these approaches are viable, each focuses on a single, isolated job. These approaches do not necessarily consider how that single job fits into the overall work flow or structure of the organization. Thus, to use these techniques effectively, we have to understand the organization as a whole. Without this big-picture appreciation, we might redesign a job in a way that might be good for that one job but out of line with the work flow, structure, or strategy of the organization.

Job Analysis

Job analysis refers to the process of getting detailed information about jobs.[16] Job analysis has deep historical roots. For example, in his description of the "just" state, Socrates argued that society needed to recognize three things. First, there are individual differences in aptitudes for work, meaning that individuals differ in their abilities. Second, unique aptitude requirements exist for different occupations. Third, to achieve high-quality performance, society must attempt to place people in occupations that best suit their aptitudes. In other words, for society (or an organization) to succeed, it must have detailed information about the requirements of jobs (through job analysis) and it must ensure that a match exists between the job requirements and individuals' aptitudes (through selection).[17]

Job analysis
The process of getting detailed information about jobs.

Whereas Socrates was concerned with the larger society, it is even more important for organizations to understand and match job requirements and people to achieve high-quality performance. This is particularly true in today's competitive marketplace. Thus the information gained through job analysis is of utmost importance; it has great value to both human resource and line managers.

The Importance of Job Analysis to HR Managers

Job analysis is such an important activity to HR managers that it has been called the building block of everything that personnel does.[18] This statement refers to the fact that almost every human resource management program requires some type of information that is gleaned from job analysis: selection, performance appraisal, training and development, job evaluation, career planning, work redesign, and human resource planning.[19]

Work Redesign. As previously discussed, job analysis and job design are interrelated. Often a firm will seek to redesign work to make it more efficient or effective. To redesign the work, detailed information about the existing job(s) must be available. In addition, redesigning a job will, in fact, be similar to analyzing a job that does not yet exist.

Human Resource Planning. In human resource planning, planners analyze an organization's human resource needs in a dynamic environment and develop activities that enable a firm to adapt to change. This planning process requires accurate information about the levels of skill required in various jobs to ensure that enough individuals are available in the organization to meet the human resource needs of the strategic plan.[20]

Selection. Human resource selection identifies the most qualified applicants for employment. To identify which applicants are most qualified, it is first necessary to determine the tasks that will be performed by the individual hired and the knowledge, skills, and abilities the individual must have to perform the job effectively. This information is gained through job analysis.[21]

Training. Almost every employee hired by an organization will require training. Some training programs may be more extensive than others, but all require the trainer to have identified the tasks performed in the job to ensure that the training will prepare individuals to perform their jobs effectively.[22]

Performance Appraisal. Performance appraisal deals with getting information about how well each employee is performing in order to reward those who are effective, improve the performance of those who are ineffective, or provide a written justification for why the poor performer should be disciplined. Through job analysis, the organization can identify the behaviors and results that distinguish effective performance from ineffective performance.[23]

Career Planning. Career planning entails matching an individual's skills and aspirations with opportunities that are or may become available in the organization. This matching process requires that those in charge of career planning know the skill requirements of the various jobs. This allows them to guide individuals into jobs in which they will succeed and be satisfied.

Job Evaluation. The process of job evaluation involves assessing the relative dollar value of each job to the organization to set up internally equitable pay structures. If pay structures are not equitable, employees will be dissatisfied and quit, or they will not see the benefits of striving for promotions. To put dollar values on jobs, it is necessary to get information about different jobs to determine which jobs deserve higher pay than others.[24]

The Importance of Job Analysis to Line Managers

Job analysis is clearly important to the HR department's various activities, but it may not be as clear why it is important to line managers. There are many reasons. First, managers must have detailed information about all the jobs in their work group to understand the work-flow process. Earlier in this chapter we noted the importance of understanding the work-flow process—specifically, identifying the tasks performed and the knowledge, skills, and abilities required to perform them. In addition, an understanding of this work-flow process is essential if a manager chooses to redesign certain aspects to increase efficiency or effectiveness.

Second, managers need to understand the job requirements to make intelligent hiring decisions. Very seldom do employees get hired by the human resource department without a manager's input. Managers will often interview prospective applicants and recommend who should receive a job offer. However, if the manager does not clearly understand what tasks are performed on the job and the skills necessary to perform them, the hiring decision may result in employees whom the manager "likes" but who are not capable of performing the job successfully.

Third, a manager is responsible for ensuring that each individual is performing satisfactorily (or better). This requires the manager to evaluate how well each person is performing and to provide feedback to those whose performance needs improvement. Again, this requires that the manager clearly understand the tasks required in every job.

Job Analysis Information

Nature of Information

Job description
A list of the tasks, duties, and responsibilities that a job entails.

Two types of information are most useful in job analysis: job descriptions and job specifications. A **job description** is a list of the tasks, duties, and responsibilities (TDRs) that a job entails. TDRs are observable actions. For example, a clerical job requires the jobholder to type. If you were to observe someone in that position for a day, you would certainly see some typing. When a manager attempts to evaluate job performance, it is most important to have detailed information about the work performed in the job (that is, the TDRs). This makes it possible to determine how well an individual is meeting each job requirement. Table 4.1 shows a sample job description.

TABLE 4.1
A Sample Job Description

Job Title: Maintenance Mechanic
General Description of Job: General maintenance and repair of all equipment used in the operations of a particular district. Includes the servicing of company vehicles, shop equipment, and machinery used on job sites.

1. *Essential Duty (40%): Maintenance of Equipment*
   Tasks: Keep a log of all maintenance performed on equipment. Replace parts and fluids according to maintenance schedule. Regularly check gauges and loads for deviances that may indicate problems with equipment. Perform nonroutine maintenance as required. May involve limited supervision and training of operators performing maintenance.
2. *Essential Duty (40%): Repair of Equipment*
   Tasks: Requires inspection of equipment and a recommendation that a piece be scrapped or repaired. If equipment is to be repaired, mechanic will take whatever steps are necessary to return the piece to working order. This may include a partial or total rebuilding of the piece using various hand tools and equipment. Will primarily involve the overhaul and troubleshooting of diesel engines and hydraulic equipment.
3. *Essential Duty (10%): Testing and Approval*
   Tasks: Ensure that all required maintenance and repair has been performed and that it was performed according to manufacturer specifications. Approve or reject equipment as being ready for use on a job.
4. *Essential Duty (10%): Maintain Stock*
   Tasks: Maintain inventory of parts needed for the maintenance and repair of equipment. Responsible for ordering satisfactory parts and supplies at the lowest possible cost.

Nonessential Functions
Other duties as assigned.

A **job specification** is a list of the knowledge, skills, abilities, and other characteristics (KSAOs) that an individual must have to perform the job. *Knowledge* refers to factual or procedural information that is necessary for successfully performing a task. A *skill* is an individual's level of proficiency at performing a particular task. *Ability* refers to a more general enduring capability that an individual possesses. Finally, *other characteristics* might be personality traits such as one's achievement motivation or persistence. Thus KSAOs are characteristics about people that are not directly observable; they are observable only when individuals are carrying out the TDRs of the job. If someone applied for the clerical job discussed, you could not simply look at the individual to determine whether he or she possessed typing skills. However, if you were to observe that individual typing something, you could assess the level of typing skill. When a manager is attempting to fill a position, it is important to have accurate information about the characteristics a successful jobholder must have. This requires focusing on the KSAOs of each applicant. The "Competing by Meeting Stakeholders' Needs" box illustrates the unique KSAOs of graveyard-shift workers.

Job specification
A list of the knowledge, skills, abilities, and other characteristics (KSAOs) that an individual must have to perform a job.

Sources of Job Analysis Information

In performing the job analysis, one question that often arises is, Who should make up the group of incumbents that are responsible for providing the job analysis information? Whatever job analysis method you choose, the process of job analysis entails

COMPETING BY MEETING STAKEHOLDERS' NEEDS

Staying Alive on the Graveyard Shift: Beyond the Traditional KSAOs

One area where it is difficult to balance the needs of employers, employees, and consumers is where there is a need to run operations 24 hours a day. For example, employers may have expensive equipment that for efficiency's sake cannot lie idle overnight. In other cases, the need is generated by consumers who demand services around the clock, such as security or health care. The increased globalization of work also means that consumers or coworkers are sometimes in different time zones, which can generate non-traditional working hours.

When the job description entails working night shifts, the job specifications have to reflect this. Human beings are not nocturnal animals, so working at night is not a natural activity for most people. Virtually all of the body's functions are influenced by circadian rhythms regulated by an internal biological clock. This internal clock, in turn, is influenced by patterns of sunlight and darkness, and when the two are not synchronized, bodily functions become impaired. Indeed, evidence suggests that people working the graveyard shift between 10 to 11 P.M. and 6 to 7 A.M. are more likely to have health problems than other employees doing the same work. These problems include fatigue, sleeping disorders, depression, obesity, some types of cancer, and increased risk of coronary disease. People who work at night have also been found to be more accident-prone and have higher absenteeism and turnover rates.

Fortunately, however, there seems to be wide variability in how people respond to this disruptive activity, and if this is taken into consideration when writing job specifications, some of these problems may be reduced. Research shows that people who are effective working at night tend to share a number of characteristics. First, they are "night owls," meaning that left on their own, they prefer to sleep late in the morning and stay up until very late at night. Second, they tend to be people who can sleep easily at different times of the day and like to take naps. Third, they exercise regularly and hence do not compound the physical problems associated with night work with problems caused by inactive lifestyles. Finally, effective shift workers either have few inflexible nonwork responsibilities (such as child day care) or have a dedicated support network that allows them to work irregular hours. Thus, when it comes to working the graveyard shift, worker health depends a great deal on developing the right job specifications, and dealing with nocturnality may be the most critical KSAO.

SOURCE: G. Koretz, "Perils of the Graveyard Shift: Poor Health and Low Productivity," *Business Week* (March 10, 1997), p. 22; C.R. Maiwald, J.L. Pierce, and J.W. Newstrom, "Workin' 8 P.M. to 8 A.M. and Lovin' Every Minute of It," *Workforce*, July 1997, pp. 30–36.

obtaining information from people familiar with the job. We refer to these people as *subject-matter experts* because they are experts in their knowledge of the job.

In general, it will be useful to go to the job incumbent to get the most accurate information about what is actually done on the job. This is especially the case when it is difficult to monitor the person who does the job. (As the "Competing through High-Performance Work Systems" box shows, this is becoming more prevalent with today's technology.) However, particularly when the job analysis will be used for compensation purposes, incumbents might have an incentive to exaggerate their duties. Thus, you will also want to ask others familiar with the job, such as supervisors,

COMPETING THROUGH HIGH-PERFORMANCE WORK SYSTEMS

Telework

Prior to the Industrial Revolution, most people worked either close to or inside their own homes. However, mass production technologies changed all this, separating work life from home life, as people began to travel to centrally located factories and offices. As we enter the new millennium, however, skyrocketing office space prices combined with drastically reduced prices for portable electronic computing and communication devices seem ready to reverse this trend. The broad term for doing one's work away from a centrally located office is *telework.* Studies reveal that the cost savings from such programs can top $8,000 per employee annually. Not surprisingly, given these savings, the number of teleworkers has increased dramatically over the past few years. It has been estimated that over 10 million U.S. workers now fall under this heading.

For example, at IBM, a program was initiated where each teleworker was supplied with an IBM ThinkPad Notebook Computer with a modem, fax card, mobility software, and printer as well as an extra home telephone line. Marketing employees were also supplied with cellular telephones, alphanumeric pagers, fax machines, and personal copiers. All of these workers gave up dedicated office space at IBM headquarters and instead worked either in a small shared office space (allocated on a first-come/first-served basis), at home, or (better yet) at a customer's site. Because leases at different offices were up at different times, IBM could compare the effect of telework arrangements on a large number of outcomes, where the first workers whose jobs were converted were compared to workers doing the same work in a traditional office (whose lease had not yet expired).

The results of this experiment showed that productivity for teleworkers was significantly higher than for traditional workers, especially among women. Most of this came about by reducing wasted commuting time as well as eliminating distractions caused by working in a traditional office. Part of this productivity gain also resulted from the flexibility that allowed people to work when they were at their peak efficiency (late at night or early in the morning for some) and work around nonwork obligations (such as caring for a sick child). On the negative side, some teleworkers perceived that this type of arrangement hindered teamwork; they felt isolated from informal networks of communication and missed the mentoring opportunities that went along with traditional office work. Most interestingly, some teleworkers felt that the arrangements actually made it harder to balance home and work. Many had relied on time and distance to clearly differentiate when they were engaging in one role versus another (worker versus parent) and then struggled with this distinction when time and distance were removed. Thus, as we noted at the outset of this chapter, there is no one best way of designing work. While telecommuting may improve some outcomes, it has a negative impact on others.

SOURCE: M. Werner, "Working at Home—the Right Way to Be a Star in Your Bunny Slippers," *Fortune* (March 3, 1997), pp. 165–66; P. Coy, "Home Sweet Office," *Business Week* (April 6, 1998), p. 30; E.J. Hill, B.C. Miller, S.P. Weiner, and J. Colihan, "Influences of the Virtual Office on Aspects of Work and Work/Life Balance," *Personnel Psychology* 51 (1998), pp. 667–83.

to look over the information generated by the job incumbent. This serves as a check to determine whether what is being done is congruent with what is supposed to be done in the job. Although job incumbents and supervisors are the most obvious and frequently used sources of job analysis information, other sources can be helpful, particularly for service jobs.

It is important to understand the usefulness of different sources of job analysis information because this information is only as good as the source. Research has revealed some interesting findings regarding various sources of job analysis information, particularly regarding job incumbents and supervisors.

One question is whether supervisors and incumbents agree in their job analysis ratings. Some research has demonstrated significant differences in the job analysis ratings provided from these two different sources.[25] However, other research has found greater agreement between supervisors and subordinates when rating general job duties than when rating specific tasks.[26] One conclusion that can be drawn from this research is that incumbents may provide the most accurate estimates of the actual time spent performing job tasks. However, supervisors may be a more accurate source of information about the importance of job duties.

Another question is whether a job incumbent's own performance level is related to the job analysis ratings. Although it is intuitively appealing to think that individuals who perform well in a job might give different ratings than individuals who do not perform well, research has not borne this out. One frequently cited study compared the job analysis ratings of effective and ineffective managers and found that they tended to give the same ratings despite their performance level.[27] However, more recent research has also examined the relationship between job analysis and employee performance. In this research no differences were observed between high and low performers regarding the tasks and KSAOs generated, the ratings made regarding the time spent, or importance of the tasks.[28] However, differences have been observed in the types of critical incidents generated[29] and the ratings of the level of effectiveness of various incidents.[30] Thus, research at present seems inconclusive regarding the relationship between the performance level of the job analyst and the job analysis information she or he provides.

Although the relationship between job analysis ratings and job performance is inconclusive, research has strongly demonstrated some demographic differences in job analysis information. One study found differences between males and females and between blacks and whites in the importance and time-spent ratings for a variety of tasks.[31] Similarly, another study observed minor differences between males and females and between blacks and whites in job analysis ratings. However, in this study larger differences in ratings were the result of the experience level of the job incumbent.[32] These research results imply that when conducting a job analysis, you should take steps to ensure that the incumbent group responsible for generating the job analysis information represents a variety of gender, racial, and experience-level categories.

Job Analysis Methods

There are various methods for analyzing jobs and no "one best way." In this section we discuss three methods for analyzing jobs: the position analysis questionnaire, the task analysis inventory, and the job analysis system. Although most managers may not have time to use each of these techniques in the exact manner suggested, the three provide some anchors for thinking about broad approaches, task-focused approaches, and person-oriented approaches to conducting job analysis.

Position Analysis Questionnaire (PAQ)

We lead this section off with the PAQ because this is one of the broadest and most well-researched instruments for analyzing jobs. Moreover, its emphasis on inputs, processes, relationships, and outputs is consistent with the work flow analysis approach that we used in leading off this chapter (Figure 4.1).

The PAQ is a standardized job analysis questionnaire containing 194 items.[33] These items represent work behaviors, work conditions, and job characteristics that can be generalized across a wide variety of jobs. They are organized into six sections:

1. *Information input*—Where and how a worker gets information needed to perform the job.
2. *Mental processes*—The reasoning, decision making, planning, and information processing activities that are involved in performing the job.
3. *Work output*—The physical activities, tools, and devices used by the worker to perform the job.
4. *Relationships with other persons*—The relationships with other people required in performing the job.
5. *Job context*—The physical and social contexts where the work is performed.
6. *Other characteristics*—The activities, conditions, and characteristics other than those previously described that are relevant to the job.

The job analyst is asked to determine whether each item applies to the job being analyzed. The analyst then rates the item on six scales: extent of use, amount of time, importance to the job, possibility of occurrence, applicability, and special code (special rating scales used with a particular item). These ratings are submitted to the PAQ headquarters, where a computer program generates a report regarding the job's scores on the job dimensions.

Research has indicated that the PAQ measures 32 dimensions and 13 overall dimensions of jobs (listed in Table 4.2) and that a given job's scores on these dimensions can be very useful. The significant database has linked scores on certain dimensions to scores on subtests of the General Aptitude Test Battery (GATB). Thus knowing the dimension scores provides some guidance regarding the types of abilities that are necessary to perform the job. Obviously, this technique provides information about the work performed in a format that allows for comparisons across jobs, whether those jobs are similar or dissimilar. Another advantage of the PAQ is that it covers the work context as well as inputs, outputs, and processes. (As the "Competing

TABLE 4.2
Overall Dimensions of the Position Analysis Questionnaire

Overall Dimensions
Decision/communication/general responsibilities
Clerical/related activities
Technical/related activities
Service/related activities
Regular day schedule versus other work schedules
Routine/repetitive work activities
Environmental awareness
General physical activities
Supervising/coordinating other personnel
Public/customer/related contact activities
Unpleasant/hazardous/demanding environment
Nontypical work schedules

COMPETING THROUGH GLOBALIZATION

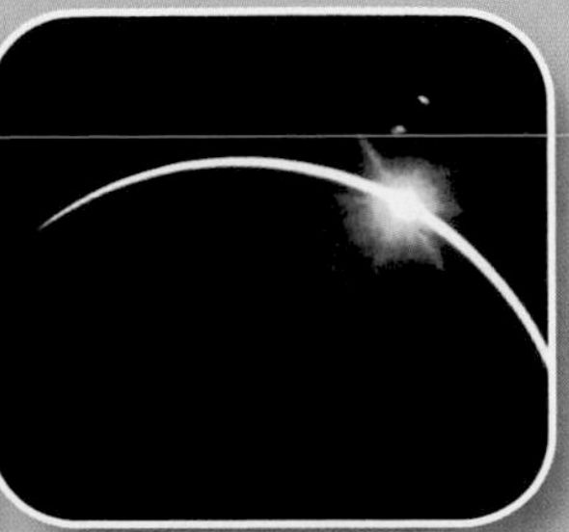

Eliminating Sweatshops at Nike: Just Do It—But How?

Over the past decade, Nike has been one of the most profitable companies in the United States. However, at a time when the company's spokesperson, Michael Jordan, was bringing in over $10 million, the young, mostly women workers in its Indonesian plants were taking home only $2.23 a day. Moreover, working conditions in Nike's Serang plant, 50 miles west of Jakarta, were far from ideal. Hundreds of workers, some children, were crowded into vast sheds where they glued, stitched, pressed, and boxed 70 million pairs of shoes a year. Overtime was mandatory for most workers, and severe forms of punishment were meted out to any worker who missed quantity or quality goals. Collusion between local management and government made organizing workers into unions both difficult and dangerous, and the high level of unemployment left workers powerless. Taken together, these labor practices helped keep costs so low and quality so high that a pair of running shoes that sells for $75 retail in the United States costs just $18.25 to manufacture.

With this type of cost and price structure, it is easy to see how Nike became so profitable. However, the ability to sustain these practices became an issue in 1996 when the U.S. media exposed these sweatshop conditions. As consumers became increasingly aware of how their sneakers were actually being made, some felt guilty, and human rights groups went so far as to organize boycotts of Nike products. Given the damage to Nike's image and future profitability, something had to be done.

At first, Nike CEO Phillip Knight defended his operations, noting that Nike pays its workers no less than its rivals do and that these workers make more than minimum wage in the host countries. Critics countered that the level of pay was below the subsistence level and much lower than what is paid by other U.S. companies such as Coca-Cola, Gillette, and Goodyear.

To end this image problem once and for all, on May 12, 1998, Knight pledged to (a) raise the minimum worker age requirement, (b) adopt U.S.-style safety and health standards, and (c) allow human rights groups to help monitor working conditions in all foreign plants. He again showed his commitment to reform six months later by raising wages 22 percent to offset the currency devaluation that rocked Indonesia in the fall of 1998. Knight used both occasions to challenge his competitors to do the same, realizing that their failure to do so would put Nike at a competitive disadvantage. Although it is currently unclear how these competitors will respond, it is obvious that Nike is at least trying to establish its image as a trendsetter in both footwear and working conditions in international locations.

SOURCE: M.L. Clifford, "Pangs of Conscience over Sweatshops," *BusinessWeek* (July 29, 1996), p. 38; L. Himelstein, "Nike Hasn't Scrubbed Its Image Yet," *BusinessWeek* (July 7, 1997), p. 44; A. Bernstein, "Nike Finally Does It," *BusinessWeek* (May 25, 1998), p. 46; A. Bernstein, "A Floor under Foreign Factories," *BusinessWeek* (November 2, 1998), pp. 126–27.

through Globalization" box shows, the context in which work takes place is the subject of much attention in recent years.)

In spite of its widespread use, the PAQ is not without problems. One problem is that to fill out the test, an employee needs the reading level of a college graduate; this disqualifies some job incumbents from the PAQ. In fact, it is recommended that only job analysts trained in how to use the PAQ should complete the questionnaire, rather than job incumbents or supervisors.[34] A second problem associated with the PAQ is that its general, standardized format leads to rather abstract characterizations of jobs. Thus it does not lend itself well to describing the specific, concrete task activities that comprise the actual job, and it is not ideal for developing job descriptions or redesigning jobs. Methods that do focus on this aspect of the work are needed if this is the goal.

Task Analysis Inventory

The **task analysis inventory** refers to several different methods, each with slight variations. However, common to these approaches is the focus on analyzing all the tasks performed in the focal job. (It is not uncommon to have over 100 tasks.)

Task analysis inventory
The process of identifying the tasks, knowledge, skills and behaviors that need to be emphasized in training.

For example, the task inventory–CODAP method[35] entails asking subject matter experts (SMEs) to generate a list of the tasks performed in a job. Once this list has been developed, the SMEs rate each task on dimensions such as the relative amount of time spent on the task, the frequency of task performance, the relative importance of the task, the relative difficulty of the task, and whether the task can be learned on the job relatively quickly. These ratings are then subjected to the CODAP computer program that organizes the tasks into dimensions of similar tasks.

Task inventories focus on providing detailed information about the work performed in a given job. The detail of the information can be helpful in developing both selection exam plans and performance appraisal criteria. Although a task inventory might indirectly suggest the types of KSAOs people might need to perform the job, these KSAOs do not come directly out of the process. Thus other approaches that do put the focus squarely on the people requirement associated with jobs have been developed.

Fleishman Job Analysis System[36]

Another job analysis technique that elicits information about the worker's characteristics is the Fleishman Job Analysis System (FJAS). This approach defines *abilities* as enduring attributes of individuals that account for differences in performance. The system is based on a taxonomy of abilities that adequately represent all the dimensions relevant to work. This taxonomy includes 52 cognitive, psychomotor, physical, and sensory abilities, listed in Table 4.3.[37]

The actual FJAS scales consist of descriptions of the ability, followed by behavioral benchmark examples of the different levels of the ability along a seven-point scale. An example of the written comprehension ability scale from the FJAS is presented in Figure 4.6.

In using the job analysis technique, SMEs are presented with each of the 52 scales. These experts indicate the point on the scale that best represents the level of that ability required in a particular job. These ratings provide an accurate picture of the ability requirements of the job. Substantial research has shown the value of this general approach for human resource activities such as career development, selection, and training.[38]

Dynamic Elements of Job Analysis

Although we tend to view jobs as static and stable, in fact, jobs tend to change and evolve over time. Those who occupy or manage the jobs often make minor, cumulative adjustments to the job that try to match either changing conditions in the environment or personal preferences for how to conduct the work.[39] Indeed, although

TABLE 4.3

Abilities Included in the Fleishman Job Analysis System

1. Oral comprehension	27. Arm–hand steadiness
2. Written comprehension	28. Manual dexterity
3. Oral expression	29. Finger dexterity
4. Written expression	30. Wrist–finger speed
5. Fluency of ideas	31. Speed of limb movement
6. Originality	32. Static strength
7. Memorization	33. Explosive strength
8. Problem sensitivity	34. Dynamic strength
9. Mathematical reasoning	35. Trunk strength
10. Number facility	36. Extent flexibility
11. Deductive reasoning	37. Dynamic flexibility
12. Inductive reasoning	38. Gross body coordination
13. Information ordering	39. Gross body equilibrium
14. Category flexibility	40. Stamina
15. Speed of closure	41. Near vision
16. Flexibility of closure	42. Far vision
17. Spatial orientation	43. Visual color discrimination
18. Visualization	44. Night vision
19. Perceptual speed	45. Peripheral vision
20. Selective attention	46. Depth perception
21. Time sharing	47. Glare sensitivity
22. Control precision	48. Hearing sensitivity
23. Multilimb coordination	49. Auditory attention
24. Response orientation	50. Sound localization
25. Rate control	51. Speech recognition
26. Reaction time	52. Speech clarity

there are numerous sources for error in the job analysis process,[40] most inaccuracy is likely to result from job descriptions simply being outdated. For this reason, in addition to statically defining the job, the job analysis process must also detect changes in the nature of jobs.

For example, in today's world of rapidly changing products and markets, some people have begun to question whether the concept of the job is simply a social artifact that has outlived its usefulness. Indeed, many researchers and practitioners are pointing to a trend referred to as "dejobbing" in organizations. This trend consists of viewing organizations as a field of work needing to be done rather than a set of discrete jobs held by specific individuals. For example, at Amazon.com, HR director Scott Pitasky notes, "Here, a person might be in the same 'job,' but three months later be doing completely different work."[41] This means Amazon.com puts more emphasis on broad worker specifications ("entrepreneurial and customer-focused") than on detailed job descriptions ("HTML programming") that may not be descriptive one year down the road. This change in the nature of work is not unique to this industry, and as the "Competing in the New Economy" box on page 158 shows, has required major changes in our thinking about the best way to match people to jobs.

These changes in the nature of work and expanded use of "project-based" organizational structures require the type of broader understanding that comes from an analysis of work flows. Because the work can change so rapidly and it is impossible to rewrite job descriptions every week, more flexibility is needed in the writing of job descriptions and specifications. However, legal requirements (as discussed in Chapter 3)

FIGURE 4.6
Example of an Ability from the Fleishman Job Analysis System

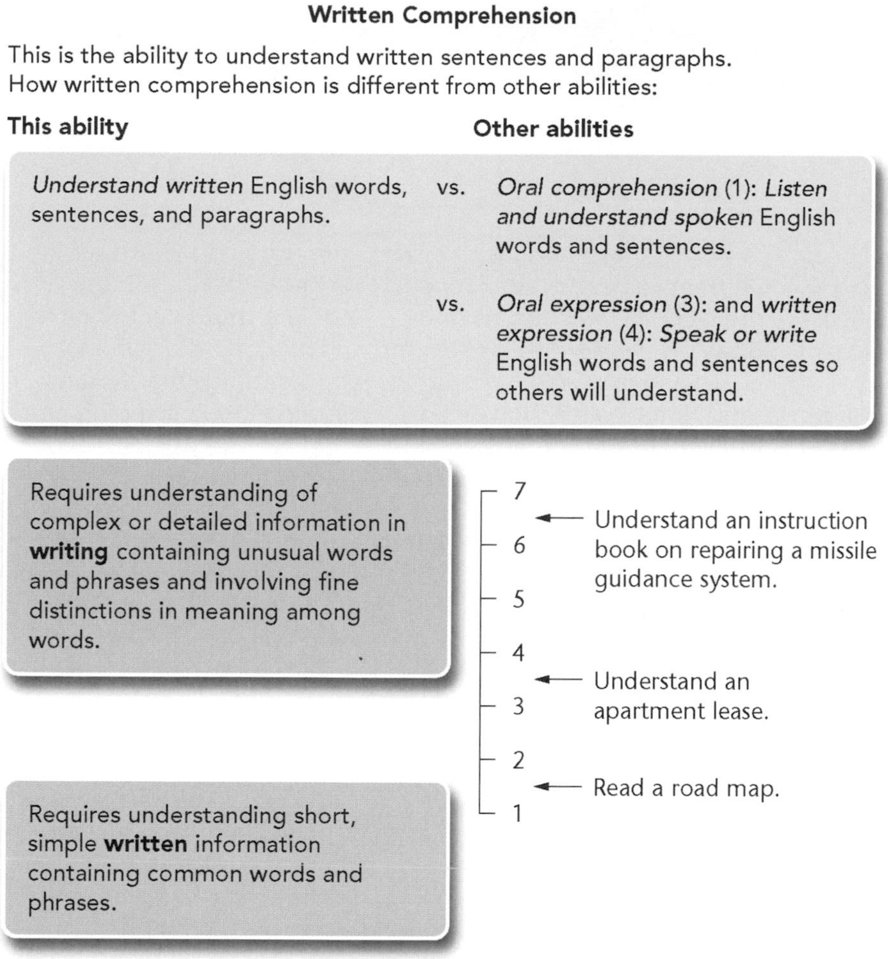

Written Comprehension

This is the ability to understand written sentences and paragraphs.
How written comprehension is different from other abilities:

This ability		Other abilities
Understand written English words, sentences, and paragraphs.	vs.	*Oral comprehension* (1): *Listen and understand spoken* English words and sentences.
	vs.	*Oral expression* (3): and *written expression* (4): *Speak or write* English words and sentences so others will understand.

Requires understanding of complex or detailed information in **writing** containing unusual words and phrases and involving fine distinctions in meaning among words.

- 7
- ← Understand an instruction book on repairing a missile guidance system.
- 6
- 5
- 4
- ← Understand an apartment lease.
- 3
- 2
- ← Read a road map.
- 1

Requires understanding short, simple **written** information containing common words and phrases.

SOURCE: E.A. Fleishman and M. D. Mumford, "Evaluating Classifications of Job Behavior: A Construct Validation of the Ability Requirements Scales," *Personnel Psychology* 44 (1991), pp. 523–76. The complete set of ability requirement scales, along with instructions for their use, may be found in E.A. Fleishman, *Fleishman Job Analysis Survey* (F-JAS) (Palo Alto, CA: Consulting Psychologists Press, 1992). Used with permission.

may discourage firms from writing flexible job descriptions. Thus firms seeking to use their employees as a source of competitive advantage must balance the need for flexibility with the need for legal documentation. This presents one of the major challenges faced by HRM departments in the next decade. Rather than a passive, job-analytic approach, these types of changes require an active approach to job design such as those discussed in our next section.

Job Design

So far we have approached the issue of managing work in a passive way, focusing only on understanding what gets done, how it gets done, and the skills required to get it done. Although this is necessary, it is a very static view of jobs, in that jobs must already exist and that they are already assumed to be structured in the one best way.

COMPETING IN THE NEW ECONOMY

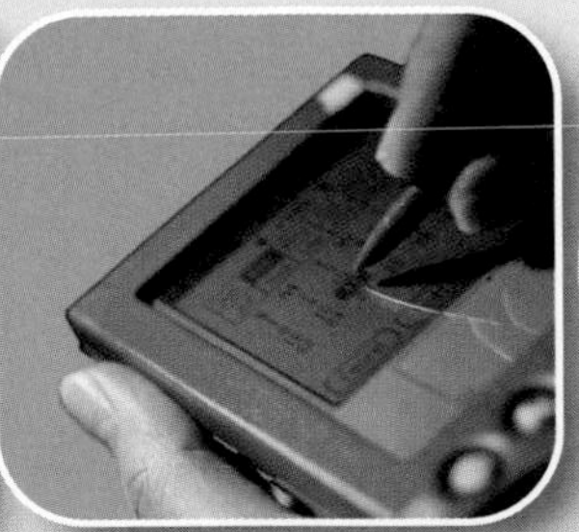

O*NET: A Framework for Jobs in the 21st Century

The Dictionary of Occupational Titles (DOT) was born during the 1930s as a vehicle for helping the new public employment system link the demand for skills and the supply of skills in the U.S. workforce. Given the high unemployment rate during the Great Depression, federal intervention was perceived as being necessary to help create a match between workers and employers. The DOT described over 12,000 jobs, as well as some of the requirements of successful job incumbents. The DOT was used by both public employment agencies and private employers to help efficiently staff jobs. It was also a valuable source for workers because it listed the skills and educational requirements they would need to have or develop for certain occupations.

Although this system served the country well for over 60 years, it became clear to U.S. Department of Labor officials that jobs in the new economy were so qualitatively different that the DOT no longer served its purpose. Technological changes in the nature of work, global competition, and a shift from stable, fixed manufacturing jobs to a more flexible, dynamic, service-based economy were quickly making the system obsolete.

For all these reasons, the Department of Labor abandoned the DOT in 1998 and developed an entirely new system for classifying jobs: the Occupational Information Network or O*NET. Instead of relying on fixed job titles and narrow task descriptions, the O*NET uses a common language that generalizes across jobs to describe the abilities, work styles, work activities, and work context required for various occupations that are more broadly defined (instead of the 12,000 jobs in the DOT, the O*NET will eventually describe only 1,000 occupations).

It is still being developed, but the O*NET is already being used by many employers and employment agencies. For example, after closing its Seattle-based headquarters, Boeing used the O*NET system to help find new jobs for the workers who were laid off because of the impending move. The state of Texas has used the O*NET to identify emerging occupations within the state whose requisite knowledge, skills, and abilities are underrepresented in the current occupational system. This information will be used to help train Texas residents for the jobs of the future. Finally, educational organizations like the Boys and Girls Club of America have used the O*NET to help design activities for children from disadvantaged backgrounds that would improve their standing on skills that are likely to be needed by future employers.

Although these examples show its value for employers, the O*NET was also designed to help job seekers. To see if you think this new system meets the goal of promoting "the effective education, training, counseling, and employment needs of the American workforce," visit its website yourself at **http://online.onetcenter.org** and see if the skills it lists for your current job or your dream job match what you know from your own experiences and expectations.

SOURCE: N.G. Peterson, M.D. Mumford, W.C. Borman, P.R. Jeanneret, and E.A. Fleishman, *An Occupational Information System for the 21st Century: The Development of O*NET* (Washington, DC: American Psychological Association, 1999); N.G. Peterson, M.D. Mumford, W.C. Borman,. P.R. Jeanneret, E.A. Fleishman, K.Y. Levin, M.A. Campion, M.S. Mayfield, F. P. Morgenson, K. Pearlman, M.K. Gowing, A.R. Lancaster, M.B. Silver, and D.M. Dye, "Understanding Work Using the Occupational Information Network (O*NET): Implications for Practice and Research," *Personnel Psychology* 54 (2001), pp. 451–92; S. Holmes, "Lots of Green Left in the Emerald City," *BusinessWeek Online* (March 28, 2000); D. Dyer, "O*NET in Action," O*NET online website.

However, a manager may often be faced with a situation in which the work unit does not yet exist, requiring jobs within the work unit to be designed from scratch. Sometimes work loads within an existing work unit are increased, or work group size is decreased while the same work load is required, a trend increasingly observed with the movement toward downsizing.[42] Finally, sometimes the work is not being performed in the most efficient manner. In these cases, a manager may decide to change the way that work is done in order for the work unit to perform more effectively and efficiently. This requires redesigning the existing jobs.

Job design is the process of defining how work will be performed and the tasks that will be required in a given job. **Job redesign** refers to changing the tasks or the way work is performed in an existing job. To effectively design jobs, one must thoroughly understand the job as it exists (through job analysis) and its place in the larger work unit's work-flow process (work-flow analysis). Having a detailed knowledge of the tasks performed in the work unit and in the job, a manager then has many alternative ways to design a job. This can be done most effectively through understanding the trade-offs between certain design approaches.

Job design
The process of defining the way work will be performed and the tasks that will be required in a given job.

Job redesign
The process of changing the tasks or the way work is performed in an existing job.

Research has identified four basic approaches that have been used among the various disciplines (such as psychology, management, engineering, and ergonomics) that have dealt with job design issues.[43] Although these four approaches comprehensively capture the historical approaches to this topic, one still needs to go below the category level to get a full appreciation of the exact nature of jobs and how they can be changed.[44] All jobs can be characterized in terms of how they fare according to each approach; thus a manager needs to understand the trade-offs of emphasizing one approach over another. In the next section we discuss each of these approaches and examine the implications of each for the design of jobs. Table 4.4 displays how jobs are characterized along each of these dimensions.

Finding and Keeping the Best Employees

One job that seems to be increasingly viewed as intrinsically satisfying to people these days is teaching. Many workers who have been laid off from the private sector, particularly in the wake of the September 11th, 2001, tragedy are looking for more meaningful work. The opportunity to work with young people in a learning context where one has some control over his or her work seems to meet this need for many. Between October 2000 and October 2001, while corporate employment contracted, the labor force for teachers expanded by 3 percent.

For example, when Patrick Bernhardt was laid off from his marketing executive position in a failing dot-com start-up, he seized the chance to switch fields and become a teacher. Bernhardt now teaches computer science at John Muir Middle School and is taking education classes at night in order to qualify for a teaching license. Employers that cannot compete for employees by paying them exorbitant salaries may be able to offset this by offering more intrinsically satisfying jobs. Bernhardt took a 50 percent pay cut when he switched jobs, noting, "This is the hardest thing I've ever done, but the sense of satisfaction makes it worth it."

SOURCE: P. Gogoi, "Going to the Head of the Class," *Business Week* (December 10, 2001), pp. 53–54.

Mechanistic Approach

The mechanistic approach has roots in classical industrial engineering. The focus of the mechanistic approach is identifying the simplest way to structure work that

TABLE 4.4

Characterizing Jobs on Different Dimensions of Job Design

The motivational job design approach

1. *Autonomy:* Does the job allow freedom, independence, or discretion in work scheduling, sequence, methods, procedures, quality control, and other types of decisions?
2. *Intrinsic job feedback:* Do the work activities themselves provide direct, clear information about the effectiveness (in terms of quality and quantity) of job performance?
3. *Extrinsic job feedback:* Do other people in the organization (such as managers and coworkers) provide information about the effectiveness (in terms of quality and quantity) of job performance?
4. *Social interaction:* Does the job provide for positive social interaction (such as teamwork or coworker assistance)?
5. *Task/goal clarity:* Are the job duties, requirements, and goals clear and specific?
6. *Task variety:* Does the job have a variety of duties, tasks, and activities?
7. *Task identity:* Does the job require completion of a whole and identifiable piece of work? Does it give the incumbent a chance to do an entire piece of work from beginning to end?
8. *Ability/skill-level requirements:* Does the job require a high level of knowledge, skills, and abilities?
9. *Ability/skill variety:* Does the job require a variety of types of knowledge, skills, and abilities?
10. *Task significance:* Is the job significant and important compared with other jobs in the organization?
11. *Growth/learning:* Does the job allow opportunities for learning and growth in competence and proficiency?

The mechanistic job design approach

1. *Job specialization:* Is the job highly specialized in terms of purpose and/or activity?
2. *Specialization of tools and procedures:* Are the tools, procedures, materials, etc., used on this job highly specialized in terms of purpose?
3. *Task simplification:* Are the tasks simple and uncomplicated?
4. *Single activities:* Does the job require the incumbent to do only one task at a time? Does it not require the incumbent to do multiple activities at one time or in very close succession?
5. *Job simplification:* Does the job require relatively little skill and training time?
6. *Repetition:* Does the job require performing the same activity or activities repeatedly?
7. *Spare time:* Is there very little spare time between activities on this job?
8. *Automation:* Are many of the activities of this job automated or assisted by automation?

continued

SOURCE: Reprinted from *Organizational Behavior,* Winter 1987, M. A. Campion, et al., "Job Design: Approaches, Outcomes, and Trade-Offs." Copyright © 1987, with permission of Elsevier Science.

maximizes efficiency. This most often entails reducing the complexity of the work to provide more human resource efficiency—that is, making the work so simple that anyone can be trained quickly and easily to perform it. This approach focuses on designing jobs around the concepts of task specialization, skill simplification, and repetition.

TABLE 4.4
Characterizing Jobs on Different Dimensions of Job Design *(concluded)*

The biological job design approach
1. *Strength:* Does the job require fairly little muscular strength?
2. *Lifting:* Does the job require fairly little lifting, and/or is the lifting of very light weights?
3. *Endurance:* Does the job require fairly little muscular endurance?
4. *Seating:* Are the seating arrangements on the job adequate (with ample opportunities to sit, comfortable chairs, good postural support, etc.)?
5. *Size difference:* Does the workplace allow for all size differences between people in terms of clearance, reach, eye height, leg room, etc.?
6. *Wrist movement:* Does the job allow the wrists to remain straight, without excessive movement?
7. *Noise:* Is the workplace free from excessive noise?
8. *Climate:* Is the climate at the workplace comfortable in terms of temperature and humidity, and is it free of excessive dust and fumes?
9. *Work breaks:* Is there adequate time for work breaks given the demands of the job?
10. *Shift work:* Does the job not require shift work or excessive overtime?
The perceptual–motor job design approach
1. *Lighting:* Is the lighting in the workplace adequate and free from glare?
2. *Displays:* Are the displays, gauges, meters, and computerized equipment used on this job easy to read and understand?
3. *Programs:* Are the programs in the computerized equipment for this job easy to learn and use?
4. *Other equipment:* Is the other equipment (all types) used on this job easy to learn and use?
5. *Printed job materials:* Are the printed materials used on this job easy to read and interpret?
6. *Workplace layout:* Is the workplace laid out so that the employee can see and hear well enough to perform the job?
7. *Information input requirements:* Is the amount of attention needed to perform this job fairly minimal?
8. *Information output requirements:* Is the amount of information that the employee must output on this job, in terms of both action and communication, fairly minimal?
9. *Information-processing requirements:* Is the amount of information that must be processed, in terms of thinking and problem solving, fairly minimal?
10. *Memory requirements:* Is the amount of information that must be remembered on this job fairly minimal?
11. *Stress:* Is there relatively little stress on this job?
12. *Boredom:* Are the chances of boredom on this job fairly small?

Scientific management was one of the earliest and best-known statements of the mechanistic approach.[45] According to this approach, productivity could be maximized by taking a scientific approach to the process of designing jobs. Scientific management first sought to identify the "one best way" to perform the job. This entailed performing time-and-motion studies to identify the most efficient movements for workers to make. Once the best way to perform the work is identified, workers should be selected based on their ability to do the job, they should be trained in the standard "one best way" to perform the job, and they should be offered monetary incentives to motivate them to work at their highest capacity.

The scientific management approach was built upon in later years, resulting in a mechanistic approach that calls for jobs to be designed so that they are very simple and lack any significant meaningfulness. By designing jobs in this way, the organization reduces its need for high-ability individuals and thus becomes less dependent on individual workers. Individuals are easily replaceable—that is, a new employee can be trained to perform the job quickly and inexpensively. The Chinese factories that we discussed in our "Competing through Globalization" box on page 141 epitomize the mechanistic approach to job design.

Motivational Approach

The motivational approach to job design has roots in organizational psychology and management literature and, in many ways, emerged as a reaction to mechanistic approaches to job design. It focuses on the job characteristics that affect psychological meaning and motivational potential, and it views attitudinal variables (such as satisfaction, intrinsic motivation, job involvement, and behavioral variables such as attendance and performance) as the most important outcomes of job design. The prescriptions of the motivational approach focus on increasing the complexity of jobs through such interventions as job enlargement, job enrichment, and the construction of jobs around sociotechnical systems.[46] Accordingly, a study of 213 different jobs found that the motivational attributes of jobs were positively related to the mental ability requirements of workers in those jobs.[47]

An example of the motivational approach is Herzberg's Two-Factor theory, which argues that individuals are motivated more by intrinsic aspects of work such as the meaningfulness of the job content than by extrinsic characteristics such as pay.[48] Herzberg argued that the key to motivating employees was not through monetary incentives but through the redesign of jobs to make their work more meaningful.

A more complete model of how job design affects employee reactions is the "Job Characteristics Model."[49] According to this model, jobs can be described in terms of five characteristics. *Skill variety* is the extent to which the job requires a variety of skills to carry out the tasks. *Task identity* is the degree to which a job requires completing a "whole" piece of work from beginning to end. *Task significance* is the extent to which the job has an important impact on the lives of other people. *Autonomy* is the degree to which the job allows an individual to make decisions about the way the work will be carried out. *Feedback* is the extent to which a person receives clear information about performance effectiveness from the work itself.

These five job characteristics determine the motivating potential of a job by affecting the three critical psychological states of "experienced meaningfulness," "responsibility," and "knowledge of results." According to the model, when the core job characteristics (and thus the critical psychological states) are high, individuals will have a high level of internal work motivation. This is expected to result in higher quantity and quality of work as well as higher levels of job satisfaction.[50]

Job design interventions emphasizing the motivational approach tend to focus on increasing the motivating potential of jobs. Much of the work on job enlargement (broadening the types of tasks performed), job enrichment (empowering workers by adding more decision-making authority to jobs), and self-managing work teams has its roots in the motivational approach to job design. The critical psychological state one needs to create in the mind of the job incumbent is that the work is meaningful and that it contributes to accomplishing goals that are important to the individual.[51] Thus, although at some point it might be necessary to pay workers, it is even more important to show job incumbents why their jobs are important.

Biological Approach

The biological approach to job design comes primarily from the sciences of biomechanics (*i.e.*, the study of body movements), work physiology, and occupational medicine, and it is usually referred to as *ergonomics*. **Ergonomics** is concerned with examining the interface between individuals' physiological characteristics and the physical work environment. The goal of this approach is to minimize physical strain on the worker by structuring the physical work environment around the way the human body works. It therefore focuses on outcomes such as physical fatigue, aches and pains, and health complaints.

Ergonomics
The interface between individuals' physiological characteristics and the physical work environment.

The biological approach has been applied in redesigning equipment used in jobs that are physically demanding. Such redesign is often aimed at reducing the physical demands of certain jobs so that anyone can perform them. In addition, many biological interventions focus on redesigning machines and technology, such as adjusting the height of the computer keyboard to minimize occupational illnesses (like carpal tunnel syndrome). The design of chairs and desks to fit posture requirements is very important in many office jobs and is another example of the biological approach to job design. For example, one study found that having employees participate in an ergonomic redesign effort significantly reduced the number and severity of cumulative trauma disorders, lost production time, and restricted duty days.[52]

Often redesigning work to make it more worker-friendly also leads to increased efficiencies. For example, at International Truck and Engine Corporation, one of the most difficult aspects of truck production was pinning the axles to the truck frame. Traditionally, the frame was lowered onto the axle and a crew of six people, armed with oversized hammers and crowbars, forced the frame onto the axle. Because the workers could not see the bolts they had to tighten under the frame, the bolts were often not fastened properly, and many workers injured themselves in the process. After a brainstorming session, the workers and engineers figured that it would be better to flip the frame upside down and attach the axles from above instead of below. The result was a job that could be done twice as fast by half as many workers, who were much less likely to make mistakes or get injured.[53]

Similarly, at 3M's plant in Tonawanda, New York, the company spent $60,000 on new ramps and forklifts specifically to help its aging workers lift crates filled with the company's product. The crates weighed over 125 pounds and were the source of numerous employee complaints. The result of this change in work processes was that productivity went up (expressed in terms of time to load trucks) and worker compensation claims in the factory went to zero in the next year—down from an average of 20 over the last five years. These positive outcomes far outstripped the cost of the changes, again illustrating how a change aimed at improving the work from an ergonomic point of view often leads to cost savings as well.[54]

Because of the new Occupational Safety Health and Administration (OSHA) regulations that went into effect in 2001, one can expect that a number of employers will soon be looking to achieve the same kind of results from ergonomically focused changes in jobs. In particular, the regulations identify five specific high-risk work practices that employers need to avoid, including jobs that require a person to (a) use a keyboard for four hours straight without a break, (b) lift more than 75 pounds, (c) kneel or squat for more than two hours a day, (d) work with the back, neck, or wrists bent more than two hours a day, or (e) use large vibrating equipment such as chainsaws or jackhammers more than 30 minutes a day.[55] Although these new rules are controversial and may change over time, the fact that employers need to be vigilant about opportunities to improve the design of work for the benefit of both workers and shareholders is not likely to change.[56]

Perceptual–Motor Approach

The perceptual–motor approach to job design has roots in human-factors literature.[57] Whereas the biological approach focuses on physical capabilities and limitations, the perceptual–motor approach focuses on human mental capabilities and limitations. The goal is to design jobs in a way that ensures they do not exceed people's mental capabilities and limitations. This approach generally tries to improve reliability, safety, and user reactions by designing jobs to reduce their information-processing requirements. In designing jobs, one looks at the least capable worker and then constructs job requirements that an individual of that ability level could meet. Similar to the mechanistic approach, this approach generally decreases the job's cognitive demands.

Jobs such as air traffic controller, oil refinery operator, and quality control inspector require a large amount of information processing. Many clerical and assembly-line jobs, on the other hand, require very little information processing. However, in designing all jobs, managers need to be aware of the information-processing requirements and ensure that these requirements do not exceed the capabilities of the least capable person who could potentially be performing the job.[58]

Trade-Offs among Different Approaches to Job Design

A recent stream of research has aimed at understanding the trade-offs and implications of these different job design strategies.[59] Many authors have called for redesigning jobs according to the motivational approach so that the work becomes more psychologically meaningful. However, one study examined how the various approaches to job design are related to a variety of work outcomes. Table 4.5 summarizes the results. For example, in this study, job incumbents expressed higher satisfaction with jobs scoring high on the motivational approach. Also, jobs scoring high on the biological approach were ones for which incumbents expressed lower physical requirements. Finally, the motivational and mechanistic approaches were negatively related to each other, suggesting that designing jobs to maximize efficiency very likely results in a lower motivational component to those jobs.

Another recent study demonstrated that enlarging clerical jobs made workers more satisfied, less bored, more proficient at catching errors, and better at providing customer service. However, these enlarged jobs also had costs, such as higher training requirements, higher basic skill requirements, and higher compensation requirements based on job evaluation compensable factors.[60] Again, it is important to recognize the trade-off between the motivational value of jobs and the efficiency with which the jobs are performed.

Finally, research has examined how job design approaches relate to compensation. Starting from the assumption that job evaluation (the process of determining the worth of jobs to organizations) links job design and market forces, researchers examined the relationship between job design approaches and both job evaluation results and pay. They found that jobs high on the motivational approach had higher job

TABLE 4.5
Summary of Outcomes from the Job Design Approaches

JOB DESIGN APPROACH	POSITIVE OUTCOMES	NEGATIVE OUTCOMES
Motivational	Higher job satisfaction Higher motivation Greater job involvement Higher job performance Lower absenteeism	Increased training time Lower utilization levels Greater likelihood of error Greater chance of mental overload and stress
Mechanistic	Decreased training time Higher utilization levels Lower likelihood of error Less chance of mental overload and stress	Lower job satisfaction Lower motivation Higher absenteeism
Biological	Less physical effort Less physical fatigue Fewer health complaints Fewer medical incidents Lower absenteeism Higher job satisfaction	Higher financial costs because of changes in equipment or job environment
Perceptual–motor	Lower likelihood of error Lower likelihood of accidents Less chance of mental overload and stress Lower training time Higher utilization levels	Lower job satisfaction Lower motivation

SOURCE: Reprinted from *Organizational Behavior,* Winter 1987, M. A. Campion, et al., "Job Design: Approaches, Outcomes, and Trade-Offs." Copyright © 1987, with permission of Elsevier Science.

evaluation scores representing higher skill requirements and that these jobs had higher pay levels. Jobs high on the mechanistic and perceptual–motor dimensions had lower skill requirements and correspondingly lower wage rates. Finally, jobs high on the biological dimension had lower physical requirements and had a weak positive relationship to wage rates. Thus, it seems reasonable to conclude that jobs redesigned to increase the motivating potential result in higher costs in terms of ability requirements, training, and compensation.[61]

To summarize, in designing jobs it is important to understand the trade-offs inherent in focusing on one particular approach to job design. Managers who seek to design jobs in a way that maximizes all the outcomes for jobholders and the organization need to be aware of these different approaches, understand the costs and benefits associated with each, and balance them appropriately to give the organization a competitive advantage.

A Look Back

The chapter opening of IBM showed how drastically restructuring the nature of work could increase both the effectiveness and efficiency of operations. The specific changes in how work was designed created a better fit between the organization and its environment, as well as between the organization and its internal strategy.

Questions

1. Based on this chapter, how would you characterize the changes that were made in terms of the degree of centralization and departmentalization?
2. What would be some characteristics of the environments or internal strategy that might force a different firm to move in the opposite structural direction?
3. How would each of these changes in structure "trickle down" and affect the jobs of individual workers?

Summary

The analysis and design of work is one of the most important components to developing and maintaining a competitive advantage. Strategy implementation is virtually impossible without thorough attention devoted to work-flow analysis, job analysis, and job design. Managers need to understand the entire work-flow process in their work unit to ensure that the process maximizes efficiency and effectiveness. To understand this process, managers also must have clear, detailed information about the jobs that exist in the work unit, and the way to gain this information is through job analysis. Equipped with an understanding of the work-flow process and the existing job, managers can redesign jobs to ensure that the work unit is able to achieve its goals while individuals within the unit benefit on the various work outcome dimensions such as motivation, satisfaction, safety, health, and achievement. This is one key to competitive advantage.

Discussion Questions

1. Assume you are the manager of a fast food restaurant. What are the outputs of your work unit? What are the activities required to produce those outputs? What are the inputs?
2. Based on Question 1, consider the cashier's job. What are the outputs, activities, and inputs for that job?
3. Consider the "job" of college student. Perform a job analysis on this job. What are the tasks required in the job? What are the knowledge, skills, and abilities necessary to perform those tasks? What environmental trends or shocks (like computers) might change the job, and how would that change the skill requirements?
4. Discuss how the following trends are changing the skill requirements for managerial jobs in the United States: (a) increasing use of computers, (b) increasing international competition, (c) increasing work–family conflicts.
5. Why is it important for a manager to be able to conduct a job analysis? What are the negative outcomes that would result from not understanding the jobs of those reporting to the manager?
6. What are the trade-offs between the different approaches to job design? Which approach do you think should be weighted most heavily when designing jobs?
7. For the cashier job in Question 2, which approach to job design was most influential in designing that job? In the context of the total work-flow process of the restaurant, how would you redesign the job to more heavily emphasize each of the other approaches?

Web Exercise

The Center for Office Technology is a national group of employers, manufacturers, and associations dedicated to improving the office work environment. Visit the website at **www.cot.org**. Review the information available on the home page. Click on the "2000 Outstanding Office Ergonomics Program Winners." The names of the two organizations who received this award are shown. Click on the name of one of the organizations to see the steps they took to improve the office environment.

Questions

1. What is ergonomics? Why is it important?

2. In this chapter we discuss four different job design dimensions: motivational, mechanistic, biological, and perceptual–motor. What steps did the company take to improve each of these job design dimensions?
3. What role did this organization play in the development of the new OSHA regulations mentioned in this chapter?

Managing People: From the Pages of *BusinessWeek*

BusinessWeek The New Factory Worker

Fred Price gropes his way downstairs in the dark, grabs a Danish, and races off to work at 4 A.M. Today is a special day for the 29-year-old North Carolina factory hand. On the job, he will schedule orders as usual for the tiny tool-and-die shop where he doubles as a supervisor when he's not bending metal himself. But at midday, test results are coming in from the state Labor Department in Raleigh. These aptitude exams for all 43 workers at Northeast Tool & Manufacturing Co., outside Charlotte, measure everything from math and mechanical skills to leadership and adaptability. And they come with a prescription. Now it appears that Price will have to pull back from the bird hunting a little and spend less time with the kids' go-cart. Like tens of thousands of factory workers across America, Fred Price is going back to school.

Growing up, Price liked to work with his hands more than his head. He would help his father fix the family's old Ford pickup, and once they rigged up a hydraulic log splitter. In high school, he excelled in shop class but sat toward the back in English and math. These days, in an economy where even factory work increasingly is defined by blips on a computer screen, more schooling is the only road ahead. Northeast Tool, for one, will use the employee tests over the next several months to develop customized training for each worker. Some will enroll at a nearby community college. Others will take remote courses through computers set up at the plant. A few will attend afternoon classes with professors brought right into the mill. Price wants to pursue a two-year degree in metallurgy, even if it means putting in long hours on weekends. "Someday I hope to manage the plant," he says.

Until recently, Americans often divided ranks in high school between shop kids such as Price, who went on to industrial or service work, and college-bound students headed for white-collar or professional jobs. They parted ways at graduation and would move into distinct categories of manual and knowledge workers.

But over the past decade, thinned-out ranks of managers have been equipping factory workers with industrial robots and teaching them to use computer controls to operate massive steel casters and stamp presses. At the same time, managers are funneling reams of information through the computers, bringing employees into the data loop. Workers are trained to watch inventories, to know suppliers and customers, costs and prices. Knowledge that long separated brain workers from hand workers is now available via computer on the factory floor. At Northeast Tool, Rusty Arant, Fred Price's manager, points to a powerful computer he rigged up to a milling machine and says, "I crammed it with memory because I want these guys to be managing the business from the shop floor."

The trend toward high-skills manufacturing began in the mid-1980s with innovative companies such as Corning, Motorola, and Xerox. They replaced rote assembly-line work with an industrial vision that requires skilled and nimble workers to think while they work. In the 1990s, what was once the industrial avant-garde is now mainstream as its practices spread across the manufacturing sector. Large, old-line companies finally are learning the lesson that investments in training boost productivity, often at less cost than capital investments. And as the big guys push suppliers and subcontractors on quality, price, and just-in-time delivery, even little shops such as Northeast Tool see high skills as essential for competition.

The result is an intensifying transformation of the American factory. The ranks of manufacturers that put a majority of their workers through different types of training have doubled or tripled in the past decade, according to surveys of large companies by the University of California's Center for Effective Organizations. At the same time, the share of the country's 19 million factory workers with a year or two of college has jumped to 25 percent vs. 17 percent in 1985, according to the Bureau of Labor Statistics. An additional 19 percent have college diplomas today, up from 16 percent a decade ago. "There's a real rise in companies' willingness to invest in their workforces," says Pamela J. Tate, president of the Council for Adult & Experiential Learning, a Chicago consulting group.

This investment, though, carries a none-too-subtle message for America's manufacturing workers: Hone your skills or risk being left behind. U.S. workers are being pushed to raise their technical savvy to the level of the best Japanese and German workers. At the same time, many are being asked to develop leadership skills and to take a role in managing that's rare in the top-down structures found in Asia and Europe.

Indeed, the old formula of company loyalty, a strong back, and showing up on time no longer guarantees job security or even a decent paycheck. Today industrial workers will thrive only if they use their wits and keep adding to their skills base. It's a rich irony: Millions of Americans who headed for the factory because they didn't like school, among other reasons, are now faced with a career-long dose of it. "It isn't whether you can hoist 100-pound sacks anymore," says Anthony Carnevale, a training expert at Educational Testing Service in Princeton, N.J. "Most of the work is mental."

Demanding as it is, the high-skills factory represents blue-collar America's best hope for retaining high wages in a world teeming with workers. Across the economy, in manufacturing and services alike, there has been a surge in demand for higher skills as employers reorganize work around new technologies and human capital investments. Recently the pressure for more capable workers has even begun to generate skills shortages in pockets around the country.

But many companies still need to catch up: Only 10 to 20 percent of large companies have adopted high-performance techniques, surveys show, including a third of large manufacturers, according to the National Association of Manufacturers. Others are actually going in the opposite direction. In industries as diverse as apparel making, telemarketing, and chicken processing, many employers continue to slice pay, avoid unions, and outsource work to lower-wage subcontractors. These trends have led to a growing inequality along skill and education lines, similar to the one cleaving society at large. So far, the net result has weighed more heavily downward, even in manufacturing, where average pay lagged inflation by 3 percent from 1989 to 1995, according to the BLS.

In this cutthroat environment, an individual worker's best chance of getting ahead now lies in advancing his or her skills whenever the opportunity arises. And plenty of workers are jumping at the chance. From downsized defense industry hands in Long Beach, California, to white-smocked pharmaceutical workers in the Delaware Valley, they are studying for new factory jobs.

This even includes veterans in old-line smokestack companies. Take Adlai John Warner, 44, who put in 25 years at Acme Metal Inc., a specialty steelmaker outside Chicago. Warner always enjoyed learning and was quick with facts—quick enough to be given top security clearance as a U.S. Marine intelligence specialist in Vietnam. He had planned to attend college when he returned to Chicago after the war. Instead, he started a family and wound up making good money as a laborer at Acme.

Warner found the work tedious. Acme, like most other manufacturers, was organized for a low-skilled force and used Warner's body but not much of his brain. Even after he jumped a few rungs on the job ladder by apprenticing as a pipe fitter, the work required more endurance than thought. Warner describes long empty days of sitting around, waiting for pipe-fitting jobs, making time and a half with gobs of overtime. Despite pay that eventually reached $60,000 a year, the boredom prompted Warner to pursue a bachelor's degree in psychology at night at Chicago State University in the hopes of moving into human resources. He got his BA in 1978, but it never led anywhere.

Meanwhile, the world was closing in on Acme. Low-cost minimills and foreign mills threatened its niche in super-high-carbon steel, which is used in knife blades, tools, and critical machine parts. Its old equipment was falling apart. In 1994 management launched a $400 million redesign of the mill with a high-tech German caster—an audacious move for a $560 million company. But operation of the finicky caster, which converts molten steel into a two-inch–thick band, is fast and dangerous. If workers can't make quick decisions, they risk a "breakout," when hot liquid steel spills from the mold all over the machinery. To date, only minimill leader Nucor Corp. and its offspring, Steel Dynamics Inc., with skilled and flexible workforces, have made money with the new technology.

In effect, Acme is betting the company on its workers' brains—and Warner has leaped at the opportunity. Last year, the company brought in scads of consultants to test those who volunteered among its 1,100 unionized ranks. They used an exhaustive battery of exams to look for reading, math, technical, and communication skills. Some workers weren't interested and took early retirement. About 750 were chosen to create an entirely new, team-oriented system. Warner qualified for an advanced job as a maintenance technician and last September promptly hit the books.

Acme set up classroom trailers next to the mill and brought in teachers from Detroit, Georgia, even Germany. The company paid Warner and 130 others to spend nine months, full-time, learning everything from metallurgy, math, and computers to a piece-by-piece study of the new machinery. The total cost to upgrade the workforce, including employee salaries, came to some $8 million, or just 2 percent of the amount Acme spent on the new caster. "We're being exposed to things we've never been exposed to before," says Warner appreciatively.

Warner and his colleagues also are involved in reinventing Acme's entire work system. In the spring, he and five other workers were selected to sit down with managers and consultants for weeks on end at a nearby Ramada Inn. There, they hung poster paper all over the walls and blackboards, marking up a scheme for the new workplace, from devising a pay system pegged to profits to redefining supervisors' roles. "The people working there have to make the decisions," says Anthony C. Capito, Acme's vice president for steel production. The new system, including the training received by Warner and his colleagues, will be put to the test when the new caster is brought on line this fall.

Workers at small manufacturers are facing similar tests. In 1985, when the then 18-year-old Fred Price landed his job at Northeast Tool, the job shop sold custom-made metal pieces primarily to local Carolina customers. Today, as regional markets meld into national and global ones, Northeast must boost quality enough to land contracts from the likes of BMW and Siemens. These companies want metal fashioned to precise tolerances that only statistical quality control methods can achieve. Many demand that suppliers be certified to tough European standards, a goal Northeast is pursuing.

All this requires more training than Price, a high school graduate, had gained through work experience. For him, the payoff comes in getting a shot at advancement and improving his $15-an-hour pay. From manager Arant's perspective, there's no choice at all. Arant plans to use his higher-skilled workforce to bid for more lucrative business and expand. If he didn't, Northeast could fall behind, as Arant thinks some rivals may do. "They'll run the machines as long as they can and then close," he predicts.

Until recently, workers such as Price probably would have been out of luck. Northeast, a flyspeck of a company with annual revenues of less than $5 million, simply wouldn't have had the wherewithal to launch its ambitious training program. And many companies, large and small, were loath to invest too much in workers, only to lose them later. Now, though, more companies feel they can't afford not to train. And Northeast, like other small companies, has been able to tap into a growing network of local and state training initiatives. Often these are cobbled together with regional or state development funds and community college training programs.

As a result, Northeast is spending just $35,000 for its entire training plan. North Carolina has set up programs to assist small companies and has helped out with staff advice, software, and access to the nearby community college. Such state programs are growing fast. "If we don't invest in higher skills, we relegate ourselves to low-wage jobs," says Eric Butler, president of Bay States Skills Corp., which coordinates training programs in Boston.

The education message rings so loudly today that some job seekers actually target high-performance employers just to get the schooling. In fact, in the post–cold war era, such companies are replacing the military as a blue-collar training ground and a way to get some college education, or its equivalent, inexpensively. Many companies are willing to sink money into training if they feel confident the employee has the profile of a lifelong learner. "We look for people who want change, who don't see it as troublesome, but as an opportunity," says David P. Jones, an official of Aon Consulting, a Chicago firm that assists manufacturers in testing and hiring.

Questions

1. Examine the changes that have been made in Fred Price's job at Northeast Tool, and then compare these to the four types of job design approaches described earlier in this chapter. If we had before-and-after measures on each of the four approaches, which would have revealed the largest change in the content of the job and which would have revealed the least: motivational, mechanistic, biological, or perceptual–motor? Knowing what you do about the trade-offs for various changes in job design, what negative outcomes might we fear from the types of changes brought about at Northeast?
2. Technological changes, like the robotization of operations at Northeast Tool, can affect the structure of organizations, which in turn can change the level of skill requirements for workers. How did robotization affect the structure of Northeast Tool and the skill requirements for Fred Price's job? Can you think of other technological advancements that have resulted in the opposite effects on worker skill requirements (such as in the fast food or retail industries)? In what sense does the competitive strategy employed by the firm influence in which direction technology is likely to affect skill levels of workers?
3. As we will see throughout this text, globalization has widespread effects on human resource practices. To what extent were the changes in jobs that came about at Northeast Tool driven by factors outside the United States? If companies like Northeast Tool did not make these types of changes to compete, what other changes might they have had to make? If Fred Price was not willing to make the types of self-improvements he is making, what other types of changes might he have had to accept? What are the national implications of these kinds of changes, and how do these changes relate to the competitive advantage of nations like the United States?

SOURCE: Reprinted from Sept. 30, 1996 issue of *BusinessWeek* by special permission.

Notes

1. J. Galbraith and R. Kazanjian, *Strategy Implementation: Structure, Systems, and Process* (St. Paul, MN: West Publishing, 1986).
2. D. Ilgen and J. Hollenbeck, "The Structure of Work: Job Design and Roles," in *Handbook of Industrial & Organizational Psychology*, 2nd ed., ed. M. Dunnette and L. Hough (Palo Alto, CA: Consulting Psychologists Press, 1991), pp. 165–208.

3. R. Harvey, "Job Analysis," in ibid., pp. 71–164.
4. R. Griffin, *Task Design: An Integrative Approach* (Glenview, IL: Scott Foresman, 1982).
5. B. Brocka and M.S. Brocka, *Quality Management: Implementing the Best Ideas of the Masters* (Homewood, IL: Business One Irwin, 1992).
6. R. Pritchard, D. Jones, P. Roth, K. Stuebing, and S. Ekeberg, "Effects of Group Feedback, Goal Setting, and Incentives on Organizational Productivity," *Journal of Applied Psychology* 73 (1988), pp. 337–60.
7. D. Bowen and E. Lawler, "Total Quality-Oriented Human Resources Management," *Organizational Dynamics* (1992), pp. 29–41.
8. M. Fefer, "Bill Gates' Next Challenge," *Fortune* (December 14, 1992), pp. 30–41.
9. D. Little, "Even the Supervisor Is Expendable: The Internet Allows Factories to Be Managed from Anywhere," *Business Week* (July 23, 2001), p. 78.
10. M.G. Morris and V. Venkatesh, "Age Differences in Technology Adoption Decisions: Implications for a Changing Workforce," *Personnel Psychology* 53 (2000), pp. 375–403.
11. G.L. Stewart and M.R. Barrick, "Team Structure and Performance: Assessing the Mediating Role of Intrateam Process and the Moderating Role of Task Type," *Academy of Management Journal* 43 (2000), pp. 135–48.
12. G.S. Van der Vegt, B.J.M. Emans, and E. Van de Vliert, "Patterns of Interdependence in Work Teams: A Two-Level Investigation of the Relations with Job and Team Satisfaction," *Personnel Psychology* 54 (2001), pp. 51–70.
13. M. Schminke, M.L. Ambrose, and R.S. Cropanzano, "The Effect of Organizational Structure on Perceptions of Procedural Fairness," *Journal of Applied Psychology* 85 (2000), pp. 294–304.
14. M. Moeller, "Remaking Microsoft: Why America's Most Successful Company Needed an Overhaul," *Business Week* (May 17, 1999), pp. 106–14.
15. K. Rebello, "Visionary-in-Chief: A Talk with Bill Gates on the World beyond Windows," *Business Week* (May 17, 1999), pp. 114–16.
16. E. McCormick, "Job and Task Analysis," in *Handbook of Industrial & Organizational Psychology*, ed. M. Dunnette (Chicago: Rand McNalley, 1976), pp. 651–96.
17. E. Primoff and S. Fine, "A History of Job Analysis," in *The Job Analysis Handbook for Business, Industry, and Government*, ed. S. Gael (New York: Wiley, 1988), pp. 14–29.
18. W. Cascio, *Applied Psychology in Personnel Management*, 4th ed. (Englewood Cliffs, NJ: Prentice-Hall, 1991).
19. P. Wright and K. Wexley, "How to Choose the Kind of Job Analysis You Really Need," *Personnel*, May 1985, pp. 51–55.
20. J. Walker, *Human Resource Strategy* (New York: McGraw-Hill, 1992).
21. R. Gatewood and H. Feild, *Human Resource Selection*, 2nd ed. (Hinsdale, IL: Dryden, 1990).
22. I. Goldstein, *Training in Organizations*, 3rd ed. (Pacific Grove, CA: Brooks/Cole, 1993).
23. K. Murphy and J. Cleveland, *Performance Appraisal: An Organizational Perspective* (Boston: Allyn & Bacon, 1991).
24. R. Harvey, L. Friedman, M. Hakel, and E. Cornelius, "Dimensionality of the Job Element Inventory (JEI): A Simplified Worker-Oriented Job-Analysis Questionnaire," *Journal of Applied Psychology* 73 (1988), pp. 639–46.
25. A. O'Reilly, "Skill Requirements: Supervisor–Subordinate Conflict," *Personnel Psychology* 26 (1973), pp. 75–80.
26. J. Hazel, J. Madden, and R. Christal, "Agreement between Worker–Supervisor Descriptions of the Worker's Job," *Journal of Industrial Psychology* 2 (1964), pp. 71–79.
27. K. Wexley and S. Silverman, "An Examination of Differences between Managerial Effectiveness and Response Patterns on a Structured Job-Analysis Questionnaire," *Journal of Applied Psychology* 63 (1978), pp. 646–49.
28. P. Conley and P. Sackett, "Effects of Using High- versus Low-Performing Job Incumbents as Sources of Job-Analysis Information," *Journal of Applied Psychology* 72 (1988), pp. 434–37.
29. W. Mullins and W. Kimbrough, "Group Composition as a Determinant of Job-Analysis Outcomes," *Journal of Applied Psychology* 73 (1988), pp. 657–64.
30. N. Hauenstein and R. Foti, "From Laboratory to Practice: Neglected Issues in Implementing Frame-of-Reference Rater Training," *Personnel Psychology* 42 (1989), pp. 359–78.
31. N. Schmitt and S. Cohen, "Internal Analysis of Task Ratings by Job Incumbents," *Journal of Applied Psychology* 74 (1989), pp. 96–104.
32. F. Landy and J. Vasey, "Job Analysis: The Composition of SME Samples," *Personnel Psychology* 44 (1991), pp. 27–50.
33. E. McCormick and R. Jeannerette, "The Position Analysis Questionnaire," in *The Job Analysis Handbook for Business, Industry, and Government*, pp. 880–901.
34. *PAQ Newsletter* (August 1989).
35. E. Primhoff, *How to Prepare and Conduct Job Element Examinations* (Washington, DC: U.S. Government Printing Office, 1975).
36. E. Fleishman and M. Reilly, *Handbook of Human Abilities* (Palo Alto, CA: Consulting Psychologists Press, 1992).
37. E. Fleishman and M. Mumford, "Ability Require-

ments Scales," in *The Job Analysis Handbook for Business, Industry, and Government*, pp. 917–35.

38. R. Christal, *The United States Air Force Occupational Research Project* (AFHRL-TR-73-75) (Lackland AFB, TX: Air Force Human Resources Laboratory, Occupational Research Division, 1974).
39. M.K. Lindell, C.S. Clause, C.J. Brandt, and R.S. Landis, "Relationship between Organizational Context and Job Analysis Ratings," *Journal of Applied Psychology* 83 (1998), pp. 769–76.
40. F.P. Morgeson and M.A. Campion, "Social and Cognitive Sources of Potential Inaccuracy in Job Analysis," *Journal of Applied Psychology* 82 (1997), pp. 627–55.
41. S. Caudron, "Jobs Disappear When Work Becomes More Important," *Workforce*, January 2000, pp. 30–32.
42. K. Cameron, S. Freeman, and A. Mishra, "Best Practices in White Collar Downsizing: Managing Contradictions," *The Executive* 5 (1991), pp. 57–73.
43. M. Campion and P. Thayer, "Development and Field Evaluation of an Interdisciplinary Measure of Job Design," *Journal of Applied Psychology* 70 (1985), pp. 29–34.
44. J.R. Edwards, J.A. Scully, and M.D. Brtek, "The Measurement of Work: Hierarchical Representation of the Multimethod Job Design Questionnaire," *Personnel Psychology* 52 (1999), pp. 305–24.
45. F. Taylor, *The Principles of Scientific Management* (New York: W.W. Norton, 1967) (originally published in 1911 by Harper & Brothers).
46. R. Griffin and G. McMahan, "Motivation through Job Design," in *OB: The State of the Science*, ed. J. Greenberg (Hillsdale, NJ: Lawrence Erlbaum Associates, 1993).
47. M. Campion, "Ability Requirement Implications of Job Design: An Interdisciplinary Perspective," *Personnel Psychology* 42 (1989), pp. 1–24.
48. F. Herzberg, "One More Time: How Do You Motivate Employees?" *Harvard Business Review* 65 (1987), pp. 109–20.
49. R. Hackman and G. Oldham, *Work Redesign* (Boston: Addison-Wesley, 1980).
50. M. Schrage, "More Power to Whom?" *Fortune* (July 23, 2001), p. 270.
51. R.C. Liden, S.J. Wayne, R.T. Sparrowe, "An Examination of the Mediating Role of Psychological Empowerment on the Relations between the Job, Interpersonal Relationships, and Work Outcomes," *Journal of Applied Psychology* 85, pp. 407–16.
52. D. May and C. Schwoerer, "Employee Health by Design: Using Employee Involvement Teams in Ergonomic Job Redesign," *Personnel Psychology* 47 (1994), pp. 861–86.
53. S.F. Brown, "International's Better Way to Build Trucks," *Fortune* (February 19, 2001), pp. 210k–210v.
54. C. Haddad, "OSHA's New Regs Will Ease the Pain—For Everybody," *Business Week* (December 4, 2000), pp. 90–94.
55. G. Flynn, "Now Is the Time to Prepare for OSHA's Sweeping New Ergonomics Standard," *Workforce*, March 2001, pp. 76–77.
56. J. Schlosser, "A Real Pain in the Workplace," *Fortune* (February 19, 2001), p. 246.
57. W. Howell, "Human Factors in the Workplace," in *Handbook of Industrial & Organizational Psychology*, 2nd ed., pp. 209–70.
58. L.C. Buffardi, E.A. Fleishman, R.A. Morath, and P.M. McCarthy, "Relationships between Ability Requirements and Human Errors in Job Tasks," *Journal of Applied Psychology* 85 (2000), pp. 551–64.
59. J.R. Edwards, J.A. Scully, and M.D. Brteck, "The Nature and Outcomes of Work: A Replication and Extension of Interdisciplinary Work-Design Research," *Journal of Applied Psychology* 85 (2000), pp. 860–68.
60. M. Campion and C. McClelland, "Interdisciplinary Examination of the Costs and Benefits of Enlarged Jobs: A Job-Design Quasi-experiment," *Journal of Applied Psychology* 76 (1991), pp. 186–98.
61. M. Campion and C. Berger, "Conceptual Integration and Empirical Test of Job Design and Compensation Relationships," *Personnel Psychology* 43 (1990), pp. 525–53.

5 Chapter
Human Resource Planning and Recruitment

Objectives
After reading this chapter, you should be able to:

1. Discuss how to align a company's strategic direction with its human resource planning.
2. Determine the labor demand for workers in various job categories.
3. Discuss the advantages and disadvantages of various ways of eliminating a labor surplus and avoiding a labor shortage.
4. Describe the various recruitment policies that organizations adopt to make job vacancies more attractive.
5. List the various sources from which job applicants can be drawn, their relative advantages and disadvantages, and the methods for evaluating them.
6. Explain the recruiter's role in the recruitment process, the limits the recruiter faces, and the opportunities available.

While most other airlines were laying off employees in the fall of 2001, Southwest Airlines was able to avoid any layoffs. Other cuts needed to be made, but the employees remained at the forefront of their company. What advantages and disadvantages may occur because of these decisions?

Enter the World of Business

Southwest Airlines: Focused on Take-Offs, Not Layoffs

In the summer of 2001, the airline industry was facing severe problems due to slumping business travel and vacationer demand. In fact, Northwest Airlines announced draconian cuts in both schedules and service; Midway Airlines declared bankruptcy in August of that year, citing "calamitous" decline in air traffic. However, as bad as things were, they soon got worse.

The September 11, 2001, terrorist attacks on New York and Washington, D.C., devastated the whole nation, but few segments of the economy felt the impact as dramatically as the already struggling airline industry. Even after reducing scheduled flights by more than 20 percent, most planes were taking off with fewer than half their seats filled, and airline shares lost a third of their value on the stock exchange. Most airlines needed to cut costs drastically in order to make ends meet, and over 100,000 employees were eventually laid off from American Airlines, United Airlines, US Airways, Continental Airlines, and America West.

Southwest Airlines bucked this trend, however. Indeed, despite the regular ups and downs of the airline industry, in its 30 years of operation, Southwest has never laid off employees; remarkably, it was able to maintain this record even during the difficult Fall 2001 period. Southwest's no-layoff policy is one of the core values that underlie its human resource strategy, and insiders stress that it is one of the main reasons why the Southwest workforce is so fiercely loyal, productive, and flexible.

The high productivity of these workers helps keep labor costs low, and these savings are passed on to consumers in the form of lower prices that are sometimes half those offered by competitors. High levels of job security also promote a willingness on the part of Southwest employees to be innovative on the job without fearing that they will be punished for any mistakes. Southwest also finds that satisfied employees help create satisfied customers and can even help in recruiting new employees when economic conditions are conducive to growth.

In order to keep this perfect no-layoff record in 2001, Southwest executives assembled into an emergency command and control center in Dallas and brainstormed methods other than layoffs that could reduce costs. Decisions were made to delay the planned purchase of new planes, as well as to scrap ongoing plans to renovate the company's headquarters. The company, which had no debt and over a billion dollars in cash, also leaned heavily on this "rainy-day" fund to help get through tough times. It was a difficult and painful process, but as CEO Jim Parker noted, "We are willing to suffer some damage, even to our stock price, to protect the jobs of our people."

SOURCE: M. Arndt, "Suddenly, Carriers Can't Get off the Ground," *BusinessWeek* (September 3, 2001), pp. 36–37; M. Arndt, "What Kind of Rescue?" *BusinessWeek* (October 1, 2001), pp. 36–37; W. Zeller, "Southwest: After Kelleher, More Blue Skies," *BusinessWeek* (April 2, 2001), p. 45; M. Conlin, "Where Layoffs Are a Last Resort," *BusinessWeek* (October 8, 2001), p. 42.

Introduction

As the opening vignette illustrates, employers do not exist in a vacuum. Two of the major ways that societal trends and events affect employers are through (1) consumer markets, which affect the demand for goods and services, and (2) labor markets, which affect the supply of people to produce goods and services. In some cases, as we saw in the opening vignette, an event in the market might drastically alter the demand for labor, leading to a potential labor surplus. In the immediate aftermath of the World Trade Center attacks, most airlines had too many workers given the slack demand for air travel. In other cases, increased demand for a product may result in an organization having a shortage of labor. For example, many information technology jobs go unfilled because the demand for people with these skills outstrips the supply. Reconciling the difference between the supply and demand for labor presents a challenge for organizations, and how they address this will affect their overall competitiveness. Most of the airlines that faced a labor surplus reacted by trimming their workforce. Southwest Airlines, on the other hand, took a different approach—one that has paid off for it in the past in terms of gaining long-term competitive advantage over the airlines.

There are three keys to effectively utilizing labor markets to one's competitive advantage. First, companies must have a clear idea of their current configuration of human resources. In particular, they need to know the strengths and weaknesses of their present stock of employees. Second, organizations must know where they are going in the future and be aware how their present configuration of human resources relates to the configuration that will be needed. Third, where there are discrepancies between the present configuration and the configuration required for the future, organizations need programs that will address these discrepancies. Under conditions of a labor surplus, this may mean creating an effective downsizing intervention. Under conditions of a labor shortage, this may mean waging an effective recruitment campaign.

This chapter looks at tools and technologies that can help an organization develop and implement effective strategies for leveraging labor market "problems" into opportunities to gain competitive advantage. In the first half of the chapter, we lay out the actual steps that go into developing and implementing a human resource plan. Through each section, we focus especially on recent trends and practices (like downsizing, employing temporary workers, and outsourcing) that can have a major impact on the firm's bottom line and overall reputation. In the second half of the chapter, we familiarize you with the process by which individuals find and choose jobs and the role of personnel recruitment in reaching these individuals and shaping their choices.

The Human Resource Planning Process

An overview of human resource planning is depicted in Figure 5.1. The process consists of forecasting, goal setting and strategic planning, and program implementation and evaluation. We discuss each of these stages in the next sections of this chapter.

Forecasting

The first step in the planning process is **forecasting,** as shown in the top portion of Figure 5.1. In personnel forecasting, the HR manager attempts to ascertain the supply of and demand for various types of human resources. The primary goal is to predict areas within the organization where there will be future labor shortages or surpluses.

Forecasting
The attempts to determine the supply of and demand for various types of human resources to predict areas within the organization where there will be future labor shortages or surpluses.

Forecasting, on both the supply and demand sides, can use either statistical methods or judgmental methods. Statistical methods are excellent for capturing historic trends in a company's demand for labor, and under the right conditions they give predictions that are much more precise than those that could be achieved through subjective judgments of a human forecaster. On the other hand, many important events that occur in the labor market, such as the World Trade Center attacks, have no historical precedent; hence, statistical methods that work from historical trends are of little use in such cases. In these situations one must rely on the pooled subjective judgments of experts, and their "best guesses" might be the only source from which to make inferences about the future. Typically, because of the complementary strengths and weaknesses of the two methods, companies that engage in human resource planning use a balanced approach that includes both statistical and judgmental components.

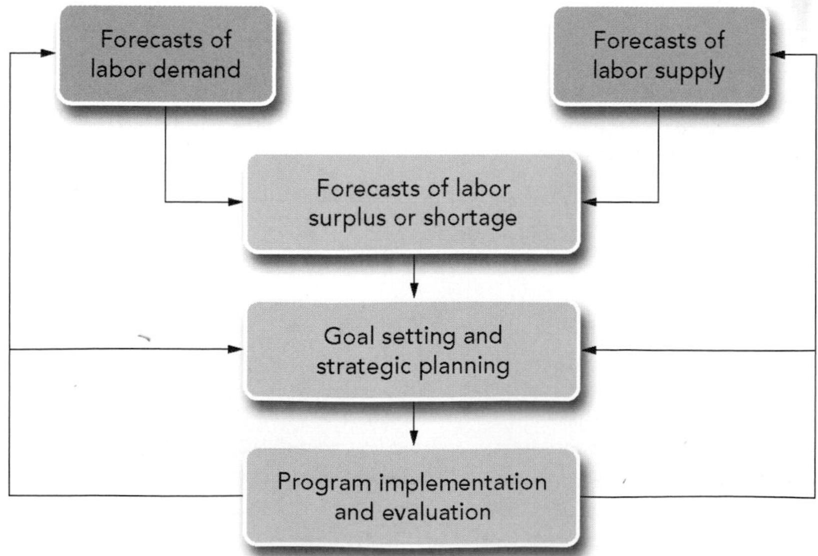

FIGURE 5.1
Overview of the Human Resource Planning Process

Determining Labor Demand

Typically, demand forecasts are developed around specific job categories or skill areas relevant to the organization's current and future state. Once the job categories or skills are identified, the planner needs to seek information that will help predict whether the need for people with those skills or in that job category will increase or decrease in the future. Organizations differ in the sophistication with which such forecasts are derived.

Leading indicator
An objective measure that accurately predicts future labor demand.

At the most sophisticated level, an organization might have statistical models that predict labor demand for the next year given relatively objective statistics on leading indicators from the previous year. A **leading indicator** is an objective measure that accurately predicts future labor demand. For example, a manufacturer of automobile parts that sells its product primarily to the Big Three automakers would use several objective statistics on the Big Three automakers for one time period to predict how much demand there would be for the company's product at a later time period. As shown in Figure 5.2, inventory levels, sales levels, employment levels, and profits at the Big Three in one year might predict the demand for labor in the production assembler job category in the next year.

For example, using historical records, one might use multiple regression techniques to assess the best predictive model for estimating demand for production assemblers from information on sales levels, inventory levels, employment levels, and profits at the Big Three. This is not a statistics book, so a detailed explanation of regression techniques is beyond our scope. Rather, we simply note here that this technique will convert information of four or more leading indicators into a single predicted value for demand for production assemblers that is optimal—at least according to the historical data.

Statistical planning models are useful when there is a long, stable history that can be used to reliably detect relationships among variables. However, these models almost always have to be complemented by subjective judgments of people who have expertise in the area. There are simply too many "once-in-a-lifetime" changes that have to be considered and that cannot be accurately captured in statistical models. For example, our small-parts manufacturer might learn that the leadership at one of the Big Three automakers changed and that the new leadership plans on closing 21 plants over the next 10 years. This event has no historical precedent, so the company might want to consult all its best managers to get their opinions on exactly how much this change would affect the demand for labor in different job categories.

Determining Labor Supply

Once a company has projected labor demand, it needs to get an indicator of the firm's labor supply. Determining the internal labor supply calls for a detailed analysis of how many people are currently in various job categories (or who have specific skills) within

FIGURE 5.2
Leading Indicators of the Demand for Labor for a Hypothetical Auto Parts Manufacturer

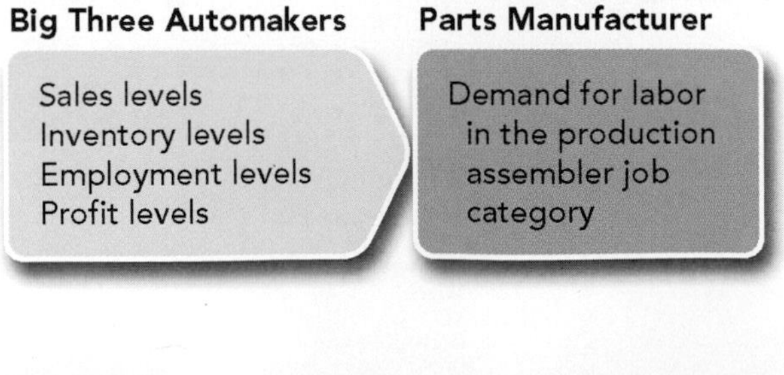

the company. This analysis is then modified to reflect changes in the near future caused by retirements, promotions, transfers, voluntary turnover, and terminations.

As in the case of labor demand, projections for labor supply can be derived either from historical statistical models or through judgmental techniques. One type of statistical procedure that can be employed for this purpose involves transitional matrices. **Transitional matrices** show the proportion (or number) of employees in different job categories at different times. Typically these matrices show how people move in one year from one state (outside the organization) or job category to another state or job category.[1]

Transitional matrix Matrix showing the proportion (or number) of employees in different job categories at different times.

Table 5.1 shows a hypothetical transitional matrix for our parts manufacturer, focusing on seven job categories. Although these matrices look imposing at first, you will see that they are easy to read and use in determining the internal labor supply. A matrix like the one in this table can be read in two ways. First, we can read the rows to answer the question "Where did people in this job category in 1998 go by 2001?" For example, 70 percent of those in the clerical job category (row 7) in 1998 were still in this job category in 2001, and the remaining 30 percent had left the organization. For the production assembler job category (row 6), 80 percent of those in this position in 1998 were still there in 2001. Of the remaining 20 percent, half (10 percent) were promoted to the production manager job category, and the other half (10 percent) left the organization. Finally, 75 percent of those in the production manager job category in 1998 were still there in 2001, while 10 percent were promoted to assistant plant manager and 15 percent left the organization.

Reading these kinds of matrices across rows makes it clear that there is a career progression within this firm from production assembler to production manager to assistant plant manager. Although we have not discussed rows 1 through 3, it might also be noted that there is a similar career progression from sales apprentice to sales representative to sales manager. In this organization, the clerical category is not part of any career progression. That is, this job category does not feed any other job categories listed in Table 5.1.

A transitional matrix can also be read from top to bottom (in the columns) to answer the question "Where did the people in this job category in 2001 come from (Where were they in 1998)?" Again, starting with the clerical job (column 7), 70 percent of the 2001 clerical positions were filled by people who were also in this position in 1998, and the remaining 30 percent were external hires (they were not part of the organization in 1998). In the production assembler job category (column 6),

TABLE 5.1

A Hypothetical Transitional Matrix for an Auto Parts Manufacturer

	2001							
1998	(1)	(2)	(3)	(4)	(5)	(6)	(7)	(8)
(1) Sales manager	.95							.05
(2) Sales representative	.05	.60						.35
(3) Sales apprentice		.20	.50					.30
(4) Assistant plant manager				.90	.05			.05
(5) Production manager				.10	.75			.15
(6) Production assembler					.10	.80		.10
(7) Clerical							.70	.30
(8) Not in organization	.00	.20	.50	.00	.10	.20	.30	

80 percent of those occupying this job in 2001 occupied the same job in 1998, and the other 20 percent were external hires. The most diversely staffed job category seems to be that of production manager (column 5): 75 percent of those in this position in 2001 held the same position in 1998; however, 10 percent were former production assemblers who were promoted, 5 percent were former assistant plant managers who were demoted, and 10 percent were external hires who were not with the company in 1998.

Matrices such as these are extremely useful for charting historical trends in the company's supply of labor. More important, if conditions remain somewhat constant, they can also be used to plan for the future. For example, if we believe that we are going to have a surplus of labor in the production assembler job category in the next three years, we note that by simply initiating a freeze on external hires, the ranks of this position will be depleted by 20 percent on their own. Similarly, if we believe that we will have a labor shortage in the area of sales representatives, the matrix informs us that we may want to (1) decrease the amount of voluntary turnover in this position, since 35 percent of those in this category leave every three years, (2) speed the training of those in the sales apprentice job category so that they can be promoted more quickly than in the past, and/or (3) expand external recruitment of individuals for this job category, since the usual 20 percent of job incumbents drawn from this source may not be sufficient to meet future needs. As with labor demand, historical precedents for labor supply may not always be reliable indicators of future trends. Thus statistical forecasts of labor supply also need to be complemented with judgmental methods.

Determining Labor Surplus or Shortage

Once forecasts for labor demand and supply are known, the planner can compare the figures to ascertain whether there will be a labor shortage or labor surplus for the respective job categories. When this is determined, the organization can determine what it is going to do about these potential problems.

Japan's Matsushita Corporation provides a good example of the benefits of accurate forecasting. Because so many of Matsushita's revenues come from exported products, a leading indicator for its labor demand is the value of the Japanese yen against other currencies. There is a strong negative correlation between the yen and sales because when the value of the yen is high, Matsushita's products are more expensive. This depresses demand for its products and, of course, its demand for Japanese labor.

In 1988 Matsushita's planners anticipated that the price of the yen would rise 30 percent by 1994, leading them to conclude if they did nothing, they would wind up having an oversupply of Japanese labor. Therefore, rather than expanding in Japan, they decided to open "export centers" all over the world. The export centers designed and produced televisions and air conditioners in Malaysia, China, and the United States, and prices of these goods were unaffected by the rising yen. By 1995 it was clear that these projections about the yen were highly accurate, and Matsushita's export centers were doing booming business.[2] Meanwhile, other Japanese companies that failed to accurately predict what would happen with this valuable leading indicator had to lay off workers—an act almost unprecedented in Japan until that time.[3]

Indeed, as the "Competing through Globalization" box shows, Japan has largely abandoned its traditional concept of lifetime employment for workers. Other countries such as France still cling desperately to policies that try to protect their workers from the ebb and flow of labor surpluses and shortage, however, often to the long-term detriment of the workers themselves.

COMPETING THROUGH GLOBALIZATION

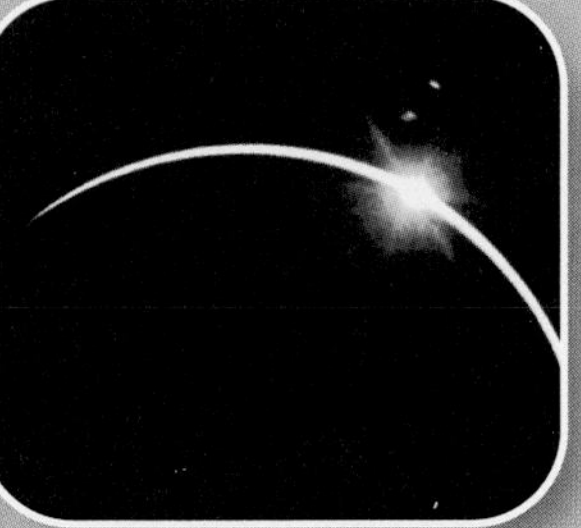

Rethinking Worker Protection: A Tale of Two Nations

At its peak in the mid 1990s, Nissan Motor Company's Murayama plant was a symbol of Japanese automaking efficiency, producing close to a half million cars a year. More recently, it has become a symbol of a new age in Japanese employment relations—when the plant was closed in September 2001 and all 5,000 workers were displaced. This incident and several other well-publicized layoffs at Honda, NEC, Toshiba, Fujitsu, and other large Japanese firms lay to rest the concept of "lifetime employment" that once characterized this country.

Even more remarkably, as Nissan was closing plants in Japan, it was expanding production of its Maxima sedan in Tennessee and was planning a new $1 billion factory to produce minivans and sport utility vehicles in Mississippi. With its home market weak and demand for its product strong in North America, it made sense for Nissan to build cars close to their buyers. Producing in the United States minimizes transportation costs and helps the firm avoid currency fluctuations. Moreover, by closing the Murayama and other less efficient plants, Nissan accelerated operating capacity and boosted profits by 21 percent relative to the same period in the year 2000.

Although moves such as this make clear economic sense, 10 years ago this practice would never have been allowed by government regulations that made worker protection a top priority. In order to climb out of its recent recession, however, Japan is rethinking its past approach and granting corporations increased opportunity to restructure themselves in ways that will promote competitiveness.

This type of open-minded approach is not necessarily spreading to other countries that have traditionally placed a premium on worker protection, however. For example, in France it is very difficult to lay off workers, with labor laws requiring lengthy negotiations and lucrative severance packages for displaced workers. Indeed, when food maker Groupe Danone moved to close two factories that employed fewer than 600 people, protesters marched through Paris calling for a boycott of the company's products.

Handcuffing French employers in this way sometimes appears to be self-defeating, however, when it comes to protecting workers. For example, although authorities were able to repeatedly block Moulinex from closing some of its plants, saving the short-term futures of 800 workers, the firm's standing against international competition continued to erode. In the end, 8,880 workers were displaced in October 2001 when Moulinex went bankrupt, and there was little or nothing the French government could do about that.

SOURCE: I. M. Kunii, "Under the Knife," *BusinessWeek* (September 10, 2001), p. 62; C. Dawson, "Saying Sayonara," *BusinessWeek* (September 24, 2001), pp. 108–109; I. M. Kunii, "Japan's Jobless Need More Than a Handout," *BusinessWeek* (September 24, 2001), p. 110; C. Matlack, "The High Cost of France's Aversion to Layoffs," *BusinessWeek* (November 5, 2001), p. 56.

Goal Setting and Strategic Planning

The second step in human resource planning is goal setting and strategic planning, as shown in the middle of Figure 5.1. The purpose of setting specific quantitative goals is to focus attention on the problem and provide a benchmark for determining the relative success of any programs aimed at redressing a pending labor shortage or surplus. The goals should come directly from the analysis of labor supply and demand and should include a specific figure for what should happen with the job category or skill area and a specific timetable for when results should be achieved.

The auto parts manufacturer, for instance, might set a goal to reduce the number of individuals in the production assembler job category by 50 percent over the next three years. Similarly, the firm might set a goal to increase the number of individuals in the sales representative job category by 25 percent over the next three years.

Once these goals are established, the firm needs to choose from the many different strategies available for redressing labor shortages and surpluses. Table 5.2 shows some of the options for a human resource planner seeking to reduce a labor surplus. Table 5.3 shows some options available to the same planner intent on avoiding a labor shortage.

This stage is critical because the many options available to the planner differ widely in their expense, speed, effectiveness, amount of human suffering, and revocability (how easily the change can be undone). For example, if the organization can anticipate a labor surplus far enough in advance, it may be able to freeze hiring and then just let natural attrition adjust the size of the labor force. If successful, an organization may be able to avoid layoffs altogether, so that no one has to lose a job. In 2001, for instance, many employers such as Texas Instruments, General Motors, Charles Schwab, Disney, Procter & Gamble, and NBC enacted hiring freezes in anticipation of a deteriorating economy. Figure 5.3 shows how the number of help wanted advertisements dropped during this period.[4]

TABLE 5.2
Options for Reducing an Expected Labor Surplus

OPTION	SPEED	HUMAN SUFFERING
1. Downsizing	Fast	High
2. Pay reductions	Fast	High
3. Demotions	Fast	High
4. Transfers	Fast	Moderate
5. Work sharing	Fast	Moderate
6. Hiring freeze	Slow	Low
7. Natural attrition	Slow	Low
8. Early retirement	Slow	Low
9. Retraining	Slow	Low

TABLE 5.3
Options for Avoiding an Expected Labor Shortage

OPTION	SPEED	REVOCABILITY
1. Overtime	Fast	High
2. Temporary employees	Fast	High
3. Outsourcing	Fast	High
4. Retrained transfers	Slow	High
5. Turnover reductions	Slow	Moderate
6. New external hires	Slow	Low
7. Technological innovation	Slow	Low

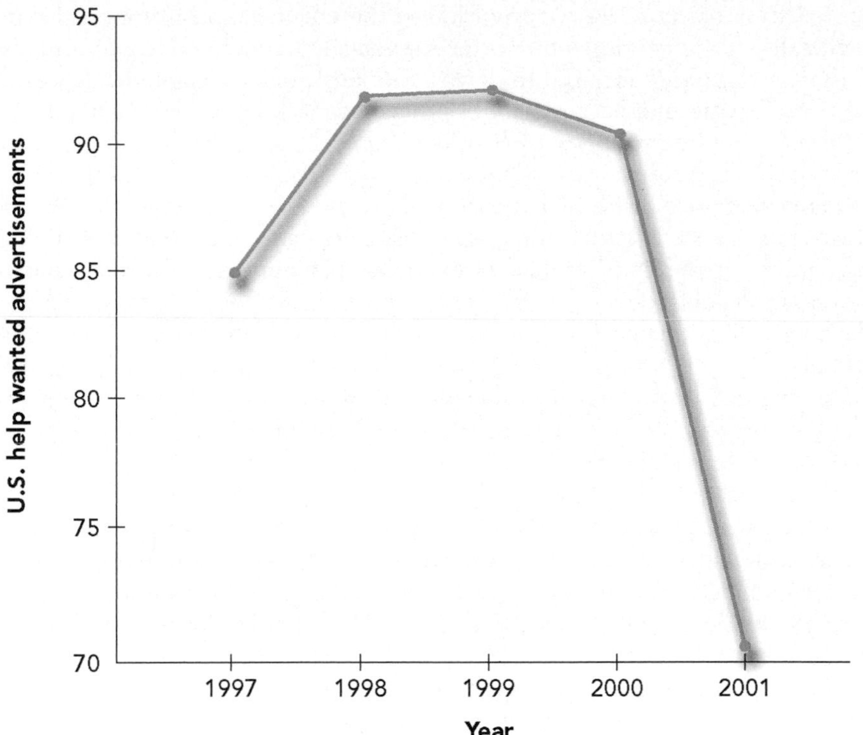

FIGURE 5.3
The Impact of Hiring Freezes on Employment Opportunities in 2001

Unfortunately for many workers, in the past decade the typical organizational response to a surplus of labor has been downsizing, which is fast but high in human suffering. The widespread use of downsizing in 2001 was a contributing factor in the largest number of personal bankruptcies ever recorded in the United States. Beyond this economic impact, the psychological impact spills over and affects families, increasing the rates of divorce, child abuse, and drug and alcohol addiction.[5] The typical organizational response to a labor shortage has been either hiring temporary employees or outsourcing, responses that are fast and high in revocability. Given the pervasiveness of these choices, we will devote special subsections of this chapter to each of these options.

Downsizing

We define **downsizing** as the planned elimination of large numbers of personnel designed to enhance organizational competitiveness. Many organizations adopted this strategic option in the late 1980s and early 1990s, especially in the United States. In fact, over 85 percent of the *Fortune* 1000 firms downsized between 1987 and 2001, resulting in more than 8 million permanent layoffs—an unprecedented figure in U.S. economic history. The jobs eliminated in these downsizing efforts should not be thought of as temporary losses due to business cycle downturns or a recession but as permanent losses due to the changing competitive pressures faced by businesses today. In fact, in over 80 percent of the cases where downsizing took place, the organizations initiating the cutbacks were making a profit at the time.[6] For example, in 1998, General Electric Company set in motion a $2 billion restructuring program even though all of GE's divisions were generating double-digit returns on investments.[7]

Downsizing
The planned elimination of large numbers of personnel designed to enhance organizational effectiveness.

Rather than trying to stem current losses, the major reasons for most downsizing efforts dealt with promoting future competitiveness. Surveys indicate four major reasons that organizations engaged in downsizing. First, many organizations were looking to reduce costs, and because labor costs represent a big part of a company's total costs, this is an attractive place to start. For example, when the Dow Jones industrial average dropped from over 11,000 points to below 9,000 in the year 2001, many Wall Street firms were faced with high overhead costs that could be eliminated only by reducing head counts. Merrill Lynch, Bank of America, Paine Webber, J. P. Morgan Chase, and Deutsche Bank all laid off roughly 10 percent of their workforce in an effort to stay profitable.[8]

Second, in some organizations, closing outdated plants or introducing technological changes to old plants reduced the need for labor. For example, at Caterpillar, as a result of changes in the way the company employs information technology, it now needs only one shift of workers to turn out a volume of engines that would have required two shifts a few years ago. To appreciate this kind of trade-off, it is instructive to examine Caterpillar's old and new methods.

A few years ago, if a customer wanted to order an engine with particular features, it had to work with Caterpillar representatives to translate what it needed into Caterpillar part numbers. The representatives would then forward the order to a shop floor supervisor, who would relay the order to workers. Workers would then order the needed parts and assemble the tools required. Now, using a computer connected to Caterpillar's Peoria, Illinois, headquarters, customers can electronically order an engine with the desired specifications in plain English over phone lines. Caterpillar's computer then translates that ordinary language into the company's internal language and ships the order directly to the workers on the factory floor. While shop floor workers read the computer printouts to figure out what engine to produce next, the computer is already sending the same message to a computer-controlled monorail system and robots that bring the workers the necessary parts, tools, and instructions about what to do. By using up-to-date information technology, Caterpillar's enhanced productivity allows it to get twice as much work out of the same number of individuals.[9]

A third reason for downsizing was that many mergers and acquisitions reduced the need for bureaucratic overhead, displacing many managers and some professional staff members. For example, the threat of health care reform in the mid-1990s prevented many pharmaceutical companies from raising prices. To maintain profitability in the face of price stagnation, many firms pursued merger strategies so that they would have more products but fewer people. For example, Rouche Holding Ltd. purchased Syntex Corporation for $5.3 billion, acquiring all its products, but then cut the Syntex payroll from 10,000 people to 5,000.[10] Similarly, outside the pharmaceutical industry, the merger between First Union Corporation and CoreStates Financial Corporation created administrative efficiencies but eliminated 12,000 jobs.[11]

A fourth reason for downsizing was that, for economic reasons, many firms changed the location of where they did business. Some of this shift was from one area of the United States to another—in particular, many organizations moved from the Northeast, the Midwest, and California to the South and mountain regions of the West. For example, Universal Studios moved many of its operations out of Los Angeles to Orlando, Florida, where the costs of producing television shows are over 40 percent less than in Los Angeles.[12] Some of this shift was also due to jobs moving out of the United States altogether. In 1998 Fruit of the Loom, citing the high costs of American labor, announced that it was going to cut 2,900 domestic jobs in the United States and move production to Mexico.[13]

Although the jury is still out on whether these downsizing efforts have enhanced organizational effectiveness, some early indications are that the results have not lived up to expectations. One study of 52 *Fortune* 100 firms shows that most firms that announce a downsizing campaign show worse, rather than better, financial performance in the following years.[14]

There seem to be a number of reasons for the failure of most downsizing efforts to live up to expectations in terms of enhancing firm performance. First, although the initial cost savings are a short-term plus, the long-term effects of an improperly managed downsizing effort can be negative. Downsizing not only leads to a loss of talent, but in many cases it disrupts the social networks needed to promote creativity and flexibility.[15] For example, in the Rouche Holding–Syntex merger discussed earlier, most employees who left did so voluntarily, taking advantage of a lucrative severance package. This "parachute" gave employees two to three years of full compensation, depending on their job level. Many felt that this strategy led to turnover among the best, most marketable scientists and managers. One former Syntex scientist asked, "What makes them think they can be successful scientifically and discover new drugs when they have lost most of their good discovery people?"[16]

Second, many downsizing campaigns let go of people who turn out to be irreplaceable assets. In fact, one survey indicated that in 80 percent of the cases, firms wind up replacing some of the very people who were let go. One senior manager of a *Fortune* 100 firm described a situation in which a bookkeeper making $9 an hour was let go; but then, when the company realized she knew many things about the company that no one else knew, she was hired back as a consultant for $42 an hour.[17] Indeed, the practice of hiring back formerly laid-off workers has become so routine that many organizations are increasingly using software formerly used for tracking job applicants to track their laid-off employees. The software creates a custom snapshot of each laid-off employee and periodically updates the file by e-mailing former workers to see what new skills they may have developed. If the organization moves from facing a labor surplus to a labor shortage, these former workers can be contacted quickly and restored to payrolls.[18]

A third reason downsizing efforts often fail is that employees who survive the purges often become narrow-minded, self-absorbed, and risk-averse. Motivation levels drop off because any hope of future promotions—or even a future—with the company dies out. Many employees also start looking for alternative employment opportunities. The negative publicity associated with a downsizing campaign can also hurt the company's image in the labor market, making it more difficult to recruit employees later. The key to avoiding this kind of reputation damage is to ensure that the need for the layoff is well explained and that procedures for implementing the layoff are fair.[19] Although this may seem to reflect common sense, organizations are often reluctant to provide this kind of information, especially if part of the reason for the layoff was top-level mismanagement.[20]

Many of these problems with downsizing efforts can be reduced with better planning, but this is hardly a panacea for increasing organizational competitiveness in the new millennium. More judicious use of all the other avenues for eliminating a labor surplus (shown in Table 5.2) is needed, but because many of these take effect slowly, without better forecasting, organizations will be stuck with downsizing as their only viable option.

Early Retirement Programs

Another popular means of reducing a labor surplus is to offer an early retirement program. As shown in Figure 5.4, the average age of the U.S. workforce is increasing. But,

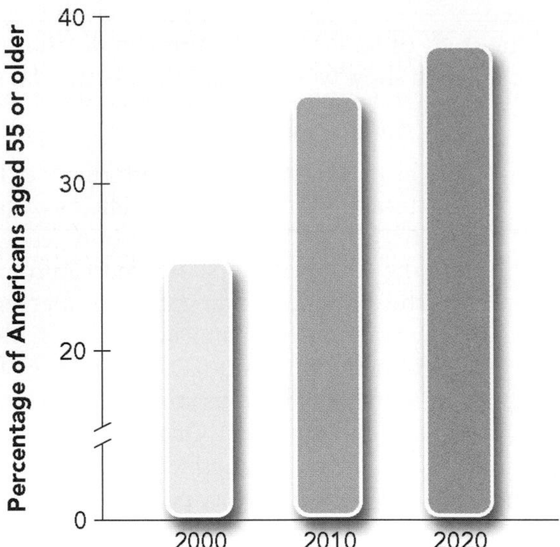

FIGURE 5.4
Aging of the U.S. Population, 2000–2020

although many baby boomers are approaching traditional retirement age, early indications are that this group has no intention of retiring any time soon.[21] Several forces fuel the drawing out of older workers' careers. First, the improved health of older people in general, in combination with the decreased physical labor in many jobs, has made working longer a viable option. Second, this option is attractive for many workers because they fear Social Security will be cut, and many have skimpy employer-sponsored pensions that may not be able to cover their expenses. Finally, age discrimination legislation and the outlawing of mandatory retirement ages have created constraints on organizations' ability to unilaterally deal with an aging workforce.

Although an older workforce has some clear advantages for employers in terms of experience and stability, it also poses problems. First, older workers are sometimes more costly than younger workers because of their higher seniority, higher medical costs, and higher pension contributions. When the value of the experience offsets these costs, then employers are fine; but if it does not, it becomes difficult to pass these costs to consumers. Second, because older workers typically occupy the best-paid jobs, they sometimes prevent the hiring or block the advancement of younger workers. This is frustrating for the younger workers and leaves the organization in a perilous position whenever the older workers decide to retire.

For example, in the 20-year period between 1978 and 1997, Cummins Engine's Columbus plant did not hire a single new full-time person at its 2,800-employee plant. By the year 2000, almost all of its hourly workers will be old enough to retire, but there will be little if any experienced talent available to take their place. The company would like to bring in younger, cheaper workers, but its hands are tied by a no-layoff contract signed with the Diesel Workers Union and by poor performance in the product market (profits having dropped 29 percent in 1996).[22]

In the face of such demographic pressures, many employers try to induce voluntary attrition among their older workers through early retirement incentive programs. These programs come in an infinite variety. Depending on how lucrative they are, they meet with varied success. Although some research suggests that these programs do induce attrition among lower-performing older workers,[23] to a large extent, such programs' success is contingent upon accurate forecasting. For example, at AT&T, CEO

Mike Armstrong wanted to cut up to 11,000 managers between 1996 and 1999. However, by as early as 1997, 14,000 managers had already opted for the package, and by 1998, AT&T went from a labor surplus in this job category to a severe labor shortage.[24]

For this and other reasons, many organizations are moving from early retirement programs to phased retirement programs. Phased retirement programs allow the organization to tap into the experience of older workers while reducing the number of hours they work (and hence reducing costs). This option is often helpful psychologically for the workers, who can ease into retirement rather than being thrust all at once into a markedly different way of life.[25]

Employing Temporary Workers

Whereas downsizing has been a popular method for reducing a labor surplus, hiring temporary workers and outsourcing has been the most widespread means of eliminating a labor shortage. Indeed, government estimates indicate that in 1997 close to 1 million people were working in temporary job arrangements in the manufacturing sector alone, and 2.3 million across the entire economy.[26] Temporary employment affords firms the flexibility needed to operate efficiently in the face of swings in the demand for goods and services. Several other advantages with temporary employment arrangements need to be noted as well.

In addition to size flexibility, the use of temporary workers frees the firm from many administrative tasks and financial burdens associated with being the "employer of record." For example, the cost of benefits at McDonnell Douglas, including health care, pension, life insurance, workers' compensation, and unemployment insurance, accounted for 40 percent of payroll expenses. It is easy to understand why McDonnell Douglas's human resource plan raised the percentage of temporary workers from 4.3 percent to 15 percent.

Second, small companies that cannot afford their own testing programs often get employees who have been tested by a temporary agency. For example, Cheryl Nelson (HR manager at Aligned Fiber Composites, a small manufacturer in Chatfield, Minnesota) notes, "We do not have a satisfactory means of testing employees in-house, so we turned to a temporary agency. We bring temporaries on for 90 days, and if they work out, and we can use them in permanent positions, we roll them onto our payroll." In fact, 17 percent of Aligned Fiber's permanent employees were once successful temporaries.[27]

Third, many temporary agencies train employees before to sending them to employers, which reduces training costs and eases the transition for both the temporary worker and the company. For example, when United Parcel Service (UPS) signed on with a temporary agency to supply data entry personnel, the agency designed a computer screen that simulated those used at UPS. A temporary worker would not be assigned to UPS without achieving a certain keystroke level. Nike, the athletic shoe company, had a similar arrangement with an agency that provided workers who packed sneakers.[28]

Finally, because the temporary worker has little experience in the host firm, she brings an objective perspective to the organization's problems and procedures that is sometimes valuable. Also, since the temporary worker may have a great deal of experience in other firms, she can sometimes identify solutions to the host organization's problems that were confronted at a different firm. For example, one temporary worker at Lord, Abbett and Company, an investment firm in New York, suggested an efficient software program for managing portfolios that she had been trained with at a different firm. Thus temporary employees can sometimes help employers to benchmark and improve their practices.

Certain disadvantages to employing temporary workers need to be overcome to effectively use this source of labor. For example, there is often tension between a firm's temporary employees and its full-time employees. Surveys indicate that 33 percent of full-time employees perceive the temporary help as a threat to their own job security. This can lead to low levels of cooperation and, in some cases, outright sabotage if not managed properly.

There are several keys to managing this problem. First, the organization needs to have bottomed out first in terms of any downsizing effort before it starts bringing in temporaries. A downsizing effort is almost like a death in the family for employees who survive, and a decent time interval needs to exist before new temporary workers are introduced into this context. Without this time delay, there will be a perceived association between the downsizing effort (which was a threat) and the new temporary employees (who may be perceived by some as outsiders who have been hired to replace old friends). Any upswing in demand for labor after a downsizing effort should probably first be met by an expansion of overtime granted to core full-time employees. If this demand persists over time, one can be more sure that the upswing is not temporary and that there will be no need for future layoffs. The extended stretches of overtime will eventually tax the full-time employees, who will then be more receptive to the prospect of hiring temporary employees to help lessen their load.

Second, if the organization is concerned about the reactions of full-time workers to the temporaries, it may want to go out of its way to hire "nonthreatening" temporaries. For example, although most temporary workers want their temporary assignments to turn into full-time work (75 percent of those surveyed expressed this hope), not all do. Some prefer the freedom of temporary arrangements. These workers are the ideal temporaries for a firm with fearful full-time workers.

Firms can also create their own nonthreatening temporary pool staffed by full-time employees who move from unit to unit. For example, AT&T Universal Card Services in Jacksonville, Florida, created its own in-house temporary agency. These internal temporaries move from one department to another, depending on the demand for services. The company has created a special database that tracks each employee's past internal assignments, and this is used to check on the relevant experience of each such internal transfer.

Of course, in attempting to convince full-time employees that they are valued and not about to be replaced by temporary workers, as the "Competing by Meeting Stakeholders' Needs" box highlights, the organization must not create the perception that temporary workers are second-class organizational citizens. As with managing the full-time employee concerns, there are several keys to managing the concerns of temporary employees. First, as far as possible, the organization should treat temporary employees the same way it treats full-time workers. For example, at Ford Motor Company in Detroit, temporary engineering employees were given the same memos, newsletters, and bulletins about the company as were regular employees, even though many of the projects they were working on had little to do with much of the organization's core business. Joe O'Hagan, principal engineer at Ford, notes, "We treated them as if they were an integral part of our team, and to be a part of our team, they had to know what everybody else knows. We worked to make sure they understood the big picture."[29]

HR staff can also prevent feelings of a two-tiered society by ensuring that the temporary agency provides benefits to the temporaries that are at least minimally compa-

COMPETING BY MEETING STAKEHOLDERS' NEEDS

Revenge of the Permatemps

Microsoft's brown bag lunches were well known throughout the organization as being an excellent place to learn about new product developments and recent corporate initiatives. David Larsen was on his way to his first of these when he was pulled aside by his supervisor and told, "We don't want you to go to those things; we want you at your computer finding bugs."

Larson was unwanted at this event because he was not a "regular" Microsoft employee but was instead one of its 5,000 temporary workers. These temporary workers performed many of the same duties as regular employees, including customer service, software testing, and programming, and had done so for many years—earning the nickname "permatemps." However, despite their years of service, these people were treated as second-class citizens throughout the corporation.

Some of the distinctions, such as wearing orange identification badges rather than blue ones worn by the regular staff, were simply embarrassing, but others were more costly. For example, permatemps were not allowed to participate in the employee stock purchase program, which allowed regular employees to buy stock at a 15 percent discount. This benefit made millionaires out of many Microsoft employees because the stock rose nearly 2,500 percent between 1992 and 2000.

These permatemps had their revenge, however, on January 9, 2000, when the U.S. Supreme Court ruled that this type of differential treatment of long-term temporary employees was illegal. In the subsequent settlement Microsoft agreed to pay $97 million to roughly 10,000 current and former permatemps to rectify the past injustice. This legal decision sent shock waves through the rest of the U.S. economy because many other employers had created similar two-tier wage structures for regular and temporary employees.

During the lawsuit Microsoft made extensive changes in the way it managed its temporary workers. First, it aggressively converted past temporary workers into regular employees by taking 35 percent of all new hires from a pool of temporary workers. Second, it established clear rules for limiting temporary assignments to one year in duration with 100 days' minimum interval between assignments. Third, the company made more judicious use of outside temporary agencies to ensure that the workers provided by those services received benefits that more closely resembled those of Microsoft workers. Although changing the internal culture of Microsoft might be more difficult, as one former permatemp noted, "Microsoft is slowly but painfully finding out that they have to treat people who work full-time, year round as regular employees."

SOURCE: M. Gimein, "The Bugs in Microsoft's Culture," *Fortune* (January 8, 2001), p. 128; T. Smits, "Microsoft 'Temps' Win Court Ruling," *USA Today Online* (January 10, 2000), p. 1; L. Davidson, "Temp Workers Want a Better Deal," *Workforce* (October 2000), pp. 44–49; J. Redman, "Microsoft Bans Long-Term Temps," *USA Today Online* (June 7, 2000), p. 1.

rable with those enjoyed by the full-time workers with whom they interact. For example, one temporary agency, MacTemps, gives its workers long-term health coverage, full disability insurance, and complete dental coverage. This not only reduces the benefit gap between the full-time and part-time workers but also helps attract the best part-time workers in the first place.

Outsourcing

Outsourcing
An organization's use of an outside organization for a broad set of services.

Whereas a temporary employee can be brought in to manage a single job, in other cases a firm may be interested in getting a much broader set of services performed by an outside organization; this is called **outsourcing.** For example, American Airlines established a contract with Johnson Controls Inc. to provide ticket agents for American's operations at 28 second-tier airports. In this case, cost control was the main reason—American paid its veteran agents at major airports $19 an hour plus benefits, the going market rate for this industry. Johnson Controls, on the other hand, pays the existing local market wage, only $8 an hour, for the 500 jobs that were handed over to it.

In other cases, outsourcing is driven by economies of scale that make it more efficient to hand over work to an outside agent. For example, several years ago Ford Motor Company had a unit that processed automobile financing applications. Now it hands this work over to Detroit-based MCN Corporation, which can do the same job with fewer people than Ford. MCN uses its dedicated computers and staff to process data for Ford (and over 25 other companies) with an efficiency that comes from a narrow focus on data entry and analysis, unfettered by the need to produce automobiles. APAC (a private telemarketing company in Cedar Rapids, Iowa) has a similar arrangement with Western Union, Compaq, Quill, Sears, and many other companies. APAC's specialty is answering the telephone, and its 4,000 operators take orders and provide information to customers of their clients. As Donald Gerryman, vice president of APAC, notes, "When you call our clients' 800 numbers, you get us."

Outsourcing is a logical choice when the firm simply does not have certain expertise and is not willing to invest the time and energy to develop it. For example, American Express Financial Advisors (AEFA) has a leadership development division that provides training services to clients based on a detailed needs analysis. Sometimes this needs analysis turns up training requirements in areas where AEFA has no established curriculum. Where once the firm might have developed such curriculum for the client, now, to keep a narrower focus, it searches for an outside supplier better able to meet this need. No new trainers are added to the AEFA payroll, and no costly curriculum development is initiated. As one manager notes, "There are just a lot of good programs out there, and we don't want to reinvent the wheel. . . . This allows us to keep ourselves very lean and focused."[30]

Outsourcing in the area of manufacturing often involves designing projects in the United States and then shipping manufacturing responsibilities overseas. Japanese and Korean firms, in particular, can often produce key components or even a finished product for 10 to 60 percent less than the cost of in-house manufacturing. For example, close to 50 percent of Chrysler's minicompact and subcompact cars are produced in Asia; Apple introduced a laptop computer produced by Sony; and Motorola set up equipment production centers in Hong Kong. Outsourcing in the service industry often means shipping data entry jobs overseas. Metropolitan Life Insurance has its medical claims analyzed in Ireland, where operating costs are about 35 percent less than in the United States. Typing mills in the Philippines are even more competitive, entering 10,000 characters for 50 cents; those in China will do the same for a mere 20 cents. Clearly, the labor supplies of countries like China, India, Jamaica, and those in Eastern Europe are creating an oversupply of labor for unskilled and low-skilled work.

Technological advancements in computer networking and transmission have speeded up the outsourcing process and have also helped it spread beyond manufacturing areas and low-skilled jobs. For example, firms that perform design engineering find that India is a fertile ground for outsourcing this type of work. India inherited a strong English-language school system from the days of British rule and has always emphasized mathematics in its schools. Yet, Indian computer scientists earn only $1,300 a month on average, compared with $5,000 per month in the United States.[31] One survey of U.S. CEOs indicated that 42 percent of communication firms, 40 percent of computer manufacturers, and 37 percent of semiconductor companies rely on outsourcing to foreign firms, and most expected these percentages to grow to the 50 percent range.[32]

Many are concerned that while this type of outsourcing may make good sense in the short term, its long-term implications for U.S. firms' competitiveness are negative. Although these firms may be reducing manufacturing costs, eventually they will find it more and more difficult to design products that can take advantage of innovations in technology. It is argued that outsourcing, if left unchecked, starts a downward spiral that prompts more and more outsourcing until the firm itself produces nothing of value. In the meantime, more and more U.S. workers get displaced. In the end, firms that do the manufacturing soon develop their own design teams and then become direct competitors with a substantial competitive advantage. For example, Toshiba once produced televisions for Sears and then introduced sets under its own brand name several years later. At that time, its marketing strategy was to simply say, "These televisions are exactly what you would get at Sears, but they cost less." Needless to say, Sears no longer produces televisions under its own brand name. Nationwide, whereas 100 percent of color television sets were manufactured by U.S. firms in 1960, by 1990 that share was down to 12 percent.[33]

Overtime and Expanding Worker Hours

Companies facing a shortage of labor may be reluctant to hire new full-time or part-time employees. Under some conditions, these firms may have the option of trying to garner more hours out of the existing labor force. Many employers opted for this strategy during the 1990s. Indeed, 6 percent of the automobiles assembled in North America in 1997 resulted from overtime production. To put this in perspective, this is equivalent to the output of an additional four auto plants running on straight time.[34]

Despite having to pay workers time-and-a-half for overtime production, employers see this as preferable to hiring and training new employees—especially if they are afraid that current demand for products or services may not extend to the future. Also, for a short time at least, many workers enjoy the added compensation. However, over extended periods, employees experience stress and frustration from being overworked in this manner. Thus it is not surprising that during the 1998 General Motors strikes, one employee demand was for the company to hire additional new workers.

Program Implementation and Evaluation

The programs developed in the strategic-choice stage of the process are put into practice in the program-implementation stage, shown at the bottom of Figure 5.1. A critical aspect of program implementation is to make sure that some individual is held accountable for achieving the stated goals and has the necessary authority and resources to accomplish this goal. It is also important to have regular progress reports on the implementation to be sure that all programs are in place by specified times and that the early returns from these programs are in line with projections.

The final step in the planning process is to evaluate the results. Of course, the most obvious evaluation involves checking whether the company has successfully avoided any potential labor shortages or surpluses. Although this bottom-line evaluation is critical, it is also important to go beyond it to see which specific parts of the planning process contributed to success or failure.

A good example of the necessary diagnostic work can be seen in Bell Atlantic's recent failed downsizing effort. Convinced in 1994 that the company would need fewer workers, but facing a union (the Communication Workers of America) that staunchly opposed layoffs, Bell Atlantic developed a high-priced buyout plan. Any worker could take advantage of the buyout program, but they had do it before their contract expired in August 1998.

By June 1998 almost a third of its unionized workforce (14,000 people) stood ready to take the company up on its offer. However, forecasts for product demand were grossly underestimated. Whereas Bell Atlantic forecasted lower demand for copper wiring, instead orders surged as many industrial and residential consumers added second lines for faxes and modems. The smaller workforce could not keep up with demand, however. Stretching the hours of the remaining employees simply did not work in many traffic-congested metropolitan areas like New York City.

So, while many experienced employees were walking away with lucrative buyouts, Bell Atlantic had to replace them with inexperienced new hires amid a labor shortage in the overall U.S. economy. To avert disaster, the company had to offer a 25 percent hike in its already generous pension plan to any employee who would stay. The overall effect was to create an extravagant bonus system that rewarded employees for either staying or leaving.[35]

The Special Case of Affirmative Action Planning

We have argued that human resource planning is an important function that should be applied to an organization's entire labor force. It is also important to plan for various subgroups within the labor force. For example, affirmative action plans forecast and monitor the proportion of various protected group members, such as women and minorities, that are in various job categories and career tracks. The proportion of workers in these subgroups can then be compared with the proportion that each subgroup represents in the relevant labor market. This type of comparison is called a **workforce utilization review.** This process can be used to determine whether there is any subgroup whose proportion in the relevant labor market is substantially different from the proportion in the job category.

Workforce utilization review
A comparison of the proportion of workers in protected subgroups with the proportion that each subgroup represents in the relevant labor market.

If such an analysis indicates that some group—for example, African Americans—makes up 35 percent of the relevant labor market for a job category but that this same group constitutes only 5 percent of the actual incumbents in that job category in that organization, then this is evidence of underutilization. Underutilization could come about because of problems in selection or from problems in internal movement, and this could be seen via the transitional matrices discussed earlier in this chapter.

This kind of review is critical for many different reasons. First, many firms adopt "voluntary affirmative action programs" to make sure underutilization does not occur and to promote diversity. These efforts seem to be particularly needed at upper levels of management, where the underutilization of African Americans is most acute.[36] Second, companies might also engage in utilization reviews because they are legally required to do so. For example, Executive Order 11246 requires that government contractors and subcontractors maintain affirmative action programs. Third, affirmative action programs can be mandated by the courts as part of the settlement of discrimination complaints. Indeed, the new Civil Rights Act was largely supportive of these kinds of court-ordered affirmative action plans.

Regardless of the motivation for adopting affirmative action planning, the steps required to execute such a plan are identical to the steps in the generic planning process discussed earlier in this chapter. That is, the company needs to assess current utilization patterns and then forecast how these are likely to change in the near future. If these analyses suggest current underutilization and if forecasts suggest that this problem is not likely to change, then the company may need to set goals and timetables for changing this situation. Certain strategic choices need to be made in the pursuit of these goals that might affect recruitment or selection practices, and then the success of these strategies has to be evaluated against the goals established earlier in the process.

The Human Resource Recruitment Process

As the first half of this chapter shows, it is difficult to always anticipate exactly how many (if any) new employees will have to be hired in a given year in a given job category. The role of human resource recruitment is to build a supply of potential new hires that the organization can draw on if the need arises. Thus **human resource recruitment** is defined as any practice or activity carried on by the organization with the primary purpose of identifying and attracting potential employees.[37] It thus creates a buffer between planning and actual selection of new employees, which is the topic of our next chapter.

Human resource recruitment
The practice or activity carried on by the organization with the primary purpose of identifying and attracting potential employees.

Recruitment activities are designed to affect (1) the number of people who apply for vacancies, (2) the type of people who apply for them, and/or (3) the likelihood that those applying for vacancies will accept positions if offered.[38] The goal of an organizational recruitment program is to ensure that the organization has a number of reasonably qualified applicants (who would find the job acceptable) to choose from when a vacancy occurs.

The goal of the recruiting is not simply to generate large numbers of applicants. If the process generates a sea of unqualified applicants, the organization will incur great expense in personnel selection (as discussed more fully in the next chapter), but few vacancies will actually be filled.

The goal of personnel recruitment is not to finely discriminate among reasonably qualified applicants either. Recruiting new personnel and selecting new personnel are both complex processes. Each task is hard enough to accomplish successfully, even when one is well focused. Organizations explicitly trying to do both at the same time will probably not do either well. For example, research suggests that recruiters provide less information about the company when conducting dual-purpose interviews (interviews focused on both recruiting and selecting applicants).[39] Also, applicants apparently remember less information about the recruiting organization after dual-purpose interviews.[40]

Because of strategic differences among companies (see Chapter 2), the importance assigned to recruitment may differ.[41] In general, however, as shown in Figure 5.5, all companies have to make decisions in three areas of recruiting: (1) personnel policies, which affect the kinds of jobs the company has to offer; (2) recruitment sources used to solicit applicants, which affect the kinds of people who apply; and (3) the charac-

FIGURE 5.5
Overview of the Individual Job Choice–Organizational Recruitment Process

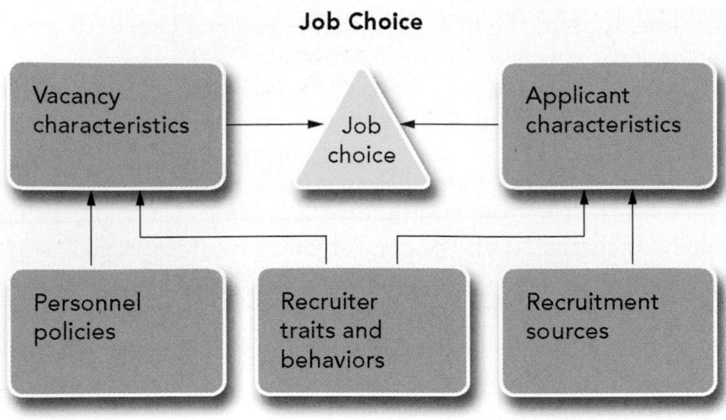

teristics and behaviors of the recruiter. These in turn, influence both the nature of the vacancies and the nature of the people applying for jobs in a way that shapes job choice decisions.[42]

Personnel Policies

Personnel policies is a generic term we use to refer to organizational decisions that affect the nature of the vacancies for which people are recruited. If the research on recruitment makes one thing clear, it is that characteristics of the vacancy are more important than recruiters or recruiting sources when it comes to predicting job choice.[43]

Internal versus External Recruiting

One desirable feature of a vacancy is that it provides ample opportunity for advancement and promotion. One organizational policy that affects this is the degree to which the company "promotes from within"—that is, recruits for upper-level vacancies internally rather than externally. Indeed, a 2001 survey of MBA students found that this was their top consideration when evaluating a company.[44]

We discuss internal versus external recruiting both here and in "Recruitment Sources" later in this chapter because this policy affects the nature of both the job and the individuals who apply. For now, we focus on the effects that promote-from-within policies have on job characteristics, noting that such policies make it clear to applicants that there are opportunities for advancement within the company. These opportunities spring not just from the first vacancy but from the vacancy created when a person in the company fills that vacancy. For example, in a company with three levels of management, a vacancy at the third level that is filled from within may "trickle down," creating a vacancy at the second level; this, in turn, creates a vacancy at the first level.

McDonald's restaurants provide a good example of the virtues of promoting from within. Phil Hagans, an African American who was once a cook at a McDonald's, now owns two franchises thanks to a program that encourages low-income managers, regardless of race, to buy franchises. Hagans's restaurants not only turn a profit, they also perform a valuable social function by providing needed employment and work experience for many inner-city youths in the Houston area. In Hagans's view, programs such as this make McDonald's "the best company for African American entrepreneurs."[45]

The retailing industry is an example of an entire sector of the economy that is increasingly being perceived as an area with good opportunities for internal advancement. This is especially the case for the superstores, such as Wal-Mart, Home Depot, and Target, where thousands of managers must be hired and promoted each year to run new outlets. Applicants who used to shun retailing jobs are now attracted to them because of the opportunities for advancement. A new college graduate who goes to Target can have responsibility for 20 employees and an $8 million department just 12 weeks out of school. These trainees, if successful, can become managers of small stores in as little as three years. Some employees who started with Target at 24 years of age are regional senior vice presidents by the time they are 30.[46]

Lead-the-Market Pay Strategies

Because pay is an important job characteristic for almost all applicants, companies that take a "lead-the-market" approach to pay—that is, a policy of paying higher-than-current-market wages—have a distinct advantage in recruiting. Pay can also make up for a job's less desirable features—for example, paying higher wages to employees who have to work midnight shifts. These kinds of specific shift differentials and other forms of more generic compensating differentials will be discussed in more detail in later chapters that focus on compensation strategies. We merely note here that "lead" policies make any given vacancy more attractive to applicants.

Increasingly, organizations that compete for applicants based on pay do so using pay forms other than wages and salary. For example, a 1997 survey indicates that close to 40 percent of employers used signing bonuses rather than higher wages to attract new hires, and up to 20 percent were providing lucrative stock option plans.[47] Bonuses and stock options are preferable for many employers because, unlike wages and salary, they tend not to compound over time and can be administered more flexibly. However, due to the recent downturn in the economy and the demise of many dot-coms, job applicants are showing less interest in stock options. As Figure 5.6 shows, between January 2000 and January 2001, the percentage of students who listed stock options as their most important incentive decreased while the number that valued flexible hours increased.[48] Indeed, the bottom seems to have dropped out of the labor market for dot-com jobs, and firms within this industry are having a difficult time recruiting any applicants for positions.

Finding and Keeping the Best Employees

In the 1990s many employers attempted to recruit employees with promises of stock option plans. However, the 2001 recession saw stock values drop sharply, thus reducing the attractiveness of this specific inducement. In addition, many people became aware of restrictions on stock option plans in the wake of the Enron bankruptcy in December 2001. Some low-level and midlevel Enron employees held stock options worth over $1 million. When Enron stock started to slide, the company prevented its employees from cashing out their options, leaving many to helplessly watch their stock become worthless. Other Enron employees whose 401(k) plans were entirely based on Enron stock (which they too could not sell) also suffered. It only made matters worse when the U.S. Security and Exchange Commission suggested that Enron's

FIGURE 5.6
Changing Nature of the "Most Important Benefit" Among New Job Applicants

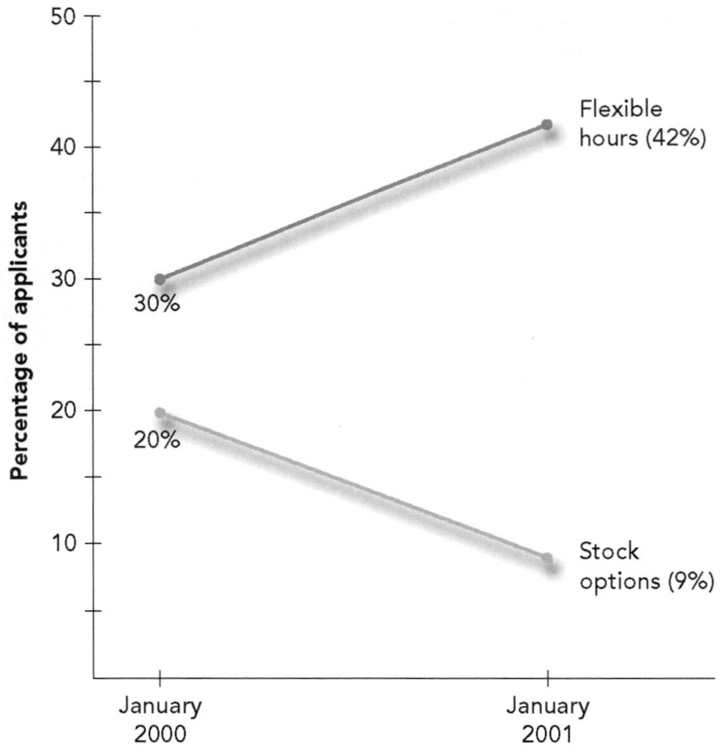

top executives illegally made more than $1 billion off stock sales just prior to the bankruptcy announcement.

For many applicants restricted stock option plans are now perceived as having limited value, and in order to attract top talent, employers are returning to more traditional inducements such as salary and other benefits. Moreover, when the traditional benefit is a 401(k) plan, smart applicants are demanding diversified funds rather than funds that are heavily skewed toward the employer's own stock.

SOURCE: W. Zellner, "The Fall of Enron," *BusinessWeek* (December 17, 2001), pp. 30–36.

Employment-at-will policies
Policies which state that either an employer or an employee can terminate the employment relationship at any time, regardless of cause.

Due process policies
Policies by which a company formally lays out the steps an employee can take to appeal a termination decision.

Employment-at-Will Policies

Employment-at-will policies state that either party in the employment relationship can terminate that relationship at any time, regardless of cause. Companies that do not have employment-at-will provisions typically have extensive due process policies. **Due process policies** formally lay out the steps an employee can take to appeal a termination decision. Recent court decisions have increasingly eroded employers' rights to terminate employees with impunity.[49] To protect themselves from wrongful discharge suits, employers have been encouraged to state explicitly, in all formal recruiting documentation, that the employment is "at will."

Some authors have gone so far as to suggest that all mention of due process should be eliminated from company handbooks, personnel manuals, and recruiting brochures.[50] Although this may have some legal advantages, job security is an important feature to many job applicants. Organizational recruiting materials that emphasize due process, rights of appeal, and grievance mechanisms send a message that job security is high; employment-at-will policies suggest the opposite. Research indicates that job applicants find companies with due process policies more attractive than companies with employment-at-will policies.[51]

Image Advertising

Organizations often advertise specific vacancies (discussed later in "Recruitment Sources"). Sometimes, however, organizations advertise just to promote themselves as a good place to work in general.[52] Image advertising is particularly important for companies in highly competitive labor markets that perceive themselves as having a bad image.[53]

The challenge and responsibility associated with a job is an attractive characteristic for many people. Dow Chemical's $60 million television campaign in the early 1990s hammered home the message "Dow lets you do great things." This message was clearly aimed at affecting the general public's view of the work at Dow. It was also an attempt to offset recurring negative publicity resulting from controversies surrounding the production of napalm (1970s), Agent Orange (1980s), and faulty breast implants (1990s).[54] This negative publicity sometimes affected Dow's ability to recruit on college campuses. The U.S. Army's "Be all that you can be" campaign pursued a similar objective. These ads focused on the challenge associated with army jobs. They also attempted to offset certain negative attributes of the work, such as the fact that, in some of its jobs at certain times, other people are systematically trying to kill you.

Although the programs described here try to promote the employer in the labor market in general, other image advertising programs target specific groups within the overall labor market. For example, many large corporations with agricultural ties, such as DuPont and Cargill, struggle to attract minority applicants. Statistics indicate, for example, that Hispanics, Asians, and African Americans constitute a mere 4 percent, 3 percent, and 3 percent of all agriculture and food scientists, respectively. Lisa Barrios, a Mexican American who grew up in Chicago, typifies many urban minorities when she notes, "I assumed everything was just farming . . . if you didn't have a rural background, then you wouldn't be able to do it." After working at a special minority internship program at Monsanto's Hybritech unit in Indiana, however, Barrios changed her major from chemical engineering to agricultural engineering.[55]

Whether the goal is to influence the perception of the public in general or specific segments of the labor market, research clearly shows that job seekers form beliefs about the nature of organizations well before they have any direct interviewing experience with those companies. Thus, it is critical for organizations to systematically assess their reputation in the labor market and redress any shortcomings they detect relative to their desired image.[56]

Recruitment Sources

The sources from which a company recruits potential employees are a critical aspect of its overall recruitment strategy. The total labor market is expansive; any single organization needs to draw from only a fraction of that total. The size and nature of the fraction that applies for an organization's vacancies will be affected by how (and to whom) the organization communicates its vacancies.[57] The type of person who is likely to respond to a job advertised on the Internet may be different from the type of person who responds to an ad in the classified section of a local newspaper. In this section we examine the different sources from which recruits can be drawn, highlighting the advantages and disadvantages of each.

Internal versus External Sources

We discussed internal versus external sources of recruits earlier in this chapter and focused on the positive effects that internal recruiting can have on recruits' perceptions of job characteristics. We will now discuss this issue again, but with a focus on how using internal sources affects the kinds of people who are recruited.

In general, relying on internal sources offers a company several advantages.[58] First, it generates a sample of applicants who are well known to the firm. Second, these applicants are relatively knowledgeable about the company's vacancies, which minimizes the possibility of inflated expectations about the job. Third, it is generally cheaper and faster to fill vacancies internally.

For example, Inova Health Systems, a Virginia-based consortium of hospitals, originally centralized its human resource functions to cut recruitment costs. Prior to consolidation, Inova's many separate hospitals were all managing their own different recruitment and selection efforts. This not only led to duplication of efforts, but in many cases one Inova facility was competing with another for the same applicants. Moreover, while no one facility had exorbitant costs, taken together they were spending \$500,000 on recruitment advertising alone. The volume of applications (close to 30,000 a year) and the large number of interviews that needed to be conducted (over 3,000) added to these costs.

One part of the consolidation plan at Inova called for creating a database that contained all the existing personnel in one file, as well as an internal computer network for promoting interhospital communication. Once the new database was constructed, it became clear how many openings in one area could be filled by internal transfers and promotions from other areas that were experiencing a labor surplus. The vacancies were posted on the internal communication network, and Inova employees were given first consideration when it came to interviewing. This policy enhanced the job satisfaction of current employees by increasing their chances of promotion and by enhancing the person–job fit via internal transfers. It also reduced the need for external hiring and the cost of generating and processing so many applications.[59]

With all these advantages, you might ask why any organization would ever employ external recruiting methods. There are several good reasons why organizations might decide to recruit externally.[60] First, for entry-level positions and perhaps even for some specialized upper-level positions, there may not be any internal recruits from which to draw. Second, bringing in outsiders may expose the organization to new ideas or new ways of doing business. Using only internal recruitment can result in a workforce whose members all think alike and who therefore may be poorly suited to innovation.[61]

Direct applicants
People who apply for a job vacancy without prompting from the organization.

Referrals
People who are prompted to apply for a job by someone within the organization.

Direct Applicants and Referrals

Direct applicants are people who apply for a vacancy without prompting from the organization. **Referrals** are people who are prompted to apply by someone within the organization. These two sources of recruits share some characteristics that make them excellent sources from which to draw.

First, many direct applicants are to some extent already "sold" on the organization. Most of them have done some homework and concluded that there is enough fit between themselves and the vacancy to warrant their submitting an application. This process is called *self-selection*. When it works effectively, it takes a great deal of pressure off the organization's recruiting and selection systems. A form of aided self-selection occurs with referrals. Many job seekers look to friends, relatives, and acquaintances to help find employment, and evoking these social networks can greatly aid the job search process for both the job seeker and the organization.[62] Current employees (who are knowledgeable of both the vacancy and the person they are referring) do their homework and conclude that there is a fit between the person and the vacancy; they then sell the person on the job. Indeed, research shows that new hires that used at least one informal source reported having greater prehire knowledge of the organization than those who relied exclusively on formal recruitment sources. Those who report having multiple sources were even better, however, in terms of both prehire knowledge about the position and subsequent turnover. In fact, the turnover rate for applicants who came from multiple recruiting sources was half that of those recruited via campus interviews or newspaper advertisements.[63]

When one figures into these results the low costs of such sources, they clearly stand out as one of the best sources of new hires. Indeed, some employers even offer financial incentives to current employees for referring applicants who are accepted and perform acceptably on the job (stay 180 days, for example).[64] Other companies play off their good reputations in the labor market to generate direct applications. For example, minorities constitute 26 percent of the 6,500 managerial and professional employees at Avon Products, and this enhances the firm's ability to recruit other minorities. As Al Smith, director of managing diversity at Avon, notes, "I get a lot of résumés from people of all cultures and ethnicities because Avon has a good reputation," and this precludes the need for expensive and sometimes unreliable outreach programs.[65]

Of course, referrals do not necessarily have to come just from current employees. The importance of good community relations to recruitment can be seen in the experience of Papa John's Pizza, which was rated number one on *BusinessWeek*'s list of 100 Best Small Companies in America. Papa John's, one of the fastest-growing companies in the United States, once relied on classified ads to find drivers and store employees. This method was highly unreliable, however, because the company did not have the facilities to develop sophisticated tests of people's skills and attitudes. Store managers are now encouraged to make professional contacts within their communities, such as with the principal or guidance counselor at the local high school, leaders of church groups, and coaches in youth sports leagues. Store managers can then use these contacts to help generate referrals among promising young applicants. These community relationships help connect Papa John's to youths who have established good reputations in their community for reliability and trustworthiness. As one industry analyst notes, "I think the greatest advantage for Papa John's is recruitment. Once you get your feet wet recruiting that way, you can move on to bigger and better things."[66]

Advertisements in Newspapers and Periodicals

Advertisements to recruit personnel are ubiquitous, even though they typically generate less desirable recruits than direct applications or referrals—and do so at greater expense. However, because few employers can fill all their vacancies with direct applications and referrals, some form of advertising is usually needed. Moreover, an employer can take many steps to increase the effectiveness of this recruitment method.

The two most important questions to ask in designing a job advertisement are, What do we need to say? and To whom do we need to say it? With respect to the first question, many organizations fail to adequately communicate the specifics of the vacancy. Ideally, persons reading an ad should get enough information to evaluate the job and its requirements, allowing them to make a well-informed judgment regarding their qualifications. This could mean running long advertisements, which costs more. However, these additional costs should be evaluated against the costs of processing a huge number of applicants who are not reasonably qualified or who would not find the job acceptable once they learn more about it.

In terms of whom to reach with this message, the organization placing the advertisement has to decide which medium it will use. The classified section of local newspapers is the most common medium. It is a relatively inexpensive means of reaching many people within a specified geographic area who are currently looking for work (or at least interested enough to be reading the classifieds). On the downside, this medium does not allow an organization to target skill levels very well. Typically, classified ads are read by many people who are either over- or underqualified for the position. Moreover, people who are not looking for work rarely read the classifieds, and thus this is not the right medium for luring people away from their current employers. Specially targeted journals and periodicals may be better than general newspapers at reaching a specific part of the overall labor market. In addition, employers are increasingly using television—particularly cable television—as a reasonably priced way of reaching people.[67]

Public Employment Agencies

The Social Security Act of 1935 requires that everyone receiving unemployment compensation be registered with a local state employment office. These state employment offices work with the U.S. Employment Service (USES) to try to ensure that unemployed individuals eventually get off state aid and back on employer payrolls. To accomplish this, agencies collect information from the unemployed about their skills and experiences.

With the passage of the Personal Responsibility and Work Opportunity Reconciliation Act of 1996, the pressure on welfare recipients to find jobs through either public employment agencies or other means has increased dramatically. This act sets a five-year limit on benefits and requires most people to land jobs in two years. It also provides incentives for organizations, in the form of federal tax credits, of up to $8,500 for each welfare recipient hired. Some credit this act with the 30 percent reduction in welfare rolls between 1994 and 1998.[68]

Employers can register their job vacancies with their local state employment office, and the agency will attempt to find someone suitable using its computerized inventory of local unemployed individuals. The agency makes referrals to the organization at no charge, and these individuals can be interviewed or tested by the employer for potential vacancies. Because of certain legislative mandates, state unemployment offices often have specialized "desks" for minorities, handicapped individuals, and Vietnam-era veterans. Thus, this is an excellent source for employers who feel they are currently underutilizing any of these subgroups.

Private Employment Agencies

Public employment agencies serve primarily the blue-collar labor market; private employment agencies perform much the same service for the white-collar labor market. Unlike public agencies, however, private employment agencies charge the organization for the referrals. Another difference between private and public employment agencies is that one doesn't have to be unemployed to use a private employment agency.

One special type of private employment agency is the so-called executive search firm (ESF). These agencies are often referred to as *headhunters* because, unlike the other sources we have examined, they operate almost exclusively with people who are currently employed. For example, when BMW sought to open its new U.S. plant, it used an executive search firm to help "liberate" Allen Kinzer and Edwin Buker from Honda. These two executives were vice presidents for Honda's U.S. operations, and BMW was looking to recreate Honda's success by recruiting them.[69]

Dealing with executive search firms is sometimes a sensitive process because executives may not want to advertise their availability for fear of their current employer's reaction. Thus, ESFs serve as an important confidentiality buffer between the employer and the recruit. ESFs are expensive to employ for both direct and indirect reasons. Directly, according to a 1997 survey, ESFs often charge one-third to half of the salary of the executive who is eventually placed.[70] Indirectly, employers who use ESFs wind up having to lure people not from unemployment but from jobs that they may be quite satisfied with. A company in a growing industry may have to offer as much as 50 percent more than the executive's current pay to prompt her to take the new job.[71]

Colleges and Universities

Most colleges and universities have placement services that seek to help their graduates obtain employment. Indeed, on-campus interviewing is the most important source of recruits for entry-level professional and managerial vacancies.[72] Organizations tend to focus especially on colleges that have strong reputations in areas for which they have critical needs (chemical engineering, public accounting, or the like).[73]

For example, 3M has a five-part college recruiting strategy. First, the company concentrates its efforts on 25 to 30 selected universities, trying not to spread itself too thin. Second, it has a commitment to these selected universities and returns each year with new openings. Third, 3M uses a large number of line managers in its recruiting interviews, because they have better real-world knowledge about the jobs and working conditions relative to more narrowly informed human resource staff. Fourth, the HR staff is used to coordinate the line managers' activities with the university's staff, making sure that the same person works with the same university year in and year out to achieve "continuity of contact." Finally, 3M strives for continuous improvement by frequently asking students they have recruited to give them feedback on the process and, where possible, to compare and contrast 3M's process with the process used by other firms recruiting at the same university.[74]

Many employers have found that to effectively compete for the best students, they need to do more than just sign prospective graduates up for interview slots. One of the best ways to establish a stronger presence on a campus is with a college internship program. For example, Dun & Bradstreet funds a summer intern program for minority MBA students and often hires these interns for full-time positions when they graduate.[75] These kinds of programs allow an organization to get early access to potential applicants and to assess their capacities directly.

Another way of increasing one's presence on campus is to participate in university job fairs. In general, a job fair is a place where many employers gather for a short time to meet large numbers of potential job applicants. Although job fairs can be held anywhere (such as at a hotel or convention center), campuses are ideal locations because of the many well-educated, yet unemployed, individuals who live there. Job fairs are a rather inexpensive means of generating an on-campus presence and can even provide one-on-one dialogue with potential recruits—dialogue that could not be achieved through less interactive media like newspaper ads.

Finally, as more organizations attempt to compete on a global level, the ability to recruit individuals who will be successful both at home and abroad is a growing concern. Many organizations feel that college campuses are one of the best places to search for this type of transportable talent. Molex Inc., for example, is a U.S. technology firm with 8,000 employees, only 2,000 of whom live in the United States. Molex derives 70 percent of its $950 million in annual sales from outside the United States, and thus the majority of workers are either expatriates, local nationals, or foreign service employees. Three critical aspects of Molex's recruitment strategy are critical to its success in attaining an internationally talented workforce.

First, Molex focuses on recruiting college students. As one manager at Molex states, "We have had more success molding younger people into this company and into overseas assignments than taking more experienced people who've worked for other companies." Second, Molex recruits many foreigners (especially MBA candidates) who are studying in the United States for assignments back in their native country. These individuals have the best of both worlds in terms of having a formal education in U.S. business practices and also understanding both the language and culture of their home country. Finally, when recruiting U.S. students, Molex requires that each person hired be fluent in both English and one other language. This commitment to multilingual competency can be seen at the national headquarters, where 15 different languages are spoken.[76]

Electronic Recruiting

The growth of the information superhighway has opened up new vistas for organizations trying to recruit talent. There are many ways to employ the Internet, and increasingly organizations are refining their use of this medium. In fact, a recent 2001 survey of HR executives indicated that electronic job boards were the most effective source of recruits for 36 percent of the respondents, well ahead of local newspapers (21 percent), job fairs (4 percent), and walk-ins and referrals (1 percent).[77]

Obviously, one of the easiest ways to get into "e-cruiting" is to simply use the organization's own Web page to solicit applications. Although this was an option on only 22 percent of the websites of the world's largest firms in 1998, by 2000 this was up to 88 percent; it is an effective and extremely cost-effective practice for large organizations.[78]

Of course, smaller and less well-known organizations may not attract any attention to their own websites, and thus for them this is not a good option. A second way for organizations to use the Web is to interact with the large, well-known job sites such as Monster.com, HotJobs.com, or Headhunter.net. These sites attract a vast array of applicants, who submit standardized résumés that can be electronically searched using key terms. Applicants can also search for companies in a similar fashion; the hope, of course, is that there may be a match between the employer and the applicant. The biggest downside to these large sites, however, is their sheer size and lack of differentiation. In fact, as one HR executive has noted regarding these sites, "The last thing you need is get a thousand résumés, 990 of which don't meet your needs."[79] (The "Competing through High-Performance Work Systems" box suggests ways for job seekers to effectively navigate the Internet for promising leads.)

Because of this limitation of the large sites, smaller, more tailored websites called "niche boards" focus on certain industries, occupations, or geographic areas. For ex-

COMPETING THROUGH HIGH-PERFORMANCE WORK SYSTEMS

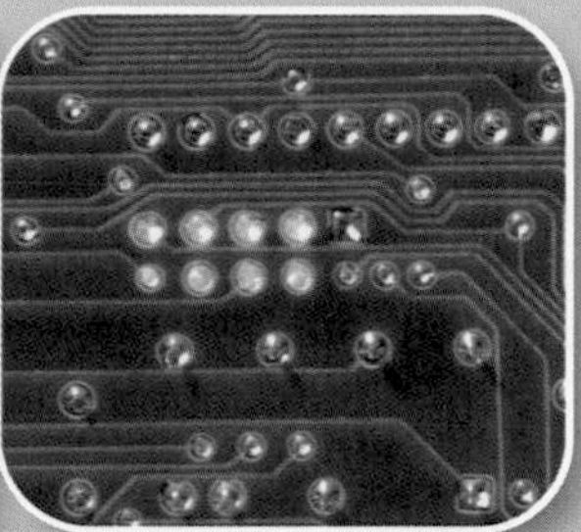

How to Spin the Web: A Job Seeker's Perspective

No area of human resource management has been impacted more by the Internet than recruiting. As employers develop more experience with this medium, they are becoming increasingly skilled in accessing both active job seekers, via large services like Monster.com and Headhunter.net, and people with specific skills they need that are not actively searching for work. A host of search engines now allow employers to search websites for specific terms that allow recruiters to unearth people on the Internet that may not even be in the job market at the present time.

Whereas the skills of recruiters using the Web get better each year, many job applicants still struggle to effectively use this medium in their own search for jobs. Web-based job seekers often make common mistakes, and avoiding these can help make the process work more effectively for both sides of the employment relationship.

One common mistake made by inexperienced Web-based job seekers is submitting a résumé loaded with graphics in the form of an e-mail attachment. Often companies afraid of contracting a computer virus will not even open attachments that accompany such letters. Moreover, even if they open the attachment, the graphics take up a great deal of space and sometimes fail to convert in the manner intended.

Second, online job seekers need to be wary of stale listings or "fake jobs." Many companies fail to remove job postings after they have filled their vacancies, and thus, when confronted with a large number of postings, applicants are wise to focus on just the most recent job listings. Monster.com supports this with its "My Agent" feature, which e-mails pertinent new listings to the job seeker as they arrive. In addition, some companies may even post jobs that do not exist just to get a sense of who is out there and what the market might be for certain skills. Overly vague job descriptions or listings posted by anonymous sources may warrant special scrutiny along these lines.

Finally, in some cases, the private searches of currently employed job seekers become public knowledge when members of their own organization download their online résumé. Unless you are using a formal outplacement service, it is rarely a good idea to seek employment using equipment owned by your current employer. Beyond this, however, certain sites like HotJobs.com allow those listing their résumé to block access so that certain companies cannot see the listing.

SOURCE: S. Gutmacher, "Secrets of Online Recruiters Exposed," *Workforce,* October 2000, pp. 44–50; N. Mangi, "Click and Hire," *BusinessWeek Online* (October 25, 2001); S. L. Bradford, "The Web Is a Great Job-Hunt Tool, But It Helps to Be an Informed Searcher," *The Wall Street Journal Sunday* (July 15, 2001), pp. 1–3.

ample, Telecommcareers.net is a site devoted to, as the name implies, the telecommunications industry. CIO.com, a companion site to *CIO Magazine*, is an occupational board that specializes in openings for chief information officers. The San Francisco Bay Area also features "craiglist.com"—a job board for applicants who live in that area and have no intentions of relocating. The best evidence regarding the growing popularity and effectiveness of these niche boards can be seen in the behaviors of the larger sites, which are scrambling to create more focused subsections of their own.[80] Clearly this dynamic area of human resource management is one where innovative, forward-thinking managers can gain competitive advantage.

Another technological innovation in recruiting that eliminates travel requirements but allows for a more personal meeting between employer and applicant is videoconferencing.[81] Used mostly on college campuses, videoconferencing allows applicants and employers to meet each other technologically "face-to-face."

Evaluating the Quality of a Source

Because there are few rules about the quality of a given source for a given vacancy, it is generally a good idea for employers to monitor the quality of all their recruitment sources. One means of accomplishing this is to develop and compare yield ratios for each source.[82] Yield ratios express the percentage of applicants who successfully move from one stage of the recruitment and selection process to the next. Comparing yield ratios for different sources helps determine which is best or most efficient for the type of vacancy being investigated. Data on cost per hire are also useful in establishing the efficiency of a given source.

Table 5.4 shows hypothetical yield ratios and cost-per-hire data for five recruitment sources. For the job vacancies generated by this company, the best two sources of recruits are local universities and employee referral programs. Newspaper ads generate the largest number of recruits, but relatively few of these are qualified for the position. Recruiting at nationally renowned universities generates highly qualified applicants, but relatively few of them ultimately accept positions. Finally, executive search firms generate a small list of highly qualified, interested applicants, but this is an expensive source compared with other alternatives.

Recruiters

The last part of the model presented in Figure 5.5 that we will discuss is the recruiter. We consider the recruiter this late in the chapter to reinforce our earlier observation

TABLE 5.4

Hypothetical Yield Ratios for Five Recruitment Sources

	RECRUITING SOURCE				
	LOCAL UNIVERSITY	RENOWNED UNIVERSITY	EMPLOYEE REFERRALS	NEWSPAPER AD	EXECUTIVE SEARCH FIRMS
Résumés generated	200	400	50	500	20
Interview offers accepted	175	100	45	400	20
Yield ratio	87%	25%	90%	80%	100%
Applicants judged acceptable	100	95	40	50	19
Yield ratio	57%	95%	89%	12%	95%
Accept employment offers	90	10	35	25	15
Yield ratio	90%	11%	88%	50%	79%
Cumulative yield ratio	90/200 45%	10/400 3%	35/50 70%	25/500 5%	15/20 75%
Cost	$30,000	$50,000	$15,000	$20,000	$90,000
Cost per hire	$333	$5,000	$428	$800	$6,000

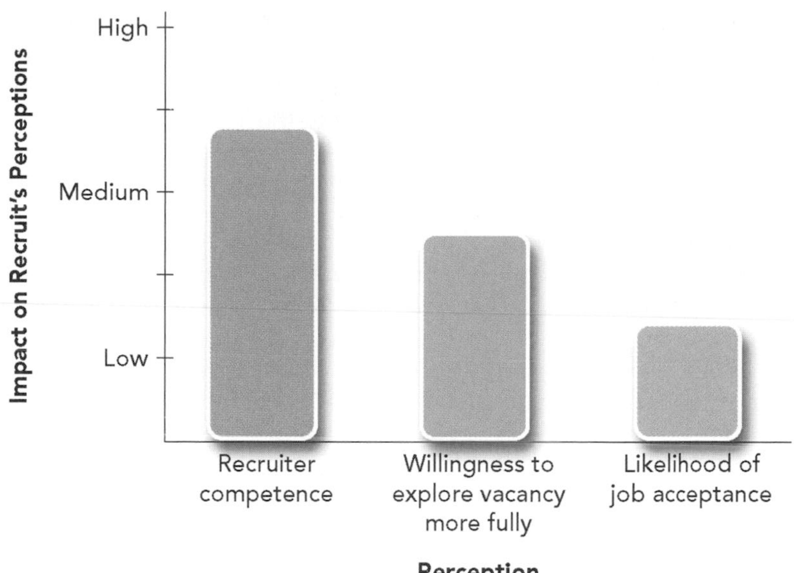

FIGURE 5.7
Relative Impact of the Recruiter on Various Recruitment Interview Outcomes

that the recruiter often gets involved late in the process. In many cases, by the time a recruiter meets some applicants, they have already made up their minds about what they desire in a job, what the current job has to offer, and their likelihood of receiving a job offer.[83]

Moreover, many applicants approach the recruiter with some degree of skepticism. Knowing that it is the recruiter's job to sell them on a vacancy, some applicants may discount what the recruiter says relative to what they have heard from other sources (like friends, magazine articles, and professors). For these and other reasons, recruiters' characteristics and behaviors seem to have less impact on applicants' job choices than we might expect. Moreover, as shown in Figure 5.7, whatever impact a recruiter does have on an applicant lessens as we move from reaction criteria (how the applicant felt about the recruiter) toward job choice criteria (whether the applicant takes the job).[84]

Recruiter's Functional Area. Most organizations must choose whether their recruiters are specialists in human resources or experts at particular jobs (supervisors or job incumbents). Some studies indicate that applicants find a job less attractive and the recruiter less credible when he is a personnel specialist.[85] This does not completely discount personnel specialists' role in recruiting, but it does indicate that such specialists need to take extra steps to ensure that applicants perceive them as knowledgeable and credible.

Recruiter's Traits. Two traits stand out when applicants' reactions to recruiters are examined. The first, which could be called "warmth," reflects the degree to which the recruiter seems to care about the applicant and is enthusiastic about her potential to contribute to the company. The second characteristic could be called "informativeness." In general, applicants respond more positively to recruiters who are perceived as warm and informative. These characteristics seem more important than such demographic characteristics as age, sex, or race, which have complex and inconsistent effects on applicant responses.[86]

Recruiter's Realism. Perhaps the most well-researched aspect of recruiting deals with the level of realism that the recruiter incorporates into his message. Since the recruiter's job is to attract candidates, there is some pressure to exaggerate the positive features of the vacancy while downplaying the negative features. Applicants are highly sensitive to negative information. Research suggests that the highest-quality applicants may be less willing to pursue jobs when this type of information comes out.[87] On the other hand, if the recruiter goes too far in a positive direction, the candidate can be misled and lured into taking the job under false pretenses. This can lead to a serious case of unmet expectations and a high turnover rate.[88] In fact, unrealistic descriptions of a job may even lead new job incumbents to believe that the employer is deceitful.[89]

Many studies have looked at the capacity of "realistic job previews" to circumvent this problem and help minimize early job turnover. On the whole, the research suggests that the effect of realistic job previews on eventual turnover is weak and inconsistent.[90] Certainly, the idea that one can go overboard in selling a vacancy to a recruit has merit. However, the belief that informing people about the negative

TABLE 5.5

Quotes from Recruits Who Were Repelled by Recruiters

One firm I didn't think of talking to initially, but they called me and asked me to talk with them. So I did, and then the recruiter was very, very rude. Yes, very rude, and I've run into that a couple of times. (engineering graduate)
I had a very bad campus interview experience . . . the person who came was a last-minute fill-in. . . . I think he had a couple of "issues" and was very discourteous during the interview. He was one step away from yawning in my face. . . .The other thing he did was that he kept making these (nothing illegal, mind you) but he kept making these references to the fact that I had been out of my undergraduate and first graduate programs for more than 10 years now. (MBA with 10 years of experience)
________ has a management training program which the recruiter had gone through. She was talking about the great presentational skills that ________ teaches you, and the woman was barely literate. She was embarrassing. If that was the best they could do, I did not want any part of them. Also, ________ and ________'s recruiters appeared to have real attitude problems. I also thought they were chauvinistic. (arts undergraduate)
________ had a set schedule for me which they deviated from regularly. Times overlapped, and one person kept me too long, which pushed the whole day back. They almost seemed to be saying that it was my fault that I was late for the next one! I guess a lot of what they did just wasn't very professional. Even at the point when I was done, where most companies would have a cab pick you up, I was in the middle of a snowstorm in Chicago and they said, "You can get a cab downstairs." There weren't any cabs. I literally had to walk 12 or 14 blocks with my luggage, trying to find some way to get to the airport. They didn't book me a hotel for the night of the snowstorm so I had to sit in the airport for eight hours trying to get another flight. . . They wouldn't even reimburse me for the additional plane fare. (industrial relations graduate student)
The guy at the interview made a joke about how nice my nails were and how they were going to ruin them there due to all the tough work. (engineering undergraduate)

SOURCE: S.L. Rynes, R.D. Bretz, Jr., and B. Gerhart, "The Importance of Recruitment in Job Choice: A Different Way of Looking," *Personnel Psychology* 44 (1991), pp. 487–521. Used by permission.

characteristics of the job will "inoculate" them to such characteristics seems unwarranted, based on the research conducted to date.[91] Thus we return to the conclusion that an organization's decisions about personnel policies that directly affect the job's attributes (pay, security, advancement opportunities, and so on) will probably be more important than recruiter traits and behaviors in affecting job choice.

Enhancing Recruiter Impact. Although research suggests that recruiters do not have much influence on job choice, this does not mean recruiters cannot have an impact. Most recruiters receive little training.[92] One research has attempted to find conditions in which recruiters do make a difference. Based on this research, an organization can take several steps to increase the impact that recruiters have on those they recruit.

First, recruiters can provide timely feedback. Applicants react very negatively to delays in feedback, often making unwarranted attributions for the delays (such as, the organization is uninterested in my application). Second, recruiters need to avoid behaviors that might convey the wrong organizational impression.[93] Table 5.5 lists quotes from applicants who felt that they had had extremely bad experiences with recruiters. Third, recruiting can be done in teams rather than by individuals. As we have seen, applicants tend to view line personnel (job incumbents and supervisors) as more credible than personnel specialists, so these kinds of recruiters should be part of any team. On the other hand, personnel specialists have knowledge that is not shared by line personnel (who may perceive recruiting as a small part of their "real" jobs), so they should be included as well.

A Look Back

The chapter opener showed how Southwest Airlines steadfastly refused to lay off workers, despite the pressure applied by the external environment. This one instance of behavior, however, was simply an extension of a long-term culture that used methods other than layoffs as a means of managing a labor surplus.

Questions

1. Based on this chapter, what steps can other firms that want to emulate Southwest take in order to avoid layoffs? That is, what are some alternatives to lay offs for avoiding a labor surplus?
2. How does the way a firm reacts to a labor shortage affect its ability to successfully manage a labor surplus?

Summary

Human resource planning uses labor supply and demand forecasts to anticipate labor shortages and surpluses. It also entails programs that can be utilized to reduce a labor surplus (such as downsizing and early retirement programs) and eliminate a labor shortage (like bringing in temporary workers or expanding overtime). When done well, human resource planning can enhance the success of the organization while minimizing the human suffering resulting from poorly anticipated labor surpluses or shortages. Human resource recruiting is a buffer activity that creates an applicant pool that the organization can draw from in the event of a labor shortage that is to be filled with new hires. Organizational recruitment programs affect applications through personnel policies (such as promote-from-within policies or due process provisions) that affect the attributes of the vacancies themselves. They can also impact the nature of people who apply for positions by using different recruitment sources (like recruiting from universities versus advertising in newspapers). Finally, organizations can use recruiters to influence individuals' perceptions of jobs (eliminating misconceptions, clarifying uncertainties) or perceptions of themselves (changing their valences for various work outcomes).

Discussion Questions

1. Discuss the effects that an impending labor shortage might have on the following three subfunctions of human resource management: selection and placement, training and career development, and compensation and benefits. Which subfunction might be most heavily impacted? In what ways might these groups develop joint cooperative programs to avert a labor shortage?
2. Discuss the costs and benefits associated with statistical versus judgmental forecasts for labor demand and labor supply. Under what conditions might either of these techniques be infeasible? Under what conditions might both be feasible, but one more desirable than the other?
3. Some companies have detailed affirmative action plans, complete with goals and timetables, for women and minorities, and yet have no formal human resource plan for the organization as a whole. Why might this be the case? If you were a human resource specialist interviewing with this company for an open position, what would this practice imply for the role of the human resource manager in that company?
4. Recruiting people for jobs that entail international assignments is increasingly important for many companies. Where might one go to look for individuals interested in these types of assignments? How might recruiting practices aimed at these people differ from those one might apply to the "average" recruit?
5. Discuss the relative merits of internal versus external recruitment. What types of business strategies might best be supported by recruiting externally, and what types might call for internal recruitment? What factors might lead a firm to decide to switch from internal to external recruitment or vice versa?

Web Exercise

In this chapter we discussed how electronic recruiting using the Web can identify and attract potential employees. Texas Instruments (TI) is using the Web not only to post job openings but to provide potential job candidates with information about the company so they can decide if their values and the working conditions they want are a "match" with those available at Texas Instruments. Go to **www.ti.com**, TI's home page on the Web. Click on "Employment" and then click on "Why Work at T.I.?". Click on "Fit Check". The "Fit Check" is a questionnaire that TI designed for potential job applicants to determine whether they "fit" with TIs environment and culture.

Questions

1. Complete the "Fit Check" as if you were interested in a job with TI.
2. What types of work environment characteristics and values are included in the "Fit Check"?
3. If the "Fit Check" indicates that a job candidate's interests and values do not match TI's, should they still consider working at TI? Explain your answer. What are some of the problems that TI might experience if a "mismatched" employee is hired?

Managing People: From the Pages of *BusinessWeek*

BusinessWeek Forget the Huddled Masses: Send Nerds

As a headhunter, George Van Derven has an unlikely connection: Russia's former state airline, Aeroflot. Not that Van Derven trades in pilots, flight mechanics, or surly Russian flight attendants. But in a former career, he sold a computerized reservation system to Aeroflot and came to know the talented programmers stashed in the back offices. When Aeroflot broke up into regional carriers in 1992, Van Derven promptly tapped its brain pool. Now, as president of Alternative Technology Resources Inc. in Sacramento, Van Derven is mining a rich lode of programming talent and busily dispatching it to understaffed computer departments throughout the Western world.

Other recruiters should be so lucky. High-tech headhunters for Andersen Consulting tramp through technical schools in Budapest and job fairs in Manila. At a recent training session for programmers in Holland, Microsoft Corp. hired bouncers to keep headhunters at bay. And a recruiter for IBM's Global Services Div., who is trying to hire 15,000 software hands this year alone, introduces himself as James R. Bunch, "as in bunch of jobs."

The Information Revolution is racing ahead of its vital raw material: brainpower. As demand explodes for computerized applications for everything from electronic commerce on the Internet to sorting out the Year 2000 glitch, companies are finding themselves strapped for programmers. In the United States alone, which accounts for two-thirds of the world's $300 billion market in software products and services, some 190,000 high-tech jobs stand open, most of them for programmers, according to the Information Technology Association.

That's sending companies scouring the globe for talent—and lifting salaries skyward. A typical programmer's wages, now some $70,000, is jumping 13 percent a year, and far higher in the hottest niches, such as Java Internet software and SAP business applications. These days, $20,000 signing bonuses are commonplace, and stock options are being handed out with as little fanfare as office supplies. If the pace keeps up, experts say, ballooning salaries could wind up damaging the global tech machine as margins are squeezed and investments postponed.

And relief is nowhere in sight. Experts predict the gap between computer science students and expected demand won't ease for a decade, if then. Too many bright young people, especially in Europe and the United States, consider programming geek work and choose other careers. In the United States, the number of computer science graduates has plummeted in the past decade or so, from 48,000 graduates in 1984 to an estimated 26,000 this year. "This is a real limiting factor to growth," says Avron Barr, a researcher at Stanford Computer Industry Project who is investigating the shortage.

Indeed, for high-tech companies, the dearth of programmers is the greatest threat to expansion in the coming year—far more menacing, they say, than an economic slump or competition in the marketplace. And it's not just a problem for tech companies. Plenty of others are desperate for the same talent. Automakers from Tokyo to Detroit are packing more computing power into their cars and plants. Banks, brokerages, and phone companies are rushing to outdo each other with the zippiest online services, all requiring herds of nerds. Those that choose not to install the newest technology, says Owens Corning CIO Michael Radcliff, are "creating a competitive liability."

Of course, if you're willing to pay—or have the stock options to entice—you could be up to your propeller hats in programmers. In Silicon Valley, star programmers are swimming in stock options, driving Porsches, and buying homes in the pricey Los Altos hills. At Netscape Communications Corp., which plans to hire more than 1,000 programmers this year, employees receive up to $5,000 just for a successful referral, and the pampered programmers are treated to onsite massages, teeth-cleanings, and laundry service. The company lines up their 49ers tickets and books their white-water rafting vacations. All this to keep them from succumbing to a stream of calls from headhunters. "Everybody's going crazy now trying to find these folks," says Margie Mader, Netscape's human resources director.

How did the shortage get so bad? For years, tech companies had little reason to fret. In the early '90s, the industry snapped up hundreds of thousands of workers who were dropped into the job market when large corporations downsized—a source now running dry.

At the same time, the very act of writing software has not speeded up despite the computer revolution and the terabytes of information hurtling around the globe. Today, even the best of programmers painstakingly turns out some 10 lines of code a day. To whip up today's software programs—even a cellular telephone requires some 300,000 lines of code—takes armies of programmers laboriously writing away. Consider this: There are 6 million software programmers and counting in the world today, 2 million of them in the United States and 1 million in Japan. As an industrial model, it's akin to pre-Gutenberg monasteries with their legions of scribbling monks.

For years, global savants pooh-poohed the pending programmer crunch by pointing to India, which boasted a seemingly bottomless reserve of techies. India, they said, would be to software what Saudi Arabia was to oil. And true, with 50,000 programmers pouring out of schools every year—twice the American total—India is a valuable labor pool.

But with global technology bursting to $3 trillion this decade—four times higher than in the '80s—India's supply simply isn't enough. And no other plentiful source of software skills appears to be on the horizon. Russia has promise, but it's limited: Few of its programmers speak English or understand business applications. China is a possibility, but it's likely to employ most of its programmers over the next decade for its own massive development projects. "I had this one programmer from China," laments one official at Electronic Data Systems Corp. "I took him through the whole immigration process, got his papers. Then he got a better offer."

Naturally, in this world of predators, there's a pecking order. Sitting on top are the fast-growth companies with hot Internet technologies. They're magnets for talented programmers, and they can pad their offers with rich stock options. Service companies such as Andersen Consulting, IBM Global Services, and Ernst & Young, which are helping companies install systems worldwide, are forced to routinely dole out six-figure salaries to programmers with experience in business applications. They compete with countless body shops—outsourcing companies that pay as much as $300,000 for skilled programmers willing to live on the road.

At the bottom of the pile are the corporate tech departments throughout the world. Many are short on money and stock options. And if they install a popular system, bringing their staff up to date on something new from, say, Oracle Corp. or the German software giant SAP, their departments get raided in no time. Don Yates became familiar with SAP's leading software package for business while helping install the system in the early '90s at Royal LePage Ltd., a real estate company in Toronto. Within a year, the 18-person department was picked clean. "I was the last one to go," says Yates, who now makes three times as much money, some $150,000, as an itinerant programmer for EMI, a Pittsburgh-based company that rents out software talent.

No surprise, then, that companies are trying any tactic, including turning to the World Wide Web. Since the Net is where most programmers spend idle hours, growing numbers of recruiters are using it to chase them down. That's where Michael L. McNeal casts his global net. McNeal, human resources chief at Cisco Systems Inc., needs to hire 1,000 people each quarter, many of them programmers. Like other recruiters, he buys ads on popular websites like the Dilbert page, which funnels traffic to Cisco's website. There the company lists some 500 current job openings. Applicants in foreign countries can hit hot buttons to translate the page into Cantonese, Mandarin, Russian. And, by filling out a short questionnaire, they can create a résumé and zap it to Cisco.

Cisco's Web page draws 500,000 job searches per month. This gives Cisco gobs of data about the job market, including which companies have interested employees. Armed with the best prospects, McNeal then turns to Cisco employees for help, asking them to call recruits, who speak the same language.

Like the others, Microsoft recruits on the Web and snaps up startups for talent—some 20 companies in 1996 alone. But to get its software up and running throughout the world, Microsoft relies on service companies, which are grossly understaffed. Microsoft calculates that its service partners are short 41,000 professionals trained to install Microsoft products. This is forcing the company to educate new recruits. With an effort known as Skills 2000, Microsoft is pushing into 350 schools and colleges around the world. It hammers out curricula that will produce more programmers, such as adding computer training in business schools.

A big part of the effort is in Europe, a major market that has 18 million unemployed workers. Microsoft's solution is to invite jobless Europeans in 11 countries into free training programs. In the past year, 3,000 Europeans have gone through the program, with 98 percent of them landing jobs.

It's in this $170 billion market for global software services, including the Big Six consulting firms, IBM Global Services, Manpower, and many others, that demand for programmers is especially hot. This is because corporations need loads of help to link far-flung operations with the latest in e-mail networks, inventory control, and finance packages. "The productive sector of the economy is becoming absolutely dependent on software systems," says reengineering author Michael Hammer. "If SAP vanished, you couldn't buy a can of Coke."

In the finance capitals of London, Tokyo, and Hong Kong, banks are installing vast new systems to adapt to Europe's single currency and Japan's financial deregulation. Meanwhile, they're working overtime to sort out the Year 2000 glitch, the dating problem companies face when the year of double zeroes rolls around. Mastech Corp., a Pittsburgh-based outsourcer, sent a handful of programmers a year ago to follow a Citibank contract from Singapore to London. Once in London, they found a wealth of other business and started importing more programmers from South Africa, Sri Lanka, India, and Australia. "We have 50 people now, and we'd hire another 50 today if we could find them," says country manager Guil Hastings.

As recruiters travel, they focus on regional specialties. The Russians are whizzes at math. India's university at Puna has a strong Japanese language program, which positions it well for Japan's Year 2000 workload. South African programmers learned to cope during the years of the anti-apartheid boycott with a motley collection of jerry-rigged mainframes. This makes them especially adept at Year 2000 work, which is targeted toward aging mainframe software.

As for programmers, the world is their oyster. In a computer lab in Austin, Texas, Natalia Bogataya and her husband, Konstantin Bobovich, both Belorussians and products of Van Derven's so-called Russian connection, labor away on a mainframe program. They've left their college-age children with relatives in Minsk and are debugging insurance software for Computer Sciences Corp. "We can't use our experience in our country," Bobovich explains, "and my wife said, 'Let's see America.'"

Why not? In today's fervid market, programmers can write their own tickets.

Questions

1. This case discusses the labor shortage associated with computer programmers that some fear will constrain worldwide economic growth as we enter the new millennium. What characteristics of the product demand market have led to the explosion in demand for pro-

grammers? What characteristics of the programming job have limited the number of people willing to develop the skills necessary to meet this demand? Which of the seven options this chapter listed for avoiding a labor shortage have been attempted by employers in this market? Which do you think will be most successful?

2. Some have argued that the shortage of programmers is partly due to employers that (a) tend to offer temporary employment arrangements rather than full-time ones to maintain flexibility, (b) discriminate against older programmers in favor of younger ones who will work longer hours, and (c) substitute low-paid immigrant workers for higher-wage American workers. To what extent does this seem to be true or false? To what extent can an actual or perceived labor shortage be created by employers because of their chosen business strategies?

Notes

1. D.W. Jarrell, *Human Resource Planning: A Business Planning Approach* (Englewood Cliffs, NJ: Prentice-Hall, 1993).
2. B. Schlender, "Matsushita Shows How to Go Global," *Fortune* (July 11, 1994), pp. 159–66.
3. P. Smith, "Salariless Man," *The Economist* (September 16, 1995), p. 79.
4. M. Conlin, "Suddenly, It's the Big Freeze," *BusinessWeek* (April 16, 2001), pp. 38–39.
5. M. Conlin, "Savaged by the Slowdown," *BusinessWeek* (September 17, 2001), pp. 74–77.
6. W.F. Cascio, "Whither Industrial and Organizational Psychology in a Changing World of Work?" *American Psychologist* 50 (1995), pp. 928–39.
7. D. Greising, "It's the Best of Times—Or Is It?" *BusinessWeek* (January 12, 1998), pp. 35–38.
8. A. Serwer, "What's Hot on Wall Street in 2001? Cost Cutting and Layoffs," *Fortune* (February 19, 2001), pp. 34–36.
9. M. Magnet, "The Productivity Payoff Arrives," *Fortune* (July 27, 1994), pp. 79–84.
10. R.T. King, "Is Job Cutting by Drug Makers Bad Medicine?" *The Wall Street Journal* (August 23, 1995), pp. B1–B3.
11. Greising, "It's the Best of Times."
12. K. Labich, "The Geography of an Emerging America," *Fortune* (June 27, 1994), pp. 88–94.
13. Greising, "It's the Best of Times."
14. K.P. DeMeuse, P.A. Vanderheiden, and T.J. Bergmann, "Announced Layoffs: Their Effect on Corporate Financial Performance," *Human Resource Management* 33 (1994), pp. 509–30.
15. P.P. Shaw, "Network Destruction: The Structural Implications of Downsizing," *Academy of Management Journal* 43 (2000), pp. 101–12.
16. King, "Is Job Cutting by Drug Makers Bad Medicine?"
17. W.F. Cascio, "Downsizing: What Do We Know? What Have We Learned?" *Academy of Management Executive* 7 (1993), pp. 95–104.
18. J. Schu, "Internet Helps Keep Goodwill of Downsized Employees," *Workforce*, July 2001, p. 15.
19. D. Skarlicki, J.H. Ellard, and B.R.C. Kellin, "Third Party Perceptions of a Layoff: Procedural, Derogation, and Retributive Aspects of Justice," *Journal of Applied Psychology* 83 (1998), pp. 119–27.
20. R. Folger and D.P. Skarlicki, "When Tough Times Make Tough Bosses: Managerial Distancing as a Function of Layoff Blame," *Academy of Management Journal* 41 (1998), pp. 79–87.
21. R. Stodghill, "The Coming Job Bottleneck," *BusinessWeek* (March 24, 1997), pp. 184–85.
22. Ibid.
23. S. Kim and D. Feldman, "Healthy, Wealthy, or Wise: Predicting Actual Acceptances of Early Retirement Incentives at Three Points in Time," *Personnel Psychology* 51 (1998), pp. 623–42.
24. P. Wechsler, "AT&T Managers Rush out the Door," *BusinessWeek* (June 15, 1998), p. 53.
25. D. Fandray, "Gray Matters," *Workforce*, July 2000, pp. 27–32.
26. L. Schiff, "Manufacturing's Hidden Asset: Temporary Employees," *Fortune* (November 10, 1997), pp. 28–29.
27. S. Caudron, "Contingent Work Force Spurs HR Planning," *Personnel Journal*, July 1994, pp. 52–59.
28. G. Flynn, "Contingent Staffing Requires Serious Strategy," *Personnel Journal*, April 1995, pp. 50–58.
29. S. Caudron, "Are Your Temps Doing Their Best?" *Personnel Journal*, November 1995, pp. 32–38.
30. T. Cothran, "Outsourcing on the Inside Track," *Training*, May 1995, pp. 31–37.
31. K. Bradsher, "American Workers Watch as Jobs Go Overseas," *International Herald Tribune* (August 29, 1995), pp. C1–C2.
32. R.A. Bettis, S.P. Bradley, and G. Hamel, "Outsourcing and Industrial Decline," *Academy of Management Executive* 6 (1992), pp. 7–22.
33. Ibid.

34. G. Koretz, "Overtime versus New Factories," *BusinessWeek* (May 4, 1998), p. 34.
35. A. Bernstein, "Bell Atlantic North Faces a Monstrous Labor Crunch," *BusinessWeek* (June 8, 1998), p. 38.
36. G.N. Powell and D.A. Butterfield, "Effect of Race on Promotions to Top Management in a Federal Department," *Academy of Management Journal* 40 (1997), pp. 112–28.
37. A.E. Barber, *Recruiting Employees* (Thousand Oaks, CA: Sage, 1998).
38. J.A. Breaugh, *Recruitment: Science and Practice* (Boston: PWS-Kent, 1992).
39. C.K. Stevens, "Antecedents of Interview Interactions, Interviewers' Ratings, and Applicants' Reactions," *Personnel Psychology* 51 (1998), pp. 55–85.
40. A.E. Barber, J.R. Hollenbeck, S.L. Tower, and J.M. Phillips, "The Effects of Interview Focus on Recruitment Effectiveness: A Field Experiment," *Journal of Applied Psychology* 79 (1994), pp. 886–96.
41. J.D. Olian and S.L. Rynes, "Organizational Staffing: Integrating Practice with Strategy," *Industrial Relations* 23 (1984), pp. 170–83.
42. R. Kanfer, C.R. Wanberg, and T.M. Kantrowitz, "Job Search and Employment: A Personality–Motivational Analysis and Meta-Analytic Review," *Journal of Applied Psychology* 86 (2001), pp. 837–55.
43. G.T. Milkovich and J.M. Newman, *Compensation* (Homewood, IL: Richard D. Irwin, 1990).
44. S.J. Marks, "After School," *Human Resources Executive* (June 15, 2001), pp. 49–51.
45. J. Kaufman, "A McDonald's Owner Becomes a Role Model for Black Teenagers," *The Wall Street Journal* (August 23, 1995), p. A1.
46. K. Helliker, "Sold on the Job: Retailing Chains Offer a Lot of Opportunity, Young Managers Find," *The Wall Street Journal* (August 25, 1995), p. A1.
47. K. Clark, "Reasons to Worry about Rising Wages," *Fortune* (July 7, 1997), pp. 31–32.
48. Jobtrack.com, "Changing Views on Valued Benefits" (June 30, 2001), p. 1.
49. M. Leonard, "Challenges to the Termination-at-Will Doctrine," *Personnel Administrator* 28 (1983), pp. 49–56.
50. C. Schowerer and B. Rosen, "Effects of Employment-at-Will Policies and Compensation Policies on Corporate Image and Job Pursuit Intentions," *Journal of Applied Psychology* 74 (1989), pp. 653–56.
51. M. Magnus, "Recruitment Ads at Work," *Personnel Journal* 64 (1985), pp. 42–63.
52. S.L. Rynes and A.E. Barber, "Applicant Attraction Strategies: An Organizational Perspective," *Academy of Management Review* 15 (1990), pp. 286–310.
53. Breaugh, *Recruitment*.
54. J. Bussey, "Dow Chemical Tries to Shed Tough Image and Court the Public," *The Wall Street Journal* (November 20, 1987), p. 1.
55. R. Thompson, "More Diversity in Agriculture: A Hard Row," *The Wall Street Journal* (September 19, 1995), p. B1.
56. D.M. Cable, L. Aiman-Smith, P. Mulvey, and J.R. Edwards, "The Sources and Accuracy of Job Applicants' Beliefs about Organizational Culture," *Academy of Management Journal* 43 (2000), pp. 1076–85.
57. M.A. Conrad and S.D. Ashworth, "Recruiting Source Effectiveness: A Meta-analysis and Re-examination of Two Rival Hypotheses" (paper presented at the annual meeting of the Society of Industrial/Organizational Psychology, Chicago, 1986).
58. Breaugh, *Recruitment*.
59. P. A. Savill, "HR at Inova Reengineers Recruitment Process," *Personnel Journal*, June 1995, pp. 109–14.
60. Breaugh, *Recruitment*.
61. R.S. Schuler and S.E. Jackson, "Linking Competitive Strategies with Human Resource Management Practices," *Academy of Management Executive* 1 (1987), pp. 207–19.
62. C.R. Wanberg, R. Kanfer, and J.T. Banas, "Predictors and Outcomes of Networking Intensity among Job Seekers," *Journal of Applied Psychology* 85 (2000), pp. 491–503.
63. C.R. Williams, C.E. Labig, and T.H. Stone, "Recruitment Sources and Posthire Outcomes for Job Applicants and New Hires: A Test of Two Hypotheses," *Journal of Applied Psychology* 78 (1994), pp. 163–72.
64. A. Halcrow, "Employers Are Your Best Recruiters," *Personnel Journal* 67 (1988), pp. 42–49.
65. G. Flynn, "Do You Have the Right Approach to Diversity?" *Personnel Journal*, October 1995, pp. 68–75.
66. B.P. Sunoo, "Papa John's Rolls Out Hot HR Menu," *Personnel Journal*, September 1995, pp. 38–47.
67. Breaugh, *Recruitment*.
68. K.H. Hammonds, "Welfare to Work: A Good Start," *BusinessWeek* (June 1, 1998), pp. 102–4.
69. J. Mitchell, "BMW Names 2 Honda Executives to Oversee New U.S. Assembly Plant," *The Wall Street Journal* (November 29, 1992), p. B4.
70. J. Reingold, "Casting for a Different Set of Characters," *BusinessWeek* (December 8, 1997), pp. 38–39.
71. J. Greenwald, "Invasion of the Body Snatchers," *Time* (April 23, 1984), p. 41.
72. P. Smith, "Sources Used by Employers When Hiring College Grads," *Personnel Journal*, February 1995, p. 25.
73. J.W. Boudreau and S.L. Rynes, "Role of Recruitment in Staffing Utility Analysis," *Journal of Applied Psychology* 70 (1985), pp. 354–66.
74. D. Anfuso, "3M's Staffing Strategy Promotes Produc-

tivity and Pride," *Personnel Journal*, February 1995, pp. 28–34.

75. L. Winter, "Employers Go to School on Minority Recruiting," *The Wall Street Journal* (December 15, 1992), p. B1.
76. C.M Solomon, "Navigating Your Search for Global Talent," *Personnel Journal*, May 1995, p. 94–97.
77. J. Smith, "Is Online Recruiting Getting Easier?" *Workforce* (September 2, 2001), p. 25.
78. C. Timberlake, "Corporate Web Sites Increasingly Offer Chances to Apply for Open Jobs Online," *The Wall Street Journal* (October 30, 2001), p. 1.
79. S. Bills, "A Wider Net for Hiring," *CNN/Money Online* (July 26, 2000), p. 1.
80. A. Salkever, "A Better Way to Float Your Resume," *BusinessWeek Online* (October 9, 2000), pp. 1–2.
81. K.O. Magnusen and K.G. Kroeck, "Video Conferencing Maximizes Recruiting," *HRMagazine*, August 1995, pp. 70–72.
82. R. Hawk, *The Recruitment Function* (New York: American Management Association, 1967).
83. C.K. Stevens, "Effects of Preinterview Beliefs on Applicants' Reactions to Campus Interviews," *Academy of Management Journal* 40 (1997), pp. 947–66.
84. C.D. Fisher, D.R. Ilgen, and W.D. Hoyer, "Source Credibility, Information Favorability, and Job Offer Acceptance," *Academy of Management Journal* 22 (1979), pp. 94–103; G.N. Powell, "Applicant Reactions to the Initial Employment Interview: Exploring Theoretical and Methodological Issues," *Personnel Psychology* 44 (1991), pp. 67–83; N. Schmitt and B.W. Coyle, "Applicant Decisions in the Employment Interview," *Journal of Applied Psychology* 61 (1976), pp. 184–92.
85. M.S. Taylor and T.J. Bergman, "Organizational Recruitment Activities and Applicants' Reactions at Different Stages of the Recruitment Process," *Personnel Psychology* 40 (1984), pp. 261–85; Fisher, Ilgen, and Hoyer, "Source Credibility."
86. L.M. Graves and G.N. Powell, "The Effect of Sex Similarity on Recruiters' Evaluations of Actual Applicants: A Test of the Similarity–Attraction Paradigm," *Personnel Psychology* 48 (1995), pp. 85–98.
87. R.D. Bretz and T.A. Judge, "Realistic Job Previews: A Test of the Adverse Self-Selection Hypothesis," *Journal of Applied Psychology* 83 (1998), pp. 330–37.
88. J.P. Wanous, *Organizational Entry: Recruitment, Selection and Socialization of Newcomers* (Reading, MA: Addison-Wesley, 1980).
89. P. Hom, R.W. Griffeth, L.E. Palich, and J.S. Bracker, "An Exploratory Investigation into Theoretical Mechanisms Underlying Realistic Job Previews," *Personnel Psychology* 51 (1998), pp. 421–51.
90. G.M. McEvoy and W.F. Cascio, "Strategies for Reducing Employee Turnover: A Meta-analysis," *Journal of Applied Psychology* 70 (1985), pp. 342–53; S.L. Premack and J.P. Wanous, "A Meta-analysis of Realistic Job Preview Experiments," *Journal of Applied Psychology* 70 (1985), pp. 706–19.
91. P.G. Irving and J.P. Meyer, "Reexamination of the Met-Expectations Hypothesis: A Longitudinal Analysis," *Journal of Applied Psychology* 79 (1995), pp. 937–49.
92. R.W. Walters, "It's Time We Become Pros," *Journal of College Placement* 12 (1985), pp. 30–33.
93. S.L. Rynes, R.D. Bretz, and B. Gerhart, "The Importance of Recruitment in Job Choice: A Different Way of Looking," *Personnel Psychology* 44 (1991), pp. 487–522.

Chapter 6 Selection and Placement

Objectives

After reading this chapter, you should be able to:

1. Establish the basic scientific properties of personnel selection methods, including reliability, validity, and generalizability.

2. Discuss how the particular characteristics of a job, organization, or applicant affect the utility of any test.

3. Describe the government's role in personnel selection decisions, particularly in the areas of constitutional law, federal laws, executive orders, and judicial precedent.

4. List the common methods used in selecting human resources.

5. Describe the degree to which each of the common methods used in selecting human resources meets the demands of reliability, validity, generalizability, utility, and legality.

The need for background checks when hiring new employees is greater than ever. Companies like Kroll Associates help employers detect and respond to problematic applicants being considered for jobs. Hiring an investigative agency such as this one, or performing psychological testing could save a company time, money, and legal problems in the long run.

Enter the World of Business

Never Having to Say "You Never Know"

Seymour Schlager had an impressive résumé. He had both MD and JD degrees, as well as a PhD in microbiology. He had experience as a director of established AIDS research at Abbott Laboratories, and as an entrepreneur in a small, upstart pharmaceutical company. He seemed like a perfect fit for the medical director job open at Becton Dickinson, a large medical device company, and was hired on the spot.

One fact about Schlager that did not come out of the application process was that he was convicted of attempted murder in 1991 and had spent several years in prison as a result of this crime. While any reader of this book could type Schlager's name into almost any Internet search engine and uncover at least one of the 24 articles written about his case—some of which were front-page material in the *Chicago Tribune*—apparently no one at Becton Dickinson felt this was necessary.

Although this is an extreme case, the practice of stretching, shading, spinning, and outright lying on one's résumé is hardly uncommon, and when one is in the business of hiring complete strangers, it pays to "be afraid—be very afraid." Although many firms fail to perform routine background checks on their hires, organizations that provide such checks can point to some startling statistics. For example, Kroll Associates, one of the leading investigative agencies for top-level executives, notes that of the 70 background checks it did in the year 2000, 39 percent turned up problems such as fraud, bankruptcy, and SEC violations that were serious enough to nix the employment offers being considered.

One reason for the lack of "due diligence" on the part of employers is that in a labor shortage, too many are in a rush to secure top talent. For example, when the firm Christian and Timbers narrowed the search for the new CEO of Pinpoint Networks Inc. down to six candidates, rather than let the firm finish its work, the young founders of this company were so infatuated with the résumé of one applicant that they immediately took over and closed the search. Unfortunately, when it became clear 13 weeks later that the new CEO, Anthony J. Blake, was not who he claimed to be, it was too late. Without a seasoned CEO, Pinpoint blew the opportunity to attract venture capital when it was still available. When the technology sector tanked later that year, Pinpoint was forced to lay off over a third of its workforce.

Experiences such as these are prompting other employers to slow down the hiring process so that they have a much better idea of exactly whom they are asking to join their organizational family. Some firms do not only background checks but also extensive psychological testing to ensure that a person is who he or she claims to be and also fits the culture of the organization. You never know what these kinds of investigations will uncover—unless, of course, you fail to perform them.

SOURCE: G. David, "You Just Hired Him: Should You Have Known Better," *Fortune* (October 29, 2001), pp. 205–6; D. Foust, "When the CEO Is Too Good to Be True," *BusinessWeek* (July 16, 2001), pp. 62–63; C. Daniels, "Does This Man Need a Shrink?" *Fortune* (February 5, 2001).

Introduction

Any organization that intends to compete through people must take the utmost care with how it chooses organizational members. As one can see from our opening vignette, personnel selection decisions made by the organization are instrumental to its ability to survive, adapt, and grow. The competitive aspects of selection decisions become especially critical when organizations are confronted with tight labor markets or when competitors tap the same labor market. If one company systematically skims off the best applicants, the remaining companies must make do with what is left.

The purpose of this chapter is to familiarize you with ways to minimize errors in employee selection and placement and, in doing so, improve your company's competitive position. The chapter first focuses on five standards that should be met by any selection method. The chapter then evaluates several common selection methods according to those standards.

Selection Method Standards

Personnel selection is the process by which companies decide who will or will not be allowed into their organizations. Several generic standards should be met in any selection process. We focus on five: (1) reliability, (2) validity, (3) generalizability, (4) utility, and (5) legality. The first four build off each other in the sense that the preceding standard is often necessary but not sufficient for the one that follows. This is less the case with legal standards. However, a thorough understanding of the first four standards helps us understand the rationale underlying many legal standards.

Reliability

Much of the work in personnel selection involves measuring characteristics of people to determine who will be accepted for job openings. For example, we might be interested in applicants' physical characteristics (like strength or endurance), their cognitive abilities (such as mathematical ability or verbal reasoning capacity), or aspects of their personality (like their initiative or integrity). Whatever the specific focus, in the end we need to quantify people on these dimensions (assign numbers to them) so we can order them from high to low on the characteristic of interest. Once people are ordered in this way, we can decide whom to hire and whom to reject.

Reliability
The consistency of a performance measure; the degree to which a performance measure is free from random error.

One key standard for any measuring device is its reliability. We define **reliability** as the degree to which a measure is free from random error.[1] If a measure of some supposedly stable characteristic such as intelligence is reliable, then the score a person receives based on that measure will be consistent over time and in different contexts.

True Scores and the Reliability of Measurement

Most measuring done in personnel selection deals with complex characteristics like intelligence, integrity, and leadership ability. However, to appreciate some of the complexities in measuring people, we will consider something concrete in discussing these concepts: the measurement of height. For example, if we were measuring an applicant's height, we might start by using a 12-inch ruler. Let's say the first person we measure turns out to be 6 feet 1 and 4⁄16 inches tall. It would not be surprising to find out that someone else measuring the same person a second time, perhaps an hour later, found this applicant's height to be 6 feet and 12⁄16 inches. The same applicant, measured a third time, maybe the next day, might be measured at 6 feet 1 and 8⁄16 inches tall.

As this example makes clear, even though the person's height is a stable characteristic, we get slightly different results each time he is assessed. This means that each time the person is assessed, we must be making slight errors. If a measurement device were perfectly reliable, there would be no errors of measurement. If we used a measure of height that was not as reliable as a ruler—for example, guessing someone's height after seeing her walk across the room—we might see an even greater amount of unreliability in the measure. Thus *reliability* refers to the measuring instrument (a ruler versus a visual guess) rather than to the characteristic itself.

Because one never really knows the true score for the person being measured, there is no direct way to capture the "true" reliability of the measure. We can estimate reliability in several different ways, however; and because most of these rely on computing a correlation coefficient, we will briefly describe and illustrate this statistic.

The *correlation coefficient* is a measure of the degree to which two sets of numbers are related. The correlation coefficient expresses the strength of the relationship in numerical form. A perfect positive relationship (as one set of numbers goes up, so does the other) equals +1.0; a perfect negative relationship (as one goes up, the other goes down) equals –1.0. When there is no relationship between the sets of numbers, the correlation equals .00. Although the actual calculation of this statistic goes beyond the scope of this book (see any introductory statistics book or spreadsheet program), it will be useful for us to conceptually examine the nature of the correlation coefficient and what this means in personnel selection contexts.

When assessing the reliability of a measure, for example, we might be interested in knowing how scores on the measure at one time relate to scores on the same measure at another time. Obviously, if the characteristic we are measuring is supposedly stable (like intelligence or integrity) and the time lapse is short, this relationship should be strong. If it were weak, then the measure would be inconsistent—hence unreliable. This is called assessing *test–retest reliability*.

Plotting the two sets of numbers on a two-dimensional graph often helps us to appreciate the meaning of various levels of the correlation coefficient. Figure 6.1, for example, examines the relationship between student scholastic aptitude in one's junior and senior years in high school, where aptitude for college is measured in three ways: (1) via the scores on the Scholastic Aptitude Test (SAT), (2) via ratings from a high school counselor on a 1-to-100 scale, and (3) via tossing dice. In this plot, each X on the graphs represents a person whose scholastic aptitude is assessed twice (in the junior and senior years), so in Figure 6.1a, X_1 represents a person who scored 1580 on the

FIGURE 6.1A

Measurements of a Student's Aptitude

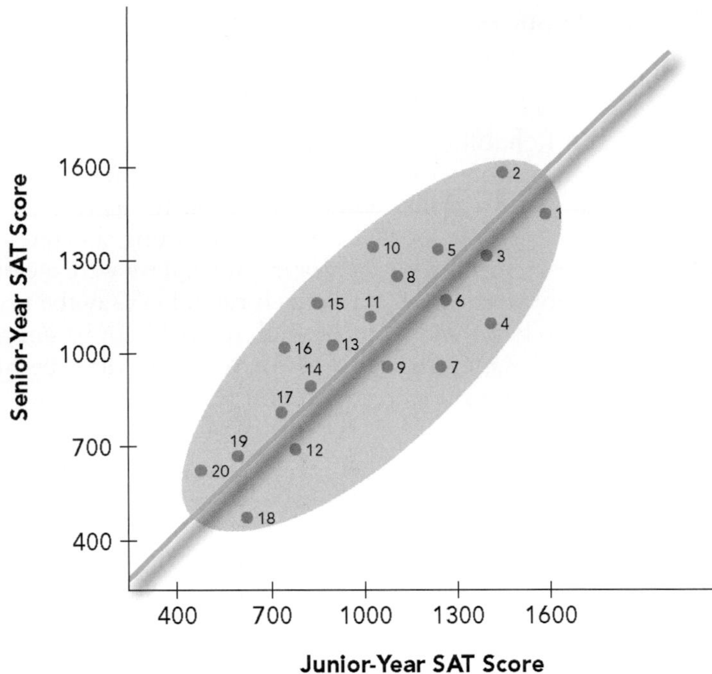

SAT in the junior year and 1500 in the senior year; X_{20} represents a person who scored 480 in the junior year and 620 in the senior year.

Figure 6.1a shows a very strong relationship between SAT scores across the two years. This relationship is not perfect in that the scores changed slightly from one year to the next, but not a great deal. Indeed, if there were a perfect 1.0 correlation, the plot would show a straight line at a 45-degree angle. The correlation coefficient for this set of data is in the .90 range. In this case, .90 is considered the test–retest estimate of reliability.

Turning to Figure 6.1b, we see that the relationship between the high school counselors' ratings across the two years, while still positive, is not as strong. That is, the counselors' ratings of individual students' aptitudes for college are less consistent over the two years than their test scores. The correlation, and hence test–retest reliability, of this measure of aptitude is in the .50 range.

Finally, Figure 6.1c shows a worst-case scenario, where the students' aptitudes are assessed by tossing two six-sided dice. As you would expect, the random nature of the dice means that there is virtually no relationship between scores taken in one year and scores taken the next. Hence, in this instance, the correlation and test–retest estimate of reliability are .00. Although no one would seriously consider tossing dice to be a measure of aptitude, it is worth noting that research shows that the correlation of overall ratings of job applicants' suitability for jobs based on unstructured interviews is very close to .00. Thus, one cannot assume a measure is reliable without actually checking this directly. Novices in measurement are often surprised at exactly how unreliable many human judgments turn out to be.

Standards for Reliability

Regardless of what characteristic we are measuring, we want highly reliable measures. Thus, in the previous example, when it comes to measuring students' aptitudes for

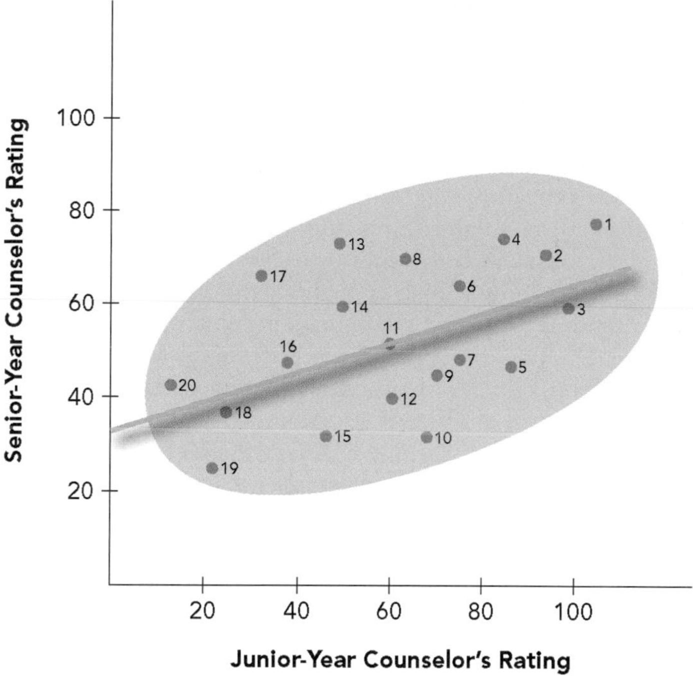

FIGURE 6.1B

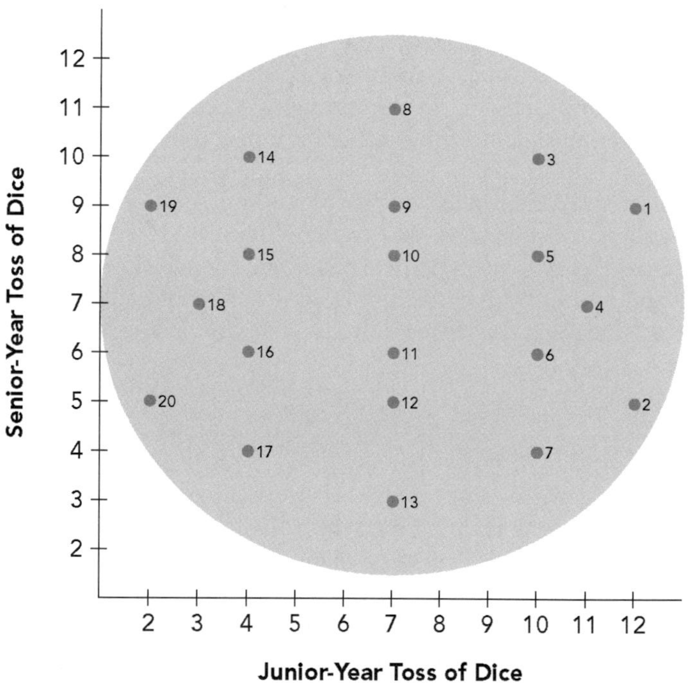

FIGURE 6.1C

college, the SAT is more reliable than counselor ratings, which in turn are more reliable than tossing dice. But in an absolute sense, how high is high enough—.50, .70, .90? This is a difficult question to answer specifically because the required reliability depends in part on the nature of the decision being made about the people being measured.

For example, let's assume some college admissions officer was considering several students depicted in Figures 6.1a and 6.1b. Turning first to Figure 6.1b, assume the admissions officer was deciding between Student 1 (X_1) and Student 20 (X_{20}). For this decision, the .50 reliability of the ratings is high enough because the difference between the two students is so large that one would make the same decision for admission regardless of the year in which the rating was taken. That is, Student 1 (with scores of 100 and 80 in the junior and senior year, respectively) is always admitted and Student 20 (with scores of 12 and 42 for junior and senior years, respectively) is always rejected. Thus, although the ratings in this case are not all that reliable in an absolute sense, their reliability is high enough for this decision.

On the other hand, let's assume the same college admissions officer was deciding between Student 1 (X_1) and Student 2 (X_2). Looking at Figure 6.1a, it is clear that even with the highly reliable SAT scores, the difference between these students is so small that one would make a different admission decision depending on what year one obtained the score. Student 1 would be selected over Student 2 if the junior-year score was used, but Student 2 would be chosen over Student 1 if the senior-year score was used. Thus, even though the reliability of the SAT exam is high in an absolute sense, it is not high enough for this decision. Under these conditions, the admissions officer needs to find some other basis for making the decision regarding these two students (like high school GPA or rank in graduating class).

Although these two scenarios clearly show that no specific value of reliability is always acceptable, they also demonstrate why, all else being equal, the more reliable a measure is, the better. For example, turning again to Figures 6.1a and 6.1b, consider Student 9 (X_9) and Student 14 (X_{14}). One would not be able to make a decision between these two students based on scholastic aptitude scores if assessed via counselor ratings, because the unreliability in the ratings is so large that scores across the two years conflict. That is, Student 9 has a higher rating than Student 14 in the junior year, but Student 14 has a higher rating than Student 9 in the senior year.

On the other hand, one would be able to base the decision on scholastic aptitude scores if assessed via the SAT, because the unreliability of the SAT scores is so low that scores across the two years point to the same conclusion. That is, Student 9's scores are always higher than Student 14's scores. Clearly, all else being equal, the more reliable the measure, the more likely it is that we can base decisions on the score differences that it reveals.

Validity
The extent to which a performance measure assesses all the relevant—and only the relevant—aspects of job performance.

Validity

We define **validity** as the extent to which performance on the measure is related to performance on the job. A measure must be reliable if it is to have any validity. On the other hand, we can reliably measure many characteristics (like height) that may have no relationship to whether someone can perform a job. For this reason, reliability is a necessary but insufficient condition for validity.

Criterion-related validity
A method of establishing the validity of a personnel selection method by showing a substantial correlation between test scores and job-performance scores.

Criterion-Related Validation

One way of establishing the validity of a selection method is to show that there is an empirical association between scores on the selection measure and scores for job performance. If there is a substantial correlation between test scores and job-performance scores, **criterion-related validity** has been established. For example, Figure 6.2 shows the relationship between 2000 scores on the Scholastic Aptitude

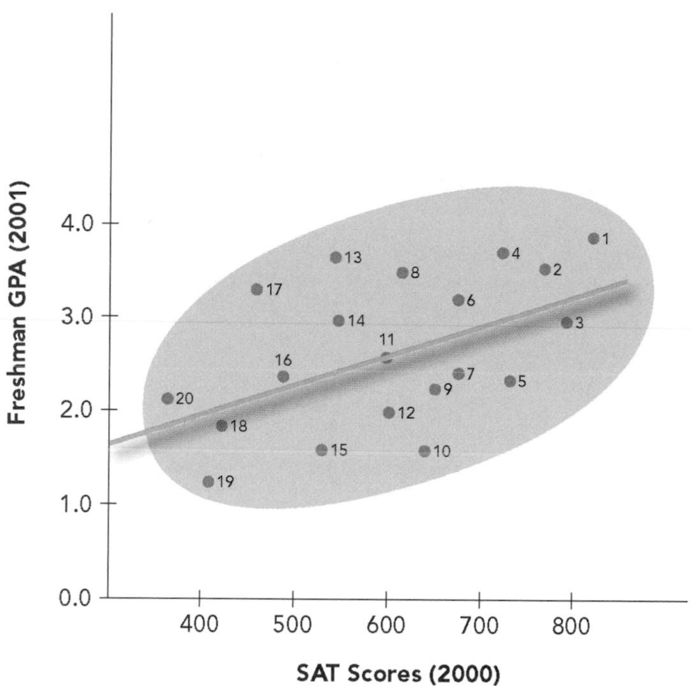

FIGURE 6.2
Relationship between 2000 SAT Scores and 2001 Freshman GPA

Test (SAT) and 2001 freshman grade point average (GPA). In this example, there is roughly a .50 correlation between the SAT and GPA. This .50 is referred to as a *validity coefficient*. Note that we have used the correlation coefficient to assess both reliability and validity, which may seem somewhat confusing. The key distinction is that the correlation reflects a reliability estimate when we are attempting to assess the same characteristic twice (such as SAT scores in the junior and senior years), but the correlation coefficient reflects a validity coefficient when we are attempting to relate one characteristic (SAT) to performance on some task (GPA).

Predictive validation
A criterion-related validity study that seeks to establish an empirical relationship between applicants' test scores and their eventual performance on the job.

Criterion-related validity studies come in two varieties. **Predictive validation** seeks to establish an empirical relationship between test scores taken prior to being hired and eventual performance on the job. Predictive validation requires one to administer tests to job applicants and then wait for some time after test administration to see how a subset of those applicants (those who were actually hired) performed.

Concurrent validation
A criterion-related validity study in which a test is administered to all the people currently in a job and then incumbents' scores are correlated with existing measures of their performance on the job.

Because of the time and effort required to conduct a predictive validation study, many employers are tempted to use a different design. **Concurrent validation** assesses the validity of a test by administering it to people already on the job and then correlating test scores with existing measures of each person's performance. The logic behind this strategy is that if the best performers currently on the job perform better on the test than those who are currently struggling on the job, the test has validity. (Figure 6.3 compares the two types of validation study.)

Despite the extra effort and time needed for predictive validation, it is superior to concurrent validation for a number of reasons, First, job applicants (because they are seeking work) are typically more motivated to perform well on the tests than are current employees (who already have jobs). Second, current employees have learned many things on the job that job applicants have not yet learned. Therefore, the correlation between test scores and job performance for current employees may not be the same as the correlation between test scores and job performance for less

FIGURE 6.3
Graphic Depiction of Concurrent and Predictive Validation Designs

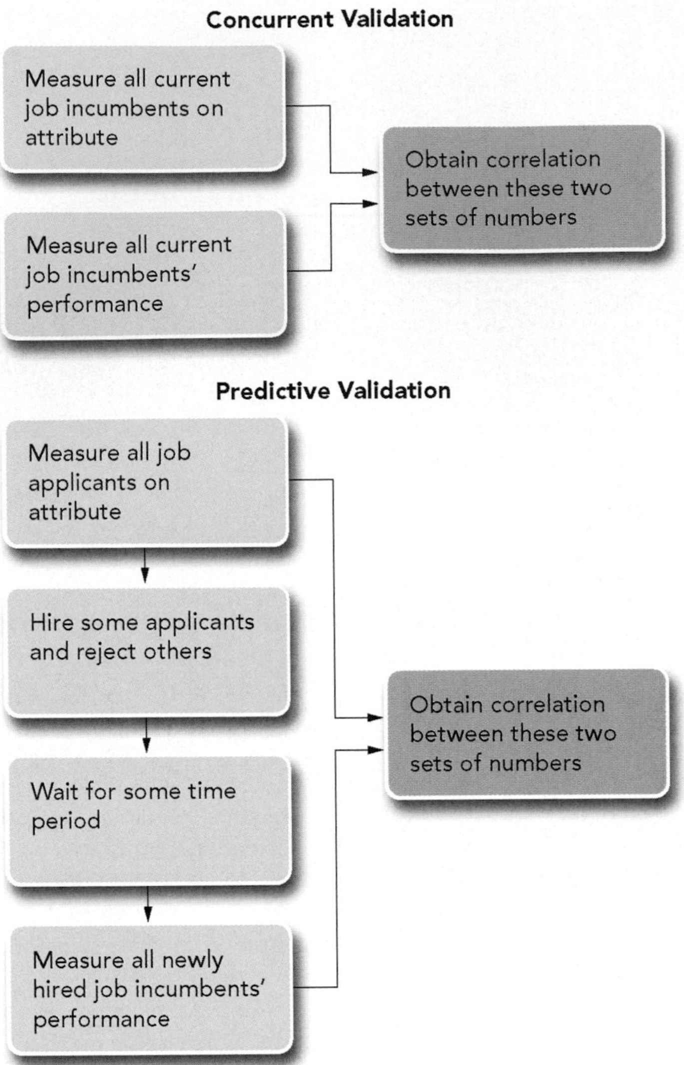

knowledgeable job applicants. Third, current employees tend to be homogeneous—that is, similar to each other on many characteristics.[2] Thus, on many of the characteristics needed for success on the job, most current employees will show restriction in range. This restricted range makes it hard to detect a relationship between test scores and job-performance scores because few of the current employees will be very low on the characteristic you are trying to validate. For example, if emotional stability is required for a nursing career, it is quite likely that most nurses who have amassed five or six years' experience will score high on this characteristic. Yet to validate a test, you need both high test scorers (who should subsequently perform well on the job) and low test scorers (who should perform poorly on the job). Thus, although concurrent studies can sometimes help one anticipate the results of predictive studies, they do not serve as substitutes.[3]

Obviously, we would like our measures to be high in validity; but as with the reliability standard, we must also ask, how high is high enough? When trying to deter-

TABLE 6.1

Required Level of Correlation to Reach Statistical Significance as a Function of Sample Size

SAMPLE SIZE	REQUIRED CORRELATION
5	.75
10	.58
20	.42
40	.30
80	.21
100	.19

mine how much validity is enough, one typically has to turn to tests of statistical significance. A test of statistical significance answers the question, "How likely is it that a correlation of this size could have come about through luck or chance?"

Table 6.1 shows how big a correlation between a selection measure and a measure of job performance needs to be to achieve statistical significance at a level of .05 (that is, there is only a 5 out of 100 chance that one could get a correlation this big by chance alone). Although it is generally true that bigger correlations are better, the size of the sample on which the correlation is based plays a large role as well. Because many of the selection methods we examine in the second half of this chapter generate correlations in the .20s and .30s, we often need samples of 80 to 90 people.[4] A validation study with a small sample (such as 20 people) is almost doomed to failure from the start. Thus, many companies are too small to use a criterion-related validation strategy for most, if not all, of their jobs.

Content Validation

When sample sizes are small, an alternative test validation strategy, content validation, can be used. **Content validation** is performed by demonstrating that the items, questions, or problems posed by the test are a representative sample of the kinds of situations or problems that occur on the job.[5] A test that is content valid exposes the job applicant to situations that are likely to occur on the job, and then tests whether the applicant currently has sufficient knowledge, skill, or ability to handle such situations.

Content validation
A test-validation strategy performed by demonstrating that the items, questions, or problems posed by a test are a representative sample of the kinds of situations or problems that occur on the job.

For example, one general contracting firm that constructed tract housing needed to hire one construction superintendent.[6] This job involved organizing, supervising, and inspecting the work of many subcontractors involved in the construction process. The tests developed for this position attempted to mirror the job. One test was a scrambled subcontractor test, where the applicant had to take a random list of subcontractors (roofing, plumbing, electrical, fencing, concrete, and so on) and put them in the correct order that each should appear on the site. A second test measured construction error recognition. In this test, the applicant went into a shed that was specially constructed to have 25 common and expensive errors (like faulty wiring and upside-down windows) and recorded whatever problems she could detect. Because the content of these tests so closely parallels the content of the job, one can safely make inferences from one to the other.

Although criterion-related validity is established by empirical means, content validity is achieved primarily through a process of expert judgment. One means of quantifying the degree of content validity is to use the content-validation ratio (CVR). To

TABLE 6.2
Required Level of Content-Validation Ratio to Reach Statistical Significance as a Function of the Number of Judges

NUMBER OF JUDGES	REQUIRED CONTENT-VALIDATION RATIO
5	.99
8	.75
10	.62
15	.49
30	.33

calculate this ratio, various individuals considered experts on the job are assembled. These people review each test (or item) and then categorize each test in terms of whether the skill or knowledge the test assesses is essential to the job. The content-validation ratio is then calculated from the formula

$$\text{CVR} = \frac{n_e - N/2}{N/2}$$

where n_e is the number of judges who rate the item "essential" and N is the number of judges. CVR equals 1.0 when all judges believe the item is essential and –1.0 when all judges believe it is nonessential. A CVR of .00 means there is complete disagreement on the degree to which the item is essential. Table 6.2 shows the level of CVR needed to achieve statistical significance as a function of the number of judges.[7]

The ability to use content validation in small sample settings makes it generally more applicable than criterion-related validation. However, content validation has two limitations.[8] First, one assumption behind content validation is that the person who is to be hired must have the knowledge, skills, or abilities at the time she is hired. Thus it is not appropriate to use content validation in settings where the applicant is expected to learn the job in a formal training program conducted after selection.

Second, because subjective judgment plays such a large role in content validation, it is critical to minimize the amount of inference involved on the part of judges. Thus the judges' ratings need to be made with respect to relatively concrete and observable behaviors (for example, "applicant detects common construction errors" or "arranges optimal subcontractor schedules"). Content validation would be inappropriate for assessing more abstract characteristics such as intelligence, leadership capacity, and integrity.

Generalizability

Generalizability
The degree to which the validity of a selection method established in one context extends to other contexts.

Generalizability is defined as the degree to which the validity of a selection method established in one context extends to other contexts. There are three primary "contexts" over which we might like to generalize: different situations (jobs or organizations), different samples of people, and different time periods. Just as reliability is necessary but not sufficient for validity, validity is necessary but not sufficient for generalizability.

It was once believed, for example, that validity coefficients were situationally specific—that is, the level of correlation between test and performance varied as one went from one organization to another, even though the jobs studied seemed to be identical. Subsequent research has indicated that this is largely false. Rather, tests tend to show similar levels of correlation even across jobs that are only somewhat similar (at least for tests of intelligence and cognitive ability). Correlations with these kinds of tests change as one goes across widely different kinds of jobs, however. Specifically, the more complex the job, the higher the validity of many tests.[9]

It was also believed that tests showed differential subgroup validity, which meant that the validity coefficient for any test–job performance pair was different for people of different races or genders. This belief was also refuted by subsequent research, and, in general, one finds very similar levels of correlations across different groups of people.[10]

Because the evidence suggests that test validity often extends across situations and subgroups, *validity generalization* stands as an alternative for validating selection methods for companies that cannot employ criterion-related or content validation. Validity generalization is a three-step process. First, the company provides evidence from previous criterion-related validity studies conducted in other situations that shows that a specific test (such as a test of emotional stability) is a valid predictor for a specific job (like nurse at a large hospital). Second, the company provides evidence from job analysis to document that the job it is trying to fill (nurse at a small hospital) is similar in all major respects to the job validated elsewhere (nurse at a large hospital). Finally, if the company can show that it uses a test that is the same as or similar to that used in the validated setting, then one can "generalize" the validity from the first context (large hospital) to the new context (small hospital).[11]

Utility

Utility is the degree to which the information provided by selection methods enhances the bottom-line effectiveness of the organization.[12] Strategic approaches to human resource management place a great deal of importance in determining the financial worth of their human capital, and great strides have been made in assessing this value.[13] In general, the more reliable, valid, and generalizable the selection method is, the more utility it will have. On the other hand, many characteristics of particular selection contexts enhance or detract from the usefulness of given selection methods, even when reliability, validity, and generalizability are held constant.

Utility
The degree to which the information provided by selection methods enhances the effectiveness of selecting personnel in real organizations.

Figures 6.4a and 6.4b, for example, show two different scenarios where the correlation between a measure of extroversion and the amount of sales revenue generated by a sample of sales representatives is the same for two different companies: Company A and Company B. Although the correlation between the measure of extroversion and sales is the same, Company B derives much more utility or practical benefit from the measure. That is, as indicated by the arrows proceeding out of the boxes (which indicate the people selected), the average sales revenue of the three people selected by Company B (Figure 6.4b) is $850,000 compared to $780,000 from the three people selected by Company A (Figure 6.4a).

The major difference between these two companies is that Company B generated twice as many applicants as Company A. This means that the selection ratio (the percentage of people selected relative to the total number of people tested) is quite low for Company B (3/20) relative to Company A (3/10). Thus the people selected by Company B have higher amounts of extroversion than those selected by Company A; therefore, Company B takes better advantage of the relationship between extroversion and sales. Although this might be somewhat offset by the cost of recruiting and measuring 20 more people, this added cost is probably trivial relative to the difference in revenue shown in this example ($70,000). Thus the utility of any test generally

FIGURE 6.4A

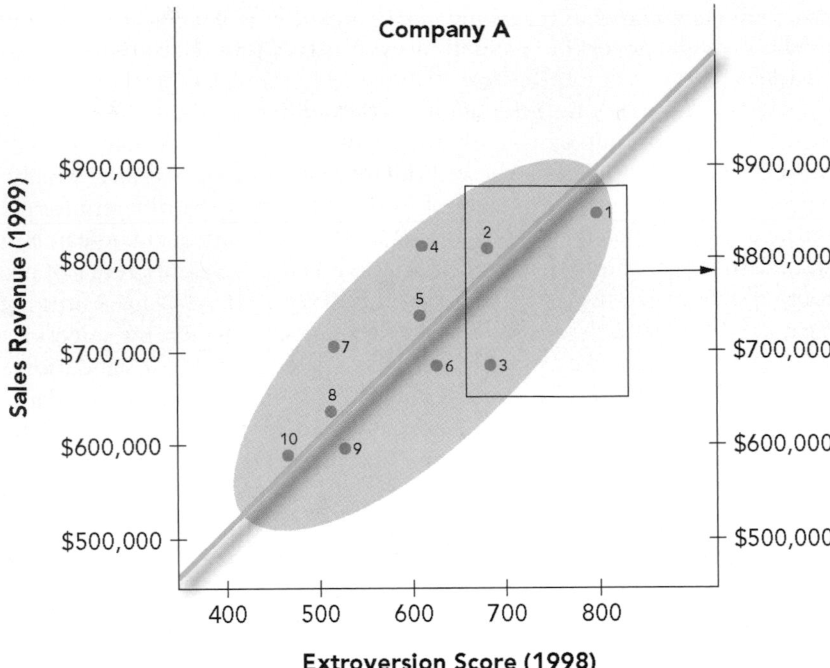

FIGURE 6.4B

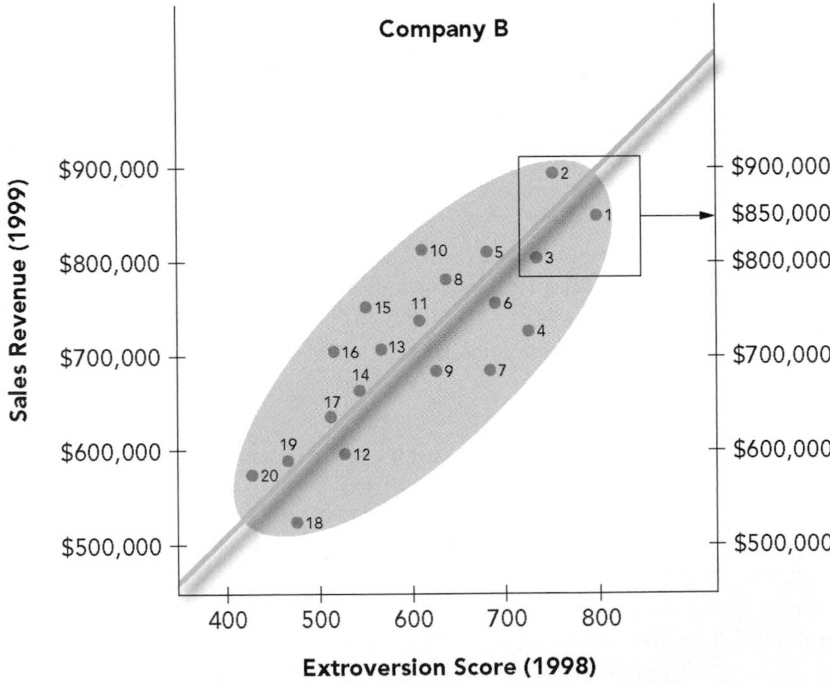

increases as the selection ratio gets lower, so long as the additional costs of recruiting and testing are not excessive.

Many other factors relate to the utility of a test. For example, the value of the product or service produced by the job incumbent plays a role: the more valuable the product or service, the more value there is in selecting the top performers. The cost of the test, of course, also plays a role. More expensive tests will on average have less utility unless they produce more valid predictions. Often, however, if many people are tested, and the product or service being delivered has a great deal of value, the cost of testing is more than offset by the gains in utility.

Legality

The final standard that any selection method should adhere to is *legality*. All selection methods should conform to existing laws and existing legal precedents. Many issues related to selecting employees safely under U.S. law were discussed generically in Chapter 3. Our treatment there was broad and dealt with legal aspects in all areas of human resource management. In this chapter we focus more narrowly on issues that relate directly to personnel selection, bypassing constitutional amendments and focusing more squarely on federal legislation and executive orders.

Federal Legislation

Three primary federal laws form the basis for a majority of the suits filed by job applicants. First, the Civil Rights Act of 1991 (discussed in Chapter 3), an extension of the Civil Rights Act of 1964, protects individuals from discrimination based on race, color, sex, religion, and national origin with respect to hiring as well as compensation and working conditions. The 1991 act differs from the 1964 act in three important areas.

First, it establishes employers' explicit obligation to establish the business necessity of any neutral-appearing selection method that has had adverse impact on groups specified by the law. This is typically done by showing that the test has significant criterion-related or content validity. Second, it allows the individual filing the complaint to have a jury decide whether he or she may recover punitive damages (in addition to lost wages and benefits) for emotional injuries caused by the discrimination.[14] This can generate large financial settlements as well as poor public relations that can hinder the organization's ability to compete. One recent example of this can be seen at Coca-Cola, and this is highlighted in the "Competing by Meeting Stakeholders' Needs" box. Finally, it explicitly prohibits the granting of preferential treatment to minority groups. For example, it specifically prohibits adjusting scores upward on tests just because someone is in a group with lower average scores (sometimes referred to as *race norming*). Adjusting scores in this way has been found to have a number of negative effects, not only on the attitudes of white males, but on the proposed beneficiaries of such preferential treatment. Research shows that when selection decisions are perceived as being based partially on group membership, it undermines the confidence and hurts the job performance of the women or minority group members the program was designed to help.[15]

The Age Discrimination in Employment Act of 1967 is also widely used in personnel selection. This act mirrors the Civil Rights Act of 1964 in its protections and, as amended in 1978, covers job applicants over the age of 40. The act does not protect younger workers (thus there is never a case for "reverse discrimination" here), and like the most recent civil rights act, it allows for jury trials and punitive damages. This act outlaws almost all "mandatory retirement" programs (company policies that dictate that everyone who reaches a set age must retire).

Litigation brought forward under this act surged by over 200 percent between 1991 and 2001. Two trends have combined to generate this increase: the general aging of the workforce and recent attempts by organizations to downsize. Together these trends

COMPETING BY MEETING STAKEHOLDERS' NEEDS

Coca-Cola: Its Problems with Diversity Are the Real Thing

The battle between Coca-Cola and Pepsico is an ongoing struggle for supremacy in the lucrative soft drink market. However, while Pepsico has been consistently rated one of the best places for minorities to work, Coca-Cola has struggled with race relations throughout its recent history.

For example, to compensate for its past discriminatory practices, Coca-Cola has had to offer $1 billion over five years to minority-owned suppliers, banks, and retailers beginning in the year 2000. At the same time, the company's African American employees were suing for $176 million in retaliation for discrimination in pay and promotion policies, and an external group, headed by Larry Jones, was organizing a consumer boycott of Coke products because of alleged mistreatment of African American employees.

Then, in what was the last straw for many, a Coca-Cola senior African American executive, Carl Ware, retired after being passed over for a promotion that was considered well overdue by outside observers. Ware, a veteran at Coke, had played a critical role in the local Atlanta community, where Coke is headquartered, and was instrumental in terms of helping Coke break into the African market. Many attribute the fact that operating revenue from Africa rose over 40 percent between 1998 and 2000 to Ware's efforts.

The negative publicity associated with all these events was simply too much for Coca-Cola's board of directors: four months after he made the decision to overlook Ware's career, the board terminated the career of then-CEO M. Douglas Ivestor. Ivestor was replaced with Douglas Daft, who immediately committed to helping the company mend fences with African American employees and suppliers. He talked Ware out of retirement and placed him in charge of Coke's Diversity Advisory Council, a new unit dedicated to promoting minority hiring and career development. Whether these steps will be enough to earn the trust of minorities has yet to be seen. However, what is clear is that until Coke mends its internal conflicts, it will never be able to focus squarely on its true threat—Pepsico.

SOURCE: E. LeBlanc, L. Vanderkam, and K. Vella Zarb, "America's 50 Best Companies for Minorities," *Fortune* (July 10, 2000), pp. 190–200; D. Foust, "Coke: Say Goodbye to the Good Ol' Boy Culture," *BusinessWeek* (May 29, 2000), p. 58; D. Foust, "Will Coke Go Better with Carl Ware?" *BusinessWeek* (January 24, 2000), p. 138; A. Harrington, "Prevention Is the Best Defense," *Fortune* (July 10, 2000), p. 188.

have displaced many older workers, who have brought age discrimination suits against their former employers. The long list of companies sued under this act includes CBS Inc., McDonnell Douglas, Northwest Airlines, Disney, and Martin Marietta.[16]

Finally, the Americans with Disabilities Act (ADA) of 1991 protects individuals with physical and mental disabilities (or with a history of the same). It extends the Vocational Rehabilitation Act of 1973, requiring employers to make "reasonable accommodation" to disabled individuals whose handicaps may prevent them from performing essential functions of the job as currently designed. "Reasonable accommodation" could include restructuring jobs, modifying work schedules, making facilities accessible, providing readers, or modifying equipment. Largely due to this act, the percentage of disabled people participating full-time in the U.S. workforce has increased from under 45 percent in 1986 to over 55 percent in 2001.[17]

Employers need not make accommodations that cause "undue hardship." In other words, if the accommodation is "unduly costly, extensive, substantially disruptive, or fundamentally alters the nature of the job," the employer need not comply. Undue hardship can also be established if the employer can show that hiring the applicant will directly threaten the safety of that person or others he or she encounters on the job despite attempts at accommodation.

This act also restricts many preemployment inquiries.[18] For instance, it is legal to ask an applicant, "Can you meet the attendance requirements for this job?" but it is not legal to ask, "How many days did you miss work in your last job because you were sick?" because the latter question might reveal a disability. The ADA also prohibits tests that might reveal a psychological or physical disability. (These would fall under the heading of "illegal medical examinations.") If a manager is uncertain whether a test would be considered medical, she should review the test to determine whether it must be interpreted by a medical professional or whether the behavior or trait assessed by the test is so fundamental to the job that it can be interpreted by any line manager.

Executive Orders

As noted in Chapter 3, the executive branch of the government also regulates hiring decisions through the use of executive orders. Executive Order 11246 parallels the protections provided by the Civil Rights Act of 1964 but goes beyond the 1964 act in two important ways. First, not only do the executive orders prohibit discrimination, they actually mandate that employers take affirmative action to hire qualified minority applicants. The executive orders also allow the government to suspend all business with a contractor while an investigation is being conducted (rather than waiting for an actual finding), which puts a great deal of pressure on employers to comply with these orders. Executive orders are monitored by the Office of Federal Contract Compliance Procedures (OFCCP), which issues guidelines (like the Affirmative Action Program Guidelines published by the Bureau of National Affairs in 1983) to help companies comply.

Finding and Keeping the Best Employees

Given the events that took place toward the end of 2001, it may come as little surprise that one group that has been singled out most for employment discrimination has been Arab Americans. Between October 1, 2001, and December 1, 2001, the Equal Employment Opportunity Commission (EEOC) investigated over 100 cases of discrimination against Arab Americans. Many of these charges come from workers in the security and airlines industries who are, for obvious reasons, especially sensitive about this topic.

For example, Mamdouh Bayoumy was offered a job at the Boeing plant in San Antonio, but the company then reneged on its offer after the September 11th hijackings and terrorist attacks on the World Trade Center and Pentagon. Even though Bayoumy had a 10-year track record of work in the United States, numerous glowing references from past employers, and no history of criminal activity, Boeing claimed it "could not secure his background." Although organizations clearly need to protect their customers and workers from terrorism, the blanket refusal to consider any Arab American job applicants is not just bad business practice—it's illegal.

SOURCE: M. Conlin, "Taking Precautions—or Harassing Workers?" *BusinessWeek* (December 3, 2001), p. 84.

Types of Selection Methods

The first half of this chapter laid out the five standards by which we can judge selection measures. In the second half of this chapter, we examine the common selection methods used in various organizations and discuss their advantages and disadvantages in terms of these standards.

Interviews

A selection interview has been defined as "a dialogue initiated by one or more persons to gather information and evaluate the qualifications of an applicant for employment."[19] The selection interview is the most widespread selection method employed in organizations.

Unfortunately, the long history of research on the employment interview suggests that, without proper care, it can be unreliable, low in validity,[20] and biased against a number of different groups.[21] Moreover, interviews are relatively costly because they require at least one person to interview another person, and these persons have to be brought to the same geographic location. Finally, in terms of legality, the subjectivity embodied in the process often makes applicants upset, particularly if they fail to get a job after being asked apparently irrelevant questions. The Supreme Court ruled in *Watson* v. *Fort Worth Bank and Trust* that subjective selection methods like the interview must be validated by traditional criterion-related or content-validation procedures.[22]

Fortunately, more recent research has pointed to a number of concrete steps that one can employ to increase the utility of the personnel selection interview.[23] First, HR staff should keep the interview structured, standardized, and focused on accomplishing a small number of goals. That is, they should plan to come out of each interview with quantitative ratings on a small number of dimensions that are observable (like interpersonal style or ability to express oneself) and avoid ratings of abilities that may be better measured by tests (like intelligence). In the words of one experienced interviewer for Johnson and Son Inc., "Gut feelings count, but the goal is controlled subjectivity."[24] For the most part, interviews tap the applicants' personality characteristics and interpersonal style. However, they can also delve into the person's job knowledge and skill, and interviews show higher predictive validity when focused on these latter factors.

Situational interview
An interview procedure where applicants are confronted with specific issues, questions, or problems that are likely to arise on the job.

Second, ask questions dealing with specific situations that are likely to arise on the job, and use these to determine what the person is likely to do in that situation. These types of **situational interview** items have been shown to have quite high predictive validity.[25] Situational judgment items come in two varieties, as shown in Table 6.3. Some items are "experience-based" and require the applicant to reveal an actual experience he or she had in the past when confronting the situation. Other items are "future-oriented" and ask what the person is likely to do when confronting a certain hypothetical situation in the future. Research suggests that these types of items can both show validity but that experience-based items often outperform future-oriented items.[26] These types of tests also tend to work well in combination with some of the other methods discussed later in this chapter because they seem to tap something unique about each candidate.[27]

Ameritech Cellular Services uses these types of situational questions in its interview procedures. Interviewees answer questions that directly relate to past experiences and future behaviors. As James Reicks, director of human resources, notes, "We're shifting toward competency-based systems which really zero in on the attri-

TABLE 6.3

Examples of Experience-Based and Future-Oriented Situational Interview Items

Experience-based	
Motivating employees:	"Think about an instance when you had to motivate an employee to perform a task that he or she disliked but that you needed to have done. How did you handle that situation?"
Resolving conflict:	"What was the biggest difference of opinion you ever had with a coworker? How did you resolve that situation?"
Overcoming resistance to change:	"What was the hardest change you ever had to bring about in a past job, and what did you do to get the people around you to change their thoughts or behaviors?"
Future-oriented	
Motivating employees:	"Suppose you were working with an employee whom you knew greatly disliked performing a particular task. You needed to get this task completed, however, and this person was the only one available to do it. What would you do to motivate that person?"
Resolving conflict:	"Imagine that you and a coworker disagree about the best way to handle an absenteeism problem with another member of your team. How would you resolve that situation?"
Overcoming resistance to change:	"Suppose you had an idea for change in work procedures that would enhance quality, but some members of your work group were hesitant to make the change. What would you do in that situation?"

butes of a candidate. We're looking for specific examples of how they succeeded in previous jobs rather than examining their entire work history."[28]

It is also important to use multiple interviewers who are trained to avoid many of the subjective errors that can result when one human being is asked to rate another. Limiting the subjectivity of the process is central to much of this training, and research suggests that it is best to ask interviewers to be "witnesses" of facts that can later be integrated via objective formulas, as opposed to being "judges" allowed to idiosyncratically weigh how various facts should be combined to form the final recommendation.[29] That is, interviewers need to be made aware of their own biases, prejudices, and other personal features that may color their perceptions of others.[30] For example, at Levi Strauss, the human resource department makes sure women and minorities play a large role in interviewing job applicants to ensure their perspective is included.[31] Many employers are now videotaping interviews and then sending the tapes (rather than the applicants) around from place to place. This is seen by some as a cost-effective means of allowing numerous raters to evaluate the candidate under standard conditions.[32]

References and Biographical Data

Just as few employers would think of hiring someone without an interview, nearly all employers also use some method for getting background information on applicants before an interview. This information can be solicited from the people who know the candidate through reference checks.

The evidence on the reliability and validity of reference checks suggests that these are, at best, weak predictors of future success on the job.[33] The main reason for this low validity is that the evaluations supplied in most reference letters are so positive that it is hard to differentiate applicants. As Northwestern Bell's district manager of management employment notes, "They all say, 'This is the greatest individual the world has ever seen, the next president, at least.' . . . It isn't always accurate."[34]

This problem with reference letters has two causes. First, the applicant usually gets to choose who writes the letter and can thus choose only those writers who think the highest of her abilities. Second, because letter writers can never be sure who will read the letters, they may fear that supplying damaging information about someone could come back to haunt them. This fear is well placed. Over 10,000 such lawsuits have been filed since 1983. In 70 percent of these cases, the recipient of the bad reference prevails, and the average award is over $500,000. (The record is $1.9 million.)[35]

Intuit Corporation, the Menlo Park, California, software company that produces *Quicken*, tries to get around these problems by requesting references in bulk—sometimes asking for as many as 12 letters of reference. The first two or three people listed invariably have nothing but positive things to say about the candidate, but, according to Sharyn Vacunich, staffing manager for Intuit, once you get beyond those people, you hear more than just positive things.[36]

The evidence on the utility of biographical information collected directly from job applicants is much more positive, especially for certain occupational categories such as clerical and sales jobs[37] and for particular outcomes like turnover.[38] The low cost of obtaining such information significantly enhances its utility, especially when the information is used in conjunction with a well-designed follow-up interview that complements, rather than duplicates, the biographical information bank.[39]

The biographical information form also provides a written document that the organization can verify via outside checks. For example, APCOA Inc. (a Cleveland-based company that operates parking facilities at 400 urban sites and 70 airports in 42 states) conducts a battery of checks. Depending on the position, this investigation can include driving records, credit history, criminal record, and education and employment verification. According to Bobbi Navarro, a human resource staff member at APCOA, "The perception is [that] a parking company would never spend the time and energy to do all this, but if you're committed to excellence, then it's absolutely necessary. The hiring process can set you apart from the competition, and nowadays, you have to know who the people are who work for you. The risk is just too great to ignore."[40]

Physical Ability Tests

Although automation and other advances in technology have eliminated or modified many physically demanding occupational tasks, many jobs still require certain physical abilities or psychomotor abilities.[41] In these cases, tests of physical abilities may be relevant not only to predicting performance but to predicting occupational injuries and disabilities as well.[42] There are seven classes of tests in this area: ones that evaluate (1) muscular tension, (2) muscular power, (3) muscular endurance, (4) cardiovascular endurance, (5) flexibility, (6) balance, and (7) coordination.[43]

The criterion-related validities for these kinds of tests for certain jobs are quite strong.[44] Unfortunately, these tests, particularly the strength tests, are likely to have an adverse impact on some applicants with disabilities and many female applicants. For example, roughly two-thirds of all males score higher than the highest-scoring female on muscular tension tests.[45] In the wake of the September 11th, 2001, terrorist attacks on New York and Washington, recruiting offices faced a surge of applicants for the armed services. However, due to high physical standards associated with being in the military, the actual number of these new applicants that could be selected was very small. In the end, the number of new enlistments was largely unaffected by the patriotic response to the terrorist attacks.[46]

There are two key questions to ask in deciding whether to use these kinds of tests. First, is the physical ability essential to performing the job and is it mentioned prominently enough in the job description? Neither the Civil Rights Act nor the ADA requires employers to hire individuals who cannot perform essential job functions, and both accept a written job description as evidence of the essential functions of the job.[47] Second, is there a probability that failure to adequately perform the job would result in some risk to the safety or health of the applicant, coworkers, or clients? The "direct threat" clause of the ADA makes it clear that adverse impact against those with disabilities is warranted under such conditions.

Cognitive Ability Tests

Cognitive ability tests differentiate individuals: based on their mental rather than physical capacities. Cognitive ability has many different facets, although we will focus only on three dominant ones.[48] **Verbal comprehension** refers to a person's capacity to understand and use written and spoken language. **Quantitative ability** concerns the speed and accuracy with which one can solve arithmetic problems of all kinds. **Reasoning ability,** a broader concept, refers to a person's capacity to invent solutions to many diverse problems.

Cognitive ability tests
Tests that include three dimensions: verbal comprehension, quantitative ability and reasoning ability.

Verbal comprehension
Refers to a person's capacity to understand and use written and spoken language.

Quantitative ability
Concerns the speed and accuracy with which one can solve arithmetic problems of all kinds.

Reasoning ability
Refers to person's capacity to invent solutions to many diverse problems.

Some jobs require only one or two of these facets of cognitive ability. Under these conditions, maintaining the separation among the facets is appropriate. However, many jobs that are high in complexity require most, if not all, of the facets, and hence one general test is often as good as many tests of separate facets.[49] Highly reliable commercial tests measuring these kinds of abilities are widely available, and they are generally valid predictors of job performance. The validity of these kinds of tests is related to the complexity of the job, however, in that one sees higher criterion-related validation for complex jobs than for simple jobs.[50] The predictive validity for these tests is also higher in jobs that are dynamic and changing over time and thus require adaptability on the part of the job incumbent.[51] Given the changing nature of economy, the adaptability of workers has become a critical concern of many employers. People who are high in adaptability have been found to skilled at (a) handling emergencies, (b) managing stress, (c) solving problems, (d) learning new technologies, and (e) dealing with culturally diverse populations.[52]

One of the major drawbacks to these tests is that they typically have adverse impact on African Americans. Indeed, the size of the differences is so large that some have advocated abandoning these types of tests for making decisions regarding who will be accepted for certain schools or jobs.[53] In the past, the difference between the means for blacks and whites meant that an average black would score at the 16th percentile of the distribution of white scores.[54] The notion of race norming, alluded to earlier, was born of the desire to use these high-utility tests in a manner that avoided adverse impact. Although race norming was made illegal by the recent amendments to the Civil Rights Act, some have advocated the use of banding to both achieve the benefits of testing and minimize its adverse impact. The concept of *banding* suggests that similar groups of people whose scores differ by only a small amount all be treated as having the same score. Then, within any band, preferential treatment is given to minorities. Most observers feel preferential treatment of minorities is acceptable when scores are tied, and banding simply broadens the definition of what constitutes a tied score.[55]

For example, in many classes a score of 90–100 percent may constitute a 4.0 for the course. This means that even though someone scoring 99 outperformed someone with a score of 91, each gets the same grade (a 4.0). Banding uses the same logic for all kinds of tests. Thus, if one was going to use the grade in the class as a selection standard, this would mean that the person with the 91 is equal to the person with the 99 (that is, they both score a 4.0), and if their scores are tied, preference should be given to the minority. Like race norming, banding is very controversial, especially if the bands are set too wide.[56]

Personality Inventories

While ability tests attempt to categorize individuals relative to what they can do, personality measures tend to categorize individuals by what they are like. Two recent reviews of the personality literature independently arrived at five common aspects of personality.[57] We refer to these five major dimensions as "the Big Five," and they include (1) extroversion, (2) adjustment, (3) agreeableness, (4) conscientiousness, and (5) inquisitiveness. Table 6.4 lists each of these with a corresponding list of adjectives that fit each dimension.

Although it is possible to find reliable, commercially available measures of each of these traits, the evidence for their validity and generalizability is mixed at best.[58] Conscientiousness is one of the few factors that displays any validity across a number of different job categories, and many real-world managers rate this as one of the most important characteristics they look for in employees.[59] People high in conscientiousness show more stamina at work, which is helpful in many occupations. For example, at the highest levels of management, many CEOs of the largest companies—such as Herb Kelleher of Southwest Airlines, Tony O'Reilly of H.J. Heinz, and Wolfgang Schmitt of Rubbermaid—report working 80 to 90 hours a week and get by on as little as 5 to 6 hours of sleep each night.[60] Conscientiousness seems to be a particularly good predictor when teamed with tests of mental ability because there is a stronger relationship between this trait and performance when ability is high.[61]

Although conscientiousness is the only dimension of personality that seems to show predictive validity across all situations, there are contexts where other components of the Big Five relate to job performance. First, extroversion and agreeableness seem to be related to performance in jobs such as sales or management; it is easy to see why these types of attributes would be required for such jobs.[62] These two factors also seem to be predictive of performance in team contexts, although in many cases it is the score of the lowest team member that determines the whole group outcome. That is, one highly disagreeable, introverted, or unconscientious member can ruin an

TABLE 6.4
The Five Major Dimensions of Personality Inventories

Dimension	Adjectives
1. Extroversion	Sociable, gregarious, assertive, talkative, expressive
2. Adjustment	Emotionally stable, nondepressed, secure, content
3. Agreeableness	Courteous, trusting, good-natured, tolerant, cooperative, forgiving
4. Conscientiousness	Dependable, organized, persevering, thorough, achievement-oriented
5. Inquisitiveness	Curious, imaginative, artistically sensitive, broad-minded, playful

COMPETING IN THE NEW ECONOMY

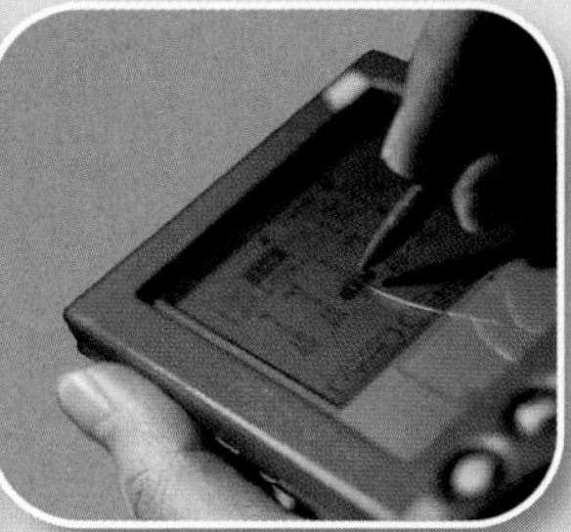

Personality Plays a More Prominent Role

One key feature of the new economy is the complexity and dynamic nature of both consumer markets and labor markets. Dynamic consumer markets mean there is less value in top-down strategic planning and a more critical need for collaborative problem solving. The shortage of high-skilled workers means that leaders can no longer rule by threat and intimidation, but instead must be able to nurture and retain highly valued colleagues. Managing this complexity also tends to outstrip the skills of any one person and demands a team-based approach to work with the emphasis on cooperation and interdependence.

Unfortunately, traditional business school education in the 1980s and early 1990s emphasized individual achievements over teamwork and technical skills over interpersonal skills. The result has been a cadre of managers whose past training makes them ill-suited for the challenges of the new economy. A recent analysis of data collected for a *Fortune* article on "Why CEOs Fail" indicates that in a majority of cases it was attributable to a lack of "people skills." Indeed, as one senior manager has noted, "Before it was all about what you as an individual could achieve and get credit for. Now you have to give up personal ownership—which goes against all my education in business school."

Instead of aggressive lone wolves looking out for number one, companies are instead seeking team players that can achieve results working with others that may share different backgrounds or skills. For example, when Hewlett Packard was looking for a new CEO, the company was facing many of these new economy pressures as it tried to transform itself from a stodgy hardware company that told people what to do, to a more nimble, Web-based firm that empowered workers to be creative. In order to accomplish this goal in its hiring process, Hewlett Packard turned to personality tests.

Prior to being hired as the new CEO at Hewlett Packard, Carly Fiorina and all the other finalists for this job had to respond to a two-hour, 900-question personality test, and this is becoming increasingly common in contemporary organizations. The personality tests go beyond skills and experiences and try to tap into the common behavioral styles people tend to use in interacting with others, evaluating traits such as agreeableness, extroversion, conscientiousness, and emotional stability. The measures also capture how people typically process information and the implications this has for working with others. As one manager has noted with respect to working in teams, "Sometimes you have to put down that voice in the back of your head screaming 'me, me, me.'" Although this is a commendable sentiment, people employing personality tests do so in order to select people who have no such voices in their head.

SOURCE: H. Mintzberg and J. Lampel, "Do MBAs Make Better CEOs? Sorry, Dubya, It Ain't Necessarily So," *Fortune* (February 19, 2001), p. 244; F. Russo, "State of Aggression: The Ways of Type A's May Not Pay," *Time Magazine* (July 2, 2001), pp. 32–35; W.F. Wagner, "All Skill, No Finesse," *Workforce*, June 2000, p. 116; P. Mendels, "Do You Have a Personality for Success," *BusinessWeek Online*, October 13, 2000, p. 1–3.

entire team.[63] Indeed, as the "Competing in the New Economy" box shows, there are several reasons why firms are increasingly turning to personality tests for staffing.

Finally, the validity for almost all of the Big Five factors in terms of predicting job performance also seems to be higher when the scores are not obtained from the applicant but are instead taken from other people.[64] The lower validity associated with self-reports of personality can be traced to two factors. First, people sometimes lack insight into what their own personalities are actually like (or how they are perceived by others), so their scores are inaccurate or unreliable. Second, applicants can sometimes fake their responses to personality items.[65] The evidence suggests that faking may be particularly an issue with the traits of conscientiousness and emotional stability because of the transparent nature of how these items would be used in decision making.[66]

Work Samples

Work-sample tests and job-performance tests attempt to simulate the job in miniaturized form. For example, many organizations use an "in-basket" test when assessing people who are applying for managerial jobs. In an in-basket test, job candidates are asked to respond to memos that typify the problems confronted by those who already hold the job. The key in this and other forms of work-sample tests is the behavioral consistency between the requirements of the job and the requirements of the test.[67]

Work-sample tests tend to be job specific—that is, tailored individually to each different job in each organization. On the positive side, this has resulted in tests that demonstrate a high degree of criterion-related validity. In addition, the obvious parallels between the test and the job make content validity high. In general, this reduces the likelihood that rejected applicants will challenge the procedure through litigation. Available evidence also suggests that these tests are low in adverse impact.[68]

As the Competing through Globalization box shows, work-sample tests, because they get directly at the ability to do the job, are particularly useful when hiring non-U.S. citizens, for whom background information may be hard to collect or interpret.

With all these advantages come two drawbacks. First, by their very nature the tests are job-specific, so generalizability is low. Second, partly because a new test has to be developed for each job and partly because of their nonstandardized formats, these tests are relatively expensive to develop. It is much more cost-effective to purchase a commercially available cognitive ability test that can be used for a number of different job categories within the company than to develop a test for each job. For this reason, some have rated the utility of cognitive ability tests higher than work-sample tests, despite the latter's higher criterion-related validity.[69] On the other hand, technological developments in the area of communications have reduced the cost of many different kinds of work-sample tests. For example, many work-sample tests can now be delivered online from a remote location, creating some economies of scale.[70]

Assessment center
A process in which multiple raters evaluate employees' performance on a number of exercises.

In the area of managerial selection, work-sample tests are typically the cornerstone in assessment centers. Generically, the term **assessment center** is used to describe a wide variety of specific selection programs that employ multiple selection methods to rate either applicants or job incumbents on their managerial potential. Someone attending an assessment center would typically experience work-sample tests such as an in-basket test and several tests of more general abilities and personality. Because assessment centers employ multiple selection methods, their criterion-related validity tends to be quite high. Research indicates that one of the best combinations of selection methods includes work-sample tests with a highly structured interview and a measure of general cognitive ability. The validity coefficient expected from such a combined battery often exceeds .60.[71]

Honesty Tests and Drug Tests

Many problems that confront society also exist within organizations, which has led to two new kinds of tests: honesty tests and drug-use tests. Many companies formerly

COMPETING THROUGH GLOBALIZATION

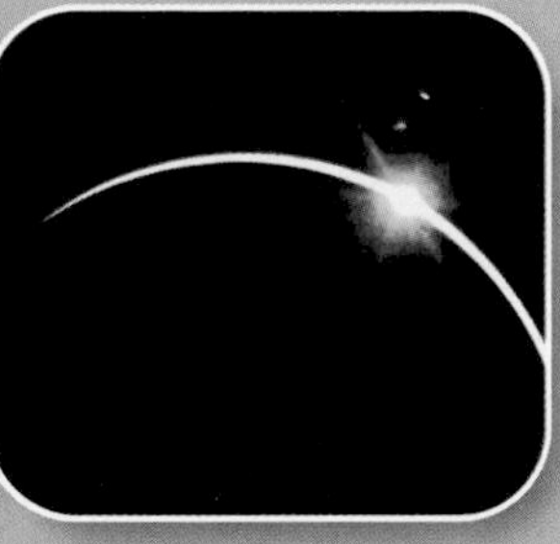

Hiring Foreign Nationals for U.S. Firms

Although the majority of firms in the United States hire U.S. citizens, the search for the world's best talent may require crossing U.S. borders. This is increasingly common in industries such as software development, engineering, pharmaceuticals, and aerospace, where high-ability, low-cost talent can be found in Russia, India, Taiwan, Singapore, China, and Korea. However, hiring foreign nationals for U.S. firms is not as easy as you might think. There are a number of barriers to overcome when hiring non-U.S. citizens.

For example, documenting and verifying the credentials of foreign nationals is difficult. If the applicant has attended a non-U.S. university, how does the institution and the degree awarded compare to what would be found in the United States? To get around overseas educational idiosyncrasies, some companies like Mobil Corporation conduct their own screening tests for basic skills in reading and math. Other companies—such as the Knowledge Company in Fairfax, Virginia—employ work-sample tests, where, for example, an applicant for an engineering job would be asked to submit drawings and plans for a certain product, which would be evaluated by experts.

Also, the typical criminal background check is difficult because, except for the most serious crimes, there is little information within the United States regarding crimes committed in other countries. Beyond this, the American Foreign Corrupt Practices Act even bars U.S. entry of foreign businesspeople who might have bribed government officials in their home countries—even if that is not against the law in those countries.

Finally, even if one is able to obtain the necessary data for making an informed hiring decision with respect to a foreign national, the U.S. Department of Labor requires the employer to show that (1) the employment of this person will not adversely affect wages and working conditions of U.S. citizens who work in similar occupations and (2) no U.S. citizens are willing and able to do the work at that specific time.

Taken altogether, these and other hurdles associated with hiring foreign nationals make this a difficult though not impossible proposition. Since many companies are not able or willing to go through this effort, here is yet another area where one organization can gain competitive advantage over another. Indeed, as Texas Instruments' William Glickman notes, "If American firms are going to compete successfully in the years ahead, they must look everywhere for those with the best ability."

SOURCE: C.J. Bachler, "Global Inpats—Don't Let Them Surprise You," *Personnel Journal*, June 1996, pp. 54–65; R. Horn, "Give Me Your Huddled . . . High Tech Ph.D.s: Are High Skilled Foreigners Displacing U.S. Workers?" *BusinessWeek* (November 6, 1995), pp. 161–62; S. Greengard, "Gain the Edge in the Knowledge Race," *Personnel Journal*, August 1996, pp. 52–56.

employed polygraph tests, or lie detectors, to evaluate job applicants, but this changed with the passage of the Polygraph Act in 1988. This act banned the use of polygraphs in employment screening for most organizations. However, it did not eliminate the problem of theft by employees. As a result, the paper-and-pencil honesty testing industry was born.

Paper-and-pencil honesty tests typically ask applicants directly about their attitudes toward theft or their past experiences with theft. Some sample items are shown in Table 6.5. Given the recent development of these tests, there is not a great deal of independent evidence (evidence not generated by those who publish and sell the

TABLE 6.5
Sample Items from a Typical Integrity Test

1. It's OK to take something from a company that is making too much profit.
2. Stealing is just a way of getting your fair share.
3. When a store overcharges its customers, it's OK to change price tags on merchandise.
4. If you could get into a movie without paying and not get caught, would you do it?
5. Is it OK to go around the law if you don't actually break it?

SOURCE: From *Inc.: The Magazine for Growing Companies.* Copyright © 1992 by Goldhirsh Group/Inc. Publishing. Reproduced with permission of Goldhirsh Group/Inc. Publishing via Copyright Clearance Center.

tests) on their reliability and validity. A large-scale independent review of validity studies conducted by the publishers of many integrity tests suggests they can predict both theft and other disruptive behaviors.[72] One of the few predictive studies conducted by someone other than a publisher of honesty tests also suggests that these tests predict theft in convenience store settings.[73] Another positive feature of these tests is that one does not see large differences attributable to race or sex, so they are not likely to have adverse impact on these demographic groups.[74]

As is the case with measures of personality, some people are concerned that people confronting an honesty test can fake their way to a passing score. The evidence suggests that people instructed to fake their way to a high score (indicating honesty) can do so. However, it is not clear that this affects the validity of the predictions made using such tests. That is, it seems that despite this built-in bias, scores on the test still predict future theft. Thus, the effect of the faking bias is not large enough to detract from the test's validity.[75]

Although it is always a good rule to locally evaluate the reliability and validity of any selection method, because of the novelty of these kinds of measures this may be even more critical with honesty tests. For example, Nordstrom, the large department store chain, uses the Reid Survey to screen for violent tendencies, drug use, and dishonesty. Originally, the test was only one of many factors that went into the final hiring decision, so there were some people hired who were not recommended by the Reid test. Follow-up studies showed that the turnover rate for those recommended by the Reid test was only 22 percent, compared with 44 percent of those who did not pass the test but were hired anyway. Since the test costs only $5 to administer, this represents a major cost saving in the stores using the test.[76]

As with theft, there is a growing perception of the problems caused by drug use among employees. Indeed, 79 percent of *Fortune* 1,000 chief executives cited substance abuse as a significant problem in their organizations, and 50 percent of medium-size and large organizations test applicants for drug use.[77] Because the physical properties of drugs are invariant and subject to highly rigorous chemical testing, the reliability and validity of drug tests are very high.

The major controversies surrounding drug tests involve not their reliability and validity but whether they represent an invasion of privacy, an unreasonable search and seizure, or a violation of due process. Urinalysis and blood tests are invasive procedures, and accusing someone of drug use is a serious matter. For these reasons, as illustrated in the "Competing through High-Performance Work Systems" box, employers are looking for alternatives to drug testing.

COMPETING THROUGH HIGH-PERFORMANCE WORK SYSTEMS

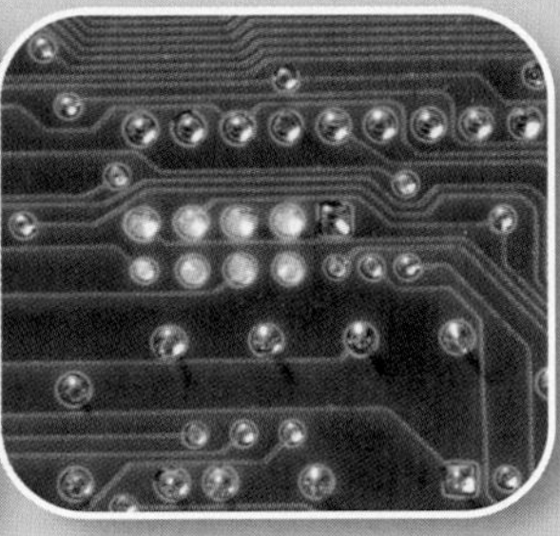

Impairment Tests: Ready or Not, Here They Come

Making workplaces safe for both workers and consumers is a critical responsibility, and for years this has been the primary defense of those that have advocated mandatory drug-testing programs conducted by employers. Ever since President Ronald Reagan urged the creation of drug-free workplaces in 1986, the nation has witnessed a steady increase in the percentage of employers who relied on urine tests. Steady, that is, until 1996. After peaking at 81 percent in that year, the percentage of employers relying on drug testing has steadily decreased to less than 70 percent in 2001.

There are several reasons for the decline in drug testing over the last few years. For one, many employees and groups such as the American Civil Liberties Union feel that the tests are invasive and violate a person's right to privacy. Second, the labor shortage in some sectors of the economy has prevented many employers from making a blanket rejection decision with respect to all recreational drug users—especially if their off-work behavior has no impact in terms of on-the-job performance. Third, research conducted by the National Academy of Sciences has debunked several of the fundamental assumptions upon which such testing is justified—most significantly, that testing reduces on-the-job accidents and injuries. Indeed, one spokesperson for this group has noted that drug testing is "a pathetic excuse for a safety program, because it misses 95 percent of the problem—most people who have accidents on the job are not drug users but instead [have accidents] caused by alcohol or fatigue."

Finally, and most importantly, consensus is growing within the scientific, legal, and business communities that "impairment testing" is a far superior approach for addressing these kinds of problems. Also going under the heading of "fitness for duty testing," impairment-testing programs measure whether a worker is alert and mentally capable of performing critical tasks right now—and does not get into whether this is due to illegal drugs, alcohol, prescription drugs, nonprescription drugs, or simple fatigue.

A typical test looks like a high-tech video game: the employee looks into a dark viewport and tries to follow a randomly moving point of light with his or her eyes. The equipment analyzes the person's performance and compares it to a baseline to see if the person is fit for duty at that moment. Results are available in as little as two minutes, and because it measures involuntary physical responses, it is impossible to cheat on the test—which is something one cannot say regarding a drug test.

Although the high cost of the technology has limited the widespread adoption of this technique, the price of impairment tests has been coming down each year. Moreover, in many high-stakes industries, if a technology can prevent the occurrence of only one or two errors, it more than pays for itself over time. To get a feel for how you would do on such a test, check one out at **http://www.pmifit.com**. Are you fit to be reading this textbook right now?

SOURCE: E. Beck, "Is the Time Right for Impairment Testing?" *Workforce*, February 2001, pp. 69–71; J. Farley, "Better Than Caffeine," *USA Today* (March 9, 2001), p. C1; J. Hamilton, "A Video Game That Tells If Employees Are Fit for Work," *BusinessWeek* (June 3, 1991), pp. 34–35.

Employers considering the use of drug tests would be well advised to make sure that their drug-testing programs conform to some general rules. First, these tests should be administered systematically to all applicants for the same job. Second, testing seems

TABLE 6.6

A Summary of Personnel Selection Methods

METHOD	RELIABILITY	VALIDITY	GENERALIZABILITY	UTILITY	LEGALITY
Interviews	Low when unstructured and when assessing nonobservable traits	Low if unstructured and nonbehavioral	Low	Low, especially because of expense	Low because of subjectivity and potential interviewer bias; also, lack of validity makes job-relatedness low
Reference checks	Low, especially when obtained from letters	Low because of lack of range in evaluations	Low	Low, although not expensive to obtain	Those writing letters may be concerned with charges of libel
Biographical information	High test–retest, especially for verifiable information	High criterion-related validity; low in content validity	Usually job-specific, but have been successfully developed for many job types	High; inexpensive way to collect vast amounts of potentially relevant data	May have adverse impact; thus often develop separate scoring keys based on sex or race
Physical ability tests	High	Moderate criterion-related validity; high content validity for some jobs	Low; pertain only to physically demanding jobs	Moderate for some physical jobs; may prevent expensive injuries and disability	Often have adverse impact on women and people with disabilities; need to establish job-relatedness
Cognitive ability tests	High	Moderate criterion-related validity; content validation inappropriate	High; predictive for most jobs, although best for complex jobs	High; low cost and wide application across diverse jobs in companies	Often have adverse impact on race, especially for African Americans, though decreasing over time
Personality inventories	High	Low criterion-related validity for most traits; content validation inappropriate	Low; few traits predictive for many jobs	Low, although inexpensive for jobs where specific traits are relevant	Low because of cultural and sex differences on most traits, and low job-relatedness in general
Work-sample tests	High	High criterion and content validity	Usually job-specific, but have been successfully developed for many job types	High, despite the relatively high cost to develop	High because of low adverse impact and high job-relatedness
Honesty tests	Insufficient independent evidence	Insufficient independent evidence	Insufficient independent evidence	Insufficient independent evidence	Insufficient history of litigation, but will undergo scrutiny
Drug tests	High	High	High	Expensive, but may yield high payoffs for health-related costs	May be challenged on invasion-of-privacy grounds

more defensible for jobs that involve safety hazards associated with failure to perform. Test results should be reported back to the applicant, who should be allowed an avenue of appeal (and perhaps retesting). Tests should be conducted in an environment that is as unintrusive as possible, and results from those tests should be held in strict confidence. Finally, when testing current employees, the program should be part of a wider organizational program that provides rehabilitation counseling.[78]

A Look Back

The chapter opener about the Becton Dickinson fraud case showed how important it is for organizations to become very familiar with people prior to hiring them. People are not always whom they claim to be, and what might seem like a good fit after a short, unstructured interview could turn out disastrously for firms that fail to delve more deeply into the backgrounds, traits, and skills of job applicants.

Questions

1. Based on this chapter, what are the best methods of obtaining information about job applicants?
2. What are the best characteristics to look for in applicants, and how does this depend on the nature of the job?
3. If you could use only two of the methods described in this chapter and could assess only two of the characteristics discussed, which would you choose, and why?

Summary

In this chapter we examined the five critical standards with which all personnel selection methods should conform: reliability, validity, generalizability, utility, and legality. We also looked at nine different selection methods currently used in organizations and evaluated each with respect to these five standards. Table 6.6 summarizes these selection methods and can be used as a guide in deciding which test to use for a specific purpose. Although we discussed each type of test individually, it is important to note in closing that there is no need to use only one type of test for any one job. Indeed, managerial assessment centers use many different forms of tests over a two- or three-day period to learn as much as possible about candidates for important executive positions. As a result, highly accurate predictions are often made, and the validity associated with the judicious use of multiple tests is higher than for tests used in isolation.

Discussion Questions

1. We examined nine different types of selection methods in this chapter. Assume that you were just rejected for a job based on one of these methods. Obviously, you might be disappointed and angry regardless of what method was used to make this decision, but can you think of two or three methods that might leave you most distressed? In general, why might the acceptability of the test to applicants be an important standard to add to the five we discussed in this chapter?
2. Videotaping applicants in interviews is becoming an increasingly popular means of getting multiple assessments of that individual from different perspectives. Can you think of some reasons why videotaping interviews might also be useful in evaluating the interviewer? What would you look for in an interviewer if you were evaluating one on videotape?
3. Distinguish between concurrent and predictive validation designs, discussing why the latter is preferred over

the former. Examine each of the nine selection methods discussed in this chapter and determine which of these would have their validity most and least affected by the type of validation design employed.

4. Some have speculated that in addition to increasing the validity of decisions, employing rigorous selection methods has symbolic value for organizations. What message is sent to applicants about the organization through hiring practices, and how might this message be reinforced by recruitment programs that occur before selection and training programs that occur after selection?

Web Exercise

Saville & Holdsworth (SHL) is an international human resource consulting firm that provides assessment solutions for companies. To learn more about SHL, visit their home page at **www.shlusa.com**. This site provides examples of test questions used by employers in the employee selection process. Click on "Practice Test and Feedback." Go to the bottom of the page and click on "Example Questions." Review each of the four categories of sample questions by clicking on them (verbal, numerical, diagrammatic, personality).

Questions

1. How would you validate verbal tests? numerical tests? diagrammatic tests? personality tests?
2. Why might job candidates question the validity of personality test items such as those you reviewed?

Managing People: From the Pages of *BusinessWeek*

BusinessWeek It's Not Easy Making Pixie Dust

We are in the Utilidor—a series of tunnels below Disney World's Magic Kingdom theme park in Orlando. The tunnel complex is generally off-limits to outsiders, but not to 41 visiting managers whose companies have anted up $2,295 a head so they can learn about Walt Disney Co.'s approach to people management.

This underground city is a beehive of activity. Employees rush through the gray concrete tunnels, scrambling to put on costumes and assume their roles upstairs. Golf carts speed by with supplies. Makeup artists prepare an array of Cinderella and Snow White wigs.

Before coming to this 3½-day seminar, I was skeptical. The program sounded like little more than a dream junket: three nights at the resort's most elegant hotel, plus four-day passes to Disney's theme parks. Besides, I thought, what could any manager possibly learn at Disney World? By the end of the first day's activities, however, my note pad was brimming with ideas and lessons dished out by Disney staff.

My colleagues, most of them human-resource managers, take the program seriously. Most are facing a slew of challenges in need of Disney-style magic. A delivery manager at Anheuser–Busch Cos. is trying to make his drivers more responsive to retailers. Personnel managers at a fast-growing bagel chain in Florida worry about maintaining standards as they beef up the chain's ranks. And an employee trainer at South Africa's state-owned transportation conglomerate is looking for ways to streamline the company's hiring process.

Disney's reputation for cleanliness, attention to detail, and helpful employees is what has drawn them here. "Everyone knows how wonderful Disney is, so you figure they must be doing something right," says Kathleen Scappini, who works for Multi-Media in West Hartford, Conn. That "something right" is what Disney refers to as the "pixie-dust" formula, with four key ingredients—employee selection, training, support, and benefits. Our seminar, "Disney's Approach to People Management," promises to reveal how the company motivates employees.

Instructors, called facilitators, tell us that we cannot count on Tinkerbell. "The solutions are not complicated," assures Jeff Soluri, a Disney instructor. "It's attention to detail and hard-nosed business practices that produce the magic."

If there is pixie dust, it starts with the hiring process. One of the first activities is a field trip to Disney's "casting center," a Venetian-style castle where job candidates view a video before being interviewed. The short film informs job seekers about the company's strict appearance guidelines (one ring per hand and no tattoos, please) and the rigors of the work. By being blunt and detailed, Disney says, it's able to weed out incompatible candidates at the first crack.

The critical part of the process, though, is employee training. New hires, who average less than $10 an hour, are treated to a visual company history. They are told that they are not just employees but pivotal "cast members" in a "show." From street sweepers to monorail pilots, each cast member must go out of his way to make the resort seem unreal. No matter how tired workers are or how deeply guests may try their patience, they must never lose composure. To do so, the company tells its cast, is to risk alienating a guest, spoiling the illusion, and damaging Disney's standing in entertainment and American culture.

Between excursions, participants share what they have learned—and what they might use. Disney staffers with wireless microphones dart Oprah-like through a conference room seeking comments. They get plenty. John Lealos, the Anheuser-Busch manager, says he wants to incorporate more of an appreciative, team feel into his unit's corporate culture. "If we can get that kind of atmosphere at our company, the productivity will go up," he says. Hugo Strydom, the training manager at South Africa's Transit Ltd., intends to use a Disney-style orientation to weed out weak candidates in a major hiring blitz.

Questions

1. This case reveals a great deal about what Disney looks for in a job applicant as well as what it does (realistic job previews) to get unsuitable job candidates to remove themselves from the process. If you were called in as a consultant to help Disney with its personnel selection and placement process, what sorts of tests, measures, and methods that were covered in this chapter would you use to further screen job applicants?
2. If you wanted to prove to Disney that the tests, measures, and methods you introduced were actually helping it gain competitive advantage, what type of evidence would you collect, and how would you present this evidence?

Notes

1. J.C. Nunnally, *Psychometric Theory* (New York: McGraw-Hill, 1978).
2. B. Schneider, "An Interactionist Perspective on Organizational Effectiveness," in *Organizational Effectiveness: A Comparison of Multiple Models*, ed. K.S. Cameron and D.A. Whetton (Orlando, FL: Academic Press, 1983), pp. 27–54.
3. N. Schmitt, R.Z. Gooding, R.A. Noe, and M. Kirsch, "Meta-Analysis of Validity Studies Published between 1964 and 1982 and the Investigation of Study Characteristics," *Personnel Psychology* 37 (1984), pp. 407–22.
4. J. Cohen, *Statistical Power Analysis for the Behavioral Sciences* (New York: Academic Press, 1977).
5. C.H. Lawshe, "Inferences from Personnel Tests and Their Validity," *Journal of Applied Psychology* 70 (1985), pp. 237–38.
6. D.D. Robinson, "Content-Oriented Personnel Selection in a Small Business Setting," *Personnel Psychology* 34 (1981), pp. 77–87.
7. C.H. Lawshe, "A Quantitative Approach to Content Validity," *Personnel Psychology* 28 (1975), pp. 563–75.
8. P.R. Sackett, "Assessment Centers and Content Validity: Some Neglected Issues," *Personnel Psychology* 40 (1987), pp. 13–25.
9. F.L. Schmidt and J.E. Hunter, "The Future of Criterion-Related Validity," *Personnel Psychology* 33 (1980), pp. 41–60; F.L. Schmidt, J.E. Hunter, and K. Pearlman, "Task Differences as Moderators of Aptitude Test Validity: A Red Herring," *Journal of Applied Psychology* 66 (1982), pp. 166–85; R.L. Gutenberg, R.D. Arvey, H.G. Osburn, and R.P. Jeanneret, "Moderating Effects of Decision-Making/Information Processing Dimensions on Test Validities," *Journal of Applied Psychology* 68 (1983), pp. 600–8.
10. F.L. Schmidt, J.G. Berner, and J.E. Hunter, "Racial Differences in Validity of Employment Tests: Reality or Illusion," *Journal of Applied Psychology* 58 (1974), pp. 5–6.
11. Society for Industrial and Organizational Psychology, *Principles for the Validation and Use of Personnel Selection Procedures* (College Park, MD: University of Maryland Press, 1987).
12. J.W. Boudreau, "Utility Analysis for Decisions in Human Resource Management," in *Handbook of Industrial & Organizational Psychology*, ed. M.D. Dunnette and L.M. Hough (Palo Alto, CA: Consulting Psychologists Press, 1992).
13. E. Zimmerman, "What Are Employees Worth?" *Workforce*, February 2001, p. 36.
14. K.F. Ebert, "New Civil Rights Act Invites Litigation," *Personnel Law Update* 6 (1991), p. 3.
15. M.E. Heilman, W.S. Battle, C.E. Keller, and R.A. Lee, "Type of Affirmative Action Policy: A Determinant of Reactions to Sex-Based Preferential Selection," *Journal of Applied Psychology* 83 (1998), pp. 190–205.
16. R. Ableson, "Fighting Discrimination Takes Will and Cash," *Taipei Times* (July 2, 2001), pp. 21–22.
17. B.P. Sunoo, "Accommodating Workers with Disabilities," *Workforce*, February 2001, p. 93.
18. B.S. Murphy, "EEOC Gives Guidance on Legal and Illegal Inquiries under ADA," *Personnel Journal*, August 1994, p. 26.

19. R.L. Dipboye, *Selection Interviews: Process Perspectives* (Cincinnati, OH: South-Western Publishing, 1991).
20. J.E. Hunter and R. H. Hunter, "Validity and Utility of Alternative Predictors of Job Performance," *Psychological Bulletin* 96 (1984), pp. 72–98.
21. R. Pingitore, B.L. Dugoni, R.S. Tindale, and B. Spring, "Bias against Overweight Job Applicants in a Simulated Interview," *Journal of Applied Psychology* 79 (1994), pp. 909–17.
22. *Watson* v. *Fort Worth Bank and Trust,* 108 Supreme Court 2791 (1988).
23. M.A. McDaniel, D.L. Whetzel, F.L. Schmidt, and S.D. Maurer, "The Validity of Employment Interviews: A Comprehensive Review and Meta-Analysis," *Journal of Applied Psychology* 79 (1994), pp. 599–616; A.I. Huffcutt and W.A. Arthur, "Hunter and Hunter (1984) Revisited: Interview Validity for Entry-Level Jobs," *Journal of Applied Psychology* 79 (1994), pp. 184–90.
24. J. Solomon, "The New Job Interview: Show Thyself," *The Wall Street Journal* (December 4, 1989), p. B4.
25. M.A. McDaniel, F.P. Morgeson, E.B. Finnegan, M.A. Campion, and E.P. Braverman, "Use of Situational Judgment Tests to Predict Job Performance: A Clarification of the Literature," *Journal of Applied Psychology* 86 (2001), pp. 730–40.
26. M.A. Campion, J.E. Campion, and J.P. Hudson, "Structured Interviewing: A Note of Incremental Validity and Alternative Question Types," *Journal of Applied Psychology* 79 (1994), pp. 998–1002; E.D. Pulakos and N. Schmitt, "Experience-Based and Situational Interview Questions: Studies of Validity," *Personnel Psychology* 48 (1995), pp. 289–308.
27. J. Clavenger, G.M. Perreira, D. Weichmann, N. Schmitt, and V.S. Harvey, "Incremental Validity of Situational Judgment Tests," *Journal of Applied Psychology* 86 (2001), pp. 410–17.
28. S. Greengard, "Are You Well Armed to Screen Applicants?" *Personnel Journal,* December 1995, pp. 84–95.
29. Y. Ganzach, A.N. Kluger, and N. Klayman, "Making Decisions from an Interview: Expert Measurement and Mechanical Combination," *Personnel Psychology* 53 (2000), pp. 1–21.
30. G. Stasser and W. Titus, "Effects of Information Load and Percentage of Shared Information on the Dissemination of Unshared Information during Group Discussion," *Journal of Personality and Social Psychology* 53 (1987), pp. 81–93.
31. A. Cuneo, "Diverse by Design," *BusinessWeek* (June 6, 1992), p. 72.
32. T. Libby, "Surviving the Group Interview," *Forbes* (March 24, 1986), p. 190; Dipboye, *Selection Interviews*, p. 210.
33. Hunter and Hunter, "Validity and Utility."
34. L. McDonnell, "Interviews and Tests Counting More as Past Employers Clam Up," *Minneapolis Tribune* (May 3, 1981).
35. J.B. Copeland, "Revenge of the Fired," *Newsweek* (February 16, 1987), pp. 46–47.
36. Greengard, "Are You Well Armed to Screen Applicants?"
37. Hunter and Hunter, "Validity and Utility"; R.R. Reilly and G.T. Chao, "Validity and Fairness of Some Alternative Employee Selection Procedures," *Personnel Psychology* 35 (1982), pp. 1–62.
38. F.A. Mael and B.E. Ashforth, "Loyal from Day One: Biodata, Organizational Identification, and Turnover among Newcomers," *Personnel Psychology* 48 (1995), pp. 309–33.
39. T.W. Dougherty, D.B. Turban, and J.C. Callender, "Confirming First Impressions in the Employment Interview: A Field Study of Interviewer Behavior," *Journal of Applied Psychology* 79 (1994), pp. 659–65.
40. Greengard, "Are You Well Armed to Screen Applicants?"
41. L.C. Buffardi, E.A. Fleishman, R.A. Morath, and P.M. McCarthy, "Relationships between Ability Requirements and Human Errors in Job Tasks," *Journal of Applied Psychology* 85 (2000), pp. 551–64.
42. J.R. Hollenbeck, D.R. Ilgen, and S.M. Crampton, "Lower-Back Disability in Occupational Settings: A Human Resource Management View," *Personnel Psychology* 42 (1992), pp. 247–78.
43. J. Hogan, "Structure of Physical Performance in Occupational Tasks," *Journal of Applied Psychology* 76 (1991), pp. 495–507.
44. B.R. Blakely, M.A. Quinones, M.S. Crawford, and I.A. Jago, "The Validity of Isometric Strength Tests," *Personnel Psychology* 47 (1994), pp. 247–74.
45. J. Hogan, "Physical Abilities," in *Handbook of Industrial & Organizational Psychology,* 2nd ed., ed. M.D. Dunnette and L.M. Hough (Palo Alto, CA: Consulting Psychologists Press, 1991).
46. M. Williams, "Many Americans Try to Enlist in Military; Not Many Make It," *The Wall Street Journal* (October 25), pp. 1–2.
47. Americans with Disabilities Act of 1990, S. 933, Public Law 101-336 (1990).
48. Nunnally, *Psychometric Theory*.
49. M.J. Ree, J.A. Earles, and M.S. Teachout, "Predicting Job Performance: Not Much More Than g," *Journal of Applied Psychology* 79 (1994), pp. 518–24.
50. L.S. Gottfredson, "The g Factor in Employment," *Journal of Vocational Behavior* 29 (1986), pp. 293–96; Hunter and Hunter, "Validity and Utility"; Gutenberg et al., "Moderating Effects"; Schmidt, Berner, and Hunter, "Racial Differences in Validity."
51. J.A. LePine, J.A. Colquitt, and A. Erez, "Adaptability to Changing Task Contexts: Effects of General

Cognitive Ability, Conscientiousness, and Openness to Experience," *Personnel Psychology* 53 (2000), pp. 563–93.

52. E.D. Pulakos, S. Arad, M.A. Donovan, K.E. Plamondon, "Adaptability in the Workplace: Development of a Taxonomy of Adaptive Performance," *Journal of Applied Psychology* 85 (2000), pp. 612–24.
53. R.J. Barro, "Why Colleges Shouldn't Dump the SAT," *BusinessWeek* (April 9, 2001), p. 20.
54. A.R. Jenson, "g: Artifact or Reality?" *Journal of Vocational Behavior* 29 (1986), pp. 301–31.
55. D.A. Kravitz and S.L. Klineberg, "Reactions to Versions of Affirmative Action among Whites, Blacks, and Hispanics," *Journal of Applied Psychology* (2000), pp. 597–611.
56. M.A. Campion, J.L. Outtz, S. Zedeck, F.S. Schmidt, J.E. Kehoe, K.R. Murphy, and R.M. Guion, "The Controversy over Score Banding in Personnel Selection: Answers to 10 Key Questions," *Personnel Psychology* 54 (2001), pp. 149–85.
57. M.R. Barrick and M.K. Mount, "The Big Five Personality Dimensions and Job Performance: A Meta-Analysis," *Personnel Psychology* 44 (1991), pp. 1–26; L.M. Hough, N.K. Eaton, M.D. Dunnette, J.D. Camp, and R.A. McCloy, "Criterion-Related Validities of Personality Constructs and the Effect of Response Distortion on Test Validities," *Journal of Applied Psychology* 75 (1990), pp. 467–76.
58. G.M. Hurtz and J.J. Donovan, "Personality and Job Performance: The Big Five Revisited," *Journal of Applied Psychology* 85 (2000), pp. 869–79.
59. W.S. Dunn, M.K. Mount, M.R. Barrick, and D.S. Ones, "Relative Importance of Personality and General Mental Ability on Managers' Judgments of Applicant Qualifications," *Journal of Applied Psychology* 80 (1995), pp. 500–9.
60. L. Smith, "Stamina: Who Has It, Why You Need It and How You Get It," *Fortune* (November 28, 1994).
61. P.M. Wright, K.M. Kacmar, G.C. McMahan, and K. Deleeuw, "$P = f(M \times A)$: Cognitive Ability as a Moderator of the Relationship between Personality and Job Performance," *Journal of Management* 21 (1995), pp. 1129–39.
62. M. Mount, M.R. Barrick, and J.P. Strauss, "Validity of Observer Ratings of the Big Five Personality Factors," *Journal of Applied Psychology* 79 (1994), pp. 272–80.
63. M.R. Barrick, G.L. Stewart, M.J. Neubert, and M.K. Mount, "Relating Member Ability and Personality to Work Team Processes and Team Effectiveness," *Journal of Applied Psychology* 83 (1998), pp. 377–91; J.L. LePine, J.R. Hollenbeck, D.R. Ilgen, and J. Hedlund, "Effects of Individual Differences on the Performance of Hierarchical Decision Making Teams: Much More Than g," *Journal of Applied Psychology* 82 (1997), pp. 803–11.
64. Mount, Barrick, and Strauss, "Validity of Observer Ratings."
65. J.G. Rosse, M.D. Stecher, J.L. Miller, and R.A. Levin, "The Impact of Response Distortion on Preemployment Personality Testing and Hiring Decisions," *Journal of Applied Psychology* 83 (1998), pp. 634–44.
66. L.A. McFarland and A.M. Ryan, "Variance in Faking across Noncognitive Measures," *Journal of Applied Psychology* 85 (2000), pp. 812–21.
67. P.F. Wernimont and J.P. Campbell, "Signs, Samples and Criteria," *Journal of Applied Psychology* 46 (1968), pp. 417–19.
68. N. Schmitt and A.E. Mills, "Traditional Tests and Job Simulations: Minority and Majority Performance and Test Validities," *Journal of Applied Psychology* 86 (2001), pp. 451–58.
69. Hunter and Hunter, "Validity and Utility."
70. G. Nicholson, "Automated Assessments for Better Hire," *Workforce*, December 2000, pp. 102–09.
71. F.L. Schmidt and J.E. Hunter, "The Validity and Utility of Selection Methods in Personnel Psychology: Practical and Theoretical Implications of 85 Years of Research Findings," *Psychological Bulletin* 124 (1998), pp. 262–74.
72. D.S. One, C. Viswesvaran, and F.L. Schmidt, "Comprehensive Meta-Analysis of Integrity Test Validities: Findings and Implications for Personnel Selection and Theories of Job Performance," *Journal of Applied Psychology* 78 (1993), pp. 679–703.
73. H.J. Bernardin and D.K. Cooke, "Validity of an Honesty Test in Predicting Theft among Convenience Store Employees," *Academy of Management Journal* 36 (1993), pp. 1097–1106.
74. D.S. Ones and C. Viswesvaran, "Gender, Age, and Race Differences on Overt Integrity Tests: Results across Four Large-Scale Job Applicant Data Sets," *Journal of Applied Psychology* 83 (1998), pp. 35–42.
75. M.R. Cunningham, D.T. Wong, and A.P. Barbee, "Self-Presentation Dynamics on Overt Integrity Tests: Experimental Studies of the Reid Report," *Journal of Applied Psychology* 79 (1994), pp. 643–58.
76. Greengard, "Are You Well Armed to Screen Applicants?"
77. M. Freudenheim, "Workers Substance Abuse Increasing, Survey Says," *The New York Times* (December 13, 1988), p. 2; J.P. Guthrie and J.D. Olian, "Drug and Alcohol Testing Programs: The Influence of Organizational Context and Objectives" (paper presented at the Fourth Annual Conference of the Society for Industrial/Organizational Psychology, Boston, 1989).
78. K.R. Murphy, G.C. Thornton, and D.H. Reynolds, "College Students' Attitudes toward Drug Testing Programs, *Personnel Psychology* 43 (1990), pp. 615–31.

Chapter 7 Training

Objectives

After reading this chapter, you should be able to:

1. Discuss how training can help companies gain a competitive advantage.
2. Explain the role of the manager in identifying training needs and supporting training on the job.
3. Conduct a needs assessment.
4. Evaluate employees' readiness for training.
5. Discuss the strengths and weaknesses of presentation, hands-on, and group training methods.
6. Explain the potential advantages of e-learning for training.
7. Design a training session to maximize learning.
8. Choose an appropriate evaluation design based on training objectives and analysis of constraints.
9. Design a cross-cultural preparation program.
10. Develop a program for effectively managing diversity.

Tires Plus provides intensive training and educational programs for their employees. In doing so, employees are motivated to stay with the company and work toward advancement. What other strategic goals might these training programs achieve for the company?

Enter the World of Business

Training Helps the Rubber Hit the Road at Tires Plus

The mission at Tires Plus's headquarters and its 150 stores located in the midwestern United States is to encourage employees to be the same at work as they are in other areas of their lives. Once a struggling company, Tires Plus's annual growth rate has exceeded 20 percent over the past five years. It is now a $200 million company, the sixth largest independent tire retailer, and it hopes to expand nationally and double in size in the next 10 years. Cofounder Tom Gegax insists that growth will not come at the expense of employees or customers. One of the company's most important goals is to ensure that the business strategy promotes employee growth, loyalty, and fairness as economic and social concepts. Tires Plus makes great effort to differentiate itself from old-fashioned tire shops. Many customers enter the store expecting the same service and dirty service areas they have experienced at some other tire shops—but they are pleasantly surprised. Salespeople wear white shirts and ties, and they immediately greet customers. Showrooms are clean and organized; each store has a customer lounge with television sets, tables, and play areas for children. Fast, friendly service is the norm. Customers are encouraged to walk into the shop to watch the mechanics at work. Its business expansion goals will require Tires Plus to expand recruiting efforts and develop its workforce while facing a tight labor market. Tires Plus is investing in training to help reach its goals. As one of the company's trainers notes, "The more information and education we can give people, the better equipped they'll be to advance within the company. And if they're moving up, hopefully they'll see opportunities to expand with us."

The company's intensive training and internal promotion programs motivate employees hoping to advance in their careers. It's all part of Tires Plus's effort to reduce turnover and improve customer relations. Approximately 1,700 Tires Plus employees spend about 60,000 hours annually in formal training programs offered by Tires Plus University, at a cost of $3 million. The company's training facility includes a 250-seat auditorium, replicas of store showrooms and service shops, a computer lab, media center, and four full-time trainers. New hires receive a week of product, sales, or mechanical training depending on their positions. Employees spend hours in classrooms and in simulated tire shops, learning how to create a service environment that encourages customers to return and recommend the company to their friends. Tires Plus career tracks help employees develop into mechanics and store managers—an effort that has helped recruit new employees, retain current employees, and fill leadership positions in the company. The company also devotes time and money to giving employees opportunities to advance, which helps retention and recruitment. For example, a tire technician who wants to become a mechanic can take an 11-week course at Tires Plus University, learning all the basics of the mechanic's job. After formal training he or she works with an on-the-job mentor until ready to work alone as a mechanic. The course is free, and the prospective mechanic gets paid a full salary while participating in training. Employees with potential to be managers are given 80 hours' leadership training.

The company's large time and financial investment in training has helped the company meet its strategic goals. Store surveys show a 96 percent customer satisfaction rate. Tires Plus's annual turnover rate is 8 percent—a high rate but about 20 percent lower than competitors in the automotive service industry and half that of retailers.

SOURCE: K. Dobbs, "Tires Plus Takes the Training High Road," *Training*, April 2000, pp. 57–63.

Introduction

The opening vignette about Tires Plus illustrates how companies use training to support their business strategies and gain competitive advantage. Besides helping employees learn job skills, training helps the company retain and motivate employees. From the company's perspective, training is strategic for business goals related to human resources as well as productivity, customer service, and innovation. Employees are aware that training is essential to their future marketability; as a result, they choose companies to work for based on opportunities for learning. Companies that do not provide training will not be able to attract and retain high-quality employees. Company leaders like Tom Gegax realize that the growing amount of information about customers, products, and technologies makes training important. Also, training investments can give companies a competitive edge with savvy customers who take their business to companies that provide quality and service. Michael Dell, CEO of Dell Computer, has directed that the role of training in the company be expanded.[1] The role of Dell Learning is to align training and learning with key business initiatives, make learning available to everyone who needs it, ensure that employees understand the skills required for success, and provide consistency in training content and delivery. Dell understands that training is important to keep the company ahead of competitors that could take away his business. He emphasizes that the success of Dell depends on how fast it can learn new technologies and apply them to serving customers. Why do Dell, Tires Plus, and many other companies believe that an investment in training can help them gain a competitive advantage? Training can

- Increase employees' knowledge of foreign competitors and cultures, which is critical for success in foreign markets.
- Help ensure that employees have the basic skills to work with new technology, such as robots and computer-assisted manufacturing processes.

- Help employees understand how to work effectively in teams to contribute to product and service quality.
- Ensure that the company's culture emphasizes innovation, creativity, and learning.
- Ensure employment security by providing new ways for employees to contribute to the company when their jobs change, their interests change, or their skills become obsolete.
- Prepare employees to accept and work more effectively with each other, particularly with minorities and women.[2]

In this chapter we emphasize the conditions through which training practices can help companies gain competitive advantage and how managers can contribute to a high-leverage training effort and create a learning organization. The chapter begins by discussing a systematic and effective approach to training design. Next we review training methods and training evaluation. The chapter concludes with a discussion of issues such as cross-cultural preparation, managing diversity, and socializing employees.

High-Leverage Training Strategy: A Systematic Approach

In general, **training** refers to a planned effort by a company to facilitate employees' learning of job-related competencies. These competencies include knowledge, skills, or behaviors that are critical for successful job performance. The goal of training is for employees to master the knowledge, skill, and behaviors emphasized in training programs and to apply them to their day-to-day activities. Recently it has been acknowledged that to offer a competitive advantage, training has to involve more than just basic skill development.[3] Training is moving from a primary focus on teaching employees specific skills to a broader focus of creating and sharing knowledge.[4] That is, to use training to gain a competitive advantage, a firm should view training broadly as a way to create intellectual capital. Intellectual capital includes basic skills (skills needed to perform one's job), advanced skills (such as how to use technology to share information with other employees), an understanding of the customer or manufacturing system, and self-motivated creativity.

Traditionally most of the emphasis on training has been at the basic and advanced skill levels. But some estimate that soon up to 85 percent of the jobs in the United States and Europe will require extensive use of knowledge. This requires employees to share knowledge and creatively use it to modify a product or serve the customer, as well as to understand the service or product development system.

Many companies have adopted this broader perspective, which is known as high-leverage training. **High-leverage training** is linked to strategic business goals and objectives, uses an instructional design process to ensure that training is effective, and compares or benchmarks the company's training programs against training programs in other companies.[5]

High-leverage training practices also help to create working conditions that encourage continuous learning. **Continuous learning** requires employees to understand the entire work system including the relationships among their jobs, their work units, and the company. (Continuous learning is similar to the idea of system understanding mentioned earlier.)[6] Employees are expected to acquire new skills and knowledge, apply them on the job, and share this information with other employees. Managers identify training needs and help to ensure that employees use training in their work.

Training
A planned effort to facilitate the learning of job-related knowledge, skills, and behavior by employees.

High-leverage training
Training practice that links training to strategic business goals, has top management support, relies on an instructional design model, and is benchmarked to programs in other organizations.

Continuous learning
A learning system that requires employees to understand the entire work process and expects them to acquire new skills, apply them on the job, and share what they have learned with other employees.

TABLE 7.1

Key Features of a Learning Organization

FEATURE	DESCRIPTION
Continuous learning	Employees share learning with each other and use their jobs as a basis for applying and creating knowledge.
Knowledge generation and sharing	Systems are developed for creating, capturing, and sharing knowledge.
Critical systematic thinking	Employees are encouraged to think in new ways, see relationships and feedback loops, and test assumptions.
Learning culture	Learning is rewarded, promoted, and supported by manager and company objectives.
Encouragement of flexibility and experimentation	Employees are encouraged to take risks, innovate, explore new ideas, try new processes, and develop new products and services.
Valuing of employees	System and environment focus on ensuring the development and well-being of every employee.

SOURCE: Adapted from M.A. Gephart, V.J. Marsick, M.E. Van Buren, and M.S. Spiro, "Learning Organizations Come Alive," *Training and Development* 50 (1996), pp. 34–45. Reprinted with permission.

To facilitate the sharing of knowledge, managers may use informational maps that show where knowledge lies within the company (for example, directories that list what a person does as well as the specialized knowledge she possesses) and use technology such as groupware or the Internet that allows employees in various business units to work simultaneously on problems and share information.[7]

Learning organization
An organization whose employees are continuously attempting to learn new things and apply what they have learned to improve product or service quality.

High-leverage training practices are one characteristic of companies considered to be learning organizations. A **learning organization** is one whose employees are continuously attempting to learn new things and apply what they have learned to improve product or service quality. Improvements do not stop when formal training is completed.[8] A learning organization is also a company that has an enhanced capacity to learn, adapt, and change. Training processes are carefully scrutinized and aligned with company goals.[9] In a learning organization, training is seen as one part of a system designed to create intellectual capital.

System-level learning
A company's ability to preserve what is learned over time.

The essential features of a learning organization appear in Table 7.1. Note that the learning organization emphasizes that learning occurs not only at the individual employee level (as we traditionally think of learning), but also at the group and organizational levels. The learning organization emphasizes system-level learning. **System-level learning** refers to the company's ability to preserve what is learned over time. That is, despite the fact that employees (and even divisions) of the company may no longer exist, their knowledge is still available. Two features of Table 7.1's learning organization relate directly to system-level learning. Continuous learning and knowledge generation encourage employees to share information with each other. How might this occur? There are several ways to create and share knowledge:

1. Use technology and software such as LOTUS Discovery System 1.0 and e-mail, or create a company intranet that allows people to store information and share it with others.
2. Publish directories that list what employees do, how they can be contacted, and the type of knowledge they have.[10]

3. Develop informational maps that identify where specific knowledge is stored in the company.
4. Create a chief information officer position for cataloging and facilitating the exchange of information in the company.
5. Require employees to give presentations to other employees about what they have learned from training programs they have attended.
6. Allow employees to take time off from work (e.g., sabbaticals) to acquire knowledge or study problems.
7. Create an online library of learning resources such as journals, technical manuals, training opportunities, and seminars.

Finding and Keeping the Best Employees

Viant, a consulting company specializing in building e-businesses, is designed to be a learning organization that successfully manages knowledge.[11] Viant consultants work and create in a community of shared learning, mutual respect, and energetic collaboration, where inspiration happens and innovation results. This type of environment attracts talented consultants and increases the loyalty and commitment of current employees. New employees begin their careers at the home office in Boston learning about the company. They learn team skills and Viant's consulting strategy and tools, are exposed to the company culture, and meet the company's upper management team. Viant has an open-office arrangement that encourages interaction between work teams by setting up snack areas that intersect where teams are working. The company's nonhierarchical structure promotes the free flow of ideas and values expertise over titles. Viant's leadership team includes rotating "fellows" nominated by peers. Performance reviews emphasize growth in employees' skill level, while knowledge sharing is rewarded with stock options. Viant rewards employees for how they contribute to the company and the culture, including how they share knowledge, master new skills, take ownership, and mentor and teach. At Viant, before every project, consultants complete a brief document that describes the knowledge they need, what knowledge from other projects can be used, what they will need to create, and what lessons they hope to learn that they can share with other consultants. The documents end up in Viant's internal website. Every six weeks the company's internal knowledge management group prepares and posts online a summary of what has been learned. To further stimulate knowledge, Viant management has created the role of "project catalyst" for its consultants. Project catalysts are assigned to multiple projects; their job is to challenge and question the teams to push them to think of innovative solutions and insightful approaches and ideas for business problems.

How does knowledge management translate into Viant's business practices? Viant's team helped BlueTape build and launch a digital entertainment business. BlueTape's first offering is sputnik7, an online interactive music video channel for Web- and music-savvy trendspotters. The technologists on the sputnik7.com team pushed current technology to its limits, delivering inline, synchronized streaming media through a Web browser. They weren't stopped by not knowing if something could be done—they questioned processes and technology and experimented.

Designing Effective Training Systems

A key characteristic of training systems that contribute to competitiveness is that they are designed according to the instructional design process.[12] **Instructional design process** refers to a systematic approach for developing training programs. Table 7.2

Instructional design process
A systematic approach for developing training programs.

TABLE 7.2
Components of Instructional Design

1. Assessing needs
   - Organizational analysis
   - Person analysis
   - Task analysis
2. Ensuring employees' readiness for training
   - Attitudes and motivation
   - Basic skills
3. Creating a learning environment
   - Identification of learning objectives and training outcomes
   - Meaningful material
   - Practice
   - Feedback
   - Observation of others
   - Administering and coordinating program
4. Ensuring transfer of training
   - Self-management strategies
   - Peer and manager support
5. Selecting training methods
   - Presentational methods
   - Hands-on methods
   - Group methods
6. Evaluating training programs
   - Identification of training outcomes and evaluation design
   - Cost–benefit analysis

presents the six steps of this process, which emphasizes that effective training practices involve more than just choosing the most popular or colorful training method.

Step 1 is to assess needs to determine if training is needed. Step 2 involves ensuring that employees have the motivation and basic skills to master training content. Step 3 addresses whether the training session (or the learning environment) has the factors necessary for learning to occur. Step 4 is to ensure that trainees apply the content of training to their jobs. This requires support from managers and peers for the use of training content on the job as well as getting the employee to understand how to take personal responsibility for skill improvement. Step 5 involves choosing a training method. As we shall see in this chapter, a variety of training methods are available ranging from traditional on-the-job training to newer technologies such as the Internet. The key is to choose a training method that will provide the appropriate learning environment to achieve the training objectives. Step 6 is evaluation—that is, determining whether training achieved the desired learning outcomes and/or financial objectives.

Needs assessment
The process used to determine if training is necessary.

The first step in the instructional design process, **needs assessment,** refers to the process used to determine if training is necessary. Figure 7.1 shows the causes and outcomes resulting from needs assessment. As we see, many different "pressure points" suggest that training is necessary. These pressure points include performance problems, new technology, internal or external customer requests for training, job redesign, new legislation, changes in customer preferences, new products, or employees' lack of basic skills. Note that these pressure points do not guarantee that training is the correct solution. Consider, for example, a delivery truck driver whose job is to de-

FIGURE 7.1

The Needs Assessment Process

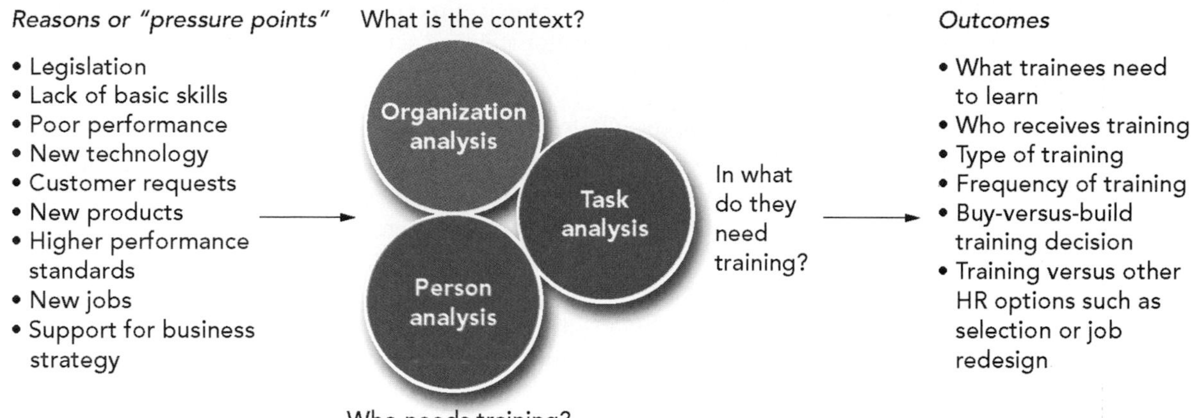

liver anesthetic gases to medical facilities. The driver mistakenly hooks up the supply line of a mild anesthetic to the supply line of a hospital's oxygen system, contaminating the hospital's oxygen supply. Why did the driver make this mistake, which is clearly a performance problem? The driver may have done this because of a lack of knowledge about the appropriate line hookup for the anesthetic, anger over a requested salary increase that his manager recently denied, or mislabeled valves for connecting the gas supply. Only the lack of knowledge can be addressed by training. The other pressure points require addressing issues related to the consequence of good performance (pay system) or the design of the work environment.

Needs assessment typically involves organizational analysis, person analysis, and task analysis.[13] Organizational analysis considers the context in which training will occur. That is, **organizational analysis** involves determining the business appropriateness of training, given the company's business strategy, its resources available for training, and support by managers and peers for training activities.

Person analysis helps identify who needs training. **Person analysis** involves (1) determining whether performance deficiencies result from a lack of knowledge, skill, or ability (a training issue) or from a motivational or work-design problem, (2) identifying who needs training, and (3) determining employees' readiness for training. **Task analysis** includes identifying the important tasks and knowledge, skill, and behaviors that need to be emphasized in training for employees to complete their tasks.

In practice, organizational analysis, person analysis, and task analysis are usually not conducted in any specific order. However, because organizational analysis is concerned with identifying whether training fits with the company's strategic objectives and whether the company wants to devote time and money to training, it is usually conducted first. Person analysis and task analysis are often conducted at the same time because it is often difficult to determine whether performance deficiencies are a training problem without understanding the tasks and the work environment.

What outcomes result from a needs assessment? As shown in Figure 7.1, needs assessment shows who needs training and what trainees need to learn, including the tasks in which they need to be trained plus knowledge, skill, behavior, or other job requirements. Needs assessment helps determine whether the company will purchase training from a vendor or consultant or develop training using internal resources.

Organizational analysis
A process for determining the business appropriateness of training.

Person analysis
A process for determining whether employees need training, who needs training, and whether employees are ready for training.

Task analysis
The process of identifying the tasks, knowledge, skills, and behaviors that need to be emphasized in training.

Organizational Analysis

Managers need to consider three factors before choosing training as the solution to any pressure point: the company's strategic direction, the training resources available, and support of managers and peers for training activities.

Support of Managers and Peers

Various studies have found that peer and manager support for training is critical. The key factors to success are a positive attitude among peers and managers about participation in training activities; managers' and peers' willingness to tell trainees how they can more effectively use knowledge, skills, or behaviors learned in training on the job; and the availability of opportunities for the trainees to use training content in their jobs.[14] If peers' and managers' attitudes and behaviors are not supportive, employees are not likely to apply training content to their jobs.

Company Strategy

Concentration strategy
A strategy focusing on increasing market share, reducing costs, or creating and maintaining a market niche for products and services.

Internal growth strategy
A focus on new market and product development, innovation, and joint ventures.

External growth strategy
An emphasis on acquiring vendors and suppliers or buying businesses that allows a company to expand into new markets.

Disinvestment strategy
An emphasis on liquidation and divestiture of businesses.

In Chapter 2 we discussed the importance of business strategy for a company to gain a competitive advantage. The plan or goal that the company chooses to achieve strategic objectives has a major impact on whether resources (money, trainers' time, program development) should be devoted to addressing a training pressure point.

Table 7.3 describes four business strategies—concentration, internal growth, external growth, and disinvestment—and highlights the implications of each for training practices.[15] Each strategy differs based on the goal of the business. A **concentration strategy** focuses on increasing market share, reducing costs, or creating and maintaining a market niche for products and services. Southwest Airlines has a concentration strategy. It focuses on providing short-haul, low-fare, high-frequency air transportation. It utilizes one type of aircraft (the Boeing 737), has no reserved seating, and serves no meals. This has enabled Southwest to keep costs low and revenues high. An **internal growth strategy** focuses on new market and product development, innovation, and joint ventures. For example, the merger between two publishing companies, McGraw-Hill and Richard D. Irwin, created one company with strengths in the U.S. and international college textbook markets. An **external growth strategy** emphasizes acquiring vendors and suppliers or buying businesses that allow the company to expand into new markets. For example, General Electric, a manufacturer of lighting products and jet engines, acquired the National Broadcast Corporation (NBC), a television and communications company. A **disinvestment strategy** emphasizes liquidation and divestiture of businesses. For example, General Mills sold its restaurant businesses, including Red Lobster.

Preliminary research suggests a link between business strategy and amount and type of training.[16] As shown in Table 7.3, training issues vary greatly from one strategy to another. For example, divesting companies need to train employees in job-search skills and focus on cross-training remaining employees who may find themselves in jobs with expanding responsibilities. Companies focusing on a market niche (a concentration strategy) need to emphasize skill currency and development of their existing workforce. For example, Transocean Offshore Inc., a contractor that drills offshore oil wells for oil companies such as BP Amoco, was formed from the merger of Norwegian and U.S drilling companies.[17] Transocean has decided to focus exclusively on deep-water drilling. Contracts for these jobs last four or five years, longer than contracts for other types of well drilling (such as shallow-water wells). New

TABLE 7.3
Implications of Business Strategy for Training

STRATEGY	EMPHASIS	HOW ACHIEVED	KEY ISSUES	TRAINING IMPLICATIONS
Concentration	• Increase market share • Reduce operating costs • Create or maintain market niche	• Improve product quality • Productivity improvement or technical process innovation • Customize products or services	• Skill currency • Development of existing workforce	• Team building • Cross-training • Specialized programs • Interpersonal skill training • On-the-job training
Internal growth	• Market development • Product development • Innovation • Joint ventures	• Market existing products/add distribution channels • Global market expansion • Modify existing products • Create new or different products • Expand through joint ownership	• Creating new jobs and tasks • Innovation	• Support or promote high-quality communication of product value • Cultural training • Develop organizational culture that values creative thinking and analysis • Technical competence in jobs • Manager training in feedback and communication • Conflict negotiation skills
External growth (acquisition)	• Horizontal integration • Vertical integration • Concentric diversification	• Acquire firms operating at same stage in product market chain (new market access) • Acquire businesses that can supply or buy products • Acquire firms that have nothing in common with acquiring firm	• Integration • Redundancy • Restructuring	• Determine capabilities of employees in acquired firms • Integrate training systems • Methods and procedures of combined firms • Team building
Disinvestment	• Retrenchment • Turnaround • Divestiture • Liquidation	• Reduce costs • Reduce assets • Generate revenue • Redefine goals • Sell off all assets	• Efficiency	• Motivation, goal setting, time management, stress management, cross-training • Leadership training • Interpersonal communications • Outplacement assistance • Job-search skills training

technology and new ships are needed for the deep-water drilling. The *Discoverer Enterprise* is one of the biggest and most technologically sophisticated offshore drilling ships. The ship has numerous workstations, computer systems, and automated drilling systems. As a result, the company has to provide training for specialized job skills as well as training for general rig safety. Traditionally, training is not part of the oil-drilling business due to the boom–bust business cycle, where every business decision depends on the price of crude oil. Most companies provide basic safety training but are reluctant to invest in training for employees who may be laid off when the price of oil drops. Because of the merger and new business focus, Transocean is one of the first drilling contractors to recognize the importance of training. The company developed job descriptions for each oil rig position (such as roughneck and derrickman); these job descriptions were used to build on-the-job training programs. The company is even using computer-based training modules to supplement training via videos and workbooks.

It is important to identify the prevailing business strategy to ensure that the company allocates enough of its budget to training, that employees receive training on relevant topics, and that employees get the right amount of training.[18]

A good example of how training can contribute to business strategy is evident in the changes made by SunU, the training and development organization of Sun Microsystems, a manufacturer of computer workstations and workstation software.[19] SunU realigned its training philosophy and the types of training conducted to be more linked to the strategy of Sun Microsystems. Sun Microsystems was in a constantly evolving business due to new technologies, products, and product markets (an internal growth strategy). SunU found that its customers wanted training services that could be developed quickly, could train many people, and would not involve classroom training. Because of the internal growth strategy, Sun Microsystems was also interested in maintaining and improving the knowledge and competence of its current workforce.

To better align the training function with the needs generated by the business strategy, SunU took several steps. First, SunU developed a new approach to determining the knowledge and skills that the employees needed to meet business goals. SunU identified several basic competencies (such as customer relations). A team of trainers at SunU constantly reviews these competencies and discusses them with key senior managers. For example, in the customer service competency, vice presidents and directors of sales and marketing are interviewed to identify training needs. As a result of this process SunU learned more about the business needs and was able to develop relevant training. To deliver training quickly to many trainees without relying on the classroom, SunU developed videoconferencing programs that allow simultaneous training at several sites without requiring trainees to travel. To help maintain and improve the knowledge and abilities of its employees, SunU developed a desktop library that enables all employees to access CD-ROMs containing up-to-date information on technologies and products as well as profiles of customers and competitors.

Training Resources

It is necessary to identify whether the company has the budget, time, and expertise for training. For example, if the company is installing computer-based manufacturing equipment in one of its plants, it has three possible strategies to have computer-literate employees. First, the company can use internal consultants to train all affected employees. Second, the company may decide that it is more cost-effective to identify computer-literate employees by using tests and work samples. Employees who fail the test or perform below standards on the work sample can be reassigned to other jobs. Choosing this strategy suggests that the company has decided to devote resources to selection and placement rather than training. Third, if it lacks time or expertise, the company may decide to purchase training from a consultant.

Many companies identify vendors and consultants who can provide training services by using requests for proposals.[20] A **request for proposal (RFP)** is a document that outlines for potential vendors and consultants the type of service the company is seeking, the type and number of references needed, the number of employees who need to be trained, funding for the project, the follow-up process used to determine level of satisfaction and service, the expected completion date of the project, and the date when proposals must be received by the company. The request for proposal may be mailed to potential consultants and vendors or posted on the company's website. The request for proposal is valuable because it provides a standard set of criteria against which all consultants will be evaluated. The RFP also helps eliminate the need to evaluate outside vendors who cannot provide the needed services.

Request for proposal (RFP)
A document that outlines for potential vendors and consultants the type of service the company is seeking, references needed, number of employees who should be trained, project funding, the follow-up process, expected completion date, and the date when proposals must be received by the company.

Usually the RFP helps identify several vendors who meet the criteria. The next step is to choose the preferred provider. Table 7.4 provides examples of questions to ask vendors.

When using a consultant or other outside vendor to provide training services, it is also important to consider the extent to which the training program will be customized to the company's needs or whether the consultant provides training services based on a generic framework that it applies to many different organizations. For example, Towers Perrin, a well-known, successful New York consulting firm, told several clients that it would study their companies in detail and customize a diversity training program to fit their needs. However, six companies (including Nissan USA, Thompson Consumer Electronics, and Harris Bank) were given the same 18 recommendations (such as separate the concept of affirmative action from that of managing diversity)![21]

How long should you expect it to take a vendor or consultant to develop a training program? The answer is, it depends.[22] Some consultants estimate that development time ranges from 10 to 20 hours for each hour of instruction. Highly technical content requiring more frequent meeting with subject matter experts can add 50 percent more time. For training programs using new technology (such as a CD-ROM) development time can range from 300 to 1,000 hours per hour of program time, depending on how much animation, graphics, video, and audio are included, how much new content needs to be developed, the number of practice exercises and type

TABLE 7.4
Questions to Ask Vendors and Consultants

Questions
How much and what type of experience does your company have in designing and delivering training?
What are the qualifications and experiences of your staff?
Can you provide demonstrations or examples of training programs you have developed?
Would you provide references of clients for whom you worked?
What evidence do you have that your programs work?

SOURCE: From R. Zemke and J. Armstrong, "Evaluating Multimedia Developers." Reprinted with permission from the November 1996 issue of *Training Magazine*.

of feedback to be provided to trainees, and the number of "branches" to different instructional sequences.

Person characteristics
An employee's knowledge, skills, abilities, and attitudes.

Input
Instructions that tell the employee what, how, and when to perform; also the support they are given to help them to perform.

Output
A job's performance standards.

Consequences
The incentives that employees receive for performing well.

Feedback
Information that employees receive while they are performing concerning how well they are meeting objectives.

Person Analysis

Person analysis helps the manager identify whether training is appropriate and which employees need training. In certain situations, such as the introduction of a new technology or service, all employees may need training. However, when managers, customers, or employees identify a problem (usually as a result of a performance deficiency), it is often unclear whether training is the solution.

A major pressure point for training is poor or substandard performance—that is, a gap between employees' current performance and their expected performance. Poor performance is indicated by customer complaints, low performance ratings, or on-the-job accidents or unsafe behavior. Another potential indicator of the need for training is if the job changes so current performance levels need improvement or employees must complete new tasks.

Figure 7.2 shows the factors that influence employees' performance and learning. These factors include person characteristics, input, output, consequences, and feedback.[23] **Person characteristics** refer to the employees' knowledge, skill, ability, and attitudes. **Input** relates to the instructions that tell employees what, how, and when to perform. Input also refers to the support given to employees to help them perform. This support includes resources such as equipment, time, or budget. Support also includes feedback and reinforcement from managers and peers. **Output** refers to the job's performance standards. **Consequences** are the incentives employees receive for performing well. **Feedback** is the information employees receive while they are performing.

From a manager's perspective, to determine if training is needed, for any performance problem you need to analyze characteristics of the performer, input, output, con-

FIGURE 7.2
Factors That Influence Employee Performance and Learning

Person characteristics
- Ability and skill
- Attitudes and motivation

Input
- Understand need to perform
- Necessary resources (equipment, etc.)
- Interference from other job demands
- Opportunity to perform

Output
- Standard to judge successful performers

Consequences
- Positive consequences/incentives to perform
- Few negative consequences to perform

Feedback
- Frequent and specific feedback about how the job is performed

→ Performance and learning

SOURCE: G. Rummler, "In Search of the Holy Performance Grail," *Training and Development*, April 1996, pp. 26–31. Reprinted with permission.

sequences, and feedback. How might this be done? Based on the model in Figure 7.2, you should ask several questions to determine if training is the likely solution to a performance problem.[24] Assess whether

1. The performance problem is important and has the potential to cost the company a significant amount of money from lost productivity or customers.
2. Employees do not know how to perform effectively. Perhaps they received little or no previous training or the training was ineffective. (This problem is a characteristic of the person.)
3. Employees cannot demonstrate the correct knowledge or behavior. Perhaps they were trained but they infrequently or never used the training content (knowledge, skills, etc.) on the job. (This is an input problem.)
4. Performance expectations are clear (input) and there are no obstacles to performance such as faulty tools or equipment.
5. There are positive consequences for good performance, whereas poor performance is not rewarded. For example, if employees are dissatisfied with their compensation, their peers or a union may encourage them to slow down their pace of work. (This involves consequences.)
6. Employees receive timely, relevant, accurate, constructive, and specific feedback about their performance (a feedback issue).
7. Other solutions such as job redesign or transferring employees to other jobs are too expensive or unrealistic.

If employees lack the knowledge and skill to perform and the other factors are satisfactory, training is needed. If employees have the knowledge and skill to perform, but input, output, consequences, or feedback are inadequate, training may not be the best solution. For example, if poor performance results from faulty equipment, training cannot solve this problem, but repairing the equipment will! If poor performance results from lack of feedback, then employees may not need training, but their managers may need training on how to give performance feedback.

Task Analysis

A task analysis, defined on page 255, identifies the conditions in which tasks are performed. The conditions include identifying equipment and the environment the employee works in, time constraints (deadlines), safety considerations, or performance standards. Task analysis results in a description of work activities, including tasks performed by the employee and the knowledge, skills, and abilities required to successfully complete the tasks. A *job* is a specific position requiring the completion of specific tasks. A *task* is a statement of an employee's work activity in a specific job. There are four steps in task analysis:

1. Select the job(s) to be analyzed.
2. Develop a preliminary list of tasks performed on the job by interviewing and observing expert employees and their managers and talking with others who have performed a task analysis.
3. Validate or confirm the preliminary list of tasks. This involves having a group of subject matter experts (job incumbents, managers, and so on) answer in a meeting or on a written survey several questions regarding the tasks. The types of questions that may be asked include the following: How frequently is the task performed? How much time is spent performing each task? How important or critical

TABLE 7.5
Sample Task Statement Questionnaire

Name Date
Position

Please rate each of the task statements according to three factors: the *importance* of the task for effective performance, how *frequently* the task is performed, and the degree of *difficulty* required to become effective in the task. Use the following scales in making your ratings.

Importance	*Frequency*
4 = Task is critical for effective performance.	4 = Task is performed once a day.
3 = Task is important but not critical for effective performance.	3 = Task is performed once a week.
2 = Task is of some importance for effective performance.	2 = Task is performed once every few months.
1 = Task is of no importance for effective performance.	1 = Task is performed once or twice a year.
0 = Task is not performed.	0 = Task is not performed.

Difficulty

4 = Effective performance of the task requires extensive prior experience and/or training (12–18 months or longer).
3 = Effective performance of the task requires minimal prior experience and training (6–12 months).
2 = Effective performance of the task requires a brief period of prior training and experience (1–6 months).
1 = Effective performance of the task does not require specific prior training and/or experience.
0 = This task is not performed.

Task	*Importance*	*Frequency*	*Difficulty*
1. Ensuring maintenance on equipment, tools, and safety controls			
2. Monitoring employee performance			
3. Scheduling employees			
4. Using statistical software on the computer			
5. Monitoring changes made in processes using statistical methods			

is the task for successful performance of the job? How difficult is the task to learn? Is performance of the task expected of entry-level employees?[25]

Table 7.5 presents a sample task analysis questionnaire. This information is used to determine which tasks will be focused on in the training program. The person or committee conducting the needs assessment must decide the level of ratings across dimensions that will determine that a task should be included in the training program. Tasks that are important, frequently performed, and of moderate-to-high levels of difficulty should be trained. Tasks that are not important and are infrequently performed will not be trained. It is difficult for managers and trainers to decide if tasks that are important, are performed infrequently, and require minimal difficulty should be included in training. Managers and trainers must determine whether important tasks—regardless of how frequently they are performed or their level of difficulty—will be included in training.

4. Identify the knowledge, skills, or abilities necessary to successfully perform each task. This information can be collected using interviews and questionnaires. Information concerning basic skill and cognitive ability requirements is critical for determining if certain levels of knowledge, skills, and abilities will be prerequisites for entrance to the training program (or job) or if supplementary training in

underlying skills is needed. For training purposes, information concerning how difficult it is to learn the knowledge, skill, or ability is important—as is whether the knowledge, skill, or ability is expected to be acquired by the employee before taking the job.[26]

Example of a Task Analysis

Each of the four steps of a task analysis can be seen in this example from a utility company. Trainers were given the job of developing a training system in six months.[27] The purpose of the program was to identify tasks and knowledge, skills, abilities, and other considerations that would serve as the basis for training program objectives and lesson plans.

The first phase of the project involved identifying potential tasks for each job in the utility's electrical maintenance area. Procedures, equipment lists, and information provided by subject matter experts (SMEs) were used to generate the tasks. SMEs included managers, instructors, and senior technicians. The tasks were incorporated into a questionnaire administered to all technicians in the electrical maintenance department. The questionnaire included 550 tasks. Figure 7.3 shows sample items from the questionnaire for the electrical maintenance job. Technicians were asked to rate each task on importance, difficulty, and frequency of performance. The rating scale for frequency included zero. A zero rating indicated that the technician rating the task had never performed the task. Technicians who rated a task zero were asked not to evaluate the task's difficulty and importance.

FIGURE 7.3

Sample Items from Task Analysis Questionnaires for the Electrical Maintenance Job

Job: Electrical Maintenance Worker

		Task Performance Ratings		
Task #s	**Task description**	**Frequency of performance**	**Importance**	**Difficulty**
199-264	Replace a light bulb	0 1 2 3 4 5	0 1 2 3 4 5	0 1 2 3 4 5
199-265	Replace an electrical outlet	0 1 2 3 4 5	0 1 2 3 4 5	0 1 2 3 4 5
199-266	Install a light fixture	0 1 2 3 4 5	0 1 2 3 4 5	0 1 2 3 4 5
199-267	Replace a light switch	0 1 2 3 4 5	0 1 2 3 4 5	0 1 2 3 4 5
199-268	Install a new circuit breaker	0 1 2 3 4 5	0 1 2 3 4 5	0 1 2 3 4 5
		Frequency of performance 0=never 5=often	**Importance** 1=negligible 5=extremely high	**Difficulty** 1=easiest 5=most difficult

SOURCE: E.F. Holton III and C. Bailey, "Top to Bottom Curriculum Redesign," *Training & Development*, March 1995, pp. 40–44. Reprinted with permission.

Customized software was used to analyze the ratings collected via the questionnaire. The primary requirement used to determine whether a task required training was its importance rating. A task rated "very important" was identified as one requiring training regardless of its frequency or difficulty. If a task was rated moderately important but difficult, it also was designated for training. Tasks rated unimportant, not difficult, and done infrequently were not designated for training.

The list of tasks designated for training was reviewed by the SMEs to determine if it accurately described job tasks. The result was a list of 487 tasks. For each of the 487 tasks, two SMEs identified the necessary knowledge, skills, abilities, and other factors required for performance. This included information on working conditions, cues that initiate the task's start and end, performance standards, safety considerations, and necessary tools and equipment. All data were reviewed by plant technicians and members of the training department. More than 14,000 knowledge, skill, ability, and other considerations were clustered into common areas. An identification code was assigned to each group that linked groups to task and knowledge, skill, ability, and other factors. These groups were then combined into clusters that represented qualification areas. That is, the task clusters related to linked tasks that the employees must be certified in to perform the job. The clusters were used to identify training lesson plans and course objectives; trainers also reviewed the clusters to identify prerequisite skills.

Ensuring Employees' Readiness for Training

The second step in the instructional design process is to evaluate whether employees are ready to learn. *Readiness for training* refers to whether (1) employees have the personal characteristics (ability, attitudes, beliefs, and motivation) necessary to learn program content and apply it on the job and (2) the work environment will facilitate learning and not interfere with performance.

Motivation to learn The desire of the trainee to learn the content of a training program.

Although managers are not often trainers, they play an important role in influencing employees' readiness for training. **Motivation to learn** is the desire of the trainee to learn the content of the training program.[28] Various research studies have shown that motivation is related to knowledge gain, behavior change, or skill acquisition in training programs.[29] Managers need to ensure that employees' motivation to learn is as high as possible. They can do this by ensuring employees' self-efficacy; understanding the benefits of training; being aware of training needs, career interests, and goals; understanding work environment characteristics; and ensuring employees' basic skill levels. Managers should also consider input, output, consequences, and feedback because these factors influence motivation to learn.

Self-efficacy

Self-efficacy The employees' belief that they can successfully learn the content of a training program.

Self-efficacy is the employees' belief that they can successfully learn the content of the training program. The training environment is potentially threatening to many employees who may not have extensive educational experience or who have little experience in the particular area emphasized by the training program. For example, training employees to use equipment for computer-based manufacturing represents a potential threat, especially if employees are intimidated by new technologies and do not have confidence in their ability to master the skills needed to use a computer. Research has demonstrated that self-efficacy is related to performance in training programs.[30] Managers can increase employees' self-efficacy level by

1. Letting employees know that the purpose of training is to try to improve performance rather than to identify areas in which employees are incompetent.
2. Providing as much information as possible about the training program and purpose of training prior to the actual training.
3. Showing employees the training success of their peers who are now in similar jobs.
4. Providing employees with feedback that learning is under their control and they have the ability and the responsibility to overcome any learning difficulties they experience in the program.

Understanding the Benefits or Consequences of Training

Employees' motivation to learn can be enhanced by communicating to them the potential job-related, personal, and career benefits they may receive as a result of attending the training program. These benefits may include learning a more efficient way to perform a process or procedure, establishing contacts with other employees in the firm (networking), or increasing opportunities to pursue different career paths. The communication from the manager about potential benefits should be realistic. Unmet expectations about training programs have been shown to adversely affect motivation to learn.[31]

Awareness of Training Needs, Career Interests, and Goals

To be motivated to learn in training programs, employees must be aware of their skill strengths and weaknesses and of the link between the training program and improvement of their weaknesses.[32] Managers should make sure that employees understand why they are asked to attend training programs, and they should communicate the link between training and improvement of skill weaknesses or knowledge deficiencies. This can be accomplished by sharing performance appraisal information with employees, holding career development discussions, or having employees complete self-evaluations of their skill strengths and weaknesses and career interests and goals.

If possible, employees need to choose programs to attend and must perceive how actual training assignments are made to maximize motivation to learn. Several recent studies have suggested that giving trainees a choice regarding which programs to attend and then honoring those choices maximizes motivation to learn. Giving employees choices but not necessarily honoring them can reduce motivation to learn.[33]

Work Environment Characteristics

Employees' perceptions of two characteristics of the work environment—situational constraints and social support—are critical determinants of motivation to learn. *Situational constraints* include lack of proper tools and equipment, materials and supplies, budgetary support, and time. *Social support* refers to managers' and peers' willingness to provide feedback and reinforcement.[34]

To ensure that the work environment enhances trainees' motivation to learn, managers need to

1. Provide materials, time, job-related information, and other work aids necessary for employees to use new skills or behavior before participating in training programs.
2. Speak positively about the company's training programs to employees.

3. Let employees know they are doing a good job when they use training content in their work.
4. Encourage work group members to involve each other in trying to use new skills on the job by soliciting feedback and sharing training experiences and situations in which training content was helpful.
5. Give employees time and opportunities to practice and apply new skills or behaviors to their work.

Basic Skills

Basic skills
Reading, writing, and communication skills needed to understand the content of a training program.

Employees' motivation to learn in training activities can also be influenced by the degree to which they have **basic skills**—cognitive ability and reading and writing skills needed to understand the content of training programs. Recent forecasts of the skill levels of the U.S. workforce indicate that managers will likely have to work with employees who lack those skills.[35]

Managers need to conduct a literacy audit to determine employees' basic skill levels. Table 7.6 shows the activities involved in a literacy audit.

Cognitive ability
Includes three dimensions: verbal comprehension, quantitative ability, and reasoning ability.

Cognitive Ability. Research shows that cognitive ability influences learning and job performance. **Cognitive ability** includes three dimensions: verbal comprehension, quantitative ability, and reasoning ability.[36] *Verbal comprehension* refers to the person's capacity to understand and use written and spoken language. *Quantitative ability* refers to how fast and accurately a person can solve math problems. *Reasoning ability* refers to the person's capacity to invent solutions to problems. Research shows that cogni-

TABLE 7.6
Performing a Literacy Audit

Step 1.	Observe employees to determine the basic skills they need to succeed in their jobs. Note the materials employees use on the job, the tasks performed, and the reading, writing, and computations completed by employees.
Step 2.	Collect all materials that are written and read on the job and identify computations that must be performed to determine the necessary level of basic skill proficiency. Materials include bills, memos, and forms such as inventory lists and requisition sheets.
Step 3.	Interview employees to determine the basic skills they believe are needed to do the job. Consider the basic-skill requirements of the job yourself.
Step 4.	Determine whether employees have the basic skills needed to successfully perform their jobs. Combine the information gathered by observing and interviewing employees and evaluating materials they use on their jobs. Write a description of each job in terms of reading, writing, and computation skills needed to perform successfully.
Step 5.	Develop or buy tests that ask questions relating specifically to the employees' jobs. Ask employees to complete the tests.
Step 6.	Compare test results with the description of the basic skills required for the job (from step 5). If the level of employees' reading, writing, and computation skills does not match the basic skills required by the job, then a basic skills problem exists.

SOURCE: U.S. Department of Education, U.S. Department of Labor. *The Bottom Line: Basic Skills in the Workplace* (Washington, DC: 1988), pp. 14–15.

tive ability is related to successful performance in all jobs.[37] The importance of cognitive ability for job success increases as the job becomes more complex.

For example, a supermarket cashier needs low to moderate levels of all three dimensions of cognitive ability to successfully perform that job. An emergency room physician needs higher levels of verbal comprehension, quantitative ability, and reasoning ability than the cashier. The supermarket cashier needs to understand denominations of money to give customers correct change. The cashier also needs to invent solutions to problems. (For example, how does the cashier deal with items that are not priced that the customer wants to purchase?) The cashier also needs to be able to understand and communicate with customers (verbal comprehension). The physician also needs quantitative ability, but at a higher level. For example, when dealing with an infant experiencing seizures, the physician needs to be able to calculate the correct dosage of medicine (based on an adult dosage) to stop the seizures after considering the child's weight. The physician has to be able to quickly diagnose the situation and determine what actions (blood tests, X-rays, respiratory therapy) are necessary. The physician also needs to communicate clearly to the patient (or its parents) the treatment and recovery process.

Cognitive ability influences job performance and ability to learn in training programs. If trainees lack the cognitive ability level necessary to perform job tasks, they will not perform well. Also, trainees' level of cognitive ability can influence whether they can learn in training programs.[38] Trainees with low levels of cognitive ability are more likely to fail to complete training or (at the end of training) receive low grades on tests to measure how much they have learned.

As discussed in Chapter 6, to identify employees without the cognitive ability to succeed on the job or in training programs, companies use paper-and-pencil cognitive ability tests. Determining a job's cognitive ability requirement is part of the task analysis process discussed earlier in this chapter.

Reading Ability. Lack of the appropriate reading level can impede performance and learning in training programs. Material used in training should be evaluated to ensure that its reading level does not exceed that required by the job. **Readability** refers to the difficulty level of written materials.[39] A readability assessment usually involves analysis of sentence length and word difficulty.

Readability
The difficulty level of written materials.

If trainees' reading level does not match the level needed for the training materials, four options are available. First, determine whether it is feasible to use video or on-the-job training, which involves learning by watching and practicing rather than by reading. Second, employees without the necessary reading level could be identified through reading tests and reassigned to other positions more congruent with their skill levels. Third, again using reading tests, identify employees who lack the necessary reading skills and provide them with remedial training. Fourth, determine whether the job can be redesigned to accommodate employees' reading levels. The fourth option is certainly most costly and least practical. Therefore, alternative training methods need to be considered, or you can elect a nontraining option. Nontraining options include selecting employees for jobs and training opportunities on the basis of reading, computation, writing, and other basic skill requirements.

Many companies are finding that employees lack the basic skills needed to successfully complete training programs. For example, a training program for 1,800 hourly employees at Georgia-Pacific (a paper manufacturer) was ineffective.[40] Employees reported that they understood the training content, but once they left training and returned to their jobs, they couldn't successfully perform maintenance tasks.

In trying to determine the cause of the failed training, employees' basic skills were tested. Tests revealed that many employees had difficulty reading and writing. As a result, they were unable to understand the materials used in training. This translated into reduced learning and poor job performance.

To help ensure that employees have the basic skills needed to succeed in training, Georgia-Pacific developed a basic skills assessment and training program. The first step involved assessment (or measurement) of employees' basic skills. A test of reading and math skills was given to employees. People who scored at or above a ninth grade reading level were eligible to attend training programs. Those with literacy levels below ninth-grade were counseled to attend basic skills training. Because Georgia-Pacific's primary concern was how to convince employees to attend training, the company had to establish trust with the employees. In general, employees who lack basic skills are embarrassed to admit they have difficulty and are afraid that their lack of literacy will cost them their jobs. To alleviate these fears, employees received confidential counseling about their test results, they were not required to start basic skills training immediately after the assessment, and the company did not put information regarding test results (pass or fail) in employees' personnel files.

A local community college supplied the basic skills training. Classes were set up close to Georgia-Pacific's plants so employees could attend classes before or after their work shifts. There was no charge for the classes. Now the workforce has the necessary basic skills. To ensure that new employees do not lack basic skills, Georgia-Pacific has changed its hiring qualifications. The company does not accept applications from anyone who hasn't completed a specific 18-month schedule of courses at the community college.

Creating a Learning Environment

Learning permanently changes behavior. For employees to acquire knowledge and skills in the training program and apply this information in their jobs, the training program must include specific learning principles. Educational and industrial psychologists and instructional design specialists have identified several conditions under which employees learn best.[41] Table 7.7 shows the events that should take place for learning to occur in the training program and their implications for instruction.

Objective
The purpose and expected outcome of training activities.

Employees Need to Know Why They Should Learn. Employees learn best when they understand the objective of the training program. The **objective** refers to the purpose and expected outcome of training activities. There may be objectives for each training session as well as overall objectives for the program. Training objectives based on the training needs analysis help employees understand why they need training. Objectives are also useful for identifying the types of training outcomes that should be measured to evaluate a training program's effectiveness.

A training objective has three components:

1. A statement of what the employee is expected to do (performance or outcome).
2. A statement of the quality or level of performance that is acceptable (criterion).
3. A statement of the conditions under which the trainee is expected to perform the desired outcome (conditions).[42]

For example, a training objective for a retail customer service training program might be "After training, the employee will be able to express concern [performance] to all irate customers by a brief (fewer than 10 words) apology, only after the customer has stopped talking [criteria] and no matter how upset the customer is [conditions]."

TABLE 7.7

Instructional Events and Their Implications for the Learning Environment

INSTRUCTIONAL EVENTS	IMPLICATIONS
Informing the learner of the lesson objective	Provide a demonstration of the performance to be expected. Indicate the kind of verbal question to be answered.
Presenting stimuli with distinctive features	Emphasize the features of the subject to be perceived. Use formatting and figures in text to emphasize features.
Limiting the amount to be learned	Chunk lengthier material. Provide a visual image of material to be learned. Provide practice and overlearning to aid the attainment of automatization.
Providing learning guidance	Provide verbal cues to proper combining sequence. Provide verbal links to a larger meaningful context. Use diagrams and models to show relationships among concepts.
Elaborating the amount to be learned	Vary the context and setting for presentation and recall of material. Relate newly learned material to previously learned information. Provide a variety of contexts and situations during practice.
Providing cues that are used in recall	Suggest cues that elicit the recall of material. Use familiar sounds or rhymes as cues.
Enhancing retention and learning transfer	Design the learning situation to share elements with the situation of use. Provide verbal links to additional complexes of information.
Providing feedback about performance correctness	Provide feedback on degree of accuracy and timing of performance. Confirm that original expectancies were met.

SOURCE: Adapted from R.M. Gagne, "Learning Processes and Instruction," *Training Research Journal* 1 (1995/96), pp. 17–28.

Good training objectives provide a clear idea of what the trainees are expected to do at the end of training. Standards of satisfactory performance (such as speed, time constraints, products, or reactions) that can be measured or evaluated should be included. Any resources (equipment, tools) that the trainees need to perform the action or behavior specified in the objective need to be described. The conditions under which performance of the objective is expected to occur also need to be described. These conditions can relate to the physical work setting (at night), mental stresses (an angry customer), or equipment failure (malfunctioning landing gear on an airplane).

Employees Need Meaningful Training Content. Employees are more likely to learn when the training is linked to their current job experiences and tasks—that is, when it is meaningful to them.[43] To enhance the meaningfulness of training content, the message should be presented using concepts, terms, and examples familiar to trainees. Also, the training context should mirror the work environment. The *training context* refers to the physical, intellectual, and emotional environment in which the training occurs. For example, in a retail salesperson customer service program, the meaningfulness of the material will be increased by using scenarios of unhappy customers actually encountered by salespersons in stores. Recent research indicates that besides linking training to current job experiences, learning can be enhanced by letting trainees choose their practice strategy and other characteristics of the learning environment.[44]

Practice
Having the employee demonstrate what they have learned in training.

Overlearning
Trainees practice what they have learned several times.

Employees Need Opportunities to Practice. **Practice** involves having the employee demonstrate the learned capability (such as cognitive strategy or verbal information) emphasized in the training objectives under the conditions and performance standards specified by the objective. Effective practice actively involves the trainee, includes overlearning (repeated practice), takes the appropriate amount of time, and includes the appropriate unit of learning (amount of material). Practice also needs to be relevant to the training objectives.

Learning will not occur if employees practice only by talking about what they are expected to do. For example, using the objective for the customer service course previously discussed, practice would involve having trainees participate in role playing with unhappy customers (customers upset with poor service, poor merchandise, or exchange policies). Trainees need to continue to practice even if they have been able to perform the objective several times **(overlearning).** Overlearning helps the trainee become more comfortable using new knowledge and skills and increases the length of time the trainee will retain the knowledge, skill, or behavior.

Trainers need to be sure that instruction does not exceed employees' short-term and long-term memory capacities. Research suggests that no more than four to five items can be attended to at one time. If a lengthy procedure or process is to be taught, instruction needs to be delivered in shorter sessions or chunks in order not to exceed memory limits.[45] Visual images are another way to reduce demands on memory. Finally, automatizing (making performance of a task so automatic that it requires little thought or attention to be performed) is another way to reduce memory demands. For example, it would be difficult for a jet engine mechanic to perform some of the later parts of a maintenance procedure unless the earlier steps (such as removing the cover of the turbines) have been automatized. The more automatization of a procedure that occurs, the more memory is freed up to concentrate on other learning and thinking. Automatization occurs through overlearning; that is, learners are given extra learning opportunities even after they have demonstrated that they can perform adequately.

It is also important to consider whether to have only one practice session or to use distributed (multiple) practice sessions. Distributed practice sessions have been shown to result in more efficient learning of skills than continuous practice.[46] With factual information, the less meaningful the material and the greater its length or difficulty, the better distributed practice sessions are for learning.

A final issue related to practice is how much of the training should be practiced at one time. One option is that all tasks or objectives should be practiced at the same time (whole practice). Another option is that an objective or task should be practiced individually as soon as each is introduced in the training program (part practice). It is probably best to employ both whole and part practice in a training session. Trainees should have the opportunity to practice individual skills or behaviors. If the skills or behaviors introduced in training are related to one another, the trainee should demonstrate all of them in a practice session after they are practiced individually.

For example, one objective of the retail customer service training is learning how to handle an unhappy customer. Salespersons are likely to have to learn three key behaviors: (1) greeting disgruntled customers, (2) understanding their complaints, and then (3) identifying and taking appropriate action. Practice sessions should be held for each of the three behaviors (part practice). Then another practice session should be held so that trainees can practice all three skills together (whole practice). If trainees were given the opportunity only to practice the behaviors individually, it is unlikely they would be able to deal with an unhappy customer.

For practice to be relevant to the training objectives, several conditions must be met.[47] Practice must be related to the training objectives. The trainer should identify what trainees will be doing when practicing the objectives (performance), the criteria for attainment of the objective, and the conditions under which they may perform. These conditions should be present in the practice session. Next, the trainer needs to consider the adequacy of the trainees' performance. That is, how will trainees know whether their performance meets performance standards? Will they see a model of desired performance? Will they get a checklist or description of desired performance? Can the trainees decide if their performance meets standards, or will the trainer or a piece of equipment compare their performance with standards?

If trainees' performance does not meet standards, the trainer must also decide if they will understand what is wrong and how to fix it. That is, trainers need to consider if trainees can diagnose and correct their performance or if they will need help from the trainer or a fellow trainee.

Employees Need Feedback. *Feedback* is information about how well people are meeting the training objectives. To be effective, feedback should focus on specific behaviors and be provided as soon as possible after the trainees' behavior.[48] Also, positive trainee behavior should be verbally praised or reinforced. Videotape is a powerful tool for giving feedback. Trainers should view the videotape with trainees, provide specific information about how behaviors need to be modified, and praise trainee behaviors that meet objectives.

Employees Learn by Observing, Experience, and Interacting with Others. According to social learning theory, people learn by observing and imitating the actions of models. For the model to be effective, the desired behaviors or skills need to be clearly specified, and the model should have characteristics (such as age or position) similar to the target audience.[49] After observing the model, trainees should have the opportunity to reproduce the skills or behavior shown by the model in practice sessions.

Communities of practice are groups of employees who work together, learn from each other, and develop a common understanding of how to get work accomplished.[50] The idea of communities of practice suggests that learning occurs on the job as a result of social interaction. Communities of practice also take the form of discussion boards, list servers, or other forms of computer-mediated communication in which employees communicate electronically. In doing so, each employee's knowledge can be accessed relatively quickly. It is as if employees are having a conversation with a group of experts. Every company has naturally occurring communities of practice that develop as a result of relationships employees develop to accomplish work and the design of the work environment. For example, Oticon Inc., a Danish hearing aid manufacturer, replaced its formal organizational structure with a flexible work environment and project-based work processes.[51] Self-directed teams are formed and disband as required by the work. Most of Oticon's 1,500 employees work on several projects at one time. At Oticon, the physical workspace encourages the development of communities of practice. Oticon workers are given mobile workstations with drawerless desks and networked computers; their workspace is wherever they choose to park their workstations while on a project. Workers are encouraged to network and learn from colleagues.

Communities of practice
Employees who work together, learn from each other, and have a common understanding of how to get work accomplished.

Employees Need the Training Program to Be Properly Coordinated and Arranged. Training coordination is one of several aspects of training administration. **Training administration** refers to coordinating activities before, during, and after the program.[52] Training administration involves

Training administration
Coordinating activities before, during, and after a training program.

1. Communicating courses and programs to employees.
2. Enrolling employees in courses and programs.
3. Preparing and processing any pretraining materials such as readings or tests.
4. Preparing materials that will be used in instruction (copies of presentations, cases).
5. Arranging the training facility and room.
6. Testing equipment that will be used in instruction.
7. Having backup equipment (paper copies of slides, an extra overhead projector bulb) should equipment fail.
8. Providing support during instruction.
9. Distributing evaluation materials (tests, reaction measures, surveys).
10. Facilitating communications between trainer and trainees during and after training (for example, coordinating exchange of e-mail addresses).
11. Recording course completion in the trainees' training records or personnel files.

Good coordination ensures that trainees are not distracted by events (such as an uncomfortable room or poorly organized materials) that could interfere with learning. Activities before the program include communicating to trainees the purpose of the program, the place it will be held, the name of a person to contact if they have questions, and any preprogram work they are supposed to complete. Books, speakers, handouts, and videotapes need to be prepared. Any necessary arrangements to secure rooms and equipment (such as VCRs) should be made. The physical arrangement of the training room should complement the training technique. For example, it would be difficult for a team-building session to be effective if the seats could not be moved for group activities. If visual aids will be used, all trainees should be able to see them. Make sure that the room is physically comfortable with adequate lighting and ventilation. Trainees should be informed of starting and finishing times, break times, and location of bathrooms. Minimize distractions such as telephone messages. If trainees will be asked to evaluate the program or take tests to determine what they have learned, allot time for this activity at the end of the program. Following the program, any credits or recording of the names of trainees who completed the program should be done. Handouts and other training materials should be stored or returned to the consultant. The end of the program is also a good time to consider how the program could be improved if it will be offered again.

Transfer of training
The use of knowledge, skills, and behaviors learned in training on the job.

Transfer of Training

Transfer of training refers to on-the-job use of knowledge, skills, and behaviors learned in training. As Figure 7.4 shows, transfer of training is influenced by the climate for transfer, manager support, peer support, opportunity to use learned capabilities, technology support, and self-management skills. As we discussed earlier, learning is influenced by the learning environment (such as meaningfulness of the material and opportunities for practice and feedback) and employees' readiness for training (for example, their self-efficacy and basic skill level). If no learning occurs in the training program, transfer is unlikely.

Climate for transfer
Trainees' perceptions of characteristics of the work environment (social support and situational constraints) that can either facilitate or inhibit use of trained skills or behavior.

Climate for Transfer

One way to think about the work environment's influence on transfer of training is to consider the overall climate for transfer. **Climate for transfer** refers to trainees' per-

FIGURE 7.4
Work Environment Characteristics Influencing Transfer of Training

ceptions about a wide variety of characteristics of the work environment that facilitate or inhibit use of trained skills or behavior. These characteristics include manager and peer support, opportunity to use skills, and the consequences for using learned capabilities.[53] Research has shown that transfer of training climate is significantly related to positive changes in behaviors following training.

Manager Support

Manager support refers to the degree to which trainees' managers (1) emphasize the importance of attending training programs and (2) stress the application of training content to the job. Table 7.8 shows what managers should do to support training. For example, trainers at the California Housing Partnership train project managers of rental housing on how to schedule complex tasks. Unfortunately, many trainees do not implement the scheduling system because when they return to their community agencies, their managers are not convinced that the scheduling system is worthwhile.[54]

The greater the level of manager support, the more likely that transfer of training will occur.[55] The basic level of support that a manager should provide is acceptance

TABLE 7.8
What Managers Should Do to Support Training

Understand the content of the training.
Know how training relates to what you need employees to do.
In performance appraisals, evaluate employees on how they apply training to their jobs.
Support employees' use of training when they return to work.
Ensure that employees have the equipment and technology needed to use training.
Prior to training, discuss with employees how they plan to use training.
Recognize newly trained employees who use training content.
Give employees release time from their work to attend training.
Explain to employees why they have been asked to attend training.
Give employees feedback related to skills or behavior they are trying to develop.

SOURCE: Based on A. Rossett, "That Was a Great Class, but . . ." *Training and Development*, July 1997, p. 21.

allowing trainees to attend training. The highest level of support is to participate in training as an instructor (teaching in the program). Managers who serve as instructors are more likely to provide lower-level support functions such as reinforcing use of newly learned capabilities, discussing progress with trainees, and providing opportunities to practice. Managers can also facilitate transfer through use of action plans. An **action plan** is a written document that includes the steps that the trainee and manager will take to ensure that training transfers to the job. The action plan includes (1) a goal identifying what training content will be used and how it will be used (project, problem); (2) strategies for reaching the goal, including resources needed; (3) strategies for getting feedback (such as meetings with the manager); and (4) expected outcome (what will be different?). The action plan includes a schedule of specific dates and times when the manager and trainee agree to meet to discuss the progress being made in using learned capabilities on the job.

Action plan
Document summarizing what trainee and manager will do to ensure training transfers to the job.

At a minimum, special sessions should be scheduled with managers to explain the purpose of the training and set expectations that they will encourage attendance at the training session, provide practice opportunities, reinforce use of training, and follow up with employees to determine the progress in using newly acquired capabilities.

Peer Support

Transfer of training can also be enhanced by creating a support network among the trainees.[56] A **support network** is a group of two or more trainees who agree to meet and discuss their progress in using learned capabilities on the job. This could involve face-to-face meetings or communications via e-mail. Trainees can share successful experiences in using training content on the job; they can also discuss how they obtained resources needed to use training content or how they coped with a work environment that interfered with use of training content.

Support network
Trainees who meet to discuss progress in using learned capabilities.

A newsletter might be written to show how trainees are dealing with transfer of training issues. Distributed to all trainees, the newsletter might feature interviews with trainees who were successful in using new skills. Managers may also provide trainees with a mentor—a more experienced employee who previously attended the same training program. The mentor, who may be a peer, can provide advice and support related to transfer of training issues (such as how to find opportunities to use the learned capabilities).

Opportunity to Use Learned Capabilities

Opportunity to use learned capabilities **(opportunity to perform)** refers to the extent to which the trainee is provided with or actively seeks experience with newly learned knowledge, skill, and behaviors from the training program. Opportunity to perform is influenced by both the work environment and trainee motivation. One way trainees can use learned capabilities is through assigned work experiences (problems or tasks) that require their use. The trainees' manager usually plays a key role in determining work assignments. Opportunity to perform is also influenced by the degree to which trainees take personal responsibility to actively seek out assignments that allow them to use newly acquired capabilities.

Opportunity to perform
Trainee is provided with or seeks experience using newly learned knowledge, skills, or behavior.

Opportunity to perform includes breadth, activity level, and task type.[57] *Breadth* includes the number of trained tasks performed on the job. *Activity level* is the number of times or the frequency with which trained tasks are performed on the job. *Task type* refers to the difficulty or criticality of the trained tasks that are actually performed on the job. Trainees given many opportunities to use training content on the job are more likely to maintain learned capabilities than trainees given few opportunities.[58]

Opportunity to perform can be measured by asking former trainees to indicate (1) whether they perform a task, (2) how many times they perform the task, and (3) the extent to which they perform difficult and challenging tasks. Individuals who report low levels of opportunity to perform may be prime candidates for "refresher courses" (courses designed to let trainees practice and review training content). Refresher courses are necessary because these persons have likely experienced a decay in learned capabilities since they haven't had opportunities to perform. Low levels of opportunity to perform may also indicate that the work environment is interfering with using new skills. For example, the manager may not support training activities or give the employee the opportunity to perform tasks using skills emphasized in training. Finally, low levels of opportunity to perform may indicate that training content is not important for the employee's job.

Technological Support

Electronic performance support systems (EPSSs) are computer applications that can provide, as requested, skills training, information access, and expert advice.[59] EPSSs may be used to enhance transfer of training by giving trainees an electronic information source that they can refer to as needed as they attempt to apply learned capabilities on the job.

Electronic performance support systems (EPSS)
Computer applications that can provide (as requested) skills training, information access, and expert advice.

For example, Atlanta-based poultry processor Cagle's Inc. uses an EPSS for employees who maintain the chicken-processing machines.[60] Because the machines that measure and cut chickens are constantly increasing in sophistication, it is impossible to continually train technicians so that they know the equipment's details. However, technicians are trained on the basic procedures they need to know to maintain these types of machines. When the machines encounter a problem, the technicians rely on what they have learned in training as well as on the EPSS, which provides more detailed instructions about the repairs. The EPSS also tells technicians the availability of parts and where in inventory to find replacement parts. The EPSS consists of a postage stamp–size computer monitor attached to a visor that magnifies the screen. The monitor is attached to a three-pound computer about half the size of a portable compact disc player. Attached to the visor is a microphone that the technician uses to give verbal commands to the computer. The EPSS helps employees diagnose and fix the machines very quickly. This is important given that the plant processes more than 100,000 chickens a day, and chicken is a perishable food product! The "Competing through High-Performance Work Systems" box shows how technology is used to support training.

Self-Management Skills

Training programs should prepare employees to self-manage their use of new skills and behaviors on the job.[61] Specifically, within the training program, trainees should set goals for using skills or behaviors on the job, identify conditions under which they might fail to use them, identify the positive and negative consequences of using them, and monitor their use of them. Also, trainees need to understand that it is natural to encounter difficulty in trying to use skills on the job; relapses into old behavior and skill patterns do not indicate that trainees should give up. Finally, because peers and supervisors on the job may be unable to reward trainees using new behaviors or

COMPETING THROUGH HIGH-PERFORMANCE WORK SYSTEMS

Technology Provides a Human Touch to Every Question

Some companies are utilizing technology to help support training efforts when employees return to their jobs. Ernie is what's known as a *virtual representative* or *v-rep*. When mechanics at a Ford Motor Company car dealership encounter a problem, they contact Ernie. Ernie is not a real person—he is a robot! He is friendly as well as smart. The mechanics type in a question, and Ernie's picture appears on the screen. He answers the question and can provide a link to an internal website with more detailed explanations from service manuals. Before Ernie, when service technicians had a question, they would have to sort through detailed technical manuals or call a hotline, both of which are time-consuming. Ernie includes information from all the latest service manuals and is tied into Ford's worldwide diagnostic system. If Ernie can't answer, he will automatically sequence to call the management center, where a real person will try to provide an answer. The goal is for Ernie to be able to answer up to 80 percent of the questions; currently Ernie handles 15 percent. To evaluate Ernie's effectiveness, Ford reviews the conversation logs to see how many problems Ernie solves. Ford also uses an online survey to find out how satisfied technicians were with Ernie's answers. The biggest advantage of Ernie is that the technicians can get faster answers at any time of day or night.

SOURCE: From wire reports, "Ford Mechanics Get Real Technical Answers from Virtual Assistants," *Columbus Dispatch* (August 24, 2001), p. E2.

to provide feedback automatically, trainees need to create their own reward system and ask peers and managers for feedback.

Selecting Training Methods

A number of different methods can help employees acquire new knowledge, skills, and behaviors. Figure 7.5 shows the percentage of companies using different training methods. The figure shows that lectures and videotapes are the most frequently used training methods. Other common methods include case studies and role plays. Companies are also beginning to use new technologies for training. Although face-to-face classroom instruction is used by almost all companies, new technologies are gaining in popularity. The use of training technologies is expected to increase dramatically in the next decade as technology improves and becomes cheaper, companies recognize the potential cost savings of delivering training via desktop computers, and the need for customized training increases as the economy moves from a one-size-fits-all approach to mass customization in the delivery of goods and services.[62] As Figure 7.5 shows, over 76 percent of companies are using CD-ROM training, 51 percent are using the Internet, and 2 percent use virtual reality. New technologies also allow employees to see, feel, and hear how equipment, other trainees, and the environment respond to their behaviors. Despite the increased use of new technologies, most training still includes classroom instruction. (Approximately 75 percent of total training

FIGURE 7.5

Overview of Use of Instructional Methods

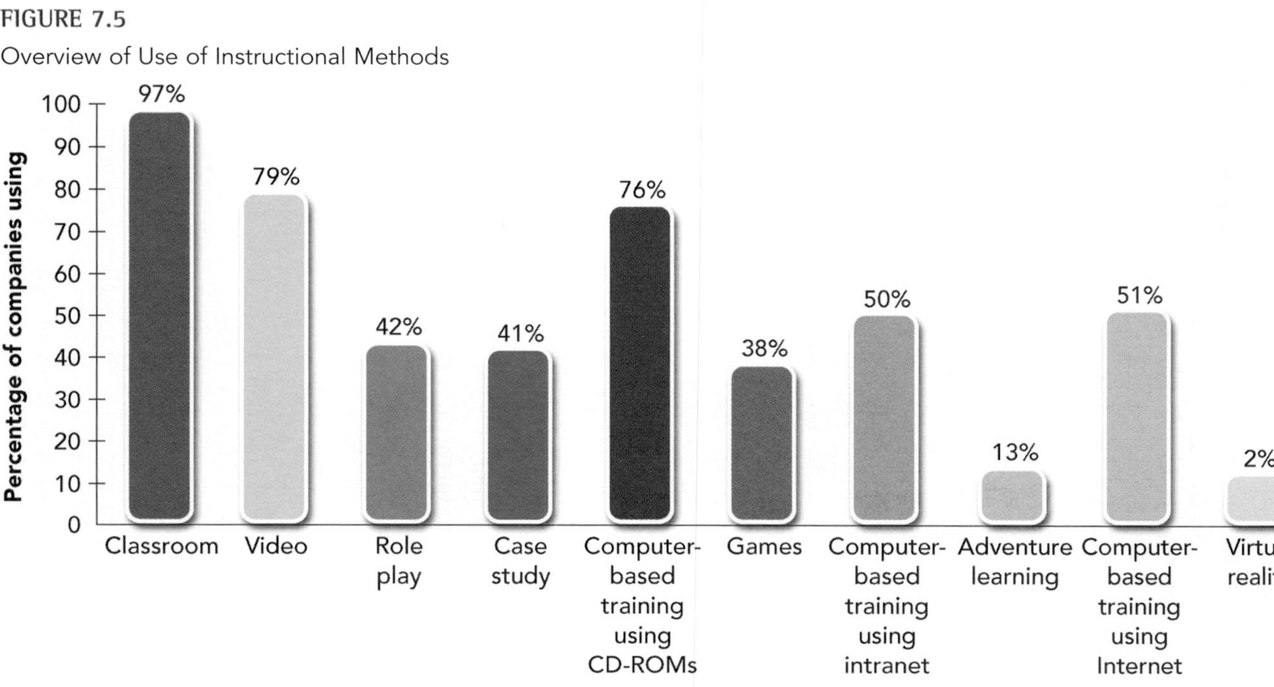

SOURCE: "Industry Report 2000." Reprinted with permission from the October 2000 issue of *Training Magazine*.

time involves classroom instruction compared to 20 percent involving new technologies.)[63] As you will see later in this chapter, new training technologies are unlikely to totally replace face-to-face instruction. Rather, face-to-face instruction will be combined with new training technologies (a combination known as *blended training*) to maximize learning.

New training technologies can lower delivery costs and increase flexibility in delivery.[64] For example, training delivered by an instructor at a central location requires employees to spend time away from their regular jobs and incurs employee travel costs. Lower delivery costs can be realized by using satellite-based training or distance learning in which training programs are transmitted via satellite to several locations. Also, use of CD-ROM or Web-based training gives employees the flexibility to participate in training on a 24-hour basis at home or work through use of a personal computer. Linking training to personal computers also gives employees more responsibility for their own training. Such technology includes characteristics that can enhance learning that often are not found in traditional instructor-led programs (immediate feedback, multiple practice opportunities, and opportunities for the employees to learn at their own pace).

However, having state-of-the-art instructional technology should not be the guiding force in choosing a training method. The specific instructional method used should be based on the training objectives. Instructional methods can be crudely grouped into three broad categories: presentation methods, hands-on methods, and group-building methods.[65]

Presentation Methods

Presentation methods
Training methods in which trainees are passive recipients of information.

Presentation methods refer to methods in which trainees are passive recipients of information. Presentation methods include traditional classroom instruction, distance learning, and audiovisual techniques. These are ideal for presenting new facts, information, different philosophies, and alternative problem-solving solutions or processes.

Classroom Instruction. Classroom instruction typically involves having the trainer lecture a group. In many cases the lecture is supplemented with question-and-answer periods, discussion, or case studies. Classroom instruction remains a popular training method despite new technologies such as interactive video and computer-assisted instruction. Traditional classroom instruction is one of the least expensive, least time-consuming ways to present information on a specific topic to many trainees. The more active participation, job-related examples, and exercises that the instructor can build into traditional classroom instruction, the more likely trainees will learn and use the information presented on the job.

Distance Learning. Distance learning is used by geographically dispersed companies to provide information about new products, policies, or procedures, as well as skills training and expert lectures.[66] Distance learning features two-way communication between people. Distance learning includes simultaneous learning in which trainees attend programs where they can communicate with the trainer and other trainees at other locations. It includes audioconferencing, videoconferencing, and docuconferencing (which allows employees to collaborate on a shared document via computers). Distance learning also includes individualized personal computer–based training.[67] Course materials and instruction may be distributed using the Internet or a CD-ROM. Trainees and trainers interact via e-mail, electronic bulletin boards, or conferencing systems.

Videoconferencing usually includes a telephone link so that trainees viewing the presentation can call in questions and comments to the trainer. Also, satellite networks allow companies to link up with industry-specific and educational courses for which employees receive college credit and job certification. IBM, Digital Equipment, and Eastman Kodak are among the many firms that subscribe to the National Technological University, which broadcasts courses throughout the United States that technical employees need to obtain advanced degrees in engineering.[68]

An advantage of distance learning is that the company can save on travel costs. It also allows employees in geographically dispersed sites to receive training from experts who would not otherwise be available to visit each location. For example, the research and development group at 3M found considerable cost savings by using videoconferencing to conduct an eight-week class on imaging technology that involved instructors from Europe and the United States.[69] Without videoconferencing the class would have cost $100,000, making it too expensive. With videoconferencing the course cost only $13,000.

The major disadvantage of distance learning is the potential for lack of interaction between the trainer and the audience. That's why a communications link between employees and the trainer is so important. Also, on-site instructors or facilitators should be available to answer questions and moderate question-and-answer sessions.

Audiovisual Techniques. *Audiovisual instruction* includes overheads, slides, and video. As Figure 7.5 shows, video is one of the most popular instructional methods.[70] It has been used for improving communications skills, interviewing skills, and customer-service skills and for illustrating how procedures (such as welding) should be followed. Video is, however, rarely used alone. It is usually used in conjunction with lectures to show trainees real-life experiences and examples. Video is also a major component of behavior modeling and, naturally, interactive video instruction. Morse Bros., located in Tangent, Oregon, is one of only a few ready-mix firms in the Northwest that provide regular training for their drivers. Drivers play a key role in determining the success of the business. Excessive idling at construction sites, avoiding rollovers at construction sites, and product training can reduce costs and raise customer satisfaction. Morse Bros. produces training videos, which are presented by mentor-drivers. The mentor-driver's job is to select the weekly video, schedule viewing sessions, keep attendance records, and guide a wrap-up discussion following each video. The mentor-drivers are trained to call attention to key learning points covered in the video and relate the topics to issues the drivers deal with on the job. Because training sessions are scheduled early in the morning at the beginning of the drivers' shift, time is limited. Videos seldom run more than 10 minutes. For example, one called *Another Pair of Eyes* trains drivers to observe test procedures used by testing agencies at job sites. Samples are tested several times a month. A sample that fails can leave the company liable for demolition and removal of the concrete structure. Morse Bros. provides training on test procedures because samples often fail a test due to contamination (such as dirt) that gets into the test cylinder. At each training session, drivers answer several questions related to the content of the program. At the end of a session, drivers and the mentor-driver discuss anything that might be interfering with the quality of the product or timeliness of delivery. Mentor-drivers then share this information with company managers.[71]

The use of video in training has a number of advantages. First, the trainer can review, slow down, or speed up the lesson, which permits flexibility in customizing the session depending on trainees' expertise. Second, trainees can be exposed to equipment, problems, and events that cannot be easily demonstrated, such as equipment malfunctions, angry customers, or emergencies. Third, trainees get consistent instruction; program content is not affected by the interests and goals of a particular trainer. Fourth, videotaping trainees allows them to see and hear their own performance without the interpretation of the trainer. As a result, trainees cannot attribute poor performance to the bias of external evaluators such as the trainer or peers.

Most problems in video result from the creative approach used.[72] These problems include too much content for the trainee to learn, poor dialogue between the actors (which hinders the credibility and clarity of the message), overuse of humor or music, and drama that makes it confusing for the trainee to understand the important learning points emphasized in the video.

Hands-on Methods

Hands-on methods
Training methods that actively involve the trainee in learning.

Hands-on methods are training methods that require the trainee to be actively involved in learning. Hands-on methods include on-the-job training, simulations, business games and case studies, behavior modeling, interactive video, and Web-based training. These methods are ideal for developing specific skills, understanding how skills and behaviors can be transferred to the job, experiencing all aspects of completing a task, and dealing with interpersonal issues that arise on the job.

On-the-Job Training (OJT). Companies spend between $90 billion and $180 billion annually on informal on-the-job training, compared with $30 billion on formal off-the-job training.[73] OJT can be useful for training newly hired employees, upgrading the skills of experienced employees when new technology is introduced, cross-training employees within a department or work unit, and orienting transferred or promoted employees to their new jobs. The basic philosophy of OJT is that employees learn through observing peers or managers performing the job and trying to imitate their behavior. While OJT takes various forms, including apprenticeships and self-directed training programs, all effective OJT programs include the following:

1. A policy statement that describes the purpose of OJT and emphasizes the company's support for it.
2. A clear specification of who is accountable for conducting OJT. If managers conduct OJT, this is mentioned in their job descriptions and is part of their performance evaluation.
3. A thorough review of OJT practices (program content, types of jobs, length of program, cost savings) at other companies in similar industries.
4. Training of managers and peers in the principles of structured OJT.
5. Availability of lesson plans, checklists, procedure manuals, training manuals, learning contracts, and progress report forms for use by employees who conduct OJT.
6. Evaluation of employees' levels of basic skills (reading, computation, writing) before OJT.[74]

For example, Borden's Inc.'s North American Pasta Division's OJT program has many of these characteristics.[75] Not all managers and peers are used as trainers. Borden's invests in trainer selection, training, and rewards to ensure OJT's effectiveness. Employees and managers interested in being instructors are required to apply for the positions. Those chosen as instructors are required to complete a demanding train-the-trainer course. The course involves classroom training as well as time on the manufacturing floor to learn how to operate machinery such as pasta machines and correctly teach other employees to use the equipment. Borden's also builds accountability into the OJT program. Trainees complete a checklist requiring them to verify that the trainer helped them learn the skills needed and used effective instructional techniques.

Self-directed learning
A program in which employees take responsibility for all aspects of learning.

Self-directed learning involves having employees take responsibility for all aspects of learning—when it is conducted and who will be involved. For example, at Corning Glass, new engineering graduates participate in an OJT program called SMART (self-managed, awareness, responsibility, and technical competence).[76] Each employee seeks the answers to a set of questions (such as "Under what conditions would a statistician be involved in the design of engineering experiments?") by visiting plants and research facilities and meeting with technical engineering experts and managers. After employees complete the questions, they are evaluated by a committee of peers who have already completed the SMART program. Evaluations have shown that the program cuts employees' start-up time in their new jobs from six weeks to three weeks. It is effective for a number of reasons. It encourages active involvement of the new employees in learning and allows flexibility in finding time for training. It has a peer-review evaluation component that motivates employees to complete the questions correctly. And, as a result of participating in the program, employees make contacts throughout the company and better understand the technical and personal resources available within the company.

There are several advantages and disadvantages of self-directed learning.[77] It allows trainees to learn at their own pace and receive feedback about the learning performance. For the company, self-directed learning requires fewer trainers, reduces costs associated with travel and meeting rooms, and makes multiple-site training more realistic. Self-directed learning provides consistent training content that captures the knowledge of experts. Self-directed learning also makes it easier for shift employees to gain access to training materials. A major disadvantage of self-directed learning is that trainees must be willing and comfortable learning on their own; that is, trainees must be motivated to learn. From the company perspective, self-directed learning results in higher development costs, and development time is longer than with other types of training programs. Self-directed learning will likely be more common in the future as companies seek to train staff flexibly, to take advantage of technology, and to encourage employees to be proactive in their learning rather than driven by the employer.[78]

The Four Seasons Regent Hotel and Resorts is a luxury hotel operations and management group with 22,000 employees worldwide, including approximately 13,000 in international locations. The Four Seasons faced the challenge of opening a new hotel and resort at Jambaran Bay, Bali. To address training needs, the human resources staff created a self-directed learning center. The Self Access Learning Center emphasizes communication skills as well as English language skills. Its purpose is to teach skills and improve employees' confidence in their communications. The center includes video recorders, training modules, books, and magazines. Besides English, the center also teaches Japanese (the language of 20 percent of hotel visitors) and provides training for foreign managers in Bahasa Indonesian, the native language of Indonesia. The training process begins by administering an English test to potential employees to gauge the level of English training they need. As employees complete each level of the training, they receive a monetary incentive.

How has the training paid dividends? Travel experts rated the Four Seasons Bali as one of the top hotels in the world. Business has increased steadily since the hotel opened, with guests from North America, Europe, Asia, Australia, and South America. As a result of the training, the Four Seasons is prepared for expansion. As the hotel industry expands in Asia, the Four Seasons now has a trained and talented staff that can be used to meet human resource needs as new resorts are developed. Four Seasons learned that the company must combine the training needs of the local culture with the standards of the company's culture to create a successful international business.[79]

Apprenticeship
A work-study training method with both on-the-job and classroom training.

Apprenticeship is a work-study training method with both on-the-job training and classroom training.[80] To qualify as a registered apprenticeship program under state or federal guidelines, at least 144 hours of classroom instruction and 2,000 hours, or one year, of on-the-job experience are required.[81] Apprenticeships can be sponsored by individual companies or by groups of companies cooperating with a union. The majority of apprenticeship programs are in the skilled trades, such as plumbing, carpentry, electrical work, and bricklaying.

Apprenticeship programs are more widely used in Western European countries (such as Germany and Denmark) than in the United States.[82] In these countries, apprenticeship is linked with employment, education, and training systems; it is a system that provides youths with the schooling needed to obtain work in the skill trades. The U.S. government is considering establishing a federally directed apprenticeship program to ease the school-to-work transition for youths who are not motivated or skilled enough to attend college. Such a program may help to alleviate the shortage of skilled workers that many manufacturers are experiencing.[83]

One advantage of an apprenticeship program is that learners earn pay while they learn. This is important because the programs can last for several years. (Learners' wages increase automatically as their skills improve.) Also, apprenticeships are usually effective learning experiences because they involve learning why and how a task is performed in classroom instruction provided by local trade schools, high schools, and community colleges. OJT involves assisting a certified tradesperson (a journeyman) at the work site.

One disadvantage of apprenticeship programs is that minorities' and women's access to these programs has been restricted because of unions' and employers' choice of men for entry-level jobs.[84] Another is that there is no guarantee jobs will be available when the program is completed.

For example, the German apprenticeship model has recently had its problems.[85] German businesses such as Siemens and Daimler Benz have been experiencing high wage and welfare costs, so they are creating most new jobs outside the country. These firms want flexible workers who will upgrade their skills, rather than employees from the apprenticeship program who are well trained in just one trade or occupation. As a result, the availability of apprenticeships for trainees has declined.

Simulation
A training method that represents a real-life situation, allowing trainees to see the outcomes of their decisions in an artificial environment.

Simulations. A **simulation** is a training method that represents a real-life situation, with trainees' decisions resulting in outcomes that mirror what would happen if the trainee were on the job. Simulations, which allow trainees to see the impact of their decisions in an artificial, risk-free environment, are used to teach production and process skills as well as management and interpersonal skills.

Simulators need to have identical elements to those found in the work environment. The simulator needs to respond exactly as the equipment would under the conditions and response given by the trainee. For this reason simulators are expensive to develop and need constant updating as new information about the work environment is obtained.

Simulators replicate the physical equipment that employees use on the job. For example, at Motorola's Programmable Automation Literacy Lab, employees who may never have worked with computers or robots learn to operate them.[86] Before entering the lab, employees are given a two-hour introduction to factory automation, which introduces new concepts, vocabulary, and computer-assisted manufacturing. The simulator allows trainees to become familiar with the equipment by designing a product (a personalized memo holder). Also, trainees do not have to be afraid of the impact of wrong decisions; errors are not as costly as they would be if the trainees were using the equipment on an actual production line. Success in simple exercises with the robot and computer increases employees' confidence that they can work successfully in an automated manufacturing environment.

Simulations are also used to develop managerial skills. Looking Glass© is a simulation designed to develop both teamwork and individual management skills.[87] In this program, participants are assigned different roles in a glass company. On the basis of memos and correspondence, each participant interacts with other members of the management team over six hours. Participants' behavior and interactions in solving the problems described in correspondence are recorded and evaluated. At the conclusion of the simulation, participants are given feedback regarding their performance.

A recent development in simulations is the use of virtual reality technology. **Virtual reality** is a computer-based technology that provides trainees with a three-dimensional learning experience. Using specialized equipment or viewing the virtual model on the computer screen, trainees move through the simulated environment and interact with its components.[88] Technology is used to stimulate multiple senses of the trainee.[89] Devices relay information from the environment to the senses. For example, audio interfaces, gloves that provide a sense of touch, treadmills, or motion platforms are used to create a realistic, artificial environment. Devices also communicate information about the trainee's movements to a computer. These devices allow the trainee to experience the perception of actually being in a particular environment. For example, Motorola's advanced manufacturing courses for employees learning to run the Pager Robotic Assembly facility use virtual reality. Employees are fitted with a head-mount display that allows them to view the virtual world, which includes the actual lab space, robots, tools, and the assembly operation. The trainees hear and see the actual sounds and sights as if they were using the real equipment. Also, the equipment responds to the employees' actions (such as turning on a switch or dial).

Virtual reality
Computer-based technology that provides trainees with a three-dimensional learning experience. Trainees operate in a simulated environment that responds to their behaviors and reactions.

Business Games and Case Studies. Situations that trainees study and discuss (case studies) and business games in which trainees must gather information, analyze it, and make decisions are used primarily for management skill development. Games stimulate learning because participants are actively involved and they mimic the competitive nature of business. The types of decisions that participants make in games include all aspects of management practice, including labor relations (such as agreement in contract negotiations), marketing (the price to charge for a new product), and finance (financing the purchase of new technology). For example, Market Share, part of a marketing management course at Nynex Corporation, requires participants to use strategic thinking such as competitive analysis to increase market share.[90] The playing board is divided into different segments representing the information industry (cable, radio, and so on). Teams of two or three players compete to gain market share by determining where the team will allocate its efforts and challenge opponents' market share.

Documentation on learning from games is anecdotal.[91] Games may give team members a quick start at developing a framework for information and help develop cohesive groups. For some groups (such as senior executives) games may be more meaningful training activities (because the game is realistic) than presentation techniques such as classroom instruction.

Cases may be especially appropriate for developing higher-order intellectual skills such as analysis, synthesis, and evaluation. These skills are often required by managers, physicians, and other professional employees. Cases also help trainees develop the willingness to take risks given uncertain outcomes, based on their analysis of the situation. To use cases effectively, the learning environment must let trainees prepare and discuss their case analyses. Also, face-to-face or electronic communication among trainees must be arranged. Because trainee involvement is critical for the effectiveness of the case method, learners must be willing and able to analyze the case and then communicate and defend their positions.

There are a number of available sources for preexisting cases. It is especially important to review preexisting cases to determine how meaningful they will be to the trainee. Preexisting cases on a wide variety of problems in business management (human resource management, operations, marketing, advertising, and so forth) are available from Harvard Business School, The Darden Business School at the University of Virginia, McGraw-Hill publishing company, and various other sources.

Behavior Modeling. Research suggests that behavior modeling is one of the most effective techniques for teaching interpersonal skills.[92] Each training session, which typically lasts four hours, focuses on one interpersonal skill, such as coaching or communicating ideas. Each session presents the rationale behind key behaviors, a videotape of a model performing key behaviors, practice opportunities using role playing, evaluation of a model's performance in the videotape, and a planning session devoted to understanding how the key behaviors can be used on the job. In the practice sessions, trainees get feedback regarding how closely their behavior matches the key behaviors demonstrated by the model. The role playing and modeled performance are based on actual incidents in the employment setting in which the trainee needs to demonstrate success.

Interactive Video. Interactive video combines the advantages of video and computer-based instruction. Instruction is provided one-on-one to trainees via a monitor connected to a keyboard. Trainees use the keyboard or touch the monitor to interact with the program. Interactive video is used to teach technical procedures and interpersonal skills. The training program may be stored on a videodisc or compact disc (CD-ROM). For example, Federal Express's 25-disc interactive video curriculum includes courses related to customer etiquette, defensive driving, and delivery procedures.[93] As Federal Express discovered, interactive video has many advantages. First, training is individualized: employees control what aspects of the training program they want to view. They can skip ahead when they feel competent, or they can review topics. Second, employees receive immediate feedback concerning their performance. Third, training is more convenient for both employers and employees. Regardless of employees' work schedules, they can have access to the equipment, which is located at their work site. From the employer's standpoint, the high cost of developing interactive video programs and purchasing the equipment is offset by the reduction in instructor costs and travel costs related to a central training location. At Federal Express, interactive video has made it possible to train 35,000 customer-contact employees in 650 locations nationwide, saving the company millions of dollars. Without interactive video, it would have been impossible for Federal Express to deliver consistent, high-quality training. The main disadvantage of interactive video is the high cost of developing the courseware. This may be a particular problem for courses in which frequent updates are necessary.[94]

E-Learning. **E-learning** or online learning refers to instruction and delivery of training by computers through the Internet or company intranets.[95] E-learning includes Web-based training, distance learning, virtual classrooms, and use of CD-ROMs. E-learning can include task support, simulation training, distance learning, and learning portals. There are three important characteristics of e-learning. First, e-learning involves electronic networks that enable information and instruction to be delivered, shared, and updated instantly. Second, e-learning is delivered to the trainee via computers with Internet technology. Third, it focuses on learning solutions that go beyond traditional training to include information and tools that improve performance.

E-learning
Instruction and delivery of training by computers through the Internet or company intranet.

Figure 7.6 depicts the features of e-learning, which include collaboration and sharing, links to resources, learner control, delivery, and administration. As Figure 7.6 shows, e-learning not only provides training content but lets learners control what they learn, the speed at which they progress through the program, how much they practice, and even when they learn. E-learning also allows learners to collaborate or interact with other trainees and experts, and it provides links to other learning

FIGURE 7.6
Characteristics of E-Learning

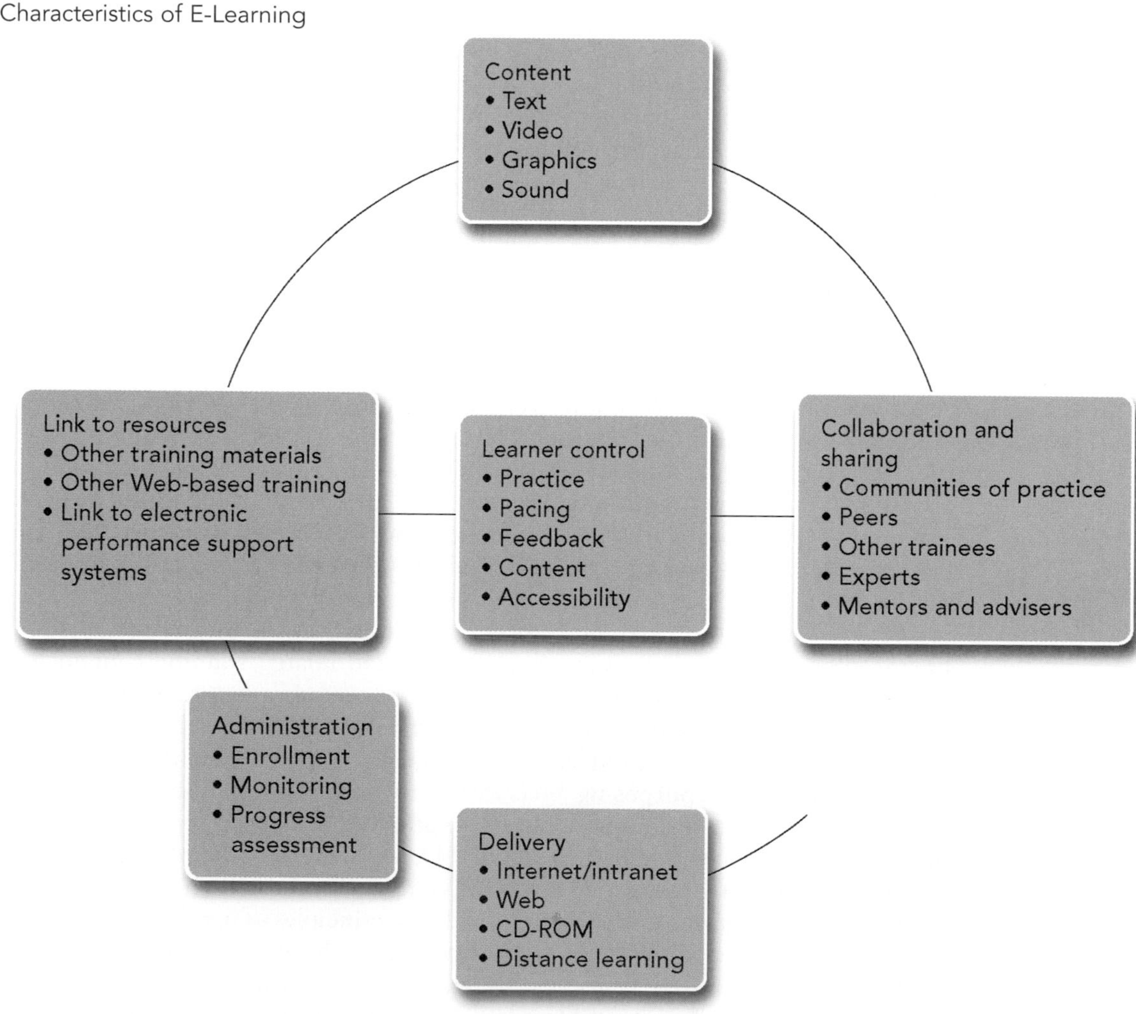

resources such as reference materials, company websites, and other training programs. Text, video, graphics, and sound can present course content. E-learning may also include various aspects of training administration such as course enrollment, testing and evaluating trainees, and monitoring learning progress. Various delivery methods can be incorporated into e-learning including distance learning, CD-ROM, and the Internet.

These features of e-learning give it advantages over other training methods. E-learning initiatives are designed to contribute to strategic business objectives.[96] E-learning supports company initiatives such as attracting customers, devising new ways to operate such as e-business, or quickly developing products or new services. E-learning may involve a larger audience than traditional training programs, which focused on employees; it may involve partners, suppliers, vendors, and potential customers.

Learning is enhanced through e-learning because trainees are more engaged through the use of video, graphics, sound, and text, which appeal to multiple senses of the learner. Also, e-learning requires that learners actively participate in practice, questions, and interaction with other learners and experts.

Besides enhancing the training experience, e-learning can reduce training costs and time. E-learning brings training to geographically dispersed employees at their locations, reducing travel costs. Consider how Merrill Lynch uses e-learning.[97] Traditionally, thousands of Merrill Lynch employees have received training in basic financial planning, advanced concepts of investing, and other topics at the company's residential training center near Princeton, New Jersey. With about 1,000 new client associates who support financial consultants in the branch offices joining the company each year, Merrill Lynch couldn't bring them all to the residential training facility or send trainers to each branch location. As a result, Merrill Lynch created the Learning Network, which includes online training, databases of stories of successful financial consultants, online job aids, and performance support tools. In addition, the Learning Network allows financial consultants to personalize their learning network home page, customizing their own learning plans. The ability of all employees to access e-learning has changed the role of classroom instruction. Previously classroom training delivered all training content, but now prerequisite training is provided on the Learning Network for every classroom session. The design of classroom and e-learning components is coordinated, ensuring little redundancy. E-learning provides fundamental information, examples, best practices, consulting experiences, and key communications from the company. The classroom component focuses on applications, practice, and personalized coaching from employees who serve as instructors. Future plans are for the Learning Network to deliver live, interactive presentations. Improved search capabilities will allow users to find related training content anywhere in the company and in websites outside the company. Future e-learning content will be built by employees, customized to their needs.

Repurposing
Directly translating instructor-led training online.

Effective e-learning is grounded on a thorough needs assessment and complete learning objectives. **Repurposing** refers to directly translating an instructor-led, face-to-face training program online. Online learning that merely repurposes an ineffective training program will remain ineffective. Unfortunately, in their haste to develop online learning, many companies are repurposing bad training! The best e-learning combines the advantages of the Internet with the principles of a good learning environment. Effective online learning takes advantage of the Web's dynamic nature and ability to use many positive learning features, including linking to other training sites and content through the use of hyperlinks, providing learner control, and allowing the trainee to collaborate with other learners. **Learner control** refers to the ability of trainees to actively learn through self-pacing, exercises, exploring links to other material, and conversations with other trainees and experts. That is, online learning allows activities typically led by the instructor (presentation, visuals, slides), trainees (discussion, questions), and group interaction (discussion of application of training content) to be incorporated into training without trainees or the instructor having to be physically present in a training room. Effective online learning gives trainees meaningful content, relevant examples, and the ability to apply content to work problems and issues. Also, trainees can practice and receive feedback through problems, exercises, assignments, and tests.

Learner control
Ability of trainees to actively learn through self-pacing, exercises, links to other materials, and conversations with other trainees and experts.

Group-Building Methods. **Group-building methods** help trainees share ideas and experiences, build group or team identity, understand the dynamics of interpersonal relationships, and get to know their own strengths and weaknesses and those of their coworkers. Various training techniques are available to improve work group or team performance, to establish a new team, and to improve interactions among different teams. All involve examination of feelings, perceptions, and beliefs about the functioning of the team; discussion; and development of plans to apply what was learned in training to the team's performance in the work setting.

Group-building methods
Training techniques that help trainees share ideas and experiences, build group identity, understand the dynamics of interpersonal relationships, and get to know their own strengths and weaknesses and those of their coworkers.

Adventure Learning. **Adventure learning** develops teamwork and leadership skills using structured outdoor activities.[98] Adventure learning appears to be best suited for developing skills related to group effectiveness, such as self-awareness, problem solving, conflict management, and risk taking. Adventure learning may involve strenuous, challenging physical activities such as dogsledding or mountain climbing. It can also use structured individual and group outdoor activities such as climbing walls, going through rope courses, making trust falls (in which each trainee stands on a table and falls backward into the arms of fellow group members), climbing ladders, and traveling from one tower to another using a device attached to a wire that connects the two towers.

Adventure learning
Learning focused on the development of teamwork and leadership skills using structured outdoor activities.

For example, a Chili's restaurant manager in adventure learning was required to scale a three-story-high wall.[99] About two-thirds away from the top of the wall the manager became very tired. She successfully reached the top of the wall using the advice and encouragement shouted from team members on the ground below. When asked to consider what she learned from the experience, she reported that the exercise made her realize that reaching personal success depends on other people. At her restaurant, everyone has to work together to make the customers happy.

For adventure learning programs to succeed, the exercises should be related to the types of skills that participants are expected to develop. Also, after the exercises, a skilled facilitator should lead a discussion about what happened in the exercise, what was learned, how the exercise relates to the job situation, and how to set goals and apply what was learned on the job.[100]

Does adventure learning work? Rigorous evaluations of the impact of adventure learning on productivity and performance have not been conducted. However, participants often report that they gained a greater understanding of themselves and the ways they interact with their coworkers. One key to the success of an adventure learning program may be the insistence that whole work groups participate together so that group dynamics that inhibit effectiveness can emerge and be discussed.

The physically demanding nature of adventure learning and the requirement that trainees often have to touch each other in the exercises may increase the company's risk for negligence claims due to personal injury, intentional infliction of emotional distress, and invasion of privacy. Also, the Americans with Disabilities Act (discussed in Chapter 3) raises questions about requiring employees with disabilities to participate in physically demanding training experiences.[101]

Team Training. Team training coordinates the performance of individuals who work together to achieve a common goal. Such training is an important issue when information must be shared and individuals affect the overall performance of the group. For example, in the military as well as the private sector (think of nuclear power plants or commercial airlines), much work is performed by crews, groups, or teams. Success depends on coordination of individual activities to make decisions, team performance, and readiness to deal with potentially dangerous situations (like an overheating nuclear reactor).

Cross-training
Team members understand and practice each other's skills.

Coordination training
Trains the team in how to share information and decisions.

Team leader training
Training the team manager or facilitator.

Team training strategies include cross-training and coordination training.[102] In **cross-training** team members understand and practice each other's skills so that members are prepared to step in and take another member's place. **Coordination training** trains the team in how to share information and decisions to maximize team performance. Coordination training is especially important for commercial aviation and surgical teams, who monitor different aspects of equipment and the environment but must share information to make the most effective decisions regarding patient care or aircraft safety and performance. **Team leader training** refers to training the team manager or facilitator. This may involve training the manager how to resolve conflict within the team or help the team coordinate activities or other team skills.

Team training usually involves multiple methods. For example, a lecture or video may disseminate knowledge regarding communication skills to trainees. Role plays or simulations may let trainees practice the communication skills emphasized in the lecture. Boeing utilized team training to improve the effectiveness of teams used to design the Boeing 777.[103] At Boeing, 250 teams with 8 to 15 members each worked on the design of the aircraft. Team members included engineers with different specialties (such as design engineers and production engineers), reliability specialists, quality experts, and marketing professionals. This type of team is known as a *concurrent engineering team* because employees from all the business functions who are needed to design the aircraft work together at the same time. Concurrent engineering team members must understand how the process or product they are working on fits with the finished product. Because each 777 aircraft contains millions of parts, it is important that they fly together!

Boeing's team training approach began with an extensive orientation emphasizing how team members were supposed to work together. Following orientation, the teams were given their work assignments. Trainers helped the teams work through issues and problems as needed; that is, trainers were available to help the teams if they requested help in communication skills, conflict resolution, and leadership.

Research suggests that effective teams develop procedures to identify and resolve errors, coordinate information gathering, and reinforce each other.[104]

Action learning
Teams work on an actual business problem, commit to an action plan, and are accountable for carrying out the plan.

Action Learning. In **action learning** teams or work groups get an actual business problem, work on solving it and commit to an action plan, and are accountable for carrying out the plan.[105] Typically, action learning involves between 6 and 30 employees; it may also include customers and vendors. There are several variations on the composition of the group. In one variation the group includes a single customer for the problem being dealt with. Sometimes the groups include cross-functional team members (members from different company departments) who all have a stake in the problem. Or the group may involve employees from multiple functions who all focus on their own functional problems, each contributing to helping solve the problems identified. For example, Whirlpool used action learning to recover overpaid duty on compressors the company was importing from Brazil. Members of the procurement group formed a team to implement Whirlpool's strategies for cost reduction and inventory control. The team developed a process for recovering the duty, saving Whirlpool hundreds of thousands of dollars a year.

Action learning is widespread in Europe but is just starting in the United States. Although action learning has not been formally evaluated, the process appears to maximize learning and transfer of training because it involves real problems. Also, action learning can identify dysfunctional team dynamics that can get in the way of effective problem solving.

Evaluating Training Programs

Examining the outcomes of a program helps in evaluating its effectiveness. These outcomes should be related to the program objectives, which help trainees understand the purpose of the program. **Training outcomes** can be categorized as cognitive outcomes, skill-based outcomes, affective outcomes, results, and return on investment.[106]

Training outcomes
A way to evaluate the effectiveness of a training program based on cognitive, skill-based, affective, and results outcomes.

Cognitive Outcomes

Cognitive outcomes determine the degree to which trainees are familiar with principles, facts, techniques, procedures, or processes emphasized in the training. Cognitive outcomes measure what trainees learned in the program, typically via paper-and-pencil tests.

Cognitive outcomes
Determine the degree to which trainees are familiar with principles, facts, techniques, procedures, or processes emphasized in training.

Skill-Based Outcomes

Skill-based outcomes—technical or motor skills and behaviors—include acquisition or learning of skills (skill learning) and use of skills on the job (skill transfer). The extent to which trainees have learned skills can be evaluated by observing their performance in work samples such as simulators. Skill transfer is usually determined by observation. For example, a resident medical student may perform surgery while the surgeon carefully observes, giving advice and assistance as needed. Peers and managers may also rate trainees' behavior or skills based on their observations.

Skill-based outcomes
Include acquisition or learning of skills and use of skills on the job.

Affective Outcomes

Affective outcomes include attitudes and motivation. One type of affective outcome is trainees' reactions toward the training program. **Reaction outcomes** are trainees' perceptions of the program including the facilities, trainers, and content. (Reaction outcomes are often referred to as a measure of "creature comfort.") This information is typically collected at the program's conclusion. Reactions are useful for identifying what trainees thought was successful and what inhibited learning.

Affective outcomes
Include attitudes and motivation.

Reaction outcomes
Trainees' perceptions of the program, including facilities, trainers, and content.

Reaction outcomes are typically collected via a questionnaire that usually asks questions like the following: "How satisfied are you with the training program?" "Did the session meet your personal expectations?" "How comfortable did you find the classroom?" Keep in mind that while reactions provide useful information, they usually relate only weakly to learning or transfer of training.

Other affective outcomes that might be evaluated include tolerance for diversity, motivation to learn, safety attitudes, and customer service orientation. Affective outcomes can be measured using surveys. The specific attitude of interest depends on the program objectives. For example, attitudes toward equal employment opportunity laws might be an appropriate outcome to use in evaluating a diversity training program.

Results

Results
Used to determine training's payoff for the company.

Results are used to determine training's payoff for the company. Examples of results include reduced costs related to employee turnover or accidents, increased production, and improvements in product quality or customer service. For example, to evaluate a program designed to teach delivery van drivers safe driving practices, Federal Express tracked drivers' accidents and injuries over a 90-day period after they had completed the training.[107]

Return on Investment

Return on investment (ROI)
Comparing training's monetary benefits with its costs.

Direct costs
Training costs including salaries and benefits for all employees involved in training; program material and supplies, equipment or classroom rentals or purchases, and travel costs.

Indirect costs
Costs not directly related to the design, development, or delivery of the training program.

Benefits
What the company gains from the training program.

Return on investment (ROI) refers to comparing the training's monetary benefits with its cost. Training costs include direct and indirect costs.[108] **Direct costs** include salaries and benefits for all employees involved in training, including trainees, instructors, consultants, and employees who design the program; program material and supplies; equipment or classroom rentals or purchases; and travel costs. **Indirect costs** are not related directly to the design, development, or delivery of the training program. They include general office supplies, facilities, equipment, and related expenses; travel and expenses not directly billed to one program; training department management and staff salaries not related to any one program; and administrative and staff support salaries. **Benefits** refer to what the company gains from the training program. Later in the chapter we will show a detailed example of how to determine the costs, benefits, and return on investment from a training program.

Which training outcomes measure is best? The answer depends on the training objectives. For example, if the instructional objectives identified business-related outcomes such as increased customer service or product quality, then results outcomes should be included in the evaluation. Both reaction and cognitive outcomes are usually collected before the trainees leave the training site. As a result, these measures do not help determine the extent to which trainees actually use the training content in their jobs (transfer of training). Skill-based, affective, and results outcomes measured following training can be used to determine transfer of training—that is, the extent to which training has changed behavior, skills, or attitudes or directly influenced objective measures related to company effectiveness (such as sales).

Reasons for Evaluating Training

Many companies are beginning to invest millions of dollars in training programs to gain a competitive advantage. Firms with high-leverage training practices not only invest large sums of money in developing and administering training programs but also evaluate training programs. Why should training programs be evaluated?

1. To identify the program's strengths and weaknesses. This includes determining whether the program is meeting the learning objectives, the quality of the learning environment, and whether transfer of training to the job is occurring.
2. To assess whether the content, organization, and administration of the program

(including the schedule, accommodations, trainers, and materials) contribute to learning and the use of training content on the job.

3. To identify which trainees benefited most or least from the program.
4. To gather marketing data by asking participants whether they would recommend the program to others, why they attended the program, and their level of satisfaction with the program.
5. To determine the financial benefits and costs of the program.
6. To compare the costs and benefits of training to nontraining investments (such as work redesign or better employee selection).
7. To compare the costs and benefits of different training programs to choose the best program.

Walgreens is a good example of a company that has reconsidered the role of training based on evaluation data. A Walgreens training course for new technicians was developed to replace on-the-job training they received from the pharmacists who hired them. This course involved 20 hours of classroom training and 20 hours of supervision on the job. Because the company has several thousand stores, large amounts of money and time were invested in the training, so the company decided to evaluate the program.

The evaluation consisted of comparing technicians who had completed the program with some who had not. Surveys about new employees' performance were sent to the pharmacists who supervised the technicians. Some questions related to speed of entering patient and drug data into the store computer and how often the technician offered customers generic drug substitutes. The results showed that formally trained technicians were more efficient and wasted less of the pharmacist's time than those who received traditional on-the-job training. Sales in pharmacies with formally trained technicians exceeded sales in pharmacies with on-the-job–trained technicians by an average of $9,500 each year.[109]

Evaluation Designs

A number of different evaluation designs can be applied to training programs.

Pretest/Posttest with Comparison Group. This method compares a group of employees who receive training and a group who do not. Outcome measures are collected from both groups before and after training. If improvement is greater for the training group than the comparison group, this provides evidence that training is responsible for the change.

Pretest/Posttest. This method is similar to the pretest/posttest comparison group design but has one major difference: no comparison group is used. The lack of a comparison group makes it difficult to rule out the effects of business conditions or other factors as explanations for changes. This design is often used by companies that want to evaluate a training program but are uncomfortable with excluding certain employees or that intend to train only a small group of employees.

Posttest Only. In this method only training outcomes are collected. This design can be strengthened by adding a comparison group (which helps to rule out alternative explanations for changes). The posttest-only design is appropriate when trainees (and the comparison group, if one is used) can be expected to have similar levels of knowledge, behavior, or results outcomes (same number of sales, equal awareness of how to close a sale) prior to training.

Time Series. In the time-series method, training outcomes are collected at periodic intervals before and after training. (In the other evaluation designs we have discussed, training outcomes are collected only once before and after training.) A comparison group can also be used with a time-series design. One advantage of the time-series design is that it allows analysis of the stability of training outcomes over time. This type of design is frequently used to evaluate training programs that focus on improving readily observable outcomes (such as accident rates, productivity, and absenteeism) that vary over time. For example, a time-series design was used to evaluate the extent to which a training program helped improve the number of safe work behaviors in a food manufacturing plant.[110] Observations of safe work behaviors were made for 25 weeks. Training directed at increasing the number of safe behaviors was introduced after approximately five weeks. The number of safe acts observed varied across the observation period. However, the number of safe behaviors increased after training and remained stable across the observation period.

There is no one appropriate evaluation design. Several factors need to be considered in choosing one:[111]

- Size of the training program.
- Purpose of training.
- Implications if a training program does not work.
- Company norms regarding evaluation.
- Costs of designing and conducting an evaluation.
- Need for speed in obtaining program effectiveness information.

For example, if a manager is interested in determining how much employees' communications skills have changed as a result of a behavior-modeling training program, a pretest/posttest comparison group design is necessary. Trainees should be randomly assigned to training and no-training conditions. These evaluation design features give the manager a high degree of confidence that any communication skill change is the result of participating in the training program.[112] This type of evaluation design is also necessary if the manager wants to compare the effectiveness of two training programs.

Evaluation designs without pretesting or comparison groups are most appropriate if the manager is interested in identifying whether a specific level of performance has been achieved (for example, can employees who participated in behavior-modeling training adequately communicate their ideas?). In this situation the manager is not interested in determining how much change has occurred.

Arthur Andersen's evaluation strategy for a training course delivered to the company's tax professionals is a good example of how company norms regarding evaluation and the purpose of training influence the type of evaluation design chosen.[113] Arthur Andersen views training as an effective method for developing human resources. Training is expected to provide a good return on investment. The company used a combination of affective, cognitive, behavior, and results criteria to evaluate a five-week course designed to prepare tax professionals to understand state and local tax law. The course involved two weeks of self-study and three weeks of classroom work. A pretest/posttest comparison design was used. Before they took the course, trainees took a test to determine their knowledge of state and local tax laws and completed a survey designed to assess their self-confidence in preparing accurate tax returns. The evaluators also identified the trainees' (accountants') billable hours related to calculating state and local tax returns and the revenue generated by the activity. After the course, evaluators again identified billable hours and surveyed trainees' self-confidence. The evaluation indicated that the accountants were spending more time doing state and local tax work. Also, the trained accountants produced more revenue doing state and local tax work than accountants who had not yet received the training (comparison group). There was a significant improvement in the accountants' confidence following training, and they were more willing to promote their expertise in state and local tax preparation. After 15 months the amount of revenue gained by the company more than offset the cost of training; on average, the increase in revenue for the trained tax accountants was more than 10 percent.

Determining Return on Investment

Cost–benefit analysis is the process of determining the economic benefits of a training program using accounting methods, which involves determining training costs and benefits. Training cost information is important for several reasons:

Cost–benefit analysis
The process of determining the economic benefits of a training program using accounting methods.

1. To understand total expenditures for training, including direct and indirect costs.
2. To compare the costs of alternative training programs.
3. To evaluate the proportion of money spent on training development, administration, and evaluation, as well as to compare monies spent on training for different groups of employees (such as exempt versus nonexempt).
4. To control costs.[114]

Determining Costs. As we discussed earlier, training costs include direct and indirect costs.[115] One method for comparing costs of alternative training programs is the resource requirements model.[116] This model compares equipment, facilities, personnel, and materials costs across different stages of the training process (training design, implementation, needs assessment, development, and evaluation). The resource requirements model can help determine overall differences in costs between training programs. Also, costs incurred at different stages of the training process can be compared across programs.

Determining Benefits. To identify the potential benefits of training, the company must review the original reasons for the training. For example, training may have been conducted to reduce production costs or overtime costs or to increase repeat business. A number of methods may help identify the benefits of training:

1. Technical, academic, and practitioner literature summarizes the benefits that have been shown to relate to a specific training program.
2. Pilot training programs assess the benefits for a small group of trainees before a company commits more resources.
3. Observing successful job performers can help a company determine what they do differently than unsuccessful job performers.[117]
4. Trainees and their managers can provide estimates of training benefits.

Making the Analysis. A cost–benefit analysis is best explained by an example.[118] A wood plant produced panels that contractors used as building materials. The plant employed 300 workers, 48 supervisors, seven shift superintendents, and a plant manager. The business had three problems. First, 2 percent of the wood panels produced each day were rejected because of poor quality. Second, the production area was experiencing poor housekeeping, such as improperly stacked finished panels that would fall on employees. Third, the number of preventable accidents was higher than the industry average. To correct these problems, supervisors were trained in performance management, interpersonal skills related to quality problems and poor work habits of employees, and rewarding employees for performance improvement. The supervisors, shift superintendents, and plant manager attended training. Training was conducted in a hotel close to the plant. The training program, purchased from a consultant, used videotape. Also, the instructor for the program was a consultant. Costs were determined as shown in Table 7.9. Benefits of the training were identified by considering why training was conducted (quality of panels, housekeeping, accidents). Table 7.10 shows how benefits were determined.

Legal Issues

Certain training situations can make an employer vulnerable to legal actions.[119]

Employee Injury During Training. On-the-job training and simulations often use work tools and equipment (welder, printing press) that could cause injury if incorrectly used. Workers' compensation laws in many states make employers responsible for paying employees their salary and/or providing them with a financial settlement for injuries received during any employment-related activity such as training. Managers should ensure that employees are warned of potential dangers from incorrectly using equipment and that safety equipment is used.

TABLE 7.9
Training Program Costs

Direct costs	
Instructor	$ 0
In-house instructor (12 days @ $125 per day)	1,500
Fringe benefits (25% of salary)	375
Travel expenses	0
Materials ($60 × 56 trainees)	3,360
Classroom space and audiovisual equipment (12 days @ $50 per day)	600
Refreshments ($4 per day × 3 days × 56 trainees)	672
Total direct costs	$ 6,507
Indirect costs	
Training management	$ 0
Clerical and administrative salaries	750
Fringe benefits (25% of salary)	187
Postage, shipping, and telephone	0
Pre- and posttraining learning materials ($4 × 56 trainees)	224
Total indirect costs	$ 1,161
Development costs	
Fee for program purchase	$ 3,600
Instructor training	
Registration fee	1,400
Travel and lodging	975
Salary	625
Benefits (25% of salary)	156
Total development costs	$ 6,756
Overhead costs	
General organizational support, top management time (10% of direct, indirect, and development costs)	$ 1,443
Total overhead costs	$ 1,443
Compensation for trainees	
Trainees' salaries and benefits (based on time away from job)	$16,969
Total training costs	$32,836
Cost per trainee	$ 587

TABLE 7.10

Determination of Training Benefits

OPERATIONAL RESULTS AREA	HOW MEASURED	RESULTS BEFORE TRAINING	RESULTS AFTER TRAINING	DIFFERENCES (+ OR –)	EXPRESSED IN
Quality of panels	Percentage rejected	2 percent rejected—1,440 panels per day	1.5 percent rejected—1,080 panels per day	.5 percent—360 panels	$720 per day $172,800 per year
Housekeeping	Visual inspection using 20-item checklist	10 defects (average)	2 defects (average)	8 defects	Not measurable in $
Preventable accidents	Number of accidents	24 per year	16 per year	8 per year	$48,000 per year
	Direct cost of accidents	$144,000 per year	$96,000 per year	$48,000 per year	

$$\text{ROI} = \frac{\text{Return}}{\text{Investment}} = \frac{\text{Operational results}}{\text{Training costs}} = \frac{\$220{,}800}{\$32{,}836} = 6.7$$

Total savings: $220,800 per year

SOURCE: Adapted from D.G. Robinson and J. Robinson, "Training for Impact," *Training & Development Journal,* August 1989, pp. 30–42.

Employees or Others Injured Outside a Training Session. Managers should ensure that trainees have the necessary level of competence in knowledge, skills, and behaviors before they are allowed to operate equipment or interact with customers. Even if a company pays for training to be conducted by a vendor, it is still liable for injuries or damages resulting from the actions of poorly, incorrectly, or incompletely trained employees.

Breach of Confidentiality or Defamation. Managers should ensure that information placed in employees' files regarding performance in training activities is accurate. Also, before discussing an employee's performance in training with other employees or using training performance information for promotion or salary decisions, managers should tell employees that training performance will be used in that manner.

Reproducing and Using Copyrighted Material in Training Classes without Permission. *Copyrights* protect the expression of an idea (such as a training manual for a software program) but not the ideas that the material contains (such as the use of help windows in the software program). Copyrights also prohibit others from creating a product based on the original work and from copying, broadcasting, or publishing the product without permission.

The use of videotapes, learning aids, manuals, and other copyrighted materials in training classes without obtaining permission from the owner of the material is illegal. Managers should ensure that all training materials are purchased from the vendor or consultant who developed them or that permission to reproduce materials has been obtained. For example, Wilson Learning Corporation—a major developer and distributor of training-related products—holds the copyright to its sales training materials. To use the product, clients must pay Wilson Learning a fee and agree to attend a training seminar to familiarize them with the materials.

Excluding Women, Minorities, and Older Employees from Training Programs. Women, minorities, and older employees can be illegally excluded from training programs by not being made aware of opportunities for training or purposeful exclusion from enrolling in training programs. Managers and trainers must ensure that stereotypes do not influence (1) decisions about whom to send to training programs or (2) to whom training opportunities are communicated. For example, stereotypes such as "older workers are resistant to change" and "women are not aggressive enough for managerial positions" may result in excluding qualified women and older workers from training programs.

Not Ensuring Equal Treatment of All Employees While in Training. Equal treatment of all trainees means that conditions of the learning environment such as opportunities for practice, feedback, and role playing are available for all trainees regardless of their background. Also, trainers should avoid jokes, stories, and props that might create a hostile learning environment.

Requiring Employees to Attend Programs That Might Be Offensive. Allstate Insurance has been the focus of several religious discrimination lawsuits by insurance agents who found Scientology principles emphasized in agent training programs to be offensive and counter to their religious beliefs (for example, employees who met their sales goals were not to be questioned no matter how they behaved, but persons who failed to meet their sales goals deserved to be harassed and treated poorly).[120]

Revealing Discriminatory Information During a Training Session. At Lucky Store Foods, a California supermarket chain, notes taken by a trainer during a diversity training program were used as evidence of discrimination.[121] In the training session supervisors were asked to verbalize their stereotypes. Some comments ("women cry more," "black women are aggressive") were derogatory toward women and minorities. The plaintiff in the case used the trainer's notes as evidence that the company conducted the training session to avoid an investigation by the Equal Employment Opportunity Commission. The case was settled out of court.

Not Accommodating Trainees with Disabilities. As we discussed in Chapter 3, the *Americans with Disabilities Act (ADA) of 1990* prohibits individuals with disabilities from being discriminated against in the workplace.

Reasonable accommodation
Making training facilities accessible and usable by persons with disabilities.

In the context of training, **reasonable accommodation** refers to making training facilities readily accessible to and usable by individuals with disabilities. Reasonable accommodation may also include modifying instructional media, adjusting training policies, and providing trainees with readers or interpreters. Employers are not required to make reasonable accommodations if the person does not request them. Employers are also not required to make reasonable accommodations if persons are not qualified to participate in training programs (for example, if they lack the prerequisite certification or educational requirements).

One example of how the ADA might influence training activities involves adventure learning. Adventure learning experiences demand a high level of physical fitness. Employees who have a disability cannot be required to attend adventure learning training programs or penalized for not participating in such programs.[122] If it does not cause an undue hardship, employees should be offered an alternative program for developing the learned capabilities emphasized in the adventure learning program.

It is impossible to give specific guidelines regarding the type of accommodations that trainers and managers should make to avoid violating the ADA. It is important to identify if the training is related to "essential" job functions. That is, are the tasks or knowledge, skills, and abilities that are the focus of training fundamental to the position? To the extent that the disability makes it difficult for the person to receive training necessary to complete essential job functions, managers must explore whether it is possible to make reasonable accommodations.

Cross-Cultural Preparation

As we mentioned in Chapter 1, companies today are challenged to expand globally. Because of the increase in global operations, employees often work outside their country of origin or work with employees from other countries. An **expatriate** works in a country other than his or her country of origin. For example, Microsoft is headquartered in the United States but has facilities around the world. To be effective, expatriates in the Microsoft Mexico operations in Mexico City must understand the region's business and social culture. Because of a growing pool of talented labor around the world, greater use of host-country nationals is occurring.[123] A key reason is that a host-country national can more easily understand the values and customs of the workforce than an expatriate can. Also, training and transporting U.S. employees and their families to a foreign assignment and housing them there tend to be more expensive than hiring a host-country national. We discuss international human resource management in detail in Chapter 15. Here the focus is on understanding how to prepare employees for expatriate assignments.

Expatriate
Employee sent by his or her company to manage operations in a different country.

Cross-cultural preparation educates employees (expatriates) and their families who are to be sent to a foreign country. To successfully conduct business in the global marketplace, employees must understand the business practices and the cultural norms of different countries.

Cross-cultural preparation
The process of educating employees (and their families) who are given an assignment in a foreign country.

Steps in Cross-Cultural Preparation

To prepare employees for cross-cultural assignments, companies need to provide cross-cultural training. Most U.S. companies send employees overseas without any preparation. As a result, the number of employees who return home before completing their assignments is higher for U.S. companies than for European and Japanese companies.[124] U.S. companies lose more than $2 billion a year as a result of failed overseas assignments.

To succeed overseas, expatriates (employees on foreign assignments) need to be

1. Competent in their areas of expertise.
2. Able to communicate verbally and nonverbally in the host country.
3. Flexible, tolerant of ambiguity, and sensitive to cultural differences.
4. Motivated to succeed, able to enjoy the challenge of working in other countries, and willing to learn about the host country's culture, language, and customs.
5. Supported by their families.[125]

One reason for U.S. expatriates' high failure rate is that companies place more emphasis on developing employees' technical skills than on preparing them to work in other cultures. Research suggests that the comfort of an expatriate's spouse and family is the most important determinant of whether the employee will complete the assignment.[126] Studies have also found that personality characteristics are related to expatriates' desire to terminate the assignment and performance in the assignment.[127] Expatriates who were extroverted (outgoing), agreeable (cooperative and tolerant),

COMPETING THROUGH GLOBALIZATION

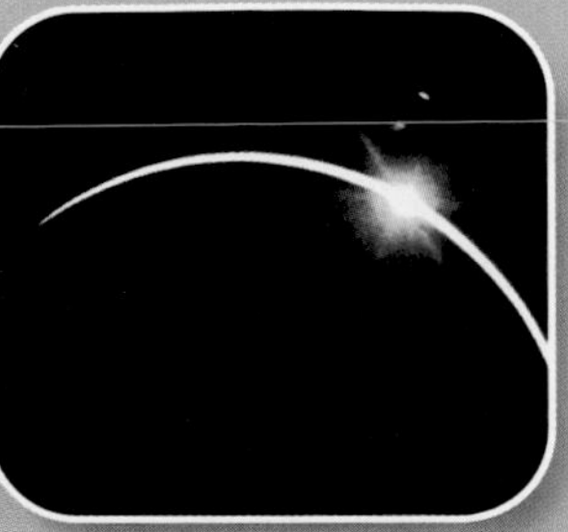

Supportive Benefits and Technology Ease the Transition to Foreign Assignments

One major reason that employees refuse expatriate assignments is that they can't afford to lose their spouses' income or are concerned that their spouses' careers will be derailed if they are out of the workforce for a few years. Some "trailing" spouses decide to use the time to pursue education that could contribute to their long-term career goals. But it is difficult to find these opportunities in an unfamiliar place. Companies are providing creative benefits to ensure that the assignments do not break up marriages and families. For example, the London-based president for Xerox Corporation receives a mobility allowance for hotels and travel that allows him to return to the family home in Paris on weekends. Companies are also offering higher salaries and shorter assignments and are helping spouses find jobs. Pfizer, the pharmaceutical company, provides a $10,000 allowance that the spouse can use in many different ways. A person at the expatriate location helps the spouse with professional development and locating educational or other resources. In countries where the spouse is allowed to work, Pfizer tries to find him or her a job within the company. Pfizer also provides cross-cultural counseling and language assistance and tries to connect the family with the expatriate community.

Because of the difficulty in getting employees to accept foreign assignments and the low success rate of such assignments, companies are creating "virtual" expatriate positions. Virtual expatriates manage an operation abroad without being located permanently in that country. The employees travel to the overseas location and use videoconferencing and communications technology to manage the operation. Virtual expatriates eliminate exposing the families to the culture shock of an overseas move; they also allow employees to manage globally while keeping in closer touch with the home office. Virtual expatriates are also less expensive than traditional expatriates, who can cost companies over three times as much as a host national employee. One disadvantage of virtual expatriates is that visiting a foreign operation sporadically may lengthen the time needed to build a local management team and slow problem solving because of the lack of a strong personal relationship with local employees.

SOURCE: Based on J. Flynn, "E-mail, Cell Phones, and Frequent-Flier Miles Let 'Virtual' Expats Work Abroad but Live at Home," *The Wall Street Journal* (October 25, 1999), p. A26; J. Flynn, "Multinationals Help Career Couples Deal with Strains Affecting Expatriates," *The Wall Street Journal* (August 8, 2000), p. A19; C. Solomon, "The World Stops Shrinking," *Workforce*, January 2000, pp. 48–51; C. Solomon, "Unhappy Trails," *Workforce*, August 2000, pp. 36–41.

and conscientious (dependable, achievement oriented) were more likely to want to stay on the assignment and perform well. This suggests that cross-cultural training may be effective only when expatriates' personalities predispose them to be successful in assignments in other cultures.

The key to a successful foreign assignment appears to be a combination of training and career management for the employee and family. The "Competing through Globalization" box above shows how companies are using technology and providing benefits to support expatriates and their families. Foreign assignments involve three phases: predeparture, on-site, and repatriation (preparing to return home). Training is necessary in all three phases.

Predeparture Phase

Before departure, employees need to receive language training and an orientation to the new country's culture and customs. It is critical that the family be included in orientation programs.[128] Expatriates and their families need information about housing, schools, recreation, shopping, and health care facilities in the areas where they will live. Expatriates also must discuss with their managers how the foreign assignment fits into their career plans and what types of positions they can expect upon return.

Cross-cultural training methods range from presentational techniques, such as lectures that expatriates and their families attend on the customs and culture of the host country, to actual experiences in the home country in culturally diverse communities.[129] Experiential exercises, such as miniculture experiences, allow expatriates to spend time with a family in the United States from the ethnic group of the host country.

Research suggests that the degree of difference between the United States and the host country (cultural novelty), the amount of interaction with host country citizens and host nationals (interaction), and the familiarity with new job tasks and work environment (job novelty) all influence the "rigor" of the cross-cultural training method used.[130] Hands-on and group building methods are most effective (and most needed) in assignments with a high level of cultural and job novelty that require a good deal of interpersonal interaction with host nationals.

On-Site Phase

On-site training involves continued orientation to the host country and its customs and cultures through formal programs or through a mentoring relationship. Expatriates and their families may be paired with an employee from the host country who helps them understand the new, unfamiliar work environment and community.[131]

Repatriation Phase

Repatriation prepares expatriates for return to the parent company and country from the foreign assignment. Expatriates and their families are likely to experience high levels of stress and anxiety when they return because of the changes that have occurred since their departure. Employees should be encouraged to self-manage the repatriation process.[132] Before they go on the assignment they need to consider what skills they want to develop and the types of jobs that might be available in the company for an employee with those skills. Because the company changes and colleagues, peers, and managers may leave while the expatriate is on assignment, they need to maintain contact with key company and industry contacts. Otherwise, on return the employees' reentry shock will be heightened due to having to deal with new colleagues, a new job, and a company culture that may have changed. This includes providing expatriates with company newsletters and community newspapers and by ensuring that they receive personal and work-related mail from the United States while they are on foreign assignment. It is also not uncommon for employees and their families to have to readjust to a lower standard of living in the United States than they had in the foreign country, where they may have enjoyed maid service, a limousine, private schools, and clubs. Salary and other compensation arrangements should be worked out well before employees return from overseas assignments.

Repatriation
The preparation of expatriates for return to the parent company and country from a foreign assignment.

Aside from reentry shock, many expatriates decide to leave the company because the assignments they are given upon returning to the United States have less responsibility, challenge, and status than their foreign assignments.[133] As noted earlier, career planning discussions need to be held before the employees leave the United States to ensure that they understand the positions they will be eligible for upon repatriation.

Monsanto has a successful repatriation program. Monsanto is an agricultural, chemical, and pharmaceutical company with 50 expatriates and 35 international employees working in the United States. Preparation for repatriation begins before the employee leaves the United States. Employees and both their sending and receiving managers develop an agreement about their understanding of the assignment and how it fits into the company's business objectives. Expectations regarding the assignment and how the knowledge gained will be used when the employee returns are specified. In Monsanto's program expatriates share their experiences with American peers, superiors, and subordinates. The program also gives repatriating employees a way to work through personal difficulties. After their return, expatriates meet with several colleagues of their choice for a debriefing segment. The debriefing segment includes a trained counselor who discusses all the important aspects of the repatriation and helps the employee understand what he or she is experiencing. The debriefing not only helps the returning expatriate but also helps educate peers and colleagues to better understand different cultural issues and business environments.[134]

Managing Workforce Diversity

The goals of diversity training are (1) to eliminate values, stereotypes, and managerial practices that inhibit employees' personal development and therefore (2) to allow employees to contribute to organizational goals regardless of their race, sexual orientation, gender, family status, religious orientation, or cultural background.[135] Because of Equal Opportunity Employment laws, companies have been forced to ensure that women and minorities are adequately represented in their labor force. That is, companies have focused on ensuring equal access to jobs. **Managing diversity** involves creating an environment that allows all employees to contribute to organizational goals and experience personal growth. This includes access to jobs as well as fair and positive treatment of all employees. This requires the company to develop employees so that they are comfortable working with others from a wide variety of ethnic, racial, and religious backgrounds. Managing diversity may require changing the company culture. It includes the company's standards and how employees are treated, competitiveness, results orientation, innovation, and risk taking.

Managing diversity
The process of creating an environment that allows all employees to contribute to organizational goals and experience personal growth.

As Chapter 1 said, management of diversity has been linked to innovation, improved productivity, and lower employee turnover and other costs related to human resources.[136] For example, Voice Processing Corporation benefits from having employees with different language skills and cultural orientations.[137] Diversity gives the company an edge in producing and marketing software that enables computers to process voice commands.

Managing Diversity through Adherence to Legislation

One approach to managing diversity is through affirmative action policies and by making sure that human resource management practices meet standards of equal employment opportunity laws.[138] This approach rarely changes employees' values, stereotypes, and behaviors that inhibit productivity and personal development. Figure 7.7 shows the cycle of disillusionment resulting from managing diversity by rely-

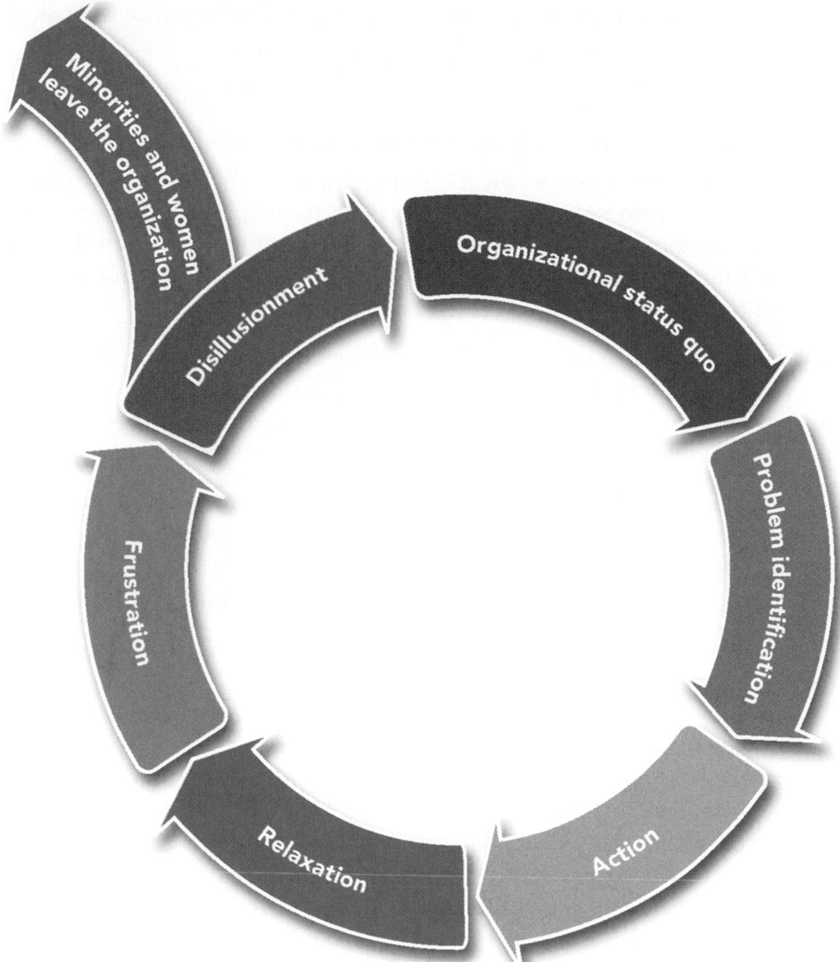

FIGURE 7.7
Cycle of Disillusionment Resulting from Managing Diversity through Adherence to Legislation

SOURCE: *HR Magazine* by Cresencio Torres and Mary Bruxelles. Copyright © 1992 by Society for Human Resource Management. Reproduced with permission of Society for Human Resource Management via Copyright Clearance Center.

ing solely on adherence to employment laws. The cycle begins when the company realizes that it must change policies regarding women and minorities because of legal pressure or a discrepancy between the number or percentage of women and minorities in the company's workforce and the number available in the broader labor market. To address these concerns, a greater number of women and minorities are hired by the company. Managers see little need for additional action because women and minority employment rates reflect their availability in the labor market. However, as women and minorities gain experience in the company, they may become frustrated. Managers and coworkers may avoid providing coaching or performance feedback to women and minorities because they are uncomfortable interacting with individuals from different gender, ethnic, or racial backgrounds. Coworkers may express beliefs that women and minorities are employed only because they received special treatment (hiring standards were lowered).[139] As a result of their frustration, women and minorities may form support groups to voice their concerns to management. Because of the work atmosphere, women and minorities may fail to fully utilize their skills and leave the company.

Managing Diversity through Diversity Training Programs

The preceding discussion is not to suggest that companies should be reluctant to engage in affirmative action or pursue equal opportunity employment practices. However, affirmative action without additional supporting strategies does not deal with issues of assimilating women and minorities into the workforce. To successfully manage a diverse workforce, companies need to ensure that

- Employees understand how their values and stereotypes influence their behavior toward others of different gender, ethnic, racial, or religious backgrounds.
- Employees gain an appreciation of cultural differences among themselves.
- Behaviors that isolate or intimidate minority group members improve.

Diversity training
Training designed to change employee attitudes about diversity and/or develop skills needed to work with a diverse workforce.

This can be accomplished through diversity training programs. **Diversity training** refers to training designed to change employee attitudes about diversity and/or develop skills needed to work with a diverse workforce. Diversity training programs differ according to whether attitude or behavior change is emphasized.[140]

Attitude Awareness and Change Programs

Attitude awareness and change program
Program focusing on increasing employees' awareness of differences in cultural and ethnic backgrounds, physical characteristics, and personal characteristics that influence behavior toward others.

Attitude awareness and change programs focus on increasing employees' awareness of differences in cultural and ethnic backgrounds, physical characteristics (such as disabilities), and personal characteristics that influence behavior toward others. The assumption underlying these programs is that, by increasing their awareness of stereotypes and beliefs, employees will be able to avoid negative stereotypes when interacting with employees of different backgrounds. The programs help employees consider the similarities and differences between cultural groups, examine their attitudes toward affirmative action, or analyze their beliefs about why minority employees are successful or unsuccessful in their jobs. Many of these programs use videotapes and experiential exercises to increase employees' awareness of the negative emotional and performance effects of stereotypes, values, and behaviors on minority group members. For example, 3M conducts workshops in which managers are asked to assess their attitudes toward stereotypical statements about race, age, and gender.[141] The participants select two stereotypes they hold and consider how these stereotypes affect their ability to manage. One of the most popular video training packages, Copeland Griggs Productions' "Valuing Diversity Training Program," involves three days of training that focus on managing differences, diversity in the workplace, and cross-cultural communications.

The attitude awareness and change approach has been criticized for several reasons.[142] First, by focusing on group differences, the program may communicate that certain stereotypes and attitudes are valid. For example, in diversity training a male manager may learn that women employees prefer to work by building consensus rather than by arguing until others agree with their point. He might conclude that the training has validated his stereotype. As a result, he will continue to fail to give women important job responsibilities that involve heated negotiations with customers or clients. Second, encouraging employees to share their attitudes, feelings, and stereotypes toward certain groups may cause employees to feel guilty, angry, and less likely to see the similarities among racial, ethnic, or gender groups and the advantages of working together.

Behavior-Based Programs

Behavior-based programs focus on changing the organizational policies and individual behaviors that inhibit employees' personal growth and productivity. These programs can take three approaches.

Behavior-based program
A program focusing on changing the organizational policies and individual behaviors that inhibit employees' personal growth and productivity.

One approach of these programs is to identify incidents that discourage employees from working up to their potential. Groups of employees are asked to identify specific promotion opportunities, sponsorship, training opportunities, or performance management practices that they believe were handled unfairly. Their views regarding how well the work environment and management practices value employee differences and provide equal opportunity may also be collected. Specific training programs may be developed to address the issues presented in the focus groups.

Another approach is to teach managers and employees basic rules of behavior in the workplace.[143] For example, managers and employees should learn that it is inappropriate to use statements and engage in behaviors that have negative racial, sexual, or cultural content. Companies that have focused on teaching rules and behavior have found that employees react less negatively to this type of training than to other diversity training approaches.

A third approach is **cultural immersion:** sending employees directly into communities where they have to interact with persons from different cultures, races, and nationalities. The degree of interaction varies but may involve talking with community members, working in community organizations, or learning about religious, cultural, or historically significant events. AT&T uses cultural immersion as part of its diversity program.[144] AT&T sends teams of managers into areas of the United States where they have to learn to interact with people from a specific culture. For example, AT&T sent six managers to Harlem, New York, an eclectic community including Asian Americans, African Americans, Hispanic Americans, and Puerto Rican Americans. The managers were required to go on a scavenger hunt requiring them to learn about the people, community, and culture. For example, the team had to find a Harlem bilingual community directory, a Jamaican meat patty, and soul food. Success in the scavenger hunt required the team to interact with street vendors and total strangers.

Cultural immersion
A behavior-based diversity program that sends employees into communities where they interact with persons from different cultures, races, and nationalities.

Characteristics of Successful Diversity Efforts

Is a behavior-based or an attitude awareness and change program most effective? Increasing evidence shows that attitude awareness programs are ineffective and that one-time diversity training programs are unlikely to succeed. For example, R. R. Donnelley & Sons suspended its diversity awareness training program even though the company has spent more than $3 million on it as a result of a racial discrimination lawsuit.[145]

At various training sessions participants were encouraged to voice their concerns. Many said that they were experiencing difficulty in working effectively due to abuse and harassment. The managers attending the training disputed the concerns. Also, after training, an employee who applied for an open position was rejected, because, she was told, she had been too honest in expressing her concerns during the diversity training session. Although R. R. Donnelley held many diversity training sessions, little progress was made in increasing the employment and promotion rates of women and minorities. Because of the low ratio of black employees to white employees, many black employees were asked to attend multiple training sessions to ensure diverse groups, which they resented. The company declined to release data requested by shareholders that it provided to the Equal Employment Opportunity Commission regarding female and minority representation in jobs throughout the company. The firm also failed to act on recommendations made by company-approved employee "diversity councils."

More generally, a survey of diversity training efforts found that[146]

- The most common area addressed through diversity is the pervasiveness of stereotypes, assumptions, and biases.
- Fewer than one-third of companies do any kind of long-term evaluation or follow-up. The most common indicators of success were reduced grievances and lawsuits, increased diversity in promotions and hiring, increased self-awareness of biases, and increased consultation of HRM specialists on diversity-related issues.
- Most programs lasted only one day or less.
- Three-fourths of the survey respondents indicated that they believed the typical employee leaves diversity training with positive attitudes toward diversity. However, over 50 percent reported that the programs have no effect over the long term.

Table 7.11 shows the characteristics associated with the long-term success of diversity programs. It is critical that a diversity program be tied to business objectives. For example, cultural differences affect the type of skin cream consumers believe they need or the fragrance they may be attracted to. Understanding cultural differences is part of understanding the consumer (which is critical to the success of companies such as Avon). Top management support can be demonstrated by creating a structure to support the initiative.

As you may remember from Chapter 1, managing diversity at Texaco goes beyond attending workshops.[147] Table 7.12 shows that managing diversity includes both HRM activities and business initiatives. Managers are held accountable for diversity goals in their performance evaluations. There is considerable evidence that the program is transforming the culture. During the first six months of 1999, minorities accounted for 44 percent of new hires and 22 percent of promotions. Texaco paid over $500 million to minority-owned vendors. Many training experts suggest that the company is a model for managing diversity.

TABLE 7.11
Characteristics Associated with Diversity Programs' Long-Term Success

- Top management provides resources, personally intervenes, and publicly advocates diversity.
- The program is structured.
- Capitalizing on a diverse workforce is defined as a business objective.
- Capitalizing on a diverse workforce is seen as necessary to generate revenue and profits.
- The program is evaluated.
- Manager involvement is mandatory.
- The program is seen as a culture change, not a one-shot program.
- Managers and demographic groups are not blamed for problems.
- Behaviors and skills needed to successfully interact with others are taught.
- Managers are rewarded on progress toward meeting diversity goals.

SOURCE: S. Rynes and B. Rosen, "What Makes Diversity Programs Work?" *HR Magazine*, October 1994, pp. 67–73; S. Rynes and B. Rosen, "A Field Survey of Factors Affecting the Adoption and Perceived Success of Diversity Training," *Personnel Psychology* 48 (1995), pp. 247–70; J. Gordon, "Different from What? Diversity as a Performance Issue," *Training*, May 1995, pp. 25–33.

TABLE 7.12

Texaco's Diversity Effort

Recruitment and Hiring
- Ask search firms to identify wider arrays of candidates.
- Enhance the interviewing, selection, and hiring skills of managers.
- Expand college recruitment at historically minority colleges.

Identifying and Developing Talent
- Form a partnership with INROADS, a nationwide internship program that targets minority students for management careers.
- Establish a mentoring process.
- Refine the company's global succession planning system to improve identification of talent.
- Improve the selection and development of managers and leaders to help ensure that they are capable of maximizing team performance.

Ensuring Fair Treatment
- Conduct extensive diversity training.
- Implement an alternative dispute resolution process.
- Include women and minorities on all human resources committees throughout the company.

Holding Managers Accountable
- Link managers' compensation to their success in creating "openness and inclusion in the workplace."
- Implement 360-degree feedback for all managers and supervisors.
- Redesign the company's employee attitude survey and begin using it annually to monitor employee attitudes.

Improving Relationships with External Stakeholders
- Broaden the company's base of vendors and suppliers to incorporate more minority- and women-owned businesses.
- Increase banking, investment, and insurance business with minority- and women-owned firms.
- Add more independent, minority retailers and increase the number of minority managers in company-owned gas stations and Xpress Lube outlets.

SOURCE: D. Hellriegel, S.E. Jackson, and J.W. Slocum, Jr., *Management*, 8th ed. (Cincinnati, OH: South-Western College Publishing, 1999). Originally adapted from V.C. Smith, "Texaco Outlines Comprehensive Initiatives," *Human Resource Executive*, February 1997, p. 13; A. Bryant, "How Much Has Texaco Changed? A Mixed Report Card on Anti-bias Efforts," *The New York Times* (November 2, 1997), pp. 3–1, 3–16, 3–17; and "Texaco's Worldforce Diversity Plan," as reprinted in *Workforce*, March 1997, supp. from D. Daft and R. Noe, *Organizational Behavior* (Fort Worth, TX: Dryden Press, 2001), p. 58.

As you can see from this discussion, successful diversity programs involve more than just effective training. Top management support, diversity policies and practices, training and development, and administrative structures, such as conducting diversity surveys and evaluating managers' progress on diversity goals, are needed.[148]

Welfare-to-Work Programs

Companies are seeking to hire people from nontraditional sources, such as welfare roles, to meet their labor needs. The "Competing in the New Economy" box shows how Intel is trying to develop strong ties with another source of employees, community colleges,

COMPETING IN THE NEW ECONOMY

Recession Suspends Hiring but Supporting Education Avoids Future Labor Shortage

Because of a downturn in business, Intel has eliminated 5,000 jobs, delayed raises, and reduced spending on travel, overtime, and consultants. Still, Intel spent several thousand dollars to send five employees and 12 community college presidents and deans on a three-day trip through New Mexico and Texas. The trip included a tour of Intel's Albuquerque computer chip plant and visits to four community colleges. Why would Intel's cost-cutting spare this college tour? Skilled workers needed to operate chip plants are scarce. Intel will resume hiring in the future, but training programs will not be able to keep up with the demand for skilled employees. As an Intel manager said, "If we don't invest now, the students won't be there when we need them." Intel is investing in community colleges by lobbying state governments for bigger budgets and donating equipment. For example, Intel spent $1.2 million on a small chip-making plant at Albuquerque's community college.

Intel did not take an interest in community colleges 10 years ago. But as the need for unskilled workers declined due to relocating these jobs overseas or replacing them with automation, Intel needed a more skilled workforce. Now, even new hires at Intel need math, physics, and chemistry, and all new hires must have at least two years of college. How seriously does Intel take its investment in community colleges? An Intel worker recently questioned why the company was collecting trash less often but still spending on science contests for high school students. Chief Executive Craig Barrett responded, "There are certain things that Intel does that provide returns to the company on a long-term basis."

SOURCE: D. Wessel, "Intel Cost-Cutting Spares a College Tour," *The Wall Street Journal* (June 14, 2000), p. A1.

to help prepare its future workforce. Training plays an important part in both preparing the workforce and helping nontraditional employees succeed on the job.

TJX Companies was desperate to fill jobs in its retail stores.[149] TJX Companies is the parent of off-price clothing retailers T.J. Maxx and Marshalls. Turnover is typically a problem in retailing. The company was used to 100 percent annual turnover of store jobs. To find employees, TJX has taken people off the welfare rolls. The company pays CIC Enterprises to create and run a job hotline tied to agencies that help prepare welfare recipients for work. A store manager for a T.J. Maxx or Marshalls in any city can call a toll-free number at any time to request candidates for job openings. For every 10 calls made to the hotline, 8 have produced a job candidate who has been hired. TJX also started a program with Morgan Memorial Goodwill Industries in Boston. This program gives welfare recipients three weeks of classroom training followed by an internship at a store. Those who complete the internship are guaranteed jobs. A case manager follows up on program graduates for at least a year, helping solve child care and transportation problems.

TJX has received many benefits from hiring former welfare recipients. TJX reports that the retention rate for welfare-to-work hires is above retention for traditional hires. The welfare-to-work hires are looking for full-time jobs, in comparison to the typical retail employee looking for short-term, part-time work.

Socialization and Orientation

Organizational socialization is the process by which new employees are transformed into effective members of the company. As Table 7.13 shows, effective socialization involves being prepared to perform the job effectively, learning about the organization, and establishing work relationships. Socialization involves three phases: anticipatory socialization, encounter, and settling in.[150]

Organizational socialization
The process used to transform new employees into effective company members.

Anticipatory Socialization

Anticipatory socialization occurs before the individual joins the company. Through **anticipatory socialization,** expectations about the company, job, working conditions, and interpersonal relationships are developed through interactions with representatives of the company (recruiters, prospective peers, and managers) during recruitment and selection. The expectations are also based on prior work experiences in similar jobs.

Anticipatory socialization
Process that helps individuals develop expectations about the company, job, working conditions, and interpersonal relationships.

Potential employees need realistic job information. A **realistic job preview** provides accurate information about the attractive and unattractive aspects of the job, working conditions, company, and location to ensure that employees develop appropriate expectations. This information should come early in recruiting and selection. It is usually given in brochures, in videos, or by the company recruiter during an interview. Although research specifically investigating the influence of realistic job previews on employee turnover is weak and inconsistent, we do know that unmet expectations resulting from recruitment and selection relate to dissatisfaction and turnover.[151] As we will see, employees' expectations about a job and a company may be formed by interactions with managers, peers, and recruiters rather than from specific messages about the job.

Realistic job preview
Provides accurate information about the unattractive and attractive aspects of the job, working conditions, company, and location.

TABLE 7.13
What Employees Should Learn and Develop through the Socialization Process

History	The company's traditions, customs, and myths; background of members
Company goals	Rules, values, or principles directing the company
Language	Slang and jargon unique to the company; professional technical language
Politics	How to gain information regarding the formal and informal work relationships and power structures in the company
People	Successful and satisfying work relationships with other employees
Performance proficiency	What needs to be learned; effectiveness in using and acquiring the knowledge, skills, and abilities needed for the job.

SOURCE: Based on G.T. Chao, A.M. O'Leary-Kelly, S. Wolf, H. Klein, and P.D. Gardner, "Organizational Socialization: Its Content and Consequences," *Journal of Applied Psychology* 79 (1994), pp. 730–43.

Encounter

Encounter phase Phase of socialization that occurs when an employee begins a new job.

The **encounter phase** occurs when the employee begins a new job. No matter how realistic the information provided during interviews and site visits, individuals beginning new jobs will experience shock and surprise.[152] Employees need to become familiar with job tasks, receive appropriate training, and understand company practices and procedures.

Challenging work plus cooperative and helpful managers and peers have been shown to enhance employees' learning a new job.[153] New employees view managers as an important source of information about their jobs and the company. Research suggests that the nature and quality of the new employee's relationship with the manager has a significant impact on socialization.[154] In fact, the negative effects of unmet expectations can be reduced by the new employee having a good relationship with her or his manager! Managers can help create high-quality work relationships by helping new employees understand their roles, providing information about the company, and understanding the stresses and issues that new employees experience.

Settling In

Settling-in phase Phase of socialization that occurs when employees are comfortable with job demands and social relationships.

In the **settling-in phase,** employees begin to feel comfortable with their job demands and social relationships. They begin to resolve work conflicts (like too much work or conflicting job demands) and conflicts between work and nonwork activities. Employees are interested in the company's evaluation of their performance and in learning about potential career opportunities within the company.

Employees need to complete all three socialization phases to fully contribute to the company. For example, employees who do not feel that they have established good working relationships with coworkers will likely spend time and energy worrying about those relationships rather than being concerned with product development or customer service. Employees who experience successful socialization are more motivated, more committed to the company, and more satisfied with their jobs.[155]

Orientation programs play an important role in socializing employees. Orientation involves familiarizing new employees with company rules, policies, and procedures. Table 7.14 shows the content of orientation programs. Typically, a program includes information about the company, department in which the employee will be working, and community.

Although the content of orientation programs is important, the process of orientation cannot be ignored. Too often, orientation programs consist of completing payroll forms and reviewing personnel policies with managers or human resource representatives. The new employee, a passive recipient of information, has little opportunity to ask questions or interact with peers and managers.

Effective orientation programs actively involve the new employee. Table 7.15 shows the characteristics of effective orientation. An important characteristic of effective orientation is that peers, managers, and senior coworkers are actively involved in helping new employees adjust to the work group.[156]

Before being assigned to their plant locations, new engineers at Pillsbury, for example, have a one-year headquarters assignment.[157] A mentor (a senior engineer), shows them the technical engineering resources available within the company. The mentor also helps them become familiar with the community and deal with relocation issues. New engineers attend seminars in which engineers from different divisions (frozen foods, for example) explain the role of engineering. New employees also meet key Pillsbury players in engineering management.

TABLE 7.14
Content of Orientation Programs

I.	**Company-level information**
	Company overview (e.g., values, history, mission)
	Key policies and procedures
	Compensation
	Employee benefits and services
	Safety and accident prevention
	Employee and union relations
	Physical facilities
	Economic factors
	Customer relations
II.	**Department-level information**
	Department functions and philosophy
	Job duties and responsibilities
	Policies, procedures, rules, and regulations
	Performance expectations
	Tour of department
	Introduction to department employees
III.	**Miscellaneous**
	Community
	Housing
	Family adjustment

SOURCE: J.L. Schwarz and M.A. Weslowski, "Employee Orientation: What Employers Should Know," *The Journal of Contemporary Business Issues,* Fall 1995, p. 48. Used with permission.

TABLE 7.15
Characteristics of Effective Orientation Programs

Employees are encouraged to ask questions.
Program includes information on both technical and social aspects of the job.
Orientation is the responsibility of the new employee's manager.
Debasing or embarrassing new employees is avoided.
Formal and informal interactions with managers and peers occur.
Programs involve relocation assistance (such as house hunting or information sessions on the community for employees and their spouses).
Employees are told about the company's products, services, and customers.

Similarly, new employees and their managers are actively involved in orientation at Corning Glass.[158] Corning Glass was experiencing turnover among its high-potential new employees. Employees were leaving the company because they felt the company had a sink-or-swim attitude toward new hires. As a result, Corning designed a new orientation process including

- *Manager preparation*. Hiring managers are given guidelines and checklists that specify the steps they should take before and after the arrival of new employees.
- *Guided self-learning*. Managers are encouraged to spend the first two weeks orienting new employees to the job and the company rather than focusing on their regular job duties. Each new employee gets a workbook about the company's customers,

suppliers, objectives, and culture; The employee decides how to complete the workbook questions (interviews, visits to the company resource center, and so on). The manager and employee jointly review the answers to the workbook questions. If the employee needs more information, the learning period is extended.
- *Organization acculturation. During their first three months, employees attend* seminars on Corning's philosophy, culture, and values.

Retention data suggest that the orientation program is a success. It has increased new employee retention 25 to 35 percent in comparison with employees who did not take the new program.

Training and Pay Systems

Training is increasingly being linked to employees' compensation through the use of skill-based pay systems. (We discuss skill-based pay systems in detail in Chapter 11, "Pay Structure Decisions.") In skill-based pay systems, employees' pay is based primarily on the knowledge and skills they possess rather than the knowledge and skills necessary to successfully perform their current jobs.

Skill-based pay systems have several implications for training systems. Because pay is directly tied to the amount of knowledge and skill employees have obtained, employees will be motivated to attend training programs. This means that the volume of training conducted, as well as training costs, will increase. Skill-based pay systems require continual evaluation of employees' skills and knowledge to ensure that employees are competent in the skills acquired in training programs.

A Look Back

As the chapter opener highlighted, Tires Plus uses training to support the company's business strategy. Tires Plus provides extensive training, has its own university (Tires Plus University), and uses mentors to help employees apply what they have learned in training to their jobs.

Questions

1. Suppose a manager asked you to determine whether training was supporting a company's business strategy. How would you conduct this type of analysis?
2. What kind of information would you need?

Summary

Technological innovations, new product markets, and a diverse workforce have increased the need for companies to reexamine how their training practices contribute to learning. In this chapter we discussed a systematic approach to training, including needs assessment, design of the learning environment, consideration of employee readiness for training, and transfer-of-training issues. We reviewed numerous training methods and stressed that the key to successful training was to choose a method that would best accomplish the objectives of training. We also emphasized how training can contribute to effectiveness through establishing a link with the company's strategic direction and demonstrating through cost–benefit analysis how training contributes to profitability. Managing diversity and cross-cultural preparation are two training issues that are relevant given company needs to capitalize on a diverse workforce and global markets.

Discussion Questions

1. Noetron, a retail electronics store, recently invested a large amount of money to train sales staff to improve customer service. The skills emphasized in the program include how to greet customers, determine their needs, and demonstrate product convenience. The company wants to know whether the program is effective. What outcomes should it collect? What type of evaluation design should it use?
2. "Melinda," bellowed Toran, "I've got a problem and you've got to solve it. I can't get people in this plant to work together as a team. As if I don't have enough trouble with the competition and delinquent accounts, now I have to put up with running a zoo. It's your responsibility to see that the staff gets along with each other. I want a human relations training proposal on my desk by Monday." How would you determine the need for human relations training? How would you determine whether you actually had a training problem? What else could be responsible?
3. Assume you are general manager of a small seafood company. Most training is unstructured and occurs on the job. Currently, senior fish cleaners are responsible for teaching new employees how to perform the job. Your company has been profitable, but recently wholesale fish dealers that buy your product have been complaining about the poor quality of your fresh fish. For example, some fillets have not had all the scales removed and abdomen parts remain attached to the fillets. You have decided to change the on-the-job training received by the fish cleaners. How will you modify the training to improve the quality of the product delivered to the wholesalers?
4. A training needs analysis indicates that managers' productivity is inhibited because they are reluctant to delegate tasks to their subordinates. Suppose you had to decide between using adventure learning and interactive video for your training program. What are the strengths and weaknesses of each technique? Which would you choose? Why? What factors would influence your decision?
5. To improve product quality, a company is introducing a computer-assisted manufacturing process into one of its assembly plants. The new technology is likely to substantially modify jobs. Employees will also be required to learn statistical process control techniques. The new technology and push for quality will require employees to attend numerous training sessions. Over 50 percent of the employees who will be affected by the new technology completed their formal education over 10 years ago. Only about 5 percent of the company's employees have used the tuition reimbursement benefit. How should management maximize employees' readiness for training?
6. A training course was offered for maintenance employees in which trainees were supposed to learn how to repair and operate a new, complex electronics system. On the job, maintenance employees were typically told about a symptom experienced by the machine operator and were asked to locate the trouble. During training, the trainer would pose various problems for the maintenance employees to solve. He would point out a component on an electrical diagram and ask, "What would happen if this component was faulty?" Trainees would then trace the circuitry on a blueprint to uncover the symptoms that would appear as a result of the problem. You are receiving complaints about poor troubleshooting from maintenance supervisors of employees who have completed the program. The trainees are highly motivated and have the necessary prerequisites. What is the problem with the training course? What recommendations do you have for fixing this course?
7. What factors contribute to the effectiveness of Web training programs?

Web Exercise

Go to **www.webbasedtraining.com**. This website provides guidelines for creating Web-based training, lists of resources and tools, and example online learning lessons and programs. Click on "RESOURCES"; under "RESOURCES" click on "WBT Online." Choose one of the online learning programs shown. For the program you choose (a) describe the purpose of the program, include a copy of the program's screens and its Web address,

(b) identify what features are effective for learning and (c) provide recommendations for improving the program. Your instructor will advise you to either e-mail your report or provide a paper copy.

Managing People: From the Pages of *BusinessWeek*

BusinessWeek Look Who's Building Online Classrooms

Since investment moguls such as Michael Milken began granting huge sums of money to online education ventures in the late 1990s, debates about e-learning have focused on its impact on traditional universities or K–12 schools. Would traditional universities be forced out of business? Would kindergarten students watch a teacher on a screen all day, instead of sitting in a circle with one at story time?

Given such questions, primary schools and universities have been cautious about getting into the e-learning game. But corporations have been far more adventurous. In fact, e-learning is becoming commonplace in offices and workplaces across the country, spawning a multimillion-dollar industry. The trend isn't limited to just tech courses. Online programs now teach so-called "soft" skills, such as leadership, coaching, and global teamwork.

The new learning models have the potential to make education a high priority on the job. After all, analysts write volumes on the value of having an educated, skilled, and speedy workforce. When a lesson can be transmitted quickly to managers and sales teams worldwide through an e-learning program, it begins to show on the bottom line. Says James Moore, Sun Microsystems' director of workforce: "If you look at product development at Sun, by the time I got everyone trained [the traditional way, the product] would be obsolete."

Is e-learning here to stay? BusinessWeek Online explores this question in a series that looks at the companies investing heavily in adult learning on the job. Later parts of this series will examine how private e-learning companies are trying to cash in on the potential boom and will look at how companies are affected by the change.

While no reliable estimates on the current U.S. market for corporate education exist, by 2003 the Net-based corporate education market should be worth a hefty $11.4 billion, according to International Data Corp. The stack of dough could be that tall thanks to a conversion by training directors to use the Net to teach employees. It saves money and time, and managers can pack more information into a lesson, missionaries say.

Publicly traded e-learning companies—long victims of a skeptical market—are beginning to report improved earnings, too. Chris J. Nguyen, CEO of Baltimore's Caliber Learning Network (CLBR), says when his company reports quarterly earnings on July 26, investors can expect sequential growth over the first quarter of 2000. SmartForce (SMTF), a Redwood (California) e-learning company that focuses on adults, saw revenues increase to $36.4 million in the second quarter of 2000. And in San Francisco, DigitalThink (DTHK), an e-learning company offering programs for corporations, also reported stronger earnings in its fiscal first quarter of 2001, ending June 30. The $6.3 million in earnings is a 433 percent increase since last year. That's right, 433 percent.

"Our customers want learning strategies to integrate all the learning that goes on in their organization with the corporate strategy," says John W. Humphrey, chairman of Forum Corp., a 30-year-old private-sector provider of leadership training. FT Knowledge, an e-learning company spun off from British publishing giant Pearson, announced earlier in July that it will acquire Forum for $90 million. The move points to a race among old economy training groups to use the Web to meet company needs. The idea is to mix e-learning with some classroom sessions, using content from varied sources—executives, university professors, or private training companies.

Other online learning companies are struggling to stay on top of demand. General Manager Robert Brodo of 15-year-old SMG Net, the online business unit of SMG Strategic Management Group in Philadelphia, says each of the company's 40 top clients—Boeing is its largest—has had a conversation about bringing courses online. Eighty percent are implementing courses such as SMG's "simulated company." In the two-day simulation, execs can play out five to six years of business experience. "We can't keep up with the demand, and it's scary when you have to tell a customer that you can't start a project for them until October and November." Privately held SMG says it will generate revenues of $31 million in 2000—$5 million from online programs. Next year, Brodo estimates $48 million to $50 million in revenues. "The growth is from online corporate universities," he says.

Cushing Anderson, program manager for learning-services research at International Data Corp., is in the process of researching how companies are using e-learning for everyone from managers to sales teams and programmers. In 1999, 6 percent of all corporate training was done online, he says. Anderson's preliminary findings show that doubling to 12 percent this year. In 2001, that figure should double again. "Large companies tend to be more adventurous and have larger budgets" to put courses online, he says, though most buy programs from outside vendors.

That isn't the case at IBM. Nancy J. Lewis, IBM's director of management development worldwide, says Big Blue will move its training programs online for 5,000 new managers, saving the company $16 million in 2000, half of which has already been realized. She adds that producing five times the content at a third of the cost has helped convince all of IBM's training units to adopt the model. Her unit alone has reduced its staff from about 500 trainers worldwide to 70 this year.

IBM is so confident about its training that the company has packaged its programs to sell to customers—a side business that is already bringing in "small amounts of revenue" says Lewis's second in command, Robert MacGregor. If IBM's models for e-corporate universities works, it could become a profitable new business.

Heads of training and development have grander plans than simply offering a course online. They expect to change adults' learning habits. Pippa Wicks, CEO of FT Knowledge, says in January 2001 the company will launch a new learning program called Insight Forum. "You do your job through the training program," she says. For instance, a customer service manager would use the program to perform her daily tasks and then receive feedback about her decisions. Employees could take the training individually, or entire departments can share information in open sessions. FT Knowledge says it is already billing an unnamed company $3,500 an hour to link a handful of its execs with one of FT's management gurus for advice via videoconferencing.

Los Altos (California)-based Pensare, a four-year-old e-learning company, has a different vision. The company uses a model that lets employees, not trainers, decide what they need to learn, and when. "Tell [employees] what they need to do to help [execute] company strategy, then say, 'what do you think you need to know to help us?'" says Pensare cofounder Dean Hovey.

Online learning, delivered quickly and in a setting where the information can be commonly shared, will make the training process more engaging and less of a chore, experts say. And it'll give companies an advantage over competitors. 3Com, for one, places a high value on e-learning. "I've got senior people saying that they want more [online training]," says Geoff Roberts, 3Com's director of education. 3Com's agility with technology makes it imperative to train not only internal employees but also its customers. "We're selling into a market where 80 percent of the people don't understand the industry," he says, adding that 3Com's investment in e-learning is fed from the company's marketing budget, not training.

As companies convert lessons to be delivered over intranets, one massive obstacle remains: unless it's mandatory, most employees drop out of training. "Getting 2 percent to 3 percent [of a workforce to sign on] can't happen," says Forum's Humphrey. "There have to be more breakthroughs to make learning less intrusive to the worker." His suggestion to clients: make lessons relevant.

The good news is that generation-Y workers—recent college grads—are more comfortable using the Web. In 2003, analysts expect 95 percent of college students to use the Internet; only 41.7 percent did in 1996. This means college grads entering the workforce in 2003, and beyond, may be more receptive to e-learning. In fact, they may expect it. In 1998, 700,000 students were enrolled in distance learning programs. By 2002, 2.2 million will be, according to Credit Suisse First Boston analysts.

The plans sound grand. More and more companies will log their workers on to lessons on the Net. But getting the 45-year-old manager or executive to adopt e-learning models as easily as they've grown to employ e-mail is a challenge. No matter how fancy the program, if no one logs on, it'll be a hard to convince any CFO that investing in e-learning is worth it.

QUESTIONS

1. What features are necessary for online learning to be effective? Explain.
2. Online learning blurs the distinction between training and work. Trainees are expected to be motivated to complete online learning during breaks in their workday or on their personal time. As a manager, is this realistic? How would you "schedule" online learning for your employees?

SOURCE: Reprinted from July 25, 2000 issue of *BusinessWeek* by special permission.

Notes

1. J. Meister, "The CEO-Driven Learning Culture," *Training and Development*, June 2000, pp. 52–70.
2. I.I. Goldstein and P. Gilliam, "Training Systems Issues in the Year 2000," *American Psychologist* 45 (1990), pp. 134–43.
3. J.B. Quinn, P. Anderson, and S. Finkelstein, "Leveraging Intellect," *Academy of Management Executive* 10 (1996), pp. 7–27.
4. T.T. Baldwin, C. Danielson, and W. Wiggenhorn, "The Evolution of Learning Strategies in Organizations: From Employee Development to Business Redefinition," *Academy of Management Executive* 11,

pp. 47–58; J.J. Martocchio and T.T. Baldwin, "The Evolution of Strategic Organizational Training," in *Research in Personnel and Human Resource Management* 15, ed. G.R. Ferris (Greenwich, CT: JAI Press, 1997), pp. 1–46.

5. A.P. Carnevale, "America and the New Economy," *Training and Development Journal*, November 1990, pp. 31–52.
6. J.M. Rosow and R. Zager, *Training: The Competitive Edge* (San Francisco: Jossey-Bass, 1988).
7. L. Thornburg, "Accounting for Knowledge," *HR Magazine* (October 1994), pp. 51–56; T.A. Stewart, "Mapping Corporate Brainpower," *Fortune* (October 30, 1995), p. 209.
8. D. Senge, "The Learning Organization Made Plain and Simple," *Training and Development Journal*, October 1991, pp. 37–44.
9. M.A. Gephart, V.J. Marsick, M.E. Van Buren, and M.S. Spiro, "Learning Organizations Come Alive," *Training and Development* 50 (1996), pp. 35–45; C.M. Solomon, "HR Facilitates the Learning Organization Concept," *Personnel Journal* (November 1994), pp. 56–66; T.A. Stewart, "Getting Real about Brainpower," *Fortune* (November 27, 1995), pp. 201–3; L. Thornburg, "Accounting for Knowledge," *HR Magazine*, October 1994, pp. 51–56.
10. Gephart, Marsick, Van Buren, and Spiro, "Learning Organizations Come Alive."
11. T. Stewart, "The House That Knowledge Built," *Fortune* (October 2, 2000), pp. 278–80; Viant's Website, **www.viant.com**.
12. R. Noe, *Employee Training and Development*, 2nd ed. (Burr Ridge, IL: Irwin/McGraw-Hill, 2001).
13. I.L. Goldstein, E.P. Braverman, and H. Goldstein, "Needs Assessment," in *Developing Human Resources*, ed. K.N. Wexley (Washington, DC: Bureau of National Affairs, 1991), pp. 5–35 to 5–75.
14. J.Z. Rouillier and I.L. Goldstein, "Determinants of the Climate for Transfer of Training" (presented at Society of Industrial/Organizational Psychology meetings, St. Louis, MO, 1991); J.S. Russell, J.R. Terborg, and M.L. Powers, "Organizational Performance and Organizational Level Training and Support," *Personnel Psychology* 38 (1985), pp. 849–63; H. Baumgartel, G.J. Sullivan, and L.E. Dunn, "How Organizational Climate and Personality Affect the Payoff from Advanced Management Training Sessions," *Kansas Business Review* 5 (1978), pp. 1–10.
15. A.P. Carnevale, L.J. Gainer, and J. Villet, *Training in America* (San Francisco: Jossey-Bass, 1990); L.J. Gainer, "Making the Competitive Connection: Strategic Management and Training," *Training and Development*, September 1989, pp. s1–s30.
16. S. Raghuram and R.D. Arvey, "Business Strategy Links with Staffing and Training Practices," *Human Resource Planning* 17 (1994), pp. 55–73.
17. D. Stamps, "Deep Blue Sea," *Training*, July 1999, pp. 39–43.
18. Carnevale, Gainer, and Villet, *Training in America*.
19. P.A. Smith, "Reinventing SunU," *Training and Development* (July 1994), pp. 23–27.
20. B. Gerber, "How to Buy Training Programs," *Training*, June 1989, pp. 59–68.
21. D.A. Blackmon, "Consultants' Advice on Diversity Was Anything but Diverse," *The Wall Street Journal* (March 11, 1997), pp. A1, A16.
22. R. Zemke and J. Armstrong, "How Long Does It Take? (The Sequel)," *Training*, May 1997, pp. 69–79.
23. G. Rummler, "In Search of the Holy Performance Grail," *Training and Development*, April 1996, pp. 26–31; D.G. Langdon, "Selecting Interventions," *Performance Improvement* 36 (1997), pp. 11–15.
24. R.F. Mager and P. Pipe, *Analyzing Performance Problems: Or You Really Oughta Wanna*, 2nd ed. (Belmont, CA: Pittman Learning, 1984); A.P. Carnevale, L.J. Gainer, and A.S. Meltzer, *Workplace Basics Training Manual*, 1990 (San Francisco: Jossey-Bass, 1990); G. Rummler, "In Search of the Holy Performance Grail."
25. C.E. Schneier, J.P. Guthrie, and J.D. Olian, "A Practical Approach to Conducting and Using Training Needs Assessment," *Public Personnel Management*, Summer 1988, pp. 191–205.
26. I. Goldstein, "Training in Organizations," in *Handbook of Industrial/Organizational Psychology*, 2nd ed., ed. M.D. Dunnette and L.M. Hough (Palo Alto, CA: Consulting Psychologists Press, 1991), vol. 2, pp. 507–619.
27. E.F. Holton III and C. Bailey, "Top-to-Bottom Curriculum Redesign," *Training and Development*, March 1995, pp. 40–44.
28. R.A. Noe, "Trainees' Attributes and Attitudes: Neglected Influences on Training Effectiveness," *Academy of Management Review* 11 (1986), pp. 736–49.
29. T.T. Baldwin, R.T. Magjuka, and B.T. Loher, "The Perils of Participation: Effects of Choice on Trainee Motivation and Learning," *Personnel Psychology* 44 (1991), pp. 51–66; S.I. Tannenbaum, J.E. Mathieu, E. Salas, and J.A. Cannon-Bowers, "Meeting Trainees' Expectations: The Influence of Training Fulfillment on the Development of Commitment, Self-Efficacy, and Motivation," *Journal of Applied Psychology* 76 (1991), pp. 759–69.
30. M.E. Gist, C. Schwoerer and B. Rosen, "Effects of Alternative Training Methods on Self-Efficacy and Performance in Computer Software Training," *Jour-*

nal of Applied Psychology 74 (1989), pp. 884–91; J. Martocchio and J. Dulebohn, "Performance Feedback Effects in Training: The Role of Perceived Controllability," *Personnel Psychology* 47 (1994), pp. 357–73; J. Martocchio, "Ability Conceptions and Learning," *Journal of Applied Psychology* 79 (1994), pp. 819–25.

31. W.D. Hicks and R.J. Klimoski, "Entry into Training Programs and Its Effects on Training Outcomes: A Field Experiment," *Academy of Management Journal* 30 (1987), pp. 542–52.
32. R.A. Noe and N. Schmitt, "The Influence of Trainee Attitudes on Training Effectiveness: Test of a Model," *Personnel Psychology* 39 (1986), pp. 497–523.
33. M.A. Quinones, "Pretraining Context Effects: Training Assignments as Feedback," *Journal of Applied Psychology* 80 (1995), pp. 226–38; Baldwin, Magjuka, and Loher, "The Perils of Participation."
34. L.H. Peters, E.J. O'Connor, and J.R. Eulberg, "Situational Constraints: Sources, Consequences, and Future Considerations," in *Research in Personnel and Human Resource Management*, ed. K.M. Rowland and G.R. Ferris (Greenwich, CT: JAI Press, 1985), vol 3, pp. 79–114; E.J. O'Connor, L.H. Peters, A. Pooyan, J. Weekley, B. Frank, and B. Erenkranz, "Situational Constraints Effects on Performance, Affective Reactions, and Turnover: A Field Replication and Extension," *Journal of Applied Psychology* 69 (1984), pp. 663–72; D.J. Cohen, "What Motivates Trainees?" *Training and Development Journal* (November 1990), pp. 91–93; Russell, Terborg, and Powers, "Organizational Performance."
35. A.P. Carnevale, "America and the New Economy," *Training and Development Journal,* November 1990, pp. 31–52.
36. J. Nunally, *Psychometric Theory* (New York: McGraw-Hill, 1978).
37. L. Gottsfredson, "The g Factor in Employment," *Journal of Vocational Behavior* 19 (1986), pp. 293–96.
38. M.J. Ree and J.A. Earles, "Predicting Training Success: Not Much More Than g," *Personnel Psychology* 44 (1991), pp. 321–32.
39. D.R. Torrence and J.A. Torrence, "Training in the Face of Illiteracy," *Training and Development Journal*, August 1987, pp. 44–49.
40. M. Davis, "Getting Workers Back to the Basics," *Training and Development,* October 1997, pp. 14–15.
41. C.E. Schneier, "Training and Development Programs: What Learning Theory and Research Have to Offer," *Personnel Journal* (April 1974), pp. 288–93; M. Knowles, "Adult Learning," in *Training and Development Handbook,* 3rd ed., ed. R.L. Craig (New York: McGraw-Hill, 1987), pp. 168–79; R. Zemke and S. Zemke, "30 Things We Know for Sure about Adult Learning," *Training* (June 1981), pp. 45–52; B.J. Smith and B.L. Delahaye, *How to Be an Effective Trainer,* 2nd ed. (New York: Wiley, 1987).
42. B. Mager, *Preparing Instructional Objectives*, 2nd ed. (Belmont, CA: Lake Publishing, 1984); B.J. Smith and B.L. Delahaye, *How to Be an Effective Trainer,* 2nd ed. (New York: John Wiley and Sons, 1987).
43. K.A. Smith-Jentsch, F.G. Jentsch, S.C. Payne, and E. Salas, "Can Pretraining Experiences Explain Individual Differences in Learning?" *Journal of Applied Psychology* 81 (1996), pp. 110–16.
44. J.K. Ford, D.A. Weissbein, S.M. Guly, and E. Salas, "Relationship of Goal Orientation, Metacognitive Activity and Practice Strategies with Learning Outcomes and Transfer," *Journal of Applied Psychology* 83 (1998), pp. 218–33.
45. J.C. Naylor and G.D. Briggs, "The Effects of Task Complexity and Task Organization on the Relative Efficiency of Part and Whole Training Methods," *Journal of Experimental Psychology* 65 (1963), pp. 217–24.
46. W. McGehee and P.W. Thayer, *Training in Business and Industry* (New York: Wiley, 1961).
47. R.M. Mager, *Making Instruction Work* (Belmont, CA: David Lake, 1988).
48. R.M. Gagne and K.L. Medsker, *The Condition of Learning* (Fort Worth, TX: Harcourt-Brace, 1996).
49. P.J. Decker and B.R. Nathan, *Behavior Modeling Training: Principles and Applications* (New York: Praeger, 1985).
50. D. Stamps, "Communities of Practice," *Training*, February 1997, pp. 35–42.
51. T. Tetenbaum and H. Tetenbaum (2000) "Office 2000: Tear Down the Walls," *Training* 37(2), pp. 58–64.
52. Smith and Delahaye, *How to Be an Effective Trainer;* M. Van Wart, N.J. Cayer, and S. Cook, *Handbook of Training and Development for the Public Sector* (San Francisco: Jossey-Bass, 1993)
53. J.B. Tracey, S.I. Tannenbaum, and M.J. Kavanaugh, "Applying Trained Skills on the Job: The Importance of the Work Environment," *Journal of Applied Psychology* 80 (1995), pp. 239–52; P.E. Tesluk, J.L. Farr, J.E. Mathieu, and R.J. Vance, "Generalization of Employee Involvement Training to the Job Setting: Individual and Situational Effects," *Personnel Psychology* 48 (1995), pp. 607–32; J.K. Ford, M.A. Quinones, D.J. Sego, and J.S. Sorra, "Factors Affecting the Opportunity to Perform Trained Tasks on the Job," *Personnel Psychology* 45 (1992), pp. 511–27.
54. A. Rossett, "That Was a Great Class, but . . . ," *Training and Development,* July 1997, pp. 19–24.

55. J.M. Cusimano, "Managers as Facilitators," *Training and Development* 50 (1996), pp. 31–33.
56. C.M. Petrini, ed., "Bringing It Back to Work," *Training and Development Journal*, December 1990, pp. 15–21.
57. Ford, Quinones, Sego, and Sorra, "Factors Affecting the Opportunity to Perform Trained Tasks on the Job."
58. Ibid.; M.A. Quinones, J.K. Ford, D.J. Sego, and E.M. Smith, "The Effects of Individual and Transfer Environment Characteristics on the Opportunity to Perform Trained Tasks," *Training Research Journal* 1 (1995/96), pp. 29–48.
59. G. Stevens and E. Stevens, "The Truth about EPSS," *Training and Development* 50 (1996), pp. 59–61.
60. "In Your Face EPSSs," *Training*, April 1996, pp. 101–2.
61. R.D. Marx, "Relapse Prevention for Managerial Training: A Model for Maintenance of Behavior Change," *Academy of Management Review* 7 (1982), pp. 433–41; G.P. Latham and C.A. Frayne, "Self-Management Training for Increasing Job Attendance: A Follow-up and Replication," *Journal of Applied Psychology* 74 (1989), pp. 411–16.
62. M. Van Buren and W. Woodwell, Jr., *The 2000 ASTD Trends Report: Staying Ahead of the Winds of Change* (Alexandria, VA: American Society for Training and Development, 2000).
63. D. McMurrer, M. Van Buren, and W. Woodwell, Jr., *The 2000 ASTD State of the Industry Report* (Alexandria, VA: American Society for Training and Development, 2000).
64. "Top Training Facilities," *Training*, March 1995, special section, H.; U. Gupta, "TV Seminars and CD-ROMs Train Workers," *The Wall Street Journal* (January 3, 1996), pp. B1, B6.
65. C. Lee, "Who Gets Trained in What?" *Training*, October 1991, pp. 47–59; W. Hannum, *The Application of Emerging Training Technology* (San Diego, CA: University Associates, 1990); B. Filipczak, "Make Room for Training," *Training*, October 1991, pp. 76–82; A.P. Carnevale, L.J. Gainer, and A.S. Meltzer, *Workplace Basics Training Manual* (San Francisco: Jossey-Bass, 1990).
66. Hannum, *Application of Emerging Training Technology*; "Putting the Distance into Distance Learning," *Training*, October 1995, pp. 111–18.
67. P.A. Galagan, "Think Performance: A Conversation with Gloria Gery," *Training and Development*, March 1994, pp. 47–51.
68. Rosow and Zager, *Training: The Competitive Edge*.
69. M. Nadeau, "Reach out and Touch Someone," *Personnel Journal*, May 1995, pp. 120–24; B. Filipczak and B. Leonard, "Distance Learning: Work & Training Overlap," *HR Magazine*, April 1996, pp. 40–48.
70. C. Lee, "Who Gets Trained in What?"; A.P. Carnevale, L.J. Gainer, and A.S. Meltzer, *Workplace Basics Training Manual* (San Francisco: Jossey-Bass, 1990).
71. T. Skylar, "When Training Collides with a 35-Ton Truck," *Training*, March 1996, pp. 32–38.
72. R.B. Cohn, "How to Choose a Video Producer," *Training*, July 1996, pp. 58–61.
73. A.P. Carnevale, "The Learning Enterprise," *Training and Development Journal*, February 1989, pp. 26–37.
74. W.J. Rothwell and H.C. Kanzanas, "Planned OJT Is Productive OJT," *Training and Development Journal*, October 1990, pp. 53–56.
75. B. Filipczak, "Who Owns Your OJT?" *Training*, December 1996, pp. 44–49.
76. D.B. Youst and L. Lipsett, "New Job Immersion without Drowning," *Training and Development Journal*, February 1989, pp. 73–75; G.M. Piskurich, *Self-Directed Learning* (San Francisco: Jossey-Bass, 1993).
77. G.M. Piskurich, "Self-Directed Learning," in *The ASTD Training and Development Handbook*, 4th ed., pp. 453–72; G.M. Piskurich, "Developing Self-Directed Learning," *Training and Development*, March 1994, pp. 31–36.
78. P. Warr and D. Bunce, "Trainee Characteristics and the Outcomes of Open Learning," *Personnel Psychology* 48 (1995), pp. 347–75.
79. C.M. Solomon, "When Training Doesn't Translate," *Workforce* 76, no. 3 (1997), pp. 40–44.
80. R.W. Glover, *Apprenticeship Lessons from Abroad* (Columbus, OH: National Center for Research in Vocational Education, 1986).
81. Commerce Clearing House, Inc., *Orientation–Training* (Chicago, IL: Personnel Practices Communications, Commerce Clearing House, 1981), pp. 501–905.
82. M. McCain, "Apprenticeship Lessons from Europe," *Training and Development*, November 1994, pp. 38–41.
83. R. Narisetti, "Manufacturers Decry a Shortage of Workers while Rejecting Many," *The Wall Street Journal* (September 8, 1995), pp. A1, A4.
84. *Eldredge* v. *Carpenters JATC* (1981). 27 Fair Employment Practices. Bureau of National Affairs, 479.
85. K.L. Miller and K.N. Anhalt, "Without Training, I Can't Start My Real Life," *BusinessWeek* (September 16, 1996), p. 60.
86. A.F. Cheng, "Hands-on Learning at Motorola," *Training and Development Journal*, October 1990, pp. 34–35.
87. M.W. McCall Jr. and M.M. Lombardo, "Using Sim-

ulation for Leadership and Management Research," *Management Science* 28 (1982), pp. 533–49.
88. N. Adams, "Lessons from the Virtual World," *Training*, June 1995, pp. 45–48.
89. N. Adams, "Lessons from the Virtual World."
90. A. Richter, "Board Games for Managers," *Training and Development Journal*, July 1990, pp. 95–97.
91. M. Hequet, "Games That Teach," *Training*, July 1995, pp. 53–58.
92. G.P. Latham and L.M. Saari, "Application of Social Learning Theory to Training Supervisors through Behavior Modeling," *Journal of Applied Psychology* 64 (1979), pp. 239–46.
93. D. Filipowski, "How Federal Express Makes Your Package Its Most Important," *Personnel Journal*, February 1992, pp. 40–46.
94. Hannum, *Application of Emerging Training Technology*.
95. M. Rosenberg, *E-Learning: Strategies for Delivering Knowledge in the Digital Age* (New York: McGraw-Hill, 2001).
96. P. Galagan, "The E-Learning Revolution," *Training and Development*, December 2000, pp. 24–30; D. Khirallah, "A New Way to Learn," *Information Week Online*, May 22, 2000.
97. Rosenberg, *E-Learning: Strategies for Delivering Knowledge in the Digital Age*.
98. R.J. Wagner, T.T. Baldwin, and C.C. Rowland, "Outdoor Training: Revolution or Fad?" *Training and Development Journal*, March 1991, pp. 51–57; C.J. Cantoni, "Learning the Ropes of Teamwork," *The Wall Street Journal* (October 2, 1995), p. A14.
99. C. Steinfeld, "Challenge Courses Can Build Strong Teams," *Training and Development*, April 1997, pp. 12–13.
100. P.F. Buller, J.R. Cragun, and G.M. McEvoy, "Getting the Most out of Outdoor Training," *Training and Development Journal*, March 1991, pp. 58–61.
101. C. Clements, R.J. Wagner, C.C. Roland, "The Ins and Outs of Experiential Training," *Training and Development*, February 1995, pp. 52–56.
102. Ibid.
103. P. Froiland, "Action Learning," *Training*, January 1994, pp. 27–34.
104. R.L. Oser, A. McCallum, E. Salas, and B.B. Morgan, Jr., "Toward a Definition of Teamwork: An Analysis of Critical Team Behaviors," Technical Report 89-004 (Orlando, FL.: Naval Training Research Center, 1989).
105. P. Froiland, "Action Learning," *Training*, January 1994, pp. 27–34.
106. K. Kraiger, J.K. Ford, and E. Salas, "Application of Cognitive, Skill-Based, and Affective Theories of Learning Outcomes to New Methods of Training Evaluation," *Journal of Applied Psychology* 78 (1993), pp. 311–28; J.J. Phillips, "ROI: The Search for Best Practices," *Training and Development*, February 1996, pp. 42–47; D.L. Kirkpatrick, "Evaluation of Training," in *Training and Development Handbook*, 2nd ed., ed. R. L. Craig (New York: McGraw-Hill, 1976), pp. 18-1 to 18-27.
107. J.J. Phillips, "Was It the Training?" *Training and Development*, March 1996, pp. 28–32; Phillips, "ROI: The Search for Best Practices."
108. D.A. Grove and C. Ostroff, "Program Evaluation," in *Developing Human Resources*, ed. K.N. Wexley (Washington, DC: Bureau of National Affairs, 1991), pp. 5-185 to 5-220.
109. B. Gerber, "Does Your Training Make a Difference? Prove It!" *Training*, March 1995, pp. 27–34.
110. J. Komaki, K.D. Bardwick, and L.R. Scott, "A Behavioral Approach to Occupational Safety: Pinpointing and Reinforcing Safe Performance in a Food Manufacturing Plant," *Journal of Applied Psychology* 63 (1978), pp. 434–45.
111. A.P. Carnevale and E.R. Schulz, "Return on Investment: Accounting for Training," *Training and Development Journal*, July 1990, pp. S1–S32; P.R. Sackett and E.J. Mullen, "Beyond Formal Experimental Design: Toward an Expanded View of the Training Evaluation Process," *Personnel Psychology* 46 (1993), pp. 613–27; S.I. Tannenbaum and S.B. Woods, "Determining a Strategy for Evaluating Training: Operating within Organizational Constraints," *Human Resource Planning* 15 (1992), pp. 63–81; R.D. Arvey, S.E. Maxwell, and E. Salas, "The Relative Power of Training Evaluation Designs under Different Cost Configurations," *Journal of Applied Psychology* 77 (1992), pp. 155–60.
112. D.A. Grove and C.O. Ostroff, "Program Evaluation," in *Developing Human Resources*, ed. K.N. Wexley (Washington, DC: BNA Books, 1991), pp. 185–219.
113. Gerber, "Does Your Training Make a Difference? Prove It."
114. Carnevale and Schulz, "Return on Investment."
115. Ibid.; G. Kearsley, *Costs, Benefits, and Productivity in Training Systems* (Boston: Addison-Wesley, 1982).
116. Ibid.
117. D.G. Robinson and J. Robinson, "Training for Impact," *Training and Development Journal*, August 1989, pp. 30–42.
118. Ibid.
119. J.K. McAfee and L.S. Cote, "Avoid Having Your Day in Court," *Training and Development Journal*, April 1985, pp. 56–60.

120. R. Sharpe, "In Whose Hands? Allstate and Scientology," *The Wall Street Journal* (March 22, 1995), pp. A1, A4.
121. Bureau of National Affairs, "Female Grocery Store Employees Prevail in Sex-Bias Suit against Lucky Stores," *BNAs Employee Relations Weekly* 10 (1992), pp. 927–38; *Stender* v. *Lucky Store Inc.*, DC Ncalifornia, No. c-88-1467, 8/18/92.
122. J. Sample and R. Hylton, "Falling Off a Log—and Landing in Court," *Training*, May 1996, pp. 67–69.
123. B. Ettorre, "Let's Hear It for Local Talent," *Management Review*, October 1994, p. 9; S. Franklin, "A New World Order for Business Strategy," *Chicago Tribune* (May 15, 1994), sec. 19, pp. 7–8.
124. R.L. Tung, "Selection and Training of Personnel for Overseas Assignments," *Columbia Journal of World Business* 16 (1981), pp. 18–78.
125. W.A. Arthur, Jr., and W. Bennett, Jr., "The International Assignee: The Relative Importance of Factors Perceived to Contribute to Success," *Personnel Psychology* 48 (1995), pp. 99–114; G.M. Spreitzer, M.W. McCall, Jr., and Joan D. Mahoney, "Early Identification of International Executive Potential," *Journal of Applied Psychology* 82 (1997), pp. 6–29.
126. J.S. Black and J.K. Stephens, "The Influence of the Spouse on American Expatriate Adjustment and Intent to Stay in Pacific Rim Overseas Assignments," *Journal of Management* 15 (1989), pp. 529–44.
127. P. Caligiuri, "The Big Five Personality Characteristics as Predictors of Expatriate's Desire to Terminate the Assignment and Supervisor-Rated Performance," *Personnel Psychology* 53 (2000), pp. 67–88.
128. E. Dunbar and A. Katcher, "Preparing Managers for Foreign Assignments," *Training and Development Journal*, September 1990, pp. 45–47.
129. J.S. Black and M. Mendenhall, "A Practical but Theory-Based Framework for Selecting Cross-Cultural Training Methods," in *Readings and Cases in International Human Resource Management*, ed. M. Mendenhall and G. Oddou (Boston: PWS-Kent, 1991), pp. 177–204.
130. S. Ronen, "Training the International Assignee," in *Training and Development in Organizations*, ed. I.L. Goldstein (San Francisco: Jossey-Bass, 1989), pp. 417–53.
131. P.R. Harris and R.T. Moran, *Managing Cultural Differences* (Houston: Gulf Publishing, 1991).
132. H. Lancaster, "Before Going Overseas, Smart Managers Plan Their Homecoming," *The Wall Street Journal* (September 28, 1999), p. B1; A. Halcrow, "Expats: The Squandered Resource," *Workforce*, April 1999, pp. 42–48.
133. Harris and Moran, *Managing Cultural Differences*.
134. C.M. Solomon, "Repatriation: Up, Down, or Out?" Personnel Journal, January 1995, pp. 28–37; D.R. Briscoe, *International Human Resource Management* (Englewood Cliffs, NJ: Prentice-Hall, 1994).
135. S.E. Jackson and Associates, *Diversity in the Workplace: Human Resource Initiatives* (New York: Guilford Press, 1992).
136. T.C. Cox, *Cultural Diversity in Organizations* (San Francisco: Berrett-Kohler, 1993), pp. 24–27.
137. M. Selz, "Small Company Goes Global with Diverse Workforce," *The Wall Street Journal* (October 12, 1994), p. B2.
138. R.R. Thomas, "Managing Diversity: A Conceptual Framework," in *Diversity in the Workplace* (New York: Guilford Press), pp. 306–18.
139. M.E. Heilman, C.J. Block, and J.A. Lucas, "Presumed Incompetent? Stigmatization and Affirmative Action Efforts," *Journal of Applied Psychology* 77 (1992), pp. 536–44.
140. B. Gerber, "Managing Diversity," *Training*, July 1990, pp. 23–30; T. Diamante, C.L. Reid, and L. Ciylo, "Making the Right Training Moves," *HR Magazine*, March 1995, pp. 60–65.
141. C.M. Solomon, "The Corporate Response to Workforce Diversity," *Personnel Journal*, August 1989, pp. 43–53; A. Morrison, *The New Leaders: Guidelines on Leadership Diversity in America* (San Francisco: Jossey-Bass, 1992).
142. S.M. Paskoff, "Ending the Workplace Diversity Wars," *Training*, August 1996, pp. 43–47; H.B. Karp and N. Sutton, "Where Diversity Training Goes Wrong," *Training*, July 1993, pp. 30–34.
143. Paskoff, "Ending the Workplace Diversity Wars."
144. A. Brown, "Cultural Immersion Part of Diversity Exercise," *The Columbus Dispatch* (January 17, 2000), "Business Today," p. 3.
145. A. Markels, "Diversity Program Can Prove Divisive," *The Wall Street Journal* (January 30, 1997), pp. B1–B2; "R.R. Donnelley Curtails Diversity Training Moves," *The Wall Street Journal* (February 13, 1997), pp. B3.
146. S. Rynes and B. Rosen, "A Field Study of Factors Affecting the Adoption and Perceived Success of Diversity Training," *Personnel Psychology* 48 (1995), pp. 247–70.
147. H. Rosin, "Cultural Revolution at Texaco," *The New Republic* (February 2, 1998), pp. 15–18; K. Labich, "No more Crude at Texaco," *Fortune* (September 6, 1999), pp. 205–12.
148. C.T. Schreiber, K.F. Price, and A. Morrison, "Workforce Diversity and the Glass Ceiling: Practices, Barriers, Possibilities," *Human Resource Planning* 16 (1994), pp. 51–69.
149. A. Harrington, "How Welfare Worked for T.J. Maxx," *Fortune* (November 13, 2000), pp. 453–56.

150. D.C. Feldman, "A Contingency Theory of Socialization," *Administrative Science Quarterly* 21 (1976), pp. 433–52; D.C. Feldman, "A Socialization Process That Helps New Recruits Succeed," *Personnel* 57 (1980), pp. 11–23; J.P. Wanous, A.E. Reichers, and S.D. Malik, "Organizational Socialization and Group Development: Toward an Integrative Perspective," *Academy of Management Review* 9 (1984), pp. 670–83; C.L. Adkins, "Previous Work Experience and Organizational Socialization: A Longitudinal Examination," *Academy of Management Journal* 38 (1995), pp. 839–62; E.W. Morrison, "Longitudinal Study of the Effects of Information Seeking on Newcomer Socialization," *Journal of Applied Psychology* 78 (1993), pp. 173–83.
151. G.M. McEnvoy and W.F. Cascio, "Strategies for Reducing Employee Turnover: A Meta-Analysis," *Journal of Applied Psychology* 70 (1985), pp. 342–53.
152. M.R. Louis, "Surprise and Sense Making: What Newcomers Experience in Entering Unfamiliar Organizational Settings," *Administrative Science Quarterly* 25 (1980), pp. 226–51.
153. R.F. Morrison and T.M. Brantner, "What Enhances or Inhibits Learning a New Job? A Basic Career Issue," *Journal of Applied Psychology* 77 (1992), pp. 926–40.
154. D.A. Major, S.W.J. Kozlowski, G.T. Chao, and P.D. Gardner, " A Longitudinal Investigation of Newcomer Expectations, Early Socialization Outcomes, and the Moderating Effect of Role Development Factors," *Journal of Applied Psychology* 80 (1995), pp. 418–31.
155. D.C. Feldman, *Managing Careers in Organizations* (Glenview, IL: Scott–Foresman, 1988).
156. Ibid.; D. Reed-Mendenhall and C.W. Millard, "Orientation: A Training and Development Tool," *Personnel Administrator* 25, no. 8 (1980), pp. 42–44; M.R. Louis, B.Z. Posner, and G.H. Powell, "The Availability and Helpfulness of Socialization Practices," *Personnel Psychology* 36 (1983), pp. 857–66; C. Ostroff and S.W.J. Kozlowski, Jr., "Organizational Socialization as a Learning Process: The Role of Information Acquisition," *Personnel Psychology* 45 (1992), pp. 849–74; D.R. France and R.L. Jarvis, "Quick Starts for New Employees," *Training and Development* (October 1996), pp. 47–50.
157. Pillsbury engineering orientation program.
158. D.B. Youst and L. Lipsett, "New Job Immersion without Drowning," *Training and Development*, February 1989, pp. 73–75.

Creative Staffing Solutions Pair Workers with Employers

One of the greatest challenges for any company is to find the right workers to fill its needs, whether it's someone who can operate heavy machinery or someone who can give great haircuts. In the recent labor market, even with an economic downturn, high-tech firms have had difficulty finding enough employees who are skilled in information technology to fill their open positions. In addition, these companies have needs that are different from firms in other industries. First, they are often looking for people who are willing to work part-time or on a temporary basis to develop and complete a particular project. Second, that temporary basis differs from "traditional" temporary assignments, which often last a week or two while a permanent employee is ill or on vacation. Instead, high-tech companies want people who can stay on the job for six months or a year. Third, these firms seek workers with particular skills and aptitudes in information technology. "Scarcity of qualified candidates, competition from high-profile employers, and the potential for IT professionals to earn more as professional contractors were cited as top barriers for recruiting IT workers," states a recent study conducted by the American Electronics Association (AEA). In a tight labor market, where can high-tech firms find these perfect employees?

Creative Staffing Solutions, a temporary and alternative staffing firm, provides such workers to companies. "Temping," as it used to be called, is now a $40 billion industry as more and more companies turn to staffing agencies for help. Companies are willing to pay for these employees. "For high-tech workers, this is an employees' market," notes Marc Brailov of the American Electronics Association. "It is very important for Internet companies to create and offer incentives to attract and retain employees." That's where Creative Staffing Solutions (CSS) comes in.

Founded by Mel Rhone in 1996, CSS, a minority-owned firm based in Philadelphia, now has clients ranging from small companies to large organizations such as AT&T, Hershey's, and Lockheed Martin. CSS specializes in finding IT professionals, engineers, computer programmers, and other high-tech workers for its clients. On one side of the process, a CSS manager meets with and interviews the HR manager at the client firm to determine the firm's needs. On the other side, CSS managers screen, interview, and test prospective job candidates to determine their suitability for positions. CSS checks a candidate's work history and tests grammar and spelling, math, computer skills, and so forth. Recently CSS made it possible for job hunters to post their résumés on the CSS website, where staffing managers can review them. In addition, CSS's staffing managers peruse Internet job sites in search of potential matches.

According to CSS managers, the alternative staffing solution meets the needs of both the company and the worker. Firms obtain screened, highly skilled, and motivated workers for a designated period. And currently many high-tech firms prefer to hire temporary workers because the IT economy is very volatile. They like to hire people to complete a special project, such as development of a new computer system. Workers also benefit. "You get to make your own schedule," remarks CSS staffing manager Joy Thomas. Because CSS tests and trains candidates, people who want to improve their job skills can find plenty of opportunity through the company. Some workers are looking to change careers but are afraid to make a total commitment without knowing whether they will like the new field. Filling a temporary position can give them a good taste of what the field will be like. Occasionally CSS sends a worker to fill one temporary position at a company, and the person moves on to a completely different job at the firm. The arrangement gives both parties convenience and flexibility.

Creative Staffing Solutions continues to find ways to grow its own business. Now with an in-house staff of 11 people, Mel Rhone wants to expand. Recently the company received a loan of $100,000 from the eSpeed Loans program, which is funded by ePhiladelphia, a group that represents technology companies headquartered in Philadelphia. CSS plans to use the funding to purchase hardware and software, as well as to hire more staff to train workers for all levels of technology-related jobs. Rhone, like others, foresees a future in which temporary and alternative staffing will be routine in American industry, and he wants his company to be ready to grab every opportunity that comes its way. A study by the National Association of Temporary and Staffing Services found that 90 percent of companies surveyed employ temporary help. "Companies are incorporating temp workers in long-term plans, whereas 15 years ago they used temps just to fill occasional holes," remarks Richard Wahlquist, executive vice president of the association. The same holds true for today's workers. "The way Americans seek work has fundamentally shifted—so many young adults look to temp agencies first, to get a taste of different fields, that we are a central part of the job search process," says Wahlquist. Creative Staffing Solutions intends to remain part of the process as well.

Questions

1. In addition to job websites and its own site, where else might Creative Staffing Solutions look for potential job candidates?
2. How can Creative Staffing Solutions create a learning environment for job candidates before they accept a position or while they are between positions?
3. As you consider your career, would you try working through a temporary agency such as CSS? Why or why not?
4. What difficulties might Creative Staffing Solutions have to deal with in using electronic job and résumé postings?

SOURCE: Creative Staffing Solutions website, **www.cssrecruiting.com**, accessed November 28, 2001; J. Lyman, "Uncle Sam May Help Train IT Geeks," *E-Commerce Times* (April 30, 2001), **www.ecommercetimes.com**; C. Macavinta, "Study: High-Tech Worker Shortage Persists," *CNet News.com* (April 26, 2001), **http://news.cnet.com**; J. Kuriantzick, "A Temporary Boom in the Job Market," *U.S. News & World Report* (March 19, 2001), **www.usnews.com**; P. Key, "Author/Innovator Gives Penn Large Gift," *Philadelphia Business Journal* (January 19, 2001), **http://philadelphia.bcentral.com**; R. Naraine, "Tech Worker Shortage Remains Despite Layoffs," *Internet.com News* (January 10, 2001), **www.atnewyork.com**.

PART 3

Assessment and Development of HRM

Chapter 8 Performance Management

Objectives
After reading this chapter, you should be able to:

1. Identify the major determinants of individual performance.
2. Discuss the three general purposes of performance management.
3. Identify the five criteria for effective performance management systems.
4. Discuss the four approaches to performance management, the specific techniques used in each approach, and the way these approaches compare with the criteria for effective performance management systems.
5. Choose the most effective approach to performance measurement for a given situation.
6. Discuss the advantages and disadvantages of the different sources of performance information.
7. Choose the most effective source(s) for performance information for any situation.
8. Distinguish types of rating errors and explain how to minimize each in a performance evaluation.
9. Identify the characteristics of a performance measurement system that follows legal guidelines.
10. Conduct an effective performance feedback session.

Ford had to reassess its forced ranking system. Facing potential legal problems, the company was challenged to adopt a new performance ranking system. What type of performance management system might be more effective than the one described here?

Enter the World of Business

The Top, the Middle, and the Below Average: The Trials and Tribulations of Ford Motors' Performance Management Process

In many U.S. companies, including Ford Motors, General Electric, Microsoft, and Hewlett-Packard, performance evaluation systems, known as *forced ranking systems* in which employees are ranked against each other, have generated lawsuits and negative publicity and have caused poor employee morale. In these systems a certain percentage of employees have to receive above average, average, or below average rankings. For example, at General Electric managers are to place employees into top (20 percent), middle (70 percent), and bottom (10 percent) categories. The bottom 10 percent usually receive no bonuses and can be terminated.

Ford Motors believed the system was necessary to overhaul its culture and build a younger, more ethnically diverse management team that could succeed in the new economy, in which change and new technology must be accepted. This was not the first time that Ford tried to get poor performers to leave the company. In the late 1990s Ford tried another program to persuade poorly performing salaried employees to voluntarily resign or retire early. Although the program was voluntary, managers were advised to tell buyout candidates that management believed they should leave the company.

Ford Motors Performance Management Process involved grading 1,800 middle managers as A, B, or C. Managers who received a C for one year received no bonus; two years at the C level meant possible demotion and termination. Ten percent of the managers were to be graded as C. The system caused several lawsuits, pressuring the company to change. Fifty-seven employees were party to two lawsuits charging the performance management system was discriminatory because it adversely affected older employees. That is, a larger proportion of older workers received C grades. The American Association of Retired Persons was also considering joining the lawsuit.

As a result of threatened lawsuits, Ford abandoned the major elements of its performance management process, including the practice of assigning a fixed percentage of managers every year to a C category that resulted in no bonus, no merit raise, and perhaps no job. The system has been modified because it harmed teamwork and morale. The percentage of managers to receive a C has now been reduced to 5 percent, and the A, B, and C letter grades have been replaced by "Top Achiever," "Achiever," and "Improvement Required." Employees ranked "Improvement Required" are given coaching and counseling to improve their performance.

Deteriorating relations with employees partly resulting from the performance management caused CEO Jacques Nasser and the head of human resources to leave Ford. William Clay Ford Jr., Ford's new CEO, is actively trying to settle the lawsuits. He has been quoted as saying that having employees sue the company founded by his great-grandfather "breaks my heart."

SOURCE: M. Boyle, "Performance Reviews: Perilous Curves Ahead," *Fortune* (May 28, 2001), pp. 187–88; N. Shirouzu, "Ford Stops Using Letter Rankings to Rate Workers," *The Wall Street Journal* (July 11, 2001), pp. B1, B4; N. Shirouzu, "Nine Ford Workers File Bias Suit Saying Ratings Curb Older Staff," *The Wall Street Journal* (February 15, 2001), p. B14; N. Shirouzu and J.B. White, "Ford Assesses Job Ratings Amid Bias Suit," *The Wall Street Journal* (July 9, 2001), pp. A3, A14; T.D. Schellhardt and S.K. Goo, "At Ford, Buyout Plan Has a Twist," *The Wall Street Journal* (July 22, 1998), pp. B1, B6; N. Shirouzu "Ford Is in Talks on Settling Bias Lawsuits," *The Wall Street Journal* November 2, 2001), p. A4.

Introduction

Companies that seek competitive advantage through employees must be able to manage the behavior and results of all employees. The opening vignette illustrates that one of the most difficult challenges is how to get managers to distinguish between good, average, and poor performers. Ford Motors had decided to rely on a performance appraisal system that forced managers to evaluate some employees as poor performers. The system was met with great resistance because it impelled managers to make artificial distinctions between employees to correctly use the system. Also, such a system makes sense only if those being ranked perform the exact same job. In this chapter we will discuss characteristics that performance appraisal systems need for administrative purposes such as this. For example, Ford must ensure that the system is job-related; the rationale for performance evaluations is well-documented, and managers have to discuss improvements with employees in the "Improvement Required" category.

Traditionally, the formal performance appraisal system has been viewed as the primary means for managing employee performance. Performance appraisal was an administrative duty performed by managers and was primarily the responsibility of the human resource function. Managers view performance appraisal as an annual ritual—they quickly complete the form and use it to catalog all the negative information they have collected on an employee over the previous year. Because they may dislike confrontation and not feel that they know how to give effective evaluations, some managers spend as little time as possible giving employees feedback. Not surprisingly, most managers and employees dislike performance appraisals! The major reasons for this dislike include the lack of ongoing review, lack of employee involvement, and lack of recognition for good performance.[1]

Some have argued that all performance appraisal systems are so flawed that they are manipulative, abusive, autocratic, and counterproductive. Table 8.1 shows some

TABLE 8.1
Problems and Possible Solutions in Performance Management

PROBLEM	SOLUTION
Discourages teamwork	Make collaboration a criterion on which employees will be evaluated.
Evaluators are inconsistent or use different criterion and standards	Provide training for managers; have the HR department look for patterns on appraisals that suggest bias or over- or underevaluation.
Only valuable for very good or very poor employees	Evaluate specific behaviors or results to show specifically what employees need to improve.
Encourages employees to achieve short-term goals	Include both long-term and short-term goals in the appraisal process.
Manager has complete power over the employee	Managers should be appraised for how they appraise their employees.
Too subjective	Evaluate specific behavior or results.
Produces emotional anguish	Focus on behavior; do not criticize employees; conduct appraisal on time.

SOURCE: Based on J.A. Siegel, "86 Your Appraisal Process?" *HR Magazine,* October 2000, pp. 199–202.

of the criticism of performance appraisals and how the problems can be fixed. It is important to realize that the deficiencies shown in Table 8.1 are not the result of evaluating employee performance. Rather, they result from how the appraisal system is developed and used. As we will see in this chapter, if done correctly, performance appraisal can provide several valuable benefits to both employees and the company. An important part of appraising performance is to establish employee goals, which should be tied to the company's strategic goals. The performance appraisal process tells top performers that they are valued by the company. It requires managers to at least annually communicate to employees their performance strengths and deficiencies. A good appraisal process ensures that all employees doing similar jobs are evaluated according to the same standards. A properly conducted appraisal can help the company identify the strongest and weakest employees. It can help legally justify many HRM decisions such as promotions, salary increases, discipline, and layoffs. Annually, *Fortune* magazine ranks the most globally admired companies. The Hay Group, which produces the Global Most Admired report for *Fortune*, says the companies on the list have chief executive officers who understand that performance measurement is about learning how to motivate people and link performance to rewards.[2] Many of the executives report that performance measurement encourages collaboration and cooperation. They believe performance measures help companies focus on operational excellence, customer loyalty, and development of people.

We believe that performance appraisal is only one part of the broader process of performance management. We define **performance management** as the process through which managers ensure that employees' activities and outputs are congruent with the organization's goals. Performance management is central to gaining competitive advantage.

Performance management
The means through which managers ensure that employees' activities and outputs are congruent with the organization's goals.

Our performance management system has three parts: defining performance, measuring performance, and feeding back performance information. First, a performance

Performance appraisal
The process through which an organization gets information on how well an employee is doing his or her job.

Performance feedback
The process of providing employees information regarding their performance effectiveness.

management system specifies which aspects of performance are relevant to the organization, primarily through *job analysis* (discussed in Chapter 4). Second, it measures those aspects of performance through **performance appraisal,** which is only one method for managing employee performance. Third, it provides feedback to employees through **performance feedback** sessions so they can adjust their performance to the organization's goals. Performance feedback is also fulfilled through tying rewards to performance via the compensation system (such as through merit increases or bonuses), a topic to be covered in Chapters 11 and 12.

In this chapter we examine a variety of approaches to performance management. We begin with a model of the performance management process that helps us examine the system's purposes. Then we discuss specific approaches to performance management and the strengths and weaknesses of each. We also look at various sources of performance information. The errors resulting from subjective assessments of performance are presented, as well as the means for reducing those errors. Then we discuss some effective components to performance feedback. Finally, we address components of a legally defensible performance management system.

An Organizational Model of Performance Management

For many years, researchers in the field of HRM and industrial–organizational psychology focused on performance appraisal as a measurement technique.[3] The goal of these performance appraisal systems was to measure individual employee performance reliably and validly. This perspective, however, tended to ignore some important influences on the performance management process. Thus we begin this section by presenting the major purposes of performance management from an organizational rather than a measurement perspective. To do this, we need to understand the process of performance. Figure 8.1 depicts our process model of performance.

As the figure shows, individuals' attributes—their skills, abilities, and so on—are the raw materials of performance. For example, in a sales job, an organization wants someone who has good interpersonal skills and knowledge of the products. These raw materials are transformed into objective results through the employee's behavior. Employees can exhibit behaviors only if they have the necessary knowledge, skills, abilities, and other characteristics. Thus, employees with good product knowledge and interpersonal skills can talk about the advantages of various brands and can be friendly and helpful (not that they necessarily display those behaviors, only that they *can* display them). On the other hand, employees with little product knowledge or interpersonal skills cannot effectively display those behaviors. The objective results are the measurable, tangible outputs of the work, and they are a consequence of the employee's or the work group's behavior. In our example, a salesperson who displays the correct behaviors will likely make a number of sales.

Another important component in our organizational model of the performance management system is the organization's strategy. The link between performance management and the organization's strategies and goals is often neglected. Chapter 2 pointed out that most companies pursue some type of strategy to attain their revenue, profit, and market share goals. Divisions, departments, work groups, and individuals within the company must align their activities with these strategies and goals. If they are not aligned, then the likelihood of achieving the goals becomes small. How is this link made in organizations? Primarily by specifying what needs to be accomplished

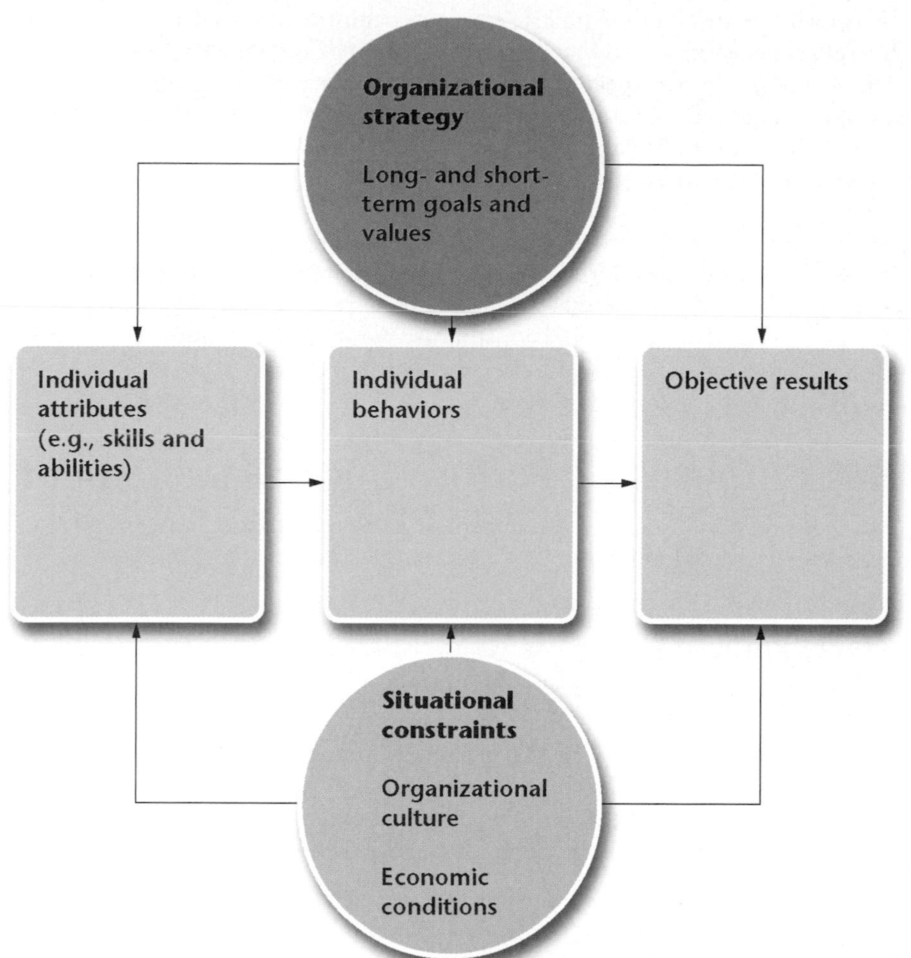

FIGURE 8.1
Model of Performance Management in Organizations

and what behaviors must be exhibited for the company's strategy to be implemented. This link is being recognized as necessary more and more often, through the increasing popularity of **performance planning and evaluation (PPE) systems.** PPE systems seek to tie the formal performance appraisal process to the company's strategies by specifying at the beginning of the evaluation period the types and level of performance that must be accomplished to achieve the strategy. Then at the end of the evaluation period, individuals and groups are evaluated based on how closely their actual performance met the performance plan. In an ideal world, performance management systems would ensure that all activities support the organization's strategic goals.

Performance planning and evaluation (PPE) system
Any system that seeks to tie the formal performance appraisal process to the company's strategies by specifying at the beginning of the evaluation period the types and level of performance that must be accomplished in order to achieve the strategy.

Finally, our model notes that situational constraints are always at work within the performance management system. As discussed previously, an employee may have the necessary skills and yet not exhibit the necessary behaviors. Sometimes the organizational culture discourages the employee from doing effective things. Work group norms often dictate what the group's members do and the results they produce. On the other hand, some people are simply not motivated to exhibit the right behaviors. This often occurs if the employees do not believe their behaviors will be rewarded with pay raises, promotions, and so forth. Finally, people may be performing effective behaviors, and yet the right results do not follow. For example, an outstanding salesperson may not have a large dollar volume because the economy is bad and people are not buying.

Thus, as you can see in Figure 8.1, employees must have certain attributes to perform a set of behaviors and achieve some results. To gain competitive advantage, the attributes, behaviors, and results must be tied to the company's strategy. It is also important to note that constraints within the work environment often preclude employees from performing. Table 8.2 provides recommendations for an effective performance management system. Regardless of the job or company, effective performance management systems measure performance criteria (such as behaviors or sales) as precisely as possible. Effective performance management systems also serve a strategic function by linking performance criteria to internal and external customer requirements. Effective performance management systems include a process for changing the system based on situational constraints. We will next examine the purposes of performance management systems.

Purposes of Performance Management

The purposes of performance management systems are of three kinds: strategic, administrative, and developmental.

Strategic Purpose

First and foremost, a performance management system should link employee activities with the organization's goals. One of the primary ways strategies are implemented is through defining the results, behaviors, and, to some extent, employee characteristics that are necessary for carrying out that strategy, and then developing measurement and feedback systems that will maximize the extent to which employees exhibit the characteristics, engage in the behaviors, and produce the results. To achieve this

TABLE 8.2
Recommendations for Designing an Effective Performance Management System

Strive for precision in defining and measuring performance.

- Define performance with a focus on valued outcomes. Use outcomes that can be defined in terms of relative frequencies of behavior.
- Include performance criteria that include various ways that employees can add value to a product or service (such as quantity, quality, timeliness, cost-effectiveness, and interpersonal impact).
- Include measures of work behaviors that add value above and beyond what is necessary to perform the job (such as assisting coworkers or taking the initiative to repair broken equipment).

Link performance dimensions to meeting internal and external customer requirements.

- Internal customer definitions of performance should be linked to external customer satisfaction.

Measure and correct for the impact of situational constraints.

- Monitor actual and perceived constraints through interviews, surveys, and observation.

SOURCE: Adapted from Exhibit 2.1 in H.J. Bernardin, C.M. Hagan, J.S. Kane, and P. Villanova, "Effective Performance Management: A Focus on Precision, Customers, and Situational Constraints," in *Performance Appraisal: State of the Art in Practice*, ed. J.W. Smither (San Francisco: Jossey-Bass, 1998), p. 56. Used by permission of Jossey-Bass, Inc., a subsidiary of John Wiley & Sons, Inc.

strategic purpose, the system must be flexible, because when goals and strategies change, the results, behaviors, and employee characteristics usually need to change correspondingly. However, performance management systems do not commonly achieve this purpose. A survey indicates that only 13 percent of the companies questioned were using their performance appraisal system to communicate company objectives.[4] In addition, surveys of HRM practitioners regarding the purposes of performance appraisal suggest that most systems focus on administrative and developmental purposes.[5]

Performance management systems can also be useful for communicating corporate culture and values in companies whose business operations are becoming more global. (See the "Competing through Globalization" box on the next page.)

Administrative Purpose

Organizations use performance management information (performance appraisals, in particular) in many administrative decisions: salary administration (pay raises), promotions, retention–termination, layoffs, and recognition of individual performance.[6] Despite the importance of these decisions, however, many managers, who are the source of the information, see the performance appraisal process only as a necessary evil they must go through to fulfill their job requirements. They feel uncomfortable evaluating others and feeding those evaluations back to the employees. Thus, they tend to rate everyone high or at least rate them the same, making the performance appraisal information relatively useless. For example, one manager stated, "There is really no getting around the fact that whenever I evaluate one of my people, I stop and think about the impact—the ramifications of my decisions on my relationship with the guy and his future here. . . . Call it being politically minded, or using managerial discretion, or fine-tuning the guy's ratings, but in the end, I've got to live with him, and I'm not going to rate a guy without thinking about the fallout."[7]

Developmental Purpose

A third purpose of performance management is to develop employees who are effective at their jobs. When employees are not performing as well as they should, performance management seeks to improve their performance. The feedback given during a performance evaluation process often pinpoints the employee's weaknesses. Ideally, however, the performance management system identifies not only any deficient aspects of the employee's performance but also the causes of these deficiencies—for example, a skill deficiency, a motivational problem, or some obstacle holding the employee back.

Managers are often uncomfortable confronting employees with their performance weaknesses. Such confrontations, although necessary to the effectiveness of the work group, often strain everyday working relationships. Giving high ratings to all employees enables a manager to minimize such conflicts, but then the developmental purpose of the performance management system is not fully achieved.[8]

The purposes of an effective performance management system are to link employee activities with the organization's strategic goals, furnish valid and useful information for administrative decisions about employees, and give employees useful developmental feedback. Fulfilling these three purposes is central to gaining competitive advantage through human resources. A vital step in performance management is to develop the measures by which performance will be evaluated. Thus we next discuss the issues involved in developing and using different measures of performance.

COMPETING THROUGH GLOBALIZATION

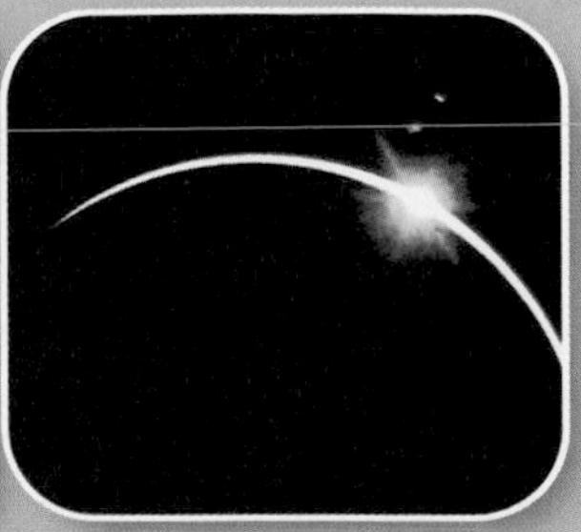

Evaluation Helps Build Unity across Cultures and Jobs

General Semiconductor has a workforce that is spread from North America to Asia and includes employees who speak five languages. Although General Semiconductor is headquartered on Long Island, New York, only 200 of its 5,600 employees are located in the United States. General Semiconductor makes power magnet components for the high-tech industry. These components power everything from automobiles to cell phones to dishwashers. It manufactures over 17 million parts each day from facilities in Europe, Taiwan, Ireland, and China.

The company's interest in growth created the need to identify a core set of company values and make sure these values were adhered to at all of the worldwide facilities. The company has eight values that are referred to as "culture points." They include integrity; a passion for customer satisfaction; respect for, responsiveness to, and empowerment of employees; technology and innovation; continual improvement; teamwork; job satisfaction; and a winning, competitive spirit. A leadership and problem-solving program developed by the company's HRM staff was used to spread these values throughout the company. The company also developed a program called People Plus that involves a 360-degree review of each employee, including an employee self-assessment matched with feedback from managers, peers, and subordinates chosen by the employee. Once the evaluations are completed, each employee meets with a psychologist to discuss the evaluations and make recommendations on how to improve the weaknesses identified.

Employees believe that that the program brings the company together despite its global locations. The program focuses on identifying the unique talents and contributions of every employee. It also helps employees understand how others on the work team view them. The positive results of the program are measurable. Two years after the program was implemented, a survey of the senior management group showed that of 39 development areas, 36 showed improvement. The program has also contributed to a very stable workforce with a low turnover rate across all locations. This has helped General Semiconductor take pride in having the most knowledgeable and well-trained employees in its industry.

SOURCE: C. Cole, "Eight Values Bring Unity to a Worldwide Company," *Workforce*, March 2001, pp. 44–45; General Semiconductor website, www.generalsemiconductor.com, September 2, 2001.

Performance Measures Criteria

In Chapter 4 we discussed how, through job analysis, one can analyze a job to determine exactly what constitutes effective performance. Once the company has determined, through job analysis and design, what kind of performance it expects from its employees, it needs to develop ways to measure that performance. This section presents the criteria underlying job performance measures. Later sections discuss approaches to performance measurement, sources of information, and errors.

Although people differ about criteria to use to evaluate performance management systems, we believe that five stand out: strategic congruence, validity, reliability, acceptability, and specificity.

Strategic Congruence

Strategic congruence is the extent to which a performance management system elicits job performance that is congruent with the organization's strategy, goals, and culture. If a company emphasizes customer service, then its performance management system should assess how well its employees are serving the company's customers. Strategic congruence emphasizes the need for the performance management system to guide employees in contributing to the organization's success. This requires systems flexible enough to adapt to changes in the company's strategic posture.

Strategic congruence
The extent to which the performance management system elicits job performance that is consistent with the organization's strategy, goals, and culture.

Many companies such as Hewlett-Packard, Federal Express, and Coca-Cola have introduced measures of critical success factors (CSFs) into their performance management systems.[9] CSFs are factors in a company's business strategy that give it a competitive edge. Companies measure employee behavior that relates to attainment of CSFs, which increases the importance of these behaviors for employees. Employees can be held accountable and rewarded for behaviors that directly relate to the company attaining the CSFs.

Take, for example, a drug company whose business strategy is to penetrate the North American market for dermatology compounds.[10] The company needs to shorten the drug development cycle, attract and retain research and development talent, and maximize the effectiveness of research teams. These are core competencies of the business; performance measures are linked directly to the core competencies. These include number of dermatology compound submissions to the Food and Drug Administration (FDA), number of compound approvals by the FDA, turnover of senior engineers, and team leadership and collaboration. The sources for information regarding these performance measures include FDA decisions, team member feedback on surveys, and turnover rates. Team and individual accountabilities are directly linked to the performance measures. For example, research teams' performance goals include FDA submission and approval of three compounds.

Most companies' appraisal systems remain constant over a long time and through a variety of strategic emphases. However, when a company's strategy changes, its employees' behavior needs to change too.[11] The fact that they often do not change may account for why many managers see performance appraisal systems as having little impact on a firm's effectiveness.

Validity

Validity is the extent to which a performance measure assesses all the relevant—and only the relevant—aspects of performance. This is often referred to as "content validity." For a performance measure to be valid, it must not be deficient or contaminated. As you can see from Figure 8.2 on the next page, one of the circles represents "true" job performance—all the aspects of performance relevant to success in the job. On the other hand, companies must use some measure of performance, such as a supervisory rating of performance on a set of dimensions or measures of the objective results on the job. Validity is concerned with maximizing the overlap between actual job performance and the measure of job performance (the green portion in the figure).

Validity
The extent to which a performance measure assesses all the relevant—and only the relevant—aspects of job performance.

A performance measure is deficient if it does not measure all aspects of performance (the cranberry portion in the figure). An example is a system at a large university that assesses faculty members based more on research than teaching, thereby relatively ignoring a relevant aspect of performance.

A contaminated measure evaluates irrelevant aspects of performance or aspects that are not job related (the gold portion in the figure). The performance measure

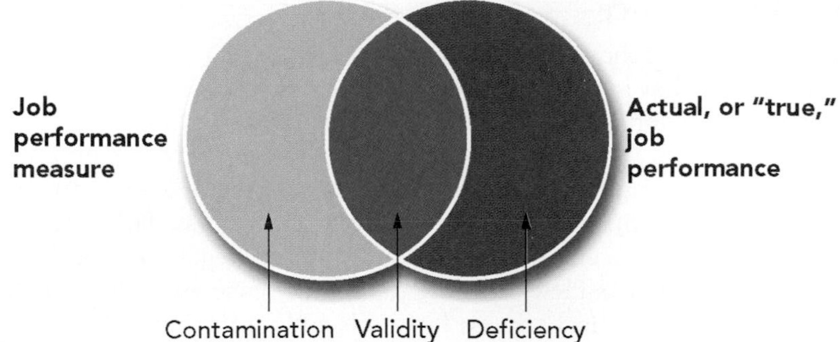

FIGURE 8.2
Contamination and Deficiency of a Job Performance Measure

should seek to minimize contamination, but its complete elimination is seldom possible. An example of a contaminated measure is the use of actual sales figures for evaluating salespersons across very different regional territories. Often sales are highly dependent upon the territory (number of potential customers, number of competitors, economic conditions) rather than the actual performance of the salesperson. A salesperson who works harder and better than others might not have the highest sales totals because the territory simply does not have as much sales potential as others. Thus, these figures alone would be a measure that is strongly affected by things beyond the control of the individual employee.

Reliability

Reliability
The consistency of a performance measure; the degree to which a performance measure is free from random error.

Reliability refers to the consistency of a performance measure. One important type of reliability is *interrater reliability:* the consistency among the individuals who evaluate the employee's performance. A performance measure has interrater reliability if two individuals give the same (or close to the same) evaluations of a person's job performance. Evidence seems to indicate that most subjective supervisory measures of job performance exhibit low reliability.[12] With some measures, the extent to which all the items rated are internally consistent is important (*internal consistency reliability*).

In addition, the measure should be reliable over time (*test–retest reliability*). A measure that results in drastically different ratings depending on when the measures are taken lacks test–retest reliability. For example, if salespeople are evaluated based on their actual sales volume during a given month, it would be important to consider their consistency of monthly sales across time. What if an evaluator in a department store examined sales only during May? Employees in the lawn and garden department would have high sales volumes, but those in the men's clothing department would have somewhat low sales volumes. Clothing sales in May are traditionally lower than other months. One needs to measure performance consistently across time.

Acceptability

Acceptability
The extent to which a performance measure is deemed to be satisfactory or adequate by those who use it.

Acceptability refers to whether the people who use a performance measure accept it. Many elaborate performance measures are extremely valid and reliable, but they consume so much of managers' time that they refuse to use it. Alternatively, those being evaluated by a measure may not accept it.

Acceptability is affected by the extent to which employees believe the perform-

TABLE 8.3
Categories of Perceived Fairness and Implications for Performance Management Systems

FAIRNESS CATEGORY	IMPORTANCE FOR PERFORMANCE MANAGEMENT SYSTEM	IMPLICATIONS
Procedural fairness	Development	• Give managers and employees opportunity to participate in development of system. • Ensure consistent standards when evaluating different employees. • Minimize rating errors and biases.
Interpersonal fairness	Use	• Give timely and complete feedback. • Allow employees to challenge the evaluation. • Provide feedback in an atmosphere of respect and courtesy.
Outcome fairness	Outcomes	• Communicate expectations regarding performance evaluations and standards. • Communicate expectations regarding rewards.

SOURCE: Adapted from S.W. Gilliland and J.C. Langdon, "Creating Performance Management Systems That Promote Perceptions of Fairness," in *Performance Appraisal: State of the Art in Practice,* ed. J.W. Smither (San Francisco: Jossey-Bass, 1998), pp. 209–43. Used by permission of Jossey-Bass, Inc., a subsidiary of John Wiley & Sons, Inc.

ance management system is fair. As Table 8.3 shows, there are three categories of perceived fairness: procedural, interpersonal, and outcome fairness. The table also shows specifically how the performance management system's development, use, and outcomes affect perceptions of fairness. In developing and using a performance management system, managers should take the steps shown in the column labeled "Implications" in Table 8.3 to ensure that the system is perceived as fair. Research suggests that performance management systems that are perceived as unfair are likely to be legally challenged, be used incorrectly, and decrease employee motivation to improve.[13]

Specificity

Specificity is the extent to which a performance measure tells employees what is expected of them and how they can meet these expectations. Specificity is relevant to both the strategic and developmental purposes of performance management. If a measure does not specify what an employee must do to help the company achieve its strategic goals, it does not achieve its strategic purpose. Additionally, if the measure fails to point out employees' performance problems, it is almost impossible for the employees to correct their performance.

Specificity
The extent to which a performance measure gives detailed guidance to employees about what is expected of them and how they can meet these expectations.

The "Competing through High-Performance Work Systems" box shows how a web-based appraisal system can improve the strategic congruence, validity, acceptability, and specificity of a performance management system.

COMPETING THROUGH HIGH-PERFORMANCE WORK SYSTEMS

Using the Web to Move Engineers' Competencies Forward

Otis Elevator Co., a wholly owned subsidiary of United Technologies Corporation, is the world's largest manufacturer, installer, and servicer of elevators, escalators, moving walkways, and similar transportation systems. The executive leader of Otis's worldwide engineering group wanted to avoid the problems that plagued past performance management systems. Too much paper and time were required, and employees did not feel the evaluations were helpful. Also, the company had just started to extensively use project teams and wanted to evaluate managerial competencies needed to successfully manage the teams. The performance evaluation system had to accurately assess managers' team leadership and project management competencies and had to hold managers accountable for achieving the business results of engineering projects. In addition to team leadership competencies and business results, Otis also wanted to evaluate the engineering managers' leadership skills. Because engineering managers were unaccustomed to being evaluated on their leadership skills, Otis wanted the system to provide feedback in a way that helped managers learn and develop leadership competencies.

The company decided to build an evaluation system that could be accessed via the Internet and the company's intranet. Engineering managers' direct reports, peers, and customers, as well as their managers, would be included in the evaluation process. The specific evaluation instrument used has 75 behavioral items that measure seven facets of team leadership (communications, leading change, customer relationships, people development, team building, process/task knowledge, and innovation and creativity). A simple, user-friendly website gives employees access to the instrument. After employees access the website, they use a personal identification number to go to a screen that explains the instrument and provides instructions. Employees can practice their evaluations and review and change their ratings before submitting them. The evaluations are anonymous. One person can be evaluated in about 20 minutes. Once all ratings for an engineering manager are received, the results are compiled and individual profiles showing the results are provided within three days. The profiles that the engineering managers receive show their actual ratings and compare them to those of an "ideal" leader. The profiles also summarize how employees were rated by peers, subordinates, managers, and customers. By reducing the time needed to complete evaluations and give feedback, managers now have more specific information about their leadership strengths and weaknesses and more time to work on their weaknesses before their next evaluation.

SOURCE: G.D. Huet-Cox, T.M. Nielsen, and E. Sundstrom, "Get the Most from 360-Degree Feedback: Put It on the Internet," *HR Magazine*, May 1999, pp. 92–103.

Approaches to Measuring Performance

The model of performance management presented in Figure 8.1 shows that we can manage performance by focusing on employee attributes, behaviors, or results. In addition, we can measure performance in a relative way, making overall comparisons among individuals' performance. Finally, we can develop a performance measurement system that incorporates some variety of the preceding measures, as evidenced by the quality approach to measuring performance. Various techniques combine these approaches. In this section we explore these approaches to measuring and managing performance, discussing the techniques that are associated with each approach and evaluating these approaches against the criteria of strategic congruence, validity, reliability, acceptability, and specificity.

The Comparative Approach

The comparative approach to performance measurement requires the rater to compare an individual's performance with that of others. This approach usually uses some overall assessment of an individual's performance or worth and seeks to develop some ranking of the individuals within a work group. At least three techniques fall under the comparative approach: ranking, forced distribution, and paired comparison.

Ranking

Simple ranking requires managers to rank employees within their departments from highest performer to poorest performer (or best to worst). *Alternation ranking,* on the other hand, consists of a manager looking at a list of employees, deciding who is the best employee, and crossing that person's name off the list. From the remaining names, the manager decides who the worst employee is and crosses that name off the list—and so forth.

Ranking is one method of performance appraisal that has received specific attention in the courts. In the *Albermarle* v. *Moody* case, the validation of the selection system was conducted using employee rankings as the measure of performance. The court actually stated, "There is no way of knowing precisely what criteria of job performance that supervisors were considering, whether each supervisor was considering the same criteria—or whether, indeed, any of the supervisors actually applied a focused and stable body of criteria of any kind."[14]

Forced Distribution

The *forced distribution* method also uses a ranking format, but employees are ranked in groups. This technique requires the manager to put certain percentages of employees into predetermined categories as depicted in Table 8.4. The example in the table shows how Merck combines the performance of the division with individual performance to recommend the distributions of employees that should fall into each category. For example, among poorly performing divisions (Not Acceptable), only 1 percent of employees should receive the highest rating (TF = Top 5 percent), whereas among top-performing divisions (Exceptional), 8 percent of employees should receive the highest rating. In some situations, the forced distribution method forces managers to categorize employees based on distribution rules, not on their performance. For example, even if a manager's employees are all above average performers, the manager is forced to rate some employees as "Not Acceptable."

Ford Motors' forced ranking system (a type of forced distribution system) was discussed in the chapter opener. Proponents of forced distribution systems argue that they guard against managers who are afraid to fire poor performers. Critics say they make managers penalize a good but not great employee who is part of an outstanding team. A mediocre employee in a struggling work team can come out looking like an

TABLE 8.4

Proposed Guidelines for Targeted Distribution of Performance Ratings

Targeted Employee Rating Distribution, by Divisional Performance

		PERFORMANCE RATING FOR DIVISIONS				
PERFORMANCE RATING FOR EMPLOYEES	RATING TYPE	EX EXCEPTIONAL	WD WITH DISTINCTION	HS HIGH STANDARD	RI ROOM FOR IMPROVEMENT	NA NOT ACCEPTABLE
TF Top 5%	Relative	8%	6%	5%	2%	1%
TQ Top quintile	Relative	20%	17%	15%	12%	10%
OU Outstanding	Absolute					
VG Very good	Absolute	71%	75%	75%	78%	79%
GD Good	Absolute					
LF Lower 5%	Relative					
NA Not acceptable	Absolute	1%	2%	5%	8%	10%
PR Progressing		Not Applicable				

SOURCE: Reprinted with permission of The Conference Board, New York City. Data supplied by Merck & Co.; chart by Kevin J. Murphy, University of Rochester.

outstanding employee. Also, it is difficult to rank employees into distinctive categories when criteria are subjective or when it is difficult to differentiate employees on the criteria (such as teamwork or communication skills).

Paired Comparison

The *paired comparison* method requires managers to compare every employee with every other employee in the work group, giving an employee a score of 1 every time he or she is considered the higher performer. Once all the pairs have been compared, the manager computes the number of times each employee received the favorable decision (that is, counts up the points), and this becomes the employee's performance score.

The paired comparison method tends to be time-consuming for managers and will become more so as organizations become flatter with an increased span of control. For example, a manager with 10 employees must make 45 ($10 \times 9/2$) comparisons. However, if the group increases to 15 employees, 105 comparisons must be made.

Evaluating the Comparative Approach

The comparative approach to performance measurement is an effective tool in differentiating employee performance; it virtually eliminates problems of leniency, central tendency, and strictness. This is especially valuable if the results of the measures are to be used in making administrative decisions such as pay raises and promotions. In addition, such systems are relatively easy to develop and in most cases easy to use; thus, they are often accepted by users.

One problem with these techniques, however, is their common failure to be linked to the strategic goals of the organization. Although raters can evaluate the extent to which individuals' performances support the strategy, this link is seldom made explicit. In addition, because of the subjective nature of the ratings, their actual validity and reliability depend on the raters themselves. Some firms use multiple evaluators to reduce the biases of any individual, but most do not. At best, we could conclude that their reliability and validity are modest.

These techniques lack specificity for feedback purposes. Based only on their relative rankings, individuals are completely unaware of what they must do differently to improve their ranking. This puts a heavy burden on the manager to provide specific feedback beyond that of the rating instrument itself. Finally, many employees and managers are less likely to accept evaluations based on comparative approaches. Evaluations depend on how employees' performance relates to other employees in a group, team, or department (normative standard) rather than on absolute standards of excellent, good, fair, and poor performance.

The Attribute Approach

The attribute approach to performance management focuses on the extent to which individuals have certain attributes (characteristics or traits) believed desirable for the company's success. The techniques that use this approach define a set of traits—such as initiative, leadership, and competitiveness—and evaluate individuals on them.

Graphic Rating Scales

The most common form that the attribute approach to performance management takes is the *graphic rating scale*. Table 8.5 shows a graphic rating scale used in a manufacturing company. As you can see, a list of traits is evaluated by a five-point (or some other number of points) rating scale. The manager considers one employee at a time, circling the number that signifies how much of that trait the individual has. Graphic rating scales can provide a number of different points (a discrete scale) or a continuum along which the rater simply places a check mark (a continuous scale).

The legal defensibility of graphic rating scales was questioned in the *Brito* v. *Zia* (1973) case. In this case Spanish-speaking employees had been terminated as a result of their performance appraisals. These appraisals consisted of supervisors' rating sub-

TABLE 8.5

Example of a Graphic Rating Scale

The following areas of performance are significant to most positions. Indicate your assessment of performance on each dimension by circling the appropriate rating.

PERFORMANCE DIMENSION	RATING				
	DISTINGUISHED	EXCELLENT	COMMENDABLE	ADEQUATE	POOR
Knowledge	5	4	3	2	1
Communication	5	4	3	2	1
Judgment	5	4	3	2	1
Managerial skill	5	4	3	2	1
Quality performance	5	4	3	2	1
Teamwork	5	4	3	2	1
Interpersonal skills	5	4	3	2	1
Initiative	5	4	3	2	1
Creativity	5	4	3	2	1
Problem solving	5	4	3	2	1

ordinates on a number of undefined dimensions such as volume of work, quantity of work, job knowledge, dependability, and cooperation. The court criticized the subjective appraisals and stated that the company should have presented empirical data demonstrating that the appraisal was significantly related to actual work behavior.

Mixed-Standard Scales

Mixed-standard scales were developed to get around some of the problems with graphic rating scales. To create a mixed-standard scale, we define the relevant performance dimensions and then develop statements representing good, average, and poor performance along each dimension. These statements are then mixed with the statements from other dimensions on the actual rating instrument. An example of a mixed-standard scale is presented in Table 8.6.

As we see in the table, the rater is asked to complete the rating instrument by indicating whether the employee's performance is above (+), at (0), or below (–) the statement. A special scoring key is then used to score the employee's performance for each dimension. Thus, for example, an employee performing above all three statements receives a 7. If the employee is below the good statement, at the average statement, and above the poor statement, a score of 4 is assessed. An employee below all three statements is given a rating of 1. This scoring is applied to all the dimensions to determine an overall performance score.

Note that mixed-standard scales were originally developed as trait-oriented scales. However, this same technique has been applied to instruments using behavioral rather than trait-oriented statements as a means of reducing rating errors in performance appraisal.[15]

Evaluating the Attribute Approach

Attribute-based performance methods are the most popular methods in organizations. They are quite easy to develop and are generalizable across a variety of jobs, strategies, and organizations. In addition, if much attention is devoted to identifying those attributes relevant to job performance and carefully defining them on the rating instrument, they can be as reliable and valid as more elaborate measurement techniques.

However, these techniques fall short on several of the criteria for effective performance management. There is usually little congruence between the techniques and the company's strategy. These methods are used because of the ease in developing them and because the same method (list of traits, comparisons) is generalizable across any organization and any strategy. In addition, these methods usually have very vague performance standards that are open to different interpretations by different raters. Because of this, different raters often provide extremely different ratings and rankings. The result is that both the validity and reliability of these methods are usually low.

Virtually none of these techniques provides any specific guidance on how an employee can support the company's goals or correct performance deficiencies. In addition, when raters give feedback, these techniques tend to elicit defensiveness from employees. For example, how would you feel if you were told that on a five-point scale, you were rated a "2" in maturity? Certainly you might feel somewhat defensive and unwilling to accept that judgment, as well as any additional feedback. Also, being told you were rated a "2" in maturity doesn't tell you how to improve your rating.

TABLE 8.6

An Example of a Mixed-Standard Scale

Three traits being assessed:	Levels of performance in statements:
Initiative (INTV)	High (H)
Intelligence (INTG)	Medium (M)
Relations with others (RWO)	Low (L)

Instructions: Please indicate next to each statement whether the employee's performance is above (+), equal to (0), or below (–) the statement.

Trait	Level	Statement	Rating
INTV	H	1. This employee is a real self-starter. The employee always takes the initiative and his/her superior never has to prod this individual.	+
INTG	M	2. While perhaps this employee is not a genius, s/he is a lot more intelligent than many people I know.	+
RWO	L	3. This employee has a tendency to get into unnecessary conflicts with other people.	0
INTV	M	4. While generally this employee shows initiative, occasionally his/her superior must prod him/her to complete work.	+
INTG	L	5. Although this employee is slower than some in understanding things, and may take a bit longer in learning new things, s/he is of average intelligence.	+
RWO	H	6. This employee is on good terms with everyone. S/he can get along with people even when s/he does not agree with them.	–
INTV	L	7. This employee has a bit of a tendency to sit around and wait for directions.	+
INTG	H	8. This employee is extremely intelligent, and s/he learns very rapidly.	–
RWO	M	9. This employee gets along with most people. Only very occasionally does s/he have conflicts with others on the job, and these are likely to be minor.	–

Scoring Key:

STATEMENTS			SCORE
HIGH	MEDIUM	LOW	
+	+	+	7
0	+	+	6
–	+	+	5
–	0	+	4
–	–	+	3
–	–	0	2
–	–	–	1

Example score from preceding ratings:

	STATEMENTS			SCORE
	HIGH	MEDIUM	LOW	
Initiative	+	+	+	7
Intelligence	0	+	+	6
Relations with others	–	–	0	2

The Behavioral Approach

The behavioral approach to performance management attempts to define the behaviors an employee must exhibit to be effective in the job. The various techniques define those behaviors and then require managers to assess the extent to which employees exhibit them. We discuss five techniques that rely on the behavioral approach.

Critical Incidents

The *critical incident* approach requires managers to keep a record of specific examples of effective and ineffective performance on the part of each employee. Here's an example of an incident described in the performance evaluation of an appliance repair person:

> A customer called in about a refrigerator that was not cooling and was making a clicking noise every few minutes. The technician prediagnosed the cause of the problem and checked his truck for the necessary parts. When he found he did not have them, he checked the parts out from inventory so that the customer's refrigerator would be repaired on his first visit and the customer would be satisfied promptly.

These incidents give specific feedback to employees about what they do well and what they do poorly, and they can be tied to the company's strategy by focusing on incidents that best support that strategy. However, many managers resist having to keep a daily or weekly log of their employees' behavior. It is also often difficult to compare employees because each incident is specific to that individual.

Behaviorally Anchored Rating Scales

A *behaviorally anchored rating scale (BARS)* builds on the critical incidents approach. It is designed to specifically define performance dimensions by developing behavioral anchors associated with different levels of performance.[16] An example of a BARS is presented in Figure 8.3. As you can see, the performance dimension has a number of examples of behaviors that indicate specific levels of performance along the dimension.

To develop a BARS, we first gather a large number of critical incidents that represent effective and ineffective performance on the job. These incidents are classified into performance dimensions, and the ones that experts agree clearly represent a particular level of performance are used as behavioral examples (or anchors) to guide the rater. The manager's task is to consider an employee's performance along each dimension and determine where on the dimension the employee's performance fits using the behavioral anchors as guides. This rating becomes the employee's score for that dimension.

Behavioral anchors have advantages and disadvantages. They can increase interrater reliability by providing a precise and complete definition of the performance dimension. A disadvantage is that they can bias information recall—that is, behavior that closely approximates the anchor is more easily recalled than other behavior.[17] Research has also demonstrated that managers and their subordinates do not make much of a distinction between BARS and trait scales.[18]

Behavioral Observation Scales

A *behavioral observation scale (BOS)* is a variation of a BARS. Like a BARS, a BOS is developed from critical incidents.[19] However, a BOS differs from a BARS in two basic

FIGURE 8.3
Task-BARS Rating Dimension: Patrol Officer

Preparing for Duty

7 — Always early for work, gathers all necessary equipment to go to work, fully dressed, uses time before roll call to review previous shift's activities and any new bulletins, takes notes of previous shift's activity mentioned during roll call.

6 — Always early for work, gathers all necessary equipment to go to work, fully dressed, checks activity from previous shifts before going to roll call.

5 — Early for work, has all necessary equipment to go to work, fully dressed.

4 — On time, has all necessary equipment to go to work, fully dressed.

3 — Not fully dressed for roll call, does not have all necessary equipment.

2 — Late for roll call, does not check equipment or vehicle for damage or needed repairs, unable to go to work from roll call, has to go to locker, vehicle, or home to get necessary equipment.

1 — Late for roll call majority of period, does not check equipment or vehicle, does not have necessary equipment to go to work.

SOURCE: Adapted from R. Harvey, "Job Analysis," in *Handbook of Industrial & Organizational Psychology,* 2nd ed., ed. M. Dunnette and L. Hough (Palo Alto, CA.: Consulting Psychologists Press, 1991), p.138.

TABLE 8.7
An Example of a Behavioral Observation Scale (BOS) for Evaluating Job Performance

Overcoming Resistance to Change						
(1) Describes the details of the change to subordinates.						
Almost Never	1	2	3	4	5	Almost Always
(2) Explains why the change is necessary.						
Almost Never	1	2	3	4	5	Almost Always
(3) Discusses how the change will affect the employee.						
Almost Never	1	2	3	4	5	Almost Always
(4) Listens to the employee's concerns.						
Almost Never	1	2	3	4	5	Almost Always
(5) Asks the employee for help in making the change work.						
Almost Never	1	2	3	4	5	Almost Always
(6) If necessary, specifies the date for a follow-up meeting to respond to the employee's concerns.						
Almost Never	1	2	3	4	5	Almost Always
		Total = ________				

Below Adequate	Adequate	Full	Excellent	Superior
6–10	11–15	16–20	21–25	26–30

Scores are set by management.

SOURCE: G. Latham and K. Wexley, *Increasing Productivity through Performance Appraisal*, p. 56. © 1994, 1981 Addison-Wesley Publishing Co., Inc. Reprinted by permission of Addison-Wesley Longman Publishing Company, Inc.

ways. First, rather than discarding a large number of the behaviors that exemplify effective or ineffective performance, a BOS uses many of them to more specifically define all the behaviors that are necessary for effective performance (or that would be considered ineffective performance). Instead of using, say, 4 behaviors to define 4 levels of performance on a particular dimension, a BOS may use 15 behaviors. An example of a BOS is presented in Table 8.7.

A second difference is that rather than assessing which behavior best reflects an individual's performance, a BOS requires managers to rate the frequency with which the employee has exhibited each behavior during the rating period. These ratings are then averaged to compute an overall performance rating.

The major drawback of a BOS is that it may require more information than most managers can process or remember. A BOS can have 80 or more behaviors, and the manager must remember how frequently an employee exhibited each of these behaviors over a 6- or 12-month rating period. This is taxing enough for one employee, but managers often must rate 10 or more employees.

A direct comparison of BOS, BARS, and graphic rating scales found that both managers and employees prefer BOS for differentiating good from poor performers, maintaining objectivity, providing feedback, suggesting training needs, and being easy to use among managers and subordinates.[20]

Organizational Behavior Modification

Organizational behavior modification (OBM) entails managing the behavior of employees through a formal system of behavioral feedback and reinforcement. This system builds on the behaviorist view of motivation, which holds that individuals' future behavior is determined by past behaviors that have been positively reinforced. The

FIGURE 8.4
Increases in Record Keeping as a Result of OBM

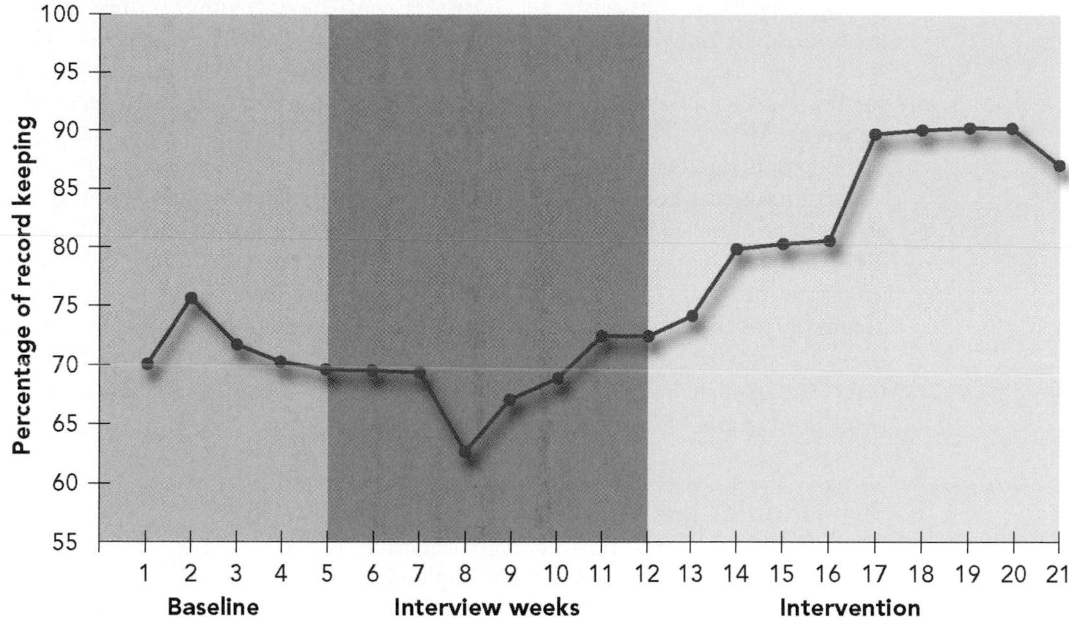

SOURCE: Based on K.L. Langeland, C.M. Johnson, and T.C. Mawhinney, "Improving Staff Performance in a Community Mental Health Setting: Job Analysis, Training, Goal Setting, Feedback, and Year of Data," *Journal of Organizational Behavior Management* 18 (1998), pp. 211–43.

techniques vary, but most have four components. First, they define a set of key behaviors necessary for job performance. Second, they use a measurement system to assess whether these behaviors are exhibited. Third, the manager or consultant informs employees of those behaviors, perhaps even setting goals for how often the employees should exhibit those behaviors. Finally, feedback and reinforcement are provided to employees.[21]

OBM techniques have been used in a variety of settings. For example, OBM was used to increase the rates and timeliness of critical job behaviors by showing the connection between job behaviors and the accomplishments of a community mental health agency.[22] Job behaviors were identified that related to administration, record keeping, and service provided to clients. Feedback and reinforcement improved staff performance. Figure 8.4 shows increases in staff performance in record keeping following the feedback and reinforcement intervention. "Baseline" refers to measures of record keeping prior to the intervention. "Interview" refers to record keeping when interviews were being conducted with staff to better explain their jobs. Similar results have been observed with the frequency of safety behaviors in a processing plant.[23]

Assessment Centers

Although assessment centers are usually used for selection and promotion decisions, they have also been used as a way of measuring managerial performance.[24] At an **assessment center,** individuals usually perform a number of simulated tasks, such as leaderless group discussions, in-basket management, and role playing. Assessors

Assessment centers
A process in which multiple raters evaluate employees' performance on a number or exercises.

observe the individuals' behavior and evaluate their skill or potential as managers. We discuss assessment centers more in Chapter 9.

The advantage of assessment centers is that they provide a somewhat objective measure of an individual's performance at managerial tasks. In addition, they allow specific performance feedback, and individualized developmental plans can be designed. For example, ARCO Oil & Gas Corporation sends its managers through assessment centers to identify their individual strengths and weaknesses and to create developmental action plans for each manager.

An interesting public sector application of assessment centers is in the state government of North Carolina. Managers there can be assessed to become "certified middle managers." This process includes an assessment center at the beginning of the certification program, from which an individualized developmental action plan is created. The developmental plan, implemented over approximately two years, consists of training and on-the-job developmental experiences. At the end of the two years, the manager attends the certification assessment center. Those who successfully meet the criteria set forth then become certified.

Evaluation of the Behavioral Approach

The behavioral approach can be very effective. It can link the company's strategy to the specific behavior necessary for implementing that strategy. It provides specific guidance and feedback for employees about the performance expected of them. Most of the techniques rely on in-depth job analysis, so the behaviors that are identified and measured are valid. Because those who will use the system develop the measures, the acceptability is also often high. Finally, with a substantial investment in training raters, the techniques are reasonably reliable.

The major weaknesses have to do with the organizational context of the system. Although the behavioral approach can be closely tied to a company's strategy, the behaviors and measures must be constantly monitored and revised to ensure that they are still linked to the strategic focus. This approach also assumes that there is "one best way" to do the job and that the behaviors that constitute this best way can be identified. One study found that managers seek to control behaviors when they perceive a clear relationship between behaviors and results. When this link is not clear, they tend to rely on managing results.[25] The behavioral approach might be best suited to less complex jobs (where the best way to achieve results is somewhat clear) and least suited to complex jobs (where there are multiple ways, or behaviors, to achieve success).

The Results Approach

The results approach focuses on managing the objective, measurable results of a job or work group. This approach assumes that subjectivity can be eliminated from the measurement process and that results are the closest indicator of one's contribution to organizational effectiveness.[26] We will examine two performance management systems that use results: management by objectives and the productivity measurement and evaluation system.

Management by Objectives

Management by objectives (MBO) is popular in both private and public organizations.[27] The original concept came from the accounting firm of Booz, Allen, and Hamilton and was called a "manager's letter." The process consisted of having all the sub-

TABLE 8.8
An Example of a Management by Objectives (MBO) Measure of Job Performance

KEY RESULT AREA	OBJECTIVE	% COMPLETE	ACTUAL PERFORMANCE
Loan portfolio management	Increase portfolio value by 10% over the next 12 months	90	Increased portfolio value by 9% over the past 12 months
Sales	Generate fee income of $30,000 over the next 12 months	150	Generated fee income of $45,000 over the past 12 months

ordinate managers write a letter to their superiors, detailing what their performance goals were for the coming year and how they planned to achieve them. Harold Smiddy applied and expanded this idea at General Electric in the 1950s, and Douglas McGregor has since developed it into a philosophy of management.[28]

In an MBO system, the top management team first defines the company's strategic goals for the coming year. These goals are passed on to the next layer of management, and these managers define the goals they must achieve for the company to reach its goals. This goal-setting process cascades down the organization so that all managers set goals that help the company achieve its goals.[29] These goals are used as the standards by which an individual's performance is evaluated.[30]

MBO systems have three common components.[31] They require specific, difficult, objective goals. (An example of MBO-based goals used in a financial service firm is presented in Table 8.8.) The goals are not usually set unilaterally by management but with the managers' and subordinates' participation. And the manager gives objective feedback throughout the rating period to monitor progress toward the goals.

Research on MBO has revealed two important findings regarding its effectiveness.[32] Of 70 studies examined, 68 showed productivity gains, while only 2 showed productivity losses, suggesting that MBO usually increases productivity. Also, productivity gains tend to be highest when there is substantial commitment to the MBO program from top management: an average increase of 56 percent when commitment was high, 33 percent when commitment was moderate, and 6 percent when commitment was low.

Clearly, MBO can have a very positive effect on an organization's performance. Considering the process through which goals are set (involvement of staff in setting objectives), it is also likely that MBO systems effectively link individual employee performance with the firm's strategic goals.

Finding and Keeping the Best Employees

For example, Pier 1 Imports was able to give store managers and salespeople access to real-time sales totals and analyses, telling them exactly how they were doing compared with, say, the previous day or month. Instead of creating a sweatshop atmosphere, as some critics worried, employees took the figures as a challenge. "The more information you give the associates, the more ownership they feel in the store's performance," says Dave Self, a regional manager for 33 Pier 1 stores.

Pier 1 employees agree. "It adds to the excitement," claims Alicia Winchell, an assistant manager. During the day, clerks at the store rotate their use of a backroom computer that gives them up-to-the-minute sales data. They learn not only how many items were sold and at what price but also how many people entered the store and the percentage of those who bought something. They know how many items are new and how many were imported from overseas. These figures help managers and sales staff create better value for customers, paying close attention to everyone who walks in the door. Paula Hankins, a store manager, spent a half hour one day helping an interior designer select some small decorations. The designer hadn't planned to spend $250 that day but said that Hankins "did a great job pointing out what I wanted."

Pier 1 management makes an important distinction about the data: they are an informational tool, not an instrument of discipline. If a store fails to meet a certain short-term goal, "It's not like they're blaming us for it," says employee Kim Smith. Results provide valuable insight into the whole performance management picture.[33]

Productivity Measurement and Evaluation System (ProMES)

The main goal of ProMES is to motivate employees to higher levels of productivity.[34] It is a means of measuring and feeding back productivity information to personnel.

ProMES consists of four steps. First, people in an organization identify the products, or the set of activities or objectives, the organization expects to accomplish. The organization's productivity depends on how well it produces these products. At a repair shop, for example, a product might be something like "quality of repair." Second, the staff defines indicators of the products. Indicators are measures of how well the products are being generated by the organization. Quality of repair could be indicated by (1) return rate (percentage of items returned that did not function immediately after repair) and (2) percentage of quality-control inspections passed. Third, the staff establishes the contingencies between the amount of the indicators and the level of evaluation associated with that amount. Fourth, a feedback system is developed that provides employees and work groups with information about their specific level of performance on each of the indicators. An overall productivity score can be computed by summing the effectiveness scores across the various indicators.

Because this technique is somewhat new, it has been applied in only a few situations. However, research thus far strongly suggests it is effective in increasing productivity. (Figure 8.5 illustrates the productivity gains in the repair shop described previously.) The research also suggests the system is an effective feedback mechanism. However, users found it time-consuming to develop the initial system. Future research on ProMES needs to be conducted before we draw any firm conclusions, but the existing research indicates that this may be a useful performance management tool.

Evaluation of the Results Approach

The results approach minimizes subjectivity, relying on objective, quantifiable indicators of performance. Thus, it is usually highly acceptable to both managers and employees. Another advantage is that it links an individual's results with the organization's strategies and goals.

However, objective measurements can be both contaminated and deficient—contaminated because they are affected by things that are not under the employee's control, such as economic recessions, and deficient because not all the important aspects of job performance are amenable to objective measurement. Another disadvantage is that individuals may focus only on aspects of their performance that are measured, neglecting those that are not. For example, if the large majority of employees' goals relate to productivity, it is unlikely they will be concerned with customer service. One study

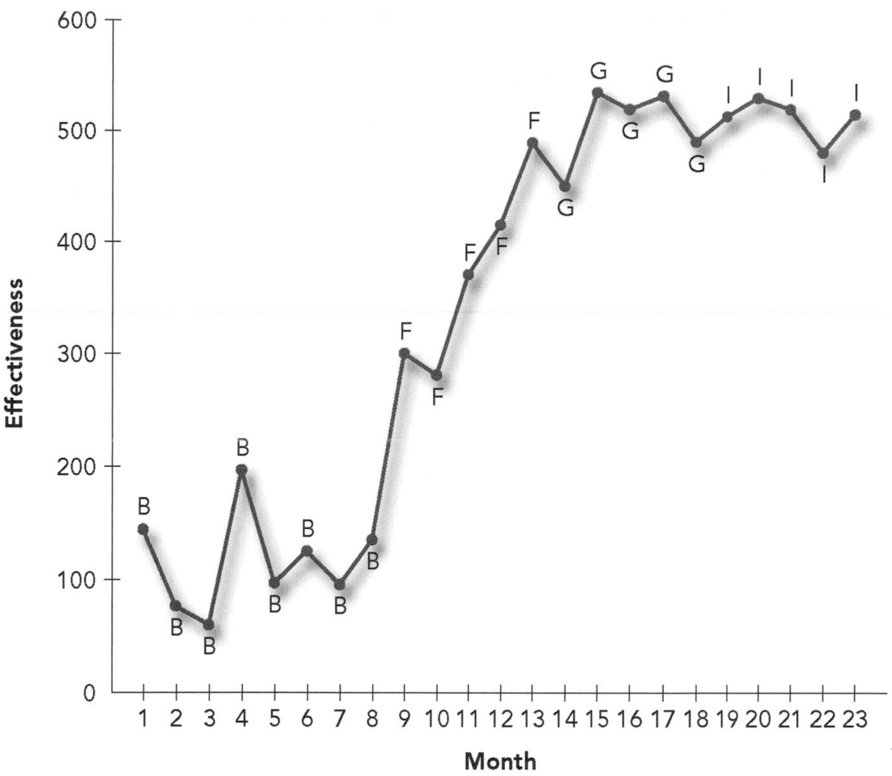

FIGURE 8.5
Increases in Productivity for a Repair Shop Using ProMES Measures

SOURCE: R. Pritchard, S. Jones, P. Roth, K. Stuebing, and S. Ekeberg, "The Evaluation of an Integrated Approach to Measuring Organizational Productivity," *Personnel Psychology* 42 (1989), pp. 69–115. Used by permission.

found that objective performance goals led to higher performance but that they also led to less helping of coworkers.[35] A final disadvantage is that, though results measures provide objective feedback, the feedback may not help employees learn how they need to change their behavior to increase their performance. If baseball players are in a hitting slump, simply telling them that their batting average is .190 may not motivate them to raise it. Feedback focusing on the exact behavior that needs to be changed (like taking one's eye off the ball or dropping one's shoulder) would be more helpful.[36]

The Quality Approach

Thus far we have examined the traditional approaches to measuring and evaluating employee performance. Two fundamental characteristics of the quality approach are a customer orientation and a prevention approach to errors. Improving customer satisfaction is the primary goal of the quality approach. Customers can be internal or external to the organization. A performance management system designed with a strong quality orientation can be expected to

- Emphasize an assessment of both person and system factors in the measurement system.
- Emphasize that managers and employees work together to solve performance problems.

- Involve both internal and external customers in setting standards and measuring performance.
- Use multiple sources to evaluate person and system factors.[37]

Based on this chapter's earlier discussion of the characteristics of an effective performance management system, it should be apparent to you that these characteristics are not just unique to the quality approach but are characteristics of an effective appraisal system!

Advocates of the quality approach believe that most U.S. companies' performance management systems are incompatible with the quality philosophy for a number of reasons:

1. Most existing systems measure performance in terms of quantity, not quality.
2. Employees are held accountable for good or bad results to which they contribute but do not completely control.
3. Companies do not share the financial rewards of successes with employees according to how much they have contributed to them.
4. Rewards are not connected to business results.[38]

Sales, profit margins, and behavioral ratings are often collected by managers to evaluate employees' performance. These are person-based outcomes. An assumption of using these types of outcomes is that the employee completely controls them. However, according to the quality approach, these types of outcomes should not be used to evaluate employees' performance because they do not have complete control over them (that is, they are contaminated). For example, for salespersons, performance evaluations (and salary increases) are often based on attainment of a sales quota. It is assumed that salespersons' abilities and motivation are directly responsible for their performance. However, quality approach advocates argue that better determinants of whether a salesperson reaches the quota are "systems factors" (such as competitors' product price changes) and economic conditions (which are not under the salesperson's control).[39] Holding employees accountable for outcomes affected by systems factors is believed to result in dysfunctional behavior, such as falsifying sales reports, budgets, expense accounts, and other performance measures, as well as lowering employees' motivation for continuous improvement.

Quality advocates suggest that the major focus of performance evaluations should be to provide employees with feedback about areas in which they can improve. Two types of feedback are necessary: (1) subjective feedback from managers, peers, and customers about the personal qualities of the employee and (2) objective feedback based on the work process itself using statistical quality control methods.

Performance feedback from managers, peers, and customers should be based on such dimensions as cooperation, attitude, initiative, and communication skills. Performance evaluation should include a discussion of the employee's career plans. The quality approach also strongly emphasizes that performance appraisal systems should avoid providing overall evaluations of employees (like ratings such as excellent, good, poor). Categorizing employees is believed to encourage them to behave in ways that are expected based on their ratings. For example, "average" performers may not be motivated to improve their performance but rather may continue to perform at the expected level. Also, because employees do not have control over the quality of the system in which they work, employee performance evaluations should not be linked to compensation. Compensation rates should be based on prevailing market rates of pay, seniority, and business results, which are distributed equitably to all employees.

Statistical process control techniques are very important in the quality approach.

These techniques provide employees with an objective tool to identify causes of problems and potential solutions. These techniques include process-flow analysis, cause-and-effect diagrams, Pareto charts, control charts, histograms, and scattergrams.

Process-flow analysis identifies each action and decision necessary to complete work, such as waiting on a customer or assembling a television set. Process-flow analysis is useful for identifying redundancy in processes that increase manufacturing or service time. For example, one business unit at Owens-Corning was able to confirm that customer orders were error-free only about 25 percent of the time (an unacceptable level of service). To improve the service level, the unit mapped out the process to identify bottlenecks and problem areas. As a result of this mapping, one simple change (installing an 800 number for the fax machine) increased overall accuracy of orders as well as transaction speed.[40]

In *cause-and-effect diagrams*, events or causes that result in undesirable outcomes are identified. Employees try to identify all possible causes of a problem. The feasibility of the causes is not evaluated, and as a result, cause-and-effect diagrams produce a large list of possible causes.

A *Pareto chart* highlights the most important cause of a problem. In a Pareto chart, causes are listed in decreasing order of importance, where *importance* is usually defined as the frequency with which that cause resulted in a problem. The assumption of Pareto analysis is that the majority of problems are the result of a small number of causes. Figure 8.6 shows a Pareto chart listing the reasons managers give for not selecting current employees for a job vacancy.

Control charts involve collecting data at multiple points in time. By collecting data at different times, employees can identify what factors contribute to an outcome and when they tend to occur. Figure 8.7 shows the percentage of employees hired internally for a company for each quarter between 1993 and 1995. Internal hiring increased dramatically during the third quarter of 1994. The use of control charts helps employees understand the number of internal candidates who can be expected to be

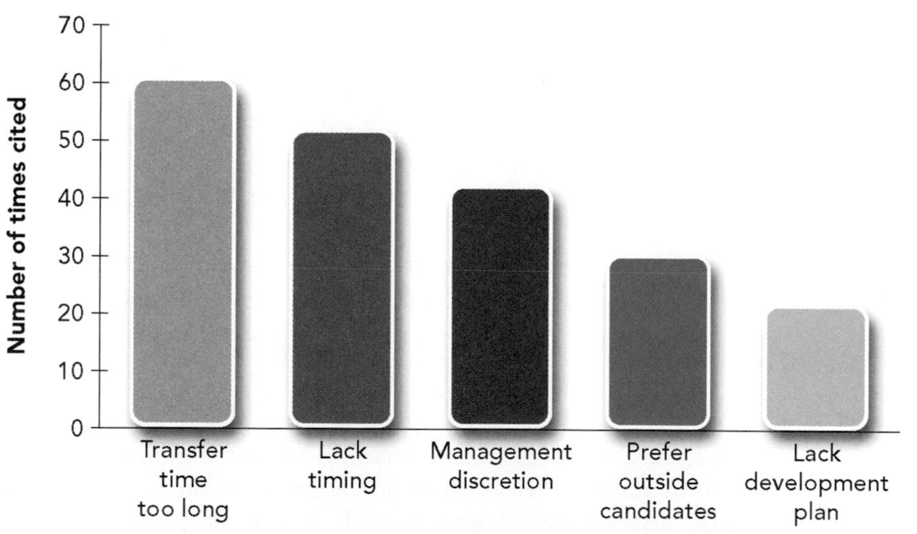

FIGURE 8.6
Pareto Chart

SOURCE: "Seven Basic Quality Tools" by Carla Carter, *HR Magazine*, January 1992, p. 83. Reprinted with permission of Society for Human Resource Management via Copyright Clearance Center.

FIGURE 8.7
Control Chart

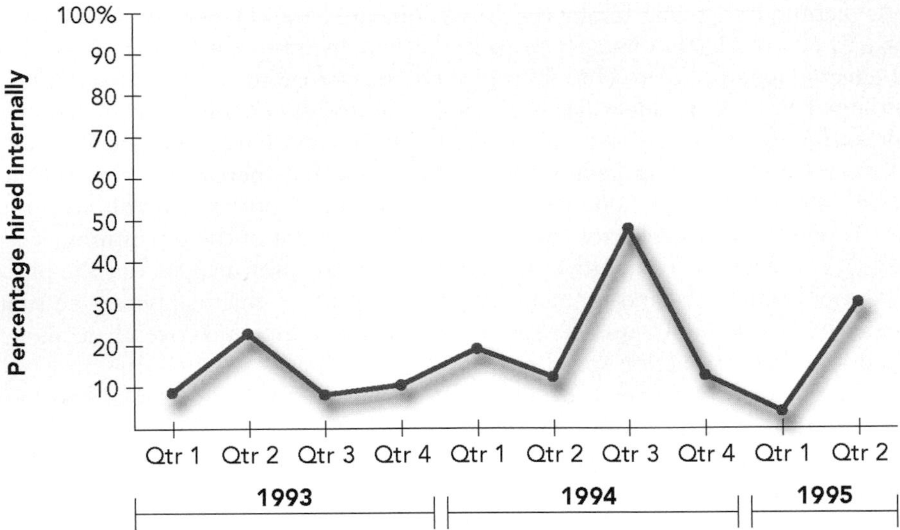

SOURCE: "Seven Basic Quality Tools" by Carla Carter, *HR Magazine*, January 1992, p. 82. Reprinted with permission of Society for Human Resource Management via Copyright Clearance Center.

FIGURE 8.8
Histogram

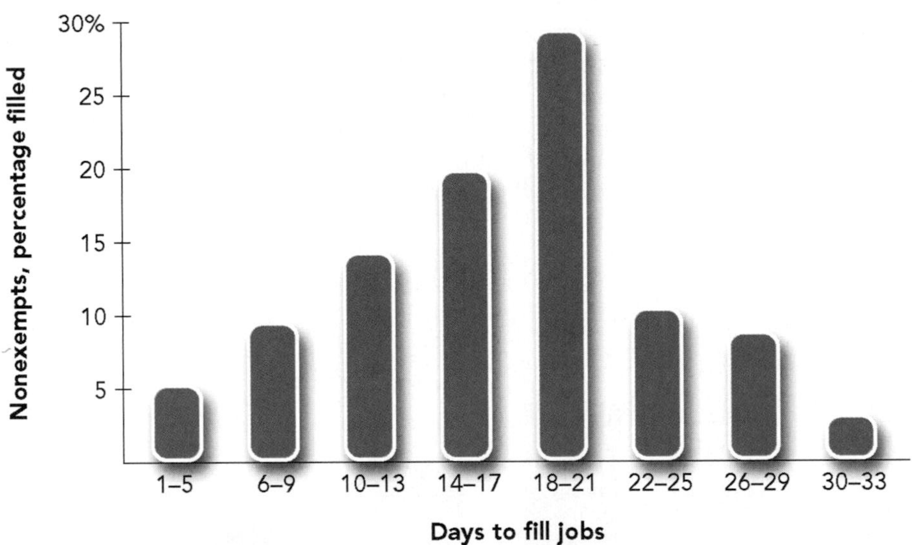

SOURCE: "Seven Basic Quality Tools" by Carla Carter, *HR Magazine*, January 1992, p. 83. Reprinted with permission of Society for Human Resource Management via Copyright Clearance Center.

hired each year. Also, the control chart shows that the amount of internal hiring conducted during the third quarter of 1994 was much larger than normal.

Histograms display distributions of large sets of data. Data are grouped into a smaller number of categories or classes. Histograms are useful for understanding the amount of variance between an outcome and the expected value or average outcome. Figure 8.8 is a histogram showing the number of days it took a company to fill nonexempt job vacancies. The histogram shows that most nonexempt jobs took from 17 to 21 days to fill, and the amount of time to fill nonexempt jobs ranged from 1 to 33 days. If an HR manager relied simply on data from personnel files on the number of days it took to fill nonexempt positions, it would be extremely difficult to understand the variation and average tendency in the amount of time to fill the positions.

Scattergrams show the relationship between two variables, events, or different pieces of data. Scattergrams help employees determine whether the relationship between two variables or events is positive, negative, or zero.

Evaluation of the Quality Approach

The quality approach relies primarily on a combination of the attribute and results approaches to performance measurement. However, traditional performance appraisal systems focus more on individual employee performance, while the quality approach adopts a systems-oriented focus.[41] Many companies may be unwilling to completely abandon their traditional performance management system because it serves as the basis for personnel selection validation, identification of training needs, or compensation decisions. Also, the quality approach advocates evaluation of personal traits (such as cooperation), which are difficult to relate to job performance unless the company has been structured into work teams.

In summary, organizations can take five approaches to measuring performance: comparative, attribute, behavioral, results, and quality. Table 8.9 summarizes the various approaches to measuring performance based on the criteria we set forth earlier and illustrates that each approach has strengths and weaknesses. As the quality approach illustrates, the most effective way of measuring performance is to rely on a combination of two or more alternatives. For example, performance management systems in many companies evaluate the extent to which managers reach specific performance goals or results as well as evaluate their behavior. Figure 8.9 on page 355 shows an example of a performance management system that evaluates behavior and results. The results (project development) are linked to the goals of the business. The performance standards include behaviors that the employee can demonstrate to reach the results. The system provides for feedback to the employee and holds both the employee and manager accountable for changing behavior.

Choosing a Source for Performance Information

Whatever approach to performance management is used, it is necessary to decide whom to use as the source of the performance measures. Each source has specific strengths and weaknesses. We discuss five primary sources: managers, peers, subordinates, self, and customers.

Managers

Managers are the most frequently used source of performance information. It is usually safe to assume that supervisors have extensive knowledge of the job requirements and that they have had adequate opportunity to observe their employees—in other words, that they have the ability to rate their employees. In addition, because

TABLE 8.9

Evaluation of Approaches to Performance Measurement

APPROACH	CRITERIA				
	STRATEGIC CONGRUENCE	VALIDITY	RELIABILITY	ACCEPTABILITY	SPECIFICITY
Comparative	Poor, unless manager takes time to make link	Can be high if ratings are done carefully	Depends on rater, but usually no measure of agreement used	Moderate; easy to develop and use but resistant to normative standard	Very low
Attribute	Usually low; requires manager to make link	Usually low; can be fine if developed carefully	Usually low; can be improved by specific definitions of attributes	High; easy to develop and use	Very low
Behavioral	Can be quite high	Usually high; minimizes contamination and deficiency	Usually high	Moderate; difficult to develop, but accepted well for use	Very high
Results	Very high	Usually high; can be both contaminated and deficient	High; main problem can be test–retest—depends on timing of measure	High; usually developed with input from those to be evaluated	High regarding results, but low regarding behaviors necessary to achieve them
Quality	Very high	High, but can be both contaminated and deficient	High	High; usually developed with input from those to be evaluated	High regarding results, but low regarding behaviors necessary to achieve them

supervisors have something to gain from the employees' high performance and something to lose from low performance, they are motivated to make accurate ratings.[42] Finally, feedback from supervisors is strongly related to performance and to employee perceptions of the accuracy of the appraisal if managers attempt to observe employee behavior or discuss performance issues in the feedback session.[43]

Problems with using supervisors as the source of performance information can occur in particular situations. In some jobs, for example, the supervisor does not have an adequate opportunity to observe the employee performing his job duties. For example, in outside sales jobs, the supervisor does not have the opportunity to see the salesperson at work most of the time. This usually requires that the manager occasionally spend a day accompanying the salesperson on sales calls. However, on those occasions the employee will be on best behavior, so there is no assurance that performance that day accurately reflects performance when the manager is not around.

FIGURE 8.9

Example of a Performance Management System That Includes Behavior and Results

Accountabilities and Key Results	Performance Standards	Interim Feedback	Actual Results	Performance Rating	Areas for Development	Action
Key result areas that the employee will accomplish during the review period. Should align with company values, business goals, and job description.	How the key result area will be measured (quality, cost, quantity). Focus on work methods and accomplishments.	Employee and manager discuss performance on an ongoing basis.	Review actual performance for each key result.	Evaluate performance on each key result. 1 = Outstanding 2 = Highly effective 3 = Acceptable 4 = Unsatisfactory	Specific knowledge, skills, and behaviors to be developed that will help employee achieve key results.	What employee and manager will do to address development needs.
Project Development Manage the development of project scope, cost estimate studies, and schedules for approval.	Develop preliminary project material for approval within four weeks after receiving project scope. Eighty percent of new projects receive approval. Initial cost estimates are within 5% of final estimates.	Preliminary project materials are developed on time.	By end of year, approvals were at 75%, 5% less than standard.	3	Increase knowledge of project management software.	Read articles, research, and meet with software vendors.

Also, some supervisors may be so biased against a particular employee that to use the supervisor as the sole source of information would result in less-than-accurate measures for that individual. Favoritism is a fact of organizational life, but it is one that must be minimized as much as possible in performance management.[44] Thus, the performance evaluation system should seek to minimize the opportunities for favoritism to affect ratings. One way to do this is not to rely on only a supervisor's evaluation of an employee's performance.

While managers are the most frequently used source of performance information, it is ironic that upper level managers or chief executive officers, whose decisions affect all of the company's shareholders, rarely receive performance evaluation. This situation is beginning to change. For example, Thomas Loarie (chairman and CEO of KeraVision Inc., a vision correction company in California) is evaluated by the company's six directors.[45] The six nonmanagement directors evaluate Loarie each August during a retreat that lasts two or three days. The process is separate from that used to set his annual compensation. Directors use a 17-item questionnaire that focuses on four key areas: company performance, leadership, team building and management succession, and leadership of external stakeholders such as customers. The board rated him lower than he expected on involving its members. As a result of the appraisal, he has taken steps to get the board involved in setting the company's objectives. He has encouraged more interactions between senior managers and board members.

Although CEOs view appraisals such as Loarie's with anxiety, these appraisals are helpful in building an understanding with the board of directors. Such feedback is also useful for changing the CEO's strategy and policies, likely improving the bottom line. This translates into benefits for employees and shareholders alike!

Peers

Another source of performance information is the employee's coworkers. Peers are an excellent source of information in a job such as law enforcement, where the supervisor does not always observe the employee. Peers have expert knowledge of job requirements, and they often have the most opportunity to observe the employee in day-to-day activities. Peers also bring a different perspective to the evaluation process, which can be valuable in gaining an overall picture of the individual's performance. In fact, peers have been found to provide extremely valid assessments of performance in several different settings.[46]

One disadvantage of using peer ratings is the potential for friendship to bias ratings.[47] Little empirical evidence suggests that this is often a problem, however. Another disadvantage is that when the evaluations are made for administrative decisions, peers often find the situation of being both rater and ratee uncomfortable. When these ratings are used only for developmental purposes, however, peers react favorably.[48]

Subordinates

Subordinates are an especially valuable source of performance information when managers are evaluated. Subordinates often have the best opportunity to evaluate how well a manager treats employees. One recent study found that managers viewed receiving upward feedback more positively when receiving feedback from subordinates who were identified, but subordinates preferred to provide anonymous feedback. When subordinates were identified, they inflated their ratings of the manager.[49]

One problem with subordinate evaluations is that they give subordinates power over their managers, thus putting the manager in a difficult situation.[50] This can lead to managers' emphasizing employee satisfaction over productivity. However, this happens only when administrative decisions are made from these evaluations. As with peer evaluations, it is a good idea to use subordinate evaluations only for developmental purposes. To assure subordinates that they need not fear retribution from their managers, it is necessary to use anonymous evaluations and at least three subordinates for each manager.

Self

Although self-ratings are not often used as the sole source of performance information, they can still be valuable.[51] Obviously, individuals have extensive opportunities to observe their own behavior, and they usually have access to information regarding their results on the job.

One problem with self-ratings, however, is a tendency toward inflated assessments. This stems from two sources. If the ratings are going to be used for administrative decisions (like pay raises), it is in the employees' interests to inflate their ratings. And there is ample evidence in the social psychology literature that individuals attribute their poor performance to external causes, such as a coworker who they think has not provided them with timely information. Although self-ratings are less inflated when supervisors provide frequent performance feedback, it is not advisable to use them for administrative purposes.[52] The best use of self-ratings is as a prelude to the performance feedback session to get employees thinking about their performance and to focus discussion on areas of disagreement.

Customers

Service industries are expected to account for virtually all job growth between 1996 and 2006.[53] As a result, we would expect many companies to move toward involving customers in their evaluation systems. One writer has defined *services* this way: "Services is something which can be bought and sold but which you cannot drop on your foot."[54] Because of the unique nature of services—the product is often produced and consumed on the spot—supervisors, peers, and subordinates often do not have the opportunity to observe employee behavior. Instead, the customer is often the only person present to observe the employee's performance and thus is the best source of performance information.

Many companies in service industries have moved toward customer evaluations of employee performance. Marriott Corporation provides a customer satisfaction card in every room and mails surveys to a random sample of customers after their stay in a Marriott hotel. Whirlpool's Consumer Services Division conducts both mail and telephone surveys of customers after factory service technicians have serviced their appliances. These surveys allow the company to evaluate an individual technician's customer-service behaviors while in the customer's home.

Using customer evaluations of employee performance is appropriate in two situations. [55] The first is when an employee's job requires direct service to the customer or linking the customer to other services within the company. Second, customer evaluations are appropriate when the company is interested in gathering information to determine what products and services the customer wants. That is, customer evaluations serve a strategic goal by integrating marketing strategies with human resource activities and policies. Customer evaluations collected for this purpose are useful for both evaluating the employee and helping to determine whether changes in other HRM activities (such as training or the compensation system) are needed to improve customer service.

The weakness of customer surveys is their expense. Printing, postage, telephone, and labor can add up to hundreds of dollars for the evaluation of one individual. Thus many companies conduct such evaluations only once a year for a short time.

In conclusion, the best source of performance information often depends on the particular job. One should choose the source or sources that provide the best opportunity to observe employee behavior and results. The "Competing by Meeting Stakeholders' Needs" box shows how Synergy, Inc., includes multiple evaluations in the performance measurement system. Table 8.10 summarizes this information for most jobs. Often, eliciting performance information from a variety of sources results in a performance management process that is accurate and effective. In fact, one recent popular trend in organizations is called **360-degree appraisals.**[56] This technique consists of having multiple raters (boss, peers, subordinates, customers) provide input into a manager's evaluation. The major advantage of the technique is that it provides a means for minimizing bias in an otherwise subjective evaluation technique. It has been used primarily for strategic and developmental purposes and is discussed in greater detail in Chapter 9.[57]

360-degree appraisal
A performance appraisal process for managers that includes evaluations from a wide range of persons who interact with the manager. The process includes self-evaluations as well as evaluations from the manager's boss, subordinates, peers, and customers.

Rater Errors in Performance Measurement

Research consistently reveals that humans have tremendous limitations in processing information. Because we are so limited, we often use "heuristics," or simplifying mechanisms, to make judgments, whether about investments or about people.[58] These heuristics, which appear often in subjective measures of performance, can lead to rater errors. Performance evaluations may also be purposefully distorted. We discuss rater errors and appraisal politics next.

TABLE 8.10
Frequency of Observation for Various Sources of Performance Information

	SOURCE				
	SUPERVISOR	PEERS	SUBORDINATES	SELF	CUSTOMERS
Task					
Behaviors	Occasional	Frequent	Rare	Always	Frequent
Results	Frequent	Frequent	Occasional	Frequent	Frequent
Interpersonal					
Behaviors	Occasional	Frequent	Frequent	Always	Frequent
Results	Occasional	Frequent	Frequent	Frequent	Frequent

SOURCE: Adapted from K. Murphy and J. Cleveland, *Performance Appraisal: An Organizational Perspective* (Boston: Allyn & Bacon, 1991).

COMPETING BY MEETING STAKEHOLDERS' NEEDS

Timely Feedback Leads to an Evaluation Program That Gets High Marks

Synergy, Inc., headquartered in a Philadelphia suburb, provides incentive compensation plan management software for large companies. An important part of Synergy's culture is open communications and continuous feedback—not just between employee and manager but also between client and employee and between employees.

When the company consisted of only seven employees, Synergy had a very informal appraisal process. The seven employees would sit around a table and discuss performance issues. The informal appraisal process is no longer realistic because Synergy has grown to 260 employees. To maintain positive teamwork, Synergy has developed a unique employee evaluation program. One of the most important features is that Synergy employees are evaluated every quarter instead of the typical once-a-year evaluation. Management believes that to change behavior more frequent feedback is necessary.

For their evaluations, employees are given a numerical score from 1 to 5 in addition to written comments. To motivate employees to improve their numbers, the evaluations are linked to compensation. The evaluation determines up to 40 percent of the quarterly bonus, which can be from 5 to 100 percent of an employee's base pay. Another important feature of the evaluation system is that employees can receive feedback from their managers, colleagues, and employees and managers in other departments. All feedback is anonymous except that provided by an employee's manager. Staff members are even encouraged to give feedback to managers and executives. Customers also contribute feedback to Synergy teams they work with. The feedback from multiple sources shows employees that others besides their managers see their performance similarly. The feedback also builds managers' confidence in their own evaluations when it matches the evaluations of others. If other evaluators disagree or identify possible barriers that inhibited performance, a manager may reconsider an evaluation.

One challenge of the evaluation program is that it requires a major commitment from both employees and managers to make it work. Employees can write comments for as many as 20 other employees in addition to their own self-evaluations and setting personal performance goals. For managers the process may take an entire week each quarter. But despite this large effort, the system has had some positive payoffs. Because the system gives managers plenty of opportunities to help employees improve, Synergy has terminated only 10 employees in the past eight years. Employees also appreciate the program because it helps them focus on what is important for themselves and for Synergy's success.

SOURCE: P. Kiger, "Frequent Employee Feedback Is Worth the Cost and Time," *Workforce*, March 2001, pp. 62–65.

Similar to Me

"Similar to me" is the error we make when we judge those who are similar to us more highly than those who are not. Research has demonstrated that this effect is strong, and when similarity is based on demographic characteristics such as race or sex, it can result in discriminatory decisions.[59] Most of us tend to think of ourselves as effective, and so if others are like us—in race, gender, background, attitudes, or beliefs—we assume that they too are effective.

Contrast

Contrast error occurs when we compare individuals with one another instead of against an objective standard. Consider a completely competent performer who works with a number of peers who are outstanding. If the competent employee receives lower-than-deserved ratings because of the outstanding colleagues, that is contrast error.

Distributional Errors

Distributional errors are the result of a rater's tendency to use only one part of the rating scale. *Leniency* occurs when a rater assigns high (lenient) ratings to all employees. *Strictness* occurs when a manager gives low ratings to all employees—that is, holds all employees to unreasonably high standards. *Central tendency* reflects that a manager rates all employees in the middle of the scale. These errors pose two problems. First, they make it difficult to distinguish among employees rated by the same person. Second, they create problems in comparing the performance of individuals rated by different raters. If one rater is lenient and the other is strict, employees of the strict rater will receive significantly fewer rewards than those rated by the lenient rater.

Halo and Horns

These errors refer to a failure to distinguish among different aspects of performance. *Halo error* occurs when one positive performance aspect causes the rater to rate all other aspects of performance positively—for example, professors who are rated as outstanding researchers because they are known to be outstanding teachers. *Horns error* works in the opposite direction: one negative aspect results in the rater assigning low ratings to all the other aspects.

Halo and horns errors preclude making the necessary distinctions between strong and weak performance. Halo error leads to employees believing that no aspects of their performance need improvement. Horns error makes employees frustrated and defensive.

Reducing Rater Errors

Two approaches to reducing rating errors have been offered.[60] *Rater error training* attempts to make managers aware of rating errors and helps them develop strategies for minimizing those errors.[61] These programs consist of having the participants view videotaped vignettes designed to elicit rating errors such as "contrast." They then make their ratings and discuss how the error influenced the rating. Finally, they get tips to avoid committing those errors. This approach has been shown to be effective for reducing errors, but there is evidence that reducing rating errors can also reduce accuracy.[62]

Rater accuracy training, also called *frame-of-reference training*, attempts to emphasize the multidimensional nature of performance and thoroughly familiarize raters with the actual content of various performance dimensions. This involves providing examples of performance for each dimension and then discussing the actual or "correct" level of performance that the example represents.[63] Accuracy training seems to increase accuracy, provided that in addition the raters are held accountable for ratings, job-related rating scales are used, and raters keep records of the behavior they observe.[64]

Appraisal Politics

Appraisal politics refer to evaluators purposefully distorting a rating to achieve personal or company goals. Research suggests that several factors promote appraisal politics. These factors are inherent in the appraisal system and the company culture. Appraisal politics are most likely to occur when raters are accountable to the employee being rated, there are competing rating goals, and a direct link exists between performance appraisal and highly desirable rewards. Also, appraisal politics are likely to occur if top executives tolerate distortion or are complacent toward it, and if distortion strategies are part of "company folklore" and are passed down from senior employees to new employees.

Appraisal politics
A situation in which evaluators purposefully distort ratings to achieve personal or company goals.

It is unlikely that appraisal politics can be completely eliminated. Unfortunately, there is little research on the best methods to eliminate appraisal politics. To minimize appraisal politics, managers should keep in mind the characteristics of a fair appraisal system shown in Table 8.3. In addition, managers should

- Train raters on the appropriate use of the process as discussed previously.
- Build top management support for the appraisal system and actively discourage distortion.
- Give raters some latitude to customize performance objectives and criteria for their ratees.
- Recognize employee accomplishments that are not self-promoted.
- Make sure constraints such as budget do not drive the process.
- Make sure appraisal processes are consistent across the company.
- Foster a climate of openness to encourage employees to be honest about weaknesses.[65]

Performance Feedback

Once the expected performance has been defined and employees' performances have been measured, it is necessary to feed that performance information back to the employees so they can correct any deficiencies. The performance feedback process is complex and provokes anxiety for both the manager and the employee. Table 8.11 provides examples of feedback that managers have given employees. You be the judge as to these statements' effectiveness in improving employees' performance!

Few of us feel comfortable sitting in judgment of others. The thought of confronting others with what we perceive to be their deficiencies causes most of us to shake in our shoes. If giving negative feedback is painful, receiving it can be excruciating—thus the importance of the performance feedback process.

The Manager's Role in an Effective Performance Feedback Process

If employees are not made aware of how their performance is not meeting expectations, their performance will almost certainly not improve. In fact, it may get worse. Effective managers provide specific performance feedback to employees in a way that elicits positive behavioral responses. To provide effective performance feedback managers should consider the following recommendations.

Feedback Should Be Given Frequently, Not Once a Year. There are two reasons for this. First, managers have a responsibility to correct performance deficiencies

TABLE 8.11
Examples of Performance Feedback

Since my last report; this employee has reached rock bottom and has started to dig.
His men would follow him anywhere, but only out of morbid curiosity.
I would not allow this employee to breed.
This associate is really not so much of a "has-been," but more of a "definitely won't-be."
Works well when under constant supervision and cornered like a rat in a trap.
When she opens her mouth, it seems that this is only to change whichever foot was previously in there.
He would be out of his depth in a parking-lot puddle.
This young lady has delusions of adequacy.
He sets low personal standards, then consistently fails to achieve them.
This employee should go far—and the sooner he starts, the better.
This employee is depriving a village somewhere of an idiot.

SOURCE: Y. Harari, *The Daily Dose* (**www.harari.org/index.html**), July 22, 1997. Reprinted with permission.

immediately on becoming aware of them. If performance is subpar in January, waiting until December to appraise the performance could mean an 11-month productivity loss. Second, a major determinant of how effectively a feedback session goes is the extent to which the subordinate is not surprised by the evaluation. An easy rule to follow is that employees should receive such frequent performance feedback that they already know almost exactly what their formal evaluation will be.

Create the Right Context for the Discussion. Managers should choose a neutral location for the feedback session. The manager's office may not be the best place for a constructive feedback session because the employee may associate the office with unpleasant conversations. Managers should describe the meeting as an opportunity to discuss the role of the employee, the role of the manager, and the relationship between them. Managers should also acknowledge that they would like the meeting to be an open dialogue.

Ask the Employee to Rate His or Her Performance before the Session. Having employees complete a self-assessment before the feedback session can be very productive. It requires employees to think about their performance over the past rating period, and it encourages them to think about their weaknesses. Although self-ratings used for administrative decisions are often inflated, there is evidence that they may actually be lower than supervisors' ratings when done for developmental purposes. Another reason a self-assessment can be productive is that it can make the session go more smoothly by focusing discussion on areas where disagreement exists, resulting in a more efficient session. Finally, employees who have thought about past performance are more able to participate fully in the feedback session.

Encourage the Subordinate to Participate in the Session. Managers can take one of three approaches in performance feedback sessions. In the "tell-and-sell" approach, managers tell the employees how they have rated them and then justify these ratings. In the "tell-and-listen" approach, managers tell employees how they have rated them and then let the employees explain their side of the story. In the "problem-solving" approach, managers and employees work together to solve performance problems in an atmosphere of respect and encouragement. In spite of the research demonstrating the superiority of the problem-solving approach, most managers still rely on the tell-and-sell approach.[66]

When employees participate in the feedback session, they are consistently satisfied with the process. (Recall our discussion of fairness earlier in this chapter.) Participation includes allowing employees to voice their opinions of the evaluation, as well as discuss performance goals.[67] One study found that, other than satisfaction with one's supervisor, participation was the single most important predictor of satisfaction with the feedback session.[68]

Recognize Effective Performance through Praise. One usually thinks of performance feedback sessions as focusing on the employee's performance problems. This should never be the case. The purpose of the session is to give accurate performance feedback, which entails recognizing effective performance as well as poor performance. Praising effective performance provides reinforcement for that behavior. It also adds credibility to the feedback by making it clear that the manager is not just identifying performance problems.

Focus on Solving Problems. A common mistake that managers make in providing performance feedback is to try to use the session as a chance to punish poorly performing employees by telling them how utterly lousy their performance is. This only reduces the employees' self-esteem and increases defensiveness, neither of which will improve performance.

To improve poor performance, a manager must attempt to solve the problems causing it. This entails working with the employee to determine the actual cause and then agreeing on how to solve it. For example, a salesperson's failure to meet a sales goal may be the result of lack of a proper sales pitch, lack of product knowledge, or stolen sales by another salesperson. Each of these causes requires a different solution. Without a problem-solving approach, however, the correct solution might never be identified.

Focus Feedback on Behavior or Results, Not on the Person. One of the most important things to do when giving negative feedback is to avoid questioning the employee's worth as a person. This is best accomplished by focusing the discussion on the employee's behaviors or results, not on the employee. Saying "You're screwing up! You're just not motivated!" will bring about more defensiveness and ill feelings than stating "You did not meet the deadline that you agreed to because you spent too much time on another project."

Minimize Criticism. Obviously, if an individual's performance is below standard, some criticism must take place. However, an effective manager should resist the temptation to reel off a litany of offenses. Having been confronted with the performance problem, an employee often agrees that a change is in order. However, if the manager continues to come up with more and more examples of low performance, the employee may get defensive.

Agree to Specific Goals and Set a Date to Review Progress. The importance of goal setting cannot be overemphasized. It is one of the most effective motivators of performance.[69] Research has demonstrated that it results in increased satisfaction, motivation to improve, and performance improvement.[70] Besides setting goals, the manager must also set a specific follow-up date to review the employee's performance toward the goal. This provides an added incentive for the employee to take the goal seriously and work toward achieving it.

What Managers Can Do to Manage the Performance of Marginal Employees

As we emphasized in the previous discussion, employees need performance feedback to improve their current job performance. As we will discuss in Chapter 9, "Employee Development," performance feedback is also needed for employees to develop their knowledge and skills for the future. In addition to understanding how to effectively give employees performance feedback, managers need to be aware of what types of actions are likely to improve and maintain that performance. For example, giving performance feedback to marginal employees may not be sufficient for improving their performance. **Marginal employees** are those employees who are performing at a bare minimum level due to a lack of ability and/or motivation to perform well.[71]

marginal employee
An employee performing at a barely acceptable level due to lack of ability and/or motivation to perform well. Performance is not due to poor work conditions.

Table 8.12 shows actions for the manager to take with four different types of employees. As the table highlights, managers need to take into account whether employees lack ability, motivation, or both in considering ways to improve performance. To determine an employee's level of ability, a manager should consider if he or she has the knowledge, skills, and abilities needed to perform effectively. Lack of ability may be an issue if an employee is new or the job has recently changed. To determine employees' level of motivation, managers need to consider if employees are doing a job they want to do and if they feel they are being appropriately paid or rewarded. A sudden negative change in an employee's performance may indicate personal problems.

TABLE 8.12
Ways to Manage Employees' Performance

		ABILITY	
		HIGH	**LOW**
Motivation	**High**	Solid performers • Reward good performance • Identify development opportunities • Provide honest, direct feedback	Misdirected effort • Coaching • Frequent performance feedback • Goal setting • Training or temporary assignment for skill development • Restructured job assignment
	Low	Underutilizers • Give honest, direct feedback • Provide counseling • Use team building and conflict resolution • Link rewards to performance outcomes • Offer training for needed knowledge or skills • Manage stress levels	Deadwood • Withholding pay increases • Demotion • Outplacement • Firing • Specific, direct feedback on performance problems

SOURCE: Based on M. London, *Job Feedback* (Mahwah, NJ: Lawrence Erlbaum Associates, 1997), pp. 96–97. Used by permission.

Employees with high ability and motivation are likely good performers (*solid performers*). Table 8.12 emphasizes that managers should not ignore employees with high ability and high motivation. Managers should provide development opportunities to keep them satisfied and effective. Poor performance resulting from lack of ability but not motivation (*misdirected effort*) may be improved by skill development activities such as training or temporary assignments. Managers with employees who have the ability but lack motivation (*underutilizers*) need to consider actions that focus on interpersonal problems or incentives. These actions include making sure that incentives or rewards that the employee values are linked to performance and making counseling available to help employees deal with personal problems or career or job dissatisfaction. Chronic poor performance by employees with low ability and motivation (*deadwood*) indicates that outplacement or firing may be the best solution.

Developing and Implementing a System That Follows Legal Guidelines

We now discuss the legal issues and constraints affecting performance management. Because performance measures play a central role in such administrative decisions as promotions, pay raises, and discipline, employees who sue an organization over these decisions ultimately attack the measurement systems on which the decisions were made. Two types of cases have dominated: discrimination and unjust dismissal.

In discrimination suits, the plaintiff often alleges that the performance measurement system unjustly discriminated against the plaintiff because of race or gender. Many performance measures are subjective, and we have seen that individual biases can affect them, especially when those doing the measuring harbor racial or gender stereotypes.

In *Brito* v. *Zia*, the Supreme Court essentially equated performance measures with selection tests.[72] It ruled that the *Uniform Guidelines on Employee Selection Procedures* apply to evaluating the adequacy of a performance appraisal instrument. This ruling presents a challenge to those involved in developing performance measures, because a substantial body of research on race discrimination in performance rating has demonstrated that both white and black raters give higher ratings to members of their own racial group, even after rater training.[73] There is also evidence that the discriminatory biases in performance rating are worse when one group makes up a small percentage of the work group. When the vast majority of the group is male, females receive lower ratings; when the minority is male, males receive lower ratings.[74]

In the second type of suit, an unjust dismissal suit, the plaintiff claims that the dismissal was for reasons other than those the employer claims. For example, an employee who works for a defense contractor might blow the whistle on the company for defrauding the government. If the company fires the employee, claiming poor performance, the employee may argue that the firing was, in fact, because of blowing the whistle on the employer—in other words, that the dismissal was unjust. The court case will likely focus on the performance measurement system used as the basis for claiming the employee's performance was poor.

Because of the potential costs of discrimination and unjust dismissal suits, an organization needs to determine exactly what the courts consider a legally defensible performance management system. Based on reviews of such court decisions, we offer the following characteristics of a system that will withstand legal scrutiny.[75]

1. The system should be developed by conducting a valid job analysis that ascertains the important aspects of job performance. The requirements for job success should be clearly communicated to employees.
2. The system should be based on either behaviors or results; evaluations of ambiguous traits should be avoided.
3. Raters should be trained in how to use the system rather than simply given the materials and left to interpret how to conduct the appraisal.
4. There should be some form of review by upper-level managers of all the performance ratings, and there should be a system for employees to appeal what they consider to be an unfair evaluation.
5. The organization should provide some form of performance counseling or corrective guidance to help poor performers improve their performance before being dismissed. Both short- and long-term performance goals should be included.
6. Multiple raters should be used, particularly if an employee's performance is unlikely to be seen by only one rating source such as manager or customer. At a minimum, employees should be asked to comment on their appraisals. There should be a dialogue between the manager and the employee.

Use of Technology for Performance Management: Electronic Monitoring

Employees' performance ratings, disciplinary actions, and work-rule violations can be stored in electronic databases. Personal computers are also increasingly being used for monitoring the actual performance and productivity of service employees.[76] For example, at a General Electric customer service center, agents answer over 14,000 telephone inquiries per day. The agents' calls are recorded and reviewed to help the agents improve customer service. American Airlines also monitors calls to its reservation centers. Managers can hear what the agents tell customers and see what agents enter on their personal computer screens. One disadvantage of monitoring is that employees sometimes find it demoralizing, degrading, and stressful. To avoid the potential negative effect of performance monitoring, managers must communicate why employees are being monitored. Nonmanagement employees also need to monitor and coach less experienced employees.

Legislation regarding computer monitoring may occur in the future. Both the U.S. House and Senate have considered legislation designed to protect employees' rights from being violated by computer monitoring (The Privacy for Consumers and Workers Act).

Using Performance Management Applications for Decision Making

Performance management applications are available to help managers monitor performance problems.[77] Software is available to help the manager customize performance rating forms for each job. The manager determines the performance standard for each job and rates each employee according to the appropriate standards. The manager receives a report summarizing the employees' strengths and weaknesses. The report also shows how different the employee's performance was from the established standard.

Performance diagnosis applications ask the manager for information about performance problems (e.g., Has the employee been trained in the skills that caused the performance problem?) and the work environment (e.g., Does the employee work under time pressure?). The software analyzes the information and provides solutions to consider in dealing with the performance problem.

A Look Back

The chapter opener on Ford Motors Inc. highlighted the problems that can occur with a forced ranking appraisal system that is used to differentiate above-average, average, and below-average managers. Companies remain challenged to find a performance management system that is acceptable to managers yet allows them to make important administrative decisions (like promotions, salary increases, and terminations).

Questions

1. Based on what was covered in the chapter, what type of performance system would you recommend that Ford adopt to improve managers' performance and ability to deal with future business challenges?
2. What advantages will your system have over Ford's current system?

Summary

Measuring and managing performance is a challenging enterprise and one of the keys to gaining competitive advantage. Performance management systems serve strategic, administrative, and developmental purposes—their importance cannot be overestimated. A performance measurement system should be evaluated against the criteria of strategic congruence, validity, reliability, acceptability, and specificity. Measured against these criteria, the comparative, attribute, behavioral, results, and quality approaches have different strengths and weaknesses. Thus, deciding which approach and which source of performance information are best depends on the job in question. Effective managers need to be aware of the issues involved in determining the best method or combination of methods for their particular situations. In addition, once performance has been measured, a major component of a manager's job is to feed that performance information back to employees in a way that results in improved performance rather than defensiveness and decreased motivation. Managers should take action based on the causes for poor performance: ability, motivation, or both. Managers must be sure that their performance management system can meet legal scrutiny, especially if it is used to discipline or fire poor performers.

Discussion Questions

1. What are examples of administrative decisions that might be made in managing the performance of professors? Developmental decisions?
2. What would you consider the strategy of your university (e.g., research, undergraduate teaching, graduate teaching, a combination)? How might the performance management system for faculty members fulfill its strategic purpose of eliciting the types of behaviors and results required by this strategy?
3. If you were developing a performance measurement system for faculty members, what types of attributes would you seek to measure? Behaviors? Results?
4. What sources of performance information would you use to evaluate faculty members' performance?
5. The performance of students is usually evaluated with an overall results measure of grade point average. How is this measure contaminated? How is it deficient? What other measures might you use to more adequately evaluate student performance?
6. Think of the last time you had a conflict with another

Chapter 9 Employee Development

Objectives
After reading this chapter, you should be able to:

1. Discuss current trends in using formal education for development.
2. Relate how assessment of personality type, work behaviors, and job performance can be used for employee development.
3. Develop successful mentoring programs.
4. Explain how job experiences can be used for skill development.
5. Tell how to train managers to coach employees.
6. Discuss the steps in the development planning process.
7. Explain the employees' and company's responsibilities in planning development.
8. Discuss what companies are doing for management development issues including succession planning, melting the glass ceiling, and helping dysfunctional managers.

The Opportunity Knocks program at First USA gives employees the resources to research career management literature, develop new skills, and speak to advisers about their career plans. Would a program like this help you be more optimistic about your career prospects in your company?

Enter the World of Business

Developing Employees Reduces Risk for First USA Bank

First USA Bank is the largest issuer of Visa credit cards. The company offers high-value credit cards for consumers and businesses under its own name, that of its parent (Bank One), the First Card name, and on behalf of several thousand marketing partners. These partners include leading U.S. corporations, universities, sports franchises, and financial institutions. First USA is based in Wilmington, Delaware, and has 11,000 employees.

First USA offers its employees a way to help identify their career dreams and what they can do to achieve them. The company's Opportunity Knocks program was designed in 1998 as a direct result of employee attitude survey results showing that employees were dissatisfied with their jobs and pessimistic about their future job and career prospects within First USA. The goals of the Opportunity Knocks program are to improve job satisfaction, reduce turnover, and increase the number of employees promoted. First USA also wants its employees to take charge of their own careers and to realize that promotions are not the only desirable career path. For example, lateral moves within the company help employees develop a greater range of experience and perspective by working at a different job at the same level. First USA has adopted "five P's" as the core philosophy of the program—person, perspective, place, possibility, and plan. The person, or individual employee, needs to understand his or her skills, values, and interests and communicate them so that career development is possible. Employees conduct self-assessments and seek feedback on them by talking to peers and managers (perspective). Employees need to understand not only First USA and their jobs but also developments in the industry, profession, and workplace requiring changes in employees' skills (place). Employees need to consider different possibilities within First USA: moving laterally or vertically or enriching the current job. And, employees need plans for developing new skills and competencies that will help them reach their career goals. The program includes career management skills workshops, and at each worksite career resource centers were set up with business publications, career management literature, and computers for preparing résumés. First USA also hired employment development advisers to counsel employees about their careers.

The program has had many positive benefits. Internal promotions at First USA have increased by 50 percent. When First USA repeated the employee attitude survey, it found that employee satisfaction with career development issues had increased more than 25 percent. The turnover rate among employees who participated in the Opportunity Knocks program was approximately 65 percent lower than that of employees who did not participate.

SOURCE: Based on P. Kiger, "At First USA Bank, Promotions and Job Satisfaction Are Up," *Workforce*, March 2001, pp. 54–56.

Introduction

As the First USA Bank example illustrates, development is a key component of a strategy to retain employees and prepare them for career opportunities within the company. Employee development is a necessary component of a company's efforts to compete in the new economy, to meet the challenges of global competition and social change, and to incorporate technological advances and changes in work design. As we noted in Chapter 1, employee commitment and retention are directly related to how employees are treated by their managers.

Finding and Keeping the Best Employees

To "win the war for talent," managers need to be able to identify high-potential employees, make sure their talents are used, and reassure them of their value before they become dissatisfied and leave the company. Managers also need to be able to listen. Although new employees need strong direction and bosses who can make quick decisions, they expect to be able to challenge managers' thinking and be treated with respect and dignity. Because of their skills, many employees are in high demand and can easily leave for a competitor. American Express, a financial services company, is teaching managers how to establish mentoring relationships with employees,[1] and the retention rates of skilled employees are considered in managers' performance reviews. At Autodesk Inc., a software developer, an intranet-based program teaches managers how to understand employee values and interests and how to use job experiences, such as opportunities in other departments, to develop employees.[2] Managers complete a development plan for each employee with development activities and a timeline for completion. Increased globalization of product markets compels companies to help their employees understand cultures and customs that affect business practices. Because more of employees' responsibilities are organized on a project or customer basis (rather than on a functional basis) and due to the increased use of work teams, employees need to develop a broader range of technical and interpersonal skills. Employees must also be able to perform roles traditionally reserved for managers. Legislation (such as the Civil Rights Act of 1991), labor market forces, and a company's social responsibility dictate that employers give women and minorities access to development activities that will prepare them for managerial positions. Because companies (and their employees) must constantly learn and change to meet customer needs and compete in new markets, the emphasis placed on both training and development has increased.

This chapter begins by discussing the relationship between development, training, and careers. Second, we look at development approaches, including formal education, assessment, job experiences, and interpersonal relationships. The chapter emphasizes the types of skills, knowledge, and behaviors that are strengthened by each development method. Choosing an approach is one part of development planning. Before one or multiple developmental approaches are used, the employee and the company must have an idea of the employee's development needs and the purpose of development. Identifying the needs and purpose of development is part of its planning. The third section of the chapter describes the steps of the development planning process. Employee and company responsibilities at each step of the process are emphasized. The chapter concludes with a discussion of special issues in employee development, including succession planning, dealing with dysfunctional managers, and using development to help women and minorities move into upper-level management positions (referred to as "melting the glass ceiling").

The Relationship between Development, Training, and Careers

Development and Training

Development refers to formal education, job experiences, relationships, and assessment of personality and abilities that help employees prepare for the future. Because it is future-oriented, it involves learning that is not necessarily related to the employee's current job.[3] Table 9.1 shows the differences between training and development. Traditionally, training focuses on helping employees' performance in their current jobs. Development prepares them for other positions in the company and increases their ability to move into jobs that may not yet exist.[4] Development also helps employees prepare for changes in their current jobs that may result from new technology, work designs, new customers, or new product markets. Chapter 7 emphasized the strategic role of training. As training continues to become more strategic (that is, related to business goals), the distinction between training and development will blur.

Development
The acquisition of knowledge, skills, and behaviors that improve an employee's ability to meet changes in job requirements and in client and customer demands.

Development and Careers

Traditionally, careers have been described in various ways.[5] Careers have been described as a sequence of positions held within an occupation. For example, a university faculty member can hold assistant, associate, and full professor positions. A career has also been described in the context of mobility within an organization. For example, an engineer may begin her career as a staff engineer. As her expertise, experience, and performance increase, she may move through advisory engineering, senior engineering, and senior technical positions. Finally, a career has been described as a characteristic of the employee. Each employee's career consists of different jobs, positions, and experiences.

TABLE 9.1
Comparison between Training and Development

	TRAINING	DEVELOPMENT
Focus	Current	Future
Use of work experiences	Low	High
Goal	Preparation for current job	Preparation for changes
Participation	Required	Voluntary

Protean career
A career that is frequently changing due to both changes in the person's interests, abilities, and values and changes in the work environment.

Psychological contract
The expectations that employers and employees have about each other.

Psychological success
The feeling of pride and accomplishment that comes from achieving life goals.

The new concept of the career is often referred to as a "protean career."[6] A **protean career** is a career that frequently changes based on changes in the person's interests, abilities, and values and also in the work environment. Compared to the traditional career view, employees here take major responsibility for managing their careers. For example, an engineer may decide to take a sabbatical from her position to work in management at the United Way Agency for a year. The purpose of this assignment could be to develop her managerial skills as well as help her personally evaluate if she likes managerial work more than engineering.

Changes in the psychological contract between employees and their companies have influenced the development of the protean career.[7] A **psychological contract** is the expectations that employers and employees have about each other. Traditionally, the psychological contract emphasized that the company would provide continued employment (job security) and advancement opportunities if the employee remained with the company and performed well. Pay increases and status were linked directly to vertical movement in the company (promotions).

The protean career has several implications for employee development. The goal of the new career is **psychological success:** the feeling of pride and accomplishment that comes from achieving life goals that are not limited to achievements at work (such as raising a family and having good physical health). Psychological success is more under the employee's control than the traditional career goals, which were not only influenced by employee effort but were controlled by the availability of positions in the company. Psychological success is self-determined rather than solely determined through signals the employee receives from the company (like salary increase and promotion). Psychological success appears to be especially important to the new generation of persons entering the workforce. "Generation X" is often unimpressed with status symbols, wants flexibility in doing job tasks, and desires meaning from work.[8]

Employees need to develop new skills rather than rely on a static knowledge base. This has resulted from companies' need to be more responsive to customers' service and product demands. The types of knowledge an employee needs have changed.[9] In the traditional career, "knowing how" (having the appropriate skills and knowledge to provide a service or produce a product) was critical. Although knowing how remains important, employees also need to "know why" and "know whom." Knowing why refers to understanding the company's business and culture so the employee can develop and apply knowledge and skills that can contribute to the business. Knowing whom refers to relationships the employee may develop to contribute to company success. These relationships may include networking with vendors, suppliers, community members, customers, or industry experts. Learning to know whom and know why requires more than formal courses and training programs. Learning and development in the protean career are increasingly likely to involve relationships and job experiences rather than formal courses.

The emphasis on continuous learning and learning beyond knowing how as well as changes in the psychological contract are altering the direction and frequency of movement within careers (career pattern).[10]

Traditional career patterns consisted of a series of steps arranged in a linear hierarchy, with higher steps related to increased authority, responsibility, and compensation. Expert career patterns involve a lifelong commitment to a field or specialization (such as law, medicine, or management). These types of career patterns will not disappear. Rather, career patterns involving movement across specializations or disciplines (a spiral career pattern) will become more prevalent. These new career patterns mean that developing employees (as well as employees taking control of their own careers) will require providing them with the opportunity to (a) determine their interests, skill strengths, and weaknesses and (b) based on this information, seek appropriate development experiences that will likely involve job experiences and relationships as well as formal courses.

The most appropriate view of a career is that it is "boundaryless."[11] It may include movement across several employers or even different occupations. Statistics indicate that the average employment tenure for all American workers is only five years.[12] For example, Craig Matison, 33 years old, took a job with Cincinnati Bell Information System, a unit of Cincinnati Bell Corporation that manages billing for phone and cable companies.[13] Although he has been on the job only six months, he is already looking to make his next career move. Not wanting to stay on the technical career path, he regularly explores company databases for job postings, looking for sales and marketing opportunities within the company. A career may also involve identifying more with a job or profession than with the present employer. A career can also be considered boundaryless in the sense that career plans or goals are influenced by personal or family demands and values. Finally, *boundaryless* may refer to the fact that career success may be tied not to promotions but to achieving goals that are personally meaningful to the employee rather than those set by parents, peers, or the company.

As this discussion shows, to retain and motivate employees companies need to provide a system to identify and meet employees' development needs. This is especially important to retain good performers and employees who have potential for managerial positions. This system is often known as a **career management** or **development planning system.** We will discuss these systems in detail later in the chapter.

Career management system
A system to retain and motivate employees by identifying and meeting their development needs. (Also called *development planning systems.*)

Approaches to Employee Development

Four approaches are used to develop employees: formal education, assessment, job experiences, and interpersonal relationships.[14] Many companies combine these approaches. For example, the New York City–based Metropolitan Transportation Authority (MTA) found that it needed a system for developing employees for first-level management positions.[15] As a result, the Future Managers Program (FMP) was created. The goal of the program was to develop first-level managers who understood the transportation business and operations. Employees in the FMP survive a rigorous selection process involving interviews and assessment centers. The FMP uses assessment, courses, job experiences, and relationships to develop managers, combining classroom instruction with job rotation. Classroom instruction provides a learning foundation, whereas job rotation exposes employees to a wide variety of on-the-job experiences. Class time is devoted to case study analysis, team building, and developing skills in problem solving, delegation, leadership, and communications. Working in groups, students complete projects that involve real issues such as creating a customer service brochure in Chinese. Examples of job rotation assignments include working at Grand Central Terminal, working with the system road foreman, and working in the operations control center. Job rotation familiarizes employees with different aspects of operations so they are prepared to move into new areas when positions become available.

Because future managers often confront new situations, mentors help trainees understand the agency's culture and answer their questions. The students receive continued feedback on their performance throughout the program based on supervisory and peer evaluations.

Does the program work? Although they are not guaranteed jobs after completing the program, the majority of graduates have received jobs they targeted after graduation. The long-term success of the program will be determined by analyzing graduates' career progression in the MTA.

Keep in mind that although much development activity is targeted at managers, all levels of employees may be involved in development. For example, grocery store clerks usually receive performance appraisal feedback (a development activity related to assessment). As part of the appraisal process they are asked to complete individual development plans outlining (1) how they plan to change their weaknesses and (2) their future plans (including positions or locations desired and education or experience needed). Next we explore each type of development approach.

Formal Education

Formal education programs Employee development programs, including short courses offered by consultants or universities, executive MBA programs, and university programs.

Formal education programs include off-site and on-site programs designed specifically for the company's employees, short courses offered by consultants or universities, executive MBA programs, and university programs in which participants actually live at the university while taking classes. These programs may involve lectures by business experts, business games and simulations, adventure learning, and meetings with customers. Many companies (such as Motorola, IBM, GE, Metropolitan Financial, and Dow) have training and development centers that offer one- or two-day seminars as well as week-long programs. For example, General Electric's Management Development Institute in Crotonville, New York, teaches courses in manufacturing and sales, marketing, and advanced management training.[16] Tuition ranges from $800 for a half-week conference to $14,000 for a four-week executive development course. Tuition is paid by the employee's business unit. Table 9.2 shows the types of development programs used at GE and their target audiences.

TABLE 9.2

Examples of Development Programs at General Electric

PROGRAM	DESCRIPTION	TARGET AUDIENCE	COURSES
Executive development sequence	Courses emphasize strategic thinking, leadership, cross-functional integration, competing globally, customer satisfaction.	Senior professionals and executives identified as high-potential	Manager development Global business management Executive development
Core leadership program	Courses develop functional expertise, business excellence, management of change.	Managers	Corporate entry leadership Professional development New manager development Experienced manager
Professional development program	Courses emphasize preparation for specific career path.	New employees	Audit staff Financial management Human resources Technical leadership

SOURCE: Based on website http://www.ge.com/ibcrucl8.htm.

TABLE 9.3
Example of Institutions for Executive Education

PROVIDER (LOCATION)	1998–99 REVENUE (MILLIONS)	FIVE-YEAR GROWTH	PERCENTAGE OF CUSTOMIZED PROGRAMS	NUMBER OF PROGRAMS
Harvard (Boston)	$65.0	124%	25%	69
Pennsylvania, Wharton School (Philadelphia)	40.1	151	29	89
Michigan (Ann Arbor, Michigan)	25.3	29	17	79
Center for Creative Leadership (Greensboro, North Carolina)	50.6	120	47	244
INSEAD (Fontainebleau, France)	40.0	60	41	124

SOURCE: M. Schneider, J. Reingold, and N. Enbar, Cambria Consulting, "*BusinessWeek*'s Top 20 for Nondegree Study," *BusinessWeek Online* (October 18, 1999), www.businessweek.com.

Table 9.3 shows examples of institutions for executive education. There are several important trends in executive education. More and more companies and universities are using distance learning (which we discussed in Chapter 7) to reach executive audiences.[17] For example, Duke University's Fuqua School of Business offers an electronic executive MBA program. Using their personal computers, students "attend" CD-ROM video lectures as well as traditional face-to-face lectures. They can download study aids and additional video and audio programs. Students discuss lectures and work on team projects using computer bulletin boards, e-mail, and live chat rooms. They use the Internet to research specific companies and class topics. They also travel to Europe, China, and South America for classes and meetings with local business owners. The "Competing in the New Economy" box shows how IBM is using the Web for its management development program.

Another trend in executive education is for companies and the education provider (business school or other educational institution) to create short custom courses with content designed specifically for the audience. For example, in the Global Leadership Program run by Columbia University's business school, executives work on real problems they face in their jobs. A manager for window maker Pella Corporation left the program with a plan for international sales.[18]

The final important trend in executive education is to supplement formal courses from consultants or university faculty with other types of development activities. Avon Products' "Passport Program" is targeted at employees the company thinks can become general managers.[19] To learn Avon's global strategy, they meet for each session in a different country. The program brings a team of employees together for six-week periods spread over 18 months. Participants are provided with general background of a functional area by university faculty and consultants. The team then works with senior executives on a country project, such as how to penetrate a new market. The team projects are presented to Avon's top managers.

COMPETING IN THE NEW ECONOMY

E-Learning Helps Build Management Talent

To succeed in the new economy, companies need to identify employees with managerial talent and help managers develop skills needed to be more effective. To attract and retain talented employees who are in short supply, companies must offer training and development opportunities on the Web to meet the needs of a geographically dispersed workforce dealing with many work demands. IBM's "Basic Blue for Managers" program uses e-learning and face-to-face classroom experiences. The program helps managers understand their responsibilities in managing performance, employee relations, diversity, and multicultural issues. It moves the learning of all basic management skills to the Web, using classroom experiences for more complex management issues. It also gives managers and their bosses greater responsibility for development, while the company provides support in the form of unlimited access to development activities and support networks. The learning model includes four levels:

- Management quick views: These provide practical information on over 40 common management topics related to how to conduct business, leadership and management competencies, productivity, and HRM issues.
- Interactive learning modules and simulations: These interactive simulations emphasize people and task management. Employees learn by viewing videos, interacting with models and problem employees, deciding how to deal with a problem, issue, or request, and getting feedback on their decisions. Case studies are also available for review.
- Collaborative learning: The learner can connect on the company intranet with tutors, team members, customers, or other learners to discuss problems, issues, and approaches to share learning.
- Learning labs: Five-day class workshops build on the learning acquired during the previous phases of e-learning. The workshops emphasize peer learning and the development of a learning community. Through challenging activities and assignments managers gain increased awareness of themselves, their work teams, and IBM.

The program recognizes the roles of the boss as coach, supporter, and role model. The boss is involved in the program through providing coaching and feedback, on-the-job learning experiences, assessment of the manager's development needs and progress, and assistance to complete individual development plans.

IBM believes that by utilizing e-learning and the classroom environment, managers participate in self-directed learning, try out skills in a "safe" environment, and gain access to communities of learning and just-in-time learning. The advantages of e-learning are complemented by the strengths of an interactive classroom experience and support from the manager's boss to create the best development program possible.

SOURCE: N. Lewis and P. Orton, "The Five Attributes of Innovative E-Learning," *Training and Development*, June 2000, pp. 47–51.

Managers who attend the Center for Creative Leadership development program take psychological tests; receive feedback from managers, peers, and direct reports; participate in group-building activities (like adventure learning, discussed in Chapter 7); receive counseling; and set improvement goals and write development plans.[20]

Most companies consider the primary purpose of education programs to be providing the employee with job-specific skills.[21] Unfortunately, there has been little research on the effectiveness of formal education programs. In a study of Harvard University's Advanced Management Program, participants reported that they had acquired valuable knowledge from the program (like how globalization affects a company's structure). They said the program broadened their perspectives on issues facing their companies, increased their self-confidence, and helped them learn new ways of thinking and looking at problems.[22]

Assessment

Assessment involves collecting information and providing feedback to employees about their behavior, communication style, or skills.[23] The employees, their peers, managers, and customers may provide information. Assessment is most frequently used to identify employees with managerial potential and to measure current managers' strengths and weaknesses. Assessment is also used to identify managers with the potential to move into higher-level executive positions, and it can be used with work teams to identify the strengths and weaknesses of individual team members and the decision processes or communication styles that inhibit the team's productivity.

Assessment
Collecting information and providing feedback to employees about their behavior, communication style, or skills.

Companies vary in the methods and the sources of information they use in developmental assessment. Many companies appraise employee performance. Companies with sophisticated development systems use psychological tests to measure employees' skills, personality types, and communication styles. Self, peer, and managers' ratings of employees' interpersonal styles and behaviors may also be collected. Popular assessment tools include the Myers-Briggs Type Indicator, assessment centers, benchmarks, performance appraisal, and 360-degree feedback.

Myers-Briggs Type Indicator®

Myers-Briggs Type Indicator (MBTI) is the most popular psychological test for employee development. As many as 2 million people take the MBTI in the United States each year. The test consists of more than 100 questions about how the person feels or prefers to behave in different situations (such as "Are you usually a good 'mixer' or rather quiet and reserved?"). The MBTI is based on the work of Carl Jung, a psychologist who believed that differences in individuals' behavior resulted from preferences in decision making, interpersonal communication, and information gathering. The MBTI identifies individuals' preference for energy (introversion versus extroversion), information gathering (sensing versus intuition), decision making (thinking versus feeling), and lifestyle (judging versus perceiving).[24] The energy dimension determines where individuals gain interpersonal strength and vitality. Extroverts (E) gain energy through interpersonal relationships. Introverts (I) gain energy by focusing on personal thoughts and feelings. The information-gathering preference relates to the actions individuals take when making decisions. Individuals with a Sensing (S) preference tend to gather facts and details. Intuitives (I) tend to focus less on facts and more on possibilities and relationships between ideas. Decision-making preferences differ based on the amount of consideration the person gives to others' feelings in making a decision. Individuals with a Thinking (T) preference tend to be objective in making decisions. Individuals with a Feeling (F) preference tend to evaluate the impact of potential decisions on others and be more subjective in making a decision. The lifestyle preference reflects an individual's tendency to be

Myers-Briggs Type Indicator (MBTI)
A psychological test used for team building and leadership development that identifies employees' preferences for energy, information gathering, decision making, and lifestyle.

flexible and adaptable. Individuals with a Judging (J) preference focus on goals, establish deadlines, and prefer to be conclusive. Individuals with a Perceiving (P) preference tend to enjoy surprises, like to change decisions, and dislike deadlines.

Sixteen unique personality types result from the combination of the four MBTI preferences. (See Table 9.4.) Each person has developed strengths and weaknesses as a result of using these preferences. For example, individuals who are Introverted, Sensing, Thinking, and Judging (known as ISTJs) tend to be serious, quiet, practical, orderly, and logical. These persons can organize tasks, be decisive, and follow through on plans and goals. ISTJs have several weaknesses because they have not used the opposite preferences: Extroversion, Intuition, Feeling, and Perceiving. Potential weaknesses for ISTJs include problems dealing with unexpected opportunities, appearing too task-oriented or impersonal to colleagues, and making overly quick decisions.

The MBTI is used for understanding such things as communication, motivation, teamwork, work styles, and leadership. For example, it can be used by salespeople or executives who want to become more effective at interpersonal communication by learning about their own personality styles and the way they are perceived by others. The MBTI can help develop teams by matching team members with assignments that allow them to capitalize on their preferences and helping employees understand how the different preferences of team members can lead to useful problem solving.[25] For example, employees with an Intuitive preference can be assigned brainstorming tasks. Employees with a Sensing preference can evaluate ideas.

Research on the validity, reliability, and effectiveness of the MBTI is inconclusive.[26] People who take the MBTI find it a positive experience and say it helps them change their behavior. MBTI scores appear to be related to one's occupation. Analysis of managers' MBTI scores in the United States, England, Latin America, and Japan suggests that a large majority of all managers have certain personality types (ISTJ, INTJ, ESTJ, or ENTJ). However, MBTI scores are not necessarily stable over time. Studies in which the MBTI was administered at two different times found that as few as 24 percent of those who took the test were classified as the same type the second time.

The MBTI is a valuable tool for understanding communication styles and the ways people prefer to interact with others. Because it does not measure how well employees perform their preferred functions, it should not be used to appraise performance or evaluate employees' promotion potential. Furthermore, MBTI types should not be viewed as unchangeable personality patterns.

Assessment center
A process in which multiple raters evaluate employees' performance on a number of exercises.

Leaderless group discussion
Process in which a team of five to seven employees solve an assigned problem together within a certain time period.

Interview
Employees are questioned about their work and personal experiences, skills, and career plans.

Assessment Center

At an **assessment center** multiple raters or evaluators (assessors) evaluate employees' performance on a number of exercises.[27] An assessment center is usually an off-site location such as a conference center. From 6 to 12 employees usually participate at one time. Assessment centers are primarily used to identify if employees have the personality characteristics, administrative skills, and interpersonal skills needed for managerial jobs. They are also increasingly being used to determine if employees have the necessary skills to work in teams.

The types of exercises used in assessment centers include leaderless group discussions, interviews, in-baskets, and role plays.[28] In a **leaderless group discussion,** a team of five to seven employees is assigned a problem and must work together to solve it within a certain time period. The problem may involve buying and selling supplies, nominating a subordinate for an award, or assembling a product. In the **interview,** employees answer questions about their work and personal experiences, skill strengths

TABLE 9.4

The 16 Personality Types Used in the Myers-Briggs Type Indicator Assessment

	SENSING TYPES (S)		INTUITIVE TYPES (N)	
	THINKING (T)	FEELING (F)	FEELING (F)	THINKING (T)
Introverts (I) Judging (J)	**ISTJ** Quiet, serious, earn success by thoroughness and dependability. Practical, matter-of-fact, realistic, and responsible. Decide logically what should be done and work toward it steadily, regardless of distractions. Take pleasure in making everything orderly and organized—their work, their home, their life. Value traditions and loyalty.	**ISFJ** Quiet, friendly, responsible, and conscientious. Committed and steady in meeting their obligations. Thorough, painstaking, and accurate. Loyal, considerate, notice and remember specifics about people who are important to them, concerned with how others feel. Strive to create an orderly and harmonious environment at work and at home.	**INFJ** Seek meaning and connection in ideas, relationships, and material possessions. Want to understand what motivates people and are insightful about others. Conscientious and committed to their firm values. Develop a clear vision about how best to serve the common good. Organized and decisive in implementing their vision.	**INTJ** Have original minds and great drive for implementing their ideas and achieving their goals. Quickly see patterns in external events and develop long-range explanatory perspectives. When committed, organize a job and carry it through. Skeptical and independent, have high standards of competence and performance—for themselves and others.
Perceiving (P)	**ISTP** Tolerant and flexible, quiet observers until a problem appears, then act quickly to find workable solutions. Analyze what makes things work and readily get through large amounts of data to isolate the core of practical problems. Interested in cause and effect, organize facts using logical principles, value efficiency.	**ISFP** Quiet, friendly, sensitive, and kind. Enjoy the present moment, what's going on around them. Like to have their own space and to work within their own time frame. Loyal and committed to their values and to people who are important to them. Dislike disagreements and conflicts, do not force their opinions or values on others.	**INFP** Idealistic, loyal to their values and to people who are important to them. Want an external life that is congruent with their values. Curious, quick to see possibilities, can be catalysts for implementing ideas. Seek to understand people and to help them fulfill their potential. Adaptable, flexible, and accepting unless a value is threatened.	**INTP** Seek to develop logical explanations for everything that interests them. Theoretical and abstract, interested more in ideas than in social interaction. Quiet, contained, flexible, and adaptable. Have unusual ability to focus in depth to solve problems in their area of interest. Skeptical, sometimes critical, always analytical.
Extroverts (E) Perceiving (P)	**ESTP** Flexible and tolerant, they take a pragmatic approach focused on immediate results. Theories and conceptual explanations bore them—they want to act energetically to solve the problem. Focus on the here-and-now, spontaneous, enjoy each moment that they can be active with others. Enjoy material comforts and style. Learn best through doing.	**ESFP** Outgoing, friendly, and accepting. Exuberant lovers of life, people, and material comforts. Enjoy working with others to make things happen. Bring common sense and a realistic approach to their work, and make work fun. Flexible and spontaneous, adapt readily to new people and environments. Learn best by trying a new skill with other people.	**ENFP** Warmly enthusiastic and imaginative. See life as full of possibilities. Make connections between events and information very quickly, and confidently proceed based on the patterns they see. Want a lot of affirmation from others, and readily give appreciation and support. Spontaneous and flexible, often rely on their ability to improvise and their verbal fluency.	**ENTP** Quick, ingenious, stimulating, alert, and outspoken. Resourceful in solving new and challenging problems. Adept at generating conceptual possibilities and then analyzing them strategically. Good at reading other people. Bored by routine, will seldom do the same thing the same way, apt to turn to one new interest after another.
Judging (J)	**ESTJ** Practical, realistic, matter-of-fact. Decisive, quickly move to implement decisions. Organize projects and people to get things done, focus on getting results in the most efficient way possible. Take care of routine details. Have a clear set of logical standards, systematically follow them and want others to also. Forceful in implementing their plans.	**ESFJ** Warmhearted, conscientious, and cooperative. Want harmony in their environment, work with determination to establish it. Like to work with others to complete tasks accurately and on time. Loyal, follow through even in small matters. Notice what others need in their day-by-day lives and try to provide it. Want to be appreciated for who they are and for what they contribute.	**ENFJ** Warm, empathetic, responsive, and responsible. Highly attuned to the emotions, needs, and motivations of others. Find potential in everyone, want to help others fulfill their potential. May act as catalysts for individual and group growth. Loyal, responsive to praise and criticism. Sociable, facilitate others in a group, and provide inspiring leadership.	**ENTJ** Frank, decisive, assume leadership readily. Quickly see illogical and inefficient procedures and policies, develop and implement comprehensive systems to solve organizational problems. Enjoy long-term planning and goal setting. Usually well informed, well read, enjoy expanding their knowledge and passing it on to others. Forceful in presenting their ideas.

SOURCE: Reproduced with special permission of the publisher, Consulting Psychologists Press, Inc., Palo Alto, CA 94303, from *Manual: A Guide to the Development and Use of the Myers-Briggs Type Indicator* by Isabel Briggs-Myers and Mary H. McCaulley.

In-basket
A simulation of the administrative tasks of a manager's job.

Role plays
A participant taking the part or role of a manager or other employee.

and weaknesses, and career plans. An **in-basket** is a simulation of the administrative tasks of the manager's job. The exercise includes a variety of documents that may appear in the in-basket on a manager's desk. The participants read the materials and decide how to respond to them. Responses might include delegating tasks, scheduling meetings, writing replies, or completely ignoring the memo! **Role plays** refer to the participant taking the part or role of a manager or other employee. For example, an assessment center participant may be asked to take the role of a manager who has to give a negative performance review to a subordinate. The participant is told about the subordinate's performance and is asked to prepare for and actually hold a 45-minute meeting with the subordinate to discuss the performance problems. The role of the subordinate is played by a manager or other member of the assessment center design team or company. The assessment center might also include interest and aptitude tests to evaluate an employee's vocabulary, general mental ability, and reasoning skills. Personality tests may be used to determine if employees can get along with others, their tolerance for ambiguity, and other traits related to success as a manager.

Assessment center exercises are designed to measure employees' administrative and interpersonal skills. Skills typically measured include leadership, oral and written communication, judgment, organizational ability, and stress tolerance. Table 9.5 shows an example of the skills measured by the assessment center. As we see, each exercise gives participating employees the opportunity to demonstrate several different skills. For example, the exercise requiring scheduling to meet production demands evaluates employees' administrative and problem-solving ability. The leaderless group discussion measures interpersonal skills such as sensitivity toward others, stress tolerance, and oral communication skills.

Managers are usually used as assessors. The managers are trained to look for employee behaviors that are related to the skills that will be assessed. Typically, each as-

TABLE 9.5

Examples of Skills Measured by Assessment Center Exercises

	EXERCISES				
	IN-BASKET	SCHEDULING EXERCISE	LEADERLESS GROUP DISCUSSION	PERSONALITY TEST	ROLE PLAY
SKILLS					
Leadership (Dominance, coaching, influence, resourcefulness)	X		X	X	X
Problem solving (Judgment)	X	X	X		X
Interpersonal (Sensitivity, conflict resolution, cooperation, oral communication)			X	X	X
Administrative (Organizing, planning, written communications)	X	X	X		
Personal (Stress tolerance, confidence)			X	X	X

X indicates skill measured by exercise.

TABLE 9.6
Skills Related to Managerial Success

Resourcefulness	Can think strategically, engage in flexible problem solving, and work effectively with higher management.
Doing whatever it takes	Has perseverance and focus in the face of obstacles.
Being a quick study	Quickly masters new technical and business knowledge.
Building and mending relationships	Knows how to build and maintain working relationships with coworkers and external parties.
Leading subordinates	Delegates to subordinates effectively, broadens their opportunities, and acts with fairness toward them.
Compassion and sensitivity	Shows genuine interest in others and sensitivity to subordinates' needs.
Straightforwardness and composure	Is honorable and steadfast.
Setting a developmental climate	Provides a challenging climate to encourage subordinates' development.
Confronting problem subordinates	Acts decisively and fairly when dealing with problem subordinates.
Team orientation	Accomplishes tasks through managing others.
Balance between personal life and work	Balances work priorities with personal life so that neither is neglected.
Decisiveness	Prefers quick and approximate actions to slow and precise ones in many management situations.
Self-awareness	Has an accurate picture of strengths and weaknesses and is willing to improve.
Hiring talented staff	Hires talented people for the team.
Putting people at ease	Displays warmth and a good sense of humor.
Acting with flexibility	Can behave in ways that are often seen as opposites.

SOURCE: Adapted with permission from C.D. McCauley, M.M. Lombardo, and C.J. Usher, "Diagnosing Management Development Needs: An Instrument Based on How Managers Develop," *Journal of Management* 15 (1989), pp. 389–403.

sessor observes and records one or two employees' behaviors in each exercise. The assessors review their notes and rate each employee's level of skills (for example, 5 = high level of leadership skills, 1 = low level of leadership skills). After all employees have completed the exercises, the assessors discuss their observations of each employee. They compare their ratings and try to agree on each employee's rating for each of the skills.

As we mentioned in Chapter 6, research suggests that assessment center ratings are related to performance, salary level, and career advancement.[29] Assessment centers may also be useful for development because employees who participate in the process receive feedback regarding their attitudes, skill strengths, and weaknesses.[30] In some organizations, such as Eastman Kodak, training courses and development activities related to the skills evaluated in the assessment center are available to employees.

Benchmarks
An instrument designed to measure the factors that are important to managerial success.

Benchmarks

Benchmarks© is an instrument designed to measure the factors that are important to being a successful manager. The items measured by Benchmarks are based on research that examines the lessons executives learn at critical events in their careers.[31] This includes items that measure managers' skills in dealing with subordinates, acquiring resources, and creating a productive work climate. Table 9.6 shows the 16 skills and perspectives believed to be important for becoming a successful manager. These skills and perspectives have been shown to be related to performance evaluations, bosses' ratings of promotability, and actual promotions received.[32] To get a complete picture of managers' skills, the managers' supervisors, their peers, and the managers themselves all complete the instrument. A summary report presenting the self-ratings and ratings by others is provided to the manager, along with information about how the ratings compare with those of other managers. A development guide with examples of experiences that enhance each skill and how successful managers use the skills is also available.

Performance Appraisals and 360-Degree Feedback Systems

Performance appraisal
The process through which an organization gets information on how well an employee is doing his or her job.

Upward feedback
A performance appraisal process for managers that includes subordinates' evaluations.

360-degree feedback systems
A performance appraisal system for managers that includes evaluations from a wide range of persons who interact with the manager. The process includes self-evaluations as well as evaluations from the manager's boss, subordinates, peers, and customers.

As we mentioned in Chapter 8, **performance appraisal** is the process of measuring employees' performance. Performance appraisal information can be useful for employee development under certain conditions.[33] The appraisal system must tell employees specifically about their performance problems and how they can improve their performance. This includes providing a clear understanding of the differences between current performance and expected performance, identifying causes of the performance discrepancy, and developing action plans to improve performance. Managers must be trained in frequent performance feedback. Managers also need to monitor employees' progress in carrying out action plans.

A recent trend in performance appraisals for management development is the use of upward feedback and 360-degree feedback. Dow Chemical, Hallmark, Honeywell, Raychem, and AT&T use this appraisal process. **Upward feedback** refers to appraisal that involves collecting subordinates' evaluations of managers' behaviors or skills. The 360-degree feedback process is a special case of upward feedback. In **360-degree feedback systems,** employees' behaviors or skills are evaluated not only by subordinates but by peers, customers, their bosses, and themselves. The raters complete a questionnaire asking them to rate the person on a number of different dimensions. Table 9.7 shows an example of the type of skill and items used in a questionnaire designed for a 360-degree feedback system. Here "Communicating information and ideas" is the dimension of the manager's behavior being evaluated. Each of the five items relates to specific aspects of written and oral communications (such as clarity of messages). Typically raters evaluate the degree to which each particular item is a strength or if development is needed.

The results of a 360-degree feedback system show how the manager was rated on each item. The results also show how self-evaluations differ from evaluations from the other raters. Typically managers review their results, seek clarification from the raters, and set specific development goals based on the strengths and weaknesses identified.[34] Table 9.8 shows the type of activities involved in development planning using 360-degree feedback.[35] Consider how U.S. West used development planning with 360-degree feedback.[36] The 360-degree feedback results showed that one manager tended to avoid confrontation. Knowing this helped her focus her training and development activity on role plays and discussions that would help her become more comfortable with confrontation. She left the program with an individualized list of training and development activities linked directly to the skill she needed to improve.

The benefits of 360-degree feedback include collecting multiple perspectives of managers' performance, allowing employees to compare their own personal evaluations with the views of others, and formalizing communications about behaviors and skills ratings between employees and their internal and external customers. For ex-

TABLE 9.7

Sample Dimension and Items from a 360-Degree Feedback Instrument.

Communicating information and ideas
Person makes points effectively to a resistant audience.
Person is skilled at public speaking.
Person is good at disseminating information to others.
Person has good writing skills.
Person writes understandable, easy-to-read memos.

TABLE 9.8

Activities in Development Planning

1. **Understand strengths and weaknesses.**
   Review ratings for strengths and weaknesses.
   Identify skills or behaviors where self and others' (manager, peer, customer) ratings agree and disagree.
2. **Identify a development goal.**
   Choose a skill or behavior to develop.
   Set a clear, specific goal with a specified outcome.
3. **Identify a process for recognizing goal accomplishment.**
4. **Identify strategies for reaching the development goal.**
   Establish strategies such as reading, job experiences, courses, and relationships.
   Establish strategies for receiving feedback on progress.
   Establish strategies for reinforcing the new skill or behavior.

ample, Robert Allen, a high-level AT&T executive, now more freely airs his opinions in executive committee meetings based on the feedback he received from his subordinates as part of a 360-degree feedback system. Several studies have shown that performance improves and behavior changes as a result of participating in upward feedback and 360-degree feedback systems.[37]

Potential limitations of 360-degree feedback include the time demands placed on the raters to complete the evaluations, managers seeking to identify and punish raters who provided negative information, the need to have a facilitator help interpret results, and companies' failure to provide ways that managers can act on the feedback they receive (development planning, meeting with raters, taking courses).

In effective 360-degree feedback systems, reliable or consistent ratings are provided, raters' confidentiality is maintained, the behaviors or skills assessed are job-related (valid), the system is easy to use, and managers receive and act on the feedback.[38]

Technology allows 360-degree questionnaires to be delivered to the raters via their personal computers. This increases the number of completed questionnaires returned, makes it easier to process the information, and speeds feedback reports to managers.

Regardless of the assessment method used, the information must be shared with the employee for development to occur. Along with assessment information, the employee needs suggestions for correcting skill weaknesses and using skills already learned. These suggestions might be to participate in training courses or develop skills through new job experiences. Based on the assessment information and available development opportunities, employees should develop action plans to guide their self-improvement efforts.

Job Experiences

Job experience The relationships, problems, demands, tasks, and other features that employees face in their jobs.

Most employee development occurs through **job experiences:**[39] relationships, problems, demands, tasks, or other features that employees face in their jobs. A major assumption of using job experiences for employee development is that development is most likely to occur when there is a mismatch between the employee's skills and past experiences and the skills required for the job. To succeed in their jobs, employees must stretch their skills—that is, they are forced to learn new skills, apply their skills and knowledge in a new way, and master new experiences.[40] For example, to prepare employees to grow overseas business markets, companies are using international job experiences.

Most of what we know about development through job experiences comes from a

TABLE 9.9

Job Demands and the Lessons Employees Learn from Them

Making transitions	*Unfamiliar responsibilities:* The manager must handle responsibilities that are new, very different, or much broader than previous ones. *Proving yourself:* The manager has added pressure to show others she can handle the job.
Creating change	*Developing new directions:* The manager is responsible for starting something new in the organization, making strategic changes in the business, carrying out a reorganization, or responding to rapid changes in the business environment. *Inherited problems:* The manager has to fix problems created by a former incumbent or take over problem employees. *Reduction decisions:* Decisions about shutting down operations or staff reductions have to be made. *Problems with employees:* Employees lack adequate experience, are incompetent, or are resistant.
Having high level of responsibility	*High stakes:* Clear deadlines, pressure from senior managers, high visibility, and responsibility for key decisions make success or failure in this job clearly evident. *Managing business diversity:* The scope of the job is large with responsibilities for multiple functions, groups, products, customers, or markets. *Job overload:* The sheer size of the job requires a large investment of time and energy. *Handling external pressure:* External factors that affect the business (e.g., negotiating with unions or government agencies; working in a foreign culture; coping with serious community problems) must be dealt with.
Being involved in nonauthority relationships	*Influencing without authority:* Getting the job done requires influencing peers, higher management, external parties, or other key people over whom the manager has no direct authority.
Facing obstacles	*Adverse business conditions:* The business unit or product line faces financial problems or difficult economic conditions. *Lack of top management support:* Senior management is reluctant to provide direction, support, or resources for current work or new projects. *Lack of personal support:* The manager is excluded from key networks and gets little support and encouragement from others. *Difficult boss:* The manager's opinions or management style differs from those of the boss, or the boss has major shortcomings.

SOURCE: C.D. McCauley, L.J. Eastman, and J. Ohlott, "Linking Management Selection and Development through Stretch Assignments," *Human Resource Management* 84 (1995), pp. 93–115.

series of studies conducted by the Center for Creative Leadership.[41] Executives were asked to identify key career events that made a difference in their managerial styles and the lessons they learned from these experiences. The key events included those involving the job assignment (such as fixing a failing operation), those involving interpersonal relationships (getting along with supervisors), and the specific type of transition required (situations in which the executive did not have the necessary background). The job demands and what employees can learn from them are shown in Table 9.9.

One concern in the use of demanding job experiences for employee development is whether they are viewed as positive or negative stressors. Job experiences that are seen as positive stressors challenge employees to stimulate learning. Job challenges viewed as negative stressors create high levels of harmful stress for employees exposed to them. Recent research findings suggest that all of the job demands, with the exception of obstacles, are related to learning.[42] Managers reported that obstacles and job demands related to creating change were more likely to lead to negative stress than the other job demands. This suggests that companies should carefully weigh the potential negative consequences before placing employees in development assignments involving obstacles or creating change.

Although the research on development through job experiences has focused on executives and managers, line employees can also learn from job experiences. As we noted earlier, for a work team to be successful, its members now need the kinds of skills that only managers were once thought to need (such as dealing directly with customers, analyzing data to determine product quality, and resolving conflict among team members). Besides the development that occurs when a team is formed, employees can further develop their skills by switching work roles within the team.

Figure 9.1 shows the various ways that job experiences can be used for employee

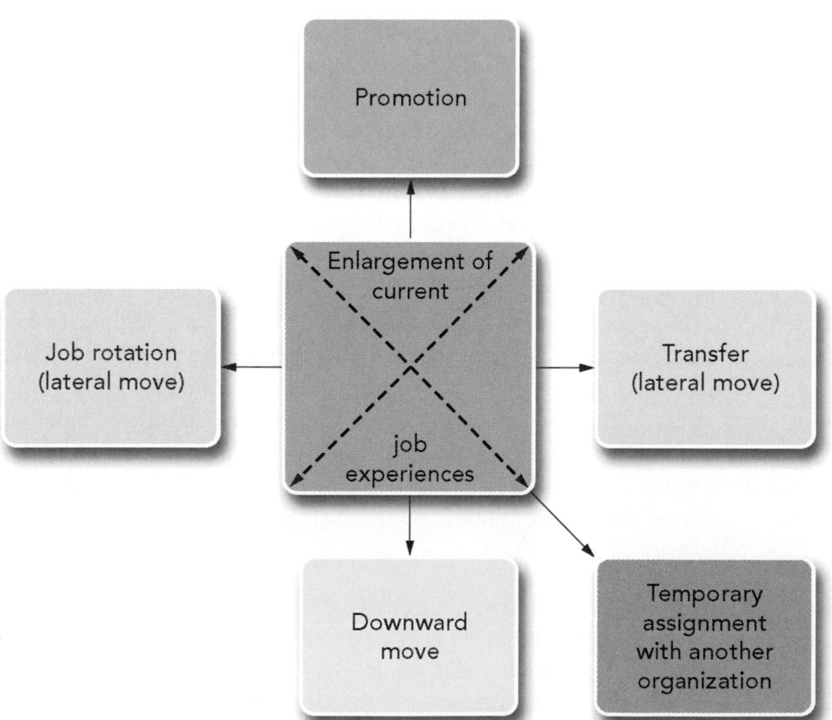

FIGURE 9.1
How Job Experiences Are Used for Employee Development

development. These include enlarging the current job, job rotation, transfers, promotions, downward moves, and temporary assignments with other companies.

Enlarging the Current Job

Job enlargement
Adding challenges or new responsibilities to an employee's current job.

Job enlargement refers to adding challenges or new responsibilities to employees' current jobs. This could include special project assignments, switching roles within a work team, or researching new ways to serve clients and customers. For example, an engineering employee may join a task force developing new career paths for technical employees. Through this project work, the engineer may lead certain aspects of career path development (such as reviewing the company's career development process). As a result, the engineer not only learns about the company's career development system, but uses leadership and organizational skills to help the task force reach its goals.

Job Rotation

Job rotation
The process of systematically moving a single individual from one job to another over the course of time. The job assignments may be in various functional areas of the company or movement may be between jobs in a single functional area or department.

Job rotation gives employees a series of job assignments in various functional areas of the company or movement among jobs in a single functional area or department. For example, at United Technologies Corporation the job rotation program in finance is within the finance function because employees need to understand all aspects of budgeting. Greyhound Financial Corporation has a job rotation program known as "muscle-building" for high-potential executive managers.[43] Managers are put in departments where they have to perform tasks different from those they have performed in the past. They maintain their titles and compensation levels while moving through the assignments, which vary in status. The time employees spend in each job varies depending on the assignment's purpose. In the Greyhound program, assignments last two years.

Job rotation helps employees gain an overall appreciation of the company's goals, increases their understanding of different company functions, develops a network of contacts, and improves problem-solving and decision-making skills.[44] Job rotation has also been shown to be related to skill acquisition, salary growth, and promotion rates. But there are several potential problems with job rotation for both the employee and the work unit. The rotation may create a short-term perspective on problems and solutions in rotating employees and their peers. Employees' satisfaction and motivation may be adversely affected because they find it difficult to develop functional specialties and they don't spend enough time in one position to receive a challenging assignment. Productivity losses and work load increases may be experienced by both the department gaining a rotating employee and the department losing the employee due to training demands and loss of a resource.

The characteristics of effective job rotation systems are shown in Table 9.10. As we see, effective job rotation systems are linked to the company's training, development, and career management systems. Also, job rotation should be used for all types of employees, not just those with managerial potential.

Transfer
The movement of an employee to a different job assignment in a different area of the company.

Transfers, Promotions, and Downward Moves

Upward, lateral, and downward mobility is available for development purposes in most companies.[45] In a **transfer,** an employee is assigned a job in a different area of the company. Transfers do not necessarily increase job responsibilities or compensation. They

TABLE 9.10

Characteristics of Effective Job Rotation Systems

1. Job rotation is used to develop skills as well as give employees experience needed for managerial positions.
2. Employees understand specific skills that will be developed by rotation.
3. Job rotation is used for all levels and types of employees.
4. Job rotation is linked with the career management process so employees know the development needs addressed by each job assignment.
5. Benefits of rotation are maximized and costs are minimized through managing timing of rotations to reduce work load costs and helping employees understand job rotation's role in their development plans.
6. All employees have equal opportunities for job rotation assignments regardless of their demographic group.

SOURCE: Based on L. Cheraskin and M. Campion, "Study Clarifies Job Rotation Benefits," *Personnel Journal,* November 1996, pp. 31–38.

are likely lateral moves (a move to a job with similar responsibilities). **Promotions** are advancements into positions with greater challenges, more responsibility, and more authority than in the previous job. Promotions usually include pay increases.

Promotions
Advances into positions with greater challenge, more responsibility, and more authority than the employee's previous job.

Transfers may involve relocation within the United States or to another country. This can be stressful not only because the employee's work role changes, but if the employee is in a two-career family, the spouse must find new employment. Also, the family has to join a new community. Transfers disrupt employees' daily lives, interpersonal relationships, and work habits.[46] People have to find new housing, shopping, health care, and leisure facilities, and they may be many miles from the emotional support of friends and family. They also have to learn a new set of work norms and procedures; they must develop interpersonal relationships with their new managers and peers; and they are expected to be as productive in their new jobs as they were in their old jobs even though they may know little about the products, services, processes, or employees for whom they are responsible.

Because transfers can provoke anxiety, many companies have difficulty getting employees to accept them. Research has identified the employee characteristics associated with a willingness to accept transfers:[47] high career ambitions, a belief that one's future with the company is promising, and a belief that accepting a transfer is necessary for success in the company. Employees who are not married and not active in the community are generally most willing to accept transfers. Among married employees, the spouse's willingness to move is the most important influence on whether an employee will accept a transfer.

A **downward move** occurs when an employee is given less responsibility and authority.[48] This may involve a move to another position at the same level (lateral demotion), a temporary cross-functional move, or a demotion because of poor performance. Temporary cross-functional moves to lower-level positions, which give employees experience working in different functional areas, are most frequently used for employee development. For example, engineers who want to move into management often take lower-level positions (like shift supervisor) to develop their management skills.

Downward move
A job change involving a reduction in an employee's level of responsibility and authority.

Because of the psychological and tangible rewards of promotions (such as increased feelings of self-worth, salary, and status in the company), employees are more willing to accept promotions than lateral or downward moves. Promotions are more readily available when a company is profitable and growing. When a company is restructuring or experiencing stable or declining profits—especially if numerous employees are interested in promotions and the company tends to rely on the external labor market to staff higher-level positions—promotion opportunities may be limited.[49]

Unfortunately, many employees have difficulty associating transfers and downward moves with development. They see them as punishments rather than as opportunities to develop skills that will help them achieve long-term success with the company. Many employees decide to leave a company rather than accept a transfer. Companies need to successfully manage transfers not only because of the costs of replacing employees but because of the costs directly associated with them. For example, GTE spends approximately $60 million a year on home purchases and other relocation costs such as temporary housing and relocation allowances.[50] One challenge companies face is learning how to use transfers and downward moves as development opportunities—convincing employees that accepting these opportunities will result in long-term benefits for them.

To ensure that employees accept transfers, promotions, and downward moves as development opportunities, companies can provide

- Information about the content, challenges, and potential benefits of the new job and location.
- Involvement in the transfer decision by sending the employees to preview the new location and giving them information about the community.
- Clear performance objectives and early feedback about their job performance.
- A host at the new location to help them adjust to the new community and workplace.
- Information about how the job opportunity will affect their income, taxes, mortgage payments, and other expenses.
- Reimbursement and assistance in selling and purchasing or renting a place to live.
- An orientation program for the new location and job.
- Information on how the new job experiences will support the employee's career plans.
- Assistance for dependent family members, including identifying schools and child care and elder care options.
- Help for the spouse in identifying and marketing skills and finding employment.[51]

Temporary Assignments with Other Organizations

Externship
When a company allows an employee to take a full-time operational role at another company.

Externship refers to a company allowing employees to take a full-time operational role at another company. Mercer Management, a consulting firm, uses externship to develop employees interested in gaining experience in a specific industry.[52] Mercer Management promises to employ the externs after their assignments end. For example, one employee who has been a Mercer consultant for five years is now vice president of Internet services for Binney & Smith, the maker of Crayola crayons. A year ago he was consulting on an Internet project for Binney & Smith. But he wanted to actually implement his recommendations rather than just give them to the client and move on to another project—so he started working at Binney & Smith. He remains on Mercer Management's payroll, though his salary comes from Binney & Smith. Mercer believes that employees who participate in the externship program will remain committed to the company because they have had the opportunity to learn and grow professionally and have not had to disrupt their personal and professional lives with a job search. Although externships give employees other employment options and some employees will leave, Mercer believes that it not only is a good development strategy but also helps in recruitment. The externship program signals to potential employees that Mercer is creative and flexible with its employees.

First Chicago National Bank and Kodak participated in an employee exchange program so that the two companies could better understand each other's business and how to improve the services provided.[53] For example, a First Chicago employee helped Kodak's business imaging division identify applications for compact disc technology. A Kodak employee helped First Chicago understand areas within the bank that could benefit from imaging technology.

Temporary assignments can include a **sabbatical** (a leave of absence from the company to renew or develop skills). Employees on sabbatical often receive full pay and benefits. Sabbaticals let employees get away from the day-to-day stresses of their jobs and acquire new skills and perspectives. Sabbaticals also allow employees more time for personal pursuits such as writing a book or spending more time with young children. Sabbaticals are common in a variety of industries ranging from consulting firms to the fast food industry.[54] Morningstar Inc., the mutual fund tracking company, provides a six-week paid sabbatical every four years for all employees.[55] A Morningstar manager who had recently been promoted to the role of exhibit/conference manager took an extra year before taking his sabbatical. He spent half his sabbatical on the beach in California and another three weeks pursuing his passion for modern dance. How employees spend their sabbaticals varies from company to company. Some employees may work for a nonprofit service agency; others may study at a college or university or travel and work on special projects in non-U.S. subsidiaries of the company.

Sabbatical
A leave of absence from the company to renew or develop skills.

Interpersonal Relationships

Employees can also develop skills and increase their knowledge about the company and its customers by interacting with a more experienced organization member. Mentoring and coaching are two types of interpersonal relationships that are used to develop employees.

Mentoring

A **mentor** is an experienced, productive senior employee who helps develop a less experienced employee (the protégé). Most mentoring relationships develop informally as a result of interests or values shared by the mentor and protégé. Research suggests that employees with certain personality characteristics (like emotional stability, the ability to adapt their behavior based on the situation, and high needs for power and achievement) are most likely to seek a mentor and be an attractive protégé for a mentor.[56] Mentoring relationships can also develop as part of a planned company effort to bring together successful senior employees with less experienced employees.

Mentor
An experienced, productive senior employee who helps develop a less-experienced employee.

Developing Successful Mentoring Programs. Although many mentoring relationships develop informally, one major advantage of formalized mentoring programs is that they ensure access to mentors for all employees, regardless of gender or race. An additional advantage is that participants in the mentoring relationship know what is expected of them.[57] One limitation of formal mentoring programs is that mentors may not be able to provide counseling and coaching in a relationship that has been artificially created.[58]

TABLE 9.11

Characteristics of Successful Formal Mentoring Programs

1. Mentor and protégé participation is voluntary. Relationship can be ended at any time without fear of punishment.
2. The mentor–protégé matching process does not limit the ability of informal relationships to develop. For example, a mentor pool can be established to allow protégés to choose from a variety of qualified mentors.
3. Mentors are chosen on the basis of their past record in developing employees, willingness to serve as a mentor, and evidence of positive coaching, communication, and listening skills.
4. The purpose of the program is clearly understood. Projects and activities that the mentor and protégé are expected to complete are specified.
5. The length of the program is specified. Mentor and protégé are encouraged to pursue the relationship beyond the formal period.
6. A minimum level of contact between the mentor and protégé is specified.
7. Protégés are encouraged to contact one another to discuss problems and share successes.
8. The mentor program is evaluated. Interviews with mentors and protégés give immediate feedback regarding specific areas of dissatisfaction. Surveys gather more detailed information regarding benefits received from participating in the program.
9. Employee development is rewarded, which signals managers that mentoring and other development activities are worth their time and effort.

Table 9.11 presents the characteristics of a successful formal mentoring program. Mentors should be chosen based on interpersonal and technical skills. They also need to be trained. For example, New York Hospital–Cornell Medical Center developed a mentoring program for housekeeping employees. Each mentor has between 5 and 10 protégés to meet with on a quarterly basis. To qualify as mentors, employees have to receive outstanding performance evaluations, demonstrate strong interpersonal skills, and be able to perform basic cleaning tasks and essential duties of all housekeeping positions including safety procedures (such as handling infectious waste).

Mentors undergo a two-day training program that emphasizes communication skills. They are also taught how to convey information about the job and give directions effectively without criticizing employees.[59]

Career support
Coaching, protection, sponsorship, and providing challenging assignments, exposure, and visibility.

Psychosocial support
Serving as a friend and role model, providing positive regard and acceptance, and creating an outlet for a protégé to talk about anxieties and fears.

Benefits of Mentoring Relationships. Both mentors and protégés can benefit from a mentoring relationship. Research suggests that mentors provide career and psychosocial support to their protégés. **Career support** includes coaching, protection, sponsorship, and providing challenging assignments, exposure, and visibility. **Psychosocial support** includes serving as a friend and a role model, providing positive regard and acceptance, and creating an outlet for the protégé to talk about anxieties and fears. Additional benefits for the protégé include higher rates of promotion, higher salaries, and greater organizational influence.[60]

Mentoring relationships provide opportunities for mentors to develop their interpersonal skills and increase their feelings of self-esteem and worth to the organization. For individuals in technical fields such as engineering or health services, the protégé may help them gain knowledge about important new scientific developments in their field (and therefore prevent them from becoming technically obsolete). For example, General Electric recently launched an initiative in e-business. However, many veteran managers faced the challenge of trying to understand how to effectively use the Internet. Jack Welch, former CEO of General Electric, created a mentoring program for his top 600 managers.[61] The program involves having younger employees who have more experience with the Internet serving as mentors for the top managers. Welch generated interest in the program by getting his own mentor, who is approximately half his age and has much less business experience than he does—but is a Web expert who runs the company's website. The purpose of the program is to help managers become familiar with competitors' websites, experience the difficulty of ordering products online, and understand what the best websites are doing right. Welch started the program because he believes that e-business knowledge is generally inversely related to age and position in the company hierarchy. GE managers meet with their mentors for Web lessons, where they critique websites, discuss articles and books about e-commerce they have have been given to read, and ask the mentors questions. The sessions benefit both the mentors and the protégés. The protégés learn about the Web, and the mentoring sessions make the younger employees more comfortable talking to their bosses. The mentors also learn about the skills that a manager needs to run a large business operation (such as the ability to communicate with different people).

Purposes of Mentoring Programs. Mentor programs socialize new employees, increase the likelihood of skill transfer from training to the work setting, and provide opportunities for women and minorities to gain the exposure and skills needed to evolve into managerial positions. Consider the New York Hospital–Cornell Medical Center mentoring program. The program is designed to help new employees more quickly learn housekeeping duties and understand the culture of the hospital. One benefit of the program is that new employees' performance deficiencies are more quickly corrected. Although the formal mentoring of new employees lasts only two weeks, mentors are available to provide support many months later.

At E. I. Du Pont de Nemours and Company's corporate headquarters, Steve Croft and Janet Graham have met at least once a month for the past seven years to share problems, information, and advice as part of Du Pont's mentoring program.[62] He is a planning manager in Du Pont's research division. She is an administrative assistant in the toxicology lab where Steve used to work. From a list of volunteers, protégés choose mentors (managers and executives) whose skills and experience they want to learn about. Croft, the mentor, has answered Graham's questions about corporate programs and given her the opportunity to meet scientists and managers in the company. Graham has also learned more about the role of other departments in the company and budgetary priorities. Croft too has benefited from the relationship. He has learned about how management decisions affect employees. For example, when the toxicology lab was forced to begin to charge departments for its services (rather than being supported from the company's general fund), Croft learned about employees' reactions and anxieties from Graham.

Because of the lack of potential mentors or a formal reward system supporting mentoring, and the belief that the quality of mentorships developed in a formal program is poorer than informal mentoring relationships, some companies have initiated group mentoring programs. In **group mentoring programs,** a successful senior employee is paired with a group of four to six less experienced protégés. One potential advantage of the mentoring group is that protégés can learn from each other as well as from a more experienced senior employee. The leader helps protégés understand the organization, guides them in analyzing their experiences, and helps them clarify career directions. Each member of the group may complete specific assignments, or the group may work together on a problem or issue.[63]

Group mentoring program
A program pairing a successful senior employee with a group of four to six less experienced protégés.

Coaching

Coach
A peer or manager who works with an employee to motivate her, help her develop skills, and provide reinforcement and feedback.

A **coach** is a peer or manager who works with an employee to motivate him, help him develop skills, and provide reinforcement and feedback. There are three roles that a coach can play.[64] Part of coaching may be one-on-one with an employee (such as giving feedback). Another role is to help employees learn for themselves. This involves helping them find experts who can assist them with their concerns and teaching them how to obtain feedback from others. Third, coaching may involve providing resources such as mentors, courses, or job experiences that the employee may not be able to gain access to without the coach's help. For example, companies are using coaching specifically to groom future chief executive officers.[65] Best Buy, a consumer-electronics retailer, is directly addressing younger managers' weaknesses in personality and management style before they are put into higher-level management positions and have problems. Best Buy has invested nearly $10 million on coaches for all top managers. Once a month, top executives spend a few hours with an industrial psychologist who helps them work through leadership issues. For example, one manager discussed with his coach how to balance the needs of some of his subordinate management team members, who are more comfortable in the roles of a traditional retail environment, with the business need to compete with competitors online. He has to learn how to lead and push new ideas (such as forging record industry partnerships) without being authoritarian, dominating discussions, or making quick decisions.

To develop coaching skills, training programs need to focus on four issues related to managers' reluctance to provide coaching.[66] First, managers may be reluctant to discuss performance issues even with a competent employee because they want to avoid confrontation. This is especially an issue when the manager is less of an expert than the employee. Second, managers may be better able to identify performance problems than to help employees solve them. Third, managers may also feel that the employee interprets coaching as criticism. Fourth, as companies downsize and operate with fewer employees, managers may feel that there is not enough time for coaching.

Career Management and Development Planning Systems

Companies' career management systems vary in the level of sophistication and the emphasis they place on different components of the process. Steps and responsibilities in the career management system are shown in Figure 9.2.

Self-Assessment

Self-assessment refers to the use of information by employees to determine their career interests, values, aptitudes, and behavioral tendencies. It often involves psychological tests such as the Myers-Briggs Type Indicator (described earlier in the chapter), the Strong-Campbell Interest Inventory, and the Self-Directed Search. The Strong-Campbell helps employees identify their occupational and job interests; the Self-Directed Search identifies employees' preferences for working in different types of environments (like sales, counseling, landscaping, and so on). Tests may also help employees identify the relative values they place on work and leisure activities. Self-assessment can involve exercises such as the one in Table 9.12. This type of exercise helps an employee consider where she is now in her career, identify future plans, and

FIGURE 9.2
Steps and Responsibilities in the Career Management Process

TABLE 9.12
Example of a Self-Assessment Exercise

ACTIVITY	(PURPOSE)
Step 1:	***Where am I?* (Examine current position of life and career.)**
Think about your life from past and present to the future. Draw a time line to represent important events.	
Step 2:	***Who am I?* (Examine different roles.)**
Using 3 × 5 cards, write down one answer per card to the question "Who am I?"	
Step 3:	***Where would I like to be and what would I like to happen?* (This helps in future goal setting.)**
Consider your life from present to future. Write an autobiography answering three questions: What do you want to have accomplished? What milestones do you want to achieve? What do you want to be remembered for?	
Step 4:	***An ideal year in the future* (Identify resources needed.)**
Consider a one-year period in the future. If you had unlimited resources, what would you do? What would the ideal environment look like? Does the ideal environment match step 3?	
Step 5:	***An ideal job* (Create current goal.)**
In the present, think about an ideal job for you with your available resources. Consider your role, resources, and type of training or education needed.	
Step 6:	***Career by objective inventory* (Summarize current situation.)**
• What gets you excited each day? • What do you do well? What are you known for? • What do you need to achieve your goals? • What could interfere with reaching your goals? • What should you do now to move toward reaching your goals? • What is your long-term career objective?	

SOURCE: Based on J.E. McMahon and S.K. Merman, "Career Development," in *The ASTD Training and Development Handbook*, 4th ed., ed. R.L. Craig (New York: McGraw–Hill, 1996), pp. 679–97. Reproduced with permission.

gauge how her career fits with her current situation and available resources. In some companies, counselors assist employees in the self-assessment process and interpret the results of psychological tests.

Through the assessment, a development need can be identified. This need can result from gaps between current skills and/or interests and the type of work or position the employee wants. For example, a branch manager at Wells Fargo Bank for 14 years enjoyed both working with computers and researching program development issues.[67] He was having difficulty in choosing whether to pursue further work experiences with computers or enter a new career in developing software applications. Psychological tests he completed as part of the company's career assessment program confirmed his strong interests in research and development. As a result, he began his own software design company.

Reality Check

Reality check refers to the information employees receive about how the company evaluates their skills and knowledge and where they fit into the company's plans (potential promotion opportunities, lateral moves). Usually this information is provided by the employee's manager as part of performance appraisal. It is not uncommon in well-developed career management systems for the manager to hold separate performance appraisals and career development discussions. For example, in Coca-Cola USA's system, employees and managers have a separate meeting after the annual performance review to discuss the employee's career interests, strengths, and possible development activities.[68]

Goal Setting

Goal setting refers to the process of employees developing short- and long-term career objectives. These goals usually relate to desired positions (such as becoming sales manager within three years), level of skill application (use one's budgeting skills to improve the unit's cash flow problems), work setting (move to corporate marketing within two years), or skill acquisition (learn how to use the company's human resource information system). These goals are usually discussed with the manager and written into a development plan. A development plan for a product manager is shown in Figure 9.3. Development plans usually include descriptions of strengths and weaknesses, career goals, and development activities for reaching the career goal.

Action Planning

During this phase, employees determine how they will achieve their short- and long-term career goals. Action plans may involve any one or combination of development approaches discussed in the chapter (such as enrolling in courses and seminars, getting additional assessment, obtaining new job experiences, or finding a mentor or coach).[69] The development approach used depends on the needs and developmental goal.

Example of a Career Management System

United Parcel Service's (UPS's) career development system illustrates the career planning process and the strategic role it can play in ensuring that staffing needs are met.[70] UPS has 285,000 employees in 185 nations and territories who are responsible for mak-

FIGURE 9.3
Career Development Plan

Name: **Title:** Project Manager **Immediate Manager:**

Competencies
Please identify your three greatest strengths and areas for improvements.

Strengths
- Strategic thinking and execution (confidence, command skills, action orientation)
- Results orientation (competence, motivating others, perseverance)
- Spirit for winning (building team spirit, customer focus, respect colleagues)

Areas for Improvement
- Patience (tolerance of people or processes and sensitivity to pacing)
- Written communications (ability to write clearly and succinctly)
- Overly ambitious (too much focus on successful completion of projects rather than developing relationships with individuals involved in the projects)

Career Goals
Please describe your overall career goals.
- **Long-term:** Accept positions of increased responsibility to a level of general manager (or beyond). The areas of specific interest include but are not limited to product and brand management, technology and development, strategic planning, and marketing.
- **Short-term:** Continue to improve my skills in marketing and brand management while utilizing my skills in product management, strategic planning, and global relations.

Next Assignments
Identify potential next assignments (including timing) that would help you develop toward your career goals.
- Manager or director level in planning, development, product, or brand management. Timing estimated to be Spring 2003.

Training and Development Needs
List both training and development activities that will either help you develop in your current assignment or provide overall career development.
- Master's degree classes will allow me to practice and improve my written communications skills. The dynamics of my current position, teamwork, and reliance on other individuals allow me to practice patience and to focus on individual team members' needs along with the success of the projects.

Employee ______________________ **Date** ________
Immediate Manager ______________ **Date** ________
Mentor ________________________ **Date** ________

ing sure that packages are picked up and delivered on time. UPS wanted to develop its managerial ranks, which included 49,000 people worldwide, via a management development system that would ensure that managers' skills were up to date; the system had to be linked to selection and training activities. As a result, UPS designed a career management process. The process starts with the manager identifying the skills, knowledge, and experience that the work team needs to meet current and anticipated business needs. Gaps between needs and relevant qualifications of the team are identified. The manager then identifies the development needs of each team member. Next, team members complete a series of exercises that help them with self-assessment, goal setting, and development planning. The manager and employee work together to create an individual development plan. In the discussion, the manager shares performance appraisal information and analysis of team needs with the employee; that is, the manager provides a "reality check." The plan includes the employee's career goals and development actions to pursue during the next year. To ensure that the career management process helps with future staffing decisions, divisionwide career development meetings are held. Here managers report on the development needs and plans as well as their work teams' capabilities. Training and development managers attend to ensure that a realistic training plan is created. The process is repeated at higher levels of management. The ultimate result is a master plan with training activities and development plans coordinated among the functional areas.

The UPS system includes all of the steps in the career management process. The most important feature of the system is the sharing of information about individual employees, districts, and functional development and training needs and capabilities. This use of information from employees, districts, and company functions allows UPS to be better prepared to meet changing staffing needs and customer demands than many companies.

The "Competing through High-Performance Work Systems" box gives an example of how companies are using technology to give employees complete control of their career management. Several important design factors should be considered in the process of developing a career management system (see Table 9.13). Tying development of the system to business objectives and needs, top management support, and having managers and employees participate in building the system are especially important to help overcome resistance to using the system.

Example of an Employee's Use of a Career Management System

Robert Brown, a program manager in an information systems department, needs to increase his knowledge of available project management software. His performance appraisal indicates that only 60 percent of the projects he is working on are being approved due to incomplete information. (Assessment identified his development need.) As a result, Robert and his manager agree that his development goal is to increase his

TABLE 9.13

Design Factors of Effective Career Management Systems

1. System is positioned as a response to a business need.
2. Employees and managers participate in development of the system.
3. Employees are encouraged to take an active role in career management.
4. Evaluation is ongoing and used to improve the system.
5. Business units can customize the system for their own purposes (with some constraints).
6. Employees need access to career information sources (including advisers and positions available).
7. Senior management supports the career system.
8. Career management is linked to other human resource practices such as performance management, training, and recruiting systems.

SOURCE: Based on B. Baumann, J. Duncan, S.E. Former, and Z. Leibowitz, "Amoco Primes the Talent Pump," *Personnel Journal,* February 1996, pp. 79–84.

COMPETING THROUGH HIGH-PERFORMANCE WORK SYSTEMS

Using Intranets to Drive Development Planning

Technology such as intranets facilitates the process of giving employees complete control over their development while enabling them to plan their development at their convenience. For example, Ford Motor Company in Detroit, Michigan, has recognized that to be successful, its employees must be trained and developed. To facilitate the development process, Ford created the "Personal Development Roadmap" (PDR), a Web-based resource available on the company intranet that allows marketing, sales, and service employees to take control of their personal and professional development. The PDR helps employees answer three questions: What skills do I have? What skills should I have? And how do I enhance my skills?

Employees annually asses their current skills by completing an online profile. The PDR compares each employee's profile to the expected skill levels for the employee's job group. Following the self-assessment, the employee identifies the areas where he or she would like to focus development. The PDR will recommend education (Ford classes and seminars), exploration (activities outside Ford), and/or experiences (job assignments and other on-the-job opportunities) to help meet the employee's development needs. Employees can enroll in a suggested course offered by Ford through the website. The PDR also helps the employee create an annual development plan related to attaining the development needs. Ford has identified specific leader behaviors (like drive for results, innovation, desire to serve) that all salaried employees need for the company to lead in marketing, sales, and service. The PDR focuses on helping employees improve these leadership behaviors.

Although it is too early to evaluate success, Ford developed the PDR to help employees continually improve their knowledge, skill, and abilities, to align their behavior with company goals and strategies, and to take responsibility for their own performance, progress, and development.

SOURCE: Ford Motor Company brochure "Personal Development Roadmap," 1998. Courtesy Ford Motor Company.

knowledge of available project management software, which can boost his effectiveness in project management. To raise his knowledge of project management software, Robert will read articles (formal education), meet software vendors, and contact vendors' customers for evaluations of the project management software they have used (job experiences). His manager will provide the names of customers to contact. Robert and his manager set six months as the target date for completion of these activities.

Special Issues in Employee Development

Melting the Glass Ceiling

A major development issue facing companies today is how to get women and minorities into upper-level management positions—how to break the **glass ceiling.** The glass ceiling is a barrier to advancement to the higher levels of the organization. This

Glass ceiling
A barrier to advancement to higher-level jobs in the company that adversely affects women and minorities. The barrier may be due to lack of access to training programs, development experiences, or relationships (e.g., mentoring).

barrier may be due to stereotypes or company systems that adversely affect the development of women or minorities.[71] The glass ceiling is likely caused by lack of access to training programs, appropriate developmental job experiences, and developmental relationships (such as mentoring).[72] Research has found no gender differences in access to job experiences involving transitions or creating change.[73] However, male managers receive significantly more assignments involving high levels of responsibility (high stakes, managing business diversity, handling external pressure) than female managers of similar ability and managerial level. Also, female managers report experiencing more challenge due to lack of personal support (a type of job demand considered to be an obstacle that has been found to relate to harmful stress) than male managers. Managers making developmental assignments need to carefully consider whether gender biases or stereotypes are influencing the types of assignments given to women versus men.

The "Competing by Meeting Stakeholders' Needs" box shows the steps that Procter & Gamble is taking to melt the glass ceiling. Women and minorities often have trouble finding mentors because of their lack of access to the "old boy network," managers' preference to interact with other managers of similar status rather than with line employees, and intentional exclusion by managers who have negative stereotypes about women's and minorities' abilities, motivation, and job preferences.[74] Potential mentors may view minorities and women as a threat to their job security because they believe affirmative action plans give those groups preferential treatment.

Consider Deloitte & Touche's efforts to melt the glass ceiling. Deloitte & Touche is an accounting, tax, and consulting firm with offices throughout the United States. The company had been experiencing high turnover of talented women and set out to understand why this was occurring and what the company could do to stop it.[75] Table 9.14 shows Deloitte & Touche's recommendations for melting the glass ceiling. Deloitte's Initiative for the Retention and Advancement of Women grew from a task force chaired by the company's chief executive officer. Deloitte & Touche made a business case for change by showing the senior partners of the company that half of the new hires were women, and half of them left the company before becoming candidates for upper management positions (partners). Data on the problem were gathered by having every management professional in the company attend a workshop designed to explore how gender attitudes affected the work environment (and led to the loss of talented women). The workshops included discussions, videos, and case studies. For example, a case scenario involved having partners evaluate two

TABLE 9.14
Deloitte & Touche's Recommendations for Melting the Glass Ceiling

Make sure senior management supports and is involved in the program.
Make a business case for change.
Make the change public.
Gather data on problems causing the glass ceiling using task forces, focus groups, and questionnaires.
Create awareness of how gender attitudes affect the work environment.
Force accountability through reviews of promotion rates and assignment decisions.
Promote development for all employees.

SOURCE: Based on D. McCracken, "Winning the Talent War for Women," *Harvard Business Review*, November–December 2000, pp. 159–67.

COMPETING BY MEETING STAKEHOLDERS' NEEDS

Selling Women on a Career at P&G

Procter & Gamble has successfully used its marketing strategy to sell its products to women. It had been less successful in bringing women into its management ranks. A study of employee turnover found that two of every three high-performing employees who left the company were women. Because P&G promotes from within, retention of high performers is critical. Until recently, no women sat on P&G's executive committee, and few executives were female.

To uncover the reasons for women's low retention rate and lack of movement into executive positions, P&G conducted interviews and surveys. P&G found that women felt their consensus-building management styles were not valued in the company's command-and-control culture, which favors quick, aggressive decision makers. Because career planning was not openly discussed at the company, women employees reported that they didn't know where they stood with the company. Employee opinion surveys revealed that a "lack of feeling valued" was a larger issue for women than for men. Women employees realized that to be successful, they needed to put in long hours. But they wanted flexible hours, not part-time work schedules that would slow their promotion.

P&G then created a task force to study the brand management career path, the major career path to executive-level management. The team set goals to lower the female turnover rate and achieve 40 percent women at each level of brand management by the year 2005. One step of the task force was to develop a mentoring program known as Mentoring Up. The program incorporates many characteristics of effective mentoring programs. All eligible junior, female managers and male, senior managers are expected to participate. The female managers must have at least one year of tenure and be good performers. Junior protégés are matched with senior mentors based on their responses to a questionnaire. Both mentors and protégés attend an orientation session that includes a panel discussion by past participants in the program and a series of exercises probing women's workplace issues and reasons for success at P&G. The mentoring relationships require meeting at least once every two months. Mentors and protégés receive discussion guides designed to help facilitate dialogue. For example, one guide asks the mentoring pairs to explore the keys to success and failure for women and men in company leadership positions. The discussion guides also include questions designed to elicit feelings about when women feel valued. The mentor and protégés explore differences and similarities in response to these questions to identify how people like to be recognized. Two issues have frequently been raised in the mentoring relationships—the barriers that women face in achieving a balance between work and life and differences in managerial and decision-making styles between men and women.

One of the biggest benefits of the program has been that mentors and protégés have shared advice and perspectives and feel comfortable using each other to test out new ideas. Junior female managers also get exposure to top executives. This helps the executives who make promotion and succession decisions become familiar with them. The program has reduced the turnover rate of female managers by 25 percent so that it is now similar to the turnover rate for male managers.

SOURCE: Based on T. Parker-Pope, "Inside P&G, a Pitch to Keep Women Employees," *The Wall Street Journal* (September 9, 1998), pp. B1, B6; D. Zielinski, "Mentoring Up," *Training*, April 2000, pp. 34–38.

promising employees, one male and one female, with identical skills. One issue that was raised through the case analysis was that men get evaluated based on their potential, women based on their performance. Discussion suggested that the male could be expected to grow into the position through mentoring and other types of development. The female was evaluated based on performance in her current position. Her potential was not considered; rather, her past performance indicated that she was good in her current job but didn't have the necessary skills to move into executive management. The workshop also focused on how work assignments were allocated. High-profile, high-revenue assignments were important for advancement in the company. Workshop discussion showed that women were passed over for these desirable assignments because of false assumptions that male partners made about what women wanted, such as no travel. Also, women tended to get assigned to projects that were in the nonprofit, health care, and retail sectors—important segments but not as visible as areas like manufacturing, financial services, or mergers and acquisitions.

As a result of the workshops, Deloitte & Touche began discussing assignment decisions to make sure women had opportunities for highly visible assignments. Also, the company started formal career planning for both women and men. The company also sponsored networking events for women, where they had the opportunity to hear from successful women partners and meet other women at their level and higher in the company.

To measure the effectiveness of the program, Deloitte & Touche offices were given a menu of goals that they could choose from as evaluation criteria, including recruiting more women and reducing turnover. The compensation and promotability of office managers depended in part on their meeting these objectives. The company communicated to top management results on turnover and promotion rates for each office. Low-performing offices were visited by top managers to facilitate more progress.

Melting the glass ceiling takes time. Currently 14 percent of Deloitte & Touche's partners and directors are women, and women's and men's turnover rates are comparable. Reducing the turnover rate for women has saved the company an estimated $250 million in hiring and training costs. Deloitte is still striving to make sure that more women are partners and directors. In a global business world, one challenge is to extend the values of the initiative while respecting local cultural norms that might view women as less desirable employees or business partners.

Succession Planning

Many companies are losing sizable numbers of upper-level managers due to retirement and company restructurings that reduced the number of potential upper level-managers. They are finding that their middle managers are not ready to move into upper management positions due to skill weaknesses or lack of needed experience. This creates the need for succession planning. **Succession planning** refers to the process of identifying and tracking high-potential employees. Succession planning helps organizations in several different ways.[76] It requires senior management to systematically review leadership talent in the company. It assures that top-level managerial talent is available. It provides a set of development experiences that managers must complete to be considered for top management positions; this avoids premature promotion of managers who are not ready for upper management ranks. Succession planning systems also help attract and retain managerial employees by providing

Succession planning
The identification and tracking of high-potential employees capable of filling higher-level managerial positions.

them with development opportunities that they can complete if upper management is a career goal for them. **High-potential employees** are those the company believes are capable of being successful in higher-level managerial positions such as general manager of a strategic business unit, functional director (such as director of marketing), or chief executive officer (CEO).[77] High-potential employees typically complete an individual development program that involves education, executive mentoring and coaching, and rotation through job assignments. Job assignments are based on the successful career paths of the managers whom the high-potential employees are being prepared to replace. High-potential employees may also receive special assignments, such as making presentations and serving on committees and task forces.

High-potential employees
Employees the company believes are capable of being successful in high-level management positions.

Research suggests that the development of high-potential employees involves three stages.[78] A large pool of employees may initially be identified as high-potential employees, but the numbers are reduced over time because of turnover, poor performance, or a personal choice not to strive for a higher position. In stage 1, high-potential employees are selected. Those who have completed elite academic programs (like an MBA at Stanford) or who have been outstanding performers are identified. Psychological tests such as assessment centers may also be used.

In stage 2, high-potential employees receive development experiences. Those who succeed are the ones who continue to demonstrate good performance. A willingness to make sacrifices for the company is also necessary (such as accepting new assignments or relocating to a different region). Good oral and written communication skills, an ease in interpersonal relationships, and a talent for leadership are critical. In what is known as a "tournament model" of job transitions, high-potential employees who meet their senior managers' expectations in this stage advance into the next stage of the process.[79] Employees who do not meet the expectations are ineligible for higher-level managerial positions in the company.

To reach stage 3, high-potential employees usually have to be seen by top management as fitting into the company's culture and having the personality characteristics needed to successfully represent the company. These employees have the potential to occupy the company's top positions. In stage 3, the CEO becomes actively involved in developing the employees, who are exposed to the company's key personnel and are given a greater understanding of the company's culture. It is important to note that the development of high-potential employees is a slow process. Reaching stage 3 may take 15 to 20 years.

American Express Financial Services recently wanted to grow and expand but realized that it didn't have the leaders to do so.[80] The company developed a process to forecast how many and what kinds of leaders it needs, assess the current employee talent, and develop employees with managerial talent it had already identified. Because American Express Financial Services is rapidly growing, it relies on one- to two-year forecasts to find and develop people. Managers recommend talented employees to regional vice presidents. Regional and corporate vice presidents recommend these employees into assessment programs designed to measure leadership and basic managerial skills. Employees receive personalized development plans designed to improve weaknesses in knowledge, skill, or experience. Their progress is monitored by top managers, who provide coaching if needed.

Some companies' succession planning systems identify a small number of potential managers for each position. Although this approach allows development activities to be targeted to a select few highly talented managers, it also limits the company's ability to staff future managerial positions and may cause a "talent drain." That is, high-potential employees who are not on the short list for managerial positions may leave the company. American Express's approach avoids this problem by identifying and creating a large number of qualified leaders, which helps build commitment to staying with the company.

Helping Managers with Dysfunctional Behaviors

A number of studies have identified managerial behavior that can cause an otherwise competent manager to be a "toxic" or ineffective manager. Such behavior includes insensitivity to others, inability to be a team player, arrogance, poor conflict management skills, inability to meet business objectives, and inability to change or adapt during a transition.[81] For example, a skilled manager who is interpersonally abrasive, aggressive, and an autocratic leader may find it difficult to motivate subordinates, may alienate internal and external customers, and may have trouble getting ideas accepted by superiors. These managers are in jeopardy of losing their jobs and have little chance of future advancement because of the dysfunctional behavior. Typically, a combination of assessment, training, and counseling is used to help managers change the dysfunctional behavior.

One example of a program designed specifically to help managers with dysfunctional behavior is the Individual Coaching for Effectiveness (ICE) program.[82] Although such programs' effectiveness needs to be further investigated, research suggests that managers' participation in them improves skill and reduces likelihood of termination.[83] The ICE program includes diagnosis, coaching, and support activities, tailored to the manager's needs. Clinical, counseling, or industrial–organizational psychologists are involved in all phases of the ICE program. They conduct the diagnosis, coach and counsel the manager, and develop action plans for implementing new skills on the job.

The first step in the ICE program, diagnosis, involves collecting information about the manager's personality, skills, and interests. Interviews with the manager, his or her supervisor, and colleagues as well as psychological tests collect this information to determine whether the manager can actually change the dysfunctional behavior. For example, personality traits such as extreme defensiveness may make behavior change difficult. If it is determined that the manager can benefit from the program, then specific developmental objectives are set. The manager and supervisor are typically involved in this process.

The coaching phase of the program first involves presenting the manager with information about the targeted skills or behavior. This may include information about principles of effective communication or teamwork, tolerance of individual differences in the workplace, or conducting effective meetings. The second step is for the manager to participate in behavior modeling training (discussed in Chapter 7). The manager also receives psychological counseling to overcome beliefs that may inhibit learning the desired behavior.

The support phase of the program creates conditions to ensure that the manager can use the new behaviors and skills acquired in the ICE program on the job. The supervisor provides feedback to the manager and the psychologist about progress made in using the new skills and behavior. The psychologist and manager identify situations in which the manager may tend to rely on dysfunctional behavior. The coach and manager also develop action plans that outline how the manager should try to use new behavior in daily work activities.

A Look Back

The chapter opener described First USA Bank's development program designed to help employees identify their career interests and develop them within the company.

Questions

1. How might job experiences be useful for helping employees develop?
2. To be effective, what should a development plan include that an employee at First USA Bank might complete as part of the Opportunity Knocks program?

Summary

This chapter emphasized the various development methods that companies use: formal education, assessment, job experiences, and interpersonal relationships. Most companies use one or more of these approaches to develop employees. Formal education involves enrolling employees in courses or seminars offered by the company or educational institutions. Assessment involves measuring the employee's performance, behavior, skills, or personality characteristics. Job experiences include job enlargement, rotating to a new job, promotions, or transfers. A more experienced, senior employee (a mentor) can help employees better understand the company and gain exposure and visibility to key persons in the organization. Part of a manager's job responsibility may be to coach employees. Regardless of the development approaches used, employees should have a development plan to identify (1) the type of development needed, (2) development goals, (3) the best approach for development, and (4) whether development goals have been reached. For development plans to be effective, both the employee and the company have responsibilities that need to be completed.

Discussion Questions

1. How could assessment be used to create a productive work team?
2. List and explain the characteristics of effective 360-degree feedback systems.
3. Why do companies develop formal mentoring programs? What are the potential benefits for the mentor? For the protégé?
4. Your boss is interested in hiring a consultant to help identify potential managers among current employees of a fast food restaurant. The manager's job is to help wait on customers and prepare food during busy times, oversee all aspects of restaurant operations (including scheduling, maintenance, on-the-job training, and food purchase), and help motivate employees to provide high-quality service. The manager is also responsible for resolving disputes that might occur between employees. The position involves working under stress and coordinating several activities at one time. She asks you to outline the type of assessment program you believe would do the best job of identifying employees who will be successful managers. What will you tell her?
5. Many employees are unwilling to relocate because they like their current community, and spouses and children prefer not to move. Yet employees need to develop new skills, strengthen skill weaknesses, and be exposed to new aspects of the business to prepare for management positions. How could an employee's current job be changed to develop management skills?
6. What is coaching? Is there one type of coaching? Explain.
7. Why are many managers reluctant to coach their employees?
8. Why should companies be interested in helping employees plan their careers? What benefits can companies gain? What are the risks?
9. What are the manager's roles in a career management system? Which role do you think is most difficult for the typical manager? Which is the easiest role? List the reasons why managers might resist involvement in career management.

Web Exercise

Go to General Electric's website at **www.gecareers.com**. Click on either "Entry-level" or "Master's level" leadership programs. Several different leadership programs are available. Choose one program and describe it (development activities, length, participants). What type of development activities are included in the program? Compare the development activities used in the entry-level and master's level leadership programs. How are they similar? How are they different? Why might they be different?

Managing People: From the Pages of *BusinessWeek*

BusinessWeek Basic Training for CEOs

Gary C. Wendt, prepare to be scared straight. On June 21, the Conseco Inc. (CNC) chief and 19 other recently crowned CEOs will subject themselves to a one-day immersion course administered by a parade of corporate critics and longtime chief executives. Those instructors are convinced they might be the only thing standing between the newbie leaders and career disaster. Open only to CEOs who have held the post for less than three years, the course will be taught by professors from elite business schools, top professionals, and such executive suite veterans as Merck's Raymond V. Gilmartin (MRK), Tyco International's Dennis Kozlowski (TYC), and Larry Bossidy, former head of AlliedSignal. "It's a boot camp for recently appointed CEOs," quips Rajiv L. Gupta, CEO of Rohm & Haas since 1999, who leapt at the chance to enlist.

To be sure, the CEO Academy is more than just a novel experiment in executive education—it may be the poshest, most expensive boot camp ever. The brainchild of an innovative CEO roundtable, the academy was conceived as a way for recently anointed CEOs to learn the perils of life in the corner office and for old-timers to discuss the trials and tribulations of CEO life before a receptive audience. It will be held in the august Harold Pratt mansion on New York City's Upper East Side. Tuition for the one-day course is a cool $10,000. But the lessons—dealing with the land mines that can bring an early end to a CEO's career—will be just as biting as the bark of any drill sergeant.

Newly minted CEOs expecting a lovefest are in for a rude awakening. The session on shareholder relations will be led in part by Nell Minow, a corporate governance agitator who has helped build bonfires under boards reluctant to deal with poor-performing CEOs. "My goal is to teach them what they need to do to avoid hearing from people like me in real life," says Minow, who will urge the CEOs to adopt performance-based pay plans, preferred by shareholders. Says Minow, "If they are responsive [to shareholders] in good times, they will have a better chance of keeping them on their side in a downturn."

If Minow's lecture reminds the new CEOs of one set of bosses, the presentation by superlawyer Ira M. Millstein, the dean of corporate governance, will urge them to pay heed to another: their board members. Millstein believes most new CEOs "would be just as happy not to have a board at all," and give it a low priority. To snap them out of that delusion, he'll warn: "There is nothing more important than getting to know the people who can fire you."

But the highlight of the CEO Academy will no doubt occur when veteran CEOs are asked to share their experiences. G. Richard Thoman, who was fired as Xerox Corp. (XRX) CEO last May, will talk about the lessons he learned at both Xerox and IBM. Gilmartin, an outsider who reinvigorated Merck & Co., will discuss the special challenges facing CEOs who are brought in from the outside. And in an era when more than half of all mergers founder—often bringing down the CEOs who attempted them—Tyco's Kozlowski will discuss "the dark side of acquisitions." His advice to the rookie CEOs: once a deal closes, "you have a very short window to create change, so speed is of the essence."

Most of the "students" can't wait to get started. "We're most able to learn when we're new in a job," says Amgen Inc. (AMGN) CEO Kevin W. Sharer, who got the top job a year ago and expects to benefit from people like Bossidy who have years of experience heading complex organizations. For Conseco's Wendt, who also has been at the helm for a year, the academy is "a chance to think outside of the box that you find yourself in as a leader of a business." Even Gilmartin, who long ago joined the ranks of proven CEOs, says he's looking forward to "the opportunity to listen to others talk about their experiences."

And that, say the group's founders, is the whole point. The CEO Academy is the creation of the M&A Group Inc., a CEO club formed in 1999 as a forum to discuss and facilitate mergers and acquisitions among members. The group has since evolved into something more: an arena that gives the reigning kings of corporate America "an opportunity to talk about the things that keep them awake at night," says cofounder Dennis C. Carey, a partner at headhunter SpencerStuart Inc. The group has grown to 60 members, including such influential CEOs as Dell Computer's Michael S. Dell (DELL) and AT&T's C. Michael

Armstrong (T). They quickly realized new CEOs needed help getting their bearings.

The reason? Although these industry titans get paid a king's ransom whether they succeed or fail, job security is a thing of the past. "This is a high-risk job," says Kozlowski, the M&A Group's chairman. "Our ranks [turn over] about 20 percent every year." And with the honeymoon period growing ever shorter, new CEOs have little time to get up to speed. Moreover, "many new CEOs have had limited experience in running a board, or in dealing with Wall Street, the business press, and shareholders," says Carey. That's why he recruited CEOs as instructors. "I wish I'd had [the chance to attend] a forum like this when I became CEO," says Kozlowski.

Of course, the ultimate test of any boot camp is whether it reduces the casualty rate among participants. It will take years to measure the effectiveness of the academy, which the M&A Group hopes to host annually. But with more CEOs crashing and burning, it sounds like a step in the right direction.

Questions

1. What recommendations would you have for identifying and preparing managers for CEO positions? Make sure you indicate the development approach(es) you would use as well as the succession planning process.
2. What actions should companies take to ensure that women and minority managers have access to development opportunities needed to reach upper levels of management?

Notes

1. S. Caudron, "Building Better Bosses," *Workforce*, May 2000, pp. 33–39.
2. K. Dobbs, "Plagued by Turnover? Train Your Managers," *Training*, August 2000, pp. 62–66.
3. M. London, *Managing the Training Enterprise* (San Francisco: Jossey-Bass, 1989).
4. R.W. Pace, P.C. Smith, and G.E. Mills, *Human Resource Development* (Englewood Cliffs, NJ: Prentice-Hall, 1991); W. Fitzgerald, "Training versus Development," *Training and Development Journal*, May 1992, pp. 81–84; R.A. Noe, S.L. Wilk, E.J. Mullen, and J.E. Wanek, "Employee Development: Issues in Construct Definition and Investigation of Antecedents," in *Improving Training Effectiveness in Work Organizations*, ed. J.K. Ford (Mahwah, NJ: Lawrence Erlbaum, 1997), pp. 153–89.
5. J.H. Greenhaus and G.A. Callanan, *Career Management*, 2nd ed. (Fort Worth, TX: Dryden Press, 1994).
6. D.T. Hall, "Protean Careers of the 21st Century," *Academy of Management Executive* 11 (1996), pp. 8–16.
7. D.M. Rousseau, "Changing the Deal while Keeping the People," *Academy of Management Executive* 11 (1996), pp. 50–61; D.M. Rousseau and J.M. Parks, "The Contracts of Individuals and Organizations," in *Research in Organizational Behavior* 15, ed. L.L. Cummings and B.M. Staw (Greenwich, CT: JAI Press, 1992), pp. 1–47.
8. P. Sellers, "Don't Call Me a Slacker," *Fortune* (December 12, 1994), pp. 181–96.
9. M.B. Arthur, P.H. Claman, and R.J. DeFillippi, "Intelligent Enterprise, Intelligent Careers," *Academy of Management Executive* 9 (1995), pp. 7–20.
10. K.R. Brousseau, M.J. Driver, K. Eneroth, and R. Larsson, "Career Pandemonium: Realigning Organizations and Individuals," *Academy of Management Executive* 11 (1996), pp. 52–66.
11. M.B. Arthur, "The Boundaryless Career: A New Perspective of Organizational Inquiry," *Journal of Organization Behavior* 15 (1994), pp. 295–309; P.H. Mirvis and D.T. Hall, "Psychological Success and the Boundaryless Career," *Journal of Organization Behavior* 15 (1994), pp. 365–80.
12. B.P. Grossman and R.S. Blitzer, "Choreographing Careers," *Training and Development*, January 1992, pp. 67–69.
13. J.S. Lubin and J.B. White, "Throwing Off Angst, Workers Are Feeling in Control of Their Careers," *The Wall Street Journal* (September 11, 1997), pp. A1, A6.
14. R.J. Campbell, "HR Development Strategies," in *Developing Human Resources*, ed. K.N. Wexley (Washington, DC: BNA Books, 1991), 5-1–5-34; M.A. Sheppeck and C.A. Rhodes, "Management Development: Revised Thinking in Light of New Events of Strategic Importance," *Human Resource Planning* 11 (1988) pp. 159–72; B. Keys and J. Wolf, "Management Education: Current Issues and Emerging Trends," *Journal of Management* 14 (1988), pp. 205–29; L.M. Saari, T.R. Johnson, S.D. McLaughlin, and D. Zimmerle, "A Survey of Management Training and Education Practices in U.S. Companies," *Personnel Psychology* 41 (1988), pp. 731–44.
15. K. Walter, "The MTA Travels Far with Its Future Managers Program," *Personnel Journal*, August 1995, pp. 68–72.
16. T.A. Stewart, "GE Keeps Those Ideas Coming," *Fortune* (August 12, 1991), pp. 41–49; N.M. Tichy, "GE's Crotonville: A Staging Ground for a Corporate Revolution," *The Executive* 3 (1989), pp. 99–106.

17. J.A. Byrne, "Virtual Business Schools," *BusinessWeek* (October 23, 1995), pp. 64–68; T. Bartlett, "The Hottest Campus on the Internet," *BusinessWeek* (October 20, 1997), pp. 77–80.
18. J. Reingold, "Corporate America Goes to School," *Business Week* (October 20, 1997), pp. 66–72.
19. J. Reingold, "Corporate America Goes to School."
20. L. Bongiorno, "How'm I Doing," *BusinessWeek* (October 23, 1995), pp. 72, 74.
21. T.A. Stewart, "GE Keeps Those Ideas Coming," *Fortune* (August 12, 1991), pp. 41–49.
22. G.P. Hollenbeck, "What Did You Learn in School? Studies of a University Executive Program," *Human Resource Planning* 14 (1991), pp. 247–60.
23. A. Howard and D.W. Bray, *Managerial Lives in Transition: Advancing Age and Changing Times* (New York: Guilford, 1988); J. Bolt, *Executive Development* (New York: Harper Business, 1989); J.R. Hinrichs and G.P. Hollenbeck, "Leadership Development," in *Developing Human Resources*, ed. K.N. Wexley (Washington, DC: BNA Books, 1991), pp. 5-221 to 5-237.
24. S.K. Hirsch, *MBTI Team Member's Guide* (Palo Alto, CA: Consulting Psychologists Press, 1992); A.L. Hammer, *Introduction to Type and Careers* (Palo Alto, CA: Consulting Psychologists Press, 1993).
25. A. Thorne and H. Gough, *Portraits of Type* (Palo Alto, CA: Consulting Psychologists Press, 1991).
26. D. Druckman and R.A. Bjork, eds., *In the Mind's Eye: Enhancing Human Performance* (Washington, DC: National Academy Press, 1991); M.H. McCaulley, "The Myers-Briggs Type Indicator and Leadership," in *Measures of Leadership*, ed. K.E. Clark and M.B. Clark (West Orange, NJ: Leadership Library of America, 1990), pp. 381–418.
27. G.C. Thornton III and W.C. Byham, *Assessment Centers and Managerial Performance* (New York: Academic Press, 1982); L.F. Schoenfeldt and J.A. Steger, "Identification and Development of Management Talent," in *Research in Personnel and Human Resource Management*, ed. K.N. Rowland and G. Ferris (Greenwich, CT: JAI Press, 1989), vol. 7, pp. 151–81.
28. G.C. Thornton III and W.C. Byham, *Assessment Centers and Managerial Performance* (New York: Academic Press, 1982).
29. B.B. Gaugler, D.B. Rosenthal, G.C. Thornton III, and C. Bentson, "Metaanalysis of Assessment Center Validity," *Journal of Applied Psychology* 72 (1987), pp. 493–511; D.W. Bray, R.J. Campbell, and D.L. Grant, *Formative Years in Business: A Long-Term AT&T Study of Managerial Lives* (New York: Wiley, 1974).
30. R.G. Jones and M.D. Whitmore, "Evaluating Developmental Assessment Centers as Interventions," *Personnel Psychology* 48 (1995), pp. 377–88.
31. C.D. McCauley and M.M. Lombardo, "Benchmarks: An Instrument for Diagnosing Managerial Strengths and Weaknesses," in *Measures of Leadership*, pp. 535–45.
32. C.D. McCauley, M.M. Lombardo, and C.J. Usher, "Diagnosing Management Development Needs: An Instrument Based on How Managers Develop," *Journal of Management* 15 (1989), pp. 389–403.
33. S.B. Silverman, "Individual Development through Performance Appraisal," in *Developing Human Resources*, pp. 5-120 to 5-151.
34. J.S. Lublin, "Turning the Tables: Underlings Evaluate Bosses," *The Wall Street Journal* (October 4, 1994), pp. B1, B14; B. O'Reilly, "360-Degree Feedback Can Change Your Life," *Fortune* (October 17, 1994), pp. 93–100; J.F. Milliman, R.A. Zawacki, C. Norman, L. Powell, and J. Kirksey, "Companies Evaluate Employees from All Perspectives," *Personnel Journal*, November 1994, pp. 99–103.
35. Center for Creative Leadership, *Skillscope for Managers: Development Planning Guide* (Greensboro, NC: Center for Creative Leadership, 1992); G. Yukl and R. Lepsinger, "360-Degree Feedback," *Training*, December 1995, pp. 45–50.
36. S. Caudron, "Building Better Bosses," *Workforce*, May 2000, pp. 33–39.
37. L. Atwater, P. Roush, and A. Fischthal, "The Influence of Upward Feedback on Self- and Follower Ratings of Leadership," *Personnel Psychology* 48 (1995), pp. 35–59; J.F. Hazucha, S.A. Hezlett, and R.J. Schneider, "The Impact of 360-Degree Feedback on Management Skill Development," *Human Resource Management* 32 (1993), pp. 325–51; J.W. Smither, M. London, N. Vasilopoulos, R.R. Reilly, R.E. Millsap, and N. Salvemini, "An Examination of the Effects of an Upward Feedback Program over Time," *Personnel Psychology* 48 (1995), pp. 1–34.
38. D. Bracken, "Straight Talk about Multirater Feedback," *Training and Development* (September 1994), pp. 44–51.
39. M.W. McCall, Jr., M.M. Lombardo, and A.M. Morrison, *Lessons of Experience* (Lexington, MA: Lexington Books, 1988).
40. R.S. Snell, "Congenial Ways of Learning: So Near yet So Far," *Journal of Management Development* 9 (1990), pp. 17–23.
41. McCall, Lombardo, and Morrison, *Lessons of Experience;* M.W. McCall, "Developing Executives through Work Experiences," *Human Resource Planning* 11 (1988), pp. 1–11; M.N. Ruderman, P.J. Ohlott, and C.D. McCauley, "Assessing Opportunities for Leadership Development," in *Measures of Leadership*, pp. 547–62; C.D. McCauley, L.J. Estman, and P.J. Ohlott,

"Linking Management Selection and Development through Stretch Assignments," *Human Resource Management* 34 (1995), pp. 93–115.

42. C.D. McCauley, M.N. Ruderman, P.J. Ohlott, and J.E. Morrow, "Assessing the Developmental Components of Managerial Jobs," *Journal of Applied Psychology* 79 (1994), pp. 544–60.
43. M. Frase-Blunt, "Ready, Set, Rotate," *HR Magazine*, October 2001, pp. 46–53; G.B. Northcraft, T.L. Griffith, and C.E. Shalley, "Building Top Management Muscle in a Slow Growth Environment: How Different Is Better at Greyhound Financial Corporation," *The Executive* 6 (1992), pp. 32–41.
44. M. London, *Developing Managers* (San Francisco: Jossey-Bass, 1985); M.A. Campion, L. Cheraskin, and M.J. Stevens, "Career-Related Antecedents and Outcomes of Job Rotation," *Academy of Management Journal* 37 (1994), pp. 1518–42; M. London, *Managing the Training Enterprise* (San Francisco: Jossey-Bass, 1989).
45. D.C. Feldman, *Managing Careers in Organizations* (Glenview, IL: Scott-Foresman, 1988).
46. J.M. Brett, L.K. Stroh, and A.H. Reilly, "Job Transfer," in *International Review of Industrial and Organizational Psychology: 1992*, ed. C.L. Cooper and I.T. Robinson (Chichester, England: John Wiley and Sons, 1992); D.C. Feldman and J.M. Brett, "Coping with New Jobs: A Comparative Study of New Hires and Job Changers," *Academy of Management Journal* 26 (1983), pp. 258–72.
47. R.A. Noe, B.D. Steffy, and A.E. Barber, "An Investigation of the Factors Influencing Employees' Willingness to Accept Mobility Opportunities," *Personnel Psychology* 41 (1988), pp. 559–80; S. Gould and L.E. Penley, "A Study of the Correlates of Willingness to Relocate," *Academy of Management Journal* 28 (1984), pp. 472–78; J. Landau and T.H. Hammer, "Clerical Employees' Perceptions of Intraorganizational Career Opportunities," *Academy of Management Journal* 29 (1986), pp. 385–405; R.P. Duncan and C.C. Perruci, "Dual Occupation Families and Migration," *American Sociological Review* 41 (1976), pp. 252–61; J.M. Brett and A.H. Reilly, "On the Road Again: Predicting the Job Transfer Decision," *Journal of Applied Psychology* 73 (1988), pp. 614–620.
48. D.T. Hall and L.A. Isabella, "Downward Moves and Career Development," *Organizational Dynamics* 14 (1985), pp. 5–23.
49. H.D. Dewirst, "Career Patterns: Mobility, Specialization, and Related Career Issues," in *Contemporary Career Development Issues*, ed. R. F. Morrison and J. Adams (Hillsdale, NJ: Lawrence Erlbaum, 1991), pp. 73–108.
50. N.C. Tompkins, "GTE Managers on the Move," *Personnel Journal*, August 1992, pp. 86–91.
51. J.M. Brett, "Job Transfer and Well-Being," *Journal of Applied Psychology* 67 (1992), pp. 450–63; F.J. Minor, L.A. Slade, and R.A. Myers, "Career Transitions in Changing Times," in *Contemporary Career Development Issues*, pp. 109–20; C.C. Pinder and K.G. Schroeder, "Time to Proficiency Following Job Transfers," *Academy of Management Journal* 30 (1987), pp. 336–53; G. Flynn, "Heck No—We Won't Go!" *Personnel Journal*, March 1996, pp. 37–43.
52. R.E. Silverman, "Mercer Tries to Keep Employees Through Its 'Externship' Program," *The Wall Street Journal* (November 7, 2000), p. B18.
53. D. Gunsch, "Customer Service Focus Prompts Employee Exchange," *Personnel Journal*, October 1992, pp. 32–38.
54. C.J. Bachler, "Workers Take Leave of Job Stress," *Personnel Journal*, January 1995, pp. 38–48.
55. Bounds, "Give Me a Break," *The Wall Street Journal* (May 5, 2000), pp. W1, W4.
56. D.B. Turban and T.W. Dougherty, "Role of Protege Personality in Receipt of Mentoring and Career Success," *Academy of Management Journal* 37 (1994), pp. 688–702; E.A. Fagenson, "Mentoring: Who Needs It? A Comparison of Protégés' and Nonprotégés' Needs for Power, Achievement, Affiliation, and Autonomy," *Journal of Vocational Behavior* 41 (1992), pp. 48–60.
57. A.H. Geiger, "Measures for Mentors," *Training and Development Journal*, February 1992, pp. 65–67.
58. K.E. Kram, *Mentoring at Work: Developmental Relationships in Organizational Life* (Glenview, IL: Scott-Foresman, 1985); L.L. Phillips-Jones, "Establishing a Formalized Mentoring Program," *Training and Development Journal* 2 (1983), pp. 38–42; K. Kram, "Phases of the Mentoring Relationship," *Academy of Management Journal* 26 (1983), pp. 608–25; G.T. Chao, P.M. Walz, and P.D. Gardner, "Formal and Informal Mentorships: A Comparison of Mentoring Functions and Contrasts with Nonmentored Counterparts," *Personnel Psychology* 45 (1992), pp. 619–36.
59. C.M. Solomon, "Hotel Breathes Life Into Hospital's Customer Service," *Personnel Journal*, October 1995, p. 120.
60. G.F. Dreher and R.A. Ash, "A Comparative Study of Mentoring among Men and Women in Managerial, Professional, and Technical Positions," *Journal of Applied Psychology* 75 (1990), pp. 539–46; J.L. Wilbur, "Does Mentoring Breed Success?" *Training and Development Journal* 41 (1987), pp. 38–41; R.A. Noe, "Mentoring Relationships for Employee Development," in *Applying Psychology in Business: The Handbook for*

Managers and Human Resource Professionals, ed. J.W. Jones, B.D. Steffy, and D.W. Bray (Lexington, MA: Lexington Books, 1991), pp. 475–82; M.M. Fagh and K. Ayers, Jr., "Police Mentors," *FBI Law Enforcement Bulletin*, January 1985, pp. 8–13; K. Kram, "Phases of the Mentor Relationships," *Academy of Management Journal* 26 (1983), pp. 608–25; R.A. Noe, "An Investigation of the Determinants of Successful Assigned Mentoring Relationships," *Personnel Psychology* 41 (1988), pp. 457–79; B.J. Tepper, "Upward Maintenance Tactics in Supervisory Mentoring and Nonmentoring Relationships," *Academy of Management Journal* 38 (1995), pp. 1191–205; B.R. Ragins and T.A. Scandura, "Gender Differences in Expected Outcomes of Mentoring Relationships," *Academy of Management Journal* 37 (1994), pp. 957–71.

61. M. Murray, "GE Mentoring Program Turns Underlings Into Teachers of the Web," *The Wall Street Journal* (February 15, 2000), pp. B1, B16.
62. F. Jossi, "Mentoring in Changing Times," *Training*, August 1997, pp. 50–54.
63. B. Kaye and B. Jackson, "Mentoring: A Group Guide," *Training and Development* (April 1995), pp. 23–27.
64. D.B. Peterson and M.D. Hicks, *Leader as Coach* (Minneapolis, MN: Personnel Decisions, 1996).
65. J.S. Lublin, "Building a Better CEO," *The Wall Street Journal* (April 14, 2000), pp. B1, B4.
66. R. Zemke, " The Corporate Coach," *Training* (December 1996), pp. 24–28.
67. Consulting Psychologists Press, "Wells Fargo Helps Employees Change Careers," *Strong Forum* 8, no. 1 (1991), p. 1.
68. L. Slavenski, "Career Development: A Systems Approach," *Training and Development Journal*, February 1987, pp. 56–60.
69. D.T. Jaffe and C.D. Scott, "Career Development for Empowerment in a Changing Work World," in *New Directions in Career Planning and the Workplace*, ed. J.M. Kummerow (Palo Alto, CA: Consulting Psychologists Press, 1991), pp. 33–60; L. Summers, "A Logical Approach to Development Planning," *Training and Development* 48 (1994), pp. 22–31; D.B. Peterson and M.D. Hicks, *Development First* (Minneapolis, MN: Personnel Decisions, 1995).
70. Z. Leibowitz, C. Schultz, H.D. Lea, and S.E. Forrer, "Shape Up and Ship Out," *Training and Development*, August 1995, pp. 39–42.
71. U.S. Dept. of Labor, A *Report on the Glass Ceiling Initiative* (Washington, DC: U.S. Dept. of Labor, 1991).
72. P.J. Ohlott, M.N. Ruderman, and C.D. McCauley, "Gender Differences in Managers' Developmental Job Experiences," *Academy of Management Journal* 37 (1994), pp. 46–67.
73. L.A. Mainiero, "Getting Anointed for Advancement: The Case of Executive Women," *Academy of Management Executive* 8 (1994), pp. 53–67; J.S. Lublin, "Women at Top Still Are Distant from CEO Jobs," *The Wall Street Journal* (February 28, 1995), pp. B1, B5; P. Tharenov, S. Latimer, and D. Conroy, "How Do You Make It to the Top? An Examination of Influences on Women's and Men's Managerial Advancement," *Academy of Management Journal* 37 (1994), pp. 899–931.
74. U.S. Dept. of Labor, A *Report on the Glass Ceiling Initiative*; R. A. Noe, "Women and Mentoring: A Review and Research Agenda," *Academy of Management Review* 13 (1988), pp. 65–78; B.R. Ragins and J.L. Cotton, "Easier Said Than Done: Gender Differences in Perceived Barriers to Gaining a Mentor," *Academy of Management Journal* 34 (1991), pp. 939–51.
75. D. McCracken, "Winning the Talent War for Women," *Harvard Business Review*, November–December 2000, pp. 159–67.
76. W.J. Rothwell, *Effective Succession Planning*, 2nd ed. (New York: AMACOM, 2001).
77. C.B. Derr, C. Jones, and E.L. Toomey, "Managing High-Potential Employees: Current Practices in Thirty-Three U.S. Corporations," *Human Resource Management* 27 (1988), pp. 273–90.
78. Derr, Jones, and Toomey, "Managing High-Potential Employees"; K.M. Nowack, "The Secrets of Succession," *Training and Development* 48 (1994), pp. 49–54; J.S. Lublin, "An Overseas Stint Can Be a Ticket to the Top," *The Wall Street Journal* (January 29, 1996), pp. B1, B2.
79. Ibid.
80. B. Gerber, "Who Will Replace Those Vanishing Execs?" *Training*, July 2000, pp. 49–53.
81. M.W. McCall, Jr., and M.M. Lombardo, "Off the Track: Why and How Successful Executives Get Derailed," *Technical Report* no. 21 (Greensboro, NC: Center for Creative Leadership, 1983); E.V. Veslor and J.B. Leslie, "Why Executives Derail: Perspectives across Time and Cultures," *Academy of Management Executive* 9 (1995), pp. 62–72.
82. L.W. Hellervik, J.F. Hazucha, and R.J. Schneider, "Behavior Change: Models, Methods, and a Review of Evidence," in *Handbook of Industrial and Organizational Psychology*, 2nd ed., ed. M.D. Dunnette and L.M. Hough (Palo Alto, CA: Consulting Psychologists Press, 1992), vol. 3, pp. 823–99.
83. D.B. Peterson, "Measuring and Evaluating Change in Executive and Managerial Development" (paper presented at the annual conference of the Society for Industrial and Organizational Psychology, Miami, 1990).

Chapter 10

Employee Separation and Retention

Objectives

After reading this chapter, you should be able to:

1. Distinguish between involuntary and voluntary turnover, and discuss how each of these forms of turnover can be leveraged for competitive advantage.
2. List the major elements that contribute to perceptions of justice and how to apply these in organizational contexts involving discipline and dismissal.
3. Specify the relationship between job satisfaction and various forms of job withdrawal, and identify the major sources of job satisfaction in work contexts.
4. Design a survey feedback intervention program and use this to promote retention of key organizational personnel.

The turnover rate in security personnel in airports is extremely high. What could officials do to help these employees feel more secure in their jobs, increase their satisfaction, and reduce turnover?

Enter the World of Business

Feeling Insecure about Airline Security

Becoming an expert in any field takes some degree of training and on-the-job experience. When working as part of a team, it also takes some time to learn about the strengths and weaknesses of one's team members so that a unit can operate like a well-oiled machine. For this reason, turnover in just one position can drastically reduce the effectiveness of work units. However, imagine the case where the entire work unit changes *every four months!*

Although it may seem hard to believe, this was the turnover rate at the security checkpoints at Logan International Airport in September 2001, when two planes were hijacked and used as guided missiles in the attacks on the World Trade Center. And Logan was not even the worst airport in this regard. The turnover rates at both St. Louis and Atlanta were over 400 percent—meaning that the entire crew turned over every three months. Given the lack of experience that workers in these positions had on the job, as well as their lack of experience working together, it is not at all surprising that performance of these work units was abysmal. In fact, as Max Cleland, chairman of the Senate Armed Services Subcommittee on Personnel, noted, "This was our front line, and what we found is we didn't have security, we had a sieve."

A number of factors explain the incredibly high turnover rates in these jobs. First, the job is low in pay. Most airport security personnel make less than $6 an hour, well below the rate of even those who work in the airport's fast food restaurants. Second, these are dead-end jobs. There is no career progression that would lead the incumbent to think that if he or she worked hard and stuck with it, he or she could climb into some managerial position. Third, the work itself is boring and monotonous. In addition, it is performed in a context of resentment, where hurried passengers look down on the security personnel who are perceived as being beneath those they are trying to serve. Finally, there is very little job security. A person can be fired for a single mistake, and the notion that a quality job is demanded is undermined by airline pressure to keep people moving during peak departure periods.

The airlines, which are currently responsible for security, blame this situation on the economics of the industry, where costs need to be kept low in order to maintain profitability. However, most airlines need to fill 65 percent of cabin capacity to clear a profit, and even two months after the terrorist attacks, fear of flying kept the capacity levels below 35 percent, putting even greater financial pressure on the carriers. As Cleland notes, as far as the industry is concerned, "Security is No. 1 in a series of confidence-building measures that will bring people back to fly."

Many of the security measures that are being considered will be imported from Europe and Israel, which have far better records than the United States in this area. There, airline security screening is treated as a police function, and the pay, training, and benefits are all much higher than what is seen in the United States. Moreover, a close emotional attachment between the security personnel and the airlines, many of which are nationalized, makes this work seem like a patriotic duty. This type of emotional attachment never develops in the revolving door that serves as the context for airline security work in the United States.

SOURCE: M. Fish, "Airport Security: A System Driven by the Minimum Wage," *CNN.com* (October 31, 2001), pp. 1–5; M. Fish, "Many Warnings over Security Preceded Terrorist Attacks," *CNN.com* (November 1, 2001), pp. 1–3; S. Candiotti, "FBI Arrests Man Who Tried to Board Flight Armed with Knives," *CNN.com* (November 5, 2001), pp. 1–2; M. Fish, "Outside the U.S., a Different Approach to Air Security," *CNN.com* (November 1, 2001), pp. 1–2.

Introduction

Every executive recognizes the need for satisfied, loyal customers. If the firm is publicly held, it is also safe to assume that every executive appreciates the need to have satisfied, loyal investors. Customers and investors provide the financial resources that allow the organization to survive. Not every executive understands the need to generate satisfaction and loyalty among employees, however. Yet, retention rates among employees are related to retention rates among both customers[1] and investors.[2] Furthermore, as is made clear both by our opening story about airline security and by more systematic research, job satisfaction and retention are related to organizational performance.[3] Firms that fail to secure a loyal base of workers constantly place an inexperienced group of noncohesive units on the front lines of their organization, much to their own detriment.[4] This is especially the case in service industries, where confused and disgruntled workers often create large numbers of dissatisfied customers.[5] With the turnover rate at its highest point in 20 years, it is clear that many executives have been slow to pick up on the relationship between retention and organizational performance.[6] Thus, this provides yet another area where one organization can gain competitive advantage over another.

In addition to holding onto key personnel, another hallmark of successful firms is their ability and willingness to dismiss employees who are engaging in counterproductive behavior. Indeed, it is somewhat ironic that one of the keys to retaining productive employees is ensuring that these people are not being made miserable by supervisors or coworkers who are engaging in unproductive, disruptive, or dangerous behavior. For example, as we noted in Chapter 8, more companies are turning to "rank and yank" systems, where all employees are listed on performance from top to bottom, and then the bottom 5–10 percent are dismissed.[7] Former Chairman of General Electric Jack Welch has noted that "while the top and middle performers sometimes trade places, the bottom 10 percent, in our experience, tend to stay there, and delaying the inevitable in their case is a form of cruelty."[8] Welch believes strongly that culling the bottom of the organization like this makes room for new members and helps maintain the company's vitality.

Thus, to compete effectively, organizations must take steps to ensure that good performers are motivated to stay with the organization, whereas chronically low performers are allowed, encouraged, or, if necessary, forced to leave. Retaining top performers is not always easy, however. Recent developments have made this more difficult than ever. For example, the rash of layoffs and downsizings of the early and mid-1990s has reduced company loyalty. Couple this general attitude of mistrust with the tight labor markets characterizing the late 1990s, and we have a workforce that is both willing and able to leave on a moment's notice. Similarly, the increased willingness of people to sue their employer, combined with an unprecedented level of violence in the workplace, has made discharging employees legally complicated and personally dangerous.

The purpose of this chapter (the last in Part III of this book) is to focus on employee separation and retention. The material presented in Part III's previous two chapters ("Performance Management" and "Employee Development") can be used to help establish who are the current effective performers as well as who is likely to respond well to future developmental opportunities. This chapter completes Part III by discussing what can be done to retain high-performing employees who warrant further development as well as managing the separation process for low-performing employees who have not responded well to developmental opportunities.

Since much of what needs to be done to retain employees involves compensation and benefits, this chapter also serves as a bridge to Part IV, which addresses these issues in more detail. The chapter is divided in two sections. The first examines **involuntary turnover,** that is, turnover initiated by the organization (often among people who would prefer to stay). The second deals with **voluntary turnover,** that is, turnover initiated by employees (often whom the company would prefer to keep). Although both types of turnover reflect employee separation, they are clearly different phenomena that need to be examined separately.[9]

Involuntary turnover
Turnover initiated by the organization (often among people who would prefer to stay).

Voluntary turnover
Turnover initiated by employees (often whom the company would prefer to keep).

Managing Involuntary Turnover

Despite a company's best efforts in the area of personnel selection, training, and design of compensation systems, some employees will occasionally fail to meet performance requirements or will violate company policies while on the job. When this happens, organizations need to invoke a discipline program that could ultimately lead to the individual's discharge. For a number of reasons, discharging employees can be a very difficult task that needs to be handled with the utmost care and attention to detail.

First, there are legal aspects to this decision that can have important repercussions for the organization. Historically, in the absence of a specified contract, either the employer or the employee could sever the employment relationship at any time. The severing of this relationship could be for "good cause," "no cause," or even "bad cause." Over time, this policy has been referred to as the **employment-at-will doctrine.** This employment-at-will doctrine has eroded significantly over time, however. Today employees who are fired sometimes sue their employers for wrongful discharge. Some judges have been willing to consider employees who meet certain criteria regarding longevity, promotions, raises, and favorable past performance reviews as having an implied contract to dismissal only for good cause—even in the face of direct language in the company handbook that states an employment-at-will relationship.[10]

Employment-at-will doctrine
The doctrine that, in the absence of a specific contract, either an employer or employee could sever the employment relationship at any time.

A wrongful discharge suit typically attempts to establish that the discharge either (1) violated an implied contract or covenant (that is, the employer acted unfairly) or (2) violated public policy (that is, the employee was terminated because he or she refused to do something illegal, unethical, or unsafe). Courts have been quite willing to listen to such cases, and employees win settlements over 70 percent of the time. The average award is more than $500,000, and the cost for mounting a defense can be anywhere from $50,000 to $250,000.[11] Thus there is great financial risk associated with any termination decision.

In addition to the financial risks associated with a dismissal, there are issues related to personal safety. Although the fact that some former employees use the court system to get back at their former employers may be distressing, even more problematic are employees who respond to a termination decision with violence directed at the employer. Violence in the workplace has become a major organizational problem. Workplace homicide is the fastest-growing form of murder in the United States—especially for women, for whom homicide is the leading cause of death in the workplace.[12] Although any number of organizational actions or decisions may incite violence among employees, the "nothing else to lose" aspect of employee dismissal cases makes for a dangerous situation.

Given the critical financial and personal risks associated with employee dismissal, it is easy to see why the development of a standardized, systematic approach to discipline and discharge is critical to all organizations. These decisions should not be left solely to the discretion of individual managers or supervisors. In the next section we explore aspects of an effective discipline and discharge policy.

Principles of Justice

In Chapter 8 ("Performance Management") we touched on the notion of justice, particularly as this relates to the notions of outcome justice, procedural justice, and interactional justice. There we noted that employees are more likely to respond positively to negative feedback regarding their performance if they perceive the appraisal process as being fair on these three dimensions. Obviously, if fairness is important with respect to ongoing feedback, this is even more critical in the context of a final termination decision. Therefore, we will explore the three types of fairness perceptions in greater detail here, with an emphasis on how these need to be operationalized in effective discipline and discharge policies.[13] Indeed, a thorough understanding of these justice principles will make it clear why many organizations have enacted various policies regarding progressive discipline, Employee Assistance Programs (EAPs), alternative dispute resolution, and outplacement.

Outcome fairness
The judgment that people make with respect to the outcomes received relative to the outcomes received by other people with whom they identify.

As we noted earlier in Chapter 8, **outcome fairness** refers to the judgment that people make with respect to the *outcomes received* relative to the outcomes received by other people with whom they identify (referent others). Clearly, a situation where one person is losing his or her job while others are not is conducive to perceptions of outcome unfairness on the part of the discharged employee. The degree to which this potentially unfair act translates into the type of anger and resentment that might spawn retaliation in the form of violence or litigation, however, depends on perceptions of procedural and interactional justice.[14]

Procedural justice
A concept of justice focusing on the methods used to determine the outcomes received.

Whereas outcome justice focuses on the ends, procedural and interactional justice focus on means. If methods and procedures used to arrive at and implement decisions that impact the employee negatively are seen as fair, the reaction is likely to be much more positive than if this is not the case. **Procedural justice** focuses specifically on the

TABLE 10.1

Six Determinants of Procedural Justice

(1) **Consistency.** The procedures are applied consistently across time and other persons.
(2) **Bias suppression.** The procedures are applied by a person who has no vested interest in the outcome and no prior prejudices regarding the individual.
(3) **Information accuracy.** The procedure is based on information that is perceived to be true.
(4) **Correctabilty.** The procedure has built-in safeguards that allow one to appeal mistakes or bad decisions.
(5) **Representativeness.** The procedure is informed by the concerns of all groups or stakeholders (coworkers, customers, owners) affected by the decision, including the individual being dismissed.
(6) **Ethicality.** The procedure is consistent with prevailing moral standards as they pertain to issues like invasion of privacy or deception.

TABLE 10.2

Four Determinants of Interactional Justice

(1) **Explanation.** Emphasize aspects of procedural fairness that justify the decision.
(2) **Social Sensitivity.** Treat the person with dignity and respect.
(3) **Consideration.** Listen to the person's concerns.
(4) **Empathy.** Identify with the person's feelings.

methods used to determine the outcomes received. Table 10.1 details six key principles that determine whether people perceive procedures as being fair. Even given all the negative ramifications of being dismissed from one's job, the person being dismissed may accept the decision with minimum anger if the procedures used to arrive at the decision are consistent, unbiased, accurate, correctable, representative, and ethical.

Whereas procedural justice deals with how a decision was made, **interactional justice** refers to the *interpersonal nature of how the outcomes were implemented*. Table 10.2 lists the four key determinants of interactional justice. When the decision is explained well and implemented in a fashion that is socially sensitive, considerate, and empathetic, this helps defuse some of the resentment that might come about from a decision to discharge an employee. As the "Competing by Meeting Stakeholders' Needs" box on page 423 indicates, many recent layoff decisions have not been administered with this type of sensitivity.

Interactional justice
A concept of justice referring to the interpersonal nature of how the outcomes were implemented.

Finding and Keeping the Best Employees

Employees are more likely to see discipline as procedurally just when the rules by which they will be evaluated are laid out clearly in advance. For example, PPG Industries, a Pennsylvania-based manufacturer employing over 35,000 employees, uses a system called SMART Goals to create clear expectations for its workforce. SMART stands for "Specific, Measurable, Agreed upon, Realistic, and Time-bound," and these types of goals have replaced more generic self-improvement goals that used to characterize PPG's performance evaluation system.

Before the SMART Goals system was in place, a common goal for a manager might have been to "boost sales over the next year." That same goal in the SMART Goals system might be translated into "develop, by September 30th, three new customers in the Southeast Region with annual sales volume of 100,000." If over several iterations an employee consistently fails to meet these goals, the failure is clear in the eyes of both the manager and the employee. Any disciplinary action based on failing to meet these goals is likely to be seen as high in procedural justice and thus is more likely to be seen as fair by both the employee and his or her colleagues.

SOURCE: S. Scherreik, "Your Performance Review: Make It Perform," *BusinessWeek* (December 17, 2001), pp. 139–40.

Progressive Discipline

Except in the most extreme cases, employees should generally not be terminated for a first offense. Rather, termination should come about at the end of a systematic discipline program. Effective discipline programs have two central components: documentation (which includes specific publication of work rules and job descriptions that should be in place prior to administering discipline) and progressive punitive measures. Thus, as shown in Table 10.3, punitive measures should be taken in steps of increasing magnitude, and only after having been clearly documented. This may start with an unofficial warning for the first offense, followed by a written reprimand for additional offenses. At some point, later offenses may lead to a temporary suspension. Before a company suspends an employee, it may even want to issue a "last chance notification," indicating that the next offense will result in termination. Such procedures may seem exasperatingly slow, and they may fail to meet one's emotional need for quick and satisfying retribution. In the end, however, when problem employees are discharged, the chance that they can prove they were discharged for poor cause has been minimized.

Alternative dispute resolution (ADR)
A method of resolving disputes that does not rely on the legal system. Often proceeds through the four stages of open door policy, peer review, mediation, and arbitration.

Alternative Dispute Resolution

At various points in the discipline process, the individual or the organization might want to bring in outside parties to help resolve discrepancies or conflicts. As a last resort, the individual might invoke the legal system to resolve these types of conflicts, but in order to avoid this, more and more companies are turning to **alternative dispute resolution (ADR)** techniques that show promise in resolving disputes in a timely, constructive, cost-effective manner.

Alternative dispute resolution can take on many different forms, but in general, ADR proceeds through the four stages shown in Table 10.4. Each stage reflects a

TABLE 10.3
An Example of a Progressive Discipline Program

OFFENSE FREQUENCY	ORGANIZATIONAL RESPONSE	DOCUMENTATION
First offense	Unofficial verbal warning	Witness present
Second offense	Official written warning	Document filed
Third offense	Second official warning, with threat of temporary suspension	Document filed
Fourth offense	Temporary suspension and "last chance notification"	Document filed
Fifth offense	Termination (with right to go to arbitration)	Document filed

COMPETING BY MEETING STAKEHOLDERS' NEEDS

Executing Layoff Decisions: Striking a Balance

The 1990s witnessed an unprecedented expansion of the U.S. economy where many employers were fighting for every employee they could get their hands on. In 2001, when the economy started to contract and some employers needed to cut costs through layoffs, many employers seemed to have totally forgotten how to conduct a layoff.

For example, one morning in May, 5,000 employees at Inacom were told to call an 800 number. The telephone then connected them to a prerecorded message that told them they were off work, *effective immediately*. Although this tactic may seem a little cold, at least Inacom workers got into the building before being told the bad news. Workers at Chrysler learned they were laid off when they arrived at the plant entrance gates, only to find that their ID badges no longer opened the security gates. Although this must have been a surprise, at least these workers got out of their houses. When Amazon.com announced its job cuts in January 2000, it sent e-mails to people's homes telling them they did not need to report to work anymore.

Clearly, few tasks can be more unpleasant than having to tell an employee that he or she is out of work, and it is easy to understand why managers and HR professionals might rather hide under the desks when such news is being relayed rather than confronting the victim face-to-face. Moreover, it is also dangerous to allow employees who know they have been laid off free access to their ex-organization. For example, one systems administrator at a New York hospital encrypted patient files once she learned she would be laid off. She then offered to "fix" the problem in exchange for a cash payout and a no-prosecution agreement—which the hospital was forced to accept. Disgruntled employees have also been known to sue their employers or act out with violence, thus further motivating employers to "keep their distance" from the victims.

When conducting a layoff, it is critical to balance the security needs of the organization's customers and investors, on the one hand, with the needs of former and future employees on the other. In terms of procedural justice, as noted by Jeffrey Schmidt, managing director of Towers Perrin, "Employees are stakeholders, and you have to make the same justification to them that you do to investors." That is, employees have to be given a clear answer to the question "why me, why now." The employees need to see this as a critical business necessity and not a personal attack on the quality or quantity of their work. In terms of interactive justice, the news should be delivered with compassion and understanding by someone who has worked closely with the employee—such as a direct supervisor. Supervisors may need to be trained and accompanied by an HR specialist in case any questions that are beyond the supervisor's scope arise; but it is not a good idea to have the news delivered by someone who is, in the employee's perspective, an unknown bureaucrat from headquarters. As one manager has stated, if people feel like the company dealt with them in a respectful and appropriate way, they are not going to have the type of personal animosity that makes them want to go out and contact a lawyer—or worse.

SOURCE: D. Spencer, "Soothing the Sting," *Human Resource Executive* (June 1, 2001), pp. 30–34; M. Conlin, "Revenge of the Downsized Nerds," *BusinessWeek* (July 30, 2001), p. 40; M. Boyle, "The Not-So-Fine Art of the Layoff," *Fortune* (March 19, 2001), pp. 209–10.

TABLE 10.4
Stages in Alternative Dispute Resolution

Stage 1: Open door policy The two people in conflict (e.g., supervisor and subordinate) attempt to arrive at a settlement together. If none can be reached, they proceed to
Stage 2: Peer review A panel composed of representatives from the organization that are at the same level of those people in the dispute hears the case and attempts to help the parties arrive at a settlement. If none can be reached, they proceed to
Stage 3: Mediation A neutral third party from outside the organization hears the case and, via a nonbinding process, tries to help the disputants arrive at a settlement. If none can be reached, the parties proceed to
Stage 4: Arbitration A professional arbitrator from outside the organization hears the case and resolves it unilaterally by rendering a specific decision or award. Most arbitrators are experienced employment attorneys or retired judges.

somewhat broader involvement of different people, and the hope is that the conflict will be resolved at earlier steps. However, the last step may include binding arbitration, where an agreed upon neutral party resolves the conflict unilaterally if necessary.

Experience shows that ADR can be highly effective in terms of cost and time savings. For example, over a four-year period, one large company, Houston-based Brown and Root, found that legal fees dropped 90 percent after instituting ADR. Indeed, of the 2,000 disputes initiated by employees at that time, only 30 ever reached the binding arbitration stage. The cost savings are so large in some cases that employers—trying to convince skeptical employees to use the system—even provide financial assistance to hire attorneys. For example, Philip Morris provides aggrieved employees with up to \$3,500 in financial assistance to help them prepare their case. In this way they assure the employees that their rights are being respected and that they are getting a fair hearing in the process.[15] However, as the "Competing through High-Performance Work Systems" box shows, organizations that mandate arbitration have come under intense scrutiny.

Whereas ADR is effective in dealing with problems related to performance and interpersonal differences in the workplace, many of the problems that lead an organization to want to terminate an individual's employment relate to drug or alcohol abuse. In these cases, the organization's discipline and dismissal program should also incorporate an employee assistance program. Due to the increased prevalence of EAPs in organizations, we describe them in detail here.

Employee assistance programs (EAPs)
Employer programs that attempt to ameliorate problems encountered by workers who are drug dependent, alcoholic, or psychologically troubled.

Employee Assistance Programs

Drug and alcohol abuse have been estimated to cost U.S. companies nearly \$100 billion a year in lost productivity.[16] Although health care costs in general have risen sharply, treatment costs for mental and chemical dependency disorders appear to be rising even faster.[17] To lower these costs and to help get unproductive employees back on track, many employers are turning to EAPs.

An **EAP** is a referral service that supervisors or employees can use to seek professional treatment for various problems. EAPs began in the 1950s with a focus on

COMPETING THROUGH HIGH-PERFORMANCE WORK SYSTEMS

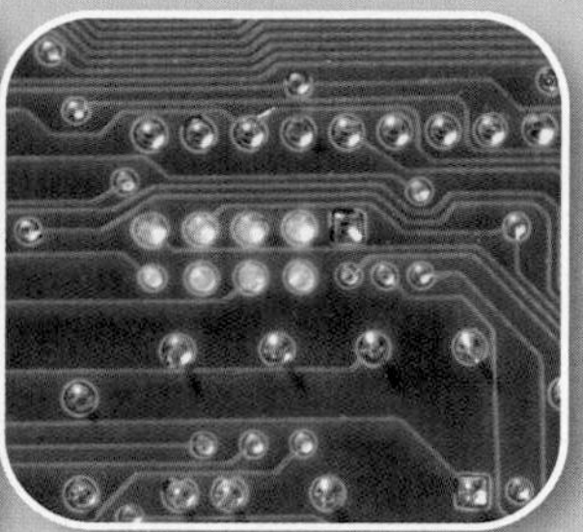

Mandatory Arbitration: Constitutional Implications of Just-in-Time Justice

Like many recent graduates just out of business school, Mary Cremin was so excited about joining a firm—here Merrill Lynch, Pierce, Fenner and Smith Inc.—that she failed to carefully read up on all the company's employment policies. When her employment was terminated in 1995 for what she perceived to be a discriminatory reason (having children), she tried to sue her employer but was surprised to learn that she was precluded from doing so by Merrill Lynch's mandatory arbitration policy. Stating that "I didn't know I signed away my constitutional rights," Cremin is now the lead plaintiff in a sexual discrimination class action suit aimed at striking down mandatory arbitration.

Many organizations began turning to alternative dispute resolution (ADR) programs in the late 1980s, when the rising incidence and cost of employee lawsuits, in terms of both time and money, prompted a search for quicker, cheaper forms of conflict resolution. ADR programs allow the employer to tap into computerized registrars of mediators and arbitrators who are managed by outside providers such as Resolute Systems Inc., JAMS/Endispute, and the American Arbitration Association. The disputants can do computer searches of potential mediators or arbitrators with various types of experience or expertise and then, when a "neutral" person acceptable to both parties is found, have their case heard outside a normal courtroom. Compared to the average time to have a civil case heard by a judge and perhaps jury (2.5 years), ADR programs are quick and less costly to invoke.

Moreover, in 1991, ADR programs got a major boost from the U.S. Supreme Court, which upheld the use of a signed contract of employment in which the employee agreed to follow mandatory arbitration procedures. In the intervening years, however, a strong backlash against mandatory arbitration has been gaining force across the country. For example, a federal judge in Boston refused to apply Merrill Lynch's policy in a sex discrimination suit by a broker prior to the Cremin case partly because arbitrators sided with brokerage firms in 93 out of 97 cases initiated by members of the New York Stock Exchange between 1993 and 1997.

Prompted by this and other cases at the U.S. Court of Appeals level, on March 2, 1998, the U.S. Supreme Court agreed to hear a case brought by a South Carolina longshoreman trying to break free of his employer's mandatory arbitration program with respect to a disability claim. If the court rules against the company, this would sharply limit the use of such policies. Many employers, seeing the writing on the wall, are not waiting for the results of this case to change their policies. For example, in November 1998, Smith Barney agreed to scale back its mandatory arbitration policy and instead rely more heavily on ADR programs that end in mediation or voluntary (rather than mandatory) arbitration.

SOURCE: D. Weimer, "Force into Arbitration? Not Any More," *BusinessWeek* (March 16, 1998), pp. 31–35; M. Lee, "See You in Court—or Mediation," *BusinessWeek* (October 12, 1998), pp. 34–36.

treating alcoholism, but in the 1980s they expanded into drug treatment as well. EAPs continue to evolve, and many are now fully integrated into companies' overall health benefits plans, serving as gatekeepers for health care utilization—especially for mental health.[18] For example, when the Campbell Soup Company incorporated mental health treatment into its EAP, claims costs associated with psychiatrists decreased 28 percent in a single year.[19] This kind of program is frequently referred to as a *carve-out plan*. In carve-out plans, mental health and chemical dependency benefits are provided by a single vendor that has responsibility for all of the company's health benefits.

EAPs vary widely, but most share some basic elements. First, the programs are usually identified in official documents published by the employer (such as employee handbooks). Supervisors (and union representatives, where relevant) are trained to use the referral service for employees whom they suspect of having health-related problems. Employees are also trained to use the system to make self-referrals when necessary. Finally, costs and benefits of the programs (as measured in positive employee outcomes such as return-to-work rates) are evaluated, typically annually.

Given EAPs' wide range of options and evolving nature, we need to constantly analyze their effectiveness. For example, there is a current debate about the desirability of costly, intensive, inpatient alcoholism and substance abuse services over less costly outpatient care. Some fear that the lower initial costs of outpatient treatment might be offset by higher long-term costs because of relapse or other forms of failure. To settle this question, General Electric performed an experiment at its plant in Lynn, Massachusetts. To evaluate the relative effectiveness of three possible treatment courses, GE researchers assessed the experiences of 227 workers who were randomly assigned to one of the three treatments: (1) compulsory hospitalization followed by participation in Alcoholics Anonymous (AA), (2) compulsory AA without hospitalization, or (3) the employee's choice of treatments (1) or (2).

The results of this study indicated that after two years, workers who received hospital care fared the best despite the fact that this option was chosen less often by the employees themselves.[20] A study of drug dependency has shown comparable results.[21] The message from these studies is clear: although both employers (for cost reasons) and employees (for convenience reasons) may be attracted to short-term, low-cost treatments, everyone might be better served by focusing on long-term costs and well-being.

Outplacement Counseling

The terminal nature of an employee discharge not only leaves the person angry, it also leads to confusion as to how to react and in a quandary regarding what happens next. If the person feels there is nothing to lose and nowhere else to turn, the potential for violence or litigation is higher than most organizations are willing to tolerate. Therefore, many organizations provide **outplacement counseling,** which tries to help dismissed employees manage the transition from one job to another.

Outplacement counseling
Counseling to help displaced employees manage the transition from one job to another.

Some organizations have their own in-house staff for conducting this counseling. In other companies, outside consultants are kept on a retainer basis to help with individual cases. Regardless, goals of outplacement programs are to help the former employee deal with the psychological issues associated with losing one's job (grief, depression, fear) while at the same time helping him or her find new employment.

Outplacement counseling is aimed at helping people realize that losing a job is not the end of the world and that other opportunities exist. Indeed, for many people, losing a job can be a critical learning experience that plants the seed for future success. For example, when John Morgridge was fired from his job as branch manager at Honeywell 20 years ago, it made him realize that his own assertiveness and need for independence were never going to cut it in a large, bureaucratic institution like Honeywell. Morgridge took his skills and went on to build computer network maker Cisco Systems, which is now worth over $1 billion.[22]

This is a success story for Morgridge, but the fact that a major corporation like Honeywell let his talent go certainly reflects a lost opportunity for the company. Retaining people who can make such contributions is a key to gaining and maintaining competitive advantage. The second half of this chapter is devoted to issues related to retention.

Managing Voluntary Turnover

In the story that opened this chapter, we showed how many of the problems associated with the poor performance of security screeners at major airports can be directly attributable to high rates of employee turnover. This is true in all organizations, and hence it is imperative for organizations to try to minimize voluntary turnover—especially among high-performing job incumbents.[23]

In this section of the chapter, we examine the job withdrawal process that characterizes voluntary employee turnover, and we illustrate the central role that job satisfaction plays in this process. We also discuss what aspects of job satisfaction seem most critical to retention and how to measure these facets. Finally, we show how survey–feedback interventions, designed around these measures, can be used to strategically manage the voluntary turnover process so that high performers are retained while marginal performers are allowed to leave.

Process of Job Withdrawal

Job withdrawal is a set of behaviors that dissatisfied individuals enact to avoid the work situation. The right side of Figure 10.1 shows a model grouping the overall set of behaviors into three categories: behavior change, physical job withdrawal, and psychological job withdrawal.

We present the various forms of withdrawal in a progression, as if individuals try the next category only if the preceding is either unsuccessful or impossible to implement. This theory of **progression of withdrawal** has a long history and many adherents.[24] Others have suggested that there is no tight progression in that any one of the categories can compensate for another, and people choose the category that is most likely to redress the specific source of dissatisfaction.[25] Either way, the withdrawal

Progression of withdrawal
Theory that dissatisfied individuals enact a set of behaviors in succession to avoid their work situation.

FIGURE 10.1
An Overall Model of the Job Dissatisfaction–Job Withdrawal Process

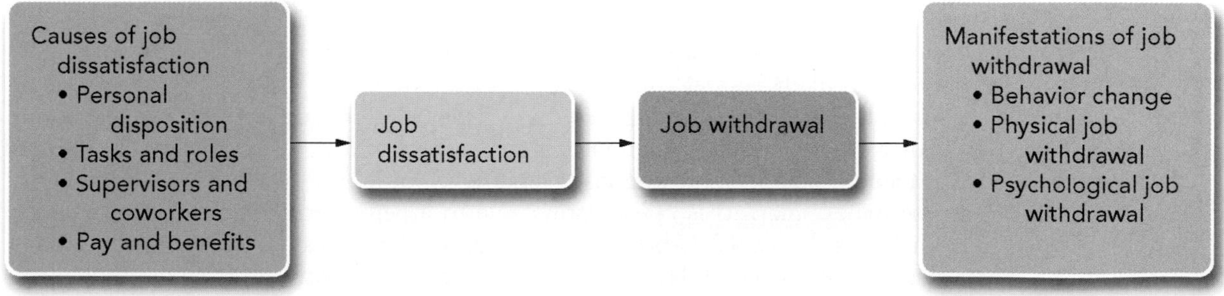

behaviors are clearly related to one another, and they are all at least partially caused by job dissatisfaction.[26]

Behavior Change

One might expect that an employee's first response to dissatisfaction would be to try to change the conditions that generate the dissatisfaction. This can lead to supervisor–subordinate confrontation, perhaps even conflict, as dissatisfied workers try to bring about changes in policy or upper-level personnel. Where employees are unionized, it can lead to an increased number of grievances being filed.[27] Although at first this type of conflict can feel threatening to the manager, on closer inspection, this is really an opportunity for the manager to learn about and perhaps solve an important problem. For example, Don McAdams, a manager at Johnsonville Foods, recalls an incident where one particular employee had been very critical of the company's incentive system. McAdams listened to the person's concerns and then asked him to head a committee charged with developing a better incentive system. At first the employee was taken aback, but he eventually accepted the challenge and became so enthusiastic about the project that he was the one who presented the new system to the general membership. Because this person was known to be highly critical of the old system, he had a high level of credibility with the other workers, who felt, "If this guy likes it, it must be pretty good." In the end, this critic-turned-champion was immensely successful in solving a specific organizational problem.[28]

Whistle-blowing
Making grievances public by going to the media or government.

Less constructively, employees can initiate change through **whistle-blowing** (making grievances public by going to the media).[29] The damage that a single well-placed whistle-blower can do to an organization was revealed at Archer Daniels Midland (ADM). Top executive Mark Whitacre, working in cooperation with the FBI, taped many conversations that were later used to charge ADM with price fixing in one of the biggest antitrust cases in the 1990s.[30]

Employees can also sue their employers when the disputed policies relate to race, sex, safe working conditions, or any other aspect of employment regulated by state or federal laws. As we have seen, such suits are costly, both financially and in terms of the firm's image, regardless of whether the firm wins or loses. Most employers would prefer to avoid litigation altogether. Keeping a majority of their employees happy is one means of achieving this.

Physical Job Withdrawal

If the job conditions cannot be changed, a dissatisfied worker may be able to solve the problem by leaving the job. This could take the form of an internal transfer if the dissatisfaction is job-specific (the result of an unfair supervisor or unpleasant working conditions). On the other hand, if the source of the dissatisfaction relates to organizationwide policies (lack of job security or below-market pay levels), organizational turnover is likely.

In addition to the overall turnover rate, we need to be concerned with the nature of the turnover in terms of who is staying and who is leaving. For example, turnover rates among minorities at the managerial level are often two to three times that of white males, and this is often attributable to a perceived lack of opportunities for promotions. Figure 10.2 shows the disparity in upper-level jobs for varying groups. Lawrence Perlman, CEO of Ceridian Corporation of Minneapolis, states, "The combination of women and people of color dropping out is really discouraging . . . it just

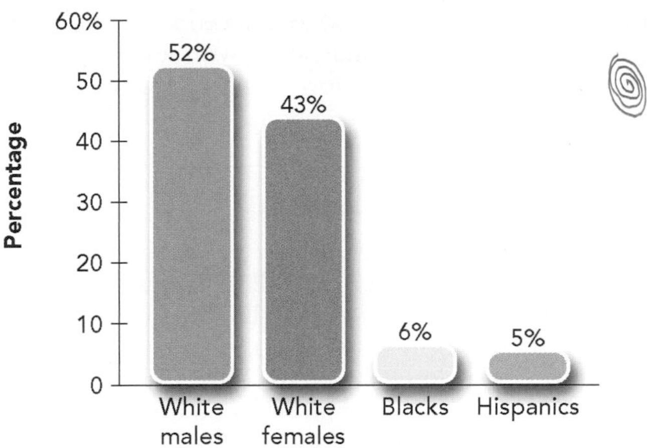

SOURCE: M. Galen, "Diversity: Beyond the Numbers Game," *BusinessWeek* (August 14, 1995), pp. 60–61.

FIGURE 10.2
Percentage of Executive and Managerial Jobs Held by Various Subgroups

isn't good business." To prevent this exodus, Ceridian set diversity goals for promotions and career-enhancing experiences. Similar steps are being taken at Polaroid, Ameritech, Texaco, and Dow Chemical.[31]

Many employees who would like to quit their jobs have to stay on if they have no other employment opportunities. Another way of physically removing oneself from the dissatisfying work is to be absent.[32] Like turnover, absenteeism is disruptive and costly to an organization. It has been estimated that absenteeism costs organizations an average of $505 per person per day for large employers and $662 per person per day for employers with fewer than 100 employees.[33] Short of missing the whole day, a dissatisfied employee may be late for work. Although not as disruptive as absenteeism, tardiness can be costly and is related to job satisfaction.[34] Tardiness can be especially costly when companies are organized around teams because the tardy individual often creates difficulties that spill over and affect the other team members.

Psychological Withdrawal

When dissatisfied employees are unable to change their situation or remove themselves physically from their jobs, they may psychologically disengage themselves from their jobs. Although they are physically on the job, their minds may be somewhere else.

This psychological disengagement can take several forms. First, if the primary dissatisfaction has to do with the job itself, the employee may display a very low level of job involvement. **Job involvement** is the degree to which people identify themselves with their jobs. People who are uninvolved with their jobs consider their work an unimportant aspect of their lives. For them, performing well or poorly on the job does not really affect their self-concept, which makes them harder to motivate.[35] Over time, job dissatisfaction leads to low job involvement.

Job involvement
The degree to which people identify themselves with their jobs.

A second form of psychological disengagement, which can occur when the dissatisfaction is with the employer as a whole, is a low level of organizational commitment. **Organizational commitment** is the degree to which an employee identifies with the organization and is willing to put forth effort on its behalf.[36] Individuals who have low organizational commitment are often just waiting for the first good opportunity to

Organizational commitment
The degree to which an employee identifies with the organization and is willing to put forth effort on its behalf.

quit their jobs. In other words, they have developed a strong intention to leave the organization. In the meantime, like individuals with low job involvement, they are often difficult to motivate. Like job involvement, organizational commitment is strongly related to job satisfaction.

Job Satisfaction and Job Withdrawal

Job satisfaction
A pleasurable feeling that results from the perception that one's job fulfills or allows for the fulfillment of one's important job values.

As we see in Figure 10.1, the key driving force behind all the different forms of job withdrawal is **job satisfaction,** which we will define as a pleasurable feeling that results from the perception that one's job fulfills or allows for the fulfillment of one's important job values.[37] This definition reflects three important aspects of job satisfaction. First, job satisfaction is a function of *values*, defined as "what a person consciously or unconsciously desires to obtain." Second, this definition emphasizes that different employees have different views of which values are important, and this is critical in determining the nature and degree of their job satisfaction. One person may value high pay above all else; another may value the opportunity to travel; another may value staying within a specific geographic region. The third important aspect of job satisfaction is perception. It is one's perception of one's present situation relative to one's values that matters. An individual's perceptions may not be a completely accurate reflection of reality, and different people may view the same situation differently.

Frame of reference
A standard point that serves as a comparison for other points and thus provides meaning.

In particular, people's perceptions are often strongly influenced by their frame of reference. A **frame of reference** is a standard point that serves as a comparison for other points and thus provides meaning. For example, an upper-level executive who offers a 6 percent salary increase to a lower-level manager might expect this to make the manager happy because inflation (the executive's frame of reference) is only 3 percent. The manager, on the other hand, might find the raise quite unsatisfactory because it is less than the 9 percent raise received by a colleague who does similar work (the manager's frame of reference). A person's frame of reference often reflects her average past experience.[38] It may also reflect her perceptions or other peoples' experience (that of her reference group).[39] Thus values, perceptions, and importance are the three components of job satisfaction. People will be satisfied with their jobs as long as they perceive that their jobs meet their important values.

Sources of Job Dissatisfaction

Many aspects of people and organizations can cause dissatisfaction among employees. Managers and HR professionals need to be aware of these because they are the levers which can raise job satisfaction and reduce employee withdrawal. Indeed, recent surveys have shown that job satisfaction in the United States has declined from 1995 to 2000, making this a particular timely concern.[40] As the "Competing in the New Economy Box" shows, keeping employees satisfied with their jobs may be a better long-term solution for managing turnover than some of the more desperate contractual measures some employers turn to.

Negative affectivity
A dispositional dimension that reflects pervasive individual differences in satisfaction with any and all aspects of life.

Personal Dispositions

Because dissatisfaction is an emotion that ultimately resides within the person, it is not surprising that many who have studied these outcomes have focused on individual differences. **Negative affectivity** is a term used to describe a dispositional dimension that

COMPETING IN THE NEW ECONOMY

Noncompete Agreements: You Can Run, But You Can't Hide

You probably believe that in a free society, every citizen has the right to enter and leave the labor market as he or she sees fit. If you do not like working for this boss or that organization, or if you feel that you are being treated unfairly or are unappreciated, you can always tell your employer, in the words of that old country song, "Take this job and shove it, I ain't working here no more." Well, in the new economy, your employer is just as likely to sing back, "You ain't working anywhere else either."

Consider the case of Debra Pilkerton, who, after just a few months of working at the Annapolis office of the TLC Laser Eye Center, had a major argument with her supervisor. She left her job after the incident, and with 23 years of experience as an optician, she quickly found work at the Baltimore Laser Eye Center. She might have been content there had she not signed a noncompete contract with TLC. After learning of her new job, lawyers from TLC wrote a letter to both her and her new employer, saying she was in violation of the contract and demanding that she be dismissed. After reading the letter and studying the contract, the Baltimore firm complied, and Pilkerton was fired from her new job.

As Jonathon Klein, general counsel to MicroStrategy Inc., a software company, notes, "In the new economy, your crown jewel is your intellectual property, which is why it is important to have provisions that protect your company's assets." In the effort to protect these assets, more and more firms are asking would-be employees to sign noncompete contracts that prohibit them from working for competing firms after quitting their jobs. Over the last 10 years the number of firms using such contracts has expanded almost tenfold. From the perspective of the employer, noncompete contracts are perceived as fair because the employer often trains the workers and provides them with the skill, information, personal contacts, and experience that make them valuable in the first place. It seems unfair for the employees to take this investment and, perhaps for a few dollars more, leave for a competing firm and make this investment work directly against the former employer.

On the other hand, it seems unfair to bind an employee to a single company, especially if the person is mistreated. Indeed, in some recent controversial noncompete cases, people have been laid off by their employers and still told that they cannot seek employment with anyone else! This has caused a major backlash against such contracts; critics argue that they are unconstitutional and border on creating indentured servitude. In fact, in one recent court case, Aetna Insurance was fined more than $1 million for terminating an employee because she refused to sign a noncompete contract.

In balancing the need for employee freedom with the employer's need to protect intellectual property, the judicious use of noncompete contracts may make sense in some cases. *Judicious use* in this context means that such contracts should be limited in time (perhaps one year) and geographical constraints (30 miles). They should also be targeted to a small set of employees whose human capital was clearly enhanced by the employer and whose movement to a competitor would do immediate, compelling damage to the former employer. Finally, the enforcement of noncompete contracts should be a last resort in the effort to retain employees, and employers should try instead to build a culture and environment where people are not motivated to leave.

SOURCE: K. Bredemeier, "In a Bind over Noncompete Clauses," *Washington Post* (March 18, 2000), p. E1; D.M. Katz, "Noncompetes: The Dark Side of the Labor Force," CFO.com (February 8, 2001), pp. 1–3; C. Hymowitz, "Firms That Cut Layoff Packages May Erode Employees' Loyalty," *The Wall Street Journal* (October 30, 2001), p. 1; K. Maher, "Noncompete Agreements Meet Rebels," *The Wall Street Journal* (October 23, 2001), pp. 1–2.

reflects pervasive individual differences in satisfaction with any and all aspects of life. Individuals who are high in negative affectivity report higher levels of aversive mood states, including anger, contempt, disgust, guilt, fear, and nervousness across all contexts (work and nonwork).[41]

People who are high in negative affectivity tend to focus extensively on the negative aspects of themselves and others.[42] They are also more likely, in a given situation, to experience significantly higher levels of distress than others—which implies that some people bring dissatisfaction with them to work. Research has shown that negative affectivity in early adolescence is predictive of overall job dissatisfaction in adulthood. There were also significant relationships between work attitudes measured over 5-year[43] and 10-year[44] periods, even for workers who changed employers and/or occupations. Thus these people may be relatively dissatisfied regardless of what steps the organization or the manager takes.

Although the causes of negative affectivity are not completely known, research that examined identical twins who were raised apart suggests that there may be a genetic component.[45] Thirty-four pairs of twins were measured for their general job satisfaction and their satisfaction with intrinsic and extrinsic aspects of the job. The researchers found a significant relationship between the ratings for each member of a pair, despite the fact that the twins were raised apart and worked at different jobs. Other research on genetic twins reared apart has shown similar effects on perceptions of the degree to which one's organization provides a supportive climate.[46]

Another construct useful in understanding dispositional aspects of job satisfaction is the notion of core self-evaluations. *Core self-evaluations* have been defined as a basic positive or negative bottom-line opinion that individuals hold about themselves. A positive core evaluation reflects the person's self-image on a number of more specific traits, including high self-esteem, high self-efficacy, internal locus of control, and emotional stability. These factors, both alone and together, have been found to be quite predictive of job satisfaction.[47]

Part of the reason why individuals with positive core self-evaluations have higher job satisfaction is that they tend to seek out and obtain jobs with more desirable characteristics, such as allowing discretion or dealing with complex tasks.[48] They also tend to take more socially approved proactive steps when it comes to trying to personally change a situation that is not to their liking. People with negative core self-evaluations tend to attribute dissatisfying features of their lives or work to the acts of other people, whom they blame for all their problems. They are less likely to work toward change, instead either doing nothing or acting aggressively toward those they blame for their misfortunes.[49]

The evidence on the linkage between these kinds of traits and job satisfaction suggests the importance of personnel selection as a way of raising overall levels of employee satisfaction. Interviews should assess the degree to which any job applicant has a history of chronic dissatisfaction with employment. If an applicant states that he was dissatisfied with his past six jobs, what makes the employer think he won't be dissatisfied with this one?

Finally, although the focus of this chapter is job dissatisfaction, we must recognize that dissatisfaction with other facets of life can spill over into the workplace. That is, a worker who is having problems with a family member may attribute some of this negative affect to the job or organization. The National Institute of Mental Health (NIMH) estimates that clinical depression affects 17.6 million Americans, including 9 percent of all male workers and 17 percent of all female workers, and costs employers over $70 billion a year.[50]

Although managers cannot be expected to become clinical psychologists, in their attempt to diagnose some work-related performance problems, the possibility of clinical depression should not be dismissed altogether, and employees can be advised to seek help from qualified professionals via a company-sponsored Employee Assistance Program.[51] For example, NIMH runs a program called DART (Depression Awareness Recognition and Treatment), which provides educational materials and management training sessions for managers of large organizations, including AT&T, Sears, Pacific Bell, and Westinghouse. Eighty percent of those suffering depression can be managed with help; the Americans with Disabilities Act covers these individuals. "Reasonable accommodation" in these cases might include several weeks of leave to adjust to medication or perhaps altering work schedules to allow for therapy sessions. The gains achieved by early recognition and treatment can be substantial. A program similar to the DART program at First Chicago Bank dropped its behavioral health care costs from 15 percent of total medical plan costs to just 8 percent.[52]

Tasks and Roles

As a predictor of job dissatisfaction, nothing surpasses the nature of the task itself.[53] Many aspects of a task have been linked to dissatisfaction. Several elaborate theories relating task characteristics to worker reactions have been formulated and extensively tested. We discussed several of these in Chapter 4. In this section we focus on three primary aspects of tasks that affect job satisfaction: the complexity of the task, the degree of physical strain and exertion on the job, and the value the employee puts on the task.[54]

With a few exceptions, there is a strong positive relationship between task complexity and job satisfaction. That is, the boredom generated by simple, repetitive jobs that do not mentally challenge the worker leads to frustration and dissatisfaction.[55] Moreover, monotony at work has been shown to have a particularly strong negative effect on women relative to men. For example, one recent study of blue-collar workers in 32 manufacturing plants showed that increased repetitive activity at work led to absenteeism rates for women that were three times the rates for men.[56]

One intervention that employees themselves often introduce to low-complexity situations is to bring personal stereo headsets to work. Many supervisors disapprove of this practice, which can be understood in situations where employees need to interact with customers. However, in simple jobs with minimal customer contact (like processing paperwork or data entry) the research actually suggests that personal stereo headsets can improve performance. For example, one study examined stereo headset use among workers in 32 jobs within a large retailing organization. The results indicated the stereo group outperformed a no-stereo control group on simple jobs (like invoice processor) but performed worse than controls on jobs high in complexity (such as accountant).[57]

The second primary aspect of a task that affects job satisfaction is the degree to which the job involves physical strain and exertion.[58] This aspect is sometimes overlooked at a time when automation has removed much of the physical strain associated with jobs. Indeed, the fact that technology has aimed to lessen work-related physical exertion indicates that such exertion is almost universally considered undesirable. Nevertheless, many jobs can still be characterized as physically demanding.

The third primary aspect is whether the object of the work promotes something valued by the worker. Over 1 million volunteer workers in the United States perform their jobs almost exclusively because of the meaning they attach to the work. Some

TABLE 10.5
Sample Items from a Standardized Job Satisfaction Scale (the JDI)

Instructions: Think of your present work. What is it like most of the time? In the blank beside each word given below, write
__Y__ for "Yes" if it describes your work
__N__ for "No" if it does NOT describe your work
__?__ if you cannot decide

Work Itself	**Pay**	**Promotion Opportunities**
_____ Routine	_____ Less than I deserve	_____ Dead-end job
_____ Satisfying	_____ Highly paid	_____ Unfair policies
_____ Good	_____ Insecure	_____ Based on ability

Supervision	**Coworkers**
_____ Impolite	_____ Intelligent
_____ Praises good work	_____ Responsible
_____ Doesn't supervise enough	_____ Boring

SOURCE: W.K. Balzar, D.C. Smith, D.E. Kravitz, S.E. Lovell, K.B. Paul, B.A. Reilly, and C.E. Reilly, *User's Manual for the Job Descriptive Index (JDI)* (Bowling Green, OH: Bowling Green State University, 1990).

TABLE 10.6
Sample Items from a Standardized Scale That Measures Overall Job Satisfaction

Instructions: Put a check beside the answer that you feel is most appropriate regarding your present job.

All in all, how satisfied are you with your job?
_____ Very satisfied
_____ Somewhat satisfied
_____ Not too satisfied
_____ Not at all satisfied

If a good friend of yours told you he or she was interested in working in a job like yours for your employer, would you recommend it to him or her?
_____ Strongly recommend this job
_____ Would have doubts about recommending this job
_____ Strongly advise against taking this job

Knowing what you know now, if you had to decide all over again to take the job you have now, what would you decide?
_____ Decide without hesitation to take the same job
_____ Would have some second thoughts about taking the same job
_____ Definitely decide not to take the same job

SOURCE: R.P. Quinn and G.L. Staines, *The 1977 Quality of Employment Survey* (Ann Arbor: Survey Research Center, Institute for Social Research, University of Michigan, 1979). Reprinted with permission.

Clearly there is no end to the number of satisfaction facets that we might want to measure, but the key in operational contexts, where the main concern is retention, is making sure that scores on whatever measures taken truly relate to voluntary turnover among valued people. For example, satisfaction with coworkers might be low, but if this aspect of satisfaction is not too central to employees, it may not translate into voluntary turnover. Similarly, in an organization that bases raises on performance, low performers might report being dissatisfied with raises, but this may not reflect any op-

Job Satisfaction from the Faces Scale
Consider all aspects of your job. Circle the face that best describes your feelings about your job in general.

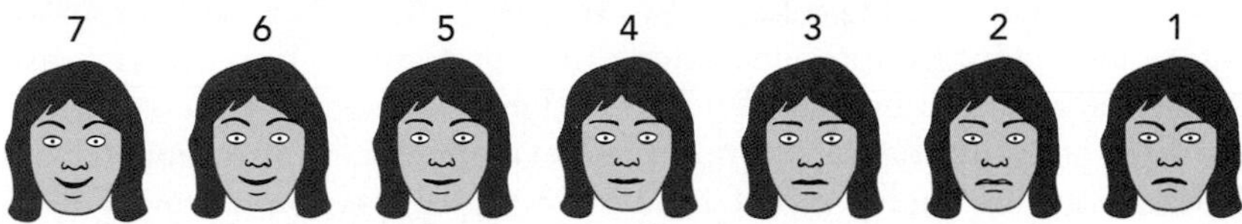

SOURCE: The faces were adapted from R.B. Dunham and J.B. Herman and published in the *Journal of Applied Psychology* 60 (1975), pp. 629–31. Copyright 1975 by the American Psychological Association. Adapted with permission.

FIGURE 10.4
Example of a Simplified, Nonverbal Measure of Job Satisfaction

erational problem. Indeed, the whole strategic purpose of many pay-for-performance plans is to create this type of dissatisfaction among low performers to motivate them to higher levels of performance.

Survey-Feedback Interventions

Regardless of what measures are used or how many facets of satisfaction are assessed, a systematic, ongoing program of *employee survey research* should be a prominent part of any human resource strategy for a number of reasons. First, it allows the company to monitor trends over time and thus prevent problems in the area of voluntary turnover before they happen. For example, Figure 10.5 shows the average profile for

FIGURE 10.5
Average Profile for Different Facets of Satisfaction over Time

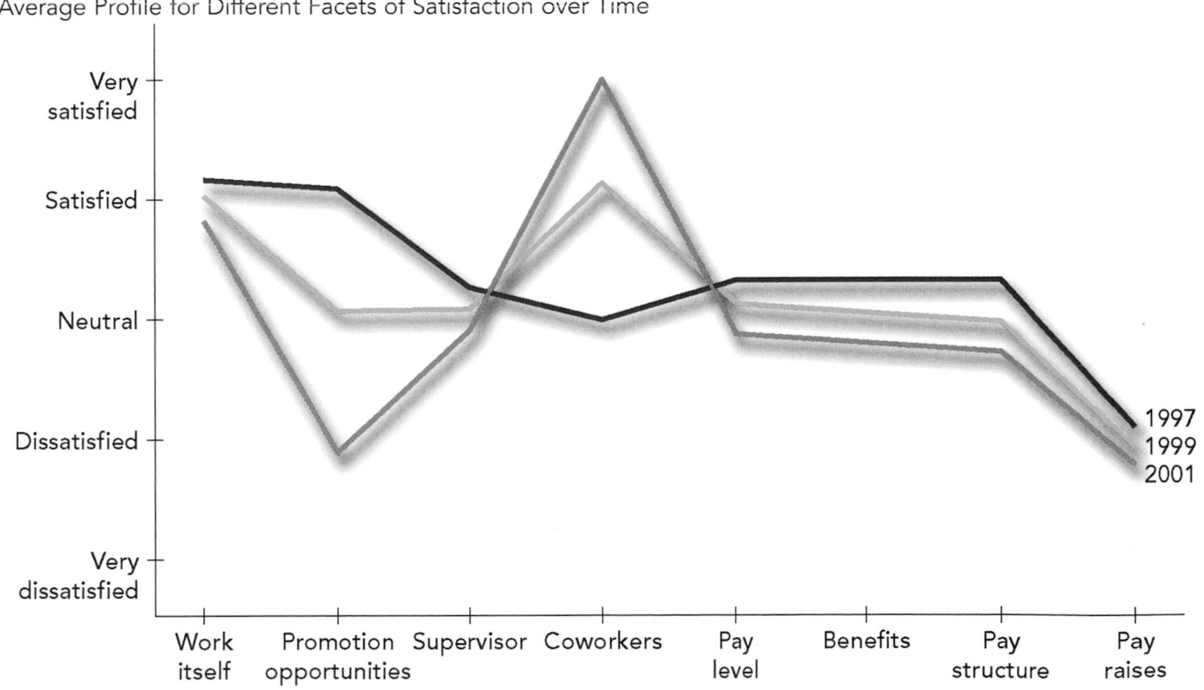

different facets of satisfaction for a hypothetical company in 1997, 1999, and 2001. As the figure makes clear, the level of satisfaction with promotion opportunities in this company has eroded over time, whereas the satisfaction with coworkers has improved. If there was a strong relationship between satisfaction with promotion opportunities and voluntary turnover among high performers, this would constitute a threat that the organization might need to address via some of the techniques discussed in our previous chapter, "Employee Development." For example, First USA Bank saw exactly this kind of profile in its 1998 job satisfaction survey of all its managers. As Jeff Brown, vice president of organizational effectiveness, noted, "We already had a sense that career development was an issue, but the survey data really threw it in our faces and made us realize we had to do something about it." This led to First USA's "Opportunity Knocks" program, an employee-led career development effort that clarified the opportunities available within the firm as well as what skills and experiences were needed to take advantage of those opportunities. As a result of this program, two years later when the survey was conducted again, satisfaction with promotion opportunities increased by 40 percent.[83]

A second reason for engaging in an ongoing program of employee satisfaction surveys is that it provides a means of empirically assessing the impact of changes in policy (such as introduction of a new performance appraisal system) or personnel (introduction of a new CEO, for example) on worker attitudes. Figure 10.6 shows the average profile for different satisfaction facets for a hypothetical organization one year before and one year after a merger. An examination of the profile makes it clear that since the merger, satisfaction with supervision and pay structure have gone down dramatically, and this has not been offset by any increase in satisfaction along other di-

FIGURE 10.6

Average Profile for Different Facets of Satisfaction before and after a Major Event

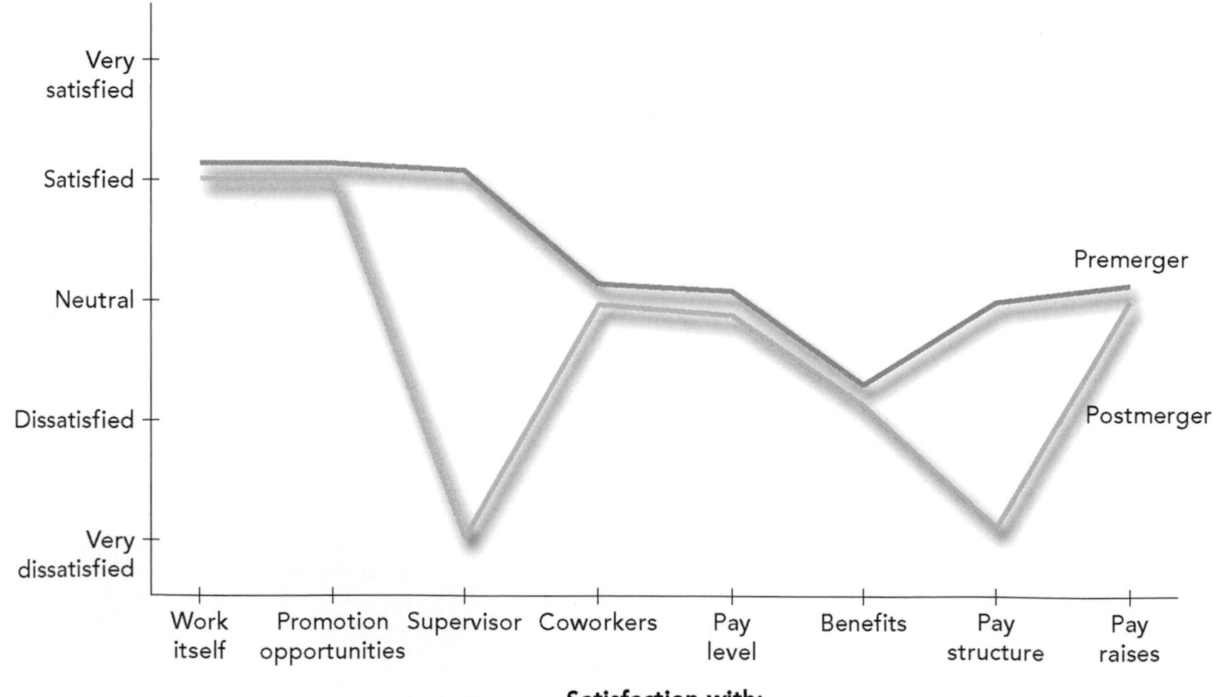

FIGURE 10.7
Average Profile for Different Facets of Satisfaction versus the Industry Average

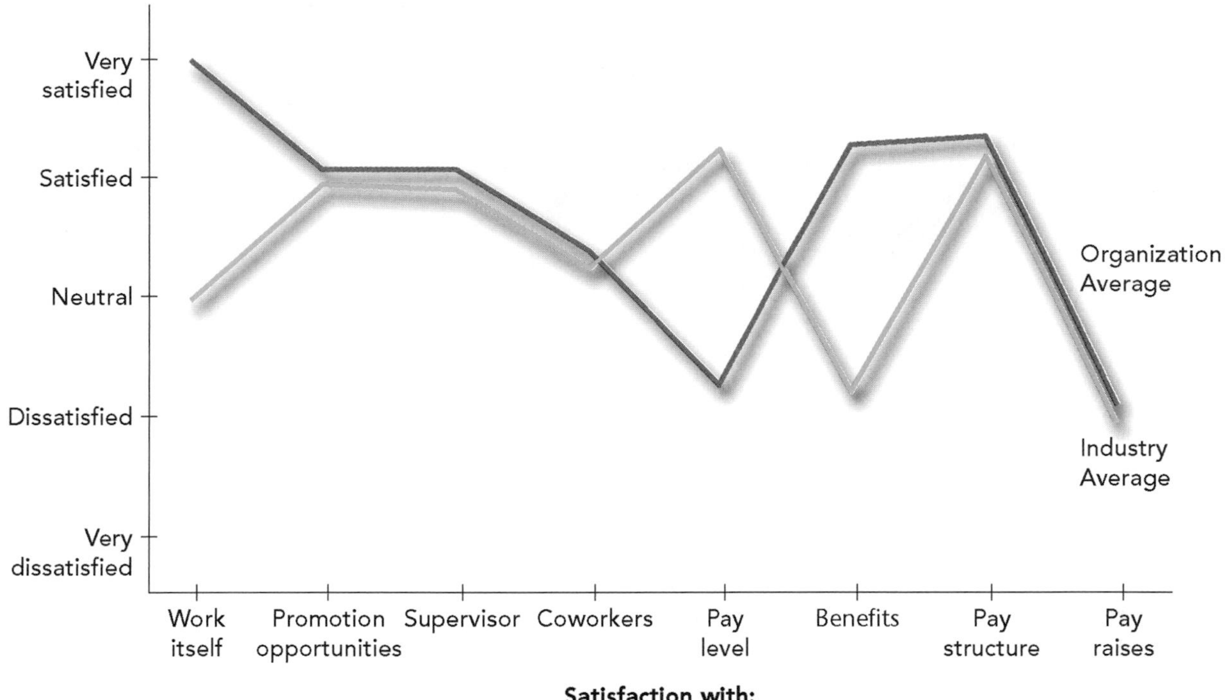

mensions. Again, this might point to the need for training programs for supervisors (like those discussed in Chapter 7) or changes in the job evaluation system (like those discussed in Chapter 11).

Third, when these surveys incorporate standardized scales like the JDI or PSQ, they often allow the company to compare itself with others in the same industry along these dimensions. For example, Figure 10.7 shows the average profile for different satisfaction facets for a hypothetical organization and compares this to the industry average. Again, if we detect major differences between one organization and the industry as a whole (on overall pay levels, for example), this might allow the company to react and change its policies before there is a mass exodus of people moving to the competition.

According to Figure 10.7, the satisfaction with pay levels is low relative to the industry, but this is offset by higher-than-industry-average satisfaction with benefits and the work itself. As we showed in Chapter 6 ("Selection and Placement"), the organization might want to use this information to systematically screen people. That is, the fit between the person and the organization would be best if the company selected applicants who reported being most interested in the nature of the work itself and benefits, and rejected those applicants whose sole concern was with pay levels.

Within the organization, a systematic survey program also allows the company to check for differences between units and hence benchmark "best practices" that might be generalized across units. For example, Figure 10.8 shows the average profile for five different regional divisions of a hypothetical company. The figure shows that satisfaction with pay raises is much higher in one of the regions relative to the others. If the overall amount of money allocated to raises was equal through the entire company, this

FIGURE 10.8
Average Profile for Different Facets of Satisfaction for Different Regional Divisions

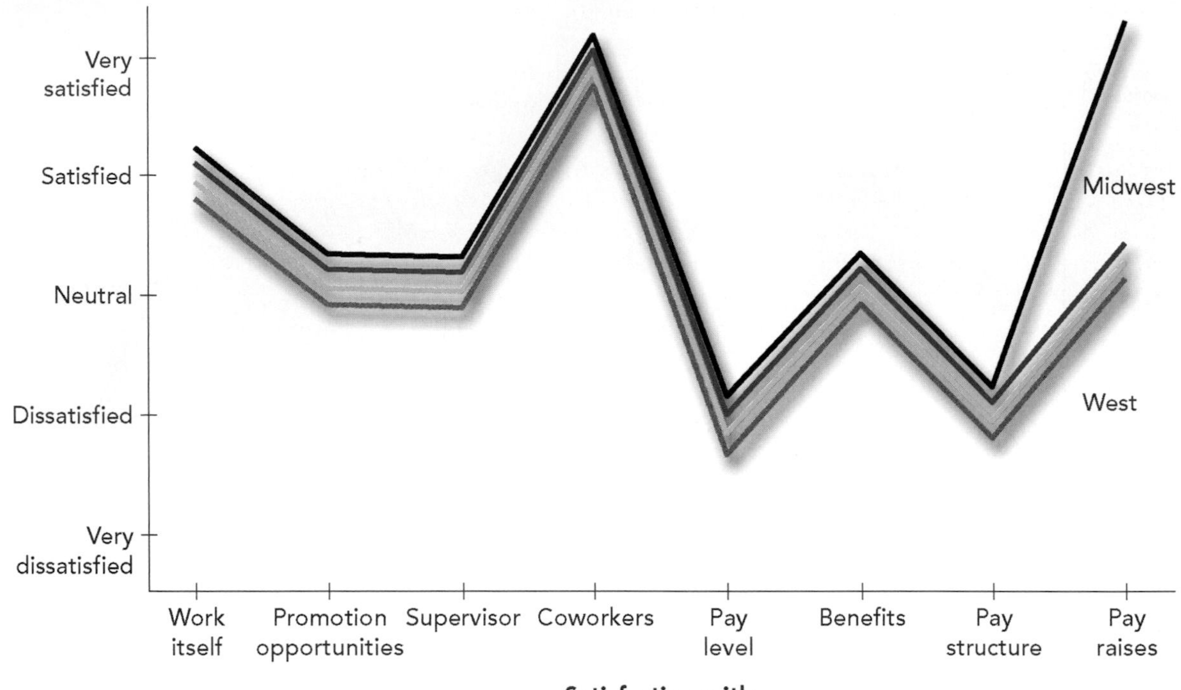

implies that the manner in which raises are allocated or communicated in the Midwest region might be something that the other regions should look into.

Voicing
A formal opportunity to complain about one's work situation.

Finally, yearly surveys give employees a constructive outlet for voicing their concerns and frustrations. Employees' ability to handle dissatisfying work experiences is enhanced when they feel they have an opportunity to air their problems. Formalized opportunities to state complaints about one's work situation have been referred to as **voicing.**[84] Research has shown that voicing gives employees an active, constructive outlet for their work frustrations.[85] For example, a study of nurses indicated that providing such voicing mechanisms as an employee attitude survey and question-and-answer sessions between employees and management enhanced worker attitudes and cut turnover.[86] The value of voicing opportunities has been expressed well by Norman Plummer, president of Monitrex (a San Francisco–based health care provider): "If you don't provide an environment for open communication, you'll suffer through revolutions rather than evolutions."[87]

Obviously a great deal can be learned from employee satisfaction surveys. It is surprising that many companies conducting regular consumer satisfaction surveys fail to show the same concern for employee satisfaction. Retention is an issue involving both customers and employees, however, and—as we noted at the outset of this chapter—the two types of retention are substantially related. For example, sales agents at State Farm Insurance stay with the company for an average of 18 to 20 years—two to three times the average tenure in this industry. This kind of tenure allows the average State Farm agent to learn the job and develop long-term customer relations that cannot be matched by competitors who may lose half of their sales staff each year. State Farm also benefits from this experienced staff by systematically surveying its agents to get their views about where customer satisfaction is high, where it is low, and what can be done to improve service.[88] The result in terms of the bottom line is that State Farm achieves 40 percent higher sales per agent compared to the competition. In addition, as an indicator of quality of service, the retention rate among State Farm customers exceeds 95 percent.[89]

Although findings such as these are leading more companies to do such surveys, conducting an organizational opinion survey is not something that should be taken lightly. Especially in the beginning, surveys such as this often raise expectations. It is critical that the organization conducting the survey be ready to act on the results. For example, at Doctor's Hospital in Manteca, California, a survey of employees' opinions revealed dissatisfaction (defined as an "unfavorable" rating by at least 35 percent of the employees) in several areas. When these results were fed back to employees, each problem area was accompanied by a corresponding action plan so that people could see how the organization intended to address the problem. In the area of career development, for instance, the survey indicated that even though the hospital reimbursed 100 percent of employee expenses for tuition, it did so at the end of the semester, and the inability to pay the money up front prevented many from using this benefit. Based on these results, the hospital now provides tuition up front along with loans to help defray nontuition costs (like child care expenses) associated with taking a class. Thus, what was once a source of dissatisfaction for employees is now a source of satisfaction.[90]

Finally, although the focus in this section has been on surveys of current employees, any strategic retention policy also has to consider surveying people who are about to become ex-employees. Exit interviews with departing workers can be a valuable tool for uncovering systematic concerns that are driving retention problems. If properly conducted, an exit interview can reveal the reasons why people are leaving, and perhaps even set the stage for their later return.[91] Indeed, in the new economy, it is now so common for people who once left their firm to return that they are given a special name—"boomerangs."[92] A good exit interview sets the stage for this phenomenon because if a recruiter is armed with information about what caused a specific person to leave (such as an abusive supervisor or a lack of family-friendly policies), when the situation changes, the person may be willing to come back.[93] Indeed, in the war for talent, the best way to manage retention is to engage in a battle for every valued employee, even in situations when it looks like the battle may have been lost.

A Look Back

The chapter opener on airline security workers showed how high rates of turnover can destroy the performance of work units. When the entire work unit changes every three months, it is impossible for individual workers to develop sufficient job experience, and successful coordination and teamwork never develop.

Questions

1. What were some of the characteristics of the airport security job that led to such poor worker attitudes and high turnover?
2. If you were charged with fixing this system, what specific steps would you take to improve the attitudes of these workers and reduce turnover?
3. What steps might you take that are costly, and what steps might you take that really do not increase costs very much?

Summary

This chapter examined issues related to employee separation and retention. Involuntary turnover reflects a separation initiated by the organization, often when the individual would prefer to stay a member of the organization. Voluntary turnover reflects a separation initiated by the individual, often when the organization would prefer that the person stay a member. Organizations can gain competitive advantage by strategically managing the separation process so that involuntary turnover is implemented in a fashion that does not invite retaliation, and voluntary turnover among high performers is kept to a minimum. Retaliatory reactions to organizational discipline and dismissal decisions can be minimized by implementing these decisions in a manner that promotes feelings of procedural and interactive justice. Voluntary turnover can be minimized by measuring and monitoring employee levels of satisfaction with critical facets of job and organization, and then addressing any problems identified by such surveys.

Discussion Questions

1. The discipline and discharge procedures described in this chapter are systematic but rather slow. In your opinion, should some offenses lead to immediate dismissal? If so, how would you justify this to a court if you were sued for wrongful discharge?
2. Organizational turnover is generally considered a negative outcome, and many organizations spend a great deal of time and money trying to reduce it. What situations would indicate that an increase in turnover might be just what an organization needs? Given the difficulty of terminating employees, what organizational policies might promote the retention of high-performing workers but voluntary turnover among low performers?
3. Three popular interventions for enhancing worker satisfaction are job enrichment, job rotation, and role analysis. What are the critical differences between these interventions, and under what conditions might one be preferable to the others?
4. If off-the-job stress and dissatisfaction begin to create on-the-job problems, what are the rights and responsibilities of the human resource manager in helping the employee to overcome these problems? Are intrusions into such areas an invasion of privacy, a benevolent and altruistic employer practice, or simply a prudent financial step taken to protect the firm's investment?
5. Discuss the advantages of using published, standardized measures in employee attitude surveys. Do employers ever need to develop their own measures for such surveys? Where would one turn to learn how to do this?

Web Exercise

Visit **www.expertss.com**. This is the website for Expert Survey Systems Inc., a company that provides employee attitude survey services to various companies. This website provides information and resources on organizational surveys. Use this website to answer the following questions.

1. Review the demo version of the 89-item Employee Opinion Survey. What aspects of the work environment are measured on this survey? What suggestions might you have for improving this survey?
2. What are the strengths and weaknesses of using the telephone or voice technology to collect survey data?
3. What are some of the methods used to share survey results with employees? Identify strengths and weaknesses for each method.

Managing People: From the Pages of *BusinessWeek*

BusinessWeek Low-Wage Lessons

At 5:30 A.M. the first workers arrive for the morning shift at the Marriott Hotel in downtown Chicago. They come from the farthest reaches of the metropolitan area and from all corners of the world: Bosnian refugees and born-in-America welfare moms, Chinese immigrants, and black teenagers don their uniforms for the day. A few yards and a world removed from the crystal chandeliers and fresh flowers their guests see, a remarkable staff of hundreds whirs into motion.

Maria Martinez picks up her room-cleaning assignments. A Mexican immigrant, she takes citizenship classes at the hotel after work. Tommie Powell, one-time welfare dad and former factory worker from the city's North Side, heads to the basement and his job in the hotel's recycling operation. Arthur Seredyn, who arrived from Poland three years ago, scrubs out the swimming pool.

Their pay: about $7 an hour. That's typical for Marriott International Inc.'s 134,417 U.S. housekeepers, laundry workers, dishwashers, and other hourly staffers. It is, Marriott says, the wage that the labor market dictates. "If we pay wages in excess of the productive contribution of our people, we will become noncompetitive ourselves," says J.W. Marriott Jr., chairman of the nation's fourth-largest hotel company.

But a low-paid workforce brings with it a host of problems: lack of education, poor work habits, inability to speak English, culture clashes, financial woes, inadequate child care, and domestic violence, for starters. People don't show up when they should; they leave without explanation. Every day in every hotel, such issues threaten employees' livelihoods—and the hotelier's.

The needs of low-wage employees once were easy to ignore. If a dishwasher quit, after all, there always was someone else happy to take the work. Not today, though. While the economy demands more and more highly educated workers, the need persists for more maids, meatpackers, and sewing machine operators. Nearly 30 percent of all U.S. employees make $7.28 an hour or less, up from 23.5 percent in 1973, according to the Economic Policy Institute. At the same time, with employment running at a low 5.2 percent rate in September, companies are hard-pressed in many places to find new workers. "It's critical that we become more skilled at managing this workforce," says Donna Klein, Marriott's director of work–life programs.

Marriott International, with a small group of other low-wage employers, is coming to terms with this challenging, increasingly important group. Paying its U.S. workers a median rate of $7.40 an hour, including overtime, the hotelier resists offering the higher wages that would attract more qualified workers. It has waged often bitter battles, moreover, against attempts at unionization. Instead, it has embraced a host of informal and formal solutions—including employee stock options, a social-services referral network, day care, and welfare-to-work training classes—designed to keep workers on the job and keep guests satisfied.

On one level, these are predictable responses as employers try to avert pay raises amid signs of a labor crunch. "They'll do a host of things before putting money into people's pockets," says Harvard University economist Richard B. Freeman. And critics insist that Marriott simply is taking advantage of vulnerable workers who can't get jobs elsewhere. But while its approach may hark back in some ways to the paternalistic labor strategies of old company towns, it has also launched something new: an attempt to forge a more lasting, more productive relationship with lower-wage workers. Employers "have returned full circle to a social contract with employees," notes Faith A. Wohl, director of the U.S. General Service Administration's Office of Workplace Initiatives.

"A LOT OF BABYSITTING." Amid ever more intense competition, Marriott will thrive only if it can wring out bigger productivity gains and provide world-class service. Its human resources strategies win such results. Even without big pay hikes, Marriott employees often exhibit loyalty and even enthusiasm for their employer, and many feel they have a chance for advancement within the company. Analysts say its employee turnover rate is well below most rivals'.

There is a cost. Historically, it has been Marriott's hotel managers and supervisors who have helped solve workers' problems—playing social worker, in effect. "Many managers spend 15 percent of their time doing social work," explains Clifford J. Ehrlich, Marriott International's senior vice president for human resources. "That's time not spent dealing with customer issues." They counsel employees confronting family problems, juggle shifts to accommodate erratic child care, or lend them money to pay pressing bills. "It's frustrating," says one Chicago area manager. "These employees need a lot of babysitting."

Yet Marriott has forged unquestionably strong bonds with many employees. "Every day I put on this uniform, just like an NBA player," proudly proclaims Thong Lee, a bartender who has worked 16 years at the Seattle Marriott. Lee has never forgotten that his boss, Sandy Olson, shut down the hotel laundry where he used to work for a day so the entire staff could attend his mother's funeral. The gesture earned Lee's loyalty for life—though the stock options the company offers all employees haven't hurt, either. Lee, who learned all the English he knows from Marriott, now owns several rental properties funded by his Marriott stock and pay.

BIG EXPANSION. Now Marriott is launching a range of corporate programs to alleviate the demands on local hotel managers—and to accommodate its aggressive growth plans. The chain expects to add 1,000 mostly franchised hotels by 2000, and managers who come aboard with franchisees may not buy into the social-worker role. At the same time, the ranks of Marriott managers have been thinned by about 5 percent in recent years. So new, institutionalized supports aim to replace the old one-on-one style. "Our philosophy hasn't changed . . . but it's a more professional approach," says J.W. Marriott.

Pathways to Independence, for example, is a company-developed class on basic work skills for former welfare recipients, offered at hotels in 15 cities. In June, the company finished rolling out the Associate Resource Line, a national toll-free referral service that hooks up its workers with local social services. In December, it will start a program in Washington, D.C., and two other sites to teach workers how to become better parents and partners. And next year, with two other hotel groups, Marriott will inaugurate Atlanta's Inn for Children, a 24-hour subsidized child care center.

Marriott also has led 28 companies—including J.C. Penney, Hyatt International, McDonald's, ConAgra, and Levi Strauss—to study ways to improve management of low-wage employees. With the help of the Families and Work Institute, a nonprofit research outfit in Manhattan, the so-called Employer Group plans to share best practices, create the first comprehensive demographic profile of this workforce, and advocate public policies that benefit low-wage workers—such as broader application of the Earned Income Tax Credit.

MISUNDERSTANDINGS. Yet companies and unions still know relatively little about low-wage workers and their needs. Marriott only began studying its hourly-wage workforce in 1993, after realizing that child care benefits launched three years earlier had left many problems of this population unresolved. It immediately found that a quarter have some literacy problems—mostly difficulties speaking English. Overall, Marriott workers speak and read 65 different languages.

Language barriers in this massive Babel can disrupt hotel operations—and worse. William D. Fleet, human resources director at the Seattle Marriott, where employees speak 17 languages, once fired a Vietnamese kitchen worker for wrongly accusing a chef of assault. Only after another employee was attacked by a kitchen worker did Fleet figure out that the Vietnamese employee had used the word chef to refer to all kitchen workers with white uniforms. The misunderstanding had led to the firing of a good staffer and delayed the arrest of a dangerous one.

Marriott managers fear the inability to speak English also may get in the way of service. "People will do the things they do well and shy away from things that make them look foolish," says Fleet. That's why he instituted a comprehensive ESL program for staffers to take on company time. After all, workers who know English interact better with guests. Teresa Ortiz, a housekeeper at the downtown San Francisco Marriott, once took a couple to the service elevator because she didn't know how to tell them how to get to the 39th floor. (An ESL graduate now, she says proudly, "I can tell them.")

More than half of the Marriotts in the U.S. offer workers ESL classes—a relatively cheap and easy productivity device. Beyond language, however, looms the far greater challenge of managing epic cultural divides. Last year, with the help of a local refugee resettlement organization, the Des Moines Marriott hired 20 Bosnian immigrants to join a 60-member housekeeping staff. The Bosnians, who easily got legal status as refugees, helped plug the holes left by Mexican workers who fled after managers installed a new screening technique for uncovering illegal immigrants. After finding a handful of undocumented workers, Marriott watched its applicant pool of predominantly Mexican workers evaporate.

While the Bosnians came to the rescue, they brought other problems. New to America, they "don't have anybody" to help them here, says hotel services director Wanda Johnson. "You figure out their phone bills, enroll their kids in school, and set up doctors' appointments." More than that, their arrival was resented by remaining Mexican workers who still were being checked for immigration status. Managers had to keep the peace by reassuring them that the company was screening workers to comply with the law, not to dump them.

When managers can overcome cultural divides, they win commitment. Sara Redwell, an assistant general manager at the North Arlington Heights (Illinois) Courtyard Hotel, started working at Marriott 12 years ago at age 23 as a housekeeper after immigrating with her mother from Mexico. While taking ESL and other college classes, she was promoted to housekeeping manager in 1990 and, last year, to her present job. There, she supervises 20 employees, most of whom are Spanish-speaking. She mentors food server Elodia Lopez, a Mexican immigrant whom she would like to promote to restaurant supervisor, by teaching her a new English phrase every day. "What Marriott gave to me, I want to give to others," she says.

Can Marriott reproduce the same dedication with human resources systems sent down from headquarters? In some ways, such standardized programs could prove more effective. Marriott's Associate Resource Line is offered in more than 100 languages—more than any one manager could handle. So far, about 7,000 staffers have called and been assigned a social worker, who finds them local help. Marriott anticipates savings of five times its $2 million investment from reduced turnover, absenteeism, and tardiness.

Gladys Chacon, a single mother who is an accounting clerk at the Chicago Downtown Marriott, found child care last year for her six-year-old, Jazmine, through the resource line. "If I hadn't found good day care, I would have had to quit my job," she says. In her previous job at a grocery, she had to stay home many days when an unreliable sitter didn't show.

The Fatherhood Project, to be launched by the Families and Work Institute in December for Marriott in Washington, will teach male employees and spouses of female ones how to become better fathers—a benefit other companies offer primarily for white-collar staffers. Surveys show that women view a more involved partner as a key stress reducer. "Less burnout at the workplace is the big payoff," says Marriott's Klein. Single fathers, such as Chicago recycling worker Tommie Powell, can take advantage of the program, too. "It's hard working full-time and having teenagers at home," says Powell, who has a 16-year-old daughter and 19-year-old son.

Powell and 600 other Marriott employees also have

benefited from Pathways to Independence. The six-week program, which could serve as a model for welfare reform, takes hold, teaches business basics, such as showing up on time, and life lessons, such as self-esteem and personal financial management. One of the few companies with such a plan, Marriott works with federally funded local organizations to split the $5,500-per-person costs. By targeting welfare recipients, it harvests an overlooked labor pool—and Pathways graduates placed in Marriott jobs have a 13 percent turnover rate, far below the company's national average.

Sabrina McWhite, who took the Pathways course last year and then left welfare, works in the kitchen at the Metro Center Marriott in Washington and wants to become a chef. A high school graduate who dropped out of the University of the District of Columbia, McWhite credits Pathways for teaching her "how to manage money correctly, how to always have backup for child care," and other responsibilities. With a regular paycheck now, she has been able to buy her four-year-old daughter a special book bag. "I feel so good I could give it to her," she says.

Still, Marriott's critics keep asking, Why can't it simply pay higher wages? "Their hypocrisy stands out," says John W. Wilhelm, secretary–treasurer of the hotel workers' union. Marriott, which insists its pay is comparable to union wages, says it has always tried to treat workers fairly. "We hire people who have never had jobs before and give them a chance," says J.W. Marriott. That's largely true. But this isn't a story about altruism. Marriott's unusual approach to the low-wage dilemma is dictated by corporate self-interest: helping workers can cut costs and lift productivity. And that goes right to the bottom line.

Questions

1. In what ways are the issues that drive retention for low-skill workers similar to or different than the issues that drive retention among high-skill workers? Other than money, what inducements may mean more to low-skill workers relative to high-skill workers? What inducements mean the same to all workers?
2. Other than turnover, how might the responses of low-skill workers to dissatisfaction regarding the job or organization be different than or similar to the responses of high-skill workers? If an organization wanted to monitor satisfaction levels among its employees, how might the nature of the monitoring program differ for high- versus low-skill workers?
3. All of the programs aimed at retaining low-skill workers described in this end-of-chapter reading cost money, and some of them cost a great deal of money. Why would these employers spend money in this way, as opposed to just raising wages and attracting a higher-skill labor force? In your opinion, are these programs a hypocritical response on the part of employers who will do anything to avoid raising wages, or are they a realistic response given the nature of this segment of the workforce?

SOURCE: Reprinted from November 11, 1996 issue of *BusinessWeek* by special permission.

Notes

1. M.L. Schmit and S.P. Allscheid, "Employee Attitudes and Customer Satisfaction: Making Theoretical and Empirical Connections," *Personnel Psychology* 48 (1995), pp. 521–36.
2. F. Reichheld, *The Loyalty Effect* (Cambridge, MA: Harvard Business School Press, 19).
3. D.J. Koys, "The Effects of Employee Satisfaction, Organizational Citizenship Behavior, and Turnover on Organizational Effectiveness: A Unit-Level Longitudinal Study," *Personnel Psychology* 54 (2001), pp. 101–14.
4. J.P. Guthrie, "High-Involvement Work Practices, Turnover, and Productivity: Evidence from New Zealand," *Academy of Management Journal* 44 (2001), pp. 180–90.
5. S.S. Masterson, "A Trickle-Down Model of Organizational Justice: Relating Employees' and Customers' Perceptions of and Reactions to Fairness," *Journal of Applied Psychology* 86 (2001), pp. 594–604.
6. K. Dobbs, "Knowing How to Keep Your Best and Brightest," *Workforce*, April 2000, pp. 57–60.
7. J. Greenwald, "Rank and Fire," *Time* (June 18, 2001), pp. 38–40.
8. D. Jones, "More Firms Cut Workers Ranked at Bottom," **USAToday.com** (May 5, 2001), pp. 1–2.
9. J.D. Shaw, J.E. Delery, C.D. Jenkins, and N. Gupta, "An Organizational-Level Analysis of Voluntary Turnover," *Academy of Management Journal* 41 (1998), pp. 511–25.
10. M. Heller, "A Return to At-Will Employment," *Workforce*, May 2001, pp. 42–46.
11. J.B. Copeland, W. Turque, L. Wright, and D. Shapiro, "The Revenge of the Fired," *Newsweek* (February 16, 1987), pp. 46–47.
12. A.Q. Nomani, "Women Likelier to Face Violence in the Workplace," *The Wall Street Journal* (October 31, 1995), p. A16.
13. N.D. Cole and G.P. Latham, "Effects of Training in Procedural Justice on Perceptions of Disciplinary Fairness by Unionized Employees and Disciplinary Subject Matter Experts," *Journal of Applied Psychology* 82 (1997), pp. 699–705.

14. D.P. Skarlicki and R. Folger, "Retaliation in the Workplace: The Roles of Distributive, Procedural, and Interactional Justice," *Journal of Applied Psychology* 82 (1997), pp. 434–43.
15. S. Caudron, "Blowing the Whistle on Employee Disputes," *Workforce*, May 1997, pp. 50–57.
16. M. McGarvey, "The Challenge of Containing Health-Care Costs," *Financial Executive* 8 (1992), pp. 34–40.
17. B.B. Pflaum, "Seeking Sane Solutions: Managing Mental Health and Chemical Dependency Costs," *Employee Benefits Journal* 16 (1992), pp. 31–35.
18. J. Smith, "EAPs Evolve to Health Plan Gatekeeper," *Employee Benefit Plan Review* 46 (1992), pp. 18–19.
19. E. Stetzer, "Bringing Sanity to Mental Health," *Business Health* 10 (1992), p. 72.
20. S. Johnson, "Results, Relapse Rates Add to Cost of Non-Hospital Treatment," *Employee Benefit Plan Review* 46 (1992), pp. 15–16.
21. C. Mulcany, "Experts Eye Perils of Mental Health Cuts," *National Underwriter* 96 (1992), pp. 17–18.
22. J. Jones, "How to Bounce Back if You're Bounced Out," *BusinessWeek* (January 27, 1998), pp. 22–23.
23. S. Branch, "You Hired 'Em. But Can You Keep 'Em?" *Fortune* (November 9, 1998), pp. 247–50.
24. D.W. Baruch, "Why They Terminate," *Journal of Consulting Psychology* 8 (1944), pp. 35–46; J.G. Rosse, "Relations among Lateness, Absence and Turnover: Is There a Progression of Withdrawal?" *Human Relations* 41 (1988), pp. 517–31.
25. C. Hulin, "Adaptation, Persistence and Commitment in Organizations," in *Handbook of Industrial & Organizational Psychology* 2nd ed., ed. M.D. Dunnette and L.M. Hough (Palo Alto, CA: Consulting Psychologists Press, 1991), pp. 443–50.
26. C. Hulin, M. Roznowski, and D. Hachiya, "Alternative Opportunities and Withdrawal Decisions," *Psychological Bulletin* 97 (1985), pp. 233–50.
27. C.E. Labig and I.B. Helburn, "Union and Management Policy Influences on Grievance Initiation," *Journal of Labor Research* 7 (1986), pp. 269–84.
28. J.Cook, "Positively Negative," *Human Resource Executive* (June 15, 2001), pp. 101–4.
29. M.P. Miceli and J.P. Near, "Characteristics of Organizational Climate and Perceived Wrongdoing Associated with Whistle-Blowing Decisions," *Personnel Psychology* 38 (1985), pp. 525–44.
30. M. Whitacre, "My Life as a Corporate Mole for the FBI," *Fortune* (September 4, 1995).
31. M. Galen, "Diversity: Beyond the Numbers Game," *BusinessWeek* (August 14, 1995), pp. 60–61.
32. R.D. Hackett and R.M. Guion, "A Re-evaluation of the Job Satisfaction–Absenteeism Relation," *Organizational Behavior and Human Decision Processes* 35 (1985), pp. 340–81.
33. J. Jones, "Absenteeism on Rise, at $505 an Employee," *Chicago Tribune* (August 29, 1995), p. 3.
34. J.G. Rosse and H.E. Miller, "Relationship between Absenteeism and Other Employee Behaviors," in *New Approaches to Understanding, Measuring, and Managing Employee Absence*, ed. P.S. Goodman and R.S. Atkin (San Francisco: Jossey-Bass, 1984).
35. R. Kanungo, *Work Alienation* (New York: Praeger Publishers, 1982).
36. R.T. Mowday, R.M. Steers, and L.W. Porter, "The Measurement of Organizational Commitment," *Journal of Vocational Behavior* 14 (1979), pp. 224–47.
37. E.A. Locke, "The Nature and Causes of Job Dissatisfaction," in *The Handbook of Industrial & Organizational Psychology*, ed. M.D. Dunnette (Chicago: Rand McNally, 1976), pp. 901–69.
38. J.W. Thibaut and H.H. Kelly, *The Social Psychology of Groups* (New York: Wiley, 1959).
39. J.S. Adams and W.B. Rosenbaum, "The Relationship between Worker Productivity to Cognitive Dissonance about Wage Inequities," *Journal of Applied Psychology* 46 (1962), pp. 161–64.
40. S. Caudron, "The Myth of Job Happiness," *Workforce*, April 2000, pp. 32–36.
41. D. Watson, L.A. Clark, and A. Tellegen, "Development and Validation of Brief Measures of Positive and Negative Affect: The PANAS Scales," *Journal of Personality and Social Psychology* 54 (1988), pp. 1063–70.
42. T.A. Judge, E.A. Locke, C.C. Durham, and A.N. Kluger, "Dispositional Effects on Job and Life Satisfaction: The Role of Core Evaluations," *Journal of Applied Psychology* 83 (1998), pp. 17–34.
43. B.M. Staw, N.E. Bell, and J.A. Clausen, "The Dispositional Approach to Job Attitudes: A Lifetime Longitudinal Test," *Administrative Science Quarterly* 31 (1986), pp. 56–78; B.M. Staw and J. Ross, "Stability in the Midst of Change: A Dispositional Approach to Job Attitudes," *Journal of Applied Psychology* 70 (1985), pp. 469–80.
44. R.P. Steel and J.R. Rentsch, "The Dispositional Model of Job Attitudes Revisited: Findings of a 10-Year Study," *Journal of Applied Psychology* 82 (1997), pp. 873–79.
45. R.D. Arvey, T.J. Bouchard, N.L. Segal, and L.M. Abraham, "Job Satisfaction: Genetic and Environmental Components," *Journal of Applied Psychology* 74 (1989), pp. 187–93.
46. S.L. Hershberger, P. Lichenstein, and S.S. Knox, "Genetic and Environmental Influences on Perceptions of Organizational Climate," *Journal of Applied Psychology* 79 (1994), pp. 24–33.
47. T.A. Judge and J.E. Bono, "Relationship of Core Self-Evaluations Traits—Self-Esteem, Generalized Self-Efficacy, Locus of Control, and Emotional Stability—

With Job Satisfaction and Job Performance: A Meta-Analysis," *Journal of Applied Psychology* 86 (2001), pp. 80–92.

48. T.A. Judge, J.E. Bono, and E.A. Locke, "Personality and Job Satisfaction: The Mediating Role of Job Characteristics," *Journal of Applied Psychology* 85 (2000), pp. 237–49.
49. S.C. Douglas and M.J. Martinko, "Exploring the Role of Individual Differences in the Prediction of Workplace Aggression," *Journal of Applied Psychology* 86 (2001), pp. 547–59.
50. E. Tanouye, "Depression Takes Annual Toll of $70 Billion on Employers," *The Wall Street Journal* (June 13, 2001), p. 1.
51. E. Tanouye, "Mental Illness in the Workplace Afflicts Bosses, Can Affect Business," *The Wall Street Journal* (June 13, 2001), pp. 1–2.
52. J. Vennochi, "When Depression Comes to Work," *Working Woman*, August 1995, pp. 43–51.
53. B.A. Gerhart, "How Important Are Dispositional Factors as Determinants of Job Satisfaction? Implications for Job Design and Other Personnel Programs," *Journal of Applied Psychology* 72 (1987), pp. 493–502.
54. E.F. Stone and H.G. Gueutal, "An Empirical Derivation of the Dimensions along Which Characteristics of Jobs Are Perceived," *Academy of Management Journal* 28 (1985), pp. 376–96.
55. L.W. Porter and R.M. Steers, "Organizational, Work and Personal Factors in Employee Absenteeism and Turnover," *Psychological Bulletin* 80 (1973), pp. 151–76.
56. S. Melamed, I. Ben-Avi, J. Luz, and M.S. Green, "Objective and Subjective Work Monotony: Effects on Job Satisfaction, Psychological Distress, and Absenteeism in Blue Collar Workers," *Journal of Applied Psychology* 80 (1995), pp. 29–42.
57. G.R. Oldham, A. Cummings, L.J. Mischel, J.M. Schmidtke, and J. Zhou, "Listen While You Work? Quasi-experimental Relations between Personal-Stereo Headset Use and Employee Work Responses," *Journal of Applied Psychology* 80 (1995), pp. 547–64.
58. Locke, "The Nature and Causes of Job Dissatisfaction."
59. L. Jones, "Xerox Is Rewriting the Book on Organization 'Architecture'," *Chicago Tribune* (December 29, 1992), pp. 3–1, 3–2.
60. S. Wellner, "What Makes Employees Want to Stick Around?" *BusinessWeek Online* (March 20, 2000), pp. 1–2.
61. G.C. Hill and K. Yamada, "Motorola Illustrates How an Aged Giant Can Remain Vibrant," *The Wall Street Journal* (December 9, 1992), p. A1.
62. J.R. Hackman and G.R. Oldham, "Motivation through the Design of Work," *Organizational Behavior and Human Performance* 16 (1976), pp. 250–79.
63. D.R. Ilgen and J.R. Hollenbeck, "The Structure of Work: Job Design and Roles," in *Handbook of Industrial & Organizational Psychology*, 2nd ed.
64. J.A. Breaugh and J.P. Colihan, "Measuring Facets of Job Ambiguity: Construct Validity Evidence," *Journal of Applied Psychology* 79 (1994), pp. 191–201.
65. B. Kaye, "Wake Up and Smell the Coffee: People Flock to Family Friendly," *BusinessWeek Online* (January 28, 2001), pp. 1–2.
66. G. Flynn, "The Legalities of Flextime," *Workforce*, October 2001, pp. 62–66.
67. S.L. Lambert, "Added Benefits: The Link between Work–Life Benefits and Organizational Citizenship Behaviors," *Academy of Management Journal* 43 (2000), pp. 801–15.
68. J.E. Perry-Smith, "Work Family Human Resource Bundles and Perceived Organizational Performance," *Academy of Management Journal* 43 (2000), pp. 1107–17.
69. M.A. Shaffer and D.A. Harrison, "Expatriates' Psychological Withdrawal from Interpersonal Assignments: Work, Non-work, and Family Influences," *Personnel Psychology* 51 (1998), pp. 87–118.
70. P.M. Caligiuri, M.M. Hyland, A.S. Bross, and A. Joshi, "Testing a Theoretical Model for Examining the Relationship between Family Adjustment and Expatriates' Work Adjustment," *Journal of Applied Psychology* 83 (1998), pp. 598–614.
71. T.J. Newton and R.S. Keenan, "Role Stress Reexamined: An Investigation of Role Stress Predictors," *Organizational Behavior and Human Decision Processes* 40 (1987), pp. 346–68.
72. B. Sorrell, "Many U.S. Employees Feel Overworked, Stressed, Study Says," **CNN.com** (May 16, 2001), pp. 1–2.
73. M. Conlin, "Revenge of the Managers," *BusinessWeek* (March 12, 2001), pp. 60–61.
74. I. Dayal and J. M. Thomas, "Operation KPE: Developing a New Organization," *Journal of Applied Behavioral Sciences* 4 (1968), pp. 473–506.
75. B.M. Meglino, E.C. Ravlin, and C.L. Adkins, "A Work Values Approach to Corporate Culture: A Field Test of the Value Congruence Process and Its Relationship to Individual Outcomes," *Journal of Applied Psychology* 74 (1989), pp. 424–33.
76. G.C. Ganster, M.R. Fusilier, and B.T. Mayes, "Role of Social Support in the Experience of Stress at Work," *Journal of Applied Psychology* 71 (1986), pp. 102–11.
77. L. Rhoades, R. Eisenberger, and S. Armeli, "Affective Commitment to the Organization: The Contribution of Perceived Organizational Support," *Journal of Applied Psychology* 86 (2001), pp. 825–36.
78. M.A. Donovan, F. Drasgow, and L.J. Munson, "The

Perceptions of Fair Interpersonal Treatment Scale: Development and Validation of a Measure of Interpersonal Treatment in the Workplace," *Journal of Applied Psychology* 83 (1998), pp. 683–92.

79. R.T. Keller, "A Test of the Path–Goal Theory of Leadership with Need for Clarity as a Moderator in Research and Development Organizations," *Journal of Applied Psychology* 74 (1989), pp. 208–12.
80. J. Lawrence, "American Airlines: A Profile in Employee Involvement," *Personnel Journal*, August 1992, p. 63.
81. H.G. Heneman and D.S. Schwab, "Pay Satisfaction: Its Multidimensional Nature and Measurement," *International Journal of Applied Psychology* 20 (1985), pp. 129–41.
82. T. Judge and T. Welbourne, "A Confirmatory Investigation of the Dimensionality of the Pay Satisfaction Questionnaire," *Journal of Applied Psychology* 79 (1994), pp. 461–66.
83. P.K. Kiger, "At First USA Bank, Promotions and Job Satisfaction Are Up," *Workforce*, March 2001, pp. 54–56.
84. A.O. Hirshman, *Exit Voice and Loyalty* (Cambridge, MA: Harvard University Press, 1970).
85. D. Farrell, "Exit, Voice, Loyalty and Neglect as Responses to Job Dissatisfaction: A Multidimensional Scaling Study," *Academy of Management Journal* 26 (1983), pp. 596–607.
86. D.G. Spencer, "Employee Voice and Employee Retention," *Academy of Management Journal* 29 (1986), pp. 488–502.
87. B. Lambert, "Give Your Company a Check-up," *Personnel Journal*, September 1995, pp. 143–46.
88. B. Schneider, S.D. Ashworth, A.C. Higgs, and L. Carr, "Design, Validity and Use of Strategically Focused Employee Attitude Surveys," *Personnel Psychology* 49 (1996), pp. 695–705.
89. M. Loeb, "Wouldn't It Be Good to Work for the Good Guys?" *Fortune* (October 14, 1996), pp. 223–24.
90. T. Gray, "A Hospital Takes Action on Employee Survey," *Personnel Journal*, March 1995, pp. 74–77.
91. J. Applegaste, "Plan an Exit Interview," CNNMoney.com (November 13, 2000), pp. 1–2.
92. M. Conlin, "Job Security, No. Tall Latte, Yes," *BusinessWeek* (April 2, 2001), pp. 62–63.
93. J. Lynn, "Many Happy Returns," CNNMoney.com (March 2, 2001), pp. 1–2.

Developing a Diverse Workforce

Most jobs start with an interview, whether it's conducted in person, by phone, or even online. Interpersonal dynamics can affect those interviews, so a human resource manager who is looking to develop a diverse workforce to meet company needs must be able to ask the right questions of a candidate and listen to the answers in an objective, controlled manner. The ultimate goal is to evaluate the candidate fairly and accurately so that he or she fits well with job requirements. As you'll see in the video, two managers for the Beck 'n' Call company are interviewing two job applicants, and how they conduct the interviews and evaluate the applicants will affect both the organization and the individuals—in the composition of the company's workforce and the way those employees later develop in their positions. Both racial and gender issues enter into play in this scenario.

The U.S. workforce is becoming increasingly diverse. Experts estimate that by 2006 the American workforce will be 72 percent Caucasian, 11 percent African American, 12 percent Hispanic, and 5 percent Asian and other ethnic or cultural groups. Companies that want to grow and remain competitive need to utilize the talents, experience, and knowledge of workers from different backgrounds and cultures. If they do not, they may miss a golden opportunity to reach a larger customer base. The customer base for Beck 'n' Call is growing more and more diverse, with African American and Hispanic communities increasing in population where Beck 'n' Call is located. So it makes sense to recruit, develop, and retain employees who can relate to this broadening customer base and meet their needs in specific ways.

Managers at all companies, whether product or service oriented, can reap the rewards of diversity for their organizations if they practice *ethnorelativism*—the belief that groups and subcultures are inherently equal. The first step toward this belief may be consciously recognizing their own tendencies toward *ethnocentrism*—the belief that their own cultures are superior. Once a person recognizes and acknowledges his or her own attitudes and stereotypical beliefs, he or she can open up to new ideas and begin to change. For instance, conducting a structured employment interview with questions that are standardized and focused on accomplishing defined goals will help promote ethnorelativism as opposed to ethnocentrism. In addition, the interview should contain questions that allow the job applicant to respond and demonstrate his or her competencies in ways that are job related, not personal. Hunches and gut feelings should play a tiny part in such an interview, because once a job applicant becomes an employee, it's the concrete evidence of performance that counts, not whether the interviewer and employer went to the same college or like the same sports teams.

After employees are hired, it is important to give them opportunities to develop their skills and advance. This practice not only enhances the employee–employer relationship but also boosts overall productivity of the company. Managers must also be aware of the possibility of a "glass ceiling," an invisible barrier that separates female employees or those of different cultural or ethnic backgrounds from top levels of the organization. One way to guard against barriers to advancement is to examine workforce composition and statistics. Do certain groups of employees top out at middle management positions? Is there a cluster of women and minorities near the bottom of the employment ladder? Is upper management made up entirely of Caucasian males? If so, why? Do all employees receive equal training and opportunities for advancement, or do some receive preferential treatment, even if it isn't obvious? Some studies indicate that companies may also have "glass walls," which are invisible barriers to important lateral moves within the company. These barriers are just as important as the glass ceiling because a glass wall can prevent an employee from receiving training or experience in certain areas that would enable him or her to move up eventually. Studies confirm the existence of the glass ceiling and glass walls; one showed recently that 97 percent of the top U.S. managers are Caucasian and 95 percent of them are male. Limiting career advancement for certain groups undermines morale at a company and reduces productivity and competitiveness. If employees believe that no matter how well they perform they will never advance, they will not try their hardest for the organization. Because a company's most important asset is its employees, it makes sense to be sure they have the opportunities to perform at the highest possible level of creativity and productivity.

A firm like Beck 'n' Call can do plenty to develop its workforce to its fullest potential: if the company hires one of the candidates in the videotaped interview, it can assign a mentor to the new hire to help her learn the ropes and identify ways to further her career within the organization. It can also offer specific training and opportunities for general education. It can make sure that its approach to assessment is fair and accurate, and it can introduce benchmarking to help the employee mark her own progress. Down the road, it could consider ways to enlarge her job. Of course, the company must review its organizational culture to be sure no glass ceiling or glass wall exists.

Thus an interview is much more important than a casual conversation about a job. It is the first step toward shaping an organization's future workforce. If it is conducted well, both parties win.

Questions

1. Evaluate the interviewers in terms of their interviewing techniques and follow-up. Did the managers conduct the interviews with unfair or discriminating practices? Did they evaluate the best person for the job fairly and accurately? What could or should they have done differently?
2. Imagine that you were interviewing either of these candidates. How would you conduct your interview? Write four or five questions that you think should be asked to find the best applicant. Which candidate do you think you would hire, and why? (Be sure to think about long-term implications for both the employee and the organization.)
3. Think of your own experience in job interviews. Based on what you now know about interviewing, in what ways might you be able to improve your own techniques for participating in an interview as a job applicant?

SOURCE: Bureau of Labor Statistics, "BLS Releases New 1996–2006 Employment Projections," **www.bls.gov/new.release/ecopro.nws.htm**; S. Nelton, "Nurturing Diversity," *Nation's Business*, June 1995, pp. 25–27.

Compensation of Human Resources

Chapter 11

Pay Structure Decisions

Objectives

After reading this chapter, you should be able to:

1. List the main decision areas and concepts in employee compensation management.
2. Describe the major administrative tools used to manage employee compensation.
3. Explain the importance of competitive labor market and product market forces in compensation decisions.
4. Discuss the significance of process issues such as communication in compensation management.
5. Describe new developments in the design of pay structures.
6. Explain where the United States stands from an international perspective on pay issues.
7. Explain the reasons for the controversy over executive pay.
8. Describe the regulatory framework for employee compensation.

Aligning compensation strategy with the organization's strategy can make a company more competitive, as was the case when Corning streamlined its salary and organizational structure.

Enter the World of Business

Changing Compensation to Support Changes in Corporate Strategy

By realigning its strategy and compensation and benefits programs, Corning Inc., once a traditional economy company, is competing successfully in the new economy. First, the company divested itself of several business units, including Corning Consumer Products. These divestitures reduced its annual revenues from $5 billion to $3 billion. Next Corning pursued a "high-octane" growth strategy in optical communications (optical fiber, cable systems, photo technologies, optical networking devices), environmental technologies, display technologies, and specialty materials. To support this shift in corporate strategy, Corning sought to support growth by creating an environment that bolstered innovation, risk taking, teaming, and speed. One major change was in its compensation system. The salary structure was streamlined from 11 grades to 5 broad bands for exempt employees and from 7 grades to 3 broad bands for nonexempt employees. In a new economy company, products have a short life cycle and change in markets is a way of life. This means that the nature of work also changes rapidly, so the detailed job descriptions and traditional promotion paths of the past may not fit this fluid environment. By changing its salary structure, Corning hopes to increase its ability to move quickly in responding to and anticipating customer needs in rapidly changing markets by encouraging flexibility, teamwork, and learning among its employees. Decentralizing more pay decisions to managers contributes to this flexibility, and giving employees an increasing stake in the success of the company by making more employees eligible for stock options contributes to the increased focus on teamwork. Finally, employee compensation is increasingly tied to individual employee learning and performance as the broad bands allow managers more flexibility to recognize outstanding achievements.

SOURCE: B. Parus, "How an Old Economy Company Became a New Economy Enterprise," *Workspan* 44:6 (June 2001), pp. 34–41.

Introduction

From the employer's point of view, pay is a powerful tool for furthering the organization's strategic goals. First, pay has a large impact on employee attitudes and behaviors. It influences the kind of employees who are attracted to (and remain with) the organization, and it can be a powerful tool for aligning current employees' interests with those of the broader organization. Second, employee compensation is typically a significant organizational cost and thus requires close scrutiny. As Table 11.1 shows, total compensation (cash and benefits) averages 23 percent of revenues and varies both within and across industries, with the ratio of companies at the 75th percentile being approximately four times that of companies at the 25th percentile across all industries.

From the employees' point of view, policies having to do with wages, salaries, and other earnings affect their overall income and thus their standard of living. Both the level of pay and its seeming fairness compared with others' pay are important. Pay is also often considered a sign of status and success. Employees attach great importance to pay decisions when they evaluate their relationship with the organization. Therefore, pay decisions must be carefully managed and communicated.

Pay structure
The relative pay of different jobs (job structure) and how much they are paid (pay level).

Pay level
The average pay, including wages, salaries, and bonuses, of jobs in an organization.

Job structure
The relative pay of jobs in an organization.

Pay decisions can be broken into two areas: pay structure and individual pay. In this chapter we focus on **pay structure,** which in turn entails a consideration of pay level and job structure. **Pay level** is defined here as the average pay (including wages, salaries, and bonuses) of jobs in an organization. (Benefits could also be included, but these are discussed separately in Chapter 13.) **Job structure** refers to the relative pay of jobs in an organization. Consider the same two jobs in two different organizations. In Organization 1, jobs A and B are paid an annual average compensation of $40,000 and $60,000, respectively. In Organization 2, the pay rates are $45,000 and $55,000, respectively. Organizations 1 and 2 have the same pay level ($50,000), but the job structures (relative rates of pay) differ.

Both pay level and job structure are characteristics of organizations and reflect decisions about jobs rather than about individual employees. This chapter's focus is on why and how organizations attach pay policies to jobs. In the next chapter we look within jobs to discuss the different approaches that can determine the pay of individual employees as well as the advantages and disadvantages of these different approaches.

Why is the focus on jobs in developing a pay structure? As the number of employees in an organization increases, so too does the number of human resource management decisions. In determining compensation, for example, each employee must be assigned a rate of pay that is acceptable in terms of external, internal, and individual

TABLE 11.1
Total Compensation as a Percentage of Revenues

INDUSTRY	PERCENTILE 10TH	50TH	75TH
Hospitals/health care	43%	46%	49%
Manufacturing	22	27	34
Insurance/health care	6	8	11
All industries	12	23	43

SOURCE: Saratoga Institute, *2000 Human Capital Benchmarking Report* (Santa Clara, CA, 2000). Reprinted with permission.

equity (defined later) and in terms of the employer's cost. Although each employee is unique and thus requires some degree of individualized treatment, standardizing the treatment of similar employees (those with similar jobs) can help greatly to make compensation administration and decision making more manageable and more equitable. Thus pay policies are often attached to particular jobs rather than tailored entirely to individual employees.

Equity Theory and Fairness

In discussing the consequences of pay decisions, it is useful to keep in mind that employees often evaluate their pay relative to that of other employees. Equity theory suggests that people evaluate the fairness of their situations by comparing them with those of other people.[1] According to the theory, a person (P) compares her own ratio of perceived outcomes O (pay, benefits, working conditions) to perceived inputs I (effort, ability, experience) to the ratio of a comparison other (o).

$$O_P/I_P <, >, \text{or} = O_o/I_o?$$

If P's ratio (O_P/I_P) is smaller than the comparison other's ratio (O_o/I_o), underreward inequity results. If P's ratio is larger, overreward inequity results, although evidence suggests that this type of inequity is less likely to occur and less likely to be sustained because P may rationalize the situation by reevaluating her outcomes less favorably or inputs (self-worth) more favorably.[2]

The consequences of P's comparisons depend on whether equity is perceived. If equity is perceived, no change is expected in P's attitudes or behavior. In contrast, perceived inequity may cause P to restore equity. Some ways of restoring equity are counterproductive, including (1) reducing one's own inputs (not working as hard), (2) increasing one's outcomes (such as by theft), (3) leaving the situation that generates perceived inequity (leaving the organization or refusing to work or cooperate with employees who are perceived as overrewarded).

Equity theory's main implication for managing employee compensation is that to an important extent, employees evaluate their pay by comparing it with what others get paid, and their work attitudes and behaviors are influenced by such comparisons. Consider the contract that shortstop Alex Rodriquez signed in 2000 with the Texas Rangers baseball team. Rodriguez will earn a minimum of $21 million to $27 million per year (plus incentives) during the 10-year span of the contract. However, two key provisions could result in him earning substantially more money. One provision states that during the 2001 to 2004 seasons, his base compensation must be at least $2 million higher than any other shortstop's in major league baseball. A second provision permits Rodriquez to void seasons after 2008 unless his 2009 and 2010 base compensation is at least $1 million higher than any position player's in major league baseball. Otherwise, Rodriguez is free to leave the Rangers. These provisions that peg Rodriguez's pay to other players' pay is a compelling example of the importance of being paid well in *relative* terms.

Another implication is that employee perceptions are what determine their evaluation. The fact that management believes its employees are paid well compared with those of other companies does not necessarily translate into employees' beliefs. Employees may have different information or make different comparisons than management.

TABLE 11.2
Pay Structure Concepts and Consequences

PAY STRUCTURE DECISION AREA	ADMINISTRATIVE TOOL	FOCUS OF EMPLOYEE PAY COMPARISONS	CONSEQUENCES OF EQUITY PERCEPTIONS
Pay level	Market pay surveys	External equity	External employee movement (attraction and retention of quality employees); labor costs; employee attitudes
Job structure	Job evaluation	Internal equity	Internal employee movement (promotion, transfer, job rotation); cooperation among employees; employee attitudes

Two types of employee social comparisons of pay are especially relevant in making pay level and job structure decisions. (See Table 11.2.) First, *external equity* pay comparisons focus on what employees in other organizations are paid for doing the same general job. Such comparisons are likely to influence the decisions of applicants to accept job offers as well as the attitudes and decisions of employees about whether to stay with an organization or take a job elsewhere. (See Chapters 5 and 10.) The organization's choice of pay level influences its employees' external pay comparisons and their consequences. A market pay survey is the primary administrative tool organizations use in choosing a pay level.

Second, *internal equity* pay comparisons focus on what employees within the same organization, but in different jobs, are paid. Employees make comparisons with lower-level jobs, jobs at the same level (but perhaps in different skill areas or product divisions), and jobs at higher levels. These comparisons may influence general attitudes of employees; their willingness to transfer to other jobs within the organization; their willingness to accept promotions; their inclination to cooperate across jobs, functional areas, or product groups; and their commitment to the organization. The organization's choice of job structure influences its employees' internal comparisons and their consequences. Job evaluation is the administrative tool organizations use to design job structures.

In addition, employees make internal equity pay comparisons with others performing the same job. Such comparisons are most relevant to the following chapter, which focuses on using pay to recognize individual contributions and differences.

We now turn to ways to choose and develop pay levels and pay structures, the consequences of such choices, and the ways two administrative tools—market pay surveys and job evaluation—help in making pay decisions.

Developing Pay Levels

Market Pressures

Any organization faces two important competitive market challenges in deciding what to pay its employees: product market competition and labor market competition.

COMPETING THROUGH HIGH-PERFORMANCE WORK SYSTEMS

What Do They Pay You?

If you have a job—or have had one in the past—how much money do you make? If you are uncomfortable discussing this subject, your employer may be happy. In fact, in a survey conducted by HRnext.com of Connecticut, one-third of 345 human resource managers polled said that their companies actually forbid workplace discussions about pay. But that number is fewer than five years ago, when more than half of employers surveyed banned such discussions, perhaps out of fear that workers would perceive inequities in their pay. In fact, many companies relaxed their grip on secrecy about pay not only because of the recent tight labor market experience but because the National Labor Relations Board has ruled that employees must be free to talk about pay in the workplace—as a conversation related to their work. Beyond the legal issues, such prohibitions do little to foster good relationships between employers and employees. "In a day of difficult retention and recruitment issues, do you really want to have policies that can be viewed as punitive?" asks Lynn Outwater, a Pittsburgh managing partner at a law firm based in New York.

The financial giant American Express is one company that is relaxing its pay discussion policy. Although the firm doesn't actively encourage pay discussions in the workplace, it is attempting to be more open about its compensation practices. For instance, employees can ask their managers for information about pay ranges or simply look up internal job postings. "It's a way to have an open dialogue within the company," says American Express spokeswoman Molly Faust. The North Side Bank & Trust Co. in Ohio has also recently dropped a ban against pay discussions. The prohibition was eliminated from the employee handbook, and the bank's human resource manager circulated a memo describing how the company's wages and salaries are determined, using such factors as education, prior experience, and seniority.

It's human nature for people to compare notes, and many experts think that it makes sense for companies to provide accurate information rather than letting rumors rule discussions. "People want to know if they're getting the best deal, so they're constantly looking to see what they're worth," notes Garth Andrus, a partner with Accenture, the large management consulting firm.

SOURCE: American Express website, www.americanexpress.com, accessed November 1, 2001; K.J. Dunham, "Employers Ease Bans on Workers Asking, 'What Do They Pay You?'" *The Wall Street Journal* (May 1, 2001), p. B10+.

Product Market Competition

First, organizations must compete effectively in the product market. In other words, they must be able to sell their goods and services at a quantity and price that will bring a sufficient return on their investment. Organizations compete on multiple dimensions (quality, service, and so on), and price is one of the most important dimensions. An important influence on price is the cost of production.

An organization that has higher labor costs than its product market competitors will have to charge higher average prices for products of similar quality. Thus, for example, if labor costs are 30 percent of revenues at Company A and Company B, but Company A has labor costs that are 20 percent higher than those of Company B, we would expect Company A to have product prices that are higher by (.30 × .20) = 6 percent. At some point, the higher price charged by Company A will contribute to a loss of its business to competing companies with lower prices (like Company B). One study, for example, found that in the early 1990s the wage and benefit cost to produce a small car was approximately $1,700 for Ford, $1,800 for Chrysler, and $2,400 for General Motors.[3] Thus, if all other costs were equal, General Motors would have to sell the same quality car for $600 to $700 more than Ford or Chrysler.

Therefore, *product market competition* places an *upper bound* on labor costs and compensation. This upper bound is more constrictive when labor costs are a larger share of total costs and when demand for the product is affected by changes in price (that is, when demand is *elastic*). Although costs are only one part of the competitive equation (productivity is just as important), higher costs may result in a loss of business. In the absence of clear evidence on productivity differences, costs need to be closely monitored.

What components make up labor costs? A major component is the average cost per employee. This is made up of both direct payments (such as wages, salaries, and bonuses) and indirect payments (such as health insurance, Social Security, and unemployment compensation). A second component of labor cost is the staffing level (number of employees). Not surprisingly, financially troubled organizations often seek to cut costs by focusing on one or both components. Staff reductions, hiring freezes, wage and salary freezes, and sharing benefits costs with employees are several ways of enhancing the organization's competitive position in the product market.

Labor Market Competition

A second important competitive market challenge is *labor market competition*. Essentially, labor market competition is the amount an organization must pay to compete against other companies that hire similar employees. These labor market competitors typically include not only companies that have similar products but also those in different product markets that hire similar types of employees. If an organization is not competitive in the labor market, it will fail to attract and retain employees of sufficient numbers and quality. For example, even if a computer manufacturer offers newly graduated electrical engineers the same pay as other computer manufacturers, if automobile manufacturers and other labor market competitors offer salaries $5,000 higher, the computer company may not be able to hire enough qualified electrical engineers. Labor market competition places a *lower bound* on pay levels.

Employees as a Resource

Because organizations have to compete in the labor market, they should consider their employees not just as a cost but as a resource in which the organization has invested and from which it expects valuable returns. Although controlling costs directly affects an organization's ability to compete in the product market, the organization's competitive position can be compromised if costs are kept low at the expense of employee productivity and quality. Having higher labor costs than your competitors is not necessarily bad if you also have the best and most effective workforce, one that produces more products of better quality.

Pay policies and programs are one of the most important human resource tools for encouraging desired employee behaviors and discouraging undesired behaviors. Therefore, they must be evaluated not just in terms of costs but in terms of the returns they generate—how they attract, retain, and motivate a high-quality workforce. For example, if the average revenue per employee in Company A is 20 percent higher than in Company B, it may not be important that the average pay in Company A is 10 percent higher than in Company B.

Deciding What to Pay

Although organizations face important external labor and product market pressures in setting their pay levels, a range of discretion remains.[4] How large the range is depends on the particular competitive environment the organization faces. Where the range is broad, an important strategic decision is whether to pay above, at, or below the market average. The advantage of paying above the market average is the ability to attract and retain the top talent available, which can translate into a highly effective and productive workforce. The disadvantage, however, is the added cost.

Under what circumstances do the benefits of higher pay outweigh the higher costs? According to **efficiency wage theory,** one circumstance is when organizations have technologies or structures that depend on highly skilled employees. For example, organizations that emphasize decentralized decision making may need higher-caliber employees. Another circumstance where higher pay may be warranted is when an organization has difficulties observing and monitoring its employees' performance. It may therefore wish to provide an above-market pay rate to ensure the incentive to put forth maximum effort. The theory is that employees who are paid more than they would be paid elsewhere will be reluctant to shirk because they wish to retain their good jobs.[5]

Efficiency wage theory
A theory stating that wages influence worker productivity.

Market Pay Surveys

To compete for talent, organizations use **benchmarking,** a procedure in which it compares its own practices against those of the competition. In compensation management, benchmarking against product market and labor market competitors is typically accomplished through the use of one or more pay surveys, which provide information on going rates of pay among competing organizations.

Benchmarking
Comparing an organization's practices against those of the competition.

The use of pay surveys requires answers to several important questions:[6]

1. Which employers should be included in the survey? Ideally, they would be the key labor market and product market competitors.
2. Which jobs are included in the survey? Because only a sample of jobs is ordinarily used, care must be taken that the jobs are representative in terms of level, functional area, and product market. Also, the job content must be sufficiently similar.
3. If multiple surveys are used, how are all the rates of pay weighted and combined? Organizations often have to weight and combine pay rates because different surveys are often tailored toward particular employee groups (labor markets) or product markets. The organization must decide how much relative weight to give to its labor market and product market competitors in setting pay.

Several factors affect decisions on how to combine surveys.[7] Product market comparisons that focus on labor costs are likely to deserve greater weight when (1) labor costs represent a large share of total costs, (2) product demand is elastic (it changes in response to product price changes), (3) the supply of labor is inelastic, and (4) employee skills are specific to the product market (and will remain so). In contrast, labor

COMPETING BY MEETING STAKEHOLDERS' NEEDS

Using Market Pay Data in Setting a Pay Strategy

Ford. The compensation committee wants the compensation of Ford executives to be competitive in the worldwide auto industry and with major U.S. companies. Each year the committee reviews a report from an outside consultant on Ford's compensation program for executives. The report discusses all aspects of compensation as well as how Ford's program compares with those of other large companies. Based on this report, its own review of various parts of the program, and its assessment of the skills, experience, and achievements of individual executives, the committee decides the compensation of executives.

The consultant develops compensation data using a survey of several leading companies picked by the consultant and Ford. General Motors and DaimlerChrysler were included in the survey. Eighteen leading companies in other industries also were included because the job market for executives goes beyond the auto industry. Companies were picked based on size, reputation, and business complexity.

The committee looks at the size and success of the companies and the types of jobs covered by the survey in determining executive compensation. One goal of Ford's compensation program over time is to approximate the survey group's average compensation, adjusted for company size and performance. At higher levels in the organization, Ford strives to provide a compensation package that is higher than the survey group's average. In 2000, Ford's executive salaries and long-term incentive awards generally were consistent with this goal. Data on bonuses for the surveyed companies are not yet available, but the committee

market comparisons may be more important when (1) attracting and retaining qualified employees is difficult and (2) the costs (administrative, disruption, and so on) of recruiting replacements are high.

As this discussion suggests, knowing what other organizations are paying is only one part of the story. It is also necessary to know what those organizations are getting in return for their investment in employees. To find that out, some organizations examine ratios such as revenues/employees and revenues/labor cost. The first ratio includes the staffing component of employee cost but not the average cost per employee. The second ratio, however, includes both. Note that comparing these ratios across organizations requires caution. For example, different industries rely on different labor and capital resources. So comparing the ratio of revenues to labor costs of a petroleum company (capital intensive, high ratio) to a bank (labor intensive, low ratio) would be like comparing apples and oranges. But within industries, such comparisons can be useful. Besides revenues, other return-on-investment data might include product quality, customer satisfaction, and potential workforce quality (such as average education levels). The "Competing by Meeting Stakeholders' Needs" box provides examples of how executive pay comparisons factor in product market, labor market, and business performance considerations.

expects Ford's 2000 bonuses to be above the average of the survey group.

Coca-Cola. The company's executive compensation policy is designed to establish an appropriate relationship between executive pay and the creation of long-term shareholder value, while motivating and retaining key employees. To achieve these goals, the company's executive compensation policy supplements annual base compensation with an opportunity to earn bonuses based on corporate performance as well as factors related to each individual's performance.

A compensation committee periodically compares base salary levels for its executives with those of other companies in the soft drink bottling industry, as well as other industries. The company strives to maintain base executive salaries at a level that will permit it to compete with other major companies for managers with comparable qualifications and abilities. The compensation committee believes that the overall compensation of the company's executive officers places them above the median compensation of similarly situated executives in all industries.

Procter & Gamble. Compensation for executives is based on the principles that compensation must (a) be competitive with other quality companies in order to help attract, motivate, and retain the talent needed to lead and grow Procter & Gamble's business; (b) provide a strong incentive for key managers to achieve the company's goals; and (c) make prudent use of the company's resources. Procter & Gamble has an enviable record of recruiting, retaining, and developing its executive talent from within—an achievement few other corporations have matched.

Executive compensation is based on performance against a combination of financial and nonfinancial measures, including business results and developing organizational capacity. In addition, executives are expected to uphold the fundamental principles embodied in the company's Statement of Purpose, Values, and Principles plus the Sustainability Report and the Environmental Quality Policy. These include a commitment to integrity, doing the right thing, maximizing the development of each individual, developing a diverse organization, and continually improving the environmental quality of products and operations. In upholding these objectives, executives not only contribute to their own success, but also help ensure that the company's business, employees, shareholders, and communities will prosper.

Excerpts from 2001 Ford, Coca-Cola, and Procter & Gamble proxy statements.

Rate Ranges

Rate ranges
Different employees in the same job may have different pay rates.

As the preceding discussion suggests, obtaining a single "going rate" of market pay is a complex task that involves a number of subjective decisions; it is both an art and a science. Once a market rate has been chosen, how is it incorporated into the pay structure? Typically—especially for white-collar jobs—it is used for setting the midpoint of pay ranges for either jobs or pay grades (discussed next). Market survey data are also often collected on minimum and maximum rates of pay as well. The use of ranges permits a company to recognize differences in employee performance, seniority, training, and so forth in setting individual pay (discussed in the next chapter). For some blue-collar jobs, however, particularly those covered by collective bargaining contracts, there may be a single rate of pay for all employees within the job.

Key Jobs and Nonkey Jobs

Key jobs
Benchmark jobs, used in pay surveys, that have relatively stable content and are common to many organizations.

In using pay surveys, it is necessary to make a distinction between two general types of jobs: key jobs (or benchmark jobs) and nonkey jobs. **Key jobs** have relatively stable content and—perhaps most important—are common to many organizations. Therefore, it is possible to obtain market pay survey data on them. Note, however,

TABLE 11.9

CEO Compensation: *BusinessWeek* Survey ("365 of the Country's Largest Companies")

	SALARY PLUS BONUS	LONG-TERM COMPENSATION	TOTAL COMPENSATION	CHANGE IN PAY	CHANGE IN* S&P 500	CEO/WORKER**
2000	$2.7 million[a]	$10.4 million[a]	$13.1 million	6%		484[a]
1999	2.3 million	10.1 million	12.4 million	17		475
1998	2.1 million	8.5 million	10.6 million	36	27	419
1997	2.2 million	5.6 million	7.8 million	35	31	326
1996	2.3 million	3.2 million	5.8 million	54	23	209

*Change in market value of the Standard & Poor's 500 group of companies

**Ratio of CEO pay to hourly employee pay

[a]Estimated

SOURCE: Reprinted from August 21, 1997 issue of *BusinessWeek* by special permission. Copyright © 1997 by The McGraw-Hill Companies, Inc.

TABLE 11.10

Highest-Paid CEOs

	SALARY PLUS BONUS	LONG-TERM COMPENSATION	TOTAL COMPENSATION
John Reed, Citigroup	$ 5.4 million	$287.6 million	$293.0 million
Stanford Weill, Citigroup	18.9 million	204.9 million	224.9 million
Gordon Levin, AOL Time Warner	11.2 million	152.6 million	163.8 million

SOURCE: Reprinted from April 16, 2001 issue of *BusinessWeek* by special permission. Copyright © 2001 by The McGraw-Hill Companies, Inc.

TABLE 11.11

Total Remuneration of CEOs in Selected Countries (U.S. dollars)

COUNTRY	CEO TOTAL REMUNERATION	CEO/MANUFACTURING EMPLOYEE TOTAL REMUNERATION MULTIPLE
United States	$1,404,000	31
Brazil	597,000	60
France	540,000	15
Argentina	861,000	48
Germany	422,000	11
Japan	546,000	11
Mexico	649,000	46

Notes: Data based on a company with $500 million in sales; total remuneration includes salary, bonus, company contributions, perquisites, and long-term incentives. Table 11.11 values are based on much smaller companies than those in Table 11.9, thus explaining the table differences.

SOURCE: Towers Perrin, "2000 Worldwide Total Remuneration," New York, 2000.

of perceived fairness in difficult economic times. One study, in fact, reported that business units with higher pay differentials between executives and rank-and-file employees had lower customer satisfaction, which was speculated to result from employees' perceptions of inequity coming through in customer relations.[39] Perhaps more important than how much top executives are paid is how they are paid. This is an issue we return to in the next chapter.

Government Regulation of Employee Compensation

Equal Employment Opportunity

Equal Employment Opportunity (EEO) regulation (such as Title VII and the Civil Rights Act) prohibits sex- and race-based differences in employment outcomes such as pay, unless justified by business necessity (like pay differences stemming from differences in job performance). In addition to regulatory pressures, organizations must deal with changing labor market and demographic realities. At least two trends are directly relevant in discussing EEO. First, women have gone from 33 percent of all employees in 1960 to 47 percent in 2001. Second, between 1960 and 2001, whites have gone from 90 percent to 84 percent of all employees. The percentage of white males in organizations will probably continue to decline, making attention to EEO issues in compensation even more important.

Is there equality of treatment in pay determination? Typically, the popular press focuses on raw earnings ratios. For example, in 2000, among full-time workers, the ratio of female-to-male median earnings was .76, and the ratio of black-to-white earnings was .79.[40] These percentages have generally risen over the last two to three decades, but significant race and sex differences in pay clearly remain.[41]

The usefulness of raw percentages is limited, however, because some portion of earnings differences arises from differences in legitimate factors: education, labor market experience, and occupation. Adjusting for such factors reduces earnings differences based on race and sex, but significant differences remain. With few exceptions, such adjustments rarely account for more than half of the earnings differential.[42]

What aspects of pay determination are responsible for such differences? In the case of women, it is suggested that their work is undervalued. Another explanation rests on the "crowding" hypothesis, which argues that women were historically restricted to entering a small number of occupations. As a result, the supply of workers far exceeded demand, resulting in lower pay for such occupations. If so, market surveys would only perpetuate the situation.

Comparable worth (or pay equity) is a public policy that advocates remedies for any undervaluation of women's jobs. The idea is to obtain equal pay, not just for jobs of equal content (already mandated by the Equal Pay Act of 1963) but for jobs of equal value or worth. Typically, job evaluation is used to measure worth. Table 11.12, which is based on State of Washington data from one of the first comparable worth cases, suggests that measures of worth based on internal comparisons (job evaluation) and external comparisons (market surveys) can be compared. In this case many disagreements between the two measures appear. Internal comparisons suggest that women's jobs are underpaid, whereas external comparisons are less supportive of this argument. For example, although the licensed practical nurse job receives 173 job evaluation points and the truck driver position receives 97 points, the market rate (and thus the State of Washington employer rate) for the truck driver position is $1,493 per month versus only $1,030 per month for the nurse. The truck driver is paid nearly 127 percent more than the pay policy line would predict, whereas the nurse is paid only 75 percent of the pay policy line prediction.

One potential problem with using job evaluation to establish worth independent

TABLE 11.12

Job Evaluation Points, Monthly Prevailing Market Pay Rates, and Proportion of Incumbents in Job Who Are Female

BENCHMARK TITLE	MONTHLY EVALUATION POINTS	PREVAILING RATES[a]	PREVAILING RATE AS PERCENTAGE OF PREDICTED[b]	PERCENTAGE OF FEMALE INCUMBENTS
Warehouse worker	97	$1,286	109.1%	15.4%
Truck driver	97	1,493	126.6	13.6
Laundry worker	105	884	73.2	80.3
Telephone operator	118	887	71.6	95.7
Retail sales clerk	121	921	74.3	100.0
Data entry operator	125	1,017	82.1	96.5
Intermediate clerk typist	129	968	76.3	96.7
Highway engineering tech	133	1,401	110.4	11.1
Word processing equipment operator	138	1,082	83.2	98.3
Correctional officer	173	1,436	105.0	9.3
Licensed practical nurse	173	1,030	75.3	89.5
Automotive mechanic	175	1,646	120.4	0.0
Maintenance carpenter	197	1,707	118.9	2.3
Secretary	197	1,122	78.1	98.5
Administrative assistant	226	1,334	90.6	95.1
Chemist	277	1,885	116.0	20.0
Civil engineer	287	1,885	116.0	0.0
Highway engineer 3	345	1,980	110.4	3.0
Registered nurse	348	1,368	76.3	92.2
Librarian 3	353	1,625	90.6	84.6
Senior architect	362	2,240	121.8	16.7
Senior computer systems analyst	384	2,080	113.1	17.8
Personnel representative	410	1,956	101.2	45.6
Physician	861	3,857	128.0	13.6

[a]Prevailing market rate as of July 1, 1980. Midpoint of job range set equal to this amount.

[b]Predicted salary is based on regression of prevailing market rate on job evaluation points $2.43 X job evaluation points + 936.19, r = .77.

SOURCE: Reprinted with permission of *Public Personnel Management*, published by the International Personnel Management Association.

of the market is that job evaluation procedures were never designed for this purpose.[43] Rather, as demonstrated earlier, their major use is in helping to capture the market pay policy and then applying that to nonkey jobs for which market data are not available. In other words, job evaluation has typically been used to help apply the market pay policy, quite the opposite of replacing the market in pay setting.

As with any regulation, there are also concerns that EEO regulation obstructs market forces, which, according to economic theory, provide the most efficient means of pricing and allocating people to jobs. In theory, moving away from a reliance on market forces would result in some jobs being paid too much and others too little, leading to an oversupply of workers for the former and an undersupply for the latter. In addition, some empirical evidence suggests that a comparable worth policy would not have much impact on the relative earnings of women in the private sector.[44] One limitation of such a policy is that it targets single employers, ignoring that men and women tend to work for different employers.[45] To the extent that segregation by employer contributes to pay differences between men and women, comparable worth would not be effective. In other words, to the extent that sex-based pay differences are the result of men and women working in different organizations with different pay levels, such policies will have little impact.

Perhaps most important, despite potential problems with market rates, the courts have consistently ruled that using the going market rates of pay is an acceptable defense in comparable worth litigation suits.[46] The rationale is that organizations face competitive labor and product markets. Paying less or more than the market rate will put the organization at a competitive disadvantage. Thus there is no comparable worth legal mandate in the U.S. private sector. On the other hand, by the early 1990s, almost one-half of the states had begun or completed comparable worth adjustments to public-sector employees' pay. In addition, in 1988 the Canadian province of Ontario mandated comparable worth in both the private and public sectors.

Another line of inquiry has focused on pinpointing where women's pay falls behind that of men. Some evidence indicates that women lose ground at the time they are hired and actually do better once they are employed for some time.[47] One interpretation is that when actual job performance (rather than the limited general qualification information available on applicants) is used in decisions, women may be less likely to encounter unequal treatment. If so, more attention needs to be devoted to ensuring fair treatment of applicants and new employees.[48] On the other hand, a "glass ceiling" is believed to exist in some organizations that allows women (and minorities) to come within sight of the top echelons of management, but not advance to them.

It is likely, however, that organizations will differ in terms of where women's earnings disadvantages arise. For example, advancement opportunities for women and other protected groups may be hindered by unequal access to the "old boy" or informal network. This, in turn, may be reflected in lower rates of pay. Mentoring programs have been suggested as one means of improving access. Indeed, one study found that mentoring was successful, having a significant positive effect on the pay of both men and women, with women receiving a greater payoff in percentage terms than men.[49]

Minimum Wage, Overtime, and Prevailing Wage Laws

The 1938 **Fair Labor Standards Act (FLSA)** establishes a minimum wage for jobs that now stands at $5.15 per hour. State laws may specify higher minimum wages. The FLSA also permits a subminimum training wage that is approximately 85 percent of the **minimum wage,** which employers are permitted to pay most employees under the age of 20 for a period of up to 90 days.

Fair Labor Standards Act (FLSA)
The 1938 law that established the minimum wage and overtime pay.

Minimum wage
The lowest amount that employers are legally allowed to pay; the 1990 amendment of the Fair Labor Standards Act permits a subminimum wage to workers under the age of 20 for a period of up to 90 days.

The FLSA also requires that employees be paid at a rate of one and a half times their hourly rate for each hour of overtime worked beyond 40 hours in a week. The hourly rate includes not only the base wage but also other components such as bonuses and piece-rate payments. The FLSA requires overtime pay for any hours beyond 40 in a week that an employer "suffers or permits" the employee to perform, regardless of whether the work is done at the workplace or whether the employer explicitly asked or expected the employee to do it.[50] If the employer knows the employee is working overtime but neither moves to stop it nor pays time and a half, a violation of the FLSA may have occurred. A department store was the target of a lawsuit that claimed employees were "encouraged" to, among other things, write thank-you notes to customers outside of scheduled work hours but were not compensated for this work. Although the company denied encouraging this off-the-clock work, it reached an out-of-court settlement to pay between $15 million and $30 million in back pay (plus legal fees of $7.5 million) to approximately 85,000 sales representatives it employed between 1987 and 1990.[51]

Exempt
Employees who are not covered by the Fair Labor Standards Act. Exempt employees are not eligible for overtime pay.

Executive, professional, administrative, and outside sales occupations are **exempt** from FLSA coverage. *Nonexempt* occupations are covered and include most hourly jobs. One estimate is that just over 20 percent of employees fall into the exempt category.[52] Exempt status depends on job responsibilities and salary, and the standards can be fairly complicated. For example, seven criteria, including whether two or more people are supervised and whether there is authority to hire and fire, are used to determine whether an employee is an executive. The Wage and Hour Division, Employment Standards Administration, U.S. Department of Labor, and its local offices can provide further information on these definitions.

Two pieces of legislation—the 1931 Davis-Bacon Act and the 1936 Walsh-Healy Public Contracts Act—require federal contractors to pay employees no less than the prevailing wages in the area. Davis-Bacon covers construction contractors receiving federal money of more than $2,000. Typically, prevailing wages have been based on relevant union contracts, partly because only 30 percent of the local labor force is required to be used in establishing the prevailing rate. Walsh-Healy covers all government contractors receiving $10,000 or more in federal funds.

Finally, employers must take care in deciding whether a person working on its premises is classified as an employee or independent contractor. We address this issue in Chapter 13.

A Look Back

We began this chapter by showing how one company supported a change in strategic direction through changes in its compensation strategy. Throughout this chapter, we have seen other examples of the importance of aligning compensation strategy with the organization's strategy. In addition to the Corning example, we have seen how Coca-Cola, Ford, and Procter & Gamble pay their executives in a way that supports their strategy, and we have seen how IBM realigned its pay structure to support changes to its strategy for competing in evolving markets. We have seen in this chapter that pay structure decisions influence the success of strategy execution by influencing costs, employee perceptions of equity, and the way that different structures provide flexibility and incentives for employees to learn and be productive.

Questions

1. What types of changes have the companies discussed in this chapter made to their pay structures to support execution of their business strategies?
2. Would other companies seeking to better align their pay structures with their business strategies benefit from imitating the changes made at these companies?

Summary

In this chapter we have discussed the nature of the pay structure and its component parts, the pay level, and the job structure. Equity theory suggests that social comparisons are an important influence on how employees evaluate their pay. Employees make external comparisons between their pay and the pay they believe is received by employees in other organizations. Such comparisons may have consequences for employee attitudes and retention. Employees also make internal comparisons between what they receive and what they perceive others within the organization are paid. These types of comparisons may have consequences for internal movement, cooperation, and attitudes (like organization commitment). Such comparisons play an important role in the controversy over executive pay, as illustrated by the focus of critics on the ratio of executive pay to that of lower-paid workers.

Pay benchmarking surveys and job evaluation are two administrative tools widely used in managing the pay level and job structure components of the pay structure, which influence employee social comparisons. Pay surveys also permit organizations to benchmark their labor costs against other organizations'. Globalization is increasing the need for organizations to be competitive in both their labor costs and productivity.

The nature of pay structures is undergoing a fundamental change in many organizations. One change is the move to fewer pay levels to reduce labor costs and bureaucracy. Second, some employers are shifting from paying employees for narrow jobs to giving them broader responsibilities and paying them to learn the necessary skills.

Finally, a theme that runs through this chapter and the next is the importance of process in managing employee compensation. How a new program is designed, decided on, implemented, and communicated is perhaps just as important as its core characteristics.

Discussion Questions

1. You have been asked to evaluate whether your organization's current pay structure makes sense in view of what competing organizations are paying. How would you determine what organizations to compare your organization with? Why might your organization's pay structure differ from those in competing organizations? What are the potential consequences of having a pay structure that is out of line relative to those of your competitors?
2. Top management has decided that the organization is too bureaucratic and has too many layers of jobs to compete effectively. You have been asked to suggest innovative alternatives to the traditional "job-based" approach to employee compensation and to list the advantages and disadvantages of these new approaches.
3. If major changes of the type mentioned in question 2 are to be made, what types of so-called process issues need to be considered? Of what relevance is equity theory in helping to understand how employees might react to changes in the pay structure?
4. Are executive pay levels unreasonable? Why or why not?
5. Your company plans to build a new manufacturing plant but is undecided where to locate it. What factors would you consider in choosing in which country (or state) to build the plant?
6. You have been asked to evaluate whether a company's pay structure is fair to women and minorities. How would you go about answering this question?

Web Exercise

Several websites provide salary surveys for clerical, professional, and managerial jobs. One of these sites is Job Smart. Go to **www.jobsmart.org**. Click on "Salary Info" and then "Salary Surveys." Click on "Profession-Specific Salary Surveys." From the list of professions presented, choose one that interests you. Review the information provided.

1. What is the value of this website for employers? For employees?
2. From an HRM perspective, what are the advantages of using websites such as this one to establish salary ranges and adjust the current salary structure? What are the disadvantages?

Managing People: From the Pages of *BusinessWeek*

BusinessWeek Revenge of the "Managers"

Many So-Called Supervisors Are Suing for Overtime Pay

Until recently, few people questioned the way salaried employees sweated and slaved, skipping dinners, parties, even vacations, without ever getting so much as a dime in overtime. Toiling longer and harder than anyone else in the industrialized world was simply the price of going for the white-collar gold in the new economy's office Olympics. Overtime pay was often considered a blue-collar perk for the lowly hourly crowd.

But thanks to some recent high-dollar settlements, the reinstatement of worker-friendly labor laws in California, and increased workloads throughout the 1990s, more and more workers are realizing they might be getting stiffed. The allegations are coming from all kinds of white-collar workers, including retail managers, reporters, pharmacists, sales reps, personal bankers, engineers, computer programmers, claims adjusters, and even lawyers. In growing numbers, these employees are filing suits and, in some cases, winning settlements for as many as four years of overtime pay, plus damages. In the case of General Dynamics Corp., this amounted to a $100 million award that is now on appeal. "It's exploding," says defense attorney Victor Schachter, a partner with San Francisco–based Fenwick & West LLP. "Companies that are not addressing these issues now are sitting ducks waiting to get shot at."

Already, large corporations are quietly changing their compensation structures to avoid the legal land mines. They are enlarging jobs to include work that is truly managerial or reclassifying workers as nonexempt so that they qualify for the extra pay. For others, though, it's already too late. Companies such as U-Haul, Taco Bell, PepsiCo, AutoZone, Borders Books, Pacific Bell, Bridgestone/Firestone, and Wal-Mart, to name a few, have all been slapped with overtime suits. Ironically, even the nation's chief law enforcement agency—entrusted with policing the nation's wage and hour laws—has gotten into trouble over the issue. Last year more than 9,000 former and current Justice Department lawyers used a law mandating overtime pay for federal workers to file a class action against the department.

OVERWORKED, UNDERPAID. It's not surprising that people are starting to seek revenge. The lawsuits come at a time when many of the overtired and overworked, now fearful of losing their jobs in the slowdown, are becoming fed up with what they describe as a kind of bait-and-switch tactic. By misclassifying them as managers exempt from overtime, companies can then load them up with work instead of hiring new people, avoiding the added payroll costs. In fact, some allege that all those record-breaking productivity gains of the new economy came not just on technology's back but also on theirs, especially since the boom was largely achieved without having to dole out big wage hikes to the rank-and-file. "It's unfair, and we don't deserve to be treated like that," says Joyce Moses, a former claims adjuster who is now part of a successful class action against Farmers Insurance Group.

Companies are getting into trouble in part because the nation's overtime laws were formed in the Industrial—not the Information—Age. Plus, the rules can be confusing, leaving lots of room for misinterpretation. Exemptions from overtime, federal laws state, are reserved for managers who either supervise two or more people, make big decisions affecting their corporations, or have the power to hire and fire. But in today's flat organizations, where even high-ranking executives often do their own word processing, "there's not a whole lot of people supervising other people anymore," says employment lawyer Lawrence Lorber, the former deputy assistant labor secretary under Gerald Ford.

That's why experts estimate that as many as half of U.S. corporations may be misclassifying. Company execs insist that's a huge exaggeration. They point out that managerial titles benefit workers by putting them on a road toward career advancement. The confusion arises in part because the law pertains to the primary duty of a worker, while titles don't necessarily match those duties. Take James Horner, the general manager at U-Haul's Barstow (California) moving center. According to court records filed in a class action, Horner, like other U-Haul International Inc. managers, is expected to work at least 60 hours a week with no overtime. U-Haul argues that its managers spend 50 percent or more of their time managing, but the court found that they actually spend more time doing the same kind of work as hourly employees. In January 2001 a California Superior Court judge ruled against U-Haul, though the amount of restitution is still being determined.

Though these suits are occurring across the country, most of them are being filed in California, where labor laws are stricter than the federal standards. In California, for example, a manager such as Horner has to spend more than half of his or her time managing the store and supervise two or more employees in order to qualify for exemption, whereas most states abide by the federal law, which mandates that managing must simply be the employee's primary duty.

Cookie-cutter chains like U-Haul are vulnerable to these claims, experts say, because much of the decision making happens in central offices instead of at the stores. Retail and restaurant chains are also likely to be hard hit, they say, since computers at chains like AutoZone Inc. do almost everything a manager would—except lead the AutoZone cheer before sales meetings.

CACHET. Not all workers want the extra pay they're entitled to, though. One reason companies have been left unchallenged for so long is because many employees feel their exempt status brings them a certain cachet. This prestige is something U-Haul execs, for one, try to emphasize, saying that if they treated managers more like hourly employees, they would lose status in the eyes of their spouses, friends, coworkers, and future employers. Plus, salaried positions often come with better benefits and chances for stock options.

Then again, if the slowdown continues and more workers find themselves laid off—or stuck putting in more hours with no reward—more employees may come to prefer the pay over the prestige.

Questions

1. Do you think the "cachet" of being a manager makes up for longer hours at the same pay?
2. Even though the law permits it, are there any potential drawbacks for an organization that works its managers long hours without paying them more? Are there consequences for perceived equity or motivation?
3. Do you think the government should allocate more or fewer resources to enforcing the Fair Labor Standards Act? Why?

SOURCE: Reprinted from March 12, 2001 issue of *BusinessWeek* by special permission.

Notes

1. J.S. Adams, "Inequity in Social Exchange," in *Advances in Experimental Social Psychology,* ed. L. Berkowitz (New York: Academic Press, 1965); P. S. Goodman, "An Examination of Referents Used in the Evaluation of Pay," *Organizational Behavior and Human Performance* 12 (1974), pp. 170–95.
2. J.B. Miner, *Theories of Organizational Behavior* (Hinsdale, IL: Dryden Press, 1980).
3. Steve Lohr, "Ford and Chrysler Outpace Japanese in Reducing Costs," *The New York Times* (June 18, 1992), p. D1.
4. B. Gerhart and G.T. Milkovich, "Organizational Differences in Managerial Compensation and Financial Performance," *Academy of Management Journal* 33 (1990), pp. 663–91; E.L. Groshen, "Why Do Wages Vary among Employers?" *Economic Review* 24 (1988), pp. 19–38.
5. G.A. Akerlof, "Gift Exchange and Efficiency-Wage Theory: Four Views," *American Economic Review* 74 (1984), pp. 79–83; J.L. Yellen, "Efficiency Wage Models of Unemployment," *American Economic Review* 74 (1984), pp. 200–5.
6. S.L. Rynes and G.T. Milkovich, "Wage Surveys: Dispelling Some Myths about the 'Market Wage,'" *Personnel Psychology* 39 (1986), pp. 71–90.
7. B. Gerhart and G.T. Milkovich, "Employee Compensation: Research and Practice," in *Handbook of Industrial and Organizational Psychology,* 2nd ed., ed. M.D. Dunnette and L.M. Hough (Palo Alto, CA: Consulting Psychologists Press, 1992).
8. G.T. Milkovich and J. Newman, *Compensation* (Homewood, IL: BPI/Irwin, 1990).
9. B. Gerhart, G.T. Milkovich, and B. Murray, "Pay, Performance, and Participation," in *Research Frontiers in Industrial Relations and Human Resources*, ed. D. Lewin, O.S. Mitchell, and P.D. Sherer (Madison, WI: IRRA, 1992).
10. C.H. Fay, "External Pay Relationships," in *Compensation and Benefits*, ed. L.R. Gomez-Mejia (Washington, DC: Bureau of National Affairs, 1989).
11. J.P. Pfeffer and A. Davis-Blake, "Understanding Organizational Wage Structures: A Resource Dependence Approach," *Academy of Management Journal* 30 (1987), pp. 437–55.
12. H.Z. Levine, "The View from the Board: The State of Compensation and Benefits Today," *Compensation and Benefits Review* 24 (March 1992), p. 24.
13. C.M. Solomon, "Global Compensation: Learn the ABCs," *Personnel Journal,* July 1995, p. 70; R.A. Swaak, "Expatriate Management: The Search for Best Practices," *Compensation and Benefits Review,* March–April 1995, p. 21.
14. *1997–1998 Survey of Geographic Pay Differential Policies and Practices* (Rochester, WI: Runzeimer International). Actually, data from the American Chamber of Commerce Research Association (ACCRA) estimate the cost of living in New York City (in 2001) to be 239.2, compared to 100 for the average metropolitan area.
15. E.E. Lawler III, *Pay and Organizational Development* (Reading, MA: Addison-Wesley, 1981).
16. R. Folger and M.A. Konovsky, "Effects of Procedural and Distributive Justice on Reactions to Pay Raise Decisions," *Academy of Management Journal* 32 (1989), pp. 115–30; Gerhart, Milkovich, and Murray, "Pay, Performance"; J. Greenberg, "Determinants of Perceived Fairness of Performance Evaluations," *Journal of Applied Psychology* 71 (1986), pp. 340–42; H.G. Heneman III, "Pay Satisfaction," *Research in Personnel and Human Resource Management* 3 (1985), pp. 115–39.
17. J. Greenberg, "Employee Theft as a Reaction to Underpayment of Inequity: The Hidden Cost of Pay Cuts," *Journal of Applied Psychology* 75 (1990), pp. 561–68.
18. Adams, "Inequity in Social Exchange"; C.J. Berger, C.A. Olson, and J.W. Boudreau, "The Effect of Unionism on Job Satisfaction: The Role of Work-Related Values and Perceived Rewards," *Organizational Behavior and Human Performance* 32 (1983), pp. 284–324; P. Cappelli and P.D. Sherer, "Assessing Worker Attitudes under a Two-Tier Wage Plan," *Industrial and Labor Relations Review* 43 (1990), pp. 225–44; R.W. Rice, S.M. Phillips, and D.B. McFarlin,

"Multiple Discrepancies and Pay Satisfaction," *Journal of Applied Psychology* 75 (1990), pp. 386–93.

19. Cappelli and Sherer, "Assessing Worker Attitudes."
20. This section draws freely on B. Gerhart and R.D. Bretz, "Employee Compensation," in *Organization and Management of Advanced Manufacturing*, ed. W. Karwowski and G. Salvendy (New York: Wiley, 1994), pp. 81–101.
21. R.M. Kanter, *When Giants Learn to Dance* (New York: Simon & Schuster, 1989); E.E. Lawler III, *Strategic Pay* (San Francisco: Jossey-Bass, 1990); "Farewell, Fast Track," *BusinessWeek* (December 10, 1990), pp. 192–200.
22. P.R. Eyers, "Realignment Ties Pay to Performance," *Personnel Journal*, January 1993, p. 74.
23. Lawler, *Strategic Pay;* G. Ledford, "3 Cases on Skill-Based Pay: An Overview," *Compensation and Benefits Review*, March–April 1991, pp. 11–23; G.E. Ledford, "Paying for the Skills, Knowledge, Competencies of Knowledge Workers," *Compensation and Benefits* Review, July–August 1995, p. 55.
24. Ledford, "3 Cases."
25. P.S. Adler, "Managing Flexible Automation," *California Management Review* 30, no. 3 (1988), pp. 34–56; T. Cummings and M. Blumberg, "Advanced Manufacturing Technology and Work Design," in *The Human Side of Advanced Manufacturing Technology*, ed. T.D. Wall, C.W. Clegg, and N.J. Kemp (Chichester, Great Britain: John Wiley & Sons, 1987); Y.P. Gupta, "Human Aspects of Flexible Manufacturing Systems," *Production and Inventory Management Journal* 30, no. 2 (1989), pp. 30–36; R.E. Walton and G.I. Susman, "People Policies for the New Machines," *Harvard Business Review* 87, no. 2 (1987), pp. 98–106; J.P. Womack, D.T. Jones, and D. Roos, *The Machine That Changed the World* (New York: Macmillan, 1990).
26. T.D. Wall, J.M. Corbett, R. Martin, C.W. Clegg, and P.R. Jackson, "Advanced Manufacturing Technology, Work Design, and Performance: A Change Study," *Journal of Applied Psychology* 75 (1990), pp. 691–97.
27. Womack et al., *The Machine That Changed the World*, p. 56.
28. Lawler, *Strategic Pay*.
29. Ibid.; Gerhart and Milkovich, "Employee Compensation."
30. B.C. Murray and B. Gerhart, "An Empirical Analysis of a Skill-Based Pay Program and Plant Performance Outcomes," *Academy of Management Journal* 41, no. 1 (1998), pp. 68–78.
31. Ibid.; N. Gupta, D. Jenkins, and W. Curington, "Paying for Knowledge: Myths and Realities," *National Productivity Review*, Spring 1986, pp. 107–23.
32. Data from U.S. Bureau of Labor Statistics website.
33. *Education at a Glance—OECD Indicators 2001* (Paris: OECD, 2001).
34. National Accounts (Paris: OECD, 2001); *Main Economic Indicators* (Paris: OECD, 2001).
35. C. Sparks and M. Greiner, "U.S. and Foreign Productivity and Labor Costs," *Monthly Labor Review*, February 1997, pp. 26–35.
36. E. Faltermayer, "U.S. Companies Come Back Home," *Fortune* (December 30, 1991), pp. 106ff.
37. Ibid.
38. A. Farnham, "The Trust Gap," *Fortune* (December 4, 1989), pp. 56ff.
39. D.M. Cowherd and D.I. Levine, "Product Quality and Pay Equity between Lower-Level Employees and Top Management: An Investigation of Distributive Justice Theory," *Administrative Science Quarterly* 37 (1992), pp. 302–20.
40. Bureau of Labor Statistics, *Current Population Surveys* (website).
41. P. Ryscavage and P. Henle, "Earnings Inequality in the 1980s," *Monthly Labor Review* 113, no. 12 (1990), pp. 3–16; F. D. Blau and M. A. Beller, "Trends in Earnings Differentials by Gender, 1971–1981," *Industrial and Labor Relations Review* 41 (1988), pp. 513–29; L.A. Carlson and C. Swartz, "The Earnings of Women and Ethnic Minorities, 1959–1979," *Industrial and Labor Relations Review* 41 (1988), pp. 530–46; M.W. Horrigan and J.P. Markey, "Recent Gains in Women's Earnings: Better Pay or Longer Hours?" *Monthly Labor Review* 113, no. 7 (June 1990), pp. 11–17.
42. B. Gerhart, "Gender Differences in Current and Starting Salaries: The Role of Performance, College Major, and Job Title," *Industrial and Labor Relations Review* 43 (1990), pp. 418–33; G.G. Cain, "The Economic Analysis of Labor-Market Discrimination: A Survey," in *Handbook of Labor Economics*, ed. O. Ashenfelter and R. Layard (New York: North-Holland, 1986), pp. 694–785.
43. D.P. Schwab, "Job Evaluation and Pay-Setting: Concepts and Practices," in *Comparable Worth: Issues and Alternatives*, ed. E.R. Livernash (Washington, DC: Equal Employment Advisory Council, 1980).
44. B. Gerhart and N. El Cheikh, "Earnings and Percentage Female: A Longitudinal Study," *Industrial Relations* 30 (1991), pp. 62–78; R.S. Smith, "Comparable Worth: Limited Coverage and the Exacerbation of Inequality," *Industrial and Labor Relations Review* 61 (1988), pp. 227–39.
45. W.T. Bielby and J.N. Baron, "Men and Women at Work: Sex Segregation and Statistical Discrimination," *American Journal of Sociology* 91 (1986), pp. 759–99.
46. Rynes and Milkovich, "Wage Surveys"; G.T. Milkovich

and J. Newman, *Compensation* (Homewood, IL: BPI/Irwin, 1993).

47. Gerhart, "Gender Differences in Current and Starting Salaries"; B. Gerhart and G.T. Milkovich, "Salaries, Salary Growth, and Promotions of Men and Women in a Large, Private Firm," in *Pay Equity: Empirical Inquiries*, ed. R. Michael, H. Hartmann, and B. O'Farrell (Washington, DC: National Academy Press, 1989).
48. Gerhart, "Gender Differences in Current and Starting Salaries"; B. Gerhart and S. Rynes, "Determinants and Consequences of Salary Negotiations by Graduating Male and Female MBAs," *Journal of Applied Psychology* 76 (1991), pp. 256–62.
49. D.J. Brass, "Men's and Women's Networks: A Study of Interaction Patterns and Influence in an Organization," *Academy of Management Journal* 28 (1985), pp. 327–43; B. Rosen, M. E. Templeton, and K. Kirchline, "First Few Years on the Job: Women in Management," *Business Horizons* 24, no. 12 (1981), pp. 26–29; K. Cannings and C. Montmarquette, "Managerial Momentum: A Simultaneous Model of the Career Progress of Male and Female Managers," *Industrial and Labor Relations Review* 44 (1991), pp. 212–28; R.A. Noe, "Women and Mentoring: A Review and Research Agenda," *Academy of Management Review* 13 (1988), pp. 65–78; G.F. Dreher and R.A. Ash, "A Comparative Study of Mentoring among Men and Women in Managerial, Professional, and Technical Positions," *Journal of Applied Psychology* 75 (1990), pp. 539–46.
50. A.W. Sherman Jr. and G. W. Bohlander, *Managing Human Resources* (Cincinnati: South-Western Publishing, 1992), p. 334.
51. G.A. Patterson, "Nordstrom Inc. Sets Back-Pay Accord on Suit Alleging 'Off-the-Clock' Work," *The Wall Street Journal* (January 12, 1993), p. A2.
52. R.I. Henderson, *Compensation Management: Rewarding Performance* (Englewood Cliffs, NJ: Prentice-Hall, 1989), p. 56.

12 Chapter

Recognizing Employee Contributions with Pay

Objectives

After reading this chapter, you should be able to:

1. Describe the fundamental pay programs for recognizing employees' contributions to the organization's success.
2. List the advantages and disadvantages of the pay programs.
3. List the major factors to consider in matching the pay strategy to the organization's strategy.
4. Explain the importance of process issues such as communication in compensation management.
5. Describe how U.S. pay practices compare with those of other countries.

Positive employee attitudes can help an organization better execute its strategy. Should companies reward executives for achieving positive employee attitudes?

Enter the World of Business

Paying for Good Employee Relations

Organizations understand that reaching financial objectives, or satisfying shareholders, depends to a considerable degree on how well they manage relationships with other important stakeholders such as customers and employees. One suggestion has been to link compensation, in part, to customer satisfaction and employee satisfaction. Is this a good idea in the case of employee satisfaction? There is some disagreement on this issue. Eastman Kodak has, since 1995, used employee opinion survey results as one factor in deciding executive bonuses. Likewise, United Airlines, which is employee-owned, is moving to a system where executive bonuses will depend to some degree on employee-satisfaction surveys. Although the idea of rewarding managers for good employee relations has some intuitive appeal, there may be unintended consequences. Indeed, Gordon Bethune, CEO of Continental Airlines, described such an idea as "absolutely stupid." Bethune argues, "Being an effective leader and having a company where people enjoy coming to work is not a popularity contest. When you run popularity contests, you tend to do things that may get you more points. That may not be good for shareholders and may not be good for the company." This is not to say that Bethune and Continental do not see employee relations as an important part of their competitive advantage. Continental was named the 2001 airline of the year by *Air Transport World* and number 18 on *Fortune*'s 2001 list of best companies to work for in America. And many companies use employee opinion survey results to adjust their employee relations policies as needed. Rather, the issue is whether an incentive plan that explicitly rewards employee satisfaction will produce only intended positive consequences or might also produce unintended, less desirable consequences. Eastman Kodak and United are two examples of companies that have decided some direct incentive makes sense, even if it is small relative to other factors (like financial performance) that determine executive pay. Other companies, even those that use strong employee relations as an important source of competitive advantage, have been too concerned about unintended consequences to use explicit incentives.

SOURCE: "Bottom-up Pay: Companies Regularly Survey How Employees Feel about Their Bosses, But They Rarely Use Ratings to Set Compensation," *The Wall Street Journal* (April 6, 2000), p. R5+.

Introduction

The opening vignette illustrates some of the challenges in using the employee compensation system to motivate desired outcomes. The problem is that the compensation system sometimes leads to unintended consequences, even when rewarding key goals is the intended focus. The pay system must encourage behaviors that both contribute to profits in the short run and build customer satisfaction for long-term success. However, there are different opinions on how to do that.

The preceding chapter discussed setting pay for jobs. In this chapter we focus on using pay to recognize and reward employees' contributions to the organization's success. Employees' pay does not depend solely on the jobs they hold. Instead, differences in performance (individual, group, or organization), seniority, skills, and so forth are used as a basis for differentiating pay among employees.[1]

Several key questions arise in evaluating different pay programs for recognizing contributions. First, what are the costs of the program? Second, what is the expected return (in terms of influences on attitudes and behaviors) from such investments? Third, does the program fit with the organization's human resource strategy and its overall business strategy?

Organizations have a relatively large degree of discretion in deciding how to pay, especially compared with the pay level decisions discussed in the previous chapter. The same organizational pay level (or "compensation pie") can be distributed ("sliced") among employees in many ways. Whether each employee's share is based on individual performance, profits, seniority, or other factors, the size of the pie (and thus the cost to the organization) can remain the same.

Regardless of cost differences, different pay programs can have very different consequences for productivity and return on investment. Indeed, a study of how much 150 organizations paid found not only that the largest differences between organizations had to do with how they paid but that these differences resulted in different levels of profitability.[2]

How Does Pay Influence Individual Employees?

Pay plans are typically used to energize, direct, or control employee behavior. Equity theory, described in the previous chapter, is relevant here as well. Most employees compare their own pay with that of others, especially those in the same job. Perceptions of inequity may cause employees to take actions to restore equity. Unfortunately, some of these actions (like quitting or lack of cooperation) may not help the organization.

Three additional theories also help explain compensation's effects: reinforcement, expectancy, and agency theories.

Reinforcement Theory

E. L. Thorndike's Law of Effect states that a response followed by a reward is more likely to recur in the future. The implication for compensation management is that high employee performance followed by a monetary reward will make future high performance more likely. By the same token, high performance not followed by a reward will make it less likely in the future. The theory emphasizes the importance of a person's actual experience of a reward.

Expectancy Theory

Although expectancy theory also focuses on the link between rewards and behaviors, it emphasizes expected (rather than experienced) rewards. In other words, it focuses on the effects of incentives. Behaviors (job performance) can be described as a function of ability and motivation. In turn, motivation is hypothesized to be a function of expectancy, instrumentality, and valence perceptions. Compensation systems differ according to their impact on these motivational components. Generally speaking, the main factor is instrumentality: the perceived link between behaviors and pay. Valence of pay outcomes should remain the same under different pay systems. Expectancy perceptions (the perceived link between effort and performance) often have more to do with job design and training than pay systems. A possible exception would be skill-based pay, which directly influences employee training and thus expectancy perceptions.

Expectancy theory
The theory that says a motivation is a function of valence, instrumentality, and expectancy.

Although expectancy theory implies that linking an increased amount of rewards to performance will increase motivation and performance, some authors have questioned this assumption, arguing that monetary rewards may increase extrinsic motivation but decrease intrinsic motivation. Extrinsic motivation depends on rewards (such as pay and benefits) controlled by an external source, whereas intrinsic motivation depends on rewards that flow naturally from work itself (like performing interesting work).[3] In other words, paying a child to read books may diminish the child's natural interest in reading, and the child may in the future be less likely to read books unless there are monetary incentives. Although monetary incentives may reduce intrinsic motivation in some settings (such as education), the evidence suggests that such effects are small and isolated in work settings.[4] Therefore, while it is important to keep in mind that money is not the only effective way to motivate behavior and that monetary rewards will not always be the answer to motivation problems, it does not appear that monetary rewards run much risk of compromising intrinsic motivation in most work settings.

Agency Theory

This theory focuses on the divergent interests and goals of the organization's stakeholders and the ways that employee compensation can be used to align these interests and goals. We cover agency theory in some depth because it provides especially relevant implications for compensation design.

An important characteristic of the modern corporation is the separation of ownership from management (or control). Unlike the early stages of capitalism, where owner and manager were often the same, today, with some exceptions (mostly smaller companies), most stockholders are far removed from the day-to-day operation of companies. Although this separation has important advantages (like mobility of financial capital and diversification of investment risk), it also creates agency costs—the interests of the **principals** (owners) and their **agents** (managers) may no longer converge. What is best for the agent, or manager, may not be best for the owner.

Principal
In agency theory, a person (e.g., an owner) who seeks to direct another person's behavior.

Three types of agency costs arise in managerial compensation.[5] First, although shareholders seek to maximize their wealth, management may spend money on things such as perquisites (corporate jets, for example) or "empire building" (making acquisitions that do not add value to the company but may enhance the manager's prestige or pay). Second, managers and shareholders may differ in their attitudes toward risk. Shareholders can diversify their investments (and thus their risks) more easily than managers (whose only major source of income may be their jobs), so managers are

Agent
In agency theory, a person (e.g., a manager) who is expected to act on behalf of a principal (e.g., an owner).

typically more averse to risk. They may be less likely to pursue projects or acquisitions with high potential payoff. It also suggests a preference on the part of managers for relatively little risk in their pay (high emphasis on base salary, low emphasis on uncertain bonuses or incentives). Indeed, research shows that managerial compensation in manager-controlled firms is more often designed in this manner.[6] Third, decision making horizons may differ. For example, if managers change companies more than owners change ownership, managers may be more likely to maximize short-run performance (and pay), perhaps at the expense of long-term success.

Agency theory is also of value in the analysis and design of nonmanagers' compensation. In this case, interests may diverge between managers (now in the role of principals) and their employees (who take on the role of agents).

In designing either managerial or nonmanagerial compensation, the key question is, How can such agency costs be minimized? Agency theory says that the principal must choose a contracting scheme that helps align the interests of the agent with the principal's own interests (that is, it reduces agency costs). These contracts can be classified as either behavior-oriented (such as merit pay) or outcome-oriented (stock options, profit sharing, commissions, and so on).[7]

At first blush, outcome-oriented contracts seem to be the obvious solution. If profits are high, compensation goes up. If profits drop, compensation goes down. The interests of "the company" and employees are aligned. An important drawback, however, is that such contracts increase the agent's risk. And because agents are averse to risk, they may require higher pay (a compensating wage differential) to make up for it.[8]

Behavior-based contracts, on the other hand, do not transfer risk to the agent and thus do not require a compensating wage differential. However, the principal must be able to monitor with little cost what the agent has done. Otherwise, the principal must either invest in monitoring and information or structure the contract so that pay is linked at least partly to outcomes.[9]

Which type of contract should an organization use? It depends partly on the following factors:[10]

- *Risk aversion.* Risk aversion among agents makes outcome-oriented contracts less likely.
- *Outcome uncertainty.* Profit is an example of an outcome. Agents are less willing to have their pay linked to profits to the extent that there is a risk of low profits. They would therefore prefer a behavior-oriented contract.
- *Job programmability.* As jobs become less programmable (less routine), outcome-oriented contracts become more likely because monitoring becomes more difficult.[11]
- *Measurable job outcomes.* When outcomes are more measurable, outcome-oriented contracts are more likely.
- *Ability to pay.* Outcome-oriented contracts contribute to higher compensation costs because of the risk premium.
- *Tradition.* A tradition or custom of using (or not using) outcome-oriented contracts will make such contracts more (or less) likely.

In summary, the reinforcement, expectancy, and agency theories all focus on the fact that behavior–reward contingencies can shape behaviors. However, agency theory is of particular value in compensation management because of its emphasis on the risk–reward trade-off, an issue that needs close attention when companies consider variable pay plans, which can carry significant risk.

COMPETING THROUGH GLOBALIZATION

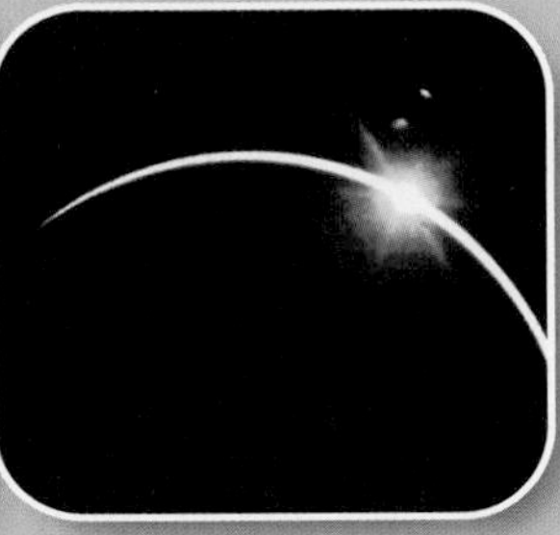

Stock Options Heat Up in Europe

One way to recognize employees' contributions to their company is to offer them stock options, which allow them to buy shares of the firm's stock in the future at a previously set price. Although this practice has been widespread in the United States for a number of years, European businesses are now embracing the idea as a method of retaining the best employees and competing in a global marketplace. In fact, European companies that have North American operations have been feeling the greatest pressure to join the stock option club for some time. For instance, executives at the French telecommunications equipment manufacturer Alacatel SA recently realized that they needed to broaden the scope of their compensation when they began to buy North American firms like Canada's Newbridge Networks. Afraid that failing to do so would mean qualified employees would quickly leave the newly acquired firm, Alacatel announced a plan that would award options to 35 percent of its engineers and middle managers outside the United States (the rate inside the United States is 75 percent).

The major difference between the way U.S. and European firms award stock options is that the European companies usually link them to specific performance goals, such as a company's share price increase compared with its competitors'. German law actually requires this, and British firms such as Barclays are beginning to enforce stricter guidelines. Belgium and Switzerland still discourage the use of stock options through high taxes, but Italy and Norway have passed legislation and tax changes that make stock options more attractive to firms and their employees. As competition in the European market increases, experts predict that companies not offering options will have a harder time recruiting the best employees.

Back in the United States, there may be a silver lining for new employees who are now receiving their options. With the faltering stock market driving prices down, these workers are now locking in low share prices that will probably earn them handsome profits in years to come as the stock market recovers. If they and their companies perform well, everyone will win.

SOURCE: "Taxation of European Stock Options," *The European Commission* (June 26, 2001), http://europa.eu.int; D. Woodruff, "Europe, a Latecomer, Embraces Options Even as Market Swoons," *The Wall Street Journal* (May 15, 2001), www.wsj.com; "Eager Europeans Press Their Noses to the Glass," *BusinessWeek Online* (April 19, 1999), www.businessweek.com.

How Does Pay Influence Labor Force Composition?

Traditionally, using pay to recognize employee contributions has been thought of as a way to influence the behaviors and attitudes of current employees, whereas pay level and benefits have been seen as a way to influence so-called membership behaviors: decisions about whether to join or remain with the organization. However, there is increasing recognition that individual pay programs may also affect the nature and composition of an organization's workforce.[12] For example, it is possible that an organization that links pay to performance may attract more high performers than an organization that does not link the two. There may be a similar effect with respect to job retention.[13]

Continuing the analysis, different pay systems appear to attract people with different personality traits and values.[14] Organizations that link pay to individual performance may be more likely to attract individualistic employees, whereas organizations relying more heavily on team rewards are more likely to attract team-oriented employees. The implication is that the design of compensation programs needs to be carefully coordinated with the business and human resource strategy. Increasingly, both in the United States and abroad, employers are seeking to establish stronger links between pay and performance.

Finding and Keeping the Best Employees

"They are the conscripts of the Information Age. Lined up headset to headset, they make pitches, take orders, and provide technical support. They get sworn at, hung up on, sometimes even thanked. But what these telephone-wielding armies do is tell people all about your business." Department of Labor data show that the number of employees working in call centers grew by 39 percent between 1996 and 2000. Other data indicate that there were 2.5 million call center workers in 1999, and this figure is expected to grow to 4 million by 2003. According to Bureau of Labor statistics, e-commerce will contribute to more, not fewer, call centers because companies will need to back up or supplement automated Web services by giving customers access to people. Each contact between a customer and a call center provides an opportunity or a risk, depending on how the exchange is handled. As Gallup Organization's director of call center retention puts it, "Everybody expects to be satisfied" when they call, so if we only meet a customer's expectations, we're "just breaking even." On the other hand, "if you dazzle me, I may tell a couple of friends. But if you make me mad, maybe I'll tell seven." Therefore, Gallup has decided that its call center employees are too important to treat as low-skilled, low-paid clerks. Instead, Gallup, which conducts polls and provides human resource consulting services, pays its top-performing call center employees as much as three times the industry average. Moreover, the higher pay at Gallup is not obtained by handling as many calls as quickly as possible, something that is common in call centers. Rather, Gallup focuses its call center pay-for-performance plan on how well customers evaluate their interactions with call center employees. Gallup's goal is to use these interactions to build brand loyalty by making customers feel better, whatever the situation. The Gallup call center strategy rests on finding and retaining superior employees in its call centers, something that its pay practices strongly support.

SOURCE: "Who's Answering the Phone? Your Company's Fortunes Hang on It." *Gallup Management Journal,* Fall 2001.

Programs

In compensating employees, an organization does not have to choose one program over another. Instead, a combination of programs is often the best solution. For example, one program may foster teamwork and cooperation but not enough individual initiative. Another may do the opposite. Used in conjunction, a balance may be attained.[15]

Table 12.1 provides an overview of the programs for recognizing employee contributions. Each program shares a focus on paying for performance. The programs differ according to three design features: (1) payment method, (2) frequency of payout, and

(3) ways of measuring performance. In a perhaps more speculative vein, the table also suggests the potential consequences of such programs for (1) performance motivation of employees, (2) attraction of employees, (3) organization culture, and (4) costs. Finally, there are two contingencies that may influence whether each pay program fits the situation: (1) management style and (2) type of work. We now discuss the different programs and some of their potential consequences in more depth.

TABLE 12.1

Programs for Recognizing Employee Contributions

	MERIT PAY	INCENTIVE PAY	PROFIT SHARING	OWNERSHIP	GAIN SHARING	SKILL-BASED
Design features						
Payment method	Changes in base pay	Bonus	Bonus	Equity changes	Bonus	Change in base pay
Frequency of payout	Annually	Weekly	Semiannually or annually	When stock sold	Monthly or quarterly	When skill or competency acquired
Performance measures	Supervisor's appraisal of individual performance	Individual output, productivity, sales	Company profit	Company stock returns	Production or controllable costs of stand-alone work unit	Skill or competency acquisition of individuals
Consequences						
Performance motivation	Relationship between pay and performance varies	Clear performance–reward connection	Stronger in smaller firms	Stronger in smaller firms	Stronger in smaller units	Encourages learning
Attraction	Over time pays better performers more	Pays higher performers more	Helps with all employees if plan pays out	Can help lock in employees	Helps with all employees if plan pays out	Attracts learning-oriented employees
Culture	Individual competition	Individual competition	Knowledge of business and cooperation	Sense of ownership and cooperation	Supports cooperation, problem solving	Learning and flexible organization
Costs	Requires well-developed performance appraisal system	Setting and maintaining acceptable standards	Relates costs to ability to pay	Relates costs to ability to pay	Setting and maintaining acceptable standards	Training and certification
Contingencies						
Management style	Some participation desirable	Control	Fits participation	Fits participation	Fits participation	Fits participation
Type of work	Individual unless group appraisals done	Stable, individual, easily measurable	All types	All types	All types	Significant skill depth or breadth

SOURCE: Adapted and modified from E.E. Lawler III, "Pay for Performance: A Strategic Analysis," in *Compensation and Benefits*, ed. L.R. Gomez-Mejia (Washington, DC: Bureau of National Affairs, 1989). Reprinted with permission.

FIGURE 12.1
Performance Dimensions for Lower to Midlevel Managers, Arrow Electronics

1. Exercises good business judgment
2. Inspires enthusiasm, energy, understanding, loyalty for company goals
3. Attracts, grows, and retains outstanding talent
4. Shows initiative
5. Has position-specific knowledge
6. Delivers results
7. Builds internal good will

SOURCE: From Compensation and Performance Evaluation at Arrow Electronics Harvard Business School Case 9-800-290. Copyright © 2000 by the President and Fellows of Harvard College.

Merit Pay

In merit pay programs, annual pay increases are usually linked to performance appraisal ratings. (See Chapter 8.) Some type of merit pay program exists in almost all organizations (although evidence on merit pay effectiveness is surprisingly scarce).[16] One reason for the widespread use of merit pay is its ability to define and reward a broad range of performance dimensions. (See Figure 12.1 for an example.) Indeed, given the pervasiveness of merit pay programs, we devote a good deal of attention to them here.

Merit increase grid
A grid that combines an employee's performance rating with the employee's position in a pay range to determine the size and frequency of his or her pay increases.

Basic Features

Many merit pay programs work off of a **merit increase grid.** As Table 12.2 indicates, the size and frequency of pay increases are determined by two factors. The first factor is the individual's performance rating (because better performers should receive higher pay). The second factor is position in range (that is, an individual's compa-ratio). So, for example, an employee with a performance rating of EX and a compa-ratio of 120 would receive a pay increase of 9 to 11 percent. By comparison, an employee with a performance rating of EX and a compa-ratio of 85 would receive an increase of 13 to

TABLE 12.2
Example of Merit Increase Grid from Merck & Co., Inc.

		SUGGESTED MERIT INCREASE PERCENTAGE			
PERFORMANCE RATING		COMPA-RATIO 80.00–95.00	COMPA-RATIO 95.01–110.00	COMPA-RATIO 110.01–120.00	COMPA-RATIO 120.01–125.00
EX	(Exceptional within Merck)	13–15%	12–14%	9–11%	To maximum of range
WD	(Merck Standard with Distinction)	9–11	8–10	7–9	—
HS	(High Merck Standard)	7–9	6–8	—	—
RI	(Merck Standard Room for Improvement)	5–7	—	—	—
NA	(Not Adequate for Merck)	—	—	—	—

SOURCE: K.J. Murphy, "Merck & Co., Inc., (B)" (Boston: Harvard Business School), Case 491-006. Copyright © 1990 by the President & Fellows of Harvard College. Reprinted with permission.

TABLE 12.3
Performance Ratings and Compa-ratio Targets

PERFORMANCE RATING		COMPA-RATIO TARGET
EX	(Exceptional within Merck)	115–125
WD	(Merck Standard with Distinction)	100–120
HS	(High Merck Standard)	90–110
RI	(Merck Standard Room for Improvement)	80–95
NA	(Not Adequate for Merck)	None

SOURCE: K.J. Murphy, "Merck & Co., Inc., (B)" (Boston: Harvard Business School), Case 491-006.

15 percent. (Note that the general magnitude of increases in such a table is influenced by inflation rates. Thus the percentage increases in such a grid would have been considerably lower in recent years.) One reason for factoring in the compa-ratio is to control compensation costs and maintain the integrity of the pay structure. If a person with a compa-ratio of 120 received a merit increase of 13 to 15 percent, she would soon exceed the pay range maximum. Not factoring in the compa-ratio would also result in uncontrolled growth of compensation costs for employees who continue to perform the same job year after year. Instead, some organizations think in terms of assessing where the employee's pay is now and where it should be, given a particular performance level. Consider Table 12.3. An employee who consistently performs at the EX level should be paid at 115 to 125 percent of the market (that is, a compa-ratio of 115 to 125). To the extent that the employee is far from that pay level, larger and more frequent pay increases are necessary to move the employee to the correct position. On the other hand, if the employee is already at that pay level, smaller pay increases will be needed. The main objective in the latter case would be to provide pay increases that are sufficient to maintain the employee at the targeted compa-ratio.

In controlling compensation costs, another factor that requires close attention is the distribution of performance ratings. (See Chapter 8.) In many organizations, 60 to 70 percent of employees fall into the top two (out of four to five) performance rating categories.[17] This means tremendous growth in compensation costs because most employees will eventually be above the midpoint of the pay range, resulting in compa-ratios well over 100. To avoid this, some organizations provide guidelines regarding the percentage of employees who should fall into each performance category, usually limiting the percentage that can be placed in the top two categories. These guidelines are enforced differently, ranging from true guidelines to strict forced-distribution requirements.

In general, merit pay programs have the following characteristics. First, they identify individual differences in performance, which are assumed to reflect differences in ability or motivation. By implication, system constraints on performance are not seen as significant. Second, the majority of information on individual performance is collected from the immediate supervisor. Peer and subordinate ratings are rare, and where they exist, they tend to receive less weight than supervisory ratings.[18] Third, there is a policy of linking pay increases to performance appraisal results.[19] Fourth, the feedback under such systems tends to occur infrequently, often once per year at the formal performance review session. Fifth, the flow of feedback tends to be largely unidirectional, from supervisor to subordinate.

Criticisms of Traditional Merit Pay Programs

Criticisms of this process have been raised. For example, W. Edwards Deming, a leader of the total quality management movement, argued that it is unfair to rate individual performance because "apparent differences between people arise almost entirely from the system that they work in, not from the people themselves."[20] Examples of system factors include coworkers, the job, materials, equipment, customers, management, supervision, and environmental conditions. These are believed to be largely outside the worker's control, instead falling under management's responsibility. Deming argued that the performance rating is essentially "the result of a lottery."[21]

Deming also argued that the individual focus of merit pay discourages teamwork: "Everyone propels himself forward, or tries to, for his own good, on his own life preserver. The organization is the loser."[22] As an example, if people in the purchasing department are evaluated based on the number of contracts negotiated, they may have little interest in materials quality, even though manufacturing is having quality problems.

Deming's solution was to eliminate the link between individual performance and pay. This approach reflects a desire to move away from recognizing individual contributions. What are the consequences of such a move? It is possible that fewer employees with individual-achievement orientations would be attracted to and remain with the organization. One study of job retention found that the relationship between pay growth and individual performance over time was weaker at higher performance levels. As a consequence, the organization lost a disproportionate share of its top performers.[23] In other words, too little emphasis on individual performance may leave the organization with average and poor performers.

Thus, although Deming's concerns about too much emphasis on individual performance are well taken, one must be careful not to replace one set of problems with another. Instead, there needs to be an appropriate balance between individual and group objectives. At the very least, ranking and forced-distribution performance-rating systems need to be considered with caution, lest they contribute to behavior that is too individualistic and competitive.

Another criticism of merit pay programs is the way they measure performance. If the performance measure is not perceived as being fair and accurate, the entire merit pay program can break down. One potential impediment to accuracy is the almost exclusive reliance on the supervisor for providing performance ratings, even though peers, subordinates, and customers (internal and external) often have information on a person's performance that is as good as or better than that of the supervisor. A 360-degree performance feedback approach (discussed in Chapter 9) gathers feedback from each of these sources.

In general, process issues appear to be important in administering merit pay. In any situation where rewards are distributed, employees appear to assess fairness along two dimensions: distributive (based on how much they receive) and procedural (what process was used to decide how much).[24] Some of the most important aspects of procedural fairness, or justice, appear in Table 12.4. These items suggest that employees desire clear and consistent performance standards, as well as opportunities to provide input, discuss their performance, and appeal any decision they believe to be incorrect.

Perhaps the most basic criticism is that merit pay does not really exist. High performers are not paid significantly more than mediocre or even poor performers in most cases.[25] For example, in the late 1980s and early 1990s, merit increase budgets often did not exceed 4 to 5 percent. Thus high performers might receive 6 percent raises, versus 3.5 to 4 percent raises for average performers. On a salary of $40,000 per

TABLE 12.4
Aspects of Procedural Justice in Pay Raise Decisions

Indicate the extent to which your supervisor did each of the following:
1. Was honest and ethical in dealing with you.
2. Gave you an opportunity to express your side.
3. Used consistent standards in evaluating your performance.
4. Considered your views regarding your performance.
5. Gave you feedback that helped you learn how well you were doing.
6. Was completely candid and frank with you.
7. Showed a real interest in trying to be fair.
8. Became thoroughly familiar with your performance.
9. Took into account factors beyond your control.
10. Got input from you before a recommendation.
11. Made clear what was expected of you.
Indicate how much of an opportunity existed, after the last raise decision, for you to do each of the following things:
12. Make an appeal about the size of a raise.
13. Express your feelings to your supervisor about the salary decision.
14. Discuss, with your supervisor, how your performance was evaluated.
15. Develop, with your supervisor, an action plan for future performance.

SOURCE: R. Folger and M.A. Konovsky, "Effects of Procedural and Distributive Justice on Reactions to Pay Raise Decisions," *Academy of Management Journal* 32 (1989), p. 115. Reprinted with permission.

year, the difference in take-home pay would not be more than about $300 per year, or about $6 per week. Critics of merit pay point out that this difference is probably not significant enough to influence employee behaviors or attitudes. Indeed, as Figure 12.2 indicates, many employees do not believe there is any payoff to higher levels of performance.

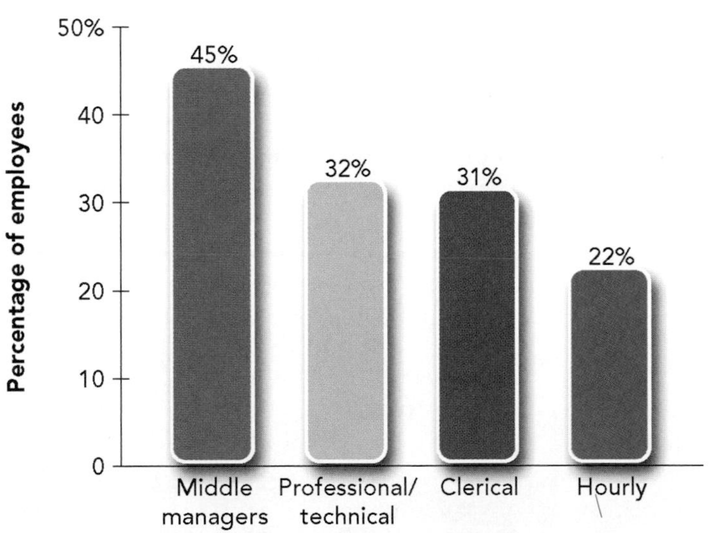

FIGURE 12.2
Percentage of Employees Who Agreed That Better Performers Get Better Increases

SOURCE: Hay Group, *The Hay Report: Compensation and Benefit Strategies for 1995 and Beyond* (Philadelphia: Hay Group, 1994). Reprinted with permission.

Of course, small differences in pay can accumulate into large differences over time. The present value of the salary advantage would be $29,489 (based on a discount rate of 5 percent). For example, over a 30-year career, an initial annual salary difference of $740 with equal merit increases thereafter of 7 percent would accumulate into a career salary advantage of $75,738.[26] Whether employees think in these terms is open to question. But even if they do not, nothing prevents an organization from explaining to employees that what may appear to be small differences in pay can add up to large differences over time. It should also be kept in mind that merit ratings are often closely linked to promotions, which in turn are closely linked to salary. Thus, even in merit pay settings where performance differences are not recognized in the short run, high performers are likely to have significantly higher career earnings.

Finally, the accumulation effect just described can also be seen as a drawback if it contributes to an entitlement mentality. Here the concern is that a big merit increase given early in an employee's career remains part of base salary "forever." It does not have to be re-earned each year, and the cost to the organization grows over time, perhaps more than either the employee's performance or the organization's profitability would always warrant. Merit bonuses (payouts that do not become part of base salary), in lieu of traditional merit increases, are thus used by some organizations instead.

Individual Incentives

Like merit pay, individual incentives reward individual performance, but with two important differences. First, payments are not rolled into base pay. They must be continuously earned and re-earned. Second, performance is usually measured as physical output (such as number of water faucets produced) rather than by subjective ratings. Individual incentives have the potential to significantly increase performance. Locke and his colleagues found that monetary incentives increased production output by a median of 30 percent—more than any other motivational device studied.[27]. Recent changes at Volkswagen have put such incentives to the test. (See the "Competing through High-Performance Work Systems" box.)

Nevertheless, individual incentives are relatively rare for a variety of reasons.[28] Most jobs (like those of managers and professionals) have no physical output measure. Instead, they involve what might be described as "knowledge work." Also, many potential administrative problems (such as setting and maintaining acceptable standards) often prove intractable. Third, individual incentives may do such a good job of motivating employees that they do whatever they get paid for and nothing else. (See the Dilbert cartoon in Figure 12.3.) Fourth, as the name implies, individual incentives typ-

FIGURE 12.3
How Incentives Sometimes "Work"

SOURCE: DILBERT reprinted by permission of United Feature Syndicate, Inc.

COMPETING THROUGH HIGH-PERFORMANCE WORK SYSTEMS

Volkswagen Drives into New Territory

Companies can use individual incentives in a variety of ways. Germany's Volkswagen has used them to revamp its relationship with workers. Traditionally, Germany maintained strict work rules under its social market economy, not allowing its companies free rein to hire and fire employees, or to determine pay or work hours. Labor groups, including the IG Metall union, have remained strong in Germany, even with recent high unemployment. But as unemployment topped 9 percent in the summer of 2001, something had to give—and Volkswagen stepped in with a proposal designed to ensure its own survival as well as that of German workers.

Europe's largest automaker offered to hire 3,500 workers to produce a new minivan at its flagship facility in Wolfsburg, Germany. The workers' wages would be about equal to others in the industry. But their opportunities for overtime pay would be limited, and they would still be responsible for keeping up the pace and quality of production. If they fell behind, they would be required to work more hours without extra pay.

IG Metall balked, but eventually an agreement was struck. Workers now will put in up to 42 hours a week before being paid overtime. They will be compensated through work-time accounts, which will allow Volkswagen to require up to 200 hours a year beyond the standard 35-hour workweek during times of peak production. Later, during off-peak production times, employees can work fewer hours, thus drawing down their work-time accounts. With this system, workers will still average a 35-hour week over the year. Their actual wages will not be reduced over the year, but the amount of overtime paid will be less. Volkswagen then gets more flexibility to gear up and scale back production when necessary.

According to the agreement, if workers fail to make Volkswagen's production targets within their normal workweeks, they'll have to work extra hours without extra pay to meet those targets. But in practice, that probably wouldn't happen because union leaders could argue that targets were missed due to company failure. "We have established an example of how one can build cars while honoring the wage standards," said Jurgen Peters, vice chairman of IG Metall. All of German industry will be watching.

SOURCE: "Giant German Union Approves Jobs Deal with Volkswagen, But Insists It's No Precedent," *Detroit News* (September 5, 2001), **http://detnews.com**; E.L. Andrews, "Accord at VW Signals a Shift for Germany," *The New York Times* (August 29, 2001), **www.nytimes.com**; B. Herman, "German Union, Volkswagen, Agree to Hiring Proposal," *Los Angeles Times* (August 29, 2001), **www.latimes.com**.

ically do not fit well with a team approach. Fifth, they may be inconsistent with the goals of acquiring multiple skills and proactive problem solving. Learning new skills often requires employees to slow or stop production. If the employees are paid based on production volume, they may not want to slow down or stop. Sixth, some incentive plans reward output volume at the expense of quality or customer service.

Therefore, although individual incentives carry potential advantages, they are not likely to contribute to a flexible, proactive, problem-solving workforce. In addition, such programs may not be particularly helpful in the pursuit of total quality management objectives.

that is seen as fair by employees, and these standards must not exclude important dimensions such as quality.

Balanced Scorecard

As the preceding discussion indicates, every pay program has advantages and disadvantages. Therefore, rather than choosing one program, some companies find it useful to design a mix of pay programs, one that has just the right chemistry for the situation at hand. Relying exclusively on merit pay or individual incentives may result in high levels of work motivation but unacceptable levels of individualistic and competitive behavior and too little concern for broader plant or organization goals. Relying too heavily on profit sharing and gainsharing plans may increase cooperation and concern for the welfare of the entire plant or organization, but it may reduce individual work motivation to unacceptable levels. However, a particular mix of merit pay, gainsharing, and profit sharing could contribute to acceptable performance on all these performance dimensions.

One approach that seeks to balance multiple objectives is the balanced scorecard (see Chapter 1), which Kaplan and Norton describe as a way for companies to "track financial results while simultaneously monitoring progress in building the capabilities and acquiring the intangible assets they would need for future growth."[46]

Table 12.7 shows how a mix of measures might be used by a manufacturing firm to motivate improvements in a balanced set of key business drivers.

TABLE 12.7

Illustration of Balanced Scorecard Incentive Concept

PERFORMANCE MEASURE	INCENTIVE SCHEDULE				
	TARGET INCENTIVE	PERFORMANCE	% TARGET	ACTUAL PERFORMANCE	INCENTIVE EARNED
Financial • Return on capital employed	$100	20%+ 16–20% 12–16% Below 12%	150% 100% 50% 0%	18%	$100
Customer • Product returns	$ 40	1 in: 1,000 + 900–999 800–899 Below 800	 150% 100% 50% 0%	1 in 876	$ 20
Internal • Cycle time reduction (%)	$ 30	9%+ 6–9% 3–6% 0–3%	150% 100% 50% 0%	11%	$ 45
Learning and growth • Voluntary employee turnover	$ 30	Below 5% 5–8% 8–12%	150% 100% 50%	7%	$ 30
Total	$200				$195

SOURCE: F.C. McKenzie and M.P. Shilling, "Avoiding Performance Traps: Ensuring Effective Incentive Design and Implementation," *Compensation and Benefits Review,* July–August 1998, pp. 57–65. Reprinted with permission.

COMPETING THROUGH HIGH-PERFORMANCE WORK SYSTEMS

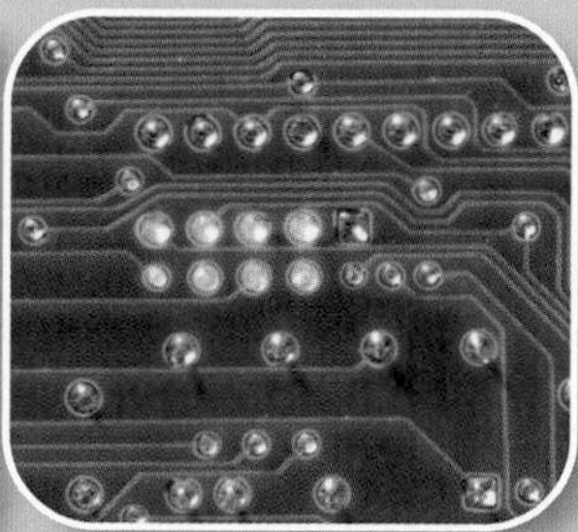

Companies Retain Employees with a Balanced Approach

Human resource managers are well aware that the people they hire are vital to the success of their companies. Compensation is often a key factor in attracting and retaining the best workers, especially during economic or marketplace volatility or during mergers and acquisitions, when people are uncertain about their futures. For example, when new dot-com firms were riding high by offering huge bonuses and stock options to encourage the best and brightest employees to join up, more traditional companies struggled to find ways to match these benefits. As the economy began a downward turn and both Internet and traditional companies began to lay off employees, workers who were left began to defect as well, looking for more secure situations. So companies faced the challenge of trying to balance cost-cutting measures with compensating employees to keep them from leaving.

Most firms have discovered that a single compensation program is not adequate to meet the needs of all employees. Human resource managers have also learned the power of listening. When AT&T laid off 500 information technology employees due to an outsourcing plan, the remaining workers were naturally skittish and began looking for more secure jobs at other companies. AT&T managers acted quickly. "We asked our people what concerns them, what bothers them, what we can do to make them more comfortable and secure about their work," says Pete D'Amato, vice president of network and local services for AT&T in Middletown, New Jersey. Workers told D'Amato and other managers that they wanted reassurance about their future in the form of training information, overtime policies, and promotion guidelines. And they wanted top executives to visit their site more often. All of these requests were relatively easy to implement. "None of this was terribly innovative," admits D'Amato. "If we can get people happier now, they'll be less likely to leave when the market picks up."

When a company makes an acquisition, a big concern is that key employees in the acquired company be retained. According to Martin Katz, a compensation consultant at William M. Mercer Inc., chief executives, financial officers, and others at the executive level typically receive retention bonuses, as do engineers, information technology, and top-performing sales employees. When AMR Corp, the parent company of American Airlines, acquired Trans World Airlines (TWA), it provided retention bonuses equal to 15–30 percent of salary to 100 key management employees at TWA. These bonuses were paid in three equal parts, one-third in January 2001 (before the formal close of the deal in April 2001), one-third in July 2001, and one-third in January 2002. Additional bonuses of 25–100 percent of salary were to be paid to this same group of executives upon successful completion of both the sale of TWA and a reorganization plan.

SOURCE: S. Clark, "Pay Fair to Maximize Employee Retention," *Bizjournals.com* (October 15, 2001), **http://bizjournals.bcentral.com**; L. Kosan, "Pay Attention for Retention," *NetworkWorldFusion News* (April 23, 2001), **www.nwfusion.com**; D.J. Hanford, "Stay. Please," *The Wall Street Journal* (April 12, 2001), **http://interactive.wsj.com**.

Managerial and Executive Pay

Because of their significant ability to influence organization performance, top managers and executives are a strategically important group whose compensation warrants special attention. In the previous chapter we discussed how much this group is paid. Here we focus on the issue of how their pay is determined.

Each year *BusinessWeek* publishes a list of top executives who did the most for their pay and those who did the least. The latter group has been the impetus for much of the attention to executive pay. The problem seems to be that in some companies, top executive pay is high every year, regardless of profitability or stock market performance. One study, for example, found that CEO pay changes by $3.25 for every $1,000 change in shareholder wealth. This relationship was interpreted to mean that "the compensation of top executives is virtually independent of corporate performance."[47]

How can executive pay be linked to organization performance? From an agency theory perspective, the goal of owners (shareholders) is to encourage the agents (managers and executives) to act in the best interests of the owners. This may mean less emphasis on noncontingent pay, such as base salary, and more emphasis on outcome-oriented "contracts" that make some portion of executive pay contingent on the organization's profitability or stock performance.[48] Among midlevel and top managers, it is common to use both short-term bonus and long-term incentive plans to encourage the pursuit of both short- and long-term organization performance objectives. Indeed, in the *BusinessWeek* survey discussed in Chapter 11, the average base salary plus short-term bonus of $2.7 million accounted for only 21 percent of average total executive compensation of $13.1 million. The remaining $10.4 million included stock options and other forms of long-term compensation.

To what extent do organizations use such pay-for-performance plans, and what are their consequences? A recent study suggests that organizations vary substantially in the extent to which they use both long-term and short-term incentive programs. The study further found that greater use of such plans among top and midlevel managers was associated with higher subsequent levels of profitability. As Table 12.8 indicates, greater reliance on short-term bonuses and long-term incentives (relative to base pay) resulted in substantial improvements in return on assets.[49]

Earlier, we saw how the balanced scorecard approach could be applied to paying manufacturing employees. It is also useful in designing executive pay. Table 12.9

TABLE 12.8

The Relationship between Managerial Pay and Organization Return on Assets

		PREDICTED RETURN ON ASSETS	
BONUS/BASE RATIO	LONG-TERM INCENTIVE ELIGIBILITY	%	$[a]
10%	28%	5.2%	$250 million
20	28	5.6	269 million
10	48	5.9	283 million
20	48	7.1	341 million

[a]Based on the assets of the average *Fortune* 500 company in 1990.

SOURCE: B. Gerhart and G.T. Milkovich, "Organizational Differences in Managerial Compensation and Financial Performance," *Academy of Management Journal* 33 (1990), pp. 663–91.

TABLE 12.9
Whirlpool's Three-Stakeholder Scorecard

STAKEHOLDER	MEASURES
Shareholder value	Economic value added Earnings per share Cash flow Total cost productivity
Customer value	Quality Market share Customer satisfaction
Employee value	High-performance culture index High-performance culture deployment Training and development diversity

SOURCE: From E.L. Gubman, *The Talent Solution,* 1998. Copyright © 1998 The McGraw-Hill Companies, Inc. Reproduced with permission of The McGraw-Hill Companies.

shows how the choice of performance measures can be guided by a desire to balance shareholder, customer, and employee objectives. Arthur Martinez of Sears refers to financial results as a lagging indicator that tells the company how it has done in the past, whereas customer and employee satisfaction are leading indicators that tell the company how its financial results will be in the future. Thus, Sears ties compensation to each type of objective. Eastman Kodak follows a similar approach. In 1996 its then-CEO, George Fisher, had his annual bonus reduced by $290,000 from its 1995 level. Why? The bonus was based on three components: shareholder satisfaction, customer satisfaction, and employee satisfaction. Relative to 1995, only shareholder satisfaction was "strong;" therefore, the bonus was reduced. George Fisher's total compensation for 1996 was still $5.5 million, the majority of which was based on stock plans. In 1997 Mr. Fisher agreed to a new contract that tied even more of his bonus to these criteria. So although Kodak does not reward only financial results, results continue to be the main driver of executive pay at Kodak. Recall that this chapter's opening vignette identified some reasons why companies continue to rely more heavily on financial results.

Finally, there has been pressure from regulators and shareholders to better link pay and performance since 1992. The Securities and Exchange Commission (SEC) has required companies to more clearly report executive compensation levels and the company's performance relative to that of competitors over a five-year period. The Omnibus Budget Reconciliation Act of 1993 eliminated the deductibility of executive pay that exceeds $1 million. However, most companies have been able to avoid the cap by taking advantage of an exemption for plans that link executive pay to company performance (such as by using stock options).

Large retirement fund investors such as TIAA-CREF and CalPERS have proposed guidelines to better ensure that boards of directors act in shareholders' best interests when making executive pay decisions, rather than being beholden to management. Some of the governance practices believed to be related to director independence from management are shown in Table 12.10. In addition, when a firm's future is at risk, the board may well need to demonstrate its independence from management by taking dramatic action, which may include removing the chief executive.

TABLE 12.10
Guidelines for Board of Directors Structure and Effective Governance

Interlocking boards	Top executives should not serve on each other's boards. Otherwise, there may be an incentive for executives to heed the Golden Rule too closely.
Outside versus inside directors	Inside directors are part of the management team and thus report to the top executive. Therefore, the number of inside directors should be kept to a minimum. Some committees, such as the nominating committee and the compensation committee, should be composed entirely of outside directors.
Outside directors meet without top executive	Such meetings permit directors to speak freely and consider actions that might be in the best interests of shareholders but unattractive to the top executive.
Director pensions	Directors with pensions may be reluctant to have conflicts with the top executive for fear of losing their directorships and thus their pensions.
Director pay	Directors should be required to own a minimum amount of stock to align their interests with those of shareholders.

SOURCE: Adapted from J.A. Byrne, "The CEO and the Board," *BusinessWeek* (September 15, 1997), p. 12.

Process and Context Issues

In Chapter 11 we discussed the importance of process issues such as communication and employee participation. Significant differences in how such issues are handled can be found both across and within organizations, suggesting that organizations have considerable discretion in this aspect of compensation management.[50] As such, it represents another strategic opportunity to distinguish one's organization from the competition.

Employee Participation in Decision Making

Consider employee participation in decision making and its potential consequences. Involvement in the design and implementation of pay policies has been linked to higher pay satisfaction and job satisfaction, presumably because employees have a better understanding of and greater commitment to the policy when they are involved.[51]

What about the effects on productivity? Agency theory provides some insight. The delegation of decision making by a principal to an agent creates agency costs because employees may not act in the best interests of top management. In addition, the more agents there are, the higher the monitoring costs.[52] Together, these suggest that delegation of decision making can be very costly.

On the other hand, agency theory suggests that monitoring would be less costly and more effective if performed by employees because they have knowledge about the workplace and behavior of fellow employees that managers do not have. As such, the right compensation system might encourage self-monitoring and peer monitoring.[53]

Researchers have suggested that two general factors are critical to encouraging such monitoring: monetary incentives (outcome-oriented contracts in agency theory) and an environment that fosters trust and cooperation. This environment, in turn, is a function of employment security, group cohesiveness, and individual rights for employees—in other words, respect for and commitment to employees.[54]

Communication

Another important process issue is communication. Earlier, we spoke of its importance in the administration of merit pay, both from the perspective of procedural fairness and as a means of obtaining the maximum impact from a merit pay program. More generally, a change in any part of the compensation system is likely to give rise to employee concerns. Rumors and assumptions based on poor or incomplete information are always an issue in administering compensation, partly because of its importance to employee economic security and well-being. Therefore, in making any changes, it is crucial to determine how best to communicate reasons for the changes to employees. Some organizations now rely heavily on videotaped messages from the chief executive officer to communicate the rationale for major changes. Brochures that include scenarios for typical employees are also used, as are focus group sessions where small groups of employees are interviewed to obtain feedback about concerns that can be addressed in later communication programs.

Pay and Process: Intertwined Effects

The preceding discussion treats process issues such as participation as factors that may facilitate the success of pay programs. At least one commentator, however, has described an even more important role for process factors in determining employee performance:

> Worker participation apparently helps make alternative compensation plans . . . work better—and also has beneficial effects of its own. . . . It appears that changing the way workers are treated may boost productivity more than changing the way they are paid.[55]

This suggestion raises a broader question: How important are pay decisions, per se, relative to other human resource practices? Although it may not be terribly useful to attempt to disentangle closely intertwined programs, it is important to reinforce the notion that human resource programs, even those as powerful as compensation systems, do not work alone.

Consider gainsharing programs. As described earlier, pay is often only one component of such programs. (See Table 12.6.) How important are the nonpay components?[56] There is ample evidence that gainsharing programs that rely almost exclusively on the monetary component can have substantial effects on productivity.[57] On the other hand, a study of an automotive parts plant found that adding a participation component (monthly meetings with management to discuss the gainsharing plan and ways to increase productivity) to a gainsharing pay incentive plan raised productivity. In a related study, employees were asked about the factors that motivated them to engage in active participation (such as suggestion systems). Employees reported that the desire to earn a monetary bonus was much less important than a number of nonpay factors, particularly the desire for influence and control in how their work was done.[58] A third study reported that productivity and profitability were both enhanced by the addition of employee participation in decisions, beyond the improvement derived from monetary incentives such as gainsharing.[59]

Organization Strategy and Compensation Strategy: A Question of Fit

Although much of our focus has been on the general, or average, effects of different pay programs, it is also useful to think in terms of matching pay strategies to organization strategies. To take an example from medicine, using the same medical treatment regardless of the symptoms and diagnosis would be foolish. In choosing a pay strategy, one must consider how effectively it will further the organization's overall business strategy. Consider again the findings reported in Table 12.8. The average effect of moving from a pay strategy with below-average variability in pay to one with above-average variability is an increase in return on assets of almost two percentage points (from 5.2 percent to 7.1 percent). But in some organizations, the increase could be smaller. In fact, greater variability in pay could contribute to a lower return on assets in some organizations. In other organizations, greater variability in pay could contribute to increases in return on assets of greater than two percentage points. Obviously, being able to tell where variable pay works and where it does not could have substantial consequences.

In Chapter 2 we discussed directional business strategies, two of which were growth (internal or external) and concentration ("sticking to the knitting"). How should compensation strategies differ according to whether an organization follows a growth strategy or a concentration strategy? Table 12.11 provides some suggested matches. Basically, a growth strategy's emphasis on innovation, risk taking, and new markets is linked to a pay strategy that shares risk with employees but also gives them the opportunity for high future earnings by having them share in whatever success the organization has. This means relatively low levels of fixed compensation in the short run but the use of bonuses and stock options, for example, that can pay off handsomely in the long run. Stock options have been described as the pay program "that built Silicon Valley," having been used by companies such as Apple, Sun Microsystems, and others.[60] When such companies become successful, everyone from top managers to secretaries can become millionaires if they own stock. Growth organizations are also thought to benefit from a less bureaucratic orientation, in the sense of having more decentralization and flexibility in pay decisions and in recognizing individ-

TABLE 12.11
Matching Pay Strategy and Organization Strategy

PAY STRATEGY DIMENSIONS	ORGANIZATION STRATEGY	
	CONCENTRATION	GROWTH
Risk sharing (variable pay)	Low	High
Time orientation	Short-term	Long-term
Pay level (short run)	Above market	Below market
Pay level (long-run potential)	Below market	Above market
Benefits level	Above market	Below market
Centralization of pay decisions	Centralized	Decentralized
Pay unit of analysis	Job	Skills

SOURCE: Adapted from L.R. Gomez-Mejia and D.B. Balkin, *Compensation, Organizational Strategy, and Firm Performance* (Cincinnati: South-Western, 1992), Appendix 4b. Reprinted with permission.

ual skills, rather than being constrained by job or grade classification systems. On the other hand, concentration-oriented organizations are thought to require a very different set of pay practices by virtue of their lower rate of growth, more stable workforce, and greater need for consistency and standardization in pay decisions.

A Look Back

At the beginning of this chapter, we saw that incentive plans can have both intended and unintended consequences. We have discussed the potential advantages and disadvantages of different types of incentive or pay for performance plans. To an important degree, pay strategy will depend on the particular goals and strategy of the organization or its units. Designing a pay for performance strategy typically seeks to balance the pros and cons of different plans by using elements of multiple plans. The main constraint on using such hybrid plans is that they should not become so complex that employees have difficulty understanding what behaviors and results will be rewarded.

Questions

1. Does money motivate? Use the theories and examples discussed in this chapter to address this question.
2. Think of a job that you have held. Design an incentive plan. What would be the potential advantages and disadvantages of your plan? If your money was invested in the company, would you adopt the plan?

Summary

Our focus in this chapter has been on the design and administration of programs that recognize employee contributions to the organization's success. These programs vary as to whether they link pay to individual, group, or organization performance. Often, it is not so much a choice of one program or the other as it is a choice between different combinations of programs that seek to balance individual, group, and organization objectives.

Wages, bonuses, and other types of pay have an important influence on an employee's standard of living. This carries at least two important implications. First, pay can be a powerful motivator. An effective pay strategy can substantially promote an organization's success; conversely, a poorly conceived pay strategy can have detrimental effects. Second, the importance of pay means that employees care a great deal about the fairness of the pay process. A recurring theme is that pay programs must be explained and administered in such a way that employees understand their underlying rationale and believe it is fair.

The fact that organizations differ in their business and human resource strategies suggests that the most effective compensation strategy may differ from one organization to another. Although benchmarking programs against the competition is informative, what succeeds in some organizations may not be a good idea for others. The balanced scorecard suggests the need for organizations to decide what their key objectives are and use pay to support them.

Discussion Questions

1. To compete more effectively, your organization is considering a profit sharing plan to increase employee effort and to encourage employees to think like owners. What are the potential advantages and disadvantages of such a plan? Would the profit sharing plan have the same impact on all types of employees? Is the size of your organization an important consideration? Why? What alternative pay programs should be considered?
2. Gainsharing plans have often been used in manufacturing settings but can also be applied in service

organizations. How could performance standards be developed for gainsharing plans in hospitals, banks, insurance companies, and so forth?

3. The opening vignette to the chapter noted that incentive plans may have unintended consequences. Why did Continental's CEO say that the proposed incentive was "absolutely stupid?" Do you agree? What is your view of the Eastman Kodak and United plans?
4. Your organization has two business units. One unit is a long-established manufacturer of a product that competes on price and has not been subject to many technological innovations. The other business unit is just being started. It has no products yet, but it is working on developing a new technology for testing the effects of drugs on people via simulation instead of through lengthy clinical trials. Would you recommend that the two business units have the same pay programs for recognizing individual contributions? Why?

Web Exercise

WorldatWork has information on compensation and benefits management, executive compensation, and international pay practices. Visit this organization at **www.worldatwork.org**. Click on "Newsline." Review the current news as well as previous postings found on this page.

1. Find articles related to stock plans. Read them.
2. What are some of the potential problems with using stock plans to reward employees or to fund their retirement benefits?

Managing People: From the Pages of *BusinessWeek*

BusinessWeek Commentary: An Options Plan Your CEO Hates

In 1998 Black & Decker Corp. CEO Nolan D. Archibald took home $36.6 million, $31.9 million of which came from the exercise of 1 million stock options he had been granted over the past nine years. The payout, while not quite massive enough to make *BusinessWeek*'s list of the top 20 best-paid executives for that year, was nothing to sneeze at. So what did Archibald do to deserve such a huge haul? Nothing earthshaking. From the time of Archibald's two grants to the time he exercised them, Black & Decker's total shareholder return trailed that of the Standard & Poor's 500 stock index, rising at a 15 percent average annualized rate, compared with 19 percent for the S&P. If Archibald had been forced to beat the market in order to cash in, his options would have been worth zilch.

In today's options-obsessed corporate climate, it doesn't take much for executives to rake in the millions. With seven-figure grants now commonplace, big bucks go to anyone who can get his stock to inch above the exercise price. Indeed, Alfred Rappaport, professor emeritus at Northwestern University's Kellogg Graduate School of Management, points out that total return to shareholders was positive for each of the 100 largest U.S. companies between 1987 and 1997.

NO COASTING. Many cynical pay watchers say that's just the way it is. If executives are taking home boatloads of cash simply because of a rising market and because boards are willing to dole out options by the bucketful, well, so be it. But that complacency could change if the market's gains continue to narrow. As of February 15, 74 of the 88 industry groups in the S&P 500 had negative returns for 2000. As a new round of shocking pay stories from this proxy season hits the presses, outrage could climb.

If that happens, it may focus attention on a controversial alternative to the standard options package. By using indexed stock options, which have no value unless the company's stock outperforms a peer group or a market index, companies can still ensure huge paydays for the true executive superheroes. Unlike the current system, however, indexed options also make sure that executives who are just floating their yachts on a rising tide get little to show for it. "Indexed options hold the executive to a higher standard," says Robin A. Ferracone, chairman of pay consultant SCA Consulting, which performed an analysis for *BusinessWeek* correlating the pay of several executives with their companies' total returns and that of the S&P 500. Had SCA used a peer group index, Archibald and the other executives might have fared somewhat differently.

Despite the support of such heavyweights as Federal Reserve Chairman Alan Greenspan and a growing clamor from a few institutional investors, indexed stock options remain very unpopular. Executives hate them because they inject more risk into the current windfall setup. Employers shun them because unlike traditional options, they require companies to take an accounting charge against earnings. Only one major company, Level 3 Communications Inc., a Broomfield (Colorado)-based telecommunications infrastructure outfit, currently uses them. "Most executives like it the way it is," says Ira M. Millstein, senior partner at law firm Weil, Gotshal & Manges and a governance expert. "Maybe when the market goes the other way, this will catch on."

How, exactly, do indexed options work? Simply put, they reward relative rather than absolute performance. Unlike premium-priced options, a more popular technique in which options are set at a higher level than the current price, indexed options have no value unless the underlying stock does better than a preset index. In a rising market, the bar is a high one. But in a declining market, an executive at a company with a falling stock price can still cash in, as long as the decline is less steep than that of his or her peers.

The difference in payout under the two types of options can be dramatic. Take the case of a hypothetical 1,000-share option grant at $10 per share that's tied to the performance of the S&P 500. If the company's stock rose by 20 percent, to $12, while the market rose 40 percent, the options would have no immediate value, since the company had underperformed. With a standard, "plain-vanilla" option, that grant would have paid $2,000. But if the overall market fell 30 percent while the stock dropped just 10 percent, to $9, that indexed grant would be worth $2,000—the difference between the index and the company performance. If the stock rose in a declining market, the payout would be yet higher.

FEW SUPPORTERS. One drawback of indexed options is that they don't pay as much as standard options when managers do outperform. If the company stock rose to $23 while the index rose to just $15, the options would be worth $8,000—compared to $13,000 with the plain-vanilla options. To make up for that shortfall, the number of indexed options granted would have to be roughly doubled, says Russell H. Miller, partner at SCA. With "grossed-up" options, that top performer would have earned $16,000 instead of $8,000. . . .

Then there's Walt Disney Co.'s Michael D. Eisner, who collected $569.8 million in fiscal 1998 from exercising a breathtaking 22 million shares granted over nine years. Had those options been indexed, he would have earned "just" $257.5 million, an amount that still would have broken all pay records at the time. With grossed-up indexed option grants, he would have made $502.1 million, a decrease from his actual haul, in part because he just barely outperformed the S&P—22 percent to 18 percent over the period. Overall, SCA says that 80 percent of the 20 best-paid CEOs in 1998 would have done better with grossed-up indexed options.

Although indexed options provide all the right incentives, they have few supporters in the mainstream corporate world, in part because they might expose some poor performers but also because they have a slew of their own problems. Start with the strangest one, an accounting anomaly that requires the value of indexed options to be calculated on a quarterly basis and charged to earnings. The Financial Accounting Standards Board (FASB) allows traditional options to avoid any charge to earnings—a free ride that has contributed mightily to the popularity of options over cash. Why the difference? Because the exercise price of indexed options fluctuates depending on the value of the index it's tied to. The FASB has ruled that indexed options must be charged to earnings every quarter so that investors can see the current option-related liabilities. Level 3 Communications' 1999 income statement reflects $111 million in expenses from its Outperform Stock Option Plan. Level 3 is currently in a quiet period and wouldn't comment on the plan.

So far Level 3 has few imitators, even though its stock has soared 212 percent since it started handing out indexed options in April 1998. The accounting charge is the biggest reason indexed options haven't caught on, though proponents argue that analysts could easily see through the charges, just as they've come to accept other oddities in a company's financials. "I think Wall Street would accept that those accounting charges were just paper charges," says Barry Bingham, director of executive compensation at Monsanto Co. Still, while Bingham finds indexed options "intriguing," Monsanto has so far experimented instead with premium priced option plans, where options are set above the current stock price but don't require relative outperformance—and carry no accounting charges.

Dilution, or the reduction in value per share from the issuance of more shares, is another drawback. Already the flood of traditional stock options has created a disturbing level of dilution. According to pay consultant Pearl Meyer & Partners Inc., the number of shares available for compensation programs as a percentage of shares outstanding was 13.7 percent in 1998 and rising. That would climb even higher with indexed options if they required bigger grants. Experts say it would be hard to get around the problem simply by rejiggering the exercise price to increase the payout for spectacular performance. That could run the risk of turning the incentive into a simple cash bonus instead of an option.

While there's hardly a groundswell of support for indexed options yet, there is a buzz around the issue that is sure to intensify if the market continues to narrow. Last year shareholder resolutions calling for indexed or performance-based options were filed at four companies, including Chubb, a longtime stock laggard, Gannett, and J.C. Penney. Sponsored by pension funds, including those of the AFL-CIO and the Communications Workers of America, the resolutions gained the support of proxy adviser Institutional Shareholder Services. "What we want to see is that they're grading themselves against a curve," says Patrick S. McGurn, director of corporate programs at Institutional Shareholder Services. The Chubb proposal received 33 percent of the vote, "a huge number for a first-time proposal," says McGurn. Now the AFL-CIO and two New York City pension funds may soon put forth similar proposals at other companies.

Still, it may take a falling market for indexed options to catch on. "What's going to trigger the interest here is when a very broad cross-section of companies starts to see either declining stock prices or flat stock prices," says Rappaport. If the market falls, traditional options will have no value at all. Companies will either have to return to cash-based pay or try wooing execs with indexed options, which could still pay off if the underlying stock falls less than the market. In fact, falling stocks could be just the thing to get widespread agreement from executives that the market's overall trends don't always reflect their companies' performance. Until that point, the pay wagons are sure to keep on rolling for executives, regardless of how well they do.

SOURCE: Reprinted from February 28, 2000 issue of *BusinessWeek* by special permission.

Questions

1. Describe how indexed options work.
2. What effect would the use of indexed options have on CEO pay in most cases?
3. In light of how indexed options would affect CEO pay, what problems might be encountered by a firm that switched to using indexed options?

Notes

1. We draw freely in this chapter on several literature reviews: B. Gerhart and G.T. Milkovich, "Employee Compensation: Research and Practice," in *Handbook of Industrial and Organizational Psychology,* vol. 3, 2nd ed., ed. M.D. Dunnette and L.M. Hough (Palo Alto, CA: Consulting Psychologists Press, 1992); B. Gerhart, G.T. Milkovich, and B. Murray, "Pay, Performance, and Participation," in *Research Frontiers in Industrial Relations and Human Resources*, ed. D. Lewin, O.S. Mitchell, and P.D. Sherer (Madison, WI: Industrial Relations Research Association, 1992); B. Gerhart and R.D. Bretz, "Employee Compensation," in *Organization and Management of Advanced Manufacturing,* ed. W. Karwowski and G. Salvendy (New York: John Wiley & Sons, 1994).
2. B. Gerhart and G.T. Milkovich, "Organizational Differences in Managerial Compensation and Financial Performance," *Academy of Management Journal* 33 (1990), pp. 663–91.
3. E. Deci and R. Ryan, *Intrinsic Motivation and Self-Determination in Human Behavior* (New York: Plenum, 1985); A. Kohn, "Why Incentive Plans Cannot Work," *Harvard Business Review,* September–October 1993.
4. R. Eisenberger and J. Cameron "Detrimental Effects of Reward: Reality or Myth?" *American Psychologist* 51, no. 11 (1996), pp. 1153–66.
5. R.A. Lambert and D.F. Larcker, "Executive Compensation, Corporate Decision Making, and Shareholder Wealth," in *Executive Compensation*, ed. F. Foulkes (Boston: Harvard Business School Press, 1989), pp. 287–309.
6. L.R. Gomez-Mejia, H. Tosi, and T. Hinkin, "Managerial Control, Performance, and Executive Compensation," *Academy of Management Journal* 30 (1987), pp. 51–70; H.L. Tosi Jr. and L.R. Gomez-Mejia, "The Decoupling of CEO Pay and Performance: An Agency Theory Perspective," *Administrative Science Quarterly* 34 (1989), pp. 169–89.
7. K.M. Eisenhardt, "Agency Theory: An Assessment and Review," *Academy of Management Review* 14 (1989), pp. 57–74.
8. R.E. Hoskisson, M.A. Hitt, and C.W. L. Hill, "Managerial Incentives and Investment in R&D in Large Multiproduct Firms," *Organizational Science* 4 (1993), pp. 325–41.
9. Eisenhardt, "Agency Theory."
10. Ibid.; E.J. Conlon and J.M. Parks, "Effects of Monitoring and Tradition on Compensation Arrangements: An Experiment with Principal–Agent Dyads," *Academy of Management Journal* 33 (1990), pp. 603–22; K.M. Eisenhardt, "Agency- and Institutional-Theory Explanations: The Case of Retail Sales Compensation," *Academy of Management Journal* 31 (1988), pp. 488–511; Gerhart and Milkovich, "Employee Compensation."
11. G.T. Milkovich, J. Hannon, and B. Gerhart, "The Effects of Research and Development Intensity on Managerial Compensation in Large Organizations," *Journal of High Technology Management Research* 2 (1991), pp. 133–50.
12. G.T. Milkovich and A.K. Wigdor, *Pay for Performance* (Washington, DC: National Academy Press, 1991); Gerhart and Milkovich, "Employee Compensation."
13. C. Trevor, B. Gerhart, and J.W. Boudreau, "Voluntary Turnover and Job Performance: Curvilinearity and the Moderating Influences of Salary Growth and Promotions," *Journal of Applied Psychology* 82 (1997), pp. 44–61.
14. R.D. Bretz, R.A. Ash, and G.F. Dreher, "Do People Make the Place? An Examination of the Attrac-

tion–Selection–Attrition Hypothesis," *Personnel Psychology* 42 (1989), pp. 561–81; T.A. Judge and R.D. Bretz, "Effect of Values on Job Choice Decisions," *Journal of Applied Psychology* 77 (1992), pp. 261–71; D.M. Cable and T.A. Judge, "Pay Performances and Job Search Decisions: A Person–Organization Fit Perspective," *Personnel Psychology* 47 (1994), pp. 317–48.

15. A. Majchrzak, *The Human Side of Factory Automation* (San Francisco: Jossey-Bass, 1988); E.E. Lawler III, *Strategic Pay* (San Francisco: Jossey-Bass, 1990); Gerhart and Milkovich, "Employee Compensation."
16. R.D. Bretz, G.T. Milkovich, and W. Read, "The Current State of Performance Appraisal Research and Practice," *Journal of Management* 18 (1992), pp. 321–52; R.L. Heneman, "Merit Pay Research," *Research in Personnel and Human Resource Management* 8 (1990), pp. 203–63; Milkovich and Wigdor, *Pay for Performance*.
17. Bretz et al., "Current State of Performance Appraisal."
18. Ibid.
19. Ibid.
20. W.E. Deming, *Out of the Crisis* (Cambridge, MA: Center for Advanced Engineering Study, Massachusetts Institute of Technology, 1986), p. 110.
21. Ibid.
22. Ibid.
23. Trevor et al., "Voluntary Turnover."
24. R. Folger and M.A. Konovsky, "Effects of Procedural and Distributive Justice on Reactions to Pay Raise Decisions," *Academy of Management Journal* 32 (1989), pp. 115–30; J. Greenberg, "Determinants of Perceived Fairness of Performance Evaluations," *Journal of Applied Psychology* 71 (1986), pp. 340–42.
25. E.E. Lawler III, "Pay for Performance: A Strategic Analysis," in *Compensation and Benefits*, ed. L.R. Gomez-Mejia (Washington, DC: Bureau of National Affairs, 1989); A.M. Konrad and J. Pfeffer, "Do You Get What You Deserve? Factors Affecting the Relationship between Productivity and Pay," *Administrative Science Quarterly* 35 (1990), pp. 258–85; J.L. Medoff and K.G. Abraham, "Are Those Paid More Really More Productive? The Case of Experience," *Journal of Human Resources* 16 (1981), pp. 186–216; K.S. Teel, "Are Merit Raises Really Based on Merit?" *Personnel Journal* 65, no. 3 (1986), pp. 88–95.
26. B. Gerhart and S. Rynes, "Determinants and Consequences of Salary Negotiations by Graduating Male and Female MBAs," *Journal of Applied Psychology* (1991), pp. 256–62.
27. E.A. Locke, D.B. Feren, V.M. McCaleb, K.N. Shaw, and A.T. Denny, "The Relative Effectiveness of Four Methods of Motivating Employee Performance," in *Changes in Working Life*, ed. K.D. Duncan, M.M. Gruenberg, and D. Wallis (New York: Wiley, 1980), pp. 363–88.
28. Gerhart and Milkovich, "Employee Compensation."
29. This idea has been referred to as the "share economy." See M.L. Weitzman, "The Simple Macroeconomics of Profit Sharing," *American Economic Review* 75 (1985), pp. 937–53. For supportive empirical evidence, see the following studies: J. Chelius and R.S. Smith, "Profit Sharing and Employment Stability," *Industrial and Labor Relations Review* 43 (1990), pp. 256S–73S; B. Gerhart and L.O. Trevor, "Employment Stability under Different Managerial Compensation Systems," working paper 1995 (Cornell University: Center for Advanced Human Resource Studies); D.L. Kruse, "Profit Sharing and Employment Variability: Microeconomic Evidence on the Weitzman Theory," *Industrial and Labor Relations Review* 44 (1991), pp. 437–53.
30. Gerhart and Milkovich, "Employee Compensation"; M.L. Weitzman and D.L. Kruse, "Profit Sharing and Productivity," in *Paying for Productivity*, ed. A.S. Blinder (Washington, DC: Brookings Institution, 1990); D.L. Kruse, *Profit Sharing: Does It Make a Difference?* (Kalamazoo, MI: Upjohn Institute, 1993).
31. "GM/UAW: The Battle Goes On," *Ward's Auto World* (May 1995), p. 40; E.M. Coates III, "Profit Sharing Today: Plans and Provisions," *Monthly Labor Review* (April 1991), pp. 19–25.
32. American Management Association, *CompFlash*, April 1991, p. 3. General Motors' Saturn division has also scaled back its reliance on profit sharing because of lower-than-expected profits.
33. American Management Association, *CompFlash*, April 1991, p. 3.
34. "Executive Compensation: Taking Stock," *Personnel* 67 (December 1990), pp. 7–8; "Another Day, Another Dollar Needs Another Look," *Personnel* 68 (January 1991), pp. 9–13.
35. Gerhart and Milkovich, "Organizational Differences in Managerial Compensation."
36. *EBRI Databook on Employee Benefits* (Washington, DC: Employee Benefit Research Institute, 1995). **www.nceo.org** (National Center for Employee Ownership website).
37. D. Jones and T. Kato, "The Productivity Effects of Employee Stock Ownership Plans and Bonuses: Evidence from Japanese Panel Data," *American Economic Review* 185, no. 3 (June 1995), pp. 391–414.
38. "Employees Left Holding the Bag," *Fortune* (May 20, 1991), pp. 83–93; M.A. Conte and J. Svejnar, "The Performance Effects of Employee Ownership Plans," in *Paying for Productivity*, pp. 245–94.
39. Conte and Svejnar, "Performance Effects of Employee Ownership Plans."
40. Ibid.; T.H. Hammer, "New Developments in Profit

Sharing, Gainsharing, and Employee Ownership," in *Productivity in Organizations*, ed. J.P. Campbell, R.J. Campbell and Associates (San Francisco: Jossey-Bass, 1988); K.J. Klein, "Employee Stock Ownership and Employee Attitudes: A Test of Three Models," *Journal of Applied Psychology* 72 (1987), pp. 319–32.

41. J.L. Pierce, S. Rubenfeld, and S. Morgan, "Employee Ownership: A Conceptual Model of Process and Effects," *Academy of Management Review* 16 (1991), pp. 121–44.
42. One study found that the value of shares was reduced annually by an amount roughly equal to 2.2 percent of pretax profits ("Unseen Apples and Small Carrots," *The Economist* (April 13, 1991), p. 75.
43. L. Hatcher and T.L. Ross, "From Individual Incentives to an Organizationwide Gainsharing Plan: Effects on Teamwork and Product Quality," *Journal of Organizational Behavior* 12 (1991), pp. 169–83; R.T. Kaufman, "The Effects of Improshare on Productivity," *Industrial and Labor Relations Review* 45 (1992), pp. 311–22; M.H. Schuster, "The Scanlon Plan: A Longitudinal Analysis," *Journal of Applied Behavioral Science* 20 (1984), pp. 23–28; J.A. Wagner III, P. Rubin, and T.J. Callahan, "Incentive Payment and Nonmanagerial Productivity: An Interrupted Time Series Analysis of Magnitude and Trend," *Organizational Behavior and Human Decision Processes* 42 (1988), pp. 47–74; M.M. Petty, B. Singleton, and D.W. Connell, "An Experimental Evaluation of an Organizational Incentive Plan in the Electric Utility Industry," *Journal of Applied Psychology* 77 (1992), pp. 427–36; J.L. McAdams, "Employee Involvement and Performance Reward Plans," *Compensation and Benefits Review*, March–April 1995, p. 45; W.N. Cooke, "Employee Participation Programs, Group-Based Incentives, and Company Performance: A Union–Nonunion Comparison," *Industrial and Labor Relations Review* 47 (1994), pp. 594–609.
44. T.L. Ross and R.A. Ross, "Gainsharing: Sharing Improved Performance," in *The Compensation Handbook*, 3rd ed., ed. M.L. Rock and L.A. Berger (New York: McGraw-Hill, 1991).
45. T.M. Welbourne and L.R. Gomez-Mejia, "Team Incentives in the Workplace," in *The Compensation Handbook*, 3rd ed.
46. R.S. Kaplan and D.P. Norton "Using the Balanced Scorecard as a Strategic Management System," *Harvard Business Review*, January–February 1996, pp. 75–85.
47. M.C. Jensen and K.J. Murphy, "Performance Pay and Top-Management Incentives," *Journal of Political Economy* 98 (1990), pp. 225–64.
48. M.C. Jensen and K.J. Murphy, "CEO Incentives—It's Not How Much You Pay, but How," *Harvard Business Review* 68 (May–June 1990), pp. 138–53.
49. Gerhart and Milkovich, "Organizational Differences in Managerial Compensation."
50. J. Cutcher-Gershenfeld, "The Impact on Economic Performance of a Transformation in Workplace Relations," *Industrial and Labor Relations Review* 44 (1991), pp. 241–60; Irene Goll, "Environment, Corporate Ideology, and Involvement Programs," *Industrial Relations* 30 (1991), pp. 138–49.
51. L.R. Gomez-Mejia and D.B. Balkin, *Compensation, Organizational Strategy, and Firm Performance* (Cincinnati: South-Western, 1992); G.D. Jenkins and E.E. Lawler III, "Impact of Employee Participation in Pay Plan Development," *Organizational Behavior and Human Performance* 28 (1981), pp. 111–28.
52. D.I. Levine and L.D. Tyson, "Participation, Productivity, and the Firm's Environment," in *Paying for Productivity*.
53. T. Welbourne, D. Balkin, and L. Gomez-Mejia, "Gainsharing and Mutual Monitoring: A Combined Agency–Organizational Justice Interpretation," *Academy of Management Journal* 38 (1995), pp. 881–99.
54. Ibid.
55. Blinder, *Paying for Productivity*.
56. Hammer, "New Developments in Profit Sharing"; Milkovich and Wigdor, *Pay for Performance;* D. J.B. Mitchell, D. Lewin, and E.E. Lawler III, "Alternative Pay Systems, Firm Performance and Productivity," in *Paying for Productivity*.
57. Kaufman, "The Effects of Improshare on Productivity"; M.H. Schuster, "The Scanlon Plan: A Longitudinal Analysis," *Journal of Applied Behavioral Science* 20 (1984), pp. 23–28; J.A. Wagner III, P. Rubin, and T.J. Callahan, "Incentive Payment and Nonmanagerial Productivity: An Interrupted Time Series Analysis of Magnitude and Trend," *Organizational Behavior and Human Decision Processes* 42 (1988), pp. 47–74.
58. C.R. Gowen III and S.A. Jennings, "The Effects of Changes in Participation and Group Size on Gainsharing Success: A Case Study," *Journal of Organizational Behavior Management* 11 (1991), pp. 147–69.
59. L. Hatcher, T.L. Ross, and D. Collins, "Attributions for Participation and Nonparticipation in Gainsharing-Plan Involvement Systems," *Group and Organization Studies* 16 (1991), pp. 25–43; Mitchell et al., "Alternative Pay Systems."
60. A.J. Baker, "Stock Options—a Perk That Built Silicon Valley," *The Wall Street Journal* (June 23, 1993), p. A20.

13 Chapter
Employee Benefits

Objectives
After reading this chapter, you should be able to:

1. Discuss the growth in benefits costs and the underlying reasons for that growth.
2. Explain the major provisions of employee benefits programs.
3. Describe the effects of benefits management on cost and workforce quality.
4. Explain how employee benefits in the United States compare with those in other countries.
5. Explain the importance of effectively communicating the nature and value of benefits to employees.
6. Describe the regulatory constraints that affect the way employee benefits are designed and administered.

Given the recent state of our economy, employees who have put too much of their investments in one place, namely their own company's stock, have a lot at risk as events at Enron and other companies have made clear.

Enter the World of Business

Not Your Father's Retirement Plan

A generation ago, a worker's pension plan was sacrosanct. An employee who stayed with a company having a strong plan would be rewarded with a comfortable retirement income. Today that security seems to be on shaky ground—if not gone altogether in some companies. Instead, today's retirement plans are increasingly of the defined contribution type, such as a 401k plan, where employees and often employers set aside money for an employee's retirement, but there are no guarantees of how much that investment will be worth in the future or whether it will provide a comfortable retirement. This depends entirely on the investment decisions that the employee makes. Thus today's retirement plans increasingly require savvy on the part of employees, particularly when it comes to owning their company's stock. If the stock soars, employees win; but if it tanks, they can lose a bundle, just when they need the money the most.

Lucent Technologies is one example. When the company was riding high, so were its employees' 401(k) investments; but in 2000, when the stock dropped 80 percent, workers who had a significant amount of their plans invested in company stock were hurt badly. "The stock was doing so well that I got greedy," laments one employee. But Lucent shares responsibility for the problem. The company's 401(k) plan for hourly employees matches every dollar contributed by an employee with 66 cents of Lucent stock. The plan also requires that an individual hold the stock for a certain number of years, which means that if the stock drops once the person hits retirement age, he or she could lose a lot of money. Also, the way the plan is structured, an employee ends up with at least 30 percent of his or her investments in Lucent stock.

But Lucent employees aren't the only ones suffering. Owens Corning, whose plan includes 44 percent of company stock, dropped 87 percent in one year. Dell, whose plan requires 88 percent in company assets, dropped 50 percent. If these employees are laid off during lean times, both their jobs and their nest eggs will be destroyed.

Although the great stock gains realized by some new economy companies may have caused many people to forget about diversification, the swift drop in stock prices at many of these companies in the last year or so has provided an abrupt, painful reminder of the importance of diversification. Unfortunately, too many companies have failed in helping their employees understand this. For example, Fidelity Investments studied 7,000 such contribution programs and learned that the average plan has more than 30 percent of its total assets invested in company stock. That's simply too many eggs in one basket. Investment writer Lewis Graham suggests lifting restrictions on the number of years an employee must hold company stock, and Fidelity learned that some companies are now capping the percentage of company stock employees can have in their plans. In addition, retirement adviser Michael Scarborough recommends that companies do a better job of educating employees about their risks and options. "The tools are out there to adequately advise employees," he remarks. "But most companies choose not to give them to employees."

Recognizing a market opportunity, Fidelity has started selling stock option services to large companies in an effort to help them sort through the administrative jumble that accompanies 401(k) plans tied to stock. Fidelity services include tracking options grants for corporate clients, providing dedicated telephone representatives for employees, offering education and calculators at its website, and posttrade record keeping. Firms seem to like the idea of having experts handle the problem. "We've got more companies in the queue than we can handle right now," says Tracy Esherick, executive vice president of Fidelity's online brokerage group. "We think there's a real opportunity here, making sure that employees have the tools they need to assess what their transaction options are."

SOURCE: B. Healy, "Taking Stock of Options," *The Boston Globe* (August 6, 2001), http://digitalmass.boston.com; L. Graham, "Company Stock Could Sink Your Ship," *BusinessWeek* (July 30, 2001), p. 86.

Introduction

If we think of benefits as a part of total employee compensation, many of the concepts discussed in the two previous chapters on employee compensation apply here as well. This means, for example, that both cost and behavioral objectives are important. The cost of benefits adds an average of 37 percent to every dollar of payroll, thus accounting for about 27 percent of the total employee compensation package. Controlling labor costs is not possible without controlling benefits costs. When Daimler Chrysler pays $1300 in health care costs per Chrysler car produced (average vehicle price of $18,600), its ability to sell automobiles at a competitive price is challenged.[1] On the behavioral side, benefits seem to influence whether potential employees come to work for a company, whether they stay, when they retire—perhaps even how they perform (although the empirical evidence, especially on the latter point, is surprisingly limited). Different employees look for different types of benefits. Employers need to regularly reexamine their benefits to see whether they fit the needs of today rather than yesterday.

Although it makes sense to think of benefits as part of total compensation, benefits have unique aspects. First, there is the question of legal compliance. Although direct compensation is subject to government regulation, the scope and impact of regulation on benefits is far greater. Some benefits, such as Social Security, are mandated by law. Others, although not mandated, are subject to significant regulation or must meet certain criteria to achieve the most favorable tax treatment; these include pensions and savings plans. The heavy involvement of government in benefits decisions reflects the central role benefits play in maintaining economic security.

A second unique aspect of benefits is that organizations so typically offer them that they have come to be institutionalized. Providing medical and retirement benefits of some sort has become almost obligatory for many employers. A large employer that did not offer such benefits to its full-time employees would be highly unusual, and the employer might well have trouble attracting and retaining a quality workforce. However, the opening vignette provides an example of how the relationship between employers and employees is changing and how it may influence the types of benefits offered. The vignette also shows how serious the consequences can be if employers and employees do not recognize the risks that particular benefits decisions may create.

A third unique aspect of benefits, compared with other forms of compensation, is their complexity. It is relatively easy to understand the value of a dollar as part of a salary, but not as part of a benefits package. The advantages and disadvantages of different types of medical coverage, pension provisions, disability insurance, and so forth are often difficult to grasp, and their value (beyond a general sense that they are good to have) is rarely as clear as the value of one's salary. Most fundamentally, employees may not even be aware of the benefits available to them; and if they are aware, they may not understand how to use them. When employers spend large sums of money on benefits but employees do not understand the benefits or attach much value to them, the return on employers' benefits investment will be fairly dismal.[2] Thus, another reason for giving more responsibility to employees for retirement planning and other benefits is to increase their understanding of the value of such benefits.

Reasons for Benefits Growth

In thinking about benefits as part of total compensation, a basic question arises: Why do employers choose to channel a significant portion of the compensation dollar away from cash (wages and salaries) into benefits? Economic theory tells us that people prefer a dollar in cash over a dollar's worth of any specific commodity because the cash can be used to purchase the commodity or something else.[3] Thus cash is less restrictive. Several factors, however, have contributed to less emphasis on cash and more on benefits in compensation. To understand these factors, it is useful to examine the growth in benefits over time and the underlying reasons for that growth.

Figure 13.1 gives an indication of the overall growth in benefits. Note that in 1929, on the eve of the Great Depression, benefits added an average of only 3 percent to every dollar of payroll. By 1955 this figure had grown to 17 percent, and it has continued to grow, now accounting for about 37 percent on top of every payroll dollar.

Many factors contributed to this tremendous growth.[4] First, during the 1930s several laws were passed as part of Franklin Roosevelt's New Deal, a legislative program aimed at buffering people from the devastating effects of the Great Depression. The Social Security Act and other legislation established legally required benefits (such as the Social Security retirement system) and modified the tax structure in such a way as to effectively make other benefits—such as workers' compensation (for work-related injuries) and unemployment insurance—mandatory. Second, wage and price controls instituted during World War II, combined with labormarket shortages, forced employers to think of new ways to attract and retain employees. Because benefits were not covered by wage controls, employers channeled more resources in this direction. Once institutionalized, such benefits tended to remain even after wage and price controls were lifted.

Third, the tax treatment of benefits programs is often more favorable for employees

FIGURE 13.1
Growth of Employee Benefits, Percentage of Wages and Salaries, 1929–99

SOURCE: U.S. Chamber of Commerce Research Center, *Employee Benefits 1990, Employee Benefits 1997, Employee Benefits 2000* (Washington, DC: U.S. Chamber of Commerce, 1991, 1997, and 2000).

Marginal tax rate
The percentage of an additional dollar of earnings that goes to taxes.

than the tax treatment of wages and salaries, meaning that a dollar spent on benefits has the potential to generate more value for the employees than the same dollar spent on wages and salaries. The **marginal tax rate** is the percentage of additional earnings that goes to taxes. Consider the hypothetical employee in Table 13.1 and the effect on take-home pay of a $1,000 increase in salary. The total effective marginal tax rate is higher for higher-paid employees and also varies according to state and city. (New York

TABLE 13.1
Example of Marginal Tax Rates for an Employee Salary of $50,000

	NOMINAL TAX RATE	EFFECTIVE TAX RATE
Federal	28.0%	28.0%
State (New York)	6.8	4.9
City (New York)	3.7	2.7
Social Security	6.2	6.2
Medicare	1.5	1.5
Total tax rate		43.3

NOTE: State and city taxes are deductible on the federal tax return, reducing their effective tax rate.

State and New York City are among the highest.) A $1,000 annual raise for the employee earning $50,000 per year would increase net pay $570 ($1,000 × [1 – .43]). In contrast, an extra $1,000 put into benefits would lead to an increase of $1,000 in "take-home benefits."

Employers, too, realize tax advantages from certain types of benefits. Although both cash compensation and most benefits are deductible as operating expenses, employers (like employees) pay Social Security tax on salaries below a certain amount ($80,400 in 2001) and Medicare tax on the entire salary, as well as other taxes like workers' compensation and unemployment compensation. However, no such taxes are paid on most employee benefits. The bottom line is that the employer may be able to provide more value to employees by spending the extra $1,000 on benefits instead of salary.

The tax advantage of benefits also takes another form. Deferring compensation until retirement allows the employee to receive cash, but at a time (retirement) when the employee's tax rate is sometimes lower because of a lower income level. More important, perhaps, is that investment returns on the deferred money typically accumulate tax free, resulting in much faster growth of the investment.

A fourth factor that has influenced benefits growth is the cost advantage that groups typically realize over individuals. Organizations that represent large groups of employees can purchase insurance (or self-insure) at a lower rate because of economies of scale, which spread fixed costs over more employees to reduce the cost per person. Insurance risks can be more easily pooled in large groups, and large groups can also achieve greater bargaining power in dealing with insurance carriers or medical providers.

A fifth factor influencing the growth of benefits was the growth of organized labor from the 1930s through the 1950s. This growth was partly a result of another piece of New Deal legislation, the National Labor Relations Act, which greatly enhanced trade unions' ability to organize workers and negotiate contracts with employers. Benefits were often a key negotiation objective. (Indeed, they still are. It is estimated that more than half of workers who struck in the early 1990s did so over health care coverage issues.)[5] Unions were able to successfully pursue their members' interests in benefits, particularly when tax advantages provided an incentive for employers to shift money from cash to benefits. For unions, a new benefit such as medical coverage was a tangible success that could have more impact on prospective union members than a wage increase of equivalent value, which might have amounted to only a cent or two per hour. Also, many nonunion employers responded to the threat of unionization by implementing the same benefits for their own employees, thus contributing to benefits growth.

Finally, employers may also provide unique benefits as a means of differentiating themselves in the eyes of current or prospective employees. In this way, employers communicate key aspects of their culture that set them apart from the rest of the pack. Table 13.2 shows some examples.

Benefits Programs

Most benefits fall into one of the following categories: social insurance, private group insurance, retirement, pay for time not worked, and family-friendly policies.[6] Table 13.3, based on Bureau of Labor Statistics (BLS) data, provides an overview of the prevalence of specific benefits programs.

TABLE 13.2
Differentiating via Benefits

CMP Media	$30,000 for infertility treatments or adoption
Fannie Mae	10 paid hours per month for volunteer work
Microstrategy	One-week Caribbean cruise each January
Eli Lilly	Free Lilly drugs (including Prozac)
Pfizer	Free Pfizer drugs (including Viagra)
Intel	Eight-week sabbatical after seven years

SOURCE: From "100 Best Companies to Work for," *Fortune*.

TABLE 13.3
Percentage of Full-Time Workers Who Participate in Selected Benefits Programs

	MEDIUM-SIZE AND LARGE PRIVATE ESTABLISHMENTS, 1997	SMALL PRIVATE ESTABLISHMENTS, 1996
Medical care	76%	64%
Dental care	59	31
Short-term disability insurance	55	29
Long-term disability insurance	43	22
Paid sick leave	56	50
All retirement	79	46
Defined benefit pension	50	15
Defined contribution plan	57	38
Life insurance	87	62
Paid leave		
Holidays	89	80
Vacation	95	86
Family leave	2	2

SOURCE: http://stats.bls.gov/ebshome.htm.

Social Insurance (Legally Required)

Social Security

Among the most important provisions of the Social Security Act of 1935 was the establishment of old-age insurance and unemployment insurance. The act was later amended to add survivor's insurance (1939), disability insurance (1956), hospital insurance (Medicare Part A, 1965), and supplementary medical insurance (Medicare Part B, 1965) for the elderly. Together these provisions constitute the federal Old Age, Survivors, Disability, and Health Insurance (OASDHI) program. Over 90 percent of U.S. employees are covered by the program, the main exceptions being railroad and federal, state, and local government employees, who often have their own plans. Note, however, that an individual employee must meet certain eligibility requirements to receive benefits. To be fully insured typically requires 40 quarters of covered employment and minimum earnings of $830 per quarter in 2001. However, the eligibility rules for survivors' and disability benefits are somewhat different.

Social Security retirement (old-age insurance) benefits for fully insured workers begin at age 65 (full benefits) or age 62 (at a permanent reduction in benefits). Although the amount of the benefit depends on one's earnings history, benefits go up very little after a certain level (the maximum monthly benefit in 2001 was $1,536); thus high earners help subsidize benefit payments to low earners. Cost-of-living increases are provided each year that the consumer price index increases.

An important attribute of the Social Security retirement benefit is that it is free from state tax in about half of the states and entirely free from federal tax. However, the federal tax code has an earnings test for those who are still earning wages. In 2001, beneficiaries ages 62–64 were allowed to make $10,680; in the year an individual reaches age 65, the earnings test is $25,000. However, as of January 2000, there is no earnings test for those 65 and older. If these amounts are exceeded, the social security benefit is reduced $1 for every $2 in excess earnings for those ages 62 to 64 and $1 for every $3 in the year a worker turns 65. Those age 65 or older face no penalty. These provisions are important because of their effects on the work decisions of those between 62 and 70. The earnings test increases a person's incentive to retire (otherwise full Social Security benefits are not received), and if she continues to work, the incentive to work part-time rather than full-time increases.

How are retirement and other benefits financed? Both employers and employees are assessed a payroll tax. In 2001, each paid a tax of 7.65 percent (a total of 15.3 percent) on the first $80,400 of the employee's earnings. Of the 7.65 percent, 6.2 percent funds OASDHI, and 1.45 percent funds Medicare (Part A). In addition, the 1.45 percent Medicare tax is assessed on all earnings.

What are the behavioral consequences of Social Security benefits? Because they are legally mandated, employers do not have discretion in designing this aspect of their benefits programs. However, Social Security does affect employees' retirement decisions. The eligibility age for benefits and the tax penalty for earnings above a certain level contribute to an outflow of employees once they reach their middle 60s. If, as some have suggested, pay rises with age more quickly than productivity does late in employees' careers, these retirements are a positive outcome for employers. Indeed, in recent years, many employers have relied heavily on early retirement incentives to reduce employment. On the other hand, when older employees leave, they take with them a great deal of experience and expertise.

Unemployment Insurance

Established by the 1935 Social Security Act, this program has four major objectives: (1) to offset lost income during involuntary unemployment, (2) to help unemployed workers find new jobs, (3) to provide an incentive for employers to stabilize employment, and (4) to preserve investments in worker skills by providing income during short-term layoffs (which allows workers to return to their employer rather than start over with another employer).

The unemployment insurance program is financed largely through federal and state taxes on employers. Although, strictly speaking, the decision to establish the program is left to each state, the Social Security Act created a tax incentive structure that quickly led every state to establish a program. The federal tax rate is currently 0.8 percent on the first $7,000 of wages. The state tax rate varies, the minimum being 5.4 percent on the first $7,000 of wages. Many states have a higher rate or impose the tax on a greater share of earnings. In 1997, Rhode Island employers incurred the highest costs, $707 per employee, whereas South Dakota was lowest at $91 per employee. The state average was $210, down from $224 in 1996.[7]

A very important feature of the unemployment insurance program is that no state imposes the same tax on every employer. Instead, the size of the tax depends on the employer's *experience rating*. Employers that have a history of laying off a large share of their workforces pay higher taxes than those who do not. In some states, an employer that has had very few layoffs may pay no state tax. In contrast, an employer with a poor experience rating could pay a tax as high as 5 to 10 percent, depending on the state.[8]

Unemployed workers are eligible for benefits if they (1) have a prior attachment to the workforce (often 52 weeks or four quarters of work at a minimum level of pay), (2) are available for work, (3) are actively seeking work (including registering at the local unemployment office), and (4) were not discharged for cause (such as willful misconduct), did not quit voluntarily, and are not out of work because of a labor dispute.

Benefits also vary by state, but they are typically about 50 percent of a person's earnings and last for 26 weeks. Extended benefits for up to 13 weeks are also available in states with a sustained unemployment rate above 6.5 percent. Emergency extended benefits are also sometimes funded by Congress. All states have minimum and maximum weekly benefit levels. In contrast to Social Security retirement benefits, unemployment benefits are taxed as ordinary income.

Because unemployment insurance is, in effect, legally required, management's discretion is limited here, too. Management's main task is to keep its experience rating low by avoiding unnecessary workforce reductions (by relying, for example, on the sorts of actions described in Chapter 5).

Workers' Compensation

Prior to enactment of these laws, workers suffering work-related injuries or diseases could receive compensation only by suing for damages. Moreover, the common-law defenses available to employers meant that such lawsuits were not usually successful. In contrast, workers' compensation laws cover job-related injuries and death.[9] These laws operate under a principle of no-fault liability, meaning that an employee does not need to establish gross negligence by the employer. In return, employers receive immunity from lawsuits. (One exception is the employer who intentionally contributes to a dangerous workplace.) Employees are not covered when injuries are self-inflicted or stem from intoxication or "willful disregard of safety rules."[10] Approximately 90 percent of all U.S. workers are covered by state workers' compensation laws, although again there are differences among states, with coverage ranging from 70 percent to over 95 percent.

Workers' compensation benefits fall into four major categories: (1) disability income, (2) medical care, (3) death benefits, and (4) rehabilitative services.

Disability income is typically two-thirds of predisability earnings, although each state has its own minimum and maximum. In contrast to unemployment insurance benefits, disability benefits are tax free. The system is financed differently by different states, some having a single state fund, most allowing employers to purchase coverage from private insurance companies. Self-funding by employers is also permitted in most states. The cost to the employer is based on three factors. The first factor is the nature of the occupations and the risk attached to each. Premiums for low-risk occupations may be less than 1 percent of payroll; the cost for some of the most hazardous occupations may be as high as 100 percent of payroll. The second factor is the state where work is located. For example, the loss of a leg may be worth $208,690 in Pennsylvania but only $31,200 in Colorado.[11] The third factor is the employer's experience rating.

The cost of the workers' compensation system to U.S. employers has grown dramatically, leading to an increased focus on ways of controlling workers' compensation costs.[12] The experience rating system again provides an incentive for employers to make their workplaces safer. Dramatic injuries (like losing a finger or hand) are less prevalent than minor ones, such as sprains and strains. Back strain is the most prevalent injury (31 percent of all injuries), costing an average of $24,000 per claim.[13] Many actions can be taken to reduce workplace injuries, such as work redesign and training.[14] Some changes can be fairly simple (such as permitting workers to sit instead of having them bend over). It is also important to hold managers accountable (in their performance evaluations) for making workplaces safer and getting employees back to work promptly following an injury. With the recent passage of the Americans with Disabilities Act, employers are under even greater pressure to deal effectively and fairly with workplace injuries. See the discussion in Chapter 3 on safety awareness programs for some of the ways employers and employees are striving to make the workplace safer.

Private Group Insurance

As we noted earlier, group insurance rates are typically lower than individual rates because of economies of scale, the ability to pool risks, and the greater bargaining power of a group. This cost advantage, together with tax considerations and a concern for employee security, helps explain the prevalence of employer-sponsored insurance plans. We discuss two major types: medical insurance and disability insurance. Note that these programs are not legally required; rather, they are offered at the discretion of employers.

Medical Insurance

Not surprisingly, public opinion surveys indicate that medical benefits are by far the most important benefit to the average person.[15] As Table 13.3 indicates, most full-time employees, particularly in medium-size and large companies, get such benefits. Three basic types of medical expenses are typically covered: hospital expenses, surgical expenses, and physicians' visits. Other benefits that employers may offer include dental care, vision care, birthing centers, and prescription drug programs. Perhaps the most important issue in benefits management is the challenge of providing quality medical benefits while controlling costs, a subject we return to in a later section.

The **Consolidated Omnibus Budget Reconciliation Act (COBRA)** of 1985 requires employers to permit employees to extend their health insurance coverage at group rates for up to 36 months following a "qualifying event" such as termination (except for gross misconduct), a reduction in hours that leads to the loss of health insurance, death, and other events. The beneficiary (whether the employee, spouse, or dependent) must have access to the same services as employees who have not lost their health insurance. Note that the beneficiaries do not get free coverage. Rather, they receive the advantage of purchasing coverage at the group rather than the individual rate.

Consolidated Omnibus Budget Reconciliation Act (COBRA)
The 1985 act that requires employers to permit employees to extend their health insurance coverage at group rates for up to 36 months following a qualifying event, such as a layoff.

Disability Insurance

Two basic types of disability coverage exist.[16] As Table 13.3 indicates, about 55 percent of employees in medium-size and large companies are covered by short-term disability plans and about 43 percent are covered by long-term disability plans. Short-term plans typically provide benefits for six months or less, at which point long-term plans take over, potentially covering the person for life. The salary replacement rate is typically between 50 and 70 percent, although short-term plans are sometimes higher. There are often caps on the amount that can be paid each month. Federal income taxation of disability benefits depends on the funding method. Where employee contributions completely fund the plan, there is no federal tax. Benefits based on employer contributions are taxed. Finally, disability benefits, especially long-term ones, need to be coordinated with other programs, such as Social Security disability benefits.

Retirement

Earlier we discussed the old-age insurance part of Social Security, a legally required source of retirement income. Although this remains the largest single component of the elderly's overall retirement income (38 percent), the combination of private pensions (17 percent) and earnings from assets (savings and other investments like stock) account for an even larger share (25 percent). The remainder of the elderly's income comes from earnings (17 percent) and other sources (3 percent).[17]

Employers have no legal obligation to offer private retirement plans, but most do. As we note later, if a private retirement plan is provided, it must meet certain standards set forth by the Employee Retirement Income Security Act.

Pension Benefit Guaranty Corporation (PBGC)
The agency that guarantees to pay employees a basic retirement benefit in the event that financial difficulties force a company to terminate or reduce employee pension benefits.

Employee Retirement Income Security Act (ERISA)
The 1974 act that increased the fiduciary responsibilities of pension plan trustees, established vesting rights and portability provisions, and established the Pension Benefit Guaranty Corporation (PBGC).

Defined Benefit

A *defined benefit plan* guarantees ("defines") a specified retirement benefit level to employees based typically on a combination of years of service and age as well as on the employee's earnings level (usually the five highest earnings years). For instance, an organization might guarantee a monthly pension payment of $1,500 to an employee retiring at age 65 with 30 years of service and an average salary over the final 5 years of $40,000. As Table 13.3 indicates, 50 percent of full-time employees in large and medium-size companies and 15 percent in small companies were covered by such plans in 1997 and 1996, respectively. This translates into less than 30 percent of employees in all companies being covered by these plans, although most salaried employees in large (mostly *Fortune* 100) companies are covered under defined benefit plans. The replacement ratio (pension payment/final salary) ranges from about 21 percent for a worker aged 55 with 30 years of service who earned $35,000 in her last year to about 36 percent for a 65-year-old worker with 40 years of service who earned the same amount. With Social Security added in, the ratio for the 65-year-old worker increases to about 77 percent.[18]

Defined benefit plans insulate employees from investment risk, which is borne by the company. In the event of severe financial difficulties that force the company to terminate or reduce employee pension benefits, the **Pension Benefit Guaranty Corporation (PBGC)** provides some protection of benefits. Established by the **Employee Retirement Income Security Act (ERISA)** of 1974, the PBGC guarantees a basic benefit, not necessarily complete pension benefit replacement, for employees who were eligible for pensions at the time of termination. It insures the retirement benefits of 43 million workers. The maximum monthly benefit is limited to the lesser of 1/12 of an employee's annual gross income during a PBGC-defined period or $3,392 in 2001. The PBGC is funded by an annual contribution of $19 per plan participant, plus an additional variable rate premium for underfunded plans that can reach $72 per participant.[19] Note that the PBGC does not guarantee health care benefits.

Defined Contribution

Unlike defined benefit plans, *defined contribution plans* do not promise a specific benefit level for employees upon retirement. Rather, an individual account is set up for each employee with a guaranteed size of contribution. The advantage of such plans for employers is that they shift investment risk to employees and present fewer administrative challenges because there is no need to calculate payments based on age and service and no need to make payments to the PBGC.[20] As Table 13.3 indicates, 57 percent of medium-size and large companies and 38 percent of small companies have such plans. Note that in small companies defined contribution plans are much more prevalent than defined benefit plans, perhaps because of employers' desire to avoid long-term obligations or perhaps because small companies, which tend to be younger, tend to adopt defined contribution plans. Many companies have both defined benefit and defined contribution plans.

There is a wide variety of defined contribution plans, a few of which are briefly described here. One of the simplest is a money purchase plan, under which an employer specifies a level of annual contribution (such as 10 percent of salary). At retirement age, the employee is entitled to the contributions plus the investment returns. The term "money purchase" stems from the fact that employees often use the money to purchase an annuity rather than taking it as a lump sum. Profit sharing plans and employee stock ownership plans are also often used as retirement vehicles. Both permit contributions (cash and stock, respectively) to vary from year to year, thus allowing employers to avoid fixed obligations that may be burdensome in difficult financial times. Section 401(k) plans (named after the tax code section) permit employees to defer compensation on a pretax basis. Annual contributions in 2000 were limited to $10,500 but will increase to $11,000 in 2002 and increase by $1,000 annually through 2005 and by $500 annually thereafter through 2010.[21]

Defined contribution plans continue to grow in importance. An important implication is that they put the responsibility for wise investing squarely on the shoulders of the employee. These investment decisions will become more critical because 401(k) plans continue to grow rapidly, and by the year 2012 they alone are expected to provide as much as 50 percent of total retirement income (up from about 15 percent in 1992).[22] Several factors affect the amount of income that will be available to an employee upon retirement. First, the earlier the age at which investments are made, the longer returns can accumulate. As Figure 13.2 shows, an annual investment of $3,000 made between ages 21 and 29 will be worth much more at age 65 than a similar investment made between ages 31 and 39. Second, different investments have different historical rates of return. Between 1946 and 1990, the average annual return was 11.4 percent for stocks, 5.1 percent for bonds, and 5.3 percent for cash (bank savings accounts).[23] As Figure 13.2 shows, if historical rates of return were to continue, an investment in a mix of 60 percent stock, 30 percent bonds, and 10 percent cash between the ages of 21 and 29 would be worth almost four times as much at age 65 as would the same amount invested in a bank savings account. A third consideration is the need to counteract investment risk by diversification because stock and bond prices can be volatile in the short run. Although stocks have the greatest historical rate of return, that is no guarantee of future performance, particularly over shorter time periods. Thus some investment advisers recommend a mix of stock, bonds, and cash, as shown in Figure 13.2, to reduce investment risk. Younger investors may wish to have more stock, while those closer to retirement age typically have less stock in their portfolios.

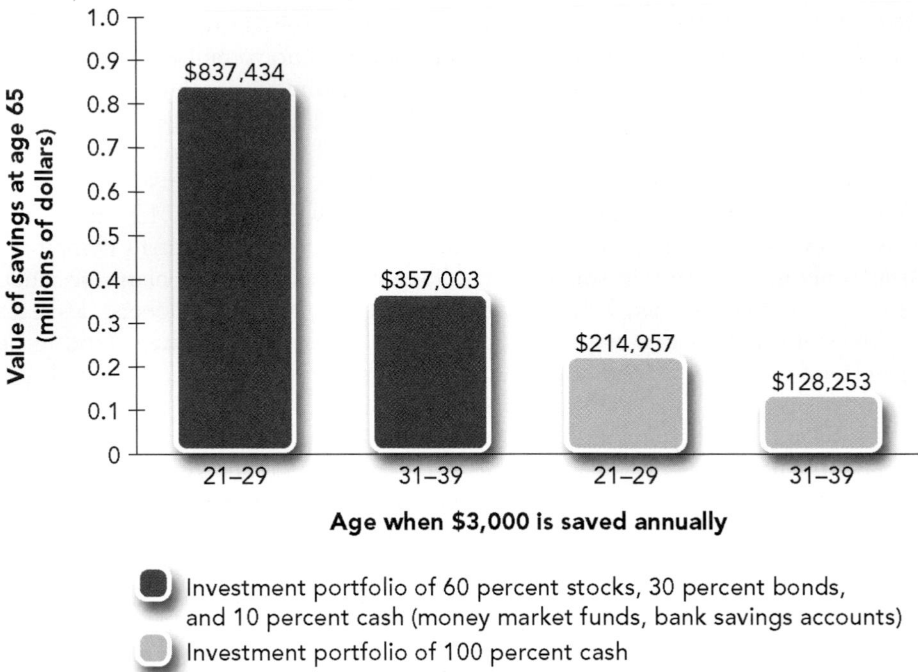

FIGURE 13.2
The Relationship of Retirement Savings to Age When Savings Begins and Type of Investment Portfolio

Funding, Communication, and Vesting Requirements

ERISA does not require organizations to have pension plans, but those that are set up must meet certain requirements. In addition to the termination provisions discussed earlier, plans must meet certain guidelines on management and funding. For example, employers are required to make yearly contributions that are sufficient to cover future obligations. (As noted previously, underfunded plans require higher premiums.) ERISA also specifies a number of reporting and disclosure requirements involving the IRS, the Department of Labor, and employees.[24] Employees, for example, must receive within 90 days after entering a plan a **summary plan description (SPD)** that describes the plan's funding, eligibility requirements, risks, and so forth. Upon request, an employer must also make available to an employee an individual benefit statement, which describes the employee's vested and unvested benefits. Obviously, employers may wish to provide such information on a regular basis anyway as a means of increasing the understanding and value employees attach to their benefits.

Summary plan description (SPD)
A reporting requirement of the Employee Retirement Income Security Act (ERISA) that obligates employers to describe the plan's funding, eligibility requirements, risks, and so forth within 90 days after an employee has entered the plan.

ERISA guarantees employees that when they become participants in a pension plan and work a specified minimum number of years, they earn a right to a pension upon retirement. These are referred to as *vesting rights*.[25] Vested employees have the right to their pension at retirement age, regardless of whether they remain with the employer until that time. Employee contributions to their own plans are always completely vested. The vesting of employer-funded pension benefits must take place under one of two schedules. Employers may choose to vest employees after five years; until that time, employers can provide zero vesting if they choose. Alternatively, employers may vest employees over a three- to seven-year period, with at least 20 percent vesting in the third year and each year thereafter. These two schedules represent minimum requirements; employers are free to vest employees more quickly. These are the two choices relevant to the majority of employers. However, so-called "top-heavy" plans, where pension benefits for "key" employees (like highly paid top managers) exceed a certain share of total pension benefits, require faster vesting for non-key employees. On the other hand, multi-employer pension plans need not provide vesting until after 10 years of employment.

These requirements were put in place to prevent companies from terminating employees before they reach retirement age or before they reach their length-of-service requirements in order to avoid paying pension benefits. It should also be noted that transferring employees or laying them off as a means of avoiding pension obligations is not legal either, even if such actions are motivated partly by business necessity.[26] On the other hand, employers are free to choose whichever of the two vesting schedules is most advantageous. For example, an employer that experiences high quit rates during the fourth and fifth years of employment may choose five-year vesting to minimize pension costs.

The traditional defined benefit pension plan discourages employee turnover or delays it until the employer can recoup the training investment in employees.[27] Even if an employee's pension benefit is vested, it is usually smaller if the employee changes employers, mainly because the size of the benefit depends on earnings in the final years with an employer. Consider an employee who earns $30,000 after 20 years and $60,000 after 40 years.[28] The employer pays an annual retirement benefit equal to 1.5 percent of final earnings times the number of years of service. If the employee stays with the employer for 40 years, the annual benefit level upon retirement would be $36,000 (.015 × $60,000 × 40). If, instead, the employee changes employers after 20 years (and has the same earnings progression), the retirement benefit from the first employer would be $9,000 (.015 × $30,000 × 20). The annual benefit from the second employer would be $18,000 (.015 × $60,000 × 20). Therefore, staying with one employer for 40 years would yield an annual retirement benefit of $36,000, versus a combined annual retirement benefit of $27,000 ($9,000 + $18,000) if the employee changes employers once. It has also been suggested that pensions are designed to encourage long-service employees, whose earnings growth may eventually exceed their productivity growth, to retire. This is consistent with the fact that retirement benefits reach their maximum at retirement age.[29]

The fact that in recent years many employers have sought to reduce their workforces through early retirement programs is also consistent with the notion that pensions are used to retain certain employees while encouraging others to leave. One early retirement program approach is to adjust years-of-service credit upward for employees willing to retire, resulting in a higher retirement benefit for them (and less monetary incentive to work). These workforce reductions may also be one indication of a broader trend toward employees becoming less likely to spend their entire careers with a single employer. On one hand, if more mobility across employers becomes necessary or desirable, the current pension system's incentives against (or penalties for) mobility may require modification. On the other hand, perhaps increased employee mobility will reinforce the continued trend toward defined contribution plans [like 401(k)s], which have greater portability (ease of transfer of funds) across employers.[30]

International Comparisons

About 45 percent of the U.S. private-sector labor force is covered by pension plans, compared with 100 percent in France, 92 percent in Switzerland, 42 percent in Germany, and 39 percent in Japan. Among those covered by pensions, U.S. workers are significantly less likely to be covered by defined benefit plans (28 percent) than Japanese workers (100 percent) or German workers (90 percent).

Pay for Time Not Worked

At first blush, paid vacation, holidays, sick leave, and so forth may not seem to make economic sense. The employer pays the employee for time not spent working, receiving no tangible production value in return. Therefore, some employers may see little direct advantage. Perhaps for this reason, a minimum number of vacation days is mandated by law in Western Europe. As many as 30 days of vacation is not uncommon for relatively new employees in Europe. By contrast, there is no legal minimum in the United States, but 10 days is typical for large companies. U.S. workers must typically be with an employer for 20 to 25 years before they receive as much paid vacation as their Western European counterparts. In both the United States and Western Europe, around 10 paid holidays are typical, regardless of length of service.[31]

Sick leave programs often provide full salary replacement for a limited period of time, usually not exceeding 26 weeks. The amount of sick leave is often based on length of service, accumulating with service (one day per month, for example). Sick leave policies need to be carefully structured to avoid providing employees with the wrong incentives. For example, if sick leave days disappear at the end of the year (rather than accumulate), a "use it or lose it" mentality may develop among employees, contributing to greater absenteeism. Organizations have developed a number of measures to counter this.[32] Some allow sick days to accumulate, then pay employees for the number of sick days when they retire or resign. Employers may also attempt to communicate to their employees that accumulated sick leave is better saved to use as a bridge to long-term disability, because the replacement rate (the ratio of sick leave or disability payments to normal salary) for the former is typically higher. Sick leave payments may equal 100 percent of usual salary, whereas the replacement ratio for long-term disability might be 50 percent, so the more sick leave accumulated, the longer an employee can avoid dropping to 50 percent of usual pay when unable to work.

Although vacation and other paid leave programs help attract and retain employees, there is a cost to providing time off with pay, especially in a global economy. The fact that vacation and other paid leave practices differ across countries contributes to the differences in labor costs described in Chapter 11. Consider that, on average, in manufacturing, German workers work 500 fewer hours per year than their U.S. counterparts, who work 1,978 hours per year. Even Japanese workers, previously known for their long hours, now work less than U.S. workers. (See Figure 13.3.) In other words, German workers are at work approximately 13 fewer weeks per year than their Japanese counterparts. It is perhaps not surprising then that German manufacturers have looked outside Germany in many cases for alternative production sites.

Family and Medical Leave Act
The 1993 act that requires employers with 50 or more employees to provide up to 12 weeks of unpaid leave after childbirth or adoption; to care for a seriously ill child, spouse, or parent; or for an employee's own serious illness.

Family-Friendly Policies

To ease employees' conflicts between work and nonwork, organizations may use *family-friendly policies* such as family leave policies and child care. Although the programs discussed here would seem to be targeted to a particular group of employees, these programs often have "spillover effects" on other employees, who see them as symbolizing a general corporate concern for human resources, thus promoting loyalty even among employee groups that do not use the programs.[33]

Since 1993 the **Family and Medical Leave Act** requires organizations with 50 or more employees within a 75-mile radius to provide as much as 12 weeks of unpaid

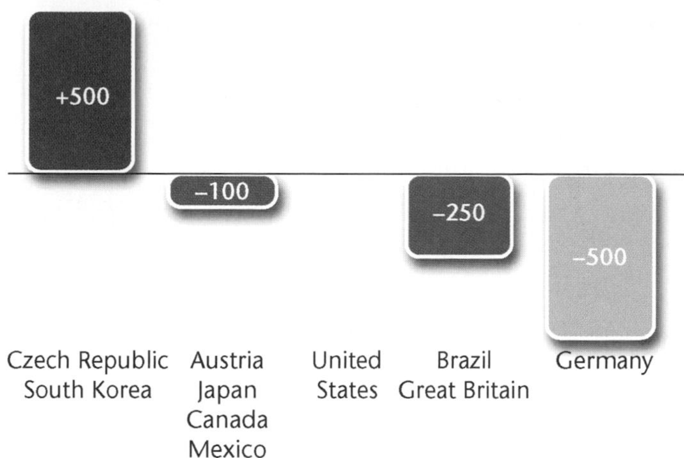

SOURCE: *Key Indicators of the Labor Market 2001–2002* (Geneva, Switzerland: International Labour Office, 2001).

FIGURE 13.3
Normal Annual Hours Worked in Manufacturing Relative to United States

leave after childbirth or adoption; to care for a seriously ill child, spouse, or parent; or for an employee's own serious illness.[34] Employees are guaranteed the same or a comparable job on their return to work. Employees with less than one year of service or who work under 25 hours per week or who are among the 10 percent highest paid are not covered.

Many employers had already taken steps to deal with this issue, partly to help attract and retain key employees. As noted by one source, only "about 4 percent of American families fit the stereotypical image of a father who works outside the home and a mother who stays home and takes care of the children."[35]

The United States still offers significantly less unpaid leave than most Western European countries and Japan. Moreover, paid family leave remains rare in the United States (fewer than 5 percent are eligible for paid leave, despite some state laws), in even sharper contrast to Western Europe and Japan, where it is typically mandated by law.[36] Until the passage of the Americans with Disabilities Act, the only applicable law was the Pregnancy Discrimination Act of 1978, which requires employers that offer disability plans to treat pregnancy as they would any other disability.

Early experience with the Family and Medical Leave Act suggests that a majority of those opting for this benefit fail to take the full allotment of time. This is especially the case among female executives. Many of these executives find they do not enjoy maternity leave as much as they expected they would and miss the challenges associated with their careers. Others fear that their careers would be damaged in the long run by missing out on opportunities that might arise while they are out on leave.[37]

Child Care

U.S. companies increasingly provide some form of child care support to their employees. This support comes in several forms that vary in their degree of organizational involvement.[38] The lowest level of involvement, offered by 36 percent of companies, is when an organization supplies and helps employees collect information about the cost and quality of available child care. At the next level, organizations provide vouchers or discounts for employees to use at existing child care facilities (5 percent of companies). At the highest level, firms provide child care at or near their worksites (9 percent of companies). Toyota's Child Development Program provides 24-hours-a-day care for children of workers at its Georgetown, Kentucky, plant. This facility is designed to meet the needs of employees working evening and night shifts who want their children to be on the same schedule. In this facility, the children are kept awake all night. At the end of the night shift, the parents pick up their children and the whole family goes home to bed.[39]

An organization's decision to staff its own child care facility should not be taken lightly. It is typically a costly venture with important liability concerns. Moreover, the results, in terms of reducing absenteeism and enhancing productivity, are often mixed. One reason for this is that many organizations are "jumping on the day care bandwagon" without giving much thought to the best form of assistance for their specific employees.[40] Organizations that fail to do an adequate needs assessment often wind up purchasing the wrong alternative. For example, one *Fortune* 500 company found that less than 2 percent of its workforce used a flexible spending account that had been adopted as the chief company policy on child care. The waste and inefficiency of this practice could have been avoided had a more thorough needs analysis been conducted before the program was implemented.[41]

As an alternative example, Memphis-based First Tennessee Bank, which was losing 1,500 days of productivity a year because of child care problems, considered creating its own on-site day care center. Before acting, however, the company surveyed its employees. This survey indicated that the only real problem with day care occurred when the parents' regular day care provisions fell through because of sickness on the part of the child or provider. Based on these findings, the bank opted to establish a sick-child care center, which was less costly and smaller in scope than a full-time center and yet still solved the employees' major problem. As a result, absenteeism dropped so dramatically that the program paid for itself in the first nine months of operation.[42]

Finding and Keeping the Best Employees

PriceWaterhouseCoopers (PWC), the accounting and consulting firm, has seen many of its clients turn to cost cutting as the economy slows. That, in turn, has led PWC to examine its own expenses, including those in the area of employee benefits. But that overhaul has not touched one key benefit: flexible work arrangements. Employees are still free to leave work early or to telecommute to help them balance work and nonwork responsibilities. Even as employers slash jobs and cut small perquisites such as free food and drinks, they continue to provide programs that help employees juggle work and personal lives—mostly because they believe these programs help retain valued workers, who are being asked to do more as workforce reductions eliminate positions but not necessarily work. At Cisco Systems, which has also faced difficult financial times, telecommuting continues to be a core benefit, and its day care center at company headquarters in San Jose, California, continues to operate at capacity. Cisco feels that these benefits enhance productivity, which is all the more important given difficult times. These companies are looking ahead to a future that will once again bring growth; they want to be ready by retaining a group of dedicated and productive employees to take advantage of that opportunity when it comes.

SOURCE: "Benefits and the Bottom Line," *The News and Observer,* Raleigh, NC (October 14, 2001).

Managing Benefits: Employer Objectives and Strategies

Although the regulatory environment places some important constraints on benefits decisions, employers retain significant discretion and need to evaluate the payoff of such decisions.[43] As discussed earlier, however, this evaluation needs to recognize that employees have come to expect certain things from employers. Employers who do not meet these expectations run the risk of violating what has been called an "implicit contract" between the employer and its workers. If employees believe their employers feel little commitment to their welfare, they can hardly be expected to commit themselves to the company's success.

Clearly, there is much room for progress in the evaluation of benefits decisions. Despite some of the obvious reasons for benefits—group discounts, regulation, and minimizing compensation-related taxes—organizations do not do as well as they could in spelling out what they want their benefits package to achieve and evaluating how well they are succeeding. Research suggests that most organizations do not have written benefits objectives.[44] Obviously, without clear objectives to measure progress, evaluation is difficult (and less likely to occur). Table 13.4 provides an example of one organization's written benefits objectives.

TABLE 13.4

One Company's Written Benefits Objectives

- To establish and maintain an employee benefit program that is based primarily on the employees' needs for leisure time and on protection against the risks of old age, loss of health, and loss of life.
- To establish and maintain an employee benefit program that complements the efforts of employees on their own behalf.
- To evaluate the employee benefit plan annually for its effect on employee morale and productivity, giving consideration to turnover, unfilled positions, attendance, employees' complaints, and employees' opinions.
- To compare the employee benefit plan annually with that of other leading companies in the same field and to maintain a benefit plan with an overall level of benefits based on cost per employee that falls within the second quintile of these companies.
- To maintain a level of benefits for nonunion employees that represents the same level of expenditures per employee as for union employees.
- To determine annually the costs of new, changed, and existing programs as percentages of salaries and wages and to maintain these percentages as much as possible.
- To self-fund benefits to the extent that a long-run cost savings can be expected for the firm and catastrophic losses can be avoided.
- To coordinate all benefits with social insurance programs to which the company makes payments.
- To provide benefits on a noncontributory basis except for dependent coverage, for which employees should pay a portion of the cost.
- To maintain continual communications with all employees concerning benefit programs.

SOURCE: *Employee Benefits,* 3rd ed., Burton T. Beam, Jr., and John J. McFadden. © 1992 by Dearborn Financial Publishing, Inc. Published by Dearborn Financial Publishing, Inc., Chicago.

TABLE 13.5
Employee Benefits by Category, Cost and Total Compensation

	PERCENTAGE OF PAYROLL	COST IN DOLLARS
Legally required	9.1%	$3,458
Retirement and savings plans	6.8	2,584
Medical and other insurance	9.7	3,686
Payments for time not worked	10.7	4,066
Miscellaneous[a]	0.7	266
Total Benefits	36.8	14,060

[a] Includes employee services and extra cash payment categories.

SOURCE: Adapted from the U.S. Chamber of Commerce Research Center, *2000 Employee Benefits Study* (Washington, DC: U.S. Chamber of Commerce, April 2001).

Surveys and Benchmarking

As with cash compensation, an important element of benefits management is knowing what the competition is doing. Survey information on benefits packages is available from private consultants and, somewhat less regularly, the Bureau of Labor Statistics.[45] BLS data of the sort in Table 13.3 and the more detailed information on programs and provisions available from consultants are useful in designing competitive benefits packages. To compete effectively in the product market, cost information is also necessary. A widely used source is the annual survey conducted by the U.S. Chamber of Commerce, which provides information on benefits costs for specific categories as well as breakdowns by industry and organization size. Table 13.5 shows some of these data for 2000.

Cost Control

In thinking about cost control strategies, it is useful to consider several factors. First, the larger the cost of a benefit category, the greater the opportunity for savings. Second, the growth trajectory of the benefit category is also important: even if costs are currently acceptable, the rate of growth may result in serious costs in the future. Third, cost containment efforts can only work to the extent that the employer has significant discretion in choosing how much to spend in a benefit category. Much of the cost of legally required benefits (like Social Security) is relatively fixed, which constrains cost reduction efforts. Even with legally required benefits, however, employers can take actions to limit costs because of "experience ratings," which impose higher taxes on employers with high rates of unemployment or workers' compensation claims.

One benefit—medical and other insurance—stands out as a target for cost control for two reasons. Its costs are substantial; they have, except for the past few years, been growing rapidly, and this growth is expected to continue. Second, employers have many options for attacking costs and improving quality.

Health Care: Controlling Costs and Improving Quality

As Table 13.6 indicates, the United States spends more on health care than any other country in the world. U.S. health care expenditures have gone from 5.3 percent of the

TABLE 13.6
Health Care Costs and Outcomes in Various Countries

	LIFE EXPECTANCY	INFANT MORTALITY RATE[a]	HEALTH EXPENDITURES AS A PERCENTAGE OF GDP
Japan	81	3.9	7.4%
Korea	74	7.9	6.0[b]
Canada	79	5.1	9.3
United Kingdom	78	5.6	6.9
France	79	4.5	9.6
Germany	77	4.8	10.6
Mexico	72	26.2	4.7[b]
United States	77	6.8	14.0

[a]Per 1,000 live births.
[b]1997

SOURCE: Organization for Economic Cooperation and Development, *OECD Health Data 99* (Paris: 1999); U.S. Census Bureau, International Database, www.census.gov.

gross national product ($27 billion) in 1960 to 14 percent (approximately $1 trillion) in 1998. Yet the percentage of full-time workers receiving job-related health benefits has declined, with over 40 million Americans uninsured as of 1999.[46] The United States also compares poorly with Japan and Western Europe on measures of life expectancy and infant mortality.

Unlike workers in most Western European countries, who have nationalized health systems, the majority of Americans receiving health insurance get it through their (or a family member's) employers.[47] Consequently, health insurance, like pensions, discourages employee turnover because not all employers provide health insurance benefits.[48] Not surprisingly, the fact that many Americans receive coverage through their employers has meant that many efforts at controlling costs and increasing quality and coverage have been undertaken by employers. These efforts, broadly referred to as managed care, fall into six major categories: (1) plan design, (2) use of alternative providers, (3) use of alternative funding methods, (4) claims review, (5) education and prevention, and (6) external cost control systems.[49] Examples appear in Table 13.7.

Health maintenance organization (HMO)
A health care plan that provides benefits on a prepaid basis for employees who are required to use only HMO medical service providers.

Preferred provider organization (PPO)
A group of health care providers who contract with employers, insurance companies, and so forth to provide health care at a reduced fee.

One trend in plan design has been to shift costs to employees through the use of deductibles, coinsurance, exclusions and limitations, and maximum benefits.[50] These costs can be structured such that employees act on incentives to shift to less expensive plans.[51] Another trend has been to focus on reducing, rather than shifting, costs through such activities as preadmission testing and second surgical opinions. The use of alternative providers like **health maintenance organizations (HMOs)** and **preferred provider organizations (PPOs)** has also increased. HMOs differ from more traditional providers by focusing on preventive care and outpatient treatment, requiring employees to use only HMO services, and providing benefits on a prepaid basis. Many HMOs pay physicians and other health care workers a flat salary instead of using the traditional fee-for-service system, under which a physician's pay may depend on the number of patients seen. Paying on a salary basis is intended to reduce incentives for physicians to schedule more patient visits or medical procedures than

TABLE 13.7

Ways Employers Use Managed Care to Control Health Care Costs

Plan design
Cost shifting to employees
Deductibles
Coinsurance
Exclusions and limitations
Maximum benefits
Cost reduction
Preadmission testing
Second surgical opinions
Coordination of benefits
Alternatives to hospital stays (such as home health care)
Alternative providers
Health maintenance organizations (HMOs)
Preferred provider organizations (PPOs)
Alternative funding methods
Self-funding
Claims review
Health education and preventive care
Wellness programs
Employee assistance programs (EAPs)
Encouragement of external control systems
National Council on Health Planning and Development
Employer coalitions

SOURCE: Adapted from B.T. Beam Jr. and J.J. McFadden, *Employee Benefits,* 3rd ed. (Chicago: Dearborn Financial Publishing, 1992).

might be necessary. (Of course, there is the risk that incentives will be reduced too much, resulting in inadequate access to medical procedures and specialists.) PPOs are essentially groups of health care providers that contract with employers, insurance companies, and so forth to provide health care at a reduced fee. They differ from HMOs in that they do not provide benefits on a prepaid basis and employees often are not required to use the preferred providers. Instead, employers may provide incentives for employees to choose, for example, a physician who participates in the plan. In general, PPOs seem to be less expensive than traditional delivery systems but more expensive than HMOs.[52] Another trend in employers' attempts to control costs has been to vary required employee contributions based on the employee's health and risk factors rather than charging each employee the same premium.

Employee Wellness Programs. Employee wellness programs (EWPs) focus on changing behaviors both on and off work time that could eventually lead to future health problems. EWPs are preventive in nature; they attempt to manage health care costs by decreasing employees' needs for services. Typically, these programs aim at specific health risks such as high blood pressure, high cholesterol levels, smoking, and obesity. They also try to promote positive health influences such as physical exercise and good nutrition.

EWPs are either passive or active. Passive programs use little or no outreach to individuals, nor do they provide ongoing support to motivate them to use the resources. Active wellness centers assume that behavior change requires not only awareness and opportunity but support and reinforcement.

One example of a passive wellness program is a health education program. Health education programs have two central goals: raising awareness levels of health-related issues and informing people on health-related topics. In these kinds of programs, a health educator usually conducts classes or lunchtime lectures (or coordinates outside speakers). The program may also have various promotions (like an annual mile run or a "smoke-out") and include a newsletter that reports on current health issues. Health education programs are the most common form of employee wellness program.[53]

Another kind of passive employee wellness program is a fitness facility. In this kind of program, the company sets up a center for physical fitness equipped with aerobic and muscle-building exercise machines and staffed with certified athletic trainers. The facility is publicized within the organization, and employees are free to use it on their own time. Aetna, for example, has created five state-of-the-art health clubs that serve over 7,500 workers.[54] Northwestern Mutual Life's fitness facilities are open 24 hours a day to its 3,300 employees.[55] Health education classes related to smoking cessation and weight loss may be offered in addition to the facilities.

Although fitness facility programs are usually more expensive than health education programs, both are classified as passive because they rely on individual employees to identify their problems and take corrective action. In contrast, active wellness centers assume that behavior change also requires encouragement and assistance. One kind of active wellness center is the outreach and follow-up model. This type of wellness center contains all the features of a passive model, but it also has counselors who handle one-on-one outreach and provide tailored, individualized programs for employees. Typically, tailored programs obtain baseline measures on various indicators (weight, blood pressure, lung capacity, and so on) and measure individuals' progress relative to these indicators over time. The programs set goals and provide small, symbolic rewards to individuals who meet their goals.

This encouragement needs to be particularly targeted to employees in high-risk categories (like those who smoke, are overweight, or have high blood pressure) for two reasons. First, a small percentage of employees create a disproportionate amount of health care costs; therefore, targeted interventions are more efficient. Second, research shows that those in high-risk categories are the most likely to perceive barriers (like family problems or work overload)[56] to participating in company-sponsored fitness programs. Thus untargeted interventions are likely to miss the people that most need to be included.

Research on these different types of wellness centers leads to several conclusions.[57] First, the costs of health education programs are significantly less than those associated with either fitness facility programs or the follow-up model. Second, as indicated in Figure 13.4, all three models are effective in reducing the risk factors associated with cardiovascular disease (obesity, high blood pressure, smoking, and lack of exercise). However, the follow-up model is significantly better than the other two in reducing the risk factors.

Whether the added cost of follow-up programs compared with health education programs is warranted is a judgment that only employers, employees, and unions can make. However, employers like Sony and Quaker Oats believe that incentives are worth the extra cost, and their employees can receive up to several hundred dollars for reducing their risk factors. There appears to be no such ambiguity associated with the fitness facility model, however. This type of wellness center costs as much or more than the follow-up model but is only as effective as the health education model. Providing a fitness facility that does not include systematic outreach and routine long-term follow-up to assist people with risk factors is not cost-effective in reducing

FIGURE 13.4
The Cost and Effectiveness of Three Different Types of Employee Wellness Designs

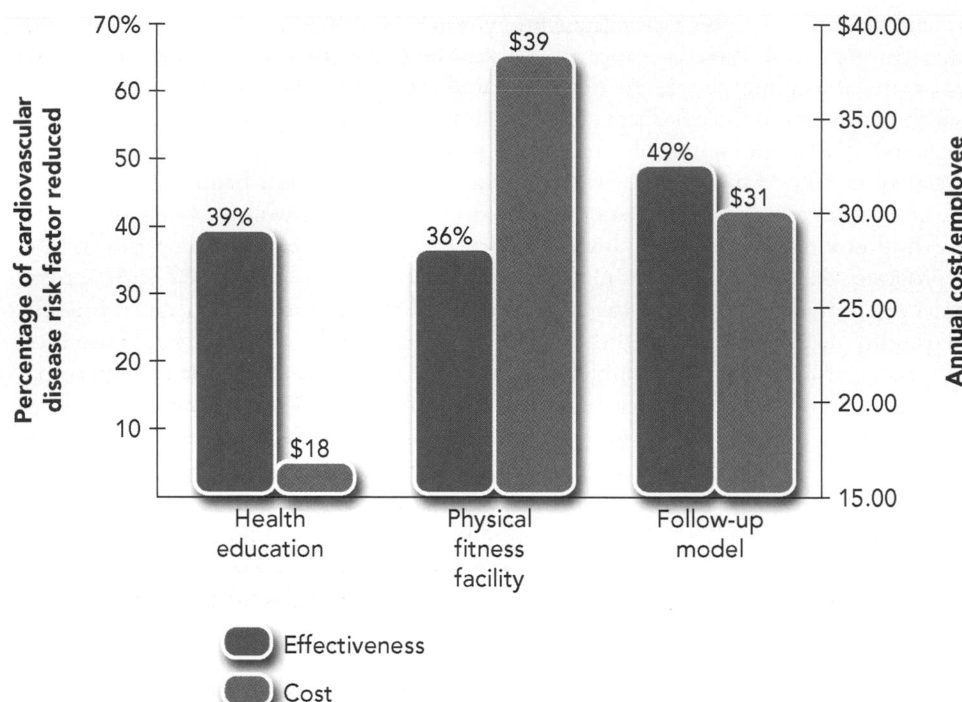

SOURCE: J.C. Erfurt, A. Foote, and M.A. Heirich, "The Cost Effectiveness of Worksite Wellness Programs for Hypertension Control, Weight Loss, Smoking Cessation and Exercise," *Personnel Psychology* 45 (1992), pp. 5–27. Used with permission.

health risks. "Attendants may sit in the fitness center like the 'Maytag repairman' waiting for people to come."[58]

Health Care Costs and Quality: Progress and Prospects. Efforts to control health care cost growth have borne fruit. Whereas from 1980 through 1993 there was double-digit annual growth in health care costs, between 1993 and 1996 employer expenditures on health care actually fell by nearly 20 percent. However, these reductions proved to be temporary, as costs increased 24 percent from 1996 to 2000, with costs in 2001 alone projected to grow 11.5 percent by Hewitt Associates. A report by the Health Care Financing Administration projects that health care spending in the United States will continue to grow. Why? Because 85 percent of working Americans with health care are already covered by managed care, so few additional savings can be obtained by further switches. Moreover, many managed care companies have existed on small profit margins, but this cannot continue indefinitely.

Two important phenomena are often encountered in cost control efforts. First, piecemeal programs may not work well because steps to control one aspect (such as medical cost shifting) may lead employees to "migrate" to other programs that provide medical treatment at no cost to them (like workers' compensation). Second, there is often a so-called Pareto group, which refers to a small percentage (perhaps 20 percent) of employees being responsible for generating the majority (often 60 to 80 percent) of health care costs. Obviously, cost control efforts will be more successful to the extent that the costs generated by the Pareto group can be identified and managed effectively.[59]

Although cost control will continue to require a good deal of attention, there is a growing emphasis on monitoring health care quality, which has been described as "the next battlefield." A major focus is on identifying best medical practices by measuring and monitoring the relative success of alternative treatment strategies using large-scale databases and research.[60] In addition, employers increasingly cooperate with one another to develop "report cards" on health care provider organizations to facilitate better choices by their employers and to receive improved health care. General Motors, Ford, and Chrysler, for example, have developed this type of system and made it Web-accessible.[61]

Staffing Responses to Control Benefits Cost Growth

Employers may change staffing practices to control benefits costs. First, because benefits costs are fixed (in that they do not usually go up with hours worked), the benefits cost per hour can be reduced by having employees work more hours. However, there are drawbacks to having employees work more hours. The Fair Labor Standards Act (FLSA) requires that nonexempt employees be paid time-and-a-half for hours in excess of 40 per week. Yet the decline in U.S. work hours tapered off in the late 1940s; work hours have actually gone up since then. It is estimated that Americans were working the equivalent of one month longer in 1987 than they were in 1969, and these higher levels continued into the 1990s.[62] Increased benefits were identified as one of the major reasons for this.

A second possible effect of FLSA regulations (though this is more speculative) is that organizations will try to have their employees classified as exempt whenever possible. The growth in the number of salaried workers (many of whom are exempt) may also reflect an effort by organizations to limit the benefits cost per hour without having to pay overtime. A third potential effect is the growth in part-time employment and the use of temporary workers, which may be a response to rising benefits costs.[63] Part-time workers are less likely to receive benefits than full-time workers although labor market shortages in recent years have reduced this difference.[64] Benefits for temporary workers are also usually quite limited.

Third, employers may be more likely to classify workers as independent contractors rather than employees, which eliminates the employer's obligation to provide legally required employee benefits. However, the Internal Revenue Service (IRS) scrutinizes such decisions carefully, as Microsoft and other companies have discovered. Microsoft was compelled to reclassify a group of workers as employees (rather than as independent contractors) and to grant them retroactive benefits. The IRS looks at several factors, including the permanency of the relationship between employer and worker, how much control the employer exercises in directing the worker, and whether the worker offers services to only that employer. Permanency, control, and dealing with a single employer are viewed by the IRS as suggestive of an employment relationship.

Nature of the Workforce

Although general considerations such as cost control and "protection against the risks of old age and loss of health and life" (see Table 13.4) are important, employers must also consider the specific demographic composition and preferences of their current workforces in designing their benefits packages.

At a broad level, basic demographic factors such as age and sex can have important consequences for the types of benefits employees want. For example, an older workforce is more likely to be concerned about (and use) medical coverage, life insurance, and pensions. A workforce with a high percentage of women of childbearing age may

COMPETING THROUGH HIGH-PERFORMANCE WORK SYSTEMS

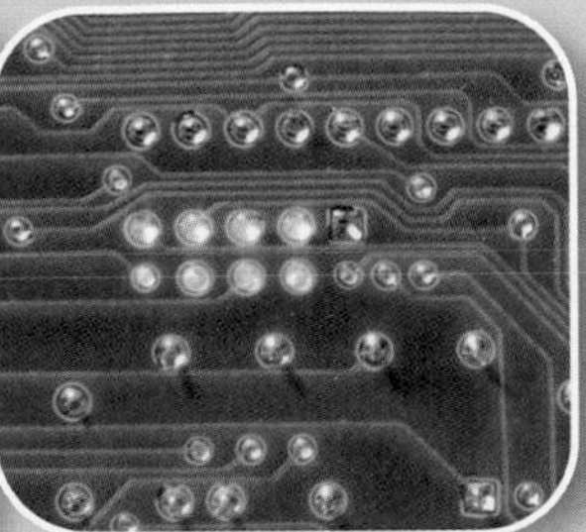

What Health Care Benefits Do Employees Want?

Today's employers face an increasingly complicated challenge as they try to determine what kinds of benefits their employees want and need. With more workers staying on the job past traditional retirement age, with more parents looking for flexible hours and other benefits, and with everyone trying to save money on a tight budget, it can be an employer's nightmare to figure out what's best for everyone.

One trend whose time has come is a consumer-oriented benefits plan, particularly for health care. Under these plans, patients—employees—would be more involved in their own treatment decisions than they have in the past. These decisions, of course, affect costs. But experts believe that educating people to make their own choices is a win–win situation. "When people are more engaged in their care, they end up using fewer resources because they have a sense of comfort and control," notes Jonathan Lord, chief clinical strategy and innovation officer for Humana, a managed care company that plans to use the Internet to engage patient–consumers directly.

WellPoint, another managed care company, discovered through surveys and other research that when premiums went up, healthy customers—especially individuals or members of small groups—simply dropped coverage instead of paying the price. So the firm decided to find out what people really wanted before redesigning their program. "In the past, we'd ask what people want covered, we'd give it to actuaries, they'd price it, and that's what we'd sell. This [new] program is about defining what people are willing to spend out of pocket, especially people who are healthy, then creating benefits that fit within those price points. It's the opposite of what we used to do." WellPoint came up with two plans: PlanScape for individual insurance purchasers and FlexScape for groups of 2 to 50. With PlanScape, the higher the monthly premium is, the richer the customer's benefits package will be and the lower the out-of-pocket expenses will be. FlexScape, on the other hand, lets an employee become a retail purchaser, choosing from among a series of benefit packages offered by the employer.

A third trend involves employers who are now insisting on health care plans that provide disease management programs. Textron, General Motors, Coca-Cola, and Georgia Power are among the large companies now in this category. These programs include home telephone calls to patients from nurses, checking on everything from blood pressure to weight gain. Why is this significant? "Sixty percent of my costs over the next decade will be basically in a dozen to 18 chronic diseases," remarks Allen Feezor, head of health benefits for the California Public Employees' Retirement System. His system alone employs 1.2 million insured workers.

SOURCE: M.D. Dalzell, "Where Will Health Plans Find the Next Generation of Savings?" *Managed Care*, September 2001, **www.managedcaremag.com**; M. Freudenheim, "A Changing World Is Forcing Changes on Managed Care," *The New York Times* (July 2, 2001), **www.nytimes.com**.

care more about disability leave. Young, unmarried men and women often have less interest in benefits generally, preferring higher wages and salaries.

Although some general conclusions about employee preferences can be drawn based on demographics, more finely tuned assessments of employee benefit preferences need to be done. One approach is to use marketing research methods to assess

COMPETING BY MEETING STAKEHOLDERS' NEEDS

Companies Learn That It Pays to Keep Employees Fit

Physical fitness—or at least wellness—*does* matter, as more and more companies and their insurers are learning. A healthy workforce means better productivity and fewer workdays lost, not to mention reduced medical costs by keeping injuries and illnesses to a minimum. A study published by the Presidents' Council on Physical Fitness and Sports found that fitness programs provided by companies saved from $1.15 to $5.52 for every dollar spent.

At 3Com, the network communications company, employees spend their lunch hours at the WellCom Center, a 13,500-square foot fitness facility right on site. There they can cycle, walk a treadmill, lift weights, take a fitness class, or relax in the sauna. Or they can play a game of basketball or beach volleyball outside. Afterward, they can cool off at the juice bar with a fruit smoothie. The center is open 24 hours a day, seven days a week, to meet the needs of employees who work at all hours. More than 40 percent of the 4,200 workers at 3Com are WellCom members, and 70 percent take advantage of the center's seminars on wellness, smoking cessation, or weight loss. "A healthy workforce is good for employees and good for 3Com," says Peter Sandman, a manager of strategic planning at the company. "It helps recruiting and it helps retention, especially in a competitive environment like Silicon Valley [California]."

Applied Materials Inc. of Santa Clara, California, conducted its own study that showed that for fitness center participants, medical payments were reduced by 20 percent, hospital admissions were 70 percent lower, costs for accident-related disability claims were 30 percent less, and workers' compensation claims were 79 percent less than those of employees who didn't use the company's fitness center. Even a five-minute stretch break has been shown to reduce strains and sprains by as much as 65 percent. "Just moving and getting away from their PC makes them feel better," says Judy Webster, director of corporate wellness for the company.

Boeing's health care package also includes access to its fitness centers as part of its overall recreation program. "When you're happy and healthy, you're able to perform at your best," explains the aircraft manufacturer's website. The recreation program includes indoor and outdoor facilities as well as discount packages for sports and cultural events. These companies have embraced the wisdom of the old adage, "an ounce of prevention is worth a pound of cure," and it has literally paid off.

SOURCE: Boeing website, **www.boeing.com**, accessed October 30, 2001; D. Beck, "Your Company Needs Its Own Best Practices," *Career Journal* from *The Wall Street Journal* (July 30–August 5, 2001), **www.careerjournal.com**; M. Chase, "Healthy Assets," *The Wall Street Journal* (May 1. 2000), **http://interactive.wsj**.

employees' preferences the same way consumers' demands for products and services are assessed.[65] Methods include personal interviews, focus groups, and questionnaires. Relevant questions might include

- What benefits are most important to you?
- If you could choose one new benefit, what would it be?
- If you were given *x* dollars for benefits, how would you spend it?

TABLE 13.8

A Field Guide to High-Tech Perks

Company	Perk
Sun Microsystems Inc.	Headquarters offers sun rooms with pool tables, basketball and volleyball courts, fitness equipment, and showers. "All the accoutrements of a university," says spokesman Jeremy Barnish.
Yahoo! Inc.	Office attire for cofounder David Fil is typically "T-shirts, shorts, and bare feet," says Diane Hunt, director of corporate communications.
Excite Inc.	This Internet firm is a round-the-clock, seven-day-a-week operation. Technical people "easily telecommute and work outside standard business hours—including East Coast hours," says spokeswoman Melissa Walia.
Qualcomm Inc.	Employees "go off on one-month junkets," says John Major, executive vice president, who adds, "I've never seen long pants on my chief engineer."
Adobe Systems Inc.	Employees get a three-week paid sabbatical every five years. And "a really neat benefit is everybody in the building has an office with a door," says Linda White, spokeswoman.

SOURCE: Q. Hardy, "Aloft in a Career without Fetters," *The Wall Street Journal* (September 29, 1998), p. B1. Reproduced with permission via Copyright Clearance Center.

As with surveys generally, care must be taken not to raise employee expectations regarding future changes. If the employer is not prepared to act on the employees' input, surveying may do more harm than good.

The preceding discussion may imply that the current makeup of the workforce is a given, but such is not the case. As discussed earlier, the benefits package may influence the composition of the workforce. For example, a benefits package that has strong medical benefits and pensions may be particularly attractive to older people or those with families. An attractive pension plan may be a way to attract workers who wish to make a long-term commitment to an organization. Where turnover costs are high, this type of strategy may have some appeal. On the other hand, a company that has very lucrative health care benefits may attract and retain people with high health care costs. Sick leave provisions may also affect the composition of the workforce. Organizations need to think about the signals their benefits packages send and the implications of these signals for workforce composition. In this vein, the benefits shown in Table 13.8 are designed to attract a particular type of employee—those in the Silicon Valley information technology labor market.

Communicating with Employees

Effective communication of benefits information to employees is critical if employers are to realize sufficient returns on their benefits investments. Research makes it clear that current employees and job applicants often have a very poor idea of what benefits provisions are already in place and the cost or market value of those benefits. One study asked employees to estimate both the amount contributed by the employer to their medical insurance and what it would cost the employees to provide their own health insurance. Table 13.9 shows that employees significantly underestimated both the cost and market value of their medical benefits. In the case of family coverage,

TABLE 13.9

Employee Perceptions versus Actual Cost and Market Value of Employer Contributions to Employee Medical Insurance

	EMPLOYER CONTRIBUTION			MARKET VALUE[a]		
COVERAGE	ACTUAL	EMPLOYEE PERCEPTION	RATIO	ACTUAL	EMPLOYEE PERCEPTION	RATIO
Individual	$34	$23	68%	$ 61	$37	61%
Family	64	24	38	138	43	31

Note: Dollar values in table represent means across three different insurance carriers for individual coverage and three different carriers for family coverage.

[a]Defined as the amount a nonemployee would have to pay to obtain the same level of coverage.

SOURCE: Adapted from M. Wilson, G.B. Northcraft, and M.A. Neale, "The Perceived Value of Fringe Benefits," *Personnel Psychology* 38 (1985), pp. 309–20. Used with permission.

employees estimated that the employer contributed $24, only 38 percent of the employer's actual contribution. This employer was receiving a very poor return on its benefits investment: $0.38 for every $1.00 spent.[66]

The situation with job applicants is no better. One study of MBAs found that 46 percent believed that benefits added 15 percent or less on top of direct payroll. Not surprisingly, perhaps, benefits were dead last on the applicants' priority lists in making job choices.[67] A study of undergraduate business majors found similar results, with benefits ranked 15th (out of 18) in importance in evaluating jobs. These results must be interpreted with caution, however. Some research suggests that job attributes can be ranked low in importance, not because they are unimportant per se, but because all employers are perceived to be about the same on that attribute. If some employers offered noticeably poorer benefits, the importance of benefits could become much greater.

Organizations can help remedy the problem of applicants' and employees' lack of knowledge about benefits. One study found that employees' awareness of benefits information was significantly increased through several media, including memoranda, question-and-answer meetings, and detailed brochures. The increased awareness, in turn, contributed to significant increases in benefits satisfaction. Another study suggests, however, that increased employee knowledge of benefits can have a positive or negative effect, depending on the nature of the benefits package. For example, there was a negative, or inverse, correlation between cost to the employee and benefits satisfaction overall, but the correlation was more strongly negative among employees with greater knowledge of their benefits.[68] The implication is that employees will be least satisfied with their benefits if their cost is high and they are well informed.

One thing an employer should consider with respect to written benefits communication is that over 27 million employees in the United States may be functionally illiterate. Of course, there are many alternative ways to communicate benefits information. (See Table 13.10.) Nevertheless, most organizations spend less than $10 per year per employee to communicate information about benefits, and almost all of this is spent on written communication rather than on more personalized or "innovative" approaches such as benefits fairs, videos, and Web-based efforts. Considering that organizations spend an average of nearly $15,000 per worker per year on benefits, together with the complex nature of many benefits and the poor understanding of most employees, the typical communication effort seems woefully inadequate.[69] Organizations are spending less than $1 to communicate every $1,000 in benefits.

Rather than a single standard benefits package for all employees, flexible benefit

TABLE 13.10
Benefits Communication Techniques

Word of mouth	Booklets
Employee meetings	Computerized statements
Manuals	Letters to employees
Paycheck inserts	Posters
Annual reports	Check stubs
Personal counseling	Benefits fairs
Interactive computers	Annual benefits review
Television and videotapes	Slide presentations
Benefits quizzes	Telephone hot lines

SOURCE: "An Evaluation of Benefit Communication Strategy" by Michael C. Giallourakis and G. Stephen Taylor, which appeared in the 4th Quarter 1991 issue, was reprinted with permission from the *Employee Benefits Journal*, published by the International Foundation of Employee Benefit Plans, Brookfield, WI. Statements or opinions expressed in this article are those of the author and do not necessarily represent the views or positions of the International Foundation, its officers, directors, or staff.

plans (flex-plans or cafeteria-style plans) permit employees to choose the types and amounts of benefits they want for themselves. The plans vary according to such things as whether minimum levels of certain benefits (such as health care coverage) are prescribed and whether employees can receive money for having chosen a "light" benefits package (or have to pay extra for more benefits). One example is vacation, where some plans permit employees to give up vacation days for more salary or, alternatively, purchase extra vacation days through a salary reduction.

What are the potential advantages of such plans?[70] In the best case, almost all of the objectives discussed previously can be positively influenced. First, employees can gain a greater awareness and appreciation of what the employer provides them, particularly with plans that give employees a lump sum to allocate to benefits. Second, by permitting employee choice, there should be a better match between the benefits package and the employees' preferences. This, in turn, should improve employee attitudes and retention.[71] Third, employers may achieve overall cost reductions in their benefits programs. Cafeteria plans can be thought of as similar to defined contribution plans, whereas traditional plans are more like defined benefit plans. The employer can control the size of the contribution under the former, but not under the latter, because the cost and utilization of benefits is beyond the employer's control. Costs can also be controlled by designing the choices so that employees have an incentive to choose more efficient options. For example, in the case of a medical flex-plan, employees who do not wish to take advantage of the (presumably more cost-effective) HMO have to pay significant deductibles and other costs under the alternative plans.

One drawback of cafeteria-style plans is their administrative cost, especially in the initial design and start-up stages. However, software packages and standardized flex-plans developed by consultants offer some help in this regard. Another possible drawback to these plans is adverse selection. Employees are most likely to choose benefits that they expect to need the most. Someone in need of dental work would choose as much dental coverage as possible. As a result, employer costs can increase significantly as each employee chooses benefits based on their personal value. Another result of adverse selection is the difficulty in estimating benefits costs under such a plan, especially in small companies. Adverse selection can be controlled, however, by limiting coverage amounts, pricing benefits that are subject to adverse selection higher,

COMPETING IN THE NEW ECONOMY

Companies Take a Second Look at Some Really Fringe Benefits

Even though companies are still competing for high-quality, talented workers, the lure of a "chill out" room or an on-site foosball table may not be worth the cost to install and maintain it. In fact, in leaner times, firms are looking for ways to cut back on certain perks without losing their employees' trust or loyalty. "Previously, managers often had an open checkbook," says Cathy Ohmes, owner of Creative Perks LLC, a firm that offers employee services to high-tech companies in the northern Virginia area. "Now perks are more likely to be a budget line item."

Dave Stum, president of Aon Consulting's Loyalty Institute, suggests, "Organizations need to take a good, hard look at the basics before launching new and trendy benefits or other human resources packages. Start by ensuring that you offer a safe, secure work environment and equitable compensation and benefit packages. These are your foundations, and there's no building on a foundation if it's faulty." However, Jean Wilson, membership director of the Employee Services Management Association in Oak Brook, Illinois, warns that often the cost of a certain benefit is much less than that of replacing an employee who has been coaxed away by a competitor.

Cathy Ohmes recommends that firms that decide they must cut back on certain employee services communicate clearly with employees before doing so. That way, employees will be forewarned and will have a chance to absorb and understand the information. Ohmes also suggests that a company establish a "perks philosophy" that states outright how employee services fit into the company's overall compensation and benefits package, as well as its mission. Then there's no confusion about what types of services are offered and why.

Many companies are looking for new, cheaper ways to offer services instead of cutting them altogether. At Intel, human resource managers were frustrated that the company was offering lunchtime health seminars that no one was attending. Worried that many workers were already skipping meals, exercise, and sleep, managers didn't want to give up the health program. So Intel linked its intranet to the Mayo Clinic HealthQuest service, which creates personalized Web pages containing ways that an individual can improve his or her health habits—with exercise programs, healthful recipes, and the like. The site is cheaper to manage and employees are much more apt to use it. "It's all about productivity and cost control," explains Sue Adams, Intel's occupational health manager. "We really feel people will be more productive if they are healthy."

SOURCE: "Benefits for Your Workers," *Business Owner's Toolkit* (October 30, 2001), **www.toolkit.cch.com**; L. Lawrence, "Companies Still Offering Perks, But HR's Taking Another Look," *HR News*, June 2001, p. 4; B. Brady, "The Cost of Health," *Business 2.0*, January 2000, **www.business2.com**.

or using a limited set of packaged options, which prevents employees from choosing too many benefits options that would be susceptible to adverse selection.

Flexible Spending Accounts

A flexible spending account permits pretax contributions to an employee account that can be drawn on to pay for uncovered health care expenses (like deductibles or copayments). A separate account of up to $5,000 per year is permitted for pretax contributions to cover dependent care expenses. The federal tax code requires that funds in the health care and dependent care accounts be earmarked in advance and spent during the plan year. Remaining funds revert to the employer.[72] Therefore, the accounts work best to the extent that employees have predictable expenses. The major advantage of such plans is the increase in take-home pay that results from pretax payment of health and dependent care expenses. Consider again the hypothetical employee with annual earnings of $50,000 and an effective total marginal tax rate of 43 percent from Table 13.1. The take-home pay from an additional $10,000 in salary with and without a flexible dependent care account is as follows:

	NO FLEXIBLE SPENDING CARE ACCOUNT	FLEXIBLE SPENDING CARE ACCOUNT
Salary portion	$10,000	$10,000
Pretax dependent care contribution	–$ 0	–$ 5,000
Taxable salary	$10,000	$ 5,000
Tax (43 percent)	–$ 4,300	–$ 2,150
Aftertax cost of dependent care	–$ 5,000	–$ 0
Take-home pay	$ 700	$ 2,850

Therefore, the use of a flexible spending account saves the employee $2,150 per year.

General Regulatory Issues

Although we have already discussed a number of regulatory issues, some additional ones require attention.

Nondiscrimination Rules and Qualified Plans

As a general rule, all benefits packages must meet certain rules to be classified as qualified plans.[73] What are the advantages of a qualified plan? Basically, it receives more favorable tax treatment than a nonqualified plan. In the case of a qualified retirement plan, for example, these tax advantages include (1) an immediate tax deduction for employers for their contributions to retirement funds, (2) no tax liability for the employee at the time of the employer deduction, and (3) tax-free investment returns (from stocks, bonds, money markets, or the like) on the retirement funds.[74]

What rules must be satisfied for a plan to obtain qualified status? Each benefit area has different rules. It would be impossible to describe the various rules here, but some general observations are possible. Taking pensions as an example again, vesting requirements must be met. More generally, qualified plans must meet so-called nondiscrimination rules. Basically, this means that a benefit cannot discriminate in favor of "highly compensated employees." One rationale behind such rules is that the tax benefits of qualified benefits plans (and the corresponding loss of tax revenues for the U.S. government) should not go disproportionately to the wealthy.[75] Rather, the favorable tax treatment is designed to encourage employers to provide important benefits to a broad spectrum of employees. The nondiscrimination rules discourage owners or top managers from adopting plans that benefit them exclusively.

Sex, Age, and Disability

Beyond the Pregnancy Discrimination Act's requirements that were discussed earlier in the chapter, a second area of concern for employers in ensuring legal treatment of men and women in the benefits area has to do with pension benefits. Women tend to live longer than men, meaning that pension benefits for women are more costly, all else being equal. However, in its 1978 *Manhart* ruling, the Supreme Court declared it illegal for employers to require women to contribute more to a defined benefit plan than men: Title VII protects individuals, and not all women outlive all men.[76]

Two major age-related issues have received attention under the Age Discrimination in Employment Act (ADEA) and later amendments such as the Older Workers Benefit Protection Act (OWBPA). First, employers must take care not to discriminate against workers over age 40 in the provision of pay or benefits. As one example, employers cannot generally cease accrual (stop the growth) of retirement benefits at some age (like 65) as a way of pressuring older employees to retire.[77] Second, early retirement incentive programs need to meet the following standards to avoid legal liability: (1) the employee is not coerced to accept the incentive and retire, (2) accurate information is provided regarding options, and (3) the employee is given adequate time (is not pressured) to make a decision.

Employers also have to comply with the Americans with Disabilities Act (ADA), which went into effect in 1992. The ADA specifies that employees with disabilities must have "equal access to whatever health insurance coverage the employer provides other employees." However, the act also notes that the terms and conditions of health insurance can be based on risk factors as long as this is not a subterfuge for denying the benefit to those with disabilities. Employers with risk-based programs in place would be in a stronger position, however, than employers who make changes after hiring employees with disabilities.[78]

Monitoring Future Benefits Obligations

Financial Accounting Statement (FAS) 106, issued by the Financial Accounting Standards Board, became effective in 1993. This rule requires that any benefits (excluding pensions) provided after retirement (the major one being health care) can no longer be funded on a pay-as-you-go basis. Rather, they must be paid on an accrual basis, and companies must enter these future cost obligations on their financial statements.[79] The effect on financial statements can be substantial. For AT&T, a company with a large retiree population, the initial effect of adopting FAS 106 was a reduction in net income of between $5.5 billion and $7.5 billion. General Motors (GM) took a $20.8 billion reduction in net income, resulting in a total loss of $23.5 billion in 1992, the largest loss in corporate history.[80]

Financial Accounting Statement (FAS) 106
The rule issued by the Financial Accounting Standards Board in 1993 requiring companies to fund benefits provided after retirement on an accrual rather than a pay-as-you-go basis and to enter these future cost obligations on their financial statements.

Increasing retiree health care costs (and the change in accounting standards) have led companies like GM to require its white-collar employees and retirees to pay insurance premiums for the first time in its history and to increase copayments and deductibles. Survey data indicate that some companies are ending retiree health care benefits altogether, while most have reduced benefits or increased retiree contributions. Obviously, such changes hit the elderly hard, especially those with relatively fixed incomes. Not surprisingly, legal challenges have arisen. The need to balance the interests of shareholders, current employees, and retirees in this area will be one of the most difficult challenges facing managers in the future.

A Look Back

We have seen that many organizations have become less paternalistic in their employee benefits strategies. Employees now have more responsibility, and sometimes more risk, regarding their benefits choices. One change has been in the area of retirement income plans, where employers have moved toward greater reliance on defined contribution plans. Such plans require employees to understand investing; otherwise, their retirement years may not be so happy. As we saw in the beginning of the chapter, the risk to employees is especially great when defined contribution plans invest a substantial portion of their assets in company stock. One reason companies do this is because they wish to move away from an entitlement mentality and instead link benefits to company performance. However, if the company has financial problems, employees risk losing not only their jobs, but also their retirement money. Another change has been in the area of health care benefits for retirees, where companies have reduced or sometimes eliminated such benefits. Again, the responsibility for anticipating this possibility increasingly falls with employees. In the health care area, employees are being asked to increase the proportion of costs that they pay and also to use data on health care quality to make better choices about health care. Finally, although these trends characterize many employers, some employers follow different benefit strategies. SAS, the subject of the end of chapter case, provides an example.

Questions

1. Why do employers offer benefits? Is it because the law requires it, because it makes good business sense, or because it is the right thing to do? How much responsibility should employers have for the health and well-being of their employees? Take the perspective of both a shareholder and an employee in answering this question.
2. If you were advising a new company on how to design its retirement plan, what would you recommend?

Summary

Effective management of employee benefits is an important means by which organizations successfully compete. Benefits costs are substantial and continue to grow rapidly in some areas, most notably health care. Control of such costs is necessary to compete in the product market. At the same time, employers must offer a benefits package that permits them to compete in the labor market. Beyond investing more money in benefits, this attraction and retention of quality employees can be helped by better communication of the value of the benefits package and by allowing employees to tailor benefits to their own needs through flexible benefits plans.

Employers continue to be a major source of economic security for employees, often providing health insurance, retirement benefits, and so forth. Changes to benefits can have a tremendous impact on employees and retirees. Therefore, employers carry a significant social responsibility in making benefits decisions. At the same time, employees need to be aware that they will increasingly become responsible for their own economic security. Health care benefit design is changing to encourage employees to be more informed consumers, and retirement benefits will depend more and more on the financial investment decisions employees make on their own behalf.

Discussion Questions

1. The opening vignette described how relationships between employers and employees are changing. What are the likely consequences of this change? Where does the social responsibility of employers end, and where does the need to operate more efficiently begin?
2. Your company, like many others, is experiencing double-digit percentage increases in health care costs. What suggestions can you offer that may reduce the rate of cost increases?
3. Why is communication so important in the employee benefits area? What sorts of programs can a company use to communicate more effectively? What are the potential positive consequences of more effective benefits communication?
4. What are the potential advantages of flexible benefits and flexible spending accounts? Are there any potential drawbacks?
5. Although benefits account for a large share of employee compensation, many feel there is little evidence on whether an employer receives an adequate return on the benefits investment. One suggestion has been to link benefits to individual, group, or organization performance. Explain why you would or would not recommend this strategy to an organization.

Web Exercise

The Health Insurance Portability and Accountability Act (HIPAA) of 1996 is a major health care reform mandate that sets minimum standards to improve the access, portability, and renewability of health insurance coverage. Visit **www.hcfa.gov** (the Web site for HIPAA), which answers some commonly asked questions for small employers about the provisions of HIPAA. Click on HIPAA, then Employers.

Questions

1. What does *portability* mean?
2. What is a preexisting condition? How does HIPAA affect how businesses can apply preexisting condition exclusions to employees?
3. How does HIPAA benefit small employers?

Managing People: From the Pages of *BusinessWeek*

BusinessWeek Dr. Goodnight's Company Town

The war for talent has businesses transforming their corporate campuses into country clubs—offering everything from five-star lunches to concierges willing to arrange employees' lawn mowing and haircuts. But long before the words "labor crunch" put employee perks in vogue, SAS Institute Inc. founder James Goodnight was lavishing money on programmers instead of headhunters. It worked: SAS turnover is 4 percent in an industry for which 20 percent is typical. The Cary (North Carolina)-based company may compete against PeopleSoft Inc. and Oracle Corp., but SAS employees aren't asked to mimic their Silicon Valley brethren's sleep-starved lifestyle. Goodnight, a shy billionaire who until recently drove a Buick Roadmaster wagon, believes in leaving the office at 5 P.M. sharp. Dinner, he says, should be spent with your family, not at your desk.

THE PERK FACTORY. Goodnight remembers working as a programmer for NASA—a place so cheap it wouldn't even spring for workers' sodas. Insulted, he vowed to do things differently. Today he's become a Willy Wonka to his workers, creating a corporate perk factory where even the plain and peanut-filled M&M's, replenished like clockwork every Wednesday, are free. Goodnight believes that if you treat people as if they make a difference, they will. The turnover savings he reaps from his largesse are huge: an estimated $75 million a year. This means Goodnight can afford all those banana trees and cracker-and-cheese–stocked snack rooms. It may be too Stepford-like for cynics, but the T-shirt- and Teva-sporting SAS employees say they wouldn't have it any other way.

On-site benefits at the Institute include day care, Montessori school, the Atrium, and lunchtime entertainment. For $25 a month, the center will take babies after SAS's six-week paid maternity leave. Sixty percent of the employees use the on-site day care; parents can visit or pick up their kids for lunch. Employees also get private offices and open spaces for impromptu meetings and breaks.

The perks aren't limited to the on-site stuff. Goodnight offers discounts on everything from land in his ritzy subdivision to memberships at his country club. Employees make only industry-average salaries, but they get a generous year-end bonus, profit sharing, and an extra week of paid vacation at Christmas. Employees can also enjoy

Shiatsu, Swedish, and deep tissue massages—all available between meetings—right down the hall. A free clinic is also available so employees can get care at work—even when a child is ill.

WHAT THEY WANT. This is just the beginning. SAS also has a 55,000-square-foot athletic facility worthy of Olympic games—plus tennis courts, walking trails, picnic shelters, and a lake, canoes provided. In summer the place looks more like a raucous college campus than a headquarter for wireheads. After your workout, the company takes your gym clothes and returns them to you freshly laundered the next day. Hungry? Head over to the subsidized cafeteria, where it's hard to spend more than $3 for a feast.

WHAT THEY LIKE. When Goodnight decided he didn't like Cary's local high school, he built a new private college prep called Cary Academy right next to SAS. (His own son didn't want to switch schools to attend.) Employees receive a 10 percent discount off the $9,000-per-year tuition. If that's too steep, they can still enjoy a smorgasbord of free services like the car wash and detailing, farmer's market, and advice on financial planning for college and retirement. But the all-time favorite SAS perk is the seven-hour workday, which leaves time for family or personal obligations. While the Silicon Valley set grinds away, SAS's gates close shut. For Goodnight, seven hours of work a day are plenty.

WHY THEY STAY. Goodnight believes that workers' environments can inspire or depress them. To that end, he has hired a full-time ergonomics specialist and built an on-site greenhouse that provides fresh flowers. His 7,000 employees also enjoyed the $16 million in bonuses and $30 million in profit sharing shelled out last year, when the company's revenues hit $1.02 billion. The payoff: similar software companies lose and replace 1,000 people a year, while SAS loses 130. Says one SAS employee, "We're spoiled rotten."

SOURCE: Reprinted from June 19, 2000 issue of *BusinessWeek* by special permission.

Questions

1. Would you like to work at SAS? Why or why not? Would you prefer to work at SAS or at Microsoft?
2. What are the advantages and disadvantages of SAS's benefits strategy?
3. SAS is sometimes criticized for being too paternalistic. What is your opinion?

Notes

1. D. Zoia, "DCC Attacks High Health Care Costs," *Ward's Auto World*, September 1999, p. 75.
2. H.W. Hennessey, "Using Employee Benefits to Gain a Competitive Advantage," *Benefits Quarterly* 5, no. 1 (1989), pp. 51–57; B. Gerhart and G.T. Milkovich, "Employee Compensation: Research and Practice," in *Handbook of Industrial and Organizational Psychology*, vol. 3, 2nd ed., ed. M.D. Dunnette and L.M. Hough (Palo Alto, CA: *Consulting Psychologists Press*, 1992).
3. R.G. Ehrenberg and R.S. Smith, *Modern Labor Economics* (Glenview, IL: Scott, Foresman and Company, 1988).
4. B.T. Beam Jr. and J.J. McFadden, *Employee Benefits* (Chicago: Dearborn Financial Publishing, 1992).
5. Bureau of National Affairs, "Most Workers Who Struck in 1990 Did So over Health Coverage, AFL–CIO Says," *Daily Labor Report* (August 20, 1991), p. A12.
6. The organization and description in this section draws heavily on Beam and McFadden, *Employee Benefits*.
7. Bureau of National Affairs, *State Unemployment Insurance Funds* (October 2, 1997), pp. 316–17.
8. J.A. Penczak, "Unemployment Benefit Plans," in *Employee Benefits Handbook*, 3rd ed., ed. J.D. Mamorsky (Boston: Warren, Gorham & Lamont, 1992).
9. J.V. Nackley, *Primer on Workers' Compensation* (Washington, DC: Bureau of National Affairs, 1989).
10. Beam and McFadden, *Employee Benefits*, p. 59.
11. Nackley, *Primer on Workers' Compensation;* P.M. Lencsis, *Workers Compensation* (Westport, CT: Quorum Books, 1998).
12. M.D. Fefer, "What to Do about Workers' Comp," *Fortune* (June 29, 1992), pp. 80ff.
13. Ibid.
14. J.R. Hollenbeck, D.R. Ilgen, and S.M. Crampton, "Lower Back Disability in Occupational Settings: A Review of the Literature from a Human Resource Management View," *Personnel Psychology* 45 (1992), pp. 247–78.
15. Gallup-collected data are summarized in Employee Benefit Research Institute, "Health-Care Reform: Trade-offs and Implications," EBRI Issue Brief, no. 125 (Washington, DC: Employee Benefit Research Institute, April 1992).
16. Beam and McFadden, *Employee Benefits*.
17. Employee Benefits Notes, July 1992, pp. 1–3. Original data from Susan Grad, *Income of the Population 55 or Older 1988*, U. S. Dept. of Health and Human Services, Social Security Administration, Publication 13-11871 (Washington, DC: Government Printing Office, 1988).

18. L.M. Dailey and J.A. Turner, "Private Pension Coverage in Nine Countries," *Monthly Labor Review*, May 1992, pp. 40–43; Hewitt Associates, *Salaried Employee Benefits Provided by Major Employers in 1990* (Lincolnshire, IL: Hewitt Associates, 1990); W.J. Wiatrowski, "New Survey Data on Pension Benefits," *Monthly Labor Review*, August 1991, pp. 8–21.
19. M. Slate, "The Retirement Protection Act," *Labor Law Journal*, April 1995, pp. 245–50.
20. R.M. McCaffery, "Employee Benefits and Services," in *Compensation and Benefits*, ed. L.R. Gomez-Mejia (Washington, DC: Bureau of National Affairs, 1989).
21. **www.irs.gov**
22. R.A. Ippolito, "Toward Explaining the Growth of Defined Contribution Plans," *Industrial Relations* 34 (1995), pp. 1–20.
23. J. Fierman, "How Secure Is Your Nest Egg?" *Fortune* (August 12, 1991), pp. 50–54.
24. Beam and McFadden, *Employee Benefits*.
25. B.J. Coleman, *Primer on Employee Retirement Income Security Act*, 3rd ed. (Washington, DC: Bureau of National Affairs, 1989).
26. *Continental Can Company* v. *Gavalik*, summary in *Daily Labor Report* (December 8, 1987): "Supreme Court Lets Stand Third Circuit Ruling That Pension Avoidance Scheme Is ERISA Violation," No. 234, p. A-14.
27. A.L. Gustman, O.S. Mitchell, and T.L. Steinmeier, "The Role of Pensions in the Labor Market: A Survey of the Literature," *Industrial and Labor Relations* 47 (1994), pp. 417–38.
28. D.A. DeCenzo and S.J. Holoviak, *Employee Benefits* (Englewood Cliffs, NJ: Prentice-Hall, 1990).
29. E.P. Lazear, "Why Is There Early Retirement?" *Journal of Political Economy* 87 (1979), pp. 1261–84; Gustman et al., "The Role of Pensions."
30. S. Dorsey, "Pension Portability and Labor Market Efficiency," *Industrial and Labor Relations* 48, no. 5 (1995), pp. 276–92.
31. U.S. data on paid holidays are from Hewitt Associates, *Salaried Employee Benefits Provided by Major U.S. Employers* (Lincolnshire, IL: Hewitt Associates, 1990); European data are from Commerce Clearing House, *Doing Business in Europe* (New York: Commerce Clearing House, 1990).
32. DeCenzo and Holoviak, *Employee Benefits*.
33. S.L. Grover and K.J. Crooker, "Who Appreciates Family Responsive Human Resource Policies: The Impact of Family-Friendly Policies on the Organizational Attachment of Parents and Non-parents," *Personnel Psychology* 48 (1995), pp. 271–88.
34. Employee Benefit Research Institute, "The Employer's Role in Helping Working Families," *Employee Benefit Notes*, November 1991, pp. 3–5; "Most Small Businesses Appear Prepared to Cope with New Family Leave Rules," *The Wall Street Journal* (February 8, 1993), pp. B1ff.
35. "The Employer's Role in Helping Working Families." For examples of child care arrangements in some well-known companies (e.g., AT&T, Apple, Exxon, IBM, Merck), see "A Look at Child-Care Benefits," *USA Today* (March 14, 1989), p. 4B.
36. Bureau of National Affairs, *101 Key Statistics on Work and Family for the 1990s* (Washington, DC: Bureau of National Affairs, 1989), p. 29.
37. P. Hardin, "Women Execs Should Feel at Ease about Taking Full Maternity Leave," *Personnel Journal*, September 1995, p. 19.
38. "The Families and Work Institute's 1998 Business Work–Life Study," **www.familiesandwork.org**. Results based on a nationally representative survey of employers having 100 or more employees.
39. J. Fierman, "It's 2 A.M.: Let's Go to Work," *Fortune* (August 21, 1995), pp. 82–88.
40. E.E. Kossek, "Diversity in Child Care Assistance Needs: Employee Problems, Preferences, and Work-Related Outcomes," *Personnel Psychology* 43 (1990), pp. 769–91.
41. E. E. Kossek, *The Acceptance of Human Resource Innovation: Lessons from Management* (Westport, CT: Quorum, 1989).
42. G. Flynn, "Some of Your Best Ideas May Be Working against You," *Personnel Journal*, October 1995, pp. 77–83.
43. R. Broderick and B. Gerhart, "Nonwage Compensation," in *The Human Resource Management Handbook*, ed. D. Lewin, D.J.B. Mitchell, and M.A. Zadi (San Francisco: JAI Press, 1996).
44. Hennessey, "Using Employee Benefits to Gain a Competitive Advantage."
45. For example, Hewitt Associates, *Salaried Employee Benefits;* Bureau of Labor Statistics, *Employee Benefits in State and Local Governments, 1990* (Washington, DC: U.S. Government Printing Office, 1992); Bureau of Labor Statistics, *Employee Benefits in Medium and Large Establishments, 1989* (Washington, DC: U.S. Government Printing Office, 1990); Bureau of Labor Statistics, *Employee Benefits in Small Private Establishments, 1990* (Washington, DC: U.S. Government Printing Office, 1991).
46. **www.census.gov**
47. Employee Benefit Research Institute, "Health Care Reform."
48. A.C. Monheit and P.F. Cooper, "Health Insurance and Job Mobility: The Effects of Public Policy on Job-Lock," *Industrial and Labor Relations Review* 48 (1994), pp. 86–102.
49. Beam and McFadden, *Employee Benefits*.

50. American Compensation Association, "Health Care Reform Strategies," ACA *NEWS* 37, no. 9 (1994), pp. 22–24.
51. M. Barringer and O.S. Mitchell, "Workers' Preferences among Company-Provided Health Insurance Plans," *Industrial and Labor Relations Review* 48 (1994), pp. 141–52.
52. Beam and McFadden, *Employee Benefits*.
53. J.E. Fielding and P.V. Pirerchia, "Frequency of Worksite Health Promotion Activities," *American Journal of Public Health* 79 (1989), pp. 16–20.
54. S. Tully, "America's Healthiest Companies," *Fortune* (June 12, 1995), pp. 98–106.
55. G. Flynn, "Companies Make Wellness Work," *Personnel Journal*, February 1995, pp. 63–66.
56. D.A. Harrison and L.Z. Liska, "Promoting Regular Exercise in Organizational Fitness Programs: Health-Related Differences in Motivational Building Blocks," *Personnel Psychology* 47 (1994), pp. 47–71.
57. J.C. Erfurt, A. Foote, and M.A. Heirich, "The Cost-Effectiveness of Worksite Wellness Programs for Hypertension Control, Weight Loss, Smoking Cessation and Exercise," *Personnel Psychology* 45 (1992), pp. 5–27.
58. Ibid.
59. H. Gardner, unpublished manuscript (Cheyenne, WY: Options & Choices, Inc., 1995).
60. H.B. Noble, "Quality Is Focus for Health Plans," *The New York Times* (July 3, 1995), p. A1; J.D. Klinke, "Medicine's Industrial Revolution," *The Wall Street Journal* (August 21, 1995), p. A8.
61. J.B. White, "Business Plan," *The Wall Street Journal* (October 19, 1998), p. R18.
62. J. Schor, *The Overworked American: The Unexpected Decline of Leisure* (New York: Basic Books, 1991); U.S. Bureau of Labor Statistics, "Workers Are on the Job More Hours over the Course of a Year," *Issues in Labor Statistics*, February 1997.
63. G. Mangum, D. Mayall, and K. Nelson, "The Temporary Help Industry: A Response to the Dual Internal Labor Market," *Industrial and Labor Relations Review* 38 (1985), pp. 599–611; M. Montgomery, "On the Determinants of Employer Demand for Part-Time Workers," *Review of Economics and Statistics* 70 (1988), pp. 112–17; F.A. Scott, M.C. Berger, and D.A. Black, "Effects of the Tax Treatment of Fringe Benefits on Labor-Market Segmentation," *Industrial and Labor Relations Review* 42 (1989), pp. 216–29. Some conflicting evidence on part-time workers, however, is provided by C. Tilly, "Reasons for the Continued Growth in Part Time Employment," *Monthly Labor Review* 114, no. 3 (1991), pp. 10–18.
64. Hewitt Associates. **http://www.hewitt.com**.
65. Beam and McFadden, *Employee Benefits*.
66. M. Wilson, G.B. Northcraft, and M.A. Neale, "The Perceived Value of Fringe Benefits," *Personnel Psychology* 38 (1985), pp. 309–20. Similar results were found in other studies reviewed by H.W. Hennessey, P.L. Perrewe, and W.A. Hochwarter, "Impact of Benefit Awareness on Employee and Organizational Outcomes: A Longitudinal Field Experiment," *Benefits Quarterly* 8, no. 2 (1992), pp. 90–96.
67. R. Huseman, J. Hatfield, and R. Robinson, "The MBA and Fringe Benefits," *Personnel Administrator* 23, no. 7 (1978), pp. 57–60. See summary in H.W. Hennessey Jr., "Using Employee Benefits to Gain a Competitive Advantage," *Benefits Quarterly* 5, no. 1 (1989), pp. 51–57.
68. Hennessey et al., "Impact of Benefit Awareness"; the same study found no impact of the increased awareness and benefits satisfaction on overall job satisfaction. G.F. Dreher, R.A. Ash, and R.D. Bretz, "Benefit Coverage and Employee Cost: Critical Factors in Explaining Compensation Satisfaction," *Personnel Psychology* 41 (1988), pp. 237–54.
69. M.C. Giallourakis and G.S. Taylor, "An Evaluation of Benefit Communication Strategy," *Employee Benefits Journal* 15, no. 4 (1991), pp. 14–18.
70. Beam and McFadden, *Employee Benefits*.
71. For supportive evidence, see A.E. Barber, R.B. Dunham, and R.A. Formisano, "The Impact of Flexible Benefits on Employee Satisfaction: A Field Study," *Personnel Psychology* 45 (1992), pp. 55–75; E.E. Lawler, *Pay and Organizational Development* (Reading, MA: Addison-Wesley, 1981).
72. P. Biggins, "Flexible/Cafeteria Plans," in *Employee Benefits Handbook*, 3rd ed.
73. For a description of these rules, see M.M. Sarli, "Nondiscrimination Rules for Qualified Plans: The General Test," *Compensation and Benefits Review* 23, no. 5 (September–October 1991), pp. 56–67.
74. Beam and McFadden, *Employee Benefits*, p. 359.
75. Ibid., p. 355.
76. *Los Angeles Dept. of Water & Power* v. *Manhart*, 435 US SCt 702 (1978), 16 EPD, 8250.
77. S.K. Hoffman, "Discrimination Litigation Relating to Employee Benefits," *Labor Law Journal*, June 1992, pp. 362–81.
78. Ibid., p. 375.
79. Ibid.
80. W.A. Reimert, "Accounting for Retiree Health Benefits," *Compensation and Benefits Review* 23, no. 5 (September–October, 1991), pp. 49–55; D.P. Levin, "20.8 Billion G.M. Charge for Benefits," *The New York Times* (February 2, 1993), p. D4.

Compensating Workers through Pay and Benefits

Today's human resource managers face a wide range of challenges in helping their organizations determine what types of compensation and benefits best suit their employees' needs. Because of the diversity of today's workers in midsized to large organizations, the choices can be mind-boggling, but HR managers must work to get the right mix to attract and retain talented employees. Older employees are more concerned about how their retirement accounts are shaping up; working parents are desperate for child care; younger workers want opportunities to move up the ladder fast. Thus HR managers and other executives must come up with creative ways to motivate and empower employees through compensation and benefits plans.

The following companies have combined some innovative perks with traditional ones:

- The S.C. Johnson Company in Racine, Wisconsin, has a company-owned, employee-directed 146-acre park with an outdoor recreation center, child care center, softball fields, tennis courts, golf driving range, miniature golf course, and other attractions. It also offers a paid sabbatical program and an expanded maternity/paternity/adoption policy, with time off for the adoption process.
- CIGNA Insurance Company employs 33,000 people worldwide and also combines a variety of traditional and alternative benefits for its employees, from medical and dental insurance plans to a company chef who will make meals to order for employees to take home to their families at the end of the day. CIGNA also offers flexible work arrangements, health and wellness programs, and a tuition reimbursement program for workers who want to continue their education.
- Employees at Wilton Connor Packaging, Inc., in Charlotte, North Carolina, can actually bring their dirty laundry to work and have it cleaned for $1 per load. The company also offers child care services, on-site tutoring for children, and English classes for employees. In addition, Wilton Connor conducts a six-week summer school program for children of full-time employees. Workers at Wilton Connor seem to be satisfied; only two leave the company on average every year.
- Financial services firm Salomon Smith Barney provides time off for special needs, such as caring for an ailing relative; child care discounts and referral services; adoption assistance; a Volunteer Incentive Program that encourages employees to volunteer for nonprofit organizations; a Life-Works Program that is designed to help workers balance work and personal responsibilities; on-site medical attention and prescription fulfillment; and investment opportunities.
- Accenture (formerly Andersen Consulting) actually employs a concierge to run errands such as grocery shopping or dry-cleaning pickup for employees who have to stay late or can't take time out at lunch for these errands. The company also focuses on professional development of its new hires and offers Student Leadership Conferences to final-year college students in the United States, Europe, and Asia.
- Both Coca-Cola and Home Depot provide wellness and fitness programs designed to reduce stress and enhance employee health. Coca-Cola has found that employees who use these programs are not only healthier but more productive on the job. Home Depot has taken its program a step further by offering on-site classes in smoking cessation, nutrition, proper exercise, and balancing work and home life. The Center for Disease Control in Atlanta strongly recommends these types of classes for the well-being of workers.

On another front, Home Depot has recently launched a new type of class for employees: an in-house course in personal finance. The company states that the financial health of its 250,000 employees is a priority. "We want to be an employer of choice, and we see helping associates [employees] manage their finances as one more way to do that," explains Layne Thome, director of associate services for the company. "We want to win the war for talent. We see this as another tool for improving recruitment and retention." Managers were spurred to develop the course after realizing that many of the company's employees were having financial trouble. "We . . . found that associates were cashing out of their retirement accounts early and they were making early withdrawals on their stock purchase plans, which also concerned us," says Thome. "We saw we had a population in trouble." So the company has done something about it. Partnering with the Fannie Mae Foundation and the Consumer Credit Counseling Service, Home Depot has custom-developed classes for its employees.

Developing the right compensation packages for employees can help ensure low turnover and higher productivity—just what every company wants.

Questions

1. You've seen a range of advantages of the creative benefits programs just described. What might be some disadvantages?
2. What special challenges might companies such as Coca-Cola face in developing and implementing compensation packages for employees in other countries?
3. As an employee, which is more important to you: your pay or other benefits? Why? Do you think this ratio might change as you grow older and progress in your career?
4. Do you think these types of benefits have the greatest influence on attracting new employees, motivating current employees, or keeping current employees? Explain your answer.

SOURCE: S.C. Johnson website (**www.scjohnsonwax.com**), Cigna website (**www.cigna.com**), Salomon Smith Barney website (**http://careers.ssmb.com**), Accenture website (**http://careers.accenture.com**), and Home Depot website (**www.homedepot.com**), all accessed November 29, 2001; J.L. Howard, "Expansion at Westlake to Add 400 Jobs," *The Business Journal of Charlotte* (June 2, 2000), **http://charlotte.bcentral.com**.

Special Topics in Human Resource Management

14 Chapter

Collective Bargaining and Labor Relations

Objectives

After reading this chapter, you should be able to:

1. Describe what is meant by collective bargaining and labor relations.
2. Identify the labor relations goals of management, labor unions, and society.
3. Explain the legal environment's impact on labor relations.
4. Describe the major labor–management interactions: organizing, contract negotiations, and contract administration.
5. Describe new, less adversarial approaches to labor–management relations.
6. Explain how changes in competitive challenges (e.g., product market competition and globalization) are influencing labor–management interactions.
7. Explain how labor relations in the public sector differ from labor relations in the private sector.

The right to strike is one important component of bargaining power that labor unions have.

Enter the World of Business

Verizon Strikes Out against Unions

Despite a decline in overall union membership in the United States, organized labor groups that are willing and able to adapt to new industries and a new economy are surviving. Granted, not every attempt to organize young workers in high-tech fields is successful; employees at both Amazon.com and CNBC knocked down union drives. But workers at telecommunications companies such as Verizon Communications and high-tech aerospace companies like Lockheed Martin do have unions—and fairly strong ones at that. In fact, the Communications Workers of America (CWA) and the International Brotherhood of Electrical Workers (IBEW) represent about 53 percent of Verizon's 250,000 employees.

Recently both unions won on a major issue in their strike against Verizon that had its roots in the merger of Bell Atlantic, GTE, and Vodafone into Verizon. The unions wanted a chance to sign up nonunion employees from the old GTE and Vodafone companies. Verizon management tried to sidestep the issue by offering a five-year contract with large wage increases, but the unions opted instead to pursue union contracts for cable and wireless employees. Also disputed was Verizon's right to transfer work from union to nonunion units, as well as workload and overtime issues. These issues were considered especially crucial to call center workers, who were under pressure to deliver service to often-frustrated customers as quickly as possible by following set marketing scripts and to take only a two-second break between calls. In the end, the unions won the right to unionize the company's nonunion divisions as well as concessions on the other issues.

Perhaps one reason the CWA and IBEW fought so hard at Verizon is because the CWA had already lost ground at AT&T, where union membership has decreased to about 25 percent of the workforce as AT&T has merged with other companies. With such a low union membership rate, AT&T management has taken a hard line against organized labor—so much so that it has ignored a previous agreement that would allow the CWA to organize workers in nonunion divisions free of executive interference. AT&T has also refused to cooperate with any arbitration proceedings. So with the AT&T experience behind them, CWA representatives don't want to find themselves banging on closed doors at other companies.

Executives at many of these companies see organized labor as a threat to their ability to compete in a marketplace that demands a high degree of flexibility and speed. Perhaps they view the traditional union relationship as one that will saddle them with complacent workers who are happy with job security and guaranteed pay raises. But as expert Robert Kuttner writes, "Most of the economy's recent productivity gains reflect technological breakthroughs, not the downgrading of labor. How these gains are to be shared among managers, shareholders, customers, and employees is more about relative political power than economic or technical imperatives." There's no question that everyone wants a slice of the new economic pie. Both management and unions will have to learn to share if they want to survive and grow.

SOURCE: T. Wolverton, "Labor Pains," *CNET News.com* (January 16, 2001), **http://news.cnet.com**; R. Kuttner, "Verizon's Crash Course in High-Tech Unionism," *BusinessWeek* (September 11, 2000), p. 28; Y.J. Dreazen, "Old Labor Tries to Establish Role in New Economy," *The Wall Street Journal* (August 15, 2000), pp. B1, B10.

Introduction

The events at Verizon illustrate both the important role of labor relations in running a business and the influence of competitive challenges on the nature of labor relations. Deregulation in the communications industry has contributed to consolidation and rethinking of core strategies. To be more competitive, Verizon hoped to use less union labor to reduce cost and increase flexibility. In contrast, the CWA saw that its future depended on being able to organize workers in other parts of Verizon into unions. The result of the conflicting goals of Verizon and the CWA was a strike—one that lasted 18 days and idled 85,000 workers.

A strike (withholding labor) is a key union bargaining tool, and it is effective to the extent that is imposes costs on the company. Strikes also impose costs on workers, however. In the short term workers lose their income; in the longer term they may be replaced by other workers, or their jobs may disappear altogether if the strike costs the company too many customers. Therefore, Verizon and the CWA realize that they also have mutual interests. Conflict must be balanced with cooperation if they are to survive. Verizon and the CWA settled their dispute. In the process, the CWA showed that new economy workers may be interested in unions, despite past difficulties in organizing such workers. Verizon made some important concessions to make the CWA's task easier.

The Labor Relations Framework

John Dunlop, former secretary of labor and a leading industrial relations scholar, suggested in the book *Industrial Relations Systems* (1958) that such a system consists of four elements: (1) an environmental context (technology, market pressures, and the legal framework, especially as it affects bargaining power); (2) participants, including employees and their unions, management, and the government; (3) a "web of rules" (rules of the game) that describe the process by which labor and management interact and resolve disagreements (such as the steps followed in settling contract grievances); and (4) ideology.[1] For the industrial relations system to operate properly, the three participants must, to some degree, have a common ideology (like acceptance of the capitalist system) and must accept the roles of the other participants. Acceptance does not translate into convergence of interests, however. To the contrary, some degree of worker–management conflict is inevitable because, although the interests of the two parties overlap, they also diverge in key respects (such as how to divide the economic profits).[2]

Therefore, according to Dunlop and other U.S. scholars of like mind, an effective industrial relations system does not eliminate conflict. Rather, it provides institutions (and a "web of rules") that resolve conflict in a way that minimizes its costs to management, employees, and society. The collective bargaining system is one such institution, as are related mechanisms such as mediation, arbitration, and participation in decision making. These ideas formed the basis for the development in the 1940s of schools and departments of industrial and labor relations to train labor relations professionals who, working in both union and management positions, would have the skills to minimize costly forms of conflict such as strikes (which were reaching record levels at the time) and maximize integrative (win–win) solutions to such disagreements.[3]

A more recent industrial relations model, developed by Harry Katz and Thomas Kochan, is particularly helpful in laying out the types of decisions management and unions make in their interactions and the consequences of such decisions for attainment of goals in areas such as wages and benefits, job security, and the rights and responsibilities of unions and managements.[4] According to Katz and Kochan, these choices occur at three levels.

First, at the strategic level, management makes basic choices such as whether to work with its union(s) or to devote its efforts to developing nonunion operations. Environmental factors (or competitive challenges) offer both constraints and opportunities in implementing strategies. For example, if public opinion toward labor unions becomes negative during a particular time period, some employers may see that as an opportunity to rid themselves of unions, whereas other employers may seek a better working relationship with their unions. Similarly, increased competition may dictate the need to increase productivity or reduce labor costs, but whether this is accomplished by shifting work to nonunion facilities or by working with unions to become more competitive is a strategic choice that management faces.

Although management has often been the initiator of change in recent years, unions face a similar choice between fighting changes to the status quo and being open to new labor–management relationships (like less adversarial forms of participation in decision making, such as labor–management teams).

Katz and Kochan suggest that labor and management choices at the strategic level in turn affect the labor–management interaction at a second level, the functional level, where contract negotiations and union organizing occur, and at the final workplace level, the arena in which the contract is administered. In the opening vignette, Verizon's strategic-level choice to prevent nonunion employees from being organized, combined with the CWA's strategic choice to take a stand on the issue, contributed to conflict (a strike) at the functional level over a new contract. Although the relationships between labor and management at each of the three levels are somewhat interdependent, the relationship at the three levels may also differ. For example, while management may have a strategy of building an effective relationship with its unions at the strategic level, there may be significant day-to-day conflicts over work rules, grievances, and so forth at any given facility or bargaining unit (workplace level).

The labor relations framework depicted in Figure 14.1 incorporates many of the

FIGURE 14.1
A Labor Relations Framework

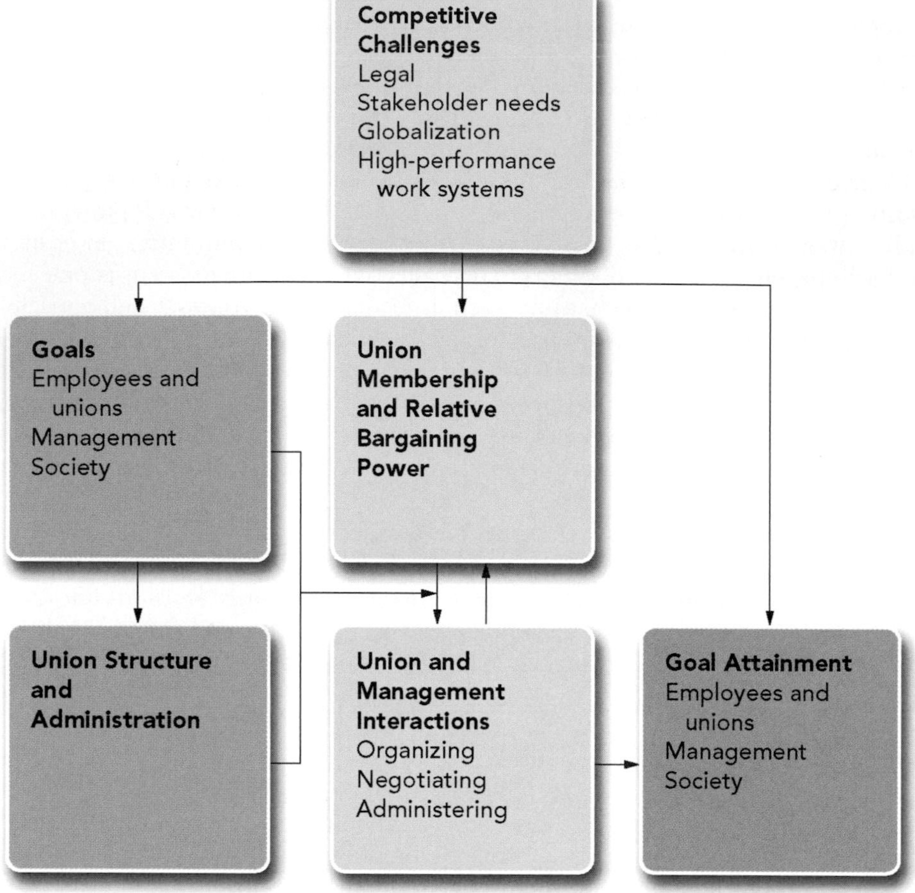

ideas discussed so far, including the important role of the environment (the competitive challenges); union, management, and societal goals; and a separation of union–management interactions into categories (union organizing, contract negotiation, contract administration) that can have important influences on one another but may also be analyzed somewhat independently. The model also highlights the important role that relative bargaining power plays in influencing goals, union–management interactions, and the degree to which each party achieves its goals. Relative bargaining power, in turn, is significantly influenced by the competitive environment (legal, social, quality, high-performance work systems, and globalization competitive challenges) and the size and depth of union membership.[5]

We now describe the components of this model in greater depth. The remainder of the chapter is organized into the following sections: the goals and strategies of society, management, and unions; union structure (including union administration and membership); the legal framework, perhaps the key aspect of the competitive environment for labor relations; union and management interactions (organizing, contract negotiation, contract administration); and goal attainment. Environmental factors (other than legal) and bargaining power are discussed in the context of these sections. In addition, two special topics, international comparisons and public sector labor relations, are discussed.

Goals and Strategies

Society

In one sense, labor unions, with their emphasis on group action, do not fit well with the individualistic orientation of U.S. capitalism. However, industrial relations scholars such as Beatrice and Sidney Webb and John R. Commons argued in the late 1800s and early 1900s that individual workers' bargaining power was far smaller than that of employers, who were likely to have more financial resources and the ability to easily replace workers.[6] Effective institutions for worker representation (like labor unions) were therefore seen as a way to make bargaining power more equal.

Labor unions' major benefit to society is the institutionalization of industrial conflict, which is therefore resolved in the least costly way. Thus, although disagreements between management and labor continue, it is better to resolve disputes through discussion (collective bargaining) than by battling in the streets. As an influential group of industrial relations scholars put it in describing the future of advanced industrial relations around the world, "Class warfare will be forgotten. The battles will be in the corridors instead of the streets, and memos will flow instead of blood."[7] In this sense, collective bargaining not only has the potential to reduce economic losses caused by strikes but may also contribute to societal stability. For this reason, industrial relations scholars have often viewed labor unions as an essential component of a democratic society.[8] These were some of the beliefs that contributed to the enactment of the National Labor Relations Act (NLRA) in 1935, which sought to provide an environment conducive to collective bargaining and has since regulated labor and management activities and interactions.

Even Senator Orrin Hatch, described by *BusinessWeek* as "labor's archrival on Capitol Hill," has spoken of the need for unions:

> There are always going to be people who take advantage of workers. Unions even that out, to their credit. We need them to level the field between labor and management. If you didn't have unions, it would be very difficult for even enlightened employers not to take advantage of workers on wages and working conditions, because of [competition from] rivals. I'm among the first to say I believe in unions.[9]

Although an industrial relations system based on collective bargaining has drawbacks, so too do the alternatives. Unilateral control by management sacrifices workers' rights. Extensive involvement of government and the courts can result in conflict resolution that is expensive, slow, and imposed by someone (a judge) with much less firsthand knowledge of the circumstances than either labor or management.

Management

One of management's most basic decisions is whether to encourage or discourage the unionization of its employees. It may discourage unions because it fears higher wage and benefit costs, the disruptions caused by strikes, and an adversarial relationship with its employees or, more generally, greater constraints placed on its decision-making flexibility and discretion. Historically, management has used two basic strategies to avoid unionization.[10] It may seek to provide employment terms and conditions that employees will perceive as sufficiently attractive and equitable so that they see little gain from union representation. Or it may aggressively oppose union representation, even where there is significant employee interest. Use of the latter strategy has increased significantly during the last 20 to 30 years.

If management voluntarily recognizes a union or if employees are already represented by a union, the focus is shifted from dealing with employees as individuals to employees as a group. Still, certain basic management objectives remain: controlling labor costs and increasing productivity (by keeping wages and benefits in check) and maintaining management prerogatives in important areas such as staffing levels and work rules. Of course, management always has the option of trying to decertify a union (that is, encouraging employees to vote out the union in a decertification election) if it believes that the majority of employees no longer wish to be represented by the union.

Labor Unions

Labor unions seek, through collective action, to give workers a formal and independent voice in setting the terms and conditions of their work. Table 14.1 shows typical provisions negotiated by unions in collective bargaining contracts. Labor unions attempt to represent their members' interests in these decisions.

A major goal of labor unions is bargaining effectiveness, because with it comes the power and influence to make the employees' voices heard and to effect changes in the workplace.[11] As the opening to this chapter suggests, the right to strike is one important component of bargaining power. In turn, the success of a strike (actual or threatened) depends on the relative magnitude of the costs imposed on management versus those imposed on the union. A critical factor is the size of union membership. More members translate into a greater ability to halt or disrupt production and also into greater financial resources for continuing a strike in the face of lost wages.

Union Structure, Administration, and Membership

A necessary step in discussing labor–management interactions is a basic knowledge of how labor and management are organized and how they function. Management has been described throughout this book. We now focus on labor unions.

National and International Unions

Most union members belong to a national or international union. Most national unions are composed of multiple local units, and most are affiliated with the American Federation of Labor and Congress of Industrial Organizations (AFL-CIO).

The largest AFL-CIO–affiliated national unions are listed in Table 14.2. (The National Education Association, with 2.5 million members, is not affiliated with the AFL-CIO.) An important characteristic of a union is whether it is a craft or industrial union. The electrical workers' and carpenters' unions are craft unions, meaning that the members all have a particular skill or occupation. Craft unions often are responsible for training their members (through apprenticeships) and for supplying craft workers to employers. Requests for carpenters, for example, would come to the union hiring hall, which would decide which carpenters to send out. Thus craft workers may work for many employers over time, their constant link being to the union. A craft union's bargaining power depends greatly on the control it can exercise over the supply of its workers.

TABLE 14.1

Typical Provisions in Collective Bargaining Contracts

Establishment and administration of the agreement
- Bargaining unit and plant supplements
- Contract duration and reopening and renegotiation provisions
- Union security and the checkoff
- Special bargaining committees
- Grievance procedures
- Arbitration and mediation
- Strikes and lockouts
- Contract enforcement

Functions, rights, and responsibilities
- Management rights clauses
- Plant removal
- Subcontracting
- Union activities on company time and premises
- Union–management cooperation
- Regulation of technological change
- Advance notice and consultation

Wage determination and administration
- General provisions
- Rate structure and wage differentials
- Allowances
- Incentive systems and production bonus plans
- Production standards and time studies
- Job classification and job evaluation
- Individual wage adjustments
- General wage adjustments during the contract period

Job or income security
- Hiring and transfer arrangements
- Employment and income guarantees
- Reporting and call-in pay
- Supplemental unemployment benefit plans
- Regulation of overtime, shift work, etc.
- Reduction of hours to forestall layoffs
- Layoff procedures; seniority; recall
- Worksharing in lieu of layoff
- Attrition arrangements
- Promotion practices
- Training and retraining
- Relocation allowances
- Severance pay and layoff benefit plans
- Special funds and study committees

Plant operations
- Work and shop rules
- Rest periods and other in-plant time allowances
- Safety and health
- Plant committees
- Hours of work and premium pay practices
- Shift operations
- Hazardous work
- Discipline and discharge

Paid and unpaid leave
- Vacations and holidays
- Sick leave
- Funeral and personal leave
- Military leave and jury duty

Employee benefit plans
- Health and insurance plans
- Pension plans
- Profit-sharing, stock purchase, and thrift plans
- Bonus plans

Special groups
- Apprentices and learners
- Workers with disabilities and older workers
- Women
- Veterans
- Union representatives
- Nondiscrimination clauses

SOURCE: From H.C. Katz and T.A. Kochan, *Collective Bargaining and Industrial Relations*, 1980. Copyright © 1980 The McGraw-Hill Companies, Inc. Reprinted with permission.

In contrast, industrial unions are made up of members who are linked by their work in a particular industry (such as steelworkers and autoworkers). Typically they represent many different occupations. Membership in the union is a result of working for a particular employer in the industry. Changing employers is less common than it is among craft workers, and employees who change employers remain members of the same union only if they happen to move to other employers covered by that union.

TABLE 14.2
Largest AFL-CIO–Affiliated Labor Unions

ORGANIZATION	NUMBER OF MEMBERS
National Education Association	2,495,826
International Brotherhood of Teamsters	1,400,700
United Food and Commercial Workers International Union	1,391,399
Service Employees International Union	1,321,790
American Federation of State, County and Municipal Employees	1,300,000
Laborers' International Union of North America	774,696
International Union, United Automobile, Aerospace and Agricultural Implement Workers of America	762,439
International Association of Machinists and Aerospace Workers	737,510
International Brotherhood of Electrical Workers	718,742
American Federation of Teachers	686,518
United Steelworkers of America	636,297
United Brotherhood of Carpenters and Joiners of America	515,986
Communications Workers of America	490,621
National Postal Mail Handlers Union	419,987
International Union of Operating Engineers	372,527
American Postal Workers Union	315,582
National Association of Letter Carriers	307,761
United Association of Journeymen and Apprentices of the Plumbing and Pipe Fitting Industry of the United States and Canada	299,136
Paper, Allied-Industrial, Chemical Employees International Union	292,160
Hotel Employees and Restaurant Employees International Union	245,327
International Association of Fire Fighters	235,527
Union of Needletrades, Industrial and Textile Employees	216,261
American Federation of Government Employees	191,171
American Association of Classified School Employees	166,512
Amalgamated Transit Union	165,678
Sheet Metal Workers International Association	142,500
Graphic Communications International Union	141,874
International Association of Bridge, Structural and Ornamental Iron Workers	126,004
United Mine Workers of America	124,803
Bakery, Confectionery, Tobacco Workers and Grain Millers International Union	121,379
Office and Professional Employees International Union	117,997
International Brotherhood of Painters and Allied Trades	113,445
International Union of Electronic, Electrical, Salaried, Machine and Furniture Workers	112,331
Transportation Communications International Union	110,652
American Federation of Musicians of the United States and Canada	110,000
Transport Workers Union of America	109,000

SOURCE: From J.A. Fossum, *Labor Relations: Development, Structure and Process,* 1992.

Whereas a craft union may restrict the number of, say, carpenters to maintain higher wages, industrial unions try to organize as many employees in as wide a range of skills as possible.

Three major unions (the United Auto Workers, the United Steelworkers, and the International Association of Machinists) had hoped to merge by the year 2000, a move that would have created a union having more than 2 million members, the largest in the AFL-CIO. AFL-CIO leadership applauded the merger as an action that would contribute to better and more powerful representation of worker interests.[12] Organized labor hopes that mergers like this will reduce competition among unions and contribute to more success in organizing new members and achieving more bargaining power for current members.[13] As of 2001, however, the ambitious merger had not taken place, and its prospects were uncertain.

Local Unions

Even when a national union plays the most critical role in negotiating terms of a collective bargaining contract, negotiation occurs at the local level as well as over work rules and other issues that are locally determined. In addition, administration of the contract is largely carried out at the local union level. Consequently, the bulk of day-to-day interaction between labor and management takes place at the local union level.

The local of an industrial-based union may correspond to a single large facility or to a number of small facilities. In a craft-oriented union, the local may cover a city or a region. The local union typically elects officers (like president, vice president, treasurer). Responsibility for contract negotiation may rest with the officers, or a bargaining committee may be formed for this purpose. Typically the national union provides assistance, ranging from background data about other settlements and technical advice to sending a representative to lead the negotiations.

Individual members' participation in local union meetings includes the election of union officials and strike votes. However, most union contact is with the shop steward, who is responsible for ensuring that the terms of the collective bargaining contract are enforced. The shop steward represents employees in contract grievances. Another union position, the business representative, performs some of the same functions, especially where the union deals with multiple employers, as is often the case with craft unions.

American Federation of Labor and Congress of Industrial Organizations (AFL-CIO)

The AFL-CIO is not a labor union but rather an association that seeks to advance the shared interests of its member unions at the national level, much as the Chamber of Commerce and the National Association of Manufacturers do for their member employers. As Figure 14.2 indicates, there are approximately 72 affiliated national and international unions and 60,000 locals. An important responsibility of the AFL-CIO is to represent labor's interests in public policy issues such as civil rights, economic policy, safety, and occupational health. It also provides information and analysis that member unions can use in their activities: organizing new members, negotiating new contracts, and administering contracts.

Union Security

The survival and security of a union depends on its ability to ensure a regular flow of new members and member dues to support the services it provides. Therefore, unions typically place high priority on negotiating two contract provisions with an employer

FIGURE 14.2
Structure of the American Federation of Labor and Congress of Industrial Organizations (AFL-CIO)

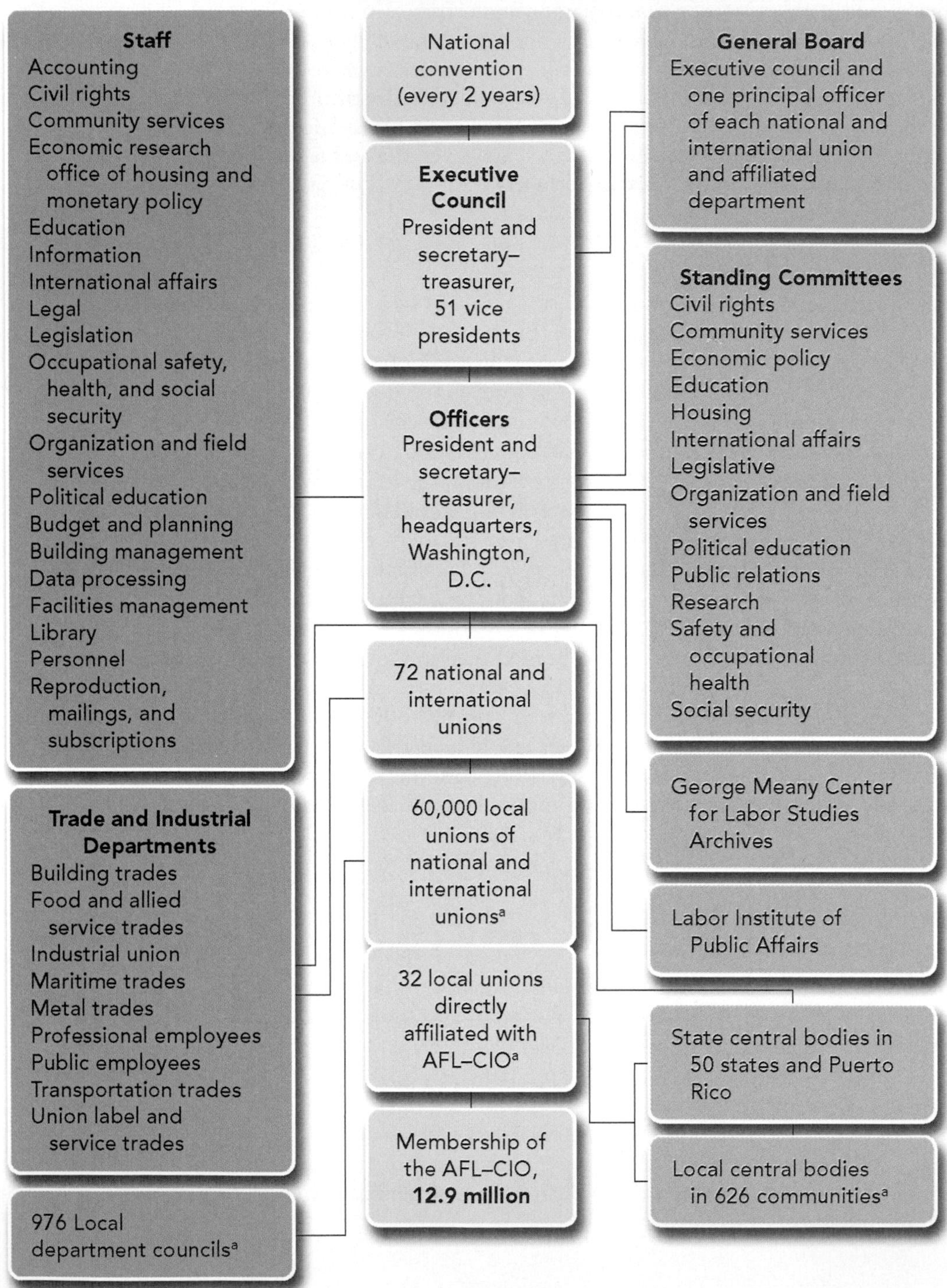

[a]1989 data.

SOURCES: J.A. Fossum, *Labor Relations*, 5th ed. (Homewood, IL: Richard D. Irwin, 1992), p. 118. Updated with data from C.D. Gifford, *Directory of U.S. Labor Organizations*, 1998 (Washington, DC: Bureau of National Affairs, 1998).

that are critical to a union's security or viability: checkoff provisions and union membership or contribution. First, under a **checkoff provision,** the employer, on behalf of the union, automatically deducts union dues from employees' paychecks.

A second union security provision focuses on the flow of new members (and their dues). The strongest union security arrangement is a **closed shop,** under which a person must be a union member (and thus pay dues) before being hired. A closed shop is, however, illegal under the NLRA. A **union shop** requires a person to join the union within a certain amount of time (30 days) after beginning employment. An **agency shop** is similar to a union shop but does not require union membership, only that dues be paid. **Maintenance of membership** rules do not require union membership but do require that employees who choose to join must remain members for a certain period of time (such as the length of the contract).

Under the 1947 Taft–Hartley Act (an amendment to the NLRA), states may pass so-called **right-to-work laws,** which make union shops, maintenance of membership, and agency shops illegal. The idea behind such laws is that compulsory union membership (or making employees pay union dues) infringes on the employee's right to freedom of association. From the union perspective, a big concern is "free riders," employees who benefit from union activities without belonging to a union. By law, all members of a bargaining unit, whether union members or not, must be represented by the union. If the union is required to offer service to all bargaining unit members, even those who are not union members, it may lose its financial viability.

Checkoff provision
A union contract provision that requires an employer to deduct union dues from employees' paychecks.

Closed shop
A union security provision requiring a person to be a union member before being hired. Illegal under NLRA.

Union shop
A union security provision that requires a person to join the union within a certain amount of time after being hired.

Agency shop
A union security provision that requires an employee to pay union membership dues but not to join the union.

Maintenance of membership
Union rules requiring members to remain members for a certain period of time (such as the length of the union contract).

Right-to-work laws
State laws that make union shops, maintenance of membership, and agency shops illegal.

Union Membership and Bargaining Power

At the strategic level, management and unions meet head-on over the issue of union organizing. Increasingly, employers are actively resisting unionization in an attempt to control costs and maintain their flexibility. Unions, on the other hand, must organize new members and hold on to their current members to have the kind of bargaining power and financial resources needed to achieve their goals in future organizing and to negotiate and administer contracts with management. For this reason we now discuss trends in union membership and possible explanations for those trends.

Since the 1950s, when union membership rose to 35 percent of employment, membership has consistently declined as a percentage of employment. It now stands at 14 percent of all employment and 9 percent of private-sector employment.[14] As Figure 14.3 indicates, this decline shows no indication of reversing (or even slowing down). If the trend continues, private-sector membership in unions may fall below 5 percent in the foreseeable future.[15]

What factors explain the decline in union membership? Several have been identified.[16]

Structural Changes in the Economy

At the risk of oversimplifying, we might say that unions have traditionally been strongest in urban workplaces (especially those outside the South) that employ middle-aged workers in blue-collar jobs. However, much recent job growth has occurred among women and youth in the service sector of the economy. Although unionizing such groups is possible, unions have so far not had much success organizing these groups in the private sector. Despite the importance of structural changes in the economy, studies show that they account for no more than one-quarter of the overall union membership decline.[17] Also, Canada, which has been undergoing similar structural

FIGURE 14.3
Union Membership Density among U.S. Wage and Salary Workers, 1973–2000

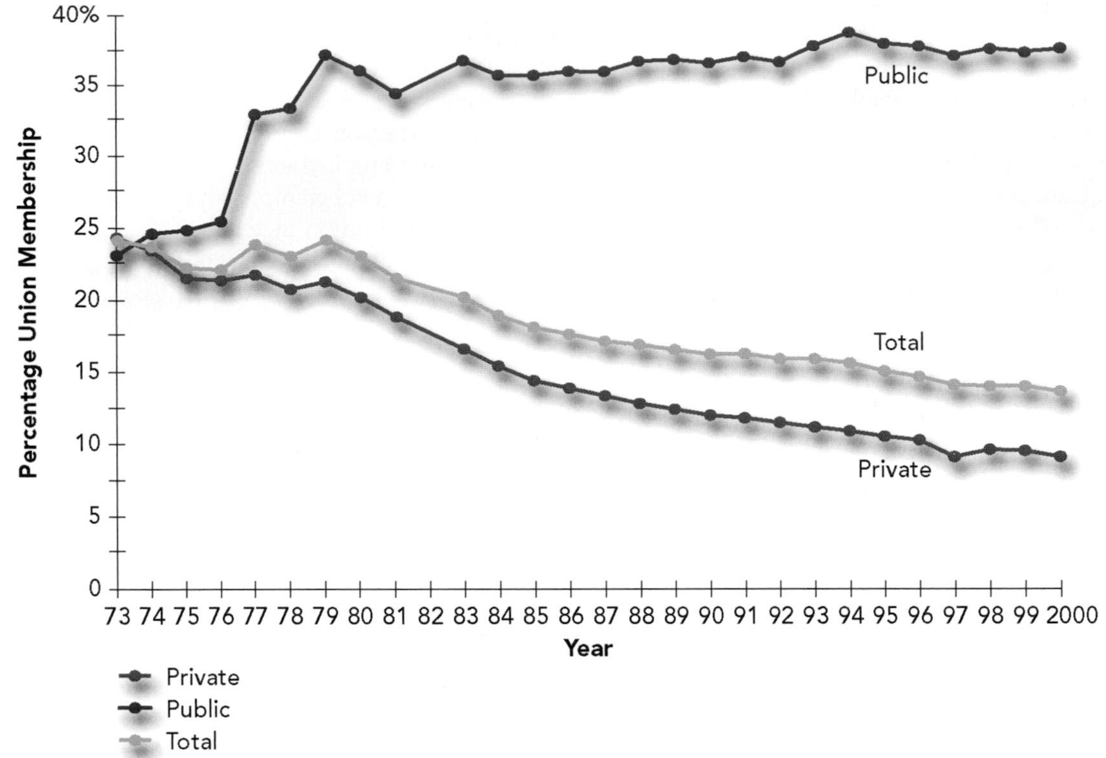

SOURCE: 1973–81—May Current Population Surveys (CPS); 1983–2000—CPS Outgoing Rotation Group (ORG) Earning Files. Values for 1982 are linearly interpolated from 1981 and 1983 values. Union Density is measured by the percentage of total, private sector, and public sector wage and salary workers who are union members. Beginning in 1977, workers belonging to "an employee association similar to a union" are included as members. From B.T. Hirsch and D.A. MacPherson, *Union Membership and Earnings Data Book 2001* (Washington, DC: The Bureau of National Affairs, Inc., 2001). Reprinted with permission.

changes, has experienced growth in union membership since the early 1960s. Growth in union membership in Canada now stands at over 30 percent of employment, compared with 16 percent in the United States.

Increased Employer Resistance

Almost one-half of large employers in a survey reported that their most important labor goal was to be union-free. This contrasts sharply with 30 years ago, when one observer wrote that "many tough bargainers [among employers] prefer the union to a situation where there is no union. Most of the employers in rubber, basic steel and the automobile industry fall in this category." The idea then was that an effective union could help assess and communicate the interests of employees to management, thus helping management make better decisions. But product-market pressures, such as foreign competition, have contributed to increasing employer resistance of unions. These changes in the competitive environment have contributed to a change in management's perspective and goals.[18]

COMPETING THROUGH GLOBALIZATION

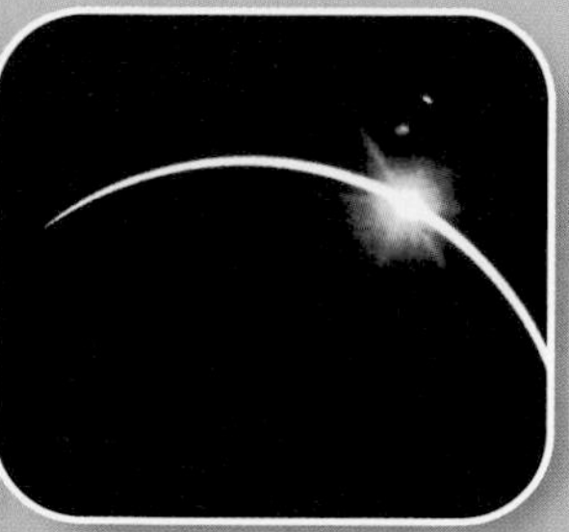

Nissan Workers Vote Down Unionization

To some it looked like a sure thing. The United Auto Workers had tried to organize Nissan's Smyrna, Tennessee, plant workers in 1989 and failed. But in 2001 those workers were older, more experienced, and looking for job security and better benefits. By August several Nissan workers had delivered large boxes of signed union cards to the local office of the National Labor Relations Board in Nashville—enough to force an official vote in October. Some plant workers openly discussed their dissatisfaction with the Japan-based company, citing workplace injuries and lack of secure retirement as primary concerns.

Nissan management did not support the organization effort. "It's our policy to maintain open and productive relationships among all employees without the interference of a third party," stated Nissan spokesperson Fred Standish. But tension between management and workers had increased dramatically since Renault of France had taken a 36 percent stake in Nissan and put its executive from Brazil, Carlos Ghosn, in charge. Ghosn, based in Tokyo, had focused entirely on cutting costs and bringing out new models during the previous two years. As part of the plan, Nissan hired more temporary workers at the Smyrna plant and reduced its health insurance benefits. Under these circumstances, it looked as though the union was a shoe-in.

But when the votes were tallied in October, the UAW lost by a wide margin. So far the UAW has not yet succeeded in organizing a Japanese-owned auto plant (a "transplant") in the United States. Why was there such a big loss in this case? One explanation may be that a week before the vote, Nissan announced plans to move the production of its top-of-the-line Maxima from Tokyo to Smyrna. That would increase production at the plant by 100,000 vehicles. In addition, Nissan committed to a $1 billion expansion at the Smyrna plant and a nearby facility that manufactures Nissan engines. "Nissan really pulled out all the stops," noted Michael Flynn, director of the Office for the Study of Automotive Transportation at the University of Michigan. "The timing of the announcement of the Maxima probably played a role."

Union representatives charged Nissan with "a campaign of fear and intimidation" while Nissan executives naturally praised the workers for their rejection of the union. "The union will probably now back off the seriousness of organizing the transplants," predicted Michael Flynn.

SOURCE: T.Y. Jones, "UAW Loses Bid to Enter Nissan Plant," *Los Angeles Times* (October 4, 2001), www.latimes.com; J. Gallagher and *Detroit Free Press* staff, "Nissan Factory Rejects Union" (October 4, 2001), www.auto.com; K. Bradsher, "Union Moves to Hold Vote at Nissan Plant in Tennessee," *The New York Times* (August 15, 2001), www.nytimes.com.

Over 30 years ago, unions were often able to organize entire industries. For example, the UAW organized all four major producers in the automobile industry (GM, Ford, Chrysler, and American Motors). The UAW usually sought and achieved the same union–management contract at each company. As a consequence, a negotiated wage increase in the industry could be passed on to the consumer in the form of higher prices. No company was undercut by its competitors because the labor cost of all major producers in the industry was determined by the same union–management

FIGURE 14.4
Employer Resistance to Union Organizing, 1950–98

NOTE: 8(a)(3) charges refer to the section of the NLRA that makes it an unfair employer labor practice to discriminate against (e.g., fire) employees who engage in union activities such as union organizing.

SOURCE: Adapted and updated from R.B. Freeman and J.L. Medoff, *What Do Unions Do?* (New York: BasicBooks, 1984). Data for 1985, 1989, 1990, 1994 and 1998 from National Labor Relations Board annual reports.

contract, and the U.S. public had little option but to buy U.S.-made cars. However, the onset of foreign competition in the automobile market changed the competitive situation as well as the UAW's ability to organize the industry.[19] U.S. automakers were slow to recognize and respond to the competitive threat from foreign producers, resulting in a loss of market share and employment.

Competitive threats have contributed to increased employer resistance to union organizing and, in some cases, to an increased emphasis on ridding themselves of existing unions. Unionized workers receive, on average, 10 percent higher pay (excluding benefits) than their nonunion counterparts. Many employers have decided that they can no longer compete with these higher labor costs, and union membership has suffered as a result.[20] One measure of increased employer resistance is the dramatic increase in the late 1960s in the number of unfair employer labor practices (violations of sections of the NLRA such as section 8(a)(3), which prohibits firing employees for union organizing, as we discuss later) even though the number of elections held did not change much. (See Figure 14.4.) The use of remedies such as back pay for workers also grew, but the costs to employers of such penalties does not appear to have been sufficient to prevent the growth in employer unfair labor practices. Not surprisingly, the union victory rate in representation elections has decreased from almost 59 percent in 1960 to about 50 percent in recent years. Since 1980, the number of elections has declined by more than 50 percent. Moreover, decertification elections have gone from about 4 percent of elections in 1960 to about 14 percent of elections in 1996.[21]

At a personal level, some managers may face serious consequences if a union successfully organizes a new set of workers or mounts a serious organizing drive. One study indicated that 8 percent of the plant managers in companies with organizing drives were fired, and 10 percent of those in companies where the union was successful were fired (compared with 2 percent in a control group).[22] Furthermore, only 3 percent of the plant managers facing an organizing drive were promoted, and none of those ending up with a union contract were promoted (compared with 21 percent of the managers in the control group). Therefore, managers are often under intense pressure to oppose unionization attempts.

Substitution with HRM

A major study of the human resource management strategies and practices among large, nonunion employers found that union avoidance was often an important employee relations objective.[23] Top management's values in such companies drive specific policies such as promotion from within, an influential personnel–human resource department, and above-average pay and benefits. These policies, in turn, contribute to a number of desirable outcomes such as flexibility, positive employee attitudes, and responsive and committed employees, which ultimately lead to higher productivity and better employee relations. In other words, employers attempt to remain nonunion by offering most of the things a union can offer, and then some, while still maintaining a productivity advantage over their competitors. Of course, one aspect of union representation that employers cannot duplicate is the independent employee voice that a union provides.

Substitution by Government Regulation

Since the 1960s, regulation of many employment areas has increased, including equal employment opportunity, pensions, and worker displacement. Combined with existing regulations, this increase may result in fewer areas in which unions can provide worker rights or protection beyond those specified by law. Yet Western European countries generally have more regulations and higher levels of union membership than the United States.[24]

Worker Views

Industrial relations scholars have long argued that the absence in the United States of a history of feudalism and of strong class distinctions found in Western Europe have contributed to a more pragmatic, business-oriented (versus class-conscious) unionism. Although this may help explain the somewhat lower level of union membership in the United States, its relevance in explaining the downward trend is not clear.

Union Actions

In some ways, unions have hurt their own cause. First, corruption in unions such as the Teamsters may have had a detrimental effect. Second, questions have been raised about how well unions have adapted to recent changes in the economic structure. Employee groups and economic sectors with the fastest growth rates tend to have the

COMPETING IN THE NEW ECONOMY

Will Unions Play a Role in High-Tech Industries?

Unions used to be the domain of auto workers, truck drivers, electricians, teachers, movie actors, and a host of other American workers. But with the changing economy, union membership has changed as well. It is now at its lowest level in 60 years. Currently there are 13 million union members, or roughly 13.5 percent of the American workforce. Will unions survive in the new economy? And if so, what kind of role will they play?

In recent years unions have turned to the information technology industry for potential growth and have been snubbed on many occasions. Perhaps this is because traditional union values seem somewhat outdated; for instance, the mostly young IT workforce isn't worried yet about job security. "The philosophy is, 'Till death do us part—until I get a better offer,'" explains Harris Miller, president of the Information Technology Association of America, an industry trade group. "That's a very different attitude from saying, 'I'll work for this steel mill for the rest of my life,' and it makes it very hard for high-tech workers to see the appeal of joining a union." The Communication Workers of America's efforts to organize at Amazon.com have failed thus far, along with a similar drive at CNBC, the cable counterpart to NBC. The failure of the latter drive is a mystery to many because cable workers are generally paid much less than their network counterparts. But local CWA vice president Bill Freeh says, "It was a very hard sell. These were workers who weren't looking for the security a union can provide. They just didn't want to jeopardize their jobs." During the organization drive, CNBC hosted pizza parties and bowling nights for employees, many of whom were recent college graduates.

But organized labor has not lost hope. "Is it hard to convince high-tech workers that they should join a union? Certainly," says Marcus Courtney, cofounder and president of WashTech, an advocacy and advice group based in Washington. "But . . . some things don't change, and one of them is that individuals have no power unless they're organized." However, some of the goals of union representation will probably change. To revitalize, unions may have to focus more on issues of quality of life for workers—such as child care or time off to take care of aging parents. "This is a sunrise industry," says Katie Quan, labor policy specialist at the Center for Labor Research and Education at the University of California at Berkeley. "It's quite important for the labor movement to get a foothold and grow with it."

SOURCE: L.M. Prencipe, "E-Mail and the Internet Are Changing the Labor/Management Power Play," *InfoWorld* (March 12, 2001), **www.infoworld.com**; T. Wolverton, "Labor Pains," *CNET News.com* (January 16, 2001), **http://news.cnet.com**; Y.J. Dreazen, "Old Labor Tries to Establish Role in New Economy," *The Wall Street Journal* (August 15, 2001), pp. B1, B10.

lowest rates of unionization.[25] Women are less likely to be in unions than men (12 percent versus 16 percent), and nonmanufacturing industries such as finance, insurance, and real estate have a lower union representation (2 percent) than does manufacturing (16 percent). The South is also less heavily organized than the rest of the country, with, for example, South Carolina having a unionization rate of 4 percent, compared with 26 percent in New York State.[26]

Legal Framework

Although competitive challenges have a major impact on labor relations, the legal framework of collective bargaining is an especially critical determinant of union membership and relative bargaining power and, therefore, of the degree to which employers, employees, and society are successful in achieving their goals. The legal framework also constrains union structure and administration and the manner in which unions and employers interact. Perhaps the most dramatic example of labor laws' influence is the 1935 passage of the Wagner Act (also known as the National Labor Relations Act or NLRA), which actively supported collective bargaining rather than impeding it. As a result, union membership nearly tripled, from 3 million in 1933 (7.7 percent of all employment) to 8.8 million (19.2 percent of employment) by 1939.[27] With increased membership came greater union bargaining power and, consequently, more success in achieving union goals.

Before the 1930s, the legal system was generally hostile to unions. The courts generally viewed unions as coercive organizations that hindered free trade. Unions' focus on collective voice and collective action (strikes, boycotts) did not fit well with the U.S. emphasis on capitalism, individualism, freedom of contract, and property rights.[28]

The Great Depression of the 1930s, however, shifted public attitudes toward business and the free-enterprise system. Unemployment rates as high as 25 percent and a 30 percent drop in the gross national product between 1929 and 1933 focused attention on employee rights and on the shortcomings of the system as it existed then. The nation was in a crisis, and President Franklin Roosevelt responded with dramatic action, the New Deal. On the labor front, the 1935 NLRA ushered in a new era of public policy for labor unions, enshrining collective bargaining as the preferred mechanism for settling labor–management disputes.

The introduction to the NLRA states:

> It is in the national interest of the United States to maintain full production in its economy. Industrial strife among employees, employers, and labor organizations interferes with full production and is contrary to our national interest. Experience has shown that labor disputes can be lessened if the parties involved recognize the legitimate rights of each in their relations with one another. To establish these rights under the law, Congress enacted the National Labor Relations Act. Its purpose is to define and protect the rights of employees and employers, to encourage collective bargaining, and to eliminate certain practices on the part of labor and management that are harmful to the general welfare.[29]

The rights of employees are set out in Section 7 of the act, including the "right to self-organization, to form, join, or assist labor organizations, to bargain collectively through representatives of their own choosing, and to engage in other concerted activities for the purpose of collective bargaining. The act also gives employees the right to refrain from any or all of such activities except [in cases] requiring membership in a labor organization as a condition of employment."[30] Examples of protected activities include

- Union organizing.
- Joining a union, whether it is recognized by the employer or not.
- Going out on strike to secure better working conditions.
- Refraining from activity on behalf of the union.[31]

Although the NLRA has broad coverage in the private sector, Table 14.3 shows that there are some notable exclusions.

TABLE 14.3
Are You Excluded from the NLRA's Coverage?

The NLRA specifically excludes from its coverage individuals who are

- Employed as a supervisor.
- Employed by a parent or spouse.
- Employed as an independent contractor.
- Employed in the domestic service of any person or family in a home.
- Employed as agricultural laborers.
- Employed by an employer subject to the Railway Labor Act.
- Employed by a federal, state, or local government.
- Employed by any other person who is not an employer as defined in the NLRA.

SOURCE: http://www.nlrb.gov/publications/engulp.html.

Unfair Labor Practices—Employers

The NLRA prohibits certain activities by both employers and labor unions. Unfair labor practices by employers are listed in Section 8(a) of the NLRA. Section 8(a)(1) prohibits employers from interfering with, restraining, or coercing employees in exercising their rights to join or assist a labor organization or to refrain from such activities. Section 8(a)(2) prohibits employer domination of or interference with the formation or activities of a labor union. Section 8(a)(3) prohibits discrimination in any aspect of employment that attempts to encourage or discourage union-related activity. Section 8(a)(4) prohibits discrimination against employees for providing testimony relevant to enforcement of the NLRA. Section 8(a)(5) prohibits employers from refusing to bargain collectively with a labor organization that has standing under the act. Examples of employer unfair labor practices are listed in Table 14.4.

Unfair Labor Practices—Labor Unions

Taft-Hartley Act, 1947
The 1947 act that outlawed unfair union labor practices.

Originally the NLRA did not list any union unfair labor practices. These were added through the 1947 **Taft–Hartley Act.** The 1959 *Landrum–Griffin Act* further regulated unions' actions and their internal affairs (like financial disclosure and conduct of elections). Section 8(b)(1)(a) of the NLRA states that a labor organization is not to "restrain or coerce employees in the exercise of the rights guaranteed in section 7" (described earlier). Table 14.5 provides examples of union unfair labor practices.

Enforcement

Enforcement of the NLRA rests with the National Labor Relations Board (NLRB), which is composed of a five-member board, the general counsel, and 33 regional offices. The basis for the NLRA is the commerce clause of the U.S. Constitution. Therefore, the NLRB's jurisdiction is limited to employers whose operations affect commerce generally and interstate commerce in particular. In practice, only purely local firms are likely to fall outside the NLRB's jurisdiction. Specific jurisdictional standards (nearly 20) that vary by industry are applied. Two examples of businesses that are covered (and the standards) are retail businesses that had more than $500,000 in annual business and newspapers that had more than $200,000 in annual business.

The NLRB's two major functions are to conduct and certify representation elections

TABLE 14.4

Examples of Employer Unfair Labor Practices

- Threatening employees with loss of their jobs or benefits if they join or vote for a union.
- Threatening to close down a plant if organized by a union.
- Questioning employees about their union membership or activities in a manner that restrains or coerces them.
- Spying or pretending to spy on union meetings.
- Granting wage increases that are timed to discourage employees from forming or joining a union.
- Taking an active part in organizing a union or committee to represent employees.
- Providing preferential treatment or aid to one of several unions trying to organize employees.
- Discharging employees for urging other employees to join a union or refusing to hire applicants because they are union members.
- Refusing to reinstate workers when job openings occur because the workers participated in a lawful strike.
- Ending operation at one plant and opening the same operation at another plant with new employees because employees at the first plant joined a union.
- Demoting or firing employees for filing an unfair labor practice or for testifying at an NLRB hearing.
- Refusing to meet with employees' representatives because the employees are on strike.
- Refusing to supply the employees' representative with cost and other data concerning a group insurance plan covering employees.
- Announcing a wage increase without consulting the employees' representative.
- Failing to bargain about the effects of a decision to close one of employer's plants.

SOURCE: National Labor Relations Board, *A Guide to Basic Law and Procedures under the National Labor Relations Act* (Washington, DC: U.S. Government Printing Office, 1991). See also **www.nlrb.gov**.

TABLE 14.5

Examples of Union Unfair Labor Practices

- Mass picketing in such numbers that nonstriking employees are physically barred from entering the plant.
- Acts of force or violence on the picket line or in connection with a strike.
- Threats to employees of bodily injury or that they will lose their jobs unless they support the union's activities.
- Fining or expelling members for crossing a picket line that is unlawful.
- Fining or expelling members for filing unfair labor practice charges or testifying before the NLRB.
- Insisting during contract negotiations that the employer agree to accept working conditions that will be determined by a group to which it does not belong.
- Fining or expelling union members for the way they apply the bargaining contract while carrying out their supervisory responsibilities.
- Causing an employer to discharge employees because they spoke out against a contract proposed by the union.
- Making a contract that requires an employer to hire only members of the union or employees "satisfactory" to the union.
- Insisting on the inclusion of illegal provisions in a contract.
- Terminating an existing contract and striking for a new one without notifying the employer, the Federal Mediation and Conciliation Service, and the state mediation service (where one exists).
- Attempting to compel a beer distributor to recognize a union (the union prevents the distributor from obtaining beer at a brewery by inducing the brewery's employees to refuse to fill the distributor's orders).
- Picketing an employer to force it to stop doing business with another employer who has refused to recognize the union (a "secondary boycott").

SOURCE: National Labor Relations Board, *A Guide to Basic Law and Procedures under the National Labor Relations Act* (Washington, DC: U.S. Government Printing Office, 1991). See also **www.nlrb.gov**.

and prevent unfair labor practices. In both realms, it does not initiate action. Rather, it responds to requests for action. The NLRB's role in representation elections is discussed in the next section. Here we discuss unfair labor practices.

Unfair labor practice cases begin with the filing of a charge, which is investigated by a regional office. A charge must be filed within six months of the alleged unfair practice, and copies must be served on all parties. (Registered mail is recommended.) If the NLRB finds the charge to have merit and issues a complaint, there are two possible actions. It may defer to a grievance procedure agreed on by the employer and union. Otherwise, a hearing is held before an administrative law judge. The judge makes a recommendation, which can be appealed by either party. The NLRB has the authority to issue cease-and-desist orders to halt unfair labor practices. It can also order reinstatement of employees, with or without back pay. Note, however, that the NLRA is not a criminal statute, and punitive damages are not available. If an employer or union refuses to comply with an NLRB order, the board has the authority to petition the U.S. Court of Appeals. The court can choose to enforce the order, remand it to the NLRB for modification, change it, or set it aside altogether.

Union and Management Interactions: Organizing

To this point we have discussed macro trends in union membership. Here we shift our focus to the more micro questions of why individual employees join unions and how the organizing process works at the workplace level.

Why Do Employees Join Unions?

Virtually every model of the decision to join a union focuses on two questions.[32] First, is there a gap between the pay, benefits, and other conditions of employment that employees actually receive versus what they believe they should receive? Second, if such a gap exists and is sufficiently large to motivate employees to try to remedy the situation, is union membership seen as the most effective or instrumental means of change? The outcome of an election campaign hinges on how the majority of employees answer these two questions.

The Process and Legal Framework of Organizing

The NLRB is responsible for ensuring that the organizing process follows certain steps. At the most general level, the NLRB holds a union representation election if at least 30 percent of employees in the bargaining unit sign authorization cards (see Figure 14.5). If over 50 percent of the employees sign authorization cards, the union may request that the employer voluntarily recognize it. If 50 percent or fewer of the employees sign, or if the employer refuses to recognize the union voluntarily, the NLRB conducts a secret-ballot election. The union is certified by the NLRB as the exclusive representative of employees if over 50 percent of employees vote for the union. If more than one union appears on the ballot and neither gains a simple majority, a runoff election is held. Once a union has been certified as the exclusive representative of a group of employees, no additional elections are permitted for one year. After the negotiation of a contract, an election cannot be held for the contract's

YES, I WANT THE IAM

I, the undersigned employee of

(Company) ______________________________

authorize the International Association of Machinists and Aerospace Workers (IAM) to act as my collective bargaining agent for wages, hours and working conditions. I agree that this card may be used either to support a demand for recognition or an NLRB election, at the discretion of the union.

Name (print) ____________ Date ____________

Home Address ____________ Phone ____________

City ____________ State ____________ Zip ____________

Job Title ____________ Dept. ____________ Shift ____________

Sign Here X ______________________________

Note: This authorization to be SIGNED and DATED in Employee's own handwriting.
YOUR RIGHT TO SIGN THIS CARD IS PROTECTED BY FEDERAL LAW.

RECEIVED BY (Initial) ____________

FIGURE 14.5
Authorization Card

SOURCE: From J.A. Fossum, *Labor Relations: Development, Structure and Process,* 2002. Copyright © 2002 The McGraw-Hill Companies, Inc. Reprinted with permission.

duration or for three years, whichever comes first. The parties to the contract may agree not to hold an election for longer than three years, but an outside party cannot be barred for more than three years.

As mentioned previously, union members' right to be represented by leaders of their own choosing was expanded under the Taft–Hartley Act to include the right to vote an existing union out—that is, to decertify it. The process follows the same steps as a representation election. A decertification election is not permitted when a contract is in effect. Research indicates that when decertification elections are held, unions typically do not fare well, losing about 70 percent of the time during the mid 1990s. Moreover, the number of such elections has increased from roughly 5 percent of all elections in the 1950s and 1960s to about 14 percent in the mid-1990s.[33]

The NLRB also is responsible for determining the appropriate bargaining unit and the employees who are eligible to participate in organizing activities. A unit may cover employees in one facility or multiple facilities within a single employer, or the unit may cover multiple employers. In general, employees on the payroll just prior to the ordering of an election are eligible to vote, although this rule is modified in some cases where, for example, employment in the industry is irregular. Most employees who are on strike and who have been replaced by other employees are eligible to vote in an election (such as a decertification election) that occurs within 12 months of the onset of the strike.

As shown in Table 14.3, the following types of employees cannot be included in bargaining units: agricultural laborers, independent contractors, supervisors, and managers. Beyond this, the NLRB attempts to group together employees who have a community of interest in their wages, hours, and working conditions. In many cases this grouping will be sharply contested, with management and the union jockeying to include or exclude certain employee subgroups in the hope of influencing the outcome of the election.

Organizing Campaigns: Management and Union Strategies and Tactics

Tables 14.6 and 14.7 list common issues that arise during most campaigns. Unions attempt to persuade employees that their wages, benefits, treatment by employers, and opportunity to influence workplace decisions are not sufficient and that the union will be effective in obtaining improvements. Management emphasizes that it has provided a good package of wages, benefits, and so on. It also argues that, whereas a union is unlikely to provide improvements in such areas, it will likely lead to certain costs for employees, such as union dues and the income loss resulting from strikes.

As Table 14.8 indicates, employers use a variety of methods to oppose unions in organizing campaigns, some of which may go beyond what the law permits, especially in the eyes of union organizers. This perception is supported by our earlier discussion, which noted a significant increase in employer unfair labor practices since the late 1960s. (See Figure 14.4.)

Why would employers increasingly break the law? Fossum suggests that the consequences (like back pay and reinstatement of workers) of doing so are "slight."[34] His review of various studies suggests that discrimination against employees involved in union organizing decreases union organizing success significantly and that the cost of back pay to union activists reinstated in their jobs is far smaller than the costs that would be incurred if the union managed to organize and gain better wages, benefits, and so forth.

Still, the NLRB attempts to maintain a noncoercive atmosphere under which employees feel they can exercise free choice. It will set aside an election if it believes that either the union or the employer has created "an atmosphere of confusion or fear of

TABLE 14.6
Prevalence of Certain Union Issues in Campaigns

UNION ISSUES	PERCENTAGE OF CAMPAIGNS
Union will prevent unfairness and will set up a grievance procedure and seniority system.	82%
Union will improve unsatisfactory wages.	79
Union strength will give employees voice in wages, working conditions.	79
Union, not outsider, bargains for what employees want.	73
Union has obtained gains elsewhere.	70
Union will improve unsatisfactory sick leave and insurance.	64
Dues and initiation fees are reasonable.	64
Union will improve unsatisfactory vacations and holidays.	61
Union will improve unsatisfactory pensions.	61
Employer promises and good treatment may not be continued without union.	61
Employees choose union leaders.	55
Employer will seek to persuade or frighten employees to vote against union.	55
No strike without vote.	55
Union will improve unsatisfactory working conditions.	52
Employees have legal right to engage in union activity.	52

SOURCE: From J.A. Fossum, *Labor Relations: Development, Structure and Process*, 1992.

TABLE 14.7

Prevalence of Certain Management Issues in Campaigns

MANAGEMENT ISSUES	PERCENTAGE OF CAMPAIGNS
Improvements not dependent on unionization.	85%
Wages good, equal to, or better than under union contract.	82
Financial costs of union dues outweigh gains.	79
Union is outsider.	79
Get facts before deciding; employer will provide facts and accept employee decision.	76
If union wins, strike may follow.	70
Loss of benefits may follow union win.	67
Strikers will lose wages; lose more than gain.	67
Unions not concerned with employee welfare.	67
Strike may lead to loss of jobs.	64
Employer has treated employees fairly and/or well.	60
Employees should be certain to vote.	54

SOURCE: From J.A. Fossum, *Labor Relations: Development, Structure and Process,* 1992. Copyright © 1992 The McGraw-Hill Companies, Inc. Reprinted with permission.

TABLE 14.8

Percentage of Firms Using Various Methods to Oppose Union Organizing Campaigns

Survey of employers	
Consultants used	41%
Unfair labor practice charges filed against employer	24
Survey of union organizers	
Consultants and/or lawyers used	70
Unfair labor practices by employer	
Charges filed	36
Discharges or discriminatory layoffs	42[a]
Company leaflets	80
Company letters	91
Captive audience speech	91[b]
Supervisor meetings with small groups of employees	92
Supervisor intensity in opposing union	
Low	14
Moderate	34
High	51

[a] This percentage is larger than the figure for charges filed because it includes cases in which no unfair labor practice charge was actually filed against the employer.

[b] Refers to management's requiring employees to attend a session on company time at which the disadvantages of union membership are emphasized.

SOURCE: R.B. Freeman and M.M. Kleiner, "Employer Behavior in the Face of Union Organizing Drives," *Industrial and Labor Relations Review* 43, no. 4 (April 1990), pp. 351–65. © Cornell University.

reprisals."[35] Examples of conduct that may lead to an election result being set aside include

- Threats of loss of jobs or benefits by an employer or union to influence votes or organizing activities.
- A grant of benefits or a promise of benefits as a means of influencing votes or organizing activities.
- An employer or union making campaign speeches to assembled groups of employees on company time less than 24 hours before an election.
- The actual use or threat of physical force or violence to influence votes or organizing activities.[36]

Associate union membership
A form of union membership by which the union receives dues in exchange for services (e.g., health insurance, credit cards) but does not provide representation in collective bargaining.

Supervisors have the most direct contact with employees. Thus, as Table 14.9 indicates, it is critical that they be proactive in establishing good relationships with employees if the company wishes to avoid union organizing attempts. It is also important for supervisors to know what not to do should a drive take place.

In response to organizing difficulties, the union movement has tried alternative approaches. **Associate union membership** is not linked to an employee's workplace and does not provide representation in collective bargaining. Instead the union provides other services, such as discounts on health and life insurance or credit cards.[37] In re-

TABLE 14.9
What Supervisors Should and Should Not Do to Stay Union-Free

WHAT TO DO:
Report any direct or indirect signs of union activity to a core management group.
Deal with employees by carefully stating the company's response to pro-union arguments. These responses should be coordinated by the company to maintain consistency and to avoid threats or promises.
Take away union issues by following effective management practice all the time: Deliver recognition and appreciation. Solve employee problems. Protect employees from harassment or humiliation. Provide business-related information. Be consistent in treatment of different employees. Accommodate special circumstances where appropriate. Ensure due process in performance management. Treat all employees with dignity and respect.
WHAT TO AVOID:
Threatening employees with harsher terms and conditions of employment or employment loss if they engage in union activity.
Interrogating employees about pro-union or anti-union sentiments that they or others may have or reviewing union authorization cards or pro-union petitions.
Promising employees that they will receive favorable terms or conditions of employment if they forgo union activity.
Spying on employees known to be, or suspected of being, engaged in pro-union activities.

SOURCE: *HR Magazine* by J.A. Segal. Copyright © 1998 by Society for Human Resource Management. Reproduced with permission of Society for Human Resource Management via Copyright Clearance Center.

turn, the union receives membership dues and a broader base of support for its activities. Associate membership may be attractive to employees who wish to join a union but cannot because their workplace is not organized by a union.

Corporate campaigns seek to bring public, financial, or political pressure on employers during the organizing (and negotiating) process.[38] For example, the Building and Construction Trades Department of the AFL-CIO successfully lobbied Congress to eliminate $100 million in tax breaks for a Toyota truck plant in Kentucky until Toyota agreed to use union construction workers and pay union wages.[39] The Amalgamated Clothing and Textile Workers Union (ACTWU) corporate campaign against J.P. Stevens during the late 1970s was one of the first and best known. The ACTWU organized a boycott of J.P. Stevens products and threatened to withdraw its pension funds from financial institutions where J.P. Stevens officers acted as directors. J.P. Stevens subsequently agreed to a contract with the ACTWU.[40]

Corporate campaigns
Union activities designed to exert public, financial, or political pressure on employers during the union-organizing process.

Unions also hope to use their financial assets to influence companies. As of 1997, union retirement funds held $1.4 trillion in corporate stock, about 14 percent of all outstanding shares. Although unions share control of these assets with company-appointed trustees, the AFL-CIO hopes to leverage these assets to influence company policies.[41]

Union and Management Interactions: Contract Negotiation

The majority of contract negotiations take place between unions and employers that have been through the process before. In most cases, management has come to accept the union as an organization that it must work with. But when the union has just been certified and is negotiating its first contract, the situation can be very different. In fact, unions are unable to negotiate a first contract in 27 to 37 percent of the cases.[42]

Labor–management contracts differ in their bargaining structures—that is, the range of employees and employers that are covered. As Table 14.10 indicates, the

TABLE 14.10
Types and Examples of Bargaining Structures

MULTIEMPLOYER (CENTRALIZED)	SINGLE EMPLOYER —MULTIPLANT	SINGLE EMPLOYER —SINGLE PLANT (DECENTRALIZED)
Craft union (narrow)		
Construction trades Longshoring Hospital association	Airline Teachers Police Firefighters Railroad	Craft union in small manufacturing plant Hospital
Industrial or multiskill union (broad)		
Coal mining (underground) Basic steel (pre-1986) Hotel association	Automobiles Steel (post-1986) Farm equipment State government Textile	Industrial union in small manufacturing plant

SOURCE: H.C. Katz and T.A. Kochan, *An Introduction to Collective Bargaining and Industrial Relations* (New York: McGraw-Hill, 1992). © 1992 The McGraw-Hill Companies, Inc. Used with permission.

COMPETING BY MEETING STAKEHOLDERS' NEEDS

A Factory's Crash Course in Economics Pays Off

As the economy slows and layoffs increase, some companies are giving employees crash courses in economics and personal finance so they will understand the tough decisions managers have to make in hard times—and learn how to plan for hard times themselves. And as a recent visit to the Outokumpu American Brass factory in this struggling industrial town of Buffalo, New York, suggests, treating blue-collar workers like thinking human beings rather than cogs in a machine can bolster workplace morale and even boost corporate profits. The plant, a renovated copper and brass factory built at the turn of the 20th century, was almost shut down in 1984 by the Atlantic Richfield Company because of flagging sales and labor unrest. But local investors bought the plant, which makes everything from brass buttons to shell casings for the Israeli Army to electrical connectors for cell phones, and quickly turned it around. In 1990 they sold it to Outokumpu Oyj, a Finnish mining and metals conglomerate, for a healthy profit.

Outokumpu officials said they reasoned that purchasing the plant, one of the largest copper and brass rolling mills in the United States, would lift their company's global presence. But officials knew they would have to raise workers' productivity over the long haul to make the investment pay off. Officials thought one way to do that would be to teach them the economic and financial basics of the company's markets and solicit their ideas on how to run the plant—a process started by the local investors. So in 1991 Outokumpu hired Cornell University's School of Industrial and Labor Relations in Buffalo to give employees what amounted to a crash course in the basics of the brass industry. At first employees were not in a cooperative mood, recalls Lou Jean Fleron, the school's director. When she went to the plant to talk about the global economy and its supposed benefits, Fleron says, she was astounded at their hostility toward their new employer. "They saw it as us against them, a takeover by this evil foreign company," she said. But the Cornell instructors persisted. In a session on global economic changes, Fleron explained that investments by foreign companies in American plants were increasing. She distributed an article

contracts differ, first, according to whether narrow (craft) or broad (industrial) employee interests are covered. Second, they differ according to whether they cover multiple employers or multiple plants within a single employer. (A single employer may have multiple plants, some union and some nonunion.) Different structures have different implications for bargaining power and the number of interests that must be incorporated in reaching an agreement.

Distributive bargaining
The part of the labor–management negotiation process that focuses on dividing a fixed economic "pie."

The Negotiation Process

Richard Walton and Robert McKersie suggested that labor–management negotiations could be broken into four subprocesses: distributive bargaining, integrative bargaining, attitudinal structuring, and intraorganizational bargaining.[43] **Distributive bargaining** focuses on dividing a fixed economic "pie" between the two sides. A wage by Robert B. Reich, the former labor secretary, outlining the benefits, including examples of how overseas capital had saved American jobs. And in round-the-clock workshops scheduled throughout the next year so that employees from all three shifts could attend, the instructors taught everything from the impact of technology on the workplace and the dynamics of international competition to the intricacies of corporate income statements and the factors that influence the pricing of commodities. . . .

The workshops are now held every three years. Before long, employees now say, they began to see the connection between the classroom discussions and their working conditions. For example, they say, after learning about manufacturing costs in developing countries and in newly industrialized countries like South Korea, they had a more sophisticated understanding of how their own wages were set. The lessons were even more basic than that. "When I first got here, nobody knew where the metal went" after it left the plant, said Verdell Hannah, a crew leader in the cast shop. "Some people didn't even know what people in the next department did." A furnace maker in favor of protectionist trade policies ended up leaving Outokumpu; now he handles business development worldwide for a high-technology textile maker.

Today management holds quarterly meetings for all 850 employees to discuss plant operations, market conditions, and investments in new equipment. And, said Warren E. Bartel, president of Outokumpu American Brass, "the questions—about pricing, competition, and customers—seem to get better every year."

In addition, Outokumpu invites customers to tour the production lines and talk to workers about the factory's products. And it has begun soliciting employees' views on ways to increase productivity. Last year, for example, management asked Brian Martinick, a 43-year-old machinist, for advice on replacing a metal-turning lathe used to repair equipment. So Martinick got together with several other machine operators to do some research and observe the performance of computer-driven lathes at other plants. . . .

From the outside, Outokumpu American Brass remains an uninspiring sight. A collection of red brick buildings and an eight-story furnace, it is surrounded by run-down shops and empty parking lots in this city's dilapidated Riverside section. But that belies what is happening inside. The factory earned a national AFL-CIO award for its labor–management cooperation four years ago. The Commerce Department uses it as a case study for effective employee involvement. The Buffalo plant has had visits from Irish zinc miners, officials from Poland, and steel company executives from Pittsburgh, who all want to know how workers and their bosses manage to get along. "I put a presentation together because all these companies were benchmarking us," says Martinick. "They came from Australia to see what we did."

SOURCE: W. Royal, "A Factory's Crash Course in Economics Pays Off," *The New York Times* (April 25, 2001), p. 9.

increase, for example, means that the union gets a larger share of the pie, management a smaller share. It is a win–lose situation. **Integrative bargaining** has a win–win focus; it seeks solutions beneficial to both sides. So if management needs to reduce labor costs, it could reach an agreement with the union to avoid layoffs in return for the union agreeing to changes in work rules that might enhance productivity.

Integrative bargaining
The part of the labor–management negotiation process that seeks solutions beneficial to both sides.

Attitudinal structuring refers to the relationship and trust between labor and management negotiators. Where the relationship is poor, it may be difficult for the two sides to engage in integrative bargaining because there is little trust that the other side will carry out its part of the deal. For example, the union may be reluctant to agree to productivity-enhancing work-rule changes to enhance job security if, in the past, it has made similar concessions but believes that management did not stick to its assurance of greater job security. Thus the long-term relationship between the two parties can have a very important impact on negotiations and their outcomes.

Attitudinal structuring
The aspect of the labor–management negotiation process that refers to the relationship and level of trust between the negotiators.

Intraorganizational bargaining
The part of the labor–management negotiation process that focuses on the conflicting objectives of factions within labor and management.

Intraorganizational bargaining reminds us that labor–management negotiations involve more than just two parties. Within management, and to an even greater extent within the union, different factions can have conflicting objectives. High-seniority workers, who are least likely to be laid off, may be more willing to accept a contract that has layoffs (especially if there is also a significant pay increase for those whose jobs are not at risk). Less senior workers would likely feel very differently. Thus negotiators and union leaders must simultaneously satisfy both the management side and their own internal constituencies. If they do not, they risk the union membership's rejecting the contract, or they risk being voted out of office in the next election. Management, too, is unlikely to be of one mind about how to approach negotiations. Some will focus more on long-term employee relations, others will focus on cost control, and still others will focus on what effect the contract will have on stockholders.

Management's Preparation for Negotiations

Clearly, the outcome of contract negotiations can have important consequences for labor costs and labor productivity and, therefore, for the company's ability to compete in the product market. Adapting Fossum's discussion, we can divide management preparation into the following seven areas, most of which have counterparts on the union side.[44]

1. *Establishing interdepartmental contract objectives:* The employer's industrial relations department needs to meet with the accounting, finance, production, marketing, and other departments and set contract goals that will permit each department to meet its responsibilities. As an example, finance may suggest a cost figure above which a contract settlement would seriously damage the company's financial health. The bargaining team needs to be constructed to take these various interests into account.
2. *Reviewing the old contract:* This step focuses on identifying provisions of the contract that might cause difficulties by hindering the company's productivity or flexibility or by leading to significant disagreements between management and the union.
3. *Preparing and analyzing data:* Information on labor costs and the productivity of competitors, as well as data the union may emphasize, needs to be prepared and analyzed. The union data might include cost-of-living changes and agreements reached by other unions that could serve as a target. Data on employee demographics and seniority are relevant for establishing the costs of such benefits as pensions, health insurance, and paid vacations. Finally, management needs to know how much it would be hurt by a strike. How long will its inventory allow it to keep meeting customer orders? To what extent are other companies positioned to step in and offer replacement products? How difficult would it be to find replacement workers if the company decided to continue operations during a strike?
4. *Anticipating union demands:* Recalling grievances over the previous contract, having ongoing discussions with union leaders, and becoming aware of settlements at other companies are ways of anticipating likely union demands and developing potential counterproposals.
5. *Establishing the cost of possible contract provisions:* Wages have not only a direct influence on labor costs but often an indirect effect on benefit costs (such as Social Security and paid vacation). Recall that benefits add 35 to 40 cents to every dol-

lar's worth of wages. Also, wage or benefit increases that seem manageable in the first year of a contract can accumulate to less manageable levels over time.

6. *Preparing for a strike:* If management intends to operate during a strike, it may need to line up replacement workers, increase its security, and figure out how to deal with incidents on the picket line and elsewhere. If management does not intend to operate during a strike (or if the company will not be operating at normal levels), it needs to alert suppliers and customers and consider possible ways to avoid the loss of their business. This could even entail purchasing a competitor's product in order to have something to sell to customers.
7. *Determining strategy and logistics:* Decisions must be made about the amount of authority the negotiating team will have. What concessions can it make on its own, and which ones require it to check with top management? On which issues can it compromise, and on which can it not? Decisions regarding meeting places and times must also be made.

Negotiation Stages and Tactics

Negotiations go through various stages.[45] In the early stages, many more people are often present than in later stages. On the union side, this may give all the various internal interest groups a chance to participate and voice their goals. This, in turn, helps send a message to management about what the union feels it must do to satisfy its members, and it may also help the union achieve greater solidarity. Union negotiators often present an extensive list of proposals at this stage, partly to satisfy their constituents and partly to provide themselves with issues on which they can show flexibility later in the process. Management may or may not present proposals of its own; sometimes it prefers to react to the union's proposals.

During the middle stages, each side must make a series of decisions, even though the outcome is uncertain. How important is each issue to the other side? How likely is it that disagreement on particular issues will result in a strike? When and to what extent should one side signal its willingness to compromise on its position?

In the final stage, pressure for an agreement increases as the deadline for a strike approaches. Public negotiations may be only part of the process. Negotiators from each side may have one-on-one meetings or small-group meetings where public-relations pressures are reduced. In addition, a neutral third party may become involved, someone who can act as a go-between or facilitator. In some cases, the only way for the parties to convince each other of their resolve (or to convince their own constituents of the other party's resolve) is to allow an impasse to occur.

Various books suggest how to avoid impasses by using mutual gains or integrative bargaining tactics. For example, *Getting to Yes* (New York: Penguin Books, 1991), by Roger Fisher and William Ury, describes four basic principles:

1. Separate the people from the problem.
2. Focus on interests, not positions.
3. Generate a variety of possibilities before deciding what to do.
4. Insist that the results be based on some objective standard.

Bargaining Power, Impasses, and Impasse Resolution

Employers' and unions' conflicting goals are resolved through the negotiation process just described. An important determinant of the outcome of this process is the relative bargaining power of each party, which can be defined as the "ability of one party to achieve its goals when faced with opposition from some other party to the bargaining process."[46] In collective bargaining, an important element of power is the relative ability of each party to withstand a strike. Although strikes are rare, the threat of a strike often looms large in labor–management negotiations. The relative ability to take a strike, whether one occurs or not, is an important determinant of bargaining power and, therefore, of bargaining outcomes.

Management's Willingness to Take a Strike

Management's willingness to take a strike comes down to two questions:

1. *Can the company remain profitable over the long run if it agrees to the union's demands?* The answer is more likely to be yes to the extent that higher labor costs can be passed on to consumers without losing business. This, in turn, is most likely when (1) the price increase is small because labor costs are a small fraction of total costs or (2) there is little price competition in the industry. Low price competition can result from regulated prices, from competition based on quality (rather than price), or from the union's organizing all or most of the employers in the industry, which eliminates labor costs as a price factor.

   Unions share part of management's concern with long-term competitiveness because a decline in competitiveness can translate into a decline in employment levels. On the other hand, the majority of union members may prefer to have higher wages, despite employment declines, particularly if a minority of the members (those with low seniority) suffer more employment loss and the majority keep their employment with higher wages.
2. *Can the company continue to operate in the short run despite a strike?* Although "hanging tough" on its bargaining goals may pay off for management in the long run, the short-run concern is the loss of revenues and profits from production being disrupted. The cost to strikers is a loss of wages and possibly a permanent loss of jobs.

Under what conditions is management most able to take a strike? The following factors are important:[47]

1. *Product demand:* Management is less able to afford a strike when the demand for its product is strong because that is when more revenue and profits are lost.
2. *Product perishability:* A strike by certain kinds of employees (farm workers at harvest time, truckers transporting perishable food, airline employees at peak travel periods) will result in permanent losses of revenue, thus increasing the cost of the strike to management.
3. *Technology:* An organization that is capital intensive (versus labor intensive) is less dependent on its employees and more likely to be able to use supervisors or others as replacements. Telephone companies are typically able to operate through strikes, even though installing new equipment or services and repair work may take significantly longer than usual.
4. *Availability of replacement workers:* When jobs are scarce, replacement workers are more available and perhaps more willing to cross picket lines. Using replacement workers to operate during a strike raises the stakes considerably for strikers who may be permanently replaced. Most strikers are not entitled to reinstatement until there are job openings for which they qualify. If replacements were hired, such openings may not occur for some time (if at all).

5. *Multiple production sites and staggered contracts:* Multiple sites and staggered contracts permit employers to shift production from the struck facility to facilities that, even if unionized, have contracts that expire at different times (so they are not able to strike at the same time).
6. *Integrated facilities:* When one facility produces something that other facilities need for their products, the employer is less able to take a strike because the disruption to production goes beyond that single facility. The just-in-time production system, which provides very little stockpiling of parts, further weakens management's ability to take a strike.
7. *Lack of substitutes for the product:* A strike is more costly to the employer if customers have a readily available alternative source from which to purchase the goods or services the company provides.

Bargaining outcomes also depend on the nature of the bargaining process and relationship, which includes the types of tactics used and the history of labor relations. The vast majority of labor–management negotiations do not result in a strike because a strike is typically not in the best interests of either party. Furthermore, both the union and management usually realize that if they wish to interact effectively in the future, the experience of a strike can be difficult to overcome. When strikes do occur, the conduct of each party during the strike can also have a lasting effect on labor–management relations. Violence by either side or threats of job loss by hiring replacements can make future relations difficult.

Impasse Resolution Procedures: Alternatives to Strikes

Given the substantial costs of strikes to both parties, procedures that resolve conflicts without strikes have arisen in both the private and public sectors. Because many public sector employees do not have the right to strike, alternatives are particularly important in that arena.

Three often-used impasse resolution procedures are mediation, fact finding, and arbitration. All of them rely on the intervention of a neutral third party, most typically provided by the Federal Mediation and Conciliation Service (FMCS), which must be notified 30 days prior to a planned change in contract terms (including a strike). **Mediation** is the least formal but most widely used of the procedures (in both the public and private sectors). One survey found it was used by nearly 40 percent of all large private sector bargaining units.[48] A mediator has no formal authority but, rather, acts as a facilitator and go-between in negotiations.

A **fact finder,** most commonly used in the public sector, typically reports on the reasons for the dispute, the views and arguments of both sides, and (in some cases) a recommended settlement, which the parties are free to decline. That these recommendations are made public may give rise to public pressure for a settlement. Even if a fact finder's settlement is not accepted, the hope is that he or she will identify or frame issues in such a way as to facilitate an agreement. Sometimes, for the simple reason that fact finding takes time, the parties reach a settlement during the interim.

The most formal type of outside intervention is **arbitration,** under which a solution is actually chosen by an arbitrator (or arbitration board). In some instances the arbitrator can fashion a solution (conventional arbitration). In other cases the arbitrator must choose either the management's or union's final offer (final offer arbitration) on either the contract as a whole or on an issue-by-issue basis. Traditionally, arbitrating the enforcement or interpretation of contract terms (rights arbitration) has

Mediation
A procedure for resolving collective bargaining impasses by which a mediator with no formal authority acts as a facilitator and go-between in the negotiations.

Fact finder
A person who reports on the reasons for the labor–management dispute, the views and arguments of both sides, and a nonbinding recommendation for settling the dispute.

Arbitration
A procedure for resolving collective bargaining impasses by which an arbitrator chooses a solution to the dispute.

been widely accepted, whereas arbitrating the actual writing or setting of contract terms (interest arbitration, our focus here) has been reserved for special circumstances. These include some public sector negotiations, where strikes may be especially costly (such as those by police or firefighters) and a very few private sector situations, where strikes have been especially debilitating to both sides (the steel industry in the 1970s).[49] One reason for avoiding greater use of interest arbitration is a strong belief that the parties closest to the situation (unions and management, not an arbitrator) are in the best position to effectively resolve their conflicts.

Union and Management Interactions: Contract Administration

Grievance Procedure

Although the negotiation process (and the occasional resulting strike) receive the most publicity, the negotiation process typically occurs only about every three years, whereas contract administration goes on day after day, year after year. The two processes—negotiation and administration—are linked, of course. Vague or incomplete contract language developed in the negotiation process can make administration of the contract difficult. Such difficulties can, in turn, create conflict that can spill over into the next negotiation process.[50] Furthermore, events during the negotiation process—strikes, the use of replacement workers, or violence by either side—can lead to management and labor difficulties in working successfully under a contract.

A key influence on successful contract administration is the grievance procedure for resolving labor–management disputes over the interpretation and execution of the contract. During World War II, the War Labor Board helped institutionalize the use of arbitration as an alternative to strikes to settle disputes that arose during the term of the contract. The soon-to-follow Taft–Hartley Act further reinforced this preference. Today the great majority of grievance procedures have binding arbitration as a final step, and only a minority of strikes occur during the term of a contract. (Most occur during the negotiation stage.) Strikes during the term of a contract can be especially disruptive because they are more unpredictable than strikes during the negotiation phase, which occur only at regular intervals.

Beyond its ability to reduce strikes, a grievance procedure can be judged using three criteria.[51] First, how well are day-to-day contract questions resolved? Time delays and heavy use of the procedure may indicate problems. Second, how well does the grievance procedure adapt to changing circumstances? For example, if the company's business turns downward and the company needs to cut costs, how clear are the provisions relating to subcontracting of work, layoffs, and so forth? Third, in multiunit contracts, how well does the grievance procedure permit local contract issues (like work rules) to be included and resolved?

Duty of fair representation
The National Labor Relations Act requirement that all bargaining unit members have equal access to and representation by the union.

From the employees' perspective, the grievance procedure is the key to fair treatment in the workplace, and its effectiveness rests both on the degree to which employees feel they can use it without fear of recrimination and whether they believe their case will be carried forward strongly enough by their union representative. The **duty of fair representation** is mandated by the NLRA and requires that all bargaining unit members, whether union members or not, have equal access to and representation by the union in the grievance procedure. Too many grievances may indicate a problem, but so may too few. A very low grievance rate may suggest a fear of

TABLE 14.11
Steps in a Typical Grievance Procedure

Employee-initiated grievance

Step 1

a. Employee discusses grievance or problem orally with supervisor.
b. Union steward and employee may discuss problem orally with supervisor.
c. Union steward and employee decide (1) whether problem has been resolved or (2) if not resolved, whether a contract violation has occurred.

Step 2

a. Grievance is put in writing and submitted to production superintendent or other designated line manager.
b. Steward and management representative meet and discuss grievance. Management's response is put in writing. A member of the industrial relations staff may be consulted at this stage.

Step 3

a. Grievance is appealed to top line management and industrial relations staff representatives. Additional local or international union officers may become involved in discussions. Decision is put in writing.

Step 4

a. Union decides on whether to appeal unresolved grievance to arbitration according to procedures specified in its constitution and/or bylaws.
b. Grievance is appealed to arbitration for binding decision.

Discharge grievance

a. Procedure may begin at step 2 or step 3.
b. Time limits between steps may be shorter to expedite the process.

Union or group grievance

a. Union representative initiates grievance at step 1 or step 2 on behalf of affected class of workers or union representatives.

SOURCE: H.C. Katz and T.A. Kochan, *Collective Bargaining and Industrial Relations*, 1980.

filing a grievance, a belief that the system is not effective, or a belief that representation is not adequate.

As Table 14.11 suggests, most grievance procedures have several steps prior to arbitration. Moreover, the majority of grievances are settled during the earlier steps of the process, which is desirable both to reduce time delays and to avoid the costs of arbitration. If the grievance does reach arbitration, the arbitrator makes the final ruling in the matter. A series of Supreme Court decisions in 1960, commonly known as the Steelworkers' Trilogy, established that the courts should essentially refrain from reviewing the merits of arbitrators' decisions and, instead, limit judicial review to the question of whether the issue was subject to arbitration under the contract.[52] Furthermore, unless the contract explicitly states that an issue is not subject to arbitration, it will be assumed that arbitration is an appropriate means of deciding the issue. Giving further strength to the role of arbitration is the NLRB's general policy of deferring to arbitration.

What types of issues most commonly reach arbitration? Data from the FMCS on a total of 3,460 grievances in 1997 show that discharge and disciplinary issues topped the list with 1,941 cases.[53] Other frequent issues include the use of seniority in promotion, layoffs, transfers, work assignments, and scheduling (684 cases); distribution of overtime or use of compulsory overtime (105 cases); and subcontracting (79 cases).

What criteria do arbitrators use to reach a decision? In the most common case—discharge or discipline—the following due process questions are important:[54]

1. *Did the employee know what the rule or expectation was and what the consequences of not adhering to it were?*
2. *Was the rule applied in a consistent and predictable way?* In other words, are all employees treated the same?
3. *Are facts collected in a fair and systematic manner?* An important element of this principle is detailed record keeping. Both employee actions (such as tardiness) and management's response (verbal or written warnings) should be carefully documented.
4. *Does the employee have the right to question the facts and present a defense?* An example in a union setting is a hearing with a shop steward present.
5. *Does the employee have the right to appeal a decision?* An example is recourse to an impartial third party, such as an arbitrator.
6. *Is there progressive discipline?* Except perhaps for severe cases, an arbitrator will typically look for evidence that an employee was alerted as early as possible that behavior was inappropriate and the employee was given a chance to change prior to some form of severe discipline, such as discharge.
7. *Are there unique mitigating circumstances?* Although discipline must be consistent, individuals differ in terms of their prior service, performance, and discipline record. All of these factors may need to be considered.

New Labor–Management Strategies

Jack Barbash has described the nature of the traditional relationship between labor and management (during both the negotiation and administration phases) as follows:

> Bargaining is a love–hate, cooperation–conflict relationship. The parties have a common interest in maximizing the total revenue which finances their respective returns. But they take on adversarial postures in debating how the revenue shall be divided as between wages and profits. It is the adversarial posture which has historically set the tone of the relationship.[55]

Although there have always been exceptions to the adversarial approach, there are signs of a more general transformation to less adversarial workplace relations (at least where the union's role is accepted by management).[56] This transformation has two basic objectives: (1) to increase the involvement of individuals and work groups in overcoming adversarial relations and increasing employee commitment, motivation, and problem solving and (2) to reorganize work so that work rules are minimized and flexibility in managing people is maximized. These objectives are especially important for companies (like steel minimills) that need to be able to shift production quickly in response to changes in markets and customer demands. The specific programs aimed at achieving these objectives include employee involvement in decision making, self-managing employee teams, labor–management problem-solving teams, broadly defined jobs, and sharing of financial gains and business information with employees.[57]

Union resistance to such programs has often been substantial, precisely because the programs seek to change workplace relations and the role that unions play. Without the union's support, these programs are less likely to survive and less likely to be effective if they do survive.[58] Union leaders have often feared that such programs will weaken unions' role as an independent representative of employee interests. Indeed, according to the NLRA, to "dominate or interfere with the formation or administration of any labor organization or contribute financial or other support to it" is an unfair labor practice. An example of a prohibited practice is "taking an active part in organizing a union or committee to represent employees."[59]

One case that has received much attention is that of Electromation, a small electrical parts manufacturer. In 1992 the NLRB ruled that the company had violated Section 8(a)(2) of the NLRA by setting up worker–management committees (typically about six workers and one or two managers) to solve problems having to do with absenteeism and pay scales.[60] The original complaint was filed by the Teamsters union, which was trying to organize the (nonunion) company and felt that the committees were, in effect, illegally competing with them to be workers' representatives. Similarly, Polaroid dissolved an employee committee that had been in existence for over 40 years in response to the U.S. Department of Labor's claim that it violated the NLRA. The primary functions of the employee committee had been to represent employees in grievances and to advise senior management on issues such as pay and company rules and regulations. In a third case, the NLRB ruled in 1993 that seven worker–management safety committees at DuPont Co. were illegal under the NLRB because they were dominated by management. The committee members were chosen by management and their decisions were subject to the approval of the management members of the committees. Finally, the committees made decisions about issues that were mandatory subjects of bargaining with the employees' elected representative—the chemical workers' union.[61] The impact of such cases will be felt both in nonunion companies, as union organizers move to fill the worker representation vacuum, and in unionized companies, as managers find they must deal more directly and effectively with their unions.

In 1994 the Commission on the Future of Worker–Management Relations (also referred to as the Dunlop Commission, after its chair, former Secretary of Labor John Dunlop) recommended that Congress clarify Section 8(a)(2) and give employers more freedom to use employee involvement programs without risking legal challenges. In 1996 the U.S. Congress passed the Teamwork for Employees and Managers Act, which supporters said would remove legal roadblocks to greater employee involvement. Critics claimed the act went too far and would bring back employer-dominated labor organizations, which existed prior to the passage of the NLRA in 1935. The Clinton administration vetoed the bill, meaning that employers will continue to face some uncertainty about legal issues. Table 14.12 provides some guidance on when the use of teams might be illegal.

TABLE 14.12
When Teams May Be Illegal

Primary factors to look for that could mean a team violates national labor law:	
Representation	Does the team address issues affecting nonteam employees? (Does it represent other workers?)
Subject matter	Do these issues involve matters such as wages, grievances, hours of work, and working conditions?
Management involvement	Does the team deal with any supervisors, managers, or executives on any issue?
Employer domination	Did the company create the team or decide what it would do and how it would function?

SOURCE: Reprinted from January 25, 1993 issue of *BusinessWeek* by special permission. Copyright © 1993 by The McGraw-Hill Companies, Inc.

Employers must take care that employee involvement meets the legal test, but the NLRB has clearly supported the legality of involvement in important cases. For example, in a 2001 ruling, the NLRB found that the use of seven employee participation committees at a Crown Cork & Seal aluminum can manufacturing plant did not violate federal labor law. The committees in question make and implement decisions regarding a wide range of issues, including production, quality, training, safety, and certain types of worker discipline. The NLRB determined that these committees were not employer-dominated labor organizations, which would have violated federal labor law. Instead of "dealing with" management in a bilateral manner where proposals are made that are either rejected or accepted by management, the teams and committees exercise authority, delegated by management, to operate the plant within certain parameters. Indeed, the NLRB noted that rather than "dealing with management," the evidence indicated that within delegated areas of authority, the teams and committees "are management." This authority was found to be similar to that delegated to a first-line supervisor. Thus the charge that the teams and committees did not have final decision-making authority (and so were not acting in a management capacity) did not weigh heavily with the NLRB, which noted, "Few, if any, supervisors in a conventional plant have authority that is final and absolute." Instead, it was noted that managers typically make recommendations that move up through "the chain of command."[62]

Although there are legal concerns to address, some evidence suggests that these new approaches to labor relations—incorporating greater employee participation in decisions, using employee teams, multiskilling, rotating jobs, and sharing financial gains—can contribute significantly to an organization's effectiveness.[63] One study, for example, compared the features of traditional and transformational approaches to labor relations at Xerox.[64] As Table 14.13 indicates, the transformational approach

TABLE 14.13
Patterns in Labor–Management Relations Using Traditional and Transformational Approaches

	PATTERN	
DIMENSION	TRADITIONAL	TRANSFORMATIONAL
Conflict resolution		
Frequency of conflicts	High	Low
Speed of conflict resolution	Slow	Fast
Informal resolution of grievances	Low	High
Third- and fourth-step grievances	High	Low
Shop-floor cooperation		
Formal problem-solving groups (such as quality, reducing scrap, employment security)	Low	High
Informal problem-solving activity	Low	High
Worker autonomy and feedback		
Formal autonomous work groups	Low	High
Informal worker autonomous activity	Low	High
Worker-initiated changes in work design	Low	High
Feedback on cost, quality, and schedule	Low	High

SOURCE: Adapted from J. Cutcher-Gershenfeld, "The Impact of Economic Performance of a Transformation in Workplace Relations," *Industrial and Labor Relations Review* 44 (1991), pp. 241–60. Reprinted with permission.

was characterized by better conflict resolution, more shop-floor cooperation, and greater worker autonomy and feedback in decision making. Furthermore, compared with the traditional approach, transformational labor relations were found to be associated with lower costs, better product quality, and higher productivity. The Commission on the Future of Worker–Management Relations concluded that the evidence is "overwhelming that employee participation and labor–management partnerships are good for workers, firms, and the national economy." National survey data also indicate that most employees want more influence in workplace decisions and believe that such influence leads to more effective organizations.[65]

Labor Relations Outcomes

The effectiveness of labor relations can be evaluated from management, labor, and societal perspectives. Management seeks to control costs and enhance productivity and quality. Labor unions seek to raise wages and benefits and exercise control over how employees spend their time at work (such as through work rules). Each of the three parties typically seeks to avoid forms of conflict (like strikes) that impose significant costs on everyone. In this section we examine several outcomes.

Strikes

Table 14.14 presents data on strikes in the United States that involved 1,000 or more employees. Because strikes are more likely in large units, the lack of data on smaller units is probably not a major concern, although such data would, of course, raise the figure on the estimated time lost to strikes. For example, for the 1960s, this estimate is .12 percent using data on strikes involving 1,000 or more employees versus .17 percent for all strikes. Although strikes impose significant costs on union members, employers, and society, it is clear from Table 14.14 that strikes are the exception rather than the rule. Very little working time is lost to strikes in the United States, and their frequency in recent years is generally low by historical standards. Does this mean that

TABLE 14.14
Work Stoppages Involving 1,000 or More Workers

YEAR	STOPPAGES	NUMBER OF WORKERS (THOUSANDS)	PERCENTAGE OF TOTAL WORKING TIME
1950	424	1,698	0.26%
1955	363	2,055	0.16
1960	222	896	0.09
1965	268	999	0.10
1970	381	2,468	0.29
1975	235	965	0.09
1980	187	795	0.09
1985	54	324	0.03
1990	44	185	0.02
1995	31	192	0.02
1999	17	73	0.01
2000	39	394	0.06

SOURCE: **http://stats.bls.gov.**

the industrial relations system is working well? Not necessarily. Some would view the low number of strikes as another sign of labor's weakness.

Wages and Benefits

In 2000, private-sector unionized workers received, on average, wages 19 percent higher than their nonunion counterparts.[66] Total compensation was 36 percent higher for union-covered employees because of an even larger effect of unions on benefits.[67] However, these are raw differences. To assess the net effect of unions on wages more accurately, adjustments must be made. We now briefly highlight a few of these.

The union wage effect is likely to be overestimated to the extent that unions can more easily organize workers who are already highly paid or who are more productive. The gap is likely to be underestimated to the extent that nonunion employers raise wages and benefits in response to the perceived "union threat" in the hope that their employees will then have less interest in union representation. When these and other factors are taken into account, the net union advantage in wages, though still substantial, is reduced to about 10 percent. The union benefits advantage is also reduced, but it remains larger than the union wage effect, and the union effect on total compensation is therefore larger than the wage effect alone.[68]

Beyond differences in pay and benefits, unions typically influence the way pay and promotions are determined. Whereas management often seeks to deal with employees as individuals, emphasizing performance differences in pay and promotion decisions, unions seek to build group solidarity and avoid the possibly arbitrary treatment of employees. To do so, unions focus on equal pay for equal work. Any differences among employees in pay or promotions, they say, should be based on seniority (an objective measure) rather than on performance (a subjective measure susceptible to favoritism). It is very common in union settings for there to be a single rate of pay for all employees in a particular job classification.

Productivity

There has been much debate regarding the effects of unions on productivity.[69] Unions are believed to decrease productivity in at least three ways: (1) the union pay advantage causes employers to use less labor and more capital per worker than they would otherwise, which reduces efficiency across society; (2) union contract provisions may limit permissible workloads, restrict the tasks that particular workers are allowed to perform, and require employers to use more employees for certain jobs than they otherwise would; and (3) strikes, slowdowns, and working-to-rule (slowing down production by following every workplace rule to an extreme) result in lost production.[70]

On the other hand, unions can have positive effects on productivity.[71] Employees, whether members of a union or not, communicate to management regarding how good a job it is doing by either the "exit" or "voice" mechanisms. "Exit" refers to simply leaving the company to work for a better employer. "Voice" refers to communicating one's concerns to management without necessarily leaving the employer. Unions are believed to increase the operation and effectiveness of the voice mechanism.[72] This, in turn, is likely to reduce employee turnover and its associated costs. More broadly, voice can be seen as including the union's contribution to the success of labor–management cooperation programs that make use of employee suggestions and increased involvement in decisions. A second way that unions can increase productivity is (perhaps ironically) through their emphasis on the use of seniority in pay, promotion, and layoff decisions. Although management typically prefers to rely more heavily on performance in such decisions, using seniority has a potentially important advantage—namely, it reduces competition among workers. As a result, workers may be less reluctant to share their knowledge with less senior workers because they do not have to worry about less senior workers taking their jobs. Finally, the introduction of a union may have a "shock effect" on management, pressuring it into tightening standards and accountability and paying greater heed to employee input in the design and management of production.[73]

Although there is evidence that unions have both positive and negative effects on productivity, most studies have found that union workers are more productive than nonunion workers. Nevertheless, it is generally recognized that most of the findings on this issue are open to a number of alternative explanations, making any clear conclusions difficult. For example, if unions raise productivity, why has union representation of employees declined over time, even within industries?[74] A related concern is that unionized establishments are more likely to survive where there is some inherent productivity advantage unrelated to unionism that actually offsets a negative impact of unionism. If so, these establishments would be overrepresented, whereas establishments that did not survive the negative impact of unions would be underrepresented. Consequently, any negative impact of unions on productivity would be underestimated.

Profits and Stock Performance

Even if unions do raise productivity, a company's profits and stock performance may still suffer if unions raise costs (such as wages) or decrease investment by a greater amount. Evidence shows that unions have a large negative effect on profits and that union coverage tends to decline more quickly in firms experiencing lower shareholder returns, suggesting that some firms become more competitive partly by reducing union strength.[75] Similarly, one study finds that each dollar of unexpected increase in collectively bargained labor costs results in a dollar reduction in shareholder wealth. Other research suggests that investment in research and development is lower in unionized firms.[76] Strikes, although infrequent, lower shareholder returns in both the struck companies and firms (like suppliers) linked to those companies.[77] These research findings describe the average effects of unions. The consequences of more innovative union–management relationships for profits and stock performance are less clear.

Finding and Keeping the Best Employees

In 1973 Harley-Davidson, a privately held Milwaukee company that manufactures motorcycles, was in dire straits. The company struggled to survive and was sold to a group of company executives in the early 1980s. Its financial problems continued until 1985, when it found a venture capitalist to back it just one hour before the bank had threatened to take the company if it did not repay its loan. In 1986 the company went public. In the late 1980s it invested heavily in equipment, technology, and engineering. It then turned its attention to investing in people.

According to Lou Kiefer, international high-performance work organization conversion coordinator for the International Association of Machinists and Aerospace Workers (IAM), Harley-Davidson focused on changing the culture from a "conglomerate multinational mentality that focuses on the exploitation of technology and jobs" to one in which the company and union could work together. A cooperative agreement was created that specified employment security for workers and joint labor–management decision making in areas such as organization redesign, employee training and development, work team design, and continuous improvement. The union is also a partner in areas such as capital investment and customer relations. For example, everyone would be involved in what were once deemed management prerogatives—responsive product development, staying close to the customer, and giving customers what they need. Employees would go to motorcycle rallies and talk with customers to see what they needed and wanted. Marketing innovations would come about using input from production people. About 65 percent of company employees are riders, many of them women, reflecting the growing number of female riders generally. Adaptations are being made in hand controls to make them more comfortable for these customers.

Bill Gray, vice president of human resources at Harley-Davidson, emphasizes the importance of sharing technical and financial information with virtually all employees—having no secrets. Harley's books are open to all company comers; the only stipulation is that they must agree in writing not to trade company stock so that no one can ever be accused of insider trading.

It's important to determine costs jointly, and Gray says you need a "a flexible collective bargaining agreement that allows people to move fluidly through the business and understand many aspects of it." It's also important to have leadership that motivates employees. Anybody in the company who is committed to making a difference can assume these leadership roles.

Kiefer also stresses the importance of looking jointly at costs and production: "We know that if we increase productivity and lower costs, we're not working ourselves out of a job, which is what happened in a lot of cases where top-down TQM was brought in and the work was reorganized and reengineered." This "leaned out" the business, he says, without "growing it."

The labor–management partnership started at Harley-Davidson continues to thrive today. The company and the IAM agreed to a seven-year contract in April 2001 that continues both the joint labor–management decision-making process and the employment security provision. (Most collective bargaining contracts are much shorter—three years on average.) Harley has also worked in cooperation with the IAM to plan and undertake a major expansion of production in its York, Pennsylvania, facility. Finally, Harley-Davidson announced in October 2001 that it expected record profits for 2001—notable in a year marked by economic recession. In summary, Harley-Davidson and the IAM have worked together to create an environment where finding and keeping the best talent is a competitive advantage that allows the company to be financially successful and workers to contribute to and share in this success.

SOURCE: Presentation, "Eighth Biennial National Labor–Management Conference," *Monthly Labor Review*, January 1999, pp. 29–45; "Companies Breaking Records in Hard Times," *Milwaukee Journal Sentinel* (October 13, 2001).

The International Context

Except for China, Russia, and the Ukraine, the United States has more union members than any other country. Yet, as Table 14.15 indicates, aside from France and Korea, the United States has the lowest unionization rate (union density) of any country in the table. Even more striking are differences in union coverage, the percentage of employees whose terms and conditions of employment are governed by a union contract. (See Table 14.15.) In Western Europe, it is common to have coverage rates of 80 to 90 percent, meaning that the influence of labor unions far outstrips what would be implied by their membership levels.[78] Why are the unionization rate

TABLE 14.15
Union Membership and Union Coverage, Selected Countries, 1995

	MEMBERSHIP		COVERAGE
COUNTRY	NUMBER (THOUSANDS)	PERCENTAGE OF EMPLOYMENT (DENSITY)	PERCENTAGE OF EMPLOYMENT
United States	16,360	14	12
Canada	4,128[a]	37	37[b]
Japan	12,410[b]	24	25
Korea	1,615	13	—
Germany	9,300	29	90[b]
France	1,758	9	90
United Kingdom	7,280	33	37
Sweden	3,180[c]	91	85
Mexico	7,000[d]	43	—
Argentina	3,200	39	73
Brazil	15,205	44[d]	—

[a]1993.
[b]1996.
[c]1994.
[d]1991.
SOURCE: International Labour Office, *World Labour Report, 1997–98* (Geneva, Switzerland, 2001).

and coverage comparatively low? One explanation is that the United States does not have as strong a history of deep class-based divisions in society as other countries do. For example, labor and social democratic political parties are commonplace in Western Europe, and they are major players in the political process. Furthermore, the labor movement in Western Europe is broader than that in the United States. It extends not just to the workplace but—through its own or closely related political parties—directly into the national political process.

What is the trend in union membership rates and coverage? In the United States, we have seen earlier that the trend is clearly downward, at least in the private sector. Although there have also been declines in membership rates in many other countries, coverage rates have stayed high in many of these countries. In the United States, deregulation and competition from foreign-owned companies have forced companies to become more efficient. Combined with the fact that the union wage premium in the United States is substantially larger than in other advanced industrialized countries, it is not surprising that management opposition would be higher in the United States than elsewhere.[79] This, in turn, may help explain why the decline in union influence has been especially steep in the United States.

It seems likely that—with the growing globalization of markets—labor costs and productivity will continue to be key challenges. The European Community's movement toward a common market and the North American Free Trade Agreement among the United States, Canada, and Mexico both suggest that goods, services, and production will continue to move more freely across international borders. Where vast differences in wages, benefits, and other costs of doing business (such as regulation) exist, there will be a tendency to move to areas that are less costly, unless skills are unavailable or productivity is significantly lower there. Unless labor unions can increase their productivity sufficiently or organize new production facilities, union influence is likely to decline.

In addition to membership and coverage, the United States differs from Western Europe in the degree of formal worker participation in decision making. Works' councils (joint labor–management decision-making institutions at the enterprise level) and worker representation on supervisory boards of directors (codetermination) are mandated by law in countries such as Germany. The Scandinavian countries, Austria, and Luxembourg have similar legislation. German works' councils make decisions about changes in work or the work environment, discipline, pay systems, safety, and other human resource issues. The degree of codetermination on supervisory boards depends on the size and industry of the company. For example, in German organizations having more than 2,000 employees, half of the board members must be worker representatives. (However, the chairman of the board, a management representative, can cast a tie-breaking vote.) In contrast, worker representation on boards of directors in the United States is still rare.[80] Thus the recent merger of Daimler-Benz and Chrysler means that former Chrysler managers will need to adapt to Germany's system of worker representation.

The works' councils exist in part because collective bargaining agreements in countries such as Germany tend to be oriented toward industrywide or regional issues, with less emphasis on local issues. However, competitive forces have led employers to increasingly opt out of centralized bargaining, even in the countries best known for centralized bargaining, like Sweden and Germany.[81]

The Public Sector

Unlike the private sector, union membership in the public sector grew in the 1960s and 1970s and remained fairly stable through the 1980s. As of 1997, 37 percent of government employees were union members, and 42 percent of all government employees were covered by a collective bargaining contract.[82] Like the NLRA in the private sector, changes in the legal framework contributed significantly to union growth in the public sector. One early step was the enactment in Wisconsin of collective bargaining legislation in 1959 for its state employees.[83] Executive Order 10988 provided collective bargaining rights for federal employees in 1962. By the end of the 1960s, most states had passed similar laws. The Civil Service Reform Act of 1978, Title VII, later established the Federal Labor Relations Authority (modeled after the NLRB). Many states have similar administrative agencies to administer their own laws.

An interesting aspect of public sector union growth is that much of it has occurred in the service industry and among white-collar employees—groups that have traditionally been viewed as difficult to organize. The American Federation of State, County, and Municipal Employees (AFSCME) with 1.3 million members, has had about 325,000 members in health care, 325,000 in clerical jobs, and over 400,000 in all white-collar occupations.[84]

In contrast to the private sector, strikes are illegal at the federal level of the public sector and in most states. At the local level, all states prohibit strikes by police (Hawaii being a partial exception) and firefighters (Idaho being the exception). Teachers and state employees are somewhat more likely to have the right to strike, depending on the state. Legal or not, strikes nonetheless do occur in the public sector. In 2000, of the 39 strikes involving 1,000 or more workers, 8 were in state and local government.

A Look Back

The membership rate, and thus influence, of labor unions in the United States and in many other countries has been on the decline in the private sector. However, as we saw in the opening to this chapter, unions recognize that one way to slow or reverse this downward trend would be to have greater success organizing workers in new economy jobs and companies. The victory of the Communications Workers of America at Verizon is an example of a major success in this sense. The question is whether labor unions will be able to duplicate this success on a broad scale. In the meantime, however, there are many companies where labor unions represent a large share of employees and thus play a major role in the operation and success of those companies. In such companies, whatever the national trend, effective labor relations are crucial for both companies and workers.

Questions

1. Many people picture labor union members as being men in blue-collar jobs in manufacturing plants. Is that accurate? Are there certain types of jobs where an employer can be fairly certain that employees will not join a union? Give examples.
2. Why do people join labor unions? Would you be interested in joining a labor union if given the opportunity? Why or why not? As a manager, would you prefer to work with a union or would you prefer that employees be unrepresented by a union? Explain.

Summary

Labor unions seek to represent the interests of their members in the workplace. Although this may further the cause of industrial democracy, management often finds that unions increase labor costs while setting limits on the company's flexibility and discretion in decision making. As a result, the company may witness a diminished ability to compete effectively in a global economy. Not surprisingly, management in nonunion companies often feels compelled to actively resist the unionization of its employees. This, together with a host of economic, legal, and other factors, has contributed to union losses in membership and bargaining power in the private sector. There are some indications, however, that managements and unions are seeking new, more effective ways of working together to enhance competitiveness while giving employees a voice in how workplace decisions are made.

Discussion Questions

1. Why do employees join unions?
2. What has been the trend in union membership in the United States, and what are the underlying reasons for the trend?
3. What are the consequences for management and owners of having a union represent employees?
4. What are the general provisions of the National Labor Relations Act, and how does it affect labor–management interactions?
5. What are the features of traditional and nontraditional labor relations? What are the potential advantages of the "new" nontraditional approaches to labor relations?
6. How does the U.S. industrial and labor relations system compare with systems in other countries, such as those in Western Europe?

Web Exercise

Many unions are merging with other U.S. as well as international unions. Visit **www.uaw.com**, the website for the United Auto Workers. This site discusses recent mergers the UAW has participated in and includes UAW news releases.

Questions

1. From the union's standpoint, what are the advantages of merging with other national unions? With international unions?
2. What are the disadvantages of these mergers from the company's perspective? Are there any advantages that a company might realize?

Managing People: From the Pages of *BusinessWeek*

BusinessWeek A World of Sweatshops

Walk through Tong Yang Indonesia (TYI) shoe factory, an 8,500-worker complex of hot, dingy buildings outside Jakarta, and company president Jung Moo Young will show you all the improvements he has made in the past two years. He did so at the behest of his biggest customer, Reebok International Ltd., to allay protests by Western activists who accuse the U.S. shoemaker of using sweatshops.

Last year Jung bought new machinery to apply a water-based solvent to glue on shoe soles instead of toluene, which may be hazardous to workers who breathe it in all day. He installed a new ventilation system after Reebok auditors found the old one inadequate. TYI bought new chairs with backs so that its young seamstresses have some support while seated at their machines—and back braces for 500 workers who do heavy lifting. In all, TYI, which has $100 million in annual sales, spent $2 million of its own money to satisfy Reebok. But to Jung's surprise, it was a sound investment. "We should make it all back after three years," he says. "The workers are more productive, and the new machinery is more efficient."

WINDOW DRESSING. TYI's efforts show how much progress Western consumer goods companies can make in cleaning up sweatshop conditions. In the early 1990s many companies adopted codes of conduct requiring contractors to fix harsh or abusive conditions. Based on recent visits to factories in Asia, several companies—such as Reebok (RBK), Nike (NKE), Liz Claiborne (LIZ), and Mattel (MAT)—have finally begun enforcing their codes in the past year or two.

In fact, more than a dozen companies have joined efforts to create an industrywide system for verifying that consumer goods sold in the United States are made under humane conditions. The most ambitious effort involves the Fair Labor Association, which grew out of a presidential task force of companies and human rights groups. It plans to send outside monitors to factories worldwide to ensure that they meet minimum standards on everything from health and safety to workers' rights to join unions.

The problem is that such companies are the exceptions. Although many multinationals operate facilities in Asia and Latin America that are as well run as any in the West, far too many still buy from factories where practices are appalling—especially in such labor-intensive sectors as garments, shoes, and toys. And many companies that claim to adhere to labor codes are still in the window-dressing stage.

Then there are the tougher issues that even companies such as Reebok haven't yet grappled with. How can companies respect workers' rights to collectively bargain in China, say, which bans free unions and often doesn't enforce its own labor laws, impressive as they are on paper? Nor have most Western companies improved wages, which are often below what even governments like Indonesia define as enough to support a family.

Investigators for U.S. labor and human rights groups estimate that Asia and Latin America have thousands of sweatshops, which do everything from force employees to work 16-hour days to cheat them out of already meager wages, that make products for U.S. and European companies. "It would be extremely generous to say that even 10 percent of [Western companies charged with abuses] have done anything meaningful about labor conditions," says S. Prakash Sethi, a Baruch College business professor who helped set up a monitoring system for Mattel at its dozen factories in China, Indonesia, Mexico, and elsewhere. Abuses may actually be proliferating. Price hikes in U.S. retail garments have lagged inflation since 1982, and Asian factory owners complain they are under intense pressure to find new ways to squeeze out costs. "American retailers are driving down prices, which ends up squeezing labor," says Robert Antoshak, vice president at garment industry consultant Werner International in Reston, Virginia.

When accused by activists of buying from sweatshops, brand-name marketers have tended to dismiss the claims. But there's reason to believe the activists are often right.

A recent (October 2, 2000) *BusinessWeek* probe found that Wal-Mart Stores Inc. (WMT) bought Kathie Lee Gifford handbags in a Chinese factory where guards beat workers and owners deducted up to 70 percent of their pay for food and lodging. The National Labor Committee, a New York watchdog group, first made that charge in a May 2000 report on 16 Chinese factories used by Western companies. Each broke Chinese labor laws or the buyers' own codes, it says.

Some of the U.S. companies cited in the report, including Timberland Co. (TBL) and New Balance, say they reexamined the Chinese factories and found most of the charges to be accurate. But others, including Huffy Corp. (HUF) and Stride Rite Corp. (SRR), refused to discuss the subject or let *BusinessWeek* visit their factories. Meanwhile, a yearlong study by labor experts from Harvard and four other universities found that 13 factories making collegiate logo clothing for U.S. companies in seven developing countries were guilty of nonpayment of wages, lax safety, and excessive overtime.

TIP OF THE ICEBERG. Liz Claiborne Inc.'s attempt to improve conditions at a factory in Guatemala shows how hard it is for companies to clean up sweatshops. In 1998 the U.S. apparel giant began working with the Commission for the Verification of Corporate Codes of Conduct (Coverco), a group of Guatemalan and U.S. church and humanitarian activists, to monitor one of its suppliers, identified by local sources as Choi Shin, a Korean-owned factory near Guatemala City. Liz Claiborne released Coverco's report last year but declined to give out the factory's name or let *BusinessWeek* inside it.

Coverco found a litany of problems. Choi Shin couldn't refute workers' claims that they didn't receive proper overtime payments or promised production bonuses. Workers lacked adequate protection when handling hazardous chemicals. Toilets and canteens were unsanitary. Some managers screamed at workers or pressured those who complained to resign. And many women, who comprise 88 percent of the plant's workers, said they were denied time off for doctors' appointments. One pregnant worker who had a note from her doctor about a high-risk pregnancy was not allowed to leave until five hours after she complained of pain. She lost the baby.

Coverco says the plant is slowly improving due to Liz Claiborne's pressure. But Choi Shin is the tip of an iceberg. "The majority of [garment-exporting] plants have similar problems," says Coverco general coordinator Homero Fuentes.

The inability to form free unions means that workers often lack the leverage to make much beyond subsistence wages. The Modas Uno Korea plant in the Guatemala City suburb of Villanueva stopped paying workers on time in August 2000 and fired 22 who complained to the Labor Ministry. On September 2, 2000, workers stormed the plant demanding back pay—and the company relented. Workers who stayed on said they were offered sewing machines instead of severance pay when the factory shut down in early October. "They make you work more hours than they pay you for," says Albina de Perez, a fired worker who earned $25 a week at the plant. No one answered Modas's phone lines to respond to questions.

OUSTED MANAGERS. At least corporate responsibility programs seem to be showing faster progress in some countries, such as Indonesia, where suppression of labor activism has abated since the 1998 downfall of strongman President Suharto. Golden Adishoes, a run-down shoe factory near Jakarta, agreed to a host of improvements Reebok demanded as a condition for starting production there last summer. And the monitoring team assembled by Baruch's Sethi brought numerous changes to Mattel's two Barbie factories near Jakarta, clean and air-conditioned facilities that employ nearly 12,000 workers. Last year Mattel removed hazardous solvents from the production process, says Tracey Rogers, manager of one Barbie factory. Mattel also began promoting workers who pass annual skills tests to higher-paying jobs. Rogers meets with 400 randomly selected workers every other week to hear their concerns. "I'll be honest," says Rogers. "This process has been good for us."

Even Nike, the bête noir of labor activists, is finally making changes. Take Nikomas Gemilang, a sprawling, 50-building minicity near Jakarta that employs 22,500 workers making shoes for Nike and Adidas (ADDDY). It is owned by Taiwan's Pou Chen Corp., the world's largest shoe manufacturer. At Nike's urging, Nikomas set a higher wage scale for senior workers and ousted managers who had yelled abuses at workers. The factory also improved safety and food in company dorms, which house 13,000 workers.

Pou Chen Chief Operating Officer Eric Chi says Nikomas is building a shopping mall, hospital, cinema, and day care center, which is needed because 85 percent of workers are female. "We've heard about all this coming, and we hope conditions here will be better next year," says Yune, a woman in her early 20s who has worked and lived at Nikomas for five years.

Such improvements, however, are unlikely to quell Western protesters who insist multinationals exploit workers. Only a few U.S. companies submit to independent audits. And workers' pay, even if it's better than average for that country, is still pitiful considering the nearly 40 percent gross profit margins Nike and Reebok earn. TYI pays about 22 cents an hour, just over Indonesia's minimum wage. It gets around $13 for every pair of shoes it makes for Reebok, paying only $1 for labor. Still, TYI says that after paying for materials and overhead, its margins are just 10 percent. It can't just hike its price to Reebok. "They look for suppliers who sell for the lowest price," says a TYI manager. "If we aren't cheap enough, they'll go to Vietnam or somewhere else." The big profits go to shoe companies and retailers: the shoes typically sell for $60 to $70 a pair.

Given the huge oversupply of cheap labor in many developing nations, more widespread gains in the workplace are unlikely until workers can organize unions to demand changes—or unless there is a system to punish violators of international codes. Even under the programs set up by Nike and Mattel, they are free to sell their goods in the United States if it turns out they were made under abusive conditions. But their experiments suggest that not every factory has to be a sweatshop to make the global economy work.

Questions

1. Why should American companies care about work conditions overseas?
2. Are these kinds of working conditions necessary for poorer countries to attract jobs?
3. Why do people work under such conditions?
4. What is the best way to improve conditions? How did working conditions improve over time in the United States?

Notes

1. J.T. Dunlop, *Industrial Relations Systems* (New York: Holt, 1958).
2. C. Kerr, "Industrial Conflict and Its Mediation," *American Journal of Sociology* 60 (1954), pp. 230–45.
3. In 1946 roughly 1.5 percent of working time was lost to strikes. This compares with 0.3 percent of working time lost in the period 1950–79. See A.M. Glassman and T.G. Cummings, *Industrial Relations: A Multidimensional View* (Glenview, IL: Scott, Foresman, 1985), p. 64; W.H. Holley Jr. and K.M. Jennings, *The Labor Relations Process* (Chicago: Dryden Press, 1984), p. 207.
4. T.A. Kochan, *Collective Bargaining and Industrial Relations* (Homewood, IL: Richard D. Irwin, 1980), p. 25; H.C. Katz and T.A. Kochan, *An Introduction to Collective Bargaining and Industrial Relations* (New York: McGraw-Hill, 1992), p. 10.
5. Katz and Kochan, *An Introduction to Collective Bargaining*.
6. S. Webb and B. Webb, *Industrial Democracy* (London: Longmans, Green, 1987); J. R. Commons, *Institutional Economics* (New York: Macmillan, 1934).
7. C. Kerr, J.T. Dunlop, F. Harbison, and C. Myers, "Industrialism and World Society," *Harvard Business Review*, February 1961, pp. 113–26.
8. T.A. Kochan and K.R. Wever, "American Unions and the Future of Worker Representation," in *The State of the Unions*, ed. G. Strauss et al. (Madison, WI: Industrial Relations Research Association, 1991).
9. "Why America Needs Unions, but Not the Kind It Has Now," *BusinessWeek* (May 23, 1994), p. 70.
10. Katz and Kochan, *An Introduction to Collective Bargaining*.
11. J. Barbash, *The Elements of Industrial Relations* (Madison, WI: University of Wisconsin Press, 1984).
12. "Auto, Steel, Machinists Unions Announce Accord to Merge by 2000," *Daily Labor Report* (July 28, 1995), p. AA-1.
13. Ibid.; A.Q. Nomani, "Struggling to Survive, Unions Battle Unions to Build Memberships," *The New York Times* (October 28, 1995), p. A1.
14. Bureau of National Affairs, "Proportion of Union Members Declines to Low of 15.8 Percent," *Daily Labor Report* (February 9, 1993), pp. B3–B7.
15. B.T. Hirsch, *Labor Unions and the Economic Performance of Firms* (Kalamazoo, MI: W.E. Upjohn Institute, 1991); R.B. Freeman, "Contraction and Expansion: The Divergence of Private Sector and Public Sector Unionism in the United States," *Journal of Economic Perspectives* 2 (1988), pp. 63–88; G.N. Chaison and D.G. Dhavale, "A Note on the Severity of the Decline in Union Organizing Activity," *Industrial and Labor Relations Review* 43 (1990), pp. 366–73.
16. Katz and Kochan, *An Introduction to Collective Bargaining*. Katz and Kochan in turn build on work by J. Fiorito and C.L. Maranto, "The Contemporary Decline of Union Strength," *Contemporary Policy Issues* 3 (1987), pp. 12–27.
17. G.N. Chaison and J. Rose, "The Macrodeterminants of Union Growth and Decline," in *The State of the Unions*.
18. T.A. Kochan, R.B. McKersie, and J. Chalykoff, "The Effects of Corporate Strategy and Workplace Innovations in Union Representation," *Industrial and Labor Relations Review* 39 (1986), pp. 487–501; Chaison and Rose, "The Macrodeterminants of Union Growth"; J. Barbash, *Practice of Unionism* (New York: Harper,

1956), p. 210; W.N. Cooke and D.G. Meyer, "Structural and Market Predictors of Corporate Labor Relations Strategies," *Industrial and Labor Relations Review* 43 (1990), pp. 280–93; T.A. Kochan and P. Cappelli, "The Transformation of the Industrial Relations and Personnel Function," in *Internal Labor Markets*, ed. P. Osterman (Cambridge, MA: MIT Press, 1984).

19. Kochan and Cappelli, "The Transformation of the Industrial Relations and Personnel Function."
20. S.B. Jarrell and T.D. Stanley, "A Meta-Analysis of the Union–Nonunion Wage Gap," *Industrial and Labor Relations Review* 44 (1990), pp. 54–67; P.D. Lineneman, M.L. Wachter, and W.H. Carter, "Evaluating the Evidence on Union Employment and Wages," *Industrial and Labor Relations Review* 44 (1990), pp. 34–53.
21. National Labor Relations Board annual reports.
22. R.B. Freeman and M.M. Kleiner, "Employer Behavior in the Face of Union Organizing Drives," *Industrial and Labor Relations Review* 43 (1990), pp. 351–65.
23. F.K. Foulkes, "Large Nonunionized Employers," in *U.S. Industrial Relations 1950–1980: A Critical Assessment*, eds. J. Steiber et al. (Madison, WI: Industrial Relations Research Association, 1981).
24. Katz and Kochan, *An Introduction to Collective Bargaining*.
25. E.E. Herman, J.L. Schwarz, and A. Kuhn, *Collective Bargaining and Labor Relations* (Englewood Cliffs, NJ: Prentice–Hall, 1992), p. 32. Note that the percentage of employed workers increased less quickly because employment grew 18 percent during the same period.
26. BLS website; AFL-CIO website.
27. Herman et al., *Collective Bargaining*, p. 33.
28. Kochan, *Collective Bargaining and Industrial Relations*, p. 61.
29. National Labor Relations Board, *A Guide to Basic Law and Procedures under the National Labor Relations Act* (Washington, DC: U.S. Government Printing Office, 1991).
30. Ibid.
31. Ibid.
32. H.N. Wheeler and J.A. McClendon, "The Individual Decision to Unionize," in *The State of the Unions*.
33. National Labor Relations Board annual reports.
34. J.A. Fossum, *Labor Relations*, 5th ed. (Homewood, IL: Richard D. Irwin, 1992), p. 149.
35. National Labor Relations Board, *A Guide to Basic Law*, p. 17.
36. Ibid.
37. Herman et al., *Collective Bargaining;* P. Jarley and J. Fiorito, "Associate Membership: Unionism or Consumerism?" *Industrial and Labor Relations Review* 43 (1990), pp. 209–24.
38. Katz and Kochan, *An Introduction to Collective Bargaining;* R.L. Rose, "Unions Hit Corporate Campaign Trail," *The Wall Street Journal* (March 8, 1993), p. B1.
39. P. Jarley and C.L. Maranto, "Union Corporate Campaigns: An Assessment," *Industrial and Labor Relations Review* 44 (1990), pp. 505–24.
40. Katz and Kochan, *An Introduction to Collective Bargaining*.
41. A. Bernstein, "Working Capital: Labor's New Weapon?" *BusinessWeek* (September 27, 1997).
42. Chaison and Rose, "The Macrodeterminants of Union Growth."
43. R.E. Walton and R.B. McKersie, *A Behavioral Theory of Negotiations* (New York: McGraw-Hill, 1965).
44. Fossum, *Labor Relations*, p. 262; see also C.S. Loughran, *Negotiating a Labor Contract: A Management Handbook*, 2nd ed. (Washington, DC: Bureau of National Affairs, 1990).
45. C.M. Steven, *Strategy and Collective Bargaining Negotiations* (New York: McGraw-Hill, 1963); Katz and Kochan, *An Introduction to Collective Bargaining*.
46. Kochan, *Collective Bargaining and Industrial Relations*.
47. Fossum, *Labor Relations*, pp. 183–84.
48. Kochan, *Collective Bargaining and Industrial Relations*, p. 272.
49. Herman et al., *Collective Bargaining*.
50. Katz and Kochan, *An Introduction to Collective Bargaining*.
51. Kochan, *Collective Bargaining and Industrial Relations*, p. 386.
52. *United Steelworkers* v. *American Manufacturing Co.*, 363 U.S. 564 (1960); *United Steelworkers* v. *Warrior Gulf and Navigation Co.*, 363 U.S. 574 (1960); *United Steelworkers* v. *Enterprise Wheel and Car Corp.*, 363 U.S. 593 (1960).
53. Original data from U.S. Federal Mediation and Conciliation Service, *Fiftieth Annual Report, Fiscal Year 1997* (Washington, DC: U.S. Government Printing Office, 1997); **www.fmcs.gov.**
54. J.R. Redecker, *Employee Discipline: Policies and Practices* (Washington, DC: Bureau of National Affairs, 1989).
55. Barbash, *The Elements of Industrial Relations*, p. 6.
56. T.A. Kochan, H.C. Katz, and R.B. McKersie, *The Transformation of American Industrial Relations* (New York: BasicBooks, 1986), chap. 6.
57. J.B. Arthur, "The Link between Business Strategy and Industrial Relations Systems in American Steel Minimills," *Industrial and Labor Relations Review* 45 (1992), pp. 488–506; M. Schuster, "Union Management Cooperation," in *Employee and Labor Relations*, ed. J.A. Fossum (Washington, DC: Bureau of National Affairs, 1990); E. Cohen-Rosenthal and C. Burton, *Mutual Gains: A Guide to Union–Management*

Cooperation, 2nd ed. (Ithaca, NY: ILR Press, 1993); T.A. Kochan and P. Osterman, *The Mutual Gains Enterprise* (Boston: Harvard Business School Press, 1994); E. Applebaum and R. Batt, *The New American Workplace* (Ithaca, NY: ILR Press, 1994).
58. A.E. Eaton, "Factors Contributing to the Survival of Employee Participation Programs in Unionized Settings," *Industrial and Labor Relations Review* 47, no. 3 (1994), pp. 371–89.
59. National Labor Relations Board, *A Guide to Basic Law*.
60. A. Bernstein, "Putting a Damper on That Old Team Spirit," *BusinessWeek* (May 4, 1992), p. 60.
61. Bureau of National Affairs, "Polaroid Dissolves Employee Committee in Response to Labor Department Ruling," *Daily Labor Report* (June 23, 1992), p. A-3; K.G. Salwen, "DuPont Is Told It Must Disband Nonunion Panels," *The Wall Street Journal* (June 7, 1993), p. A-2.
62. "NLRB 4-0 Approves Crown Cork & Seal's Use of Seven Employee Participation Committees." *HR News* (September 3, 2001).
63. Kochan and Osterman, *Mutual Gains;* J.P. MacDuffie, "Human Resource Bundles and Manufacturing Performance: Organizational Logic and Flexible Production Systems in the World Auto Industry," *Industrial and Labor Relations Review* 48, no. 2 (1995), pp. 197–221; W.N. Cooke, "Employee Participation Programs, Group-Based Incentives, and Company Performance: A Union–Nonunion Comparison," *Industrial and Labor Relations Review* 47, no. 4 (1994), pp. 594–609; C. Doucouliagos, "Worker Participation and Productivity in Labor-Managed and Participatory Capitalist Firms: A Meta-Analysis," *Industrial and Labor Relations Review* 49, no. 1 (1995), pp. 58–77.
64. J. Cutcher-Gershenfeld, "The Impact of Economic Performance of a Transformation in Workplace Relations," *Industrial and Labor Relations Review* 44 (1991), pp. 241–60.
65. R.B. Freeman and J. Rogers, *Proceedings of the Industrial Relations Research Association*, 1995.
66. **http://stats.bls.gov**.
67. Ibid.
68. Jarrell and Stanley, "A Meta-Analysis"; R.B. Freeman and J. Medoff, *What Do Unions Do?* (New York: BasicBooks, 1984).
69. J.T. Addison and B.T. Hirsch, "Union Effects on Productivity, Profits, and Growth: Has the Long Run Arrived?" *Journal of Labor Economics* 7 (1989), pp. 72–105.
70. R.B. Freeman and J.L. Medoff, "The Two Faces of Unionism," *Public Interest* 57 (Fall 1979), pp. 69–93.
71. L. Mishel and P. Voos, *Unions and Economic Competitiveness* (Armonk, NY: M.E. Sharpe, 1991).
72. Freeman and Medoff, "Two Faces."
73. S. Slichter, J. Healy, and E.R. Livernash, *The Impact of Collective Bargaining on Management* (Washington, DC: Brookings Institution, 1960); Freeman and Medoff, "Two Faces."
74. Freeman and Medoff, *What Do Unions Do?*; Herman et al., *Collective Bargaining;* Addison and Hirsch, "Union Effects on Productivity"; Katz and Kochan, *An Introduction to Collective Bargaining;* Lineneman et al., "Evaluating the Evidence."
75. B.E. Becker and C.A. Olson, "Unions and Firm Profits," *Industrial Relations* 31, no. 3 (1992), pp. 395–415; B.T. Hirsch and B.A. Morgan, "Shareholder Risks and Returns in Union and Nonunion Firms," *Industrial and Labor Relations Review* 47, no. 2 (1994), pp. 302–18.
76. Addison and Hirsch, "Union Effects on Productivity." See also B.T. Hirsch, *Labor Unions and the Economic Performance of Firms* (Kalamazoo, MI: W.E. Upjohn Institute, 1991); J.M. Abowd, "The Effect of Wage Bargains on the Stock Market Value of the Firm," *American Economic Review* 79 (1989), pp. 774–800; Hirsch, *Labor Unions*.
77. B.E. Becker, and C.A. Olson, "The Impact of Strikes on Shareholder Equity," *Industrial and Labor Relations Review* 39, no. 3 (1986), pp. 425–38; O. Persons, "The Effects of Automobile Strikes on the Stock Value of Steel Suppliers," *Industrial and Labor Relations Review* 49, no. 1 (1995), pp. 78–87.
78. C. Brewster, "Levels of Analysis in Strategic HRM: Questions Raised by Comparative Research," Conference on Research and Theory in HRM, Cornell University, October 1997.
79. C. Chang and C. Sorrentino, "Union Membership in 12 Countries," *Monthly Labor Review* 114, no. 12 (1991), pp. 46–53; D.G. Blanchflower and R.B. Freeman, "Going Different Ways: Unionism in the U.S. and Other Advanced O.E.C.D. Countries" (Symposium on the Future Role of Unions, Industry, and Government in Industrial Relations. University of Minnesota), cited in Chaison and Rose, "The Macrodeterminants of Union Growth," p. 23.
80. J.P. Begin and E.F. Beal, *The Practice of Collective Bargaining* (Homewood, IL: Richard D. Irwin, 1989); T.H. Hammer, S.C. Currall, and R.N. Stern, "Worker Representation on Boards of Directors: A Study of Competing Roles," *Industrial and Labor Relations Review* 44 (1991), pp. 661–80; Katz and Kochan, *An Introduction to Collective Bargaining;* H. Gunter and G. Leminsky, "The Federal Republic of Germany," in *Labor in the Twentieth Century*, ed. J.T. Dunlop and W. Galenson (New York: Academic Press, 1978), pp. 149–96.
81. "Adapt or Die," *The Economist* (July 1, 1995), p. 54;

G. Steinmetz, "German Firms Sour on Stem That Keeps Peace with Workers: Centralized Bargaining, a Key to Postwar Gains, Inflates Costs, Companies Fear," *The Wall Street Journal* (October 17, 1995), p. A1.

82. Herman et al., *Collective Bargaining*, p. 348; B.T. Hirsch and D.A. MacPherson, *Union Membership and Earnings Data Book 1994* (Washington, DC: Bureau of National Affairs, 1995).

83. J.F. Burton and T. Thomason, "The Extent of Collective Bargaining in the Public Sector," in *Public Sector Bargaining*, ed. B. Aaron, J.M. Najita, and J.L. Stern (Washington, DC: Bureau of National Affairs, 1988).

84. **www.afscme.org**.

Chapter 15 Managing Human Resources Globally

Objectives
After reading this chapter, you should be able to:

1. Identify the recent changes that have caused companies to expand into international markets.
2. Discuss the four factors that most strongly influence HRM in international markets.
3. List the different categories of international employees.
4. Identify the four levels of global participation and the HRM issues faced within each level.
5. Discuss the ways companies attempt to select, train, compensate, and reintegrate expatriate managers.

While globalization continues to increase and more companies are doing business overseas, recent world events may place an added responsibility on managers of expatriate employees in terms of motivation, behaviors, and family considerations.

Enter the World of Business

Terrorism and Global Human Resource Management

Globalization has continued to increase as companies expand their operations in a number of countries, employing an increasingly global workforce. Although this process has resulted in a number of positive outcomes, it has also occasionally presented new types of problems for firms to face.

On September 11, 2001, terrorists with Middle Eastern roots (alleged to be part of Osama bin Laden's al-Qaida network) hijacked four U.S. planes, crashing two of them into the World Trade Center's twin towers and one into the Pentagon (a fourth was crashed in Pennsylvania in a scuffle with passengers). President Bush and U.K. Prime Minister Tony Blair, after their demands that the Taliban government in Afghanistan turn over bin Laden and his leaders were ignored, began military action against that country on October 7, 2001. At the writing of this chapter, we do not know what the end result of this action will be, but we do know that both the terrorist acts and the subsequent war on terrorism have created a host of issues for multinational companies.

First, companies doing business overseas, particularly in Muslim-dominated countries such as the Arab states and Indonesia, must manage their expatriate workforce (particularly U.S. and British citizens) in what has the potential to become hostile territory. These employees fear for their security, and some have asked to return to their home countries.

Second, companies with global workforces must manage across what have become increasingly nationalistic boundaries. Those of us in the United States may view the terrorist attacks as an act of war and our response as being entirely justified. However, those in the Arab world, while not justifying the terrorist attacks, may similarly feel that the military response toward Afghanistan is hostile aggression. One executive at a global oil company noted the difficulty in managing a workforce that is approximately 25 percent Arab. He stated that many of the Arab executives have said, "While we know that you are concerned about the events of September 11, you should know that we are equally concerned about the events of October 7."

Introduction

The environment in which business competes is rapidly becoming globalized. More and more companies are entering international markets by exporting their products overseas, building plants in other countries, and entering into alliances with foreign companies. Of the world's largest organizations, 23 have their headquarters outside the United States. Of the top 100 organizations, 59 have their headquarters in the United States, followed by Europe with 38. Japan is currently home to 11 of the 50 largest banks in the world, whereas the United States is home to only 6.[1]

A survey of 12,000 managers from 25 different countries indicates how common international expansion has become, both in the United States and in other countries.[2] Of the U.S. managers surveyed, 26 percent indicated that their companies had recently expanded internationally. Among the larger companies (10,000 or more employees), 45 percent had expanded internationally during the previous two years. Currently, exports account for 11 percent of the gross domestic product in the United States, and they have been growing at a rate of 12 percent a year since 1987.[3]

Indeed, most organizations now function in the global economy. Thus U.S. businesses are entering international markets at the same time foreign companies are entering the U.S. market.

What is behind the trend toward expansion into global markets? Companies are attempting to gain a competitive advantage, which can be provided by international expansion in a number of ways. First, these countries are new markets with large numbers of potential customers. For companies that are producing below their capacity, they provide a means of increasing sales and profits. Second, many companies are building production facilities in other countries as a means of capitalizing on those countries' lower labor costs for relatively unskilled jobs. For example, many of the *maquiladora* plants (foreign-owned plants located in Mexico that employ Mexican laborers) provide low-skilled labor at considerably lower cost than in the United States. In 1999, the average manufacturing hourly wage in Mexico was $2.12.[4]

According to a survey of almost 3,000 line executives and HR executives from 12 countries, international competition is the number one factor affecting HRM. The globalization of business structures and globalization of the economy ranked fourth and fifth, respectively.[5] Deciding whether to enter foreign markets and whether to develop plants or other facilities in other countries, however, is no simple matter, and many human resource issues surface.

This chapter discusses the human resource issues that must be addressed to gain competitive advantage in a world of global competition. This is not a chapter on international human resource management (the specific HRM policies and programs companies use to manage human resources across international boundaries).[6] The chapter focuses instead on the key factors that must be addressed to strategically manage human resources in an international context. We discuss some of the important events that have increased the global nature of business over the past few years. We then identify some of the factors that are most important to HRM in global environments. Finally, we examine particular issues related to managing expatriate managers. These issues present unique opportunities for firms to gain competitive advantage.

Current Global Changes

Several recent social and political changes have accelerated the movement toward international competition. The effects of these changes have been profound and far-reaching. Many are still evolving. In this section we discuss the major developments that have accentuated the need for organizations to gain a competitive advantage through effectively managing human resources in a global economy.

European Economic Community

European countries have managed their economies individually for years. Because of the countries' close geographic proximity, their economies have become intertwined. This created a number of problems for international businesses; for example, the regulations of one country, such as France, might be completely different from those of another country, such as Germany. In response, most of the European countries agreed to participate in the European Economic Community, which began in 1992. The EEC is a confederation of most of the European nations that agree to engage in free trade with one another, with commerce regulated by an overseeing body called the European Commission (EC). Under the EEC, legal regulation in the participating countries has become more, although not completely, uniform. Assuming the EEC's trend toward free trade among members continues, Europe has become one of the largest free markets in the world. In addition, as of 1999, all of the members of the European Economic Community share a common currency, the euro. This ties the members' economic fates even more closely with one another.

North American Free Trade Agreement (NAFTA)

NAFTA is an agreement among Canada, the United States, and Mexico that has created a free market even larger than the European Economic Community. The United States and Canada already had a free trade agreement since 1989, but NAFTA brought Mexico into the consortium. The agreement has been prompted by Mexico's increasing willingness to open its markets and facilities in an effort to promote economic growth.[7] As previously discussed, the *maquiladora* plants exemplify this trend. In addition, some efforts have been made to expand the membership of NAFTA to other Latin American countries, such as Chile.

NAFTA has increased U.S. investment in Mexico because of Mexico's substantially lower labor costs for low-skilled employees. This has had two effects on employment in the United States. First, many low-skilled jobs went south, decreasing employment opportunities for U.S. citizens who lack higher-level skills. Second, it has increased employment opportunities for Americans with higher-level skills beyond those already being observed.[8]

The Growth of Asia

An additional global market that is of economic consequence to many firms lies in Asia. Whereas Japan has been a dominant economic force for over 20 years, recently countries such as Singapore, Hong Kong, and Malaysia have become significant economic forces. In addition, China, with its population of over 1 billion and trend toward opening its markets to foreign investors, presents a tremendous potential market for goods. In fact, a consortium of Singaporean companies and governmental agencies has jointly developed with China a huge industrial township in eastern China's Suzhou city that will consist of ready-made factories for sale to foreign companies.[9] Although Asia has recently been the victim of a large-scale economic recession termed the "Asian flu," it is fully expected to regain its stature as an attractive market for products and investment over the next few years.

General Agreement on Tariffs and Trade (GATT)

GATT is an international framework of rules and principles for reducing trade barriers across countries around the world. It currently consists of over 100 member nations. The most recent round of GATT negotiations resulted in an agreement to cut tariffs (taxes on imports) by 40 percent, reduce government subsidies to businesses, expand protection of intellectual property such as copyrights and patents, and establish rules for investing and trading in services. It also established the World Trade Organization (WTO) to resolve disputes among GATT members.

These changes—the European Economic Community, NAFTA, the growth of Asia, and GATT—all exemplify events that are pushing companies to compete in a global economy. These developments are opening new markets and new sources of technology and labor in a way that has never been seen in history. However, this era of increasing international competition accentuates the need to manage human resources effectively to gain competitive advantage in a global marketplace. This requires understanding some of the factors that can determine the effectiveness of various HRM practices and approaches.

Factors Affecting HRM in Global Markets

Companies that enter global markets must recognize that these markets are not simply mirror images of their home country. Countries differ along a number of dimensions that influence the attractiveness of direct foreign investment in each country. These differences determine the economic viability of building an operation in a foreign location, and they have a particularly strong impact on HRM in that operation. Researchers in international management have identified a number of factors that can affect HRM in global markets, and we focus on four factors, as depicted in Figure 15.1: culture, education–human capital, the political–legal system, and the economic system.[10]

FIGURE 15.1
Factors Affecting Human Resource Management in International Markets

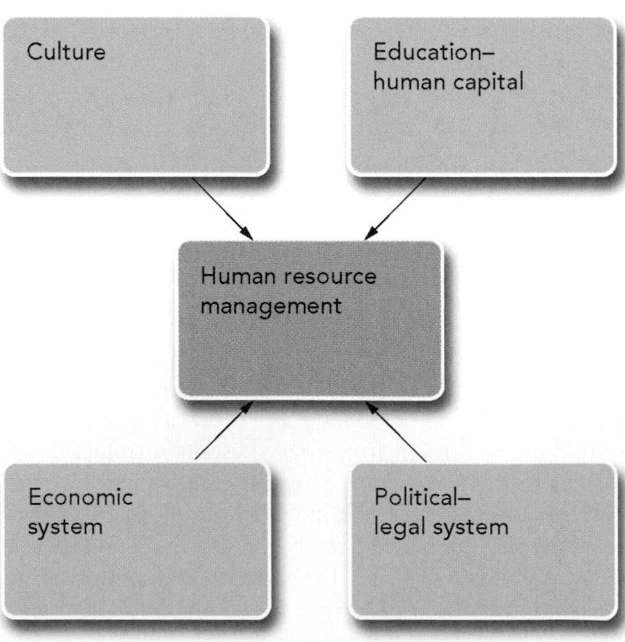

Culture

By far the most important factor influencing international HRM is the culture of the country in which a facility is located. *Culture* is defined as "the set of important assumptions (often unstated) that members of a community share."[11] These assumptions consist of beliefs about the world and how it works and the ideals that are worth striving for.[12]

Culture is important to HRM for two reasons. First, it often determines the other three factors affecting HRM in global markets. Culture can greatly affect a country's laws, in that laws are often the codification of right and wrong as defined by the culture. Culture also affects human capital, because if education is greatly valued by the culture, then members of the community try to increase their human capital. Finally, as we will discuss later, cultures and economic systems are closely intertwined.[13]

However, the most important reason that culture is important to HRM is that it often determines the effectiveness of various HRM practices. Practices found to be effective in the United States may not be effective in a culture that has different beliefs and values.[14] For example, U.S. companies rely heavily on individual performance appraisal, and rewards are tied to individual performance. In Japan, however, individuals are expected to subordinate their wishes and desires to those of the larger group. Thus, individual-based evaluation and incentives are not nearly as effective there and, in fact, are seldom observed among Japanese organizations.[15]

In this section we examine a model that attempts to characterize different cultures. This model illustrates why culture can have a profound influence on HRM.

Hofstede's Cultural Dimensions

In a classic study of culture, Geert Hofstede identified four dimensions on which various cultures could be classified.[16] In a later study he added a fifth dimension that aids in characterizing cultures.[17] The relative scores for 10 major countries are provided in Table 15.1. **Individualism–collectivism** describes the strength of the relation between an individual and other individuals in the society—that is, the degree to which people act as individuals rather than as members of a group. In individualist cultures, such as the United States, Great Britain, and the Netherlands, people are expected to look after their own interests and the interests of their immediate families. The individual is expected to stand on her own two feet rather than be protected by the group. In collectivist cultures, such as Colombia, Pakistan, and Taiwan, people are expected to look after the interest of the larger community, which is expected to protect people when they are in trouble.

Individualism–collectivism
One of Hofstede's cultural dimensions; describes the strength of the relation between an individual and other individuals in a society.

The second dimension, **power distance,** concerns how a culture deals with hierarchical power relationships—particularly the unequal distribution of power. It describes the degree of inequality among people that is considered to be normal. Cultures with small power distance, such as those of Denmark and Israel, seek to eliminate inequalities in power and wealth as much as possible, whereas countries with large power distances, such as India and the Philippines, seek to maintain those differences.

Power distance
One of Hofstede's cultural dimensions; describes how a culture deals with hierarchical power relationships.

Differences in power distance often result in miscommunication and conflicts between people from different cultures. For example, in Mexico and Japan individuals are always addressed by their titles (Señor Smith or Smith-san, respectively). Individuals from the United States, however, often believe in minimizing power distances by using first names. Although this is perfectly normal, and possibly even advisable in the United States, it can be offensive and a sign of disrespect in other cultures.

TABLE 15.1

Cultural Dimension Scores for 10 Countries

	PD[a]	ID	MA	UA	LT
United States	40 L[b]	91 H	62 H	46 L	29 L
Germany	35 L	67 H	66 H	65 M	31 M
Japan	54 M	45 M	95 H	92 H	80 H
France	68 H	71 H	43 M	86 H	30[c] L
Netherlands	38 L	80 H	14 L	53 M	44 M
Hong Kong	68 H	25 L	57 H	29 L	96 H
Indonesia	78 H	14 L	46 M	48 L	25[c] L
West Africa	77 H	20 L	46 M	54 M	16 L
Russia	95[c] H	50[c] M	40[c] L	90[c] H	10[c] L
China	80[c] H	20[c] L	50[c] M	60[c] M	118 H

[a]PD = power distance; ID = individualism; MA = masculinity; UA = uncertainty avoidance; LT = long-term orientation.

[b]H = top third; M = medium third; L = bottom third (among 53 countries and regions for the first four dimensions; among 23 countries for the fifth).

[c]Estimated.

SOURCE: From *Academy of Management Executive* by G. Hofstede. Copyright © 1993 by Academy of Management. Reproduced with permission of Academy of Management via Copyright Clearance Center.

Uncertainty avoidance
One of Hofstede's cultural dimensions; describes how cultures seek to deal with an unpredictable future.

Masculinity–femininity dimension
One of Hofstede's cultural dimensions; describes the division of roles between the sexes within a society.

Long-term–short-term orientation
One of Hofstede's cultural dimensions; describes how a culture balances immediate benefits with future rewards.

The third dimension, **uncertainty avoidance,** describes how cultures seek to deal with the fact that the future is not perfectly predictable. It is defined as the degree to which people in a culture prefer structured over unstructured situations. Some cultures, such as those of Singapore and Jamaica, have weak uncertainty avoidance. They socialize individuals to accept this uncertainty and take each day as it comes. People from these cultures tend to be rather easygoing and flexible regarding different views. Other cultures, such as those of Greece and Portugal, socialize their people to seek security through technology, law, and religion. Thus these cultures provide clear rules as to how one should behave.

The **masculinity–femininity** dimension describes the division of roles between the sexes within a society. In "masculine" cultures, such as those of Germany and Japan, what are considered traditionally masculine values—showing off, achieving something visible, and making money—permeate the society. These societies stress assertiveness, performance, success, and competition. "Feminine" cultures, such as those of Sweden and Norway, promote values that have been traditionally regarded as feminine, such as putting relationships before money, helping others, and preserving the environment. These cultures stress service, care for the weak, and solidarity.

Finally, the fifth dimension comes from the philosophy of the Far East and is referred to as the **long-term–short-term orientation.** Cultures high on the long-term orientation focus on the future and hold values in the present that will not necessarily provide an immediate benefit, such as thrift (saving) and persistence. Hofstede found that many Far Eastern countries such as Japan and China have a long-term orientation. Short-term orientations, on the other hand, are found in the United States, Russia, and West Africa. These cultures are oriented toward the past and present and promote respect for tradition and for fulfilling social obligations.

The current Japanese criticism of management practices in the United States illustrates the differences in long-term–short-term orientation. Japanese managers, traditionally exhibiting a long-term orientation, engage in 5- to 10-year planning. This leads them to criticize U.S. managers, who are traditionally much more short-term in orientation because their planning often consists of quarterly to yearly time horizons.

These five dimensions help us understand the potential problems of managing employees from different cultures. Later in this chapter we will explore how these cultural dimensions affect the acceptability and utility of various HRM practices. However, it is important to note that these differences can have a profound influence on whether a company chooses to enter a given country. One interesting finding of Hofstede's research was the impact of culture on a country's economic health. He found that countries with individualist cultures were more wealthy. Collectivist cultures with high power distance were all poor.[18] Cultures seem to affect a country's economy through their promotion of individual work ethics and incentives for individuals to increase their human capital. Figure 15.2 maps the countries Hofstede studied on the two characteristics of individualism–collectivism and economic success.

Implications of Culture for HRM

Cultures have an important impact on approaches to managing people. As we discuss later, the culture can strongly affect the education–human capital of a country, the political–legal system, and the economic system. As Hofstede found, culture also has a profound impact on a country's economic health by promoting certain values that either aid or inhibit economic growth.

More important to this discussion, however, is that cultural characteristics influence the ways managers behave in relation to subordinates, as well as the perceptions of the appropriateness of various HRM practices. First, cultures differ strongly on such things as how subordinates expect leaders to lead, how decisions are handled within the hierarchy, and (most important) what motivates individuals. For example, in Germany, managers achieve their status by demonstrating technical skills, so employees look to them to assign their tasks and resolve technical problems. In the Netherlands, on the other hand, managers focus on seeking consensus among all parties and must engage in an open-ended exchange of views and balancing of interests.[19] Clearly, these methods have different implications for selecting and training managers in the different countries.

Second, cultures strongly influence the appropriateness of HRM practices. For example, as previously discussed, the extent to which a culture promotes an individualistic versus a collectivist orientation will impact the effectiveness of individually oriented human resource management systems. In the United States, companies often focus selection systems on assessing an individual's technical skill and, to a lesser extent, social skills. In collectivist cultures, on the other hand, companies focus more on assessing how well an individual will perform as a member of the work group.

Similarly, cultures can influence compensation systems. Individualistic cultures such as those found in the United States often exhibit great differences between the highest- and lowest-paid individuals in an organization, with the highest-paid individual often receiving 200 times the salary of the lowest. Collectivist cultures, on the other hand, tend to have much flatter salary structures, with the top-paid individual receiving only about 20 times the overall pay of the lowest-paid one.

Cultural differences can affect the communication and coordination processes in organizations. Collectivist cultures, as well as those with less of an authoritarian orientation, value group decision making and participative management practices more highly than do individualistic cultures. When a person raised in an individualistic culture must work closely with those from a collectivist culture, communication problems and conflicts often appear. Much of the emphasis on "cultural diversity" programs in organizations focuses on understanding the cultures of others in order to better

FIGURE 15.2

The Position of the Studied Countries on Their Individualism Index (IDV) versus Their 1970 National Wealth

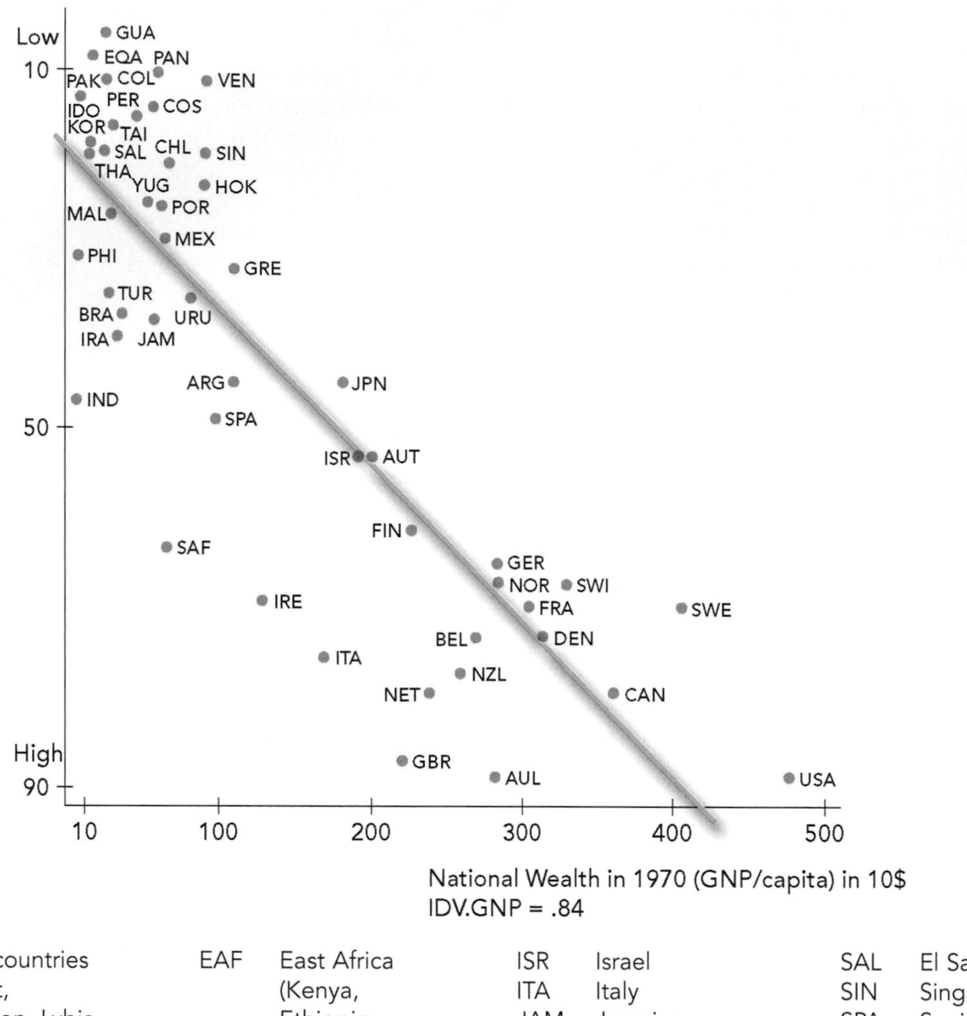

ARA	Arab countries (Egypt, Lebanon, Lybia, Kuwait, Iraq, Saudi Arabia, U.A.E.)	EAF	East Africa (Kenya, Ethiopia, Zambia)
ARG	Argentina	EQA	Equador
AUL	Australia	FIN	Finland
AUT	Austria	FRA	France
BEL	Belgium	GBR	Great Britain
BRA	Brazil	GER	Germany
CAN	Canada	GRE	Greece
CHL	Chile	GUA	Guatemala
COL	Colombia	HOK	Hong Kong
COS	Costa Rica	IDO	Indonesia
DEN	Denmark	IND	India
		IRA	Iran
		IRE	Ireland

ISR	Israel	SAL	El Salvador
ITA	Italy	SIN	Singapore
JAM	Jamaica	SPA	Spain
JPN	Japan	SWE	Sweden
KOR	South Korea	SWI	Switzerland
MAL	Malaysia	TAI	Taiwan
MEX	Mexico	THA	Thailand
NET	Netherlands	TUR	Turkey
NOR	Norway	URU	Uruguay
NZL	New Zealand	USA	United States
PAK	Pakistan	VEN	Venezuela
PAN	Panama	WAF	West Africa (Nigeria, Ghana, Sierra Leone)
PER	Peru		
PHI	Philippines		
POR	Portugal		
SAF	South Africa	YUG	Yugoslavia

SOURCE: G. Hofstede, "The Cultural Relativity of Organizational Practices and Theories," *Journal of International Business Studies* 14, no. 2 (Fall 1983), p. 89.

COMPETING THROUGH HIGH-PERFORMANCE WORK SYSTEMS

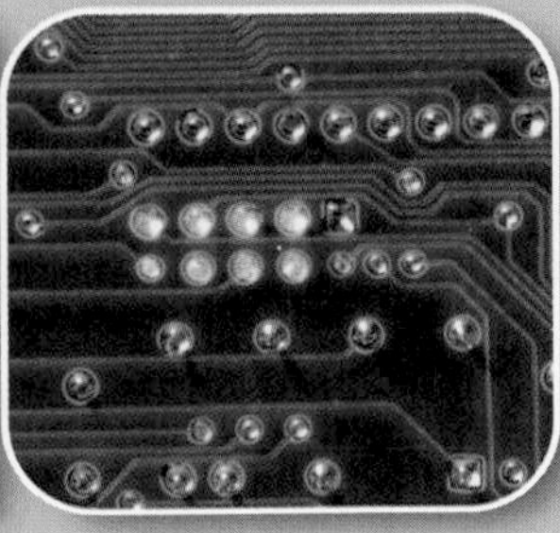

Managing in Russia

Managing employees from different cultures always presents unique problems. This is exemplified among firms trying to do business in Russia. First, many natives matured in their work habits under a communist system that was devoid of any recognition of the customer—a system in which decisions were all made by the general director. Thus, these employees, while having technical skills, are prepared neither to see the value in customer service nor to take on any decision-making authority. This presents a myriad of problems for firms seeking to develop high-performance work systems that emphasize employee involvement in decision making as a means of creating competitive advantage in the marketplace.

Second, Russia's cultural norms simply result in very different day-to-day behaviors. Take telephone skills, for example. In the United States any time you call a major company (as well as just about any small business), you are likely to have your call answered within only a few rings and then be greeted by a friendly voice saying something like "Good morning, XYZ Corporation. Where may I direct your call?" On the other hand, in Russia individuals never identify themselves or their organizations when answering the phone, and some may simply answer it by shouting "Yes?" In addition, some expatriate managers say that they have attended meetings where a phone rang repeatedly without anyone answering it. Finally, someone picked up the telephone, hung it right back up without speaking to the caller, and then left it off the hook for the rest of the meeting. They reasoned that if the call was important, the person would call back.

This highlights the need for extensive training for Russian employees working for U.S. companies. Firms that hope to compete need to invest in training employees in such broad topics as economics (understanding how markets work) all the way down to such basic skills as answering the telephone. For example, Pepsi International Bottlers provides its high-performing leaders with customized training based on evaluations of their personal strengths and weaknesses. Potential training areas are negotiation, customer focus, and business writing. This training costs roughly $3,000 per person. Clearly, the lesson is that firms that fail to upgrade Russian employees' skills and help them adapt to Western business practices will not survive for long.

SOURCE: From *HRMagazine* by M. Cooley.

communicate with them. An example of how important cultural differences can be is provided in the "Competing through High-Performance Work Systems" box.

Education–Human Capital

A company's potential to find and maintain a qualified workforce is an important consideration in any decision to expand into a foreign market. Thus a country's human capital resources can be an important HRM issue. *Human capital* refers to the productive capabilities of individuals—that is, the knowledge, skills, and experience that have economic value.[20]

Countries differ in their levels of human capital. For example, as discussed in Chapter 1, the United States suffers from a human capital shortage because the jobs being created require skills beyond those of most new entrants into the workforce.[21] In former East Germany, there is an excess of human capital in terms of technical knowledge and skill because of that country's large investment in education. However, East Germany's business schools did not teach management development, so there is a human capital shortage for managerial jobs.[22] Similarly, companies in what used to be West Germany have shifted toward types of production and service that require high-skilled workers; this is creating a human capital shortage for high-skill jobs, yet the unemployment rate remains high because of a large number of low-skilled workers.[23] However, the high skills and low wages of workers in many countries make their labor forces quite attractive.

A country's human capital is determined by a number of variables. A major variable is the educational opportunities available to the labor force. In the Netherlands, for instance, government funding of school systems allows students to go all the way through graduate school without paying.[24] Similarly, the free education provided to citizens in the former Soviet bloc resulted in high levels of human capital, in spite of the poor infrastructure and economy that resulted from the socialist economic systems. In contrast, some Third World countries, such as Nicaragua and Haiti, have relatively low levels of human capital because of a lack of investment in education.

A country's human capital may profoundly affect a foreign company's desire to locate there or enter that country's market. Countries with low human capital attract facilities that require low skills and low wage levels. This explains why U.S. companies desire to move their currently unionized low-skill–high-wage manufacturing and assembly jobs to Mexico, where they can obtain low-skilled workers for substantially lower wages. Similarly, Japan ships its messy, low-skill work to neighboring countries while maintaining its high-skill work at home.[25] Countries like Mexico, with relatively low levels of human capital, might not be as attractive for operations that consist of more high-skill jobs.

Countries with high human capital are attractive sites for direct foreign investment that creates high-skill jobs. In Ireland, for example, over 25 percent of 18-year-olds attend college, a rate much higher than other European countries. In addition, Ireland's economy supports only 1.1 million jobs for a population of 3.5 million. The combination of high education levels, a strong work ethic, and high unemployment makes the country attractive for foreign firms because of the resulting high productivity and low turnover. The Met Life insurance company set up a facility for Irish workers to analyze medical insurance claims. It has found the high levels of human capital and the high work ethic to provide such a competitive advantage that the company is currently looking for other work performed in the United States to be shipped to Ireland. Similarly, for this reason, many believe that NAFTA will result in a loss of low-skill jobs in the United States but also in an increased number of high-skill jobs in the United States. The increase in high-skill jobs would result from increased commerce between the two nations combined with the higher levels of human capital available in the United States versus Mexico.[26]

Political–Legal System

The regulations imposed by a country's legal system can strongly affect HRM. The political–legal system often dictates the requirements for certain HRM practices, such as training, compensation, hiring, firing, and layoffs. In large part, the legal system is an outgrowth of the culture in which it exists. Thus the laws of a particular country often reflect societal norms about what constitutes legitimate behavior.[27]

For example, the United States has led the world in eliminating discrimination in the workplace. Because of the importance this has in our culture, we also have legal safeguards such as equal employment opportunity laws (discussed in Chapter 3) that strongly affect the hiring and firing practices of firms. As a society, we also have strong beliefs regarding the equity of pay systems; thus the Fair Labor Standards Act (discussed in Chapter 11), among other laws and regulations, sets the minimum wage for a variety of jobs. We have regulations that dictate much of the process for negotiation between unions and management. These regulations profoundly affect the ways human resources are managed in the United States.

Similarly, the legal regulations regarding HRM in other countries reflect their societal norms. For example, in Germany employees have a legal right to "codetermination" at the company, plant, and individual levels. At the company level, a firm's employees have direct influence on the important decisions that affect them, such as large investments or new strategies. This is brought about through having employee representatives on the supervisory council (*Aufsichtsrat*). At the plant level, codetermination exists through works councils. These councils have no rights in the economic management of the company, but they can influence HRM policies on such issues as working hours, payment methods, hirings, and transfers. Finally, at the individual level, employees have contractual rights, such as the right to read their personnel files and the right to be informed about how their pay is calculated.[28]

The EEC provides another example of the effects of the political–legal system on HRM. The EEC's Community Charter of December 9, 1989, provides for the fundamental social rights of workers. These rights include freedom of movement, freedom to choose one's occupation and be fairly compensated, guarantee of social protection via social security benefits, freedom of association and collective bargaining, equal treatment for men and women, and a safe and healthful work environment, among others.

Economic System

A country's economic system influences HRM in a number of ways. As previously discussed, a country's culture is integrally tied to its economic system, and these systems provide many of the incentives for developing human capital. In socialist economic systems there are ample opportunities for developing human capital because the education system is free. However, under these systems, there is little economic incentive to develop human capital because there are no monetary rewards for increasing human capital. In addition, in former Soviet bloc countries, an individual's investment in human capital did not always result in a promotion. Rather, it was investment in the Socialist Party that led to career advancements.

In capitalist systems the opposite situation exists. There is less opportunity to develop human capital without higher costs. (You have probably observed tuition increases at U.S. universities.) However, those who do invest in their individual human capital, particularly through education, are more able to reap monetary rewards, thus providing more incentive for such investment. In the United States, individuals' salaries usually reflect differences in human capital (high-skill workers receive higher compensation than low-skill workers). In fact, research estimates that an individual's wages increase by between 10 and 16 percent for each additional year of schooling.[29]

In addition to the effects of an economic system on HRM, the health of the

TABLE 15.2

Gross Hourly Compensation in Several Countries

Germany	$26.18
Switzerland	23.56
Sweden	21.58
Austria	21.83
Netherlands	20.94
Japan	20.89
United States	19.20
France	17.98
Italy	16.60
Britain	16.56
Greece	8.91[a]
Portugal	5.48[a]
Mexico	2.12
Sri Lanka	.47[a]

[a]1998 data.

SOURCE: U.S. Department of Labor, *International Comparisons of Hourly Compensation Costs for Production Workers in Manufacturing, 1999;* Bureau of Labor Statistics, 2001.

system can have an important impact. For example, we referred earlier to lower labor costs in Mexico. In developed countries with a high level of wealth, labor costs tend to be quite high relative to those in developing countries. While labor costs are related to the human capital of a country, they are not perfectly related, as shown by Table 15.2. This table provides a good example of the different hourly labor costs for manufacturing jobs in various countries.

An economic system also affects HRM directly through its taxes on compensation packages. Thus the differential labor costs shown in Table 15.2 do not always reflect the actual take-home pay of employees. Socialist systems are characterized by tax systems that redistribute wealth by taking a higher percentage of a person's income as she moves up the economic ladder. Capitalist systems attempt to reward individuals for their efforts by allowing them to keep more of their earnings. Table 15.3 shows that a manager being paid $100,000 would take home vastly different amounts in dif-

TABLE 15.3

Maximum Marginal Federal Tax Rates

COUNTRY	INCOME TAX HIGHEST PERSONAL NATIONAL RATE
United States	40%
Germany	56%
France	54%
Britain	40%
Netherlands	60%
Sweden	55%
Italy	46%
Japan	50%
South Korea	44%

SOURCE: "America vs. the New Europe: By the Numbers," *Fortune* (December 21, 1998).

ferent countries because of the varying tax rates. Companies that do business in other countries have to present compensation packages to expatriate managers that are competitive in take-home, rather than gross, pay. HRM responses to these issues affecting expatriate managers will be discussed in more detail later in this chapter.

These differences in economies can have a profound impact on pay systems, particularly among global companies seeking to develop an international compensation and reward system that maintains cost controls while enabling local operations to compete in the war for talent. One recent study examining how compensation managers design these systems indicates that they look at a number of factors including the global firm strategy, the local regulatory/political context, institutions and stakeholders, local markets, and national culture. While they try to learn from the best practices that exist globally, they balance these approaches with the constraints imposed by the local environment.[30]

In conclusion, every country varies in terms of its culture, human capital, legal system, and economic systems. These variations directly influence the types of HRM systems that must be developed to accommodate the particular situation. The extent to which these differences affect a company depends on how involved the company is in global markets. In the next sections we discuss important concepts of global business and various levels of global participation, particularly noting how these factors come into play. The "Competing in the New Economy" box on the next page illustrates how all of these factors influence competitiveness in a global economy.

Managing Employees in a Global Context

Types of International Employees

Before discussing the levels of global participation, we need to distinguish between parent countries, host countries, and third countries. A **parent country** is the country in which the company's corporate headquarters are located. For example, the United States is the parent country of General Motors. A **host country** is the country in which the parent country organization seeks to locate (or has already located) a facility. Thus Great Britain is a host country for General Motors because GM has operations there. A **third country** is a country other than the host country or parent country, and a company may or may not have a facility there.

There are also different categories of employees. **Expatriate** is the term generally used for employees sent by a company in one country to manage operations in a different country. With the increasing globalization of business, it is now important to distinguish among different types of expatriates. **Parent-country nationals (PCNs)** are employees who were born and live in the parent country. **Host-country nationals (HCNs)** are those employees who were born and raised in the host, as opposed to the parent, country. Finally, **third-country nationals (TCNs)** are employees born in a country other than the parent country and host country but who work in the host country. Thus a manager born and raised in Brazil employed by an organization located in the United States and assigned to manage an operation in Thailand would be considered a TCN.

Research shows that countries differ in their use of various types of international employees. One study revealed that Japanese multinational firms have more ethnocentric HRM policies and practices (they tend to use Japanese expatriate managers

Parent country
The country in which a company's corporate headquarters are located.

Host country
The country in which the parent country organization seeks to locate or has already located a facility.

Third country
A country other than a host or parent country.

Expatriate
An employee sent by his or her company in one country to manage operations in a different country.

Parent-country nationals (PCNs)
Employees who were born and live in a parent country.

Host-country nationals (HCNs)
Employees who were born and raised in the host, not the parent, country.

Third-country nationals (TCNs)
Employees born in a country other than the parent or host country.

COMPETING IN THE NEW ECONOMY

Building the Canadian Economy

In this chapter we discuss some of the important factors that firms must consider when looking to expand internationally, including culture, education–human capital, the political system, and the economic system. A recent report produced by the Information Technology Association of Canada illustrates the importance of these factors. The report, titled "Toward a Culture of Innovation," provides guidance for how Canada can build a more competitive economy within the global economic landscape through building a knowledge-based society. The report suggests seven actions that track closely with the factors we have discussed.

1. *Investing strategically in education.* The report suggests that the lack of qualified workers, particularly in the IT and science fields, will both stifle economic growth and cause firms to move operations to countries where such skills are in greater abundance. The report's solution is increased public investment in education.
2. *Better business management.* The report notes that an enormous hunger for management expertise exists (again, a human capital concern), but expands the concept of leadership to making every employee a leader. The report advocates both cultivating new types of business leaders and making a leader of every decision maker in the workplace.
3. *Better access to capital.* Noting that debate exists for

more than local host-country nationals) than either European or U.S. firms. This study also found that the use of ethnocentric HRM practices is associated with more HRM problems.[31]

Levels of Global Participation

We often hear companies referred to as "multinational" or "international." However, it is important to understand the different levels of participation in international markets. This is especially important because as a company becomes more involved in international trade, different types of HRM problems arise. In this section we examine Nancy Adler's categorization of the various levels of international participation from which a company may choose.[32] Figure 15.3 depicts these levels of involvement.

Domestic

Most companies begin by operating within a domestic marketplace. For example, an entrepreneur may have an idea for a product that meets a need in the U.S. marketplace. This individual then obtains capital to build a facility that produces the product or service in a quantity that meets the needs of a small market niche. This requires recruiting, hiring, training, and compensating a number of individuals who will be involved in the production process, and these individuals are usually drawn from the whether Alexander Graham Bell invented the telephone in the United States or Canada, the report acknowledges that the financial backing for the innovation came from the United States. The report advocates building better venture capital markets to fuel investments in innovative firms.

4. *Business tax reform.* The report notes that lower business tax rates, although not as popular as personal tax reductions, will have a more important role in building Canada's economy. This includes lowering corporate tax rates, reducing tax rates on capital gains, and improving capital cost allowances for information and communications technology to encourage the adoption of these tools.
5. *Transforming the workplace.* The combination of more qualified people and increased information and communications technology will allow Canadian firms to create a more productive workplace. The report notes that in the hands of educated employees, communications and information technology can fuel productivity, agility, and innovation.
6. *Investing strategically in a national broadband network and government online.* The report notes that a broadband network linking all communities would enable Canadians to deploy new tools to exchange new ideas and new products with new markets.
7. *Brand Canada.* The report notes the need for Canada to build a brand image as strong as that of the Nike "swoosh." This brand would signify
   - Excellence in social capital and infrastructure.
   - Excellence in quality of life.
   - Excellence in applying human knowledge for the improvement of humankind.
   - Excellence in productivity.
   - Excellence in education and workplace talent.
   - Excellence in innovation and technology.
   - Excellence in work rewards and compensation.

This report illustrates the key factors that go into building an economy. As you can see, these factors highlight the importance of strategic HRM on a national as well as a firm level.

SOURCE: "Toward a Culture of Innovation," www.itac.ca.

local labor market. The focus of the selection and training programs is often on the employees' technical competence to perform job-related duties and to some extent on interpersonal skills. In addition, because the company is usually involved in only one labor market, determining the market rate of pay for various jobs is relatively easy.

FIGURE 15.3
Levels of Global Participation

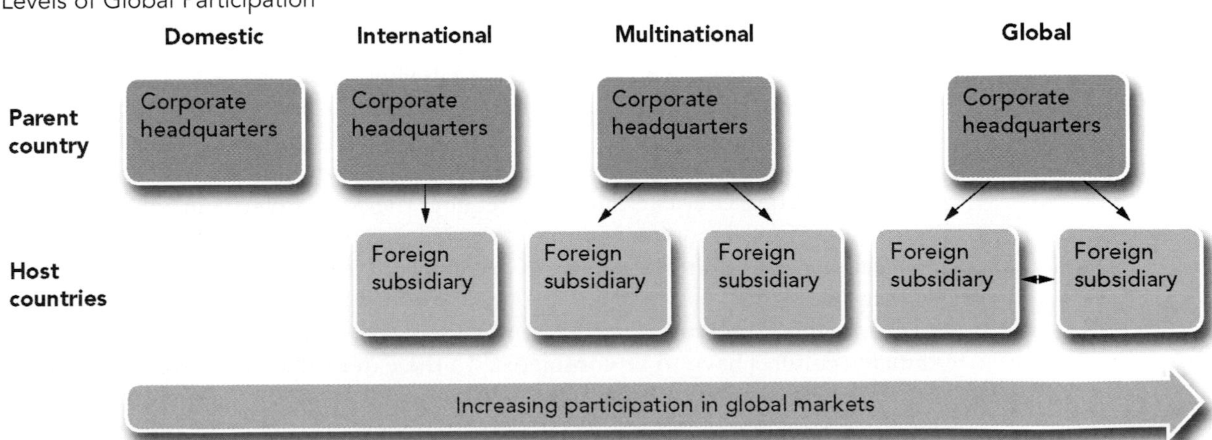

As the product grows in popularity, the owner might choose to build additional facilities in different parts of the country to reduce the costs of transporting the product over large distances. In deciding where to locate these facilities, the owner must consider the attractiveness of the local labor markets. Various parts of the country may have different cultures that make those areas more or less attractive according to the work ethics of the potential employees. Similarly, the human capital in the different areas may vary greatly because of differences in educational systems. Finally, local pay rates may differ. It is for these reasons that the U.S. economy in the past 10 years has experienced a movement of jobs from northern states, which are characterized by strong unions and high labor costs, to the Sunbelt states, which have lower labor costs and are less unionized.

Incidentally, even domestic companies face problems with cultural diversity. In the United States, for example, the representation of women and minorities is increasing within the workforce. These groups come to the workplace with worldviews that differ from those of the traditional white male. Thus we are seeing more and more emphasis on developing systems for managing cultural diversity within single-country organizations, even though the diversity might be on a somewhat smaller scale than the diversity of cultures across national boundaries.[33]

It is important to note that companies functioning at the domestic level face an environment with very similar cultural, human capital, political–legal, and economic situations, although some variation might be observed across states and geographic areas.

International

As more competitors enter the domestic market, companies face the possibility of losing market share; thus they often seek other markets for their products. This usually requires entering international markets, initially by exporting products but ultimately by building production facilities in other countries. The decision to participate in international competition raises a host of human resource issues. All the problems regarding locating facilities are magnified. One must consider whether a particular location provides an environment where human resources can be successfully acquired and managed.

Now the company faces an entirely different situation with regard to culture, human capital, the political–legal system, and the economic system. For example, the availability of human capital is of utmost importance, and there is a substantially greater variability in human capital between the United States and other countries than there is among the various states in the United States.

A country's legal system may also present HRM problems. For example, France has a relatively high minimum wage, which drives labor costs up. In Germany companies are legally required to offer employees influence in the management of the firm. Companies that develop facilities in other countries have to adapt their HRM practices to conform to the host country's laws. This requires the company to gain expertise in the country's HRM legal requirements and knowledge about how to deal with the country's legal system, and it often requires the company to hire one or more HCNs. In fact, some countries legally require companies to hire a certain percentage of HCNs for any foreign-owned subsidiary.

Finally, cultures have to be considered. To the extent that the country's culture is vastly different from that of the parent organization, conflicts, communication problems, and morale problems may occur. Expatriate managers must be trained to iden-

COMPETING THROUGH GLOBALIZATION

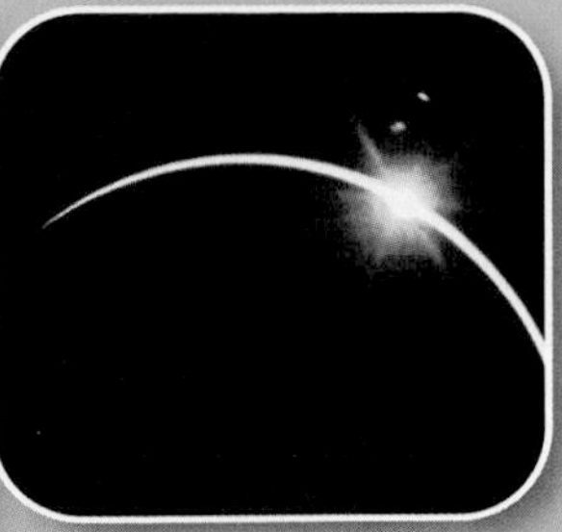

Colombia, SA, Sure Isn't Columbia, SC

Many executives at U.S. companies assume that competing in different countries will require some minor modifications in business processes and practices due to legal, political, and cultural differences, but few understand how different the business environment can truly be. Selling soft drinks in Colombia, South America, exemplifies the divergence from a traditional U.S.-based approach to selling them.

Carlos Manuel Acevedo manages a soft-drink bottling plant for Postobon—formally Gaseosas Posada Tobon, SA—in Barrancabermeja, Colombia. Soon after he arrived, the local leader of a guerrilla group known as the National Liberation Army visited and announced that he needed 50 cases of beer and 20 cases of soda. Two guerrilla groups compete for power in the local area, moving freely about the region. These guerrillas, financed by extorting Colombian and foreign-owned companies and protecting drug producers, mainly force the government to meet certain demands such as agrarian reform, rather than seeking to overthrow the government. Given that his predecessor had been gunned down by the guerrilla group in front of the plant, Mr. Acevedo quickly decided to provide the beverages at a 10 percent discount.

To minimize the risk of kidnapping, Mr. Acevedo changes the timing and site of monthly management meetings. He avoids visiting the local army bases. He denies making protection payments to the guerrillas to avoid problems, but many companies secretly do. Hijackings or torchings of delivery trucks are not common, but do occur occasionally.

In addition, competition for customers is fierce, and sales techniques differ in their approach from those in the United States. For example, one salesman for Postobon sought to make a sale with a vocational school by offering complimentary five-gallon water bottles, $600 in cash, a new kiosk, and 80 free cases of soda. The competing salesman at Coca-Cola made a similar offer, though Coca-Cola officials state that they do not normally pay cash for contracts. However, Postobon won the contract by also offering uniforms for the soccer team and newly painted lines on the school's soccer field.

tify these cultural differences, and they must be flexible enough to adapt their styles to those of their host country. This requires an extensive selection effort to identify individuals who are capable of adapting to new environments and an extensive training program to ensure that the culture shock is not devastating. The "Competing through Globalization" box illustrates just how different the environment can be in different countries.

Multinational

Whereas international companies build one or a few facilities in another country, they become multinational when they build facilities in a number of different countries, attempting to capitalize on lower production and distribution costs in different locations. The lower production costs are gained by shifting production from higher-cost locations to lower-cost locations. For example, some of the major U.S. automakers have plants all over the world. They continue to shift their production from the United States, where labor unions have gained high wages for their members, to *maquiladora* facilities in Mexico, where the wages are substantially lower. Similarly, these companies minimize distribution costs by locating facilities in Europe for manufacturing and assembling automobiles to sell in the European market. They are also now expanding into some of the former Soviet bloc countries to produce automobiles for the European market.

The HRM problems multinational companies face are similar to those international companies face, only magnified. Instead of having to consider only one or two countries' cultural, human capital, legal, and economic systems, the multinational company must address these differences for a large number of countries. This accentuates the need to select managers capable of functioning in a variety of settings, give them necessary training, and provide flexible compensation systems that take into account the different market pay rates, tax systems, and costs of living.

Multinational companies now employ many "inpatriates"—managers from different countries who become part of the corporate headquarters staff. This creates a need to integrate managers from different cultures into the culture of the parent company. In addition, multinational companies now take more expatriates from countries other than the parent country and place them in facilities of other countries. For example, a manager from Scotland, working for a U.S. company, might be assigned to run an operation in South Africa. This practice accentuates the need for cross-cultural training to provide managerial skills for interaction with individuals from different cultures.

Global

Many researchers now propose a fourth level of integration: global organizations. Global organizations compete on state-of-the-art, top-quality products and services and do so with the lowest costs possible. Whereas multinational companies attempt to develop identical products distributed worldwide, global companies increasingly emphasize flexibility and mass customization of products to meet the needs of particular clients. Multinational companies are usually driven to locate facilities in a country as a means of reaching that country's market or lowering production costs, and the company must deal with the differences across the countries. Global firms, on the other hand, choose to locate a facility based on the ability to effectively, efficiently, and flexibly produce a product or service and attempt to create synergy through the cultural differences.

This creates the need for HRM systems that encourage flexible production (thus presenting a host of HRM issues). These companies proactively consider the cultures, human capital, political–legal systems, and economic systems to determine where production facilities can be located to provide a competitive advantage. Global companies have multiple headquarters spread across the globe, resulting in less hierarchically structured organizations that emphasize decentralized decision making. This results in the need for human resource systems that recruit, develop, retain, and use managers and executives who are competent transnationally.

Transnational scope
A company's ability to make HRM decisions from an international perspective.

A transnational HRM system is characterized by three attributes.[34] **Transnational scope** refers to the fact that HRM decisions must be made from a global rather than a national or regional perspective. This creates the need to make decisions that balance the need for uniformity (to ensure fair treatment of all employees) with the need for flexibility (to meet the needs of employees in different countries). **Transnational representation** reflects the multinational composition of a company's managers. Global participation does not necessarily ensure that each country is providing managers to the company's ranks. This is a prerequisite if the company is to achieve the next attribute. **Transnational process** refers to the extent to which the company's planning and decision-making processes include representatives and ideas from a variety of cultures. This attribute allows for diverse viewpoints and knowledge associated with different cultures, increasing the quality of decision making.

Transnational representation
Reflects the multinational composition of a company's managers.

Transnational process
The extent to which a company's planning and decision-making processes include representatives and ideas from a variety of cultures.

These three characteristics are necessary for global companies to achieve cultural synergy. Rather than simply integrating foreigners into the domestic organization, a successful transnational company needs managers who will treat managers from other cultures as equals. This synergy can be accomplished only by combining selection, training, appraisal, and compensation systems in such a way that managers have a transnational rather than a parochial orientation. However, a survey of 50 companies in the United States and Canada found that global companies' HRM systems are far less transnational in scope, representation, and process than the companies' strategic planning systems and organizational structures.[35]

In conclusion, entry into international markets creates a host of HRM issues that must be addressed if a company is to gain competitive advantage. Once the choice has been made to compete in a global arena, companies must seek to manage employees who are sent to foreign countries (expatriates and third-country nationals). This causes the need to shift from focusing only on the culture, human capital, political–legal, and economic influences of the host country to examining ways to manage the expatriate managers who must be located there. Selection systems must be developed that allow the company to identify managers capable of functioning in a new culture. These managers must be trained to identify the important aspects of the new culture in which they will live as well as the relevant legal–political and economic systems. Finally, these managers must be compensated to offset the costs of uprooting themselves and their families to move to a new situation vastly different from their previous lives. In the next section we address issues regarding management of expatriates.

Managing Expatriates in Global Markets

We have outlined the major macro-level factors that influence HRM in global markets. These factors can affect a company's decision whether to build facilities in a given country. In addition, if a company does develop such facilities, these factors strongly affect the HRM practices used. However, one important issue that has been recognized over the past few years is the set of problems inherent in selecting, training, compensating, and reintegrating expatriate managers.

The importance to the company's profitability of making the right expatriate assignments should not be underestimated. Expatriate managers' average compensation package is approximately $250,000,[36] and the cost of an unsuccessful expatriate assignment (that is, a manager returning early) is approximately $100,000.[37] In spite of the importance of these assignments, U.S. organizations have been astoundingly unsuccessful in their use of expatriates. Between 16 and 40 percent of all U.S. employees sent on expatriate assignments overseas return early, a rate almost two to three times that of foreign nationals.[38] In addition, of those expatriates who remain on assignment, many are ineffective, resulting in a loss of productivity. In fact, 30 to 50 percent of U.S. expatriates are evaluated by their firms as either ineffective or marginally effective in their performance.[39]

In this final section of the chapter, we discuss the major issues relevant to the management of expatriate managers. These issues cover the selection, training, compensation, and reacculturation of expatriates.

Selection of Expatriate Managers

One of the major problems in managing expatriate managers is determining which individuals in the organization are most capable of handling an assignment in a different culture. Expatriate managers must have technical competence in the area of operations; otherwise they will be unable to earn the respect of subordinates. However, technical competence has been almost the sole variable used in deciding whom to send on overseas assignments, despite the fact that multiple skills are necessary for successful performance in these assignments.[40]

A successful expatriate manager must be sensitive to the country's cultural norms, flexible enough to adapt to those norms, and strong enough to make it through the inevitable culture shock. In addition, the manager's family must be similarly capable of adapting to the new culture. These adaptive skills have been categorized into three dimensions:[41] (1) the self dimension (the skills that enable a manager to maintain a positive self-image and psychological well-being); (2) the relationship dimension (the skills required to foster relationships with the host-country nationals); and (3) the perception dimension (those skills that enable a manager to accurately perceive and evaluate the host environment). One study of international assignees found that they considered the following five factors to be important in descending order of importance: family situation, flexibility and adaptability, job knowledge and motivation, relational skills, and extracultural openness.[42] Table 15.4 presents a series of considerations and questions to ask potential expatriate managers to assess their ability to adapt to a new cultural environment.

Little evidence suggests that U.S. companies have invested much effort in attempting to make correct expatriate selections. One researcher found that only 5 percent of the firms surveyed administered any tests to determine the degree to which expatriate candidates possessed cross-cultural skills.[43] More recent research reveals that only 35 percent of firms choose expatriates from multiple candidates and that those firms emphasize only technical job-related experience and skills in making these decisions.[44] These findings glaringly demonstrate that U.S. organizations need to improve their success rate in overseas assignments. As discussed in Chapter 6, the technology for assessing individuals' knowledge, skills, and abilities has advanced. The potential for selection testing to decrease the failure rate and productivity problems of U.S. expatriate managers seems promising.

A final issue with regard to expatriate selection is the use of women in expatriate assignments. For a long time U.S. firms believed that women would not be successful managers in countries where women have not traditionally been promoted to management positions (such as in Japan and other Asian countries). However, recent evidence indicates that this is not true. Robin Abrams, an expatriate manager for Apple Computer's Hong Kong office, states that nobody cares whether "you are wearing trousers or a skirt if you have demonstrated core competencies." In fact, some women believe that the novelty of their presence among a group of men increases their credibility with locals. Thus the number of female expatriates doubled to 12 percent from 1990 to 1995 and is expected to increase to 20 percent by the year 2000, according to one survey.[45]

TABLE 15.4

Interview Worksheet for International Candidates

Motivation

- Investigate reasons and degree of interest in wanting to be considered.
- Determine desire to work abroad, verified by previous concerns such as personal travel, language training, reading, and association with foreign employees or students.
- Determine whether the candidate has a realistic understanding of what working and living abroad requires.
- Determine the basic attitudes of the spouse toward an overseas assignment.

Health

- Determine whether any medical problems of the candidate or his or her family might be critical to the success of the assignment.
- Determine whether he or she is in good physical and mental health, without any foreseeable change.

Language ability

- Determine potential for learning a new language.
- Determine any previous language(s) studied or oral ability (judge against language needed on the overseas assignment).
- Determine the ability of the spouse to meet the language requirements.

Family considerations

- How many moves has the family made in the past among different cities or parts of the United States?
- What problems were encountered?
- How recent was the last move?
- What is the spouse's goal in this move?
- What are the number of children and the ages of each?
- Has divorce or its potential, or death of a family member, weakened family solidarity?
- Will all the children move? Why or why not?
- What are the location, health, and living arrangements of grandparents and the number of trips normally made to their home each year?
- Are there any special adjustment problems that you would expect?
- How is each member of the family reacting to this possible move?
- Do special educational problems exist within the family?

Resourcefulness and initiative

- Is the candidate independent; can he make and stand by his decisions and judgments?
- Does she have the intellectual capacity to deal with several dimensions simultaneously?
- Is he able to reach objectives and produce results with whatever personnel and facilities are available, regardless of the limitations and barriers that might arise?
- Can the candidate operate without a clear definition of responsibility and authority on a foreign assignment?
- Will the candidate be able to explain the aims and company philosophy to the local managers and workers?
- Does she possess sufficient self-discipline and self-confidence to overcome difficulties or handle complex problems?
- Can the candidate work without supervision?
- Can the candidate operate effectively in a foreign environment without normal communications and supporting services?

Adaptability

- Is the candidate sensitive to others, open to the opinions of others, cooperative, and able to compromise?
- What are his reactions to new situations, and efforts to understand and appreciate differences?
- Is she culturally sensitive, aware, and able to relate across the culture?
- Does the candidate understand his own culturally derived values?
- How does the candidate react to criticism?

continues on page 638

TABLE 15.4
Interview Worksheet for International Candidates *concluded*

Adaptability *continued*
- What is her understanding of the U.S. government system?
- Will he be able to make and develop contacts with peers in the foreign country?
- Does she have patience when dealing with problems?
- Is he resilient; can he bounce back after setbacks?

Career planning
- Does the candidate consider the assignment anything other than a temporary overseas trip?
- Is the move consistent with her progression and that planned by the company?
- Is his career planning realistic?
- What is the candidate's basic attitude toward the company?
- Is there any history or indication of interpersonal problems with this employee?

Financial
- Are there any current financial and/or legal considerations that might affect the assignment, such as house purchase, children and college expenses, car purchases?
- Are financial considerations negative factors? Will undue pressures be brought to bear on the employee or her family as a result of the assignment?

SOURCE: Reprinted with permission, pp. 55–57 from *Multinational People Management,* by D.M. Noer. Copyright © 1989 by the Bureau of National Affairs, Inc., Washington, DC 20037.

Training and Development of Expatriates

Once an expatriate manager has been selected, it is necessary to prepare that manager for the upcoming assignment. Because these individuals already have job-related skills, some firms have focused development efforts on cross-cultural training. A review of the cross-cultural training literature found support for the belief that cross-cultural training has an impact on effectiveness.[46] However, in spite of this, cross-cultural training is hardly universal. According to one 1995 survey, nearly 40 percent of the respondents offered no cross-cultural preparation to expatriates.[47]

What exactly is emphasized in cross-cultural training programs? The details regarding these programs were discussed in Chapter 7. However, for now, it is important to know that most attempt to create an appreciation of the host country's culture so that expatriates can behave appropriately.[48] This entails emphasizing a few aspects of cultural sensitivity. First, expatriates must be clear about their own cultural background, particularly as it is perceived by the host nationals. With an accurate cultural self-awareness, managers can modify their behavior to accentuate the effective characteristics while minimizing those that are dysfunctional.[49] Table 15.5 displays the ways Americans tend to be perceived by people in other countries.

Second, expatriates must understand the particular aspects of culture in the new work environment. Although culture is an elusive, almost invisible phenomenon, astute expatriate managers must perceive the culture and adapt their behavior to it. This entails identifying the types of behaviors and interpersonal styles that are considered acceptable in both business meetings and social gatherings. For example, Germans value promptness for meetings to a much greater extent than do Latin Americans.

TABLE 15.5

Americans as Others See Them

People from other countries are often puzzled and intrigued by the intricacies and enigmas of U.S. culture. Here is a selection of actual observations by foreigners visiting the United States. As you read them, ask yourself in each case whether the observer is accurate and how you would explain the trait in question.
India "Americans seem to be in a perpetual hurry. Just watch the way they walk down the street. They never allow themselves the leisure to enjoy life; there are too many things to do."
Kenya "Americans appear to us rather distant. They are not really as close to other people—even fellow Americans—as Americans overseas tend to portray. It's almost as if an American says, 'I won't let you get too close to me.' It's like building a wall."
Turkey "Once we were out in a rural area in the middle of nowhere and saw an American come to a stop sign. Though he could see in both directions for miles and no traffic was coming, he still stopped!"
Colombia "The tendency in the United States to think that life is only work hits you in the face. Work seems to be the one type of motivation."
Indonesia "In the United States everything has to be talked about and analyzed. Even the littlest thing has to be 'Why, Why, Why?' I get a headache from such persistent questions."
Ethiopia "The American is very explicit; he wants a 'yes' or 'no.' If someone tries to speak figuratively, the American is confused."
Iran "The first time . . . my [American] professor told me, 'I don't know the answer, I will have to look it up,' I was shocked. I asked myself, 'Why is he teaching me?' In my country, a professor would give the wrong answer rather than admit ignorance."

SOURCE: J. Feig and G. Blair, *There Is a Difference,* 2nd ed. (Washington, DC: Meridian House International, 1980). As cited in N. Adler, *International Dimensions of Organizational Behavior,* 2nd ed. (Boston: PWS-Kent, 1991).

Finally, expatriates must learn to communicate accurately in the new culture. Some firms attempt to use expatriates who speak the language of the host country, and a few provide language training. However, most companies simply assume that the host-country nationals all speak the parent-country's language. Although this assumption might be true, seldom do these nationals speak the parent-country language fluently. Thus expatriate managers must be trained to communicate with others when language barriers exist. Table 15.6 offers some tips for communicating across language barriers.

Effective cross-cultural training helps ease an expatriate's transition to the new work environment. It can also help avoid costly mistakes, such as the expatriate who attempted to bring two bottles of brandy into the Muslim country of Qatar. The brandy was discovered by customs; not only was the expatriate deported, the company was also "disinvited" from the country.[50]

TABLE 15.6
Communicating across Language Barriers

Verbal behavior
- *Clear, slow speech.* Enunciate each word. Do not use colloquial expressions.
- *Repetition.* Repeat each important idea using different words to explain the same concept.
- *Simple sentences.* Avoid compound, long sentences.
- *Active verbs.* Avoid passive verbs.

Nonverbal behavior
- *Visual restatements.* Use as many visual restatements as possible, such as pictures, graphs, tables, and slides.
- *Gestures.* Use more facial and hand gestures to emphasize the meaning of words.
- *Demonstration.* Act out as many themes as possible.
- *Pauses.* Pause more frequently.
- *Summaries.* Hand out written summaries of your verbal presentation.

Attribution
- *Silence.* When there is a silence, wait. Do not jump in to fill the silence. The other person is probably just thinking more slowly in the nonnative language or translating.
- *Intelligence.* Do not equate poor grammar and mispronunciation with lack of intelligence; it is usually a sign of second-language use.
- *Differences.* If unsure, assume difference, not similarity.

Comprehension
- *Understanding.* Do not just assume that they understand; assume that they do not understand.
- *Checking comprehension.* Have colleagues repeat their understanding of the material back to you. Do not simply ask whether they understand or not. Let them explain what they understand to you.

Design
- *Breaks.* Take more frequent breaks. Second-language comprehension is exhausting.
- *Small modules.* Divide the material into smaller modules.
- *Longer time frame.* Allocate more time for each module than usual in a monolingual program.

Motivation
- *Encouragement.* Verbally and nonverbally encourage and reinforce speaking by nonnative language participants.
- *Drawing out.* Explicitly draw out marginal and passive participants.
- *Reinforcement.* Do not embarrass novice speakers.

SOURCE: Used with permission of N. Adler, *International Dimensions of Organizational Behavior,* 2nd ed. (Boston: PWS-Kent, 1991).

Compensation of Expatriates

One of the more troublesome aspects of managing expatriates is determining the compensation package. As previously discussed, these packages average $250,000, but it is necessary to examine the exact breakdown of these packages. Most use a balance sheet approach to determine the total package level. This approach entails developing a total compensation package that equalizes the purchasing power of the expatriate manager with that of employees in similar positions in the home country and pro-

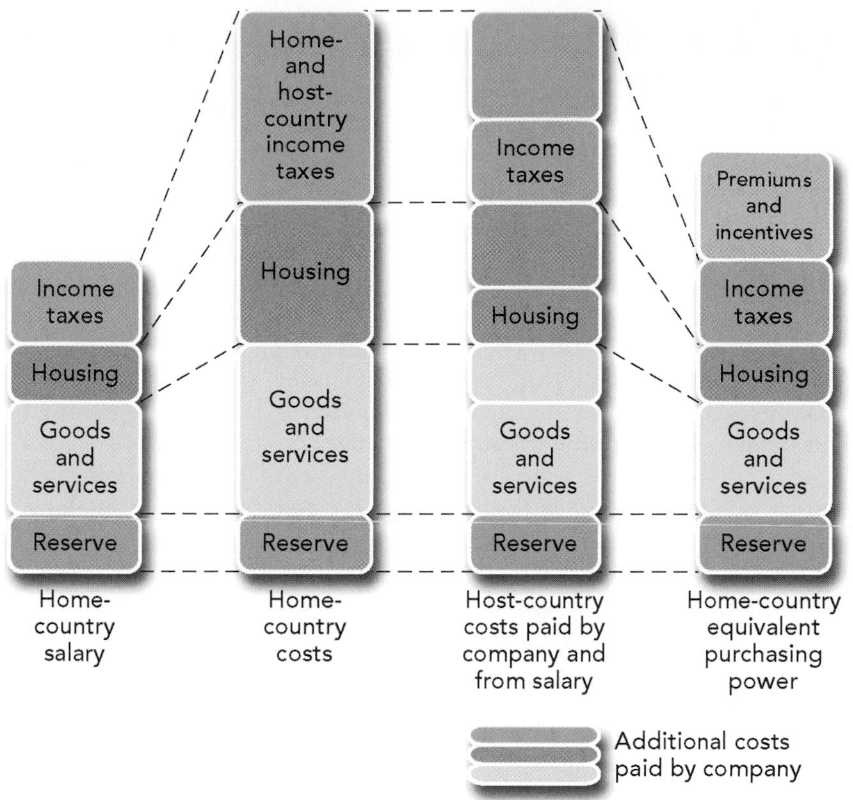

FIGURE 15.4
The Balance Sheet for Determining Expatriate Compensation

SOURCE: C. Reynolds, "Compensation of Overseas Personnel," in *Handbook of Human Resource Administration,* 2nd ed., J.J. Famularo (New York: McGraw-Hill, 1986), p. 51. Reprinted with permission.

vides incentives to offset the inconveniences incurred in the location. Purchasing power includes all of the expenses associated with the expatriate assignment. Expenses include goods and services (food, personal care, clothing, recreation, and transportation), housing (for a principal residence), income taxes (paid to federal and local governments), reserve (savings, payments for benefits, pension contributions), and shipment and storage (costs associated with moving and/or storing personal belongings). A typical balance sheet is shown in Figure 15.4.

As you can see from this figure, the employee starts with a set of costs for taxes, housing, goods and services, and reserve. However, in the host country, these costs are significantly higher. Thus the company must make up the difference between costs in the home and those in the host country, and then provide a premium and/or incentive for the employee to go through the trouble of living in a different environment. Table 15.7 provides an idea of just how much these add-ons can cost for an expatriate. As we see, these combined benefits amount to a 114 percent increase in compensation cost above the base pay.

Total pay packages have four components. First, there is the base salary. Determining the base salary is not a simple matter, however. Fluctuating exchange rates between countries may make an offered salary a raise some of the time, a pay cut at other times. In addition, the base salary may be based on comparable pay in the parent

TABLE 15.7

Average Amount of Allowance as a Percentage of Base Pay

Housing (purchase)	38%
Goods and services (cost of living)	24
Education	22
Position	17
Hardship	13

SOURCE: From *HRMagazine* by B. Fitzgerald-Turner. Copyright © 1997 by Society for Human Resource Management. Reproduced with permission of Society for Human Resource Management via Copyright Clearance Center.

country, or it may be based on the prevailing market rates for the job in the host country. Expatriates are often offered a salary premium beyond that of their present salary as an inducement to accept the expatriate assignment.

Tax equalization allowances are a second component. They are necessary because of countries' different taxation systems in high-tax countries. For example, a senior executive earning $100,000 in Belgium (with a maximum marginal tax rate of 70.8 percent) could cost a company almost $1 million in taxes over five to seven years.[51] Under most tax equalization plans, the company withholds the amount of tax to be paid in the home country, then pays all of the taxes accrued in the host country.

A third component, benefits, presents additional compensation problems. Most of the problems have to do with the transportability of the benefits. For example, if an expatriate contributing to a pension plan in the United States is moved to a different country, does the individual have a new pension in the host country, or should the individual be allowed to contribute to the existing pension in her home country? What about health care systems located in the United States? How does the company ensure that expatriate employees have equal health care coverage? For example, in one company, the different health care plans available resulted in situations where it might cost significantly less to have the employee fly to the United States to have a procedure performed rather than to have it done in the host country. However, the health plans did not allow this alternative.

Finally, allowances are often offered to make the expatriate assignment less unattractive. Cost-of-living allowances are payments that offset the differences in expenditures on day-to-day necessities between the host country and the parent country. Housing allowances ensure that the expatriate can maintain the same home-country living standard. Education allowances reimburse expatriates for the expense of placing their children in private English-speaking schools. Relocation allowances cover all the expenses of making the actual move to a new country, including transportation to and from the new location, temporary living expenses, and shipping and/or storage of personal possessions. Figure 15.5 illustrates a typical summary sheet for an expatriate manager's compensation package. The "Competing by Meeting Stakeholders' Needs" box on page 644 discusses how the war on terrorism is creating expatriate management problems.

Reacculturation of Expatriates

A final issue of importance to managing expatriates is dealing with the reacculturation process when the managers reenter their home country. Reentry is no simple feat. Culture shock takes place in reverse. The individual has changed, the company has changed, and the culture has changed while the expatriate was overseas. According

John H. Doe		1 October 2001	
Name		**Effective date**	
Singapore		Manager, SLS./Serv. AP/ME	
Location of assignment		**Title**	
Houston, Texas	1234	202	202
Home base	**Emp. no.**	**LCA code**	**Tax code**

Reason for Change: International Assignment

	Old	New
Monthly base salary		$5,000.00
Living cost allowance		$1,291.00
Foreign service premium		$ 750.00
Area allowance		- 0 -
Gross monthly salary		$7,041.00
Housing deduction		$ 500.00
Hypothetical tax		$ 570.00
Other		
Net monthly salary		$5,971.00

Prepared by	**Date**
Vice President, Human Resources	**Date**

FIGURE 15.5
International Assignment Allowance Form

to one source, 60 to 70 percent of expatriates did not know what their position would be upon their return, and 46 percent ended up with jobs that gave them reduced autonomy and authority.[52] Twenty percent of workers want to leave the company when they return from an overseas assignment, and this presents potentially serious morale and productivity problems.[53] In fact, the most recent estimates are that 25 percent of expatriate managers leave the company within one year of returning from their expatriate assignments.[54] If these repatriates leave, the company has virtually no way to recoup its substantial investment in human capital.[55]

COMPETING BY MEETING STAKEHOLDERS' NEEDS

Terrorism's Impact on Expatriate Assignments

On September 11, 2001, the world changed. The terrorist attacks killed numerous people at work that day, but the impact was not limited to them. Those who returned to work on the 12th returned to a new workplace as new people. The war in Afghanistan and continued terrorist warnings from the United States government underscore the events' impact on Americans in the United States and elsewhere in the world.

In particular, consider the situation of American citizens working as expatriates. Prior to September 11, 2001, they lived relatively normal lives free from security concerns. However, with recent threats on American interests domestically and abroad, they feel heightened insecurity, and the attractiveness of expatriate assignments has changed. The terrorist threat has reduced enthusiasm for such assignments. For example, the Global Gateway area on Monster.com is a site for Americans to look for international jobs. It recorded a 12 percent drop in visits in September from the previous month. In addition, KPMG, the accounting firm in New York, surveyed HR executives about the impact of terrorism. Of those surveyed, 4 percent said that at least half of their workforce abroad has asked to return to the United States. In particular, those working in high-risk countries such as Egypt and Pakistan are the most likely to want to return.

The result is that compensation for expatriate candidates is likely to rise quickly. Candidates can ask for "extravagant demands such as paid housing in gated communities with 24-hour security." In addition, many may ask for more frequent trips home to be with family.

SOURCE: E. Tahmincioglu, "Opportunities Mingle with Fear Overseas," *The New York Times* (October 24, 2001), p. G-1.

Finding and Keeping the Best Employees

Companies are increasingly making efforts to help expatriates through reacculturation. Two characteristics help in this transition process: communication and validation.[56] *Communication* refers to the extent to which the expatriate receives information and recognizes changes while abroad. The closer the contact with the home organization while abroad, the more proactive, effective, and satisfied the expatriate will be upon reentry. *Validation* refers to the amount of recognition received by the expatriate upon return home. Expatriates who receive recognition from their peers and their bosses for their foreign work and their future potential contribution to the company have fewer troubles with reentry compared with those who are treated as if they were "out of the loop." Given the tremendous investment that firms make in expatriate employees, usually aimed at providing global experience that will help the company, firms certainly do not want to lose expatriates after their assignments have concluded.

Finally, one research study noted the role of an expatriate manager's expectations about the expatriate assignment in determining repatriation adjustment and job performance. This study found that managers whose job expectations (constraints and demands in terms of volume and performance standards) and nonwork expectations (living and housing conditions) were met exhibited a greater degree of repatriation adjustment and higher levels of job performance.[57] Monsanto has an extensive repatriation program that begins long before the expatriate returns. The program entails providing extensive information regarding the potential culture shock of repatriation and information on how family members, friends, and the office environment might have changed. Then, a few months after returning, expatriate managers hold "debriefing" sessions with several colleagues to help work through difficulties. Monsanto believes that this program provides them with a source of competitive advantage in international assignments.[58]

A Look Back

As we discussed at the outset of the chapter, the terrorist attack on September 11, 2001, and the ensuing war on terrorism are having a profound impact on the workplace. This impact is especially strong for global companies who must manage employees from a variety of religions and nationalities and must do that across countries.

The chapter discussed some of the cultural differences that exist among countries and how these can often hinder communications between people from different cultural backgrounds. It also discussed a number of issues with regard to managing expatriates, primarily with identifying and attracting employees to accept expatriate assignments.

Questions

1. How can a global company manage the inevitable conflicts that will arise among individuals from different religious, racial, ethnic, and national groups who must work together within firms? How can these conflicts be overcome to create a productive work environment?
2. What will firms have to do differently in managing expatriates, particularly U.S. or British citizens who are asked to take assignments in predominantly Muslim countries?

Summary

Today's organizations are more involved in international commerce than ever before, and the trend will continue. Recent historic events such as the development of the EEC, NAFTA, the growth of Asia, and GATT have accelerated the movement toward a global market. Companies competing in the global marketplace require top-quality people to compete successfully. This requires that managers be aware of the many factors that significantly affect HRM in a global environment, such as culture, human capital, and the political–legal and economic systems, and that they understand how these factors come into play in the various levels of global participation. Finally, it requires that they be adept at developing HRM systems that maximize the effectiveness of all human resources, particularly with regard to expatriate managers. Managers cannot overestimate the importance of effectively managing human resources to gain competitive advantage in today's global marketplace.

Discussion Questions

1. What current trends and/or events (besides those mentioned at the outset of the chapter) are responsible for the increased internationalization of the marketplace?
2. According to Hofstede (in Table 15.1), the United

States is low on power distance, high on individuality, high on masculinity, low on uncertainty avoidance, and low on long-term orientation. Russia, on the other hand, is high on power distance, moderate on individuality, low on masculinity, high on uncertainty avoidance, and low on long-term orientation. Many U.S. managers are transplanting their own HRM practices into Russia while companies seek to develop operations there. How acceptable and effective do you think the following practices will be and why? (a) Extensive assessments of individual abilities for selection? (b) Individually based appraisal systems? (c) Suggestion systems? (d) Self-managing work teams?

3. The chapter notes that political–legal and economic systems can reflect a country's culture. The former Eastern bloc countries seem to be changing their political–legal and economic systems. Is this change brought on by their cultures, or will culture have an impact on the ability to change these systems? Why?
4. Think of the different levels of global participation. What companies that you are familiar with exhibit the different levels of participation?
5. Think of a time when you had to function in another culture (on a vacation or job). What were the major obstacles you faced, and how did you deal with them? Was this a stressful experience? Why? How can companies help expatriate employees deal with stress?
6. What types of skills do you need to be able to manage in today's global marketplace? Where do you expect to get those skills? What classes and/or experiences will you need?

Web Exercise

The introduction of a single currency, the euro, for countries who are part of the European Economic Community, has important implications for multinational companies. Germany, France, Spain, Italy, Ireland, The Netherlands, Austria, Belgium, Finland, Portugal, and Luxembourg are the first members of the European Economic Community to adopt the euro. Go to **www.shrmglobal.org**. This is the website for the Society for Human Resource Management Global Forum. As you review the website, notice that it includes publications on topics related to the global management of human resources as well as links to other websites that address global issues and provide country-specific information.

Under "Publications" click on "International Mobility Management." This is a newsletter written by Arthur Andersen. Current and back issues of the newsletter are available. To learn more about the euro and its implications for HRM click on "Expatriate Newsletter, 4th Quarter 1998."

Questions

1. Why is the introduction of the euro a significant world economic event?
2. What HR issues does the introduction of the euro present to multinational companies?

Managing People: From the Pages of *BusinessWeek*

BusinessWeek The High Cost of France's Aversion to Layoffs

It was a sad ending for appliance maker Moulinex, once considered an icon of French industry. On October 22, 2001, a bankruptcy court approved the sale of most Moulinex assets and brands to French rival SEB. Nearly two-thirds of Moulinex's 8,800 employees will lose their jobs as a result.

France's Socialist government reacted with predictable dismay, promising to help workers find new jobs. But government officials—not just the Socialists but their conservative predecessors—bear blame for the company's demise. As Moulinex slid deeper into the red over the past decade, authorities repeatedly blocked management's efforts to cut costs. In August the government rejected a plan to shutter a refrigerator factory and lay off 670 workers. Instead, the company was ordered to resume talks with unions. By then it was too late. Moulinex had racked up $120 million in losses last year on sales of $1.1 billion. Bankruptcy beckoned.

The Moulinex saga underscores a growing worry in corporate France. To stay competitive, companies need flexibility to trim their payrolls, especially now that Europe faces its steepest downturn in nearly a decade. But laying off workers in France is nightmarishly difficult. Labor laws require lengthy negotiations with unions over planned job reductions, and expensive severance packages for laid-off workers. On October 23, 2001, 56 leading French chief executives sent a letter to Prime Minister Lionel Jospin's government, warning that layoff policies were hurting

French competitiveness. "This trap must be loosened," they wrote.

French executives have reason to worry. Germany, where governments traditionally have been as layoff-averse as in France, is looking a lot more open-minded these days. Companies ranging from electronics giant Siemens (SI) to chipmaker Infineon Technologies (IFX) to Commerzbank (CRZBY) have announced thousands of job cuts with only muted government response. Such flexibility could help German companies recover more quickly when the economy improves, says Antonella Mei-Pochtler, a senior vice president at Boston Consulting Group in Munich.

In France it's another story. When consulting firm Bain & Co. recently polled chief executives of 125 leading French and German companies on their plans to weather the downturn, the German CEOs listed trimming payrolls as a top priority. But French bosses put layoffs well down their list, saying they would first cut back on purchasing, investment, and marketing. Apart from bankruptcy cases like Moulinex, virtually no companies have announced big layoffs in France this year. "We are still a civilized company," said a France Télécom (FTE) spokesman recently, denying rumors that the phone operator was planning to eliminate jobs.

HANDCUFFED. An analysis by the Organization for Economic Cooperation and Development shows that Germany's antilayoff laws are just as tough as France's. But French executives know even modest job cuts will ignite a political firestorm. Consider what happened to Groupe Danone (DA) CEO Franck Riboud last spring when he moved to close two factories employing 570 people. Riboud offered every worker a job at another factory or an attractive severance package. No matter. Protesters marched through Paris calling for a boycott of the food-maker, and the government introduced legislation, now pending, to fatten mandatory severance pay.

With unemployment creeping back up to 9 percent and national elections due next year, the pressure to protect jobs will only intensify. Already the government is pushing state-controlled Air France, which is reeling from a steep drop in traffic, to hire workers laid off by a bankrupt regional carrier, AOM-Air Liberté. "We must use every tool at our disposal," says Communist Transport Minister Jean-Claude Gayssot.

France Inc. may be ready to fight back. The October 23 letter was signed by top bosses like Thierry Desmarest of TotalFinaElf and Jean-Martin Folz of Peugeot (PEUGY). Ultimately, they warn, workers will suffer if companies cannot restructure quickly enough to save themselves. But don't take the CEOs' word on that. Just ask the ex-employees of Moulinex.

SOURCE: *BusinessWeek online*, **www.businessweek.com** (November 5, 2001).

Questions

1. Although no one likes to hear about companies laying off employees, are layoffs necessary?
2. What are some of the negative outcomes of a no-layoff policy?

Notes

1. P.J. Dowling, "Human Resource Issues in International Business," *Syracuse Journal of International Law and Commerce* 13, no. 2 (1986), pp. 255–71.
2. R.M. Kanter, "Transcending Business Boundaries: 12,000 World Managers View Change," *Harvard Business Review*, May–June 1991, pp. 151–64.
3. R. Norton, "Will a Global Slump Hurt the U.S.?" *Fortune* (February 22, 1993), pp. 63–64.
4. U.S. Department of Labor, "International Comparisons of Hourly Compensation Costs for Production Workers in Manufacturing, 1975–1999," Bureau of Labor Statistics news release, **www.aoi.gov**.
5. Towers Perrin, *Priorities for Competitive Advantage: A Worldwide Human Resource Study* (Valhalla, NY: Towers Perrin, 1991).
6. R. Schuler, "An Integrative Framework of Strategic International Human Resource Management," *Journal of Management* (1993), pp. 419–60.
7. L. Rubio, "The Rationale for NAFTA: Mexico's New 'Outward Looking' Strategy," *Business Economics* (1991), pp. 12–16.
8. H. Cooper, "Economic Impact of NAFTA: It's a Wash, Experts Say," *The Wall Street Journal*, interactive edition (June 17, 1997).
9. J. Mark, "Suzhou Factories Are Nearly Ready," *Asian Wall Street Journal* (August 14, 1995), p. 8.
10. R. Peiper, *Human Resource Management: An International Comparison* (Berlin: Walter de Gruyter, 1990).
11. V. Sathe, *Culture and Related Corporate Realities* (Homewood, IL: Richard D. Irwin, 1985).
12. M. Rokeach, *Beliefs, Attitudes, and Values* (San Francisco: Jossey-Bass, 1968).
13. L. Harrison, *Who Prospers? How Cultural Values Shape Economic and Political Success* (New York: Free Press, 1992).
14. N. Adler, *International Dimensions of Organizational Behavior*, 2nd ed. (Boston: PWS-Kent, 1991).
15. R. Yates, "Japanese Managers Say They're Adopting

Some U.S. Ways," *Chicago Tribune* (February 29, 1992), p. B1.

16. G. Hofstede, "Dimensions of National Cultures in Fifty Countries and Three Regions," in *Expectations in Cross-Cultural Psychology*, eds. J. Deregowski, S. Dziurawiec, and R.C. Annis (Lisse, Netherlands: Swets and Zeitlinger, 1983).
17. G. Hofstede, "Cultural Constraints in Management Theories," *Academy of Management Executive* 7 (1993), pp. 81–90.
18. G. Hofstede, "The Cultural Relativity of Organizational Theories," *Journal of International Business Studies* 14 (1983), pp. 75–90.
19. G. Hofstede, "Cultural Constraints in Management Theories."
20. S. Snell and J. Dean, "Integrated Manufacturing and Human Resource Management: A Human Capital Perspective," *Academy of Management Journal* 35 (1992), pp. 467–504.
21. W. Johnston and A. Packer, *Workforce 2000: Work and Workers for the Twenty-first Century* (Indianapolis, IN: Hudson Institute, 1988).
22. H. Meyer, "Human Resource Management in the German Democratic Republic: Problems of Availability and the Use of Manpower Potential in the Sphere of the High-Qualification Spectrum in a Retrospective View," in *Human Resource Management: An International Comparison*, ed. R. Peiper (Berlin: Walter de Gruyter, 1990).
23. P. Conrad and R. Peiper, "Human Resource Management in the Federal Republic of Germany," in ibid.
24. N. Adler and S. Bartholomew, "Managing Globally Competent People," *The Executive* 6 (1992), pp. 52–65.
25. B. O'Reilly, "Your New Global Workforce," *Fortune* (December 14, 1992), pp. 52–66.
26. Ibid.
27. J. Ledvinka and V. Scardello, *Federal Employment Regulation in Human Resource Management* (Boston: PWS-Kent, 1991).
28. Conrad and Peiper, "Human Resource Management in the Federal Republic of Germany."
29. R. Solow, "Growth with Equity through Investment in Human Capital," The George Seltzer Distinguished Lecture, University of Minnesota.
30. M. Bloom, G. Milkovich, and A. Mitra, "Toward a Model of International Compensation and Rewards: Learning from How Managers Respond to Variations in Local Host Contexts," working paper 00-14 (Center for Advance Human Resource Studies, Cornell University: 2000).
31. R. Kopp, "International Human Resource Policies and Practices in Japanese, European, and United States Multinationals," *Human Resource Management* 33 (1994), pp. 581–99.
32. Adler, *International Dimensions of Organizational Behavior*.
33. S. Jackson and Associates, *Diversity in the Workplace: Human Resource Initiatives* (New York: The Guilford Press, 1991).
34. Adler and Bartholomew, "Managing Globally Competent People."
35. Ibid.
36. L. Copeland and L. Griggs, *Going International* (New York: Random House, 1985).
37. K.F. Misa and J.M. Fabriacatore, "Return on Investments of Overseas Personnel," *Financial Executive* 47 (April 1979), pp. 42–46.
38. R. Tung, "Selection and Training Procedures of U.S., European, and Japanese Multinational Corporations," *California Management Review* 25, no. 1 (1982), pp. 57–71.
39. Copeland and Griggs, *Going International*.
40. M. Mendenhall, E. Dunbar, and G.R. Oddou, "Expatriate Selection, Training, and Career-Pathing: A Review and Critique," *Human Resource Management* 26 (1987), pp. 331–45.
41. M. Mendenhall and G. Oddou, "The Dimensions of Expatriate Acculturation," *Academy of Management Review* 10 (1985), pp. 39–47.
42. W. Arthur and W. Bennett, "The International Assignee: The Relative Importance of Factors Perceived to Contribute to Success," *Personnel Psychology* 48 (1995), pp. 99–114.
43. R. Tung, "Selecting and Training of Personnel for Overseas Assignments," *Columbia Journal of World Business* 16, no. 2 (1981), pp. 68–78.
44. Moran, Stahl, and Boyer, Inc., *International Human Resource Management* (Boulder, CO: Moran, Stahl, & Boyer, Inc., 1987).
45. "Work Week," *The Wall Street Journal* (September 5, 1995), p. A1.
46. J.S. Black and M. Mendenhall, "Cross-Cultural Training Effectiveness: A Review and Theoretical Framework for Future Research," *Academy of Management Review* 15 (1990), pp. 113–36.
47. B. Fitzgerald-Turner, "Myths of Expatriate Life," *HRMagazine* 42, no. 6 (June 1997), pp. 65–74.
48. P. Dowling and R. Schuler, *International Dimensions of Human Resource Management* (Boston: PWS-Kent, 1990).
49. Adler, *International Dimensions of Organizational Behavior*.
50. Dowling and Schuler, *International Dimensions of Human Resource Management*.
51. R. Schuler and P. Dowling, *Survey of ASPA/I Mem-*

bers (New York: Stern School of Business, New York University, 1988).

52. C. Solomon, "Repatriation: Up, Down, or Out?" *Personnel Journal* (1995), pp. 28–37.
53. "Workers Sent Overseas Have Adjustment Problems, a New Study Shows," *The Wall Street Journal* (June 19, 1984), p. 1.
54. J.S. Black, "Repatriation: A Comparison of Japanese and American Practices and Results," *Proceedings of the Eastern Academy of Management Bi-annual International Conference* (Hong Kong, 1989), pp. 45–49.
55. J.S. Black, "Coming Home: The Relationship of Expatriate Expectations with Repatriation Adjustment and Job Performance," *Human Relations* 45 (1992), pp. 177–92.
56. Adler, *International Dimensions of Organizational Behavior.*
57. Black, "Coming Home."
58. C. Solomon, "Repatriation: Up, Down, or Out?"

Chapter 16 Strategically Managing the HRM Function

Objectives

After reading this chapter, you should be able to:

1. Describe the roles that HRM plays in firms today and the categories of HRM activities.
2. Discuss how the HRM function can define its mission and market.
3. Explain the approaches to evaluating the effectiveness of HRM practices.
4. Describe the new structures for the HRM function.
5. Relate how process reengineering is used to review and redesign HRM practices.
6. Discuss the types of new technologies that can improve the efficiency and effectiveness of HRM.
7. Describe how outsourcing HRM activities can improve service delivery efficiency and effectiveness.

Human resource departments are constantly evolving. As technology has advanced, many of these departments have been downsized. However, the function of HRM has also transformed from having a purely administrative focus to an increasingly more strategic one. What do you think of Tom Stewart's suggestion?

Enter the World of Business

Blowing Up HRM

Fortune columnist Thomas A. Stewart wrote, "Nestling warm and sleepy in your company, like the asp in Cleopatra's bosom, is a department whose employees spend 80 percent of their time on routine administrative tasks. Nearly every function of this department can be performed more expertly for less by others. Chances are its leaders are unable to describe their contribution to value added except in trendy, unquantifiable, and wannabe terms—yet, like a serpent unaffected by its own venom, the department frequently dispenses to others advice on how to eliminate work that does not add value. It is also an organization where the average advertised salary for professional staffers increased 30 percent last year.

"I am describing, of course, your human resources department, and have a modest proposal: Why not blow it up?"

SOURCE: T. Stewart, "Taking on the Last Bureaucracy," *Fortune* (January 15, 1996), p. 105.

Introduction

Throughout this book we have emphasized how human resource management practices can help companies gain a competitive advantage. We identified specific practices related to managing the internal and external environment; designing work and measuring work outcomes; and acquiring, developing, and compensating human resources. We have also discussed the best of current research and practice to show how they may contribute to a company's competitive advantage.

As Chapter 1 said, the role of the HRM function has been evolving over time. As we see in the opening vignette, it has now reached a crossroads. Although it began as a purely administrative function, most HR executives now see the function's major role as being much more strategic. However, this evolution has resulted in a misalignment between the skills and capabilities of members of the function and the new requirements placed on it. Virtually every HRM function in top companies is going through a transformation process to create a function that can play this new strategic role while successfully fulfilling its other roles. Managing this process is the subject of this chapter. First we discuss the various activities of the HRM function. Then we examine how to develop a market- or customer-oriented HRM function. We then describe the current structure of most HRM functions. Finally, we explore measurement approaches for assessing the effectiveness of the function.

Activities of HRM

In order to understand the transformation going on in HRM, one must understand HRM activities in terms of their strategic value. One way of classifying these activities is depicted in Figure 16.1. Transactional activities (the day-to-day transactions such as benefits administration, record keeping, and employee services) are low in their strategic value. Traditional activities such as performance management, training, recruiting, selection, compensation, and employee relations are the nuts and bolts of HRM. These activities have moderate strategic value because they often form the practices and systems to ensure strategy execution. Transformational activities create long-term capability and adaptability for the firm. These activities include knowledge management, management development, cultural change, and strategic redirection and renewal. Obviously, these activities comprise the greatest strategic value for the firm.

As we see in the figure, most HRM functions spend the vast majority of their time on transactional activities, with substantially less on traditional ones and very little on transformational activities. However, virtually all HRM functions, in order to add value to the firm, must increase their efforts in the traditional and transformational activities. (See the "Competing through High-Performance Work Systems" box on page 654.) To do this, however, requires that HR executives (1) develop a strategy for the HRM function, (2) assess the current effectiveness of the HRM function, and (3) redesign, reengineer, or outsource HRM processes to improve efficiency and effectiveness. These issues will be discussed in the following sections.

Strategic Management of the HRM Function

In light of the various roles and activities of the HRM function, we can easily see that it is highly unlikely that any function can (or should) effectively deliver on all roles

FIGURE 16.1
Categories of HRM Activities and Percentages of Time Spent on Them

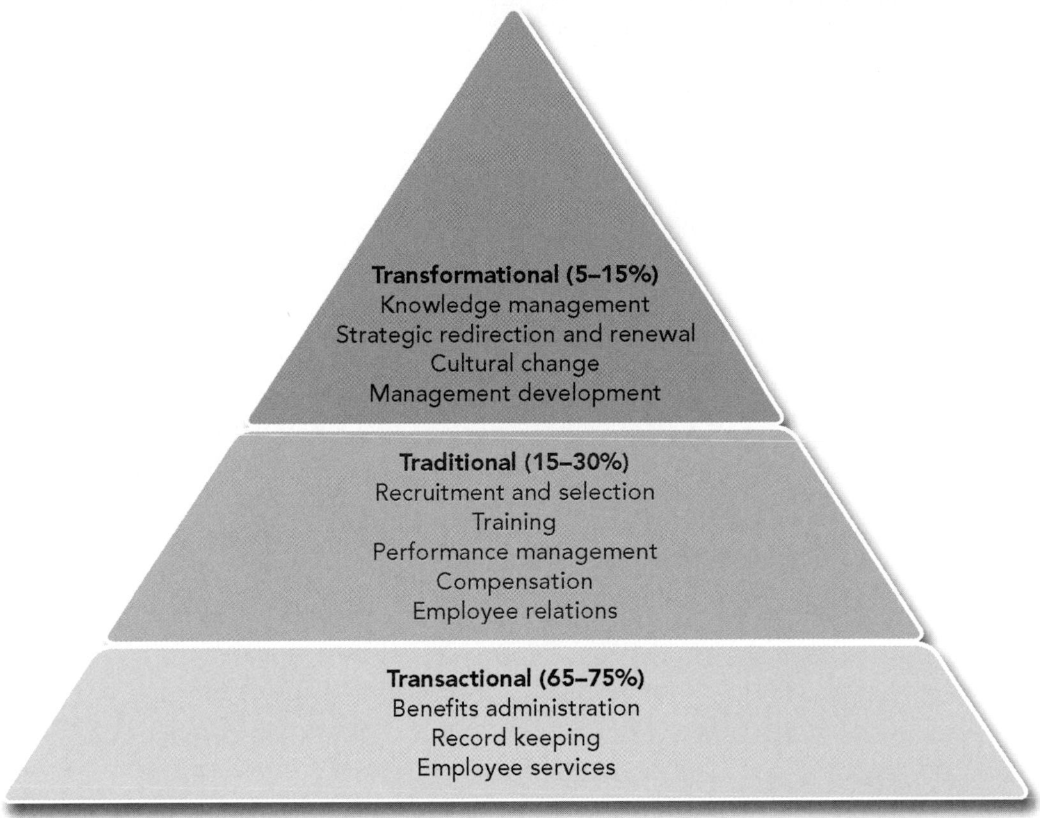

SOURCE: P. Wright, G. McMahan, S. Snell, and B. Gerhart, *Strategic Human Resource Management: Building Human Capital and Organizational Capability.* Technical report. Cornell University, 1998.

and all activities. Although this is a laudable goal, resource constraints in terms of time, money, and head count require that the HR executive make strategic choices about where and how to allocate these resources for maximum value to the firm.

Chapter 2 explained the strategic management process that takes place at the organization level and discussed the role of HRM in this process. HRM has been seen as a strategic partner that has input into the formulation of the company's strategy and develops and aligns HRM programs to help implement the strategy. However, for the HRM function to become truly strategic in its orientation, it must view itself as a separate business entity and engage in strategic management in an effort to effectively serve the various internal customers.

In this respect, one recent trend within the field of HRM, consistent with the total quality management philosophy, is for the HR executive to take a customer-oriented approach to implementing the function. In other words, the strategic planning process that takes place at the level of the business can also be performed with the HRM function. HR executives in more progressive U.S. companies have begun to view the HRM function as a strategic business unit and have tried to define that business in terms of their customer base, their customers' needs, and the technologies required to satisfy customers' needs (Figure 16.2). For example, Weyerhauser Corporation's

COMPETING THROUGH HIGH-PERFORMANCE WORK SYSTEMS

HRM Practices Add Value to the Business

Does HRM add value? According to a recent study conducted by the consulting firm Watson Wyatt, the answer is a resounding yes.

Watson Wyatt originally conducted its Human Capital Index study in 1999, surveying more than 400 U.S. and Canadian publicly traded firms, and then repeated the study in 2001. It assessed which of 43 specific HRM practices were used by each of the firms and related these to the company's market value, three- and five-year total return to shareholders, and its Tobin's Q (a measure of the firm's ability to create value beyond its physical assets). Although the 1999 study identified 30 key HRM practices that were associated with increased firm value, the question still remained, Do the practices cause firms to increase in value, or do firms that increase in value then implement the practices?

The 2001 study sought to address this question. It contained 51 companies that had been in both data collections, thus enabling the researchers to examine the direction of causality. They found that 1999 HRM practices correlated .41 with 2001 performance, but that 1999 performance correlated only .19 with 2001 HRM practices. This provides strong support for the notion that firms that increase their use of high-performance HRM practices can create value for their shareholders.

SOURCE: "Human Capital Index: Human Capital as a Lead Indicator of Shareholder Value," www.watsonwyatt.com/homepage/us/resrender.asp?id=W-488&page=1.

human resources department identified 11 characteristics that would describe a quality human resource organization; these are presented in Table 16.1.

A customer orientation is one of the most important changes in the HRM function's attempts to become strategic. It entails first identifying customers. The most obvious example of HRM customers are the line managers who require HRM services. In addition, the strategic planning team is a customer in the sense that it requires the identification, analysis, and recommendations regarding people-oriented business problems. Employees are also HRM customers because the rewards they receive from the employment relationship are determined and/or administered by the HRM department.

In addition, the products of the HRM department must be identified. Line managers want to have high-quality employees committed to the organization. The strategic planning team requires information and recommendations for the planning process as well as programs that support the strategic plan once it has been identified. Employees want compensation and benefit programs that are consistent, adequate, and equitable, and they want fair promotion decisions. At Southwest Airlines, the "People" department administers customer surveys to all clients as they leave the department to measure how well their needs have been satisfied.

Finally, the technologies through which HRM meets customer needs vary depending on the need being satisfied. Selection systems ensure that applicants selected for employment have the necessary knowledge, skills, and abilities to provide value to the organization. Training and development systems meet the needs of both line managers and employees by giving employees development opportunities to ensure they

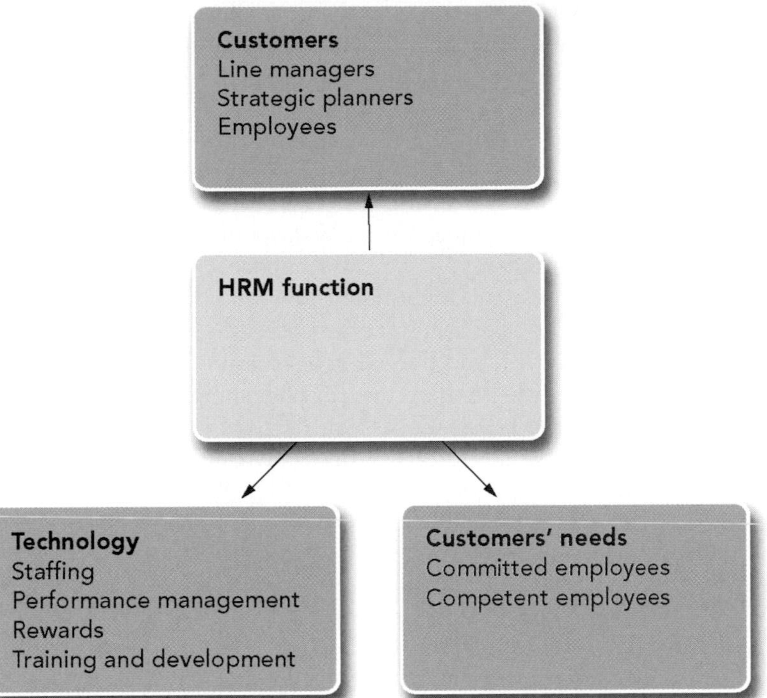

FIGURE 16.2
Customer-Oriented Perspective of the HRM Function

are constantly increasing their human capital and, thus, providing increased value to the company. Performance management systems make clear to employees what is expected of them and assure line managers and strategic planners that employee behavior will be in line with the company's goals. Finally, reward systems similarly benefit all customers (line managers, strategic planners, and employees). These systems assure line managers that employees will use their skills for organizational benefit, and

TABLE 16.1
Characteristics of HRM Quality at Weyerhauser Corporation

- Human resources products and service are linked to customer requirements.
- Customer requirements are translated into internal service applications.
- Processes for producing products and services are documented with cost/value relationships understood.
- Reliable methods and standardized processes are in place.
- Waste and inefficiency are eliminated.
- Problem solving and decision making are based on facts and data.
- Critical success variables are tracked, displayed, and maintained.
- Human resources employees are trained and educated in total quality tools and principles.
- Human resource systems have been aligned to total quality implementation strategies.
- Human resource managers provide leadership and support to organizations on large-scale organizational change.
- Human resource professionals function as "strategic partners" in managing the business and implementing total quality principles.

they provide strategic planners with ways to ensure that all employees are acting in ways that will support the strategic plan. Obviously, reward systems provide employees with an equitable return for their investment of skills and effort.

For example, Whirlpool Corporation's HR managers go through a formalized process of identifying their customer, the need/value they satisfy, and the technology used to satisfy the customer. As Whirlpool planned for start-up of a centralized service supercenter, the plan called for hiring between 100 and 150 employees to serve as call takers who receive service requests from Whirlpool appliance owners and set up service appointments from these calls. The HR manager in charge of developing a selection system for hiring these call takers identified the operations manager in charge of phone service as the HRM department's customer, the delivery of qualified phone call takers as the need satisfied, and the use of a structured interview and paper-and-pencil tests as the technologies employed. This customer service orientation may be the trend of the future. It provides a means for the HRM function to specifically identify who its customers are, what customers' needs are being met, and how well those needs are being met.

Measuring HRM Effectiveness

The strategic decision making process for the HRM function requires that decision makers have a good sense of the effectiveness of the current HRM function. This information provides the foundation for decisions regarding which processes, systems, and skills of HR employees need improvement. Often HRM functions that have been heavily involved in transactional activities for a long time tend to lack systems, processes, and skills for delivering state-of-the-art traditional activities and are thoroughly unable to contribute in the transformational arena. (The "Competing Through Globalization" box illustrates how the role of HRM is being transformed in China.) Thus diagnosis of the effectiveness of the HRM function provides critical information for its strategic management.

In addition, having good measures of the function's effectiveness provides the following benefits:[1]

- *Marketing the function:* Evaluation is a sign to other managers that the HRM function really cares about the organization as a whole and is trying to support operations, production, marketing, and other functions of the company. Information regarding cost savings and benefits is useful to prove to internal customers that HRM practices contribute to the bottom line. Such information is also useful for gaining additional business for the HRM function.
- *Providing accountability:* Evaluation helps determine whether the HRM function is meeting its objectives and effectively using its budget.

Audit approach
Type of assessment of HRM effectiveness that involves review of customer satisfaction or key indicators (like turnover rate or average days to fill a position) related to an HRM functional area (such as recruiting or training).

Approaches for Evaluating Effectiveness

There are two commonly used approaches for evaluating the effectiveness of HRM practices: the audit approach and the analytic approach.

Audit Approach

The **audit approach** focuses on reviewing the various outcomes of the HRM functional areas. Both key indicators and customer satisfaction measures are typically col-

COMPETING THROUGH GLOBALIZATION

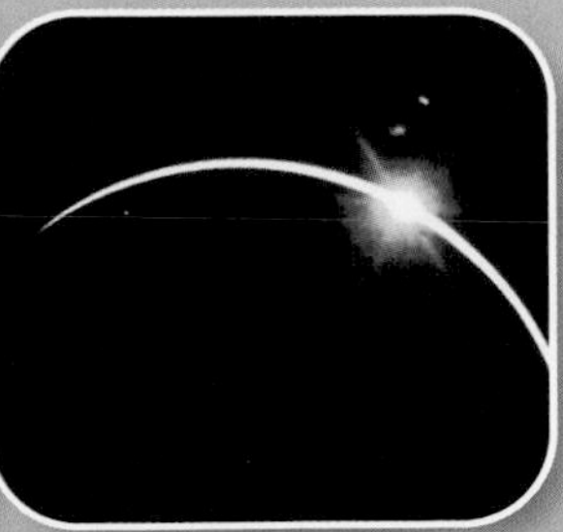

HRM's Evolving Role in China

The People's Republic of China (PRC) has become one of the most attractive business markets for foreign investors. Over the past 20 years, the PRC has registered an average annual growth rate of 9.8 percent and currently ranks seventh in the world in terms of economic strength. As the country becomes more open to foreign trade and investment, the role of HR managers has changed.

The "iron rice-bowl" concept, guaranteeing lifetime employment with an emphasis on managing employee needs through wages, housing, and medical and social insurance, used to be the dominant approach to employment. Under this concept, HRM sought to provide stable employment and maintain employees' standards of living through egalitarian reward structures. HRM also played a role in helping organizations achieve production goals assigned by the state. Managers sought to achieve these centrally dictated production goals without examining the wisdom of their actions. Absent competition, HRM was not concerned with increasing an organization's productivity, quality, or costs.

However, the recent economic transformation has similarly transformed the role of HR professionals in Chinese firms. There is now a greater focus on controlling the number and quality of employees based on business needs. Also, HRM seeks to increase the motivation level of employees through much greater use of pay incentives. In essence, HRM in China today must play the strategic partner role that we observe throughout the world.

This new role is problematic for a number of reasons. First, although China has an enormous population, there is still a tremendous lack of suitably qualified or skilled personnel. Second, the institutional system is so entrenched that it often is difficult to implement new policies and practices. For example, variable pay incentives are necessary and desired, but the old egalitarian culture makes them difficult to implement.

In any case, the PRC provides an incredibly rich case study in the transformation of both an economy and the HRM profession.

SOURCE: H. Mitsuhashi, H. Park, P. Wright, and R. Chua, "Line and HR Executives' Perceptions of HR Effectiveness in Firms in the People's Republic of China," *International Journal of Human Resource Management* 11(2) 2000, pp. 197–216.

lected. Table 16.2 lists examples of key indicators and customer satisfaction measures for staffing, equal employment opportunity, compensation, benefits, training, performance management, safety, labor relations, and succession planning. The development of electronic employee databases and information systems has made it much easier to collect, store, and analyze the functional key indicators (more on this later in the chapter) than in the past, when information was kept in file folders.

We previously discussed how HRM functions can become much more customer-oriented as part of the strategic management process. If, in fact, the function desires to be more customer-focused, then one important source of effectiveness data can be the customers. Just as firms often survey their customers to determine how effectively the customers feel they are being served, the HRM function can survey its internal customers.

TABLE 16.2

Examples of Key Indicators and Customer Satisfaction Measures for HRM Functions

KEY INDICATORS	CUSTOMER SATISFACTION MEASURES
Staffing	
Average days taken to fill open requisitions Ratio of acceptances to offers made Ratio of minority/women applicants to representation in local labor market Per capita requirement costs Average years of experience/education of hires per job family	Anticipation of personnel needs Timeliness of referring qualified workers to line supervisors Treatment of applicants Skill in handling terminations Adaptability to changing labor market conditions
Equal employment opportunity	
Ratio of EEO grievances to employee population Minority representation by EEO categories Minority turnover rate	Resolution of EEO grievances Day-to-day assistance provided by personnel department in implementing affirmative action plan Aggressive recruitment to identify qualified women and minority applicants
Compensation	
Per capita (average) merit increases Ratio of recommendations for reclassification to number of employees Percentage of overtime hours to straight time Ratio of average salary offers to average salary in community	Fairness of existing job evaluation system in assigning grades and salaries Competitiveness in local labor market Relationship between pay and performance Employee satisfaction with pay
Benefits	
Average unemployment compensation payment (UCP) Average workers' compensation payment (WCP) Benefit cost per payroll dollar Percentage of sick leave to total pay	Promptness in handling claims Fairness and consistency in the application of benefit policies Communication of benefits to employees Assistance provided to line managers in reducing potential for unnecessary claims
Training	
Percentage of employees participating in training programs per job family Percentage of employees receiving tuition refunds Training dollars per employee	Extent to which training programs meet the needs of employees and the company Communication to employees about available training opportunities Quality of introduction/orientation programs

continues

One important internal customer is the employees of the firm. Employees often have both direct contact with the HRM function (through activities such as benefits administration and payroll) and indirect contact with the function through their involvement in activities such as receiving performance appraisals, pay raises, and training programs. Many organizations such as AT&T, Motorola, and General Electric use their regular employee attitude survey as a way to assess the employees as users–customers of the HRM programs and practices.[2] However, the problem with assessing effectiveness only from the employees' perspective is that often they are responding not from the standpoint of the good of the firm, but, rather, from their own individual perspective. For example, employees notoriously and consistently express

TABLE 16.2

Examples of Key Indicators and Customer Satisfaction Measures for HRM Functions *concluded*

KEY INDICATORS	CUSTOMER SATISFACTION MEASURES
Employee appraisal and development	
Distribution of performance appraisal ratings Appropriate psychometric properties of appraisal forms	Assistance in identifying management potential Organizational development activities provided by HRM department
Succession planning	
Ratio of promotions to number of employees Ratio of open requisitions filled internally to those filled externally	Extent to which promotions are made from within Assistance/counseling provided to employees in career planning
Safety	
Frequency/severity ratio of accidents Safety-related expenses per $1,000 of payroll Plant security losses per square foot (e.g., fires, burglaries)	Assistance to line managers in organizing safety programs Assistance to line managers in identifying potential safety hazards Assistance to line managers in providing a good working environment (lighting, cleanliness, heating, etc.)
Labor relations	
Ratio of grievances by pay plan to number of employees Frequency and duration of work stoppages Percentage of grievances settled	Assistance provided to line managers in handling grievances Efforts to promote a spirit of cooperation in plant Efforts to monitor the employee relations climate in plant
Overall effectiveness	
Ratio of personnel staff to employee population Turnover rate Absenteeism rate Ratio of per capita revenues to per capita cost Net income per employee	Accuracy and clarity of information provided to managers and employees Competence and expertise of staff Working relationship between organizations and HRM department

SOURCE: Reprinted with permission excerpts from Chapter 1.5, "Evaluating Human Resource Effectiveness," pp. 187–227, by Anne S. Tsui and Luis R. Gomez-Mejia, from *Human Resource Management: Evolving Roles and Responsibilities;* edited by Lee Dyer. Copyright © 1988 by The Bureau of National Affairs, Inc., Washington DC 20037.

dissatisfaction with pay level (who doesn't want more money?), but to simply ratchet up pay across the board would put the firm at a serious labor cost disadvantage.

Thus, many firms have gone to surveys of top line executives as a better means of assessing the effectiveness of the HRM function. The top-level line executives can see how the systems and practices are impacting both employees and the overall effectiveness of the firm from a strategic standpoint. This can also be useful for determining how well HR employees' perceptions of their function's effectiveness align with the views of their line colleagues. For example, a study of 14 firms revealed that HR executives and line executives agreed on the relative effectiveness of HR's delivery of services such as staffing and training systems (that is, which were most and least effectively delivered) but not on the absolute level of effectiveness. As Figure 16.3 shows, HR executives' ratings of their effectiveness in different roles also diverged

FIGURE 16.3
Comparing HR and Line Executives' Evaluations of the Effectiveness of HRM Roles

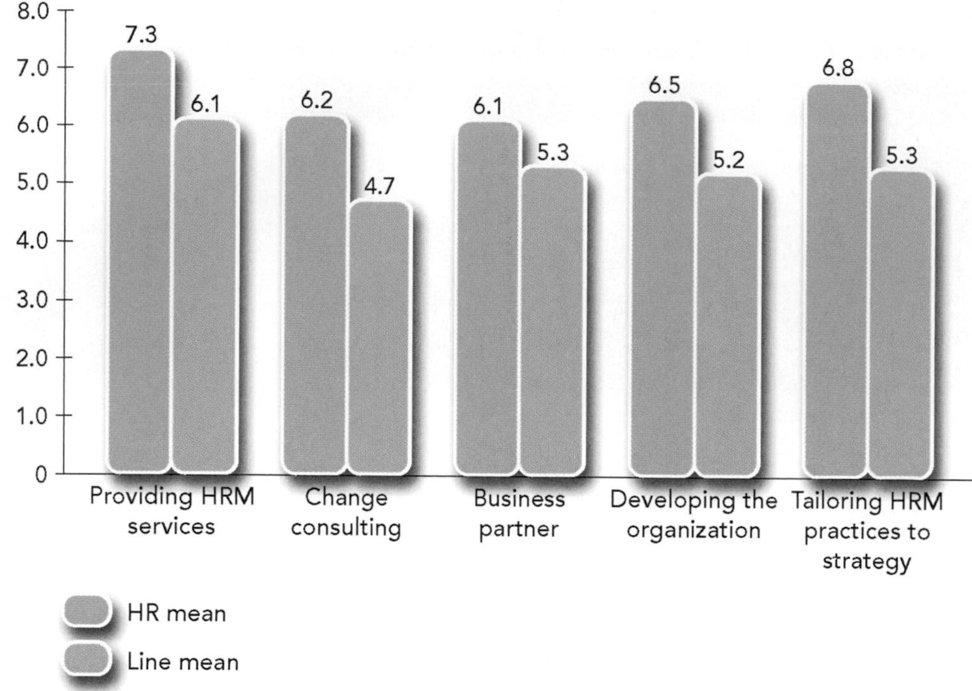

SOURCE: P. Wright, G. McMahan, S. Snell, and B. Gerhart. "Comparing Line and HR Executives' Perceptions of HR Effectiveness: Services, Roles, and Contributions." CAHRS (Center for Advanced Human Resource Studies) working paper 98-29, School of ILR, Cornell University, Ithaca, NY.

significantly from line executives'. In addition, line executives viewed HRM as being significantly less effective with regard to HRM's actual contributions to the firm's overall effectiveness, as we see in Figure 16.4.[3]

The Analytic Approach

Analytic approach
Type of assessment of HRM effectiveness that involves determining the impact of, or the financial cost and benefits of, a program or practice.

The **analytic approach** focuses on either (1) determining whether the introduction of a program or practice (like a training program or a new compensation system) has the intended effect or (2) estimating the financial costs and benefits resulting from an HRM practice. For example, in Chapter 7 we discussed how companies can determine a training program's impact on learning, behavior, and results. Evaluating a training program is one strategy for determining whether the program works. Typically, in an overall evaluation of effectiveness, we are interested in determining the degree of change associated with the program.

The second strategy involves determining the dollar value of the training program, taking into account all the costs associated with the program. Using this strategy, we are not concerned with how much change occurred but rather with the dollar value (costs versus benefits) of the program. Table 16.3 lists the various types of cost–benefit analyses that are done. The human resource accounting approach attempts to place a dollar value on human resources as if they were physical resources (like plant and equipment) or financial resources (like cash). Utility analysis attempts

FIGURE 16.4

Comparing HR and Line Executives' Evaluations of the Effectiveness of HRM Contributions

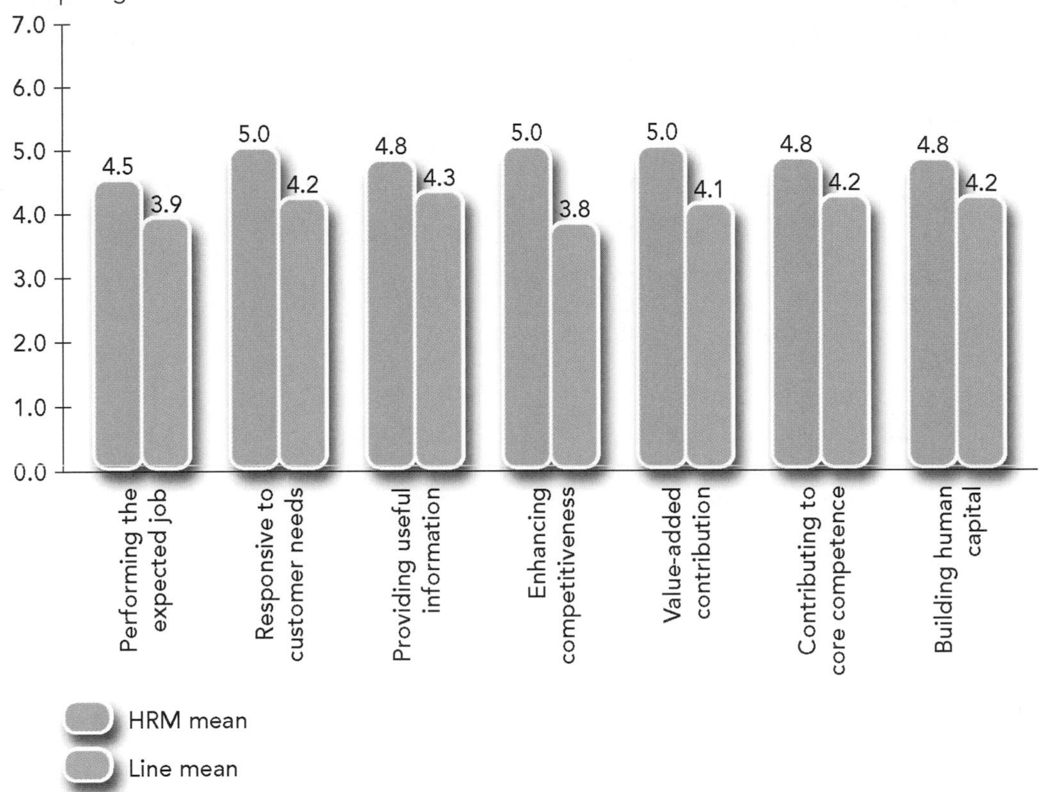

SOURCE: P. Wright, G. McMahan, S. Snell, and B. Gerhart. "Comparing Line and HR Executives' Perceptions of HR Effectiveness: Services, Roles, and Contributions." CAHRS (Center for Advanced Human Resource Studies) working paper 98-29, School of ILR, Cornell University, Ithaca, NY.

TABLE 16.3

Types of Cost–Benefit Analysis

Human resource accounting
- Capitalization of salary
- Net present value of expected wage payments
- Returns on human assets and human investments

Utility analysis
- Turnover costs
- Absenteeism and sick leave costs
- Gains from selection programs
- Impact of positive employee attitudes
- Financial gains of training programs

SOURCE: Based on A.S. Tsui and L.R. Gomez-Mejia, "Evaluating HR Effectiveness," in *Human Resource Management: Evolving Roles and Responsibilities*, ed. L. Dyer (Washington, DC: Bureau of National Affairs, 1988), pp. 1–196.

TABLE 16.4

Effectiveness and Cost-Effectiveness of Two Wellness Programs for Four Cardiovascular Disease Risk Factors

	SITE C	SITE D
Annual direct program costs, per employee per year	$30.96	$38.57
Percentage of cardiovascular disease risks[a] for which risk was moderately reduced or relapse prevented	48%	51%
Percentage of preceding entry per annual $1 spent per employee	1.55%	1.32%
Amount spent per 1% of risks reduced or relapse prevented	$.65	$.76

[a]High blood pressure, overweight, smoking, and lack of exercise.

SOURCE: J.C. Erfurt, A. Foote, and M.A. Heirich, "The Cost-Effectiveness of Worksite Wellness Programs," *Personnel Psychology* 45 (1992), p. 22.

to estimate the financial impact of employee behaviors (such as absenteeism, turnover, job performance, and substance abuse).

For example, wellness programs are a popular HRM program for reducing health care costs through reducing employees' risk of heart disease and cancer. One study evaluated four different types of wellness programs. Part of the evaluation involved determining the costs and benefits associated with the four programs over a three-year period.[4] A different type of wellness program was implemented at each site. Site A instituted a program involving raising employees' awareness of health risks (distributing news articles, blood pressure testing, health education classes). Site B set up a physical fitness facility for employees. Site C raised awareness of health risks and followed up with employees who had identified health risks. Site D provided health education and follow-up counseling and promoted physical competition and health-related events. Table 16.4 shows the effectiveness and cost-effectiveness of the Site C and Site D wellness models.

The analytic approach is more demanding than the audit approach because it requires the detailed use of statistics and finance. A good example of the level of sophistication that can be required for cost–benefit analysis is shown in Table 16.5. This table shows the types of information needed to determine the dollar value of a new selection test for entry-level computer programmers.

Improving HRM Effectiveness

Once a strategic direction has been established and HRM's effectiveness evaluated, leaders of the HRM function can explore how to improve its effectiveness in contributing to the firm's competitiveness. Returning briefly to Figure 16.1, which depicted the different activities of the HRM function, often the improvement focuses on two aspects of the pyramid. First, within each activity, HRM needs to improve both the efficiency and effectiveness in performing each of the activities. Second, often there is a push to eliminate as much of the transactional work as possible (and some of the traditional work) to free up time and resources to focus more on the higher–value-added transformational work. Redesign of the structure (reporting relationships) and processes (through outsourcing and information technology) enables the function to achieve these goals simultaneously. Figure 16.5 (on page 664) depicts this process.

TABLE 16.5

Example of Analysis Needed to Determine the Dollar Value of a Selection Test

Cost–benefit information		
Current employment	4,404	
Number separating	618	
Number selected	618	
Average tenure	9.69 years	
Test information		
Number of applicants	1,236	
Testing cost per applicant	$10	
Total test cost	$12,360	
Average test score	.80 SD	
Test validity	.76	
SD_y (per year)[a]	$10,413	
Computation		
Quantity	= Average tenure × Applicants selected	
	= 9.69 years × 618 applicants	
	= 5,988 person-years	
Quality	= Average test score × Test validity × SD_y	
	= .80 × .76 × $10,413	
	= $6,331 per year	
Utility	= (Quantity × Quality) – Costs	
	= (5,988 person-year × $6,331 per year) – $12,360	
	= $37.9 million	

[a]SD_y = Dollar value of one standard difference in job performance. Approximately 40% of average salary.

SOURCE: From J.W. Boudreau, "Utility Analysis," in *Human Resource Management: Evolving Roles and Responsibilities,* ed. L. Dyer (Washington, DC: Bureau of National Affairs, 1988), p. 150; F.L. Schmidt, J.E. Hunter, R.C. McKenzie, and T.W. Muldrow, "Impact of Valid Selection Procedures on Work-Force Productivity," *Journal of Applied Psychology* 64 (1979), pp. 609–26.

Restructuring to Improve HRM Effectiveness

Traditional HRM functions were structured around the basic HRM subfunctions such as staffing, training, compensation, appraisal, and labor relations. Each of these areas had a director who reported to the VP of HRM, who often reported to a VP of finance and administration. However, for the HRM function to truly contribute strategically to firm effectiveness, the senior HR person must be part of the top management team (reporting directly to the chief executive officer), and there must be a different structural arrangement within the function itself.

A recent generic structure for the HRM function is depicted in Figure 16.6 (on page 665). As we see, the HRM function effectively is divided into three divisions: the centers for expertise, the field generalists, and the service center.[5] The centers for expertise usually consist of the functional specialists in the traditional areas of HRM such as recruitment, selection, training, and compensation. These individuals ideally act as consultants in the development of state-of-the-art systems and processes for use in the organization. The field generalists consist of the HRM generalists who are assigned to a business unit within the firm. These individuals usually have dual reporting relationships to both the head of the line business and the head of HRM (although the line business tends to take priority). They ideally take responsibility for

FIGURE 16.5
Improving HRM Effectiveness

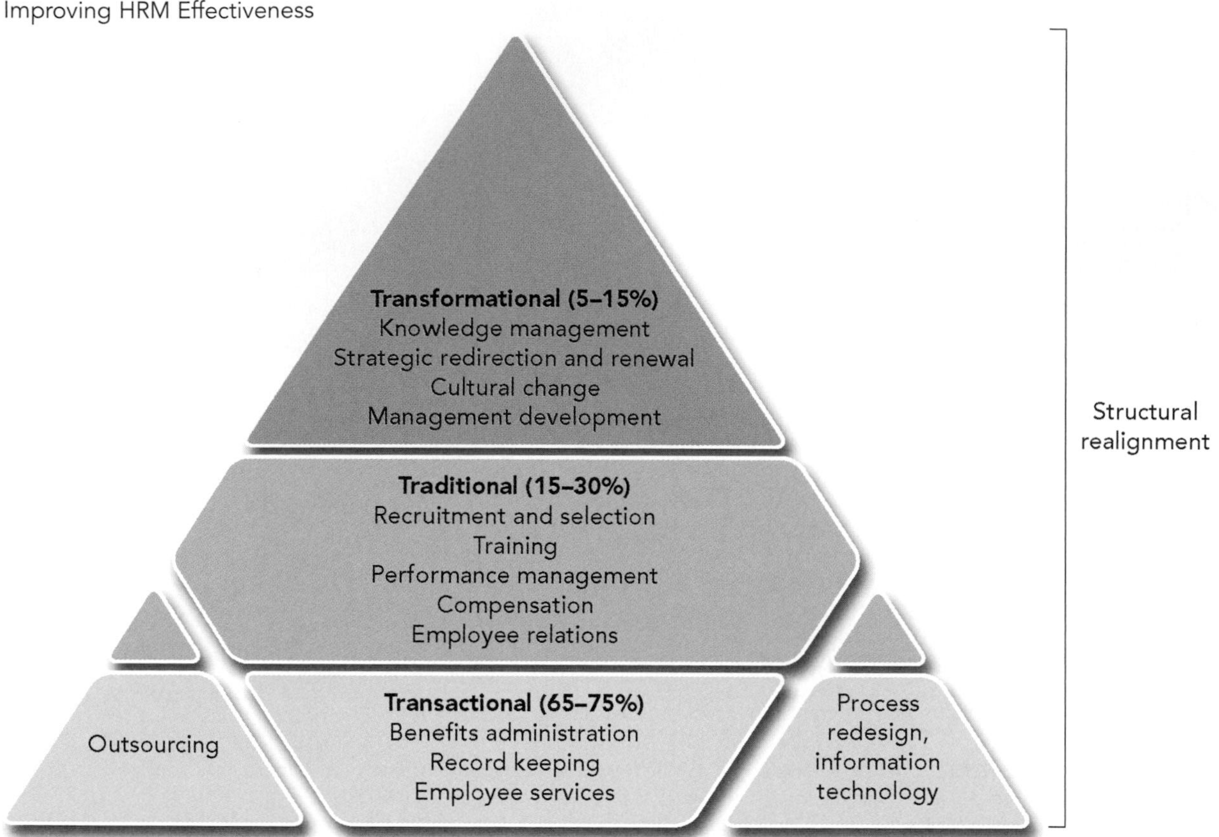

helping the line executives in their business strategically address people issues, and they ensure that the HRM systems enable the business to execute its strategy. Finally, the service center consists of individuals who ensure that the transactional activities are delivered throughout the organization. These service centers often leverage information technology to efficiently deliver employee services. For example, organizations such as Chevron have created call-in service centers where employees can dial a central number where service center employees are available to answer their questions and process their requests and transactions.

Such structural arrangements improve service delivery through specialization. Center for expertise employees can develop current functional skills without being distracted by transactional activities, and generalists can focus on learning the business environment without having to maintain expertise in functional specializations. Finally, service center employees can focus on efficient delivery of basic services across business units.

Outsourcing to Improve HRM Effectiveness

Restructuring the internal HRM function and redesigning the processes represent internal approaches to improving HRM effectiveness. However, increasingly HR executives are seeking to improve the effectiveness of the systems, processes, and services

Historical HRM organization structure

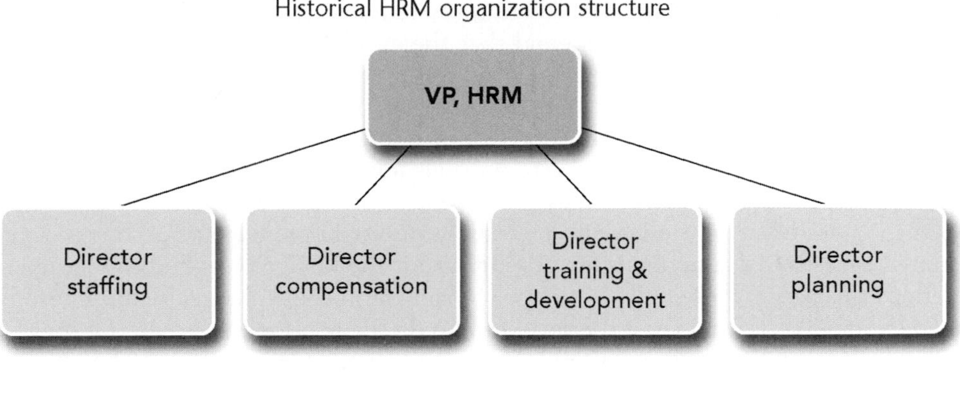

New HRM organization structure

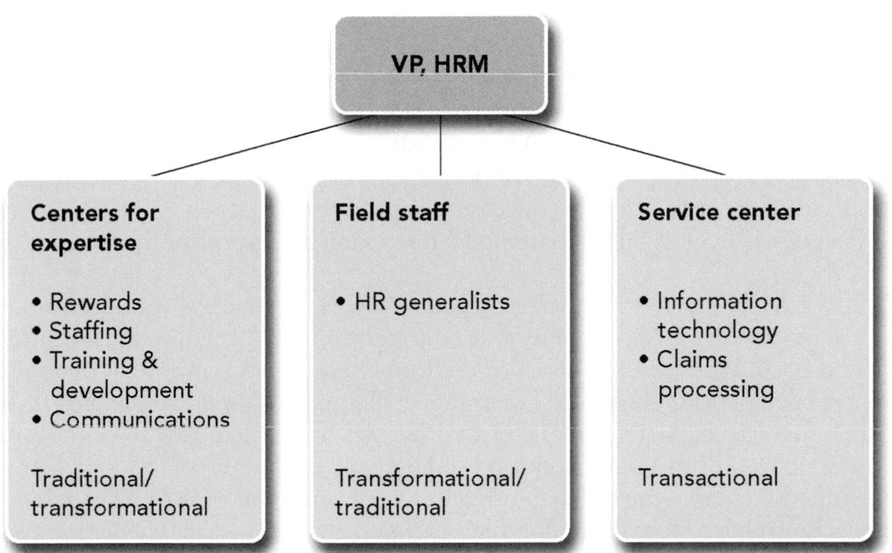

FIGURE 16.6
Old and New Structures for the HRM Organization

SOURCE: P. Wright, G. McMahan, S. Snell, and B. Gerhart, *Strategic Human Resource Management: Building Human Capital and Organizational Capability.* Technical report. Cornell University, 1998.

the function delivers through outsourcing. **Outsourcing** entails contracting with an outside vendor to provide a product or service to the firm, as opposed to producing the product using employees within the firm.

Outsourcing
An organization's use of an outside organization for a broad set of services.

Why would a firm outsource an HRM activity or service? Usually this is done for one of two reasons: Either the outsourcing partner can provide the service more cheaply than it would cost to do it internally, or the partner can provide it more effectively than it can be performed internally. Early on, firms resorted to outsourcing for efficiency reasons. Why would using an outsourced provider be more efficient than having internal employees provide a service? Usually it is because outsourced providers are specialists who are able to develop extensive expertise that can be leveraged across a number of companies.

For example, consider a relatively small firm that seeks to develop a pension system for employees. To provide this service to employees, the HRM function would need to learn all of the basics of pension law. Then it would need to hire a person with specific expertise in administering a pension system in terms of making sure that employee contributions are withheld and that the correct payouts are made to retired employees. Then the company would have to hire someone with expertise in investing pension funds. If the firm is small, requirements of the pension fund might not fill the time (80 hours per week) of these two new hires. Assume that it takes only 20 total hours a week for these people to do their jobs. The firm would be wasting 60 hours of employee time each week. However, a firm that specializes in providing pension administration services to multiple firms could provide the 20 hours of required time to that firm and three other firms for the same cost as had the firm performed this activity internally. Thus the specialist firm could charge the focal firm 50 percent of what it would cost the small firm to do the pensions internally. Of that 50 percent, 25 percent (20 hours) would go to paying direct salaries and the other 25 percent would be profit. Here the focal firm would save 50 percent of its expenses while the provider would make money.

Now consider the aspect of effectiveness. Because the outsourced provider works for a number of firms and specializes in pensions, its employees develop state-of-the-art knowledge of running pension plans. They can learn unique innovations from one company and transfer that learning to a new company. In addition, employees can be more easily and efficiently trained because all of them will be trained in the same processes and procedures. Finally, due to the experience in providing constant pension services, the firm is able to develop a capability to perform these services that could never be developed by two individuals working 25 percent of the time on these services.

What kind of services are being outsourced? Firms primarily outsource transactional activities and services of HRM such as pension and benefits administration as well as payroll. However, a number of traditional and some transformational activities have been outsourced as well. For example, Compaq Computer outsourced a large portion of its staffing activities. The firm contracted with a company to conduct all of the interviewing of its hourly crew and some managerial employees. Compaq found that while the cost was higher than it might have been if the work had been done internally, it provided more flexibility to quickly and efficiently react (not having to lay off employees) if its hiring needs decreased. The "Competing by Meeting Stakeholders' Needs" box describes the increasing trend toward outsourcing all of the administrative tasks of HRM.

Improving HRM Effectiveness through Process Redesign

In addition to structural arrangements, process redesign enables the HRM function to more efficiently and effectively deliver HRM services. Process redesign often uses information technology, but information technology applications are not a requirement. Thus we will discuss the general issue of process reengineering and then explore information technology applications that have aided HRM in process redesign.

Reengineering
Review and redesign of work processes to make them more efficient and improve the quality of the end product or service.

Reengineering is a complete review of critical work processes and redesign to make them more efficient and able to deliver higher quality. Reengineering is especially critical to ensuring that the benefits of new technology can be realized. Applying new technology to an inefficient process will not improve efficiency or effectiveness. Instead, it will increase product or service costs related to the introduction of the new technology.

Reengineering can be used to review the HRM department functions and processes, or it can be used to review specific HRM practices such as work design or the performance management system. The reengineering process involves the four

COMPETING BY MEETING STAKEHOLDERS' NEEDS

Outsourcing of HRM: Panacea or Problem?

Many aspects of HRM have been outsourced over the years, including payroll and benefits. However, a more recent trend has been toward outsourcing all of the administrative functions of HRM. Bank of America, BP-Amoco, British Telecommunications, and Nortel Networks have handed over the administration of day-to-day operations to external partners. Often 50–60 percent of the HRM costs and responsibilities are outsourced, leaving executive and graduate recruitment and strategic management of human resources in-house.

The trend is marketed as a cost- and time-saving approach that will provide best people practices, improve the quality of HRM service to employees, and enable the firm to concentrate on its core activities. Many firms that have outsourced much of HRM notice a greater focus on customer service and quality, more flexibility, and a more strategic partnership. However, critics of the approach warn that a number of potential pitfalls await firms that follow this road.

First, the cost savings certainly do not appear in the short term. Whereas the outsourced provider must make the technology investments, the firm must invest in managing the relationship with that external provider while rethinking what the new role of strategic HRM will be within the firm. Although in theory outsourcing the administrative aspects of HRM will free up remaining HR professionals to focus on strategic activities, many times the existing HR employees do not possess the skills to be strategic contributors. Thus additional investments in upgrading the remaining HR workforce occur.

Second, firms can become dependent on the single provider, enabling that supplier to subsequently raise costs down the road. Also, inevitably conflicts arise regarding priorities.

Finally, outsourcing of HRM may send the wrong signal to employees. If the company hands much of the management of people over to an outside vendor, employees may interpret this as a sign that the firm does not take people issues seriously.

In spite of these potential problems, however, the trend toward more outsourcing of HRM will continue. This trend highlights the need for HR professionals within firms to develop skills in the strategic management of human resources, because those with only administrative skills may end up working for external providers.

SOURCE: A. Maitland, "No Such Thing as a Quick Fix: Outsourcing the HR Function," *Financial Times* (October 26, 2001).

steps shown in Figure 16.7: identify the process to be reengineered, understand the process, redesign the process, and implement the new process.[6]

Identifying the Process

Managers who control the process or are responsible for functions within the process (sometimes called "process owners") should be identified and asked to be part of the reengineering team. Team members should include employees involved in the process (to provide expertise) and those outside the process, as well as internal or external customers who see the outcome of the process.

FIGURE 16.7
The Reengineering Process

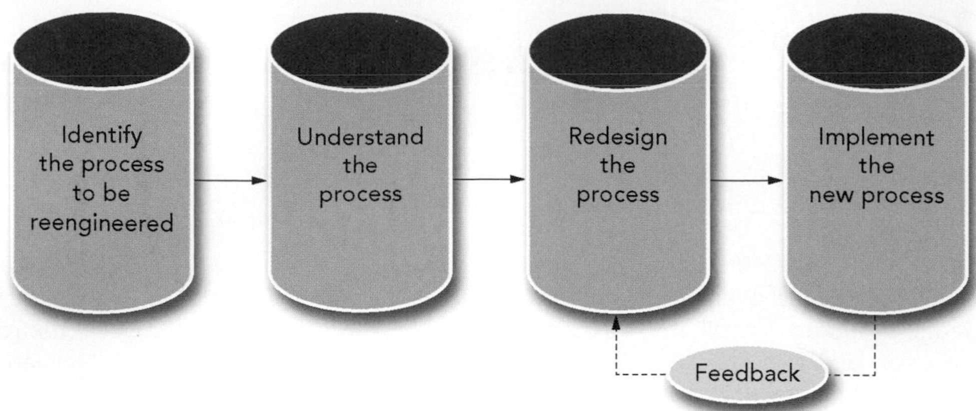

Understanding the Process

Several things need to be considered when evaluating a process:

- Can jobs be combined?
- Can employees be given more autonomy? Can decision making and control be built into the process through streamlining it?
- Are all the steps in the process necessary?
- Are data redundancy, unnecessary checks, and controls built into the process?
- How many special cases and exceptions have to be dealt with?
- Are the steps in the process arranged in their natural order?
- What is the desired outcome? Are all of the tasks necessary? What is the value of the process?

Various techniques are used to understand processes. *Data-flow diagrams* are useful to show the flow of data among departments. Figure 16.8 shows a data-flow diagram for payroll data and the steps in producing a paycheck. Information about the employee and department are sent to the general account. The payroll check is issued based on a payment voucher that is generated from the general accounting ledger. *Data-entity relationship diagrams* show the types of data used within a business function and the relationship among the different types of data. In *scenario analysis,* simulations of real-world issues are presented to data end users. The end users are asked to indicate how an information system could help address their particular situations and what data should be maintained to deal with those situations. *Surveys* and *focus groups* collect information about the data collected, used, and stored in a functional area, as well as information about time and information-processing requirements. Users may be asked to evaluate the importance, frequency, and criticality of automating specific tasks within a functional area. For example, how critical is it to have an applicant tracking system that maintains data on applicants' previous work experience? *Cost–benefit analyses* compare the costs of completing tasks with and without an automated system or software application. For example, the analysis should include the costs in terms of people, time, materials, and dollars; the anticipated costs of software and hardware; and labor, time, and material expenses.[7]

Redesigning the Process

During the redesign phase, the team develops models, tests them, chooses a prototype, and determines how to integrate the prototype into the organization.

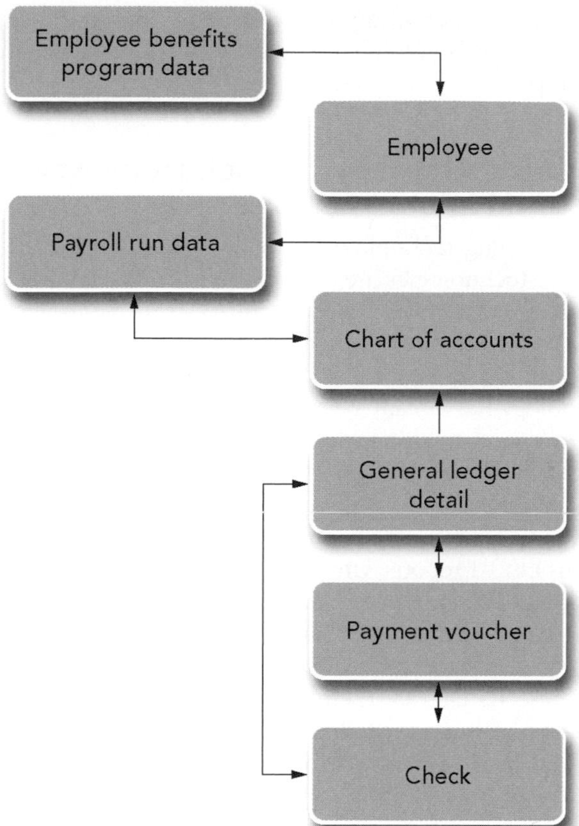

FIGURE 16.8
A Data-Flow Diagram for Payroll Data

Implementing the Process

The company tries out the process by testing it in a limited, controlled setting before expanding companywide. For example, J.M. Huber Corporation, a New Jersey–based conglomerate that has several operating divisions scattered throughout the United States, used reengineering to avoid installing new software onto inefficient processes.[8] HR staff began by documenting and studying the existing work flow and creating a strategy for improving efficiency. Top management, midlevel managers, and human resources staff worked together to identify the processes that they most wanted to improve. They determined that the most critical issue was to develop a client–server system that could access data more easily than the mainframe computer they were currently using. Also, the client–server system could eliminate many of the requisitions needed to get access to data, which slowed down work. The HRM department's efforts have streamlined record-keeping functions, eliminated redundant steps, and automated manual processes. The fully automated client–server system allows employees to sign up and change benefits information using an interactive voice-response system that is connected to the company's database. In addition, managers have easier access to employee's salary history, job descriptions, and other data. If an employee is eligible for a salary increase and the manager requests a change and it is approved, the system will process it (without entry by a clerical worker), and the changes will be seen on the employee's paycheck. Results of the reengineering effort are impressive. The redesigned processes have reduced the number of problems that HRM has to give to other departments by 42 percent, cut work steps by 26 percent, and eliminated 20 percent of the original work. Although the company is spending over $1 million to make the technology work, it estimates that the investment should pay for itself in five years.

Improving HRM Effectiveness Through Using New Technologies—HRM Information Systems

New technologies Current applications of knowledge, procedures, and equipment that have not been previously used. Usually involves replacing human labor with equipment, information processing, or some combination of the two.

Transaction processing Computations and calculations used to review and document HRM decisions and practices.

Decision support systems Problem-solving systems which usually include a "what-if" feature that allows users to see how outcomes change when assumptions or data change.

Expert systems Computer systems incorporating the decision rules of people recognized as experts in a certain area.

Several new and emerging technologies can help improve the effectiveness of the HRM function. **New technologies** are current applications of knowledge, procedures, and equipment that have not been used previously. New technology usually involves automation—that is, replacing human labor with equipment, information processing, or some combination of the two.

In HRM, technology has already been used for three broad functions: transaction processing, reporting, and tracking; decision support systems; and expert systems.[9] **Transaction processing** refers to computations and calculations used to review and document HRM decisions and practices. This includes documenting relocation, training expenses, and course enrollments and filling out government reporting requirements (such as EEO-1 reports, which require companies to report information to the government regarding employees' race and gender by job category). **Decision support systems** are designed to help managers solve problems. They usually include a "what if" feature that allows users to see how outcomes change when assumptions or data change. These systems are useful, for example, for helping companies determine the number of new hires needed based on different turnover rates or the availability of employees with a certain skill in the labor market. **Expert systems** are computer systems incorporating the decision rules of people deemed to have expertise in a certain area. The system recommends actions that the user can take based on the information provided by the user. The recommended actions are those that a human expert would take in a similar situation (such as a manager interviewing a job candidate). We discuss expert systems in more detail later in this chapter.

The newest technologies being applied to HRM include interactive voice technology, the Internet, client–server architecture, relational databases, imaging, and development of specialized software, CD-ROM, and laser disc technology. These technologies improve effectiveness through increasing access to information, improving communications, improving the speed with which HRM transactions and information can be gathered, and reducing the costs and making it easier to administer HRM functions such as recruiting, training, and performance management. Technology enables

- Employees to gain complete control over their training and benefits enrollments (more self-service).
- The creation of a paperless employment office.
- Streamlining the HRM department's work.
- Knowledge-based decision support technology, which allows employees and managers to access knowledge as needed.
- Employees and managers to select the type of media they want to use to send and receive information.
- Work to be completed at any time and place.
- Closer monitoring of employees' work.[10]

As Dilbert shows in Figure 16.9 managers who cannot use or fail to use new technologies will be at a competitive disadvantage.

FIGURE 16.9
The Competitive Advantage of Technology

SOURCE: DILBERT reprinted by permission of United Feature Syndicate, Inc.

There is evidence that new technology is related to improvements in productivity. Improvements in productivity have been credited largely to downsizing, restructuring, and reengineering. But technology is also responsible because new technology has allowed companies to find leaner, more flexible ways of operating.[11] A study of companies in a variety of industries found that investments in computers provided a better return than investments in other kinds of capital.[12] Technology requires companies to have appropriately skilled and motivated people and streamlined work processes. In some cases technology is replacing human capital.[13] For example, Statewide, the regional telephone unit of Pacific Telesis Group, used to dispatch about 20,000 trucks a day to fix customers' lines. New technology has enabled the company to find broken lines using computer signals. As a result, now fewer truck dispatches (and fewer drivers) are necessary.

Interactive Voice Technology

Interactive voice technology uses a conventional personal computer to create an automated phone-response system. This technology is especially useful for benefits administration. For example, at Hannaford Brothers, a supermarket chain spread through the Northeastern United States, the HRM department installed an interactive voice-response system that allows employees to get information on their retirement accounts, stock purchases, and benefits plans by using the touchtone buttons on their phone.[14] Employees can also directly enroll in programs and speak to an HRM representative if they have questions. As a result of the technology, the company was able to reduce the size of the HRM staff and more quickly serve employees' benefits needs.

The Internet

The **Internet** is a widely used tool for communications, a method for sending and receiving communications quickly and inexpensively, and a way to locate and gather resources, such as software and reports.[15] According to one survey, 11 percent of the North American population over age 16 are on the Internet, and 17.6 million people use the World Wide Web (which we discuss later).[16] To gain access to the Internet, you need a personal computer with a direct connection via an existing network or a modem to dial into the Internet. Educational institutions, government agencies, and commercial service providers such as Prodigy, CompuServe, and America Online provide access to the Internet.

Internet
A tool used for communications and to locate and gather resources such as software and reports.

Managers can communicate with other managers at their location or across the globe, leave messages or documents, and get access to *rooms* that are designated for conversation on certain topics (the Americans with Disabilities Act, for example). Various *newsgroups* exist, which are bulletin boards dedicated to areas of interest, where you can read, post, and respond to messages and articles. Internet sites can have *home pages*—mailboxes that identify the person or company and contain text, images, and sounds.

World Wide Web Service on the Internet that provides browser software allowing the user to explore the items (home pages) on the Web.

The **World Wide Web** is a user-friendly service on the Internet. It provides browser software that enables the user to explore its items (like *Mosaic* and *Netscape*). Every home page on the Web has an address or *uniform resources locator (URL)*. Many organizations are creating websites to provide financial information to investors, advertise products and services, give the latest news releases about the company, and post position openings.[17] The Internet is a valuable source of information on a wide range of HRM topics available from professional societies, schools, and government agencies. On the accompanying website for this book website addresses related to HRM topics are provided.

One manager at Hydro Quebec, a large Canadian utility, used the Internet to research topics related to TQM and business process reengineering. When the company wanted information on diversity and women's issues, the manager logged into a Cornell University website and quickly downloaded two dozen reports dealing with the topic. When the company needed to develop a satisfaction survey, the manager used the Internet to identify similar-sized companies that had conducted comprehensive surveys. Within one day, 30 HR professionals, including managers at Federal Express and United Parcel Service, responded. The manager has also networked with HR managers at Motorola, IBM, and other companies.[18]

Networks and Client–Server Architecture

Network A combination of desktop computers, computer terminals and mainframes or minicomputers that share access to databases and a method to transmit information throughout the system.

Client–server architecture Computer design that provides a method to consolidate data and applications into a single host system (the client).

Traditionally, different computer systems (with separate databases) are used for payroll, recruiting, and other human resource management functions. A **network** is a combination of desktop computers, computer terminals, and mainframes or minicomputers that share access to databases and a means to transmit information throughout the system. A common form of network involves client–server architecture. **Client–server architecture** provides the means of consolidating data and applications into a single system (the client).[19] The data can be accessed by multiple users. Also, software applications can be stored on the server and "borrowed" by other users. Client–server architecture allows easier access to data, faster response time, and maximum use of the computing power of the personal computer.

For example, a pharmaceutical company with 50,000 employees worldwide has used client–server technology to create an employee information system that integrates data from six databases.[20] The available data include financial, operational, and human resource information. A manager at a European location can compare her plant's human resource costs with those for the entire company or a plant in Ohio, and at the same time senior management can use the same data to compare the productivity of the Ohio plant with a plant in Maine.

Relational Databases

Databases contain several data files (topics), which are made up of employee information (records) containing data fields. A data field is an element or type of information such as employee name, Social Security number, or job classification.

In a **relational database** information is stored in separate files, which look like tables. These files can be linked by common elements (fields) such as name, identification number, or location. This contrasts with the traditional file structure, in which all data associated with an employee was kept in one file. In the relational database shown in Figure 16.10, employees' personal information is located in one file and salary information in another, but both topics of information can be accessed via the employees' Social Security numbers.

Relational database
A database structure that stores information in separate files that can be linked by common elements.

Users of relational databases can file and retrieve information according to any field or multiple fields across different tables or databases. They provide an easy way to organize data. Also, the number of data fields that can be kept for any employee using a relational database is limitless. The ability to join or merge data from several different tables or to view only a subset of data is especially useful in human resource management. Databases that have been developed to track employee benefit costs, training courses, and compensation, for example, contain separate pieces of employee information that can be accessed and merged as desired by the user. Relational technology also allows databases to be established in several different locations. Users in one plant or division location can access data from any other company location. Consider an oil company. Human resources data—such as the names, salaries, and skills of employees working on an oil rig in the Gulf of Mexico—can be stored at company headquarters. Databases at the oil rig site itself might contain employee name, safety equipment issued, and appropriate skill certification. Headquarters and oil rig managers can access information on each database as needed.

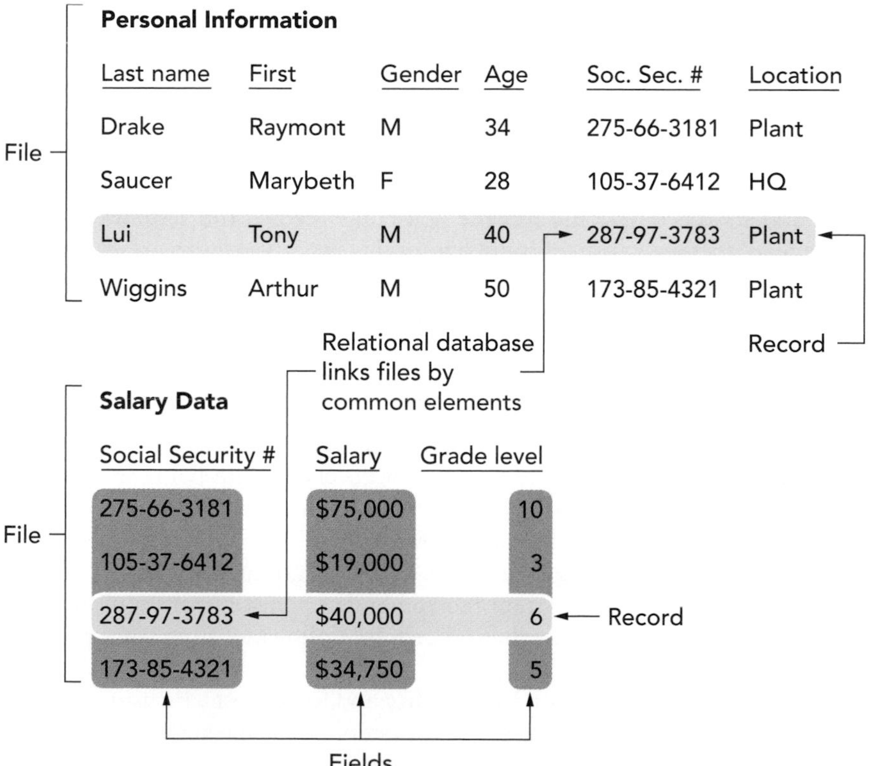

FIGURE 16.10
Example of a Relational Database

Imaging

Imaging
A process for scanning documents, storing them electronically, and retrieving them.

Imaging refers to scanning documents, storing them electronically, and retrieving them.[21] Imaging is particularly useful because paper files take a large volume of space and are difficult to access. Imaging has been used in applicant tracking and in benefits management. Applicants' résumés can be scanned and stored in a database so they will be available for access at a later date. Some software applications (such as *Resumix*) allow the user to scan the résumé based on key items such as job history, education, or experience. At Warner-Lambert, the compensation and benefits department provides HR-related services for over 15,000 retirees.[22] Eight employees retire or die each month; approximately 100 employees terminate each month. This "exit" activity created a tremendous volume of paper for each employee, as well as requests for data from analysts in the department. It was very time-consuming and inefficient to locate the data and refile them. Using imaging, the compensation and benefits department was able to better serve its customers by reducing the time needed to locate a file or handle a phone inquiry from a retiree, providing the ability for sharing files among analysts simultaneously, eliminating the need to refile, and reducing the physical space needed to store the files.

Expert Systems

As we discussed earlier, expert systems are technologies that mimic a human expert. Expert systems have three elements:

- A knowledge base that contains facts, figures, and rules about a specific subject.
- A decision-making capability that draws conclusions from those facts and figures to solve problems and answer questions.
- A user interface that gathers and gives information to the person using the system.

The use of expert systems in HRM is relatively new. Some companies use expert systems to help employees decide how to allocate their money for benefits, help managers schedule the labor requirements for projects, and assist managers in conducting selection interviews. Pic 'n Pay stores (a chain of shoe stores) uses an expert system for the initial job interview. Candidates call a toll-free phone number. The candidates then respond to 100 questions, and the computer records the responses and scores them. At headquarters, a team of trained interviewers evaluates the responses and designs a list of follow-up questions, which are administered by the hiring manager. The expert system reduced employee turnover by 50 percent and reduced losses due to theft by 39 percent. Also, hiring of minorities has risen 8 percent, implying that decision biases may be less significant using the expert system.[23]

A large international food processor uses an expert system called *Performer*, designed to provide training and support to its plant operators. One of the problems the company was facing was determining why potato chips were being scorched in the fryer operation. An operator solved the problem using *Performer*. He selected the "troubleshooting" menu, then "product texture/flavor," then "off oil flavor." The program listed probable causes, beginning with high oxidation during frying. The operator chose that cause, and the system recommended adjusting the cooking line's oil flush, providing detailed steps for that procedure. Following those steps resolved the problem.[24]

Expert systems can deliver both high quality and lower costs. By using the decision processes of experts, the system enables many people to arrive at decisions that reflect the expert's knowledge. An expert system helps avoid the errors that can result from fatigue and decision biases. The efficiencies of an expert system can be realized if it can be operated by fewer employees or less skilled (and likely less costly) employees than the company would otherwise require.

Groupware

Groupware (electronic meeting software) is a software application that enables multiple users to track, share, and organize information and to work on the same document simultaneously.[25] A groupware system combines such elements as electronic mail, document management, and an electronic bulletin board. The most popular brand of groupware is *Lotus Notes*.

Groupware
Software that enables multiple users to track, share, and organize information and to work on the same database or document simultaneously.

Companies have been using groupware to improve business processes such as sales and account management, to improve meeting effectiveness, and to identify and share knowledge in the organization. (See our earlier discussion of creating a learning organization in Chapter 7.) Monsanto uses *Lotus Notes* to link salespeople, account managers, and competitor-intelligence analysts.[26] The database contains updated news on competitors and customers, information from public news sources, salespeople's reports, an in-house directory of experts, and attendees' notes from conventions and conferences. Many companies are also creating their own "intranet," a private company network that competes with groupware programs such as *Lotus Notes*. Intranets are cheaper and simpler to use than groupware programs but pose potential security problems because of the difficulty of keeping people out of the network.[27]

Software Applications for HRM

Today nearly 1,000 personal computer–based human resource applications are available.[28] Because of the wide variety, several publications that deal exclusively with human resource management (like *HRMagazine* and *Personnel Journal*) devote one issue a year to reviewing software applications. In the following sections we review the software applications available in the areas of staffing, human resource planning, training and career development, performance management, and compensation and benefits.

Staffing Applications

Common software applications used in the area of staffing include applicant tracking, recruitment practices tracking, help in meeting equal employment opportunity reporting requirements, and aid in maintaining databases of employee information.

Applicant Recruiting and Tracking

Applicant tracking helps a company maintain its information about job candidates and identify suitable candidates for particular positions. An effective applicant tracking system does the following:

1. Retrieves applications by name, Social Security number, or other identifiers.
2. Tracks all the events in the application process (like interviews and tests).
3. Allows the user to determine how long an application has remained active.

4. Contains the information needed to meet equal employment opportunity reporting requirements, such as name, gender, race, and date of application.
5. Tracks data entry (allows for entry of only essential applicant information).
6. Simplifies the recruiter's function (provides basic data needed to schedule interviews, generate reports, and reduce the list of job candidates).
7. Allows evaluation of recruiting strategy (such as by identifying which sources of advertising bring in the best candidates or the cost-effectiveness of visiting various college campuses).
8. Permits customization (allows additional types of data to be added to the file, such as test results or job offers).
9. Increases the applicant pool (potential job candidates can be identified and tracked earlier; qualified candidates can be tracked after a position is filled).
10. Increases selection criteria by allowing simultaneous searches based on several types of criteria, such as skills, work history, and educational background.[29]

Equal Employment Opportunity and Affirmative Action Reporting Requirements

To comply with equal employment opportunity requirements, companies have to provide reports to the federal government. The most common is the EEO-1 report, which shows the number of employees by race and gender within nine job categories (professional, office and clerical, craft workers, and so on). A section of an EEO report is shown in Figure 16.11. The EEO-1 report is usually submitted annually to the Equal Employment Opportunity Commission. All government contractors and any employers who have been found to engage in illegal hiring practices are also required to file affirmative action reports. To complete either kind of report, employers need to

1. Describe the workforce by job category and job classification.
2. Evaluate the adverse impact of employment practices on representatives of protected classes (such as women and minorities) in the workforce.
3. Determine the availability of jobs for qualified members of protected classes.
4. Evaluate the company's utilization of qualified protected class members.
5. Describe the company's goals and timetables for implementing equal employment opportunity or affirmative action initiatives.
6. Monitor those initiatives.[30]

Because of EEO and affirmative action reporting requirements, employers need to keep track of job candidates' and employees' race and gender and the percentages of women and minorities in the internal and external workforce by job category. Collecting this information into databases makes it easier to track affirmative action and EEO-related statistics. Many software packages are available that generate the necessary EEO and affirmative action reports (one of the most popular being *ABRA 2000 Human Resource System*).

Developing a Master Employee Database

Companies usually keep data about employees in one large file. Information in the master employee database can be used for many purposes: administering payroll, tracking compensation and benefit costs, human resource planning, and meeting EEO reporting requirements. The master employee database usually includes information

FIGURE 16.11

Section D—Employment Data of EEO-1 Report

Number of Employees		Male						Female						
		Overall Total	White	Black	Hispanic	Asian	American Indian		White	Black	Hispanic	Asian	American Indian	
		A	B	C	D	E	F	A	B	C	D	E	F	G
Officials and Managers	1													
Professionals	2													
Technicians	3													
Sales Workers	4													
Office and Clerical	5													
Craft Workers (Skilled)	6													
Operatives (Semiskilled)	7													
Laborers (Unskilled)	8													
Service Workers	9													
Total	10													
Total employment reported in previous EEO-1 report	11													

Formal on-the-Job Training															
	White-Collar	12													
	Production														

SOURCE: Adapted from V.R. Ceriello, *Human Resource Management* (New York: Lexington Books, 1991), p. 420.

such as the employee's name, Social Security number, job status (full- or part-time), hiring date, position, title, rate of pay, citizenship status, job history, job location, mailing address, birth date, and emergency contacts.

Using Staffing Applications for Decision Making

Information related to applicant recruiting and tracking can help managers make recruiting practices more efficient and productive. For example, managers can evaluate the yield of recruiting sources. Those sources that produce the greatest number of applicants who are offered and accept positions are targeted for subsequent recruiting efforts, and low-yield sources are abandoned. Managers can also determine which recruiters are providing the most successful employees. EEO reporting and adverse-impact analyses can help managers evaluate the extent to which women and minority employees are gaining access to managerial and other highly compensated and valued positions in the company.

At Nike, recruitment has become less costly and time-consuming because the company uses an applicant tracking system.[31] Before the automated system was implemented, job applicants had to submit a separate résumé for each job they were interested in. The old system also lacked the capability to process and store data from unsolicited job applications. Most of the 35,000 unsolicited applications Nike received were thrown away. Using *Resumix*, the applicant tracking program mentioned earlier, the company uses imaging technology to quickly enter every résumé it receives into the system. *Resumix* also lets managers cross-reference résumés. Using *Resumix*, Nike has lowered the time and cost of employee recruitment. The company is running fewer newspaper ads, and the ads are more general, generating a greater variety of candidates. *Resumix* has also reduced the time needed to fill positions.

Human Resource Planning Applications

Succession planning
The identification and tracking of high-potential employees capable of filling higher-level managerial positions.

Forecasting
The attempt to determine the supply of and demand for various types of human resources to predict areas within the organization where there will be future labor shortages or surpluses.

Two principal computer applications are related to human resource planning: succession planning and forecasting.[32] **Succession planning** ensures that the company has employees who are prepared to move into positions that become available because of retirement, promotion, transfers, terminations, or expansion of the business. **Forecasting** includes predicting the number of employees who have certain skills and the number of qualified individuals in the labor market.

Because human resource planning uses company-specific calculations to determine future employee turnover, growth rates, and promotion patterns, human resource planning applications usually require more customization than applications for other human resource functions. They usually contain several data files, including a starting population file, exit rate file, growth rate file, and promotion patterns. The starting population file lists employees by job classification within each job family. These file lists usually include all active, regular, full-time employees. However, starting population files may include only specific populations of employees. Starting population data that may be used include job grade, gender, race or ethnicity, age, service, training, and experience information. Starting population lists that are limited to specific populations of employees are used to identify the mobility patterns of these employee groups. Exit rate data include promotion patterns, training completion rates, turnover rates, and hiring rates. Growth rate data include the percentage increase in the number of employees within the job or demographic characteristic of interest. Promotion patterns include the rate of movement into and out of each position.

Information regarding starting population and exit and growth rates is useful for conducting workforce profile analysis and workforce dynamics analysis.[33]

Workforce Profile Analysis

To determine future labor supply and demand, it is necessary to identify the characteristics of the current workforce, a process known as a workforce profile review. The software can be used to generate reports that provide information regarding employee demographics (such as age), the number of employees in each job classification, and the interaction between demographics and company characteristics (such as the average age of employees within each job classification or division of the company).

Workforce Dynamics Analysis

A workforce dynamics analysis involves analyzing employee movement over time. Promotion, demotion, transfer, and turnover data are used. Employee movement data can also be used to forecast the effects of layoffs or hiring on the future workforce. Workforce dynamics analysis provides the following kinds of information:

1. Number of new hires, transfers, and promotions by job classification or department.
2. The total number of promotions, or the number of promotions from a specific job to another job or from one division to another division.
3. The number of employees the company will need in the future.
4. The number of employees who will be available to fill future job openings.

Using Human Resource Planning Applications for Decision Making

The workforce profile review provides managers with information regarding

1. Divisions or departments that have the greatest concentration of employees who are nearing retirement age.
2. Job classifications in which too few employees are ready for promotion.
3. Job classifications in which there are few women or minorities.
4. Job classifications or departments that have large groups of employees who lack basic skills.

An example of a human resource planning application is Cyborg Systems' *Workforce Planning* module.[34] This application, which can be run on either a mainframe or a personal computer, retains data on employees' skills and work experience, education, job history, and termination and separation. It permits integration with payroll applications so that data can be shared between the databases. It reports on the number of people hired, terminated, transferred, and promoted by pay class. It also reports on the net change and percentage change in hiring, termination, or transfers during each business cycle, month, or other time frame chosen by the user.

Managers can use information about employee movement, skills, and job openings to make decisions about where employees should be deployed to help the company successfully execute its business strategy.

Performance Management Applications

Employees' performance ratings, disciplinary actions, and work rule violations can be stored in electronic databases. Personal computers are also increasingly being used for monitoring the actual performance and productivity of service employees.[35] For example, at a General Electric customer service center, agents answer over 14,000 telephone inquiries per day. The agents' calls are recorded and reviewed to help the agents improve customer service. American Airlines also monitors the telephone calls that come into its reservation centers. Managers can hear what the agents tell customers and see what agents enter on their personal computer screens. One of the disadvantages of monitoring is that employees sometimes find it demoralizing, degrading, and stressful. To avoid this potential negative effect of performance monitoring, managers must communicate why employees are being monitored. Nonmanagement employees also need to be involved in monitoring and coaching less experienced employees. Legislation regarding computer monitoring may occur in the future. Both the U.S. House and Senate have considered legislation designed to protect employees' rights from being violated by computer monitoring (the Privacy for Consumers and Workers Act).

Using Performance Management Applications for Decision Making

Performance management applications are available to help managers tailor performance rating systems to jobs and to assist the manager in identifying solutions to performance problems.[36] Software is available to help the manager customize performance rating forms for each job. The manager determines the performance standard for each job and rates each employee according to the appropriate standards. The manager receives a report summarizing the employees' strengths and weaknesses. The report also shows how different an employee's performance was from the established standard.

Performance diagnosis applications ask the manager for information about performance problems (Has the employee been trained in the skills that caused the performance problem?) and the work environment (Does the employee work under time pressure?). The software analyzes the information and describes solutions to consider in dealing with the performance problem.

Training and Career Development Applications

Training applications have been used primarily to track information related to training administration (such as course enrollments, tuition reimbursement summaries, and training costs), employee skills, and employees' training activities. Important database elements for training administration include training courses completed, certified skills, and educational experience. Georgia Power, a utility company, uses a database system that tracks internal training classes, available classroom space, instructor availability, costs, and the salaries of training class members.[37] Figure 16.12 illustrates a screen showing training costs for an accounting department. Cost information can be used by managers to determine which departments are exceeding their training budgets. This information can be used to reallocate training dollars during the next budget period. Databases are also available that provide professional employees, such as engineers and lawyers, with access to summaries of journal articles, legal cases, and books to help these employees keep up to date.[38]

Career development applications assess the employees' career interests, work values, and career goals. The computer tells employees about positions in the company that meet their interests and values. Company information systems may also have ca-

Cost Center: Accounting

Total Budget: 4500

	Budget	Expenditure	Variance
Course	3500	1000	2500
Accommodation	600	00	600
Meals	300	00	300
Travel	100	00	100
Total	4500	1000	3500

FIGURE 16.12 Example of a Training Budget Screen

SOURCE: Adapted from Spectrum Human Resource Systems Corporation, "TD/2000: Training and Development System: Sample Screens and Reports" (Denver, CO).

reer development plans for each employee. These may include information such as skill strengths, projected training and development needs, target positions, and ratings of readiness for managerial or other positions.

Using Training and Career Development Applications for Decision Making

Managers can use skills inventories to ensure that they are getting the maximum benefit out of their training budget. Using skills inventories, managers can determine which employees need training and can suggest training programs that are appropriate for their job and skill levels. Skills inventories are also useful for identifying employees who are qualified for promotions and transfers. Finally, they can also help managers quickly build employee teams with the necessary skills to respond to customer needs, product changes, international assignments, or work problems.

Career development applications can help improve the effectiveness of managers' career development discussions with employees. They also help employees determine their interests, goals, and work values, which is often a difficult and uncomfortable task for managers. By having employees complete a self-assessment of interests, goals, and values, managers and employees can have a more efficient and effective career development discussion that focuses on developing career plans and helping employees progress toward their career goals.

Career development applications also can help managers advise employees on available development opportunities (such as new jobs). For example, 3M has an internal search system that helps managers identify qualified internal candidates for job openings and a job information system that gives employees access to information about internal job openings and the opportunity to nominate themselves for openings.[39]

Compensation and Benefits Applications

Applications in compensation and benefits include payroll, job evaluation, salary surveys, salary planning, international compensation, and benefits management.

Payroll

Meeting a payroll involves calculating and reporting federal, state, and local taxes; computing gross pay, deductions, and net pay for each pay period; arranging for transfer of money into appropriate accounts; distributing payments and records to employees; and reporting dollars allocated to payroll and benefits to the accounting function. Several issues have to be considered in designing or choosing a payroll system. The company must decide whether payroll will be administered in-house or by a service bureau. The company must also decide the extent of integration between payroll and other human resource information systems.

In many companies payroll is done by a service bureau, a company that provides payroll services to other organizations. One of the advantages of a service bureau is that it ensures that the company's payroll meets federal, state, and local laws. It also provides a level of computer expertise that may be unavailable within the company. Many service bureaus have developed other human resource applications that integrate with their payroll systems. However, a problem arises when a company wants to use human resource applications that have not been developed by the service bureau. The service bureau may be unable or unwilling to integrate its payroll system with other applications.

Besides deciding whether to have its payroll done by a service bureau, managers have to decide whether payroll will be integrated with other human resource data systems. In an integrated payroll system, the information in the payroll system is shared with other databases. In most companies payroll is not linked to other human resource information systems. However, the trend is toward integrated systems because of the reduced costs resulting from sharing databases. Another advantage of an integrated payroll is that it cuts down on the storage of redundant information, thus speeding up the computer. Tesseract Corporation's payroll system is completely integrated with both its human resource manager and its benefits systems. Information needed for salary planning and compliance with government regulations can be shared between the systems. The integration of payroll with other systems raises important security issues because access to payroll data needs to be restricted to certain employees.

Job Evaluation

Job evaluation involves determining the worth of each job and establishing pay rates. In computerized job evaluation, jobs are given points, and the relative worth of each job is determined by the total number of points.[40] Managers and employees complete surveys that ask them to rate their jobs' level of problem solving, interaction with customers, and other important compensable factors. The survey data are entered into the computer. A summary of the survey responses is generated and checked for accuracy (for example, jobs high in complexity should also have high ratings of required job knowledge). The computer calculates a point value to assign each job to a salary grade.

Salary Surveys

Salary surveys are sent to competing companies to gain information about compensation rates, pay levels, or pay structures. The information gathered may include salary ranges, average salary of job incumbents, and total compensation of job incumbents. Software designed specifically for this purpose collects, records, analyzes, and generates reports comparing company salary ranges with those of competitors.

Salary Planning

Salary planning anticipates changes in employees' salaries because of seniority or performance. Salary planning applications calculate merit increase budgets and allocate salary increases based on merit or seniority. They also allow users to see what effect changes in the amount of money devoted to merit, seniority, or cost-of-living wage increases would have on compensation budgets.

Home Box Office (HBO) has a proactive approach toward compensation.[41] The company believes that all employees should understand their salary, why it was assigned, and what type of merit increase they can expect. Merit increases are based on performance ratings. The information service staff helps the human resource department administer the performance reviews by providing an evaluation report for each employee. The report includes the employee's current salary and performance evaluations from previous years. The information systems staff also assists in the bonus administration program, converting each employee's performance ratings into a bonus rating, developing calculation worksheets, entering data, and providing a wide range of reports that are needed to determine the amount of money available for merit raises. One of the software products related to the bonus system is a report that estimates and calculates bonuses for employees and confirms the approved bonus.

International Compensation

Software applications also perform U.S. and foreign tax calculations necessary to determine the costs of international assignments. Many international compensation applications can also calculate salary levels and cost-of-living differentials between U.S. and foreign cities.

Benefits Management

Benefits can be classified into three types: time benefits (sick leave, parental leave), risk benefits (various forms of health and long-term disability insurance that help employees and their families in case of injury or death), and security benefits (retirement and savings programs).[42] Benefits management includes tracking coverage for employees and former employees, producing reports on changes in benefits coverage, and determining employee eligibility for benefit plans. Software is available to help administer flexible benefits programs, pensions, retirement planning, and defined benefit and defined contribution plans. These applications can track the employee's enrollment in each part of the benefit plan, track claims, communicate premium costs to employees, calculate taxes, and determine employee eligibility for coverage. Siemens Corporation uses a flexible benefit software application that allows employees from all 40 Siemens companies to enroll in and inquire about their benefits plans by using a touchtone telephone.[43] Benefits software applications can reduce the time it takes to process changes in employees' benefit plans. They also allow employers to track current benefit expenses and project future benefits costs.

Benefits software applications can also help companies comply with federal legislation regarding benefits. For example, the Comprehensive Omnibus Budget Reconciliation Act (COBRA) requires companies to offer health benefits to terminated and retired employees. The company must ensure that all eligible former employees and their dependents have been notified of their option of continuing health care benefits; it must also track who accepts and who declines coverage and determine when COBRA coverage has expired.[44] Software is available that automates the recordkeeping and reporting requirements necessary to comply with COBRA.

Using Compensation and Benefits Applications for Decision Making

The software applications mentioned provide graphic depictions of pay ranges and salary lines. They allow managers to quickly see the effects of changes in compensation rates and policies. Compensation and benefit applications can be useful for determining the impact of different percentages of pay increases on total compensation costs. Managers can use job evaluation data to determine which jobs are over- or underpaid in comparison with other jobs in the company. Hypothetical pay ranges can be constructed based on different compensation strategies. For example, the costs of a "lead the market" strategy can be determined before the company decides on this compensation approach.

Managers can also use compensation information to adjust an individual employee's compensation. For example, managers can determine whether employee performance ratings are related to merit increases and can identify the employee's position within the pay range.

Improving HRM Effectiveness through New Technologies—E-HRM

Over the past 5–10 years, as HRM functions sought to play a more strategic role in their organizations, the first task was to eliminate transactional tasks in order to free up time to focus on traditional and transformational activities. As indicated in Figure 16.5, outsourcing of many of these activities provided one mechanism for reducing this burden. However, more relevant today is the focus on the use of information technology to handle these tasks. Early on this was achieved by the development and implementation of information systems that were run by the HRM function but more recently have evolved into systems that allow employees to serve themselves. Thus, for example, employees can access the system and make their benefit enrollment, changes, or claims online. Clearly, technology has freed HRM functions from transactional activities to focus on more strategic actions. The "Competing in the New Economy" box illustrates how Oracle Corporation has leveraged e-HRM to transform its HRM function.

However, the speed requirements of e-business force HRM functions to explore how to leverage technology for the delivery of traditional and transformational HRM

COMPETING IN THE NEW ECONOMY

ing Technology Efficiency

The promise and the challenge of e-business technology are that it enables firms to review and reengineer traditional processes that exist within the firm, even those of HRM programs. Some companies, such as Oracle Corporation, have discovered that when they rise to this challenge, they fulfill the promise of vast efficiency improvements, particularly in the area of HRM. It has saved over a billion dollars using its own e-business software, and a significant part of that savings has come through the transformation of HRM.

Oracle is the world's second largest independent software company, and because of its growing global workforce it must manage administrative activities as smoothly and efficiently as possible. It is utilizing automation to achieve a cost-effective "B2E" (business to employee) relationship that enhances both employee productivity and workforce return on investment.

Much of Oracle's HRM transformation has come about through moving routine, day-to-day administrative tasks online. This has allowed its HR professionals to focus on more productive activities such as recruiting, staffing, training, and compensation. "It's been a remarkable journey," stated senior VP of HR Joyce Westerdahl. "Before setting out on this e-biz transformation, Oracle carefully measured and audited the work that was taking place within the HR organization worldwide. We discovered that about 60 percent of the work that HR people were doing involved simple administrative tasks. With self-service capabilities, we've been able to break away from the routine and focus more on the strategic issues."

Using its HRM information system, Oracle has been able to

- Deliver 100 percent Internet-architected, self-service tools for all managers and employees.
- Automate virtually every routine transaction by intr… applicat… elf-service automation… work-flow
- Consolidate mu… disparate HRM syste… around the world.
- Reduce administrative costs, thus enabling Oracle to increase the ratios of HR administrative staff to employees. Its previous ratio of one HR administrative staff person for every 800 employees is now one for every 3,000 employees.

Such efficiencies have enabled Oracle to run HRM at a zero growth budget even when the firm is growing 10 percent a year. "Our B2E strategies have brought us great success," says Westerdahl. "We will continue to add more and more capabilities to empower employees and managers with the tools and knowledge they need to be as effective and as productive as possible."

SOURCE: C. Collett, "Business to Employee: Automating the HR Function," *CMA Management* 75, no. 7 (October 1, 2001), p. 20.

activities. This does not imply that over time all of HRM will be executed over the Web, but that a number of HRM activities currently delivered via paper or face-to-face communications can be moved to the Web with no loss (and even gains) in effectiveness and efficiency. This is illustrated by Figure 16.13. We explore some examples next.

FIGURE 16.13
Change in Delivery

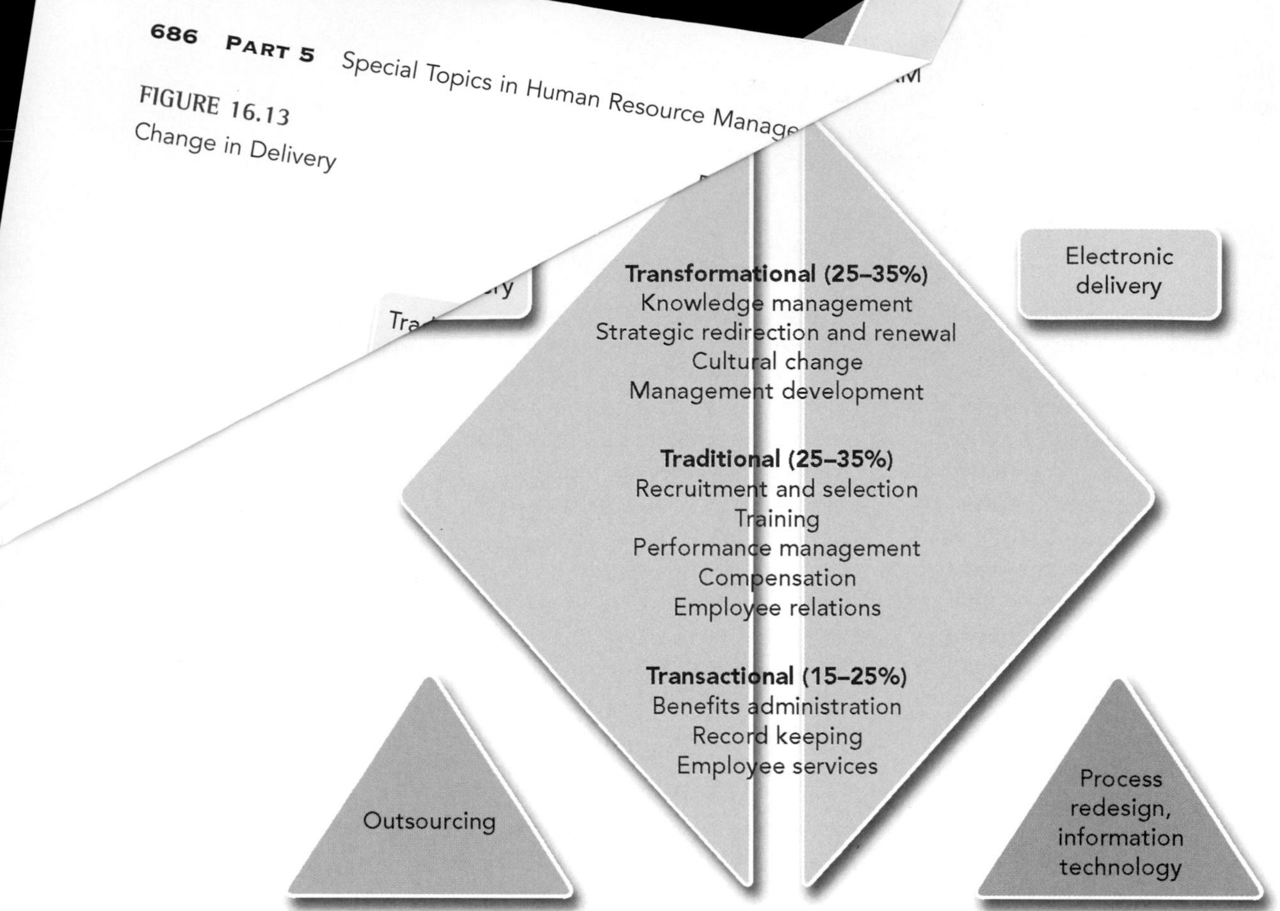

Recruitment and Selection

Traditional recruitment and selection processes have required considerable face-to-face communications with recruitment firms and potential employees, labor-intensive assessment devices, and significant monitoring of managerial decisions to ensure that hiring patterns and decisions do not run afoul of regulatory requirements. However, technology has transformed these processes.

For example, online recruiting accounted for one of every eight hires last year, according to k-force.com's poll of 300 U.S. companies. IBM employees now fill out forms on the Web to identify contract help they need, and that information is immediately sent to 14 temp agencies. Within an hour agencies respond with résumés for review, allowing IBM to cut hiring time from 10 days to 3 and save $3 million per year.

In addition, firms such as Q-Hire in Austin, Texas, provide online testing services. Applicants for positions at a firm are directed to a website where they complete an assessment device. Their scores are immediately compared to an ideal profile, and this profile comparison is communicated to the company screening manager. Firms can gather considerable amounts of relevant information about potential employees long before they ever need to set foot on company premises.

Finally, technology has enabled firms to monitor hiring processes to minimize the potential for discriminatory hiring decisions. For example, as noted in Chapter 3,

Home Depot was accused of forcing femal[illegible] cashier jobs while reserving the customer service jobs for males. While [illegible]ult, as part of their consent decree Home Depot uses technology to identi[illegible] have skills for jobs they are not applying for based on key words in their re[illegible]dition, the technology forces managers to interview diverse candidate sets be[illegible] decisions.

Compensation and Rewards

Compensation systems in organizations probably reflect the most pervasive [illegible] bureaucracy within HRM. In spite of the critical role they play in attracting, mot[illegible]vating, and retaining employees, most systems consist of rigid, time-consuming, and ineffective processes. Managers fill out what they believe to be useless forms, ignore guidelines, and display a general disdain for the entire process.

Leveraging technology may allow firms to better achieve their compensation goals with considerably less effort. For example, one problem many merit or bonus pay plans face is that managers refuse to differentiate among performers, giving everyone similar pay increases. This allows them to spend less time thinking about how to manage (rate and review) performance as well as minimizes the potential conflict they might face. Thus employees do not see linkages between performance and pay, resulting in lower motivation among all employees and higher turnover among top performers (and possibly lower turnover among bottom performers). To minimize this, Cypress Semiconductors requires managers to distinguish between equity and merit and forces distributions with regard to both concepts.[45] For example, equity means that the top-ranked performer in any group of peers should make 50 percent more than the lowest-ranked performer, and people with comparable performance should receive comparable salaries. With regard to merit, there must be at least a 7 percent spread between the lowest and highest pay raises (if the lowest raise is 3 percent, then the highest must be at least 10 percent). If ratings and raises are input into a system, the firm can monitor and control the rating process to ensure that adequate differentiations are made consistent with the policy.

Training and Development

Exploring different vehicles for delivering training (PC, video, and the like) certainly is not a new concept. In addition, a number of firms have begun delivering training via the Web. Their experience suggests that some types of training can be done effectively via the Internet or an intranet, whereas others might not. For example, companies such as IBM and Dell both boast that they have developed Internet-based training for some parts of their workforce.

Interestingly, the challenge of speedy delivery of HRM services brings the concept of Internet-based training to the forefront. In today's competitive environment, firms compete to attract and retain both customers and talented employees. How well a firm develops and treats existing employees largely determines how well it achieves these outcomes. Yet the challenges of speed, project focus, and changing technology create environments that discourage managers from managing their people, resulting in a situation where employees may not feel respected or valued.

This presents a challenge to firms to provide both the incentive and the skills for managers to treat employees as assets rather than commodities. Consider how Internet-based training might facilitate this. Assume that you work for Widget.com, a fast-growing, fast-paced e-business. You arrive at work Monday morning, and your e-mail contains a high-priority me... It is your Monday morning ch... will track whether you lin... a digital video of your... vantage, and that... is to make yo... utes lear... poin...

...n attachment or a link to a URL. ...CEO, and you know that the system ...this challenge. When you link to it, you see ...ou how people are Widget.com's competitive ad- ...n't feel valued, they leave. Thus his challenge to you ...feel valued today. To do so, you will in the next 10 min- ...xpress appreciation to an employee. You receive six learning ...erve a digitized video model performing the learning points; you re- ...earning points again and take a quiz. You then see the CEO giving you the ...challenge: that in the next 15 minutes you are to take one of your employees aside and express your appreciation using the skill you just developed.

Notice the advantages of this process. First, it was not time-consuming like most three-day or one-week training programs. The entire process (training and demonstration with a real employee) took less than 30 minutes; you have developed a skill; and an employee now probably feels better about the organization. It communicated a real organizational value or necessary competency. It didn't require any travel expenses to a training facility. It did not overwhelm you with so much information that you would be lucky to remember 10 percent of what you were exposed to. Finally, it was a push, rather than pull, approach to training. The firm did not wait for you to realize you had a deficiency and then go search and sign up for training. It pushed the training to you.

Thus technology allows firms to deliver training and development for at least some skills or knowledge faster, more efficiently, and probably more effectively. It can quickly merge training, communication, and immediate response to strategic contingencies.

Finding and Keeping the Best Employees

Creating and nurturing a committed workforce presents a tremendous challenge to firms today. To do so requires that firms monitor commitment levels, identify potential obstacles to commitment, and respond quickly to eliminate those obstacles. In large part, attitude surveys have constituted the platform from which these activities were managed in the past.

Consider the traditional attitude survey. Surveys are administered to employees over a period of four to six weeks. The data are entered and analyzed, requiring another six to eight weeks. A group interprets the results to identify the major problem areas, and task forces are formed to develop recommendations; this process easily takes another four to six months. Finally, decisions must be made about implementing the task force recommendations. In the end, at best employees might see responses to their concerns 12 to 18 months after the survey—and then the survey administrators cannot understand why employees think that completing the survey is a waste of time.

Now consider how technology can shorten that cycle. E-pulse represents one attempt to create a platform for almost real-time attitude surveys. Developed by Theresa Welbourne at the University of Michigan, E-pulse is a scalable survey device administered online. Normally three questions are asked regarding how employees feel about work, but more questions can be added to get feedback on any specific issue. The survey goes out online, and when employees complete it, the data are immediately entered and analyzed. In essence, the part of the process that took four months in the past has been reduced to a day.

Next the firm can decide how it . could be broken down by business, site, o going to the leader of the chosen unit of anal the information. For example, it ceive almost immediate feedback about the attitu with the relevant information general manager about his or her business unit. The su nce, a supervisor could re- spond immediately, even if only to communicate that she or h r her work group, or a ists and will take action soon. r manager can re- s a problem ex-

One must recognize that although the technology provides for faste more systemic approach will ensure better and smarter HRM. For example, only a nating the information to the supervisors and managers may be faster, but unless mi- individuals possess good problem-solving and communication skills, they may either ignore the information or, worse yet, exacerbate the problem with inappropriate responses. As we noted with regard to training, this systemic approach requires knocking down traditional functional walls to deliver organizational solutions rather than functional programs. Thus the challenge is to get beyond viewing the technology as a panacea or even as a functional tool, but rather as a catalyst for transforming the HRM organization.

Benefits applications are useful for evaluating the costs of changes in benefits availability and how changes in the characteristics of the employee population (such as age or gender) may affect benefits costs. The implications of different types of early retirement programs on benefits costs can also be considered before a program is offered.

TABLE 16.6
HR Salaries
2001 Median Total

JOB TITLE	CASH COMPENSATION	% CHANGE FROM 2000
Top HR management executive (with industrial relations responsibilities)	$210,000	7.4%
Human resource director	117,700	5.1
Organization development/training manager	92,000	6.9
Compensation manager	90,000	4.7
Human resource manager	88,800	2.6
HRIS manager	85,000	8.1
Benefits manager	84,100	5.2
Employment and recruiting manager	80,800	5.3
Payroll manager	68,000	8.7
Senior generalist	65,500	3.9
Senior compensation analyst	60,000	5.4
Managerial/professional recruiter	59,200	7.4
HRIS specialist	52,000	6.1
Generalist	50,000	2.0
Compensation analyst	45,000	2.0
Trainer	44,500	5.4
General recruiter	42,800	8.6
Entry-level generalist	40,000	5.3
Human resource assistant	30,100	3.2
Payroll clerk	29,300	2.1

SOURCE: P. Schaefer, "HR Compensation: A Mixed Bag," *HRMagazine* 46, no. 10 (2001), p. 56.

A Look Back

Blowing up HRM has becom[illegible] in the field since Tom Stewart wrote his original essay. He receive[illegible]er of responses from thought leaders in HRM who reacted to his su[illegible] Interestingly, those responses seemed to concur with his thesis. M[illegible]e field suggested that he was correctly criticizing "old HRM," which [illegible]tedly consists of predominantly transactional activities and is charac[illegible] by an overwhelmingly bureaucratic mindset.

[illegible], as we have seen in this chapter, HRM has been in a process of transi[illegible]tion from transactional to transformational activities, and from playing [illegible]e role of a bureaucratic "cop" to becoming a strategic business partner. This transformation was driven by the war for talent during the late 1990s and into 2000, which heightened firms' concerns about being able to attract and retain highly skilled technology and managerial professionals. This brought recruitment to the forefront and illustrated the important role of HRM. In addition, much of the transformation of HRM has been enabled by state-of-the-art e-HRM technologies, which have become integral to HRM. This is illustrated by Table 16.6, which presents the average 2001 salaries for a variety of HR professionals as well as their average increase since 2000. As you can see, the HRIS specialists and recruiters were among those receiving the largest increases in pay between 2000 and 2001.

Tom Stewart's suggestion to blow up HRM has been heard and followed. HRM in today's top companies looks nothing like HRM of 20 years ago. This change presents a tremendous opportunity for those seeking careers in the HRM profession.

Questions

1. How has the field of HRM responded to the challenge Tom Stewart laid out to blow up HRM?
2. What do you think is the future of HRM? Is it a positive one or a negative one? Why?

Summary

The roles required of the HRM function have changed as people have become recognized as a true source of competitive advantage. This has required a transformation of the HRM function from focusing solely on transactional activities to an increasing involvement in strategic activities. In fact, according to a recent study, 64 percent of HR executives said that their HRM function is in a process of transformation.[47] The strategic management of the HRM function will determine whether HRM will transform itself to a true strategic partner or simply be blown up.

In this chapter we have explored the various changing roles of the HRM function. HRM today must play roles as an administrative expert, employee advocate, change agent, and strategic partner. The function must also deliver transactional, traditional, and transformational services and activities to the firm, and it must be both efficient and effective. HR executives must strategically manage the HRM function just as the firm must be strategically managed. This requires that HRM develop measures of the function's performance through customer surveys and analytical methods. These measures can form the basis for planning ways to improve performance. HRM performance can increase through new structures for the function, through using reengineering and information technology, and through outsourcing.

Discussion Questions

1. Tom Stewart, in the opening vignette, suggested that HRM be blown up. Do you agree? Why or why not? Which parts should be blown up and how?
2. Why have the roles and activities of the HRM function changed over the past 20 to 30 years? What has been driving this change? How effectively do you think HRM has responded?
3. How can the processes for strategic management discussed in Chapter 2 be transplanted to manage the HRM function?
4. Why do you think that few companies take the time to determine the effectiveness of HRM practices? Should a company be concerned about evaluating HRM practices? Why? What might people working in the HRM function gain by evaluating the function?
5. How might imaging technology be useful for recruitment? For training? For benefits administration? For performance management?
6. Employees in your company currently choose and enroll in benefits programs after reading communications brochures, completing enrollment forms, and sending them to their HR rep. A temporary staff has to be hired to process the large amount of paperwork that is generated. Enrollment forms need to be checked, sorted, batched, sent to data entry, keypunched, returned, and filed. The process is slow and prone to errors. How could you use process reengineering to make benefit enrollment more efficient and effective?
7. Some argue that outsourcing an activity is bad because the activity is no longer a means of distinguishing the firm from competitors. (All competitors can buy the same service from the same provider, so it cannot be a source of competitive advantage.) Is this true? If so, why would a firm outsource any activity?

Web Exercise

Hewlett-Packard (HP) is one of the world's largest computer companies and producer of test and measurement instruments. HP is well known for its printers that set the standard for technology, performance, and reliability. HP also manufactures medical electronic equipment, instruments and systems for chemical analysis, handheld calculators, and electronic components. With 125,000 employees worldwide, HP is headquartered in Palo Alto, California. HP is consistently recognized as one of the best companies to work for. Visit its website at **www.hp.com**. Click on "company information" and "about hp." Review HP's corporate objectives (click on "corporate objectives") and the company's commitment to diversity and work life (click on "diversity @ hp").

Questions

1. What are HP's corporate objectives?
2. What human resource practices help HP reach its corporate objectives?

Managing People: From the Pages of *BusinessWeek*

BusinessWeek Gap: Missing That Ol' Mickey Magic

Bad fashion calls and an exodus of execs have Mickey Drexler's retail empire hurting

For most of us, polo shirts peaked in popularity back in the mid-1990s. But somehow, fashion guru Millard S. "Mickey" Drexler became captivated by them last year. The chief executive of Gap Inc. insisted that his Gap-brand stores carry deep inventories in an unusually wide palette of colors. Gap merchandising managers, unable to dissuade him from the idea, produced data suggesting that three or four colors account for the vast majority of sales. But Drexler was adamant, saying he didn't want to miss a sale to an XXL customer who wanted the shirt in purple. While Gap defends the plan as having "brought fashion to a basic item," the offbeat colors bombed. Stores wound up with mounds of marked-down polo shirts.

Call it another losing bet for Mickey Drexler. Long hailed as the merchant king whose inspired wager on khaki pants ignited a huge growth spurt in the late 1990s, Drexler recently has been on a ruinous losing streak. Gap's once-reliable growth engine has seized up: sales at stores open at least a year plummeted by 17 percent in both August and September. As Drexler acknowledges, each of the company's three core brands—Gap, Banana Republic, and Old Navy—has come untethered from the tight rapport with consumers that accounted for its earlier prosperity. Aggravating those tensions are the CEO's dogged insistence on adding new stores while trying to fix the fundamentals, plus management turnover, in particular last year's exodus of some seasoned executives who knew when to rein in Drexler's impulses.

Now, many analysts and investors, who long trusted that Drexler, 57, would once again pull a rabbit out of his hat as he did during a downturn in the mid-1990s, fear that he has lost his magic. Even in a tough retail environment, Gap's declining same-store sales are worse than those of its peers, having fallen 11 percent so far this year after declining 5 percent in 2000. In contrast, Abercrombie & Fitch Co.'s are down 7 percent, while American Eagle Outfitters Inc.'s are up 4.4 percent. Emme P. Kozloff, an analyst at Sanford C. Bernstein & Co., expects Gap to lose $216.6 million in the third quarter, including a charge of $140 million to $150 million related to an adjustment in tax rates. That follows five consecutive quarters of declining profits. Says Kozloff, "The Street has relied way too much on the 'Mickey will fix it' idea. It's amazing that people give him the benefit of the doubt." Increasingly, however, they don't: Gap's shares are trading around $14, down from $35 in May and slightly more than one-quarter of their high in February 2000.

While some observers figure the nation's more sober mood could spur a shift from rhinestone-encrusted jeans and other novelties to more tried-and-true styles, Gap won't necessarily benefit. Its customers have been fleeing to discounters, such as Kohl's and Target, and youth-oriented chains, such as American Eagle, that offer similar goods. "Somewhere along the line, Gap just lost it," says New York retail consultant Wendy Liebmann.

Drexler scoffs at that and refuses to concede that he doesn't get it anymore. "I'm absolutely still in touch, talking to customers every day, looking at product every day, involved in the creative processes," he says. And so far, Gap board members and the company's founding Fisher family continue to express full support. "I don't know of a merchant better than Mickey," says director Adrian D.P. Bellamy, chairman of Gucci Group. "He's going through a difficult time, but I believe Mickey will lead the company to better days ahead." Board member and Apple Computer Inc. CEO Steven P. Jobs insists there's no talk of replacing Drexler: "The question's not even in the ballpark."

But talk to some of the legions of executives who have left Gap over the past couple of years and you get a different assessment. *BusinessWeek* spoke to 10 former executives, none of whom would be identified, who painted a disturbing picture of a manager whose short attention span and impulsive flip-flopping has cost the company dearly in both dollars and strategic detours. Drexler's erratic style arguably didn't matter so much during the flush times, when Gap could afford the inefficiency and waste that sudden changes of heart create. Besides, his guesses were more often right than wrong. Old Navy, launched in 1994, soared to $1 billion in sales in only five years on the strength of low-cost, whimsical fashions aimed at teens and their parents.

Former execs say Drexler still insists, though, on running the chain in a hands-on style and relying to an alarming degree on gut decisions. Critics contend that the company "is too big to be run by an entrepreneurial, possessed genius," as one alumnus puts it. It hasn't been unusual for Drexler to approve, say, gingham-check skirts for the Gap chain only to cool on them once they arrive from the factory, says a former manager. The skirts were shipped to Gap's outlet stores, forcing the regular stores to overemphasize core denim styles to fill the void. "When you see the denim stretched out in the store and think it sure looks kind of basic, it means Mickey fell out of love with something," the exec says. . . . "He'll pull the plug on things," says the former exec. "It's part of his emotional style." Gap dismisses such complaints, saying such changes are "part of the normal give and take of the business."

CONCRETE FLOORS? Some of the flip-flops have strained relations not just among Drexler's staff but also with external partners whose goodwill Gap needs to cultivate. Drexler created an internal uproar last summer when he greenlighted a change in design for new Gap stores without making sure that company real estate specialists assigned to negotiate with mall developers had been informed. The real estate team then had to go back to developers to persuade them to accept the new design, which uses concrete floors and open ceilings rather than the maple floors and finished ceilings that had been promised. . . .

Of course, creative types often have disruptive personalities. Board member Jobs, no stranger to an impulsive management style, defends Drexler—who sits on Apple's board—on those grounds. "I think Mickey Drexler is a creative person," Jobs says. "As a creative person, he's not a robot—he's a human being with moods. When he sees something he doesn't like, he says so." Drexler sees that as a requirement in an ever-changing industry. "I do like to introduce newness at the edges of the business all the time," he says. "That might be read as mercurial or inconsistent, but you can't get the new ideas without challenging current ideas."

To be sure, some of Drexler's staff find his style motivating. "Creative people really like working with him because he's emotional, passionate," says Amy Schoening, senior vice president and chief marketing officer at Gap. She recalls Drexler's insistence two years ago that Banana Republic cast some older people in its catalog, over the objections of Schoening and her staff. Now, she concedes the "inclusive" move generated goodwill among those older customers. Dennis Connors, who left his post as

Gap's chief information officer in 1999, adds, "People who blame Mickey, they have to grow up. It's a fast-paced company. The cycle times for fashion are getting shorter and shorter."

REACHING OUT. Problem is, in the past, there were plenty of veteran managers and staffers around who could talk Drexler out of going too far out on a limb. Today many of those veterans have left the company. Of the 23 corporate and divisional officers named in Gap's 1999 annual report, 8 have departed for various reasons, including 4 of the 5 officers in the Gap division. True, Drexler gets good marks for some of his replacements. That's particularly the case with nine-year board member John M. Lillie, who was put on the payroll in January as vice chairman and assigned to such crucial matters as manufacturing and distribution systems and cost-cutting, none of them Drexler's forte. . . .

Still, it may take a while for the new execs to decode Drexler—to "lip-read" him, as company insiders say. An edict to order 50,000 more shirts might be meant literally, or it could just be a metaphor for taking risks. "You have to figure out when he's serious and when he's emotionally going off," explains a former Gap exec. Meanwhile, staffers often end up playing guessing games in which they debate what they think the CEO wants, says another former manager. And with some of the newcomers arriving from very different corporate cultures, the learning curve may be steep. "They all could potentially have what it takes to run their businesses, but do they have experience in their positions? No," says Karen Hiatt, an analyst at Gap shareholder Dresdner RCM Global Investors.

With all three chains facing big problems, there's no time to waste. . . . The biggest problem, though, is at the core Gap chain, which in its peak years appealed to everyone from teens to baby boomers with its huge selection of khakis and wearable tops. Drexler took a serious wrong turn in 1999, pushing Gap into fashions that were too young-looking for its clientele. Today, he has gotten rid of the oodles of pink capri pants and cargo pants in favor of items with broader appeal that he hopes reflect "casual style." But that emphasis still seems to span irreconcilable genres. Earlier this year, Drexler declared Gap's target market to be 20- to 30-year-olds who crave fashion. So for the fall season, he ditched much of Gap's basic-style merchandise and took a stab at offering trendier, more cutting-edge fashions, such as belted sweaters and super-dark denim jeans and handbags. That's a risky move that has Gap vying in apparel's most treacherous segment against more agile competitors, such as American Eagle, which can revamp its merchandise mix in half the time Gap needs to respond to shifting tastes. Gap's plummeting same-store sales this fall suggest that Drexler is off-base again.

With Lillie in place, Gap has finally committed to realistic cost-cutting. One of Lillie's more dramatic moves was a first-ever layoff of 1,040 employees in July. Yet Drexler continued to increase his store count by over 20 percent in both 1999 and 2000. He has backed off a bit on the pace of expansion—from 10 percent for next year, to 5 percent to 7 percent—but some analysts wonder why he's expanding at all. Drexler insists there's still opportunity to be tapped but admits he's evaluating 2002 leases that haven't already been signed.

Drexler's loyal supporters on the board say he's merely executing the strategy they set. "We all agreed to put the foot on the accelerator" for the massive expansion, says director Bellamy. But with Gap heading for what looks like a wreck of a year, more investors wonder if Drexler has both hands on the wheel.

SOURCE: *BusinessWeek online* (November 9, 2001).

Questions

1. What are some of the HRM issues inherent in Gap's recent problems?
2. How would an effective strategic HRM function contribute to putting Gap back on track?

Notes

1. A.S. Tsui and L.R. Gomez-Mejia, "Evaluating HR Effectiveness," in *Human Resource Management: Evolving Roles and Responsibilities*, ed. L. Dyer (Washington, DC: Bureau of National Affairs, 1988), pp. 1-187–1-227.
2. D. Ulrich, "Measuring Human Resources: An Overview of Practice and a Prescription for Results," *Human Resource Management* 36, no. 3 (1997), pp. 303–20.
3. P. Wright, G. McMahan, S. Snell, and B. Gerhart, "Comparing Line and HR Executives' Perceptions of HR Effectiveness: Services, Roles, and Contributions," CAHRS (Center for Advanced Human Resource Studies) working paper 98-29, School of ILR, Cornell University, Ithaca, NY.
4. J.C. Erfurt, A. Foote, and M.A. Heirich, "The Cost-Effectiveness of Worksite Wellness Programs," *Personnel Psychology* 15 (1992), p. 22.
5. P. Wright, G. McMahan, S. Snell, and B. Gerhart, *Strategic HRM: Building Human Capital and Organizational Capability*, Technical report. Cornell University, Ithaca, NY, 1998.

6. T.B. Kinni, "A Reengineering Primer," *Quality Digest*, January 1994, pp. 26–30; "Reengineering Is Helping Health of Hospitals and Its Patients," *Total Quality Newsletter*, February 1994, p. 5; R. Recardo, "Process Reengineering in a Finance Division," *Journal for Quality and Participation*, June 1994, pp. 70–73.
7. L. Quillen, "Human Resource Computerization: A Dollar and Cents Approach," *Personnel Journal*, July 1989, pp. 74–77.
8. S. Greengard, "New Technology Is HR's Route to Reengineering," *Personnel Journal*, July 1994, pp. 32c–32o.
9. R. Broderick and J.W. Boudreau, "Human Resource Management, Information Technology, and the Competitive Edge," *Academy of Management Executive* 6 (1992), pp. 7–17.
10. S.E. O'Connell, "New Technologies Bring New Tools, New Rules," *HRMagazine*, December 1995, pp. 43–48; S.F. O'Connell, "The Virtual Workplace Moves at Warp Speed," *HRMagazine*, March 1996, pp. 51–57.
11. E. Brynjolfsson and L. Hitt, "The Productivity Paradox of Information Technology," *Communications of the* ACM, December 1993, pp. 66–77.
12. "Seven Critical Success Factors for Using Information Technology," *Total Quality Newsletter*, February 1994, p. 6.
13. J.E. Rigdon, "Technological Gains Are Cutting Costs in Jobs and Services," *The Wall Street Journal* (February 24, 1995), pp. A1, A5, A6.
14. S. Greengard, "How Technology Is Advancing HR," *Personnel Journal*, September 1993, pp. 80–90.
15. S. Greengard, "Catch the Wave as HR Goes Online," *Personnel Journal*, July 1995, pp. 54–68; M.I. Finney, "It's All in the Knowing How," *HRMagazine*, July 1995, pp. 36–43; "A Survey of the Internet," *The Economist* (special section July 1, 1995), pp. 3–18; A. Doran, "The Internet: The New Tool for the HR Professional," *The Review*, August–September 1995, pp. 32–35; A.L. Sprout, "The Internet Inside Your Company," *Fortune* (November 27, 1995), pp. 161–68.
16. J. Sandberg, "On-Line Population Reaches 24 Million in North America," *The Wall Street Journal* (October 30, 1995), p. B2.
17. S. Greengard, "Home, Home on the Web," *Personnel Journal*, March 1996, pp. 26–33.
18. S. Greengard, "Catch the Wave."
19. T.L. Hunter, "How Client/Server Is Reshaping the HRIS," *Personnel Journal*, July 1992, pp. 38–46; B. Busbin, "The Hidden Costs of Client/Server," *The Review*, August–September 1995, pp. 21–24.
20. D. Drechsel, "Principles for Client/Server Success," *The Review*, August–September 1995, pp. 26–29.
21. A.L. Lederer, "Emerging Technology and the Buy–Wait Dilemma: Sorting Fact from Fantasy," *The Review*, June–July 1993, pp. 16–19.
22. D.L. Fowler, "Imaging in HR: A Case Study," *The Review*, October–November 1994, pp. 29–33.
23. "Dial a Job Interview," *Chain Store Age Executive*, July 1994, pp. 35–36.
24. P.A. Galagan, "Think Performance: A Conversation with Gloria Gery," *Training and Development*, March 1994, pp. 47–51.
25. J. Clark and R. Koonce, "Meetings Go High-Tech," *Training and Development*, November 1995, pp. 32–38; A.M. Townsend, M.E. Whitman, and A.R. Hendrickson, "Computer Support Adds Power to Group Processes," *HRMagazine*, September 1995, pp. 87–91.
26. T.A. Stewart, "Getting Real about Brainpower," *Fortune* (November 27), 1994, pp. 201–3.
27. B. Ziegler, "Internet Software Poses Big Threat to Notes, IBM's Stake in Lotus," *The Wall Street Journal* (November 7, 1995), pp. A1, A8.
28. R.B. Frantzreb, ed., *The 1993 P5 Personnel Software Census* (Roseville, CA: Advanced Personnel Systems, 1993).
29. P. Anthony, "Track Applicants, Track Costs," *Personnel Journal*, April 1990, pp. 75–81; L. Stevens, "Resume Scanning Simplifies Tracking," *Personnel Journal*, April 1993, pp. 77–79.
30. V.R. Ceriello and C. Freeman, *Human Resource Management Systems* (Lexington, MA: Lexington Books, 1991).
31. J. Cohan, "Nike Uses *Resumix* to Stay Ahead in the Recruitment Game," *Personnel Journal*, November 1992, p. 9 (supplement).
32. S.E. Forrer and Z.B. Leibowitz, *Using Computers in Human Resources* (San Francisco: Jossey-Bass, 1991); Ceriello and Freeman, *Human Resource Management Systems*.
33. M.J. Kavanaugh, H.G. Guental, and S.I. Tannenbaum, *Human Resource Information Systems* (Boston: PWS-Kent, 1990).
34. Cyborg Systems Inc., advertising brochure titled "The Solution Series," 1992.
35. G. Bylinsky, "How Companies Spy on Employees," *Fortune* (November 4, 1991), pp. 131–40.
36. Forrer and Leibowitz, *Using Computers in Human Resources*.
37. Ibid.
38. L. Granick, A.Y. Dessaint, and G.R. VandenBos, "How Information Systems Can Help Build Professional Competence," in *Maintaining Professional Competence*, ed. S.L. Willis and S.S. Dubin (San Francisco: Jossey-Bass, 1990), pp. 278–305.
39. Personal communication, Susan Runkel, *Career Resources* (April 18, 1992).

40. F.H. Wagner, "The Nuts and Bolts of Computer-Assisted Job Evaluation," *The Review*, October–November 1991, pp. 16–22.
41. M. Coleman-Carlone, "HBO's Program for Merit Pay," *Personnel Journal*, May 1990, pp. 86–90.
42. Ceriello and Freeman, *Human Resource Management Systems*.
43. H. Glatzer, "Top Secret—Maybe," *Human Resource Executive* 7 (1993), pp. 26–29.
44. Kavanaugh et al., *Human Resource Information Systems*.
45. C. O'Reilly and P. Caldwell, *Cypress Semiconductor (A): Vision, Values, and Killer Software* (Stanford University Case Study, HR-8A, 1998).
46. T. Stewart, "Human Resources Bites Back," *Fortune* 133(9) (May 13, 1996), p. 175.
47. S. Csoka and B. Hackett, *Transforming the HR Function for Global Business Success*, Report 1209-19RR, New York: The Conference Board, 1998.

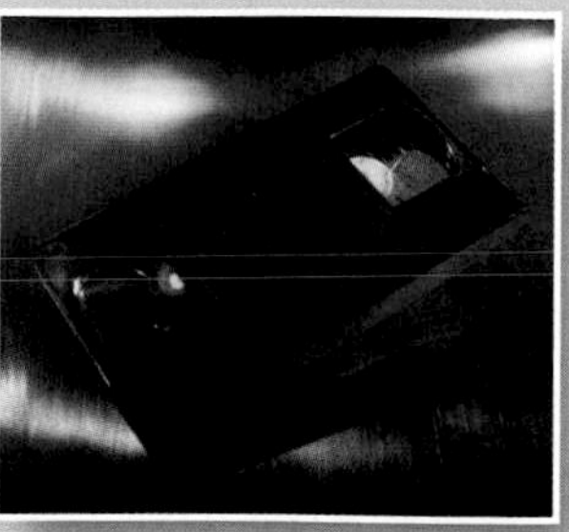

Workplace Ergonomics Is Good Business

During the Industrial Revolution a century ago, workplace injuries were so commonplace that they were simply considered one of the hazards of having a job. Children and adults were often maimed or disfigured in factory accidents. Today strict regulations cover safety in the workplace, guided by the U.S. Department of Labor's Occupational Safety and Health Administration (OSHA). But during the past couple of decades, as industry itself has changed, a different type of injury has emerged: musculoskeletal disorders (MSDs). MSDs are injuries resulting from overexertion and repetitive motion, such as constantly lifting heavy loads or grabbing and twisting a piece of machinery. People who sit at computer workstations all day are susceptible to MSDs as well, particularly carpal tunnel syndrome, which affects the nerves of the hand, wrist, and arm. According to OSHA, about one third of repetitive stress injuries, or 600,000, are serious enough to require time off the job, which means that businesses pay for these injuries not only in medical costs but in lost productivity. They can also contribute to high employee turnover. No one disputes that these injuries occur. But various experts, industry leaders, and politicians argue about how severe the injuries are, who should pay for them, what should be done about them, and who takes ultimate responsibility for the safety of workers.

One aspect of the whole issue of workplace injuries is ergonomics: "the applied science of equipment design, intended to reduce operator fatigue and discomfort, or as OSHA puts it, the science of fitting the job to the worker," explains news correspondent Gwen Ifill. Ergonomics involves everything from developing new equipment, including desk chairs that support the back properly and flexible splints to support the wrist while typing, to designing better ways to use the equipment, such as the proper way to hold a computer mouse. Ergonomic standards are "about helping real people suffering real problems, problems like back injuries and carpal tunnel syndrome, tendonitis—not minor aches or pains, but serious, life-altering injuries," notes Alexis Herman, former secretary of labor.

Several years ago OSHA proposed new guidelines for better ergonomic standards, targeting jobs where workers perform repetitive tasks, whether they are in processing poultry or delivering packages. The proposal required employers that received reports from workers who were suffering from MSDs to respond promptly with an evaluation and follow-up health care. Workers who needed time off could receive 90 percent of their pay and 100 percent of their benefits. Not surprisingly, arguments for and against the proposal broke out. OSHA spokesperson Charles Jeffers claimed that the guidelines "will save employers $9 billion every year from what they've currently been spending on these problems." Peg Seminario of the AFL-CIO noted that the guidelines did not go far enough because they did not cover "workers in construction, agriculture, or maritime, who have very serious problems." Pat Cleary of the National Association of Manufacturers argued that "there's a central flaw here and that is that there is no . . . consensus in the scientific or medical community about the causes of ergonomics injuries." Debates over the proposed rules' merit were further clouded by the Small Business Administration's prediction that implementing the standards would cost industries $18 billion; OSHA had forecast a mere $4.2 billion.

Just before he left office, President Bill Clinton signed the bill into law, which was overturned by incoming President George Bush and the new Congress. Calling the workplace safety regulations "unduly burdensome and overly broad," Bush signed a measure to roll back the new rules.

Where do these actions leave workers and businesses in regard to workplace injuries? Legally, businesses are not required to redesign work systems or continue full pay and benefits for an extended period after a work-related injury. But if the goal of a company is to find and keep the best employees, perhaps developing good ergonomic practices makes good business sense. The high cost of treatment and turnover, not to mention lowered productivity, points toward prevention as a competitive strategy. "Good ergonomics in the office should not be a big burden in a company and may be a way to retain good employees," notes Peter Budnick, president and CEO of ErgoWeb Inc., an ergonomics consulting firm in Utah. Gary Allread, program director at the Institute for Ergonomics at The Ohio State University, remarks, "In my opinion, there's enough research out there to show that implementing some of these types of controls can significantly reduce workers' compensation costs. . . . [But] there are also a lot of companies that aren't as concerned about the health and welfare of their employees, so they're not attuned to the things that can be done" to minimize workplace repetitive stress injuries. In fact, they may not even realize that shifting an employee's computer screen from the side to directly in front of the employee could actually prevent an injury.

So perhaps the more savvy companies can use good ergonomics as a competitive strategy—to retain the best workers, boost morale, and even enhance productivity. "Employers have every incentive to protect employees," says Tim Hammonds, president of the Food Marketing Institute. To that end, many supermarkets and grocery stores have already put ergonomics programs in place to prevent workplace injuries—with or without federal regulations.

Questions

1. Do you agree or disagree that ergonomics in the workplace should be covered by federal regulations? Explain your answer.
2. Choose a job with which you are familiar and discuss the possibilities for repetitive stress injuries that could occur on this job and ways they could be prevented.
3. Imagine that you are the human resources manager for a company that hires workers for the job selected in question 2. What steps might you encourage company officials to take to identify and prevent potential MSDs?

SOURCE: "Ergonomics Rules," *Workforce* (June 19, 2001), **www.workforce.com**; J.Jones, "Bush Expected to Rescind OSHA Rules," *InfoWorld* (March 22, 2001), **www.cnn.com**; M. Allen, "Bush Signs Repeal of Ergonomics Rules," *Washington Post* (March 21, 2001), **www.washingtonpost.com**; J. Kuhnhenn, "House Joins Senate in Repeal of Workplace Ergonomics Rules," *San Jose Mercury News*, **www.siliconvalley.com**; K. Kiely, "House Votes to Repeal Ergonomics Rules," *USA Today* (March 7, 2001), **www.usatoday.com**; D. Espo, "Senate Votes to Repeal Ergonomics Rules," *ABCNews.com* (March 6, 2001), **www.abcnews.go.com**; P. Thibodeau, "OSHA Releases Final Version of Workplace Ergonomics Rules," *Computerworld* (November 13, 2000), **www.computerworld.com**; video transcript, "Working Better," *Online NewsHour* (November 22, 1999), **www.pbs.org**.

Glossary

Acceptability The extent to which a performance measure is deemed to be satisfactory or adequate by those who use it.

Action learning Teams work on an actual business problem, commit to an action plan, and are accountable for carrying out the plan.

Action plan A written document that includes the steps the trainee and manager will take to ensure that training transfers to the job.

Action steps The part of a written affirmative plan that specifies what an employer plans to do to reduce underutilization of protected groups.

Adventure learning Learning focused on the development of teamwork and leadership skills by using structured outdoor activities.

Affective outcomes Outcomes such as attitudes and motivation on the job.

Agency shop A union security provision that requires an employee to pay union membership dues but not to join the union.

Agent In agency theory, a person (e.g., a manager) who is expected to act on behalf of a principal (e.g., an owner).

Alternative dispute resolution (ADR) A method of resolving disputes that does not rely on the legal system. Often proceeds through the four stages of open door policy, peer review, mediation, and arbitration.

Alternative work arrangements Independent contractors, on-call workers, and contract company workers who are not employed full-time by the company.

Americans with Disabilities Act (ADA) A 1990 act prohibiting individuals with disabilities from being discriminated against in the workplace.

Analytic approach Type of assessment of HRM effectiveness that involves determining the impact of, or the financial costs and benefits of, a program or practice.

Anticipatory socialization Socialization that occurs before an individual joins a company. Includes expectations about the company, job, working conditions, and interpersonal relationships.

Appraisal politics A situation in which evaluators purposefully distort a rating to achieve personal or company goals.

Apprenticeship A work-study training method with both on-the-job and classroom training.

Arbitration A procedure for resolving collective bargaining impasses by which an arbitrator chooses a solution to the dispute.

Assessment Collecting information and providing feedback to employees about their behavior, communication style, or skills.

Assessment center A process in which multiple raters evaluate employees' performance on a number of exercises.

Associate union membership A form of union membership by which the union receives dues in exchange for services (e.g., health insurance, credit cards) but does not provide representation in collective bargaining.

Attitude awareness and change program Program focusing on increasing employees' awareness of differences in cultural and ethnic backgrounds, physical characteristics, and personal characteristics that influence behavior toward others.

Attitudinal structuring The aspect of the labor–management negotiation process that refers to the relationship and level of trust between the negotiators.

Audiovisual instruction Includes overheads, slides, and video.

Audit approach Type of assessment of HRM effectiveness that involves review of customer satisfaction or key indicators (e.g., turnover rate, average days to fill a position) related to an HRM functional area (e.g., recruiting, training).

Balanced scorecard A means of performance measurement that gives managers a chance to look at their company from the perspectives of internal and external customers, employees, and shareholders.

Basic skills Reading, writing, and communication skills needed to understand the content of a training program.

Behavior-based program A program focusing on changing the organizational policies and individual behaviors that inhibit employees' personal growth and productivity.

Benchmarking Comparing an organization's practices against those of the competition.

Benchmarks© An instrument designed to measure the factors that are important to success.

Benefits In reference to training evaluation, refers to what the company gains from the training program.

Bona fide occupational qualification (BFOQ) A job qualification based on race, sex, religion, and so on that an employer asserts is a necessary qualification for the job.

Career management system A system to retain and motivate employees by identifying and meeting their development needs (also called *development planning system*).

Career support Coaching, protection, sponsorship, and providing challenging assignments, exposure, and visibility.

Centralization Degree to which decision-making authority resides at the top of the organizational chart.

Checkoff provision A union contract provision that requires an employer to deduct union dues from employees' paychecks.

Client–server architecture Computer design that provides a method to consolidate data and applications into a single host system (the client).

Closed shop A union security provision requiring a person to be a union member before being hired. Illegal under NLRA.

Coach A peer or manager who works with an employee to motivate her, help her develop skills, and provide reinforcement and feedback.

Cognitive ability tests Tests that include three dimensions: verbal comprehension, quantitative ability, and reasoning ability.

Cognitive outcomes Outcomes used to determine the degree to which trainees are familiar with principles, facts, techniques, procedures, or processes emphasized in a training program.

Communities of training Groups of employees who work together, learn from each other, and develop a common understanding of how to get work accomplished.

Compa-ratio An index of the correspondence between actual and intended pay.

Compensable factors The characteristics of jobs that an organization values and chooses to pay for.

Competitiveness A company's ability to maintain and gain market share in its industry.

Concentration strategy A strategy focusing on increasing market share, reducing costs, or creating and maintaining a market niche for products and services.

Concurrent validation A criterion-related validity study in which a test is administered to all the people currently in a job and then incumbents' scores are correlated with existing measures of their performance on the job.

Consolidated Omnibus Budget Reconciliation Act (COBRA) The 1985 act that requires employers to permit employees to extend their health insurance coverage at group rates for up to 36 months following a qualifying event, such as a layoff.

Content validation A test validation strategy performed by demonstrating that the items, questions, or problems posed by a test are a representative sample of the kinds of situations or problems that occur on the job.

Coordination training Training a team in how to share information and decision-making responsibilities to maximize team performance.

Corporate campaigns Union activities designed to exert public, financial, or political pressure on employers during the union-organizing process.

Cost–benefit analysis The process of determining the economic benefits of a training program using accounting methods.

Criterion-related validity A method of establishing the validity of a personnel selection method by showing a substantial correlation between test scores and job performance scores.

Cross-cultural preparation The process of educating employees (and their families) who are given an assignment in a foreign country.

Cross-training Training in which team members understand and practice each other's skills so that members are prepared to step in and take another member's place should he or she temporarily or permanently leave the team.

Cultural immersion A behavior-based diversity program that sends employees into communities where they interact with persons from different cultures, races, and nationalities.

Decision support systems Problem-solving systems that usually include a "what-if" feature that allows users to see how outcomes change when assumptions or data change.

Delayering Reducing the number of job levels within an organization.

Departmentalization Degree to which work units are grouped based on functional similarity or similarity of workflow.

Development The acquisition of knowledge, skills, and behaviors that improve an employee's ability to meet changes in job requirements and in client and customer demands.

Direct applicants People who apply for a job vacancy without prompting from the organization.

Direct costs Training costs including salaries and benefits for all employees involved in training; program material and supplies; equipment or classroom rentals or purchases; and travel costs.

Disparate impact A theory of discrimination based on facially neutral employment practices that disproportionately exclude a protected group from employment opportunities.

Disparate treatment A theory of discrimination based on different treatment given to individuals because of their race, color, religion, sex, national origin, age, or disability status.

Distributive bargaining The part of the labor–management negotiation process that focuses on dividing a fixed economic "pie."

Diversity training Training designed to change employee attitudes about diversity and/or develop skills needed to work with a diverse workforce.

Downsizing The planned elimination of large numbers of personnel, designed to enhance organizational effectiveness.

Downward move A job change involving a reduction in an employee's level of responsibility and authority.

Due process policies Policies by which a company formally lays out the steps an employee can take to appeal a termination decision.

Duty of fair representation The National Labor Relations Act requirement that all bargaining unit members have equal access to and representation by the union.

Efficiency wage theory A theory stating that wage influences worker productivity.

E-learning Instruction and delivery of training by computers through the Internet or company intranet.

Electronic business (e-business) Any business that a company conducts electronically.

Electronic human resource management (e-HRM) The processing and transmission of digitized information used in HRM.

Employee assistance programs (EAPs) Employer programs that attempt to ameliorate problems encountered by workers who are drug dependent, alcoholic, or psychologically troubled.

Employee Retirement Income Security Act (ERISA) The 1974 act that increased the fiduciary responsibilities of pension plan trustees, established vesting rights and portability provisions, and established the Pension Benefit Guaranty Corporation (PBGC).

Employee stock ownership plan (ESOP) An employee ownership plan that provides employers certain tax and financial advantages when stock is granted to employees.

Employment-at-will doctrine The doctrine that, in the absence of a specific contract, either an employer or employee could sever the employment relationship at any time.

Empowering Giving employees the responsibility and authority to make decisions.

Encounter phase The phase that occurs when an employee begins a new job.

Equal employment opportunity (EEO) The government's attempt to ensure that all individuals have an equal opportunity for employment, regardless of race, color, religion, sex, age, disability, or national origin.

Equal Employment Opportunity Commission (EEOC) The government commission established to ensure that all individuals have an equal opportunity for employment, regardless of race, color, religion, sex, age, disability, or national origin.

Ergonomics The interface between individuals' physiological characteristics and the physical work environment.

Exempt Employees who are not covered by the Fair Labor Standards Act. Exempt employees are not eligible for overtime pay.

Expatriate Employee sent by his or her company to manage operations in a different country.

Expectancy theory The theory that says motivation is a function of valence, instrumentality, and expectancy.

Expert systems Computer systems incorporating the decision rules of people recognized as experts in a certain area.

External analysis Examining the organization's operating environment to identify strategic opportunities and threats.

External growth strategy An emphasis on acquiring vendors and suppliers or buying businesses that allow a company to expand into new markets.

External labor market Persons outside the firm who are actively seeking employment.

Externship When a company allows an employee to take a full-time operational role at another company.

Fact finder A person who reports on the reasons for a labor–management dispute, the views and arguments of both sides, and a nonbinding recommendation for settling the dispute.

Fair Labor Standards Act (FLSA) The 1938 law that established the minimum wage and overtime pay.

Family and Medical Leave Act The 1993 act that requires employers with 50 or more employees to provide up to 12 weeks of unpaid leave after childbirth or adoption; to care for a seriously ill child, spouse, or parent; or for an employee's own serious illness.

Financial Accounting Statement (FAS) 106 The rule issued by the Financial Accounting Standards Board in 1993 requiring companies to fund benefits provided after retirement on an accrual rather than a pay-as-you-go basis and to enter these future cost obligations on their financial statements.

Forecasting The attempts to determine the supply of and demand for various types of human resources to predict areas within the organization where there will be future labor shortages or surpluses.

Formal education programs Employee development programs, including short courses offered by consultants or universities, executive MBA programs, and university programs.

Four-fifths rule A rule that states that an employment test has disparate impact if the hiring rate for a minority group is less than four-fifths, or 80 percent, of the hiring rate for the majority group.

Frame of reference A standard point that serves as a comparison for other points and thus provides meaning.

Gainsharing A form of group compensation based on group or plant performance (rather than organizationwide profits) that does not become part of the employee's base salary.

General duty clause The provision of the Occupational Health and Safety Act that states an employer has an overall obligation to furnish employees with a place of employment free from recognized hazards.

Generalizability The degree to which the validity of a selection method established in one context extends to other contexts.

Glass ceiling A barrier to advancement to higher-level jobs in the company that adversely affects women and minorities. The barrier may be due to lack of access to training programs, development experiences, or relationships (e.g., mentoring).

Goals What an organization hopes to achieve in the medium- to long-term future.

Goals and timetables The part of a written affirmative action plan that specifies the percentage of women and minorities that an employer seeks to have in each job group and the date by which that percentage is to be attained.

Group-building methods Training methods that help trainees share ideas and experiences, build group identity, understand the dynamics of interpersonal relationships, and get to know their own strengths and weaknesses and those of their coworkers.

Group mentoring program A program pairing a successful senior employee with a group of four to six less experienced protégés.

Groupware Software application that enables multiple users to track, share, and organize information and to work on the same database or document simultaneously.

Hands-on methods Training methods that require the trainee to be actively involved in learning.

Health maintenance organization (HMO) A health care plan that provides benefits on a prepaid basis for employees who are required to use only HMO medical service providers.

High-leverage training Training practice that links training to strategic business goals, has top management support, relies on an instructional design model, and is benchmarked to programs in other organizations.

High-performance work systems Work systems that maximize the fit between employees and technology.

High-potential employees Employees the company believes are capable of being successful in high-level management positions.

Host country The country in which the parent-country organization seeks to locate or has already located a facility.

Host-country nationals (HCNs) Employees born and raised in a host, not parent, country.

Human resource information system (HRIS) A system used to acquire, store, manipulate, analyze, retrieve, and distribute information related to human resources.

Human resource management (HRM) The policies, practices, and systems that influence employees' behavior, attitudes, and performances.

Human resource recruitment The practice or activity carried on by the organization with the primary purpose of identifying and attracting potential employees.

Imaging A process for scanning documents, storing them electronically, and retrieving them.

In-basket A simulation of the administrative tasks of a manager's job.

Indirect costs Costs not directly related to the design, development, or delivery of the training program.

Individualism–collectivism One of Hofstede's cultural dimensions; describes the strength of the relation between an individual and other individuals in a society.

Intellectual capital Creativity, productivity, and service provided by employees.

Instructional design process A systematic approach for developing training programs.

Integrative bargaining The part of the labor–management negotiation process that seeks solutions beneficial to both sides.

Interactional justice A concept of justice referring to the interpersonal nature of how the outcomes were implemented.

Internal analysis The process of examining an organization's strengths and weaknesses.

Internal growth strategy A focus on new market and product development, innovation, and joint ventures.

Internal labor force Labor force of current employees.

Internet A tool used for communications and to locate and gather resources such as software and reports.

Interview Situation in which potential employees are asked questions about their work and personal experiences, skills, and career plans.

Intraorganizational bargaining The part of the labor–management negotiation process that focuses on the conflicting objectives of factions within labor and management.

Involuntary turnover Turnover initiated by the organization (often among people who would prefer to stay).

ISO 9000:2000 A series of quality assurance standards developed by the International Organization for Standardization in Switzerland and adopted worldwide.

Job analysis The process of getting detailed information about jobs.

Job description A list of the tasks, duties, and responsibilities that a job entails.

Job design The process of defining the way work will be performed and the tasks that will be required in a given job.

Job enlargement Adding challenges or new responsibilities to an employee's current job.

Job enrichment Ways to add complexity and meaningfulness to a person's work.

Job evaluation An administrative procedure used to measure internal job worth.

Job experience The relationships, problems, demands, tasks, and other features that employees face in their jobs.

Job hazard analysis technique A breakdown of each job into basic elements, each of which is rated for its potential for harm or injury.

Job involvement The degree to which people identify themselves with their jobs.

Job redesign The process of changing the tasks or the way work is performed in an existing job.

Job rotation The process of systematically moving a single individual from one job to another over the course of time. The job assignments may be in various functional areas of the company or movement may be between jobs in a single functional area or department.

Job satisfaction A pleasurable feeling that results from the perception that one's job fulfills or allows for the fulfillment of one's important job values.

Job specification A list of the knowledge, skills, abilities, and other characteristics (KSAOs) that an individual must have to perform a job.

Job structure The relative pay of jobs in an organization.

Key jobs Benchmark jobs, used in pay surveys, that have

relatively stable content and are common to many organizations.

Knowledge worker Employees who own the means of producing a product or service.

Leaderless group discussion Process in which a team of five to seven employees solve an assigned problem together within a certain time period.

Leading indicator An objective measure that accurately predicts future labor demand.

Learner control Ability of trainees to actively learn through self-pacing, exercises, links to other materials, and conversations with other trainees and experts.

Learning organization An organization whose employees are continuously attempting to learn new things and apply what they have learned to improve product or service quality.

Long-term–short-term orientation One of Hofstede's cultural dimensions; describes how a culture balances immediate benefits with future rewards.

Maintenance of membership Union rules requiring members to remain members for a certain period of time (e.g., the length of the union contract).

Malcolm Baldrige National Quality Award An award established in 1987 to promote quality awareness, to recognize quality achievements of U.S. companies, and to publicize successful quality strategies.

Managing diversity The process of creating an environment that allows all employees to contribute to organizational goals and experience personal growth.

Marginal tax rate The percentage of an additional dollar of earnings that goes to taxes.

Masculinity–femininity dimension One of Hofstede's cultural dimensions; describes the division of roles between the sexes within a society.

Mediation A procedure for resolving collective bargaining impasses by which a mediator with no formal authority acts as a facilitator and go-between in the negotiations.

Mentor An experienced, productive senior employee who helps develop a less experienced employee.

Merit increase grid A grid that combines an employee's performance rating with his or her position in a pay range to determine the size and frequency of his or her pay increases.

Minimum wage The lowest amount that employers are legally allowed to pay; the 1990 amendment of the Fair Labor Standards Act permits a subminimum wage to workers under the age of 20 for a period of up to 90 days.

Motivation to learn The desire of the trainee to learn the content of a training program.

Myers-Briggs Type Indicator (MBTI) A psychological test used for team building and leadership development that identifies employees' preferences for energy, information gathering, decision making, and lifestyle.

Needs assessment The process used to determine if training is necessary.

Negative affectivity A dispositional dimension that reflects pervasive individual differences in satisfaction with any and all aspects of life.

Network A combination of desktop computers, computer terminals, and mainframes or minicomputers that share access to databases and a method to transmit information throughout the system.

New technologies Current applications of knowledge, procedures, and equipment that have not been previously used. Usually involves replacing human labor with equipment, information processing, or some combination of the two.

Nonkey jobs Jobs that are unique to organizations and that cannot be directly valued or compared through the use of market surveys.

Occupational Safety and Health Act (OSHA) The 1970 law that authorizes the federal government to establish and enforce occupational safety and health standards for all places of employment engaging in interstate commerce.

Opportunity to perform The trainee is provided with or actively seeks experience using newly learned knowledge skills, or behavior.

Organizational analysis A process for determining the business appropriateness of training.

Organizational commitment The degree to which an employee identifies with the organization and is willing to put forth effort on its behalf.

Organizational socialization The process by which new employees are transformed into effective members of a company.

Outcome fairness The judgment that people make with respect to the outcomes received relative to the outcomes received by other people with whom they identity.

Outplacement counseling Counseling to help displaced employees manage the transition from one job to another.

Output A job's performance standards.

Outsourcing An organization's use of an outside organization for a broad set of services.

Overlearning The continuation of practice even after trainees have been able to perform the objective several times.

Parent country The country in which a company's corporate headquarters is located.

Parent-country nationals (PCNs) Employees who were born and live in a parent country.

Pay grades Jobs of similar worth or content grouped together for pay administration purposes.

Pay level The average pay, including wages, salaries, and bonuses, of jobs in an organization.

Pay-policy line A mathematical expression that describes the relationship between a job's pay and its job evaluation points.

Pay structure The relative pay of different jobs (job structure) and how much they are paid (pay level).

Pension Benefit Guaranty Corporation (PBGC) The agency that guarantees to pay employees a basic retirement benefit in the event that financial difficulties force a company to terminate or reduce employee pension benefits.

Performance appraisal The process through which an organization gets information on how well an employee is doing his or her job.

Performance feedback The process of providing employees with information regarding their performance effectiveness.

Performance management The means through which managers ensure that employees' activities and outputs are congruent with the organization's goals.

Performance planning and evaluation (PPE) system Any system that seeks to tie the formal performance appraisal process to the company's strategies by specifying at the beginning of the evaluation period the types and level of performance that must be accomplished in order to achieve the strategy.

Person analysis A process for determining whether employees need training, who needs training, and whether employees are ready for training.

Power distance One of Hofstede's cultural dimensions; concerns how a culture deals with hierarchical power relationships—particularly the unequal distribution of power.

Practice Having the employee demonstrate what he or she has learned in training.

Predictive validation A criterion-related validity study that seeks to establish an empirical relationship between applicants' test scores and their eventual performance on the job.

Preferred provider organization (PPO) A group of health care providers who contract with employers, insurance companies, and so forth to provide health care at a reduced fee.

Presentation methods Training methods in which trainees are passive recipients of information.

Principal In agency theory, a person (e.g., the owner) who seeks to direct another person's behavior.

Procedural justice A concept of justice focusing on the methods used to determine the outcomes received.

Profit sharing A compensation plan in which payments are based on a measure of organization performance (profits) and do not become part of the employees' base salary.

Progression of withdrawal Theory that dissatisfied individuals enact a set of behaviors to avoid the work situation.

Promotions Advances into positions with greater challenge, more responsibility, and more authority than the employee's previous job.

Protean career A career that is frequently changing due to both changes in the person's interests, abilities, and values and changes in the work environment.

Psychological contract The expectations that employers and employees have about each other.

Psychological success The feeling of pride and accomplishment that comes from achieving life goals.

Psychsocial support Serving as a friend and role model, providing positive regard and acceptance, and creating an outlet for a protégé to talk about anxieties and fears.

Quantitative ability Concerns the speed and accuracy with which one can solve arithmetic problems of all kinds.

Range spread The distance between the minimum and maximum amounts in a pay grade.

Rate ranges Different employees in the same job may have different pay rates.

Reaction outcomes Trainees' perceptions of a training program including the facilities, trainers, and content.

Readability The difficulty level of written materials.

Realistic job preview Provides accurate information about the attractive and unattractive aspects of a job, working conditions, company, and location to ensure that potential employees develop appropriate expectations.

Reasonable accommodation Making facilities readily accessible to and usable by individuals with disabilities.

Reasoning ability Refers to a person's capacity to invent solutions to many diverse problems.

Recruitment The process of seeking applicants for potential employment.

Reengineering Review and redesign of work processes to make them more efficient and improve the quality of the end product or service.

Referrals People who are prompted to apply for a job by someone within the organization.

Relational database A database structure that stores information in separate files that can be linked by common elements.

Reliability The consistency of a performance measure; the degree to which a performance measure is free from random error.

Repatriation The preparation of expatriates for return to the parent company and country from a foreign assignment.

Repurposing Directly translating instructor-led training online.

Results Measurements used to determine a training program's payoff for a company.

Return on investment (ROI) A measure comparing a training program's monetary benefits with its cost.

Right-to-work laws State laws that make union shops, maintenance of membership, and agency shops illegal.

Role What an organization expects from an employee in terms of what to do and how to do it.

Role ambiguity Uncertainty about what an organization expects from an employee in terms of what to do and how to do it.

Role analysis technique A method that enables a role occupant and other members of the role occupant's role set to specify and examine their expectations for the role occupant.

Role behaviors Behaviors that are required of an individual in his or her role as a job holder in a social work environment.

Role conflict Recognition of incompatible or contradictory demands by the person occupying the role.

Role overload A state in which too many expectations or demands are placed on a person.

Role play A participant taking the part or role of a manager or other employee.

Role underload A state in which too few expectations or demands are placed on a person.

Sabbatical A leave of absence from the company to renew or develop skills.

Safety awareness programs Employer programs that attempt to instill symbolic and substantive changes in the organization's emphasis on safety.

School-to-work Programs including basic skills training and joint training ventures with universities, community colleges, and high schools.

Selection The process by which an organization attempts to identify applicants with the necessary knowledge, skills, abilities, and other characteristics that will help it achieve its goals.

Self-directed learning A program in which employees take responsibility for all aspects of learning.

Self-efficacy The employees' belief that they can successfully learn the content of a training program.

Self-service Giving employees online access to human resources information.

Settling-in phase Phase of socialization that occurs when employees are comfortable with job demands and social relationships.

Simulation A training method that represents a real-life situation, allowing trainees to see the outcomes of their decisions in an artificial environment.

Six Sigma process System of measuring, analyzing, improving, and controlling processes once they meet quality standards.

Skill-based outcomes Include acquisition or learning of skills and use of skills on the job.

Skill-based pay Pay based on the skills employees acquire and are capable of using.

Specificity The extent to which a performance measure gives detailed guidance to employees about what is expected of them and how they can meet these expectations.

Standard deviation rule A rule used to analyze employment tests to determine disparate impact; it uses the difference between the expected representation for minority groups and the actual representation to determine whether the difference between the two is greater than would occur by chance.

Stock options An employee ownership plan that gives employees the opportunity to buy the company's stock at a previously fixed price.

Strategic choice The organization's strategy; the ways an organization will attempt to fulfill its mission and achieve its long-term goals.

Strategic congruence The extent to which the performance management system elicits job performance that is consistent with the organization's strategy, goals, and culture.

Strategic human resource management (SHRM) A pattern of planned human resource deployments and activities intended to enable an organization to achieve its goals.

Strategy formulation The process of deciding on a strategic direction by defining a company's mission and goals, its external opportunities and threats, and its internal strengths and weaknesses.

Strategy implementation The process of devising structures and allocating resources to enact the strategy a company has chosen.

Succession planning The identification and tracking of high-potential employees capable of filling higher-level managerial positions.

Summary plan description A reporting requirement of the Employee Retirement Income Security Act (ERISA) that obligates employers to describe the plan's funding, eligibility requirements, risks, and so forth within 90 days after an employee has entered the plan.

Support network A group of two or more trainees who agree to meet and discuss their progress in using learned capabilities on the job.

Taft-Hartley Act The 1947 act that outlawed unfair union labor practices.

Task analysis inventory The process of identifying the tasks, knowledge, skills, and behaviors that need to be emphasized in training.

Team leader training Training of the team manager or facilitator.

Technic of Operations Review (TOR) Method of determining safety problems via an analysis of past accidents.

Third country A country other than a host or parent country.

Third-country nationals (TCNs) Employees born in a country other than a parent or host country.

360-degree feedback appraisal A performance appraisal process for managers that includes evaluations from a wide range of persons who interact with the manager. The process includes self-evaluations as well as evaluations from the manager's boss, subordinates, peers, and customers.

Total quality management (TQM) A cooperative form of doing business that relies on the talents and capabilities of both labor and management to continually improve quality and productivity.

Training A planned effort to facilitate the learning of job-related knowledge, skills, and behavior by employees.

Training administration Coordinating activities before, during, and after a training program.

Training outcomes A way to evaluate the effectiveness of a training program based on cognitive, skill-based, affective, and results outcomes.

Transaction processing Computations and calculations used to review and document HRM decisions and practices.

Transfer The movement of an employee to a different job assignment in a different area of the company.

Transfer of training The use of knowledge, skills, and behaviors learned in training on the job.

Transitional matrix Matrix showing the proportion or number of employees in different job categories at different times.

Transnational process The extent to which a company's planning and decision-making processes include representatives and ideas from a variety of cultures.

Transnational representation Reflects the multinational composition of a company's managers.

Transnational scope A company's ability to make HRM decisions from an international perspective.

Uncertainty avoidance One of Hofstede's cultural dimensions; describes how cultures seek to deal with an unpredictable future.

Union shop A union security provision that requires a person to join the union within a certain amount of time after being hired.

Utility The degree to which the information provided by selection methods enhances the effectiveness of selecting personnel in real organizations.

Utilization analysis A comparison of the race, sex, and ethnic composition of an employer's workforce with that of the available labor supply.

Validity The extent to which a performance measure assesses all the relevant—and only the relevant—aspects of job performance.

Verbal comprehension Refers to a person's capacity to understand and use written and spoken language.

Virtual reality Computer-based technology that provides trainees with a three-dimensional learning experience. Trainees operate in a simulated environment that responds to their behaviors and reactions.

Voicing A formal opportunity to complain about one's work situation.

Voluntary turnover Turnover initiated by employees (often whom the company would prefer to keep).

Whistle-blowing Making grievances public by going to the media or government.

Workforce utilization review A comparison of the proportion of workers in protected subgroups with the proportion that each subgroup represents in the relevant labor market.

World Wide Web Service on the Internet that provides browser software allowing the user to explore the items (home pages) on the Web.

Photo Credits

Page 3	The Container Store
Page 53	© George Hall/CORBIS
Page 91	The Home Depot
Page 135	White.Packert/Getty Images
Page 177	Courtesy of Southwest Airlines
Page 217	Janis Christie/Getty Images
Page 249	Courtesy of Tires Plus
Page 325	© Alon Reininger/Contact Press Images/PictureQuest
Page 375	Steve McAlister Productions/Getty Images
Page 417	Jack Hollingsworth/Getty Images
Page 457	Russell Thurston/Getty Images
Page 493	Anton Vengo/SuperStock
Page 527	Nick Rowe/Getty Images
Page 567	© AFP/CORBIS
Page 617	© Julie Houck/Stock, Boston Inc./PictureQuest
Page 651	EyeWire Collection/Getty Images

Name Index

Subject Index

COMPETING IN THE NEW ECONOMY

COMPETING BY MEETING STAKEHOLDER'S NEEDS